*Firmly I Believe And Truly*

Pope St Gregory the Great, Apostle of the English, detail from the reredos painted by James Gillick in 2008 for the church of SS. Gregory and Augustine, Oxford. Photograph courtesy of Brother Lawrence Lew OP. St Gregory's, as the church is popularly known, was the parish church of Graham Greene and J. R. R. Tolkien. Monsignors Ronald Knox and Vernon Johnson preached at its Corpus Christi processions in the 1940s.

# Firmly I Believe And Truly

## The Spiritual Tradition of Catholic England
### 1483–1999

COMPILED, EDITED, AND INTRODUCED BY

JOHN SAWARD

JOHN MORRILL

MICHAEL TOMKO

OXFORD

UNIVERSITY PRESS

UNIVERSITY PRESS

Great Clarendon Street, Oxford OX2 6DP

Oxford University Press is a department of the University of Oxford.
It furthers the University's objective of excellence in research, scholarship,
and education by publishing worldwide in

Oxford New York

Auckland Cape Town Dar es Salaam Hong Kong Karachi
Kuala Lumpur Madrid Melbourne Mexico City Nairobi
New Delhi Shanghai Taipei Toronto

With offices in

Argentina Austria Brazil Chile Czech Republic France Greece
Guatemala Hungary Italy Japan Poland Portugal Singapore
South Korea Switzerland Thailand Turkey Ukraine Vietnam

Oxford is a registered trade mark of Oxford University Press
in the UK and in certain other countries

Published in the United States
by Oxford University Press Inc., New York

Introduction and Selection © John Saward, John Morrill, and Michael Tomko 2011

The moral rights of the author have been asserted
Database right Oxford University Press (maker)

First published 2011

British Library Cataloguing in Publication Data

Data available

Library of Congress Cataloging in Publication Data

Data available

Typeset by SPI Publisher Services, Pondicherry, India
Printed in Great Britain
on acid-free paper by
CPI Antony Rowe, Chippenham, Wiltshire

ISBN 978-0-19-929122-9

1 3 5 7 9 10 8 6 4 2

In memory of Frances

Come to her assistance, all you saints of God;
meet her, all you angels of God;
receive her soul, and present it now before its Lord.
May Jesus Christ receive thee,
and the angels conduct thee to thy place of rest.
May they receive her soul, and present it now before its Lord.

*The Roman Ritual*, translated by John Gother (+ 1704)

# Foreword

'English' is a language and a culture, a landscape and a literature, which cannot be fully understood without an appreciation of the Catholic faith. Indeed that faith has been a constant formative influence on every aspect of English life, from village to city, in conflict and persecution, in peace and times of plenty, in politics and in sovereignty.

I salute the editors of this anthology for making the voice of this Catholic faith accessible, in so many of its different expressions. This is a valuable and timely publication.

As is stated in the General Introduction, the Catholic faith is the 'religion of the invisible made visible, and the Eternal entering time', and therefore 'must insert itself, express itself, within the concrete conditions and specific cultures in which human beings live' (p. xxi). The selection of English Catholic writers to be found here is, therefore, widespread and varied, embracing many different aspects of life. For Catholic faith is not a project apart from the business of daily living, but rather informing, inspiring, and sustaining every worthy human effort at serving the common good of our society.

The writers presented here are all thoroughly English. And they are thoroughly Catholic, both in the sense of finding life and truth in the Catholic Church and in knowing that they share and express a truth of life that unites them to others beyond their shores and beyond their age. They know themselves to be part of a fine symphony of faith and life, pointing to a wholeness within the human family of which contemporary efforts for 'social inclusion' are a partial expression.

This volume represents a powerful testimony to our times. Here are witnesses to the goodness, compassion, selfless generosity, hope, and perseverance to which the Catholic faith gives rise. This evidence simply outweighs the truncated versions of religious faith as divisive, small-minded, and gullible, so often put forward by today's pundits. Part of the purpose of this book is to make this evidence more easily available. For this it is most welcome.

Anyone who wishes to understand English Catholicism, and all who wish to be encouraged and nurtured in that faith, will welcome this publication. I do, most certainly.

✠ VINCENT NICHOLS

Archbishop of Westminster
15 August 2009
The Assumption of Our Lady

# Acknowledgements

We are most grateful to His Grace the Archbishop of Westminster, Vincent Nichols, for writing the foreword, and for encouraging us at every stage of this long-drawn-out project. Among colleagues and friends we should like especially to thank Professor Eamon Duffy, Fr Dermot Fenlon, Dr Kevin Hughes, Br Lawrence Lew OP, Monsignor Vaughan Morgan, Dr William Oddie, Fr James Pereiro, Dr Thomas W. Smith, and Dr Helena Tomko. We owe a particular debt of gratitude to the Hutton Trust and the Theodore Trust for their generous support over the last five years, and to Villanova University for a *Veritas* faculty research grant. We must also thank Marie Kelly, P. J. Gorre, Sue Stefanski, and Douglas Wisneiski for helping in the preparation of the typescript, and our editors at Oxford University Press, Lucy Qureshi, Tom Perridge, and Lizzie Robottom, for their heroic patience.

All three editors acknowledge their deep gratitude to the *Oxford Dictionary of National Biography*, which has made their work far easier and rendered it much more reliable.

We are also grateful to the following publishers and organizations for their kind permission to quote from works for which they hold the copyright:

Agenda Editions, for David Jones, *The Roman Quarry and Other Sequences*, ed. Harman Grisewood and René Hague (London, 1981).

The John Bradburne Memorial Society for the poems of John Bradburne.

Cambridge University Press, for David Knowles OSB, *The Religious Orders in England*, vol. iii (Cambridge, 1979).

Members of the Congregation of Jesus in Augsburg for permission to reproduce the painting of the Spilled Chalice from the series of 'The Painted Life' of Venerable Mary Ward in their trusteeship.

The Catholic Truth Society, for David Knowles OSB, *Humanae Vitae: Peter Has Spoken* (London, 1968) and W. A. Pantin's Speech to the CTS Congress, Brighton, 1938.

By kind permission of the Continuum International Publishing Group, we have taken texts from the following books, originally published by Burns & Oates: M. C. D'Arcy SJ (*Belief and Reason* (1944), *The Mass and Redemption* (1926), *Of God and Man* (1964)); David Knowles OSB (*The English Mystical Tradition* (new edition, 1964)); Ronald A. Knox (*Occasional Sermons* (1960), *Pastoral Sermons* (1960)); ed. Shane Leslie, *Letters of Herbert Cardinal Vaughan to Lady Herbert of Lea, 1867 to 1903* (1942); Vincent McNabb OP (*The Craft of Prayer* (1935), *God's Good Cheer* (1937), *Mary of Nazareth* (1939), *Nazareth or Social Chaos* (1933), *Some Mysteries of Jesus Christ* (1941), *Stars of Comfort* (1957)); C. C. Martindale SJ ('The Sacramental System', in *The Teaching of the Catholic Church*, ed. G. D. Smith (1948)); R. H. J. Steuart SJ (*The Two Voices* (1952), *Spiritual Teaching* (1952)); Ferdinand Valentine OP (*Father Vincent McNabb OP* (1955)); and Anscar Vonier OSB (*Collected Works* (1952 & 1953), *A Key to the Doctrine of the Eucharist* (1925), *Sketches and Studies in Theology* (1940), 'Angels', in *The Teaching of the Catholic Church*, ed. G. D. Smith (1948)). By kind permission of the same publisher we have also made use of the following books and contributions to collections of essays, originally published by Sheed and Ward: Hilaire Belloc (*Essays of a Catholic Layman in England* (1931)); Christopher Dawson (*Enquiries into Religion and Culture* (1933), *The Making of*

*Europe* (1948), *The Judgement of the Nations* (1943)); Eric Gill (*Beauty Looks After Herself* (1933)); John Carmel Heenan, *The People's Priest* (1951); Caryll Houselander (*The Passion of the Infant Christ* (1949), *The Reed of God* (1945), *This War is the Passion* (1945), *The Risen Christ* (1958), *The Letters of Caryll Houselander* (1965)); Vernon Johnson (*One Lord, One Faith* (1929) and *Spiritual Childhood* (1953)); David Knowles OSB ('St Wulstan of Worcester', in *The English Way*, edited by Maisie Ward (1933)); Ronald Knox (*The Creed in Slow Motion* (1950), *A Retreat for Priests* (1946), *The Mass in Slow Motion* (1948)); Arnold Lunn (*Now I See* (1934), *And Yet So New* (1958), *Within that City* (1936), 'Alpine Mysticism and "Cold Philosophy"', in *For Hilaire Belloc* (1942)); C. C. Martindale SJ (*Christianity is Christ* (1935), *The Words of the Missal* (1932)); David Mathew ('Blessed John Fisher', in *The English Way*, edited by Maisie Ward (1933)); Gervase Mathew OP ('St Bede', in *The English Way*, edited by Maisie Ward (1933)); J. B. Morton (*By the Way* (1936)); W. A. Pantin ('The Pre-Conquest Saints of Canterbury', in *For Hilaire Belloc* (1942)); F. J. Sheed (*Theology and Sanity* (1947), *A Map of Life* (1933), *Theology for Beginners* (1958)); R. H. J. Steuart SJ (*March, Kind Comrade* (1931)); Gerald Vann OP (*The Temptations of Christ* (1957)); Maisie Ward (foreword to *The English Way* (1933), *The Splendour of the Rosary* (1945)), Hubert van Zeller OSB (*Approach to Prayer* (1958), *Approach to Penance* (1958)).

Darton, Longman & Todd, for Basil Hume OSB, *The Mystery of the Incarnation* (London, 1999).

Faber & Faber, for David Jones, *Anathémata* (London, 1952) and *The Sleeping Lord and Other Fragments* (London, 1974), and for *Dai Greatcoat: A Self-Portrait of David Jones in His Letters*, ed. René Hague (London, 1980).

Very Revd Fr John Farrell OP, Prior Provincial of the English Dominicans, for texts from the journal *Blackfriars* and Blackfriars Publications.

Gracewing, for John Dove SJ, *Strange Vagabond of God: The Story of John Bradburne* (Swords: Poolbeg Press, 1983).

*The Letters of J. R. R. Tolkien*, edited by Humphrey Carpenter, reprinted by permission of HarperCollins Publishers Ltd, © J. R. R. Tolkien, 1981; translation of the poem, 'Pearl' (*Sir Gawain and the Green Knight, Pearl, and Sir Orfeo*. Translated by J. R. R. Tolkien, new edition (New York: Ballantyne Books, 1980); the poem 'Mythopoeia' (J. R. R. Tolkien, *Tree and Leaf including the poem Mythopoeia*. Introduction by Christopher Tolkien (Boston: Houghton Mifflin, 1989) reprinted by permission of HarperCollins Publishers Ltd, © J. R. R. Tolkien.

David Higham Associates, for Graham Greene, *The End of the Affair* (New York: Penguin, 1979), *The Lawless Roads* (London: William Heinemann & The Bodley Head, 1978), and 'The Paradox of a Pope' in Greene's *Collected Essays* (New York: Viking, 1979).

Sr Christina Kenworthy-Brown for permission to draw upon sections of her edition of *Mary Ward, A Briefe Relation with Autobiographical Fragments and a Selection of Letters*, published by Boydell for the Catholic Record Society (2008).

Barbara Levy Literary Agency for the poems of Siegfried Sassoon: 'Arbor Vitae 1959', 'A Prayer at Pentecost 1960', 'Compline May 1962', 'A Prayer in Old Age 23 September 1964'.

Liverpool University Press, for *Blundell's Diary and Letter Book, 1702–1728*, ed. Margaret Blundell (Liverpool, 1952).

Penguin Books Ltd for Evelyn Waugh, *Brideshead Revisited* (revised edition, Harmondsworth, 1962) and *Helena* (Harmondsworth, 1963).

Viking Penguin, a division of Penguin Group (USA) Inc. for Graham Greene, *The End of the Affair*, copyright 1951, renewed © 1979 by Graham Greene.

Random House Group Ltd for Leonard Cheshire, *The Face of Victory* (London: Hutchinson, 1961).

A. P. Watt Ltd on behalf of the Trustees of the Maurice Baring Will Trust, for the poems by Maurice Baring, and for *Daphne Adeane* (London: Heinemann, 1926).

The Wylie Agency for Evelyn Waugh, *The Diaries of Evelyn* Waugh, ed. Michael Davie (London: Weidenfeld & Nicolson, 1976) and *Edmund Campion*, new edition (London: Hollis & Carter, 1947).

Although every effort has been made to trace and contact copyright holders prior to publication, this has not been possible in every case. If notified, the publishers will be pleased to rectify any errors or omissions at the earliest opportunity.

# Contents

PART 2 · 1688–1850

# PART 3 · 1850–1999

# List of Illustrations

# Authors and Texts:
# Principles of Selection

The authors represented in *Firmly I Believe and Truly* were Catholic according to the Church's own definition of that name and dignity, namely, those who ended their lives fully incorporated into the Catholic Church, that is, in the profession of the Church's faith, the actual reception of the Church's last Sacraments (or the capacity to receive them), and a juridical bond of communion with the hierarchical Church governed by the Successor of St Peter and the bishops in communion with him.[1] We have therefore excluded authors, such as George Tyrrell, who died without recanting their heterodox opinions and seeking reconciliation with the Church.

Four further principles guided our selection. The first is that the texts chosen were all composed within the Catholic lifetime of their authors. Nothing has been selected, therefore, from the writings of converts, such as Newman and Chesterton, dating from before the time of their reception, nor have we included works written in times of separation from Catholic unity by men like Bishops Gardiner and Tunstall, who, though dying at peace with the Holy See, previously followed Henry VIII into schism. Those received on their deathbeds, such as Robert Stephen Hawker and Oscar Wilde, have also been left out, since their work, however Catholic some of it may seem, was produced when they were still outside full communion.

The second principle was the inclusion, so far as possible, of work that appeared in print rather than in manuscript. We begin, therefore, with work published by Caxton in the 1480s. We realize how lively manuscript culture was, especially in the penal times, and consequently have made a few judicious exceptions to this principle, especially so as to allow more female voices to appear, since they were disproportionately denied access to print (see, for example, our extracts from the writings of the Venerable Mary Ward). The principle of working with English Catholic writing in the age of print not only facilitates our portrayal of the international reach and historical depth of English Catholicism, but also helps convey the way in which the texts in our first two periods, often published with great inconvenience and even peril, enabled English Catholics to achieve their own sense of community, often under persecution and in exile, and to present themselves to their neighbours in the broader English reading public.

---

[1] 'Fully incorporated into the society of the Church are those who, possessing the Spirit of Christ, accept all the means of salvation given to the Church together with her entire organization, and who—by the bonds constituted by the profession of faith, the Sacraments, ecclesiastical government, and communion—are joined in the visible structure of the Church of Christ, who rules her through the Supreme Pontiff and the bishops' (*The Catechism of the Catholic Church*, n. 837, citing the Second Vatican Council, Dogmatic Constitution on the Church, *Lumen gentium*, n. 14).

The third principle was publication in the English language. Since we are reflecting a tradition, we have taken this to mean that work translated within the lifetime of the author, or within two generations of its composition, in Latin could be included. The only modern translations are our own, and are found only where short phrases or single sentences in Latin, normally from Scripture or from the Fathers, are to be found within an English language work. Because we hope this book will be used devotionally as well as for study, we have modernized the spelling and punctuation of all our texts. This becomes less and less obtrusive as we move through the centuries, but for the period 1484–1700 this is a very extensive change. It has involved not only standardization of spelling and punctuation, but the bringing of all passages, even fairly recent ones, into line with *The Oxford Style Manual*. Obsolete words have been glossed in square brackets or footnoted when a longer gloss was required. We made two pragmatic exceptions to the general rule of modernization: first, we left text that was in the second person singular (e.g. 'thou livest', 'thy God') in both pronoun and verb forms; secondly, we used the modern short form for 'Saint' or 'S.', namely, 'St'.

The fourth principle was that the works selected should both represent and contribute to the making of an English tradition. We have limited our selections to authors who lived and worked in England, or whose work was directed at those living in that kingdom. We include a number of authors who were born outside England, but only where they became influential members of the Church in England. We have excluded other English-language authors, writing in or for the Church in Ireland, Scotland, or Wales. Out of respect for the richness of those traditions, we have deferred their works to future anthologies and other editors. We have, however, gladly noted examples of interdependence, as at St Winefride's well in Holywell or in the writings of the Irish Dominican Vincent McNabb and the Anglo-Welsh poet David Jones.

Chesterton defined tradition as the 'democracy of the dead'. Our constituency is likewise composed of men and women who have departed this life, and whose date of death falls between 1482 and 1999. We are not suggesting that the tradition of English Catholic writing has not survived into these early years of the twenty-first century. Rather, we are making the prudential judgement that an interval of reception and assessment needs to follow death in order to determine a Catholic writer's contribution to the Tradition. Moreover, since a work such as this must have a cut-off point of some kind, the end of the second millennium of Christianity seemed to us to be a most fitting one. Within these historical limits, we have striven to keep a good balance in chronology and genre (poetry and prose, books and pamphlets, homilies, personal letters, etc.), and as far as possible between men and women, clergy and laity, and the diverse traditions of the major religious orders.

As regards content, our texts are broader than the term 'spirituality', as presently understood, would signify. Spiritual doctrine, for the Catholic, presupposes the doctrine of the faith, the liturgy and Sacraments of the Church, and the practice of Christian morality in fidelity to the Commandments. Moreover, since the Catholic believes himself to be supported in his following of Christ by the example, merits, and prayers of the saints in Heaven, their earthly lives are an intrinsic part of the patrimony upon which he draws. All of these elements, which make up the Christ-given wholeness that is Catholicity, will be represented in the anthology. Catholic doctrines and devotions are here, but so, too, are Catholic philosophy, social thought, biography, history, and literature, including humour and satire. Within each period, the reader will notice a pattern of historical circularity and cross-reference: Tudor Catholics looking back to the age of the Fathers; Georgian Catholics honouring the martyrs of the previous two centuries; twentieth-century Catholics remembering the saints of Anglo-Saxon times. These intersections bear witness to an essential fact: the history of the Catholic Church in England reaches across the ages and beyond the Alps, beginning with the mission of St Augustine of Canterbury, or perhaps we should say with that remote evangelization of the Romano-British symbolized by the old story of Joseph of Arimathea landing at Glastonbury.

# General Introduction

Firmly I believe and truly,
God is Three and God is One;
And I next acknowledge duly
Manhood taken by the Son.[1]

Before he dies, Gerontius makes a profession of his faith, beginning with the
mysteries of the Triune God and the Incarnation, within which everything else in
the creed is enfolded.[2] The protagonist of Cardinal Newman's poem, made a
musical masterpiece by Elgar, is an ordinary Catholic in his final moments in this
life and in his movement towards Particular Judgement and Purgatory in the next.
In the infirmity of his deathbed, as he suffers the 'emptying out of each constituent
| And natural force, by which [he] came to be', he reaches out to the Reality that is
infinitely greater than himself: *Sanctus fortis, Sanctus Deus*, 'Holy Mighty One,
Holy God'. He believes not merely *firmly*, in assertion of a subjective conviction,
but *truly*, by assent to the objective truth of what God has revealed and entrusted
to the Catholic Church. Gerontius wants to die, as he has lived, as a faithful
Catholic who loves Christ:

And I hold in veneration,
For the love of Him alone,
Holy Church as His creation
And her teachings as His own.

Both in death and in life, Newman's Gerontius is a representative Catholic,
namely (according to the Second Vatican Council), someone who believes what
the Catholic Church believes, who receives her Sacraments, and who lives in
communion with her pastors.[3] Yet what does it mean to be both English *and*
Catholic? On the one hand, there is a tension between these two identities. For
English Catholics, the Reformation and the subsequent establishment of the penal
laws introduced both a myriad of political complexities and a series of persecutions that resonate in the 'dungeon, fire, and sword' of Frederick Faber's hymn,
'Faith of our Fathers'.[4] In every century, though in different forms, English
Catholics had to make sense of the ways their duties to Church and conscience

---

[1] John Henry Cardinal Newman, *The Dream of Gerontius*, See pp. 457–8 below.
[2] In his treatise on faith in the *Summa theologiae*, St Thomas Aquinas says that the things that pertain *per
se* to faith are the things of which we hope to have the vision in Heaven, namely, the 'majesty of the divinity'
and the 'mystery of Christ's humanity' (cf. *Summa theologiae* 2a2ae q. 1, a. 8).
[3] These are the three criteria given by the Second Vatican Council for full incorporation into the society of
the Church (cf. The Dogmatic Constitution on the Church, *Lumen gentium*, n. 14).
[4] For the political, social, and cultural fate of Catholicism in England at the time of the Reformation, see
Eamon Duffy, *The Stripping of the Altars: Traditional Religion in England, c.1400–c.1580* (New Haven: Yale
University Press, 1992) and Christopher Haigh, *English Reformations: Religion, Politics, and Society under the
Tudors* (Oxford: Clarendon Press, 1993). For a discussion of these recent historical reassessments, see John
Aberth and Gregory Randolph, 'England's Counter-Reformation: The Changing Historiography on English
Religious History', *Downside Review* 117 (1999), 273–92.

were often opposed to their ties to nation and neighbour. They had to face what England had become while harbouring their own cultural memories of England as 'Mary's Dowry' and of 'the faith of the holy Roman Church' once 'delivered to [them] inviolate' by Augustine and his brethren,[5] who were sent from Rome in the sixth century by Pope Gregory the Great, *Apostolus anglorum*. On the other hand, Newman counsels English Catholics to view their home country with a 'special warmth of attachment'. He calls on them to 'drink in its particular spirit' and to 'glory in the characteristic tokens of a Divine Presence':

Christendom is divided into a great number of districts, each with its own character and interests; each has its own indigenous saints; each has its own patrons, its holy men, its benefactors, its patterns. Each region or province has those within it to whom it has given birth, and who in time become its teachers; who form its traditions, mould its character, and thereby separate and discriminate it from other regions. And thus it is that each part of the Catholic Church has excellences of its own which other parts have not, and is as distinct from the rest in genius and in temper as it is in place.[6]

Just as Alban Butler, the eighteenth-century author of the *Lives of the Saints*, could describe the characteristic virtues of the individual saints as setting forth 'in some degree' particular aspects of Christ's 'plenitude of all virtue and sanctity',[7] so Catholics believe that the special qualities of Catholic thought and devotion in individual countries have been inspired by the boundless riches of Christ in his Church, and that the universal can be found in the particular, because the eternal Word, by and for whom all things were made, was made flesh in one place and at a given time.

Gerontius's act of faith in the Incarnation, *And I next acknowledge duly | Manhood taken by the Son*, articulates the major premise for Catholicism's sacramental understanding of how a religion of the invisible made visible, and the Eternal entering time, must insert itself, express itself, within the concrete conditions and specific cultures in which human beings live their lives on earth. In 1933 it inspired Maisie Ward to edit a collection of essays that anticipates this project in scope and purpose:

Because [Catholic Christianity] is universal, it is in every country, but because it is sacramental, it is intensely local, found in each country, not a spirit only but a spirit clothed in material form. St Gregory [the Great] ... once counselled St Augustine not to destroy the temples which had been used for pagan worship but to consecrate them to Christ. So, too, the Englishman was not to be changed *for* but *into* the Christian. The Mediaevals were wont to paint the Infancy and the Passion of Our Lord in the setting of their own lives, and William Langland 'saw Christ walking in the fields in the dress of an English labourer'. In Langland, says Christopher Dawson, 'Catholic faith and national feeling are fused in a single flame'.[8]

---

[5] 'Be mindful of our fathers, Eleutherius, Celestine, and Gregory, bishops of the holy City; of Augustine, Columba, and Aidan, who *delivered to us inviolate the faith of the holy Roman Church*' (from the prayer, O merciful God, let the glorious intercession of thy saints assist us', to be recited in England at Benediction on the second Sunday of the month, *Ritus servandus in solemni expositione et benedictione Sanctissimi Sacramenti* (London: Burns & Oates, 1955), 29).

[6] John Henry Cardinal Newman, 'Sermon 13. The Tree beside the Waters', in *Sermons Preached on Various Occasions* (London: Burns & Oates, 1881), 247–9.

[7] Alban Butler, *The Lives of the Fathers, Martyrs, and other Principal Saints*, 4 vols. (London, 1759), iv. 460.

[8] Maisie Ward, *The English Way* (London and New York: Sheed & Ward, 1933), 7.

The searing experience of living with the Reformation, marked by widespread religious conflict throughout Christian Europe, gave the medieval fusion of 'Catholic faith and national feeling' new qualities. English Catholics lived under an alliance of Church and State hostile to much that was, and is, at the core of Catholic faith. The suffering endured in the escalating cycle of Catholic resistance and Protestant repression, the official attempts to suppress the Communion of Saints that bound together the living and the faithful departed, the systematic exclusion of Catholics from most aspects of public life, and the exile of Catholics abroad for education and formation in sacred ministry—all of these resulted in an English Catholic experience that was distinctive. Nevertheless, that 'single flame' still illuminates the history of the Church in England, beginning with the fortitude under persecution evinced in the period represented in the first part of this book (pp. 1 ff.), the circumspection and modesty characterizing the Age of Challoner (cf. Part 2, pp. 251 ff.), and the revived sense of self-confidence after the restoration of the hierarchy (cf. Part 3, pp. 445 ff.).

All our authors were natives of England, or, as in the examples of Vincent McNabb or Dominic Barberi, were dedicated participants in English Catholic life. Every state of Christian life—clerical, religious, and lay—is represented in this book, as is every kind of writing: prayers and meditations, sermons and letters, poetry and hymnody, novels and drama, biography and historiography, polemics and apologetics, humour and satire, as well as theology in all its departments. There are women as well as men, and the accents of almost every county can be heard.

*Firmly I believe and truly...* The Englishmen and women in this anthology adhered to the faith of the Catholic Church, what they take to be *Christ's* Church, not by political enforcement or contemporary definition, but by divine institution and perpetual recognition, the Church of the Apostles and Martyrs, of the Fathers and Doctors; as St Thomas More puts it in his *Confutacyon* of Tyndale, Christ's 'known Catholic Church'.[9] More would not have died at the hands of Henry VIII, nor would others later have suffered martyrdom, exile, and exclusion, for a Catholic Church that they viewed merely as a venerable English institution. As St Bede never tires of reminding his readers, the Church of the English was founded from Rome by the Pope himself. For this historical and theological reason, our anthology begins, beyond the Protestant Reformation, with authors of the late fifteenth century. For while scarred and shaped, sometimes glorified, sometimes refined, by the experience of the Reformation and its legacy, the Catholic Church in England is not simply a product of the 'Counter-Reformation'

---

[9] 'The faith of the known Catholic Church, that correcteth the false faith of the false preachers and heretics, is the same faith which the holy doctors of Christ's Church in every age have believed and taught' (*The Confutation of Tyndale's Answer*, Book IV; ed. Louis A. Schuster et al., *The Complete Works of St Thomas More*, vol. viii, part 1 (New Haven and London: Yale University Press, 1973), 390). More sees the Catholic Church as an all-embracing solidarity in contrast to the elitism and individualism of Tyndale's church: 'The very Church is none other but this that he denieth, that is, to wit, the common known Catholic people, clergy, layfolk, and all which whatsoever their living be ... do stand together and agree in the confession of one true Catholic faith, with all old holy doctors and saints, and good Christian people beside that are already passed this fifteen hundred year before, against Arius, Otho, Lambert, Luther, and Wycliffe, Zwingli, Hutten, Hus, and Tyndale and all the rabble of such erroneous heretics' (ibid. 480 f.).

with a history of only 450 years.[10] Despite the tensions between the 'old' Catholics, who kept the faith in the penal times, and the enthusiastic new converts of the mid-nineteenth century, and even though not all have looked with equal attention and warmth on what was said and done 'beyond the mountains', English Catholicism has remained truly Catholic, universal in both time and space: culturally, intellectually, and devotionally indebted to its medieval past, rooted in communion with the Church throughout the world. In its veneration of ancient English saints and sites and its continuing exchange of ideas and energies with the Church in Europe, English Catholic religious culture has transcended the borders of mortality and nationality.

The purpose of *Firmly I Believe and Truly* is, first, to give readers of our own time, non-Catholic as well as Catholic, convenient access to a rich but often overlooked religious culture within England. Cardinal Newman may have been convinced that 'English Literature will ever *have been* Protestant',[11] but his own work is the refutation of his thesis, for while for him 'Swift and Addison' were 'the most native and natural of our writers', his own prose, so clear and close to the rhythms of ordinary speech, has served for the generations that have come after him as a model of the way to write well in our language. Think also of the literary achievements of Chaucer and More, Robert Southwell and Richard Crashaw, Alexander Pope and John Dryden, Gerard Manley Hopkins and Francis Thompson; remember the twentieth-century writing of G. K. Chesterton and Hilaire Belloc, of Graham Greene and Evelyn Waugh, of J. R. R. Tolkien, recently named the 'author of the century'.[12] At the very least, then, we can say without fear of contradiction that there is a strong Catholic current running through the English literature of the modern age, and it is that current to which we intend to give a new outlet.[13]

Our second goal, reflected in our subtitle, 'The Spiritual Tradition of Catholic England', is to open up to a new generation of readers, both Catholic and non-Catholic, the work of the masters of English Catholic writing. Some of our authors were canonized saints; others had failings and eccentricities that were more conspicuous than their sanctity. Writing in the eighteenth century, Alban Butler warned that for many the world was 'a whirlpool of business, pleasure, and sin' whose 'torrent is always beating upon their hearts, ready to break in, and bury them under its flood, unless frequent pious reading and consideration oppose a strong sense to its waves'. In our own fast-paced world, how much more pressing

---

[10] For such a view, see John Bossy, *The English Catholic Community 1570–1850* (London: Darton, Longman & Todd, 1975), which argues that English Catholicism is a species of nonconformist dissent from the Anglican Establishment, not essentially different from Methodism or Unitarianism. English Catholicism, according to Bossy, is formed after the Reformation, insularly disconnected from influence from the continent and beyond, and discontinuous with the medieval Church. For a critical assessment of this position, see Eamon Duffy's *Peter and Jack: Roman Catholics and Dissent in Eighteenth-Century England* (London: Dr Williams's Trust, 1982).

[11] *The Idea of a University* (London and New York: Longmans, 1907), 314.

[12] Tom Shippey, *J. R. R. Tolkien: The Author of the Century* (New York: Houghton Mifflin, 2000), pp. vii–xxvii.

[13] Based on Newman's own accomplishments as a prose stylist, Ian Ker has labelled Newman's eloquent argument 'curiously self-falsifying'. See *The Catholic Revival in English Literature* (Leominster: Gracewing, 2003), 1.

is Butler's counsel and recommendation of devotional reading and reflection: 'The more deeply a person is immersed in...tumultuous cares, so much the greater ought to be his solicitude to find leisure to breathe, after the fatigues and dissipation of business and company; to plunge his heart, by secret prayer, in the ocean of the divine immensity, and by pious reading, to afford his soul some spiritual reflection'.[14] In *Firmly I Believe and Truly*, we hope to provide resources for such a contemplative task, in which 'the mind is instructed and enlightened, and the affections of the heart are purified and inflamed'. This, again, is a call to which Gerontius bears witness:

> And I hope and trust most fully
> In that Manhood crucified,
> And each thought and deed unruly
> Do to death, as He has died.

The third aim of our anthology is to offer a modern *enchiridion*. In the fifth century, drawing on Greek models for his own *Enchiridion*,[15] St Augustine of Hippo agreed to provide for his disciple Laurentius

a sort of handbook, something for you to keep beside you, containing answers to questions: What ought one chiefly to pursue? What, in view of the different heresies, ought one to shun? To what extent may reason contend in the cause of religion? What lack of harmony is there with reason when faith stands alone? What is first and last to be held, the sum of all doctrine? What is the sure and proper foundation of the Catholic faith? Now, without doubt, you will know the answers to all these questions, when you have a sure knowledge of the objects of our faith, our hope, and our love, for these are what is supreme in religion, or rather in these alone is religion to be found.[16]

Over five centuries, English Catholic responses to these fundamental questions have sought to exhibit radiant truth in doctrine, heroic goodness in human lives, and more than earthly beauty in literary art. In representing the tradition of More's 'known' Church of Christ, Newman's 'One Fold of the Redeemer',[17] and the 'Thing' awaiting Chesterton at the end of his adventure in orthodoxy, we want to provide our own handbook for anyone who wishes to understand the faith, hope, and love summed up in the affirmation of Gerontius: *Firmly I believe and truly*.

---

[14] Alban Butler, *The Lives of the Fathers, Martyrs, and other Principal Saints*, 4 vols. (London, 1756), i, p. iv.

[15] The editors of *Love's Redeeming Work*, an anthology of Anglican writing that has served as a model for our own Catholic compilation, describe their work as 'handbook for faithful living, a resource for wisdom on leading an intelligent, humble, and grateful life of discipleship'. See *Love's Redeeming Work: The Anglican Quest for Holiness*, ed. Geoffrey Rowell, Kenneth Stevenson, and Rowan Williams (Oxford: Oxford University Press, 2003), p. xiii.

[16] *Enchiridion ad Laurentium, sive De fide, spe, et caritate*, cap. 4; Patrologia Latina 40. 232–3.

[17] See p. 452 below.

# PART I

## 1483–1688

'The Spilled Chalice', one in the series of 'a painted life' of Venerable Mary Ward in the trusteeship of the Congregation of Jesus, Augsburg. Reproduced by permission of the Congregation of Jesus in Augsburg, and with the assistance of Sister Christina Kenworthy-Browne of the Bar Convent in York.

This picture (painted after her and death and still in the possession of the Community she founded) shows a crucial episode in the life of Venerable Mary Ward. The original inscription reads (in translation from the German): 'When Mary Ward's confessor was saying Mass in London in 1650, it happened by divine permission that he inadvertently spilt the chalice. This wrought such a change in him that when Mary, after Mass, respectfully handed him the towel to dry his hands, he said to her with tears streaming from his eyes:"I will never more hinder your religious design, but further you all I can."'

# 'Dungeon, Fire and Sword': The Creation of an Enduring Tradition

The first three works ever printed in the English language on specifically religious subjects all came out during the short and contentious reign of Richard III. And they set the scene for the whole of the first part of this book. By 1483 William Caxton had published romances and histories in English and liturgical and devotional books in Latin and French. And then in quick succession he published what we present below: a twelfth-century monk's vision of purgatory; a prayer begging for forgiveness in and through confession, communion, and the intercession of 'Our Lady Saint Mary, and all the holy company of Heaven'; and the story of the creation of a major pilgrimage site in the seventh century.[1] English Catholicism in the late fifteenth century was vibrant, deeply aware of both its English past and also how firmly it was embedded in the Western Latin Church which it would not fail to call 'Universal'. It was above all a Church where the doctrine of the communion of the saints, the dead praying for the living and the living praying for the dead, was at the heart of its devotional life. Despite all the horrors of the Reformation and the subsequent persecutions, this focus was never to be lost.

This first part of the book has, as its prelude, a selection of spiritual writings up to Henry VIII's schism. It notes the anxieties of leading churchmen like John Colet, the humanist dean of St Paul's in London, about clerical abuse,[2] but it focuses on the rich sacramental life and commitment to the communion of the saints that Eamon Duffy has demonstrated so powerfully in his writings.[3] This is followed by what could be called the struggle for control of the hearts and minds of Englishmen, beginning with the testimony of the two most prominent victims of Henry VIII's legal tyranny, St John Fisher and St Thomas More.[4] What the selections make clear is that the closer they came to death, the firmer became their faith and trust in God.[5] This is followed by extracts from official and non-official

---

[1] See below, pp. 3–11.

[2] See below, pp. 25–7.

[3] E. Duffy, *The Stripping of the Altars: Traditional Religion in England, c.1400–c.1580* (New Haven and London: Yale University Press, 1992); and E. Duffy, *Marking the Hours: English People and their prayers, 1240–1570* (New Haven and London: Yale University Press, 2006).

[4] See below, pp. 31–40, 52–63.

[5] For Fisher, the best all-round biography is M. Dowling, *Fisher of Men: A Life of John Fisher, 1469–1535* (New York: St Martin's Press, 1999); but see also R. Rex, *The Theology of John Fisher* (Cambridge: Cambridge University Press, 1991). For More, there is a vast literature. The classic biography is R. W. Chambers, *Thomas More* (London: Jonathan Cape, 1935). For one that is informed and deeply sympathetic, E. E. Reynolds, *The Field is Won: The Life and Death of Saint Thomas More* (Milwaukee: Bruce Publishing Co., 1968) or, more recently, L. Martz, *Thomas More: The Search for the Inner Man* (New Haven: Yale University Press, 1990). An excellent recent study of a key relationship is J. Guy, *A Daughter's Love: Thomas and Margaret More* (London: Fourth Estate, 2008). The two contemporary lives have been made available by the Early English Text Society: W. Roper, *The Lyfe of Sir Thomas Moore, Knighte*, ed. E. V. Hitchcock (Early English Text Society, original series, 197, 1935); N. Harpsfield, *The Life and Death of Sr Thomas Moore, Knight*, ed. E. V. Hitchcock (Early English Text Society, original ser., 186, 1932). There is an exemplary modern edition of all More's writings,

writings from the attempted Restoration under Mary I. Here examples of powerful preaching and catechetical teaching are laid out alongside some of the documents framing the largely successful Marian attempt to restore the sacraments and devotional life of the nation,[6] even though all this had to go along with her acceptance of the impossibility of reclaiming the things that the first Reformation had plundered in an orgy of greed: the lands, monastic churches, and charitable activities of 800 religious houses, the chantry chapels and parish guilds, the great shrines and pilgrimage centres.[7] Perhaps because the legacy of the past was in so many places reduced to the 'bare ruined choirs'[8] standing gaunt against the sunlit landscape, there was an even greater emphasis in Catholic writing on memorializing that legacy in print and in prayer.[9] Thus, Thomas Stapleton, sometime Fellow of New College Oxford and prebend of Chichester, spent his early years in Catholic exile (1559–1656) translating Bede's *The History of the Church of England* into English with an irenical preface begging Elizabeth to return the Church in England to its rightful place within the universal church.[10] Meanwhile Elizabeth, determined, as she put it, not to make windows into men's souls, created a church which 'looked Catholic and sounded Protestant'[11] and which a vast majority of the population, with varying degrees of heaviness of heart, found they could worship in.

All that was to change in 1570. What triggered the change was a revolt at the end of 1569 by Catholics who could accept neither Elizabeth as their Queen, nor the Church of England as a true Church.[12] Catastrophically, after much hesitation and in defiance of the general papal principle of playing it long, Pope Pius V issued a bull to help the rebels to broaden the basis of their support by declaring that Elizabeth was a heretic tyrant.[13] By the time the Bull arrived the rebellion had failed, but the government response had not been finalized, and it triggered a much fiercer reaction than had been planned. It led to decades of persecution and horror for those who separated from the Church of England. The Queen, Council, and Parliament now set out to force those who publicly worshipped in the Established

St Thomas More, *The Yale Edition of the Complete Works of St Thomas More*, 15 vols. (New Haven and London: Yale University Press, 1963–97).

[6] For a full recent account, see E. Duffy, *Fires of Faith: Catholic England under Mary Tudor* (New Haven and London: Yale University Press, 2009).

[7] See below, pp. 167–8.

[8] The phrase is from Shakespeare's Sonnet 73, and refocused as the title of a book by Dom David Knowles, *Bare Ruined Choirs: The Dissolution of the English Monasteries* (Cambridge: Cambridge University Press, 1976). But for a full account and analysis of the consequences, see A. Walsham, *The Reformation of the Landscape* (Oxford: Oxford University Press, 2011).

[9] For the oral and manuscript tradition, see A. Shell, *Oral Culture and Catholicism in Early Modern England* (Cambridge: Cambridge University Press, 2007). Chapter 1 of the book takes up the theme of ruined abbeys and sacrilege.

[10] See below, pp. 97–9.

[11] C. Russell, 'The Reformation and the Creation of the Church of England, 1500–1640, in J. Morrill, *The Oxford Illustrated History of Tudor and Stuart Britain* (Oxford: Oxford University Press, 1996), 280—referring to clerical vestments (Catholic not reformed) and liturgical actions during the Holy Communion service (and in the use of the sign of the cross etc.)

[12] By far the best and most pertinent discussion is K. Kesselring, *The Northern Rebellion of 1569: Faith, Politics, and Politics in Elizabethan England* (Basingstoke: Palgrave Macmillan, 2007).

[13] See below, pp. 104–6.

Church while privately seeking out Catholic rites when opportunity presented itself to choose where their allegiance truly lay. It created a recusant community.[14] And Parliament approved, and the Crown and its agents irregularly enforced, a penal code designed to terrorize the recusant community.[15] It was directed first and foremost at the clergy trained in the seminaries established abroad: in Rome, France, and Spain and the Low Countries. Simply to be a priest ordained outside England and owing allegiance to the See of Rome, was deemed to be treason, and all such seminary priests found in England and Wales were to be mutilated and butchered as traitors. In just seventeen years more than 120 were executed and 150 imprisoned.[16] Between 1580 and 1606, some forty were severely tortured under warrants issued by the Privy Council (not to establish their guilt, but to secure evidence against those who had assisted them or to discover the whereabouts of other priests).[17] Those who harboured priests were subject to sometimes long periods in prison, and a few were executed.[18] The 'penal laws' imposed oaths that disqualified Catholics from public life (office in central or local government and in parliament, education at the universities and the inns of court etc).[19] In fact, by

[14] The classic accounts are J. C. H. Aveling, *The Handle and the Axe: The Catholic Recusants in England from the Reformation to Emancipation* (London: Blond & Briggs, 1976); J. Bossy, *The English Catholic Community 1570–1850* (London: Darton, Longman, Todd, 1975). The latter is to read alongside important revisionist articles by Christopher Haigh, especially 'The Continuity of Catholicism in the English Reformation', *Past and Present*, 93 (1981), 37–69. There is an excellent short students' introduction by M. Mullett, *Catholicism in Britain and Ireland 1558–1829* (Basingstoke: Palgrave Macmillan, 1998).

[15] For an account of these laws and some pointed comparisons with the later penal laws in Ireland, see J. Morrill, 'The Causes of the Popery Laws: Paradoxes and Inevitabilities', *Eighteenth Century Ireland: Iris an dá chultúr* (2010), forthcoming.

[16] Taking the longer period of 1570–1603, in all 800 English and Welsh seminary priests were ordained: 144 were executed, 180 imprisoned, most of them released and/or deported, 50 defected to Protestantism, 150 remained on the continent in other mission fields or in seminary work, and 280 served in England, under threat but not apprehended (although in many cases the authorities knew where they were). For an explanation, see below.

[17] The best discussion of the legal use of torture in England is J. Langbeim, *Torture and the Law of Proof: Europe and England in the Ancien Regime* (Chicago: Chicago UP, 1977).

[18] The most (in)famous example was St Margaret Clitherow, who was crushed to death with heavy stones (*peine forte et dure*) for refusing to plead to a charge of harbouring priests in York (1585). This was the standard penalty for such refusal but it was so clearly unjust that it became a cause célèbre. None of her own words survives and the highly fabricated account of her martyrdom by Fr John Mush was not published until modern times. For the received account of her martyrdom in the eighteenth century, see below, An outstanding analysis of her story and its polemical consequences is being published by Peter Lake and Michael Questier, *The Trials of Margaret Clitherow* (in press).

[19] The text of the Oath of Supremacy (1559) is accurately made available online at <http://www.luminarium.org/encyclopedia/actsupremacyeliza.htm>; and the Oath of Allegiance (1606) at <http://history.wisc.edu/sommerville/361/oath%20allegiance.htm>. The Oath of Supremacy required that 'I, A. B., do utterly testify and declare in my conscience that the Queen's Highness is the only supreme governor of this realm, and of all other her Highness's dominions and countries, as well in all spiritual or ecclesiastical things or causes, as temporal, and that no foreign prince, person, prelate, state or potentate hath or ought to have any jurisdiction, power, superiority, pre-eminence or authority ecclesiastical or spiritual within this realm' while the Act of Allegiance added clauses (written to exclude casuistical interpretation) explicitly denouncing papal claims made in *Regnans in excelsis*. The Test Acts (1672, 1678) required of all seeking public office an explicit denial of the doctrine of transubstantiation. The most important recent discussion of the Oath of Allegiance, supplanting much previous work, is J. Sommerville, 'Papalist Political Thought and the Controversy over the Jacobean Oath of Allegiance', in E. Shagan (ed.), *Catholics and the 'Protestant Nation': Religious Politics and Identity in Early Modern England* (Manchester: Manchester University Press, 2005) a book with several other important essays on themes in this book.

statute refusing the Oath of Supremacy three times could have led to execution, but successive rulers prohibited the repeated tender of the Oath. The penal laws provided for crippling fines for those convicted of attending the Mass or possessing Catholic religious objects (sacred vessels for the Mass, crucifixes, rosaries, etc.), and two levels of fine (twelve pence a week or £20 a month) for any head of household who failed to attend worship in his or her parish church. Interestingly when the higher level of fines were introduced, the lower ones were not repealed and it was the lower ones which were usually collected even from the gentry and nobility. There were laws that prevented Catholics from moving more than five miles from their home without a licence, and these laws were occasionally enforced and were available to vindictive local magistrates at all times.

Catholics lived under the threat of these laws for about 100 years; and although penalties for religious observance became less and less frequent and harsh from 1650 onwards, discrimination and exclusion from public life existed until well into the nineteenth century and cultural prejudice for longer still. But the period of really sharp persecution lasted for less than thirty years, from 1580 to 1606. In the period 1607–52, less than one priest a year was executed; no priest was condemned to death in Britain under the Cromwellian Protectorate[20] and none in the Restoration, except during the Popish Plot panics of 1679–81.[21] About one in ten of all the priests ordained on the Continent between 1570 and 1690 and who served in the English mission were executed; about 20 per cent were imprisoned and/or deported; about two-thirds lived in constant fear but were in fact unmolested.[22] Except in the years 1641–52, a large majority of the priests who arrived after 1610 were now able to move freely if discreetly around the country and to celebrate the sacraments in private houses; fewer and fewer Catholics were locked up decade by decade; recusancy fines were collected at the lower rate, and indeed many Catholics (all those willing to do so) bought a kind of season ticket, a dispensation from the laws requiring attendance at church. Increasingly the state saw these as a source of revenue rather than an attempt to compel attendance. The laws were never repealed (except that the recusancy laws were repealed between 1650 and 1660), but they were less and less enforced. Catholic homes would be (roughly) searched for arms whenever there was a security scare, and a number of priests rounded up, interrogated, and usually released, but it is a mistake to think of the reign of terror, of dungeon, fire, and sword, as lasting for a century or more. It lasted, to put it brutally, as long as some Catholics engaged in acts designed to overthrow Elizabeth, by assassination or insurrection and to promote regime change. The response of the Protestant state was disproportionate but not irrational. The regime always acted in the knowledge that it had to target the militants

---

[20] St John Southworth was indeed executed in 1654, but under a sentence passed in 1627. See below, pp. 235–8. And for a fuller discussion, see John Morrill, 'Southworth, John [St John Southworth] (1592–1654)', *Oxford Dictionary of National Biography*, Oxford University Press, 2004 <http://www.oxforddnb.com/view/article/67460, accessed 1 March 2010>.

[21] For the executions in 1678–81, see J. Miller, *Popery and Politics in England 1660–1688* (Cambridge: Cambridge University Press, 1973).

[22] J. Morrill, 'Confrontation and Collusion: The State and the Catholic Community in the Penal Times' forthcoming, in a festschrift.

without radicalizing the moderate majority.[23] It knew that its main problem lay with foreign-trained clergy more than with the one-fifth of the nobility, one-tenth of the gentry, and perhaps one in thirty of the population who embraced the Catholic faith. It considered and abandoned (as in a bill debated in parliament in 1593) even more draconian laws including the removal of children from convicted recusant fathers for education in Protestant households, the confiscation of property for persistent recusancy, and fines on householders who did not compel their family and servants to attend parish worship. Almost all those things which made the Irish Penal Code of 1690–1720 so vindictive were considered and rejected by the Elizabethan regime as too vindictive. They did not do all they could have done to terrorize Catholics, and enforcement was consciously piecemeal.[24]

And Catholic response was itself considered and piecemeal. Successive popes resisted suggestions that they appoint bishops to English sees, and until the worst of the persecution was over, they did not appoint bishops *in partibus infidelium* with pastoral oversight of England, preferring instead to appoint secular priests to the anomalous position of 'archpriest'. The successors of Pope St Pius V did not cancel his Bull *Regnans in Excelsis*, but they released all English Catholics from the obligation to act in accordance with its demand for non-obedience to heretic monarchs in civil matters. Although the spiritual directors at the English College in Rome trained priests to take a tough stance on 'church popery' or insincere and occasional lay participation in protestant worship (and rites of passage) as a means of mitigating the law, Pope Clement VIII granted Anne of Denmark a dispensation to attend the chapel royal and to have her and James VI and I's children baptized as Protestants. The vast majority of Catholics struggled to distinguish between a secular obedience to Elizabeth and her Stuart successors and a religious obedience to the See of Rome in all matters of faith and morals. Catholic laity had to draw two jagged lines: on the extent of compromise with the state, and on the degree of compromise with their priests and confessors.[25]

All this provides the context for the material offered in this book, which tries faithfully to portray the theory and practice of English Catholic piety in the penal times. As we will see, it records the heroism of the martyrs, it records the attempts of men and women to accept and to grow through both suffering and discrimination, it shows some remarkable examples of living faith in action. It shows a faith completely secure in its rootedness in time and place. But alongside that it shows the stresses and strains of a community under internal as well as external stress. Thus we find arguments for accepting the brokenness of the world and for living in that broken world as it is, not as we would want it to be. Cardinal William Allen and Robert Parsons SJ prevaricated about the extent of their collusion in international plans to overthrow Elizabeth and claimed to accept Elizabeth as de facto if

---

[23] For a recent discussion of this 'quadrille' as he puts it between Protestant state and catholic commissioners, see P. Collinson, 'The Politics of Religion and the Religion of Politics in Elizabethan England', *Historical Research*, 82/215 (2009), 74–92, where he speaks of the 'quadrille' between the ministers of state and the leaders of the Catholic mission.

[24] Morrill, 'Popish Laws', forthcoming.

[25] For this paragraph, see A. Walsham, *Church Papists: Catholicism, Conformity and Confessional Polemic in Early Modern England* (London: Royal Historical Society Studies in History, 1993); and M. Questier, *Catholicism and Community in Early Modern England: Politics, Aristocratic Patronage and Religion c.1550–1640* (Cambridge: Cambridge University Press, 2006).

not de jure Queen of England.[26] They permitted Catholic priests on the mission to travel without their breviaries as a way of reducing the risk of arrest; and to eat meat on Fridays when at table with heretics in certain circumstances.[27] Many priests in the confessional and in their spiritual counsel acknowledged that it was too much to expect ordinary Catholics to bring complete ruin on themselves and their posterity, and condoned occasional attendance at protestant services so long as ears stayed closed, hearts stony. Some Catholics had their children baptized twice, and treated the Protestant wedding rite as forming a contract that the state could accept and the Catholic rite as the covenant between the consenting couple and God. Most Catholics were able to bury their dead in the middle of the night (with the collusion of Protestant ministers and churchwardens) in ground consecrated centuries before (even some priests including, it is said, Augustine Baker OSB were buried in Anglican churchyards); but where that was not possible, they consented to Protestant burial and separate Catholic Requiem. Catholics took oaths which the Pope and the leaders of the English mission had made clear could not be taken because they believed that oaths forced on conscience were not binding in the absence of true consent.[28] As we have suggested, almost all Catholics compromised to an extent, some much more than others.

There was always a party amongst the clergy with strong lay support that sought an accommodation with the state. This generally took the form of a search for a new oath, binding in nature, that would replace the oaths of supremacy and allegiance and that would unequivocally promise political obedience to the Protestant state in return for freedom of worship. Attempts at such deals can be found from the 1590s onwards and reached a peak in the mid-seventeenth century when the theologically liberal 'Blackloists' controlled the Chapter, the ruling council of secular priests.[29] Their efforts were always frowned on by Rome and never came as close to realization as they believed possible; but that was not clear to those engaged in serious negotiations. This is part of the Catholic story, and is part of the calculation of those living under prejudice and the threat of spasmodic persecution. It is therefore reflected in the pages that follow.

There was then a debate at the heart of the Catholic mission between on the one hand those who believed that ultimately only the blood of the martyrs could atone for the apostasy of England and who willingly laid down their lives in that cause when their attempts to evade capture failed, and on the other hand those

[26] Eamon Duffy, in his superb life of Cardinal Allen for the *Oxford Dictionary of National Biography* shows how Allen schemed for the overthrow of Elizabeth but was very careful not to share knowledge of any of his 'treasons' with the priests he sent on the mission. So he at once maintained that they were simple pastors while at the same time planning in detail for the post-revolution creation of a Catholic confessional state with himself as Archbishop of Canterbury, Papal Legate *and* Lord Chancellor. Eamon Duffy, 'Allen, William (1532–1594)', *Oxford Dictionary of National Biography*, Oxford University Press, Sept 2004; online edn., Oct 2008 <http://www.oxforddnb.com/view/article/391>, accessed 26 Feb. 2010.

[27] See the fascinating cases of conscience edited by P. J. Holmes. *Elizabethan Casuistry* (Catholic Record Society, 1981), 67–71.

[28] For all this, see Bossy, *English Catholic Community*, esp. chs. 6–8; Aveling, *The Handle and the Axe*, chs. 4–8; Walsham, *Church Papists*, *passim*.

[29] The standard printed study is by B. Southgate, *Covetous for Truth: The Life and Work of Thomas White, 1593–1676* (Dordrecht: Kluwer, 1993). Blacklo was the pen name of Thomas White. For a revelatory study that takes the subject much further see, Anthony Brown, 'Anglo-Irish Gallicanism, c.1635–c.1685' (Univ. of Cambridge Ph.D. thesis, 2004).

who were willing to make a series of accommodations with successive rulers in order to ensure that the Catholic communities of England should have the sacraments available to them on a regular base. They too embraced the possibility of death by torture and they taught the rigid separation of Catholics from the demands of the Protestant state, but they saw the teaching as unrealistic and they softened that teaching in their daily practice; and as a result they were not targeted by the state. 'The man who lives in the world as though the world is the way he hopes it is going to be, is a crank!' was Clem Attlee's response to left-wing criticism when he sent his son to be privately educated at Haileybury.[30] It was a mindset that always has and always will exist; and many Catholics then as now lived in the world as it was, not as it should be, and sought and seek to build the kingdom by nudges not by dramatic confrontation, by small sacrifices not massive ones.[31]

The story we tell is that story. It is a very English story. The penal times were hard times, and yet it is almost certain that there was never a decade between the 1570s and 1680s when the number of English Catholics and indeed the proportion of the population who were Catholic was not growing. The number of people embracing exclusion from public life and actual or probable persecution (for new converts would be targeted by the authorities) is a testimony to the witness of those already Catholic, and to the power and conviction of the written testimony in the thousands of books and pamphlets written and published by the Catholic community. If most had to be published abroad and smuggled into England, and if much of it was written by priests and religious abroad, it addressed the situation in England. Conversion, as in the case of Benjamin Carier, a court preacher before he was reconciled, often involved engagement with the facts of the English Reformation and its wretched contamination with greed in the 1530s and 1540s.[32] It often had to do with the *locus* of authority. It also had to do with the impressive Biblicism of Catholic apologists, above all it had to do with a deeply rooted sacramentalism. But if one word sums up the source of the inexorable Catholic growth it would be Catholic witness, and not just the disturbing witness of the men dragged from the torture chambers to Tyburn to be half-hanged, emasculated, eviscerated, and cut into pieces, but also the quiet witness of neighbours or relations, so obviously trying to maintain loyalty both to monarch and pope and what each represented. Here in part 1 of *Fully I Believe and Truly* we present the words of the mission's leaders, from William Allen and Robert Parsons in the late sixteenth century to the vicars apostolic John Leyburn and Bonaventure Giffard at the end of the seventeenth century;[33] the words of five devotional books printed over the course of 150 years which reveal the prayer life of so many members of the Catholic community,[34] the words of martyrs and

---

[30] Quoted in *The Times*, 13 Jan. 2007, accessible at <http://www.timesonline.co.uk/tol/life_and_style/education/article1292400.ece>.

[31] Questier, *Catholicism and Community*; P. Holmes, *Resistance and Compromise: The Political Thought of Elizabethan Catholics* (Cambridge: Cambridge University Press, 1982).

[32] See below, pp. 180–2. C. Kenworthy-Browne, *Mary Ward (1585–1645): A Briefe Relation—with Autobiographical Fragments and a Selection of Letters* (Woodbridge: Boydell and Brewer for the Catholic Record Society, 2008).

[33] See below, pp. 110–12, 139–50, 245–9.

[34] See below, pp. 134–7, 162–6, 227–8, 241–5.

enclosed nuns, of many poets, of priests from all the major orders with English missions, of laymen mainly as they lay in prison. We include the conversion narrative not only of Benjamin Carier but of the first wife of the future King James II (Anne, duchess of York).[35] Behind the richness of theological tradition and engagement, is what will probably strike most readers as a pessimism about the human condition that is deeply Augustinian but alleviated and redeemed by a profound sense of sacramental grace and by what Protestantism had almost completely rejected, a deep sense of the communion of saints, and especially of the powerful intercession of Our Lady and the saints for all those struggling to overcome the burden of this-worldly obsessions. For all the ferocious disagreements within the Catholic community (and they were really ferocious; and amongst the millions of words written polemically in the period 1570–1690, probably more than half were directed at internal, not external, opponents) what anchored Catholic faith and practice was a deep sense of time and place. When John Wilson set out to commemorate the Elizabethan martyrs he began with a calendar of British saints from the time of Christ to the Norman period, one for every day of the year;[36] when Thomas Stapleton wanted to say what it was to be a Catholic in England, he translated Bede's *History*.[37] The great mystics of the medieval English tradition (above all Walter Hilton and *The Cloud of Unknowing*) were retranslated, but so were the great mystics and teachers of continental Catholicism. You Catholics were a hounded minority in late Tudor and Stuart England, the literature said in sum, but in the greater scheme of things, in the long history of your people and in the history of the world, you are the One Holy, Catholic, and Apostolic Church.

---

[35] See below, pp. 180–2, 239–41.
[36] See below, pp. 172.
[37] See below, pp. 95–104.

# William Caxton
*c.*1420–1492

Caxton spent a quarter of a century trading in cloth before he fell in love with a new technology he encountered on his visits to the Netherlands. At the age of about 55, in 1475 or 1476, he brought the first printing press to England and set it up in premises within the precincts of Westminster Abbey. He produced just over 100 works during the remaining years of his life, most of them in English. He specialized in popular histories, romances, and fables, but he also published some liturgical books in Latin, including the Ordinal of the Sarum rite in 1477. Most of Caxton's works were book length, but some were single sheets produced at the behest of others—such as advertisements for Indulgences. One very beautiful example of these ephemera is this anonymous prayer, published on a single-sheet and intended for daily use, in 1484. It is the first work of Catholic spirituality printed in the English language.

## A Prayer for Forgiveness

O glorious Jesu, o meekest Jesu, O most sweetest Jesu, I pray that I may have true confession, contrition and satisfaction or I die. And that I may see and receive thy holy body, God and Man, Saviour of all mankind, Christ Jesu without sin; and that thou wilt, my Lord God, forgive me all my sins for thy glorious wounds and passion; and that I may end my life in the true faith of all-Holy Church; and in perfect love and charity with my even Christian as thy creature. And I commend my soul into thy holy hands through the glorious help of thy blessed mother of mercy, Our Lady Saint Mary, and all the holy company of Heaven. Amen.

The holy Body of Christ Jesu be my salvation of body and soul. Amen. The Glorious blood of Christ Jesu bring my soul and body into the everlasting bliss. Amen. I cry God mercy; I cry God mercy; I cry God mercy; welcome my maker; welcome my redeemer; welcome my Saviour; I cry thee mercy with heart contrite of my great unkindness that I have had unto thee.

O the most sweetest spouse of my soul Christ Jesu, desiring heartily evermore for to be with thee in mind and will. And to let none earthly thing be so nigh mine heart as thou, Christ Jesu. And that I dread not for to die for to go to the Christ Jesu. And that I may evermore say unto thee with a glad cheer: my Lord, my God, my sovereign Saviour Christ Jesu. I beseech thee heartily, take me sinner unto thy great mercy and grace. For I love thee with all my heart, with all my mind, with all my might; and no thing so much in earth nor above earth as I do thee, my sweet Lord Christ Jesu. And for that I have not loved thee and worshipped thee above all thing as my Lord, my God and my Saviour Christ Jesu, I beseech thee with meekness and heart contrite, of mercy and of forgiveness of my great unkindness for the great love that thou showest for me and all mankind, what time thou offerest thy glorious body God and man unto the Cross, there to be crucified and wounded. And unto thy glorious heart a sharp spear, there running out plenteously blood and water for the redemption and salvation of me and all mankind. And thus having remembrance steadfastly in my heart of thee, my Saviour Christ Jesu, I doubt not but thou wilt be full nigh and comfort me both bodily and ghostly with thy glorious presence and at the last bring me unto thy everlasting bliss, the which shall never have end. Amen. (1)

NOTES AND SOURCES

1. Anon. *O glorious Ihesu, O meekest Jhesu* (1484)

**Adam of Eynsham(*c.*1155–*c.*1233) as published by William Caxton**

After a decade of works rooted in classical and popular vernacular literature—including the works of Chaucer—Caxton branched out into vernacular religious publication, beginning with the translation of a popular medieval account of visions experienced by Adam, a young monk in the Benedictine Abbey of Eynsham (close to Oxford). Adam of Eynsham (c.1155–c.1233) went on to become Abbot and to write a commissioned *Magna Vita* or biography of his patron and friend, Bishop Hugh of Lincoln, a life which promoted the cause of Hugh (canonized by Pope Honorius III in 1220). Adam's vision of Purgatory and paradise (but not of Hell) had circulated widely in manuscript in England during the thirteenth, fourteenth and fifteenth centuries, and was published by Caxton with his own prologue, in 1484. Here are the prologue and the evocative preliminary description of Adam's vision.

# Adam of Eynsham's Vision

The revelation that followeth here in this book treateth how a certain devout person the which was a monk in the abbey of Eynsham was rapt in spirit by the will of God and laid by the hand of Saint Nicholas the space of two days and two nights to see and know the pains of Purgatory and the joys of paradise and in what state the souls were that were in Purgatory and also in paradise. Soothly in both these places he saw and knew many persons both men and women, the which he knew well before when they lived in this world and spake with them there, mouth to mouth, in both the places as he found them, as it followeth well after in this book. This revelation was not showed to him only for him but also for the comfort and profiting of all Christian people that no man should doubt or mistrust of another life and world, the which every man and woman must go to and like as they deserve here in this world by here living so there to be rewarded. And as for the truth of this revelation, no man nor woman ought to doubt in any wise. For any man well read and understanding the beginning with the ending shall so largely see it approved in great miracles by Almighty God showed unto the same person that same time that all reasons and motions of infidelity, the which riseth oftentimes of man's sensuality, shall outwardly be excluded and quenched and greatly shall cause all Christian people that heareth it to dread God and love Him, and also to praise Him in His works. For such another revelation and so open was never shewed in this land nor in any other that we read of . . .

Here beginneth a marvellous revelation that was showed of Almighty God by Saint Nicholas to a monk of Evesham in the days of King Richard the First in the year of our Lord 1196.

In a Monastery called Eynsham there was a certain young man turned with faithful devotion from this world's vanity to the life of a monk the which about the beginning of his conversion fell into a great and grievous sickness and by the space of fifteen months was sore laboured with great feebleness and weakness of body. Also his stomach abhorred so greatly meat and drink that sometime by the space of nine days or more he might receive nothing but a little wan water. And what sum everything of leech-craft or physic any man did to him for his comfort or his amendment nothing him helped but all turned contrary. Therefore he lay sick in his bed greatly destitute of bodily strength so that he might not move himself from one place to another but by help of servants. Also in the last months of his sickness, he was more sorely diseased and enfeebled than ever he was before. Nevertheless then coming on the Feast of Easter [1196], suddenly he began somewhat to amend in his bodily mights and with his staff walked about the infirmary. Soothly on this eve of Maundy Thursday in the which night the office and service of our Lord Jesu Christ's Passion was solemnly sung with great devotion, he went with his staff to the church [together] with his brethren, the which by cause of sickness rested also with him in the infirmary where the night service and lauds were offered up to Our Lord. And there by the respect of heavenly grace so great compunction and sweetness, he received that his holy devotion exceeded measure wherefore he might not contain him from weeping and lauding God from midnight until six of the bell in the morning what for remembering with worship and joy the mercies of Our Lord, the which he hath done for mankind, and also remembering with sore weeping his offences and sins done in former times and the hurt and the state of his present imperfection. (1)

NOTES AND SOURCES

1. [Adam of Eynsham], *The Prologe of this Reuelation* (1483).

## A twelfth century life of St Winifred published by William Caxton

St Winifred (or Gwenfrewi), flourished around the year 650. She was a niece of St Beuno, by whom she was educated, and she lived a chaste and holy life in North Wales, near St Asaph. The well close to where she lived became the most important Holy Well in medieval Wales, and she was accepted as a saint by local people and then by the Church as a whole from soon after her death. Her body was translated to Shrewsbury in 1138, and to coincide with that, two exemplary lives were written about her,[1] one in Welsh, the other in Norman French. Caxton took one of the many manuscript copies of the latter of these and translated it into English for his edition, published in 1485—to coincide with the Tudors (a Welsh family) assuming the throne of England. The emphasis is on her purity of life and—a crucial part of medieval spirituality—a good, well-prepared death.[2]

# St Winifred's Exemplary Life

Here beginneth the life of the holy and Blessed Virgin saint Winifred. In the west end of Great Britain, which now is called England is a province which is named Wales. This said province was sometime inhabited by saints of many and diverse merits and embellished and decorate unto this day with innumerable prerogatives in many wises, amongst whom there was an holy and devout man named Beuno, a man of high merit and this holy man led religious life and was a monk in the

---

[1] The Welsh version tells of her death defending her virginity against a lascivious prince, Caradog ab Alog, who cut off her head as she fled from him. Where her head fell, the sacred spring miraculously appeared. The Welsh poem is a plea for her body to remain where she lived and died, this version for its removal to somewhere where more pilgrims could access it.

[2] For later accounts of her life, following the alternative tradition in which Winifred died protecting her virginity, see below, pp. 283–5.

said England. He edified churches and ordained certain brethren and priests for to serve God in many places, and it was so that by divive providence he was warned and admonished to desire and ask of a mighty man named Tyfid[3] a certain place to build on a church for his health which he diligently demanded and the said Tyfid granted to him gladly and with good will and also committed to him his daughter named Winifred whom he would tender for to be instruct and taught, praying him to beseech almighty God that he would dispose her conversation to the will and honour of Him...

On a night as she was in her oratory, Our Lord let her have knowledge of the day of her obit and departing out of this life which should hastily ensue and follow. And anon as she understood and felt herself called and visited by the grace of God, she with an holy devotion began to make her ready unto the joys that she was called to, then continually in the nights she was praying in the Church and in the day time she virtuously occupied herself in all things belonging to her cure and charge. And when this rumour came to the knowledge of Saint Ethelwyn, he anon was in great anguish and wailing for the departing of this holy virgin whom he entirely loved, knowing certainly that she was endowed with special grace, and desired for her singular well that as long as she should in the pilgrimage of this life endure that he might dwell and abide with her. And this he desired with great devotion. Then after this the Blessed Virgin began to suffer great sickness in all her body. And as the langour and malady was vehement and increased daily, she knew verily that she approached toward her last end. Then she lifted up her mind toward Almighty God and humbly prayed him to have mercy on her and that he would be the keeper and warden of her soul and that the devil should have no part of her. Then she did do call to her the holy Confessor Saint Elerius[4] the abbot which houseled her with the blessed body of Our Lord. Then the day of the kalends of November she began to wax feeble by the dissolution of her body but for all that she rested not for all her pain and sickness to preach and inform them that were assistant with holy and blessed exhortations. Then when she was enfeebled with overmuch pain of grievous sicknesses and felt well that on the morn she should depart and finish her bodily life, she called to her St Elerius and prayed him that her body might be buried and put in the sepulchre by the body of St Theonia his mother which request the holy man granted benignly. And then the holy virgin intending with all her whole heart in prayer unto Almighty God the day of the third None of November she commended her spirit into the hands of her maker to be associate unto the celestial company of saints. Then the holy man, commending her soul unto God, began to procure busily and make all thing ready that he saw appertain to the exequies of the Blessed Virgin; and when all was done that appertained to her funeral service, he buried her in the place that she desired, and with great wailings and lamentations her body was laid in the sepulchre. And in the same place the said body lay unto the time of King Stephen, King of England, in whose time by divine revelations and miracles before going, the

---

[3] Tyfid ab Eiludd, who owned land in the Sychnant Valley, in which Winifred's Holy Well stands. Beuno became a personal chaplain to Tyfid, saying Mass for him and his family and he received land in exchange for his services.

[4] Elerius founded a double monastery in the Vale of Clwyd, of which Theonia became the abbess.

bones of the Blessed Virgin were translated unto the abbey of Shrewsbury, where much people coming by the suffrages and merits of many asking remedy of their infirmities and sicknesses have been healed and made all whole.

Thus endeth the martyrdom of this blessed saint, Saint Winifred, which passion and decollation was the one and twentieth day of June. (1)

NOTES AND SOURCES

1. Robert, Prior of Shrewsbury, *The Lyf of the Holy Blessed Vyrgyn Saynt Wenefryde* (1485), unpag.

## Wynkyn de Worde                                                    (d. 1534/5)

When William Caxton returned to England with his printing press in 1475/6, he brought with him Wynkyn de Worde, a young man from Lorraine who was for the remaining years of his life his assistant and eventually, from 1492, his successor, initially continuing Caxton's printing from the precincts of Westminster Abbey, and then—after a spell in Fleet Street—in the churchyard of St Paul's Cathedral, which was to remain the centre of English printing for 300 years. Between 1492 and his death in 1534/5 de Worde published more than 1,000 titles, with a stronger emphasis than Caxton had had on religious works (although in the last ten years he was strongly drawn to schismatical works). He published texts created in England that had been widely circulated in manuscript and in Latin, such as the fourteenth-century Augustinian Walter Hilton's *Scala perfectionis*, better known today as *The Ladder of Perfection*, and continental works such as this anonymous devotional *Treatise of Love* translated from the French and published in 1493 (our first extract). The second extract, whose full title correctly identifies the content, also comes from one of his earliest independent publications. It is an adaptation of an earlier, manuscript translation of a Latin text with Carthusian links, and was originally a guide for a female religious written by her spiritual adviser.

### Wake and Pray

The profitable book for man's soul, and right comfortable to the body, and especially in adversity and tribulation, which book is called 'the chastising of God's children'

That holy men and good men been more tempted than others, and how our Lord playeth with his children by example of the mother and her child, and what joy and mirth is in our Lord's presence.

*Vigilate et orate ut non intretis in temptacione.* Wake and pray that you enter not into temptation. These been the words of our Lord Jesu Christ, the which need none other declaration than the same understanding of these self-same words. Therefore I leave divisions of matters plainly to write, as God will give me grace, somewhat of temptations and of remedy against them to your ghostly comfort. Take now then good heed of these holy words: wake and pray that you fall not into temptation. You shall understand continual and busy prayer: when he says 'wake and pray' and when it be that you enter not into temptation, you shall understand that you be not overcome with temptation. Thus have you then by the teaching of our Lord a special remedy against all temptation and that is busy prayer. Prayeth then busily in all time of need. But now to our purpose, take heed what our Lord says. He says not pray that you be not tempted but says that you fall not into temptation. That good Lord knoweth well by his grace and ordinance how profitable it is to good men and women much to be tempted and to be troubled, yet seemeth by his words which he speaketh by the Prophet to a man or to a woman that is troubled: 'I am with him in his tribulation, I shall deliver him and I shall glorify him.' Of this we have example of our holy fathers which grievously were tempted as you shall hereafter. And among all of our glorious lady [*sic*] which passed all other in holiness and most was troubles. Therefore he is deceived that weneth [*sic*] he be holy for he is not tempted. For sooth it is good men and women that travail to be perfect [have] been more tempted than other which be wretched of living. And a cause why is for a mountain the higher it is there is the greater wind, in the same manner, the higher a man's living is the stronger is the temptation of his ghostly enemy. Wherefore if men and women of religion or of any perfection feel no temptations then ought they sorest [= most sorely] to dread, for then they be most tempted when they feel themselves not tempted. Therefore, says St Gregory, then are thou most assailed when thou feelest thyself not assailed.

Also when our Lord suffereth us to be tempted in our beginning, he playeth with us as the mother with the child which sometimes flee-eth away and hideth and suffereth the child to weep and cry and busily to seek her with sobbing and weeping; but thence cometh the mother suddenly with merry cheer and laughing be-clipping her child and kissing and wipeth away the tears. Thus fareth our Lord with us as for a time he withdraweth his grace and comfort from us insomuch that in his absence we been all cold and dry, sweetness have we none nor savour in devotion, slow we been to pray or to travail, the wretched soul suddenly is changed and made full heavy and full of sorrow and care. Then is the body sluggish and the heart full hard and all our spirits so dull that the life of our body is to us noisome. All that we hear or see though it be good yet for the time it is not...

I have rehearsed here shortly what manner of sorrow we have in absence. For you shall have it more openly after. But sayeth now what Joy cometh and matter of Joy by his blessed presence. Anon at his coming the soul waxeth light and joyful, the conscience is clear and much in rest, the spirits that were dull and had been quick and ready to travail and all thing that was hard and sharp and impossible to seeming, anon they wax soft and sweet and all manner of exercise in fasting and in waking and all good works of such exercise is turned into mirth for great desire and love. The soul is filled with charity and all manner of cleanness. She is fed with such ghostly sweetness that for such great liking in ghostly feeding, all outward things been almost forgotten. Thence cometh so merry meditations with plenty of tears of compassion, tears of compunction, tears of love and of devotion and though there come no tears there come other visitations that pass all worldly mirth and therewith so great plenty of grace that what is asked it is granted, what is sought is found and the gate of grace is opened to all that ask thence to enter. (1)

## A Meditation on the Crucifixion

This treatise is of love and speaketh of four of the most special loves that have been in the world and sheweth verily and perfectly by great reasons and causes, how the marvellous and bounteous love that our Lord Jesu Christ had to many souls exceedeth by far all other loves...

Sorrow Inestimable, O anguish singular, he was palmed, that is the true palm of victory, he was crowned with thorns that came to break the thorns of sin. He was sore bound that came to loose them that were in bonds; he was hanged on the cross that raiseth them that had been overthrown; the well of life had thirst, the bread of angels had hunger. And what more? Discipline was beaten, health was wounded, life for a time was dead to slay death without end. There was never none heard of creature that received by many fold so great harm in reward of his great goodness. And then to remember his benignity and his great debonaire [=graciousness of manner] whereof Holy Church maketh great sorrow in a hymn of the Passion, and piteously complaineth that so gracious a body was so cruelly stricken with a spear and pierced so deep with great nails...

When a man see-eth other folk make sorrow, he is more apt to sorrow with them. In like wise behold how many examples were of sorrow when our Lord Jesu Christ died. The unreasonable creatures made sorrow; the sun withdrew his light hiding his beams and became all dark; the hard stones all to break, thus as though they had compassion of their creator; the veil of the temple cleft in two as if it were for anguish of the spouse of Holy Church, whose body was so piteously entreated; the bodies of dead folk arose for example of that sorrow. And that men ought to remember that death with great compassion: and also it is a great example of pity and sorrow the lamentable complaint that his blessed and sorrowful mother made for the death of her sweet son when she was left alone of all friends except for St John to whose keeping she was delivered, beholding then her dear child dead upon the cross hanging between two thieves. Well might she make then the most sorrowful complaint that ever was made...

It may be thought full great sorrow was in his blessed mother when the creatures that felt not made so great sorrow as is before rehearsed. There can no tongue say, nor heart think, how marvellous great sorrows and piteous torments was in the heart of that Blessed Virgin Mary... Now sweet virgin you have yielded with esurience [=great desire] this, that in the birth of your son was changed against nature: for in his birth felt you no sorrow nor pain, but in his death felt you the thousand-fold of sorrows. The mother was near unto the cross at the death of Jesu Christ which she conceived by the Holy Ghost, but she failed both speech and voice which sorrow had taken from her.

O the true word of the very just Simeon,[5] for then was your promise fulfilled of the sword of sorrow when that Blessed Virgin Mary was there present and her sweet son hanged on the cross. She lay at the earth as dead pale and discoloured but her soul lived, as in dying; and yet was she not dead but living as a deadly creature, the sorrows tormented her soul so cruelly that she desired much more to die than live. For after the death of her sweet child full painfully and deadly lived she though she were not utterly dead. That day was she therein full marvellous sorrow awaiting when the blessed body of our Lord Jesu Christ should be taken down off the cross. She wept in saying and said in weeping, Alas, alas, who shall

---

[5] The devout Jew who 'looked forward to the deliverance of Israel' and had been promised he would not die until he had seen 'the Lord's Christ'. When Mary came to Temple for her Purification forty days after the birth of Jesus, Simeon greeted her and his song of prophetic joy, the *nunc dimittis*, read daily at Night Prayer, is the most beautiful of the New Testament canticles (Luke 2: 25–35).

yield to me your sorrowful mother the dead body of her dear love and child, O you cruel Jews, you have accomplished now your desire, wherefore I require you take down this holy body off the cross and yield him to his woeful mother. She being near to the cross beholding full piteously her sweet son Jesu there hanging, then rose she up on her feet and with full great pain pressed her to the cross, where she might best embrace the blessed body of Jesu Christ, to whom she had sometime given suck with her own sweet breasts, but she might not reach him. And then enforced she here with all her power to stretch her as high as she might reach to touch some part of him: wherewith she overthrew to the earth and lay there a great while in marvellous sorrows. But yet again the great fervertness of love made her to arise, coveting her dear son: And enforced her with all her power to draw him to her...

O how grievous martyrdom! O how deep and often sighs! O how this virginal heart was painfully tormented! And this holy soul that was all dissolved in sorrow and this colour that before was fresh as the rose was become so piteously pale; and she all besplattered with the precious blood of her sweet son whereof great plenty fell upon the earth which she with her holy mouth kissed so entirely that she broke the wawes [sic] and clots of that precious blood touching the earth, so wonderfully was she tormented with full great sorrows. O was not this more like a sorrowful dying than a life? And while she was in these torments came a noble man that was named Joseph [of Arimathea] which was truly in his heart a disciple to Jesus; and he went all hardly to Pilate and asked the body of Jesu Christ, which was granted to him. Then took he another man with him that was called Nicodemus. So came they to Golgotha where our Lord was crucified and brought with them their instruments to take out the nails of his hands and feet, and to take him down off the cross. And when that Blessed Virgin saw that they would take him down, she rose up as well as she might for all her sorrow to help them to her power. That one took out the nails and that other sustained his body that it should not fall to the earth and his blessed mother took him by the arm, and as soon as he was taken down, his sweet mother took him in her arms full sorrowfully kissing and clipping him so piteously weeping that she all to wet his blessed visage with her sorrowful tears...

And thence after she had long continued in this travail and torment with sorrowful sighs and weeping, then came Joseph and Nicodemus to wrap up his blessed body in a clean cloth of sandal [= a thin rich silken material] and to lay it in a fair new sepulchre of stone. Thither came thousand thousands of angels to the burying of their Lord...(2)

NOTES AND SOURCES

1. Anon, *The prouffytable boke for manes soule, and right comfortable to the body, and specyally in aduersitee* [and] *tribulacyon, whiche boke is called The chastising of goddes chyldren* (1493), unpag.

2. Anon., *This tretyse is of loue and spekyth of iiij of the most specyall louys that ben in the worlde and shewyth veryly and perfitely bi gret resons and causis, how the meruelous [and] bounteuous loue that our lord Ihesu cryste had to mannys soule excedyth to ferre alle other loues... Whiche tretyse was translatid out of frenshe into englyshe, the yere of our lord M cccc lxxxxiij, by a persone that is vnperfight insuche werke* (1493), unpag.

# Richard Pynson 1448–1529

Richard Pynson was born in Normandy and trained as a glover before transferring to the print trade and settling in London, where he printed more than 500 works specializing in law texts and in Books of Hours and devotional works, all in Latin. *The Holy House of Walsingham*, a work of piety in twenty seven-line stanzas of English verse, is unusual for him. Its publication indicates the central place of Walsingham as a pilgrimage site for 400 years up to the vindictive destruction of the Holy House in 1538. The poem tells the story of the visions experienced by the Lady Richeldis in 1061 and the subsequent miraculous building of the replica of the house in Nazareth where the Blessed Virgin Mary had been visited by Gabriel and had consented to carry the Son of God in her womb. Around this 'Holy House', an Augustinian Priory had been built and it had become a national and indeed international centre of pilgrimage and miraculous healing. Seven English kings had made regular visits, not least Henry VII, who visited it at key moments of his reign, for example before he set out to crush the rebellion that sought to put Lambert Simnel on the throne in 1487. He came there too in 1506 accompanied by his own aged mother, Margaret Beaufort. Henry's journey coincided with the departure of the Controller of his household on a pilgrimage to Jerusalem to which Henry aspired but which his duties prevented. So he sent Sir Richard Guildford as his surrogate to the Holy Land, and he went to Walsingham to plead for pardon for his sins. He was accompanied not only by his mother, but by his son and heir, the future Henry VIII, who was, as king, to return to give thanks for the birth of his first son in 1511 (the child soon died) and again in 1522. But it was one of the first great shrines to suffer in the iconoclasm associated with the dissolution of the monasteries. The Holy House was smashed to pieces in 1538 and the statue of Our Lady was one of several burnt on Thomas Cromwell's orders in Chelsea, mockingly close to the home of St Thomas More, perhaps as part of a campaign to denigrate him. In our first text, we see the poet encouraging pilgrimage to Walsingham and informing potential pilgrims of the wonderful nature of the place. This is followed by an extract from a substantial (120-page) account of a pilgrimage journey from England to the Holy Land that was clearly intended as an aid to meditation and reflection for men and women who knew the Gospels really well. It is the story which can be linked with the story of Henry VII's final visit to Walsingham. Sir Richard Guildford was one of the civil servants closest to Henry VII, serving as the Controller of his Household from 1494 to 1506. Unfortunately, he got caught up in the infighting within the Royal Household and his enemies had him imprisoned in 1505. Henry offered him a deal: a pardon in exchange for undertaking the pilgrimage that Henry VII yearned to make himself to the Holy Land and to pray for Henry in the Holy Places. On the Wednesday of Holy Week 1506 (8 April), as Henry set out for Walsingham, Guildford and his party (including the Augustinian Prior of Guisborough in North Yorkshire) set sail from Rye for France and then onward across Europe. By the end of August they were nearing Jerusalem, travelling up from Jaffa. The third extract offers an account of their first impressions of Jerusalem, and of a subsequent pilgrimage to Mt Sion and a week later to sites within Jerusalem itself, where the pilgrimage had a very dramatic denouement…

## The Holy House of Walsingham

Of this chapel see here the foundation,
Builded the year of Christ's incarnation
A thousand complete sixty and one,
The time of Saint Edward King of this region.

Behold and see you ghostly folks all,
Which to this place have devotion.
When you to Our Lady asking succour call
Desiring here her help in your tribulation.
Of this her chapel you may see the foundation
If you will this table oversee and read,
How by miracle it was founded indeed.

A noble widow sometime lady of this town
Called Richeldis, living full virtuous,
Desired of Our Lady a petition,
Her to honour with some work bounteous.
This Blessed Virgin and Lady most gracious
Granted her petition, as I shall after tell
Unto her worship to edify this chapel.

In spirit Our Lady to Nazareth her led,
And showed her the place where Gabriel her greet.
Lo daughter consider, to her Our Lady said,
Of this place take thou surely the <u>met</u>,                 [= measure]
Another like this at Walsingham thou set
Unto my laud and singular honour,
All that me seek there shall find succour.

Where shall be had in a memorial,
The great joy of my salutation.
First of my joy's ground and original,
Root of mankind's gracious redemption
When Gabriel gave to me relation
To be a mother through humility
And God's son conceived in virginity.

This vision showed thrice to this devout woman,
In mind well she marked both length and breadth.
She was full glad and thanked Our Lady then
Of her great grace never destitute in need.
This foresaid house in haste she thought to speed
Call to her artificers full wise
This chapel to forge as Our Lady did devise...

The widow thought it most likely of congruence,
This house on the first soil to build and erect,
Of this who list to have experience,
A chapel of Saint Laurence standeth now there
Fast by twain wells experience doth thus <u>lere</u>          [= learn]
There she thought to have set this chapel,
Which was begun by Our Lady's counsel.

The carpenters began to set the fundament
This heavenly house to erect on high
But soon their works showed inconvenient,
For no piece with other would agree with geometry.
Then were they all sorry and full of agony
That they could not ken neither measure nor mark
To join together their own proper work.

They went to rest and laid all things on side,
As they on their mistress had a commandment.
She thought Our Lady that first was her guide
Would convey this work after her own intent.
Her men to rest as for that night she sent,
And prayed Our Lady with devout exclamation
As she had begun to perform that habitation.

All night the widow remaining in this prayer,
Our Blessed Lady with heavenly ministers
Herself being chief artificer
Erected this said house with angels' hands;
And not only raised it but set it where it is
That is two hundred foot and more in distance
From the first place books make remembrance.

Early when the artificers came to their travail,
Of this said chapel to have made an end
They found each part conjoined <u>sans fail</u>,                    [= unerringly]
Better than they could conceive it in mind.
Thus each man home again did wend
And this holy matron thanked Our Lady
Of her great grace shewed here specially.

And since here Our Lady hath shewed many miracle,
Innumerable now here for to express
To such as visit this <u>habitacle</u>,                    [= dwelling place]
Ever like new to them that call her in distress.
Four hundred years and more the chronicle to witness
Hath endured this noble pilgrimage,
Where grace is daily showed to me of every age.

Many sick been here cured by Our Lady's might,
Dead again revived of this is no doubt,
Lame made whole, and blind restored to sight,
Mariners vexed with tempest safe to port brought,
Deaf, wounded and lunatic that hither have sought
And also lepers here recovered have be[en],
By Our Lady's grace of their infirmity.

Folk that of fiends have had encumbrance,
And of wicked spirits also much vexation,
Have here be delivered from every such chance,
And soul's greatly vexed with ghostly temptation.
Lo here the chief solace against all tribulation
To all that be sick bodily or ghostly,
Calling to Our Lady devoutly.

Therefore every pilgrim give your attendance;
Our Lady here to serve with humble affection,
Yourself you apply to do her pleasance,
Remembering the great joy of her Annunciation,
Therewith conceiving this brief compilation,
Though it halt in metre and eloquence,
It is here written to do reverence...

O gracious lady, glory of Jerusalam,
Cypress of Sion, and joy of Israel,
Rose of Jericho, and star of Bethlehem,
O glorious lady our asking not repel
In mercy all women ever thou dost excel.
Therefore Blessed Lady grant thou this great grace
To all that thee devoutly visit in this place.
Amen (1)

## A Pilgrimage to the Holy Land in 1506

About two miles from Ramah is the town of Lydda where Saint George suffered martyrdom and was beheaded and in the same town in which Saint Peter healed Aeneas of the palsy, Ramah is from Jaffa ten miles and from Jerusalem thirty miles and upon the right hand going from Ramah to Jerusalem about twenty miles from Ramah is the Castle of Emmaus, where the eleven[6] disciples knew our Saviour in the breaking of bread after his Resurrection as is well known by the Gospel etc. A little from thence upon a hill called Mount Joy lieth Samuel the Prophet and a little thereby is the town of Ramathaim where Samuel was born and of this town was Joseph of Arimathea owned the new tomb or monument that our Saviour Christ was buried in and a little over midway on the left hand is the Vale of Terebinth [Elah] where David slew Goliath etc.

Sunday at night we took our journey towards Jerusalem and because both my master prior of Gisborough were sore sick, therefore with great difficulty and outrageous cost we purveyed camels for them and certain Mamluks to conduct them in safety to Jerusalem which intreated us very evil and took much more for their pain than their covenant was.

---

[6] This is of course an error. In Luke 24, two disciples (one named as Cleopas, the other unnamed) were travelling from Jerusalem to Emmaus when they met the risen Jesus and only recognized him in the breaking of bread. They then returned to Jerusalem to share their experience with the Eleven.

Upon Monday that was the last day of August about two or three o'clock at afternoon we come to Jerusalem and were received into the Latin Hospital, called by some men the Hospital of St John, and there we rested us that night which hospital is right nigh the Temple of the Holy Sepulchre. And there the Greyfriars of Mt Sion ministered wine unto us every day twice, and lent us carpets to lie upon, for the which every pilgrim recompensed the said friars at their devotion and power. As for bread and other victuals was brought unto for our money by persons of divers sorts; and always the warden of the said friars or some of his brethren by his assignment daily accompanied us informing and showing unto us the holy places within the Holy Land. (2)

## A Pilgrimage to Mount Sion

Tuesday the first day of September that was the next morrow after that we came to Jerusalem, we went early to Mount Sion, and by the way we visited some Holy places: first the place where the Jews would have arrested and taken away the holy body of our Blessed Lady when the apostles bear her to the vale of Jehoshaphat to be buried;[7] and thereby we come unto a place where Saint Peter after he had denied our Lord thrice went out of the house of Caiaphas into a cave and wept bitterly; and a little from thence we come into the Church of the Angels where sometime was the house of Annas the Bishop[8] into the which our Saviour Christ was first led from the Mount of Olives where he suffered many injuries and specially there he took a buffet of one of the Bishop's servants saying, 'Is that how you answer the Bishop etc'.

From there we went to a Church of Saint Saviour, where sometime stood the great house of Caiaphas where as our Blessed Saviour was scorned, his face covered and bobbied [sic] and most grievously betimes there suffered many afflictions all the night. There is also a little cave where they shut him in the time the Jews had taken their counsel and determined what they would do with him, and it is yet called *carcer dei* [the prison of the Lord]. There is also in the same place the most part of a great stone that the Angel as we read removed from the door of the Sepulchre; and it is now the stone of the high Altar in the same church. Another part of the same stone lyeth yet before the Sepulchre door.

And there without the door in the Court on the left hand is a tree with many stones about it, where the ministers of the Jews and St Peter with them warmed themselves by the fire ...

... Sunday the sixth day of September we went all to Mount Sion to Mass. The same day we dined with the warden and friars there where we had a right honest dinner. Then we rose from the board, the Warden rose from the board, and took a basin full of folded papers with relics in each of them, and so he went along the

---

[7] The Valley of Jehoshophat was widely believed to be the precise site of Christ's Second Coming. So his mother would be the first to be raised. There were two traditions about the death of Our Lady; one (accepted by the Orthodox) that she died on Mt Sion and the other (held by most in the Western Church) that she escorted St John the Beloved Apostle to Ephesus and died there. Unsurprisingly the guardians of the shrines in Jerusalem, Western or Eastern, favoured the former, but it is interesting that the author of this narrative accepts it without comment.

[8] A curious anachronism for 'high priest'.

cloister where we sat at the table, and dealt to every pilgrim as he passed a paper with relics of the holy places about Jerusalem which we took as devoutly as we could with thanks accordingly.

The Saturday before Master Prior of Gisborough deceased about two or three o'clock at afternoon and the same night he was had to Mount Sion and there buried. And this same Sunday at night about one or two o'clock after midnight my master Sir Richard Guildford whom God assoil [= pardon] deceased and was had the same morning to mount Sion afore day. And the same Monday, the eve of our Lady's nativity all the pilgrims came to Mount Sion to the burying of my said Master Guildford where was done by the friars as much solemn service as might be done for him etc. The same afternoon we went to Bethany which is beyond the Mount of Olives about four miles from Jerusalem. There we entered into an old church and saw the grave or monument in which Lazarus lay four days dead as the Gospel sheweth, whom our Saviour raised from death to life. Not far from thence is Simon the Leper's house which prayed our Lord to eat with him and where as he sat Mary Magdalene brought alabaster of an ointment and sat at our Lord's feet and without ceasing wash his feet with her tears, wiping them with her hair and anointed him with her precious ointment, and there our Saviour Christ forgave the sins of the said Mary Magdalene . . . (3)

[*After many adventures, including a shipwreck, the party got back to England a year later, in August 1507.*] (4)

NOTES AND SOURCES

1. Anon. *Of this chapell se here the fundacyon bylded the yere of crystes incarnacyon a thousande complete syxty and one the tyme of sent edward kyng of this region* (1496), unpag.
2. *This is the begynnynge, and contynuaunce of the pylgrymage of Sir Richarde Guylforde Knyght [and] controuler vnto our late soueraygne lorde kynge Henry the. vij. And howe he went with his seruauntz and company towardes Iherusalem* (1511), unpag.
3. Ibid.
4. Ibid.

# John Colet, Dean of St Paul's Cathedral (London)   *c.*1467–1519

John Colet was an influential educational reformer and friend of Erasmus. Following an extended visit to France and Italy in the 1490s, he became a firm supporter of the 'new learning' or Christian humanism, and especially of the combination of Neoplatonist philosophy and ascetic Christian piety characteristic of Florence. He was—in the judgement of both Erasmus and Thomas More—an outstanding preacher, but the text of only one of his sermons has survived. Our first extract comes from that sermon, delivered to Convocation meeting at St Paul's in 1511, published in Latin in 1512 and in an English translation made by his friend Thomas Lupset in 1530–1. It follows the common style at the time of avoiding doctrinal emphasis but pressing on the clergy the need for absolute purity of life and, more strikingly, restraint in temporal matters, in order to justify the Church in her claims to liberty from state interference and obedience from the people. The sermon was many times reprinted over the next 200 years. Our second Colet extract comes from one of his most popular works, his *Daily Devotions, or The Christians morning and evening sacrifice digested into prayers and meditations, for every day in the week, and other occasions: with some short directions for a Godly life*, consisting of prayers and psalms for each day of the week and special prayers for a variety of purposes—e.g. sickness, perseverance, evil imaginings. Here we have extracted his definition of prayer and his prayers of preparation for the receiving of holy communion, and the prayer for use by families at the end of a day. By 1700 it had appeared in more than twenty editions.

## An Exhortation to the Clergy in Convocation

Be not conformed to this world, but be you reformed by the renewing of your mind; that you may prove what is that good will of God, well-pleasing and perfect (Rom. 12: 2).[9]

This the Apostle wrote to all Christian men, but most chiefly to Priests and Bishops. Priests and Bishops are the light of the world. For he said unto them, *you are the light of the world*: and he said also, *If the light that is in you be darkness, how great is that darkness?* that is, If Priests and Bishops (who should be as lights) run in the dark way of the world, how dark then shall the secular people be? Wherefore St Paul said chiefly to Priests and Bishops, *Be you not conformed to this world, but be you reformed.* In which words the Apostle doth two things: First he *forbids*, that we be not conformed to this world, and made carnal: and then he *commands*, that we be reformed in the spirit of God, and become spiritual. Intending to follow this order, I shall speak first of Conformation, and then of Reformation. *Be not conformed to this world.* By the word *world*, the Apostle meaneth the ways and manner of secular living; which chiefly consist in four evils of this world, that is, in devillish pride, carnal lust, worldly covetousness, and secular business. These are in the world as St John witnesseth (cf 1 John 2: 16). For he saith, *All that is in the world is either the lust of the flesh, the lust of the eyes, or the pride of life.* These same things now *are* and *reign* in the Church and ecclesiastical persons; so that we may seem truly to say, All that is in the Church is either the lust of the flesh, the lust of the eyes, or pride of life.

And first to speak of *pride of life.* How much greediness and appetite of honour and dignity is seen nowadays in Clergymen? How run they (yea almost out of breath) from one benefice to another, from the less to the greater, from the lower to the higher? Who seeth not this, and who seeing sorroweth not? And most of those which are in these dignities, carry their heads so high, and are so stately, that they seem not to be put in the humble Bishopric of Christ, but rather in the high Lordship and power of the world; not knowing, or not minding what Christ the master of all meekness said unto his disciples (whom he called to be Bishops and Priests); *The princes of the Gentiles exercise dominion over them, and those that be in authority have power; but do ye not so. Whosoever will be chief among you highest in dignity) let him be your servant. The Son of Man came not to be ministred unto, but to minister* (Matt. 20: 5), etc. By which words our Saviour doth plainly teach, that a prelacy in the Church is nothing else but a ministration; that an high dignity in an Ecclesiastical person, ought to be nothing but a meek service.

The second secular evil is carnal *concupiscence.* And hath not this vice grown and increased in the Church so far, that in this most busy age, the far greater number of priests mind nothing but what doth delight and please their senses?

---

[9] Here and throughout, we have modernized biblical citation into a standard form and not followed the particular forms given in our original texts.

They give themselves to feasts and banqueting, spend their time in vain babbling, are addicted to hunting and hawking, and in a word drowned in the delights of this world; diligent only in progging [= hunting, searching] for those lusts they set by. Against which sort of men St Jude exclaims in his Epistle, saying, *Woe unto them which have gone the way of Cain: they are foul and beastly, feasting in their meats, without fear feeding themselves; floods of the wild sea, foaming out their own shame: unto whom the storm of darkness is reserved for everlasting* [Jude 1: 12–13].

*Covetousness* is the third secular evil, which St John calls the *lust of the eyes*, and St Paul, *idolatry*. This abominable pestilence hath so entered into the minds of almost all priests, hath so blinded the eyes of their understanding, that we see nothing but that which seems to bring unto us some gain. What other thing seek we nowadays in the Church, except fat benefices, and high promotions?...We care not how vast our charge of souls be, how many or how great benefices we take, so they be of large value. O covetousness, covetousness! St Paul justly called thee *the root of all evil* [1 Tim. 6: 10]. Of thee cometh this heaping of benefices upon benefices. Of thee so great pensions assigned, from many benefices resigned. Of thee so much suing for tithes, for offerings, for mortuaries, for delapidations, by the right and title of the Church, for which things we contend as eagerly as for our lives. *All* [are] *evil...*

The fourth secular evil that spotteth the face of the Church, is *continual secular occupation;* wherein Priests and Bishops nowadays do busy themselves, becoming the servants rather of men than God, the warriors rather of this world, than of Jesus Christ. For the Apostle Paul writeth to Timothy (2 Tim. 2: 3.) that no man who is a good soldier of Christ, or that warreth for God, entangleth himself with the affairs of this life, is turmoiled with secular business. The warfare of God's soldier is not carnal, but spiritual. Our warring is to pray devoutly, to read and study Scriptures diligently, to preach the word of God sincerely, to administer the Holy Sacraments rightly, and offer sacrifice for the people. For we are mediators and intercessors unto God for men: which St Paul witnesseth writing to the Hebrews, *Every Bishop*, saith he, *taken of men, is ordained for men in those things that be unto God, that he may offer gifts and sacrifices for sins* [Heb. 5: 1]. Wherefore those Apostles, that were the first Priests and Bishops, did so much abhor all manner of meddling in secular things, that they would not minister the meat that was necessary to poor people, although it were a great work of virtue...

In this age we are sensible of the contradiction of lay people. But they are not so much contrary to us, as we are to ourselves. Their contrariness hurteth not us so much, as the contrariness of our own evil life; which is contrary both to God and Christ; who said, *He that is not with me is against me.* We are also nowadays troubled with heretics (men intoxicated with strange opinions) but the heresies of them are not so pestilent and pernicious to us and the people, as the *naughty lives of priests*, which (if we believe St Bernard) is *a kind of heresy; nay, the chief of all, and most perilous.* For that holy Father preaching in a certain convocation to the priests of his time, had these words in his sermon: *many men are Catholic in their speaking and preaching, which are heretics in their works and actions. For what the heretics do by evil teaching, the same do these men by ill example; viz. they lead the people out of the right way, and bring them into error of life. And these men are so much worse than hereticks, by how much their works prevail more than their words.* This that holy Father St Bernard spoke, with a fervent spirit, against the sect of evil priests in his time. By which words he sheweth plainly, that there be two kinds of heresies; one arising from perverse teaching, and the other from naughty life: of which two this latter is far worse, and more perilous; reigning (now) in priests, who do not live like themselves: not priestly, but secularly, to the utter and miserable destruction of the Church of God. Wherefore you Fathers, you priests, and all you of the clergy, at last rouse and look up from this your sleep in this forgetful world; and being well awaked, hear St Paul crying unto you, *Be you not conformed to this world.* Thus much for the first part. (1)

## What Prayer Is

Prayer is an humble request either of the heart, or tongue, or both unto God, proceeding from our belief and acknowledgement of his power, as God, and of his goodness, as our Father in Jesus Christ, to supply all our necessities, with thanksgiving unto him for any blessing received.

The parts of a prayer are usually three:

- 1. humble confession.
- 2. petition or supplication.
- 3. hearty thanksgiving.

### 1. CONFESSION

Which is an humble and penitent repetition of our sins and wickedness, with an acknowledgment of punishments and miseries thereby deserved, and with an earnest desire and prayer for absolution, and that for Jesus Christ alone.

Epigraphs:

He that covereth his sins shall not prosper, but whoso confesseth and forsaketh them, shall have mercy. (Prov. 28: 13)

I said I will confess my transgressions to the Lord, and thou forgavest the iniquity of my sin (Ps. 32: 5)[10]

If we confess our sins, He is faithful and just to forgive us our sins, and to cleanse us from all unrighteousness (1 John 1: 19)

My misdeeds prevail against me; O be thou merciful to my sins (Ps. 67: 3)

### 2. PETITION

Petition or supplication is that part of prayer, in which we beseech God, the Author of all good, and punisher of all ill, for all the mercies, comforts, graces, and blessings of this life, and the life to come, and for deliverance from all fears, ills, dangers, and punishments of this life, and the life to come, for ourselves and others, and all for the merits of Christ Jesus alone, and his mediation.

---

[10] Colet does not use the Vulgate numbering of the psalms, but the Hebrew one later accepted by Protestants. (This was doubtless because of his humanistic interest in texts in their original language). We have silently amended (in this case from Psalm 31 to Psalm 32) for the sake of consistency across the whole of this book.

Epigraphs:

Hearken unto my voice, O Lord, when I cry unto thee: have mercy upon me, and hear me (Ps. 27: 7)

Hear me, O God, in the multitude of thy mercies: even in the truth of thy Salvation (Ps. 68: 14)

Who can tell how oft he offendeth? O cleanse me from my secret faults (Ps. 19)

Have mercy upon me, O God, after thy great goodness; according to the multitude of thy mercies do away mine offences (Ps. 50: 1)

Whosoever shall call on the name of the Lord shall be saved (Rom. 10)

### 3. HEARTY THANKSGIVING

Thanksgiving is an humble joyful acknowledgment and expression of our thanks unto Almighty God for any mercy or blessing received, or promised; and for preservation and deliverance from any calamity, danger, or distress, with denial of our own merits of the least of these, and a magnifying of the greatness and goodness of God unto us in and through Jesus Christ.

Epigraphs:

Give thanks unto the Lord and call upon his name (Ps. 105: 1)

Whatsoever ye do in word or deed, do all in the name of the Lord Jesus, giving thanks to God the Father, and by him (Col. 3: 17)

My mouth shall daily speak of thy righteousness and salvation, for I know no end thereof (Ps. 71: 15)

O that men would therefore praise the Lord for his goodness, and declare the wonders he doth for the children of men: that they would offer unto him the sacrifice of thanksgiving (Ps. 107: 21–2)

O Lord thou art my God, I will exalt thee, I will praise thy name, for thou hast done wonderful things (Isa. 25: 1)

What shall I render unto the Lord for all his benefits he hath done unto me? I will take the cup of salvation, and call upon the name of the Lord . . . [Ps. 117: 13] (2)

## A Prayer before the Receiving of Holy Communion

O Most holy and heavenly God and Father, which by the immortal seed of thy Word hast begotten us to be thy children, and with the same (as with milk) dost nourish us purely as new born babes, as also with the divine mysteries of thy holy Sacraments (as by a visible word) dost confirm and strengthen us in faith and righteousness; and having so adopted us into thy family, continually feedest and nourishest us unto eternal life: we humbly beseech thee so to prepare our souls to the due receiving thereof worthily, that we may thereby effectually feel, taste, and feed on thy Son Jesus Christ (the true manna and bread that came down from Heaven) that we may by him have eternal life: pardon (O Lord) pardon our unpreparedness in coming to the participation of so holy and divine mysteries: Make thy Word and Sacraments always so powerful and effectual in our ears and hearts that we may thereby be sanctified and renewed unto all holy obedience unto thy will in the mortification of our sinful corruptions, and renewing of thy perfect image in us (unto holiness, righteousness, sobriety, truth, knowledge, faith, and temperance) through his most powerful and glorious Resurrection. Establish our conscience in the assurance of our salvation, by the remission of our sins in the blood of thy Son, which was shed for us on the Altar of the Cross (as a sacrifice of expiation, to cleanse away all sin). O Lord, seal and confirm this covenant of grace in our hearts by these holy Sacraments (pledges of thy grace and love towards us) that at no time we may stagger at thy promises, nor fall away from hope and confidence in thee; but being hereby incorporated into one Body, we may partake of one Spirit, and grow in love one towards another (as members of the same mystical Body) that we may forgive one another, as thou hast forgiven us. O Lord, make us ever thankful for thy manifold and great mercies, in providing unto us such means and helps of our salvation; and grant that we may not put any confidence in external actions and exercises thereof (in any hope to be justified thereby) but that we may thereby exalt our minds to heavenly and spiritual contemplations, and by faith be firmly united to thee our Head in Heaven, to be made one with thee, and thou with us: and howsoever heretofore we have transgressed and defiled our selves, as well with our natural impurities, and actual impieties, henceforth (being now washed and purified in the blood of the Lamb which was sacrificed for us) we may have our conversation in Heaven; and being new creatures in Christ, may have new thoughts, desires, and delights, (far from the lusts of our former ignorance) and may live ever unto him and with him, who sitteth at thy right hand, our Redeemer and Advocate, and shall return to be our Judge, to justify and acquit us before thee; to whom, with thee, and the Holy Ghost, be all praise, etc. (3)

## An Evening Prayer for a Private Family

O Eternal God and heavenly Father, which hast made of one blood all mankind, and breathed into us the breath of life, and assigned times and length of our life in this world, which thou continuest according to thy good pleasure; and if thou withdrawest thy hand, we soon perish, and are returned to dust, whence we were taken: we will therefore show forth thy power in the evening, and magnify thy goodness for saving us this day from dangers, and from our birth, in the whole course of our lives, hitherto preserving us; for thou art a God of patience, pity, and much forgiveness; showing mercy unto thousands, and blotting out all our offences. O Lord, we pray thee set not before thine eyes the horrible confusion, uncleanness, and wickedness of our hearts (being replenished with loathsome darkness, of ignorance, errors, doubtings, and distrust) yea, our vile hearts have been turned away from thee, and all the powers of our souls and bodies are filthily defiled and weakened with wickedness; only we cry aloud unto thee, favourably to consider the troubles and sorrows of our hearts, to strengthen our infirmities, and to pardon our most horrible offences: for we are wounded and weak and cannot be holpen but only through thy exceeding great mercy. There is no health in our flesh, because of thy displeasure, neither is there any peace or rest in our souls, by reason of our sin; yet hear thou us (O Lord) for thy Holy name's sake, for Jesus Christ his sake, pardon and forgive us all our sins that we have committed against thee this day; and grant us thy grace, that we may amend our lives, and unfeignedly serve thee in the several duties of our callings, to thy glory, and the comfort of our own souls; remit our punishments, restore us to thy wonted favour, and receive us into thy most gracious protection, and keep us this night and evermore, that the devil may have no power over us, nor the sin of wickedness may be able to hurt us. Whether we sleep or wake, live or die, we are always thine, thou art our Creator and Redeemer; guard us about with the armies of thy Holy Angels in our habitations; expel and remove far away from us wicked spirits (our mortal enemies) and graciously protect us from our persecutors which lay snares to subdue us: Do thou (O God) assist us, that we may peaceably sleep and rest in thee: hide us in thy Tabernacle from the strife of all men, and we will fear no evil, for thou that keepest us, dost neither slumber nor sleep: thy rod and thy staff do always comfort and defend us: Let thy mercy (O God) prevent [= go before] and follow us all the days of our lives, that we may dwell in thy house of defence in longness of days, praising thee evermore, Father, Son, and Holy Ghost, one true, gratious, and everlasting God, ruling and reigning world without end.

Our Father which art in Heaven, hallowed etc

Lighten our darkness we beseech thee, O Lord, and by thy great mercy defend us from all perils and dangers of this night, for the love of thy only Son, our Lord and Saviour, Jesus Christ.

Let thy mighty, hand and outstretched arm, O Lord, be still our defence; thy mercy and loving kindness in Jesus Christ thy dear Son our Salvation; thy true and holy word our instruction; thy Grace and holy Spirit our comfort and consolation, to the end, and in the end, So be it. Amen. (4)

NOTES AND SOURCES

1. John Colet, *A sermon of conforming and reforming made in the Convocation at St Pauls Church in London* (1531, checked against a reprint issued in 1661), unpag.
2. John Colet, *Daily devotions, or, The Christians morning and evening sacrifice digested into prayers and meditations, for every day in the week, and other occasions: with some short directions for a godly life* (taken from a reprint of 1693), unpag.
3. Ibid.
4. Ibid.

# Margaret Beaufort, Countess of Richmond          1443–1509

Margaret Beaufort was descended from King Edward III through his fourth son John of Gaunt and then through the line of the Beauforts, dukes of Somerset. As wife to Jasper Tudor she was the mother of Henry VII and grandmother of Henry VIII. She was one of the most learned and pious women of her age, and one of the greatest educational philanthropists of the Renaissance, responsible for the foundation of Christ's and St John's Colleges in Cambridge, both centres of the 'new learning' (Christian humanism). She was also a great supporter of the infant printing industry, and several of her own translations were amongst the earliest religious works published in the English language. An early example is her translation of this work ascribed to Denis the Carthusian and entitled *The Mirror of Gold for the Sinful Soul* (published by Richard Pynson in 1506, and several times reprinted in the following decades), Margaret's translation is free and ecstatic.

## Of the Joys of Paradise

It is written by Saint Paul in an epistle that he sent to the Corinthians in the fifth Chapter that the eye of man hath not seen nor the ear heard nor heart can think the joys that our lord God hath and prepared to his friends and lovers. O poor wretched and sinful soul, give heed diligently what joys, how great joys and how many they be which be prepared in heaven to the lovers of God to the intent that all things in this world may be to the vile and abject, for certainly it is to be known that the joys of Heaven be so great and many in number that all arithmeticians by their numbers cannot number nor measure them nor all the grammarians and rhetoricians with all their fair speeches can or may declare them. For as it is said before, neither eye may see them nor ear hear, nor the heart of man may comprehend them. For certainly in the glory eternal, all the saints shall enjoy them in the vision of God. Above them, they shall enjoy the beauty of heaven and of other spiritual creatures; they shall enjoy within them the glorification of the body and nigh unto them the association and company of angels and men. A worthy doctor named Anselm putteth and declareth seven yests [sic] of the soul that the just people shall have in the celestial beatitude. First he putteth the yests [sic] of the body as beauty, lightness, strength, liberty and health. Of the beauty of just people, saith this doctor, it shall be seven times more shining than the Sun is now, the which witnesseth the Scripture saying thus: the virtuous persons shall shine as the Sun. In the realm of their father [sic] sweetness shall so accompany just livers that it shall make them semblable or like to the angels of Heaven which—from Heaven unto the Earth and from the Earth unto Heaven—transport themselves lighter and suddenlier than the moving of a finger. Of the which sweetness is made a familiar example by the beams of the Sun the which rising in the East, attaineth and touchest the farthest part of the West, that by the said example we may have true hope and trust.... And therefore I pray and require thee that nothing exceed thy soul which hath taken the similitude of the angels given of Almighty God unto it. Wherefore it must needs follow that likewise as we may receive the power and similitude of angels, so we may have the surety and liberty of them, for certainly like as unto angels may there be no letting nor gainsaying in this world but, at their own will. In likewise shall there be no one obstacle nor let to hinder us nor wall nor enclosure to keep us out nor yet element which unto our will may withstand or annoy. (1)

NOTES AND SOURCES

1. Denis the Carthusian (trans. Margaret Beaufort, Countess of Richmond and Derby), *The Mirroure of Golde for the Synfull Soul* (1506) unpag.

## St John Fisher                                                    1469–1535

St John Fisher is one of the towering figures of the sixteenth century. He was to die as one of the first martyrs of the Reformation period for his refusal to acknowledge Henry VIII as Supreme Head of the Church. But for many years he had been an influential and powerful figure in Church and State. He had been a leading counsellor to Margaret Beaufort, mother of Henry VII, and her guide and adviser as the foundress of both Christ's College and St John's College, Cambridge. As Bishop of Rochester, he was an exemplary pastor and was a noted preacher, not least when Henry VIII and Cardinal Wolsey became concerned about the spread of Lutheranism in the early 1520s. His writings (almost all in Latin) are voluminous; our selection is designed to show the range of his interests and concerns. We begin our extracts with the sermon Fisher preached to mark the passing of the first month after the death of his friend and patron Margaret Beaufort

(1443–1509). Here is noble piety in its purest essence on the eve of the Reformation. We then draw on a sermon Fisher preached seventeen years later. Fisher was very much the preacher on major occasions preferred by the King and by his Cardinal Legate Thomas Wolsey. In 1526, there occurred the trial of the first Englishmen to take 'the heresies of Martin Luther that famous heretic', and for the keeping and retaining of his books against the ordinance of Pope Leo X. In the presence of King and Cardinal, Fisher was called upon to preach the sermon from the great open-air pulpit known as Paul's Cross, just outside St Paul's Cathedral in London. It called upon the heretics to abjure their heresy but stopped short of calling for them to be burnt at the stake, for centuries the penalty for heresy. As heresy spread, the use of the ultimate sanction was invoked, and the century of persecution began. This English version of Fisher's sermon was printed in 1526. Next, we have a work not published until later. It is the English translation of a work written by Fisher in the 1520s and first issued under the title *A Godly treatise declaring the benefits, fruits, and great commodities of prayer and also the true use thereof. Written in Latin, forty years past, by an Englishman of great virtue [and] learning. And lately translated into English. 1560.* The translation was almost certainly commissioned by Cardinal Pole in Mary's reign. It was published in 1560 with Fisher's name omitted (but implied) and dated defiantly as a work written before Henry VIII's schism. Finally, we have a long and powerful extract from the *Spiritual Consolation* written on the eve of his execution for treason. Two men (and only two men) at the centre of power defied Henry VIII's determination to make himself Supreme Head of the Church of England in order to put aside his first wife Katherine of Aragon and to marry Ann Boleyn out of lust and a yearning to provide for the succession to the throne: John Fisher and Thomas More. John Fisher was even more heroic than More in his forthrightness. He was willing publicly to defend the cause of Queen Katherine, and to defy Henry's attempt to force all those in public office—including the Bishops—to take an oath recognizing his Royal Supremacy. In 1535, Fisher was put on trial for his defiance and sentenced to death. Facing death, he wrote this *Spirituall Consolation*, composed for his sister Elizabeth (who was a nun) and probably intended only for her eyes. It begins with a plea with her to read it 'by yourself in secret manner'. However, it was copied and made widely available in Catholic circles, especially in the 1550s, and was finally published in 1578.

## In Memoriam Margaret Beaufort

Hereafter followeth a mourning remembrance had at the month mind of the noble princess Margaret Countess of Richmond and Derby mother unto King Henry VII and grand-dame to our sovereign Lord that now is, upon whose soul Almighty God have mercy.

This holy Gospel late read[11] containeth in it a dialogue that is to say a communication betwixt the woman of blessed memory called Martha and Our Saviour Jesu which dialogue I would apply unto this noble princess late deceased, in whose remembrance this office and observances be done at this time. And three things by the leave of God I will intend. First to show wherein this noble princess may well be likened and compared unto the blessed woman Martha. Second how we may complain unto Our Saviour Jesu for the painful death of her body like as Martha died for the death of her brother Lazarus. Third the comfortable answer of Our Saviour

---

[11] Not given in the printed text, but presumably Luke 10: 38–42.

Jesu unto her again. In the first shall stand her praise and commendation. In the second our mourning for the loss of her. In the third our comfort again.

First I say that the comparison of them two may be made in four things—in nobleness of person, in discipline of their bodies, in ordering of their souls to God, in hospitality-keeping and charitable dealing to their neighbours. In which four the noble woman Martha (as say the doctors entreating this Gospel and her life) was singularly to be commended and praised, wherefore let us consider likewise whether in this noble countess may anything like be found. First the blessed Martha was a woman of noble blood to whom by inheritance belonged the castle of Bethany and this nobleness of blood they have which descended of noble lineage. Beside this there is a nobleness of manners without which the nobleness of blood is much defaced, for as Boethius[12] saith: if ought be good in the nobleness of blood, it is for that thereby the noble men and women should be ashamed to go out of kind from the virtuous manners of their ancestry before. Yet also there is another nobleness which ariseth in every person by the goodness of nature whereby full often such as come of right poor and ignoble father and mother have great abilities of nature to noble deeds. Above all these same there is a foremanner of nobleness which may be called an increased nobleness as by marriage and affinity of more noble persons such as were of less condition may increase in their degree of nobleness. In every of these I suppose this countess was noble. First she came of noble blood lineally descending of King Edward III within the 4th degree of the same. Her father was John duke of Somerset, her mother was called Margaret right noble as well in manners as in blood, to whom she was a very daughter in all noble manners, for she was bounteous and liberal to every person of her knowledge or acquaintance. Avarice and covetousness she most hated, and sorrowed it full much in all persons but especially in any that belonged unto her.

She was also of singular easiness to be spoken unto and [with] full courtesy answer she would make to all that came unto her, of marvellous gentleness she was unto all folks but especially unto her own whom she trusted and loved right tenderly. Unkind she would not be unto no creature nor forgetful of any kindness or service done to her before which is no little part of true nobleness. She was not vengeable nor cruel but ready anon to forget and to forgive injuries done unto her at the least desire or motion made unto her for the same. Merciful also and piteous she was unto such as was grieved and wrongfully troubled; and to them that were in poverty or sickness or any other misery. To God and to the Church full obedient and tractable searching his honour and pleasure full busily. Awareness of herself she had always to eschew everything that might dishonest any noble woman or distain her honour in any condition...

The holy Martha is magnified for her Godly hospitality and charitable dealing to her neighbours. Much business there is in keeping hospitality. And therefore Our Lord said unto her: Martha, Martha, the household servants must be put in some good order. The strangers of honesty which of their courtesy resorteth for to visit the sovereign must be considered. And the suitors also which cometh

---

[12] Anicius Manlius Severinus Boethius (c.480–c.524) was a Christian theologian of high patrician status (descended from Emperors and the son of a consul). He himself was consul in 510. His best-known work is the *Consolation of Philosophy*. He was executed for conspiracy in 524 or 525.

compelled by necessity to seek help and succour in their cause must be heard. And the poor and needy especially would be relieved and comforted. First her own household with marvellous diligence and wisdom this noble princess ordered providing reasonable statutes and ordinances for them which by her officers she commanded to be read four times a year. And oftentimes by herself she would so lovingly encourage every of them to do well, and sometime by other mean persons. If any factions or bands were made secretly amongst her head officers, she with great policy did bolt it out and likewise if any strife or controversy she would with great discretion study the reformation thereof…

For the poor creatures albeit she did not receive into her house Our Saviour in his own person as the blessed Martha did, she nevertheless received them that doth represent his person. Of whom he saith himself: poor folks, to the number of twelve, she daily and nightly kept in her house, giving them lodging, meat and drink and clothing, visiting them as often as she conveniently might; and in their sickness visiting them and comforting them and ministering unto them with her own hands. And when it pleased God to call any of them out of this wretched world she would be present to see them depart and to learn to die; and likewise bring them unto the earth which as Bonaventure affirmeth is of greater merit than if she had done all this to the self person of our saviour Jesu and the other servants and ministers of our Lord. Whom she heard were of any devotion and virtue full glad she was at all times when she might get them to whom she would likewise show the comfort that she could. Suppose not you that if she might have gotten Our Saviour Jesu in his own person but she would as desirously and as fervently have ministered unto him as ever did Martha when thus much she did until his servants for his sake.

Thus it may appear some comparison of the blessed Martha and of this noble princess which was the first promised. (1)

## Fisher on Heresy

*Respice fides tua te salvum fecit.*

These words are written in the Gospel read in the church this Quinquagesima Sunday. They may thus be Englished: Open thine eyes, thy faith hath made thee safe. In this Gospel St Luke telleth a miracle the which Our Saviour did show upon a blind man. He saith that a blind man sitting nigh to the way heard a noise of people passing by and inquired what that was. It was told him that Jesus of Nazareth passed that way. He gave faith unto this word and cried for mercy saying: Jesu the son of David have mercy upon me. Part of this people went before Our Saviour in the way and part came after him. They that went before (as the Gospel saith) rebuked the blind man and he much rather cried for mercy, saying: the son of David have mercy upon me. Our Saviour standing commanded this man to be brought unto him. And when he was brought to his presence, Our Saviour asked him what he would. O sir, said this man, that I might have my sight again. Then did Our Saviour this miracle upon him and said these words above rehearsed: open thine eyes, thy faith hath made thee safe. And forthwith this blind man was restored to his sight and followed Our Saviour in the way with the other people.

By this word and other such Martin Luther hath taken occasion of many great errors: whereby he hath blinded many a Christian soul and brought them out of the way saying that only faith doth justify us and sufficeth to our salvation, whereby many a one little regardeth any good works but only resteth unto faith.

This Gospel therefore may sufficiently instruct any reasonable man what faith suffiseth and what not: for it marvellously pertaineth to this purpose if we with any diligence observe and mark every mystery thereof.

First let us consider this multitude in itself where many went before Our Saviour Jesu and many followed after: and he in the midst of them all. Those that went before him betoken unto us the fathers and the people of the Old Testament, the which did pass the course of this world before the birth of Our Saviour Christ; those that followed after do signify the fathers and the people of the New Testament the which succeeded the birth of Christ. Both these make but one people: for they be all of one faith...

But now to us the laws of Saviour Christ be made easy by the abundance of grace and by the dulcetness of love which the Holy Ghost hath put in our hearts as St Paul saith: the love of God is spread in our hearts by the Holy Ghost the which is given unto us. And this is a great pre-eminence that we have above that people. This multitude that followeth Christ in the way and is in passage is the succession of Christ's church which hath continued and shall continue unto the world's end even like a flood that passeth continually the waters go past but yet the flood continueth and retaineth still the name of the flood: so the succession of Christ's church ever continueth and is called the Church Catholic though the people yearly renew. Thus much that I have said for this multitude among which Our Saviour Christ was. Now let us also briefly consider what this blind man doth mean and signify.

This man doth betoken unto us the heretics, and that for four conditions above rehearsed in this Gospel. And here my brethren that now be abjured, take heed.

First, here I say that this man was singular by himself: and so the heretics study to be singular in their opinions. Singularity and pride is the ground of all heresy. When a man studieth to be singular in his opinion and will not conform himself unto the multitude of good person then falleth he into heresies. Second, this man was blind and had lost his sight. And the heretics by the error of false doctrines and of perverse heresies be blinded in their hearts and have not the clear light of faith. Third, this man sat out of the right way and walked not: And so likewise these heretics sit out of the right way and walk not in the journey toward Heaven. Fourth, this man was divided from this people among whom Christ Jesu was; and so be the heretics likewise: they be divided from the Church of Christ with whom Our Saviour Christ continueth unto the world's end. Thus we perceive I suppose that this man which was singular and blind and sat out of the way divided from Christ for these four conditions representeth the heretics.

In the third place we may by this easily conceive what great diversity is between the Church Catholic and the heretics. First, they that be of this multitude and of the Church Catholic they be of one mind and opinion concerning the substance of our faith to agree together in one doctrine. The heretics be singular and have opinions by themselves: and they be repugnant not only with the church but with themselves among themselves as we shall show hereafter. It is a very truth that one wise man hath said: Every truth agreeth with others: but falsehood is both repugnant against himself and against the truth. Second: the church is in the clear brightness of faith, the heretics be blinded by their false and erroneous opinions. For as truth giveth a light and a brightness, so falsehood blindeth and bringeth into darkness. Third: The Church is in the right way; the heretics be out of the right way. Fourth: The Church walketh and profiteth in their journey toward the country of Heaven; the heretics sit in the seat of pestilence and profit nothing in this journey but rather sinketh deeper and deeper toward the pit of Hell. Fifth: the Church hath in it the presence of Christ and shall have continually unto the world's end; the heretics be divided from Christ in this present time and so finally shall be excluded from the sight of his face for ever. All these five differences be so manifest in this Gospel that we need not much declaration for the same.

Now in the fourth place let us discuss how this blind man was restored unto his sight: to the intent that we may perceive how an heretic may be restored to the true faith of Christ's church. This blind man by four manner of ways was brought unto his sight. First he hearing and enquiring the very truth of that multitude which passed forby: he heard the people which was in passage and of them he learned what Jesus of Nazareth was. So must heretics do if he will be restored unto the true faith. For nowhere the true doctrine of Jesu can be learned but in the church. Here must the word of God be learned. And this is wonderfully expressed in this Gospel by mystery. It is certain that the people of the Jews when that manna was sent unto them from above and they saw it in the likeness of the coriander seed, they made this same question which this blind man now doth ask: what is that? And of this question that seed took this name and was called manna. Now manna betokeneth in figure the word of God. Who therefore so ever will learn the true doctrine of the word of God, he must enquire it of this multitude that walketh in the right way: that is to say of the church catholic. Doubtless out of the church this truth cannot be learned. Second: this man cried for mercy; so must the heretic do. He must beseech Our Saviour Christ to enlighten his heart by clear faith and to remove from his heart the blindness of all errors and heresy. Third: Our Saviour did command that this blind man should be brought unto him: and so must the heretics be reduced unto the ways of the church. But by whom commandeth Our Saviour that thus they shall be reduced? Truly by them that be set in spiritual authority: as now that most reverend father in God my Lord Legate [Thomas Wolsey] having this most sovereign authority hath endeavoured himself for these men here present and others which were out of the way to reduce them in to the ways of the church. The heretics contend that it shall not be lawful thus to do: but they would have every man left unto their liberty. But doubtless it may not be so; for the nature of man is more prone to all naughtiness rather than to any goodness; and therefore many must be compelled according as the Gospel saith in another place: If every man should have liberty to say what he would we should have a marvellous world. No man should steer [= to travel a set course] anywhere for heresies. And therefore St Paul considering the pronity of man's heart to be infected with heresies, giveth often warning that we shall in any wise eschew the perilous infections of these heretics. And the same St Paul often pronounceth excommunication against them that sow these perverse doctrines among the Christian people. Wherefore it is not lawful that any man shall have liberty to speak in these matters concerning our faith whatsoever that he list: but he must be compelled to conform him unto the wholesome doctrine of the church.

Fourth this blind man when he was brought unto Our Saviour yet had he not his [sight unto] than he did fully assent with his whole will unto the same. And to that purpose Our Saviour asked him what he would? And so made him to confess his full assent. Thus must the heretic do that will have his spiritual sight: he must fully assent unto the doctrine of Christ's church. He may be compelled to come bodily but if he come not also with the feet of his soul and fully assent unto the church, he cannot have this true faith. The faith of the church is not made our faith but by our assent, which assent cometh of us and is the womb of our soul. And therefore it is not absolutely said: that is to say *thy* faith. The faith of the church (which by thine assent is made thy faith) doth make thee safe. (2)

## Fisher on daily prayer and contrition

A certain monk, one of the old Fathers, being demanded how he fulfilled that saying or commandment of Christ, *Oportet semper orare*, a man must always pray, made this answer: when I have (saith he) finished and said my daily prayers, the time that remaineth I use to bestow in labouring with my hands, as far forth as the ability and strength of my body doth permit, whereby it cometh to pass, that daily I gain somewhat, with the which I may relieve not only myself, but also some other poor people. And they (saith he) pray for me, as oft as by the unquietness and trouble of my body, I cannot pray for myself; and by this mean, he did believe that he satisfied the commandment. And he had the holy Scripture agreeable with his opinion, which saith (Ecclesiastes 29) Hide thy alms in the bosom of the poor, and that shall pray for thee. See, then, how the holy Scripture confirmeth that our alms doth pray for us: and therefore, if a man apply his mind to show mercy and pity to his neighbours, if he seek to defend the orphans and fatherless children, if he labour to comfort the widows which be destitute of all consolation, if he be careful to deliver those that be oppressed with violence, from injury and wrong. Finally, if he show himself ready to help to his power, any that want succour or relief, so that besides all this he neglect not the ordinary appointed times for prayer, by the Church of God, he may well be judged to have fulfilled the former words of Our Saviour. For that man doth pray always, either by himself, or else by his alms and charitable deeds, which supplieth all the want that appeareth in his own prayer. In this wise then, may the words of Christ aforesaid, be understanded, wherein he teacheth us always to continue in prayer, which is as much to say, always to live and do well, which doth some time happen to men, yea when they be sleeping. For as oft as we do sleep or wake, walk or sit still, eat or drink, be vexed or be in quiet, or what else soever we do or suffer, if all these doings be with a true faith referred to the honour and glory of God, no doubt they appertain to the increase of a good and perfect life. For if it were not so, Saint Paul would not have willed the Corinthians, that whatsoever they did, they should intend and direct the same, to the glory of God, saying unto them (1 Cor. 10: 31): whether you eat or drink, or what thing else soever you do, do all to the honour of God. And surely, if God be moved with our words and speaking, to be gracious unto us, he will be much more stirred to the same, by our good works and well doing, forasmuch as works do now supply the place of words. And therefore the favour of God is turned towards us by our good works, which we do to this end, and of purpose to please his divine Majesty; for they do express the vehemency of prayer, and that much more mightily than the prayers themself. Therefore, whosoever referreth all that he doth or suffereth, only to the glory of God, he surely prayeth continually, and doth at all times satisfy this aforesaid precept of Christ. For we may justly say, that he doth continue always in prayer, which always directeth his works and doings, to the honour and glory of God.

But albeit this saying, *Oportet semper orare*, may be understanded in this sense; yet notwithstanding, because Christ hath of purpose appointed a difference between praying and working, and declareth a great diversity between alms, prayer, and fasting, therefore we shall now add unto these two, a third understanding of the same. St Paul doth admonish the people of Thessalonica that they should pray incessantly (1 Thess. 5) and in many places of his Epistles, he declareth that he did without ceasing remember divers in his prayers. Moreover in the Acts of the Apostles (ch. 12) it is written that whilst Peter was detained prisoner and in captivity, the Church of God made continual prayer, and intercession for him. By the which words it is manifest and apparent, that every true Christian man doth pray in every action and work he doth, yea although he sleep. The which thing cannot be true in any wise except we do by prayer understand the continual desire of the heart which is always strong, and hath his continual motion in man's mind. For like as a man being bound in prison with weighty fetters of iron is compelled by the tedious weariness of those miseries and afflictions which he endureth, vehemently to desire and earnestly seek for liberty. And if he have once conceived any manner of hope of his deliverance, he then incessantly longeth, wisheth, and desireth to be loosed from those painful bands. Verily even so every Christian man (which is not ignorant, how grievously and fiercely he is invaded and daily assaulted by the flesh, the world, and the devil, and how divers and manifold miseries and calamities he sustaineth in this vale of wretchedness, to how many, and therewith how great perils and daily dangers his life is subjected and set forth) is enforced every moment to desire the aid and help of God his grace, by the which, at the last he being delivered from those calamities and great evils, may ascend into the beautiful sight and beholding of God himself, and the most happy fruition of everlasting felicity. And this earnest desire is in the Scripture oftentimes understood for a loud cry in the ears of Almighty God, as where the Prophet saith (Psalm 9) God hath heard the vehement desire of the poor. For doubtless, the earnest desire of those that be vexed and punished in mind and soul, doth speedily break in and maketh a ready way to the presence of God himself, and raiseth a wonderful outcry and noise into his ears: and therefore forasmuch as such and the like desire, never ceaseth in the hearts of good men, but is continually occupied, and moved by grace, so that they do always desire and long for the succour and aid of God, his might and power, and that whether they sleep, wake, eat, drink, or whatsoever thing else they do, these men may justly be judged always to pray, and that without any intermission. For the declaration whereof, St Augustine sayth thus (Epistle 121). To pray (saith he) without ceasing, what else is it, but incessantly to desire of God to lead a good and honest life? Let us always crave and beg this grace of God, and then we do always pray. Thus far Saint Augustine. And without this hearty desire, it is not any noise or sound of words, be it never so long that can stir up the ears of almighty God. But if that be fervent (although there be no sound of any one word heard) it doth most easily penetrate, and obtaineth undelayedly a thorough and gracious audience at the hand of God, as shall more largely and plainly be showed afterward. Therefore whosoever shall in this wise understand the word of our Saviour aforesaid, in my judgement, shall think most rightly. And in another sense, a man cannot easily conceive how he may, or is in any wise able continually without ceasing to pray: but by the fervency of this desire, which is never quenched in the hearts of good men, prayer is always and incessantly made before God, and we do continually knock at the gates of the mercy of God, begging of him his grace and divine assistance. It is therefore very true which Christ our Saviour did say, *Oportet semper orare*, we must always pray, and never give over. (Luke 18) ...

Whether the prayer of the heart only be more fruitful than that wherein the mouth and heart also is occupied.

It resteth now to be discussed whether that prayer be more beneficial to man which he maketh with his heart only, or that which is both uttered from his heart and with his mouth. And here I make this protestation, that I do in no wise purpose or intend anything to say in the dispraise or otherwise, to the derogation of open prayer by words, which is either admitted by custom and the use thereof, or appointed by the ordinance of the Church, or enjoined unto any man by penance or by any means vowed, or in heart by promise taken in hand, whereby any man standeth bound to recite and say his prayers. But yet I do think that a man which is free from any such bond, and enjoyeth full and perfect liberty in Christ, and is studious of the most pure and healthful manner of prayer, shall be oftentimes more hindered by the continual use of praying inwards, than by the exercise of his heart alone, in making of his prayer unto God. For as St Augustine in an Epistle (12, ch. 10) [says]: this work is many times more perfectly wrought by the sighing of the heart than by pronouncing of the mouth, more effectually done by the inward working than by outward speaking. But if the work of prayer be more perfectly performed by the sighing of the heart than with the utterance of the mouth, then must it needs follow that the prayer of the heart, from the which those sighings break forth, be more profitable than the praying with the mouth, whereby words only be uttered. And that may of right be judged for as St Cyprian (*De oratione dominica, Serm. 6.*) doth witness, God giveth ear not to the voice of man's mouth, but to the cry of his heart, neither is he to be moved with words, which see-eth all thoughts. And therefore any simple poor man, which being with great humility prostrate to the ground, lying like a most vile abject, confessing himself a sinner, opening his own miseries, and showing forth the most secret griefs of his heart before the sight of God uttering no words at all, but only pouring forth abundance of tears and sighs of his heart, that man (no doubt) shall most speedily obtain his request of God: which thing did most manifestly appear in Anna the mother of Samuel. For this Anna (as it is written in the first book of the Kings) did most earnestly require of God, being barren, to have a child, for the obtaining whereof, she did frequent the Temple, and there by daily prayer she continually craved the goodness of God, that in her request he would be gracious unto her: And yet did she not frame her prayer in words, but only in her heart. For the Scripture testifieth, that she spake to God with her heart, and that no word was heard that came from her, only her lips moved. To conclude, by this her prayer (of heart I say, without speech outwardly pronounced) she obtained the thing she required of God, and had a son, which she so greatly desired, and had begged of God, with many sighs and abundance of weeping tears, and yet no words by her mouth uttered.

St Jerome agreeth with this, expounding this place of Saint Matthew (chapter 6), when thou doest pray, enter into thy chamber and shutting fast thy door, pray unto thy heavenly father. It seemeth unto me (saith St Jerome) that this is rather a precept, that we keeping secretly in the thought of our hearts, and having our voice suppressed with silence, should so make our prayers unto God, which we also read in the book of the kings, that Anna did, where it is written that her lips only moved, but no voice was heard. This much Saint Jerome writeth. And surely this manner of prayer, doth vehemently move the ears of the mercy of God, and doth mightily bow them speedily to hear us: yea, and as St Paul witnesseth, the holy spirit of God is the guide and the director of this manner of prayer, saying (Romans 8) what we should pray, as we ought to pray, we know not: but the Spirit himself maketh request for us, with unspeakable moanings and sighings. The meaning whereof is, that we do not sufficiently know in what manner we ought to demand anything of God, but the very spirit of God inwardly raising up our hearts, maketh us with unspeakable moan and intercession to require of God, that thing which is most profitable for us. And yet do I not deny, but that any devout man may right well begin his prayer as he list, with words pronounced by his mouth, but so soon as he shall perceive his heart to be any thing kindled and inspired with a sweet delectation coming from the spirit of God, than shall it be most commodious to him, leaving his prayer in words, to follow and give heed to the leading of the spirit of God, and with silence to yield himself wholly to his direction and order.

For as I have said a little before, the end which we ought to appoint upon in prayer is specially the ferventness of charity, by the which at the last our minds be kindled, when with most diligent prayer our hearts be strongly raised, and our minds be highly lifted up unto the beholding of God. And therefore whensoever we may perceive ourselves to have attained unto this end, then must we apply all our endeavour and diligence, that as much as may be, the same be continued in us, which thing shall doubtless much better proceed, by the guiding and operation of the holy spirit, than by any words uttered by our never so great industry and diligence. And therefore we must now with all our power follow the motion and driving of the spirit of God, whithersoever it will lead us, and so need not to utter any more words. In like manner as if a man when after much travail, he hath passed the seas, and hath obtained harbour and his desired haven, leaving his ship which brought him to the haven, intendeth now to the end and purpose for the which he arrived and thinketh now no more of his ship, even so verily, he that by the use of pronounced prayer, as by a mean, is carried into the inward consolation of the mind, and cometh to the spiritual fervency in God, ought now to have his principal care and study bent on this, that this heat in no wise wax cold, and leaving now the prayer of the mouth, he must follow the spirit of God, the minister of this fervent devotion, whithersoever it doth drive him. And now let him not use any more his own words, but only those which be suggested inwardly in the heart by that Holy Spirit of God, and let him ask that of God with vehement and fervent devotion of mind, without any pronunciation or sound of words. But to the end thou mayest more plainly and assuredly perceive, that this manner of prayer, which is done by the spirit and mind is much more excellent than that which is uttered in words, hear what our Saviour Christ saith in the Gospel (John 4) God is a spirit, and they that adore him, must adore him in spirit and truth. Lo, as God is a most spiritual thing, even so requireth he a most spiritual sacrifice. And therefore that prayer is more grateful unto him, which is offered by the spirit and the mind, than the only gross utterance of the voice, which cannot be framed without the bodily breath. And let not this move thee, that 'adore' [*Adorare*] is named in that place, and not 'pray' [*Orare*], for the one of them shall never well be without the other, but when God is prayed unto, then is he also adored, and when he is adored, he is also prayed unto. (3)

## A Dying Man Offers Spiritual Consolation

Alas, alas, I am unworthily taken, all suddenly death hath assailed me, the pains of his stroke be so sore and grievous that I may not long endure them, my last home I perceive well is come. I must now leave this mortal body, I must now depart hence out of this world never to return again into it. But whether I shall go, or where I shall become, or what lodging I shall have this night, or in what company I shall fall, or in what country I shall be received, or in what manner I shall be entreated, God knoweth for I know not. What if I shall be damned in the perpetual prison of Hell, where be pains endless and without number? Grievous it shall be to them that be damned for ever, for they shall be as men in most extreme pains of death, ever wishing and desiring death, and yet never shall they die. It should be now unto me much weary, one year continually to lie upon a bed were it never so soft, how weary then shall it be to lie in the most painful fire so many thousand of years without number? And to be in that most horrible company of devils most terrible to behold, full of malice and cruelty. O wretched and miserable creature that I am, I might so have lived and so ordered my life by the help and grace of my Lord Christ Jesu, that this hour might have been unto me much joyous and greatly desired. Many blessed and Holy saints were full joyous and desirous of this hour, for they knew well that by death their souls should be translated into a new life: to the life of all joy and endless pleasure, from the streights and bondage of this corruptible body, into a very liberty and true freedom among the company of Heaven, from the miseries and grievances of this wretched world, to be above with God in comfort inestimable that can not be spoken nor thought. They were assured of the promises of Almighty God which had so promised to all them that be his faithful servants. And sure I am that if I had truly and faithfully served him unto this hour, my soul had been partner of these promises. But unhappy and ungracious creature that I am, I have been negligent in his service, and therefore now my heart doeth waste in sorrows seeing the nighness of death, and considering my great sloth and negligence. I thought full little thus sudden to have been trapped: But (alas) now death hath prevented me, and hath unwarily attached me, and suddenly oppressed me with his mighty power, so that I know not whither I may turn me for succour, nor where I may seek now for help, nor what thing I may do to get any remedy: If I might have leisure and space to repent me and amend my life, not compelled with this sudden stroke but of my own free will and liberty, and partly for the love of God, putting aside all sloth and negligence. I might then safely die without any dread, I might then be glad to depart hence and leave my manifold miseries and encumbrances of this world.

But how may I think that my repentance or mine amendment cometh now of mine own free will, since I was before this stroke so cold and dull in the service of my Lord God? Or how may I think that I do this more rather for his love, than for fear of his punishment, when if I had truly loved him, I should more quickly and more diligently have served him heretofore? Me seemeth now that I cast away my sloth and negligence compelled by force. Even as a merchant that is compelled by a great tempest in the sea to cast his merchandise out of the ship, it is not to be supposed that he would cast away his riches of his own free will, not compelled by the storm? And even so likewise do I if this tempest of death were not now raised upon me, it is full like that I would not have cast from me my sloth and negligence. O would to God that I might now have some farther respect, and some longer time to amend myself of my free will and liberty. O if I might entreat death to spare me for a season, but that will not be, death in no wise will be entreated, delay he will none take, respect he will none give, if I would give him all the riches of this world, no if all my lovers and friends would fall upon their knees and pray him for me. No if I and they would wéep (if it were so possible) as many tears as there be in the seas drops of water, no piety may restrain him. (Alas) when opportunity of time was, I would not use it well, which if I had done, it would now be unto me more precious than all the treasures of a realm. For then my soul as now should have been clothed with good works innumerable, the which should make me not to be ashamed when I should come to the presence of my Lord God, where now I shall appear loaden with sin miserably, to my confusion and shame...

But as for my good deeds that should be available in the sight of God: (alas) they be few or none that I can think to be available, they must bee done principally and purely for his love. But my deeds when of their kind they were good, yet did I linger them by my folly. For either I did them for the pleasure of men, or to avoid the shame of the world, or else for my own affection, or else for dread of punishment. So that seldom I did any good deed in that purity and straightness that it ought of right to have been done. And my misdeeds, my lewd deeds that be shameful and abominable be without number, not one day of all my life, no not one hour I trow, was so truly expended to the pleasure of God, but many deeds, words, and thoughts, miscaped me in my life. (Alas) little trust then may I have upon my deeds. And as for the prayers of my friends such as I shall leave behind me, of them many peradventure be in the same need that I am in. So that where their own prayers might profit themselves, they cannot so profit another. And many of them will bee full negligent, and some forgetful of me. And no marvell for who should have been more friendly unto me than mine own self?... My purpose therefore dear sister is to minister unto you some common considerations which if you will often resort unto by due remembrance, and so by diligent prayer call upon Almighty God for his love, you shall now by his grace attain it.

The first consideration may be this: First consider by your own mind and reason, that Almighty God of his own singular goodness and free will did create you and make you of nought, whereunto he was not bound by any necessity, nor drawn by any commodity that might rise upon him by your creation. No other thing moved him but his very goodness and special favour that he bear unto you, long or ever he did make you. This, good sister, take for a very truth and firmly believe it, for so it is in very deed innumerable creatures more than ever were made or ever shall be made, he might have made if it had been so pleasing unto him. For how many, suppose you, married men and married women have been and shall be hereafter in this world, that never had nor never shall have any children, yet they full gladly would have had, and by possibility of nature might have had many, if it had so pleased Almighty God to have made and to have given unto them children. But all those be left unmade, and amongst them he might have left you also unmade, and never have put his hand to the making of you, if he had so would...

The second consideration is this, where there is many manner of beings, some creatures have a goodly being, some have an ungoodly being. It is a more goodly being margarite [= a pearl] or a precious stone, than of a pebble stone, of the fair bright gold, than of rusty iron, of a goodly pheasant than of a venomous serpent, of a pretty fawn than of a foul toad, of a reasonable soul, than of an unreasonable beast. And it is not to be doubted but Almighty God might have given to any of them, what being so ever he would, and might have transformed each of those into the nature and kind of any of the other at his pleasure and will. For of the stones he might make men, as in the Gospel Our Saviour doth affirm, Almighty God is of power to make of these stones the children of Abraham. And contrariwise he might of men have made stones as the wife of Lot was turned into a salt stone. And in likewise me or you or any other man or woman, he might have made a stone, or a Serpent, or a Toad, for his pleasure. There is no creature so foul, so horrible, or so ungoodly, but he might put you in the same condition that the most loathly of them be put in, and them, in contrariwise he might have put in the same condition that you be in. Consider now by your reason, that if you had been made in the likeness of an Owl, or of an Ape, or of a Toad, how deformed you should have been, and in how wretched and miserable condition. And thank your Lord God that hath given you a more excellent nature, yea, such a nature as excelleth in nobleness, in dignity, all other bodily natures: for it is made to the very likeness and image of Almighty God: whereunto none other bodily creature doth reach near...

The seventh consideration is this: where now it appeareth unto you, that if you will give your love freely, there is none so worthy to have it as Jesu, the Son of the Virgin Mary. I will further show unto you that if you will not freely give it, but you will look peradventure to have some thing again, yet there is none so well worthy to have it as he is, for if another will give more for it than he, I will not be against it, take your advantage. But sure I am there is none other to whom your love is so dear, and of so great price as it is unto him, nor any that will come nigh unto that, that he hath given or will give. If his benefits and kindness showed towards you, whereof I speak somewhat before, were by you well pondered, they be no small benefits, and especially the love of so great a prince, and that he would thus love you, and prefer you before so many innumerable creatures of his, and that when there was in you no love, and when you could not skill of love [sic]: yea, and that, that more is, when you were enemy unto him yet he loved you, and so wonderfully that for your love and to wash you from sin, and to deliver your soul from the extreme peril he shed his most precious blood, and suffered the most shameful, the most cruel, and the most painful death of the cross, his head to be pierced with thorns, his hands and feet to be through-holed with nails, his side to be lanced with a spear, and all his most tender body to be torn and rent with whips and scourges. Believe this for a very truth, good sister, that for your sake he suffered all, as if there had been no more in all the world but only your self, which I will declare more largely unto you in the next consideration following. Believe it in the mean time certainly, for so it is indeed, and if you believe it not, you do a great injury and show a full unkindness unto him that thus much hath done for you. And if this belief truly settle in your heart, it is to me a marvel if you can content your heart without the love of him, of him I say, that thus dearly hath loved you, and doth love you still. For what other lover will do thus much for your love? What creature in all the world will die for your sake? What one person will depart with one drop of his heart blood for your sake? when then the son of God, the prince of Heaven, the Lord of Angels hath done this for your sake, which thing no other creature will do, what frost could have un-gelled your heart, that it may not relent against so great an heat of love? if he so excellent in all nobleness should have given you but one favourable countenance from the Heavens above, it had been a more precious benefit than ever you could recompense by your love again. It were impossible for your love to recompense that one thing...

The eighth consideration is this: that albeit, there are many others which also are beloved of Christ Jesu, yet the love that he showeth to them, nothing diminisheth his love towards you, as if there were no more beloved of him in all the kind of man. This may evidently be showed unto you by this example following. If before any image of Our Saviour were disposed and set in a long row many glasses, some great and some little, some high and some low, a convenient distance from the image, so that every of them might receive a presentment of the image, it is no doubt but in every of these glasses should appear the very likeness of the same image I will not say but this likeness should be longer in the great glasses than in the less, and clearer in the better cleansed glasses, and in them that were nigh unto the image, than in the other that were not so well cleansed, and much farther of. But as to the likeness itself it shall be as full and as whole in every one glass as though there were but one. Now to my purpose, if you consider likewise that all the good souls that be scourged from deadly sin, be in the manner of glasses set in an order to receive the love of Our Saviour Christ Jesu. Such souls as by true penance doing, by sighing, by weeping, by praying, by watching, by fasting, and by other like, be the better scoured and cleansed from the spots and malice of deadly sin, they be the brighter glasses and more clearly receive this love, and such also be near unto Our Saviour, for nothing putteth us far from him but only sin. And therefore they that have more diligently scoured their souls from the rust of sin, be nearer unto him, than the other that so have not done. Such souls also as of their part enforce themselves to a great love and to a more ample fervour, they do enlarge the capacity of their souls, to receive a more large abundance of love again, those that less enforce them, have a less capacity in receiving, and therefore so much the less they receive of this love...

The ninth consideration is this, where peradventure you would object to me again and say: brother, if it be thus as you say, that my Lord Jesu loveth me so much, and is so mindful of me, and so fervently intendeth my weal, what need me to care whatsoever I do, he will not cast me away, he will not forsake me nor suffer me to perish. Good sister without doubt as I have said, Our Saviour Christ Jesu is in love towards you, and he is mindful and more loving towards you than I can express. And sure you may be, that he will never cast you away, nor forsake you, if you before cast not yourself away, nor forsake yourself. But if you give any place to sin in your soul, and suffer it to enter upon you, verily then you forsake your self and cast yourself away, and willingly destroy yourself, that is your deed and not his: for he never forsaketh any creature unless they before have forsaken themselves. And if they will forsake themselves were they never in so great favour with him before, they then incontinently lose his favour, the which thing well appeareth in his first spiritual creatures, the noble angels Lucifer and his company, which were created in excellent brightness, and were much in the favour of Almighty God, they presumptuously offended him in pride for the which not only, they lost his favour, but also their marvellous brightness became incontinently horrible, foul, and were expelled out of the glorious Kingdom of Heaven that they were in, and thrown into perpetual darkness into the prison of Hell. The first man Adam also who was created in singular honour, and was put into paradise a place full of gladness, there to live in comfort of all pleasure, the which was done to him for a singular love that Almighty God had towards him, yet anon as he fell to sin he was in like manner expelled out from that pleasure, and sent into this miserable world to endure misery and pain. If those noble creatures which were lift up into so great favour with Almighty God, so lightly by their misdemeanor in sin, lost his gracious favour, let none other creature think but if they admit any sin to their soul, they shall be likewise excluded out of his favour.

The tenth consideration is this: it were well done and much it should further this cause if you truly esteem of how little value your love is, how vain, how light, and how triflous a thing it is, and how few there be that would much regard it, or set much price thereby, for few there be or none to whom it may do any profit or avail. Contrariwise you should consider the love of your spouse the sweet Jesu, how excellent it is, how sure, how fast, how constantly abiding, how many have much specially regarded it, martyrs innumerable both men and women for his love have shed their blood, and have endured every kind of martyrdom were it never so cruel, were it never so terrible. No pain, no tormenting, might compel them to forsake his love: so desirous were they of his love, that rather than they would forgo it, they gave no force of the loss of all this world beside, and their own life also...

The final conclusion of all. Now then, good Sister, I trust that these considerations, if you often read them with good deliberation, and truly imprint them in your remembrance, they will somewhat inflame your heart with the love of Christ Jesu, and that love once established in you, all the other points and ceremonies of your religion shall be easy unto you, and no whit painful, you shall then comfortably do every thing that to good religion appertaineth, without any great weariness. Nevertheless if it so fortune that you at any time begin to feel any dullness of mind quicken it again by the meditation of death, which I send you here before, or else by some effectual prayer, earnestly calling for help and succour upon the most sweet Jesu, thinking as it is indeed, that is your necessity, and that no where else you can have any help but of him. And if you will use these short prayers following, for every day in the week once, I think it shall be unto you profitable. For thus you may in your heart shortly pray what company so ever you be amongst...

The Prayers be these.

O blessed Jesu make me to love thee entirely.

O blessed Jesu I would fain but without thy help I can not. [*sic*]

O blessed Jesu let me deeply consider the greatness of thy love towards me.

O blessed Jesu give unto me grace heartily to thank thee for thy benefits.

O blessed Jesu give me good will to serve thee, and to suffer.

O sweet Jesu give me a natural remembrance of thy passion.

O sweet Jesu possess my heart, hold and keep it only to thee.

These short prayers if you will often say, and with all the power of your soul and heart, they shall marvellously kindle in you this love so that it shall be always fervent and quick, the which is my especial desire to know in you. For nothing may be to my comfort more than to hear of your furtherance and profiting in God and in good religion, the which our blessed Lord grant you for his great mercy. Amen.(4)

NOTES AND SOURCES

1. John Fisher, *Here after foloweth a mornynge remembrau[n]ce had at the moneth mynde of the noble prynces Margarete countesse of Rychemonde [et] Darbye moder vnto kynge Henry the. vii. [et] grandame to oure souerayne lorde that nowe is* (1509) unpag.

2. John Fisher, *A sermon had at Paulis by the comandment of the most reuerend father in god my lorde legate, and sayd by Ioh bysshop of Rochester, vpon quiquagesom sonday, concernyng certayne heretickes* (1526), unpag.

3. John Fisher, *A Godlie treatisse declaryng the benefites, fruites, and great commodities of prayer and also the true vse therof. Written in Latin, fourtie yeres past, by an Englyshe man, of great vertue [and] learnyng. And lately translated into Englyshe. 1560* (1560), unpag.

4. John Fisher, *A spirituall consolation, written by Iohn Fyssher Bishoppe of Rochester, to hys sister Elizabeth, at suche tyme as hee was prisoner in the Tower of London. Uery necessary, and commodious for all those that mynde to leade a vertuous lyfe: also to admonishe them, to be at all tymes prepared to dye, and seemeth to bee spoken in the person of one that was sodainly preue[n]ted by death* (1578), unpag.

# Nicholas Harpsfield                                              1519–1574

Nicholas Harpsfield became a member of the More circle while a Fellow of New College Oxford, where he was to remain until the aggressively Protestant phase of the reign of Edward VI when he withdrew—along with Sir Thomas More's nephew William Rastell—to Louvain. Together they planned the edition of More's works, in English and in Latin, which appeared in 1557 and 1564. Harpsfield was additionally commissioned by William Roper, effectively by then More's literary executor, to write a model life of More for the first volume. It is from this that our extract comes. Harpsfield was to be a highly effective Archdeacon of Canterbury under Mary I, and a keen pursuer of heretics (hence his unflinching account of More as heresy-hunter in his *Life*). Imprisoned early in Elizabeth's reign for obstructing the implementation of her church settlement and for refusing the revised Oath of Supremacy, he spent the last fifteen years in prison, writing long Latin tracts in defence of Mary, and in defiance of all aspects of the Reformation.

## The Private Life of Sir Thomas More

True it is also, that notwithstanding the like calumniations and false slanders of his adversaries, he lived and died also afterwards (though these men defame him with a new-found kind of treason) most innocently and most honourably. The full declaration of which his life and death doth now remain to be by us opened and declared.

But inasmuch as we have many other things touching this man worthy to be remembered, we will interlace them before. And as we have hitherto prosecuted his public doings in the common affairs of the realm, himself being the highest magistrate, after the King, in the same, and will hereafter also in convenient place declare what account be rendered to the prince and magistrates, being afterwards a private man, of his public doings. So will we now in the meanwhile recount unto you, first his private, secret and domestical life and trade with his wife, children, family and others. And then because the world well knew him and so took him, and the testimony of learned men and his own books withal bear good and substantial record thereof, for a great excellent learned man, we will not altogether pretermit [= neglect to mention] his said books, but speak so much as shall seem to serve the turn.

First then will we lay before you a description of some part of his said private life and doings. In whom this is principally to be considered, as the root and head of all his well doings, that always he had a special and singular regard and respect to Godward, and to keep his conscience whole, sincere and upright. And this among other was one of his good, virtuous and godly properties, conditions and customs, that when he entered into any matter or office of importance, as when he was chosen to be one of the King's Privy Council, when he was sent ambassador, appointed Speaker of the Parliament, made Lord Chancellor, or when he took any weighty matter or affair upon him, he would go to the Church and be confessed, he would hear Mass and be houseled [i.e., he would receive holy communion].

He used, yea, being Lord Chancellor, to sit and sing in the choir with a surplice on his back. And when that the Duke of Norfolk, coming at a time to Chelsea to dine with him, fortuned to find him in his attire and trade, going homeward after service, arm in arm with him, said after this fashion: 'God body, God body, my Lord Chancellor, a parish clerk, a parish clerk! You dishonor the King and his office'; 'nay', quoth Sir Thomas More, smiling upon the Duke, 'your Grace may not think that the King, your master and mine, will with me, for serving God *his* master, be offended, or there account his office dishonoured.' Wherein Sir Thomas did very godly and devoutly, and spake very truly and wisely. What would the Duke have said if he had seen that great and mighty Emperor Charles the Great, playing the very same part; or King David, long before, hopping and dancing naked before the ark?

He was sometimes for godly purposes desirous to be solitary, and to sequester himself from worldly company. And therefore the better to satisfy and accomplish this his godly desire, he built a good distance from his mansion house at Chelsea, a place called the New Building, wherein there was a chapel, a library and a gallery. In which, as his use was upon other days to occupy himself in prayer and study together, so on the Friday there usually continued he from morning to evening, spending his time alone in devout prayers and spiritual exercises.[13]

As to the poor, for God's sake he was good and pitiful, so used he another rare and singular form of alms of his own body, as to punish the same with whips, the cords knotted. And albeit by reason he would not be noted of singularity, he

[13] The text says 'onely', which I take as 'alone' not 'only' and have so modernized.

conformed himself outwardly to other men for his apparel, according to his state and vocation, yet how little he inwardly esteemed such vanities, it well appeared by his shirt of hair that he wore secretly next his body; whereof no person was privy but his daughter only, Mistress Margaret Roper, whom for her secrecy he above all other trusted, causing her, as need arose, to wash the same shirt of hair, saving that it chanced once that as he sat at supper in the summer, singly in his doublet and hose, wearing upon the said secret shirt of hair a plain linen shirt without ruff or collar, that a young gentlewoman, Mistress More, sister of the said Margaret, chancing to espy the same, began to laugh at it. His daughter Margaret, not ignorant of his manner, perceiving the same, privily told him of it. And he, being sorry that she saw it, presently amended it.

As he was not ambitious and greedy of honour and worldly preferment, and one that in twenty years service to the King never craved of him anything for himself, and as he, after that he was by his well-deserving and by the King's free and mere goodness advanced and promoted, did not look up on high and solemnly set by himself with the contempt and disdain of other, so was he nothing grieved but rather glad (for, as I have showed, he did procure it) when he was rid of the chancellorship. And whereas upon Holy Days during his high office, one of his gentlemen, when service at the Church was done, ordinarily used to come to my Lady his wife's pew and say unto her: 'Madam, my Lord is gone'. The next holy-day after the surrender of his office and departure of his gentleman, he came unto my Lady his wife's pew himself, and making a low curtsy, said unto her 'Madam, my Lord is gone.'

As prosperity did nothing lift him up with haughtiness and pride, so no mischance or trouble that very heavily fell upon him afterwards could infringe or break his great patience and constancy, as we shall declare hereafter more at large. A little before he was made Lord Chancellor, it chanced his barns and all his corn at Chelsea by reckless negligence to be burnt and consumed by fire, and some of his neighbours' houses; whereof he being at Court and understanding, wrote to his wife a comfortable letter, willing her, their children and all their family to repair to the Church to give God thanks, who might have taken away the residue they had besides. And willed diligent search and inquiry to be made what damage his poor neighbours had taken thereby, which, he said, should be recompensed and restored (as it was) to the uttermost farthing. (1)

NOTES AND SOURCES

1. *Harpsfield's Life of More*, ed. E. V. Hitchcock (Early English Text Society, 1932), 63–7.

# William Roper 1498–1572

William Roper was married to Thomas More's daughter Margaret and he produced one of the two near-contemporary biographies of St Thomas with all the advantages of having lived in his household 'xvi years or more'. Thomas and William's fathers had been great friends so the bonds were close and their mutual love and admiration undoubted. This friendship is impressive, for intellectually they were far apart. Early in his married life, Roper became a 'marvellous zealous Protestant'; and only Cardinal Wolsey's leniency ('for love borne to Sir Thomas') spared him the penalties of heresy. More spent many hours in intellectual debate but got nowhere: he gave up on argument and turned to prayer, which worked. Roper returned to Catholic orthodoxy. But Roper was 'neither humanist nor Hellenist or a theologian but a conservative lawyer'[14] and when crunch time came in the 1530s and Thomas refused the oath of supremacy, Roper took it without any quibble or dissembling. It is important to realize that not the least of More's dark nights in the Tower was his wife's and his son-in-law's (though not Margaret's) incomprehension at his refusal of the oath. With the death of Margaret in 1544, Roper became the trustee of More's papers and memory. He worked with Nicholas Harpsfield and William Rastell to produce the great edition of More's works which was to appear in the 1550s. When the others moved to Louvain during English Protestantism's first heyday under Edward VI, Roper gritted his teeth and stayed in England to make (lots of) money to support them and their work. He commissioned not only the *English Works* of More (1557) and the *Latin Works* (1564) but the biography from Nicholas Harpsfield. He remained in England until his death, publicly sworn to the Protestant regime, privately doing all he could for Catholics and Catholicism. He wrote his own memoir of More, including the following extract.

## More in the Tower Observed

After he had remained in the Tower about a month, his daughter Roper (having greatly desired to see her Father) made earnest suit, and got leave to visit him: at whose coming after the saying of the seven Psalms and Litanies, which he was ever accustomed to say with her) before they fell into discourse of any other matter, among other speeches he said unto her: I believe Meg, that they who have put me here think they have done me a great displeasure: But I assure thee on my faith (mine own good daughter) if it had not been for my wife and you my Children, whom I accompt the chief part of my charge, I would not have failed long ere now, to have enclosed myself in a straiter room than this. But since I am come hither, without mine own desert, I trust that God of his goodness will disburden me of my care, and with his gracious help supply my want amongst you. And I find no cause (I thank God, Meg) to reckon myself in worse case here, than in mine own house. For methinks in this case, God maketh me even a wanton, setting me upon his knee, and dandling me.

Sir Thomas More being now prisoner in the Tower, and one day looking forth at his window, saw a Father of Sion (named Mr Reynolds) and three monks of the Charterhouse, going out of the Tower to execution, for that they had refused the Oath of Supremacy whereupon, he languishing it were with desire to bear them company said unto his daughter then present: Look, dost thou not see that these blessed Fathers be now going as cheerfully to their deaths, as Bridegrooms to their marriages? By which thou mayest see (mine own dear daughter) what a great difference there is between such as have spent all their days in a religious, hard, and penitential life, and such as have, in this world, like wretches (as thy poor Father here hath done) consumed all their time in pleasure and ease...

Now Sir Thomas More had continued almost six weeks in the Tower, before the Lady his wife could obtain licence to visit him. Who at her first coming to him

[14]  H. R.Trevor-Roper, 'Roper, William (1495×8–1578)', *Oxford Dictionary of National Biography*, Oxford University Press, 2004; online edn., May 2005, <http://www.oxforddnb.com/view/article/24074>, accessed 29 Jan. 2010.

(like a good simple worldly woman) bluntly saluted him in this manner: What
[sic] a good-care *Mr More*, I marvel that you, who have been always hitherto taken
for so wise a man, will now so play the fool to lie here in this close filthy prison,
and be content to be thus shut up amongst mice and rats, when you might be
abroad at your liberty, with the favour and goodwill both of the King and his
Council, if you would but do as all the Bishops, and best learned of the realm have
done? And since you have at Chelsea a right fair house, your Library, your Books,
your Garden, your Orchard, and all other necessaries handsome about you where
also you might, in the company of me your wife, Children and household be
merry; muse what in God's name you mean thus fondly to tarry here?

    After he had a while quietly heard her, with a cheerful countenance he said unto
her. I pray thee good Alice, tell me one thing. What is that, quoth she? Is not this
house as near Heaven as mine own? Whereto after her accustomed homely
fashion not liking such speeches she answered: Tille-valle [*sic*]. (1)

NOTES AND SOURCES

1.  William Roper, *The Mirrour of Vertue in Worldly Greatnes. Or The life of Syr Thomas More Knight,
    sometime Lo. Chancellour of England* (1626), 126–8, 133–5, 137–8.

## Margaret Roper                                                    1505–1544

Margaret Roper was the daughter of Sir Thomas More and a woman of extraordinary learning
as well as of courage. At the age of 18 she read, for curiosity, Erasmus's edition of the letters of
St Cyprian and noticed an error in Erasmus's Latin and the misattribution of a letter actually
written by Novatian (a heretic and schismatic) but ascribed by Erasmus to Cyprian. Erasmus
was delighted to be caught out and, by way of tribute, wrote for her a witty dialogue about a
young woman outwitting a foolish abbot. She, in her turn, then set out to translate one of his
recent works, a treatise on the *Pater Noster*. It is probably the only work by a woman as young
as 19 to have been published in the sixteenth century. Margaret was the only one of More's
family to stand by him completely when to the world at large he was a pariah. She visited him
and wrote to him as he languished in the Tower, waiting upon Henry VIII's capricious will. Not
once but twice she pushed herself through the armed guards as More was being dragged
away after his condemnation, for a final embrace and blessing; and it was Margaret who was
to haggle with the keeper of Tower Bridge over how much money it would take for him to
hand over to her her father's boiled and tarred head (rather than just casting it into the
Thames) when the time came for the head of another victim of Henry's justice to be displayed
on the bridge. The head is thought to have been buried with her in 1544. Our extracts begin
with part of the preface by Richard Hyrde, Sir Thomas More's physician and already the
translator of the Spanish humanist Jean-Luis Vives's tract on the education of women. Then
we have Margaret's translation of Erasmus's commentary on one of the petitions of the Lord's
prayer. It has been described as 'instilling a familiar, cosy, domestic idiom into the idea of a
loving, merciful God', full of 'inspired techniques of translation'[15] that gets the essence and
the true spirit of Erasmus's luminous Latin. No wonder Erasmus was enraptured by her, and
her father so proud of her. It has a prophetic side to it...

[15]  J. Guy, *A Daughter's Love: Thomas and Margaret More* (London: Fourth Estate, 2008), 150–1.

## A Commendation of Female Learning

I have heard many men put great doubt whether it should be expedient and requisite or not a woman to have learning in books of Latin and Greek. And some utterly affirm that it is not only neither necessary nor profitable but also very noisome and jeopardous: alleging for their opinion that the frail kind of women being inclined of their own courage unto vice and mutable at every novelty if they should have skill in many things that be written in the Latin and Greek tongue compiled and made with great craft and eloquence where the matter is happily sometime more sweet unto the ear than wholesome for the mind, it would of likelihood both enflame their stomachs a great deal the more to that vice that men say they be too much given unto of their own nature already and instruct them also with more subtlety and conveyance to set forward and accomplish their forward intent and purpose. But these men that so say do in my judgement either regard but little what they speak in this matter or else as they be for the more part unlearned, they envy it and take it sore to heart that other should have that precious jewel which they neither have themselves nor can find in their hearts to take the pain to get ... And as for the translation herein, I dare be bold to say it that who so list and well can confer and examine the translation with the original, he shall not fail to find that she hath showed herself not only erudite and elegant in either tongue, but hath also used such wisdom, such discreet and substantial judgement in expressing lively the Latin as a man may peradventure miss in many things translated and turned by them that bear the name of rightwise and very well learned men; and the labour that I have had with it about the printing I yield wholly and freely give unto you in whose good manners and virtue as in a child I have so great affection ... (1)

## A Meditation on the Lord's Prayer

*Et ne nos in ducas in tentationem* [And lead us not into temptation]. O good Father in Heaven, albeit there is nothing that we greatly fear, having the merciful unto us [sic] and while mutual love and charity each with other maketh us thy children of more strength against every evil assault; yet when we consider how weak and frail the nature of man is, and how ignorant also we be whom thy goodness will judge and think worthy the continuance in thy love to the end of this life in which as long as we are a thousand manner of ways we be steered to fall and ruin. Therefore we cannot be utterly seeker and careless: all this life is round about beset with the devil's snares; he never ceaseth tempting us which was not afraid with crafty subtleties to set upon thy son Jesus. We call to mind how grievously the fiend assaulted thy servant Job; we remember how Saul was first thy elect and chosen servant and within a while after cast out of thy light; we cannot forget how David whom you called a man even after thine own appetite was drawn to that great villainy of sin that he mingled adultery with manslaughter; we consider how Solomon, whom in the beginning of his rule thou gavest wisdom above all men, was brought to that madness and folly that he died sacrifice to strange and utter Gods. We remember also what befell the chief and head of thine apostles which after that he had so valiantly professed that he would die with his master notwithstanding thrice forswear his master. These and such many other when we consider, we cannot but fear and bear the jeopardy of temptation: and thy fatherly love would us always to be in this fear because we should not sluggishly and slothfully begin to trust in our own help but defend and arm ourselves against every sort of temptation with sober temperance, watch and prayer.

Whereby we should neither provoke our enemy, remembering our own feebleness, nor be overthrown in the storm of temptation, trusting to thy aid without which we are able to do right, naught you sufferest among temptation to fall either to prove and make steadfast the sufferance and patience of thy children, as Job and Abraham were tempted, or else by such scourges to correct and chasten our offences: but how often soever thou sufferest this, we pray thee thou wilt bring that same temptation to good and lucky end and give us strength equal to the mountenaunce [= extent, quantity] and weight of the evils that come upon us, it is no little jeopardy whensoever we be threatened with loss of our goods, with banishment, rebukes, imprisonment, with bands and bodily tormenting and horrible and fearful death. But we are in no less peril at all when prosperity too much laugheth on us than when we be overmuch feared with trouble and adversity. They are an innumerable sort which fall on every side: some for fear of punishment do sacrifice to wicked devils; some overthrown and astonished with evils and vexations, do blaspheme thy most holy name; and again some drowned with overmuch worldly wealth set at naught and despise thy gifts of grace and return again into their old and former filthiness as the son that the Scripture speaketh of, which after time he had spent and revelled out all his father's substance by unthrifty and ungracious rule was brought to that misery and wretchedness that he envied the swine their chaff. We know well, good father, that our adversary hath no power over us at all but by thy sufferance; wherefore we be content to be put to whatsoever jeopardy it pleaseth thee so it will like thy gentleness to measure our enemy's assault and our strength for so though we be sometime in the first meeting too weak yet thy wisdom in the conclusion will turn it to our wealth. So thy most dear and honourable son was ever wont to overcome the devil—thus the flesh; and thus the world—so that when he seemed most to be oppressed he then most specially triumphed; and he fought for us; he overcame for us; and triumphed for us. Let us also overcome by his example with thy help and by the holy ghost proceeding from both for ever. Amen. (2)

NOTES AND SOURCES

1. *A deuoute treatise vpon the Pater noster, made fyrst in latyn by the moost famous doctour mayster Erasmus Roterodamus, and tourned in to englisshe by a yong vertuous and well lerned gentylwoman of. xix. yere of age* (1526), unpag.
2. Ibid.

## St (and Sir) Thomas More           1478–1535

Thomas More was indeed, as Erasmus, the greatest intellectual of the day, called him, 'a man for all seasons'. The son of a lawyer and judge, Thomas was himself a lawyer, a statesman, a scholar, a prolific author, one drawn both to the cloister and to family life, a man unflinchingly drawn to martyrdom when faced with the choice between faith and political expediency. More drafted the rebuttal to Luther's view of the Sacraments issued in Henry VIII's name that earned the King the papal title *Fidei Defensor*. In the end it was the ghost writer not the front man who lived up to that title. It is hard to think of anyone in this period of polymaths whose life was so varied and so grounded in faith. Two experiences in his early life appear to control all that happened afterwards. First, there are his years from the age of 11 in the household of the humanist-leaning John Morton, Archbishop of Canterbury and Lord Chancellor to Henry VII, a place of debate and great learning, visited by the greatest intellectuals—Erasmus included—and internationally minded politicians of the day, a place of great debate and learning. Secondly, following two years of study in Oxford and during his extended training in both Roman and common law, there are his four years sharing the life and daily prayer of the London Charterhouse. He was torn between life in the world and life in the cloister. His first thought on how to unite the two was, as he told Erasmus, life as a Franciscan. His father's relentless pressure led him to opt for the law and for marriage, to a household open to the learned and the witty, in which he rejoiced in bringing up his daughters, against all convention, to be as learned as he had been at their age. But the call of the cloister never left him, and informed his devotional life. Indeed the extraordinary flowering of his thought and writing in harsh imprisonment in the Tower was clearly a consequence of the freedom he had there to live the life of the ascetic. His training in law and in letters brought him to the King's attention and more especially the attention of Cardinal Wolsey, another great humanist, who was however far from an ascetic and combined a deep compassion for the poor with an untroubled enjoyment of the sins of the flesh. More became one of Henry VIII's counsellors in 1518, and served him as legal officer, envoy, and parliamentary manager for eleven years until Wolsey's fall from power for failing to secure Henry's divorce and remarriage to Anne Boleyn. More found himself thrust into the hottest seat in government, succeeding Wolsey as Lord Chancellor. For four years his selfless devotion to office found expression in radical law reform, preferential action for the poor, and the pursuit of heresy and the punishment of heretics. He allowed others to pursue the King's 'Great Matter' and neither helped nor hindered the King's furious assault on the clergy as surrogates for the Pope on account of papal obstruction of his dynastic lusts. But with the formal breach from Rome, and with the introduction of the Oath of Supremacy that required a renunciation of papal jurisdiction over the Church in England, More found an issue which he could not dodge. Loss of office was not sufficient: the king needed to show lesser folk that he would not tolerate dissent. Lord Chancellor More and Bishop John Fisher were to be made scapegoats. Both refused the oath, and although More (unlike Fisher) refused to say why he refused it (relying on the common law dogma that 'silence implies consent') evidence was procured (it is assumed by perjured evidence) that he had privately denied the king's authority and after a show trial he was condemned to death and beheaded within the walls of the Tower of London. He was in the Tower for just over a year, but in that year, devotional works poured out of him, hundreds of thousands of words. Our first extract comes from Sir Thomas More's *Utopia*, first printed in Latin in 1516 and here taken from Ralph Robynson's rapturous translation, published in 1556. It describes More's fictional encounter in Antwerp (where More actually was in 1515 on a diplomatic errand) with one Raphael Hythloday, said to have travelled to the Americas with Amerigo Vespucci. It describes the fictional island of Utopia and analyses its social, cultural, and institutional forms. Book 1, however contains an extended discussion of whether the good humanist should seek public office (as More did) or devote himself to scholarship and the writing of wise books, as advocated by Hythloday (and by More's friend Erasmus), surely the man More was writing for. It has been described as 'a book of serious thought, considerable wit, genuine literary imagination, and profound ambiguity'.[16] We offer an extract in which More defends the life to which he had just committed himself. The next extract comes from a work, whose full title is self-sufficient: *A dialogue of Sir Thomas More knight: one of the council of our sovereign Lord the King, Chancellor of his duchy of Lancaster. Wherein be treated divers matters, as of the veneration [and] worship of images [and] relics, praying to saints, [and] going o[n] pilgrimage. With many other things touching the pestilent sect of Luther and Tyndale* (1529). It was published when Protestantism was still a nasty irritant and not yet a serious threat to the position of the Catholic Church or the practice or consciences of members of the church established.

The third selection comes from the *Dialogue Concerning Heresies* (1529). More has sometimes been accused of being vindictive in his pursuit of heretics, and of rushing to judgement against them. It is certainly true that he did not challenge the conventional wisdom of his age that heretics were a gangrene in the body politic and needed to be cut out and the wounds they occasioned cauterized (hence the penalty of burning), and that he himself encouraged the prosecution of a number of heretics. His fierce and ascetic faith left him in doubt. But in *A Dialogue Concerning Heresies*, he meditated on the issues raised, and here, at the heart of his treatise (chapter 12) he offers his defence of 'the burning of heretics, and that it is lawful, necessary and well done'. As with so much of his writing, it takes the form of a response to an anonymous interlocutor. The fourth set of extracts comes from *A Brief Form of Confession Instructing all Christian Folk how to Confess their Sins*, a rare example of a layman giving instruction on sacramental preparation. We include the introduction and then, as he goes systematically through the Ten Commandments as a tool for examining the conscience, we include his reflections on the sixth commandment. Here, in the midst of More the humanist Christian, More the lawyer keeps intruding himself. The fifth extract is from More's unfinished *Treatise upon the Passion of Christ Made in the Year of our Lord* 1534. The lengthy series of meditations working their way through the Passion narrative each ends with a prayer, and we include those prayers appended to the various meditations on the Last Supper. The sixth and seventh extracts comes from *A Godly Instruction* (1534). As More prepared himself for death, he had to deal with the feelings of rage against those who had wronged him. Here was the lawyer in him pleading that he might let his heart melt to forgive his greatest (albeit unnamed) enemy, most likely Sir Richard Rich (for securing his conviction by giving perjured evidence) or just possibly the king he had served so loyally and who had betrayed him so cruelly. The eighth extract demonstrates the centrality of More not only as saint and martyr and his courageous witness to the faith, but also of the importance of his *words* in shaping English Catholic piety. In many of the books of prayers and devotions published for the recusant community between the late sixteenth and the eighteenth centuries, More's prayers at the end of his life are included, some embellished by later editors. We include some of them from a Book of Prayers published in 1650 (see below). The final extract is from More's final letter, on the eve of his execution, written to his daughter and soul-mate Meg. No other member of his family could understand why he was determined not to bend to the tyrant's demands. But she understood and she stood by him. We offer here his final, tender words to her.

---

[16] Ed. D. H. Sacks, *Utopia by Sir Thomas More* (Boston/New York: Bedford Series in History and Culture, 1999), p. ix.

## Humanist Counsel

'This is what I meant', quoth [Hythloday], 'when I said philosophy had no place among kings.'

'Indeed', quoth I, 'this scholastic philosophy hath not, which thinketh all things meet for every place. But there is another philosophy more civil which knoweth, as you would say, her own stage, and thereafter ordering and behaving herself in the play that she hath on hand, playeth her part accordingly with comeliness, uttering nothing out of due order and fashion. And this is the philosophy that you must use. Or else, whilst a comedy of Plautus is playing and vile bondmen scoffing and trifling among themselves, if you should suddenly come upon the stage in a philosopher's apparel and rehearse out of *Octavia* the place wherein Seneca disputeth with Nero, had it not been better for you to have played the dumb person than by rehearsing that which served neither for the time nor place to have such a tragical comedy or gallimaufry? For by bringing in other stuff that nothing appertaineth to the present matter, you must needs mar and pervert the play that is in hand, though the stuff that you bring be much better. What part soever you have taken upon you, play that as well as you can and make the best of it, and do not, therefore, disturb and bring out of order the whole matter, because that other which is merrier and better cometh to your remembrance.'

'So the case standeth in a commonwealth, and so it is in the consultations of kings and princes. If evil opinions and haughty persuasions cannot be utterly and quite plucked out of their hearts, if you cannot even as you would remedy vices which use and custom hath confirmed, yet for this cause you must not leave and forsake the commonwealth. You must not forsake the ship in a tempest because you cannot rule and keep down the winds. No, nor you must not labour to drive into their heads new and strange informations, which you know well shall be nothing regarded with them that be of clean contrary minds. But you must with a crafty wile and subtle train study and endeavour yourself, as much as in you lies, to handle the matter wittily and handsomely for the purpose, and that which you cannot turn to go so to order it that it be not very bad, for it is not possible for all things to be well unless all men were good, which I think will not be yet these good many years.' (1)

## On Pilgrimages

The author declareth in the conprobation of pilgrimages that it is the pleasure of God to be specially sought and worshipped in some one place before another. And albeit that we cannot attain to the knowledge of the cause why God doth so yet the author proveth by great authority that God by miracle testifyeth it is so...

Then he asked me whereby was I so sure of that; whereupon I demanded him that if it so were that the thing standing in debate and question, it would like Our Lord to show a miracle [*sic*] for the proof of the one part. Would you not, quod I, reckon than the question were decided and the doubt assoiled [= to set free, discharge, or release] and that part sufficiently proved. Yes, marry, quod he, that would I. Well, quod I, then is this matter out of doubt long ago. For God hath proved my part in diverse pilgrimages by the working of many more than a thousand miracles one time and other. In the Gospel of John the fifth chapter where we read that the angel moved the water and whoso next went in was cured of his disease, was it not a sufficient proof that God would they should come thither for their health, albeit no man can tell why he sent the angel rather thither and there did his miracles than in another water? But whensoever Our Lord hath in any place wrought a miracle although he nothing do it for that place, but for the honour of that saint whom he will have honoured in that place, or for the faith that he findeth with some that prayeth in that place or for the increase of faith which he findeth failing and decayed in that place needing the show of some miracles for the reviving whatsoever the cause be...

Because pilgrimage be among other proofs testified by miracles, the messenger doth make objection against those miracles partly lest they be feigned and untrue, partly lest they be done by the devil if they be done at all ... First sith you men may and happily do of miracles make many a lie, we must not prove this matter by the miracles, but if we first prove it the miracles were true. And over this if they were done indeed yet since the angel of darkness may transform and transfigure himself into an angel of light, how shall we know whether the miracle were done by God to the increase of Christian devotion or done by the craft of the devil to the advancement of misbelief and idolatry in setting men's hearts upon stocks and stones instead of saints or upon saints themselves that are but creatures instead of God himself.

I answered him that the force of my tale was not the miracles but the thing that I hold stronger than any miracles which, as I said in the beginning, I reckon so sure and fast and therewith so plain and evident unto every Christian man. It needeth no other proof, and the thing is as I laid afore, the faith of Christ's Church by the common consent whereof these matters be decided and well known that the worship of saints and images been allowed, approbate and accustomed for good Christian and meritorious virtues. And the contrary opinion not only reproved by many holy doctors but also condemned for heresies by sundry general councils... (2)

## On Heresy and Heretics

The fear of these outrages and mischiefs to follow upon such sects and heresies with the proof that men have had in some countries thereof have been the cause that princes and people have been constrained to punish heresies by terrible death whereas else more easy ways had been taken with them. And therefore here will I somewhat answer the points which you have moved at our first meeting, when you said that many men thought it a hard and an uncharitable way taken by the clergy to put men convicted of heresy sometime to shame, sometime to death and that Christ so far abhorred all such violence that he would not any of his flock should fight in any wise neither in defence of themselves or any other not so much as in defence of Christ for which he blamed Saint Peter [Matt. 26: 52–4] but that we should all live after him in sufferance and patience so far forth that folk thought as you said that we should not fight in defence of ourselves against the Turks and infidels...

For since we should nothing so much regard as the honour of God and increasing of the Christian faith and winning of men's souls to heaven, we should seem to dishonour God if we mistrusted that his faith preached among others indifferently, without disturbance should not be able to prosper. And believing that it were, we should hinder the profit if we would refuse the condition where there be many more to be won to Christ on that side than to be lost from him on this side. But yet as for heretics rising among ourselves and springing of ourselves be in no wise suffered but to be oppressed and overwhelmed from the beginning. For by any covenant with them, Christendom can nothing win. For as many as we suffer to fall to them we lose from Christ. And by all them we cannot win to Christ one the more though we won them all home again for they our own before. And yet as I said for all that in the beginning never were they by any temporal punishment of their bodies any thing sharply handled till that they began to be violent themselves.

We read that in the time of St Augustine the great doctor of the church, the heretics of Africa called the Donatists fell to force and violence—robbing, beating, tormenting and killing such as they took of the true Christian flock as the Lutherans have in Germany. For avoiding whereof that holy man St Augustine which long had with great pains borne and suffered their malice, only writing and preaching in reproof of their errors and had not only done them no temporal harm but also had letted [= hindered, impeded] and resisted others that would have done it, did yet at the last for the peace of good people both suffer and exhort the count Boniface and other to repress them with force and afear them with bodily punishment...

For here you shall understand that it is not the clergy that laboureth to have them punished by death. Well may it be that as we be all men and not angels, some of them may have sometime either over-fervent mind and indiscrete zeal, or perchance an angry or cruel heart by which they may offend God in the self-same deed whereof they should else greatly merit. But surely the order of the spiritual law therein is both good, reasonable, piteous and charitable and nothing desiring the death of any man therein. For the first fault he is abjured, forsweareth all heresies, doth such penance for his fault as the bishop assigneth him; and in such wise graciously received again into the favour and suffrages of Christ's church. But and if he taken eftsoons with the same crime again then is he put out of the Christian flock by excommunication. And because that being such his conversation were perilous amongst Christian men, the Church refuseth him and thereof the clergy giveth knowledge to the temporality not exhorting the prince or any man else either to kill him or punish him, but only in the presence of the temporal officer the spirituality not delivereth him but leaveth him to the secular hand and foresaketh him as one excommunicate and removed out of the Christian flock. And though the Church be not light and sudden in receiving him again, yet at the time of his death upon his request with tokens of repentance, he is absolved and received again. (3)

## Preparing for Confession

He that will well and duly make his Confession must first of all call himself to accompt certain hours or days, according to the time that he hath last been shriven, and so with all diligence call to mind and remembrance his own sins and offences.

And let him not go to the feet of his ghostly Father trusting only upon that which he shall ask or enquire of him. For a thing of such importance, as is for a man to reconcile himself unto God, ought not to be done slightly, and (as a man

would say) at all adventure, or upon any sudden light occasion: but of sad and set
purpose, and upon good advice taken before, entering first into particular accompt with God and with a man's own conscience in his secret chamber and
closest place, considering that there he goeth to give accompt of his life unto God,
and unto the Priest in his name.

The which accompt cannot be made in such sort as it ought to be, except there go a
diligent examination and discussing of the bonds and burdens, charges and dis-
charges of our conscience, the which are our sins. And therefore the Priest, if he will
do well his duty, ought not to admit and receive any penitent that is unprovided in
this point, unless it be in extreme necessity. For it is a plain contempt of the
Sacrament of penance, and of the judgement of God which is exercised therein...

For to know and understand well what sins are to be called to mind for to repent us
of the same, and to confess them: it is to be noted, that the sins which a man doth
commit of his own will, are of two kinds, the one are venial, the other mortal. The
venial, are those sins and negligences into which almost hourly and at every little
occasion we do fall through our weakness: as are jesting, laughing overmuch, idle
talk, hastiness and sudden anger for a trifle, or to make a leasing without damage to
our neighbour. And generally almost all the evil motions that we have, being either
without full deliberation or consent; or at least without contempt of God, or any
notable irreverence of him, or any notable harm of ourselves, or of our neighbours.

All these, and such as these, are called venial sins, for that God our Lord having
respect to our weakness, doth easily pardon and forgive us the same and doth not
bind us to any other than temporal pain for them...

It remaineth therefore, those mortal and deadly sins only (or such as be
doubtful whether they be mortal, or no) be those, whereof we must make accompt
particularly in the Sacrament of Confession and penance, to the end to repent us
of them, and to rehearse and open them in shrift wholly and plainly. And although
it be a very hard thing to know the same, yet as far as the matter and present
consideration can admit, it is to be understood that that deed or negligence is a
deadly sin, in which of purpose and advisedly with notable contempt of God, or
manifest harm of ourself or our neighbour, any of the ten commandments are
broken, or else when we do anything against that, which our own conscience doth
teach us, in such sort, as is above said: as for example, to despise God and to
despair of his mercy, to forswear, or swear falsely, to steal anything of value, not to
give alms, if we be able, to such as we know to be in necessity.

These and suchlike, which are manifest and plain mortal or deadly sins, and
also such as in respect of their quality or quantity are doubtful to the penitent, or
to the Ghostly Father, so that they cannot well be judged, whether they be mortal
or venial, must of necessity, as we have said, be called to mind and rehearsed
of the party penitent, for to repent himself and confess the same. For if any one of
these be willingly left out in Confession, the party penitent doth hazard himself, in
not making his shrift in such sort as he ought, and so should thereby commit a
grievous sin...

Albeit that the ten commandments of our Lord be such, that some do forbid us
the evil and some do command us the good: yet for all that, each Christian man
ought to know, that each one of the commandments doth both these two all at
once: that is to say, forbid vice and command the virtue that is contrary to the
same vice...

### ON THE SIXTH AND NINTH COMMANDMENT

Thou shalt not commit adultery, nor any fornication, nor desire any other man's wife, nor have any carnal access or behaviour unto her.

### WHAT IS COMMANDED IN THIS PRECEPT

To be chaste, to be moderate and sober in eating and drinking, honest in words and all outward gestures, to wear our clothes and apparel in all decent, sad and grave wise, without wanton devices, and honesty, according to our degree and calling. We are also here commanded to procure and seek all the means and remedies that we can, whereby to drive away and avoid the foul sin of lechery, and of all unclean and beastly vice.

### WHAT IS FORBIDDEN IN THIS COMMANDMENT, AND HOW IT IS BROKEN

This Commandment is broken, in having any carnal access and copulation, howsoever it be, save with a man's own wife. And here the party penitent in his confession must express in what wise he hath offended in this sin of lechery, in all that he shall find himself guilty and faulty against this Commandment. And though he may not name any person particularly with whom he hath sinned, yet he must particularly declare with what manner of persons he hath offended our Lord. For the quality of the persons doth alter the nature of the sin: as if it be with one that is a common woman, or otherwise a harlot who is not assured by contract to any other man it is called *Simplex fornicatio*, single fornication; if with a Virgin or maiden, it is deflowering; if with a married wife, or an espoused woman, it is adultery; if it be done with force and violence it is rape; if with any of our kin within the fourth degree of consanguinity or alliance, it is called incest; if with any that is religious, or in a hallowed place, it is sacrilege: if it be with a beast in any manner of wise, it is called the sin of bestiality or beastliness.

Also a man sinneth against this Commandment in any accessories that go before, or go together with it, or ensue upon such acts: as, in beholding and casting of wanton looks, in touching and wanton handling in any manner of wise, in sending messages and messengers to and fro, or letters, gifts, presents, tokens, and suchlike enticements, as apparel, or any thing longing thereto, or in the wearing and using of his own clothes and garments to procure wanton affection, in minstrelsy, songs, sweet savours and odours, or any like inventions of amorous devices, that are but allurements tending all to such carnal delights and pleasures.

Again, this Commandment is broken in misusing a man's own wife by unhonest conversation with her, or committing any thing against the due order of nature, or by using her any way perilously while she is with child, or within the time of her natural and monthly course, or on high feasts and fasting days.

Again, in making any contract of matrimony, or in making and celebrating marriage against the orders and laws of the Church, or against the decrees and precepts of our Bishops and pastors. Item by overmuch eating and drinking for such fleshly purpose, or by eating of meats or taking of things that provoke and stir up the body to such fleshly motions. Finally in leading or keeping company with any person to any such act, or giving counsel, or dissembling and holding our peace, or not letting and staying the same by any mean we can, or helping toward any of all that aforesaid by deed, word, or by any signs ... and (to conclude) in all manner of dishonesty, and uncleanness of fleshly lust and appetite, or any thing longing thereunto, this Commandment is violated and broken. (4)

## Prayerful Meditations on the Last Supper

Good Lord, give us thy grace, not to read or hear this Gospel of thy bitter passion with our eyes and ears in manner of a pastime, but that it may with compassion so sink into our hearts, that it may stretch to the everlasting profit of our souls ...

Good Lord, which upon the sacrifice of the paschal lamb, didst so clearly destroy the first begotten children of the Egyptians that Pharaoh was thereby forced to let the children of Israel depart out of his bondage, I beseech thee give me the grace in such faithful wise to receive the very sweet paschal lamb, the very blessed body of our sweet Saviour thy Son, that the first suggestions of sin by thy power killed in my heart, I may safe depart, out of the danger of the most cruel Pharaoh, the devil ...

Good Lord, give me grace so to spend my life that when the day of my death shall come, though I feel pain in my body, I may feel comfort in my soul; and with faithful hope in thy mercy, in due love toward thee and charity toward the world, I may through thy grace, part hence in to thy glory ...

Gracious God, give me thy grace so to consider the punishment of that false great council that gathered together against thee, that I be never to thy displeasure partner, nor give mine assent to follow the sinful device of any wicked counsel ...

O my sweet Saviour Christ, whom thine own wicked disciple [Judas] entangled with the devil, through vile wretched covetousness betrayed, inspire I beseech thee, the marvel of thy majesty, with the love of thy goodness, so deep into mine heart, that in respect of the least point of thy pleasure, my mind may set always this whole wretched world at nought ...

O my sweet Saviour Christ, which of thine undeserved love towards mankind so kindly wouldst suffer the painful death of the cross, suffer not me to be cold nor lukewarm in love again toward thee ...

Almighty Jesu Christ, which wouldst for our example observe the law that thou camest to change, and being maker of the whole earth would have yet no dwelling place therein, give us the grace so to keep thine holy law, and so to reckon ourselves for no dwellers but for pilgrims upon the earth, that we may long and make haste, walking with faith in the way of virtuous works. To come to the glorious country, wherein thou hast bought its inheritance for ever with thine own precious blood ...

Almighty Jesu my sweet Saviour Christ, which wouldst vouchsafe thine own almighty hands to wash the feet of thy twelve Apostles, not only of the good but of the very traitor too, vouchsafe good Lord of thine excellent goodness, in such wise to wash the foul feet of mine affections, that I never have such pride enter into my heart, as to disdain either in friend or foe, with meekness and charity for the love of thee, to defile mine hands with washing of their feet ...

Our most dear Saviour Christ, which after the finishing of the old Paschal sacrifice, hast instituted the new Sacrament of thine own Body and Blood for a memorial of thy bitter passion, give us such faith therein, such fervent devotion thereto, that our souls may take fruitful ghostly food thereby ... (5)

# A Godly Instruction

Bear no malice nor evil will to no man living. For either that man is good or nought. If he be good and I hate him, then am I nought. If he be nought, and die nought, either he shall amend and go to God; or abide nought, and die nought and go to the devil. And then let me remember that if he shall be saved, he shall not fail (if I be saved too, as I trust to be) to love me very heartily, and I shall then in likewise love him. And why should I now then hate one for this while, which shall hereafter love me for evermore? And why should I be now an enemy to him, with whom I shall in time coming be coupled in eternal friendship? And on the other side, if he shall continue nought and be damned, then is there so outrageous eternal sorrow towards him, that I may well think myself a dreadful cruel wretch, if I would not now rather pity his pain than malign his person. If one would say that we may well with good conscience wish an evil man harm, lest he should do harm to other folk as are innocent and good, I will not now dispute upon that point for the root hath more branches, to be well weighed and considered than I can now conveniently write (having no other pen than a coal). But verily thus will I say, that I will give counsel to every good friend of mine, but if he be put in such a room, as to punish an evil man lie-eth in his charge by reason of his office, else leave the desire of punishing unto God and unto such other folk as are so grounded in charity, and so fast cleave to God, that no secret shrewd cruel affection, under the cloak of a just and a virtuous zeal, can creep in and undermine them. But let us that are no better than men of a mean sort, ever pray for such merciful amendment in other folk, as our own conscience showeth us that we have need in ourselves . . . (6)

# A Godly Meditation

Give me Thy grace, good Lord, to set the world at naught; to set my mind fast upon Thee; and not to hang upon the blast of men's mouths. To be content to be solitary; not to long for worldly company; little and little utterly to cast off the world, and rid my mind of all the business thereof; not to long to hear of any worldly things, but that the hearing of worldly phantasies may be to me displeasant.

Gladly to be thinking of God; piteously to call for His help; to lean unto the comfort of God; busily to labour to love Him. To know mine own vileness and wretchedness; to humble and meeken myself under the mighty hand of God. To bewail my sins past; for the purging of them patiently to suffer adversity; gladly to bear my purgatory here; to be joyful of tribulations; to walk the narrow way that leadeth to life. To bear the cross with Christ; to have the last things in remembrance; to have ever afore mine eye my death that is ever at hand; to make death no stranger to me; to foresee and consider the everlasting fire of hell; to pray for pardon before the Judge come. To have continually in mind the passion that Christ suffered for me; for His benefits uncessantly to give Him thanks. To buy the time again, that I before have lost; to abstain from vain confabulations; to eschew light, foolish mirth; and gladness; recreations not necessary to cut off; of worldly substance, friends, liberty, life and all, to set the loss at right nought for the winning of Christ. To think my most enemies my best friends; for the brethren of Joseph could never have done him so much good with their love and favour as they did him with their malice and hatred. These minds are more to be desired of every man than all the treasure of all the princes and kings, Christian and heathen, were it gathered and laid together all upon one heap. (7)

## Prayers in the Tower

Good Lord give me grace in all my fear and agony to have recourse to that great fear and wonderful agony that thou, my sweet Saviour, haddest at the Mount of Olivet, before thy most bitter passion, and in the meditation thereof to conceive ghostly comfort and consolation, profitable for my soul. Almighty God, take from me all vainglorious thoughts, all appetites of mine own praise, all envy, covetousness, gluttony, sloth, all luxury, all wrathful affections, all appetite for revenging, all desire or delight in other folk's harm, all pleasure in provoking any person to wrath or anger, all delight of exprobation and insultation against any person, in their affliction or calamity. And give me, good Lord, an humble, lowly, peaceable, charitable, kind, tender and pitiful mind and in all my thoughts to have a taste of thy holy spirit.

Give me, good Lord, a full faith, a firm hope, and a fervent charity, a love to thee, good Lord, incomparable above the love to myself, and that I love nothing to thy displeasure, but everything in order to thee.

Give me, good Lord, a longing to be with thee, not for the avoiding of the calamities of this wretched world, nor so much for the avoiding of the pains of Purgatory, nor the pains of Hell, nor so much for the attaining of the joys of heaven, in respect of mine own commodity, as even for a very love of thee.

And pardon me, good Lord, that I am so bold to ask so high petitions, being so vile a sinful wretch, and so unworthy to obtain the lowest; but yet good Lord, such they be as I am bound to wish for, and should be nearer the effectual desire of them, if my manifold sins were not the let, from which O glorious Trinity, vouchsafe of thy goodness to wash me with that blessed blood that issued out of thy tender body (O sweet Saviour Christ) in the divers torments of thy most bitter passion.

Take from me, good Lord, this lukewarm fashion, or rather key cold manner of meditation, and this dullness in praying unto thee; and give me thy grace to long for thy holy Sacraments and especially to rejoice in the presence of thy very Blessed Body (sweet Saviour Christ) in the holy Sacrament of the altar; and duly to thank thee for thy gracious visitation to me therewith; and at that high memorial, with tender compassion to remember and consider thy most bitter passion.

And make us all, good Lord, virtually participant of that holy Sacrament this day and every day, make us all lively members, sweet Saviour Christ, of thy holy mystical body, the Catholic Church. Amen. (8)

## More's Final Letter to his Beloved Daughter Margaret (Meg)

... That you fear your own frailty, Marget, nothing misliketh me. God give us both twain the grace of our own self, and whole to depend and hang upon the hope and strength of God. The blessed apostle Saint Paul found such lack of strength in himself that in his own temptation he was fain twice to call and cry out unto God, to take that temptation from him. And yet sped he not of his prayer, in the manner that he required. For God of his high wisdom, seeing that it was (as himself saith) necessary for him to keep him from pride that else he might peradventure have fallen in, would not at his thrice praying, by and by take it from him, but suffered him to be panged in the pain and thereof, giving him yet at the last this comfort against his fear of falling (*Sufficit tibi gratia mea*).[17] By which words it well seemeth that the temptation was so strong (whatsoever kind of temptation it was) that he was very feared of falling [from grace] through the feebleness of resisting that he began to feel in himself. Wherefore for his comfort God answered *sufficit tibi gratia mea*) putting him in surety, that were of himself never so feeble and faint, nor never so likely to fall, yet the grace of God was sufficient to keep him up and make him stand. And our Lord said further (*virtus in infirmitate proficitur* [my strength will be found in my weakness—2 Cor. 12: 9]). The more weak a man is, the more is the strength of God in safeguard declared. And so St Paul saith *Omnia possum in eo qui me confortat* [I have strength for anything through him who gives me power—Phil. 4: 13] . . . (9)

NOTES AND SOURCES

1. Thomas More, *A frutefull, pleasaunt, and wittie worke, of the beste state of a publique weale, and of the newe yle, called Utopia written in Latine, by . . . Syr Thomas More knyght, and translated into Englishe by Raphe Robynson* (1556), fos. 36ᵛ–38ʳ. Transcription taken from this, but checked against the excellent modern edition of Robynson's translation, with corrected spelling and punctuation and published as *Utopia by Sir Thomas More*, ed. D. H. Sacks (Boston: Bedford Series in History and Culture, 1999).
2. Thomas More, *A dialogue of Sir Thomas More knight . . . wherein be treated divers matters, as of the veneration [and] worship of images [and] relics, praying to saints, [and] going o[n] pilgrimage* (1529), pp. xi–xii.
3. Thomas More, *Dialogue Concerning Heresies and Matters of Religion*, in *The Workes of Sir Thomas More Knyght, sometime Lorde Chancellour of England, wrytten by him in the Englysh tonge*, ed. W. Rastell (1557), [104–288].
4. Thomas More, *A brief form of confession instructing all Christian folk how to confess their sins* (1576), 'preparing for confession', unpag.; 'sixth and ninth commandments' at pp. 27–30.
5. Thomas More, *Treatise upon the Passion of Christ Made in the Year of our Lord 1534*, in *The Workes of Sir Thomas More Knyght, sometime Lorde Chancellour of England, wrytten by him in the Englysh tonge*, ed. W. Rastell (1557), 1292–324.
6. Thomas More, *A Godly Instruction* (1534), in *The Workes of Sir Thomas More Knyght*, 1405.
7. Ibid. 1416–17.
8. *A manual of godly prayers and litanies newly annexed, taken out of many famous authors and distributed according to the days of the week, with a large and ample exercise for the morning and evening, whereunto are added the hymns and prayers for the principal feasts of the year, with a brief form of confession and the order to help at Mass* (1650), 478–82.
9. *The Workes of Sir Thomas More Knyght*, 1449–50.

# Royal Injunctions                                              1554

Mary's restoration of Catholicism was patient and sensitive. Its most (in)famous aspect was the burning of 282 heretics, a policy instituted in 1555, and justified by the need to prevent the spread of heresy and the consequent eternal damnation of all those infected by heresy. The only effective remedy for treating infected wounds in the pre-modern world was to cauterize them; and this is how that same world dealt with the infection of heresy. The burning of relapsed and defiant heretics was uncharacteristic of a regime determined to win hearts and minds by a programme of gradual restoration. What was to be done about priests who had broken their vows of chastity, or with those ordained since the schism from the Holy See? As

[17] 'my grace will suffice for you': 2 Cor. 12: 7–10.

far as rites and ceremonies—even the calendar—were concerned, was the clock to be put back to the time of the schism, or were changes introduced by Henry VIII in the later years of his reign to be allowed to continue? The basic Marian premiss was that everything done in and since 1534 and based on statute and under royal supremacy was to remain in force unless specifically repealed by another Parliament. Mary herself acted as Supreme Head of the Church (with dispensations from Rome) until the Henrician statutes were repealed. The classic dilemma—what does a Catholic do when the positive (secular) law conflicts with ecclesiastical law—was decided by Mary in terms of compromise. We seek to ameliorate the world we live in, so she seems to say, not live in it as though it was already, or could immediately become, what we would wish it to be. The silence of these injunctions about the confiscated lands of the religious houses is eloquent in this respect. Mary changes what she can change and strives to achieve, in a spirit lacking vengeance, the most essential thing: the availability and proper administration of the Sacraments.

## Injunctions

1. That every bishop and his officers, with all other having ecclesiastical jurisdiction, shall with all speed and diligence, and all manner of ways to them possible, put in execution all such canons and ecclesiastical laws heretofor in the time of King Henry VIII used within this realm of England and the dominions of the same, not being directly and expressly against the laws and statutes of this realm.

2. Item, that no bishop, or any his officer, or other person aforesaid, hereafter in any of their ecclesiastical writings in process, or other extra-judicial acts, do use to put in this clause or sentence: 'Regia auctoritate fulcitus.' [upheld (or authenticated) by royal authority]

3. Item, that no bishop, or any his officers, or other person aforesaid, do hereafter exact or demand in the administration of any person to any ecclesiastical promotion, order, or office, any oath touching the primacy or succession, as of late, in few years past, has been accustomed and used.

4. Item, that every bishop and his officers, with all other persons aforesaid, have a vigilant eye, and use special diligence and foresight, that no persons be admitted or received to any ecclesiastical function, benefice, or office, being a sacramentary, infected or defamed with any notable kind of heresy or other great crime; and that the said bishop do stay, and cause to be stayed, as much as lie-eth in him, that benefices and ecclesiastical promotions do not notably decay, or take hindrance, by passing or confirming of unreasonable leases.

5. Item, that every bishop, and all other persons aforesaid, do diligently travail for the repressing of heresies and notable crimes, especially in the clergy, duly correcting and punishing the same.

6. Item, that every bishop and all other persons aforesaid, do likewise travail for the condemning and repressing of corrupt and naughty opinions, unlawful books, ballads, and other pernicious and hurtful devices, engendering hatred among the people, and discord among the same; and that schoolmasters, preachers, and teachers do exercise and use their offices and duties without teaching, preaching, or setting forth any evil or corrupt doctrine; and that, doing the contrary, they may be, by the bishop and his said officers, punished and removed.

7. Item, that every bishop, and all the other persons aforesaid, proceeding summarily, and with all celerity and speed, may and shall deprive, or declare deprived, and remove, according to their learning and discretion, all such persons from their benefices and ecclesiastical promotions, who, contrary to the state of their order and the laudable custom of the Church, have married and used women as their wives, or otherwise notably and slanderously disordered or abused themselves; sequestering also, during the said process, the fruits and profits of the said benefices and ecclesiastical promotions.

8. Item, that the said bishop, and all other persons aforesaid, do use more lenity and clemency with such as have married, whose wives be dead, than with others, whose women do yet remain in life; and likewise such priests as, with the consents of their wives or women, openly in the presence of the bishop, do profess to abstain, to be used the more favourably: in which case, after penance effectually done, the bishop, according to his discretion and wisdom, may, upon just consideration, receive and admit them again to their former administration, so it be not in the same place; appointing them [= the wives] such a portion to live upon, to be paid out of their benefice, whereof they be deprived, by discretion of the said bishop, or his officers, as they shall think may be spared of the said benefice.

9. Item, that every bishop, and all persons aforesaid, do foresee that they suffer not any religious man, having solemnly professed chastity, to continue with his woman or wife; but that all such persons, after deprivation of their benefice or ecclesiastical promotion, be also divorced every one from the said woman, and due punishment otherwise taken for the offence therein.

10. Item, that every bishop, and all other persons aforesaid, do take order and direction, with the parishioners of every benefice, where priests do want, to repair to the next parish for divine service; or to appoint for a convenient time, till other better provision may be made, one curate to serve *alternis vicibus* in divers parishes, and to allot to the said curate for his labours some portion of the benefice that he so serves.

11. Item, that all and all manner of processions of the Church be used, frequented, and continued after the old order of the Church, in the Latin tongue.

12. Item, that all such holy days and fasting days be observed and kept, as was observed and kept in the latter time of King Henry VIII.

13. Item, that the laudable and honest ceremonies which were wont to be used, frequented, and observed in the Church, be also hereafter frequented, used and observed.

14. Item, that children be christened by the priest, and confirmed by the bishops, as heretofore hath been accustomed and used.

15. Item, touching such persons as were heretofore promoted to any orders after the new sort and fashion of order, considering they were not ordered in very deed, the bishop of the diocese finding otherwise sufficiency and ability in those men, may supply that thing which wanted in them before; and then, according to his discretion, admit them to minister.

16. Item, that, by the bishop of the diocese, a uniform doctrine be set forth by homilies, or otherwise, for the good instruction and teaching of all people;

and that the said bishop, and other persons aforesaid, do compel the parishioners to come to their several churches, and there devoutly to hear divine service, as of reason they ought.

17. Item, that they examine all schoolmasters and teachers of children, and finding them suspect in any wise, to remove them, and place Catholic men in their rooms, with a special commandment to instruct their children, so as they may be able to answer the priest at the Mass, as has been accustomed.

18. Item, that the said bishop, and all other the persons aforesaid, have such regard, respect, and consideration of and for the setting forth of the premises with all kind of virtue, Godly living, and good example, with repressing also and keeping under of vice and unthriftiness, as they and every of them may be seen to favour the restitution of true religion; and also to make an honest account and reckoning of their office and cure to the honour of God, our good contention, and the profit of this realm and dominions of the same. (1)

NOTES AND SOURCES

1. H. Gee and J. Hardy (eds.), *Documents Illustrative of English Church History* (London: Macmillan, 1914), 380–3.

# Reginald Cardinal Pole       1500–1558

Reginald Pole was a prince in both Church and State. As Papal Legate, he presided over the first session of the Council of Trent, and indeed was almost elected Pope in the conclave of 1549–50. As the grandson of George, Duke of Clarence, brother to both Edward IV and Richard III, he was in fact the Yorkist claimant to the English throne. He had gone into exile in 1532, denouncing Henry's schism. Pope Paul III made him a Cardinal in 1536. Henry responded by imprisoning, and eventually executing, his mother and brothers. In the 1530s he was seen as being at the heart of the liberal, humanist, reforming wing of the Catholic Church, and in due course his close links with this group led him into trouble with Pope Paul IV, who was convinced that the ideas of Pole's circle were heretical. In 1557 the Pope summoned him to Rome to face interrogation and trial. Mary refused to let him go, but could not prevent the Pope from suspending him and thus paralysing his extraordinary programme of renewal for the Marian Church. Reginald Pole's visitation articles, printed for circulation to all the parishes in his diocese of Canterbury (and a model for all the other sees in his province) give a clear sense of his priorities in re-establishing true religion after the Edwardian disruptions.

## Restoring the Faith

Item, whether the divine service in the church at times, days and hours be observed and kept duly or no.

Item, whether the parsons, vicars, and curates do comely and decently in their manners and doings behave themselves or no.

Item, whether they do reverently and duly minister the Sacraments and sacramentaries or no.

Item, whether any of their parishioners do die without ministration of the Sacraments through the negligence of their curates or no.

Item whether the said parsons, vicars or curates do haunt taverns or alehouses, increasing thereby infamy and slander or no.

Item whether they be diligent in teaching the widows how to christen in time of necessity, according to the canons of the Church or no.

Item whether they see that the font be comely kept and have holy water always ready for children to be christened.

Item if they do keep a book of all the names of them that be reconciled to the duty of the church.

Item whether there be any priests that late unlawfully had women under pretended marriage; and hitherto are not reconciled and to declare their names and dwelling places.

Item, whether they do diligently teach their parishioners the articles of the faith and the ten commandments.

Item, whether they do decently observe those things that do concern the service of the church and all those things that tend to a good and a Christian life, according to the canons of the Church.[18]

Item, whether the common schools be well kept and that the schoolmasters be diligent in teaching and be also Catholic and men of good and upright judgement, and that they be examined and approved by the Ordinary.

Item, whether any do take upon them to minister the goods of those that be dead without authority from the Ordinary.

Item, whether the poor people in every parish be charitably provided for.

Item, whether there do burn a lamp or candle before the Sacrament; and if there do not, that then it be provided for with expedition.

Item, whether infants and children be brought to be confirmed in convenient time.

Item, whether any do keep or have custody of any erroneous or unlawful books.

Item, whether any do withhold any money or goods bequeathed to the amending of the highways or any other charitable deed.

Item, whether there be any put away their wives or any wives to withdraw themselves from their husbands being not legally divorced.

Item, whether any do violate or break the Sundays and Holy Days doing their daily labours and exercises upon the same.

Item, whether the taverns or alehouses upon the Sundays and Holy days in the time of Mass, Mattins and Evensong do keep open their doors and do receive people into their houses to drink and eat and thereby neglect their duties in coming to church.

---

[18] At this point, in all existing copies a page is omitted, and items 12–19 are lost, except that 19 ends at the top of the next page, intriguingly, '...lie to them that fall sick, with light and with a little sacring bell.' They then continue with the numbers omitted for another page.

Item, whether any have or do deprave or contemn the authority or jurisdiction of the Pope's Holiness or the See of Rome.

Item, whether any minstrels or any other persons do use to sing any songs against the Holy Sacraments or any other rites and ceremonies of the Church.

Item, whether there be any hospitals within your parishes, or whether the foundations of them be duly and truly observed and kept; and whether the charitable contributions of the same be done accordingly.

Item whether any goods, plate, jewels or possessions, be taken away or withheld from the said hospitals and by whom.

God save the King and Queen. (1)

NOTES AND SOURCES

1. *Articles to be enquyred of in thordinary visitation of the most reuerende father in God, the Lord Cardinall Pooles grace Archbyshop of Cannterbury wythin hys Dioces of Cantorbury* (1556).

## Bishop Edmund Bonner                                        *c*.1497–1569

Bishop Bonner was a canon lawyer and diplomat who was appointed to the see of Hereford (1538) and translated to London (1539) as one of the 'Henrician conservatives' who accepted the royal supremacy and the break with Rome, but who did not embrace Protestant teaching or forms of worship. This stance was uncomfortable but possible under Henry VIII, but under the regimes acting in the name of Henry's son and successor, Edward VI, it became altogether impossible, and so in 1550 Bonner was deprived and imprisoned for his refusal to preach against transubstantiation. Restored immediately after the accession of Mary in 1553, he was one of the leading and most active restorers of Catholicism. He was again deprived in 1559 for refusing the Oath of Supremacy, and he spent his last ten years in prison in constant expectation of execution. Demonizsed by John Foxe, in his *Actes and Monuments*, as the most vicious of persecutors, he was in fact initially reluctant to pursue a violent approach to heretics or heresy. According to the teachings of the Catholic Church, virtually every person in England had fallen into heresy and schism during the reign of King Edward VI. In order to be reconciled such individuals would normally have to confess to their bishop (since the crimes of heresy and schism could only be forgiven by the bishop). But since the number of those needing to confess was so great, in February 1554 Bishop Bonner of London gave faculties to all pastors and curates (who themselves had already confessed and been reconciled) to absolve their parishioners from the crimes of heresy and schism. This confession and recon- ciliation was not to be automatic. Bishop Bonner also addressed the situation of certain members of the laity who might require additional instruction to understand how they had fallen into error. Our first extract come from a declaration issued in 1554 and to be read in every parish. It indicates that Bonner was able and willing to employ as agents of healing and reconciliation even those priests who had served Edward VI to the very end. It is also interesting to see how he addresses the problem of those unwilling to abandon Protestant teachings, which until recently had been the articles of faith of the state Church. Our other extracts are from the remarkable series of primers that Bonner published (and of which he was in part the author) as systematic expositions of key Catholic texts and beliefs (the Apostles' Creed, the Seven Sacraments, the Ten Commandments, the eight Beatitudes) followed by a series of thirteen homilies to be ready in that majority of parishes in which the clergy were not licensed to preach. These homilies included seven on Catholic teaching on God, Man, and Salvation, three on authority in the Church, and three on the Sacrament of the Altar. We include here the introduction to the Apostles' Creed and exposition of one of its clauses, and these are followed by an extract from his teaching on transubstantiation. Bonner's *A Profitable and Necessary Doctrine with Certain Homilies Adjoined* (1555) is consciously modelled on Henry VIII's *King's Book* of 1543, and reinforces the Marian case for continuity with the reign of Mary's father (when, it was claimed, sound doctrine went along with disordered ecclesiology) in reaction to the Protestantization of England under Edward VI. In the traditional manner, Bonner broke up the Creed into twelve sections and explored each in turn, in about 1,000 words per section.

Amidst all else, Bonner remained focused on building for the long term. And so he authorized and allowed to be published in his own name a primer for school children that began with reading and writing exercises and then moved on this 'honest Godly instruction', a series of daily prayers for use in the home and at Mass. Many of them are familiar enough, but there is still much of interest in the translations of familiar Latin prayers into the vernacular (as in the grace before meals or in the listing of the seven works of mercy). These provide our final extracts.

## Bishop Bonner's Absolution of his Subjects

Edmund, by the permission of God, Bishop of London, unto all and singular the lay people of my diocese, do send greetings in our Saviour Jesus Christ.

Whereas this noble realm of England, dividing itself from the unity of the Catholic Church and from the agreement in religion with all other Christian realms, has been, besides many other miseries and plagues which God's indignation has power upon it, grievously also vexed and sore infected with many and sundry sorts of sects of heretics, as Arians, Anabaptists, Libertines, Zwinglians, Lutherans, and many others, all which sects be most repugnant and contrary one against another, and all against God's truth and Christ's Catholic faith; whereupon has grown such slander to the realm, such malice and disagreement among ourselves the inhabitants thereof, such treasons, tumults, and insurrections against our prince, such blasphemy and dishonour unto God as no man's tongue or pen is able to express. It has pleased the goodness of God to cast his eye of mercy and clemency upon us, and to move the Pope's Holiness to send his most Godly messenger, the Most Reverend Father in God, the Lord Cardinal Pole legate *de latere*, to bring us the glad tidings of peace and reconciliation, and to reduce and bring home unto the fold the lost sheep that was gone astray; whose message as it has been honourably received of the King and Queen's Majesties, even so the Lords spiritual and temporal, and Commons at the last Parliament has received it, revoking all laws (the which in the time of schism were promulgated against the authority of the Pope's Holiness) and restoring the same and the Church of Rome to all that power which they had in this realm before the said schism; the which reconciliation was also most gladly and joyfully embraced, as well of all the clergy and convocation of the Province of Canterbury as also many other persons; and being so great and necessary to be extended to every person of the realm, it has pleased the said Lord Legate's grace to give, and impart unto me the said Bishop of London, for my said diocese, and to all such as I shall appoint in that behalf, power and authority to absolve and reconcile all and every person thereof, as well of the clergy as of the laity, and as well men as women, the which will renounce their errors, and (being penitent) will humbly require to be restored to the unity of the Catholic Church, as by the letters of the said Lord legate's grace sent unto me, and from me sent unto every which of the archdeacons within my diocese, more at large may and does appear.

And forasmuch as in mine own person, as well for the multitude of people as distance of places, I cannot minister this benefit unto every private person myself; and for that also the holy time of Lent is now at hand, in which every true Christian man ought to come unto his own pastor and curate to be of him confessed, and to receive at his hand wholesome counsel, penance, and absolution; these are therefore as well to give knowledge hereof unto every one of you, as also to signify and declare, that for that purpose I have, by the said authority, chosen, named and deputed, and so by these presents do choose, name and depute all and singular pastors and curates having cure of souls within my diocese, and being themselves reconciled herein, that they and every of them, by authority hereof, shall have full power and authority to absolve all such as be lay persons of their parishes, from heresy and schism, and from the confines of the church into the which they be fallen by occasion thereof, and also to reconcile unto the Church all such which shall declare themselves penitent and desirous to enjoy the benefit of the said reconciliation.

And whereas divers pastors and curates in sundry parishes peradventure be not able to satisfy the minds and appease the consciences of some of their parishioners in cases that shall trouble them, I have therefore given also authority to every archdeacon of my diocese, within his archdeaconry, to name and appoint certain of the best learned in every deanery of their archdeaconry, to supply that lack, so that every man so troubled may repair to any one of them within the said deanery whom he shall like best, to be instructed and appeased in that behalf. And also I have appointed that if, this being done, there shall yet remain any scruple in the party's conscience and himself not satisfied, then the said party to repair unto one of my archdeacons or chaplains, unto whom his mind shall be most inclined unto, or else to repair unto my own self, to be resolved in his said scruple or doubt, and to receive and take such order therein, as to one of the said archdeacons, or unto me shall therein appear to be most expedient.

Further certifying and declaring unto you, that I have given commandment herein to all my archdeacons, that they admonish and command every pastor and curate within their archdeaconries, that they having knowledge hereof, do in the first holy day next then following, at the mass time when the multitude of people is present, declare all these things unto their parishioners, and exhort them that they esteem this grace accordingly, and reconcile themselves to the Church before the first Sunday after Easter next ensuing, which thing I also do command by the tenure hereof, with intimation that the said time being past and they not so reconciled, every one of them shall have process made against him, according to the canons as the case shall require; for which purpose the pastors and curates of every parish shall be commanded by their archdeacon to certify to me in writing of every man's and woman's name that is not so reconciled.

Further, herewith I do signify and declare unto you, that our Holy Father the Pope Julius, the third of that name, like a most tender and natural father, hearing of the return and recovery of his prodigal child, this realm of England, has himself made much joy and gladness here-at, and also all other true Christian realms have done the like; exhorting you therefore in our Lord, not to be unthankful yourselves or negligent in this behalf, but diligently to seek for it, joyfully to embrace it, and fruitfully use it; remembering withal the admonition and charge which came from me the last year, concerning your coming to confession in Lent and receiving of the Sacrament at Easter, which admonition to all effects and purposes I have now here for repeated and renewed, charging you and also all your curates therewith.

And because all our duty is earnestly and devoutly to pray for the prosperous estate of our sovereigns, the King and Queen of this realm, I do finally require and pray you as heartily as I can, to pray for their Majesties accordingly, and especially that it may please Almighty God to send unto Her Grace a good time, and to make her a glad mother, which cannot be but unto us all great joy, much comfort, and inestimable profit.

Given at London, the nineteenth day of the month of February, in the year of our Lord God after the computation of the Church of England 1554, and of my translation the sixteenth.

*The form of absolution to be kept by the pastors and curates in private confessions concerning this reconciliation:*

Our Lord Jesus Christ absolve you, and by the apostolic authority to me granted and committed, I absolve you from the sentences of excommunication, and from all other censures and pains, into the which you be fallen by reason of heresy or schism or any other wise; and I restore you unto the unity of our holy mother the Church, and to the communion of all the Sacraments, dispensing with you for all manner of irregularity. And by the same authority, I absolve you from all your sins, in the name of the Father, and of the Son, and of the Holy Ghost. Amen.

God save the King and Queen. (1)

## The Creeds

Here followeth the exposition and declaration of this Creed. As concerning this Creed, there are five points generally to be marked and observed:

First that all Christian people ought and must constantly believe, maintain and defend all those things to be true which be comprehended in this Creed and in the other two Creeds whereof the one is to be said at Mass being established by ancient General Councils, and the other was made by the great clerk and holy man Athanasius. And likewise we must also constantly believe, maintain and defend all other things which are comprehended in the whole body and canon of the Bible.

Second that all things contained in this Creed, or in any of the other two Creeds, or in the whole body and canon of the said bible are so necessary to be believed for man's salvation, that whosoever will not constantly believe those things, or will obstinately believe the contrary of them, cannot (in that state remaining) be the true and very members of Christ and his spouse the Church, but either are very infidels or heretics and members of the devil with whom (if they repent not) they shalbe perpetually damned.

Thirdly, that all Christian people ought, and must not, only believe, maintain, and defend, all the said things as most certain and infallible truths of God's word, never by any contrary opinion, or authority to be altered, or convelled [= overthrown, refuted] but also must take and interpret, all the same things, according to the same sense, understanding and meaning, which the Holy Ghost hath given thereto, and which also the approved Doctors of the Catholic Church, have received and agreeably defended.

Fourthly, that all true Christian people, must utterly refuse, and condemn all those opinions which were of long time past condemned in the four holy Councils. That is to say: in the Council of Niceae, Constantinople, Ephesus, and Chalcedon.

Fifthly and finally. That although all things as they are now particularly used in the Catholic Church here in Earth, are not so distinctly, particularly, and expressly in all words, fashions, circumstances, and points, set forth, taught and expressed in Scripture, yet the pith, the substance, the matter, the foundation and ground, with the effect thereof in general words are not only comprehended and contained in Scripture, but also by express words confirmed by other sufficient authority. And seeing the Catholic Church hath so received, believed, allowed, and approved, the said things, time out of mind, therefore it shalbe a very great presumption and an uncomely part, for any man to control or contemn any such things so received, believed, allowed and approved by the said Catholic Church, and in so doing the same is indeed not worthy to be taken or reputed for a faithful member or obedient child of the said Church, but for an arrogant, naughty, and very wicked person... (2)

## From an Exposition of the Apostles' Creed

*Suffered under Pontius Pilate, was crucified, dead and buried and descended into Hell*... And finally, concerning the descent or going down of Christ into Hell (which is the last point of this article) you shall know that though to some men, upon some vain and foolish grounds, imaginations and devices, it may seem an absurdity, and a thing unseemly, that Christ, being virtue itself, and all perfection and power, should descend into Hell, which is a place of wicked persons, and of punishment for them, and a place finally from whence there is no regress, nor yet redemption in, and who saith if Christ descended into Hell, he would both there suffer punishment and also not return from thence, nor redeem there. Yet if these men would consider how diversely in Scripture Hell is taken (and withal would consider the will and omnipotency of Christ, who is God and Man, and who can do all things in Heaven, earth and Hell, that pleaseth him to do (nothing to him being impossible) and finally would consider withal, what the Catholic Church ever from the beginning hath in this behalf believed and taught, taking her belief of Christ and his doctrine generally and specially set forth in Scripture, this thing should not appear to them so strange, or so incredible as percase [= by chance] it doth. And therefore let us with the Scripture and the Catholic Church firmly and steadfastly believe that our Saviour Christ, after he was crucified and dead upon the Cross, did descend into Hell (his body remaining and lying in the grave) and did lose the pains or sorrows thereof, in which it was not possible that he should beholden nor yet to see corruption at all. And he did also conquer and oppress both the devil and Hell and also death itself, whereunto all mankind was condemned by the fall of our forefather Adam into sin. A proof whereof is taken out of Zacharias chapter 9, Hosea chapter 13, Luke chapter 1, Matthew chapter 12,

Acts, chapter 2, and Paul to the Ephesians chapter 4 and in other diverse places of Scripture.

Now the process of the life of our blessed Saviour Jesu Christ, thus declared, with his passion, death, burial and descent into Hell, it is especially to be noted, and to be believed for a certain truth, that our Saviour, in all the time of his most bitter and grievous passion, and in suffering his most painful and cruel death, not only did most patiently, without resistance and like an innocent lamb, endure and sustain for our redemption all the pains and injuries and all the opprobries and ignominies which were done to him; but also that he did willingly and gladly suffer this cross and this kind of death for our example, that we should follow the steps of him in patience and humility, and that we should bear our own cross, as he did bear his, and that we should also hate and abhor all sin, knowing for certainty that whosoever doth not in his heart hate and abhor sin, but rather accounteth the breach and violation of God's commandment but as a light matter and of small weight and importance he esteemeth not the price and value of the passion and death of Christ, according to the dignity and worthiness thereof ... (3)

## The Sacrament of the Altar

By all these most evident testimonies of ancient fathers, it appeareth, that in the Sacrament of the Altar are truly and really contained the Body and Blood of our Saviour Jesus Christ, according to the said institution of Christ. But because Christ took bread into His hands, and Saint Paul also calleth the Sacrament bread, and that thereupon the heretics have grounded their opinion that the thing contained in the said Sacrament is nothing but bread, it shall be meet to open and declare this matter further, and in what sort the Sacrament may be called bread: for the understanding whereof you must know that albeit our Saviour Christ took very material bread into His hands, yet by His omnipotent power he changed the nature and substance of bread, into the substance of His body. And likewise he changed the substance of wine into the substance of His blood, saying: This is my Body, This is my Blood.

And this is evidently proved first by the six [chapter of] John, where our Saviour Christ himself thus saith: 'the bread that I will give unto you is my flesh, which flesh I will give for the life of the world.' In which words it is most manifest that Christ promised two things: the one that he would give a bread that should be His flesh, and the other is, that he would give that flesh for the life of the world: now if Christ gave not at His maundy a bread that was His flesh, and on good Friday gave the flesh upon the cross for the life of the world, then he kept not His promise, for in no place else he did it, therefore either must we say that Christ made a promise and performed it not (which is a wicked thing to think or say of Christ), either else must we say that keeping His promise he did at His maundy give a kind of bread which was His very flesh indeed contained under the form of bread, and that the same flesh he gave the day following under the visible form of flesh upon the cross: and so he performed both His promises, that is to say giving a bread or food that was His flesh, and also giving that flesh for the life of the world. And for a more plain and full declaration of Christ's words herein, you shall note, that in the said sixth of Saint John, there is mention made of four kinds of bread.

First of the bread wherewith he miraculously fed five thousand in the wilderness, which was indeed very material bread and made of barley.

Secondly, there is mention made of a bread called manna, which was a kind of food that God sent from above, to the children of Israel, when they in the wilderness did travail toward the land of promise, which though it be there called bread, yet bread indeed made of any kind of grain or corn it was not.

Thirdly, there is mention made of bread, which is the Second Person in Trinity, that is to say, the Son of God sent down by His Father from Heaven hither into earth to be incarnate.

Fourthly, there is mention made of bread that our Saviour Christ promised to give, which is His flesh, and the self-same in substance which suffered for us upon the cross, and yet there called bread though indeed no material bread in substance. And as for the calling of it bread it is not material, for the Godhead of Christ, and also manna, in the said chapter are called bread, and yet no bread in substance. And here is not to be omitted that where our Saviour Christ speaketh of the foresaid four kinds of bread he doeth not speak of them all in one fashion, for touching the first saith, that he himself a little before had given that bread unto the people and touching the second, the Jews did boast that it was given by Moses to their forefathers in [the] wilderness. Likewise, concerning the third, Christ doth affirm that it was at that present sent from the Father of Heaven down to the Earth. But touching the fourth, he said that it should be of His own giving unto them, and that in time to come, yea and further that the same should be His flesh, and lest any man might mistake this His saying, in such spiritual or mystical sense, as thereby to exclude the very substance of His flesh and body, he addeth (to take away all doubt and cavil) that it should be the same flesh which should be given for the life of the world, as appeareth before. And hereby may you learn that by this word 'bread' mentioned in the sixth chapter of St John, and as it is here taken in this fourth acception, and in the other two next going before, our Saviour Christ doth mean nothing else but a food, and a food may it be though there be no substance of material bread at all.

After which sort is the word bread to be understood in the tenth and eleventh chapters of the first epistle of Saint Paul to the Corinthians, where diverse times also he useth this word *panis*, which ought to be englished food.

And that in very deed there is not the substance of material bread remaining in the Sacrament of the altar, ye shall beside those thinges which you have heard all ready out of the Scripture hear also out of the auncient and catholic fathers... Doest thou see bread? doest thou see wine? do they pass into the sewage from us, as other meats do? God forbid that any man should so think. For even as the wax which is cast into the fire, is made like unto the fire, and no substance of the said wax then remaineth, or is left, even so do thou think here, the mystery's meaning the substance of the bread and the wine to be by the substance of Christ's body consumed. (4)

## An Honest Godly Instruction

Forasmuch, as it is a meritorious deed, to instruct youth in virtuous things, which youth, of itself, is propense and ready, without any teacher, to take, and embrace vice, unthriftiness, and all manner [of] naughtiness, it is thought good (seeing of late days, the youth of this realm hath been nuzzled with ungodly Catechisms, and pernicious evil doctrine, which is to be feared) they will not forget, in as much as the new vessel long doth keep the scent or savour of the first liquor wherewith it was seasoned ... And that also the youth must have some honest introduction and entry in things convenient for them to learn, that is to say: both to know the letters, with joining of them together, and thereby the sooner made apt to go further, both in reading, and also in writing) it is thought good I say, seeing the elder age is provided for in necessary doctrine already set forth, that the said youth should also have some help herein. For which purpose here briefly is set forth for them as well letters of diverse sorts, commonly used in this realm, as also syllables, and joining of the said letters together. And as for words, sentences, and matters, such is here in this behalf set also forth, as is judged to be most necessary, apt, and requisite for the said youth to learn. As first to know how to bless themselves morning and evening, to say also the *Pater noster* the *Ave Maria*, the Creed, the *Confiteor*, with the rest to answer the Priest at Mass: to say grace at dinner and supper; to say the *de profundis*; to know and learn upon the book, and by heart, the ten commandments of almighty God, given in the old law; the two commandments of God, expressed in the Gospel; the seven principal virtues; the seven works of mercy bodily; the seven works of mercy ghostly or spiritual; the seven gifts of the Holy Ghost; the eight beatitudes; the seven Sacraments; to know by the book, and thereby to avoid, the seven deadly sins. All these things (jointly, in Latin and in English, for the youth, to learn thereby to read both the tongues) are set forth by the Bishop of London, to be taught by all the schoolmasters unto the youth within his said Diocese of London. Straightly charging, and commanding, all the said schoolmasters, and all manner of other persons, within his said diocese, neither to teach, learn, read, or use, any other manner of ABC Catechism, or rudiments, then this, made for the first instruction of youth ...

The manner of blessing: In the name of the Father, † and of the Son, † and of the Holy Ghost. † So be it.

Into thy hands O Lord I do commit my spirit; thou O Lord, the God of truth, hast redeemed me. So be it.

By this sign of the cross let every wicked thing flee far away, and by the same sign, let everything that is good be saved.

By the sign of the holy cross, † O Lord our God deliver us from our enemies. So be it.

O Jesu of Nazareth King of the Jews, Son of God, have mercy upon me. So be it ...

To help the priest at Mass.

The versicle: And let us not be led into temptation. The answer. But deliver us from evil.

The versicle. Confess to our Lord that he is good. The answer. For his mercy is for ever.

### THE *CONFITEOR*:

I do confess to God, to blessed Mary, to all saints, and to you that I have sinned very greatly in thought, in speech, in omission, and in deeds by mine own fault. Therefore I pray holy Mary, all the saints of God, and you, to pray for me.

THE *MISEREATUR*:

Almighty God, have mercy upon you, and forgive you all your sins, deliver you from all evil, save, and confirm you in goodness, and bring you to everlasting life. So be it.

The versicle: Our help is in the name of our Lord. The answer: Who hath made Heaven, and earth.

The versicle: The name of our Lord be blessed. The answer: From henceforth, now, and for evermore.

Three Lord have mercy upon us.

Three Christ have mercy upon us.

Three Lord have mercy upon us.

The versicle: Our Lord be with you. The answer: And with thy spirit.

The anthem: the words following are of the holy Gospel of Matthew, Mark, Luke, John.

The Answer: Glory be to thee O Lord

Versicle: by all the worlds of worlds. Answer: So be it...

Versicle. Lift up your hearts. Answer: We so have unto our Lord

Versicle: Let us give thanks unto God our Lord. Answer: It is worthy and right so to do...

Versicle. Go you, the Mass is done.

Versicle. Bless we our Lord. Answer: We give thanks to God.

Grace before dinner.

Versicle: Bless you Answer: Our Lord doth bless.

Blessing: All that on the table are set or shall be, the right hand of God bless. In the name of the Father, and of the Son, and of the Holy Ghost. So be it.

Grace after dinner

The versicle: For such a feast let us bless our Lord. The answer: We give thanks to God.

The anthem

Mother, pray to thy Son, that after this exile, he will give joy unto us without end So be it.

Versicle: After the birth of thy Child, thou didst remain a virgin inviolate.

Answer: O Mother of God, pray for us.

Let us pray: The Son of God the Father, for the merits and prayers of his Godly

Mother, bless us. Answer: So be it.

The souls of all the faithful being departed, by the mercy of God rest in peace. So be it...

THE MANNER OF PRAYING FOR THE DEAD

From the depth have I called unto thee, O Lord, Lord hear thou my prayer. Let thine ears be attentive unto the voice of my prayer. If thou, O Lord wilt narrowly look upon sins, O Lord, who may sustain it. But with thee there is mercy, and for thy law have I a-biden thee, O Lord. My soul hath a-biden in his word, my soul hath trusted in our Lord. From the morning watch until night, let Israel trust in our Lord.

For with our Lord there is mercy, and plentiful redemption is with him. And he shall redeem Israel from all his iniquities!

Lord have mercy upon us. Christ have mercy upon us. Lord have mercy upon us. Our father etc. Let us not be led etc. But deliver us etc.

Versicle: Grant to them O Lord, eternal rest. Answer: And let everlasting light shine upon them.

Versicle: From the gate of Hell. Answer: Lord deliver their souls.

Versicle: I believe to see the good things of our Lord. Answer: in the land of the living.

Versicle Lord hear my prayer. Answer: and let my cry come unto thee.

Let us pray.

Incline, O Lord, thine ear unto our prayers, in which we, being humble suitors, do desire thy mercy, that thou wilt set, or place the souls of thy men, and women servants (whom thou hast commanded to depart from this world) in the region of peace, and light, and that thou wilt command them to bee companions of thy saints, through our Lord Jesus Christ thy Son, who liveth and reigneth God with thee, in unity of the Holy Ghost, by all worlds of worlds. So be it.

The souls of all faithful departed through the mercy of God rest in peace. So be it. The Ten Commandments of Almighty God (Exodus 20).

   i. Thou shalt not have strange Gods before me.

  ii. Thou shalt not make to thee any graven thing, nor any likeness of any thing that is in Heaven above or in earth beneath, nor of them that be in waters under the earth. Thou shalt not adore them, nor honour them with Godly honour.

 iii. Thou shalt not take the name of thy Lord God in vain.

iiii. Remember that thou keep holy the Sabbath day.

  v. Honour thy father and mother.

 vi. Thou shalt not kill.

vii. Thou shalt not commit adultery.

viii. Thou shalt not steal.

 ix. Thou shalt not bear false witness against thy neighbour.

  x. Thou shalt not covet thy neighbour's house, nor desire thy neighbour's wife, nor his servant, nor his maiden, nor his ox, nor his ass, nor anything that is his.

The two commandments of the Gospel.

   i. Thou shalt love thy Lord God with all thy heart, and in all thy soul, and in all thy mind.

  ii. Thou shalt love thy neighbour as thy self.

The seven principal or highest virtues.

    i. Faith. Which also be called divine.

   ii. Hope. Which also be called divine.

  iii. Charity Which also be called divine.

 iiii. Justice.

   v. Prudence. which are called also cardinal.

  vi. Temperance which are called also cardinal.

 vii. Fortitude or strength which are called also cardinal.

The seven works of mercy bodily

   i. To give to eat unto the hungry.

  ii. To give drink unto the thirsty.

 iii. To receive into lodging or harbour the guests, or strangers that be needy.

iiii. To clothe the naked

  v. To visit the sick.

 vi. To visit and redeem the captives.

vii. To bury the dead.

The seven works of mercy spiritual or ghostly

   i. To correct sinners.

  ii. To teach the ignorant.

 iii. To give good counsel to them that be doubting.

iiii. To pray for the health of thy neighbour.

  v. To comfort the sorrowful.

 vi. To suffer patiently injuries.

vii. To forgive offenders.

The seven gifts of the Holy Ghost.

   i. Fortitude or strength.

  ii. Counsel.

 iii. Science.

iiii. Fear of God.

  v. Understanding.

 vi. Piety.

vii. Wisdom.(5)

NOTES AND SOURCES

1. *Concilia Magnae Britanniae et Hiberniae*, ed. David Wilkins (London: 1737), iv. 114–15.
2. Edmund Bonner, *A Profitable and Necessarye Doctrine with Certain Homilies Adjoining* (1555), fos. 9–11.
3. Ibid., fos. 16–19.
4. Ibid. [unpag., section headed 'Exposition of the Sacrament of the Altar '].
5. Edmund Bonner, *Certaine Short Questions and Answeres very profitable and necessary for young children* (1582 edn.), unpag.

# Bishop Thomas Watson                                    1513–1584

Thomas Watson was Bishop of Lincoln under Mary I and one of the best and most widely published of the preachers of the time. He had served in the Henrician and Edwardian Churches, mainly as a chaplain to the leading Henrician conservative Stephen Gardiner—accepting the schism from Rome but otherwise holding to most of what the Catholic Church believed (as understood by its liberal, humanist wing). Thus, when Gardiner was imprisoned for opposing the strong Protestant tide waxing in and after 1549, Watson went to prison with him. He came to the fore as soon as Mary acceded to the throne, preaching a notable sermon at Paul's Cross to celebrate her success in defeating the Protestant coup in favour of Lady Jane Grey; and another at the opening of the first Convocation of the reign. He was quickly promoted to be Master of St John's College, Cambridge (his old college, founded by Lady Margaret Beaufort as advised by St John Fisher), Dean of Durham, and then (from December 1556) Bishop of Lincoln. Many of his sermons survive in print or in manuscript. Of his printed sermons, the most notable are a series expounding the Sacraments. We offer here extracts from the first—*Of the Number of the Sacraments of Christ's Church*—and the thirteenth—*Of the Necessity and Commodity of Penance in General.*

## On the Number of the Sacraments

The Catholic Church of God, good people, doth extend her doctrine concerning the matter of our belief, not only to the Articles of our Creed, and such points, as by revelation from God it teacheth us to believe of God, and the works of our Saviour Christ, which he did or suffered for the redemption and salvation of man: but also to the holy Sacraments of God, by the worthy using whereof, he powereth abundantly his manifold graces into our souls, and by them maketh us people meet to receive the fruits and benefits of his passion. And as you have been instructed, partly concerning the articles of our faith, so it is expedient you be likewise instructed concerning the holy Sacraments of his church: to the intent you might not only know the manner of God's working in curing of your souls, but also prepare and dispose yourselves to the fruitful receiving of his medicines which be ministered to every man by his holy Sacraments. And therefore at this time by God's help I intend to declare unto you the number of the Sacraments of Christ's church, and also the effect of them all in general, and at other times every one of them in special.

It is to be believed upon pain of damnation, that there be seven Sacraments of Christ's Holy Church, institute and ordained of our Saviour Christ, in his New Testament or law, which be, Baptism, confirmation, the Sacrament of the Altar, penance, extreme unction, order, and matrimony. The first five be ordained for the making good and the perfection of every man and woman, as by Baptism we are justified and made members of Christ's mystical body; by confirmation we are increased and strengthened in grace; by the Sacrament of Christ's Body and Blood we are nourished to everlasting life, and made fat with God; by penance we are restored to our former rightwiseness and goodness, if in case we fall after Baptism; by extreme unction we are made whole spiritually, and also corporally, if it be thought to God expedient to our souls. All these five Sacraments be ordained to begin or restore our rightwiseness, and to bring it to perfectness for our salvation. The other two last be ordained for the common state of the whole Church, as matrimony to increase and multiply the Church corporally by generation: and Order to multiply the whole Church spiritually by regeneration, and also by the ministry of God's word, Sacraments, and discipline, to rule and govern it, after the will of Almighty God. And whereas the holy Scriptures in many places compare a man's life to a war (as Job 7; 1 Tim. 1; 2 Cor. 10), we may very well by that same similitude, understand the number and division of God's Sacraments, and the true effect of the same. For Christ our Lord and king, who hath for us overcome the devil, the flesh, the world, Hell, death, and all his enemies and ours, laboureth to make all us for whom he hath prepared triumph, and the inheritance in the Kingdom of Heaven, to be his soldiers, and by his power and help to fight against the said enemies, and to overcome them in our own persons, and so to attain the promised reward ... (1)

## On Penance

Our Lord and Saviour Jesus Christ which came into this world to call and save sinners, (1 Tim. 1; Luke 5; 2 Pet. 3) dealing patiently with them, not willing any man to perish, but all men to be converted and turned to him by penance: after that John Baptist, whom God sent before his face to prepare his way by preaching of penance, was apprehended and cast into prison: than (I say) our Saviour Christ began to preach the Gospel of his grace and glory, after this form, saying: Do penance, for the Kingdom of Heaven draweth near: (Matt. 4) teaching us both by his word and deed, and like as John Baptist goeth before, whose ministry was to preach penance, and Jesus cometh after, by whose death we have redemption and remission of sin: even so in the heart of every sinner, the effect of John's preaching which is true and unfeigned penance must go before, that the effect of Christ's passion, which is grace, mercy, and remission of sins, may come after.

And as this doctrine of penance was first of all other taught by our Saviour himself, and by John his most holy prophet, as a thing most necessary for the instruction and salvation of all men: even so his holy apostles in the beginning of their preaching, observed the same matter and form of doctrine, as Saint Peter in his first sermon made at Jerusalem in the day of Pentecost, when he had opened the work of the Holy Ghost in the gift of tongues, and thereby took occasion to set forth the mystery of Jesus Christ, at the last end his doctrine to the people, which were smitten with compunction of heart by his words, was this: do penance, and be every one of you baptised in the name of Jesus Christ, (Acts 2) for the remission of your sins, and you shall receive the gift of the Holy Ghost. And in his next sermon written in the third chapter of the Acts, he taught the same doctrine in these words: do you therefore penance, and be converted, that your sins may be taken away. Saint Paul also calleth the doctrine of penance the foundation of all other doctrines in the heart of a Godly man, (Hebrews ch. 6 out of which do spring such other virtues as bring a man to the perfection of a Christian life. Likewise Saint John Evangelist began with the same doctrine of penance, writing in his Revelation to the seven Churches that were in Asia, saying thus to the church of Ephesus in the person of Christ: 'Remember from whence thou hast fallen, and do penance, and do the first works, or else I shall come to thee soon, and shall remove thy candlestick from his place, except thou do penance' (Apoc. 2: 5). And this doctrine also did all the other Apostles first and principally set forth to all them that received the faith of Christ as most necessary for their salvation, being taught and commanded so to do by our Saviour Christ himself, when before his Ascension he opened to them their wits and understandings to understand the Scriptures, saying to them, that it was so written that Christ so should suffer and rise from death the third day, (Luke ch. 23) and that penance should be preached in his name and remission of sin, throughout all people, beginning at Jerusalem. For which cause and consideration, I as a minister of our Saviour Christ, to whom he hath committed the word and ministry of reconciliation, (2 Cor. 5) using as it were his embassy to exhort you to be reconciled to him, intending to teach you at this time what things to do for the saving of your souls, and the attaining of everlasting life: have thought it most expedient for satisfying of my duty in following the example and commandment of our master Christ and his Apostles, and for your erudition to be taught the straight path and high beaten way for our Christian religion, to speak of penance, and first to declare the necessity and commodity of the same, and then in order the parts of it, and how to do it in such manner as it may be acceptable to almighty God, and a mean to attain his mercy and remission of sin.

First of all consider you (good people) that penance is a gift of God, as the Scripture saith. God hath given and granted penance to the Gentiles for life and salvation. (Acts 21). And it is God that standeth at the door of our heart and knocketh, by whose inspiration we have the beginning of our conversion, (Apoc. 3) without whom we be not able and sufficient of ourselves, as of ourselves to think any good thought ... God of his mere mercy and fatherly affection, doth bear with the sins of men, and differeth to avenge and punish them justly according to their deserts, patiently looking for their conversion and penance, by means whereof he might remit their offences, deliver them from many dangers, give unto them plenty of grace, and conduct them to the fruition of his glory. For if God should by and by punish all offenders neither Zacchaeus should have had space to have done penance, nor yet St Matthew, nor many other, being taken away to eternal death before the time of their penance. But our most meek Father calling every one to penance, doth abide and tarry for us, which patience whosoever abuseth and contemneth by remaining still in his former sins, according to the hardness and obstinacy of his own heart, doth store up to himself God's indignation in the day of God's anger and just judgement, (Rom. 1) ...

The second way of doing penance is for venial sin after Baptism, and is daily done or ought to be done throughout a man's whole life, so long as we be in this weak, frail, mortal, and sinful flesh. For which cause we knock upon our breasts, saying: forgive us our trespasses, as we forgive them that trespass against us. For we require not to have those sins forgiven us, which we be sure were forgiven in

Baptism before, but those which through our frailty and sensuality by little and little continually creep upon us, which being many if they were all gathered together against us, and we contemned to avoid them in time, they would so grieve and oppress us, as one mortal sin. For what difference is it to have a man's ship drowned at once with one great surge and wave of the sea, or to suffer the water to enter into small holes by little and little till the ship by contemning to draw the poop be full, and so sink and be drowned? For the which cause we fast, do alms and pray, wherein when we say, (Matt. 6) forgive us as we forgive, we declare that we have something to be forgiven, by which words we humble our souls, and cease not after a certain manner to do daily penance.

The third way of doing penance, is for such deadly sins after Baptism, as be prohibited by Gods ten commandments, of which the Apostle saith, all they that do such, shall not possess the Kingdom of Heaven. And this penance ought to be more grievous and painful, because the fault is great, causing a deadly wound in our souls, as adultery, murder, or sacrilege. But although the wound be great, grievous, and deadly: yet Almighty God as a good Physician, after the suggestion of sin by the devil, the delectation of the flesh, the consent of our mind and freewill, and also the doing of the sin indeed, as though we had lain in grave stinking four days as Lazarus did, doth not so leave us, but cryeth: Come forth, O Lazarus, and by and by misery gave place to mercy, death to life. Lazarus cometh forth and is bounden as men be in confession of their sin doing penance, of this speaketh Saint Paul to the Corinthians, (2 Cor. 11) saying: I am afraid lest when I shall come again, God do humble and afflict me among you, and least I lament and mourn for many of them that have sinned before, and have not done penance for their fornication and unclean life they have used...

Wherefore I do exhort every man and woman in the name of our Lord Jesus Christ, as they tender the health and salvation of their souls, to be diligent and careful to use this special remedy ordained of God for remission of sin, neither contemning his justice, nor despairing of his mercy, which two be the lets of true penance, and enemies to the grace of God in remission of sin. (Ps. 7) For God is a just, mighty, and patient judge, forbearing and forgiving the penitent sinner, judging and condemning the obstinate sinner. As the consideration of his mercy should speedily provoke us to amendment, so the fear of his just judgement should utterly take away all delays. We be in danger on both sides, both by too much hoping, and by despairing. He is deceived by hoping that saith, God is good and merciful, promising pardon when so ever we convert, therefore I will do that pleaseth me, I will give the bridle to my lusts, and satisfy the desires of my mind. On the contrary side he is deceived by despera-tion, that falling into grievous sin, and thinking them not able or worthy to be forgiven, saith to himself: I shall be damned, therefore I will do that pleaseth me, the one is in danger by presuming of God's mercy, promising to himself long life, the other is in danger by undiscreet fear of God's justice, and horror of his great and manifold sins. But every Christian man and woman ought to go circumspectly in the midst, and beware for falling on either side...(2)

NOTES AND SOURCES

1. Thomas Watson, *Holsome and catholyke doctryne concerninge the seuen Sacramentes of Chrystes Church expedient to be knowen of all men, set forth in maner of shorte sermons to bee made to the people,* | *by the reuerend father in God. Thomas byshop of Lincolne* (1558), fos. ii–iv.
2. Ibid., fos. lxxxi–lxxxiii.

# John Harpsfield 1516–1578

John was the elder brother of the better-known Nicholas Harpsfield. They followed similar careers from their childhoods in London, where their father was a prosperous mercer. Both went to Winchester and to New College, Oxford, and both remained in Oxford throughout the 1540s, John as the first Regius Professor of Greek, publishing important works on Aristotle and Virgil. Both he and Nicholas conformed to the schismatical regime, John even contributing to the official collection of homilies promulgated in 1547 (his homily was on 'the misery of all mankind'). When Oxford became too hot for theological conservatives, Nicholas fled to Louvain, while John took shelter as a prebend of Chichester Cathedral, under the discreet eye of the most conservative of the conforming bishops, George Day. When Mary came to the throne he was quickly promoted to a prebend's stall at St Paul's (as was his brother), and while Nicholas became Archdeacon of Canterbury, John became Archdeacon of London. When Bishop Bonner published his *A Profitable and Necessary Doctrine with Certain Homilies Adjoined* (1554), John contributed nine of the thirteen homilies, not only rewriting his homily on human depravity, but contributing two powerful homilies on the Mass, from the second of which, *An Homelye of Transubstantiation*, the following is drawn.

## On Transubstantiation

You must know that the presence of Our Saviour Christ in this Sacrament of the Altar, is not to the intent that Christ should be conversant with us here in this Sacrament in such sort and manner, as he was with his Apostles when he lived here on earth, that is to say, in the visible shape and form of a man, but his presence in the Sacrament is to the intent to be to us an heavenly food, and therefore he is present in the sacrament, under the forms of bread and wine, so that our outward eyes and senses are certified with the outward forms, and sensible qualities, and the whole man withal receiveth the very Body and Blood of our saviour Christ. St Augustine doth say that christen men do honour under the forms of bread and wine, which they see with their bodily eyes, the Body and Blood of our Saviour Christ, which they do not see. Eusebius Emissenus also, an ancient Father of the Greek Church, speaking of the foresaid two parts contained in the Sacrament of the Altar, saith in this manner: 'this is the thing which by all means we intend to prove, that the sacrifice of the Church doth consist, and is made of two parts that is of the visible forms of the elements, and of the invisible Body and Blood of our Saviour Christ.' St Cyprian in his treatise entitled *De coena domini* doth most plainly say that the bread which our Lord did give to his disciples was by the omnipotency of God made flesh, and was changed in nature, but not in form. The forenamed Eusebius in a sermon of his made of the Body of Christ doth further say that 'Christ the invisible priest doth turn visible creatures by his word, through his secret power, into the substance of his Body and Blood.' Now for to signify this change, to turning of bread and wine, into the substance of Christ's Body and Blood, the Catholic Church useth this word, Transubstantiation, which is as much to say, as the changing of one substance into another, neither is it to be counted unfit that there should in the Sacrament of the Altar, be the form of bread, and yet not the substance of bread, seeing God is the doer and worker thereof, to whom nothing is impossible. We read in the Chapter of

Exodus, how that when God came down from Heaven unto Mount Sinai, there was heard a sound of a trumpet, and yet material trumpet was there none. In the fourth book of the Kings, and the seventh chapter, God caused a sound to be heard in the tents of the Syrians, as if it had been of horses, chariots, and of a great army, and yet was there neither horse, chariot, nor army. In the third chapter of Daniel, it is recorded, how the three children were in the midst of the flaming furnace, and yet felt no heat, so that there was the substance of fire, and yet it did not burn which to nature is impossible, but to GOD is an easy matter. In the seventeenth chapter of Matthew we read how that Christ was transfigured, and that his face did shine as the sun, and that his apparel was made as white as snow, in the twenty third chapter of Luke, Christ appeared to two of his disciples going to Emmaus, like a stranger. In all these foresaid examples, we see as strange a work as is transubstantiation, and yet no man doubteth of them because God is the worker, nor any man asketh how this, or that could be, but believeth it, and so ought we to do, concerning the change of the substance of bread and wine into the substance of Christ's Body and Blood, and not ask how it may be. The blessed martyr Justinus affirmeth that this question, *how*, is a token of unbelief; and St Cyril, writing upon the 6th Chapter of St John, blameth the Capernaites, because they did ask how Christ was able to give them his flesh to eat. The words of St Cyril be these: 'they ask not without great impiety how can this man give us his flesh and they remember not that nothing is impossible to God, but let us (sayeth he) have firm faith in the mysteries, and let us never in so high matters either think, or ask this how. When God is the worker, let us not ask how, but let us leave the knowledge of his work to himself. St Chrysostom likewise upon the said 5th Chapter saith, that when this question, how anything is done, cometh into our minds, then withal, there cometh unbelief also. But because in Scripture the thing that we receive, when we come to the sacrament, is called bread, therefore men have fancied with themselves, that there must be the substance of material bread, deceiving themselves, by mistaking the signification of this word 'bread'. For though in our common speech we use to signify by this word, bread, that one kind of material substance which is made of corn or grain, yet in Scripture, it signifieth all kind of food, whether it be the food of the body, or the food of the soul, and so doth also the Latin word, *Panis*, else when we desire God in our *Pater noster*, to give us our daily bread, we should make an unperfect petition, which yet is a most perfect petition, whereby we ask of our heavenly father, all necessary food ...

Saint Augustine in his exposition made upon the ninety-ninth Psalm saith, that it is sin, not to honour the Body of Christ, meaning in the Sacrament of the Altar. And he also saith in the name of all men. We do honour under the forms of bread and wine, which we see, the Body and Blood of Christ, which we do not see. Wherefore, good Christian people, knowing now what is the right belief, touching the Sacrament of the altar, embrace, and follow the same, and cleave fast to the Catholic Church, the spouse of Christ, that you may be true members of Christ, to whom with the father, and the Holy Ghost, be all honour and glory, world withoute ende. Amen. (1)

NOTES AND SOURCES

1. Edmund Bonner, *A Profitable and Necessary Doctrine with Certain Homilies Adjoined* (1554), unpag.

# John Heywood

*c.1496–c.1578*

John Heywood, stalwart in his Catholic faith, is typical of the crisis of the sixteenth century. His wife was a niece to St Thomas More, his daughter the mother of John Donne the poet. Two of his sons became Jesuits; his father-in-law John Rastell became too Protestant for Henry VIII and died in prison in 1536. Heywood himself was imprisoned in 1544 for plotting to discredit Thomas Cranmer, and he was tried for treason, and only pardoned after an uncomfortable wait. He was one of the wittiest writers of comedies in the 1520s and 1530s, but after his trial he turned to safer forms, collecting English proverbs and epigrams as well as courtly poetry. His one conspicuous act of defiance was to write poems in honour of the princess Mary. When she in due course became Queen, he joined her entourage and took part in the pageant that accompanied her coronation: according to Stow's *Chronicle* 'he sat under a vine and made her an oration in Latin and English'. He also wrote (and published) a ballad in praise of her marriage to Philip II of Spain. He was given a pension of £50 a year, and in return laboured away on a 500-page political and religious allegorical poem entitled *The Spider and the Fly* in which Mary was a central figure. He tried to be one of those discreet Catholics able to subsist within the Elizabethan court, but the stricter enforcement of the Oath of Supremacy in 1564 caused him to take flight to the Low Countries where he remained until his death— probably in the Franciscan college in Louvain, in late 1578 or early 1579. His comedies, and to a lesser extent his poetry, were celebrated by the great golden poets of the Jacobethan period. Our first piece by him was, as its title tells us, *A ballad specifyng partly the manner, partly the matter, in the most excellent meeting and like marriage between our soveraign Lord, and our soveraign Lady, the King's and Queen's Highness* and printed in 1554. The second piece is a short extract from a poem published in 1562 and entitled *A Ballad against Slander and Detraction*. It gives us a sense of Heywood's gift for epigram, and his delight in language.

## Celebrating the Marriage of Philip and Mary

The eagle bird hath spread his wings
And from far off, hath taken flight
In which mean way by no lowerings
On bough or branch this bird would light
Till on the rose, both red and white
He lighteth now, most lovingly
And thereto most behovingly.

The month ensuing next to June
This bird, this flower for perch doth take
Rejoicingly himself to prune
He rouseth, ripely to awake
Upon this perch to chose his make
Concluding straight for ripe right rest
In the lion's bower, to build his nest

A bird, a beast to make to choose
Namely the beast most furious

It may seem strange, and so it does
And to this bird injurious
It seemeth a case right curious
To make construction in such sense
As may stand for this bird's defence

But mark: this lion so by name
Is properly a lamb <u>tassyne</u>                              [? = to assign]
No lion wild, a lion tame
No rampant lion masculine
The lamblike lion feminine
Whose mild meek property allures
This bird to light, and him assures

The eagle bird, the eagle's <u>eyre</u>                       [= eyrie or nest]
All other birds far surmounting
The crowned lion, matcheth fair
Crown unto crown, this bird doth bring
A queenly queen, a kingly king
Thus, like to like here matched is
What match may match more meet than this?

So meet a match in parentage
So meet a match in dignity
So meet a match in patronage,
So meet match in benignity,
So macht [sic] from all malignity
As (thanks to God given for the same)
Sealed hath been seen, thus saith the fame

This meet met match, at first meeting
In their approach together near
Lovely, lovely, lively greeting
In each to other, did so appear
That lookers on all must grant clear
Their usage of such human reach
As all might learn, but none could teach

Then in conjoining of these twain
Such sacred solemn solemnity
Such fare in feast to entertain
Such notable nobility
Such honour with such honesty
Such Joy, all these to plat in plot
Plat them who can, for I can not

But here one dainty president
Number so great, in place so small
Nations so many, so different
So suddenly met, so agreed all
Without offensive word let fall
Save sight of twain, for whom all met
No one sight there, like this to get

This lamb-like lion, and lamb-like bird
To show effect, as cause affords
For that they lamb-like be concurred
The lamb of lambs, the Lord of Lords
Let us like lambs, as most accords
Most meekly thank, in humble wise
As humble hart, may most devise

Which thanks full given most thankfully
To prayer fall we on our knees
That it may like that Lord on high
In health and wealth to prosper these
As faith for their most high degrees
And that all we, their subjects may
Them and their laws, love and obey

And that between these twain and one
The three and one, one once to send
In one to knit us every each one
And to that one, such mo at end [sic]
As his will only shall extend
Grant this good God, adding thy grace
Lo make us meet to obtain this case. (1)

## Against Slander and Detraction

When vice is sought
all vice is nought
But some vice worse than some:
And each man sees
sundry degrees
In each vice self doth come.

Now sins the least
We should detest
vice or degree in vice:
If in the most

we show our boast
That showeth us most unwise.

If I in thee
such faults once see
As no man else doth know:
to thee alone
And other none
these faults I ought to show.

Then of intent
if I invent
False tales and them display:
that is most vile
Which to exile
God calleth this down down-a. (2)

NOTES AND SOURCES

1. John Heywood, *A balade specifienge partly the maner, partly the matter, in the most excellent meetyng and lyke mariage betwene our soueraigne Lord, and our soueraigne Lady, the Kynges and Queenes highnes pende by John Heywood* (1554), single sheet.
2. John Heywood, *A Ballad against Slander and Detraction* (1562), single sheet.

## Miles Huggarde                                      fl. 1533–1557

Miles Huggarde appears from obscurity in the 1540s and disappears from view in the late 1550s. He was a London craftsman, a hosier, and indeed he was appointed court hosier to Queen Mary in November 1553. He was also one of the fiercest enemies to heresy. In 1548 the Protestant preacher Robert Crowley accused him of being implicated in the prosecution of every Protestant burnt at the stake in Smithfield between 1533 and 1546. His unrelenting hostility to Protestants extended down to 1556 when his prose satire *The Displaying of Protestants* incorporated a pitiless account of the first burnings under the revived heresy laws. He was not only unrelenting, however, but also unflinching and his published attacks on those who denied the Real Presence of Christ in the Mass, including his *Aunswer to Ballad Called the Abuse of the Blessed Sacrament*, were suppressed by the Edwardian Privy Council. His major work, *The Assault of the Sacrament of the Altar*, was not published until 1554, because—as the title page puts it—'heresy then reigning, it could not take place'. In this poem, we get a chance to hear the voice of a layman, indeed of a largely uneducated artisan, articulating his faith. The poem as a whole (in some forty pages) begins with Melchizedek's offering to Abraham, and moves via the Exodus to the institution of the Eucharist, and it denounces medieval and recent heretical denials of Christ's clear teaching. Our extract comes from the central core of the poem.

### On Transubstantiation

Even so our Moses, Christ our saviour,
Delivered his people through his red blood,
From Pharaoh, the devil and all his whole power,

Under whom man then in great danger stood:
Now when God by Moses was to man thus good
He willed man yearly for a memorial,
To eat a lamb which they named the paschal.

Then for as much as our Lord did foresee,
How the nature of man was corrupted
With forgetfulness, for the which he,
For men's commodity this ordained,
That they should eat a male lamb unspotted,
In a remembrance how they delivered were
From wicked Pharaoh as you before did hear.

In like manner our Saviour Christ Jesu,
Ordained for a perpetual memory
A lamb to be eaten our minds to renew
In daily remembrance of his mercy,
Which he procured by his death truly,
The lamb that he left was himself indeed,
As in the Evangelists plain we do read.

That Christ is the lamb it doth plain appear.
Behold the Lamb of God, Saint John doth say,
That taketh away the sins of the world clear
Which he did truly by his death that day,
That his flesh was broken, none can this deny.
Now then to Christ's maundy let us resort,
And see here what weight his words doth import.

Christ at his last supper took bread in his hand:
He blest it, and break it, and those words said,
This is my body, thus doth his words stand,
The which for you, saith he, shall be betrayed.
These were his words it can not be denied.
But he spake thus, quod I, only in figure,
That doth not, quod he, agree with Scripture.

Thou must needs grant, quod he, that Christ came here
The figures of the old law to fulfil,
Chiefly all such as of his coming were,
And that not with figures, to think so were ill,
Whoso affirmeth that, can little skill
In the Scripture, for thus writeth saint Paul,
That the law to the Jews was in figures all.

And yet this same Sacrament is a figure,

But not only of Christ's body natural,
For that it containeth, but this we read in Scripture,
That the form of bread, which we see material,
Is a figure of Christ's body mystical,
As to the Corinths we do plainly read,
To recite the words I think shall not need.

But now to note Christ's words how they were spoken
This is my body, that given for you shalbe,
Which the next day on the cross was broken
For the sins of all men, this by faith we see.
Now that Christ is truth, needs we must agree,
Well then, of the bread, truth these words did say.
Which truly was true, if he died the next day.

Thus is Christ the Lamb that continually
Is eaten of us in his memorial,
Because we should not forget his mercy,
Which by his death he purchased for us all.
This to his coming truly continue shall.
The Jews then eat the lamb in figure only,
But we eat the true lamb, the Scripture doth try.

The Manna also which came from above,
To feed God's people in the wilderness,
Doth signify this great token of love,
With which Christ doth feed his people doubtless
As the Prophets saying, here plain doth express
The bread of Angels, man hath eat, saith he,
And Christ this same bread, nameth himself to be.

I am the bread of life saith our saviour,
Which from Heaven above did truly descend,
To give life to man doth pass man's power,
I am the true bread, which doth to that extend:
Manna from hunger, did man only defend,
but who that eateth of this bread, sure of life shalbe
And the bread that I will give is my flesh, saith he.

Came his flesh from Heaven, quod I, that would I here
For I believe of truth, he took it of Mary,
And yet by your words, methinks it doth appear
That the bread was his flesh which came from a-high
I think this saying true you cannot try,
For if you can so, my faith I will forsake,

For I do believe his flesh he did here take.

Lo, here thy ignorance thou dost show to me,
Did not Christ like case, say these words plainly: truly,
No man ascendeth to Heaven but only he,
Which came down from Heaven, the Son of Man
Which is in Heaven, mark what these words doth try
The Son of Man which is in Heaven, and yet he,
Was in his manhood here, as all men might see.

To discuss that, quod I, doth far pass my wit,
Why wilt thou then, quod he, in thy faith dispute,
Thou wouldest dig a pit, and thyself fall into it,
As many other doth, themselves to confute,
But do not thou like case from this faith transmute,
And now to show thee I will take in hand,
How these two places true together stand.

But first one text I will note to the more:
What will you say saith Christ, when you shall see,
The Son of Man ascend where he was before,
Doth not this text now express unto thee,
His manhood in Heaven before that to be,
May not I say then, his flesh is that bread,
Which came from Heaven, wherewith our souls be fed?

Then took he no flesh here that I perceive well,
Yes forsooth, quod he, this doth not that disprove,
For why, St John doth write in his Gospel,
That the word was made flesh, even God's son above
By eternal generation, none can that remove,
So God and man was knit, always to remain,
But one in personage, though in natures twain:

Now since our nature unto God is knit,
Being one in person as I before did say,
To know how this should be, doth pass all men's wit
Yet that this is true, no man can deny,
But that man is God, and God is man alway:
Now then Christ's holy flesh by this unity,
May truly be said alway in Heaven to be.

Now this heavenly bread under which Christ is here
The Bread of Angels the prophet well may call,
For the food of Angels is the glory clear
Of the blessed Godhead most celestial,

With the which Godhead Christ was ever equal.
So then where Christ is, the Godhead is alway,
Then the bread of Angels we eat, we may say.

Then, quod he, here the show bread is set out
Whereof none but the priests alone might eat,
The which doth signify, no Christian man will doubt
This most blessed bread, which is of virtue great,
The show bread was used as an heavenly meat:
For none but the priests God did thereto admit,
And all the people did reverence to it.

This most heavenly meat of Christ's flesh and blood,
Being, as I said, the perfect verity,
Figured by this show bread, by which the priests stood,
Only of priests also eaten here must be:
Of priests made by order, nay so take not me,
But both priests and kings, as Peter doth us call,
Which offereth to God the sacrifice spiritual. (1)

NOTES AND SOURCES

1. Miles Huggarde, *The assault of the sacrame[n]t of the Altar containyng aswell sixe seuerall assaultes made from tyme to tyme against the sayd blessed sacrament: as also the names [et] opinions of all the heretical captaines of the same assaultes: written in the yere of oure Lorde 1549. by Myles Huggarde, and dedicated to the Quenes moste excellent maiestie, beyng then ladie Marie: in which tyme (heresie then raigning) it could take no place* (1554), unpag.

## Thomas Vaux, 2nd Lord Vaux of Harrowden        1509–1556

Thomas Vaux was the son of one of the bright young men in the court of the young Henry VIII. He himself seemed destined for a courtly and public career, and he served briefly as Governor of Jersey, but his private disapproval of Henry's divorce from Katherine of Aragon and schism from Rome caused him to sell his offices (he did not even attend Parliament between 1534 and 1554) and retire to his country seat, where he kept his head down until the accession of Mary I, returning to London to be present at her coronation. He was a friend of other conservative courtly poets including Sir Thomas Wyatt and Henry Howard, Earl of Surrey. His output was modest, and most of it has been described as 'mainly concerned with the trials of love, and strike moralizing, sententious, and occasionally religious notes'. He was feted especially and influentially by George Puttenham in his influential *The Arte of English Poesie* (1589). Probably his best religious poem is this one drawn from *The Paradise of Dainty Devices*, edited by Richard Edwards (1576).

### Bethinking Himself of his End

When I behold the bier, my last and posting horse,
That bear shall to the grave, my vile and carren corpse:
Then say I: silly wretch, why doest thou put thy trust,

In things either made of clay, that soon will turn to dust.

Doest thou not see the young, the hardy and the fair,
That now are past and gone, as though they never were:
Doest thou not see thyself, draw hourly to thy last,
As shafts which that is shot, at birds that flieth fast.

Doest thou not see how death through smiteth with his lance,
Some by war, some by plague, and some by worldly chance:
What thing is there on earth for pleasure that was made,
But goeth more swift away, than doth the summer shade.

Lo here the summer flower, that sprung this other day,
But winter weareth as fast, and bloweth clean away:
Even so shalt thou consume from youth to loathsome age,
For death he doth not spare the prince more than the page.

Thy house shall be of clay, a clot under thy head,
Until the latter day, the grave shalbe thy bed:
Until the blowing trump doth say to all and some,
Rise up out of the grave, for now the judge is come. (1)

NOTES AND SOURCES

1. R. Edwards, *The paradyse of daynty deuises aptly furnished, with sundry pithie and learned inuentions: deuised and written for the most part, by M. Edwards, sometimes of her Maiesties chappel: the rest, by sundry learned gentlemen, both of honour, and woorshippe. viz. St Barnarde. E.O. L. Vaux. D. St Iasper Heyvvood. F.K. M. Bevve. R. Hill. M. Yloop, vvith others* (1576), 81–3.

# Laurence Vaux                                      1519–1585

Laurence Vaux was a Lancashire man and a distant relation of the Vauxs of Harrowden. He was ordained priest in 1542 and served in the Collegiate Church at Manchester until its dissolution under Edward VI, and then again from its restoration in 1553 until 1559 when he fled, first to Ireland and then to the Continent. For the rest of his life, he alternated between periods in Louvain (where he became a Canon Regular of St Augustine) and intervals on the English mission. On a visit to England in 1580 he was arrested and spent his remaining years in prison, where he died in 1585. His one published work is a catechism that he first prepared for his pupils when he was keeping a school. Here are his sections on one of the articles of the Apostles' Creed, his introduction to a discussion of the *Ave Maria*, his discussion of the sacrament of Extreme Unction, and his 'plain rule of faith whereby Catholics be discerned from heretics'.

## The Communion of Saints

*What is the communion of saints?* We must believe that all good faithful Christian people whether they be in Heaven, Earth or Purgatory, be members of Christ's Mystical Body (which is the Church) and communicate and participate with one another. The saints in Heaven do pray for us on earth, and we participate of the benefit of their prayers and merits. We that be in this world do communicate one with another in prayers and the Sacrifice of the Mass, with all good spiritual things, that be done in the universal Church. We ought to pray for them that be in Purgatory, and they may participate with us of the Sacrifice of the Mass, and of our prayers, and other good deeds, and take relief and benefit thereof...(1)

## The *Ave Maria*

*Why is the* Ave Maria *used so often to be said for a prayer seeing there is no petition in it?*

Whosoever hath any suit or request that he would gladly obtain of a prince, magistrate or his superior, he will use often words that will please and delight the mind of him that his suit is to; that thereby his mind may be moved with affection and made attentive to hear the suitor, and grant his request. So all Christian people are suitors to God and ought to make suit and request for mercy, grace and godly help to attain and come to eternal glory. And forthwith our blessed Lady was pre-elected and chosen of God before all other creatures to be the Mother of Christ, both God and man, and of that glorious Virgin, Christ took his manhood, wherewith he redeemed us. Therefore it is expedient to desire the said Mother of God to pray for us, that by her intercession we may the better obtain our suit of God.

No words can be found in the holy Scripture of more efficacy and strength to move the Holy Trinity mercifully to hear our suit and grant our request, than the angelical salutation.

First what words could be more acceptable to God the Father than these words, that he himself was the author of and (as one would say) indicted in Heaven and sent them down into earth by his mighty Archangel Gabriel, when he had decreed man's redemption and salvation.

What words can be more pleasant to God the Son, the Second Person in Trinity, than these words of the Angel, whereby his blessed Incarnation is most specially remembered, that he being God, was also made man perfectly; taking his manhood of the most pure blood of the Blessed Virgin Mary and was the blessed fruit of her womb, which fruit was offered upon the Cross for our redemption, the which fruit that the blessed Virgin brought forth, is really present in the blessed Sacrament of the Altar, to feed and nourish the worthy receivers, and to bring everlasting life to them that receive worthily. And also to be as a medicine, to expel the poison of the fruit that Eve first tasted of, which brought death and condemnation to all mankind.

What words can more please God the Holy Ghost, the Third Person of the Trinity, than these words that the Angel spake to the Blessed Virgin Mary, by the which he did work the miraculous incarnation of our Saviour in the Virgin's womb? So the will of the Holy Trinity was wrought by the salutation of the Angel, to the great joy of Angels, and to the unspeakable comfort of mankind.

What words can be more joyful to the Blessed Virgin Mary, than to hear these words that the Angel saluted her with, at the conception of our Saviour Jesus Christ in her womb, when EVA was turned into AVE, declaring her to be innocent, without spot of sin, so full of grace, as never any earthly creature was. In such sort and manner to have our Lord God with her, as never any creature had...Therefore upon these considerations, the holy Church doth universally and daily use both in public and private prayer, this angelical salutation and commendeth the same to all her obedient children... (2)

## The Sacrament of the Sick

*What is the Sacrament of Extreme Unction?* Extreme unction is a sacrament, wherein the sick persons (by holy oil and the words of Christ) are relieved; that more happily they may depart out of this world, and also that their bodies may be restored to health, if it be expedient. This Sacrament is to be ministered to men and women lying in extreme sickness in peril of death, by God's visitation, and not by violence of war, or execution. And this Sacrament is not to be ministered unto infants, and such as lack reason; for none ought to receive this sacrament, but such as have reason, and humbly desire it for God's sake.

*What is the matter of Sacrament?* The matter is oil olive hallowed by the bishop, wherewith the sick is anointed upon the eyes, ears, mouth, nose, hands, and feet. A man is anointed upon the reines [= region of the kidneys] of the back, and a woman upon the belly, because concupiscence reigneth most in these parts...

*Who is the minister of this Sacrament of Extreme Unction?* The priest is the minister of this Sacrament, whom the sick ought to send for, and before that he receive this sacrament, he ought to be confessed of his mortal sins, and receive absolution of the priest and also the Sacrament of the Altar, and humbly desire before the priest for God's sake to be anointed...

*What is the most plain rule of faith, whereby Catholics be discerned from heretics?* The most plain rule to know a Catholic is: they that do profess the faith of Christ and the whole authority of the Church, and steadfastly do hold the doctrine and faith of the Church, which the doctors and pastors of the Catholic Church do define and teach to be believed, are Catholics. For he that will not obey the Church (Christ himself saith) let him be taken as a heathen and publican. He shall not have God to be his Father that will not have the Church to be his Mother. (3)

NOTES AND SOURCES

1. Laurence Vaux, *A Catechism or a Christian Doctrine Necessary for Children and the Ignorant People* (1568), 11–12.
2. Ibid. 22–3.
3. Ibid. 90–3.

# Thomas Stapleton                                      1535–1598

Thomas Stapleton was one of the most formidable theologians amongst the Elizabethan exiles. He was a Fellow of New College Oxford (1553–9) and a prebend of Chichester Cathedral (1558–9). Having gone abroad soon after Elizabeth came to the throne, he was formally deprived of his prebendary in 1563 by 'the heretic jester to whom fair Chichester had become subject' (as he described Bishop William Barlow). Born a few days after the martyrdom of St Thomas More, and named after him (as he certainly liked to think), Stapleton spent the last thirty-five years of his life in and around Louvain and Douai. In the 1560s he wrote passionately in the vernacular, clearly still hopeful that the Queen herself and all right-thinking Englishmen would abandon schism and return to obedience to Rome. After the catastrophe of *Regnans in excelsis* (see below, pp. 104–6), he abandoned all such hopes, and the honeyed words of appeal to reason, and embarked instead on decades of academic debate in Latin. Just one of them, his *De universa justificationis doctrina, hodie controversa* (1581) ran to 350,000 words and addressed all the theological issues that divided Catholics from Protestants. But in the 1560s, he still hoped that deference to Elizabeth and sound pleading could win the day. It was this which led him to translate what he called *The History of the Church of Englande. Compiled by Venerable Bede, Englishman* (1565 with new editions in 1622 and 1626). His purpose, as he explained in his preface, was to show, from an impeccable eighth-century witness, how Christianity was established in Britain, especially following the arrival of Augustine in Kent in 597. Bede's aim was 'to demonstrate the role of the Christian King, what he ought to do for the Church and what the Church could do for him'. We shall see this fully in action in the account of the Synod of Whitby (664) which we offer below. Although it has been said that the *History* was Stapleton's least polemical work, it should be better said that it was his most skilfully polemical work. By looking at how successful collaboration of Pope and monarch had brought civilization to Britain, Bede was showing what Elizabeth had to gain rather than lose by reverting to the policies of her sister. And to reinforce this, Stapleton adds two significant prefaces, one addressed, very respect-fully, to Elizabeth herself, and another to what he hopes is the open-minded reader. These are substantial treatises in themselves; together with a list of the 'differences between the primitive faith of England continued these almost thousand years and the late pretended faith of Protestants' they take up fifty pages. As Stapleton makes explicit, Bede has chronicled 'a fortress of faith first planted among us Englishmen and continued hitherto in the universal Church of Christ'. This use of Bede to deny to Protestants their favourite claim that the Church of England was truer to 'primitive' Christianity than the corrupted Catholicism of the pre- and even more post-Tridentine Catholic Church, was important for Catholic self-definition. This is a lethal subversion of much Protestant rhetoric in the 1560s, and, strikingly, it went unan-swered. We begin with an extract from the dedication 'to the right excellent and most gracious princess Elizabeth, by the grace of God Queen of England, France and Ireland, Defender of the Faith'—no holding back in those words. Then we have an extract from Stapleton's Epistle to the reader; and finally an extract from the translation itself. It is reason-ably free, but there is no attempt to further a cause. St Bede's own words do all that Stapleton wants them to do. It is in fact the most fluent and readable translation before the late nineteenth century. St Bede the Venerable (673/4–735) spent his life as a monk of Wear-mouth and Jarrow. He wrote a series of very remarkable biblical commentaries (Old and New Testament), steeped in the learning of the Latin Fathers (above all Augustine and Gregory), lives of the saints, as well as works on the use of language, computation, and numerology. In 1899 Pope Leo XIII made him a Doctor of the Church, the first Englishman honoured in that way. He was and is best remembered for his *Historia ecclesiastica gentis anglorum*, com-pleted in 731. It is a work of 85,000 words, clearly inspired by the histories of Eusebius. Our extract deals with the Synod of Whitby in 664, in which King Oswy and his son Prince Alchfrid presided over clergy of the Roman and Celtic traditions to resolve a number of questions, most prominently over the dating of Easter and over the form of the tonsure for religious. Bede records the arguments of both parties and the King's adjudication in favour of the Roman party, with momentous consequences. Although he concludes his chapter on the Synod by saying that 'all sorts and degrees, abandoning their former unperfectness, con-formed themselves to the better instructions which they had now learned', this was not quite how Colman (leader of the Celtic party) saw it: he retreated to Ireland, and became a hermit on the remote island of Inishbofin, off the Connemara coast. The heroism of his life in these reduced circumstances caused him to become a saint in the Celtic tradition, so Whitby was not all bad news for him.

## Preface to Bede's *History*

The matter of the History is such, that if it may stand with your Majesty's pleasure to view and consider the same in whole or in part, Your Highness shall clearly see as well the misinformations of a few for displacing the ancient and right Christian faith, as also the way and means of a speedy redress that may be had for the same, to the quietness of the greater part of your Majesty's most loyal and lowly subjects' consciences. In this history it shall appear in what faith your noble realm was christened, and hath almost these thousand years continued: to the glory of God, the enriching of the crown, and great wealth and quiet of the realm. In this history your highness shall see in how many and weighty points the pretended reformers of the church in your Grace's dominions have departed from the pattern of that sound and catholic faith planted first among Englishmen by holy St Augustine, our apostle, and his virtuous company, described truly and sincerely by Venerable Bede, so called in all Christendom for his passing virtues and rare learning, the author of this history. And to the intent your highness's intention bent to weightier considerations and affairs may spend no long time in espying out the particulars, I have gathered out of the whole History a number of diversities between the pretended religion of Protestants, and the primitive faith of the English Church, and have annexed them straight, joining to this our simple preface. May it please your most gracious Highness to take a short view of it, and for more ample intelligence of every particular (if it shall so like your highness) to have a recourse to the book and chapter quoted.

Beside the whole history of holy and learned St Bede, I have published a short and necessary discourse to meet with the only argument of such as will pronounce this whole book to be but a fardle [= bundle or parcel] of papistry, a witness of corrupted doctrine, a testimony of that age and time which they have already condemned for the time of no true Christianity at all: of such I say as have altered the faith we were first christened in, condemning our dear forefathers of almost these thousand years, the Christian inhabitants of your Grace's dominions. This I have done principally in two parts. In the first by express testimonies of Holy Scripture, the psalms, the prophets, and the New Testament, by removing the objections of the adversaries taken out of Holy Scripture, by the glorious success of these later 900 years in multiplying the faith of Christ through the world, last of all by clear and evident reasons I have proved that the faith of us Englishmen all these 900 years, could not possibly be a corrupted faith, traded up in superstitions, blindness, and idolatry, as it is falsely and wickedly surmised of many, but that it is the true and right Christianity no less than the first 600 years, and immediate succession of the Apostles. In the second part, where we gather a number of differences in doctrine, in ecclesiastical government, in the order and manner of proceeding, in the course and consequences of both religions, that first planted among us and so many hundred years continued, and this presently preached and pretended, I have showed by the testimonies of the most ancient and approved Fathers, of the Councils and histories of that time, that in all such differences our faith first planted and hitherto continued among us, agreeth and concurreth with the practice and belief of the first 600 years, the time approved by all men's consent for the right and pure Christianity. If it may stand with your Majesty's pleasure to weigh this double truth so clearly proved first out of God's holy word and evident reason, then out of the assured practice of the primitive church, your Grace shall quickly see a ready redress of present schisms, a compendious quieting of troubled consciences, and an open path to return to the faith, without which is no salvation. As we know right well, the meaning of your gracious Highness to be already seriously bent to have the truth tried and to be sincerely published through all your Grace's dominions, so to the end that this godly zeal may in your Majesty' most princely heart the more be kindled and confirmed, most humbly and lowly I beseech the same, to behold a few examples of the most puissant princes that have been in Christendom, which in that singular virtue have principally excelled...

Such hath always been (most gracious sovereign) the virtuous zeal of the wisest and most politic princes to extirpate heresies and false religion out of their dominions, knowing right well, that none are better subjects to the prince than such as most devoutly serve Almighty God. And again that nothing more highly pleaseth God than that a prince do further and set forth the true service and worshipping of him. Such a one was King David, of whom therefore God said: I have found David a man according to my heart's desire. And these Emperors here specified, as they tendered most the setting forth of true religion, and abolishment of the false, so prospered they most of all other in worldly respects...

To the Imperial Crown of your Majesty, the noble and glorious title of Defender of the faith hath been of late years annexed and perpetually given by the See Apostolic, for the most godly and learned work of your Highness's most noble Father, our late dread sovereign, in defence of the seven holy Sacraments of Christ's Church (of which the scholars of Geneva have taken away five) and against the wicked heresies of that lewd apostate Martin Luther. To the crown of Spain for the great zeal of king Alphonsus in extirpating the Arian heresy, above 800 years past, the title of Catholic was annexed, and continueth yet hitherto unblemished. To the crown of the French king for the passing zeal of those princes (namely of Clovis the first Christian king, of Charlemagne, of Philip Augustus) in extirpating heresies from time to time out of their dominions the title of Most Christian, hath also been appropriated from the time of Pippin and Charlemagne his son hitherto...

If it may like your most excellent Highness after the pattern and examples of these most puissant and virtuous princes to proceed in your most gracious meaning to the publishing of the true Christian faith (which is but one, and not new) through your Grace's dominions, as all Christendom heartily wisheth, the view and consideration of this present history, a worthy and most authentic witness of the first and true Christian faith planted in your Graces dominions, with that which is annexed to prove it a right and uncorrupted faith, shall not a little (I trust in God, in whose hands the hearts of princes are) move and farther your Highness's virtuous intent to the speedy achieving of that it desireth. For faith being one (as the Apostle expressly saith) that one faith being proved to be the same which was first grafted in the hearts of Englishmen, and the many faiths of Protestants being found different from the same in more than forty clear differences gathered out of this present history (which reporteth not all, but a few by occasion) it must remain undoubted, the pretended faith of Protestants to be but a bastard slip proceeding of another stock (as partly of old renewed heresies, partly of new forged interpretations upon the written text of God's word) and therefore not to be rooted in your Grace's dominions, lest in time, as heresies have done in Greece and Africa, it overgrow the true branches of the natural tree, consume the spring of true Christianity, and suck out the joys of all right religion: leaving to the realm the bark and rind only, to be called Christians. Which lamentable case the more every Christian heart abhorreth, and your Highness most gracious meaning especially detesteth, the more it is of us your Highness most lowly and loyal subjects to be wished and daily to be prayed for at the dreadful throne of God's deep mercy, that it may please his goodness so to direct the heart of Your Highness, so to inspire with his heavenly grace the most gracious meaning of your Majesty, that it may wholly and perfectly be bent to the restoring of the one catholic and apostolical faith of Christendom, to the extirpating of schism and heresy, and to the publishing of God's true service. All to the honour of Almighty God, to the contentation of your Majesty's pleasure, and to the wealth of Your Grace's dominions. The which God of his tender mercy, through the merits of his dear Son, and intercession of all blessed saints in Heaven, grant. Amen.

Your Highness's most lowly subject, and bounden orator, Thomas Stapleton. (1)

## Addressing the Reader of Bede's *History*,

The Kingdom of Heaven is compared in holy Scripture (Christian Reader) to a merchant adventurer, which seeking and travailing to find precious stones, [Matt. 13] having at length found out one of singular and most excellent value, goeth and selleth all that he hath to buy that one. What this singular and most excellent pearl is, whereunto the Kingdom of Heaven is compared, if we weigh and ponder diligently, we shall find it to be no other thing than the faith in Christ Jesus, whereby the Kingdom of Heaven is undoubtedly purchased. This pearl is of price so singular, and of value so excellent, that to get it we sell all that we have, we renounce the world, the flesh and the devil with all the pomp thereof, we cleave only to this, we profess to live and die in it. This precious pearl of faith, this singular jewel of true belief, this heavenly treasure of the right knowledge of God and of his commandments, as all nations at one time received not, [Acts 14] God of his secret and right justice suffering the nations to walk on their ways, but in several ages, and by several means, as and when it pleased God was opened and made manifest, so have all nations not only for that, sold all which they had, yielding and submitting themselves only and wholly thereto, but also have steadfastly and assuredly cleaved unto it, have by long succession preserved it, and enjoyed it. If any have in time utterly lost this most excellent and rare jewel (as we see, alas, all the south and almost all the east part of the world hath) the cause thereof hath been the alteration, and new devised furbishing of that pearl from the former and natural shape thereof, first and foremost received. Such nations and parts of the world as have in many ages and do yet keep and enjoy this rich and princely treasure, do therefore yet keep it and enjoy it because they continue and remain in it after such order and manner only, as they received it: because they keep it as they found it, because they continue it, as they begun it ...

If we have an eye to the uniformity of the Christian faith first received in all such countries as yet remain Christians, with the faith first planted and grafted among them, if we look to Italy, to France, to Spain, to the Catholic territories of Greece, of Germany, of Switzerland, to the kingdoms of Poland, of Portugal, and of other main lands in other places of the world dispersed, where the precious jewel of this faith is known and enjoyed, we shall find that all those countries have and do therefore yet continue in the same, because they vary not from the first faith received, because they mangle not the jewel given unto them, neither alter the natural shape thereof, briefly because they believe all one thing and after one sort as their first teachers and Apostles believed and taught them. For why? They have well remembered the admonitions of St Paul to the Corinthians converted by him to the faith of Christ, when he wrote unto them and said, watch and stand in the faith [1 Cor. 16]; also to Timothy by him in like manner christened, writing unto him and saying: O Timothy keep well that is committed to thy charge, avoiding profane novelties of words [1 Tim. 6]; and again to the Colossians, praising them for the faith received, if yet (saith he) you continue steadfast and grounded in the faith, if we waver not from the hope of the Gospel, which you have heard, which hath been preached in al the world [Col. 1]. All Christianized Catholic countries have well remembered these lessons of the apostle. And as many as have remembered and followed them, have remained and do yet remain in the faith of Christ, have long enjoyned and do yet enjoy this rare and inestimable jewel compared to the Kingdom of Heaven. As all other countries have so done, so have we Englishmen also these many hundred years kept and preserved sound and whole the precious pearl of right faith and belief, as long as we remained steadfast in the faith first planted and grafted among us, as long as we kept that which was committed unto us, as long as we wavered not from the Gospel first received and universally preached through all the world, as St Paul willeth us. But after we began to alter and polish after our own new devices this ancient pearl so long kept among us, so universally made of and esteemed, after we forsook the first pattern of the Christian faith delivered unto us, we have fallen in to plenty of heresies, from one heresy to another, from Lutheran to sacramentary, and so forth, we stand also in danger to fall (as other countries have done before us) from a false faith to no faith, from heresy to paganism . . .

The history which must report the faith first planted among us, shall be no story of our own devising, no late compiled matter, where both for uncertainty of things so long past, we might be much to seek, and for the case of controversies now moved, partiality might justly be suspected, but it shall be an history written in the fresh remembrance of our first apostles, written above 800 years past, written of a right learned and holy Father of Christ's church, of a countryman of ours living and flourishing shortly after the faith so planted among us. (2)

## The Lessons of the Synod of Whitby

Meanwhile, after the death of Aidan, Finan succeeded in the bishopric of Northumberland, sent and consecrated of the Scots, who in Holy Island [= Lindisfarne] builded a church meet for a bishop's see, yet not of stone, but of oaken timber and thatchwork, as the manner of Scots was. This church afterward the most reverend Father Theodore, Archbishop of Canterbury, dedicated in the honour of St Peter the Apostle. Eadbert also the bishop after of that place covered the church both the roof and the walls with lead. About this time a great controversy was moved touching the observation of Easter. The bishops of France [Gaul] and Kent affirmed that the Scots observed the Sunday of Easter contrary to the accustomed manner of the universal church. And among them one Ronan a Scot born but yet instructed in the truth in France and Italy, and therefore an earnest and stout defender of the true observation of Easter. Who coupling and disputing of this matter with Finan the bishop, induced many to the truth, and enflamed others to a further search and examination of the question, but with Finan himself he could nothing prevail, but rather exasperated him, being a hasty-natured man, and made him an open adversary to the cause. James that reverent deacon of the archbishop Paulinus, with all such as he converted to the faith, observed the true and catholic time of Easter. Eanfleda also the queen, king Oswy's wife with all her train and company observed after the same manner according as she had seen it practised in Kent, bringing with her one Romanus out of Kent, a Catholic priest. By this variance it happened oftentimes that in one year two Easters were kept. As the king breaking up his fast and solemnizing the Feast of Easter, the Queen with her company continued yet the fast, and kept Palm Sunday. Yet this diversity of observing Easter, as long as Aidan lived, was of all men tolerated, knowing very well that though in observing Easter he followed the custom of those with whom he was brought up, yet he believed as all holy men did, and kept unity and love, with all. Upon which consideration he was beloved of all men, even those which varied from him in that opinion and was reverenced not only of the mean and common sort, but also of Honorius the Archbishop of Canterbury and of Felix the bishop of the East English. But after the death of Finan, which succeeded him, Colman being made bishop sent also out of Scotland, the controversy began to increase, and other variances touching external trade of life were stirred up. By occasion whereof many began to fear and doubt, lest bearing the name of Christians [Gal. 2], they did run (as the Apostle saith) or had run in vain.

This controversy reached even to the princes themselves, to king Oswy and his son Alchfrid. For Oswy being brought up and baptized of the Scots, and skilful also of their tongue thought the manner which they observed to be the best and most agreeable to truth. Contrariwise, Alchfrid, the king's son being instructed of the learned man Wilfrid, preferred worthily his judgement before all the traditions of the Scots. This Wilfrid for better instruction and learning's sake had travelled to Rome, and lived also a long time with Dalfin the Archbishop of Lyons in France, of whom also he took benet [= minor order of exorcist] and collet [= the tonsure]. To this learned prince Alchfrid gave a monastery of forty families, in a place which is called Humpum [sic]. The Scots before were in possession of that monastery: but because after the decision of this controversy they chose rather of their own accord to depart and yield up the place than to change their accustomed manner of observing the Easter, it was given by the prince to him, who both for learning and virtue was worthy thereof. About this time Agilbert bishop of the West Saxons, a friend of prince Alchfrid and Wilfrid the Abbot came to the province of Northumberland, and stayed there with them for a space. Who in the meanwhile at the request of Alchfrid made Wilfrid a priest. He had in his company also at that time one Agatho a priest. At their presence therefore the question being renewed, and much talked of, they agreed on both sides, that in the

monastery of Stranshalch [= Whitby] where that devout and virtuous woman
Hilda was Abbess, a Synod should be kept for the deciding of this question, and
other than in controversy.

To this Synod came both the kings Oswy the father and Alchfrid the son. With
king Oswy stood bishop Colman with his clergy of Scotland, Hilda also the Abbess
with her company, among whom was Cedd that reverend bishop lately consecrated of the Scots (as we have touched before) who in that assembly was a most
diligent interpreter on both sides. For the other opinion which king Alchfrid
followed, Agilbert the bishop stood, with Agatho and Wilfrid priests. Jacobus and
also Romanus two other learned men stood of that side. First then king Oswy
(premising that it behoved those which served one God, to keep one order and
rule in serving the same, nor to vary here in celebrating the heavenly Sacraments,
who looked all for one kingdom in Heaven, but rather that the truth ought to be
searched out of all, and followed uniformly of every one) commanded his bishop
Colman first to declare what his observation was, whence he received it, and
whom he followed therein. The bishop answered and said: 'the Easter which
I observe, I have received of my forefathers, of whom I was sent hither bishop,
who all being virtuous and Godly men have after the same manner observed it.
And this observation, that you may not think it a light matter or easily to be
rejected, is the self same, which St John the Evangelist the disciple whom Jesus
specially loved with all the churches under him observed.' These and such like
words when bishop Colman had spoken, the king commanded Agilbert the
bishop to speak his mind also, and to bring forth the beginning and author of
his manner of observing Easter: unto whom Agilbert answered: 'let, I beseech you,
my scholar Wilfrid priest speak herein for me. For we and all that here sit be of
one mind, and observe herein the ecclesiastical tradition uniformly. Beside he
shall better express to your Highness the whole matter speaking himself the
English tongue, than I shall be able using an interpreter.'

Then Wilfrid, the king commanding him, spake in this wise: 'the Easter which
we observe, we have seen in like manner to have been observed at Rome, where
the blessed Apostles Peter and Paul, lived and preached, suffered, and are buried.
This manner we have seen to be observed in all Italy and France, passing through
those countries partly for study, partly on pilgrimage. This manner we know to be
observed in Africa, in Asia, in Egypt, in Greece, and through out all nations and
tongues, of all the world where the Church of Christ taketh place, after the self
same order and time, beside only these few and other of like obstinacy, the Picts I
mean and the Britons, with whom these men from the two farthermost Islands of
the Ocean sea, and yet not all that neither, do fondly contend against the whole
world.' Here Colman the bishop interrupted and said: 'I marvel much you term
our doing a fond contention wherein we follow the example of so worthy an
apostle, who only leaned upon our Lord's breast, and whose life and behaviour all
the world accompteth to have been most wise and discreet.' Unto whom Wilfrid
answered, and said: 'God forbid we should charge St John with fondness or lack of
wit. For he in his observation kept yet the decrees of Moses's law literally,
according as the whole Church followed yet in many things the Jewish manner:
for why? The apostles were not able upon the sudden to blot out all customs and
rites of the law instituted of God himself, as all that come to the faith must of
necessity abandon idols invented of the devil. And this forsooth they were forced

to bear a time withal, lest the Jews which lived among the Gentiles might be offended. For in the like consideration also St Paul did circumcise, offered blood sacrifices in the Temple, shaved his head at Corinth with Aquila and Priscilla: truly to no other intent, but that the Jews might not be offended. Upon this consideration James said unto Paul. You see brother, how many thousands of the Jews have received the Faith, and all these are yet zealous followers of the law. Notwithstanding the light of the Gospel now shining through out the world, it is not now necessary, no it is not lawful now for any Christian man to be circumcised, or to offer up bloody sacrifices of beasts. St John therefore according to the custom of the law, in the fourteenth day of the first month at the evening began to celebrate the feast of Easter, not regarding whether it fell out the Sabbath day or any other ferial day of the week [John 20]. But St Peter preaching the Gospel at Rome, remembering that our Lord arose the first day after the Sabbath, giving thereby to us certain and assured hope of our resurrection, he understood the observation of Easter in such sort, that according to the custom and commandments of the law he looked for (even as St John did) the rising of the Moon at evening, in the fourteenth day of his age, in the first month. And at the rising thereof at evening, if the morrow after were Sunday (which then was called, the first day after the Sabbath) he began in that very evening to observe the feast of Easter, as all we do even to this day, beginning on Easter eve. But if Sunday were not the next morrow after the fourteenth day of the change of the Moon, but the sixteenth, seventeeth, or any other day of the Moon until the one and twentieth, he tarried for the Sunday, and the Saturday before upon the evening he began the most holy solemnity of Easter. Thus it came to pass that Easter Sunday was kept only either the fifteenth day of the change of the Moon in the first month, or the one and twentieth, or in some day between (as the Sunday fell) and no day else . . . '

[*Debate rages to and fro, with the Scots arguing from the practice of the good and holy men of their own tradition (especially Columba/Columcille). But the following response of Wilfrid proves decisive.*]

For though your fathers were holy men could yet those few of one so small corner of the uttermost island of the earth, prejudicate the whole Church of Christ dispersed through the universal world? And if your father Columba (yea and our father, if he were the true servant of Christ) were holy and mighty in miracles, yet can he by any means be preferred to the most blessed prince of the Apostles [Matt. 16] to whom our Lord said, 'thou art Peter, and upon this rock I will build my Church, and Hell's gates shall never prevail against her: and to thee I will give the keys of the Kingdom of Heaven.' Thus when Wilfrid concluded, the king said unto bishop Colman: 'were these things indeed spoken to Peter of our Lord?' To whom the bishop answered, 'yea'. 'Can you then' (saith the king), 'give evidence of so special authority given to your father Columba?' The bishop answering 'no', the king spake unto both parties, and said: 'agree you both in this without any controversy, that these words were principally spoken unto Peter, and that unto him the keys of the Kingdom of Heaven were given?' When both had answered, yea: the king concluded and said: then I say unto you, that I will not gainsay such a porter as this is, but as far as I know, and am able, I will covet all points to obey his ordinances, lest perhaps when I come to the doors of the Kingdom of Heaven, I find none to open unto me, having his displeasure, which is so clearly proved to bear the keys thereof.' Thus when the king had said, all that sat and stood by of all sorts and degrees, abandoning their former unperfectness, conformed themselves to the better instructions which they had now learned . . . (3)

NOTES AND SOURCES

1. Thomas Stapleton, *The Historie of the Church of England. Compiled by Venerable Bede Englishman. Translated out of Latin, into English, by Thomas Stapleton Doctor in Diuinite* (1565), unpag.
2. Ibid. 1–2.
3. Ibid. 162–6.

## Pope St Pius V                               1504–1572

In 1570 Pius V (Pope from 1566 to 1572) issued a bull that declared Elizabeth I to be a heretic bastard tyrant and that released all her Catholic subjects from all obligation to obey her. Indeed it placed an obligation on them to seek to overthrow her. It was this Bull, more than anything else, which unleashed the savage persecution of Catholics: within a decade it was treason to be a seminary-trained priest or religious in England, or to protect them; heads of households were liable to severe financial penalties for non-attendance at church and lengthy imprisonment for possessing Catholic books or devotional objects. The timing of the Bull could not have been worse. Six months earlier, he might have reinforced and broadened support for the noble uprising in the North of England and the conspiracies of the Duke of Norfolk to replace Elizabeth by her Catholic cousin Mary Queen of Scots. But it arrived in England just when the Queen and her Council and Parliament were considering how punitive any new measures to be taken against Catholics should be. The bull set the tone for thirty years of confrontation, of terrorism and counter-terrorism, and this in turn was to split the Catholic community into those willing to court martyrdom and persecution, and those willing to compromise with the demands of the state and to seek out ways of serving both Caesar and God. The Bull (*Regnans in excelsis*) was soon translated into English and this is its near contemporary English form.

### *Regnans in excelsis*

The sentence declaratory of the Holy Father Pope Pius the Fifth, against Elizabeth the pretended Queen of England, and those Heretics adhering to her: And finally, all such as obey her, to be ensnared in the same.

He that rules in the Heavens above, and to whom all power is given both in Heaven and Earth, gave unto one only upon Earth, viz. to Peter, the chiefest amongst the Apostles, and to the Pope of Rome, Peter's successor, a holy, Catholic and Apostolic Church (without which there is no salvation) to govern it in the fullness of power. And this he ordained as chief above all nations and kingdoms, to pull down, destroy, dissever, cast off, plant, and erect; to combine in the unity of spirit, his faithful people, conneceted together through mutual charity, and present them whole and sound to his Saviour. Which charge, we, who through the grace of God, are thereunto called, submitting ourselves to the government of the same Church, cease not with all our best labours and endeavours, to preserve this unity and Catholic religion, which he, who was the author thereof, so suffered to be encumbered, for the trial of the faith of his, and for our correction. But the number of the ungodly is so great in power, that there is not a corner left upon the whole Earth now untainted with their wicked doctrines. Amongst which, Elizabeth, pretended Queen of England, is, above all, the shelter and refuge of error, and most noisome enemies. It is she who, after she had possessed the kingdom, usurping (monster-like) the place of the chief sovereign of the Church in England, and the principal jurisdiction and authority thereof, hath thrown into miserable ruin the whole kingdom, when it was even brought to the Catholic faith, and began to bring forth good fruits. For she with a powerful hand prohibiteth the exercise of the true religion (which was heretofore overthrown by Henry the Eighth, the forsaker thereof, and afterwards repaired with the help of this See, by Mary, lawful Queen of England, of famous memory) and embraceth the heresies of obscure persons; the royal council once composed of the English nobility, she hath broken off, oppresseth such as made profession of, and exercised the Catholic religion, re-established the wicked ministers and preachers of impiety, abolished the Sacrifice of the Mass, prayers, fastings, the dividing of the meats, the celibate, and all Catholic ceremonies, sent books over her whole kingdom, containing manifest heresies, commended to her subjects the profane mysteries and institutions which she had received, and observed from the decree of Calvin, displaced the bishops, rectors, and Catholic priests from their Churches and benefices, and disposed of them to heretics, and is bold to take upon her to judge and determine ecclesiastical affairs; forbad the prelates, the clergy, and people, to acknowledge the Roman Church, or observe her commandments, and canonical duties; enforced divers to swear obedience to her detestable ordinances, to renounce the authority due to the Roman dignity, and acknowledge her the only sovereign over temporal and spiritual things; imposed penalties and taxes upon such as were refractory to her injunctions; inflicted punishments upon those who persisted in the unity of the faith and obedience, imprisoned the prelates and governors of the Catholic Churches; where divers being, with a tedious languishing and sorrow, miserably finished their unhappy days. All which things being thus evident and apparent to all nations, and so manifestly proved by the grave testimony of divers, that there is no place left for any excuse, defence, or tergiversation. We, perceiving that these impieties and mischiefs do still multiply one by another, and that the persecution of the faithful, and the affliction of the Church doth daily increase, and wax more heavy and grievous, and finding that her heart is so obstinate and obdurate, that she hath not only despised the wholesome prayers and admonitions which the Christian princes have made for her better health and conversion, but that she hath denied passage to the nuncios, who, for this end, were sent from this siege into England; and being compelled to bear the arms of justice against her, we cannot moderate the punishment that we are bound to inflict upon her, whose ancestors merited so well of the Christian commonwealth. Being then supported by his authority, who hath placed us upon this sovereign throne of justice, howsoever incapable of so great a charge, out of the fullness of our apostolical power, do pronounce and declare the said Elizabeth an heretic, and favourer of heretics, and those who adhere unto her in the foresaid things, have incurred the sentence of anathema, and are cut off from the unity of the Body of Christ; that she is deprived of the right which she pretends to the foresaid kingdom, and of all and every seignory, royalty, and privilege thereof. And the peers, subjects, and people of the said kingdom, and all others upon what terms soever sworn unto her, freed from their oath, and from all manner of duty, fidelity, and obedience. As we do free them by the authority of these presents, and exclude the said Elizabeth from the right which she pretendeth to the said kingdom, and the rest before mentioned, commanding moreover, and enjoining all, and every the nobles, as subjects, people, and others whatsoever, that they shall not once dare to obey her, or any her directions, laws or commandments, binding under the same curse, those who do any thing to the contrary ... *Given at* Rome, *at St* Peters, *the 5 of March, in the year of the Incarnation of our Saviour 1569. and of our Pontificate the 5ᵗʰ.* (1)

NOTES AND SOURCES

1. William Camden, *Annals the True and Royal History of the Famous Empress Elizabeth Queen of England France and Ireland etc* (1625), 245–8.

# A Defence of *Regnans in excelsis* (1584)

The Bull *Regnans in excelsis* provoked savage parliamentary legislation including a new law making it treason simply to be a seminary-trained priest in England. From 1581 the great persecution began that was to see more than 120 priests hanged, drawn, and quartered (many after savage torture) in the remaining twenty-two years of Elizabeth's reign. As the arrests and executions mounted, William (later Cardinal) Allen launched a defence of the work of the clergy in *A True, Sincere and Modest Defence of English Catholics that Suffer for their Faith* (1584). But there was a fatal ambiguity in his defence. On the one hand, he wanted to defend his fellow Catholics against the charge of treason, and to plead that the seminary priests were simple pastors bringing sacramental grace to men and women of conscience; on the other he had to acknowledge that the Pope had the right and duty so clearly articulated in *Regnans in excelsis*, to act against those who persecuted God's Church. However hard he tried, he had to admit that there was no easy way of separating the rights of secular rulers over the things of Caesar from the rights of the successor of Peter over the things of God. This is an extreme example of a dilemma that has faced Christians in every period of the Church's history including our own. Allen challenges the arguments of a government tract *The Execution of Justice* (attributed to William Cecil, Lord Burghley).

## In Defence of *Regnans in excelsis*

We set forth the truth of all these actions [of those martyred] for the honour of our nation, which otherwise to her infinite shame and reproach, would be thought wholly and generally to have revolted from the Catholic faith and consented to all the absurdities and iniquities of this new regiment and religion, if none with zeal and extreme endeavour resisted such pernicious innovations. Where now as well our own people, as all strangers in the Christian world, perceiving the disorder to proceed but of the partiality of a few powerful persons abusing her Majesty's clemency and credulity, do glorify our Lord God that in so great a temptation, all the clergy in manner and so many of the laity of all sorts constantly persist in their fathers' faith to the loss of goods, lands, lives, honours and whatsoever besides ...

Secondly, we set forth these things for the memory and honour of such notable martyrs as have testified to the truth of the Catholic faith by their precious death, which was an ancient canon and custom of the primitive church, which appointed certain special persons of skill and learning, to note the days of every one's glorious confession and combat, that their memories might afterwards be solemnly celebrated for ever among Christians.

Thirdly, we do it to communicate our calamities with our brethren in faith, and the Churches of other provinces standing free from this misery, both for their warning and our comfort, and to excite in them Christian compassion towards us, that thereby and by their counsel and prayers, we may find mercy and relief at God's hand; by the example of the Oriental Churches afflicted by the Arians, which we may read in St Basil, in their like distresses, made their general complaints by often letters and messengers to the west Churches, standing more entire and void of that heresy and persecution.

Finally, we are forced to publish these things so particularly and diligently to defend the doings of the said holy confessors and their fellows in faith, against the manifold slanders and calumniations of certain heretics or politiques [= unprincipled, pragmatic politicians], unjustly charging them with treason and other great trespasses against the commonwealth...

We first affirm that the very front of title of the libel [*The execution of Justice in England for maintenance of public and Christian peace, against certain stirrers of sedition, and adherents to the traitors and enemies of the realm, without any persecution of them for questions of religion*], importing that no Catholics at all, or none of them whom they have executed, were persecuted for their religion, is a very notorious untruth and contradictory to the libeller's own words in his discourse... Secondly we say and shall clearly convince, that contrary to the pursuit of the same libel, a number have been also tormented, arraigned, condemned and executed, for mere matter of religion, and upon the transgression of new statutes only, without any relation to the old treasons, so made and set down by Parliament in Edward [III]'s time: by which they untruly avouch all our brethren were convicted. And herein to deal particularly and plainly, we allege the worthy priest and bachelor of divinity Master Cuthbert Mayne, who suffered a glorious martyrdom at Launceston in the province of Cornwall, for that the cause or cover only was an *Agnus Dei* and a printed copy of that Bull now expired which denounced to the Christian world the last Jubilee, were found about him. [He] was condemned not by any old laws (as is deceitfully pretended to abuse the simple of their own nation and strangers that know not our lamentable condition) but by a late statute enacted the 13 year of the Queen's reign, which maketh it high treason to bring from Rome any beads, sacred pictures. *Agnus Dei*-s, Bulls or (as express words of the said statute are), any writing or instrument written or printed containing anything, matter or cause whatsoever... [*many more cases offered*]

In times of heretical regiment, where politiques have all the government, though religion be sometimes pretended as a thing whereof they make their advantage forth affairs especially intended, yet indeed the first and principal care is of their temporal state, and consequently of the princes and their own wellbeing in this life. The lot whereof they often prefer with Esau, before the well of the world to come, the blessing of Jacob or the kingdom of Christ, which is his reign and regiment spiritual in the Church, the house of his glory and our salvation in earth. Contrariwise in Christian Catholic commonwealths the chief respect is and ever was (as it ought to be) of the honour of God, the good of holy Church, the salvation of souls of their people; and so to pass through these secular things as eternal joys be not lost and put in hazard.

In which difference of things you shall easily perceive that in the days of disorder and error the faults done against the prince, or so said to be done, are far more odious and punishable than whatsoever is directly done against God, against the commonwealth, than against the church; against the body than against the soul; more ado about Caesar's tribute than about God's due—as in the time and regiment of Jeroboam, when all the care was how to manage matters so that the kingdom of Israel might be severed from Judah, and so established in itself that no spiritual worship in Jerusalem might reduce the divided tribes to their former state again; and all things tending to that reunion were grievously punished, but matters of faith and religion wholly condemned...

Finding no errors, heresies or false opinions concerning God and his worship worthy to condemn us of, and being ashamed of their statutes of new treasons (as it seemeth); they have found out a new fault, and a term for the same... which they call traitorous assertions, treasonable and malicious opinions against the Queen as in a former like pamphlet, evil affection or evil disposition towards her Majesty, which is now the only and proper point they pursue against us both in judgement and writing... And for the better trial thereof, they propose unto all men whom they list make away or otherwise indanger, certain demands which in effect are these that ensue:

1. Whether the Bull of Pius V against the Queen's Majesty be a lawful sentence and ought to be obeyed by the subjects of England?

2. Whether the Queen's Majesty be a lawful Queen and ought to be obeyed by the subjects of England, notwithstanding the Bull of Pius V or any other Bull or sentence that the Pope hath pronounced or may pronounce against her Majesty?

3. Whether the Pope have or had power to authorize her subjects to rebel or take arms against her or to invade her dominions; and whether such subjects so doing, do lawfully therein?

4. Whether the Pope have power to discharge any of her Majesty's subjects of any Christian prince from their allegiance...?

Wherein if you say nothing or refuse to answer somewhat in contempt or derogation of the See Apostolic; then are you indeed no good subject but a traitor; whereby let all the princes and people Christian bear witness of our miseries and unjust afflictions who are enforced to suffer death for our only cogitations and inward opinions, unduly sought out by force and fear and yet not condemned by any Christian school in the world, nor uttered by us except upon forcing interrogatories, we having committed nothing by word or deed against our prince or laws, but doing all acts of honour and homage unto her and suffering meekly what punishment soever she would lay upon us for our religion. For so most parts of all sorts of Catholics have done both in England and Ireland for this twenty five years space, only a very few nobles of both countries taking arms for their defence in all this long time of intolerable affliction... neither took up arms upon the Bull of Pius V, nor any time since the publication thereof...

By all which we may see the notable discreet and sincere dealing of Catholics all this while about fifteen years that this sentence hath been extant and published... never writing of the matter, nor dealing in it, but to the end of pacification, public rest and security of the state, brought into brindle [= uncertainty, unsteadiness] and doubt by this unhappy alteration of religion... And this was the Catholics' honest desire and behaviour touching the excommunication ever since the publishing thereof until now of late when by their interrogatories and new order of most bloody, unlawful and unwise search of men's consciences; not deeds, words or writings but very inward opinion, thoughts and cogitations of heart, are wrung out of men by the questions before rehearsed...

Princes being not subject to superiors temporal, nor patient of correction or controlment by their inferiors, may easily fall to grievous disorders which must tend to the danger and ruin of whole countries. In respect whereof, great spirit, power, courage and freedom of speech have been from the beginning granted by God, as well ordinary to priests as extraordinary to some prophets and religious persons, in all ages and times, both of the New and Old testaments. [*This is the first of several examples*] Saul, the first temporal king that ever the Jews (being God's peculiar) had, though chosen and inspired by God, was for all that led and directed by Samuel for so long as he was in order. But afterwards for aspiring to spiritual function and other disobedience, was by God's appointment and sentence, pronounced by the said Samuel, deposed of his kingdom, and another named David anointed by him. Which Saul now after his deprivation or after, as it were, his excommunication by Samuel, was invaded by an evil spirit who provoked him to kill not only David that was now made the rightful owner of the Crown, but also to seek Samuel's death—yea and to command all the holy priests of Nob (four score and five in number, as the holy Scripture counteth) to be slain and murdered in a most pitiful wise, as traitors to him, and favourers of David the competitor of his kingdom. And so it was at last; though at the beginning his guard refused to execute so vile and horrible an act, and in this sort he remained enemy many years against God and Samuel, and kept the kingdom by tyrannical force notwithstanding his deposition.

David nonetheless in whom was the right of the crown, was lawfully up in arms, with one of the principal priests whose name was Abiathar that escaped the foresaid murder, not of such power as the pretended king; until at length the usurper (whom as St Augustine deduceth, he might lawfully have killed but would not) being slain in battle, David obtained his right, first of a part of the kingdom, and afterward of all the rest, which Isobeth did for two years by the pretended right of Saul his father usurp.

By which it is plain that the priests and prophets of God, being the executors of his sentences, and rule of the people in such doubtful and partial times of variety for claim and competency, are most subject to the hatred of usurpers, as also to death and danger for the same...

By which [several] examples of holy Scripture, we see: first that anointed and lawfully created kings may be deposed; secondly, for what causes they were deprived; thirdly, that as in the creation and consecration of kings, so also in their deprivation, God used the ministry of priests and prophets, as either ordinary or extraordinary judges or executors of his will towards them...

And finally, upon all the proofs, reasons and authorities that have gone before, we avouch, that besides God Almighty, every temporal prince christened hath his pastor also, and specially the general governor of the whole church, for his superior in earth in all causes of soul and conscience; to whose orders in matters of religion he is bound to obey under pain of damnation; and that God's just judgements are near the princes and countries whatsoever that will not obey him, but violently resist his ordinance, and by Antichristian pride do challenge power not lawful to be yielded unto them. (1)

NOTES AND SOURCES

1. William Allen, *A True, Sincere and Modest Defence of English Catholics that Suffer for their Faith* (1584), pp. preface [unpag.], 1–2, 59–63, 87–94, 208.

# William Cardinal Allen                                    1532–1594

William Allen was born the younger son of a minor Lancashire gentleman. He went up to Oriel College Oxford in 1547 and, although young, played a major part in the Marian restoration in that University. At Elizabeth's succecssion, he withdrew to the Continent for a while, but returned to his family home to recuperate from a serious illness. He was appalled by the willingness of so many contemporaries to attend Protestant services, even communion services, and he made his way back to the continent and hence to Rome where he sought Holy Orders. He was the founder of the English College at Douai, both as a house of studies of Catholic exiles and as a seminary for the new generation of priests who would lead the mission to England. More than a third of the men trained at Douai while Allen was there were to die the death of martyrs. Allen prepared them for this and for a pastoral ministry that preached rigid separation for all Catholics from Protestant practice, but which recognized (in the confessional) the limits of the possible. He himself was deeply implicated in a long series of plots to overthrow Elizabeth by armed force or assassination, but the priests sent on the mission were to be innocent of his plans. *They* were to prepare the ground for the Catholic confessional state that would follow the overthrow of her regime. His polemical writing oscillated between unambiguous support for treason by English Catholics (as in his *Admonition to the Nobility of England* in preparation for the Armada) and attempts to claim that the purposes of the mission he led were purely spiritual (e.g. *A True, Sincere and Modest Defence of English Catholics that Suffer for their Faith*). The deaths of 'his men' starting with Campion produced in him a strange mixture of rage and exaltation—he called Elizabeth 'our Herodias' who had bathed in the 'brightest and best blood' of English Catholics. He was the only Englishman made a Cardinal between Reginald Pole and Thomas Howard a hundred years later. We have already printed his defence of the papal deposing power. Here he is, more pastorally, distinguishing the grace of Baptism from the grace of penance and preparing the way for his account of Purgatory.

## Baptismal and Penitential Grace

As it is most true and the very ground of all Christian comfort, that Christ's death hath paid duly and sufficiently for the sins of all the world, by that abundant price of redemption paid upon the Cross, so it is of like credit to all faithful that no man was ever partaker of this singular benefit but in the knot and unity of his body mystical which is the Church. To the members whereof, the streams of his holy blood and beams of his grace for the remission of sin and sanctification be orderly, through the blessed Sacraments as conduits of God's mercy, though they be instituted and used as means to derive Christ's benefits and bestow his grace of redemption upon the worthy receivers. Yet like effect or force is not by the meaning of their first author and institutor, employed upon all receivers, nor given to all Sacraments. That may well appear if we mark the exceeding abundant mercy that is poured upon all men at their first incorporation and entrance into the household of the faithful, by Baptism. In which Sacrament, the merits of our master's death be so fully and largely carried down for the remission of sin, that were the life before never so laden with most horrible offences, that in his misery man may commit, yet the offender is not only pardoned of the same, but also perfectly acquired for ever of all pain or punishment (other than the common miseries of mankind) which his proper offences before committed by any means might deserve, and no less free now than the child after Baptism, which only original sin brought thither. So saith St Ambrose by these words... 'the grace of God in Baptism requireth neither of sorrow nor mourning, nor any other work, but only an hearty profession of thy faith.' Whereby he meaneth that after our sins be once thus freely wiped away in our first regeneration, there is no charge of punishment or penance for further release of the same.

But now a man that is so freely discharged of all evil and sin committed before he came into the family, if he fall into relapse, and defile the temple of God, then (as God's mercy always passeth man's malice) even in this case also he hath ordained means to repair man's fall again. That is by the Sacrament of penance which therefore St Jerome terms the second table, or refuge after shipwreck as a means that may bring man to the port of salvation, though lightly not without present damage and danger. In which blessed Sacrament though God's grace have mighty force for man's recovery and worketh abundantly both the remission of sins and the discharge of eternal punishment to the offender, yet Christ himself (the author of this Sacrament as of the rest) meant not to communicate such efficacy or force to this, as to Baptism, for the utter acquitting of all pain for sinful life deserved. For as in Baptism where man is perfectly renewed, it was seemly to set the offender at his first entrance on clear ground and make him free of all things done abroad, so it exceedingly setteth forth God's justice and nothing impaireth his mercy, to use (as in commonwealths by nature and God's prescription is practiced) with grace discipline, with justice clemency, with favour correction, and with love due chastisement of such sins as have by the household children been committed.

Now, therefore, if after thy free admission to this family of Christ, though do grievously offend, remission may then be had again but not commonly with sharp discipline seeing the father of this our holy household punisheth where he loveth, and chastiseth every child whome he receiveth, whose justice is punishment of sin, not only the wicked but also the good must much fear. Whereof St Augustine warneth us thus... 'God spareth neither the just not unjust, chastising the one as his child, punishing the other as a wicked person.' A child then of this household continuing in favour though he cannot everlastingly perish with the impenitent sinners, yet he must (being not by some special prerogative pardoned) bear the rod of his father's discipline and gladly say with the prophet... I am ready for the rods (Ps. 37). And whatsoever these wantons that are run out of this house for their own ease or other men's flattery shall forge, let us continue in perpetual cogitation of our sins forgiven and all means possible recompense our negligencies past. Let us not think but God hath somewhat to say to us even for our offences pardoned, being thus warned from his own mouth... 'But somewhat I have against thee, because thou are fallen from the first love. Remember therefore from when thou fell, do penance and begin thy former good works again.' And the consideration of this diversity betwixt remission had by Baptism and relapse by the Sacrament of penance moved [St John] Damascene to call this second remedy . . . 'a kind of Baptism full of travail, by penance and tears to be wrought.' [Apoc. 2: 4] In which God so pardoneth sins that both the sin itself and the everlasting pain due for the same being wholly by Christ's death and merits wiped away, there may yet remain the debt of temporal punishment on our part to be discharged as well for some satisfaction of God's justice against the eternal order whereof we unworthily offended as for to answer the Church of her right (as St Augustine saith) in which only all sins be forgiven. (1)

NOTES AND SOURCES

1. William Allen, *A Defense and Declaration of the Catholike Churchies Doctrine Touching Purgatory, and Prayers for the Souls Departed* (1565), fos. 21$^v$–24$^v$.

## St Edmund Campion SJ                1540–1581

Campion's career and martyrdom were to prove a turning point in the experience of English Catholics. His sufferings and death were a cause célèbre throughout Europe, with both the Protestant establishment in England and the Catholic apologists in Rome and the Low Countries appropriating it for their own purposes. In the wake of the Papal Bull of 1570 and subsequent (Catholic) plots against Elizabeth's life and title, the Protestant government became convinced that the seminary priests being sent on the English mission, and especially those who were members of the Society of Jesus, were committed to political revolution and the overthrow of Protestant monarchy. Legislation was passed in 1581 which made it treason to reconcile any subject of the Queen (and treason for any subject so reconciled) to the Catholic faith. Hitherto, priests had been hunted down and imprisoned, but there had been no great wave of executions, although one priest had been executed in 1573, another in 1577 and a third in 1578 (see below, pp. 175–7). This was to change with the trial of Campion and his colleagues. Campion, a Fellow of the newly founded St John's College from 1561 to 1570, had been one of most brilliant Oxford dons of his generation. He was chosen, on behalf of the University, to make the formal speech of welcome to Elizabeth when she visited in 1566. He was ordained as a deacon of the Church of England in 1569. But he had long been troubled about his ecclesial allegiance, and ordination intensified his doubts. He resigned his Fellowship, and moved to Dublin to work out where truth lay. By 1571 he was resolved to enter into full communion with the Catholic Church, and he made his way via London to Douai, and he was quickly appointed a professor of rhetoric at the fledgling College there. But his conscience would not be stilled, and he walked, as a penance, from Douai to Rome, and there offered himself to the Society of Jesus. They sent him to Brno and Prague for formation in Jesuit houses of study, and he was ordained priest by the Archbishop of Prague in 1578. On 19 December 1579 he was recalled by Cardinal Allen to Rome and ordered (with Robert Parsons) to head up a Catholic mission to England. Despite his own misgivings (and those of Mercurian, General of the Society) that this would be seen as political provocation by the English government, and would unleash persecution on all Catholics, Campion accepted the mission. Before departing he had a personal interview with the Pope and was granted authority to release English Catholics from the obligation of implementing the Bull of 1570. Campion's ministry in England was to last from 24 June 1580 to his arrest on 17 July 1581 and his execution on 1 December 1581. For most of that time, he knew that the government had announced its intention to 'make some example of Jesuits by punishment to the terror of others', but he calmly moved round the country, preaching and administering the Sacraments. He also issued, in Latin, ten challenges to the learned men of the Church of England, inviting them to a disputation on matters of faith and authority in the Church. There was an immediate response from one of the rising stars of the Anglican establishment, Meredith Hanmer. In July 1581 Campion was betrayed as he ministered in Berkshire, and was taken to the Tower. He was repeatedly and severely tortured over the next three months, and forced to reveal the places where he had stayed. In between the bouts of torture, he was granted his wish to hold formal disputations with teams of senior academics from the universities. They chose the topics and had days to prepare; he was denied access to his books (though in any case the tortures would have rendered him incapable of turning the pages) and given notice of the topics only on each of the days of the disputations (31 August and 18, 23, 27 September). The government then published their accounts of the proceedings, and even on that basis it is clear that the plans for further exchanges were cancelled by the government because he was doing so well. The original intention had been to bring him and six other Jesuits to trial based on the recent law making it treason to reconcile Protestants; but it was then decided to use the old 1351 statute, and to allege that he and thirteen other priests were engaged in a treasonable conspiracy to raise rebellion to overthrow the Queen and alter the government and religion. After a show trial in Westminster Hall, seven priests and a laymen were sentenced to death. As the sentence was read, Campion sang the *Te Deum*. He was executed, the sentence of hanging, drawing, and quartering vindictively extended, on 1 December 1581. With thirty-nine other martyrs of England and Wales, he was canonized by Pope Paul VI in 1970. We will follow his witness and martyrdom through a series of documents: his challenges to the Anglican establishment; his disputations in the Tower with leading Protestants; an account of his execution; a government document that shows the acute difficulty he and his fellow Catholics were in with respect to the legitimacy of Elizabeth's government, and finally some commemorative poetry. We begin with an extract from Campion's *Rationes decem quibus fretus certamen aduersariis obtulit in causa fidei* (1581). We will use not the unreliable translation prepared by Meredith Hanmer for use in his refutation *The Great Bragge and Challenge of M. Champion a Jesuit* (1581), but one made by a fellow Jesuit a generation later for distribution in England. It was entitled *Campian Englished. Or A translation of the Ten reasons in which Edmund Campian (of the Societie of Iesus) priest, insisted in his challenge, to the Uniuersities of Oxford and Cambridge Made by a priest of the Catholike and Roman Church* (1635). The ten challenges relate to sacred Scripture, the nature of the Church, the authority of General Councils, the Fathers, the lessons of history, a series of 'paradoxes and sophisms', and finally 'all kinds of witness'. Our first extract comes from this final 'challenge'. In due course, Elizabeth's advisers saw propaganda value in conceding Campion's request for a series of disputations on his challenges. And so he was brought fresh from the rack, with his finger tails torn out, to face the luminaries of the Anglican academic establishment.They chose as their topics the place of the epistle of James in the canon of Scripture, and scriptural authority more generally; the relationship of faith and works in the economy of salvation; the relationship between the Church Visible and the Church Invisible; the capacity of the visible Church to err; whether the institution narratives in the first three Gospels and St Paul's First Epistle to the Corinthians can be used to demonstrate that 'after the words of Consecration, the bread and wine are transubstantiated into the Body and Blood of Christ'; whether the Scriptures contain sufficient doctrine for our salvation; and whether faith alone justifies us with God. The Protestant champions were chosen by Bishop Aylmer of London, and the Dean of St Paul's Alexander Nowell supervised the publication of a Protestant report of the exchanges, while Christopher Barker, 'printer to the Queen's Majesty' and official printer of the English Bible, was put in charge of the print-run. We include two extracts which between them give a sense of the exchanges. In the first the protagonists are William Fulke (1538–1610), Master of Pembroke and Vice-Chancellor of Cambridge, and Roger Goad (1536/7–1589), Provost of King's College, Cambridge, two near contemporaries of Campion, and both veteran controversialists.

## Campion's Tenth Challenge

*This shall be unto you a direct way, so that fools shall not err by it,* saith the Prophet [Isa. 35], speaking of the Church. Now what man, though among the vulgar sort, is so obtuse and dull, if he bear but an eye fixed upon his salvation, who may not easily discern, and withal impath himself in the beaten way of the Church; it being so notoriously made plain, even, and tracked; he by this means declining in his gate all unhaunted footways, or craggy steps and deviations?

These points shall be made, explored and evident even to the ignorant and illiterate; as Isaiah hath prophesied; to yourselves then (if so you be constant to your own good) most explorate, and most evident.

Let us present to the eyes of our imagination, the theatre or stage of this universal all; and let our thoughts lance forth into the main ocean of everything created. All things dispute in our behalf; all things even swear the truth of our religion. Let us ascend to Heaven: there we may contemplate roses and lilies, blessed martyrs, I mean, who by shedding their blood became red, by their innocency white and candid. Such were the thirty-three Popes successively slaughtered by the heathen enemy. Such were the pastors and doctors in all countries, who in that rugged and tempestuous state of the Church, engaged their blood for the name of Christ. Such were the faithful sheep, who (in the purity of a good conscience) insisted in the steps of their shepherds. Such were all the saints now in Heaven, who through sanctimony and purity (like stars of the greatest magnitude) gloriously shined in the eyes of the multitude. Certain it is, that all these were ours when they here conversed on earth; that all these continued ours, even to their last gasp and dissolution. And but to retail some particulars out of divers hundreds, since I will not be lavish of time: On our side and party stood blessed Ignatius (whose thirst only martyrdom could quench) who did not parallel any man (no, not the King) with a bishop in matters of the Church, and who with his own pen (least otherwise they might perish) did record certain apostolical traditions, of which himself was eye-witness. On our side stood Telesphorus who commanded, that the fast of lent (first instituted by the apostles) should be kept with a more rigorous care and observation. On our side was Iranaeus who preached and confirmed the apostolical faith, even from the succession of the supreme Bishops, and the see of Rome. On our side Victor (the Pope) who by his edict or bull reduced all Asia unto obedience: which act though by many and particularly by the former Irenaeus (though otherwise a most blessed man) was censured over rigid and severe; yet not one ever questioned his authority, or traduced him, as assuming in that business any exotical or foreign Sovereignty. On our side was Polycarp, who for the deciding the question of keeping Easter-day, made a peculiar journey to Rome; whose relics being burned, the Christians of Smyrna gathered together, celebrating the memory of their Bishop with an anniversary day and most solemn feast. On our side were

Cornelius and Cyprian (that golden pair of martyrs) both great prelates, but greater the first, who sterning [= guiding, piloting] the Church of Rome, extinguished the African errors; and this other much ennobled himself through the great observancy, he bore to his most dear and friendly Superior. On our side was Sixtus upon whom, celebrating at the Altar the most dreadful Sacrifice of the Mass, seven clergymen did reverently attend. On our side St Laurence (archdeacon to the said Sixtus) who did even importune martyrdom, and whom the adversaries (for their grace is to disgrace the good) have scourged out of their Calendar, our martyrology; and yet to him above twelve hundred years since, Prudentius (once Consul of Rome) in this manner directed his prayers: in English thus:

> Servant of Christ, what power is given to thee
> The Roman joys at large do testify,
> By these great favours which thou doest afford
> To them who sue to thee in sweet accord
> Among which troop, a rustic Poet, to hear,
> His faults confessing with a trembling feare:
> O hear benignly poor Prudentius,
> Guilty of Christ's blood through sins most impious.

On our side stand those most Blessed Virgins Cecilia, Agatha, Barbara, Agnes, Lucia, Dorothea, Catherina, who (enjoying an inward calm of their passions) defended their vowed chastity, as most incontaminate and intemerate [= inviolate, undefiled, unblemished], against all assaults and tyranny of men and devils. On our side was Helena, to whom the finding of the Cross (upon which our Lord suffered) hath given so great celebrity and honour; Monica who (languishing and fainting away in devotion) in the agony of her last sickness, most religiously and earnestly implored, that prayers and sacrifice might be offered up for her at the Altar, after her death and departure; Paula, who even drunk with fervour and devotion, (a wine, which the luke-warm Christian never tasteth) did abandon her palace and fruitful demesnes, and being a stranger, posted (with a most wearisome pilgrimage) to the cave of Bethlehem, that so she might spend the remnant of her life (the poor weak blast of breath) in spiritual retires of the soul, and in bewailing her sins even in that place, where Christ in his infancy lay crying in his cradle, and swaddling clothes. On our side are Paulus, Hilarion, Antonius, those good old solitary and religious hermits; whose even speaking silence in their daily and nightly meditations, pierced the ears of God. On our side was Satyrus, a brother-german to Ambrose, who (bearing about him the most dreadful Host) suffered shipwreck; and through the strength of his faith in that most holy sacrament, escaped the danger of the sea. On our side Nicolas and Martinus, both reverend bishops, being men much exercised in watching, clothed with haircloth, and even fed with extraordinary and unpractised fasting. On our side was Benedict that Father of so many monks. Ten years space is too short a time to call to mind so many thousands, as have professed our Catholic religion: And here I forbear to repeat the names of those, whom above I have marshalled among the troops of the doctors of the Church, since I am mindful (as I may term it) of my slow speediness. He that more largely will enrich and furnish himself with the knowledge thereof, let him evolve not only the histories of ancient writers, but chiefly such grave authors, of which number almost every particular author did pick out a particular saint, that so by their pens, they might record their glorious memories. Which labour after this man hath performed, then let him in the secret and inward reflex of his soul sincerely relate to me, whether he be persuaded, that those most ancient and blessed Christians (whose sanctity the very walls and streets did in those times echo forth) were, in religion, Roman Catholics, or Lutherans. I here call to witness the throne of God, and that tribunal of justice, before which I shalbe convented to give a reason of these my reasons, and an account of this my attempted challenge, that either there is no Heaven, or that Heaven is only ours; the first we wholly execrate; upon this other then we cast our anchor.

But now on the contrary side, if it please, let us peep and look down into Hell. There lie broiling in a sempiternal conflagration and flames of fire: *Who?* ... (1)

## Debating the Real Presence

GOAD: I will proceed to the next place. You doubted also, whether it were to be found in Saint Augustine, that there is no miracle in the Sacrament. Now you may hear his own words [in] *De Trinitate bk* 3, ch. 10. As the bread ordained for this purpose, is consumed in receiving the Sacrament.[19] But because these things are known unto men, and are done by men, they may have honour or reverence as holy things, but they cannot be wondered at as things strange and miraculous. Here you have Augustine's words against miracle in the Sacrament.

CAMPION: Indeed there is no such evident miracle visibly appearing, as when Christ cured the lame, the blind, etc, but yet there is a great miracle which our faith doth acknowledge.

GOAD: Augustine speaketh simply against miracle: so that whether it be visible or invisible, both is excluded. Beside, it is perpetual in all miracles, that there must be some outward sensible sign. Further, you doubted of righteousness inherent in ourselves, which I avouched to be erroneous doctrine set forth in the late Council of Trent. The words are these, Council of Trent chap. 7. We are called and indeed are truly righteous, receiving in ourselves every man his own righteousness, according to the measure which the Holy Ghost doth divide to every one even as he will, according to every man's own proper disposition and cooperation. For that righteousness which is called ours, because we are justified by it inherent in ourselves, the self-same is the righteousness of God, because it is poured into us from God by the merit of Christ.

CAMPION: I did not doubt of inherent righteousness in ourselves, whether it were in the Council of Trent, for I defend and maintain it as the Council teacheth it: you say it is by imputation of Christ's righteousness being without us, whereby we are justified: and I say, we are justified by that righteousness which is within us, though it be not of us.

GOAD: The place which I urged against you the other day, beside many other in the Scripture, is directly against this doctrine. 2 Cor 5: 21. He hath made him to be sin for us which knew no sin, that we should be made the righteousness of God in him.

FULKE: Well, now we are to come to the question. You hold that the natural Body and Blood of Christ is contained in the Sacrament of the Lord's Supper. Your words are, Christ is present in the Sacrament substantially, very God and man in his natural body.

CAMPION: I say there is really present in the Sacrament the natural Body and Blood of Christ under that bread and cup.

---

[19]   This ungrammatical formation follows from the Latin given and then translated here: '*sicut panis ad hoc factus in accipiendo sacramento consumitur. Sed quia*...' (etc.).

*FULKE*: What mean you by these words under the bread and cup, that we may agree of terms?

*CAMPION*: You know in the bread is whiteness etc that is not in his body: make your argument.

*FULKE*: So I will. The cup is not the natural blood of Christ: *Ergo* the other part is not his natural body.

*CAMPION*: There is present in the cup, the natural blood of Christ. Go to my words.

*FULKE*: Well. The natural blood of Christ is not present in the cup: *Ergo* the natural body is not present in the other part.

*CAMPION*: The natural blood of Christ is present in the cup.

*FULKE*: Thus I disprove it.The words of Christ's institution be these: This cup is the New Testament in my Blood: but the natural blood of Christ is not the new testament in his blood: *Ergo* the natural blood of Christ is not in the cup.

*CAMPION*: The word, *Is*, is neither in the Hebrew, nor in the Greek. (2)

NOTES AND SOURCES

1. *Campian Englished. Or A translation of the Ten reasons in which Edmund Campian (of the Societie of Iesus) priest, insisted in his challenge, to the Uniuersities of Oxford and Cambridge Made by a priest of the Catholike and Roman Church* (1635), 155–66.
2. Alexander Nowell, *A true report of the disputation or rather priuate conference had in the Tower of London, with Ed. Campion Iesuite, the last of August. 1581. Set downe by the reuerend learned men them selues that dealt therein. VVhereunto is ioyned also a true report of the other three dayes conferences had there with the same Iesuite. Which nowe are thought meete to be published in print by authoritie* (1583), 54–5.

# Blessed Thomas Alfield          1552–1585

We now move forward to the day of execution, 1 December 1581. Campion was executed with two other priests, St Ralph Sherwin and St Alexander Bryan (or Brian or Briant). The following account comes from the hand of another priest, Thomas Alfield, himself martyred in 1585, who had mingled with the large crowd to witness the events of that day. He was the son of a Provost of Eton, and was himself Fellow of King's College Cambridge from 1571 to 1575. He was reconciled to the Catholic Church at Douai in September 1576, and began his priestly formation immediately. He was ordained in March 1581, and sent on the mission to England. He published what he called 'A True Report of the Death and Martyrdom of M. Campion Jesuit' in 1582 as a response to a Protestant account of Campion's death (*An advertisement and defence for truth against backbiters and especially against the whispering favorers and colorers of Campions*). Alfield was shortly afterwards arrested in London, tortured but then released after agreeing to conform to the Church of England. This he intermittently did, while helping to smuggle in and disseminate the works of Catholic leaders abroad. It was for helping to disseminate Cardinal Allen's *Modest Defence of the English Catholics* that he was once more arrested, and having refused on this occasion to conform to the Protestant Church he was hanged (but not quartered) on 6 July 1585. He was beatified in 1929. With his 'true report' of Campion's death, Alfield included four poems 'by sundry persons'. The authors are not known. We include the first and the fourth. The opening of the first is clumsy, but then it builds impressively and movingly, while reinforcing the message of Campion's loyalty to established political authority in temporal matters: 'my sovereign liege behold your subject's end, your secret foes do misinform your grace'. The fourth is the shortest of the poems published by Alfield. It brings out the attempts of the regime to turn the martyrs into political activists, and of Catholic defenders of the martyrs to make crucial (but difficult) distinctions about faith and political action. Once again, his (and the Catholic community's) loyalty to Elizabeth is emphasized in defiance of *Regnans in excelsis*).

## Campion's Death

But to my purpose, which is to intimate and publish the behaviour, speeches, and protestation of these so learned and rare men. It is not unknown that Master Edmund Campion Jesuit and Priest, a man reputed and taken, and by divers his co-equals plainly confessed, the flower of Oxford for that time he studied there, and since abroad in foreign countries one in whom our country hath had great honour, the fruit of his learning, virtue, and rare gifts, which as they were in his childhood here among us wonderful, so they were abroad, as in Italy, Germany, and Bohemia an honour to our country, a glass and mirror, a light and lantern, a pattern and example to youth, to age, to learned, to unlearned, to religious, and to the laity of all sort, state, and condition, of modesty, gravity, eloquence, knowledge, virtue, and piety, of which just and due commendation, some of our adversaries can give true and certain testimony, who after diligent sifting and enquiring of his life, manners, and demeanour, found nothing faulty, nothing worthy of blame. This man (Master Campion I say) first meekly yielded himself and his carcass to this butchery, with such humility and courage, as moved most beholders to compassion and pity. Those speeches he used in the way to divers calling and crying unto him, I leave (myself not able to make relation thereof) to common report, or to that man's testimony, who either for pity or affection wiped his face defiled with dirt, as he was drawn[20] most miserably through thick and thin, as the saying is, to the place of execution: for which charity, and happily some sudden moved affection, God reward him, and bless him. What he spake openly, that my meaning is to set down truly, myself being present and very near, as hard by Sir Francis Knowles, the Lord Howard, Sir Henry Lee and other Gentlemen then gathered there to see and hear him. And here I will omit, although it be very much material, his usage in time of imprisonment, his constant patience in his rackings, and after his condemnation by report of some very near to him, his five days fast from temporal and bodily sustenance, his abstinence from sleep and ordinary rest, which was before his death by credible report of some, continued two nights, bestowed in meditation and prayer. Who, after many conflicts and agonies, joyfully coming to receive his reward and crown, the Kingdom of Heaven, an inheritance certain to such, who in this life refuse the world, things worldly, and themselves for Christ's sake, after some small pass in the cart, with grave countenance and sweet voice stoutly spake as followeth.

*Spectaculum facti sumus deo, angeli, and hominibus* saying, these are the words of St Paul, Englished thus: 'we are made a spectacle, or a sight unto God, unto his

---

[20] One of the (painful) humiliations for those to be executed for treason was to be tied hand and foot to a wooden hurdle (without wheels) attached to the back of a horse and dragged along the cobbled streets from prison to the place of execution.

Angels, and unto men: verified this day in me, who am here a spectacle unto my Lord God, a spectacle unto his angels, and unto you men.' And here going forward in this text, was interrupted and cut off by Sir Francis Knowles and the sheriffs, earnestly urging him to confess his treason against her majesty, and to acknowledge himself guilty. To whom he answered, saying: 'you have now what you do desire, I beseech you to have patience and suffer me to speak a word or two for discharge of my conscience.' But being not suffered to go forward, gave answer to that point they always urged, that he was guiltless and innocent of all treason and conspiracy, craving credit to be given to this answer, as to his last answer made upon his death and soul; adding that touching this point both the jury might be deceived, and more also put in the evidence than was true. Notwithstanding, he forgave as he would be forgiven, desiring all them to forgive him whom he had confessed upon the rack. Further he declared the meaning of a letter sent by himself in time of his imprisonment out of the Tower, in which he wrote he would not disclose the secrets of some houses where he had been entertained, affirming on his soul, that the secrets he meant in that letter were not, as some misconstrued them, treason, or conspiracy, or any matter else any way intended against her Majesty or the state, but saying of Mass, hearing of confession, preaching, and such like duties and functions of Priests: this he protested to be true, as he would answer before God. Then he desired Sir Francis Knowles, and some other of nobility, to hear him touching one Richardson condemned about a book of his, and earnestly besought them to have consideration of that man, saying, he was not that Richardson which brought his book, and this he affirmed with vehement protestation upon his death. Then one Hearne a schoolmaster, as I learned after, read the new advertisement openly with loud voice unto the people, published only to colour so manifest and express injury. Master Campion all the time of his reading devoutly praying notwithstanding which advertisement or defence of theirs, as well because they discovered their own policy in publication thereof, as that they did also desire some better colour or faster vizard for their proceedings, pressed him to declare his opinion of Pius V's Bull concerning the excommunication of our sovereign and Queen. To which demand he gave no answer. But being asked whether he renounced the Pope, said he was a Catholic. Whereupon one inferred, saying: 'in your Catholicism (I noted the word) all treason is contained.' In fine, preparing himself to drink his last draught of Christ's cup was interrupted in his prayer by a minister, willing him to say, 'Christ have mercy upon me', or such-like prayer with him. Unto whom he looking back with mild countenance, humbly said: 'you and I are not one in religion, wherefore I pray you content yourself, I bar none of prayer, only I desire them of the household of faith to pray with me and in mine agony to say one creed.' Some also called upon him to pray in English, to whom he answered that he would pray in a language that he well understood. At the upshot of this conflict he was willed to ask the queen forgiveness, and to pray for her. He meekly answered: 'wherein have I offended her? In this I am innocent, this is my last speech, in this give me credit, I have and do pray for her.' Then did the Lord Charles Howard ask of him: for which queen he prayed, whether for Elizabeth queen. To whom he answered, 'yea for Elizabeth your queen, and my queen, unto whom I wish a long quiet reign, with all prosperity.' And so he meekly and sweetly yielded his soul unto his Saviour, protesting that he died a perfect Catholic ... (1)

## Upon the Death of M. Edmund Campion, one
## of the Society of the Holy Name of Jesus

Why do I use my paper, ink, and pen,
and call my wits to counsel what to say,
such memories were made for mortal men,
I speak of saints whose names cannot decay:
an angel's trump were fitter for to sound
their glorious death, if such on earth were found.

Pardon my want, I offer naught but will,
their register remaineth safe above,
Campion exceeds the compass of my skill,
yet let me use the measure of my love,
and give me leave in low and homely verse,
his high attempts in England to rehearse.

He came by vow, the cause to conquer sin,
his armour prayer, the word his <u>targe</u> and shield, [= buckler or light shield]
his comfort Heaven, his spoil our souls to win,
the devil his foe, the wicked world the field,
his triumph joy, his wage eternal bliss,
his captain Christ, which ever blessed is.

From ease to pain, from honour to disgrace,
from love to hate, to danger being well,
from safe abode to fears in every place,
contemning death to save our souls from Hell,
our new apostle coming to restore
the faith which <u>Austin</u> planted here before. [= St Augustine of Canterbury]

His nature's flowers were mixt with herbs of grace,
his mild behaviour tempered well with skill,
a lowly mind possessed a learned place,
a sugared speech a rare and virtuous will,
a saint-like man was set on earth below,
the seed of truth in erring hearts to sow.

With tongue and pen the truth he taught and wrote,
by force whereof they came to Christ apace,
but when it pleased God, it was his lot
he should be <u>thralled</u>, he lent him so much grace, [= brought into bondage]
his patience then did work as much or more,
as had his heavenly speeches done before.

His fare was hard, yet mild and sweet his cheer,
his prison close, yet free and loose his mind,

his torture great, yet small or none his fear,
his offers large, but nothing could him blind.
O constant man, O mind, O virtue strange,
whom want, not woe, nor fear, nor hope could change.

From rack in Tower they brought him to dispute,
bookless, alone, to answer all that came,
yet Christ gave grace, he did them all confute
so sweetly there in glory of his name,
that even the adverse part are forced to say,
that Campion's cause did bear the bell away.

This foil enraged the minds of some so far,
they thought it best to take his life away,
because they saw he would their matter mar,
and leave them shortly naught at all to say:
traitor he was with many a <u>seely slight</u>,    [= feeble] [= show of contempt]
yet packed a jury that cried guilty straight.

Religion there was treason to the queen,
preaching of penance were against the land,
priests were such dangerous men as have not been
prayers and beads were fight and force of hand,
cases of conscience bane unto the state,
so blind is error, so false a witness hate.

And yet behold these lambs be drawn to die,
treason proclaimed, the queen is put in fear,
out upon Satan, fie malice, fie,
speakest thou to them that did the guiltless hear?
can humble souls departing now to Christ,
protest untrue—avant foul fiend thou liest.

My sovereign liege behold your subject's end,
your secret foes do misinform your grace:
who in your cause their holy lives would spend
as traitors die, a rare and monstrous case,
the bloody wolf condemns the harmless sheep
before the dog, that whilst the shepherds sleep.

England look up, thy soil is stained with blood,
thou hast made martyrs many of thine own,
if thou hast grace their deaths will do thee good,

the seed will take which in such blood is sown,
and Campion's learning fertile so before,
thus watered too, must needs of force be more.

Repent thee Eliot[21] of thy Judas kiss,
I wish thy penance, not thy desperate end,
let Norton think which now in prison is,
to whom was said he was not Caesar's friend,
and let the Judge consider well in fear,
that Pilate washed his hands, and was not clear

The witness false, Sledd, Munday, and the rest,
which had your slanders noted in your book,
confess your fault beforehand it were best,
lest God do find it written when he doth look
in dreadful doom upon the souls of men,
it will be late (alas) to mend it then.

You bloody jury Lea and all the leaven,
take heed your verdict which was given in haste
do not exclude you from the joys of Heaven,
and cause you rue it when the time is past:
and every one whose malice caused him say
*Crucifige*, let him dread the terror of that day.

Fond Elderton call in thy foolish rhyme,
thy scurrilous ballads are too bad to sell,
let good men rest, and mend thyself in time,
confess in prose thou hast not metred well,
or if thy folly can not choose but fain,
write alehouse joys, blaspheme not in thy vain.

Remember you that would oppress the cause,
the Church is Christ's, his honour cannot die,
though Hell herself re-vest her grisly jaws,
and join in league with schism and heresy,
though craft devise, and cruel rage oppress,
yet skill will write and martyrdom confess.

You thought perhaps when learned Campion dies,
his pen must cease, his sugared tongue be still,
but you forgot how loud his death it cries,
how far beyond the sound of tongue and quill,
you did not know how rare and great a good
it was to write his precious gifts in blood.

---

[21] Those named in this and the following stanzas are the names of the men who betrayed him or bore false
witness against him at his trial, or were suborned jurors.

Living he spake to them that present were,
his writings took their censure of the view,
Now fame reports his learning far and near,
and now his death confirms his doctrine true,
his virtues now are written in the skies,
and often read with holy inward eyes.

All Europe wonders at so rare a man,
England is filled with rumour of his end,
London must needs, for it was present than,
when constantly three saints their lives did spend
the streets, the stones, the steps you hauled them by,
proclaim the cause for which these martyrs die.

The Tower saith the truth he did defend;
the bar bears witness of his guiltless mind;
Tyburn doth tell he made a patient end,
on every gate his martyrdom we find;
in vain you wrought that would obscure his name,
for Heaven and earth will still record the same.

Your sentence wrong pronounced of him here,
exempts him from the judgements for to come,
O happy he that is not judged there.
God grant me too to have an earthly dome,
your witness false and lewdly taken in,
doth cause he is not now accused of sin.

His prison now the city of the king,
his rack and torture joys and heavenly bliss,
for men's reproach with angels he doth sing
a sacred song which everlasting is
for shame but short and loss of small renown,
he purchase hath an ever during crown.

His quartered limbs shall join with joy again,
and rise a body brighter than the sun,
your blinded malice tortured him in vain,
For every wrench some glory hath him won,
and every drop of blood which he did spend,
hath reaped a joy which never shall have end.

Can dreary death then daunt our faith, or pain?
is't lingering life we fear to lose, or ease?
no, no, such death procureth life again,
tis only God we tremble to displease,

who kills but once, and ever still we die,
whose hot revenge torments eternally.

We cannot fear a mortal torment, we
this Martyr's blood hath moistened all our hearts,
whose parted quarters when we chance to see,
we learn to play the constant Christian's parts,
his head doth speak, and heavenly precepts give,
how we that look should frame ourselves to live.

His youth instructs us how to spend our days,
his flying bids us how to vanish sin,
his straight profession shows the narrow ways
which they must walk that look to enter in.
his home return by danger and distress,
emboldens us our conscience to profess.

His hurdle draws us with him to the cross,
his speeches there provoke us for to die,
his death doth say this life is but a loss,
his martyred blood from Heaven to us doth cry,
his first and last, and all conspire in this,
to show the way that leadeth unto bliss.

Blessed be God which lent him so much grace,
thanked be Christ which blest his martyr so,
happy is he which sees his master's face,
Cursed are they that thought to work him woe,
bounden be we to give eternal praise,
to Jesus' name which such a man did raise.
Amen. (2)

## The Complaint of a Catholic for the Death of Master Edmund Campion

O God from sacred throne behold
our secret sorrows here,
Regard with grace our helpless grief,
amend our mournful cheer.
The bodies of thy saints abroad
are set for fowls to feed,
And brutish birds devour the flesh
of faithful folk indeed.

Alas I rue to think upon
the sentence truly scanned,
No prophet any honour hath
within his native land.
Thy doleful death O Campion is
bewailed in every coast,
But we live here and little know
what creatures we have lost.

Bohemia land[22] laments the same,
Rudolphus'[23] court is sad,
With deep regard they now record
what virtues Campion had
Germania mourns, all Spain doth muse,
and so doth Italy,
And France our friend hath put in print
his passing tragedy

They that would make these men to seem
to be her highness' foes,
O Lord it is a world to see
the feignéd fraud of those.
For when they had in dastard wise
devised to dispute,
And could not find in all their craft
the cause for to confute.

And that their winnings was so well
they needed not to boast,
And that in conscience they did know
new found is lightly lost,
They subtly seek a further fetch
contrary to all reason,
To say he is not Caesar's friend,
accusing him of treason.

But shall we much lament the same,
or shall we more rejoice,
Such was the case with Christ our Lord,
such was the Jewish voice.
so were their wrathful words pronounced,
so was their sentence wrong,
For Christ did give to Caesar that
which did to him belong.

---

[22] Where Campion had had his formation as a Jesuit.
[23] The Holy Roman Emperor (1576–1612) Rudolph II, ruler of Austria-Hungary (including Bohemia).

So Christ his true disciples here
no treason do pretend,
But they by Christ and Christ his lore
their faith till death defend.
Though error have devised now
a vizard so unfit
To cloak her craft to change the case
to blear each simple wit.

Because she taught us long before
that none for points of faith
According unto Christ his lore
ought to be done to death.
Her witness were soon bewrayed, [= revealed *or* accused]
had they but once recanted
No doubt thereof they had not then
not life nor living wanted.

Thus who so ways her works and words,
with fraud shall find them fraught,
And how they now perform the same
that heretofore they taught.
God knows it is not force nor might,
not war nor warlike band,
Not shield and spear, not dint of sword,
that must convert the land.

It is the blood by martyrs shed,
it is that noble train,
That fight with word and not with sword,
and Christ their capitain.
For sooner shall you want the hands
to shed such guiltless blood,
Then wise and virtuous still to come
to do their country good.

God save *Elizabeth* our queen,
God send her happy reign,
And after earthly honours here,
the heavenly joys to gain.
And all such men as heretofore
have misinformed her Grace

God grant they may amend the same
while here they have the space. (3)

NOTES AND SOURCES

1. *A true reporte of the death and martyrdome of M. Campion Iesuite and preiste, and M. Sherwin, and M. Bryan preistes, at Tiborne the first of December 1581 Observid and written by a Catholike preist* (1582), unpag.
2. Ibid., unpag. For Evelyn Waugh's use of Alfield's account in his biography of Campion, see below.
3. Ibid., unpag.

## The Words of the Tortured 1582

Finally, we include some of the sworn statements of tortured and condemned priests bearing on the dilemma of remaining loyal to the Pope while not openly expressing agreement with *Regnans in excelsis* in its releasing of Catholics from allegiance to Queen Elizabeth. The document containing the statements was another piece of official propaganda, committed to the Queen's printer Christopher Barker. It includes the signed and witnessed statements of four out of thirteen imprisoned Catholic priests: first of Campion and the two priests who suffered with him, and then, in response to six specific questions, ten other priests (of which we include two). The priests follow the common policy of denying nothing that pertains directly to the faith, while at the same time, on the political aspects of *Regnans in excelsis*, asserting their rights, under English Common Law, to silence as a guard against self-incrimination. We include them as meditations on how Christians act and react to one another in extreme circumstances.

## The Words of the Tortured

1st August 1581.

Edmund Campion being demanded whether he would acknowledge the publishing of these things before recited by Sanders, Bristow and Allen,[24] to be wicked in the whole, or in any part: and whether he doth at this present acknowledge her Majesty to be a true and lawful Queen, or a pretended Queen, and deprived, and in possession of her Crown only *de facto*. He answereth to the first, that he meddleth neither to nor fro, and will not further answer, but requireth that they may answer. To the second he saith, that this question dependeth upon the fact of *Pius quintus*, whereof he is not to judge, and therefore refuseth further to answer.

Edmund Campion. This was thus answered and subscribed by Edmund Campion, the day and year above written, in the presence of us.

Owen Hopton, Robert Beale, John Hammond, Thomas Norton.

Alexander Bryant: he is content to affirm, that the Queen is his sovereign Lady, but he will not affirm that she so is lawfully, and ought so to be, and to be obeyed by him as her subject, if the Pope declare or command the contrary. And he saith, that that question is too high, and dangerous for him to answer... Whether the Pope have authority to withdraw from obedience to her Majesty, he knoweth not. The 7th of May 1581.

Alexander Bryant.

---

[24] Nicholas Sanders, *De visibili monarchia ecclesiae* (1571); Richard Bristow, *A briefe treatise of diuerse plaine and sure wayes to finde out the truthe in this doubtful and dangerous time of heresie conteyning sundry worthy motiues vnto the Catholike faith, or considerations to moue a man to beleue the Catholikes, and not the Heretikes* (1574); William Allen is included not because of anything he had yet written, but because of his role in coordinating Catholic defences of the Papal Bull.

Articles ministered to the Jesuits and Seminary priests, which are in the Tower, and were condemned, with their answers to the same. 13 May 1582.

1 Whether the Bull of Pius Quintus against the Queen's Majesty, be a lawful sentence, and ought to be obeyed by the subjects of England?

2 Whether the Queen's Majesty be a lawful Queen, and ought to be obeyed by the subjects of England, not withstanding the Bull of *Pius quintus*, or any other Bull or sentence that the Pope hath pronounced, or may pronounce against her Majesty?

3 Whether the Pope have or had power to authorize the Earls of Northumberland and Westmorland, and other her Majesty's subjects, to rebel or take arms against her Majesty, or to authorize Doctor Saunders, or others, to invade Ireland, or any other her dominions, and to bear arms against her, and whether they did therein lawfully or no?

4 Whether the Pope have power to discharge any of her highness's subjects, or the subjects of any Christian prince from their allegiance or oath of obedience to her Majesty, or to their prince for any cause?

5 Whether the said Doctor Sanders, in his book of the visible monarchy of the Church, and Doctor Bristow, in his book of Motives (writing in allowance, commendation, and confirmation of the said Bull of *Pius Quintus*) have therein taught, testified, or maintained a truth or a falsehood?

6 If the Pope do by his Bull or sentence pronounce her Majesty to be deprived, and no lawful Queen, and her subjects to be discharged of their allegiance and obedience unto her: and after, the Pope or any other by his appointment and authority, do invade this Realm, which part would you take, or which part ought a good subject of England to take?

Luke Kirby's Answer. To the first he saith, that the resolution of this article, dependeth upon the general question, whether the Pope may for any cause depose a prince: wherein his opinion is, that for some causes he may lawfully depose a prince, and that such a sentence ought to be obeyed. To the second, he thinketh that in some cases (as infidelity or such like), her Majesty is not to be obeyed against the Pope's Bull and sentence, for so he saith he hath read, that the Pope hath so done, *de facto*, against other princes. To the third he saith, he cannot answer it. To the fourth, that the Pope (for infidelity) hath such power, as is mentioned in this article. To the fifth, he thinketh, that both Doctor Sanders, and Doctor Bristow, might be deceived in these points of their books, but whether they were deceived or not, he referreth to God. To the last he saith, that when the case shall happen, he must then take counsel what were best for him to do.
[signed] Luke Kirby.
[witnessed] John Popham, Thomas Egerton, Daniel Lewes, John Hammond...

Thomas Ford's Answer. To the first he saith, that he cannot answer, because he is not privy to the circumstances of that Bull, but if he did see a Bull published by Gregory the thirteenth, he would then deliver his opinion thereof. To the second he saith, that the Pope hath authority to depose a prince upon certain occasions: and when such a Bull shall be pronounced against her Majesty, he will then answer what the duty of her subjects, and what her right is. To the third he saith, he is a private subject, and will not answer to any of these questions. To the fourth he saith, that the Pope hath authority upon certain occasions (which he will not name) to discharge subjects of their obedience to their Prince. To the fifth he saith, that Doctor Sanders, and Doctour Bristow, be learned men, and whether they have taught truly in their books mentioned in this article, he referreth the answer to themselves, for himself will not answer. To the last he saith, that when that case shall happen, he will make answer, and not before.

[signed] Thomas Forde.

[witnessed] John Popham, Thomas Egerton, Daniel Lewes, John Hammond ... (1)

NOTES AND SOURCES

1. *A particular declaration or testimony, of the vndutifull and traiterous affection borne against her Maiestie by Edmond Campion Iesuite, and other condemned priestes witnessed by their owne confessions: in reproofe of those slanderous bookes and libels deliuered out to the contrary by such as are malitiously affected towards her Maiestie and the state. Published by authoritie* (1582), unpag.

## Gregory Martin                                    *c.*1542–1582

Till recent times, the translation of the Scriptures most familiar to Catholics in England was the Douai (or Douay or Doway) Bible, so called because it was the work of a professor at the English College, Douai, Dr Gregory Martin, sometime Fellow of St John's College, Oxford, and friend of St Edmund Campion. He was assisted in his task by, among others, Cardinal Allen, the college president. The New Testament was published in 1582 while the college was in residence in Rheims after an outbreak of the plague in Douai. The Old Testament came out, in two volumes, in 1609/10 after the return to Douai. This new English Bible was the Catholic response to the Protestant Bibles, which had been at the centre of theological controversy over the previous fifty years. By 1582, the Bible most widely in circulation in England was the one produced by the Marian exiles in Geneva, which contained many tendentious renderings and marginalia that carried on a relentless polemic against the Catholic Church and against her doctrines, especially as regards the Sacraments. The highly Latinate Rheims New Testament was published in a quarto edition and in print for about fifty years. Ironically, several editions of it were produced by Protestant opponents, with the Rheims translation and commentary in one column and Protestant alternatives in the other. We offer here the opening of St John's Gospel with its annotations together with extracts from the introduction that indicate prudential hesitations about putting the Scriptures into untrained hands and minds, particularly at a time when so many 'false and impious' translations and commentaries were in circulation. The Rheims New Testament underwent revision, first in 1730 by Robert Witham, President of Douai, and then, some twenty years later, with the Old Testament, by Bishop Challoner (for whom, see below, pp. 310–21).

## Foreword to the Rheims New Testament

The New Testament of Jesus Christ, translated faithfully into English, out of the authentical Latin, according to the best corrected copies of the same, diligently conferred with the Greek and other editions in divers languages; with arguments of books and chapters, annotations, and other necessary helps, for the better understanding of the text, and especially for the discovery of the corruptions of divers late translations, and for clearing the controversies in religion of these days ...

Psalm 118: Give me understanding, and I will search thy law, and will keep it with my whole heart.

St Augustine: All things that are read in holy Scriptures, we must hear with great attention, to our instruction and salvation: but those things specially must be commended to memory, which make most against heretics, whose deceits cease not to circumvent and beguile all the weaker sort and the more negligent persons...

The Holy Bible long since translated by us into English, and the Old Testament lying by us for lack of good means to publish the whole in such sort as a work of so great charge and importance requireth: we have yet through God's goodness at length fully finished for thee (most Christian reader) all the NEW TESTAMENT, which is the principal, most profitable and comfortable piece of holy writ: and, as well for all other institution of life and doctrine, as especially for deciding the doubts of these days, more proper and pregnant than the other part not yet printed.

Which translation we do not for all that publish, upon erroneous opinion of necessity, that the holy Scriptures should always be in our mother tongue, or that they ought, or were ordained by God, to be read indifferently of all, could be easily understood of every one that readeth or heareth them in a known language; or that they were not often through man's malice or infirmity, pernicious and much hurtful to many; or that we generally and absolutely deemed it more convenient in itself, and more agreeable to God's word and honour or edification of the faithful, to have them turned into vulgar tongues, than to be kept and studied only in the ecclesiastical learned languages. Not for these nor any such like causes do we translate this sacred book, but upon special consideration of the present time, state, and condition of our country, unto which, divers things are either necessary or profitable and medicinable now, that otherwise in the peace of the Church were neither much requisite, nor perchance wholly tolerable...

Now since Luther's revolt also, divers learned Catholics for the more speedy abolishing of a number of false and impious translations put forth by sundry sects, and for the better preservation or reclaim of many good souls endangered thereby, have published the Bible in the several languages of almost all the principal provinces of the Latin Church, no other books in the world being so pernicious as heretical translations of the Scriptures, poisoning the people under colour of divine authority, and not many other remedies being more sovereign against the same (if it be used in order, discretion, and humility) than the true, faithful, and sincere interpretation opposed thereunto. Which causeth the holy Church not to forbid utterly any Catholic translation, though she allow not the publishing or reading of any absolutely and without exception, or limitation, knowing by her divine and most sincere wisdom, how, where, when, and to whom these her masters' and spouses' gifts are to be bestowed to the most good of the faithful. And therefore neither generally permitteth that which must needs do hurt to the unworthy, nor absolutely condemneth that which may do much good to the worthy. Whereupon, the order which many a wise man wished for before, was taken by the deputies of the late famous Council of Trent in this behalf, and confirmed by supreme authority, that the holy Scriptures, though truly and Catholicly translated into vulgar tongues, yet may not be indifferently read of all men, nor of any other then such as have express licence thereunto of their lawful ordinaries, with good testimony from their curates or confessors, that they be humble, discrete and devout persons, and like to take much good, and no harm thereby. Which prescript, though in these days of ours it cannot be so precisely observed, as in other times and places, where there is more due respect of the Church's authority, rule, and discipline, yet we trust all wise and godly persons will use the matter in the meanwhile, with such moderation, meekness, and subjection of heart, as the handling of so sacred a book, the sincere senses of God's truth therein, and the holy canons, councils, reason, and religion do require.

Wherein, though for due preservation of this divine work from abuse and profanation, and for the better bridling of the intolerable insolency of proud, curious, and contentious wits, the governors of the Church guided by God's Spirit, as ever before, so also upon more experience of the malady of this time than before, have taken more exact order both for the readers and translators in these later ages, than of old: yet we must not imagine that in the primitive Church, either every one that understood the learned tongues wherein the Scriptures were written, or other languages into which they were translated, might without reprehension, read, reason, dispute, turn and toss the Scriptures; or that our forefathers suffered every schoolmaster, scholar, or grammarian that had a little Greek or Latin straight to take in hand the holy Testament: or that the translated Bibles into the vulgar tongues, were in the hands of every husbandman, artificer, apprentice, boys, girls, mistress, maid, man: that they were sung, plays, alledged, of every tinker, taverner, rhymer, minstrel: that they were for table talk, for ale-benches, for boats and barges, and for every profane person and company. No, in those better times men were neither so ill, nor so curious of themselves, so to abuse the blessed book of Christ: neither was there any such easy means before printing was invented, to disperse the copies into the hands of every man, as now there is...

Then the scholar taught not his master, the sheep controlled not the pastor, the young student set not the doctor to school, nor reproved their fathers of error and ignorance. Or if any were in those better days (as in all times of heresy such must needs be) that had itching ears, tickling tongues and wits, curious and contentious disputers, hearers, and talkers rather than doers of God's word: such the Fathers did ever sharply reprehend, counting them unworthy and unprofitable readers of the holy Scriptures. St Jerome in his Epistle to Paulinus, after declaration that no handicraft is so base, nor liberal science so easy, that can be had without a master...nor that men presume in any occupation to teach that they never learned, Only (saith St Augustine) the art of Scripture is that which every man challengeth, this the chatting old wife, this the doting old man, this the brabbling sophister, this on every hand, men presume to teach before they learn it. Again, some with poise of lofty words devise of Scripture matters among women: othersome (fie upon it) learn of women, what to teach men, and lest that be not enough, by facility of tongue, or rather audacity, teach that to others, which they understand never a whit themselves. To say nothing of such as be of my faculty, who stepping from secular learning to holy Scriptures, and able to tickle the ears of the multitude with a smooth tale, think all they speak, to be the Law of God. This he wrote then, when this malady of arrogancy and presumption in divine matters, was nothing so outrageous as now it is.

St Gregory Nazianzus made an oration of the moderation that was to be used in these matters, where he saith, that some in his time thought themselves to have all the wisdom in the world, when they could once repeat two or three words, and them ill couched together, out of Scriptures, but he there divinely discourseth of the orders and differences of degrees: how in Christ's mystical body, some are ordained to learn, some to teach; that all are not apostles, all doctors, all interpreters, all of tongues and knowledge, not all learned in Scriptures and divinity; that the people went not up to talk with God in the mountain, but Moses, Aaron, and Eleazar: nor they neither, but by the difference of their callings...

But the case now is more lamentable: for the Protestants and such as St Paul calleth *ambulantes in astutia*, walking in deceitfulness, have so abused the people and many other in the world, not unwise, that by their false translations they have instead of God's Law and Testament, and for Christ's written will and word, given them their own wicked writing and fantasies, most shamefully in all their versions Latin, English, and other tongues, corrupting both the letter and sense by false translation, adding, detracting, altering, transposing, pointing, and all other guileful means: specially where it serveth for the advantage of their private opinions, for which, they are bold also, partly to disauthorise quite, partly to make doubtful, divers whole books allowed for canonical Scripture by the universal Church of God this thousand years and upward: to alter all the authentical and ecclesiastical words used since our Christianity, into new profane novelties of speeches agreeable to their doctrine: to change the titles of works, to put out the names of the authors, to charge the very evangelist with following untrue translation, to add whole sentences proper to their sect, into their psalms in metre, even into the very creed in rhyme. All which the poor deceived people say and sing as though they were God's own word, being in deed through such sacrilegious treachery, made the devil's word...

We therefore having compassion to see our beloved countrymen, with extreme danger of their souls, to use only such profane translations, and erroneous men's mere fantasies, for the pure and blessed word of truth, much also moved thereunto by the desires of many devout persons: have set forth, for you (benign readers) the New Testament to begin withal, trusting that it may give occasion to you, after diligent perusing thereof, to lay away at least such their impure versions as hitherto you have been forced to occupy... (1)

## The Introduction, Translation and Notes on the Gospel of John, ch. 1, verses 1–14

The preface of the Evangelist, commending Christ (as being God the Son incarnate) to the Gentiles; the Acts of Christ before his manifestation, whilst John Baptist was yet baptizing and setting out the blindness of the Jews in not receiving him...

*Note*: The Gospel at the third Mass upon Christmas Day. And every day at the end of Mass

1  In the beginning was the WORD, and the WORD was with God, and God was the WORD.

2  This was in the beginning with God.

3 All things were made by him: and without him was made nothing that which was made,

4 In him was life, and the life was the light of men:

5 and the light shineth in darkness, and the darkness did not comprehend it.

6 There was a man sent from God, whose name was John.

7 This man came for testimony: to give testimony of the light, that all might believe through him.

8 He was not the light, but to give testimony of the light.

9 It was the true light, which lighteneth every man that cometh into this world.

10 He was in the world, and the world was made by him, and the world knew him not.

11 He came into his own, and his own received him not.

12 But as many as received him, he gave them power to be made the sons of God, to those that believe in his name.

13 Who, not of blood, not of the will of flesh, nor of the will of man, but of God are born.

14 AND THE WORD WAS MADE FLESH and dwelt in us (and we saw the glory of him, glory as it were of the only-begotten of the Father) full of grace and verity.

### ANNOTATIONS CHAPTER I.

1. (*Was the word*) The Second Person in Trinity which is the natural, only, and eternal Son of God the Father, is called the WORD: not as the holy Scriptures or speeches of the Prophets and Apostles (written and spoken by God's commandment for the uttering of his divine will towards man) be called his word, but in a more divine, eminent, and ineffable sort, to express unto us in a sort, by a term agreeable to our capacity, that the Son of God so is, and so from everlasting is born of God the Father, as our prime concept (which is our internal and mental word) is and issueth out of our intelligence and mind. This WORD then, Son, or Second Person in the Holy Trinity, was and had his being then already, when other creatures (of what sort so ever) had but their beginning, and therefore cannot be a creature, as many heretics before the writing of this Gospel thought, and as the Arians after taught. And this first sentence of the Gospel not only the faithful, but the Platonics did so admire (as St Augustine writeth) that they wished it to be written in gold.

1. (*With God.*) Because a man might say, if the WORD were before any thing was created, where or how could he be? the Evangelist preventing that carnal concept, saith first, that he was with God, whose being dependeth not upon time, place, space, or any other creatures, all which were made by him. Secondly, he giveth us to understand, that the WORD hath his proper subsistence or personality distinct from God the Father, whereby Sabellius the old Heretic is refuted,

thirdly, here is insinuated the order of these two persons, one towards the other, to wit, that the Son is with and of the Father, and not the Father of the Son. Fourthly, you may confute here the blasphemy of Calvin, holding the Second Person to be God, not as of God the Father, but as of himself. And yet such are the books that our youth now read commonly in England, and that by commandment.

1. (*God was the Word*) Lest any man upon the premises, which set forth the relation and distinction of the Second Person from the first, might think that the Father only were God, the evangelist expressly teacheth, the WORD to be God. For though the words seem to lie otherwise (because we have of purpose so owed the elegancy which the evangelist himself observed in placing them so, and therefore they stand so both in Greek and Latin) yet indeed the construction is thus, *The* WORD *was God*, and (as in his first epistle the same apostle writeth) *true God*, lest any might say (as the Arians did) that he was God indeed, but not truly and naturally, but by common adoption or calling, as good men in the Church be called the sons of God. What wonderful wrangling and tergiversation the Arians used to avoid the evidence of this place, we see in St Augustine even such as the Protestants do, to avoid the like words, *This is my body*, concerning the Blessed Sacrament.

3. (*By him*) Again, by this he signifieth the eternity, divinity, omnipotency, and equality of the WORD or Son, with God the Father, because by him all things were created. All things he saith, both visible of this world: and invisible, as angels and all spiritual creatures. Whereupon it is evident also, that himself is no creature, being the creator of all: neither is sin of his creation, being a defect of a thing, rather than a thing itself, and therefore neither of nor by him.

12. (*He gave them power*) Free will to receive or acknowledge Christ, and power given to men, if they will, to be made by Christ the sons of God: but not forced or drawn thereunto by any necessity.

14. (*The Word made flesh*) This is the high and divine testimony of Christ's Incarnation and that he vouchsafed to become man, for the acknowledging of which inexplicable benefit and giving humble thanks for the same, all Christian people in the world by tradition of the Fathers prostrate themselves or kneel down, when they hear it sung or said at the holy Mass, either in this Gospel: or in the Creed by these words, ET HOMO FACTUS EST. (2)

NOTES AND SOURCES

1. *The Nevv Testament of Iesus Christ, translated faithfully into English, out of the authentical Latin, according to the best corrected copies of the same, diligently conferred vvith the Greeke and other editions in diuers languages; vvith arguments of bookes and chapters, annotations, and other necessarie helpes, for the better vnderstanding of the text, and specially for the discouerie of the corruptions of diuers late translations, and for cleering the controversies in religion, of these daies: in the English College of Rheims* (1582).
2. *Ibid.*

# A Manual of Prayers (i)                              1583

Throughout the penal times, the lay Catholic community was sustained by manuals of prayers and litanies in many different recensions and many different arrangements. We have drawn on four of them in the course of creating this anthology. We begin with a collation first published in 1583 and compiled by George Flinton. This was, the title page tells us, 'taken out of many famous authors and distributed according to the days of the week'. It provides the psalms and responsaries for daily morning and evening prayer, and hymns and prayers for the principal feasts of the year, and prayers for use before, during and after Mass. Other manuals, as we will see, add a variety of other devotions, together with translations of the great medieval hymns, such as Henry Garnet SJ's translation of Thomas Aquinas's *Pange lingua* or St Robert Southwell's translation of *Lauda, Sion*. Pre-reformation devotions are freely mixed with material from Counter-Reformation Europe, revealing that English Catholic spirituality at this time is an amalgam of the two. The 'old religion' did not die with Mary Tudor to be replaced by a new Tridentine spirituality. Flinton's *Manual of Godly Prayers* itself appeared in many editions (we have drawn on a 1613 reissue) and explicitly incorporated *Jesus: An Invocation Glorious Named the Psalter of Jesus* compiled by Richard Whitford and published in 1529. Its running motto placed in a variety of woodcut adornments was from Tobit 12, 'Prayer is good, with fasting and alms'. We include prefatory matter explaining the layout of the book and its guide to prayer, and extracts from the prayers suggested for the repose of the faithful departed. Extracts from other manuals occur at appropriate points in our anthology.

## Guide to Prayer

This is the justice of man in this life: fasting, alms-deeds, prayers. He that will have his prayer to fly to heaven, must make it two wings, alms-deeds and fasting, and it shall speedily ascend and be heard.

Most dear countrymen whose desires are to serve God in holiness of life, craving aid for the accomplishment of your religious intents at the hands of his Majesty by the merits of Christ and intercession of the Blessed Virgin Mary and all angels and saints. To the intent that you may proceed daily from one virtue to another, and to be helped by the labours of God's servants and saints (who from time to time to increase the devotions of the people, have left many holy prayers and exercises, as a treasure for to comfort and strengthen the dull soul of man) I have thought good to collect and translate certain devout prayers very fit and convenient for this time . . .

The first and second chapters are such as whereby the Christian Catholic may learn and know how to crave the aid and succour of God in all his endeavours, enterprises and actions, which that day he purposeth and meaneth to take in hand; and before he go to bed, to thank God for his benefits received that day, and to know how to examine his conscience, calling to mind the sins committed the day past, but especially in the second chapter the catholic man may learn how to behave himself at the time of the dreadful mysteries which Christian people commonly call the Mass. Further he may there learn what to crave of God, and what kinds of meditations to use in the Church, and withal how to move himself to spiritual devotions. The rest which are ten chapters are put in a general index, whereby the Catholic shall easily find what prayers are thought most convenient for every day of the week, that so he may as leisure and devotion serveth him, read either the whole, or part, as they are set down in this index following:

Read upon Sundays these chapters:

    10. Prayers to the Holy Trinity

     8. Of thanksgiving to God for his benefits

Read upon Mondays these chapters:

    11. To the Blessed Virgin Mary and to the Holy saints

     3. For obtaining remission of sins

Read upon Tuesdays these chapters:

    4. For aid and comfort in tribulations and afflictions

    5. For obtaining of God necessaries of body and soul.

Read upon Wednesdays these chapters:

    9. For the Church, our friends and others

    13. For the departed souls.

Read upon Thursdays these chapters:

    5. For obtaining of God necessaries of body and soul.

    8. Of thanksgiving to God for his benefits

Read upon Fridays these chapters:

    3. For obtaining remission of sins

    6. Prayer for the life and passion of our Saviour Jesus Christ

Read upon Saturdays these chapters:

    13. For the faithful departed

    9. For the Blessed Virgin and to the Holy saints. (1)

## Prayers for the Faithful Departed

The thirteenth chapter containing devout prayers, healthful for the departed souls.

    An exhortation by which we are showed and admonished to pray for souls, departed in the Catholic Church.

    (From St Clement) My brethren, let us pray for our brother that resteth in Jesu Christ, to the end that our good God which hath received his soul may forgive him all his sins willingly or unwillingly committed, and that he obtaining forgiveness may be received into the kingdom of the blessed, in the bosom of Abraham, Isaac and Jacob, with all those that from the beginning have pleased God and have done his will.

### COMMENDATIONS OF THE SOUL THAT IS LATELY DEPARTED

(Albertus Castella). O Lord, we commend the soul of thy servant that being lately departed this life he may live in thee and according to thy mercy, pardon him his sins which he hath committed through human frailty. We commend, O Lord, the soul of this thy servant into the hands of the most holy and most glorious Virgin Mother Mary, the mother of mercy and clemency; also into the hands of all the holy archangels, angels and celestial court of Heaven; into the hands of the holy patriarchs and prophets; into the hands of the blessed apostles, evangelists and disciples; into the hands of the martyrs and confessors; into the hands of the virgins, widows and all votaries whatsoever. And finally we commend the soul of this thy servant into the hands of all such thy blessed saints and servants as have pleased thee since the first creation of the World, that by their intercession and succour, he may be delivered from the prince of darkness, and from all dreadful torments. Grant this, O God Almighty, omnipotent and full of mercy, through the bitter passion of thy sweet son our Saviour Jesu, to whom with thee and the Holy Ghost be all honour and glory for ever and ever. Amen.

A PRAYER FOR THE FAITHFUL DEPARTED

(The Church's prayer in the Mass). O eternal and almighty God, to whom we never pray without hope of mercy: have mercy on the soul of thy servant N, and make him to be united to that company of saints, which is deceased from this life in the confession of thy name, through Christ our Lord, Amen.

ANOTHER PRAYER

(Roman Pontifical, part 3) O God, by whom all things liveth, and through whom our bodies diminisheth not in dying but are changed into better: we most humbly beseech thee to command the soul of thy servant to be received by the hands of thy holy angels, to bring him into the bosom of thy friend the patriarch Abraham, to rise again at the last great judgement day pardoning him mercifully all his sins which he hath committed, through the false deceits and suggestions of the devil, through Jesus Christ our Lord. Amen.

[*There follow prayers for 'thy father', 'thy mother', 'thy parents', thy friend', 'the living and the dead', and finally*]

A PRAYER FOR THE DEPARTED TO BE SAID AT MASS

(Ambrose, *Praecationes*). We humbly beseech thee, O holy father, for the souls of the faithful departed this life, that the Holy Sacrifice of the Mass may be to them eternal salvation, perpetual health, joy and rest everlasting, O my Lord God, let this wonderful and excellent mystery of piety and bounty be unto them this day full and perfect joy. Grant that they may be replenished with thee, the living and true bread, which descended from Heaven, and givest life to the world; and with that holy and blessed flesh of thee, the immaculate Lamb, which takest away the sins of the world, and make them drink of that fountain of thy piety, which by force of the soldier's lance issued forth from the side of Lord Jesus Christ crucified, that so being comforted they may rejoice in thy holy laud and glory. Amen. (2)

NOTES AND SOURCES

1. [George Flinton], *A Manual of Godly Prayers and Litanies* (1613 edn.), unpag.
2. Ibid., fos. 145–7, 150–1.

# Anne Dormer, Lady Hungerford     1525–1603

Many manuals were published for use with the rosary. Most were produced by priests and purport to have been produced for the use of the patrons (and especially patronesses) of those priests. An excellent example is the manual produced by John Buck for Lady Anne Hungerford. She was the daughter of Sir William Dormer and the sister of Jane Dormer, duchess of Feria and confidante of Queen Mary. In 1558 Anne contracted a disastrous marriage to Sir Walter Hungerford. By 1568 Sir Walter was seeking a divorce from Anne, claiming she was an adulteress and had tried to poison him. She defended the action and won, but so bitter was her husband that he spent three years in prison for refusing to pay her maintenance. With her sister's help, Anne was allowed to move to the Netherlands and she spent the last thirty years of her life in seclusion at Louvain and it was there that Buck produced and printed this manual for her, in 1589. We include here the introduction, the first of the sorrowful and the third of the glorious mysteries and, from an appendix, the first of 'seven short matters of meditation touching the benefits which God hath bestowed upon Mankind'.

## Praying the Rosary

Instructions for the use of the beads containing many matters of meditation or mental prayer, with diverse good advices of ghostly counsel, whereunto is added a figure or form of the beads [an engraving for each mystery] . . .

It is an ancient exercise of devout Christians in time of prayer and especially in the use of the beads, to set before the eyes of the soul some conceit or imagination of one or other matter contained in the life of our Saviour or of the Blessed Virgin Mary. And this conceit well imprinted in mind will keep it from wavering in the vain thoughts and will make it more attentive and heedful, whereby devotion is sooner kindled [and] without which prayer yieldeth small fruit. Therefore when you are disposed to pray upon the beads, you may think upon three sorts of mysteries, whereof five points in every one are joyful, five are dolorous and five are glorious, in manner following . . .

The first dolorous mystery was the sweating of blood and water which our Lord and Master suffered in the garden. And here behold Christ in the Garden kneeling upon his knees, holding up his face and hands to Heaven, and praying thrift to his Father, in this sort: *Father if it be possible, let this chalice pass from me, yet not my will but yours be done.* And mark this agony upon the impression and conceit of the great pains which he was to suffer upon the Cross for mankind. And how for very labour of sorrow he sweatheth water mixed with blood; and behold withal an angel sent from Heaven to comfort him. And with imagination, say the first *Pater Noster* and ten *Ave Marias* devoutly. Then note first how in all adversities thou must flee for succour to God. Secondly, that it is not enough to pray with thy lips, but that all thy senses and inward powers must be earnestly bent to prayer, and that with continuance. Thirdly how great need you have to pray for avoiding eternal pain which you have deserved for your sins; seeing the innocent son of God did flee to prayer for escaping or patient enduring a temporal pain, to be sustained for the redemption and delivery of others. *Fourthly,* comfortably continue in prayer and think that God in the end will hear thee, and send his holy angel to relieve thee when need shall require . . .

The third glorious mystery is the coming of the Holy Ghost. And here thou may view the Blessed Mother of God our Redeemer, together with the holy apostles and disciples beholding the wonderful Ascension of our Saviour and remaining together in one place, with humble prayer and fervent devotion attending the coming of the Holy Ghost. And thou may mark how the Holy Ghost to their great comfort came down in fiery tongues in the day of Pentecost being the fiftieth day after the Resurrection of our Saviour. And with this thought recite devoutly the third *Pater Noster* and ten *Ave Marias*. And then note his faithful performance of his promise, and their firm faith and belief in the same, and use thou that example to thy benefit. Here also for thy instruction and comfort consider six special causes of the coming of the Holy Ghost: to wit, for to rejoice the pensive; to revive the dead in sin; to sanctify the unclean; to confirm the disciples in love; to save the just; to teach the ignorant. These gifts and graces are preserved and increased in us by special means, whereof prayer with humility is one, diligent frequenting the

Sacraments with hearing divine service is another; continual exercise of works of charity is a third. For thus it giveth strength against all assaults and temptations of ghostly and bodily enemies. Therefore no peril nor persecution can annoy that person which hath the Holy Ghost...

Seven short matters of meditation touching the benefits which God hath bestowed upon mankind... Creation, Gratification, Vocation, Justification, Adoration, Gubernation and Glorification. We may consider six things touching our Creation: First how God hath predestinated us in perpetual love before the world was made; secondly, how he made man most like to himself; thirdly, how he hath given us a body of a most seemly constitution and proportion, void of all deformities and made it apt to serve him; fourthly how he hath made our soul immortal and adorned it with many qufalities most precious; fifthly thus he hath appointed for each one of us a Good Angel to guide and keep us; sixthly, he hath given us a prerogative to be born of Christian parents, not of infidels or of heretics. And of these matters you may think upon, with great profit, giving God due thanks for the same every Monday at morning, noon or night, as your leisure will permit... (1)

NOTES AND SOURCES

1. *Instructions for the vse of the beades conteining many matters of meditacion or mentall prayer, vvith diuerse good aduises of ghostly counsayle. VVere vnto is added a figure or forme of the beades portrued in a table. Compiled by Iohn Bucke for the benefit of vnlearned. And dedicated to the honorable good lady, Anne Lady Hungarforde, sister to the duchesse of Ferria* (1589), 14–15, 23–35, 38–9.

# Robert Parsons SJ 1546–1610

Robert Parsons (1546–1610) was the most energetic and prolific of all the apologists for Catholicism in the darkest days of persecution. He had a brilliant career in Oxford (Fellow and Bursar of Balliol), but resigned under the probably manufactured charge of financial irregularities. He set off to study medicine at Padua, but fell in with Jesuits en route, and was persuaded to undertake the spiritual Exercises, which changed his life. He entered the Society as a postulant in 1575, and was ordained priest, with remarkable speed, in 1578. He was sent to England as head of the Jesuit mission and took a hard line against persistent or occasional conformity to the established Church. When his friend Edmund Campion was arrested, tortured, and executed, he fled to the Continent, something he never lived down. He remained vulnerable to the oft-repeated charge that Catholics in England had to pay the price of his own uncompromising stance, maintained *in absentia*, towards the Elizabethan government. In exile he devoted himself tirelessly to managing and structuring the English mission: he was central to the creation of the seminaries in Valladolid and Seville, and the school for the children of recusants at Saint-Omer which, at the time of the French Revolution, transferred to Stonyhurst in Lancashire. He developed the distinctive syllabuses of the English colleges, and secured endowments from sympathetic monarchs. More controversially, he worked with ministers of Catholic monarchs and regents to plan invasions of England, the overthrow of Elizabeth, and the establishment of a Catholic government. He drew up detailed plans for the reconversion of England under a Catholic monarch, and lobbied successive popes to make his senior colleague William Allen first a Bishop and then a Cardinal in preparation for that day. But above all he was a tireless author. The range of his writings exceeds that of any other Catholic of the penal era. Here we can only offer a limited cross-section of his vast corpus of more than thirty published works. We begin with extracts from *A Christian Directory Guiding Men to their Eternal Salvation*. This was first published in 1582 and then in a revised, expanded version in 1585. It was reprinted in 1607, 1650, 1660, 1683, 1696, 1753 (in Dublin) and 1820 (in New York). It was translated into Welsh in 1591, and subsequently into French, Italian, and German. Most startling of all is the lightly amended version produced for Protestant use by the Calvinist author Edmund Bunny under the title *A Book of Christian Exercise*. In our first extract, we see Parsons unflinching in his recognition of the place of both justice and mercy in the work of man's redemption. The second extract, which we have entitled 'Catholic Obedience' comes from Parson's less influential, but equally effective, pastoral guide, *A Comparison of a True Roman Catholic with a Protestant*. Parsons wrote more works of controversy than of pastoral theology. He often engaged directly with the apologists thrust forward by Elizabeth and James I to defend their right to create and enforce a confessional Protestant state. Here, thirdly, we include an extract from Parsons' response to Sir Edward Coke, James's Attorney-General, who argued for the supremacy of the common law of England over all other forms of law. He was as tough on his opponents within the Catholic Church who urged accommodation with the Protestant state (the taking of oaths of allegiance, partial conformity to the Protestant church in order to avoid persecution). Our extracts from Parsons therefore end with an example of the many and sharp differences amongst the leaders of the Catholic community in exile and back in England, principally but not exclusively between the Jesuits and the seculars, with other regulars, especially the Benedictines, tending to side with the seculars. At the heart of these differences were disputes about the extent to which it was permissible for Catholics in England to obey the laws of the land when they were at odds with Catholic teaching. It is a dilemma of all times and places. Nowhere was this clearer than in the issue of whether it was permissible for Catholics to attend Protestant worship as prescribed by statute law. Here are two sharply different views on this issue, the first by Parsons, the other by Alban Langdale, chaplain in the household of Lord Montague at Cowdray in Sussex. He had been archdeacon of Chichester in Mary's reign and had taken part in the disputations with Cranmer, Latimer, and Ridley in 1554. Langdale's manuscript tract, much copied and circulated at the time, with the title, 'A Discourse Delivered to Mr Sheldon to Persuade him to Conform', came into the hands of the Elizabethan government. It is anonymous, but it was Parsons, not the government, who worked out Langdale's authorship. So here is a classic confrontation between those who believe that Catholics should seek to challenge the world by refusing any compromise, and those who believe that you have to live in the world as it is, and should seek to ameliorate it day by day, step by step. Parsons's views are expressed in his tract, *A Brief Discourse Containing Certain Reasons why Catholics Refuse to Go to Church* (1580). Parsons here refers to the case of Naaman, the Syrian general, whom Elisha cured of leprosy, and who thereby came to embrace the God of Israel as the one true God, but who still sought (and received) Elisha's permission to attend his king when he was worshipping the idol of Remmon. Parsons's point is that this exceptional case is outweighed by the authority of the Apostolic Constitutions, which insist that Catholics never attend the meetings of Jews and heretics. The precedent is however explored at length by Alban Langdale, who, as chaplain to the Montagues, was serving a family who had determined to meet most of the conditions laid down by the state, but to see their attendance at Anglican services as the lifeless husk, and their participation in Catholic worship, as the living kernel of their religious practice.

# Justice and Mercy

To the end that no man may justly complain of the severe account which God is to take of us at the last day, or of the rigour of his judgement ... it shall not be amiss to consider in this place the cause why God doth show such severity against sin and sinners; as both by that which hath been said may appear that he doth, as also by the whole course of holy Scripture, where in every place (almost) he denounceth his great hatred, wrath and indignation against the same. As where it is said of him that he hateth all those that work iniquity; and again that both the wicked man and his wickedness are hateful in his sight ...

For the better understanding of which injury, we are to consider that every time we commit a mortal sin, there doth pass through our heart and mind (though we mark it not) a certain practic discourse of our understanding and will (as there doth also in every other election) whereby we lay before us on the one side the seeming commodity of that sin which we are tempted to commit—that is to say the pleasure that allures us thereunto; and on the other part the offence of God, which is the losing of his grace and friendship by that sin, if we yield unto it. And thus having, as it were, the balance there before us, and setting God in one end thereof, and in the other, the aforesaid pleasure, we stand in the midst, deliberating and examining in a certain manner, the value and weight of both parts. And finally do make choice of the pleasure and reject Almighty God, that is we choose rather to lose the favour of God, together with his grace, and whatsoever he is worth besides, than to lack that pleasure and delectation of sin. Now then, what can be more opprobrious and horrible than this? ...

The rigorous punishment of our first parents Adam and Eve and all their posterity, for the only eating of an apple by disobedience, for which fault, besides the chastising of the offenders themselves, and all the creatures of the Earth for the same, and all their children and offspring after them, both before our redemption and after (for albeit we are delivered from the guilt of that sin, yet temporal punishment do remain upon us for the same, as hunger, thirst, cold, sickness, death, and a thousand other miseries ... )

Besides all this, I say (which is man's reason may seem severe enough), God's wrath and justice could not be sufficiently satisfied except his own only Son had come down into the world, and taken our flesh upon him, and by his pains and death made satisfaction for the same. And when he was now come into the world, and had in our flesh subjected himself unto his Father's justice, albeit the love his Father bear him were infinite, and every little pain that he endured for us, at least wise every drop of blood he shed for our cause, had been sufficient for the whole satisfaction (for that his flesh being united to his Godhead, made every such satisfactory action of his, of infinite value and merit, and consequently of infinite satisfaction, correspondent to the infinity of our parents' sin), yet to the end that God might show the greatness of his hatred and justice against the said sin, and all other, he never ceased to add affliction to affliction, and to heap torments upon body and flesh of this his most dear and blessed Son (for by Isaiah he saith, that himself was the doer thereof) until he had brought him unto that most rueful plight, that his flesh being all mangled, and most lamentably torn in pieces, retained no one drop of blood within in. He spared him not (I say) even then, when he beheld him sorrowful unto death, and bathed in that agony of blood and water, when he heard him utter those most dolorous and compassionate speeches, *O my Father, if it be possible, let this cup pass from me!* And after that again, much more pitifully upon the Cross, *O my God! Why hast thou forsaken me?* Notwithstanding all which cries and lamentations, his most merciful Father (loving him as he did) would not deliver him, but for satisfying of justice, laid upon him stripe upon stripe, pain upon pain, torment after torment, until he had rendered up his life and soul into his Father's hands; which is a wonderful and dreadful document of God's hatred against sin for our example...

What shall I look for, which have committed so many sins against him? If God hath damned so many souls for lesser sins than mine are, what will he do to me for mine, that are far greater? If God hath borne longer with me than he hath with many others whom he hath cut off, without giving them time of repentance, what reason is there that he should bear longer with me? If David and others after their sins forgiven took such pains in afflicting themselves for satisfaction of their temporal punishment in this life, what punishment remaineth for me, either here or in the world to come, for satisfaction of so many sins committed? If it be true that our Saviour saith: *that the way is hard and the gate narrow whereby men go into Heaven, and that they shall answer for every idle word before they enter therein*, what shall become of me that do live so easy a life, and do keep no account at all of my deeds and much less of my words? Of good men in old time did take such pains for their salvation, and yet Saint Peter saith the very just were scarcely saved, what a state am I in which takes no pains at all, and do live in all kind of pleasure and worldly contentations...

Our Lord God of his mercy, give us his holy grace to fear him as we should, and to make such account of his judgements and justice, as by threatening the same, he would have us do, for the avoiding of sin. And then shall we not delay the time but shall resolve ourselves to serve him, whilst he is content to accept our service, and to pardon us all our offences, if we would once firmly make this resolution from our heart... (1)

## Catholic Obedience

First, the Roman Catholic (whom *Foxe*[25] calleth papist) touching matters of faith and belief, composeth himself to that humility, as whether he be learned or ulearned, or what arguments soever he hath on the one or other side, yet presumeth he to determine nothing of himself, but remitteth that determination (if any thing be doubtful or undetermined) unto the judgement and decree of the universal Church, and governors thereof. And hence proceedeth the agreements and unity of faith, which they have held and conserved in so large a body, for so many ages, as have passed since Christ and his apostles. Whereas Protestants in this behalf following another Spirit of self-will, and self-judgement, and loosing the reins of liberty to the pregnancy of each man's wit, do hold and determine

---

[25] A reference to John Foxe whose *Book of Martyrs* (or more correctly) *Actes and Monuments of these Latter and Perillous Days* (1563, 1570, 1576) was more than any other work to shape English anti-Catholicism for 350 years.

what their own judgements for the time do think to be true, or most probable, and are subject to no authority in this behalf, but to their own Spirit; which is variable, according to the variety of arguments and probabilities that do occur. And hereof do ensue the great variety of sects and opinions among them, even in this one age since they began...

Next to this, for so much as appertaineth to life and actions, the Catholic man holdeth that we can do nothing at all of ourselves, no not so much as to think a good thought, but we must be prevented and assisted by God's holy grace, as may be showed out of the Council of Trent, which teacheth with Saint *Paul*, that our sufficiency is of Christ; yet is the force of this grace so tempered notwithstanding, as it useth no violence, nor excludeth the free concurrence of man's will, prevented and stirred up by the foresaid grace of Our Saviour, and motion of the Holy Ghost, so as freely by this help, we yield to the said good motions, and do believe in God, and his promises. And this act of faith (as you may learn out of the said Council) is the first foundation and root of all our justification, but yet not sufficient of itself, except Charity and Hope (two other theological virtues) do accompany the same. So as we do both love and hope in him, in whom we believe. And out of these, and by direction of these, do flow again other Christian virtues, called moral, for that they appertain to the direction of life and manners, which virtues do consist principally in the inward habits and acts of the mind, and from thence do proceed to the external actions and operations, whereby we exercise ourselves in keeping God's Commandments, and exercising works of piety toward our neighbour, as clothing the naked, feeding the hungry, visiting the sick, and the like. In works of devotion in like manner, as singing, and praying to God, kneeling, knocking our breasts, mortifying our bodies, by fasting, watching, and other such like. All which exterior actions are so far forth commendable and meritorious, as they proceed from the inward virtues and motions of God's Spirit.

And albeit (as St Thomas saith) these exterior acts do add nothing in substantial goodness to the inward acts, but have their merit from thence; yet, for that man consisteth both of spirit and flesh, it was reason that he should be bound to honour God with both, that is to say, both with inward acts of virtue, proceeding from God's grace and motion, and with outward virtuous acts, testifying the inward, whereby we see what an excellent Christian Common-wealth the Catholic Religion doth appoint, if it were executed according to her doctrine, to wit, that all men's minds should be replenished with all sort of virtues, towards both God and our neighbour, and that their actions should be full of all righteousness, piety and charity in exterior behaviour, so as neither in thought, word, nor deed they should offend either of them both. And thus much for the Catholic man, concerning his actions, life and manners.

But this Catholic religion doth not stay here, nor teach only in general what actions a Christian man should have, and from what internal principles of grace and virtue they should flow, but doth offer us divers particular means also how to procure, and conserve, and increase this grace, which is the fountain of all goodness: for first, it exhibiteth unto us, besides all other means of prayer, and particular endeavours of our part, seven general means and instruments left us to that purpose, by the institution of Christ himself, which are seven Sacraments, that being received with due disposition of the receiver, do always bring grace by the virtue and force of Christ's merit and institution, without dependence of the merit, or demerit of the Minister that administereth them. By use of which Sacraments, infinite grace is derived daily by Christ our Saviour unto his Church, and particular members thereof, in every state and degree of men.

Moreover, Catholic Religion not contented with these generalities, doth come yet more in particular to frame direct, and help a Christian man in the way of his salvation, even from the first hour of his birth in Christ, until his soul, departing from this world, be rendered up again into his Creator's hands. For first, he having all his sins forgiven clearly and freely by the grace of Christ received in Baptism, he is strengthened to the fight and course of a true Christian life, by the Sacrament of confirmation and imposition of hands: his soul also is fed, and nourished spiritually by the sacred food of our Saviour's body in the eucharist. Two several states of Christian life are peculiarly assisted with grace of two particular Sacraments, priests and clergymen by the Sacrament of holy orders; and married people by the Sacrament of matrimony. And for that in this large race and course of life (as Saint Paul calleth it) we often fall and offend God by reason of our infirmity; there is a most sovereign Sacrament of penance, for remedy hereof appointed by our provident Saviour, founded in the merits of his sacred passion, called by holy fathers, the second table or plank, whereon we may lay hands, and escape drowning, after the shipwreck of our pardon, grace and justification received in our Baptism, which was the first table: by which second table of penance, all sorts may rise again how often soever they fall; which Sacrament consisteth of three parts, sorrow for our sins, and confessing the same, for the remission of the guilt, and some kind of satisfaction on our behalf, for removing the temporal punishment remaining: the true use whereof bringeth such exceeding help and comfort to a Christian soul, as it is unspeakable. For that by the first two parts a man is oft brought sweetly to sorrow for his sins, to think upon them, to detest them, ask pardon of God for them, to make new purposes of better life for the time to come, to examine his conscience more particularly, and other such heavenly effects as no man can tell the comfort thereof, but he that receiveth them.

By the third part also, which is *Satisfaction*, though a man perform never so little thereof in this life, yet doth it greatly avail him, not only in respect of the grateful acceptation thereof at God's hands, for that it cometh freely of his own good will, but also for that it humbleth even the proudest mind in the sight of Almighty God: it restraineth also greatly our wicked appetites from sin for the time to come, when we know we must give a particular account, and satisfy also for our sensualities somewhat even in this world. And finally, it is the very chief sinew of Christian conversation and behaviour one towards another. For when the rich man knoweth (for example sake) that he must satisfy one way or another, and be bound by his ghostly father to make restitution so far as he is able of whatsoever he hath wrongfully taken from the poor, when the poor also are taught that they must do the like towards the rich, the son towards his father, the servant towards his master, if he have deceived him. When the murmurer in like manner knoweth that he must make actual restitution of fame (if he have defamed any) this Catholic doctrine, I say, and practice, must needs be a strong hedge to all virtuous and pious conversation among men, that believe and follow the same.

And finally, not to pass to more particularities, whereas Catholic doctrine teacheth us, that all or most disorders of this life in a sensual man (to omit the infirmities of our higher powers in like manner) do proceed originally from the fountain of concupiscence, and law of the flesh remaining in us after our Baptism, and, *ad certamen*, as holy Fathers do term it, that is to say, for our conflict and combat, to the end our life may be a true warfare, as the holy Scripture calleth it. This concupiscence, I say, or sensual motion, being the ground of our temptations, though it be not sin of itself, except we consent unto it, yet is she busy in stirring us daily to wickedness; as a Christian man's principal exercise, and diligence, ought to be in resisting her, which he may do by the help and assistance of Christ's grace (merited by his sacred passion), wherein he extinguished the guilt of this original corruption, though he left still the sting and provocation for our greater merit, and continual victory by his holy grace, in them that will strive and fight, as they may and ought to do. (2)

## On Natural and Positive Law

An answer to the fifth part of Reports lately set forth by Sir Edward Coke Knight, the King's Attorney General concerning the ancient and modern municipal laws of England, which do appertain to spiritual power and jurisdiction. By occasion whereof, and of the principal question set down in the sequent page, there is laid forth an evident, plain, and perspicuous demonstration of the continuance of Catholic religion in England, from our first Kings christened, unto these days.

Of the state of the question in general, concerning spiritual, and temporal power, and jurisdiction; their origin, and subordination one to the other: And how they stand together in a Christian commonwealth. To the end, that the prosecution, and issue of the particular controversy we have in hand, about the spiritual authority of Q. Elizabeth, may be more clear: it shall not be amiss perhaps, in this very beginning, to set down briefly, what Catholic divine, and other learned men, do write and hold of power, and jurisdiction in general, and of the origin, offspring, author, division, and parts thereof; wherein Mr Attorney is wholly silent, using no explication, or distinction at all, and consequently giveth occasion thereby to some confusion.

2. First then our divines affirm that Almighty God is author of all lawful power whatsoever, both spiritual, and temporal according to that general proposition of St Paul, there is no power but from God. For that, as it pleased his divine Majesty to impart with man other sparks of his excellencies, as wisdom, reason, knowledge, providence, and the like; so vouchsafed he also to make man partaker of his power, and authority not only to govern all other creatures of his in the world, but mankind also, and this both in body and soul, temporal, and eternal things under him in this world, as his lieutenant and substitute.

3. The differences which are between these two powers, and jurisdictions, spiritual, and temporal, ecclesiastical, and civil are divers and sundry, taken from the diversity of their ends and object; the end of spiritual power being to direct us, to everlasting salvation, both by instruction, discipline, and correction; and of the temporal or Civil, by like means, and helps, to govern well the commonwealth in peace, abundance, order, justice, and prosperity. And according to these ends, are also their objects, matter, and means. As for example, the former hath for her object spiritual things belonging to the soul, as matters of faith, doctrine, Sacraments, and such other; and thy latter handleth the civil affairs of the realm, and commonwealth, as they appertain to the temporal good, and prosperity thereof.

4. The ancient learned Father St Gregory Nazianzen in a certain oration of his, doth express the nature, and conditions of these two powers; spiritual and temporal, ecclesiastical, and civil, by the similitude of spirit and flesh, soul, and sense; which he saith, may be considered, either as two distinct commonwealths, separated the one from the other; or conjoined together in one commonwealth only. An example of the former, wherein they are separated, may be in beasts, and angels; the one having their commonwealth of sense only, without soul or spirit, and their end and objects conform thereto, which are the nourishment, and preservation of the body. And the other commonwealth of angels, being of spirit only, without flesh or body—but in man [they] are conjoined, both the one, and the other. And even so in the commonwealth of the Gentiles, was only authority political, earthly, and human, given by God to govern worldly and human things, but not spiritual for the soul. Whereas contrariwise in the primitive Christian Church, for almost 300 years together, none or few Kings being yet converted, only spiritual authority was exercised by the Apostle Christians bishops, their successors for governing the Church in ecclesiastical affairs without temporal, according to the saying of St Paul in the Acts of the Apostles speaking to bishops: The Holy Ghost hath appointed you, that are bishops to govern his Church.

5. And this spiritual jurisdiction in respect of the high end, and object thereof, above the temporal, did the same apostles by instruction of the same Holy Ghost, so highly esteem, as the same St Paul writing to the Corinthians, and reprehending them for going to law about temporal things, before the heathen magistrate, said, that in secular matters, they should appoint for judges, such as were contemptible in the Church, that is to say, men of mean account, which was spoken by him, not for that he contemned temporal power, as the heretical anabaptists out of this place would prove, (for so he should be contrary to himself, who a little before, as you have heard, avowed, that all power is from God, and in other places, that the King, and temporal magistrate, is to be honoured, and obeyed, as God's minister, and the like) but only, he saith this in comparison, the one of the other, and of their ends, and objects, so different in dignity, and worthiness, as you have heard. And this continued in the primitive church, (to wit, spiritual jurisdiction, without temporal) until Constantine the Great; and other Emperors and Kings after him, being converted to the Christian faith, entered into the said Church, retaining their temporal states, and temporal power, which before they had, but submitting themselves in spiritual, and Ecclesiastical matters, to the spiritual government and governors, which they found to have been in the same Church before their conversion.

6. Furthermore besides these differences, of the end, and objects of these two powers, the foresaid divines do show another no less considerable than the former, which is, that albeit, both of them be of God, and do proceed from him; as the author, and origin, as hath been said; yet far differently: for that ecclesiastical authority is immediately from God, and was given by Christ immediately to his apostles and bishops, as before you have heard, out of St Paul, who addeth in the same place, that Christ gave them this spiritual jurisdiction over that Church which he had bought and purchased with his blood, to make them and others, in respect of this dreadful circumstance, esteem and respect the more this spiritual jurisdiction over souls, which jurisdiction Christ also himself, God and man, did exercise in person upon earth, wholly separated from the use of all temporal

jurisdiction, notwithstanding he was Lord of all, as the same divines out of the Gospel do prove; showing thereby and by the long continuance of his Church, without the said temporal Authority, that spiritual jurisdiction is wholly independent thereof, and utterly distinct by her own nature.

7. And albeit civil power and jurisdiction be of God's institution also, and duly to be honoured in his Church and Christian commonwealth, as before we have showed; yet do they teach the same to be far otherwise derived, and received from God, than is spiritual power, that is to say, not immediately by God's own delivery thereof, but mediately rather, to wit by mediation of the law of nature, and nations. For by the law of nature, God hath ordained that there should be political government, for that otherwise no multitude could be preserved, which the law of nations assuming, hath transferred that government to one, or more, according to the particular forms thereof, as monarchy, aristocracy or democracy or mixed wherein is to be noted, that the ordination of God by the law of nature doth give political power to the multitude immediately, and by them mediately to one, or more, as hath been said. But spiritual power Christ gave immediately, and by himself, to the apostles and their successors, by these words, whatsoever you shall bind upon earth, the same shall be bound in Heaven, and whatsoever you shall loose on earth, shall be loosed in Heaven. Whereby you see a general large commission granted to them of binding and loosing whatsoever, without exception. And the like to St Peter, as head and chief, by special power and commission of those words: feed my sheep, feed my lambs, thrice repeated: signifying thereby the pre-eminence, and primacy of his pastoral authority in God's Church, as the ancient Fathers have always understood the same. For that to the office of supreme feeding is required also all other authority necessary to govern, direct, command, restrain, and punish in like manner, when need requireth.

8. About which point, is to be observed and considered attentively (say Catholic divines, and most learned lawyers) that when God almighty giveth any office; he giveth also sufficient power, and authority, every way to execute that office, as when he giveth the office of a King, or temporal magistrate, for good of the commonwealth, he giveth authority therewith, not only to direct, command, and instruct, but to punish, and compel also, yea, and to extirpate, and cut off those (when need is) that are rebellious, or otherwise deserve that punishment. And the like is to be observed in spiritual power, and jurisdiction, according to which the civil law saith: to whomsoever jurisdiction is given, to him also must we understand to be granted all those things, without which his jurisdiction cannot be fulfilled. And the canon law to the same effect: jurisdiction would seem to be of no moment, if it had not some power to compel. And finally it is a general rule given in the said canon law; that when any cause is committed to any man, he is understood to receive also full authority, in all matters belonging to that cause.

9. Out of all which, is deduced, that for so much, as Christ our Saviour, God, and Man, having purchased to himself, by the price of his own blood, a most dearly beloved Church, and committed the same as St Paul saith to be governed by his apostles, and bishops their successors, to the world's end. It must needs follow, that he hath endowed the same Church with sufficient spiritual authority, both directive and coactive, to that end, for governing our souls, no less than he hath done the temporal commonwealth for affairs of the body ... (3)

## Can Catholics Attend Protestant Services
## to Avoid Persecution?

The first reason why I being a Catholic in mind, may not go to the churches or service of the contrary religion, is because I persuading myself their doctrine to be false doctrine, and consequently venomous unto the hearer, I may not venture my soul to be infected with the same. For as it is damnable for a man to kill himself, and consequently deadly sin (without just cause) to put his body in probable danger of death, so is it much more offensive to God, to put my soul, ten thousand times of more value than my body, in danger to the deadly stroke of false doctrine and heresy, especially seeing I have no warrant of security or scaping, but rather I hear God crying to the contrary. *He that loveth danger shall perish in the same.* Neither is it for me to think that I am sure enough from being infected, for that I am grounded enough, I am learned sufficiently. For what if God take his grace from thee, and let thee fall, because thou hast not followed his counsel which is, *If thou wilt not be bitten with the snake not to sleep nigh the hedge* (Eccl. 3); *If thou wilt not be spotted, then not to touch the Pitch* (Eccl. 3). Wherefore St Paul to as good a man, as learned, as strong, as I am, gave a general rule: to avoid and file an heretical man. The like precept (Tit. 3) he gave to Timothy being a Bishop, to avoid a certain heretic by name Alexander (2 Tim. 4), and more vehemently yet he conjureth as it were the Thessalonians in the name of Jesus: *Christ, that they should withdraw themselves, from like fellows* (2 Thess. 3). The same he repeateth again to the Romans beseeching them to note (Rom. 16).and to decline from such men (1 Tim. 2). The reason of this, St Paul uttereth to Timothy *Because their speech creepeth like a canker and they have subverted the faith of certain* (Rom. 16). Again he saith to the Romans of the same men: *By sweet words and gay blessings they seduce the hearts of the Innocent.* And St Peter saith of them, *that they do allure unto them unconstant souls* (2 Pet. 2). Here now I see the Scripture carefully counselling, and commanding me to avoid the company, and speech of false teachers...

The second reason why a Catholic cannot yield to go to Church is because he cannot go without scandal, which is a sin more mentioned, more forewarned, forbidden, more detested, more threatened (Prov. 18) in the Scripture, than any sin else (2 Macc. 6, Matt. 17 and 18, Mark 9) mentioned in the same, except it be Idolatry. But in the New Testament nothing so much exaggerated, or with (Luke 17) such vehement speeches prohibited, (Rom. 14, 15) Christ signifying, that the most part (1 Cor. 8 and 10, 2 Cor. 6) of the world to be damned, were to be damned for this sin, when he cryeth (1 Thess. 5) out with that compassionable voice of his, saying. Woe be to the world (Matt. 18) by reason of scandals. Wherefore pronouncing as pitiful a sentence upon the author of these scandals he saith, Woe be to that man by whom come these scandals. And devising with himself (as it were) how to express unto our capacities, the intolerable greatness of this man's torment in Hell, for scandalizing of other men: he uttereth it in this sort. It were better for that man that a millstone were hanged about his neck, and that he were cast into the sea (Mark 9). Which saying so terrified St Paul that rather than he would scandalize any man in eating a piece of meat (a thing of itself lawful as he saith) he protested that he would never eat flesh in his life (1 Cor. 8)...

The third reason why a Catholic may not come to Church, is for that going or not going to the Church is made a sign now in England distinctive, betwixt religion and religion, that is, betwixt a Catholic and a schismatic, so that a Catholic by going thither doth directly deny his religion. For the better understanding whereof, we must note that the professor of any religion may be known by three ways: first by words, professing himself to be of that religion; secondly by works, or deeds proper to that religion; thirdly some sign or mark appointed to signify that religion. As for example, In Italy a Jew may be known, first, by his words, if he would profess himself to be of that religion. Secondly, by works proper to Judaism, as by keeping the Saturday holy day, by circumcising his children, and the like. Thirdly, by a notorious sign appointed to distinguish that religion from all others, which is, to wear on his head a yellow cap. Now, as these three are ways to profess this religion, so if a man of another religion, (for example) a Christian, should yield to use any of these things, he should sin grievously, and in effect deny his faith. And as for the first, if he should profess himself to be a Jew, it is evident that he denyeth thereby his Christianity. And as for the other two ways, it cannot be denied: for the circumcising of thy children, and the wearing of a yellow cap, doth as plainly in that country tell men that thou art a Jew, as if thou didst proclaim it at the market: even as the bush at the tavern door doth tell the goers by, that there is wine to be sold within.

But now, that the going to Church is in the realm of England a plain and an apparent sign of a schismatic, that is to say, of a conformable man (as they call him) to the Protestants' proceedings ...

The fourth cause, why a Catholic may not go to the Church is because it is schism and breaking of the unity of the Catholic church, the which, how perilous and dreadful a thing it is, all Catholics do sufficiently know. For as they firmly believe, that to oppugn the visible known Church of Christ (as all heretics continually do) is a very wicked and damnable sin; even so in like manner they believe, that to break the Unity of the same Church, and to make any rent or disunion in the same (which is the proper fault of Schismatics) is also damnable. For the which cause, St Paul doth so diligently request the Corinthians to (1 Cor. 1) avoid Schisms, saying. I beseech you brethren, by the name of our Lord Jesus Christ, that you all say one thing and that there be no schisms amongst you; and to the Ephesians, be you careful to keep unity of spirit in the bond of peace (Eph. 4). The which unity Christ himself expresseth more particularly, and more distinctly, when he requesteth of his Father, that his Christians might be one, as he and his father were one (John 17), that is to say, that as he, and his Father, did agree in all their actions, and whatsoever the one did, the other also did: so in his Church there should be one only form of belief, one form of service, one form of Sacraments, and the like (Eph 2: 4): even as there is (according to Paul) one Baptism, one bread, one faith, one Church (1 Cor. 10: 12), one Christ, one Lord, one body, one Heaven, one hope of reward (1 Tim. 2), the breaking of which unity of the Church of God, hath been always accounted a most grievous, and damnable offence ...

Howbeit, some doubt being at that time, moved by certain of the nobility of England, whether they might not lawfully without offence to Church to do some mere temporal act (as, to bear the sword before her Majesty or the like), it was debated by twelve learned men there, at the Council's appointment, and determination then given, that only for such a cause, they might go to Church. As for example, if her Majesty should appoint certain Catholics to meet at [St] Paul's, to entreat of matters of the state, and that at such time as service were said there, and this was Naaman the Syrian's case, flat, who was permitted (as most men take it) for a time, to go with his King and hold him up upon his shoulder, when he went to the temples of the idols. Now, that there hath been a general custom, rule, and canon of the Church, prohibiting [any] to go to the Churches and conventicles of heretics, it is plain, by the testimony of all antiquity. The apostles themselves in their threescore and third canon, say thus: *if any man either of the clergy, or laity, do go into the Synagogue of the Jews or into conventicles of heretics to pray, let him be deposed, and excommunicated.* This canon of the Church, was exactly afterwards kept, and is mentioned very often, by the Fathers and Councils, by occasion of the like matter. As for example, when Origen was by a certain necessity, compelled to dwell in house together with one Paul, an heretic, to whom there resorted often, not only heretics, but some simple Catholics also for the fame of his excellent eloquence: yet they writ of Origen, that he could never be induced, by any means to be present at prayers where Paul was. And the reason is put down by them to be this: for that Origen even from his youth had kept and observed most diligently the canon of the Church. Here we see, what account was made in those days of this canon of the Church...(4)

## Alban Langdale's Response

And it is plain that the prophet [Elisha] allowed [Naaman's] doings for otherwise he would plainly and directly have said it was not lawful and that if he do not forthwith dispatch himself of that service, in vain it were for him either to worship or to build an Altar in the honour of the God of Israel. Thus we see that Naaman in that place might exhibit his service to the King, that in his fact he was no idolater nor committed mortal sin, and so by a consequent it appeareth that the bare, local abiding in the profane Temple at their time of service was not of itself a mortal sin. Now compare the act of him whom we speak of with Naaman from point to point and, though he be in the church of Protestants as Naaman was with idolators, yet his profession is known, he seemeth not to dissimule. By his own acts he uttereth himself evidently, and that he doth is not to any evil end nor with intention to deceive insomuch as he abstaineth from their works and to everyone which asketh he is ready and with firm mind determined to confess his faith. He is not pertinacious nor contemptuous against any law or authority. To the contrary, he confesseth his faith, avoideth all scandal as much as he may etc. And it is to little purpose it is objected Naaman was a novice, or no scandal or little was to be given there in Syria where all were idolators, for the bare act of being in such a place is here in question...

It is commendable in them which utterly rejected (as many did) to come to their churches, but...it seemeth no good consequent in every case; good men and martyrs did this, ergo this not to do or otherwise to do is Protestantism or mortal sin. For good men and martyrs in time of persecution have gone amongst Protestants and idolaters and sometimes to their churches and temples without grudge of conscience and are not defiled with the works of Protestantism or idolatry. And thus they did as circumstances moved them for circumstances do alter cases. And that good men and martyrs in time of persecution have not forbidden the bare and naked going to churches or conferences of them, and that without blemish, it appeareth by the examples of many, whereof some are hereafter set down. We read that the apostles were mixed among the wicked Jews in the temple and there prayed amongst them, though not with them, nor such prayers as the Jews prayed, who could not brook the name of Christ, and they observed the same times of prayer . . . Gamaliel was a disciple of Christ and a companion with the apostles, yet neither did he reveal himself to the Jews nor forbear the fellowship of the Pharisees, but to the end he might pacify their fury he remained among them, even in their consultation as well touching the law of God as vouching the civil policy . . . (5)

NOTES AND SOURCES

1. Robert Parsons, *A Christian Directory Guiding Men to their Eternal Salvation* (1683 edn.), 304–31.
2. Robert Parsons, *A comparison of a true Roman Catholike with a Protestant, wherby may bee discouered the difference of their spirits not only in things belonging to faith and belief, but also concerning their lives, conversations and manners: taken out of a more ample discourse of this subject, made by that worthy and reverend Father, R. Parsons, is the 20. Chapter of his Examen of Fox his Calendar, the last six Months.* (1620), 1–10.
3. Robert Parsons, *An answer to the fifth part of Reports lately set forth by Sir Edward Coke Knight, the King's Attorney General Concerning the ancient and modern municipal laws of England, which do appertain to spiritual power and jurisdiction* (1606), 23–31.
4. Robert Parsons, *A Brief Discourse Containing Certain Reasons why Catholics Refuse to Go to Church* (1580), unpag.
5. The National Archive: PRO, SP 12/144 fos. 137$^r$–143$^r$.

# St Robert Southwell                                      1561–1595

Robert Southwell was the son of a courtier and the grandson of one of the Visitors appointed under Henry VIII to assist in the suppression of religious houses in Norfolk—one of which, the convent of St Faith at Horsham, he received as a reward. Robert was brought up in a house created from the refectory of St Faith's. He left this Protestant home at the age of 15 and made his own way to Douai, Paris, and eventually to Rome, where he joined the Jesuits in 1578. He proved to be one of the most brilliant of the students, and in 1584, simultaneously with his ordination as a priest in the Society of Jesus, he became a tutor at the English College. In May 1586, following his own wish, he was sent on the mission to England, travelling from Rome with Henry Garnet, who was later—as Jesuit Provincial—to be executed in the wake of the Gunpowder Plot. He was appointed to serve in London, and after one or two close escapes from capture, took refuge in the house of Anne Howard, Countess of Arundel (whose husband was in prison, see pp. 167–70). Here, in relative safety, Southwell served as chaplain and confessor to Lady Howard, and as a discreet pastor to many other prominent Catholics. It was here, too, that he became a prolific author of poetry and prose, much of which came out in the years after his death. His poems included two of epic length, *Mary Magdalen's Funeral Tears* and *St Peter's Complaint*, but he quickly became better known for a long series of shorter poems, six of which are included below. His prose works included a strikingly stern and formal plea to his father to repent of his schism and rejoin the Church of his birth (published under the title *Dutiful Advice of a Loving Son to his Father* [1586]), *A Short Rule for a Good Life*, written for the Countess, and an *Epistle of Comfort* for her husband, who was condemned to death for allegedly procuring a priest to say a Mass for the success of the Armada. The government made little effort to arrest him until he published *An Humble Supplication to Her Majesty*, his only political statement and a powerful defence of the official Jesuit claim that 'the whole and only intent of our coming into this realm, is no other, but to labour for the salvation of souls and in peaceable and quiet sort to confirm them in the ancient Catholic faith'. The authorities, who saw his arguments as equivocation and likely to mislead moderate opinion, were able to prevent its publication, but not its widespread circulation in manuscript. Robert Southwell was now a marked man. An attempt to move him to the country led to his betrayal on 25 June 1592. He was one of the most severely tortured of the many priests taken in the Elizabethan Terror, but his trial and execution were postponed for three years. The first of his poems reprinted here is also probably his best-known poem, and it is one of those chosen by Benjamin Britten in his *Ceremony of Carols*. It is followed by three more poems on the Incarnation and the Christ-child, which are insistent themes. Next there is a meditation about St Mary Magdalen. It is one of a pair of poems, in the earlier edition of Southwell's poems, the other one being entitled 'Marie Magdalen's complaint at Christ's death'. The final poem is a powerful meditation on the Eucharist. We end with a single extract from his *The Dutifull Advice of a Loving Son to his Aged Father*. We have drawn this down from a printing in 1632 which is about its sixth printing—it had appeared in a number of anthologies, including, oddly, as an appendix to *Sir Walter Raleighs instructions to his sonne, and to posterity Whereunto is added A religious and dutifull advice of a loving sonne to his aged father*. It was still being reprinted in the later seventeenth century. Despite the harshness of its tone, Southwell's father bore him no malice, and when Robert was imprisoned in an insanitary, rat-infested cell, his father courageously lobbied privy counsellors to get his son moved to better conditions in the Tower, where he could supply him with clean clothes, food, and religious books.

## The Burning Babe

As I in hoary Winter's night stood shivering in the snow,
Surpris'd I was with sudden heat, which made my heart to glow;
And lifting up a fearful eye, to view what fire was near,
A pretty babe all burning bright did in the air appear;
Who scorched with excessive heat, such floods of tears did shed,
As though his floods should quench his flames, which with his tears
    were bred:
Alas (quoth he) but newly born, in fiery heats I fry,
Yet none approach to warm their hearts or seal my fire, but I;
My faultless breast the furnace is, the fuel wounding thorns:
Love is the fire, and sighs the smoke, the ashes, shames and scorns;
The fuel justice layeth on, and mercy blows the coals,
The metal in this furnace wrought, are men's defiled souls:
For which, as now on fire I am to work them to their good,
So will I melt into a bath, to wash them in my blood.
With this he vanished out of sight, and swiftly shrunk away,
And straight I called unto mind, that it was Christmas day. (1)

## A Child My Choice

Let folly praise that fancy loves, I praise and love that child,
Whose heart no thought, whose tongue no word, whose hand no deed
    defiled.

I praise him most, I love him best, all praise and love is his:
While him I love, in him I live, and cannot live amiss.
Love's sweetest mark, laud's highest theme, man's most desired light,
To love him life, to leave him death, to live in him, delight.
He mine by gift, I his by debt: thus each to others due:
First friend he was, best friend he is, all times will try him true.
Though young yet wise, though small yet strong, though man yet God
    he is:
As wise he knows, as strong he can, as God he loves to bliss,
His knowledge rules, his strength defends, his love doth cherish all:
His birth our Joy, his life our light, his death our end of thrall.
Alas, he weeps, he sighs, he pants, yet do his angels sing,
Out of his tears, his sighs and throbs, doth bud a joyful spring.
Almighty babe, whose tender arms can force all foes to fly:
Correct my faults, protect my life, direct me when I die. (2)

## The Nativity of Christ

Behold the father is his daughter's son,
The bird that built the nest is hatch'd therein,
The old of years an hour hath not out-run,
Eternal life to live doth now begin,
The word is dumb, the mirth of Heaven doth weep,
Might feeble is, and force doth faintly creep.

O dying souls! behold your living spring!
O dazzled eyes! behold your sun of grace!
Dull ears attend what word this word doth bring!
Up, heavy hearts, with joy your joy embrace!
From death, from dark, from deafness, from despairs,
This life, this light, this word, this joy repairs.

Gift better than Himself God doth not know,
Gift better than his God no man can see;
This gift doth here the giver given bestow,
Gift to this gift let each receiver be:
God is my gift, himself he freely gave me,
God's gift am I, and none but God shall have me.

Man alter'd was by sin from man to beast;
Beast's food is hay, hay is all mortal flesh;
Now God is flesh, and lies in manger press'd,
As hay the brutest sinner to refresh:
Oh happy field wherein this fodder grew,
Whose taste doth us from beasts to men renew! (3)

## Christ's Childhood

Till twelve years' age, how Christ his childhood spent
All earthly pens unworthy were to write;
Such acts to mortal eyes He did present,
Whose worth not men but angels must recite:
No nature's blots, no childish faults defiled,
Where grace was guide, and God did play the child.

In springing locks lay crouchèd hoary wit,
In semblant young, a grave and ancient port;
In lowly looks high majesty did sit,
In tender tongue sound sense of sagest sort:
Nature imparted all that she could teach,
And God supplied where nature could not reach.

His mirth of modest mien a mirror was;
His sadness temper'd with a mild aspect;
His eye to try each action was a glass,
Whose looks did good approve and bad correct;
His nature's gifts, his grace, his word and deed,
Well show'd that all did from a God proceed. (4)

## Mary Magdalen's Blush

The signs of shame that stain my blushing face
Rise from the feeling of my raving fits.
Whose joy, annoy; whose guerdon is disgrace;   [= reward, requital, or
                  recompense]
Whose solace, flies; whose sorrow, never flits.
Bad seed I sowed, worse fruit is now my gain,
Soon dying mirth begat long living pain,

Now pleasure ebbs, revenge begins to flow.
One day doth wreak the wrath that many wrought;
Remorse teach my guilty thoughts to know
How cheap I sold, that Christ so dearly bought.
Faults long unfelt doth conscience now bewray,  [= expose or reveal]
Which cares must cure, and tears much wash away.

All ghostly dints that grace at me did dart,
Like stubborn rock I forced to recoil:
Lo other flights an aim I made my heart,
Whose wounds, then welcome, now have wrought my foil,
Woe worth the bow, who worth the archers might,
That drove the arrows to the mark so right.

To pull them out, to leave them in, is death:
One, to this world, one, the world to come.
Wounds may I wear, and draw a doubtful breath,
But then my wounds will work a dreadful <u>dome</u>.     [= doom or judgement]
And for a world, whose pleasures pass away:
I lose a world, whose joys are past decay.

O sense, O soul, O hap, O hoped bliss,
You woo, you wean, you draw, you drive me back,
Your craft encountering, like their combat is
That never end but with some deadly wrack.
When sense doth win, the soul doth lose the field,
And present haps make future hopes to yield.

O Heaven lament, sense robbeth thee of saints
Lament, O souls, sense spoileth you of grace.
Yet sense doth scarce deserve these hard complaints,
Love is the thief, sense but the entring place.
Yet grant I must, sense is not free from sin,
For thief he is that that thief admitteth in. (5)

## Of the Blessed Sacrament of the Altar

In paschal feast, the end of ancient rite,
An entrance to never-ending grace,
Types to the truth, dim gleams to the light,
Performing deed presaging signs did chase:
Christ's final meal was fountain of our good,
For mortal meat he gave immortal food.

That which he gave he was, oh, peerless gift!
Both God and man he was, and both he gave.
He in his hands himself did truly lift,
Far off they see whom in themselves they have;
Twelve did he feed, twelve did their feeder eat,
He made, he dress'd, he gave, he was their meat.

They saw, they heard, they felt him sitting near,
Unseen, unfelt, unheard, they him received;
No diverse thing, though diverse it appear,
Though senses fail, yet faith is not deceived;
And if the wonder of their work be new,
Believe the worker 'cause his word is true.

Here truth belief, belief inviteth love,
So sweet a truth love never yet enjoy'd;

What thought can think, what will doth best approve,
Is here obtain'd where no desire is void:
The grace, the joy, the treasure here is such,
No wit can wish, nor will embrace so much.

Self-love here cannot crave more than it finds;
Ambition to no higher worth aspire;
The eagerest famine of most hungry minds
May fill, yea far exceed, their own desire:
In sum here is all in a sum express'd,
Of which the most of every good the best.

To ravish eyes here heavenly beauties are;
To win the ear sweet music's sweetest sound;
To lure the taste the angels' heavenly fare;
To soothe the scent divine perfumes abound;
To please the touch he in our hearts doth bed,
Whose touch doth cure the deaf, the dumb, the dead.

Here to delight the will true wisdom is;
To woo the will of every good the choice;
For memory a mirror showing bliss,
Here all that can both sense and soul rejoice;
And if to all, all this it doth not bring,
The fault is in the men, not in the thing.

Though blind men see no light, the sun doth shine;
Sweet <u>cates</u> are sweet, though fever'd tastes deny it;        [= delicacies,
                                                                   dainty food]

Pearls precious are, though trodden on by swine;
Each truth is true, though all men do not try it;
The best still to the bad doth work the worst;
Things bred to bliss do make the more accursed.

The angels' eyes, whom veils cannot deceive,
Might best disclose that best they did discern;
Men must with sound and silent faith receive
More than they can by sense or reason learn;
God's power our proofs, his works our wit exceed,
The doer's might is reason of his deed.

A body is endow'd with ghostly rights;
A nature's work from nature's law is free;
In heavenly sun lie hid eternal lights,
Lights clear and near, yet them no eye can see:
Dead forms a never-dying life do shroud;
A boundless sea lies in a little cloud.

The God of hosts in slender host doth dwell,
Yea, God and man with all to either due;
That God that rules the Heavens and rifled Hell,
That man whose death did us to life renew;
That God and man that is the angels' bliss,
In form of bread and wine our nature is.

Whole may his body be in smallest bread,
Whole in the whole, yea whole in every crumb;
With which be one or ten thousand fed,
All to each one, to all but one doth come;
And though each one as much as all receive,
Not one too much, nor all too little have.

One soul in man is all in every part;
One face at once in many mirrors shines;
One fearful noise doth make a thousand start;
One eye at once of countless things defines;
If proofs of one in many nature frame,
God may in stronger sort perform the same.

God present is at once in every place,
Yet God in every place is ever one;
So may there be by gifts of ghostly grace,
One man in many rooms, yet filling none;
Sith angels may effects of bodies show,

God angels' gifts on bodies may bestow.
What God as author made he alter may;
No change so hard as making all of nought;
If Adam framed were of slimy clay,
Bread may to Christ's most sacred flesh be wrought:
He may do this that made with mighty hand
Of water wine, a snake of Moses's wand. (6)

## Advice to a Father

The prerogative of Infancy is innocency; of childhood, reverence; of manhood, maturity; and of old age, wisdom.

And seeing then that the chiefest properties of wisdom are to be mindful of things past, careful for things present, and provident for things to come, use you now the privilege of nature's talent to the benefit of your own soul, and procure hereafter to be wise in well-doing, and watchful in the foresight of future harm. To serve the world you are now unable and though you were able, yet you have little cause to be willing, seeing that it never gave you but an unhappy welcome, a hurtful entertainment, and now doth abandon you with an unfortunate farewell.

You have long sowed in a field of flint, which could bring you nothing forth but a crop of cares, and afflictions of spirit; rewarding your labours with remorse, and affording for your gain, eternal danger.

It is now more than a seasonable time to alter the course of so unthriving a husbandry and to enter into the field of God's church in which, sowing the seed of repentant sorrow, and watering them with the tears of humble contrition, you may hereafter reap a more beneficial harvest, and gather the fruits of everlasting comfort.

Remember, I pray you, that your spring is spent, your summer overpast, you are now arrived at the fall of the leaf, yea, and winter colours have long since stained your hoary head.

Be not careless (saith Saint *Augustine*) though our loving Lord bear long with offenders; for the longer he stays, not finding amendment, the sorer he will scourge when he comes to judgement; and his patience in so long forbearing, is only to lend us respite to repent, and not any wise to enlarge us leisure to sin.

He that is tossed with variety of storms, and cannot come to his desired port, maketh not much way, but is much turmoiled. So he that hath passed many years, and purchased little profit, hath had a long being, but a short life. For life is more to be measured by well-doing than by number of years, seeing that most men by many days do but procure many deaths, and other in short space attained to the life of infinite ages. What is the body without the soul, but a corrupt carcass? And what is the soul without God, but a sepulchre of sin?

If God be the way, the life, and the truth, he that goeth without him, strayeth; and he that liveth without him, die-eth; and he that is not taught by him, erreth.

Well (saith *Saint Augustine*) God is our true, and chiefest life, from whom to revolt, is to fall; to whom to return is to rise, and in whom to stay is to stand sure.

God is he from whom to depart is to die; to whom to repair, is to revive and in whom to dwell, is life for ever. Be not then of that number of those that begin not to live, till they be ready to die: and then, after a foe's desert, come to crave of God a friend's entertainment ... (7)

NOTES AND SOURCES

1. Robert Southwell, *Saint Peters Complaint Newlie Augmented with Other Poems* (1602), 74.
2. Robert Southwell, *Moeoniae. Or, Certaine Excellent Poems and Spirituall Hymnes* (1595), 46.
3. *The Poetical Works of the Rev. Robert Southwell*, ed. William B. Turnbull (London: John Russell Smith, 1856), 110–11.
4. Ibid. 118.
5. Robert Southwell, *Saint Peters Complaint Newlie Augmented with Other Poems* (1602), 35–6.
6. *Poetical Works*, ed. Turnbull, 150–3.
7. Robert Southwell, *The Dutifull Advice of a Loving Son to his Aged Father* (1632 edn.).

## Elizabeth Grymeston                                        c.1563–1604

Elizabeth had an extraordinary life. The daughter of a substantial Norfolk landowner (Martin Bernye), she was married no later than 1584 to Christopher Grymeston, Fellow and Bursar of Gonville and Caius College, Cambridge. This is doubly surprising. Fellows of Cambridge colleges had to be unmarried; and Christopher and Elizabeth were church papists. The Master and other Fellows had to cast a doubly indulgent eye over these irregularities. Finally, in 1593, Christopher had to resign. Meanwhile, Elizabeth had to endure the 'undeserved wrath' of her

mother, presumably on account of her increasingly open recusancy, and even more she had
to endure the loss of eight of the nine children she bore by Christopher. By 1604, at the age of
40, and dying of a 'languishing consumption' she had written an advice book for her one
surviving child, a son called Bernye Grymstone, and it was published (in several editions) by
Richard Verstegan. We include two chapters from this work.

## A Sinner's Glass

What is the life of a man but a continual battle and defiance with God? What have
our eyes and ears been, but open gates to send in loads of sin into our mind? What
have our powers and senses been, but tinder to take and fuel to feed the flame of
concupiscence? What hath the body been but a stews of an adulteress, but a forge
of Satan, where the fire of our affections kindled with wicked suggestions, have
inflamed the passions of our heart and made it the anvil to turn us to most ugly
shapes of deformed sensuality? What hath our soul, which is the receipt of the
Blessed Trinity, betrothed to Christ in Baptism, beautified with grace, ordained
with the fellowship of the angels to eternal bliss, what hath it been, but a most vile
broker, presenting to the will allurements of sin? What hath our will been, but a
common harlot lusting after every delight wherein she took liking? What is our
memory but a register of most detestable and abominable facts committed by us?
What hath our reason, but a captured vagabond, subdued by every passion?

> The sin that conquers grace by wicked ure [= practice, performance]
> So soils our souls as they can have no cure.

So that by this metamorphosis we are become more odious to God than the
devil himself. For the devil by creation was more beautiful than we; it was sin that
deformed him, and that sin that made him odious makes us detestable, for our
sins are worse than his, and we not so good as he. For his sin was one, and ours are
infinite; he sinned before the stipend of sin was known, our after notice and
experience of it. He sinned created in innocency, we sin restored unto it. He
persisted in malice being of God, we rejected continue in hatred against him that
recalled us. His heart was hardened against him that punished him, ours obdurate
against him that allureth us. So that our case is now such as infinite goodness
detesteth and infinite love cannot condole. The earth was created for a place of
pleasure, the air was created temperate, creatures were made to be obedient to
man, all things framed to his best content—but see how sin hath transformed
pleasure into plagues, famine and murders many in number, grievous in quality,
and ordinary in experience, which indeed are *initia doloris* [= the beginnings of
our grief], for the damned suffer death without death, decay without decay, envy
without envy. For their death ever liveth, their end ever beginneth, and their decay
never ceaseth, but are always healed to be new wounded, dying but never dead,
repaired only to be anew decayed. (1)

## The Union of Mercy and Justice

There be two feet whereon God walketh on the hearts of men, Mercy and truth
which a sinner must fall down with Mary and kiss, that in respect of God's Justice
we may retain fear, and in regard of his Mercy conceive hope. For all the ways of

God are Mercy and Truth: mercy that we may not despair, and truth that we may not presume.

> O who shall shew the countenance and gestures
> Of mercy and justice which fair sacred sisters
> With equal poise do ever balance then
> Th'unhanging projects of the king of heaven!
> Th'one stern of look, th'other mild aspecting
> Th'one pleas'd with tears, th'other blood affecting;
> Th'one bears the sword of vengeance unrelenting.
> Th'other brings pardon for the true repenting.

Because God is merciful, wilt thou build a nest of sin, as the psalmist saith, upon his back: thou can'st not sever his mercy from his justice, and then justice will sentence. Is God a just God, a terrible God, into whose hands it is a horrible thing to fall? Thou can'st not separate his justice from his mercy: she will proclaim 'the mercy of God is higher than all his works', his mercy exalteth herself above his judgements: 'for he wills that all men to be saved'. He that can that he will [*sic*], will not the death of one sinner, but that he may turn from his wickedness and live for ever; he offereth mercy to all, but never useth his justice but upon necessity. I will sing unto thee, O Lord, mercy and truth together not mercy alone, as not fearing thy judgement, nor truth alone, as despairing in thy mercies. But thy mercies shall breed a love, and thy judgements shall make me fear to impath myself in the way of sinners:

> *For hope of help still comfort gives*
> *While mercy still with justice lives* (2)

NOTES AND SOURCES

1. Elizabeth Grymeston, *Miscelanea. Meditations. Memoratiues* (1604) unpag., but chap. V.
2. Ibid., unpag., but chap. VI.

## Richard Verstegan (formerly Rowlands)          1548–1640

Richard Verstegan was the son of London cooper and the grandson of a Flemish refugee. He resumed his grandfather's name in preference to the one his father had assumed, but it was as Richard Rowlands that he matriculated at Christchurch Oxford by 1564. His conversion to Catholicism occurred while he was undergraduate and he left the University without a degree 'to avoid oaths'. He took up printing and by the late 1570s he was back in Flanders, where he became one of the main printers for the Catholic cause. From 1585 to 1609 he was a pensioner of the King of Spain. His most famous publishing venture was the *Theatrum crudelitatum haereticorum nostri temporis*, with its brilliantly conceived and executed engravings of the brutal martyrdom of Catholics in England. He played a large part in the design of these engravings; and although he was first and foremost the principal publisher to those planning the English Jesuit mission, he was also a significant author in his own right. We include here examples of his religious verse (a verse translation of one of the penitential psalms) and also an extract from his *Primer or Office of the Blessed Virgin Mary*. This was the most influential of all the manuals of prayers. First published in 1599, and with forty-two separate editions in the next century, it printed the Latin texts on the left-hand page and Verstegan's translations on the right. We include part of his preface and enough extracts from the first section of daily prayers for Our Lady, to give a sense of the whole and of the strength of the translations. *The Primer* contained translations of all the principal liturgical prayers of the church, of the Golden Litany, the Creed, as well as special prayers for all occasions.

## A Penitential Psalm

In imitation of the second penitential Psal. Beginning. *Beati quorum remisse sunt: Psalm. 31.*

> O how much blessed may they remain
> That pardon for their guilt obtain,
> And whose great ill and each offence
> Lies hid in contrite penitence.
>
> What happy state may he be in
> To whom our Lord imputes no sin,
> Whose conscience doth no guile retain
> That can himself beguile again.
>
> I did my sins in silence hold,
> In grief whereof my bones grew old,
> Meanwhile my days in plaints of pains
> Wthout redress I spent in vain.
>
> But when O Lord thy heavy hand
> No day or night I could withstand,
> But that in anguish overworn
> My conscience pricked as with a thorn.
>
> Lo then O Lord I did begin
> utter all my secret sin,
> No longer list I ought conceal
> But each injustice to reveal.
>
> Against myself I said will I
> My wrongs confess and faults defy,
> To thee O Lord, O Lord to thee
> That hast from all absolved me.
>
> And since I thus thy mercies find
> Let each of good and godly mind,
> Approach to thee in happy time
> To pray for pardon of his crime.
>
> For such as so do sink in sin
> That still they plunged lie therein,

Unable are of thee to gain
What contrite sinners can obtain.

O Lord my refuge rests in thee
When troubles do environ me
O free me then my freedom's joy
From such as seek me to annoy.

Great comforts Lord I do conceive
Thou me thy servant wilt not leave,
But wilt instruct and guide me right
And keep me ever in thy sight.

O thee that careless are of grace
Behold and see your brutish case,
And be not as the horse and mule
That live devoid of reason's rule.

And thou O Lord in mercies rife
Vouchsafe restrain their straying life
With bit and bridle make them stay
That unto thee will not obey.

Since that for those of sinful trade
Full many scourges there be made,
Well him, that doth in God repose
Whose mercies may his soul enclose.

Be therefore joyful in our Lord
All that to righteousness accord,
Let each with gladness bear his part
That hath a pure and perfect heart.

All glory be O Lord to thee
And to thy Son in like degree
As also to the holy Ghost
Perpetual and enduring most.
AMEN. (1)

## An Introduction to the Office of Our Lady

For the more utility of such of the English nation as understand not the Latin
tongue, it hath been thought convenient to publish in Latin and English the
Primer or Office of the Blessed Virgin Mary, containing nothing but matter of
prayer and devotion and therefore not offensive to any except it be in respect of
the service of God according to the ancient faith of our Christian forefathers, who
have continued in former ages (even as the most part of Christendom still

observeth) the worthy magnifying of his most blessed mother, fulfilling therein her own prophesy of such generations of faithful people as ever should call her blessed. For unto her to whom the Almighty God of Heaven did vouchsafe to send in embassy his holy archangel Gabriel, by whose mouth should first be pronounced 'Hail Mary full of grace the Lord is with thee, blessed art thou among women etc'. Well may earthly creatures showing so worthy an example and precedent, often repeat this glorious salutation, and sue for her intercession unto him with whom she now liveth in everlasting glory... The veneration of other saints and desire of their intercession hath in like manner by devout Christians been used; who, knowing them to be united with God in such charity, that they desire the salvation of all and rejoice at the conversion of sinners, do also know that God's will is such that he will be praised and glorified in his faith.

In the translation of the psalms and other parts of holy Scripture, the true sense (as is most requisite) hath been sought to be observed than any phrases in our language more affected and pleasing. The hymns in the office of our Lady as also those for the whole year (notwithstanding the difficulty) are so turned into English metre, as they may be sung unto the same tunes in English as they bear in Latin. I wish that all may be to the increase of thy devotion, to the supreme honour of the most holy, glorious and undivided Trinity, God the Father, God the Son and God the Holy Ghost; and to all laud of the Blessed Virgin and all saints
R.V.

Vouchsafe good reader to remember in thy prayers such as have assisted to the furtherance of this work. (2)

## From the Office of Our Lady

The Office of Our Lady to be said from the day after the Purification unto the evening of the Saturday before the fourth Sunday of Advent: saving that on the day of the Annunciation, it is said, as hereafter followeth in the Advent.

### AT MATTINS

Hail Mary, full of grace, our Lord is with thee: blessed art thou among women, and blessed is the fruit of thy womb Jesus. Holy Mary, Mother of God, pray for us sinners, now and in the hour of our death. Amen.

The which is always said in the beginning of the hour of our blessed lady.

V. Thou O Lord wilt open our lips

R. And my mouth shall declare thy praise

V. Incline unto my aid, O God.

R. O Lord make haste to help me.

Glory be to the Father, and to the Son, and to the Holy Ghost

Even as it was in the beginning and now and ever and world without end, Amen, Alleluia.

So Alleluia is said at all hours from the evening of Easter Eve unto the compline of the Saturday before the Sunday of Septuagessima. For then unto the evensong of Easter Eve is said.

Praise be to thee, O Lord, O king of eternal glory.

THE INVITATORY

Hail Mary full of grace, Our Lord is with thee.

And is again repeated

Hail Mary full of grace, Our Lord is with thee.

In the time of Easter is added Alleluia and in like manner in the end of the Antiphons, Versicles and Responses.

THE 94 PSALM

Come let us rejoice unto our Lord. Let us make joy to God our Saviour. Let us approach to his presence in confession, and in psalms let us make joy unto him.
  Hail Mary full of grace, Our Lord is with thee.
  For our God is a great Lord and a great King above all Gods, because our Lord repelleth not his people, for that in his hand are all the bounds of the earth. And he beholdeth the heights of the mountains.
  Our Lord is with thee
  For the sea is his and he made it; and his hands founded the dry land—come let us adore and fall down before God; let us weep before our Lord that made us; because he is the Lord our God; we are his people and the sheep of his pasture
  Hail Mary full of grace, Our Lord is with thee.
  Today if you shall hear his voice, harden not your hearts, as in the provocation according to the day of temptation in the wilderness, where your fathers tempted me, proved and saw my works
  Our Lord is with thee.
  Forty years was I nigh unto this generation and said, they always err in heart; and they have not known my ways, to whom I swear in my wrath of they shall enter into my rest.
  Hail Mary full of grace, Our Lord is with thee.
  Glory be to the Father and to the Son, and to the Holy Ghost, even as it was in the beginning and now and ever, and world without end. Amen
  Our Lord is with thee
  Hail Mary full of grace, Our Lord is with thee.

THE HYMN

> Whom earth and sea and <u>eke</u> the skies [= also]
> Adore and worship and declare
> As ruler of the triple frame
> The closure of Maria bare,[26]

---

[26] This line is hard to fathom (it translates from the Latin: 'Claustrum Mariae baiulat'). Other editions of the Primer have another translation of this hymn which conveys the sense better: 'He whom Earth, Sea and Heaven above | Worship, adore & glorify; Who the World's three-fold frame doth move, in Mary's closed womb doth lie.' *The Primer According to the Last Edition of the Roman Breuiarie* (England: English Secret Press, 1617).

Whom the sun and moon and sun and all
Do serve in their due time and space,
A maiden's inward parts do bear,
Bedewed with celestial grace.

Blest is the mother of this gift.
Whose womb as in a coffer held
The maker that surmounteth all,
Who in his hand the world doth <u>weld</u>. [= join together]

She blessed is by heavenly news
And fruitful by the Holy Ghost
From out whose womb was yielded forth
Whom nations had desired most.

Glory be unto thee, O Lord.
That born was of the Virgin pure.
With the father and holy Ghost.
All ages ever to endure. Amen.

These three psalms following are said upon the Sundays, Mondays and Thursdays, at Nocturne.

The 8: psalm ... the antiphon, 'Blessed art thou'

The 18 psalm ... the antiphon 'even as elected myrrh'

The 23 psalm, the antiphon 'Before the bed'

[*others for the other days of the week*]

Thou didst remain an inviolate Virgin after thy child-bearing. O mother of God, pray for us.

V. Grace is poured forth in thy lips

R. Therefore God has blessed thee for ever.

Our Father (in secret unto the) V. and lead us unto temptation R. And deliver us from

Evil.

### THE ABSOLUTION

V. By the prayers and merits of the ever blessed Virgin Mary and of all the saints, our Lord bring us to the Kingdom of Heaven. R.Amen

V. Bid me O Lord to Bless

The blessing. The Virgin Mary with her benign Son bless us. Amen.

[*Three alternative readings with their responsaries are given*]

The Te Deum is said from Christmas to Septuagesima Sunday and from Easter Day unto Advent (3)

NOTES AND SOURCES

1. Richard Verstegan, *Odes In imitation of the seauen penitential psalmes, with sundry other poemes and ditties tending to deuotion and pietie* (1601), 3–8.
2. *The Primer or Office of the Blessed Virgin Mary According to the Reformed Latin and with lyke graces privileged. Printed at Antwerp* (1619), title page.
3. Ibid., fos. 1–15.

# St Philip Howard, Earl of Arundel       1557–1595

St Philip Howard was the eldest son of Thomas Howard, 4th Duke of Norfolk, and of Mary Howard, née Fitzalan, heiress of the 12th Earl of Arundel. His father was executed for treason in 1572, having conspired to replace Elizabeth as queen by her cousin Mary Queen of Scots (whom he aspired to marry). Philip inherited his properties but the titles belonging to the Howards were abolished. In due course, on his mother's death, he was allowed to take the title of her father and he became 13th Earl of Arundel. He was surely and inexorably drawn into a longing to be reconciled with the Catholic Church, a conviction greatly strengthened by what he read and heard of the life and death of St Edmund Campion. He gradually withdrew from attending the services of the established Church, even when his official position in Elizabeth's household required his attendance upon her in the Chapel Royal. He was reconciled to the Catholic Church in 1584. Fearing the Queen's reaction, he planned to flee abroad, but his boat was intercepted, and he was imprisoned in the Tower. Initially heavily fined and imprisoned for recusancy, and for leaving the realm without consent, he was subsequently arraigned for treason in 1588 when Father William Bennet SJ confessed under torture that Howard had paid him to say a Mass for the success of the Armada. He was sentenced to death and stripped of all remaining titles, but Elizabeth made it clear that, if he would only once attend a Church of England service, he would be pardoned and fully restored to his lands and titles. He refused and spent his remaining years in prayer, meditation, study, and the translation, among other things, of *An Epistle of Jesus Christ to the Faithful Soule* (1595) by Johann Justus. He left in manuscript three treatises 'of the excellency and utility of virtue'. Two poetic works are also ascribed to him, the first, a meditation inspired by a visit with Elizabeth to the ruins of the shrine at Walsingham (he is named as author on a contemporary copy in the Pepys Library in Cambridge); the second a series of four meditations on death and resurrection (ascribed on the title page of its 1606 printing to St Robert Southwell, but now established as by Howard). Howard's extraordinary resolution as a prisoner and the ultimate sacrifice he made for his religious beliefs secured his beatification in 1929 and canonization in 1970. The spirit in which he journeyed towards martyrdom is summed up by a Latin inscription he etched into the wall of his cell in the Tower, which can be translated as: 'The more affliction we endure for Christ in this world, the more glory we shall obtain with Christ in the next'. The first poem ascribed to him is 'In the wrackes of Walsingham'. It is in the same metre as the medieval Pynchon Walsingham Ballad printed above (pp. 19–22), and was quickly set to a tune that itself became the basis of sets of keyboard variations by many composers, including Byrd and Bull. It was one of the most subversive songs of the Catholic underground; and is clearly evoked in the first of Ophelia's 'mad songs' in *Hamlet*, grist to the mill of those who see Shakespeare as a Nicodemite Catholic. All in all, it demonstrates the power of the 'reformation of the landscape' not simply to evoke nostalgia for a lost world, but anger and contempt for those who celebrated the wilful destruction of places suffused with holiness. A decade after his death, exacerbated by the conditions in which he was held prisoner, a 'divine poem' was published in London and ascribed to 'R.St ' (Robert Southwell), whose death on the scaffold had occurred earlier in 1595, the year of Howard's own death. But there is no doubt that this poem—or sequence of poems—was written from the cell in the Tower. It consists of four meditations, on 'the hour of death', on 'the day of judgement', on 'the pains of Hell', and on 'the joys of Heaven'. There is no reference to Purgatory, probably because of the logic of the form. In the first meditation, the dying man is made to realize too late, only as his life ebbs away, just how much he has loved earthly things 'and to this world hast made thyself a thrall'. He then has to face a stern judge who asks questions that the deceased cannot answer; and then, as if this were not bad enough, Satan turns up, 'and to the Lord doth say | O righteous judge, this wretch I ought to have | for in his life he could not you obey | but with his heart, himself to me he gave', a claim he backs up with all too much evidence. In the third poem, the author finds himself condemned to Hell, and he gives a grim account of the way every one of our senses is assailed by perpetual pain. But—like Dives in Jesus' parable of Dives and Lazarus—he is able to see what he cannot have, the joys of Heaven. What follows is the first part (about a third) of that vision of Heaven. This is a poem of rare ambition, about 5,000 words in length altogether.

## Walsingham Lamented

In the wracks of Walsingham
Whom should I choose
But the Queen of Walsingham,
to be guide to my muse?

Then thou Prince of Walsingham,
Grant me to frame
Bitter plaints to rue thy wrong,
bitter woe for thy name.

Bitter was it, oh! to see
The silly sheep
Murdered by the ravening wolves
While the shepherds did sleep!

Bitter was it, oh! to view
the sacred vine,
Whilst the gardeners played all close,
rooted up by the swine.

Bitter, bitter, oh! to behold
the grass to grow
Where the walls of Walsingham
so stately did show.

Such were the works of Walsingham
while she did stand!

Such are the wracks as now do show
of that holy land!

Level, Level with the ground
the towers do lie,
Which with their golden glittering tops
pierced out to the sky!

Where were gates, no gates are now;
the ways unknown
Where the press of friars did pass,
while her fame far was blown.

Owls do shreek where the sweetest hymns
lately were sung;
Toads and serpents hold their dens
where the Psalmers did throng.

Weep, weep, o Walsingham!
whose days are nights,
Blessing turned to blasphemies,
holy deeds to despites!

Sin is where our Lady sat,
Heaven turned is to Hell!
Satan sits where our Lord did sway
Walsingham, oh! farewell! (1)

## Of the Joys of Heaven

And first behold the beauty of the place,
Where all the saints with Christ in glory reign,
Where honour is not mixed with disgrace,
Where joy is free from task of any pain:
Where great rewards attend on good deserts,
And all delights possesseth faithful hearts.

O wicked wretch! This city now behold,
Which doth surpass the reach of any thought,
The gates are pearl, the streets are finest gold,
With precious stones the walls are wholly wrought:
Of sun and moon it needeth not the light,
For ever there the lamb is shining bright.

And from his seat a crystal river flows,
Where life doth run, and pleasures ever springs,

On every side a tree of comfort grows,
Which saving health to every nation brings:
It worketh rest, and stinteth worldly strife,
It flee-eth death, and bringeth endless life.

This goodly place all beauty doth surmount,
And all this world in largeness passeth far:
The earth itself in bigness in account
Not equal is unto the smallest star:
O worthy place whose glory doth excel!
Thrice happy they that there attains to dwell!

No saint there is but brighter seems to be
Then sun or moon whose beauties wonders breed:
What glory then so many saints to see,
Which all the stars in number far exceed!
All glorious there where glory doth abound,
O blessed state where bliss is ever found!

Archangels are but under-servants there,
And angels do their makers will obey,
The powers in joy with triumphs do appear,
The beauties shine, the thrones their beams display:
The cherubim do yield a famous light,
The seraphim with love are burning shining bright.

Here patriarchs have their joy for all their pain,
The prophets eke with endless glory blest,                    [= also]
The martyrs do a worthy crown obtain,
The virgins find a haven of happy rest:
To all their joys in glory they are met,
And now possess what long they sought to get.

Those sacred saints remain in perfect peace,
Which Christ confessed and walked in his ways,
They swim in bliss which now shall never cease,
And singing all, his name for ever praise:
Before his throne in white they daily stand,
And carry palms of triumph in their hands.

The angels then are next in their degree,
Whose order is in number to be nine,
No heart can think what joy it is to see
How all those troupes with lamps in glory shine:
The joy is more than writing can express:
O happy eyes that may these joys possess!

Above them all, the Virgin hath a place,
Which caused the world with comfort to abound:
The beams do shine in her unspotted face,
And with the stars her head is richly crowned:
In glory she all creatures passeth far:
The moon her shoes, the sun her garments are.

O Queen of Heaven! o pure and glorious sight!
Most blessed thou above all women art!
This city drunk thou makest with delight,
And with thy beams rejoicest every heart:
Our bliss was lost and that thou didst restore,
The Angels all and men do thee adore.

Lo! here the look which Angels do admire!
Lo! here the spring from whom all goodness flows!
Lo! here the sight that men and saints desire!
Lo! here the stalks on which our comfort grows!
Lo this is she whom Heaven and earth embrace,
Whom God did choose and filled full of grace.

And next to her, but in a higher throne,
Our Saviour in his manhood sitteth here:
From whom proceeds all perfect joy alone,
And in whose face all glory doth appear:
The saints' delight conceived cannot be,
When they a man the Lord of angels see.

They ravished are with joy in seeing this,
How Christ our Lord the highest place obtains:
They now behold the seat of endless bliss,
And joy to mark how he in triump reigns
What joy to men moreover can befall
Than here to see a man the Lord of all?

More joy that yields than any can devise,
A greater bliss than may in words be told,
His piercing beams doth dazzle all their eyes,
His brightness scarce his angels can behold:
The saints in him their wished comfort finds,
And now enjoy what most content their minds ... (2)

NOTES AND SOURCES

1. Taken from <http://www.walsinghamanglicanarchives.org.uk/arundelballad.htm>. We are grateful to the archive staff at the Anglican Shrine at Walsingham for assistance with this 'Ballad'.
2. [Philip Howard], *A Fourefould Meditation of the Foure Last Things* (1606), unpag.

# John Wilson                                        fl. 1608

Following the Gunpowder Plot of 1605 and the imposition of the Oath of Allegiance, the
Catholic community was deeply divided. Was it possible to take the oath with all necessary
mental reservations, or would that be mortal sin? How were Catholics to maintain a secular
allegiance to their king and a religious duty to the Church? As this debate raged, and as priests
gave conflicting advice to their subjects, one secular priest, John Wilson, published a book
that called people back to essentials. In 1608, he published an *English martyrologie, containing a summary of the lives of the glorious and renowned saints of the three kingdoms,
England, Scotland and Ireland, collected and distributed into months, after the form of a
calendar, according to every saint's festivity.* There was one (or occasionally more) from
across the first millennium for every day of the year. Not all were martyrs; all offered their lives
for Christ, but some as confessors rather than martyrs, bearing witness by steadfastness in
adversity without shedding their blood. The English saints of the past were testimony to the
need for Catholics to lead *uncompromising* lives of Christian virtue; in every age, the followers
of Christ are called to self-sacrifice. Four hundred pages of exemplary lives of these Celtic and
Anglo-Saxon saints led on, however, to a simple and austere list of those who had, as the title
page concludes, *suffered death in England for defence of the Catholic cause, since Henry
VIII's breach with the see Apostolic, unto this day.* In offering a selection here, we have
identified the peak periods in the 1530s and in the early 1580s. It is striking that Wilson is
not comfortable listing the Gunpowder Plotters as martyrs. There was too much politics in
their actions. We begin with the list for January and with the lives of those memorialized in the
first week of that month.

## The Saints for January

To the Catholics of England, Scotland and Ireland:

When I had almost brought this little work to an end (dear Catholic
countrymen), I began to think with my self, to whom, among many so dearly
affected, I might make bold to dedicate the same, thereby the better to
patronize that, which over-bold presumption had conceived. And though
the thing itself needed none other patrons or protectors than the glorious
saints themselves, of whom we are now to treat: yet because I might not
seem, in a manner, to defraud any herein of their right and interest, which
I imagined; at last I thought it most convenient that you, whose hearts and
minds are firmly fixed in the honour and veneration of so glorious and
elected wights [= creatures, beings], and for the embracing whereof you
daily suffer so great and many persecutions, should take upon you this
protection, for whose comfort and consolation principally (next after the
honour of the saints themselves) the same is published. I do not here offer
unto you any new thing (which is always commonly the custom of such to do
who dedicate their works to others) but that which so many ages since, hath
by a certain inheritance, as it were, of your forefathers, descended still, by
good right and title, unto you, and shall hereafter unto your, and all
posterity. Only this, that I have here gathered together, and restored unto
you again, that which the injury of times had violently taken from you, and

sought to abolish all memory thereof: humbly presenting the same, as a duty of my love towards you, and my dearest country. Wishing you to take in good part, what my poor endeavours have been able to produce herein for your spiritual consolation, in these your so great afflictions and pressures: with desire to be made partaker of your good prayers.

## THE CALENDAR

January

1 Mydwyn, Confessor; Elvan, Bishop

2 A Thousand holy Martyrs

3 Melorius, Martyr

4 Croniac, Confessor

5 Edward, King.

6 Peter, Confessor

7 Cedd, Confessor

8 Guithelm, Bishop

9 Britwald, Bishop, Adrian Abbot.

10 Sethrid, Virgin

11 Egwin, Bishop

12 Benedict, Abbot

13 Kentigern, Abbot

14 Beno, Confessor

15 Alfred, King

16 Henry, hermit

17 Milwid, Virgin

18 Deicola, Abbot; Ulfrid, Bishop

19 Wulstan, Bishop; Henry; Bishop

20 Elfreda, Virgin

21 Malcalline, Abbot

22 Britwald, Bishop

23 Boisil, Abbot

24 Sophias, Bishop; Cadoc, Martyr

25 Conversion of Paul; Eoglodius, Confessor

26 Theorigitha (Torgyth), Virgin

27 Palladius, Bishop

28 Arwald, Martyr

29 Gildas, Abbot

30 Amnichade, Confessor

31 Adamnan Confessor

## The first day

At Glastonbury Abbey in Somersetshire the commemoration of the saints Mydwyn and Elvan, confessors, who being two noble ancient Britons by birth, were sent by King Lucius of Brittany to Rome to Pope Eleutherius, to treat of his conversion to Christian faith, and being there both baptized by the said Pope, and St Elvan made a Bishop, they were sent back again into Brittany, together with Fugatius and Damianus, who baptized the King and the greatest part of his nation, in the year of our Lord 183. And after they had much laboured in teaching and instructing the new flock of Christ in our Island for many years, full of sanctity of life, and venerable old age, they both ended their happy days, about the year of Christ, an hundred ninety and eight, and were buried at Glastonbury, as the ancient records of that abbey do witness.

And in other places of many holy martyrs, confessors, and virgins; to whose prayers and merits, we humbly commend ourselves.

This last clause is always thus to be repeated in the end of every day.

## The second day

At Lichfield in Staffordshire the commemoration of a thousand holy martyrs, of the British nation, who newly converted to the faith of Christ, and being disciples and followers of St Amphibal, priest, that suffered in the persecution of Dioclesian Emperor, and present at his martyrdom near unto the town of St Albans in Hertfordshire, fled thence for fear of like torments; but being overtaken at Lichfield, they were all in hatred of Christian religion, there most cruelly put to death, by commandment of the President of Brittany, about the year of Christ three hundred and four. The place where they suffered, was afterward called Cadaverum campus, which is as much to say as Lichfield in English, and where the foresaid city is now built, and thereof taketh his ancient name and denomination. And in other places of many holy martyrs, confessors, and virgins, etc.

## The third day

In Cornwall the commoration of St Meliorus martyr, son to Melianus, duke of that province, who being his father's only son and heir, and secretly made a Christian, was by a brother-in-law of his called Rinaldus a pagan, cruelly murdered, partly in hatred of his faith and religion, and partly to enjoy his inheritance. He first cut off his right hand, and then his left leg, and last of all his head, about the year of Christ four hundred and eleven. His body was buried in an old Church in Cornwall, whereat in sign of his innocency, it pleased God forthwith to work many miracles; where also his relics were kept with great honour and veneration, even until our days.

## The fourth day

In Scotland the commemoration of St Croniac, confessor, who born of a very noble parentage in that kingdom, took a religious habit, and became a monk of the venerable order of St Benedict, where in all kind of sanctity of life, and monastical discipline, he ended his blessed days, about the year of Christ, six hundred and fifty. His memory is yet very famous amongst the Catholics, as well of the Scottish, as the Irish Nation; in both which kingdoms in former times, many churches and altars have been dedicated in his honour. It is here, and in many other places to be observed, that the Irish and Scottish historiographers do oftentimes disagree about the native country of divers saints mentioned in this martyrology; For that in ancient times the Island of Hibernia being called Scotia, hath caused a great confusion, especially amongst foreign writers, who for want of knowledge herein, do often confound the one nation with the other.

### The fifth day

At Westminster by London, the deposition of St Edward King and Confessor, who being yet in his Mother's womb, was elected, crowned, and anointed King by St Peter the Apostle, as it was miraculously revealed to St Britwald Bishop of Winchester, that lived at the same time. He was very famous for working of miracles, especially in curing a disease of swelling in people's throats, which was afterward thereof called the king's evil. His body being taken up thirty six years after his death, was found as flexible and uncorrupt, as when it was first buried. He was canonized for a saint by Pope Alexander the third, in the year of Christ, one thousand one hundred threescore and three. His translation was wont to be kept holy-day throughout England upon the thirteenth day of October, of whom in that place we have set down a larger narration.

### The sixth day

At Boulogne in France the commemoration of St Peter Confessor, who, being by St Augustine our English apostle ordained abbot of a new monastery near unto Canterbury, which K. Ethelbert of Kent had founded, and going over into France, was by tempest of sea, drowned near to the coast of Boulogne, where the inhabitants finding his body, buried it in an obscure place: but a certain miraculous light from Heaven being seen every night to shine thereon, the people began to inquire further what he was; and at last having intelligence from England, that it was the foresaid abbot, they took up his body, and translated it with great solemnity to Boulogne, and there with due veneration placed it in a church, whereat in sign of his sanctity and holiness of life, miracles are said to have been forthwith wrought. This happened about the year of Christ, six hundred and seven.

### The seventh day

At London the festivity of St Cedd, confessor and second bishop of that see, brother to St Chad of Lichfield, who by his continual preaching to the Mercians and East Saxons, converted many thousands to the faith of Christ, and is worthily called their apostle. The see of London being void for many years after the death of St Melitus, he was at length consecrated thereto, at the intercession of Sigeberht King of the East Saxons, who was newly converted to the Christian faith. And afterwards building a goodly monastery at a place called Lestingham in the province of the Deires, and replenishing the same with many monks, at last in great sanctity of life, full of venerable old age, he ended his blessed days, in the year of Christ, six hundred fifty and four, and was buried in his foresaid new monastery, where he deceased. St Bede recounteth, that when afterward his brother St Chad died, his soul was seen to descend from Heaven, with a troop of angels, to accompany the same to paradise ... (1)

## The Martyrs of the English Reformation

Anno Christi 1535. Henrici VIII anno 27.

John Houghton Prior of the Carthusians at London.
Augustine Webster Prior of the Carthusians at Exham.
Robert Laurence Prior of the Carthusians at Beval.

These were put to death at Tyburn the 29th of April, for denying the Kings Supremacy.

Richard Reynolds, Monk of St Bridget's Order, at Sion.
John Haile Priest, Vicar of Thistleworth.

Humprey Midlemore
William Exmew
Charterhouse Monks of London, suffered at Tyburn, 18th June
Sebastian Newdigate
John Rochester
James Warnet
Carthusians at York, 11th May

Richard Bere
Thomas Greene
John Davis
Thomas Johnson
William Greenwood
Charterhouse—Monks died in prison in June and July.
Thomas Scriven
Robert Salt
Walter Persons
Thomas Reading
William Horne, Charterhouse Monk, 4th Aug.
John Fisher Cardinal of St Vitalis, and Bishop of Rochester, at the Tower-Hill 22nd June.
Sir Thomas More, Knight, at the Tower-hill, 6th July.

Anno Christi 1536. Henry VIII, anno 28.

John Paslew Abbot of Whalley
John Castegate Monk at Lancaster, 10th March
William Haddock Monk, at Whalley, 13th March
N. N. Abbot of Sawley [= William Trafford]
George Asleby, Monk of Jervaulx at Lancaster in March
Robert Hobbes, Abbot of Woburn, together with the Prior of the same Monastery and a Priest, suffered at Woburn in Bedfordshire, in March
Doctor Mackerrell with 4 other Priests, at Tyburn, 29th March
William Thrust, Abbot of Fountains
Adam Sedbar, Abbot of Jervaulx at Tyburn in June
William Wold Prior of Burlington

[*move on to*]
Anno 1573. Elizabeth 15

Thomas Woodhouse, Priest, at Tyburn, 19th June

Anno 1577. Elizabeth 19

Cuthbert Mayne, the first Priest of the Seminaries, at Launceston in Cornwall, 29th November

Anno 1578. Elizabeth 20

John Nelson, Priest, at Tyburn, 3rd February
Thomas Sherwood, Gentleman, 7th February.

Anno 1581. Elizabeth 23

Everard Hanse, Priest, at Tyburn, 31st July
Edmund Campion, Priest of the Society of Jesus.
Alexander Briant, Priest of the same Society of Jesus at Tyburn, 1st Dec.
Ralph Sherwin, Priest

Anno 1582. Elizabeth 24

John Payne, Priest, at Chelmsford in Essex, 2nd April
Thomas Ford, Priest
John Shert, Priest at Tyburn, 28th May
Robert Johnson, Priest
Thomas Cottam, Priest of the Society of Jesus
William Filby, Priest, at Tyburn, 30th May
Luke Kirby, Priest
Laurence Johnson, Priest
William Lacy, Priest
Richard Kirkman, Priest, at York, 22nd August
James Thompson Priest, at York, in November...

[*move on to*]
Under King James.
Anno 1604, Jacobi anno 2.

Laurence Bayly, Layman, at Lancaster in March.
John Sugar, Priest
Robert Grissold, Layman, at Warwick in August

Anno 1605, Jacobi 3

Thomas Wilborne, Layman, at York.

Anno 1606, Jacobi 4

Richard Oldcorn, Priest of the Society of Jesus, at Worcester, 7th April
Ralph Ashley, Layman, at Worcester 7th April
Henry Garnet, Priest, Superior of the Society of Jesus in England, in St Paul's Churchyard, 3rd May

Anno 1607, Jacobi 5

Robert Drury, Priest, at Tyburn, 26 February

Anno 1608, Jacobi 6

Matthew Flathers, Priest at York, 21st Mar
George Gervase, Priest of the Order of St Benedict, at Tyburn, 11th April.
Thomas Garnet, Priest of the Society of Jesus, at Tyburn, 23 June. (2)

NOTES AND SOURCES

1. John Wilson, *English martyrologie, containing a summary of the lives of the glorious and renowned saints of the three kingdoms, England, Scotland and Ireland, collected and distributed into months, after the form of a calendar, according to every saint's festivity* (1608), calendar (unpag.), but first six pages.
2. Ibid., concluding catalogue of recent martyrs (unpag.).

# Henry Constable                                    1562–1613

Henry was born into a major family of the Nottinghamshire gentry. His father had a distinguished career as a soldier in Elizabeth's wars, dying as Master of Ordnance. The Constables
had embraced the Reformation. Henry was an undergraduate at Cambridge, and studied at
Lincoln's Inn and set out on a courtly and diplomatic career. Between 1583 and 1585 he was a
spokesman for the Protestant cause in Paris, and was later one of those sent north to
congratulate James VI on his marriage to Anne of Denmark and to assure James privately
that the Earl of Essex would promote his succession to the English throne. In his mid-20s, he
looked set for a stellar career at the heart of court and government. As late as 1589, he locked
literary horns (in Latin) with no less a Catholic polemicist than St Robert Bellarmine. But he
was resisting a strong call of conscience to make his peace with Rome, and his father's death
and a fresh visit to France provided the spur and opportunity. He made his move in 1594, and
for the rest of Elizabeth's reign he stayed abroad, travelling round the Continent. He made
one visit to Scotland at the time when he was writing in favour of James's right to the English
succession and expressly opposing Parsons's arguments in favour of the Infanta. When James
came to the English throne, Constable made overtures to the new king, and was allowed to
return to England. However, his active pursuit of tolerationist policies led to his spending at
least two spells in prison. He was a prolific poet, and an influential one, his sonnet sequences
in the 1590s including his seventeen 'spiritual sonnets', making him, it has been written, 'the
initiator of a Tridentine aesthetic'. Here are three sonnets in praise of the Persons of the
Trinity, one in honour of Our Lady, and a contrasting pair about St Mary Magdalene.

## To God the Father

Great God, within whose simple essence we
Nothing but that which is thyself can find,
When on thy self thou didst reflect thy mind,
Thy thought was God which took the form of thee;
And when this God, thus borne, thou lov'st, and he
Lov'd thee again, with passion of like kind,
(As lovers' sighs, which meet become one wind),
Both breath'd one spright of equal Deity.                    [= spirit]

Eternal Father, whence these two do come,
And wil'st the title of my Father have,
An heavenly knowledge in my mind engrave,
that that thy Son's true Image may become;
And sent my heart with sighs of holy Love,
That that the temple of the Spright may prove. (1)

## To God the Son

Great Prince of Heaven, begotten of that King
Who rules the kingdom that himself did make;
And of that Virgin-Queen man's shape did take,
Which from King David's royal stock did spring;
No marvel though thy birth made angels sing,
And angels' ditties shepherds' pipes awake;
And kings like shepherds, humbled for thy sake,
Kneel at thy feet, and gifts of homage bring.
For Heaven and earth, the high and low estate,
As partners of thy birth make equal claim.
Angels, because in Heaven God thee begat,
Shepherds and kings, because thy mother came
From princely race, and yet, by poverty,
Made glory shine in her humility. (2)

## To God the Holy Ghost

Eternal Spright which art in Heaven the Love
With which God and his Son each other kiss;
And who, to show who God's beloved is,
The shape and wings took'st of a loving dove;
When Christ, ascending, sent the from above
In fiery tongues, thou cam'st down unto his,
That skill in uttering heavenly mysteries,
By heat of zeal, both faith and love might move.
True God of Love, from whom all true love springs,
Bestow upon my love thy wings and fire,
My soul a spirit is, and with thy wings
May like an angel fly from earth's desire;
And with thy fire a heart inflam'd may bear,
And in thy sight a seraphim appear. (3)

## To Our Blessed Lady

In that (O Queen of Queens) thy birth was free
From guilt, which others do of grace bereave,
When in their mothers' womb they life receive,

God as his sole-born daughter loved thee.
To match thee, like thy birth's nobility,
He his Spirit for thy spouse did leave,
Of whom thou didst his only Son conceive,
And so wast link'd to all the Trinity.
Cease then, O Queens who earthly crowns do wear,
To glory in the pomp of worldly things;
If men such high respect unto you bear
Which daughters, wives, and mothers are of kings,
What honour should unto that Queen be done
Who had your God for father, spouse and son! (4)

## Two Sonnets in Honour of St Mary Magdalene

For few nights' solace in delicious bed,
Where heat of lust did kindle flames of hell:
Thou naked on naked rock in desert cell
Lay thirty years, and tears of grief did shed.
But for that time, thy heart there sorrowed,
Thou now in heaven eternally dost dwell,
And for each tear, which from thine eyes then fell,
A sea of pleasure now is rendered.
If short delights entice my heart to stray,
Let me by thy long penance learn to know
How dear I should for trifling pleasures pay:
And if I virtue's rough beginning shun,
Let thy eternal joys unto me show
What high Reward by little pain is won. (5)

Sweet Saint: Thou better canst declare to me,
What pleasure is obtained by heavenly love
Than they which other loves did never prove:
Or which in sex are differing from thee:
For like a woman spouse my soul shall be,
Whom sinful passions once to lust did move,
And since betrothed to God's son above,
Should be enamoured with his deity.
My body is the garment of my spright
While as the daytime of my life doth last:
When death shall bring the night of my delight
My soul unclothed shall rest from labors past:
And clasped in the arms of God, enjoy
By sweet conjunction, everlasting joy. (6)

NOTES AND SOURCES

1. *The Poems and Sonnets of Henry Constable* (1897), p. lxxxv.
2. Ibid., p. lxxxvi.
3. Ibid., p. lxxxvii.

4. Ibid., p. lxxxix.
5. Ibid., p. lxcii.
6. Ibid., p. ci. All six have been checked against *Spirituall Sonnettes to the Honour of God and his Sayntes by H.C.*, in T. Park (ed.), *Heliconia: Comprising a Selection of English Poetry of the Elizabethan Age Published between 1575 and 1604* (3 vols., 1815), vol. ii, separate pagination, pp. 3, 4, 5, 7, 11.

## Benjamin Carier                                            1566–1614

Benjamin Carier was one of the most prominent converts from Anglicanism in the reign of James I. He was the son of a Puritan parson, he took his BD and DD as a Fellow of Corpus Christi College, Cambridge, and very nearly became its Master in 1603. He was a domestic chaplain to Archbishop Whitgift and to James I's elder son Henry and a chaplain-in-ordinary to the King himself. In 1613, at the age of 47, he sought permission to 'take the waters' at Spa in Germany for physical ailments, but in fact he headed for Cologne and the cure of spiritual ailments. He consulted the rector of the Jesuit College there and was reconciled by him to the Church. James tried to win him back with the offer of the bishopric of Lincoln, but instead Carier wrote two long letters to James, one in Latin and one in English, which became the basis of his posthumous *A Missive to His Majesty of Great Britain . . . Containing the Motives of his Conversion to the Catholike Faith* (1615). This was regularly reprinted in the seventeenth century (as the title of the 1649 reprint has it): *A Notable Foresight of the Present Distempers both in Church and State*. This is the core of the explanation he offered of his conversion.

### A Conversion Narrative

I must confess, to God's honour and my own shame, that if it had been in my power to choose, I would never have been a Catholic. I was born and brought up in schism, and was taught to abhor a papist as much as any puritan in England doth. I had ever a great desire to justify the religion of the state, and had great hope to advance myself thereby. Neither was my hope ever so great as by your Majesty's favour it was at the very instant of my resolution for Catholic religion, and the preferment I had, together with the honour of your Majesty's service, was greater by much than without your Majesty's favour, I look for in this world. But though I was as ambitious of your Majesty's favour and as desirous of the honours and pleasures of my country as any man that is therein, yet seeing that I was not like any long while to enjoy them, and if I should for private commodity speak or write or do anything against the honour of Christ his church and against the evidence of my own conscience, I must shortly appear before the same Christ in the presence of the same his church, to give an account thereof. Therefore I neither durst any further pursue my own desire of honour, nor hazard my soul any further in the justification of that religion which I saw was impossible to be justified by any such reason as at the Day of Judgement would go for payment. And that it may appear I have not respected any thing so much in this world as my duty to your Majesty, and my love of my friends and country, I humbly beseech your Majesty to give me leave, as briefly as I can, to recount unto you the whole course of my studies and endeavours in this kind, even from the beginning of my life until this present . . .

After I came to years of discretion, by all the best means I could, to inform myself whether the religion of England were indeed the very same which being prefigured and prophesied in the Old Testament, was perfected by Our Blessed

Saviour, and delivered to his Apostles and disciples to continue, by perpetual succession in the Visible Church until his coming again; or whether it were a new one, for private purposes of statesmen invented, and by human laws established. Of this I could not choose but make some doubt, because I heard men talk much in those days of the change of religion which was then lately made in the beginning of Q[ueen] Elizabeth's reign.

I was sorry to hear of change and of a new religion, seeing me thought in reason, if true religion were eternal, then new religion could not be true. But yet I hoped that the religion was not a change or new religion, but a restitution of the old, and that the change was in the Church of Rome, which in process of time might perhaps grow to be superstitious and idolatrous; and therefore that England had done well to leave the Church of Rome and to reform itself, and for this purpose I did at my leisure and best opportunity, as I came to more judgement, read over the chronicles of England and observed all the alterations of religion that I could find therein. But when I found that the present religion of England was a plain change, and change upon change, and that there was no cause at all at the first, but only that King Henry VIII was desirous to change his old bedfellow, that he might have some heirs male behind him (for belike he feared that females would not be able to withstand the title of Scotland) and that change was continued and increased by the posterity of his later wives, I could not choose but suspect something. But yet the love of the world and hope of preferment would not suffer me to believe but that all was well and as it ought to be...

There is a statute in England, made by King Henry the eighth to make him supreme Head of the Church in spiritual and ecclesiastical causes, which statute enjoins all the subjects of England, on pain of death, to believe and swear they do believe that it is true. And yet all the world knows, if Henry the eighth could have gotten the Pope to divorce Q. Katherine, that he might marry Anne Boleyn, that statute had never been made by him, and if that title had not enabled the King to pull down abbeys and religious houses, and give them to laymen, the Lords and Commons of that time would never have suffered such a statute to be made. The statute was continued by Q. Elizabeth, to serve her own turn, and it is confirmed by your Majesty to satisfy other men. And yet your Majesty yields to the Church of Rome to be the Mother Church, and the bishop of Rome to be the chief Bishop or primate of all the Western Churches, which I do verily believe, and therefore I do also verily think he hath, or ought to have, some spiritual jurisdiction in England. And although in my younger days the fashion of the world made me swear as other men did (for which I pray God forgive me) yet I ever doubted and am resolved that no Christian man can take that Oath of Supremacy with a safe conscience, neither will I ever take it, to gain the greatest preferment in the world.

There is another statute in England, made by Queen Elizabeth and confirmed by your Majesty, which makes it death for any Englishman to be in England, being made a priest by authority derived or pretended to be derived from the Bishop of Rome; I cannot believe that I am a priest at all, unless I be made by authority derived from Gregory the Great, from whence all the Bishops of England have their being, if they have any at all.

There is another statute in like manner made and confirmed that it is death to be reconciled by a Catholic priest to the Church of Rome. I am persuaded that the Church of Rome is our Mother Church, and that no man in England can be saved that continues wilfully out of the visible unity of that church, and therefore I cannot choose but persuade the people to be reconciled thereunto, if possibly they can.

There is another statute in the like manner made and confirmed, that it is death to exhort the people of England to the Catholic Roman religion. I am persuaded that the religion prescribed and practised by the Church of Rome is the true Catholic religion, which I will particularly justify and make plain from point to point, if God give time and opportunity, and therefore I cannot choose but persuade the people thereunto.

It may be these are not all several statutes, some of them may be members of the same (for I have not my books about me to search) but I am sure all of them make such felonies and treasons as were the greatest virtues of the primitive church, and such as I must needs confess myself, I cannot choose if I live in England, but endeavour to be guilty of and then it were easy to find puritans enough to make a jury against me and there would not want a justice of the peace to give a sentence, and then they had done, that which is worse than persecution itself, they would all swear solemnly that Doctor Carier was not put to death for the Catholic religion but for felony and treason. I have no hope of protection against the cruelty of those laws if your Majesty is resolved upon no conditions whatsoever, to have no society at all or communion with the Church of Rome. And therefore while the case so stands, I dare not return home again. But I cannot be altogether out of hope of better news before I die as long as I do believe that the saints in heaven do rejoice at the conversion of a sinner to Christ and do know that your Majesty by your birth hath so great an interest in the saints in heaven, as you shall never cease to have, until you cease to be the son of such a mother, as would rejoice more than all the rest for your conversion. Wherefore I assure myself that she with all the rest do pray that your Majesty before you die may be militant in the communion of that Church wherein they are triumphant.

And in this hope am I gone before to join my prayers with theirs in the unity of the Catholic Church. And do humbly pray your Majesty to pardon me for doing that which was not in my power to avoid; and to give me leave to live, where I hope shortly to die, unless I may hope to do your Majesty service, and without the prejudice of any honest man in England, to see some unity betwixt the Church of England and her mother, the Church of Rome. (1)

NOTES AND SOURCES

1. Benjamin Carier, *A missive to His Majesty of Great Britain, King James written divers yeers since by Doctor Carier; conteining the motives of his conversion to Catholike religion; vvith a notable fore-sight of the present distempers both in the church and state of His Majesties dominions, and his advice for the prevention thereof* (1649 edn.), 1–3, 12–15.

# A Manual of Prayers (ii)                                    (1618)

Richard Broughton (1561–1635) was a Catholic convert while an undergraduate at Cambridge (c.1580). He was ordained at Rheims in 1592, and spent most of the next forty-three years on the mission in England. He was an assistant to the archpriest Richard Blackwell in 1613, and when the chapter was founded in 1623 he became vicar-general for the Midland Counties and given the title of archdeacon of Huntingdon. He served for many years at Belvoir Castle as chaplain to the Countess of Rutland. He was a fierce polemicist, but in 1618 he turned his mind to collating *A Manual of Prayers Used by the Fathers of the Primitive Church for the Most Part from the Four First Hundred Years of Christ.* It was divided thematically and we include here two of the chapters—prayers to Mary and to sacred relics. The first of these, for example, draws on prayers by SS Ephraim, John Cassian, Leander, Gregory of Nazianzen, Chrysostom, and prayers from the 6th General Council.

## Prayers to the Virgin

Chapter 3: Of the Communion of the Church Militant with the Triumphant by prayer and honour to the saints there, by us on earth: and their patronage unto us and first of the most B. Virgin Mary.

O Virgin vouchsafe, that I thy servant may praise thee. Hail most bright, and most beautiful vessel of God, Hail Lady Mary full of grace: Hail among women most blessed Virgin. Hail most shining star, from which Christ went forth. Hail most glorious light, Mother and Virgin. Hail Lady higher than all. Hail song of the cherubims, and hymn of angels. Hail peace, joy, and salvation of the world. Hail gladness of mankind. Hail praise of the Fathers, and honour of the prophets. Hail beauty of martyrs, and crown of saints, hail glory of the godly. Hail most excellent ornament of the heavenly holies. Hail most worthy miracle of the world. Hail tree of life, joy, and pleasure. Hail quiet haven, and deliveress of those that be troubled. Hail the helper of them that be in danger. Hail house of grace and consolation. Hail refuge of sinners. Hail hope of all that be virtuous, and afflicted with adversities. Hail Queen and defence both of men and women. Hail most glorious mediatrix of the world. Hail door of heaven. Hail opening of the gates of paradise. Hail key of Heavens and the kingdom of Christ.

O immaculate, unspotted, uncorrupted, chaste Virgin, spouse of God, our Lady, only hope of the despaired, help of the oppressed, and most speedy aid of those that run unto thee, and refuge of all Christians: admit my prayer, most vile, and uttered with unclean lips; and also entreat thy Son my Lord and God, with thy motherly gentleness, that he may also open unto me, those most merciful bowels of his piety: and setting aside mine innumerable sins, convert me to penance, and grant me truly to fulfil his commandments.

O merciful, gentle, and bountiful Lady, be always present unto me; in this life an earnest protection and helper, driving back mine enemies' invasions, and bringing me to salvation, and in the last moment of my life, keep my wretched soul, driving far from it the ugsome [= loathsome] sight of wicked devils, and in the terrible day of Judgement, delivering me from everlasting damnation; lastly making me heir of that inaccessible glory, of thy Son and God, which by thine intercession and favour I beseech thee again and again, most holy Lady, Mother of God, that I may obtain by thy grace, mercy and gentleness of thine only begotten Son our Lord, and God, and Saviour Jesus Christ.

As thou art the Mother of the most merciful God; so mercifully receive me a sinner: be present with me, o merciful, gentle, and bountiful Virgin.

O immaculate and blessed Mother (without sin) of thy Son, and God of all, pure, sound, most sacred; we praise thee, we bless thee, as full of grace, who broughtest forth Christ. We all prostrate ourselves to thee, we all beseech thee. Deliver us O unspotted, from all necessity, from all temptations of the devil. Be our reconciliatrix and advocate in the hour of judgement. Deliver us from the fire to command darkness: and vouchsafe us the glory of thy Son; for thou art the most holy hope of Christians with God. To whom be honour world without end. Amen.

O holy and immaculate Virgin Mary Mother of God and Mother of our Lord Jesus Christ, vouchsafe to make intercession for me, to him whose Temple thou deservedst to be.

I beseech the Intercession of blessed Mary the Virgin that my prayer may be effectual.

O holy Mother of God Virgin Mary, pray for us.

Queen of heaven and Lady of earth, ever most holy Virgin, Mother of God and our Lord Jesus Christ; pray for us and daily, yea continually make intercession for me thy servant, and for all the holy Church of God, for remission of sins, purging of vices, for increase and perfection of virtues, for the peace and health of the faithful people, for the fruits of the earth, for the stability of the Church, the order of saints, and for all servants of God, men and women, both living and departed, that by thy prayers and holy merits, God almighty may take mercy on a people full of sins, here, and for ever.

Hail O Queen, Mother of mercy, life, sweetness, and our hope all hail! We that are the banished children of *Eve* do cry unto thee. To thee we sigh groaning and weeping, in this vale of tears. Therefore O thou our advocate, turn those thy merciful eyes unto us, and show unto us after this exile, blessed Jesus the fruit of thy womb. O merciful, O full of pity, O sweet Virgin Mary. Pray for us O holy Mother of God, that we may be made worthy of the promises of Christ.

Hearken O daughter of David and Abraham, and incline thine ear to our prayers, and forget not thy people. We cry unto thee, O most holy Virgin, remember us, and render unto us for this little speech, great gifts out of the riches of thy graces, thou who art full of grace. We use these words for thy praise, if at any time hymn, if at any time praise, be offered unto thee, either by us, or any creature, to thee I say our gracious Lady, Queen, Mistress, Mother of God, ark of the sanctuary. All orders of angels and earthly things pronounce thee blessed. We exalt thee with a great and loud voice saying: Hail gracious, our Lord is with thee, O Mistress, and Lady and Queen, and Mother of God, make intercession for us.

O venerable Virgin chaste, most happy, adorned with the garment of immortality, accompted as a Goddess: be mercifully present to my prayers, receive my petitions.

O Lady grant that I may so depart forth of this life, that having thee so great a governess of it, I may always find thee for me a most acceptable patroness to thy Son. Suffer me not to be delivered over as it were to be crucified and exposed to the scorn of him that is the sworn enemy and plague of all mortal men.

O maiden equalled by none in grace, Mother and Virgin, comely above all virgins, and the greatest, who exceedest all orders of heavenly inhabitants, Queen, Lady, the good of mankind: be always a friend to mortal men, and to me every where the greatest safeguard.

O thrice blessed Mother, O light of virgins, which inhabitest the most glorious temple of heaven, free from the stains of mortality: now thou art adorned with the stole of immortality, hearken gently from above to my words, and I beseech thee O Virgin, receive my prayers.

It is worthy and just, to glorify thee, God's Mother and always most blessed and wholly undefiled Mother of God more honourable than the cherubims, and incomparably more glorious than the Seraphims, which without corruption hast brought forth God: verily we magnify thee God's Mother.

O glorious Mother of God, who brought forth true God: pray unto him to save our souls.

O Mother of God, because thou art more excellent than all creatures, we which are not able to praise thee worthily, do freely beseech thee, have mercy upon us.

Hail full of grace, our Lord is with thee. Hail organ of joy, by which the condemnation of our offence is purged, and full compensation of true joy is made. Hail truly blessed. Hail illuminated. Hail magnificent temple of divine glory. Hail consecrated palace of the king. Hail bride chamber, in which humanity was espoused to Christ. Hail elected to God before thou wert born. Hail God's Reconciliation with men. Hail treasure of life which never fadeth. Hail heaven celestial, Tabernacle of the sun of glory. Hail most ample field of God, whom none other place but thou alone, could comprehend. Hail holy virginal earth, of which the new Adam by an unspeakable framing, was formed; which should restore the old Adam to salvation.

Hail Mary full of grace our Lord is with thee; blessed art thou among women, and blessed is the fruit of thy womb; for thou hast brought forth the Saviour of our souls. It is worthy, it is worthy that we call thee who art truly blessed the Mother of God always blessed and every way irreprehensible, and the Mother of our God, more honourable than the cherubims, and more glorious than the seraphims: who without corruption, hast brought forth God the word. We truly magnify thee the Mother of God, O full of grace, to thee every creature maketh joy, the company of angels, and mankind: thou who art the sanctified temple, the spiritual paradise, the glory of virgins, of whom God received flesh, and became a child, our God who is before the world: for he made thy belly his throne, and thy womb more spacious and large, than the heavens themselves. To thee o full of grace, every creature doth gratulate; glory to thee.

O holy Mary Mother of God, pray for us, I say sinners. Amen.

O Mother of God, Queen of heaven, door of paradise, Lady of the world, begin prayers for my sin. Amen.

O my blessed Lady, and defence of mankind, the harbour and protection of them that flee unto thee. I know O my Lady Mother of God, that I have greatly offended thee. For who O my Lady hath hoped in thee and was ashamed? or what man hath faithfully asked thy help, able to all things, and hath at any time been forsaken? Verily no man at any time. Wherefore, I a sinner also and wicked person, ask thy ever-during fountain, from which cures do flow to our souls, be merciful unto me. (1)

## Reverence for Relics

Of honour and reverence to the holy bodies, and other relics of saints.

We honour the vessels of the bodies of saints, and repay unto them memory, as it were reward and wages of their virtue and magnanimity of mind.

The noble relics are pulled forth of their unnoble sepulchre. Relic worshipped, lying under the altar: Christ offered upon the altar. The trophies of victory are showed unto heaven. Let the triumphant victims succeed unto the place where Christ is the sacrifice: But he who suffered for all, upon the altar, these redeemed by his passion, under the altar. This place I had appointed for myself, for it is worthy a priest should rest there, where a priest accustomed to offer sacrifice. But I yield the right hand portion to the holy victims. This place belonged to martyrs: therefore let us bury the sacred relics, and carry them into worthy houses, and celebrate the whole day with faithful devotion.

O thrice and four times O seven times happy, that Citizen who celebrateth thee, and near-hand the seat of thy bones, who may lay himself down near them who sprinkleth the place with tears, who presseth his breast upon the earth, who offereth vows in secret.

O blessed Apostles, what thanks shall we render unto you who have laboured so much for us. O Peter, I remember thee, and I am amazed. O Paul, I call thee to mind, and ravished in mind, I am oppressed with tears. For what I may say, or what I may speak, beholding your afflictions, I know not. O Peter, thou mayest joy, to whom it was given, to enjoy the cross of Christ. Joy thou also O Paul, whose head was cut off with a sword. Let that sword be to me for a crown; and the nails of Peter, for precious stones, infixed in my diadem.

O who will grant unto me to be rolled about the body of Paul, to be fastened to his sepulchre, to see the dust of that body, fulfilling the things, which as yet were wanting in Christ, bearing the signs of his wounds.

O double renowned, we beseech thee by thy hands, block off thy prison, by those potsherds by which thou gainedst conquest, by which we that come after, with reverence kiss thy bed, have mercy upon our prayers.

Here Christ verily was crucified for our sins, and if thou wouldst deny it, this place apparent disproveth thee. Blessed is this mount Golgotha, in which now, for him that was crucified, well make joy in him, and the whole globe of the earth is filled with wood of the Cross by parcels.

When will that day be that it may be lawful for us to enter into the Sepulchre of our Saviour to weep in the Sepulchre of our Lord, and then to lick the wood of the Cross; and in mount Olivet with our Lord ascending, to be lifted in desire and mind. (2)

NOTES AND SOURCES

1. [Richard Broughton], *A Manual of Prayers Used in the Fathers* (1618), 24–32.
2. Ibid. 72–5.

# Venerable Mary Ward

1585–1645

Mary Ward was the founder of the religious order whose two branches are now known as the Congregation of Jesus and the Institute of the Blessed Virgin Mary. Whatever inner serenity she achieved in this life was constantly threatened by suspicion and hostility. She was opposed by anti-Jesuits who disliked her Ignatian spirituality as well as by the Jesuits who rejected the idea of female counterparts. She received the call to religious conversion in 1600, but was prevented by her father and her confessor from answering it until 1606. Once she had their permission to follow her vocation, she joined the Poor Clares at Saint-Omer, but continuing visions and revelations persuaded her that she was called to found an unenclosed women's religious order—proscribed by the Council of Trent—and to follow the rule of the

Jesuits in founding schools, and in exercising other active apostolates. During the next twenty years of constant restless activity, she founded houses in major cities across Europe. But her disregard for the decrees of Trent and the express order of St Ignatius against any female branch of his Society caused a powerful backlash, especially in Rome. Finally, the critics got their way. By a secret decree of the Congregation for the Propagation of the Faith of October 1629 (communicated to nuncios but not to Mary), followed up by the Papal Bull *Pastoralis Romani Pontificis* (13 January 1631), all her houses were ordered to be closed, and she was accused of heresy. She fought for her houses until she came to realize that papal authority lay behind the closure; then she ordered strict compliance. She and her leading supporters were imprisoned but cleared of heresy. Once released, she made her way to Spa, and thence to her native Yorkshire, where she set up a community of laywomen running a Catholic school. Despite proscription, and the placing of all works by and about her on the Index, her example and rule continued to gain adherents, and individual bishops began to recognize uncloistered houses based on her rule from the 1680s (although the Bull of suppression was not revoked). When Pope Benedict XIV approved the office of Chief Superior in 1749, it was on condition that he was supporting a new Foundation, and he forbade the acknowledgement of Mary Ward as Foundress. The Institute received papal approbation in Blessed Pius IX's apostolic constitution of 1877 but it was not until 1909 that St Pius X formally recognized Mary Ward as Foundress. In 1951, at the First International Congress of the Lay Apostolate, Pope Pius XII described her as 'that incomparable woman'.[27] We begin with a short autobiographical fragment describing her early calling. We move next to the *Briefe Relation*, a biography of Mary Ward written by one of her most constant companions, Mary Poyntz, who was with her at Heworth when she died. She wrote her *Relation* in the years immediately after her friends's death. Here we include Poyntz's description of the episode of the spilled chalice that caused a change of heart in her confessor and his granting her permission to answer her vocation.[28] Next we include part of Mary Ward's memorial (1629) of the history of her Institute since its foundation in 1609 and her plea for papal approval and blessing. Tragically, almost simultaneously with this petition, the Pope (Urban VIII) had agreed to a recommendation from the Curia that all the houses be suppressed in perpetuity. She emphasizes throughout how she had sought and received permission from local ordinaries and (sound Catholic) princes in the Low Countries, in Germany, Austria, and Italy. But none of this was proof against a whispering campaign sustained against her in Rome. So we next offer Mary Ward's letter to her sisters in religion following the promulgation of Pope Urban VIII's Bull *Pastoralis Romani Pontificis*. Her fortitude and obedience are deeply moving, but note the very interesting 'etc' in the letter. We then return to Mary Poyntz's *Briefe Relation* with some selections from its final sections relating to Mary Ward's prayer life. This is followed by one of Mary Ward's own prayers (1619), and an account of a retreat at Liege (also 1619). When Mary Ward died, she was living with a few of her companions from the dispersed convent communities in Heworth, Yorkshire. The vicar of Osbaldwick, Samuel Hollins, was, in the tart words of Mary Poyntz, 'honest enough to

---

[27] Because of the lack of testimonies by women religious that appeared in print within our period, we are making an exception here to our 'print only' rule, and we offer autobiographical fragments written by Mary Ward herself in English. All contemporary and autobiographical manuscript materials on Mary Ward have recently been gathered together by Christina Kenworthy-Browne CJ.

[28] We reproduce the painting of this episode at p. 1. The inscription on the picture reads (in translation): when Mary Ward's confessor was saying Mass in London in 1605, it happened by divine permission that he inadvertently spilt the chalice. This wrought such a change in him that when Mary, after Mass, respectfully handed him the towel to dry his hands, he said to her with tears streaming from his eyes: 'I will never more hinder your religious design, but further you all I can.'

be bribed' to allow her to be buried in his churchyard. These are the words placed on her tombstone (now to be found in the church itself).

## Autobiographical Fragment

My first motions to religion happened so near as I can remember about the fifteenth year of my age, occasioned as I think by a devout woman's speech who amongst pious other discourses happened upon a true story which fell forth in our country before the fail of religion. A nun, said she, having violated her virginity in such sort as the thing was verily apparent and commonly known, and first banished the monastery until she was disburdened, and afterwards admitted again (because they could not dismiss her, she having made vows); there she suffered much confusion, shame and pain. Amongst her other penance this was one, that for many years she was always at the time of prayer to lie at the threshold of the quire [= chancel] that the religious as they passed to and fro might tread upon her. This exact punishment of that vice gave a splendour to the contrary virtue, and I think on that instant my loving Lord did so touch my heart with a longing desire to dedicate myself to his divine service, as that I do not remember since any moment in which I had not rather have suffered death than betoken myself to a worldly life. O my Lord and Saviour permit me not to be proud of that which is not mine, for if your majesty had left me to myself where had I now been, nay how have carried myself this grace notwithstanding . . . (1)

## Opposition from Mary Ward's Confessor: The Spilling of the Chalice

This endeavouring for her father's goodwill lasted seven years, with her no small toil, anxiety, conflict, prayers and penances, and that no trial might be wanting, in the last year of her conflict came to her acquaintance a noble man and Catholic in virtues and qualities complete, far out of her thoughts (which was wholly on God) who sought her in marriage, but so liked and approved by all, as each one vehemently urged her, and above all her confessor, so far as to say, were she a novice in any Religion she would do God more service to come out and marry this party than to proceed . . . This assault of her spiritual father[29] was beyond measure sensible, carrying the colours of religion and zeale, in so much that she, as it were in an agony, cast her self at the feet of her dear Lord, and said 'it was He must answer for her.' Then in holy quiet, free from noise and motion of any exterior thing, she rested in herself, united with God. This was a little before Mass in the chapel in lodgings in Baldwin's Gardens in London. In this manner she remained, not minding at all what passed there, till the priest, after his recollection which had been longer than ordinary, washing his hands she, forth of her wonted great respect to all priests, especially her spiritual father, arose to give him the towel. She perceived he had wept much, then sighing said, 'Shall I live to offend my God?' and to her, 'I will never more hinder your religious design, but further you all I can,' which was to her an unspeakable Jubilee. By what means God changed this

---

[29] Traditionally thought to be Richard Holtby SJ.

good priest his heart, He alone knoweth that wrought it, but in that Mass after consecration the chalice was spilt. This priest was a very exemplary and religious Man. (2)

## Memorial to Pope Urban VIII

A number of Englishwomen who had been called by God to a state of perfection that could not be put into practice in their own country, so unhappily tainted with heresy, crossed the sea and reached Flanders, willingly giving up all the consolations that homeland and family might grant them, to seek in foreign countries the greater honour and service of God.

In the year 1609 they began to live regular religious discipline in the city of St Omer under the patronage of her Serene Highness Donna Isabella Clara Eugenia, the Spanish Infanta, and to the great content and satisfaction of the Bishop of that City...as is testified by letters of his now in Rome...

As divine grace supported them to the complete satisfaction of their souls and the number of persons who esteemed their Institute and way of life increased, they began to open colleges and noviciates at Liege, Cologne and Treves, the chief cities of Germany to which they had been urgently invited by the inhabitants.

[In 1621, Pope Gregory XV] received them graciously...

But the enemy of all good prompted some ecclesiastical and religious persons (perhaps out of certain interests and envy) to rob them of their good name by spreading lying rumours and saying among other things that the said Englishwomen were preaching in pulpits and squares and holding disputations on divine matters. Other similar false charges were made against them, quite contrary to what they really did or thought. However God allowed such lies to be too readily believed, and caused Pope Gregory XV to make a difficulty about confirming their Institute at that time...

[*More and more convents and schools for day-pupils and boarders were established in the following years.*] Therefore all the members of the said company, since it has pleased the divine goodness out of his pure mercy to make use of them for twenty years in this way of life for the edification and help of their neighbours (in so many different cities, provinces and kingdoms, favoured by so many prelates, bishops and apostolic nuncios, and under the patronage of so may ecclesiastical and secular princes) now implore our Lord His Holiness not to allow them to be cast out as women of ill repute, but to have their case examined... (3)

## A Letter of Submission

My dearest Mothers and Sisters in Christ

In the event that his Holiness, through Nuncios or other religious officials in the places where they live, forbids you to continue your religious practices and the subordination and dependence one on another, obey at once. And let your reason for thus acting be the same as mine in ordering it, that his Holiness wishes it. For the rest, love and serve as best you can Him whose love and service you have left home and family and now endure etc. What other service I can give you in this life and the next is already yours. I warmly commend my failings to your faithful devotions. (4)

## Prayer Life

Her devotion to our blessed Lady was very great and tenderly dear, confidently in all occasions she made her recourse to her. It was not a devotion in formality tied to this or that particular devotion, but as a deep apprehension of her most high quality of Mother of God etc. and that all else were as lesser titles needful to our small capacity to make us capable of the highest. She always gave her the title of blessed. She had an admirable manner to bring those she conversed with to the same. In fine [= to sum up], her honour as hath been said was what she greatly desired to give her life for, and was once very near the pinch of so doing, reprehending most undauntedly one of the Justices in Guildhall [London] for blasphemy spoken against the sacred Virgin of whose many singular and visible protections I will only recount two...

Her devotion to her good angel and all angels in general was very great, particularly to Saint Michael, Saint Gabriel and Saint Raphael, whom she served daily with some devotion, and twenty-eight angels guardian besides her own, the Pope's his, and some other princes theirs. She served an angel to have care of her letters much importing her business, their safe passage, and the danger thereof, a certain prelate having offered a great sum of money to stop all her letters, another to have care of her journeys to prevent misservices of God by the indiscretion of ours...

[On her journeys] if she had time and opportunity she did always eat before she set forth, and that was always provided overnight. At noon she nor her companions never made any meal, but her servants she was careful should. In the afternoon she took time in her devotions, saying her beads etc. Near the place where she was to lodge she said the *Te Deum* in thanksgiving for her preservation that day and a *Laudate Dominum Omnes Gentes* etc for the graces bestowed on the saints to whose protection she had commended herself. When she arrived in her chamber, she sought out some picture before which kneeling down, she made an offer of herself and all her actions to be done in that place to the greatest honour and glory of God. When order was given for supper and linen had for the beds etc she had a saint's life read, that of the day if there were any, if not some other, and for this end carried always with her the saints' lives and Roman martyrology which was also daily read. The time of meal she took occasion to say something that might edify and profit those of the inn that waited...

To conclude she was in soul and body so adorned as made appear somewhat which when one would compendiously express, called it, goodness, and in particular the old Lord Eure was wont to say, I never knew goodness till I know Mistress Ward. Good doth not leave to be good, which produceth a patience to see so many excellencies in her with such order and harmony, here put down without form or order. Yet must be sealed or concluded with her Love that sacred name of Jesus her first and last word [in the form IHS], beginning and ending all her petitions, her refuge in all dangers and protection in all evil. In fine, the mark of all that was hers, and this in the ancient form thus IHS which she always put at the top of all her letters and books which were for her own use. The dearness of her love to the Holy Name of Jesus was as to a thing that had or was to cost her dear. (5)

## Mary Ward's Own Prayer

O parent of parents, and friend of all friends, without entreaty you took me into your care and by degrees led me from all else that at length I might see and settle my love in You. What had I ever done to please You? Or what was there in me wherewith to serve You? Much less could I ever deserve to be chosen by You. O happy begun freedom, the beginning of all my good, and more worth to me than the whole world besides. Had I never hindered Your will and working in me, what degrees of grace should I now have. Yet where as yet am I? My Jesus, forgive me, remembering what You have done for me and whither You have brought me, and for this excess of goodness and love let me no more hinder Your will in me. (6)

## On Retreat at Liège in October 1619

He was very near me and within me, which I never perceived Him to be before. I was moved to ask Him with great confidence and humility, what I came to know to whit, what He was. I said, 'My God, what art Thou? I saw Him evidently and very clearly go into my heart and little by little hid Himself (and there I perceive Him to be still in the same manner, my meditation being ended an hour since). I endeavoured to go forward according to the points of the meditation, but could not, He held my heart, I could not work. I would then have asked Him something, bid Him welcome, but He would not let. I once asked, 'will you lie there and do nothing?' And another time, 'make that heart perfect and such as you would have it'; but beginning my speech in both, I could not possibly go forward, I saw plainly that His only will was that I should neither work nor talk, but hold my peace. I was weary with kneeling, having nothing to do sitting down, this idleness of all powers made me wish to sleep. I would have liked a walk, but dared not without His leave. I composed I myself handsomely to attend on such a guest, but God would have none of it; my body was weary, and yet I did nothing; my mind quiet and much contented; all noise, or other things that at other times helps devotion seemed then unpleasing. An hour was gone in the space of one quarter; I left unwillingly, remaining still in the same disposition. (7)

## An Epitaph

To love the poor, persevere in the same
And die and rise with them was all the aim
Of Mary Ward who having lived 60 years and
Eight days died the 20 of Jan 1645 (8)

NOTES AND SOURCES

1. *Mary Ward 1585–1645: A 'Briefe Relation...' with Autobiographical Fragments and a Selection of Letters*, ed. Christina Kenworthy-Browne CJ (Boydell Press for the Catholic Record Society, 2008), 117–18.

2. Ibid. 9. See the plate at p. 1, showing the spilling of the chalice. It is one of fifty paintings now kept by the Congregation of Jesuits at Augsburg, and known as *The Painted Life*. They were commissioned in the second half of the seventeenth century by Venerable Mary's early companions.

3. Kenworthy-Browne, *Mary Ward*, 149–55.

4. Ibid. 157–8.

5. Ibid. 95–101.

6. Ibid. 133; and also available at the Congregation's website at <http://www.cjengland.org/ourpages02.asp?pageid=87>.

7. <http://www.cjengland.org/ourpages02.asp?pageid=87>.

8. Copied from the photograph of her tombstone displayed on the back cover of Kenworthy-Browne, *Mary Ward*.

## Edward Dawson SJ                                    *c.*1579–1622

This is the preface described as 'a brief Method for instruction and practice of meditation' added by Richard Gibbons SJ to his translation of a major work on the life, passion, death, and resurrection of Jesus written by the leading Italian Jesuit Vincentius Bruno. The preface has been reliably ascribed to Edward Dawson SJ. He served twice on the mission in England, on the first occasion being one of forty-seven priests expelled and sentenced to perpetual banishment (1606). He was sent back for a second spell in Lincolnshire and London, but was recalled by his superiors in 1614. He spent his last years, at his own request, tending English and Irish soldiers in the Low Countries who were dying of plague. In due course he contracted it himself and died. The most startling thing about this tract is its dedication 'to the virtuous and religious gentle-women Mistress Mary Ward and the rest of her devout company in St Omers.' It was published in 1614 before her falling out with the Society of Jesus.

## The Practice of Meditation

Meditation which we treat of, is nothing else but a diligent and forcible application of the understanding, to seek and know and as it were to taste some divine matter; and whence doth arise in our affectionate powers good motions, inclinations and purposes which stir us up to the love and exercise of virtue and the hatred and avoiding of sin. It is the shortest and almost the only way to attain the Christian perfection; it is the path which all holy men (of what estate soever) have trodden. Wherefore let those who desire to enjoy their company, follow their example... True it is, that through the unhappy estate of this troublesome world, man being distracted by other thoughts, and surprised by other affections, cannot continually nor without some little violence especially at the first, enjoy this so great a happiness; yet may he, joining his own diligence to God's help, so unite himself to his creator by this exercise, that at least for some determinate time, he may enjoy him with some familiarity. It will therefore be good for those who intend to reap the fruit of this heavenly employment, to appoint unto themselves, by the counsel of someone skilful in matters of spirit, the time they mean to spend every day therein... The fittest time for meditation (according to the example of the prophet David) is the morning, when the powers of our soul are free from other objects. To be therefore better prepared, we must the night before read over that part of the book[30] or writing twice or thrice, whence we take our matter; then we divide it into three parts or points, more or fewer as we please... The hour of meditation being come, we may imagine ourselves to be invited by our good angel or by some other saints to whom we are particularly devoted, to appear in the presence of God. Wherefore,

---

[30] He recommends passages from scripture *or* 'some history as the meditations of the life and passion of Blessed Saviour, of the virtuous actions of his Blessed Mother or some other saint'.

having made the sign of the holy cross and sprinkled ourselves with holy water, we may go presently with a kind of spiritual hunger to the place where we mean to make our meditation and standing from thence a pace or two, briefly lift up our mind to Almighty God, imagining him to be so present to us (as truly he is) that he beholdeth what we are to do and doth show unto us in that very place his most venerable and glorious countenance. The presence of God is best framed in our understanding by making an act of faith, whereby we believe Almighty God to be present, that he compasseth us round about on every side, as the water compasseth the fish, and yet is also within us (as he is in all things) somewhat like the water that is entered into a sponge, and this by his divine essence, presence and power which penetrate the nature of every creature and give them needful help for their operations...Having conceived God thus present, we must next look upon our own unworthiness, and with great reverence say, with the patriarch Abraham, I will speak to the Lord, being dust and ashes, and with bended knees of our heart, kneel down before our Lord, professing the presence of the blessed Trinity, with some words fitting that purpose, as blessed be the holy and undivided Trinity or glory to the Father, to the Son, and to the Holy Ghost or Holy Holy Holy, Lord God omnipotent who was, who is and who is to come, or the like. But if through indisposition or weakness of body, we find ourselves unapt to kneel, we may, having entered into our meditation, either stand, sit or walk or use such situation of body as we shall find fittest for our infirmity; and although we should have our body well disposed to kneel, yet is we find not in our meditation the comfort we expect, we may change from the position we were in, as from kneeling to sitting, standing walking, prostrating ourselves upon our faces at our Saviour's feet, etc...Then we must proceed to the preambles or *preludiums*, which are three if the matter be historical, but if it be not of some history, they are only two. The first *preludium*...is a brief calling to mind of the mystery we are to meditate, no other ways than if we should tell it to another, without any discourse thereon at all. The second is common to all meditations, and is an imagination of seeing the places where all things we meditate on were wrought, by imagining ourselves to be really present at those places which we must endeavour to represent so lively as though we saw them indeed with our corporal eye, which to perform well it will help us much to behold beforehand some image wherein that mystery is represented...The third *preludium* in all meditations is a short but earnest prayer to God for that thing which we have proposed as the scope and end of our meditation. Having finished these *preludiums*, we must begin the first point of our meditation, exercising thereon the three powers our soul, memory, understanding and will...(1)

NOTES AND SOURCES

1. [Richard Gibbons], *An abridgment of the Meditations of the life, passion, death, and resurrection of our Lord and Sauiour Iesus Christ. Written in Italian by the R Father Vincentius Bruno of the Society of Iesus. And translated into English by R.G. of the same Society. VVherento is premised a briefe method for instruction and practice of meditation* (1614), preface, unpag., 'the practical methode of meditation'.

# William Stanney OFM                                    d. 1626

The Franciscans were one of the orders whose presence in England was most disrupted by the Elizabethan regime. Although there were always English Franciscans, they had no organization for the forty years after 1559, working alone in England or returning to the Continent and being subsumed into continental friaries. Credit for creating a coherent mission to England is usually given to Father John Gennings, but he himself received the Franciscan habit from William Stanney, the commissary for England. The mission was put on a sounder footing with the founding of St Bonaventure's College at Douai in 1618. To coincide with its opening, Stanney published his *Treatise of Penance*, one of the first books published since 1559 by an English Franciscan that was not a translation of an earlier Continental work. It is first and foremost a guide to penance for third order Francicans, a translation of the rule for the third order adapted for use in the mission field. He had written it first in 1606, in Latin and for priests, but he claimed that the number of English lay Catholics joining the third order over the previous decade was so great that he felt compelled to translate it into English and print it, because the scribal labour in making handwritten copies would be too great. Here is the first part of chapter 7, 'how great the profit is which proceedeth from penance'.

## On Purgatory and the Joys of Heaven

Knowing that profit draweth many persons sooner than sweetness or pleasure, I will now return to declare more at large the utility and benefit which proceedeth from penance. The holy abbot Pynusius speaking thereof, saith that after the general grace of Baptism and that most precious gift of martyrdom which is gotten by shedding of our blood, the most excellent are the fruits of penance, whereby is gotten and attained the purifying and cleansing of our sins. Wherefore St Peter saith, be penitent and convert, that your sins may be put out (Acts 3).

Holy Dionysius the Carthusian doth in like sort declare that great is the profit and many are the benefits which the soul receiveth from penance, for that true penance (saith he) doth deliver the soul from the bondage of Satan, and doth practise it, doth adornest with virtues and gifts of the Holy Ghost, placeth it in paradise, presenteth it to be crowned and as a mediator for it.

God himself, speaking by the mouth of his prophet Ezekiel saith: if the wicked shall do penance for all the sins which he hath done and shall keep my precepts, and shall do judgements and justice, he shall live the life and shall not die. Yea, moreover he addeth in the same place, that penance blotteth out the very memory of sin, saying that he will not so much as remember the iniquities that the penitent sinner hath done, but he shall live in the justice which he hath wrought. Especially if he exercise true justice upon himself which requireth that according to the greatness of the sin, so should the penance be correspondent thereunto. Therefore must he first judge the offence and then use condign justice upon the offender, that is himself, poor sinner, whose penance ought not to be small, when the offence is great which penance is a thing pleasing unto God, that by the foresaid prophet he saith: when the wicked man shall turn himself from his impiety and wickedness which he hath done, and shall do judgement and justice, he shall give life unto the soul. Therefore, he saith again, I will judge every one (O house of Israel) according to his ways. Convert you, therefore and do penance for all your iniquities and your iniquities shall not be your ruin. Behold here what God requireth of every sinner, that he should do condign penance, behold the other side the profit that proceedeth from penance is very great whereas it saveth from eternal death, blotteth out not only the sins but the very memory thereof also, giveth life to the soul, and preserveth it from ruin and eternal pains, which we take in doing thereof, doth deliver and preserve us from the endless pains of Hell, as witnesseth St Gregory's saying: while we are wasted and spoiled with transitory labour and pains, we are delivered from everlasting torments.

Yea such benefit cometh unto us from labour, pains, and afflictions that if we do but patiently suffer them in this life for the love of God, by their means we shall be freed from the pains in the life to come, either in Hell or Purgatory...

I beseech you how great and intolerable are the future pains of Purgatory and of Hell which of necessity one of the two the poor sinner must suffer if through God's mercy penance here doth not preserve him from those intolerable pains there. St Augustine, speaking of the pains of Purgatory, saith: this fire truly, although it be not everlasting, yet notwithstanding it is most grievous. For certainly it doth far excel all the pains that ever man suffered in this life. There was never found in flesh so great and intolerable pain, although the holy martyrs have suffered marvellous torments. Let everyone therefore (saith he) study so to correct his offences and do such penance for his sins here that after this life he be not forced to suffer such and so many intolerable pains of Purgatory.

Though the pains of Purgatory do far exceed all torments of the world and if it were possible they should be ten thousand times more, yet were they all or nothing in comparison of the least torments of Hell which shall be inflicted for any mortal sin, that the sinner doth desperately and voluntarily die in. So infinite and inexplicable are the pains of Hell, that holy Anselm saith that if all the men who ever were born since the time of Adam until this present day were now alive and great preachers and that all of them should endeavour to speak but of the least pains of Hell, yet were they not able altogether to declare the very least part of the smallest torment there. So in like sort doeth he say, that no less inenarrable[31] and impossible by all those to be declared is the greatness of the joys of Heaven which the sinner dying but in one mortal sin loseth for ever... Holy Dionysius reciteth that a certain devil being demanded (in a possessed person) how great was the joys of Heaven, answered: number the stars who answered again that he could not, so also said he, no man can number the joys of Heaven; and being demanded of returning again unto Heaven, answered—if there were a fiery burning iron pillar reaching from earth to Heaven, set with sharp razors (if I were clad with human flesh wherein I could suffer) I would draw myself up and down upon it even to the day of judgement so that I might find favour at God's hands and come unto his glory. Being demanded how long he did see God before he was cast out of Heaven, he answered, little more than the twinkling of an eye; but that I might see but so long again, that most glorious face I would willingly myself endure the pains of the damned, as well of the devils, as of men, unto the world's end.

St Bernard speaking of the beauty of God (which the holy saints having passed their times here in penance do now continually behold) saith: all do rejoice there in God, because in sight he is most worthy to be desired, in face most beautiful and sweet to enjoy, by himself he pleaseth, by himself he is sufficient for reward, nothing is sought for out of him, and in him alone is all things that can be desired. This holy saints, having declared the beauty of God himself, showeth in like sort the excellence of his kingdom and saith: there is true joy, full knowledge, all beauty

---

[31] *OED*: That cannot be narrated, told, or declared; indescribable, unspeakable.

and bliss, there is peace, goodness, light, virtue and honesty, joy, mirth, sweetness, true love and what good and pleasant thing soever can be thought is there superabundantly found ... (1)

NOTES AND SOURCES

1. William Stanney, *A Treatise of Penance with an Explication of the Rule and Manner of Living of the Brethren and Sisters of the Third Order of St Francis* (1617), 55–62.

## Anthony Browne, 2nd Viscount Montague          1574–1629

Anthony-Maria Browne, 2nd Viscount Montague (1574–1629) was the grandson and heir of the 1st Viscount, who had been on Mary's Privy Council. The family was both staunchly Catholic and staunchly loyal to successive monarchs, and they managed (with difficulty) to mainly both loyalties. Occasionally, as after Gunpowder Plot in 1605, Montague was imprisoned as a leading Catholic, and equally he was an occasional Anglican conformist to safeguard the family and his posterity. But his houses in Sussex and Southwark were always safe houses for Catholic priests on the mission and on the run. He is almost certainly the translator of a life of St Bonaventure (1221–74), Doctor of the Church, Cardinal-Bishop of Albano, and Minister General of the Friars Minor, who wrote his life of St Francis (1181/2–1226) between 1260 and 1263 and had it approved by a General Chapter of the Order as the official biography. It is typical of Montagu's cautious but determined piety that he should undertake as a mental discipline, and as a labour of love, this translation of Bonaventure, from which we include part of the final chapter, a meditation on Francis's stigmata. This text survives in a manuscript version dated 1604, and in two printed editions of 1610 and 1635.

## The Stigmata

Being to the honour of Almighty God, and to the glory of the blessed Father Saint Francis, to write those approved miracles, which were by him done, after his glorification in Heaven, from that point I thought it most especially meet, to take my beginning wherein the efficacy of the cross of Jesus is shown unto us, and wherein the glory thereof is unto us renewed. This new man Saint Francis flourished now by means of a new and admirable miracle, in that he appeared to be ennobled with a singular privilege in all former ages not granted unto any, namely to be graced and adorned with the sacred stigmata of our Lord, and in the body of this death, to be configurated unto the body of him that was crucified. Of whom, whatsoever may be said by tongue of man, shall be inferior unto his due and worthy praise. For the whole endeavour doubtless of the man of God, as well that which was public as that which was private was altogether employed about the Cross of our Lord. And to the end he might outwardly sign his body with the sign of the Cross, which was from the beginning of his conversion, imprinted in his heart, encompassing himself, within a very cross, he took upon him the habit of penance, which did plainly represent the image and form of a Cross, that even as his mind had inwardly put on that Lord himself that was crucified, so might his body also put on the ensigns and arms of the Cross. And that in what sign God Almighty had subdued the powers of the air; in the same might the army of this holy man maintain the warfare of the Lord. But from the beginning of the time wherein he first began to serve under the standard of the Crucifix, divers mysteries of the Cross did in glorious manner appear about him, as to him that shall duly consider the course of his life it may be evidently and clearly known, how by means of a sevenfold apparition of Our Lord his Cross, he was as well in thought as in affection, and act wholly by the ecstatical love of him transformed into the figure and resemblance of him that was crucified. Worthily therefore did the clemency of the highest king (beyond all estimation of man condescending, unto those that were his true lovers) design him in his body to bear the banner of his cross that he who had been forearmed with a marvellous love of the cross, might also be made admirable by a marvellous honour of the Cross. And for the irrefragable[32] establishment of this wonderful miracle, not only the testimonies of them that have both seen and felt it, being all manner of means, most worthy to be believed; but also sundry marvellous apparitions and virtuous effects, shining after his death do helpfully concur to drive all cloudish darksomeness quite away from the mind. For our most holy Lord, of happy memory, Pope Gregory the ninth (of whom that blessed man had prophetically foretold that he should be raised up to the dignity of the see apostolic) did bear in his heart, before such time, as he had enrolled that standard bearer of the Cross into the catalogue of saints, a certain scruple of doubt concerning the wound of his side. But one night (according as that happy pastor did himself with tears report) blessed Saint Francis did himself with a certain kind of disconcerted countenance in sleep appear unto him; and reproving his doubtfulness of heart lifted up his right arm, discovered the wound and required of him a phial glass to gather up the overflowing blood which issued from his side. The chief bishop offered him forthwith the phial by him required, which seemed to be with the blood that came from the side filled up to the top. And from thenceforth he began with so great a devotion to be affected, and with so zealous an emulation to be inflamed unto that sacred miracle that he could by no means endure any man by proud contradiction presumptuously to disgrace those illustrious holy signs, but he would correct him with a severe rebuke . . . (1)

NOTES AND SOURCES

1. *The life of the most holy father St Francis Wrtiten [sic], and in one booke compiled, by that famous and learned man St Bonauenture a freer minor, Cardinall of the holy Roman Church Bishop of Alba, and the Seraphicall Doctor of the Church. Now lately translated into our English tongue* (1635), 293–301.

# Sister Catherine Francis                                    fl. 1628

The translation of continental works for an English audience, especially of lives of the saints, remained a strong part of the English Catholic tradition from the sixteenth to the seventeenth centuries. We include here part of an English version of the life of St Elizabeth, Queen of Portugal (1271–1336), daughter of Pedro III of Aragon and married to King Dinis of Portugal.[33] In addition to the exemplary life described below, Elizabeth became known as the 'Peacemaker', mainly for an incident in 1323. Her only son had rebelled against his father for privileging his bastards above him. Elizabeth rode in person between the opposing armies, and so reconciled her husband and son. To mark her canonization in 1625, her life was written

---

[32] 'That cannot be refuted or disproved; incontrovertible, incontestable, indisputable' (*OED*) (alternatively, (2) 'That cannot or must not be broken; indestructible; inviolable; irresistible').

[33] Dinis (or Diniz or Denis) was King of Portugal 1279–1325 and is known as the Farmer King. Dinis and Elizabeth were married in 1283.

by the Flemish Franciscan Franciscus Paludanus. It was then translated into English by the abbess of the third order Franciscan monastery in Brussels, Catharine Greenbury (Sr Catherine Francis in religion), with a dedicatory epistle by Blessed Francis Bell (martyred 1643).

## Of a Holy Life in Marriage

This new state of life and great honour did not any ways diminish her accustomed devotions: for although this holy Queen were but 12 years of age, yet did she measure and dispose of all her affairs in due time and knew how to direct and turn all her actions to the honour of God, as her mirth into modesty, her joy into tears, her jewels and costly apparel to sharp discipline and chastising her body. She was much given to the service of God in holy contemplation, yet did she never neglect her service and due respects unto the king her husband. She kept a just account how she spent the day, rising early in the morning to read her mattins and prime; and so soon as the priests and musicians were ready to perform the divine service, she went with speed to the chapel where she heard Mass very devoutly upon her knees. And after Mass having reverently kissed the priest's hand she made her offering according to the solemnity of the day, that she might not appear with empty hands before almighty God. This being done, she read the rest of her hours: and this was her accustomed manner, all the time of her life and for the last she read the office of Our Blessed Lady, and the office of the dead. In the afternoons she went again to the chapel to hear the vespers, and to perform the rest of her office: after which she gave herself to holy contemplation wherein she shed abundance of tears that proceeded from the tenderness of her heart. She also used to read devout books which incite to virtue: and after this she exercised herself in skilful needlework, chiefly to shun idleness and to give others good example, she made with her own hands all things that were necessary for the church, she went often to confession and received the most holy Sacrament of the Altar with great devotion. (1)

## On Abstinence

OF HER GREAT ABSTINENCE, AND HOW HER FASTING
WAS CONFIRMED WITH A MIRACLE.

This holy Queen was not only a lover of prayer but also of great abstinence, accustoming herself to a very spare diet that her soul might be the more pleasing unto God. And besides the fasting days appointed by the holy church, she kept three in a week and she likewise fasted the Advent of our Lord: and from the eve of St John Baptist until the day of our Blessed Lady's Assumption, and some times she fasted the Lent of St Michael. When these fasts seemed easy to her, then did she fast the Fridays and Saturdays, with the eves of Our Lady and all the apostles, with bread and water, and she would have proceeded further in fasting but that the king her husband over-ruled her. This wise and virtuous Queen knew well that costly meals, great banquets, and fine apparel was often times the nurse of many sins. And it pleased God to show by a miracle how pleasing the sobriety and abstinence of this his hand maid was unto him; for being sick at Alacante, she was appointed by the doctor to drink wine for the recovery of her strength, but she for the love of abstinence did refuse to drink it, verily believing it was not good for her health. For not she alone, but all the Kings and Queens of Portugal were no drinkers of wine so that it pleased almighty God wonderfully to look upon her, for as her waiting woman brought her twice a cup of cold water to drink it was both times miraculously turned in to good wine. (2)

## Love for the Poor

OF HER MILDNESS TO THE POOR, LIKEWISE CONFIRMED WITH A MIRACLE.

This holy Queen was all ways found mild and very charitable towards the poor being ever willing and ready to help and comfort them in all that possibly she might, so that her liberality seemed to go above her estate, she never let any depart from her uncomforted although there came many unto her, not so much driven by corporal necessity as to receive of her some consolation and ease of their griefs by her pious counsel, and virtuous example. She had great compassion upon all strangers; and outlandish pilgrims tenderly receiving and charitably relieving them according to their necessity with money, clothes, and lodging. She gave to all cloisters as well of men as of women, to the uttermost of her power. She did much commiserate the distressed estate of poor gentlemen which through any misfortune were fallen to decay, and she sought out means to help them. Likewise this pious Queen did understand that within her realm were very many women of good account which suffered great misery for want of maintenance and thereby were in danger to fall in to sin but she employed her most trusty servants to relieve their necessity and by her means preferred many in marriage. And although her piety were always plentifully manifested to the needy, yet upon fasting days and in the holy week she exercised most charity, and apparelling herself in very poor clothes, she was present at all the ceremonies of the holy Catholic church. Upon Good Friday she washed the feet of thirteen poor men and having done she humbly kissed their feet and gave them new clothes. The like she did on Holy Thursday to thirteen poor women. It chanced that one of these poor women had a very sore foot which was grievously eaten with a canker, and being loath the princess should perceive it she drew it back, and gave her other foot to wash, but the holy Queen took the sore foot into her hand and washed it very tenderly and although it had so strong a savour that it could hardly be endured yet did she humbly kiss it, whereupon the said sore was immediately healed miraculously . . . (3)

NOTES AND SOURCES

1. *A Short Relation of the Life, Virtues and Miracles of Elizabeth Called the Peacemaker, Queen of Portugal* (1628), 8–16.
2. Ibid.
3. Ibid.

# Matthew Kellison                                        1561–1642

Matthew Kellison was born and brought up a Catholic on the estates of Lord Vaux of Harrowden (Northants). In 1581, after the arrest of Edmund Campion, he made his way to the English College at Rheims (transferred from Douai) and was ordained in Rome in 1587. He spent his whole career as a scholar in the seminaries of the Low Countries, especially as President of Douai. He engaged as a controversialist against the Protestants (*A Survey of the*

*New Religion*, 1601) and as a moderate voice in the conflicts between the Jesuits and the seculars (*The Right and Jurisdiction of the Prelate and the Prince*, a moderate statement of the case against Catholics taking the oath of allegiance). He was three times recommended for the position of bishop over English Catholics because of his irenic temperament, but three times, as Charles Dodd put it in 1742, 'Doctor Kellison's humility was an obstruction to his preferment'. As he aged, his preference for the pragmatism of the seculars over the rigorism of the Jesuits became more pronounced. His *Treatise of the Hierarchie* (1629) defending the jurisdiction of bishops *in partibus infidelium* in England, was fiercely rebutted by two Jesuits. Pope Urban VIII had to impose silence on all parties in 1631 (in his breve *Britannia*). Kellison's affability appealed to many, but led to his being accused by John Floyd SJ of resembling 'the sea-crab which looketh one way and goeth another'. The first set of extracts come from the most pastoral of his works, *A Myrrhine Poesie of the Bitter Dolours of Christ his Passion, and of the Seaven Words he Spoke on the Cross* (1639). These are followed by one of a number of Kellison's meditations on the psalms for use in the home. We include the opening of a lengthy set of meditations on a psalm of penitence.

## The Garden of Gethsemane

Our blessed Saviour after he had eaten with his disciples the paschal lamb and had also feasted them with his sacred Body and Blood, passed over the torrent of Cedron to the Mount Olivet, where was a garden called Gethsemane. David once passed this torrent with a heavy heart and weeping eyes, when he fled for fear of his son Absalom, who sought his kingdom and his life; and his whole army seeing him weep so bitterly, wept also with him. Our Blessed Saviour, the Son of David, passeth the same torrent, not to fly Judas (who of a disciple whom Christ loved as his own son was become an enemy) but to meet him, for he knew Judas would come thither, in being Christ his ordinary place of resort and retire. And his disciples followed their Master, as they were wont to do, and perceiving by his countenance that he was sad and sorrowful, they went with him and for him.

This garden into which Christ the second Adam entereth is not like to the garden of paradise, in which the first Adam was placed. That was a garden of pleasure and felicity, this of sorrows and misery. In that the first Adam sinned, in this the second Adam by suffering beginneth to satisfy for his sins and ours also, who sinned in him. In that the first Adam by his sin made us all slaves to sin, and captives to the devil; in this the second Adam beginneth his Passion, by which he redeemeth us, and setteth us at liberty. In that garden was planted the tree of corporal and temporal life, in this is Christ the tree of spiritual life. In that God brought forth of the ground all manner of trees fair to behold. In this appeareth to Christ the horrid idea or pattern of the tree of the Cross on which he was to suffer a shameful death. In that was a river which watereth it. In this were the two running fountains of Christ, his eyes, which watereth it with tears, yea as many fountains as were pores in his body, which watereth it with his sacred blood. In that, of the strong rib of Adam, Eve was framed and frail flesh was put in place of the rib. In this the Church was framed of the second Adam's rib, that is, of his divinity or fortitude, by which she was so strong, that she overcame all the assaults of the devil, all the persecutions of the tyrants, and in lieu of his fortitude, Christ took to himself our frailty, which makes him in the garden so fearful and sorrowful...

His sorrow was so great that St Matthew and St Mark say *he was sorrowful even unto death*. St Luke saith *he was in an agony*. And indeed it must needs be a very great sorrow which put him into an agony and *made him to sweat blood*. For St Luke saith this *his sweat became as drops of blood trickling down upon the earth* so that his grief caused not only his eyes to shed tears of water but also whole body to shed tears of blood at all the pores of it. But, O sweet Jesus, if sorrow will permit thee, and I may be so bold as to ask such a question, tell us what are the causes of this thy excessive sorrow or inspire us by thy grace to guess at least what they may be.

The first cause is by many and devout authors thought to have been the bloody idea or foreconceit which in the garden represented unto him the bloody tragedy of his Passion and all parts and circumstances thereof, and that so lively, clearly and particularly as though he had been now suffering that which afterwards he suffered. And this was the principal cause of his faint and bloody sweat which he sweat to cure us of our ague of sin and purge us from all evil and malignant humours of our inordinate passions and affections, and to wash away all the filth of our sins. So that whereas our sorrows and pains proceed from the body to the soul (for when the body is distempered or wounded, the soul suffereth) his sorrow and pain had a contrary course and began with a strong conceit of the mind, which he voluntarily admitted, and which was so lively and particular, that it wounded the body and made it bleed at every pore so abundantly, that as St Luke affirmeth, *the drops trickled down upon the earth*.

The second cause was because he was to suffer of all kinds of persons; to wit the Jews in the priests, scribes and Pharisees; of princes in the High Priest, Herod and Pilate; of subjects in the officers and servants of those princes; of women in the maids which caused Peter to deny him; of his friends in his apostles, who fled from him; in Judas particularly who betrayed him and in Peter who denied him; of his foes in the Jews, and Romans who all conspired against him.

Thirdly He suffered in all parts of his body, in his head by the thorns that crowned him, in his hands and feet by nails that fastened him to the cross, in his face by buffets and spittle, in his whole body by whips and scourges, and by extension of it on the cross.

Fourthly He was to suffer in all his senses; in his eyes by the tears he shed and the blood which from his head descended into them, and in the sight of his cruel tormentors and their cloudy looks and of the instruments of their cruelty, yea in the sight of the tears of his weeping mother and apostle St John and of the devout women; in his ears by the blasphemies, scurrilous and reproachful speeches and in the mocks, scoffings and taunts which he heard; in his taste by gall and vinegar, in his smell by the stinking bones on Mount Calvary, in his sense of feeling by all the corporal pains he endureth ... (1)

## Jesus' Promise from the Cross

The second word or branch: *this day thou shalt be with me in paradise*, Luke 23. Our Blessed Saviour, as he is goodness itself, so he is bountiful and liberal, yea and in a good meaning prodigal. He cannot be truly prodigal because he cannot give above his state and estate, he being King of Kings and Lord of Lords, yet he may seem to us prodigal, and even another prodigal son. For having received of his eternal Father his child's portion, to wit, our human nature, he went into a far country (as the prodigal son did) as far as earth is from Heaven and there conversing with publicans and sinners, he spent his portion, our human nature, amongst them by his many afflictions and his bloody passion which he suffered; and with it he bestowed on them also his good instructions, good lessons, good examples, miracles, and holy merits and satisfactions; and whereas his least prayer would have been sufficient to have redeemed us, he would needs shed his blood for us; and whereas one drop of blood would have sufficed, he bestowed on us frankly and freely all his blood, yea his life and death, and all he had and was; so that in a good sense it may be said, *whereto is this waste? For this might have been sold for more than three hundred pence and given to the poor* (Matt. 26, Mark 14)— that is, this had been sufficient not only to redeem man but also the devils, the poorest of all creatures if God would so disposed. And yet to show his love unto us, his hatred of sin, he would bestow all this upon us...

Paradise in Holy Scripture is taken for any place of pleasure. So was that pleasant garden called, in which God placed the first man and woman, Adam and Eve. So was the country about Jordan is said to have been like a paradise (Gen. 13) before Sodom and Gomorrah were subverted; so in diverse other places of Scripture, paradise is taken for a place pleasure. And because Christ in regard of his soul was that day to descend into the *limbus partum* where the saints of the Old Testament were detained, and to illuminate them with a clear vision of his divinity, in which consisteth happiness; that place which before was a prison he made a paradise and a place of heavenly bliss, and he telleth the good thief *that he shall this day be with me in paradise*, that is shall be partaker with him and his saints of heavenly bliss and felicity...

O how great was thy hope, holy thief, who hopest to be partaker with Christ in his glory in Heaven (for else thou wouldst not have desired it) when he was partaker with thee in thy ignominy and torments of the cross; who hoped to receive of Christ life everlasting, when he was partaker with thee in thy ignominy and torments of the cross; who hopest to receive of Christ life everlasting, when he was at the period of his temporal life. O how great was thy charity and love towards Christ, who thoughtest more of him than thy torments, who chidest thy fellow thief for blaspheming him, pronounceth him innocent before the princes of the Jews and thyself and thy fellow thief worthy of the punishment.

But how great was Christ in his goodness to this thief? How prone was he to mercy, who even at the last hour had mercy on him, and for his short confession forgave him all his sins. He is like a vessel full of water, for as that being but touched runneth over, so Christ is so full of mercy that if the sinner do but touch him with true repentance (as the thief did) he overfloweth and washeth away the sinner's sins and all the filth of them.

O how great is the force of contrition and true repentance which in a moment made St Paul of a persecutor, a preacher; St Matthew of a publican, an apostle and evangelist; St Mary Magdalen of a public sinner, a pattern of all true penitents; which made St Peter of a denier of his master before a maid servant, a confessor of him before the tyrants of the world; and of the poor fisher, a prince of the apostles; which made a thief an inhabitant of paradise and Heaven itself.

O my soul, art thou thus prone to mercy as thy sweet saviour is? Doest thou easily forgive them, that have offended thee? Doest thou not show thyself too hard and difficile [= troublesome] in this kind? If thy heart be hard to forgive, desire God with David to create in thee a clean heart, clean from all malice, soft and easy to pardon those that offend thee, for as thou forgivest, so shalt thou be forgiven ... (2)

## Jesus' Great Cry from the Cross

THE FOURTH WORD OR BRANCH, *MY GOD, MY GOD, WHY HAST THOU FORSAKEN ME* (MATT. 27).

It seemeth strange that Christ, God and man, should complain that his eternal father had left him, seeing that not only as God, but as man, he was united and linked to God by divers ties and unions which were never dissolved. As God, he was consubstantial to his Father, and so linked to him by consubstantiality, which cannot be dissolved, because he and his Father are one and the same substance. As man he was united hypostatically and personally to the second divine person, so indissolubly, that death which separated his body from his soul could not separate his human nature from his divine person. As man also he was united to God (as the blessed in Heaven are) by clear vision, which he had from the first instant of his conception, and from which neither his infancy, nor by sleep, not by his many occupations in his life time, not by all the sorrows and agonies suffered on the cross, he could be distracted. He was also a man so united to God by love and affection, which supposing clear vision, can neither in Christ nor in blessed saints and angels be dissolved, because clear vision of the divine essence and goodness doth as the divines say, necessitate the will to love God; and therefore as in all his life, yea in his agonies on the cross and even in the moment of his death, his soul still retained the clear vision of God, so it still loved God, and so through dying, he ceased for a time to live (that is till he rose on the third day to life again) yet he never ceased to love. Of what forsaking then doth Christ complain, when he saith, *my God, my God, why hast thou forsaken me?*

He complaineth that God hath forsaken him, in withdrawing the assistance of his divinity by which he might have hindered all the torments and even death which he suffered. And therefore he saith, *my God my God* by consubstantiality, *my God my God* by incarnation by which thou art Emmanuel and *Deus vobiscum*, that is God with us, *my God my God*, by clear vision, *my God my God* by fruition and eternal love; *why hast thou forsaken* my human nature, and dost not protect it against the cruelty of the Jews? *My God, my God* who hast saved Noah from the Deluge, Abraham from the Chaldees, Isaac from Abraham's sacrificing sword, the Israelites from Pharaoh and the destroying angel, Jacob from Esau, Joseph from his brethren, and his mistress's false accusations, David from Goliath and Saul, Daniel from the lions, and the three children from the burning furnace, Susanna from the adulterous and false judges, young Tobit from the fish and the evil spirit, *why hast thou forsaken me?* Why doest not thou assist me? *Me*, thy natural son, *me* the verity of these figures, *me* who never offended thee, *me* who ever loved thee, honoured thee, and obeyed thee, even unto *death*.

But although he thus complained according to flesh and blood, and the inferior part of his soul, yet according to his superior part of his soul, he was resolved to die as we have seen above; his complaining was not murmuration, but groaning amid so excessive pains. Not to contradict his Father's will, to which was ever resigned, but to show himself a true man, who feareth death; to give us courage in sickness, torments and what soever adversity, to give us example to have recourse to God, as he had, in all our corporal or spiritual distresses; to forewarn us not to think much when we seem to be left of God in our adversities.

Think, O my soul, who it is that cryeth *my God, my God, why hast thou forsaken me?* He to whom his eternal Father said, *this is my well beloved son in whom I am well pleased.* And mark that he saith not *my Father, my Father,* but *my God, my God,* because at that time he would not show himself to Christ as a Father, that he might be a Father to us . . . O eternal Father, how great is thy love towards sinners, which made thee forsake thy only begotten son for a time, that he might suffer for us, and suffering, die for our sins. O eternal son, how great also was thy love for us, which made thee willingly to be forsaken of thy Father, that thou might suffer even death for us, and suffering it, redeem us . . .

Whoever heard of one plunged in the sea, ready to be drowned and crying for help and aid to a friend, nay to a mere stranger, and not assisted? And yet Christ the Son of God, plunged in the waters of his passion, and ready to be drowned by death, cryeth not to a stranger nor a friend only, but even to his eternal Father and cannot be heard: and why, *but for our sakes.*

O sinner, thou are the cause of this: to draw thee out of the sea of sin, in which thou art plunged, the Son of God must be permitted to be drowned in the waters of his passion, O hard hearted sinner, if this love of God the Father, who would forsake this his son for thee; if the love of God the son, who was willing to be thus forsaken for thee, do not move thee to love God. O ungrateful man, if after this love thou canst find it in thy heart to love any but God, or only God . . . (3)

## On Psalm 51

Paraphrastical and devout discourses upon the psalm Miserere . . . *Rent you hearts and not your garments, and turn to the Lord your God; because he is benign and merciful, patient and of much mercy and ready to be gracious to the malice* Joel. 2

[verse 1] *Have mercy on me, O God.* The royal prophet David, having, through human frailty, committed two great offences against the divine Majesty, no less than adultery with Bathsheba and murder of her husband Uriah; and being reproved thereof by the prophet Nathan, accused by his own conscience and moved by the divine grace, he conceiveth such a detestation and horror of those sins, and is so ashamed and confounded with the horrid aspect of them, that he falleth down prostrate at the feet of his God, whom he had offended. And at first sorrow hindered his tongue from craving pardon but his eyes undertook the office of the mouth and tongue, and pleaded better for the delinquent, by tears, than his mouth could have done by tongue and words, tears being the best of orators. At length speech coming to him, he singeth, or rather sobbeth forth this doleful psalm and sonnet, and peradventure he playeth to it with his harp, but assuredly with his heart. And so maketh a sweet comfort of his heart by sorrow, of his eyes by tears and of his voice by a lamentable tune. And fearing God's justice, he flyeth to his mercy, and beginneth with that doleful note *Miserere, have mercy.* As if he had said: *Thou are just, O Lord, and thy judgement is right* (Ps. 118); but thou art also *benign and merciful, patient and of much mercy, ready to be gracious upon the*

*malice* (Joel 2). If thou wert just only, I should despair, knowing my two so great offences, which now especially I lament. If thou were merciful only, I should presume. But because thou art just and merciful, my fear is mixed with my hope, and my hope with fear, and I so fear thy justice, as I hope in your mercy. Thou art, O Lord (I confess) so just, that thou are justice itself, and this maketh me fear, but thou are also so merciful, that thou art mercy itself and this maketh me hope. That discourageth me very much, this as much encourageth, and giveth me heart to say, *Have mercy on me, O God.* If I were, O Lord, as just and holy as a saint, yet durst I not appear before the eyes of your justice which *in the angels found wickedness* (Job 4) and in whose sight *the moon doth not shine and the stars are not clean* (Job 25). But seeing that I am no saint but a wretched sinner, conceived in sin, brought up in sin, and guilty of the two mentioned and many other sins. How shall I dare to appear before thy justice? For if the just man trembleth before the tribunal of thy justice, how shall the sinner stand before it?

2. But I appeal, O Lord (saith David), from thy justice to thy mercy, not as to a higher tribunal (for thy justice and mercy are both infinite, and so equal), but as to a tribunal more benign, more clement and gentle. And although I be guilty of grievous and enormous sins, and those so great, that I regard them only and their ill deserts, I may say with Cain, *my iniquity is greater than that I may deserve pardon* (Gen. 4), yet they are not so great but thy mercy is infinitely greater, and so compared to it they are not so great, but they may deserve pardon. For if it please, O Lord, to put not only my sins, but also all the sins of men in one scale of thy divine balance and thy mercy in the other, thy mercy would outweigh and oversway them, and *as the sands of the sea, thy mercy would appear heavier* (Job 6)...

5. I confess that by sin I am become *as a horse and mule which have no understanding* (Ps. 31) and my brutish appetites, to which I have been a slave, have metamorphosed me and made me so brutish, that I am in life and conversation rather a brute beast than a reasonable creature—but yet *men and beasts thou wilt save, O Lord* (Ps. 35) and in the law delivered by Moses, though it be a law of terror, thou hadst pity even on brute beasts, and wouldst not permit the Jew to plough with an ox and an ass (Deut. 22) lest the ass should be over laboured (Exod. 23); nor to seeth [= cook] the kid in the milk of his dam [= mother] (Deut. 14), that seeming cruelty, not in a nest to kill or take the old bird with the young nor to muzzle the mouth of the ox that treadeth the corn (Deut. 22). *Have mercy on me,* though by sin more a beast than they.

6. If I were the only sinner, O Lord, thou wouldst have less reason to pardon me, but seeing *all have sinned and transgressed,* seeing that *all have declined and there is not one that doth good, no not one* (Ps. 13)—if thou shouldst exercise justice only on sinners, thou shouldst find none on whom thou couldst exercise thy mercy. If thou shouldst punish all sinners, thou shouldst have none to pardon; and so thy most grateful attribute, mercy, should never show itself. And yet none of thy divine attributes is so grateful as thy clemency. None do make thee so popular as thy mercy...

7. Rue the day and hour, yea the many days and hours in which thou hast offended God and acknowledge therein thy too deep ingratitude, because in offending him thou has offended thy creator, by whom thou hast thy natural being, by whom thou liveth and breatheth, thou has offended thy redeemer, who to ransom thee from death, the devil and sin become man for thee and suffered the

most shameful and most painful death of the Cross to give to thee here in this life a spiritual life and being by grace, and in the next life an eternal life, and being by glory. Say unto him, I ought myself wholly unto thee for my creation, and I ought myself again wholly unto thee for my redemption, and so I but one, am twice thine and twice due unto thee . . . (4)

NOTES AND SOURCES

1. Matthew Kellison, *A Myrrhine Poesie of the Bitter Dolours of Christ his Passion* (1639), 1–3.
2. Ibid. 9–11.
3. Ibid. 161–5, 182–8.
4. Matthew Kellison, *Paraphrasticall and Devout Discourses upon the Psalme Miserere* (1635), 1–12.

## Sister Gertrude Helen More OSB                    1606–1633

Helen More (Gertrude in religion) was a Benedictine nun and the great-great-grand-daughter of St Thomas More. She was the daughter of Cresacre Moore (1572–1649) who was trained in the English College at Rheims and took minor orders, but who was recalled to head the family after the death of his older brother, and published in the 1620s (there is no date on the title page) a biography of Thomas More which was a skilful interweaving of earlier lives written by William Roper, Nicholas Harpsfield, and Thomas Stapleton. Helen's tutor, Benet Jones OSB, encouraged her to become a religious, and, though at first reluctant, she agreed to test her vocation. At the age of 17 she travelled with two More cousins and four others to Douai and thence to Cambrai to become one of the founding members of a Benedictine house dedicated to Our Lady of Comfort, which would later become Stanbrook Abbey. She rebelled against the Ignatian basis of the prayer life taught to the communities in and around Douai, and in its place developed the distinctive form of prayer abstracted below. She had a relationship of mutual admiration and disagreement with the spiritual director at Cambrai, Father Augustine Baker OSB. After her death from smallpox at the age of 27, her own spiritual writings were discovered and edited for publication some by Baker (who also wrote *The Inner Life of Dame Gertrude More*) and others by Serenus Cressy OSB, who edited her *Confessio Amantis*, which interweaves Augustine's Confessions into the Divine Office. Our selections come from *The Holy Practises of a Divine Lover, or the Saintly Idiot's Devotions*, published in 1657. We include two of her twenty-one penitential exercises, some Marian meditations that are especially intense and powerful, and her meditation on 'certain temptations and lettings which souls have from their spiritual enemies in their journey to spiritual Jerusalem'.

## Two Penitential Exercises

### THE III. EXERCISE.

1. My feet have been swift to evil, and mine eyes have been dissolute to vanity, and mine ears have been always open to trifles, and toys.

2. My understanding which should have contemplated thy beauty, and have meditated both day and night on thy commandments hath considered transitory toys, and meditated day and night how to transgress thy said commandments.

3. My will was by thee invited to the love of celestial delights and delicacies, but I preferred the earth before heaven.

4. I have spread my arms which thou hast consecrated to thy love to embrace, and hug the filthy love of creatures.

5. This is, O Lord, the reward, this is the fruit which I, thy creature have yielded.

6. Alas. What can I a wretch answer if thou enterest with me into judgement, and wilt say: I have planted thee a chosen vineyard all true seed, how then O strange vineyard art thou turned in my sight into that which is depraved?

7. And if I cannot answer to this first question concerning my creation, how shall I answer the second concerning my conversation?

8. Thou O merciful God hast preserved him by thy providence who hath thought of no other thing, but how to violate thy commandments, and to set up the kingdom of sin against thee.

9. Thou hast moved that tongue which dishonoured thee, thou hast governed those members which offended thee.

10. In so much as I have not only been ungrateful for thy benefits, but used thy benefits also themselves as weapons against thee.

11. Thou hast made all creatures for my use to allure me to love thee, I have abused them, and of them have divers times taken occasion of sin.

12. I have made choice rather of the gift, than the giver.

13. I have been blinded by them, and have not lifted up mine eyes at the sight of them.

14. I have not considered how much more beautiful the Creator is, than the creature.

15. Thou hast given me all things that I should give thee myself; and all things have served me, but I never have given thee glory, or paid thy tribute.

16. Thou hast given me health, and the devil hath gathered the fruits thereof.

17. Thou hast given me strength and I have spent it in the service of thine enemy.

18. What shall I say? Wherefore have not all the calamities and miseries which I have known to have fallen upon other men and touched not me, been a sufficient argument to me that my delivery from every one of them was a peculiar benefit from thee?

19. O most gracious Lord shall I be ungrateful for these benefits?

20. If the fierceness and cruelty of lions and serpents be assuaged with benefits, why shall not thy benefits be sufficient to tame and assuage my sinful heart?

THE IV EXERCISE

1. But if so strict an account shall be demanded for these things which cost thee so little what account wilt thou ask of those which thou hast bought to thyself with thy most precious Blood.

2. How have I perverted thy counsels?

3. How have I violated the mystery of thine Incarnation?

4. Thou wert made man to make me a God, I have made myself a beast, and the slave of the devil.

5. Thou hast come down to the earth to bring me to heaven, and I have not hearkened to or acknowledged this high vocation.

6. But have persevered in wickedness, and in the dirt and mire of my baseness.

7. Thou hadst delivered me, I have cast myself again headlong into my old bondage.

8. Thou hadst raised me, I have again embraced death.

9. Thou hadst made me one body with thee, and I have joined myself again with the devil.

10. So many, and so great benefits could not do so much, as make me know thee.

11. Nor so many tokens of love, make me requite thee with Love.

12. Nor so many deserts, and gifts make me hope in thee.

13. Nor such a strict kind of justice, as appeared in thy Passion make me fear thee.

14. Thou hast humbled thyself even to the dust of the earth, I puff myself up with pride.

15. Thou didst hang naked on the Cross, I seek the world and worldly delights.

16. Thou being God wert buffeted; if any man touch my garment who am only a most vile worm, I presently become choleric.

17. What shall I say, my sweet Saviour? Behold how great thy mercy and charity is towards me.

18. Thou wouldst die to kill my sins; and I presuming in thy said mercy, goodness, and love have not feared to sin against thee, what greater impiety can be imagined?

19. I have taken occasion of thy goodness to work malice; and by that mean which thou hast used to kill sin, I have taken occasion to raise again sin in myself.

20. Because thou wert so good, I thought I might without prejudice be evil.

21. And because thy benefits were so many I thought I might without punishment render unto thee, as many injuries. (1)

## Devotion to Our Lady

AN EXERCISE OF DEVOTION TO OUR BLESSED LADY MOTHER OF GOD.

1. Hail sweet Mary: hail most sacred Virgin; whom God before all ages did choose for his most Sacred Mother.

2. Thou art betwixt God, and man: that blessed mediatrix by whom the highest things are joined to the lowest.

3. Thou art the beginning of life, the gate, or entry of grace, the safe haven of the world suffering shipwreck.

4. Obtain for me I beseech thee perfect pardon of my sins, and the perfect grace of the Holy Ghost.

5. That I may diligently worship: chastely, and fervently love thy Son my Saviour, and thee the Mother of Mercy.

6. Hail sweet Mary whom, foreshowed in sundry figurative speeches, and promised in divers oracles of the prophets; the ancient fathers did cover most earnestly.

7. O my Lady receive me for thy poor servant: adopt me O Mother for thy Son!

8. Grant that I may be numbered among them whom thou dost love (whose names are written in thy virginal breast) and whom thou dost teach, direct, help, cherish and protect.

9. Hail sweet Mary; whom God by a most honourable priviledge did preserve from sin.

10. And adorned with most singular grace: and most excellent gifts.

11. O Glorious Virgin, O Gracious Virgin, O most pure Virgin chosen amongst thousands.

12. Do not repel me wicked sinner: do not despise, and reject me defiled with the filth of sin.

13. But hear me miserable wretch crying unto thee, comfort me desiring thee, and help me trusting in thee. Amen. (2)

## On Temptations

Of certain temptations, and lettings, which souls have from their spiritual enemies in their journey to spiritual Jerusalem, and of the remedy against the same.

Now art thou in the way, and knowest how thou ought to travel, and go. Now beware of enemies that will be diligent, and busy to let thee if they can. For their interest is to put out of thy heart, the desire, and longing that thou hast to the love of Jesus, and to draw thee home again to the love of worldly vanity. There is nothing that grieveth them so much as to see thee seek after, and labour for the love of Jesus. Those enemies are principally fleshly desires, and vain fears that arise out of thine heart through the corruption of thy corporal nature, and would let, and hinder thy desire of the love of God, that so they might fully, and restingly possess thy heart; these are thy nearest enemies. Other enemies also there are, and namely the wicked Spirits who are diligent, and busy with sleights, inventions, and deceits to deceive thee. But one remedy thou hast against them all, as before I have told thee, and that is, that whatsoever they say unto thee believe them not, but hold forth on thy way, and only desire the love of Jesus. Ever answer thus; I am nothing, I covet nothing, but only the love of our Lord Jesus.

This is the best, securest, and easiest way of overcoming all temptations and scruples whatsoever answer nothing to them, be not troubled with them; but still go on thy way, and tend to the love of thy God, which will overcome all, and make all right with thee.

If thine enemies, by suggestions to thy soul, say unto thee that thou hast not made thy Confession a-right, or that there is some old sin or sins hid in thy heart that thou before knowest not; or that thou hast not as yet ever made thy Confessions a-right, or as thou shouldst have made them, and therefore would have thee turn home again, and to give over thine earnest desire of the love of God; and to go, and make a better confession. Believe not this their saying, for it is folly. For thou art rightly confessed, and so do thou surely hope, and trust thyself to be; and that thou art in the way, and that thou needest no further to look into thy conscience for confession of what is past. Hold on thy way, and ever think on Jerusalem. If they say also unto thee that thou art not worthy to have the love of God; and therefore why shouldst thou covet that which thou wilt not be able to come by, or art worthy to have. Believe them not: but hold on thy way, and say thus. Not because I am worthy, but because I am unworthy, therefore would I love God. For if that I had his love, it would make me worthy. And since that I was created for that end (which is for the loving of God) though I should never come by it, yet will I covet it, and therefore will I pray, and think how I may get it, and will labour for it. And then if thine enemies see that thou beginnest to grow bold, courageous, and resolute in thy said purpose, they begin to grow afraid of thee. Nevertheless they will not cease, or give over to seek to stay, and hinder thee as much as they can: so long as thou art holding on thy way; what on the one side with fears, and threatenings; and what on the other side with false flattery, and vain pleasings for to make thee give over thy good purposes, and to turn thee home again. And for that end they will say thus unto thee. If thou thus hold on thy desire to Jesus travelling so fervently as thou now beginnest; thou wilt fall into fancies, or into frenzy, or craze thy head, or fall into bodily sickness, as thou seeest some do by going about that which thou now dost: or thou wilt fall into poverty, or some bodily harm, or mischief, and no man able to help thee; or thou mayest fall into secret and inward temptations, or illusions of the enemy so that thou wilt not be able to help thyself about them. For it is wondrous perilous for any man, or woman to give him- or herself wholly, to the love of God, and to leave, and forsake all the world, and to covet nothing, but only the love of Him. For so many perils may fall to a man in such course of his, as he cannot so much as imagine them beforehand. And therefore turn thee home again, and leave off this desire, for thou shalt never bring it to an end; and do thou as other worldly men, or the common sort of good Christians, or even of religious do. Thus say thine enemies; but believe them not, but hold on in thy desire, and say, or answer nothing else, but that thou wouldst have Jesus and be at Jerusalem. And if they perceive that thou wilt not give over, neither for sickness, for fantasies, nor for frenzies, for doubts, nor for fears of any temptations corporal, or spiritual for poverty, nor for any mischief, or harm, for life, nor for death, but ever seekest, and longest after the said one thing, and nothing else but that one thing, and yieldest to them a deaf ear as if thou hears them not, and holdest on stiffly, and constantly, and perseverantly in prayer, and in other thy spiritual works with discretion according to the counsel of thy superior; or the advice or direction given thee by thy spiritual Father, or director, then begin they to be very angry and to go a little more near thee.

Then they begin to rob thee, and beat thee, and do thee all the shame, and mischief they can. And that they do when they cause all the deeds thou dost, be they never so well done, to be deemed, and judged by others to be evil, and turned, and taken in the worser sense, and meaning. And whatsoever it be thou wouldst do, or have done in help, relief or comfort of thy body, or of thy soul: it shall be let, or hindered by those other men, so that thou shalt be put from thy will, and contradicted in it, in all or most of those things which thou with reason desirest to have. And this thy said enemies do, to the end thou shouldst be stirred, and provoked to anger, impatience, or evil will towards thy Christian brother or sister, but against all these temptations and vexations and difficulties, and all other that may come upon thee or which thou mayest feel: use this remedy that I shall now again tell thee, as before I have told thee. Take Jesus, or his love in thy mind, and trouble thyself no further with them but think on thy lesson. That thou art nothing, that thou hast nothing, that thou covetest nothing of earthly, or transitory things, that thou desirest nothing but the love of Jesus. And in and with these exercises hold on thy way to Jerusalem. And if thou happen sometimes through thy frailty or by the evil will of some other man, or through the malice of thine enemy to be tarried, or let in thy way. Yet as soon as thou canst come again to thyself, leave of thinking of what hath past, and proceed in thy good exercises, and hold on thy way, abide not long with those thy former defects, or difficulties, for fear of thine enemies who would still hold thee in them, and in discussing of them, thereby to hinder thee from going forwards in thy way. (3)

NOTES AND SOURCES

1. Gertrude More, *The Holy Practises of a Divine Lover, or the Saintly Idiot's Devotions* (1657), 46–52.
2. Ibid. 41–52.
3. Ibid. 113–15, 223–5, 314–22.

# Augustine Baker OSB                                     1575–1641

David Baker (Augustine was his name in religion) was the son of a government official in South Wales, and Welsh was his first language. He trained as a lawyer but was reconciled to the Church in 1603 and two years later travelled to Padua and entered the novitiate in the reformed Benedictine Abbey there. Thereafter his training was highly irregular. He returned to England after just a year, and was professed on his arrival in the country. He worked as a lawyer for a while, studied on his own in solitude in the West Country (immersing himself in the classics of both late medieval English and continental mysticism) and then offered himself without more ado for the sacred priesthood, not to serve on the mission but to deepen his prayer life. Although formally a member of the Benedictine community at the Abbey of Dieulouard in Lorraine, he never resided there, but stayed in England until 1624 when he was sent to be spiritual director of the new English convent at Cambrai. His own writings largely come from this period, when he was responsible for, amongst others, the spiritual development of Sr Gertrude More. He was suspicious of the more formal approaches to prayer favoured by the Jesuits and others, and his own method, drawing heavily on his medieval reading, allowed much more freedom for the Holy Spirit to work in His own way in each person. A fellow-priest denounced him to the general chapter of the English congregation, and although he was exonerated, the chapter decided to remove both men from Cambrai. He spent some time at St Gregory's Priory Douai, but complaints flared up again, and his prior was persuaded to send him back to England to minister to the communities around the Inns of Court, and he died in that part of London in 1641 and is said to have been buried in the medieval churchyard of the Anglican parish church of St Andrew's Holborn. Sixteen years after his death, his fellow Benedictine Serenus Cressy collated his manuscripts into a single, highly structured work to which he gave the title *Sancta Sophia*. We include an extract which certainly reveals his own life of prayer and his time with the sisters at Cambrai.

## Degrees of Prayer

Several mystic authors according to the several notions that they had both of the end of a spiritual life and means conducing thereto, have by several terms made the division of its degrees. The most ancient division is into three states: 1, of beginners. 2, of proficients. 3, of such as are perfect. Yet withal they do not signify by what distinctive marks each of these states are separated from the others. But generally, in the latter times, the whole course of the spiritual life is divided: 1 into the purgative way, in which all sinful defects are purged out of the soul; 2 the illuminative way, by which divine virtues and graces are introduced; 3 the unitive way by which a soul attains unto the end of all other exercises to wit, a union with God in Spirit by perfect charity...

I shall only distinguish three degrees of prayer to wit: 1 discursive prayer or meditation; 2 the prayer of forced immediate acts or affections of the will, without discourse preparatory thereto; 3 the prayer of pure active contemplation or aspirations as it were naturally and without any force flowing from the soul, powerfully and immediately directed and moved by the Holy Spirit...

These, therefore, being the three degrees of internal prayer (the which do most properly answer to the commonly assigned ways of spirituality, the purgative, the illuminative and the unitive). Of them, the first is a prayer consisting much of the discourse of the understanding. The other two are prayers of the will, but most principally and purely the last. Of these three I shall treat in order in the following discourse (to wit 1. in pursuit of this second section of the most imperfect degree to wit, meditation; 2. in the following section of the prayer of immediate acts of the will; 3. and in the last section, of the prayer of aspirations or contemplation)...

First, therefore, it is apparent and acknowledged that general(ly) speaking, a soul from a state of negligence and secularity first entering into a spiritual course though she be supposed by virtue of that grace, by which she is moved to make so great and happy a change, to be really in the state of justification, yet there still remains in her a great measure of fear conceived from the guilt of her former sins, and withal strong inclinations to sin and vicious habits do yet abide and will do so till by long practice of virtue and piety they be abated and expelled. Moreover a world of vain sinful images do possess the soul, which distract her whensoever she sets her mind on God, calling her to attend to her formerly pleasing objects, which took up all her affections, and which do still oftimes insinuate themselves into her memory, with too much contentment to inferior nature. The which contentment though she upon reflection do resist and renounce with her superior soul, yet this resistance is oftimes so feeble that frequently she is really entangled and seduced and more often does find ground to doubt that she had given consent thereto.

Such being ordinarily the disordered condition of a soul at her first conversion, the remedy acknowledged to be proper and necessary for her is prayer. And the highest degree of prayer that for the present she is capable of is either a much distracted vocal prayer or discursive meditation, in which the understanding and imagination are chiefly employed. And the reason is because although God hath imprinted true charity in such a soul, yet seducing images so abounding, and vicious affections being as yet so predominant in sensitive nature, there is a necessity for the fortifying it to chase away the said images, and subdue such affections by storing the imagination with contrary good images, and setting on work affections contrary to these; and this is done by inventing arguments and motives (especially of fear). So that the exercises proper to a soul in this imperfect state are those of sensible contrition and remorse for sin etc caused by the consideration of the foulness of it, of the misery that attends it, the certainty and uncertainty of death, the terrors of God's judgement, the horror of Hell etc, as likewise a consideration that no less a price would serve for the reparation of a soul from sin than the bloody passion of the Son of God etc. Such matters as these are now the seasonable subjects of meditation, and the actions of mortification fit to attend such prayer are more sensible, gross and exterior, proper to repress her grosser defects.

Now when by means of such exercises the soul is become well eased from remorse and begins to be moved to the resistance and hatred of sin by the love of God rather than fear of his judgements, her discursive prayer for all that does not cease, but there is a change made only in the objects of it, because instead of the consideration of judgement, Hell etc the soul finds herself more inclined to resist sin by the motives of love, or a consideration of the charity, patience and sufferings of Our Lord, as likewise out of a comfortable meditation of the future joys promised and prepared for her. Although charity be much increased, yet not yet to such a point but that she stands in need of motives and considerations to set it on work, as likewise of good, holy, efficacious images of divine things to allure her to forget or neglect the vain images that yet do much distract her. The object of her thoughts now are the infinite joys of Heaven, the sublime mysteries of faith, the blessed humanity of Our Lord, the glorious attributes of the divinity etc. And the mortifications answerable to the present state do grow more internal, being much exercised about inward defects, which by prayer are discovered to her and corrected. Now a soul whilst she continues in this sort of prayer and mortification standing in need of a much and frequent consideration of motives, is properly said to be in the purgative way, though towards the latter end there be a mixture of the illuminative.

In the second place, when a soul by perseverance in such discursive prayer comes to find (as in time she will) that she stands in less need of inventing motives to induce her to exercise love of God, because good affections by exercise abounding and growing ripe, do with facility move themselves so near, the mere presenting of a good object to the soul suffices to make her produce a good affection. Thenceforward by little and little, the soul in prayer quits discoursing and the will immediately stirs itself towards God. And here (meditation ending) the second and more perfect degree or state of internal prayer begins, to wit the prayer of immediate acts of the will.

Now a soul living a solitary or abstracted life, and being arrived to this prayer, if she should be obliged by others, or force herself to continue meditation, she would make no progress at all. Yea on the contrary, the extreme painfulness of inventing motives (now unnecessary) and trying herself to methods and prescribed forms would be to her so distractive, so void of all taste and comfort, and so insupportable, that not being suffered to follow God's invitation calling to an exercise of the will, she will be in danger to give quite over all internal prayer. Whereas by pursuing God's call, she will every day get light to discover more and more her secret inward defects and grace to mortify and amend them. And such her mortification is exercised rather by transcending and forgetting the objects of her inordinate affections than a direct combating against them. And this state of prayer doth properly answer to that which is commonly called the illuminative way, because in it the soul with little reflection on herself or her own obscurity by reason of sin etc, tends directly and immediately to God, by whom she is enlightened and adorned by all virtues and graces. In the third place a soul after a long exercise in forced affections of the will of God represented to the understanding by images far more subtle and spiritual than formerly, yea endeavouring to contemplate Him in the darkness and obscurity of a blind and naked faith void of all distinct and express images, will by little grow so well disposed to Him that she will have less need of forcing herself to produce good affections to Him, or of prescribing to herself determinate forms of acts or affections. On the contrary, divine love will become so firmly established in the soul, so wholly and only filling and possessing it, that it will become as it were a new soul unto the soul, as constantly breathing forth fervorous acts of love and as naturally almost as the lungs do send forth breath.

And here begins the state of pure contemplation (the end of all exercises of an internal life). In this blessed state the actuations and aspirations are so pure and spiritual, that the soul herself oftentimes is not able to give an account what she does; and no wonder, since they do not proceed from any forethought or election of her own, but are suggested to her by the divine spirit entirely possessing her. And although in these most sublime and blind elevations of the will, the imagination and understanding with their images are not absolutely excluded, yet so imperceptible are their operations, that it is no wonder if many mystical writers speaking according to what they felt and experienced in themselves have said that in pure contemplation the will without the understanding was only operative. As for mortifications proper to this state, they are as inexpressible as the prayer. Indeed prayer and mortification seem to be now become the same thing. For the light in which the soul walks is so clear and wonderful that the smallest imperfections are clearly discovered and by prayer alone mortified. Prayer is the whole business of life, interrupted by sleep only and not always then neither. True it is that by other necessities of corporal nature—reflections, study, conversation or business—it may be depressed a little from the height in which it is when the soul sets itself to attend to God only; but still it continues with efficacy in the midst of all those avocations. And this is truly and properly that which mystics do style the unitive way, because herein the soul is in a continual union of spirit with God, having transcended all creatures and herself too, the which are become as it were annihilated, and God is all in all. There is no state of spirituality beyond this. But yet this state may infinitely increase in degrees of purity... (1)

NOTES AND SOURCES

1. *Sancta Sophia or Directions for the prayer of contemplation etc extracted out of more then XL treatises written by the late Ven. Father F Augustine Baker, a monke of the English Congregation of the Holy Order of S Benedict: and methodically digested by the R(ev) F(ather) Serenus Cressy of the same Order and Congregation* (1657), second part, pp. 83–92.

# Richard Crashaw                                        *c.*1613–1649

Richard Crashaw was the son of a strongly anti-Catholic Anglican clergyman and polemicist. His mother and step-mother having both died by the time he was 7 and his father when he was 12, he revealed throughout his adult life a deep craving to find the security of a warm and loving family. When (after being a scholar at Pembroke College Cambridge, 1631–5) he was elected to a Fellowship at the fanatically Laudian Peterhouse, he thought he had found it: 'his little contentful kingdom', he called it. He was a poet from an early age, and precocious in his exploration of the forms and themes of (continental) Counter-Reformation poetical forms (he was more prolific in Latin and Greek than in English). As a Laudian he was not alone in his devotion to Our Lady, including her Assumption, nor was it unprecedented in the period that he should be interested in the lives of St Teresa of Avila and St Mary Magdalen, but the intensity of his devotion is startling, arising both from a theological repugnance at all aspects of Calvinist thought and a tug towards Tridentine teaching and spirituality. Nonetheless he remained in the warm embrace of Peterhouse until the middle of the civil war, when he saw his beloved chapel, the most perfect representation of 'the beauty of holiness', and its predecessor as college chapel, St Mary the Less (of which he was curate as well as college catechist) systematically stripped of all the 'monuments of idolatry and superstition' by the state-appointed iconoclast William Dowsing. In shock he withdrew to the Continent, where he served briefly in the Household of Queen Henrietta Maria, then he moved on to Rome and to a post in the Household of Cardinal Polotto and finally to 'a little employ' at the great pilgrimage centre of Loretto, where he died shortly after arriving. His formal conversion to Catholicism took place soon after he left Cambridge. Most of the poems which follow are difficult to date, but some at least must pre-date his conversion. However, he was spiritually in the Church long before his formal reconciliation, and so their inclusion here can be defended in as much they were all included in a posthumous collection edited and published as an explicitly Catholic work by Miles Pinkney, alias Thomas Carr (q.v.) in *Carmen Deo nostro* (1652). This was dedicated to Susan Fielding, née Villiers, countess of Denbigh, daughter of Charles I's assassinated favourite, the Duke of Buckingham. Lady Denbigh was lady-in-waiting to Henrietta-Maria (while her husband was a Parliamentarian in the Civil Wars), and she was teetering on the brink of conversion, hence the final poem in our selection.

## The Crown of Thorns

*Upon the Crown of Thorns taken down from the head of our Blessed Lord,*
*all bloody*

Know'st thou This, Soldier?
'Tis a much-chang'd plant which yet
Thyself did'st set.

O who so hard a Husbandman did ever find;
A soil so kind?

Is not the soil a kind one, which returns
Roses for Thrones? (1)

## Upon the Body of our Blessed Lord, Naked and Bloody

They have left thee naked, LORD, O that they had!
This garment too I would they had denied.

Thee with thyself they have too richly clad;
Opening the purple wardrobe in thy side.

O never could there be garment too good
For thee to wear, But this, of thine own Blood. (2)

## The Hymn of St Thomas the Apostle

*The hymn of Saint Thomas in Adoration of the Blessed Sacrament*

With all the powers my poor heart hath
Of humble love and loyal Faith,
Thus low (my hidden life!) I bow to thee
Whom too much love hath bow'd more low for me.
Down down, proud sense! Discourses die.
Keep close, my soul's inquiring eye!
Nor touch nor taste must look for more
But each sit still in his own Door.

Your ports are all superfluous here,
Save that which lets in faith, the ear.
Faith is my skill. Faith can believe
As fast as love new laws can give.
Faith is my force. Faith strength affords
To keep pace with those powerful words.
And words more sure, more sweet, than they
Love could not think, truth could not say.

O let thy wretch find that relief
Thou didst afford the faithful thief.
Plead for me, love! allege and show
That faith has farther, here, to go
And less to lean on. Because than
Though hid as GOD, wounds writ thee man,
Thomas might touch; None but might see
At least the suff'ring side of thee;
And that too was thyself which thee did cover,
But here ev'n that's hid too which hides the other.

Sweet, consider then, that I
Though allow'd not hand nor eye

To reach at thy lov'd Face; nor can
Taste thee GOD, or touch thee MAN
Both yet believe; And witness thee
My LORD too and my GOD, as loud as He.
Help, lord, my hope increase;
And fill my portion in thy peace.
Give love for life; nor let my days
Grow, but in new powers to thy name and praise.

O dear memorial of that death
Which lives still, and allows us breath!
Rich, royall food! Bountiful BREAD!
Whose use denies us to the dead;
Whose vital gust alone can give
The same leave both to eat and live;
Live ever bread of loves, and be
My life, my soul, my surer self to me.

O soft self-wounding pelican!
Whose breast weeps balm for wounded man.
Ah this way bend thy benign flood
To'a bleeding heart that gasps for blood.
That blood, whose least drops sovereign be
To wash my worlds of sins from me.
Come love! Come LORD! and that long day
For which I languish, come away.
When this dry soul those eyes shall see,
And drink the unseal'd source of thee.
When Glory's sun faith's shades shall chase,
And for thy veil give me thy FACE.
Amen (3)

## The Assumption

*The Glorious Assumption of our Blessed Lady. The hymn*

Hark! she is call'd, the parting hour is come
Take thy Farewell, poor world! heaven must go home.
A piece of heav'nly earth; purer and brighter
Than the chaste stars, whose choice lamps come to light her
While through the crystal orbs, clearer than they
She climbs; and makes afar more milky way.
She's called. Hark, how the dear immortal dove
Sighs to his silver mate rise up, my love!
Rise up, my fair, my spotless one!
The winter's past, the rain is gone.
The spring is come, the flowers appear

No sweets, but thou, are wanting here.
Come away, my love!
Come away, my dove! cast off delay,
The court of heav'n is come
To wait upon thee home; Come come away!
The flowers appear.
Or quickly would, wert thou once here
The spring is come, or if it stay,
'Tis to keep time with thy delay.
The rain is gone, except so much as we
Detain in needful tears to weep the want of thee.
The winter's past.
or if he make less hast,
His answer is, why she does so.
If summer come not, how can winter go.
Come away, come away.
The shrill winds chide, the waters weep thy stay;
The fountains murmur; and each loftiest tree.
Bows low'st his heavy top, to look for thee.
Come away, my love.
Come away, my dove, cast off delay,
The court of heav'n is come
To wait upon thee home; Come come away!

She's call'd again. And will she go?
When heaven bids come, who can say no?
Heaven calls her, and she must away.
Heaven will not, and she cannot stay.
Go then; go GLORIOUS.
On the golden wings
Of the bright youth of heaven, that sings
Under so sweet a Burthen. Go,
Since thy dread son will have it so.
And while thou goest, our song and we
Will, as we may, reach after thee.
HAIL, holy Queen of humble hearts!
We in thy praise will have our parts.
Thy precious name shall be.
Thy self to us; and we
With holy care will keep it by us.
We to the last
Will hold it fast
And no ASSUMPTION shall deny us.
All the sweetest showers
Of our fairest flowers
Will we strew upon it.
Though our sweets cannot make
It sweeter, they can take

Themselves new sweetness from it.
MARIA, men and Angels sing
MARIA, mother of our KING.
LIVE, rosy princess, LIVE. And may the bright
Crown of a most incomparable light
Embrace thy radiant brows. O may the best
Of everlasting joys bathe thy white breast.
LIVE, our chaste love, the holy mirth
Of heaven; the humble pride of earth.
Live, crown of women; Queen of men.
Live mistress of our song. And when
Our weak desires have done their breast,
Sweet Angels come, and sing the rest. (4)

## To the Countess of Denbigh, for her Conversion

To the noblest and best of Ladies, the Countess of Denbigh, persuading her
to resolution in religion, and to render herself without further delay into the
communion of the Catholic Church.

What heav'n-intreated HEART is this?
Stands trembling at the gate of bliss;
Holds fast the door, yet dares not venture
Fairly to open it, and enter.
Whose DEFINITION is a doubt
Twixt life and death, twixt in and out.
Say, ling'ring fair! why comes the birth
Of your brave soul so slowly forth?
Plead your pretences O you strong
In weakness! why you choose so long
In labour of yourself to lie,
Nor daring quite to live nor die?
Ah linger not, lov'd soul! a slow
And late consent was a long no,
Who grants at last, long time tried
And did his best to have denied,
What magic bolts, what mystic bars
Maintain the will in these strange wars!
What fatal, yet fantastic, bands
Keep the free heart from it's own hands!
So when the year takes cold, we see
Poor waters their own prisoners be.
Fetter'd, and locked up fast they lie
In a sad self-captivity.
The astonished nymphs their flood's strange fate deplore,
To see themselves their own severer shore.
Thou that alone canst thaw this cold,
And fetch the heart from it's strong hold;

All mighty LOVE! end this long war,
And of a meteor make a star.
O fix this fair INDEFINITE.
And 'mongst thy shafts of sovereign light
Choose out that sure decisive dart
Which has the Key of this close heart,
Knows all the corners of't, and can control
The self-shut cabinet of an unsearched soul.
O let it be at last, love's hour
Raise this tall Trophy of thy power;
Come once the conquering way; not to confute
But kill this rebel-word, IRRESOLUTE
That so, in spite of all this peevish strength
Of weakness, she may write RESOLV'D AT LENGTH,
Unfold at length, unfold fair flower
And use the season of love's shower,
Meet his well-meaning Wounds, wise heart!
And haste to drink the wholesome dart.
That healing shaft, which heaven till now
Hath in love's quiver hid for you.
O Dart of love! arrow of light!
O happy you, if it hit right,
It must not fall in vain, it must
Not mark the dry regardless dust.
Fair one, it is your fate; and brings
Eternal worlds upon its wings.
Meet it with wide-spread arms; and see
Its seat your soul's just centre be.
Disband dull fears; give faith the day.
To save your life, kill your delay
It is love's siege; and sure to be
Your triumph, though his victory.
'Tis cowardice that keeps this field
And want of courage not to yield.
Yield then, O yield, that love may win
The Fort at last, and let life in.
Yield quickly. Lest perhaps you prove
Death's prey, before the prize of love.
This Fort of your fair self, if't be not won,
He is repulsed indeed; But you're undone. (5)

NOTES AND SOURCES

1. *Carmen Deo nostro, te decet hymnus sacred poems, collected, corrected, augmented, most humbly presented To my Lady the Countess of Denbigh by her most devoted servant In hearty acknowledgment of his immortal obligation to her goodness and charity* (1652), 64.
2. Ibid. 65.
3. Ibid. 67–9.
4. Ibid. 83–5.
5. Ibid., unpag., but at the front of the volume.

# Sir Basil Brooke                                    1576–1646

The Jesuit confessor to King Louis XIII of France, Nicholas Caussin (d. 1651) published a set of Lenten exercises under the title *Sagesse evangelique pour les sacrez entrietiens*. In 1643 they appeared in an English adaptation by Sir Basil Brooke, one of the more flamboyant of Caroline Catholics, who had converted his Shropshire estates into a hugely successful iron and coal business. He also had a monopoly on the production of new soap. He bought the O'Donnell castle in Donegal, built a new Jacobean mansion at right angles to the medieval fortress and planned to settle there as a Catholic planter. As a leading Catholic he was opposed to the attempts of Bishop Smith and the Chapter to impose discipline on the secular clergy. He prepared his edition of Caussin and dedicated it to Queen Henrietta-Maria, wife of Charles I and sister of the original dedicatee, Louis XIII. It was she who organized its republication (twice) in 1661, and it was many times reprinted between then and 1785, as *Entertainments for Lent* (later prefixed with *The Penitent*).

## A Meditation for Ash Wednesday

For the first day, upon the consideration of ashes

Thou art dust and to dust thou shalt return (Gen. 3) It is an excellent way to begin Lent with the consideration of dust, whereby nature gives us beginning; and by the same death shall put an end to all our worldly vanities. There is no better way to abate and humble the proudest of all creatures than to represent his beginning and end. The middle part of his life, like a kind of Proteus, takes upon it several shapes not understood by others; but the first and last parts of it deceive no man; for they do both begin and end in dust. It is a strange thing that man, knowing well what he hath been, and what he must be, is not confounded by himself, by observing the pride of his own life and the great disorder of his passions. The end of all creatures is less deformed that that of man. Plants in their death retain some pleasing smell of their bodies; the little rose buries itself in her natural sweetness and carnation colour. Many creatures at their death leave us their teeth, horns, feathers, skins; of which we make great use; others after death, are served up in silver and golden dishes, to feed the greatest persons in the world. Only man's dead carcass is good for nothing but to feed worms; and yet he often retains the presumptuous pride of a giant, by the exorbitance of his heart, and the cruel nature of a murderer, by the furious rage of his revenge. Surely that man must either be stupid by nature, or most wicked by his own election, who will not correct and amend himself, having still before his eyes ashes for his glass and death for his mistress.

This consideration of dust is an excellent remedy to cure vice and an assured rampart against temptation. St Paulinus saith excellently well, that holy Job was free from all temptations when he was placed upon the smoke and dust of his humility. He that lies upon the ground can fall no lower; but may contemplate all above him, and meditate how to raise himself by the hand of God, which pulls down the proud and exalts the humble. Is a man tempted with pride? The consideration of ashes will humble him. Is a man burnt with wanton love? (which is a direct fire), fire cannot consume ashes. Is he persecuted with covetousness? Ashes make the greatest leeches and bloodsuckers cast their gorges.

Everything gives way to this unvalued thing, because God is pleased to draw the instruments of his power out of the objects of our infirmities.

If we knew how to use rightly the meditation of death, we should there find the streams of life. All the world together is of no estimation to him that rightly knows the true value of a just man's death. It would be necessary that they who are taken with the curiosity of tulips should set in their gardens a plant called Naple, which carries a flower that perfectly resembles a death's head; and if the other tulips please their senses, that will instruct their reason. Before our last death we should die many other deaths, by forsaking all those creatures and affections which would lead us to sin. We should resemble those creatures, sacred to the Egyptians, called Cynocephales, that died piecemeal, and were buried long before their death; so should we bury all our concupiscences before we go to the grave, and strive to live so that when death comes he should find very little business with us.

## ASPIRATION

O Father of all essences who givest beginning of all things and art without end, this day I take ashes upon my head, thereby professing, before thee, my being nothing; and to do thee homage for that which I am, and that I ought to be, by thy great bounties. Alas! O Lord, my poor soul is confounded to see so many sparkles of pride and covetousness arise from this caitiff dust, which I am. So little do I yet learn how to live, and so late do I know how to die. O God of my life and death, I most humbly beseech thee so to govern the first in me, and so to sweeten the last for me, that, if I live, I may live only for thee, and if I must die, that I must enter into everlasting bliss, by dying in thy blessed love and favour.

## THE GOSPEL FOR ASH WEDNESDAY, ST MATTHEW 6, OF HYPOCRITICAL FASTING

When you fast, be not as the hypocrites, sad: for they disfigure their faces, that they may appear unto men to fast. Amen, I say unto you, that they have received their reward. But thou when thou dost fast, anoint thy head and wash thy face, that thou appear not to men to fast, but to thy Father which is in secret; and thy Father which see-eth in secret will repay you.

Heap not up thyselves treasures on the earth, where rust and moth do corrupt, and where thieves dig through and steal. But heap up to yourselves treasures in heaven; where neither rust nor moth doth corrupt, and where thieves do not dig through nor steal. For where thy treasure is, there is thy heart also.

## MORALITIES

It imports us much to begin Lent well, entering into those lists in which so many souls have run their course with so great strictness, having been glorious before Men. The difficulty of it is apprehended only by those who have their understandings obstructed by a violent affection to kitchen stuff. It is no more burdensome to a courageous spirit than feathers are to a bird. The cheerfulness which a man brings to a good action in the beginning does half the work. Let us wash our faces by confession. Let us perfume our head (who is Jesus Christ) by alms-deeds. Fasting is a most delicious feast to the conscience, when it is accompanied with pureness and charity; but it breeds great thirst, when it is not nourished with devotion, and watered with mercy.

What great pain is taken to get treasure, what care to preserve it, what fear to lose it, and what sorrow when it is lost? Alas, is there need of so great covetousness in life to encounter with such extreme nakedness in death? We have not the souls of giants, not the body of a whale. If God will have me poor, must I endeavour to reverse the decrees of heaven and earth, that I may become rich? To whom do we trust the safety of our treasures? To rust, to moths and thieves; were it not better we should in our infirmities depend only on God Almighty, and comfort our poverty in him who is only rich and so carry our souls to heaven, where Jesus on the day of his Ascension did place our Sovereign good. Only serpents and covetous men desire to sleep amongst treasures, as St Clement saith. But the greatest riches of the world is poverty free from covetousness. (1)

NOTES AND SOURCES

1. *Entertainments for Lent, written in French by the R.F. N. Caussin SJ, Translated into English by Sir Basil Brooke* (from the edition published in Liverpool in 1755), 5–11.

## A Manual of Prayers (iii) 1650

This edition is entitled *A manual of godly prayers and litanies newly annexed, taken out of many famous authors and distributed according to the days of the week, with a large and ample exercise for the morning and evening, whereunto are added the hymns and prayers for the principal feasts of the year, with a brief form of confession and the order to help at Mass.* It is even more extensive than previous versions: we include here a selection of hymns and the order of confession.

### Hymn and Prayers for the Nativity of St John the Baptist

That we thy servants may with joy declare
The wondrous works which thou hast undergone;
Cleanse lips which foul guilt polluted are
Holy St John

A messenger sent from the highest sky
Doth to thy father thy great birth disclose
Thy name and course of life which thou shalt try
In order shows

He doubtful of the promise from above,
Hath lost his voice, which he enjoyed before,
Thou being born, that hindrance didst remove
And speech restore

Thou saw-est when in the womb thou hidden were
The King who did within his closet dwell
Hence both thy parents through their son's desert
Great secrets tell.

Glory be to the Father and the Son
And unto thee who equal glory hast
O Holy Ghost, while ages forward run
Or time shall last. Amen.

THE ANTIPHON ON THE NATIVITY OF ST JOHN BAPTIST, CALLED
MIDSUMMER DAY, 24 OF JUNE:

The child which is born to us is more than a prophet, for this is he of whom Our
Saviour saith: amongst the born of women, a greater hath not risen before John
the Baptist.

Versicle: This child is great before the Lord

Response: For his hand is with him

THE PRAYER

O God, which diddest make this day honourable unto us, in the nativity of the
Blessed Saint John: give unto thy people the grace of spiritual joys, and direct the
minds of all the faithful, in the way of eternal salvation, through our Lord etc. (1)

# Hymn for St Peter and St Paul

*The hymn on the feast of the Apostles St Peter and St Paul, 28 June*

With golden light, and with a beauteous rosy ray
Thou light of light, thy beams through all the world hast spread.
With glorious martyrdom, decking the heavens this day,
Which pardon gives to souls which have astray been led.

Heaven's porter, and the Saint that taught the world God's word:
Judges of all true lights, of th'universal round,
Th'one conquering by the cross, the other by the word
The senate of the blessed possess, with laurel crowned.

O happy Rome, whose fame such noble princes raise
In whose most precious blood thou dye-est thy purple weeds,
By thy divine desert, not by thine own due praise,
Thy glory of the world's vain beauty far exceeds.

Unto the Trinity eternal glory be,
Honour and power and hymns of joys of heav'nly pleasure
Whose empire's force remains in perfect unity
At first, and now, and still beyond time's largest measure. Amen

THE ANTIPHON

This day Simon Peter mounted on the tree of the Cross, Alleluia, this day the
porter of the kingdom rejoicing, did pass unto Christ. This day St Paul the apostle,

the light of the world, bowing down his head for the name of Christ, was crowned with martyrdom, Alleluia.

Versicle: They showed forth the works of God

Response: And they understood the things which he wrought

### THE PRAYER:

O God, which hast consecrated this day, by the martyrdom of thy Apostles Peter and Paul: grant unto thy Church to follow their commandments in all things, by whom it received the beginning of religion, through Our Lord etc. (2)

## The Hymn and Prayer on the Feast of Saint Mary Magdalene

Father of Light, that shines above
When thou dost Magdalene behold
Thou kindlest flames of heavenly love
And thaw-est her breast, benumb'd with cold.

Wounded with love, she makes repair,
In haste t'anoint thy blessed feet;
Them washed with tears, wiped with her hair,
Her lips with many kisses greet.

Near to the Cross she boldly stands
About the grave she careful dwells
She fears not the fierce soldiers' hands
For charity all fear expels.

O Christ who art true charity,
Purge thou our souls from sinful stains,
Cause that our hearts may filled be
With grace and give us heavenly gains

To God the Father glory great
And glory to his only son
And to the Holy Paraclete
Both now and still whilst ages run. Amen

2 JULY: THE ANTIPHON ON THE FEAST OF ST MARY MAGDALENE

A woman that was a sinner in the city brought an alabaster box of ointment, and standing behind, beside the feet of our Lord, began to water his feet with her tears, and wiped them with the hairs of her head.

Versicle: God elected and forechose her

Response: He maketh her dwell in his tabernacle.

We beseech thee, O Lord, let us be assisted by the suffrages of Blessed Mary Magdalene, by whose prayers thus being entreated, did'st raise Lazarus her brother from hell to life again, after he had been four days dead, who livest and reignest etc. (3)

## Preparation for Confession

### ADVERTISEMENTS BEFORE CONFESSION

About the work of Confession, Satan (who is the mortal enemy of man's soul) lyeth ever principally in wait with many secret snares, lest he should lose that in a man's confession which before he had gained of him.

Conceal nothing in thy confession: for thou canst not deceive God, thyself thou mayest deceive if thou be not truly confessed or concealest any matter of moment, this is, as if thou heldest thy peace and were not confessed at all.

Be thou not discomforted for anything, which thy ghostly father may think of thee; let him either despise thee, or love thee (whether he pleaseth) let not this trouble thee. Study thou more to be made the friend of God, and to please him, than to seek to please men, for which respect, be sure to confess clearly all thy sins which thy conscience shall move thee unto.

In every confession so dispose thee as if thou wert to make thy last confession, and presently without delay, to depart this life and whatsoever thou wouldest confess then, fail not to confess the same now.

Commend thyself unto Almighty God, to his Blessed Mother, and to thy good angel, praying that thou mayest no way be seduced or deceived by the fraud of the devil. Also to St Mary Magdalene, and to Saint Barbara, who, as it is written, have obtained most effectual grace and favour with God, to assist in confession, all such as pray unto them for their help and assistance.

Having diligently examined thy conscience, to excite in thee contrition, and to have deep remorse and sorrow for thy sins, thou mayest from the bottom of thy heart and with effusion of tears say the prayer following:
[*three choices including*]

Most sovereign, mighty and merciful Lord, who of thine infinite love and mercy towards mankind, hast ordained in thy Church the Sacrament of Penance, as a sovereign salve to heal our spiritual wounds, and to purge us from the uncleanness wherewith we after Baptism have any way defiled our souls, I N thy most vile and ungrateful creature, having offended thee many ways and and most grievously since my last confession, purpose, through thy grace, to fly unto this Sacrament for my remedy, and according to thy divine ordinance to confess my sins unto thy servant, hoping thereby that according as thou hast promised, I shall receive a full and perfect absolution from my sins.

Give me grace therefore, O Lord, that like as of your goodness thou hast inspired into my heart a desire to apply this remedy unto my ghostly griefs. So I may in due reverence, contrition and sincerity use the same to the glory of thy name, and to the full forgiveness of my sins. Open the secrets of my soul unto me, O Lord, and make me to know all my sins and iniquities whatsoever. Give me also due sorrow and contrition for the same, and grace to unfold them to thy vicar (my ghostly physician) purely, plainly, sorrowfully and sincerely, with firm and constant purpose, through thy grace to amend my life hereafter.

O Lord, my gracious God and only comfort of my soul, seeing thou desirest that in all things I should sincerely serve thee, and I through grace, desire nothing more than to do the same, why is it, O Lord, that I do still offend thee? Why fall I so often into relapse of my former follies? Thy grace is not wanting, but my ungratefulness and inconstancy is the cause thereof, for the which I am most heartily sorry. Even now I determine to fight manfully and by and by I faint and fail in my former purpose. Rightly therefore am I in respect hereof to humble myself, and to make account, that on the earth there liveth not a more vile and wicked creature than myself. Increase in me daily thy grace and sovereign virtue of humility, I most humbly beseech thee and grant me grace that once I may perfectly know thee and know myself—thee in thy Majesty and mercy, myself in mine abominations and misery; and that at length I may fight more manfully and gain victory over mine enemies, through thy gracious help and favour, my only Redeemer and Saviour Jesus Christ, who with the Father and the Holy Ghost, reigneth one God everlastingly. Amen.

These you may repeat often before confession:

Jesu, reduce into my mind my sins and wickedness, whereby I have offended thee. Jesu grant me the spirit of perfect penance, contrition, confession and satisfaction to obtain thy grace and from filthy sin to purge me.

A table of the sins to help the ignorant or ill of memory; wherein then they would be confessed, they may find out with little labour the manifold ways of offending God.

### OF THE TEN COMMANDMENTS.

The 1st Commandment
  Not loved God above all things.
  Borne over-much love to creatures.
  Doubted or staggered in matters of faith.
  Ignorant of the Ten Commandments.
  Of the Commandments of the Church.
  Of the articles of faith.
  Murmured against God in adversity.
  Lack of confidence in God.
  Presumption of his goodness.
  Desperation of his mercy.
  Believed dreams or tellers of fortunes.
  Gone to witches or to cunning men for counsel.
  Read or kept heretical books.
  Favoured heretics.
  Conversed with them without necessity
  Hindered any one's conversion from heresy or schism.
  Not recommended myself daily to God and the saints.
  Not conformed my will in things to the divine will

The 2nd commandment ... (4)

NOTES AND SOURCES

1. *A Manual of Godly Prayers and Litanies Newly Annexed* (1650), 715–17.
2. Ibid. 717–19.
3. Ibid. 719–22.
4. Ibid. 608–12.

# Sir Kenelm Digby

1603–1665

Kenelm Digby was the son of Sir Everard Digby, one of the Gunpowder Plotters executed for treason in 1606. He was brought up as a Protestant, but reverted to Catholicism following the sudden death of his wife Venetia Stanley from a brain haemorrhage in 1633. In his early days he had been a great traveller and adventurer—with letters of marque he preyed on Spanish shipping in the Mediterranean and he visited much of North Africa and Asia Minor as well as taking part in only slightly more straightforward diplomatic ventures, like the madcap expedition of Prince Charles and his cousin John Digby to Madrid in the hope of negotiating a marriage between Charles and the Spanish Infanta in 1623–4. Venetia was one of the beauties of the age, and her death had a profound effect on him. It triggered his conversion and although his life remained one constantly on the move and had its dramatic moments (he killed a man in a duel in France in 1641 for calling Charles I 'the arrantest coward in the world' at a dinner party) he now devoted himself principally to matters of religion and natural philosophy and their connections. Whether in London, on his Buckinghamshire estates or during regular periods of voluntary or involuntary exile in France, he was really a sedentary explorer of the limits of human knowledge. He was one of the leading alchemists of his generation, and some of his experiments (e.g. those in embryology) contributed significantly to the development of science. He was a leading figure in the great debates of the mid-century into the great argument about the corporeality of the soul. He was close to the minim friar Marin Mersenne and the philosopher René Descartes (who interrogated the nature of both proof and doubt) and while in Paris, and he was a founder member of what became the Royal Society. He was very much on the side of those who sought to distinguish a perishable body from an immaterial and immortal soul. His massive *Two treatises, in the one of which the nature of bodies, in the other the nature of man's soul is looked into: in way of discovery of the immortality of reasonable souls* made him at once a widely respected and deeply suspected figure. He was a passionate supporter of the Church, although many of his ideas were idiosyncratic. He was very much the patron and inspirer of the Blackloists amongst the English Catholic clergy. The Blackloists were liberals in theology and relaxed in ecumenical conversations with Protestant men of science. But they were especially committed to an extreme Catholic erastianism. The core text is that of Thomas White, whose writings under the name 'Blacklo' gave the movement its name: *The Grounds of Obedience and Government* (1655) was written during the Protectorate. Its central message was that of submission to the de facto ruler. The political aim was to secure an accommodation, and religious liberty for Catholics and Catholic practice, and this was particularly controversial since the achievement of the objective would involve the much greater renunciation of papal teaching than even amongst those who had argued for Catholic freedom to take the oath of allegiance to the Stuarts, and it might also have been at the cost of the access of Jesuits to England. Digby pursued these political objectives enthusiastically, trying to get concessions out of the curia in 1645–7, negotiating with Cromwell and the Army in 1647 for Catholic freedom in return for guarantees of Catholic obedience, and especially in his close working relationship with both Cromwell and Cardinal Mazarin in 1654–6. Here, however, we focus on his *Discourse*

*Concerning Infallibility in Religion,* published in 1652 but recalling conversations he had had with his nephew George Digby, eldest son of the earl of Bristol and himself (in the 1640s) secretary of state to Charles I. Most of the pamphlet rehearses his arguments about how science and faith can both be enlisted to demonstrate the immortality of the soul; but here he confronts even more fundamental issues.

# On Infallibility

I come now to pay your Lordship the debt I have owed you ever since our long discourse in one of the side-chapels of St German's church; when we spent most part of the afternoon in examining and weighing, which of the several Religions that at present have course in the world, a prudent man should rationally venture his soul upon. It seemed to me that it was not a small step I had advanced in obtaining your assent to the Catholic, when your Lordship acknowledged great defects of several kinds in all others, and that ours was adorned with more comeliness and Majesty, was maintained with more orderliness and prudence, was propped with more powerful means to preserve unity among the professors, and in the general course of it was replenished with more efficacious motives to incite men to the love of God, than any of the others. But withal, you professed that there were some particulars of so hard digestion in it, as you could not win of yourself to yield your assent unto them; nor were persuaded that the authority from whence we receive our faith was infallible, but that in all those particulars it had varied and swerved from what in the beginning was taught by Christ and had been preached throughout the world by his Apostles. What I replied hereunto, seemed to your Lordship out of the ordinary track of those who nowadays use to handle controversies. And it is but just, that to so sublime a wit as yours is, arguments of a higher strain should be offered than such as are pressed to vulgar capacities. For as the ordinary sort of mankind, have their understanding, satisfied with barely looking upon God in quality of a Judge, that punisheth or rewardeth according as men have obeyed or transgressed his laws: so is the enquiry of what they are to do or believe, at an end, when those unto whose conduct God's providence hath committed them, do pronounce his decrees to them in a legislative way. But so piercing a judgement as yours that knoweth there is an orderly and natural connection between all causes and their effects, and that suspecteth, not God Almighty of having bound mankind to a mere arbitrary law for the bare showing of his authority and the exercising of their obedience; will not be appayed [= satisfied], without having some scantling [= stinting, short-changing] of the *Why;* as well as of the *What,* you are to do and to believe.

Should we therefore apprehend their lot to be the worse, that are endowed with the eminentest talents; since so much labour and pains is necessary to the quieting of their doubts; when as simple people acquiesce so easily to what they are plainly taught? Nothing less. For though it is true, the difficulty be great in overcoming their strong resistance: yet, that once done, the vigorous progress they afterwards make, recompenseth to the full the precedent pains in wrestling with their reluctant imaginations and their opposing reasons, whereas new storms are easily raised by any cross wind that shall blow upon the others flexible nature. St Augustine's long irresoluteness, his anxious seeking of truth, and his difficult rendering himself unto it, was followed and crowned with admirable perfection in his own particular, and with unspeakable advantages to the Church of God in general: so as he is the only saint in Heaven after St Paul, that hath the day of his conversion celebrated in the Church. Hence is it that I am not one of those who wonder that your Lordship is so long before you come into the fold that encloseth and secureth us. You were not whom I take you to be, if you should yield up your weapons before you were fully convinced; or be convinced before you have searched into the bottom of the question. To put you into the way of receiving an entire happy defeat in this conflict, I took the freedom to represent unto you such considerations as had been heretofore most prevalent with me, when I had great unquietness in believing what I was taught till my reason was convinced that I should do unreasonably if I gave not my assent thereunto. Not that I am so vain as to think that my proper poor stock can furnish ought that you already abound not more plentifully with. But it hath been my good fortune (that is to say, God's Grace hath been so merciful to me) that I have met with a knowing and judicious guide, to lead me through this dark and intricate labyrinth. What I had formerly derived from him for my own satisfaction in this matter, I tendered to you for yours. And wherein I fell short by delivering you but a lame copy (according to my mean skill) of so excellent an original, I referred you either to his learned writings or to his fuller conversation. For your Lordship knoweth, he beareth you so great respect, that upon any least intimation from you, he would purposely make a journey to you from any remote place to do you service. In the meantime, I endeavoured to take a survey as well as I could of the whole race that Man runneth; from the first moment of his being produced a reasonable creature, to the last period of his journey, when he is settled for ever in a state of permanency. For in such a subject, the symmetry of the whole, and the due coherence of the parts, are of great weight with prudent and solid men. This cannot be completely nor orderly done, without first settling firmly the fundamental principle, That Man's soul is immortal and incorruptible, and surviveth eternally after the death of the body. In the next place, I applied myself to show, how the different courses of living in this world, do beget in the future, different conditions of happiness or misery, each of them exceeding, beyond all conceivable proportion, the goods or evils of this life. Then, upon consideration of the difficulty, or rather impossibility, for mankind to arrive to the assured knowledge of those paths which are necessary for him to walk in to bring him to beatitude, that so his steps might be steady and bold ones; I concluded, that since God would have dealt more hardly with mankind than with all other creatures besides, if to every one of them he had assigned due and proportionable means to bring them to the utmost period of their nature, and should have left only him in the dark among inevitable precipices. It was certain he had bequeathed to him a science or art whereby to govern himself and steer his course so as to be able to arrive safely into his wished haven, and to that end which he was created for. And lastly, I urged, that since the men who live in ages after his who taught them this science (which we call religion) cannot be conceived to receive it immediately from his mouth; they would fall back to an incertitude and distressed condition equal to the former, if he had not settled as infallible a means to convey entirely to them this science, as in itself it is an infallible guide so bring them to beatitude. And thence I proceeded to establish that rule which keepeth us Catholics in unity among ourselves, and in security that we are in the right way.

This was the scope of our conference then: which comprising so many, so weighty, and so difficult points, that a few hours conversation was too scanty a time to discuss them as they ought to be; I promised to give your Lordship in writing a summary collection of some of the most important reflections I had made upon them. The doing whereof, is the subject of the following discourse. (1)

NOTES AND SOURCES

1. Kenelm Digby, *Discourse Concerning Infallibility in Religion* (1652), 3–11.

## Thomas White (Blacklo)                                1593–1676

Thomas White was a secular priest who led the liberal wing of English Catholicism from the 1630s to the 1670s. He wrote more than forty polemical works on philosophy, theology and ecclesiology under the name of Blacklo (Blacklow, Blackloe), and the group he gathered around him were parodied by the Jesuits as the 'Blackloist cabal'. Their mentor and patron was Kenelm Digby. White's targets were philosophical and scientific certainty (hence his attacks on infallibility) and papal absolutism, and he strove constantly to forge agreements in which unconditional political obedience was traded in return for religious liberty. His lifelong passion was to reconcile the new (Baconian) empirical science with a reduced core of Christian doctrine. The tract which got him into most trouble was his *The Grounds of Obedience to Government* (1655) in which he argued implicitly for Catholic obedience to the Cromwellian regime in the hope that he would extend his broad policy of religious liberty and equality to Catholics. Not for the only time, this led to formal rebuke from Rome (although he was never suspended or excommunicated, his works were all placed on the Index of proscribed works), and we offer here his defiant response to that rebuke. It was in a short pamphlet entitled *A Letter to a Person of Honour Written by Mr. Thomas White, in Vindication of Himself and his Doctrine* (1659). This is most of what he wrote.

### The Limits of Tradition

Whilst my Adversaries were content to whisper up and down their grave but empty censures of me, amongst confiding, and credulously zealous devotees (their proper auditory) or, at most, amongst unlearned men, whose busy commerce, though it direct them now and then to a large and indulgent casuist, yet doth it afford them little leisure to consult with true divinity: I contented myself likewise to leave them to the applause of such admirers, looking upon it as lost time to prepare any apology. But their confidence being now raised to that height as to presume to pour their calumnies into your ears whom God hath blest with a judgement singularly capable to discern truth, and an authority fit to bear sway amongst prudent persons; I can no longer decline the task, but humbly offer what I conceive may suffice to justify me in your candid thoughts. If this short discourse serve to dispel the mist which hath lately been cast before your eyes, I shall rejoice for both our sakes; if otherwise, for my own; hoping your charity will make me see my failings, and acknowledge them.

In the first place, my doctrine is accused of heresy, nor is my person more favourably treated; but we have heard of old, that it were impossible in the world to be innocent, if it were all one to be accused and to be guilty. That nature hath furnished us with an ear for the defendant, as well as plaintiff. This justice, then,

I beg of such as are competent judges in so great a cause; for in truth it belongeth to the supremest courts of theology to censure dogmatical tenets, which office notwithstanding, nowadays the most ignorant amongst us are the most ready to usurp.

To this calumny then I answer, That if any doctrine of mine be found to contradict any authority constantly acknowledged for infallible in the Catholic Church, I am ready to disown, and renounce it; If this profession render not a man Catholic or orthodox, I should be glad to learn what doth. To speak more plainly, if we regard the testimonies of holy Scriptures, or consent of Fathers, unless I abound therewith more than my opposers; if perusing the decrees of Councils and Popes, we find therein any thing expressly repugnant to what I have taught, lastly if in any one point I have thwarted the universal practice of the Church, let me be esteemed to have lost the cause. But withal let me beg this favour, that where the clear text condemns me not, the gloss of private expositors may not pronounce me guilty. I know no reason why any divine should forfeit the right his degree and quality gives him of interpretation, because others of the same profession dissent from him.

Secondly, the practice of the Church is urged against me, and that with louder noise, and greater confidence of victory. But let them reflect, how many such ecclesiastical practices have been laid aside, and obliterated. Who nowadays administers the Eucharist in Baptism to infants? What is become of the three immersions? Where shall we see those so much anciently reverenced solemnities during the whole Octaves of Easter and Pentecost? Is the sacred host now received into our hands? Is it brought home; or carried about us in our travails? Are both the kinds or species given to the laity in public festivities? Of all the penitential canons what else remains but a faint shadow? Prayer for the saint departed is long since laid aside. The decrees of the apostolical synod concerning blood and suffocated meats are nowhere observed. What alterations may we not find in the election of prelates, and ecclesiastical courts? Finally, in our fasts and vigils? Did they thoroughly weigh all this, they would not so violently presume, and confidently proclaim the practice of the Church to be an argument of faith: They would perceive that these practices are mutable, and consequently can yield no firm foundation of doctrine.

But what is this to my particular case, who oppose, or control no one modern ecclesiastical practice; for we are not to think whatever is generally done by all Christians must therefore immediately become an ecclesiastical custom, no more than we are to conclude that an opinion, or truth, assented to by all individual Catholics must needs become an article of their faith; For so the earth's standing still, and even Columbus his discovery of the new world might claim a place in their Creed. Such customs then alone are to be styled ecclesiastical as are grounded on ecclesiastical constitutions, on the canon laws, on the rituals, or ceremonials used by the whole Church, not on the zeal or fervour of the multitude: but of any of these we hear no mention. The very name of practice imports custom and prescription, and custom has the force of a law. But none that I know of forgets himself so far as to affirm that the practice, whose denial he obtrudes on me, induceth a necessity upon any one of putting it in execution. To conclude, they asperse not only me, but the Church her self, which professeth these concessions to be privileges, that is, grants contrary to the general rule or custom. Our supreme pastors call them graces, or indulgences which my opposers either proclaim for customs, and practices, or else speak nothing to the purpose. Thus whilst they seek to calumniate me, they unaware attack the Church, esteeming nothing so sacred as the satisfaction of their precipitate passions...

But they will have us at least to confess, that wherever the whole authority of the School is engaged in any one opinion, it must of necessity be true and beyond all opposition. The same discourse returns again upon them.

That authority is either fallible, or infallible; if fallible, then cannot any multitude of patrons whatsoever secure it from liableness to error, and it will appear impiety to deny the Church a means of clearing her sight therein? If it be pretended infallible, I ask whence are we assured thereof? If by any other authority than their own; let us beg the favour to see it produced; if by their own only, we shall then submit when they shall have extricated themselves out of the maze, or circle, in which they dance. But, to proceed; by what means can we imagine this multitude on a sudden immured with the prerogative of certitude? Philosophers, besides that of faith, acknowledge no other than such as springs from demonstration; of which kind it hath not been my fortune to encounter any; when they offer at it, I shall most willingly listen. It is a received maxim that a doctor's authority reaches no further than the force of the reason he brings, can carry it. If this be verified of each particular, how come they to deserve more collectively? Look upon their own assertions, do they not define that the judgement of three grave divines in any opinion begets a probability? Yet if I have any reason left me, three compared to many thousands nothing prejudice the universality of the contrary part; nay, many of them have thought and maintained that the judgement even of one, who hath thoroughly looked into a difficult point, may be sufficient to establish a probability against the opposite multitude. What then have I or any other offended if, after mature inspection, we have preferred the substance of reason before the shadow of popularity? Add to this, the very boast of universal consent of doctors is altogether vain; who hath examined the hundreth part of them? Who can dive into the sentiments of such as have not written, whose number notwithstanding and authority is far greater than theirs who covet to appear in print? So that, if you scan the expression, under the notion of all doctors, you will find to be understood a few only, who bear sway in the universities; a handful, God knows, out of a plentiful harvest.

They rest not yet satisfied, but accuse me at least of indiscretion, that, in a kingdom averse, and separated from the communion of the Cath[olic] Church, I have printed a book or two, from which they conceive heretics may take occasion to reproach us with intestine dissensions in religion. Though I am not one who challenges the reputation of prudent, or go about to clear my self wholly from all liableness to the opposite imbecility; yet in this place I see no ground for their crimination: do they not daily hear the heterodox party exprobrating [= making the subject of reproach] the wars which in Catholic countries are waged upon the subject of efficacious grace, and Jansenism? whatsoever falls once under the press, it little imports whether it first see light here, or in any adjacent Catholic country: Take for proofs the French provincial letters; not only vulgarly known, but rendered also into our vulgar tongue; and truly if I mistake not, the publishing such truths is more expedient here than in any part of the world; nothing being more importantly conducible to the reduction of our separatists, than the discarding superfluous controversies, and contesting with them only necessary doctrines; without engaging for the uncertain and wavering opinions of doctors as for the faith delivered us by Christ and his apostles. We find by experience, that great wits, which overrule the weaker capacities, if an assent be crudely required from them upon the accompt of sole authority and command; without reason, either for the truth of the thing itself, or at least for the necessity of believing it, they reject it with scorn, and conceive thence an extreme aversion: to these the milk of reason, that is, the conformity of faith with inferior science, must, as much as is possible, be prepared; which task hath hitherto been the aim of all my endeavours. We may observe every day that disputes undertaken without these grounds, are doubtful; and either depend upon the acuteness, and dexterity of the manager, or perhaps on pure chance; and most commonly conclude in wordish and endless perplexities. All which I would not have so understood as though I confessed my writings had found no acceptance or approbation in Catholic countries, for even thence I have received not a few congratulations. In fine [= to sum up], what needs there more to justify my printing here, than barely to say, I must perforce do it where I live and find supplies sufficient for such expenses as are necessary . . . (1)

NOTES AND SOURCES

1. *A Letter to a Person of Honour Written by Mr. Thomas White, in Vindication of Himself and his Doctrine* (1659), unpag.

## Henry Holden                                                    1596–1662

Henry Holden was the oldest of the Blackloists, the group of liberal priests who briefly (1655–9) controlled the Chapter, those originally commissioned by Bishop Richard Smith to exercise jurisdiction over the English clergy. Like Thomas White ('Blacklo') he had a strongly Gallican view of the organization of the Church, acknowledging papal primacy over matters of faith and morals, but emphasizing the autonomy of local churches in matters of practice and witness, above all in reaching local accommodations with secular authority, especially in non-Catholic lands. Here, in 1657, in *A letter written by Mr Henry Holden at Paris, touching the prohibition at Rome of Mr Blacklow's book entitled Tabulae suffragiales*, is his denunciation of the Inquisition.

### Against the Inquisition and the Index

You ask me what I now say to Mr Blacklow's doctrine since the Pope's last decree against it? Why, sir, I say I am still of the same opinion I was, specified in my last unto you of the first of August . . .

   Now, Sir, that you may not be too easily carried away with the vulgar ignorant, and take a prohibition for a condemnation of heresy; and a decree of the Congregation of Cardinals and others, called the Inquisition, for a bull of the Pope himself. I will tell you as a friend, and as (I suppose) not versed in these businesses, what understanding and truly learned men do think of these prohibitions. With this caveat nevertheless, that however easy a thing it is to get any private man's writings into the Index of forbidden books amongst us, yet ought not a Catholic to condemn or sleight these decrees, since they bear the name of a supreme superior. I will therefore inform you in a word what these prohibitions are. And upon what grounds they are generally given.

First they are only acts of a particular court or congregation in Rome, though put out in the Pope's name, as all other acts of the several courts of that city usually are. And therefore do not oblige, not are commonly held to be of any force out of the Pope's territories, unless some other state or bishop receive and publish them. Nor are these kind of decrees ever admitted in France, but often rejected by the Parlement of this town [Paris], the most famous and learned seat of judiciary in the Christian world.

Secondly, we see these decrees proceed from two causes, or rather in two cases. First, when the forbidden book contains anything contrary to the common, though only tolerated, custom of the Church, or to the ordinary practice and pretensions of the Court of Rome. Second when such books are of that nature as that the more ignorant or weaker sort of men, or the more irreligious and looser lived, may there find, or thence easily gather, whereat to be scandalized. Which to prevent belongs to the zealous solicitude of a general pastor and common father. Not that such forbidden books do always contain something contrary to our Catholic faith (which then are particularly specified as such and branded with the censure of heresy) but that they are judged by the Inquisition to be obnoxious and apt to beget evil conceits and opinions in the people's fancies; or at least prejudicial to some greater good than their divulging could produce.

Hence we see many books forbidden (as in this very decree) nothing relating to the revealed points of our Christian belief. Yea some undoubtedly containing the true grounds of all Christianity, as the Bible itself in vulgar tongues. So that the Inquisition doth principally attend in these prohibitions what may be the effect of such books through the ignorance or malice of their readers, without examining what the particular doctrine of the book may be in itself...

In the last place is thrust into this catalogue of these forbidden books, Mr Blacklow's treatise, called *Tabulae Suffragiales* with its appendix, *testerae Romanae evulgatio*. Wherein the author's principal design is to prove that great truth, and essential rule of all Christianity, to wit that our Catholic faith is to be resolved into universal tradition. As also to demonstrate the ancient opinion of our Faculty at Paris, that the Pope is not unerrable and infallible in his own singular person. But indeed he goes somewhat further, and condemns the contrary opinion as improbable, heretical and archiheretical. And therefore you need not wonder if the Inquisition have forbidden his book, without specifying his doctrine, being so opposite to their pretensions though the opinion itself (not censuring the opposite) be a common tenet of many both of our ancient and modern doctors of Paris. (1)

NOTES AND SOURCES

1. *A letter written by Mr Henry Holden at Paris, touching the prohibition at Rome of Mr Blacklow's book entitled Tabulae suffragiales* (1657), 2–7, 12–13.

# St John Southworth 1592–1654

St John Southworth was born into a Catholic family in what was by far the most solidly Catholic part of Elizabethan England, North Lancashire, and he was third member of his family in his generation to offer himself for the sacred priesthood. He entered Douai in 1613, was ordained on Holy Saturday 1618, and offered his first Mass on Easter Sunday morning. He was sent to England in December 1619 and spent most of the next thirty-five years in London. During a brief period as a mission priest in Lancashire (1627–8), he was arrested, tried, and convicted under the Elizabethan statute making it treasonable to be a Catholic priest in England. His execution was stayed, however, and he was transferred to the Clink prison in London. In 1630 he was one of twelve priests who, at the behest of the Catholic queen, and to mark the peace treaty between England and France, had their sentences commuted to perpetual banishment—with the king's 'express will and pleasure' that if they remained in or returned to England and Wales, then 'the Law should pass on every several person without further favour'. Southworth simply ignored this threat and remained in London, serving in some of the poorest areas of Clerkenwell and Westminster. He was arrested at a private house on 19 June 1654, brought twice before the common serjeant of London on 24th and 26th June, and ordered to be hanged, drawn, and quartered (under the terms of his 1630 commuted sentence), and sentence was carried out at Tyburn on the 28th. Southworth was the only Catholic priest executed during the protectorate, and the last ever to be executed simply for being a priest in England. Cromwell had no desire to make martyrs, but was powerless to prevent the sentence passed in 1628 being carried out. Cromwell did however arrange for his body, sewn together after its quartering, to be embalmed and sent to Douai— evidence of his regret at what had happened. The body remained in Douai until the College closed at the time of the French Revolution, and it was later transferred to Westminster Cathedral, where it can be venerated in one of the side chapels. He was beatified by the Vatican in 1929, and in 1970 he was proclaimed one of forty English martyr-saints of the Reformation era. This account of his speech from the scaffold before his execution was printed in 1679 by those seeking to whip up anti-popish sentiment. It is 'from the true copy found among other papers at the search of a papist's house' (evidence of manuscript circulation of dying speeches).

## His Dying Speech

On Monday the 26th he was brought to the Bar again, where he was condemned to die. After sentence given him, he desired leave to speak to the Bench, which was granted and he desired to come nearer, which he did, and falling upon his knees, said: 'O Lord I humbly thank thee who hast made me worthy to suffer for thy life.' Then standing up said: 'I thank you for all you have done, and your civilities unto. And I pray God to give you his grace, that you and all this nation may be converted to the true Roman Catholic and Apostolic faith, and to remain in Heaven for ever with Jesus Christ in glory.' The Recorder answered: 'We thank you and we join with you in the latter part, but not in the first.

Upon Wednesday the 28th, he was drawn on a hurdle between two malefactors condemned to die for High Treason, from the prison to the place of execution, where immediately before his execution, he spoke as followeth:

I am come hither to die, and would willingly speak something, if I thought the weakness of my voice would give me leave to be heard. I am a Lancashire man and am brought hither to die not for any crime I have committed against the laws, but for being a priest, and obeying the commandments of my Saviour Jesus Christ and for professing the true Roman Catholic and Apostolic Faith, in which I willingly die, and have earnestly desired the same. My study from my infancy was to find out the true and only way to serve God, and having found it, my study was to serve Him. And I have suffered much, and many years imprisonment, to obtain that which I hope ere long I shall enjoy. Almighty God sent his only Son my Lord and Saviour Jesus Christ into this world for the redemption of mankind; and although the least of his sufferings was a superabundant satisfaction, yet he rested not so contented, but himself doth by word and example give us a rule by which we should be guided: he told St Peter, *thou art a rock, and upon this rock will I build my Church, and the gates of Hell shall not prevail against it*—which is the true Roman Catholic and Apostolic Church. He gave a commandment to his disciples, saying *Go you forth, preach and teach to all nations, baptizing them in the name of the Father, the Son and the Holy Ghost.* They gave the same to their disciples and successors; and by that successive depending authority was I sent to preach and teach in this my nation. This was my mission. And deeply resenting [= to take favourably, to approve of, to meet with acceptance] my Saviour's words *he that will come after me, let him deny himself, and take up his cross and follow me* by which he meant the present persecutions of this world, I took up this cross, and practised how to suffer, and as near as I could, learned the way to perfection and am now brought hither to put it in execution, never to my knowledge, as a dying man, either speaking, writing, or persuading anything against the laws of this nation. But performing my duty, and submitting myself to my superiors, as I would have you all do, both as to spiritual and temporal. I have been many years in learning this lesson of suffering for my saviour's sake, which I am now to perform. My saviour showed me the way, for he died upon the cross for my sake, and for his sake I die upon this, which is my cross, and willingly I embrace it.

The Lord Protector [Cromwell] fought long for the liberty of the subject, and having obtained it, the people of this nation were made to believe that there should be a general liberty of conscience, and that no man's life should be taken away for matter of religion, for which only I now suffer. It hath pleased God to put the sword of justice into the Lord Protector's hand and to take it out of the King's, that he should rule the nation well; and he ought to do justice to all in equal balance, and that Catholics being free-born subjects should enjoy that liberty as others do, so long as they live obedient subjects to him, and to the laws of this nation. I plead not for myself (for I am come hither to die) but for the poor distressed Catholics I leave behind me. Almighty God hath been pleased the Lord Protector should do justice in blood and not in mercy, contrary both to his promise and duty in submission to whose power, and obedience to my superiors of the Roman Catholic Church I am brought hither, and willing to obey. All other opinions have liberty of conscience, but even now we see the poor Catholics are denied that privilege I am now to suffer for it. I see no reason why my life should be taken away, for the law should be grounded upon reason and God's Word. This law, which is man's law, is repugnant to the law of God. For my Saviour said *Go preach and teach to all nations, baptizing them in the name of the Father, the Son and the Holy Ghost*, but the innocent should not be punished for the offenders. The angels in Heaven did rebel against God through pride, but how were they punished? Not all the hierarchy of angels destroyed, but they only who offended, the other angels remained still in glory...I therefore desire the Lord Protector would grant them that Liberty of Conscience equal with their fellow subjects, and that he may so govern as may be for the honour of God, and good of all people.

And being then interrupted, ceased speaking any more aloud. (1)

NOTES AND SOURCES

1. *The Last Speech and Confession of Mr John Southworth, a Popish Priest at his Execution at Tyburn June 28 1654* (1679), 1–2.

## Miles Pinkney (alias Thomas Carre)  1599–1674

Miles Pinkney was baptized into the Church of England in Durham but was reconciled to the Catholic Church as a teenager and entered the English College at Douai before his nineteenth birthday. He was ordained priest in 1625, and he spent most of his remaining forty-nine years on the continent, supporting the work of English religious communities in France. His role in establishing the Our Lady of Sion Convent of English canonesses of St Augustine was particularly important. In this and for many years afterwards, he worked closely with Richard Smith, Bishop of Chalcedon, whose miseries as bishop for England have been noticed elsewhere. Here Pinkney, under his name in religion, Thomas Carre, offers a warm and affectionate account of Bishop Smith's work in assisting the Cardinal Archbishop of Paris. This is part of Pinkney/Carre's book *Pietas Parisiensis* (1666) a roseate retrospective account of post-Tridentine Paris, pointedly different from the rampant secularism of schismatic London.

## Bishop Smith in Paris

I remember I have frequently heard from the mouth of that most venerable old prelate Monseigneur of Chalcedon (in whose blessed company I had the honour and happiness to be for above 20 years together) who all that time, and before, was ordinarily employed by the Archbishop of Paris to give holy orders and the Sacrament of confirmation. I heard, I say, from his mouth, that the primitive times seemed to him to be renewed again in those holy young men who, said he (with much emphasis, his heart being dilated with joy and jubilee) approached to me, as though drunk with the new wine of the Acts, so did the abundance of their hearts break out in sighs and sobs, intercepting their words; and their joyful tears forcibly burst forth and watered my hands. This truth which I often heard the Bishop pour out with so much fervour and high approbation, better known to me, than to many others, as I thought fit to register down, to the honour of God, and that holy institution.

If this most happy institution, spread its fruits all over France, and even extend its flourishing branches into foreign nations too, as hereafter we shall see, how just occasion doth it not administer us highly to extol the piety and charity of the good tree when they were sprung...If I should undertake to speak of the strength and purity of his faith, the height and confidence of his hope, and the ever-burning flames of his charity, I should less want matter than time to deliver it, and withal swerve from my design, which is historically to offer a small sampling of a huge abundance and not to fall into a panegyric which would find no end. No, my aim is not to praise this saintly man, but God in him, since indeed the greatest saint is never praised as he ought, but when we praise God in the saints from all sanctity [*sic*]. Nor is it my meaning to praise his virtues at home, in whatever degree of speculation or practice he might possess them, but their profusion abroad upon his neighbours, that credit may still be given to works, not to words which are liable to deceit. All the praise of virtue can a pagan tell us, consists in action, nor is virtue any other thing, as we are taught by a better Master, than the order of charity. And where was charity ever better ordered than where human respects had no hand in the distribution, but it streamed indifferently out upon all, save only where it found difference of necessity, and there it still most abounded. (1)

NOTES AND SOURCES

1. *Pietas Parisiensis or a short description of the piety and charity commonly exercised in Paris, which represents in short the pious practices of the whole Catholic Church* (1666), 38–42.

# Anne Hyde, Duchess of York                  1637–1671

It is an astonishing fact that every wife of a Stuart King of Britain between 1603 and 1688 died a Catholic. Three of them were staunch Catholics by birth and faith—the French Queen of Charles I, the Portuguese Queen of Charles II and the Italian second wife of James VII and I. But the others, Anne of Denmark, wife of James VI and I, and Anne Hyde, first wife of James VII and II, both converted to Catholicism. Anne Hyde was the daughter of Charles II's principal adviser in exile and in the early Restoration, Edward Earl of Clarendon, and the marriage caused great rifts in the royal family. Anne had become the mistress of James, Duke of York, and was about to bear his child when Charles reluctantly gave permission for them to marry secretly. She was a fierce defender of her father who was often at odds with husband. But it was a love match, and she bore James eight children, six of whom, including five boys, were to die before the age of 4. The two surviving daughters, Mary, wife of William (III) of Orange and Anne were to rule Britain and Ireland after the Revolution of 1688 that was to overthrow their father. Anne, Duchess of York, was received into the Catholic Church in 1670, shortly after her husband, and when she was already suffering from breast cancer. This account of her conversion, first published in *A Church History of England from the Year* 1500 *to the Year* 1688 (1742), is almost certainly her own work.

## A Conversion Narrative

It is so reasonable to expect that a person always bred up in the Church of England, and as well instructed in the doctrine of it as the best divines and her capacity could make her, should be liable to many censures for leaving that, and making herself a member of the Roman Catholic Church, to which, I confess, I was one of the greatest enemies it ever had; that I chose rather to satisfy my friends by reading this paper than to have the trouble to answer all the questions that may daily be asked me. And first I do protest in the presence of Almighty God, that no person, man or woman, directly or indirectly, ever said anything to me (since I came into England) or used the least endeavour to make me change my religion. It is a blessing I owe entirely to Almighty God and, I hope, the hearing of a prayer I daily made him ever since I was in France and Flanders; where, seeing much of the devotion of the Catholics (though I had very little myself) I made it my continual request unto Almighty God that if I were not, I might before I died, be in the true religion. I did not in the least doubt but that I was so, and never had any manner of doubt until November last; when, reading a book called the *History of the Reformation* by Doctor [Peter] Heylyn which I had heard very much commended and had been told, if ever I had any doubt in religion that would settle me. Instead of which I found it a description of the horridest sacrileges in the world, and could find no reason why we left the Church but for three the most abominable ones that ever were heard amongst Christians. First, Henry VIII renounced the Pope's authority because he would not give him leave to part with his wife and marry another in her lifetime. Secondly Edward VI was a child and governed by his uncle, who made his estate out of church lands. And then Queen Elizabeth who being no lawful heiress to the crown, could have no way to keep it but by renouncing a Church that would never suffer so unlawful a thing to be done by one of her children. I confess I cannot think the Holy Ghost could ever be in such counsels; and it is very strange that if the Bishops had no design but (as they say) restoring us to the doctrine of the primitive Church, they should never think upon it until Henry VIII made the breach upon so unlawful a pretence. These scruples being raised, I began to consider the difference between the Catholics and us, and examined them, as well as I could, by the holy Scripture, which though I don't pretend to be able to understand, yet there are some things I found so easy that I cannot but wonder, I had been so long without finding them out; as of the real presence in the blessed sacrament, the infallibility of the Church, confession and praying for the dead. After this, I spoke severally to two of the best bishops in England [Sheldon of Canterbury and Blandford of Worcester] who both told me there were many things in the Roman Catholic Church which it were very much to be wished we had kept—as confession, which was, no doubt, commanded by God; that praying for the dead was one of the most ancient things in Christianity; that for their parts they did it daily, though they would not own it. And afterwards pressing one of them [Blandford] very much upon other points, he told me that if he had been bred a Catholic, he would not change his religion; but that being of another Church wherein he was sure were all things necessary to salvation, he thought it very ill to give that scandal, as to leave the Church wherein he had received his Baptism. All these discourses did but add more to the desire I had to be a Catholic, and gave me the most terrible agonies in the world within myself. For all this, fearing to be rash in a matter of that weight, I did all I could to satisfy myself, and made it my daily prayer to God to settle me in the right and so went on Christmas Day to receive in the King's chapel. After which I was more troubled than ever, and could never be quiet till I had told my desire to a Catholic, who brought a priest to me, and that was the first I ever did converse with him, upon my word. The more I spoke to him, the more I was confirmed in my design. And as tis impossible for me to doubt of the words of our blessed Saviour, who says the holy Sacrament is his Body and Blood, so I cannot believe that he who is the author of all truth, and who has promised to be with his church to the end of the world, would permit them to give that holy mystery to the laity but in one kind if it were not lawful so to do. I am not able, or if I were, would I enter into disputes with anybody. I only, in short, say this for the changing of my religion which I take God to witness, I never would have done if I had thought it possible to save my soul otherwise. I think I need not say it is for any interest in this world leads me to it: it will be plain enough in everybody. I must lose my friends and credit I have here by it; and have very well weighed which I could best part with, my share in this world or in the next. I thank God I found no difficulty in the choice. My only prayer is that the poor Catholics of this nation may not suffer for my being of their religion; that God would but give me patience to bear them and send me any afflictions in this world so I may enjoy a blessed eternal hereafter. (1)

NOTES AND SOURCES

1. *The Church History of England from the Year 1500 to the Year 1688, Chiefly with Regard to Catholics* (Brussels, 1742), 397–8.

## Manual of Prayers (iv)                1686

The last in our series of *Manuals of Prayers and Litanies Distributed According to the Days of the Week With Other Excellent Devotions Fitted for All Persons and Occasions* was printed in 1686. In this (anonymous) recension, the Calendar of feasts and memoria was adorned, month by month by a short piece of verse highlighting the major feasts of that month, and we include them here, together with 'the hymns rendered according to the corrected Latin of Pope Urban VIII…and those too in far more exact and musical numbers than the former [edition]'. Although James II was now on the throne and Catholic publishing freely available in London, this book, like its predecessors, was published on the Continent.

### Verses for the Feasts of Each Month of the Year

[JANUARY]

This month was circumcised our Lord
As the Church hath asserted;
By the wise kings he was ador'd
And St Paul was converted

[FEBRUARY]

Our Lady who from stain was free
In this month purified
Only to teach humility
And St Matthias died

[MARCH]

We celebrate St Joseph's feast
And the bless'd Annuciation
Of our dear Lady, let's then at least
Still beg their intercession

[APRIL]

St Magdalen's conversion we
In this commemorate
And good St Mark this month did die
Let us them imitate

[MAY]

St Philip and Jacob lives do loss
And gain eternal crowns
And the invention of the Cross
The month of May renowns.

[JUNE]

St John who did our Lord baptize
And Barnaby here is seen
St Peter and St Paul we solemnize
With Margaret our Scots Queen

[JULY]

St James the great of John the brother
Our Lady's Visitation,
St Anne, also her glorious Mother,
And Ignatius keep their station

[AUGUST]

St Laurence roasted is alive
St Bartholomeus is slain here
We to honour the Assumption strive
Christ glorious doth appear.

[SEPTEMBER]

Our Lady born, St Matthew dies
St Michael's dedication
Let us implore their aid, with cries
And beg their intercession.

[OCTOBER]

To Simon and Jude our prayers we send
To Luke the Evangelist
If we to imitate them intend
Surely they'll us assist

[NOVEMBER]

All saints we here do solemnize
And do all souls remember
St Andrew and St Catharine dies
In the month of November

[DECEMBER]

Xavier and St Thomas here
And the Nativity
Stephen, Sylvester, John appear
And the babes guiltless die. (1)


# Hymn for Epiphany and the Octave

Most cruel Herod, whence do's spring
Thy fear, lest Christ should come as King
He seizes not on realms below
Who realms celestial does bestow

The sages followed the bright
Preceding star they had in sight;

By light to find out light they sought
They God confessed by gifts they brought.

The Heav'nly lamb (the spotless) took
The Baptism of the crystal brook
By washing us he cleans'd the blot
Of sin, which he contracted not.

A novel kind of pow'r he shows
Ruddy the pitchers' water grows
Which bid by him to send forth wine
The water chang'd its origin

To thee glory, Christ, who hast
Thy beams upon the gentiles cast;
And like unto the Father be,
And Holy Ghost eternally. Amen. (2)

## Hymn for the Purification of the Virgin

Hail Holy Queen of humble hearts!
We in thy praise will have our parts,
*Maria*, men and angels sing
*Maria*, mother of our King
Live, princess, live and may the bright
Crown of incomparable light.
Embrace thy brows, O may the best
Of endless joys bathe thy sweet breast
Live, our chaste love, the holy mirth
Of Heaven, the humble pride of Earth;
Live, crown of women, Queen of me
Live, mistress of our song, and when
Our weak desires have done their best
Blessed angels come and sing the rest
Glory to thee, great Virgin's Son
In bosom of thy Father's bliss;
The same to thee sweet sp'rit be done
As ever shall be, was and is. Amen. (3)

## Hymn for Lent

ON THE SUNDAYS AND WEEKDAYS OF LENT, TILL PASSION SUNDAY

Benign Creator lend thine ears
To pray'rs accompanied with tears
To celebrate this sacred fast,
For forty days ordained to last.

Clear searcher of all hearts, 'tis known
To thee, how weak our strength is grown
The favour of remission deign,
To such as turn to thee again.

We have offended in excess,
Yet pardon who their faults confess;
For thy name's glory do not stick,
To give a cordial to the sick

Grant that our flesh in abstinence
May so betam'd that from offence.
Our souls may fast, not e'er let in
The food that's apt to nourish sin.

O blessed Trinity afford
O single Unity accord
The duties of this Fast to be
Fruitful to those rely on thee. Amen. (4)

## Hymn for Eastertide

ON EASTER DAY AND FROM THENCE TO THE ASCENSION OF OUR LORD

At the lamb's regal banquet where
We must in candid robes appear;
After the Red Sea passed, let's sing
A hymn of praise to Christ our King.

Whose charity (divinely good)
Makes tender of his sacred Blood
While Love doth sacrifice as priest
The body whereunto souls do feast.

The striking angel dreads the gore
He sprinkled finds about the door;

The yielding sea divides his waves,
And foes there meet their liquid graves.

Now Christ our pasch, we rightly name.
Our paschal victim is the same;
Who is to souls that purged be
Pure azym of sincerity.[= possibly, azyme, the unleavened bread of the Jews]

O heavenly sacrifice! By whom
The depths of Hell are overcome.
And death's strong bonds dissolv'd, for which
Life's Crown his temples does enrich

Christ (victor o'er infernal foes)
His conquered trophies do's expose.
And, having Heaven unlock't, enslaves
The king that rules hell's darksome caves.

That Jesu thou to souls may'st be
A paschal joy eternally,
Free from the horrid death of sin
Us to regenerate have been

Be God the Father glorified
And Christ his Son who for us died
And rose again; so likewise be
The Holy Ghost eternally. Amen. (5)

NOTES AND SOURCES

1. *A Manual of Prayers and Litainies* [sic] *Distributed According to the Dayes in the Week* (1686), sig. A6–8.
2. Ibid., pp. 464–6.
3. Ibid. 466–7.
4. Ibid. 469–70.
5. Ibid. 475–6.

# Bishop John Leyburn                                    1620–1702

Leyburn was at the heart of the English Catholic Risorgimento in the late seventeenth century. Ordained priest in 1646, he was successively secretary to Bishop Richard Smith, chaplain to Lord Montagu, secretary to the Chapter after it was purged of Blackloists, President of Douai, secretary to Cardinal Thomas Howard in Rome (the most senior English Churchman between Cardinals Pole and Wiseman), vicar apostolic for the whole of England following the accession of James II (as Bishop of Adrumetum). His visitation in 1686 led to the first confirmations since 1629—and he confirmed many thousands. As James's regime secured itself, it was decided to create four 'districts' each with its own vicar apostolic, with Leyburn as vicar apostolic for the London district. Here is the first half of the pastoral letter which he issued on behalf of the four vicars apostolic in early 1688, when James was striving to make common ground with Protestant dissenters to promote the parliamentary repeal of the Test Acts (which gave Anglicans a monopoly on public office) and the penal laws. Within a few months, James's regime came crashing down and Leyburn spent two years in the Tower before resuming a quiet pastoral ministry as the new Protestant regime turned a blind eye.

## A Pastoral Letter from the Four Catholic Bishops
## to the Lay Catholics of England

Episcopal authority, dear brethren, of which you and your Catholic ancestors have been long deprived, being lately, by a merciful providence of God, and the piety of His Majesty, restored unto you; and our persons, though unworthy of such a dignity, made choice of to bear the weight, and undergo the solicitude annexed to it: we have judged it proper, before we separate ourselves in order to a discharge of our duties in the respective counties committed to our care, to join in a common address unto you all, hoping that what comes thus directed by an united application, will make a deeper impression on your minds, and dispose you to an easier compliance with the fatherly admonitions which every one in his particular district shall think fit to be made unto you.

Your condition for many years past hath been such, as enabled you to manifest a steadfastness in your religion, rather by suffering for it in your own persons, than by contributing actively towards the planting it in the minds and hearts of your fellow-subjects. The exercise of it hath been private and precarious, tending rather towards the preservation of it in yourselves, than a propagation of it in others. But now you are in circumstances of letting it appear abroad, and of edifying your neighbours by professing it publicly, and living up to the rules prescribed by it.

We need not tell you what obligation you lie under on this account, and how unjustifiable your behaviour will be in the judgement of God and men, if it be not conformable to those rules, if the liberty you enjoy of professing your religion be not improved into practices suitable to the sanctity thereof, and if the truth of your faith be not manifested by an exemplarity in your lives.

Charity, which the apostle declares to be the end of the law is the virtue by which your faith is to operate, and be kept alive: your understandings may be united without it, but your hearts cannot. This latter union is that which maintains the former, and renders it useful towards obtaining the end for which it is bestowed upon you.

We cannot mind you of this important duty with words more expressive of what we desire, than those which the same apostle made use of to exhort the Ephesians: We conjure you, as he did them, to walk in a manner worthy of the vocation by which you are called, with all humility and meekness, with patience supporting one another in charity, solicitous for maintaining the unity of spirit in a bond of peace.

You see of how great concern this unity of spirit is unto you, by the care which the apostle takes to have it well guarded. You likewise may observe the quality of the guard which is set to secure it. The employment of ordinary guards is to secure peace, but here peace itself is appointed to be the guard: peace in the first place with God, by an entire submission to the orders of his divine providence; from which connaturally follows a peace within yourselves, and a peace with your fellow-subjects.

As peace is a secure guard to the spirit of true religion and piety, so it is by the apostle ranked in the third place amongst the fruits of the Spirit. The soul centres in God by charity, and finding there an entire satisfaction, rests in peace.

Our intention in exhorting you to a practice of charity, is not that it be confined to persons of your own religion: such confinement would be a destruction of it; for true charity hath no bounds. You must love those of your religion, because they are so; and others, that as they profess themselves to be Christians, they may become members of the Catholic Church. You must evidence your love towards these, by an inoffensiveness in your behaviour.

The memory of past hardships which you have suffered from some amongst them, may be apt to create provoking animosities, and the liberty you now enjoy may possibly tempt you to insult over those who formerly abridged you of it; but it must be your care to prevent or suppress all such irregular motions. You must endeavour to tread in the footsteps of our divine master, who was so far from making such passionate returns, that he did not forbear, even in the height of his persecutions, to signalize the excess of his charity to those who were guilty of them. St Peter puts you in mind of this, proposing the example of Christ to your imitation; who, when his enemies treated him with most outrageous language, was far from answering them in the same dialect: when he was provoked by them to the highest degree of a just indignation, he did not so much as threaten them with the exercise of his power. The same Apostle leaving us a character of true Christians, declares, That they must be unanimous, compassionate, Lovers of the Brotherhood, merciful, modest, humble, not rendering evil for evil, railing for railing; but on the contrary returning Blessings to those who treated them in this manner ... (1)

NOTES AND SOURCES

1. [John Leyburn], *A Pastoral Letter from the Four Catholic Bishops to the Lay Catholics of England* (1688), 1–4.

# Bishop Bonaventure Giffard 1642–1734

Bonaventure Giffard was one of the four vicars apostolic (and titular Bishop of Madura) appointed by the Pope in 1687 with pastoral oversight of the English Church. He was initially appointed to the Midlands District, but following the death of John Leyburn in 1702, he took on the senior role as vicar apostolic for the London district. In 1687, determined to give him a strong base from which to exercise his ministry, James II forced Giffard onto the Fellows of Magdalen College Oxford as their President, and Giffard then celebrated his appointment by confirming hundreds of Catholics in the college chapel. He was briefly imprisoned at the Revolution of 1688. He was a noted court preacher, and we offer here the opening of his Christmas homily to the royal family at Whitehall in 1687.

## A Christmas Homily

Glory in the Highest to God, and in Earth, peace to men of good-will.
These words were sung by a full choir of angels at the birth of our Saviour as we find related by St Luke ch. 2, verse 14.

A stable! A manger! A little hay! Some poor swaddling bands! O helpless infant! A desolate young maid! An ox! An ass! What great matters of glory to God, or subject of so much joy to the angels? What is there in this poor equipage that should deserve to call down these noble spirits from heaven to solemnize its triumphs upon earth? O God! How different are thy judgements from those of men? And by how opposite ways dost thou seek thy glory from those which men take to establish theirs? Men place all their glory in great riches, magnificent houses, brave apparel, sumptuous entertainments, numerous attendants, and such like supports of their vanity and misery. But all the glory God Almighty designs to draw from the great work of the world's redemption, behold, he grounds them on the poverty, humility and abjection of his eternal son. Hence, as you see, for his royal palace he has provided him a ruinous stable; for his bed of state a hard manger; for his noble and numerous attendants an ox, an ass, or at best a few poor shepherds. In fine [= to sum up]: instead of mighty treasures and great plenty of all things, the utmost extremity of poverty.

This, Christians, this is the conduct Almighty God has used with his eternal son, at his first coming into the world. This is the method he has taken to purchase that glory to himself, to give that peace and joy to men, which the angels this day publish to the world in their Christmas Carol, of *Gloria in Altissimis Deo et in terra pax hominibus bonae voluntaris*. Divine Spirit! Enlighten my mind, inspire my thoughts, help me to apprehend the design of thy eternal wisdom in this astonishing mystery. I beg this of thee, by the intercession of the Virgin Mother, who this day brought forth that heavenly child, which she conceived by the operation of thy virtue, at the same time as the angel saluted her: Ave maria and Glory in the Highest to God, and in Earth, peace to men of good-will. The glory which Almighty God had in the world before the coming of our Saviour, seems to have been much eclipsed and reduced to a very small point. For the devil who no sooner became his enemy but also turned his rival, since he could not become like to God in Heaven, resolved at least to be adored for God upon Earth. And thence (as St Gregory Nazianzen observes) he has endeavoured to possess that divinity in the opinion of men which he could not steal from the uncommunicable nature of the Maker...

And indeed if the worship of men could increase or lessen the Majesty of God, if his glory were to be calculated by the number of his adorers, one might thence think (which otherwise to imagine were a blasphemy, that Lucifer had got the upper hand. Since, if we reflect on the sad condition the whole world was in, before the birth of the Saviour, we shall find that this proud and rebellious spirit was more worshipped, more glorified by men, than his sovereign Lord and maker. For if the true God was then worshipped by the Jews, false Gods were adored by other nations. If God had some zealous prophets to pronounce his oracles, the devil had many idolatrous priests to publish his lies. If God had an Altar consecrated to his service in Jerusalem, the devil had many temples dedicated to his honour throughout the rest of the world. If God was honoured by the sacrifice of beasts, the devil was worshipped by the slaughter of men. So that we are forced to own and lament that before the coming of the Messiah, the external glory of God (which consists in the worship of Men), was shut up within the narrow compass, confined to one little corner of the earth. *Notus est in Judaea Deus.*

But on this day, God Almighty begins to do himself right. He has sent down his eternal Son to vindicate his honour, to establish his glory, to subdue his proud rival, to dispossess him of his Empire he had gained over the minds of men. St John, the faithful interpreter of his designs, tells us that tis for this that the Son of God is come into the World, to destroy the works of the devil: *In hoc apparuit filius dei, ut dissolvat opera Diaboli.*[34] And the way he has taken to do this, is as strange in itself, as it has proved efficacious to the elect. The devil grounded his glory on the deluded imaginations of his followers. To make them idolaters of his false deity, he first possessed them with an erroneous conceit of their own greatness. To persuade them to offer incense to the statues they had raised in his temples, he first taught them to adore the idols he had set up in their minds: honour, riches, pleasure are the three great Gods he placed on the Altar of their hearts; to these he makes them sacrifice all their thoughts, all their affections, their bodies and soul, their eternity, their all. He persuades them that all their glory consists in worldly greatness, all their happiness in an affluence of temporal riches, and their chief beatitude is a full enjoyment of sensual satisfaction.

To destroy this work of the devil, to disabuse men of these false notions he had imbued them with, the Son of God is come into the world after the manner in which our present solemnity represents him to us. To show us how little esteem we ought to make of all the glory and greatness of the world, he would become a child, he would appear little and abject. To quench in us that ardent thirst we have after riches, he has reduced himself to the greatest poverty imaginable. To take out of our hearts that inordinate love of ease and pleasure, he begins his life all in sufferings and mortifications.

'Tis thus that Jesus Christ most successfully establishes the glory of God, because 'tis thus that he most powerfully triumphs over those vices which keep men slaves to the devil. And hence when the angels saw him laid thus low in the manger, then it was that they began to sing Glory to God and peace to men—glory to God because Jesus is come to cure our pride by his humility, our avarice by his poverty, our excesses and intemperance by his mortifications. *Gloria in altissimis Deo.* Peace and joy to men of good-will, to men that are willing to learn of such a master; to men that are willing to be instructed by such an example; to men who are willing to be saved by such a Master. *Pax hominibus bonae voluntatis.* 'Tis thus the angels divide their canticle, and 'tis thus that I divide my present discourse ... (1)

NOTES AND SOURCES

1. Bonaventure Giffard, *A Sermon of the Nativity of Our Lord Preach'd before the King and Queen at Whitehall* (1687), 1–7.

---

[34] 1 John 3: 8—in the Rheims/Douai translation: 'for this purpose the Son of God appeared, that he might destroy the work of the devil'.

# PART 2

## 1688–1850

Painted glass panel from the first public shrine of the Sacred Heart in Great Britain, Maryvale Institute, Birmingham (1814). Reproduced with permission.

# 'This Humble Hidden State': Remembrance, Enlightenment, and Emancipation

In an awed meditation on the Christmas mystery, the hagiographer Alban Butler quietly exults in God's advent among us in a 'humble hidden state'.[1] The Christ child came without fanfare, without riches, without temporal power. He came in poverty, amid distress, in obscurity. He came in exile, even in the ancestral home of David. He came amid persecution, fleeing Herod's wrath into Egypt. Yet, for Butler, this quiet moment provides voluble testament of God's grace, power, and glory. 'To contemplate immensity shut up in a little body, omnipotence clothed with weakness, the eternal God born in time, the joy of angels bathed in tears,' writes Butler, 'is something far more wonderful than to consider God creating a world out of nothing, moving the Heavens, and weighing the universe with a finger.'[2] In redirecting his gaze to the mystery of the Nativity, Butler departs from the eighteenth-century attempt to confine Christian theology within the reductive limits of an Enlightenment framework. For Deists, God was a philosophical proposition who, it was supposed, originally had to set the universe ticking. Natural theologians, culminating with the Anglican apologist, William Paley, were preoccupied with observing the mechanics of the natural world to find evidence of divine ordering. In Butler's view, any such emphasis on distance and design is overshadowed by God's entering into His Creation at the Incarnation and by His abiding presence in the liturgy of the Church, on the faces of the martyrs and saints, and within the moral law written in the hearts of humanity. Though often overlooked, no wonder can surpass the loving gentleness and life-giving humility of God becoming man.

Like the Infant God, the unassuming spiritual beauty of English Catholicism in Butler's age has been often overlooked. In accounts of English Catholic history, the time between the 1688 flight from England of the Catholic James II to the 1850 restoration of the Catholic hierarchy of bishops, in replacement of the missionary vicars apostolic, has often been viewed as one of dormancy and decline.[3] This middle period even lacks a compelling label and is inadequately dubbed Georgian, eighteenth-century, or Enlightenment. The best sobriquet might be the 'age of Challoner' after Richard Challoner, the long-serving bishop and vicar apostolic in the London district whose service did much to define the English Catholic Church and whose simple, unobtrusive, and internalized spiritual vision in *Garden of the*

---

[1] Alban Butler, *The Lives of the Fathers, Martyrs, and other Principal Saints*, 12 vols. (Dublin, 1780), xii. 321.

[2] Ibid. 319–20.

[3] For E. I. Watkin, it is the 'most dispiriting period' of English Catholic history, and David Mathew diagnoses this 'period of dispirited discouragement' as suffering from 'acute religious depression'. See *Roman Catholicism in England from the Reformation to 1950* (London: Oxford University Press, 1957), 103, and *Catholicism in England, 1535–1935. Portrait of a Minority: Its Culture and Tradition* (London: Catholic Book Club, 1938), 128, 131.

*Soul* (1740) guided devotional practice for a century or more.[4] Two of the most enduring narratives of the life of the Church in England have contributed to this period's obscurity. Frederick Faber passes over it in silence when powerfully recalling recusant Catholics 'chained in prisons dark' in his anthemic hymn 'Faith of Our Fathers'. For Blessed John Henry Cardinal Newman, the eighteenth and early nineteenth century represented a winter that provided no hopeful harbingers of the unexpected efflorescence and revival, or 'Second Spring', of Catholicism in England. In that sermon, Newman presents Bishop John Milner, the staunch leader of the Church in England from around the turn of the nineteenth century, as the lone figure who anticipated a Victorian Catholic revival.[5] It is true that Butler's age lacks the heroic braving of the Reformation's rough winds or the triumphal tide of conversions and construction after 1850. Nevertheless, the reflective spirituality and clear, quiet devotion of this complex and uncertain period can still inspire, perhaps never more resonantly than in our own complex and uncertain days.

English Catholics of this time faced a new, but constantly shifting, political reality. The 1688 Revolution meant that a political restoration of the 'Old Religion' in England was not imminent or foreseeable. As a result, John Gother, the most influential Catholic divine in this period, wrote his voluminous 'instructions' as a manorial chaplain who had been exiled from the court. From this position, Gother emphasized virtuous endurance and long-suffering charity in his apologies for the Faith and his counsel to the faithful. While there are several writers such as Jane Barker and Thomas Tyldesley included in this anthology who passionately embraced the Jacobite cause and felt the fervour of the Rebellions of 1715 and 1745, most English Catholics followed Gother and his protégé Challoner in attempting, as best they could, to live a Christian life in a nation where 'English' and 'Protestant' were widely viewed as synonymous. At the beginning of the eighteenth century, Catholics were a religious minority who no longer faced immediate threat of persecution from 'dungeon, fire and sword'. The 'enlightened' proponent of liberty, John Locke, was not alone, however, in believing that Catholics could not be fully trusted or tolerated.[6] The Reformation-era penal code remained the law of the land, and new provisions were added under William and Mary. Even though the most draconian measures, such as capital punishment for Catholic priests, were not enforced, an array of restrictions and penalties treated English Catholics as inferior subjects and objects of suspicion.[7] Catholics could not vote, hold office, or be called to the bar; they faced double taxation and inheritance restrictions; they could not build churches or open schools. A prohibition against receiving an education and taking a university degree meant that

---

[4] For a wide-ranging account of Challoner and eighteenth-century English Catholicism, see Eamon Duffy (ed.), *Challoner and His Church: A Catholic Bishop in Georgian England* (London: Darton, Longman, & Todd, 1981).

[5] Frederick William Faber, 'Faith of Our Fathers', in *Hymns* (London, 1862), 265; John Henry Newman, 'The Second Spring', in *Sermons Preached on Various Occasions* (London: Longmans, 1921), 163–82.

[6] John Locke, *A Letter Concerning Toleration 1689*, ed. John Horton and Susan Mendus (London: Routledge, 1991), 45–7 and *An Essay Concerning Toleration 1667*, ed. J. R. Milton and Philip Milton (Oxford: Clarendon Press, 2006), 290–2.

[7] For a comprehensive, contemporary survey of the penal code, see Charles Butler, *Historical Account of the Laws against the Roman-Catholics of England* (London, 1811).

many of the authors in this section were schooled abroad (though this too was technically illegal) at the English Catholic colleges in Lisbon, Valladolid, or Rome; the Jesuit college of St Omer's near Calais (and later Bruges, then Liège); and, most prominently, the secular college of Douai in northern France. These schools, established in the heat of the Reformation, were proud of the martyrs they had sent to the English mission. In the eighteenth century, they served the mission still, sending priests who often faced great hardship in ministries that ranged from far-flung rural communities to the immigrant and native poor of London and the burgeoning industrial cities of the North. The colleges abroad were also educating the Catholic gentry, who frequently enjoyed good social relations with their Anglican peers. For instance, the Welds hosted George III and the royal family while the Throckmortons patronized the evangelical poet William Cowper.

The political outlook for Catholics was also changing by the end of the century. With the threat from the Stuarts having passed, the government offered a modest alleviation of the penal laws in 1778, but this was greeted in 1780 with the Gordon Riots, a conflagration of anti-Catholicism and popular discontent that remains England's largest urban uprising.[8] In 1785, the Prince of Wales (later George IV) clandestinely wedded an English Catholic widow, Maria Fitzherbert, but this quickly dissolved marriage helped to sour George III's previously sympathetic view of his Catholic subjects. Although a substantial Catholic Relief Act was passed in 1791, George III would personally stand in the way of Catholic Emancipation—the 1829 act that removed remaining restrictions and finally allowed Catholics in all of Britain and Ireland to sit in Parliament.[9] Yet while many Catholics, including Nicholas Wiseman, heralded Catholic Emancipation as a proud, patriotic moment that ended 'recusancy', the 1850 restoration of the hierarchy and the elevation of Wiseman to Archbishop of Westminster touched off widespread popular and elite fears, resentment, and threats of violence in the 1851 'Catholic Aggression Crisis'.[10]

There was also a new social reality for Catholics amid these swerving political events. The English Catholic community gradually changed and expanded during the eighteenth century. Population concentrations could still be found in the traditional Catholic enclave of Lancashire and in London. The aristocratic

[8] See Colin Haydon, *Anti-Catholicism in Eighteenth-Century England, c.1714–80: A Political and Social Study* (Manchester: Manchester University Press, 1993), 204–44. For the role of anti-Catholicism and the formation of British national identity, see Linda Colley, *Britons: Forging the Nation 1707–1837* (New Haven: Yale University Press, 1992).

[9] For the 1791 Relief Act, see Nigel Abercrombie, 'The First Relief Act', *Challoner and His Church: A Catholic Bishop in Georgian England*, ed. Eamon Duffy (London: Darton, Longman, & Todd, 1981), 174–93. For the classic political history of Catholic Emancipation, see G. I. T. Machin, *The Catholic Question in English Politics, 1820–1830* (Oxford: Clarendon, 1964).

[10] For the 'Catholic Aggression Crisis', see Michael Wheeler, *The Old Enemies: Catholic and Protestant in Nineteenth-Century English Culture* (Cambridge: Cambridge University Press, 2006), 1–48. For recent general accounts of the history and politics of English Catholicism in this period, see J. C. H. Aveling, *The Handle and the Axe: The Catholic Recusants in England from Reformation to Emancipation* (London: Blond, 1976), 238–359; Sheridan Gilley, 'Roman Catholicism', in *Nineteenth-Century English Religious Traditions: Retrospect and Prospect*, ed. D. G. Paz (London: Greenwood Press, 1985), 33–56; Edward R. Norman, *The English Catholic Church in the Nineteenth Century* (Oxford: Clarendon Press, 1984), and Edward R. Norman, *Roman Catholicism in England: From the Elizabethan Settlement to the Second Vatican Council* (Oxford: Oxford University Press, 1985), 39–82.

manor houses that had provided protection and chapels to surrounding communities became relatively less important as urban centres such as Liverpool and Manchester grew. A massive flow of Irish immigration also brought more and more Catholics into England.[11] On the one hand, Catholic worship was still sequestered, often taking place in barns, domestic chapels, disguised churches, and even pubs; pilgrimages were made to secluded rural shrines such as Holywell in Wales or Fernyhalgh in Lancashire. On the other hand, London could also boast the august foreign embassy chapels that served Catholics in the capital. Catholics were not usually harassed, though incidents such as the national census of papists in 1767 and the prosecution of the priest J. B. Maloney (whose sentence was commuted) could disturb the general calm. Socially, Catholicism was establishing itself alongside the other Christian communities in England, and in Lancashire Catholics and Protestant Dissenters could make common political cause.[12] Yet these irenic developments do not imply theological indifference. Religious controversy remained sharp and substantial. From the suavely conciliatory London preacher James Archer to the fiery poet Thomas Ward, there was no shortage of apologists who defended the prerogatives of the 'Old Religion', explained and justified Catholic teachings on the Sacraments and the veneration of the Blessed Virgin Mary, and attacked Henry VIII and Elizabeth I for breaking from the doctrine and authority of Rome.

In addition to these gradual shifts, English Catholicism underwent sudden transformations, perhaps none more drastic than at the time of the French Revolution. While English Catholic institutions were not initially affected, the tensions between France and England eventually superseded any accumulated good will and the college at Douai was seized. Coinciding with the 1791 Relief Act that permitted Catholic educational institutions, Ushaw College, Durham, and St Edmund's College, Ware, jointly carried on Douai's legacy in England. The foundation of the other major English Catholic colleges and seminaries—Oscott College and Stonyhurst, with its historical links to St Omer's—can also be traced back to this era. English Catholics priests and students from Douai, such as John Lingard, William Poynter, and George Leo Haydock returned home; and French Catholic clergy, such as Nicholas Alain Gilbert, were among the French émigrés who sought refuge in England and found a charitable reception from both Catholics and Protestants. Even monasteries migrated. Trappist monks fleeing France in 1791 established a community in Lulworth that also included Irish and English Catholics, who returned to France after the fall of Napoleon only to flee the 1830 Revolution for its current Irish establishment as Mount Melleray Abbey.[13] It would not be wrong to characterize this moment as an early revival of English Catholicism. The Mass was now legal, and new Catholic churches, now

---

[11] For a sociological accounts of changes among English Catholics, see John Bossy, *The English Catholic Community: 1570–1850* (Oxford: Oxford University Press, 1976) and Michael A. Mullett, *Catholics in Britain and Ireland, 1558–1828* (New York: St Martin's Press, 1998), 102–37, 165–96.

[12] For this relationship, see Eamon Duffy, *Peter and Jack: Roman Catholics and Dissent in Eighteenth Century England* (London: Dr Williams's Trust, 1982).

[13] See Aidan Bellenger, 'Revolution and Emancipation', in *Monks of England: The Benedictines in England from Augustine to the Present Day*, ed. Daniel Rees (London: SPCK, 1997), 199–212. For a contemporary account of seeing the mix of modern and ancient, French and English during a visit to the Trappist abbey, see *The Catholic Miscellany* 1.3 (March 1822), 108–9; 1.4 (April 1822), 155–6; 1.6 (June 1822), 270–1.

permitted but still required to be small and discrete, were being built. Milner commissioned a Gothic chapel in Winchester that was a precursor to the ambitious recovery of medieval architecture later launched by the pugnacious architect A.W. Pugin. Catholics also laboured to establish a journalistic presence in England that would give them standing in the public sphere, as a multitude of new Catholic periodicals competed for the role that *The Tablet* eventually occupied from the 1840s onward.[14] There were also new establishments of old orders following the legislative victory of Catholic Emancipation, the campaign for which had rallied Catholics together for a common purpose, if often with great disharmony.[15]

The campaign for legislative relief brought to the fore deeper controversies among English Catholics over the future of the Church in England that revolved around the views and activities of the Cisalpine movement. As the name implies— this side of the Alps—the Cisalpines promoted a reconstruction of Catholicism that was less Roman and more English.[16] This was a pragmatic necessity for the lawyer, man of letters, and nephew of Alban Butler, Charles Butler, who was the secretary and spokesman for the Catholic Committee (1782–92) and Cisalpine Club (1791–1829). These organizations, in which the lay aristocracy of old Catholic families was well represented, attempted to prove to the government that Catholics were loyal, modern, reasonable, and nothing like the feared image of the 'papist'. The compromises of the Cisalpines drew pointed criticism from Bishop Milner, Charles Plowden, and others for their acceptance of a government 'veto' for appointments of Catholic bishops, their agreement to the term 'Protesting Catholic Dissenter' in a proposed oath of loyalty, and their general dilution of Catholic culture and identity to gain legislative concessions and social acceptance. Related to this political movement was the more audacious intellectual programmes of the Scottish priest, poet, and biblical critic Alexander Geddes and the priest and writer Joseph Berington, whose historical and philosophical writings consistently distanced modern Catholicism from all that was medieval or scholastic.[17]

English Catholicism was also shaped by controversies emanating from abroad. English Jesuits fared better than their Continental brethren after the suppression of the Jesuits in 1773. Nevertheless, St Omer's fled from France to Bruges in 1762, and from there to Liège. The Continental Catholic colleges in particular were affected by the controversy surrounding Jansenism, a heretical interpretation of St Augustine prevalent in the Netherlands and Northern France around the turn of the eighteenth century. Jansenists drew their doctrine from the writings of the seventeenth-century Dutch bishop Jansenius, who held that the total depravity of fallen humanity had left the individual incapable of resisting either divine grace or

---

[14] See John R. Fletcher, 'Early Catholic Periodicals in England', *Dublin Review*, 198 (1936), 284–310.

[15] For the internal divisions among Catholics, see Bernard Ward, *The Eve of Catholic Emancipation*, 3 vols. (London: Longmans, 1911–12).

[16] For an overview of the movement, see Joseph P. Chinnici, *The English Catholic Enlightenment: John Lingard and the Cisalpine Movement, 1760–1850* (Shepherdstown, WV: Patmos Press, 1980).

[17] See William Johnstone (ed.), *The Bible and the Enlightenment: A Case Study of Alexander Geddes 1737–1802* (London: T & T Clark, 2002) and Eamon Duffy, 'Ecclesiastical Democnacy Detected: I (1779–1787)', *Recusant History*, 10 (1970), 193–209; 'Ecclesiastical Democracy Detected: II (1787–1796)', *Recusant History* 10 (1970) 309–31; and 'Doctor Douglass and Mister Berington: An Eighteenth-Century Retraction', *Downside Review*, 88 (July 1970), 246–9.

the temptation of earthly pleasure. For denying the dignity and freedom of humanity, this set of quasi-Calvinistic ideas, which were finally condemned by Clement XI in the bull *Unigenitus* (1713), attracted adherents who viewed morality with a despondent severity and approached the sacraments with an equally rigoristic stringency.[18] Whether it was by emphasizing the pursuit of virtue, the freely available gift of divine grace, or the nobility of the human person, the Catholic writers in this section responded in various ways to the influence of Jansenism.

Amid these religious controversies and social and political transformations, three themes can be traced among the poets, theologians, journalists, historians, apologists, and priests. First, in an age of promise and progress, but also of frustration and continuing alienation, English Catholics struggled to determine their proper attitude to the world amid the joys and challenges of the society in which they lived. St Paul counselled the Romans, 'Be not conformed to this world; but be reformed in the newness of your mind, that you may prove what is the good, and the acceptable, and the perfect will of God' (Rom. 12: 2). Finding the balance between living virtuously in the world and succumbing to a worldliness that obscures the love of God seems a perennial problem in the Christian life. It took on two particular inflections in this period. For many Catholics, living in the world meant labouring long hours, raising children, and paying crippling rents and taxes. Attending to these real duties resulted in busyness and anxiety. With the fundamental pace of life transformed in many regions by rapid industrialization, infrequent or unreliable access to the sacraments and places of worship, and a lack of contemplative monastic institutions, Catholic writers often offered counsel on how to cultivate the time, place, and energy for a spiritual life of prayer and devotion—what St Paul calls being 'reformed in the newness of your mind'. But the world offered allurements as well as hardships. Even with the many disadvantages they faced, Catholics rose to prominence, even stardom, in nearly every arena of eighteenth-century life. Alexander Pope followed John Dryden as the poet of the age; John Philip Kemble was the iconic actor of his era, and Elizabeth Inchbald one of the most successful playwrights; the scientist John Tuberville Needham was the first Catholic priest to be elected to the Royal Academy and conducted a controversy with Voltaire; Thomas Augustine Arne helped revive the opera in England, composed 'Rule Britannia', and arranged 'God Save the King'; John Chetwode Eustace was one of the most widely read travel writers for the Continental 'Grand Tour'; Charles Butler and John Lingard were two of the most significant figures in law and history respectively; and no single architect had more influence than Pugin. Looking back on the success that had arisen out of persecution and at the new possibilities for social integration for Catholics emerging in 1850, Pugin himself sounded a cautionary note: 'I fear not our enemies; I fear not our calumniators; I fear not the tyranny of state measures. I have but one fear; that is, *I fear ourselves*.'[19] In eighteenth-century Catholic polemic, the 'worldling' often replaced the 'Protestant' or the 'pagan' as the object

---

[18] For the investigation and exoneration of Douai on charges of Jansenism, see Peter Guilday, *The English Catholic Refugees on the Continent* (London: Longmans, Green, & Co., 1914), 333–4.

[19] A.W. Pugin, *An Earnest Address on the Establishment of the Hierarchy* (London: 1851), 31.

of criticism. Significantly, as Pugin articulates, this new critique was directed not against other religious camps or ideas. It was instead a message to 'be not conformed to this world' that was offered by Catholics to their fellow Catholics. The slow creep of convention, financial and social emoluments, and the distractions of modern life threatened to turn their escape from the harrowing tribulations of the Reformation into a silent apostasy.

Memory, the second recurrent theme, played a key role in this spiritual struggle. The recording of sacred history became a way of bracing oneself for the challenges of today. Challoner and Butler produced comprehensive accounts of the lives of the saints for each day of the year; Lingard tried to wrest English history from partisan, politicized Protestant interpretations by using primary sources, while Hugh Tootell (Charles Dodd) attempted to offer a critical, English Catholic perspective on Church history; against the Cisalpine denigration of the medieval past, Milner's antiquary work claimed continuity between the present community and the Middle Ages; Christopher Tootell and Philip Leigh preserved and published the traditions of Catholic pilgrimage sites, while poets and antiquaries reconstructed the meaning of monastic ruins and significant English Catholic locales; and editors and biographers like William Joseph Walter enabled the reading public better to appreciate figures such as St Robert Southwell and St Thomas More.[20] To retell the past was a way to strengthen the Catholic community by remembering its suffering and its glory. Catholic periodicals launched in this period regularly featured sections dedicated to Catholic history and retrospective poems such as 'The Exiles at Home'. This poem, published in *The Orthodox Journal*, compares British Catholics to those exiled Israelites in Psalm 136 who refuse to sing the 'songs of Sion' for their Babylonian captors:

> And sad is the fate of the mourners of Erin,
> And sad are the weepers in Albion's fair isle;
> The foe has not forced them from all that's endearing,
> Their homes have been the proud conqueror's spoil.
> But millions are bound for the faith of their fathers,
> And branded as slaves in the land of their birth;
> And the sweat of hard toil on their forehead that gathers
> Comes mixed with the tear-drops of woe to the earth.

> Full long has the boon of their freedom been sighed for,—
> Long have they wept by the streams of their home;
> Yet dear is the faith that their fathers have died for,
> It caused them their fetters, but softens their doom.
> And ages of bondage may torture and bind them,
> Force cannot change them, nor slavery tire;
> Their faith will descend to their children behind them,
> The young hearts will glow with their forefather's fire.

---

[20] For recent studies—often focusing on Lingard—of history and memory among English Catholics, see Edwin Jones, *John Lingard and the Pursuit of Historical Truth* (Brighton: Sussex Academic Press, 2001); Peter Phillips (ed.), *Lingard Remembered* (London: Catholic Record Society, 2004); and John Vidmar, *English Catholic Historians and the English Reformation, 1585-1954* (Brighton: Sussex Academic Press, 2005).

In the poem, the exiles' singing of 'the faith of their fathers' looks both backward and forward as its lament becomes a rallying cry for social justice and a promise to transmit this faith to future generations. This historical emphasis, however, was important in more than the visible realms of politics and culture. Seen through the eyes of faith, memory helps to affirm the invisible community of the living and the dead as the Church seeks the intercession of the saints and prays for the souls in Purgatory.

The relation of things unseen and seen, of faith and reason, represents a third prominent theme in the selections that follow. This is another universal and perennial issue that most recently gave rise to Pope John Paul II's 1998 encyclical *Fides et Ratio*, framed nineteenth-century theology in Europe, and provided the subject for Wiseman's lectures on science and religion.[21] In this period, what can be broadly termed the Enlightenment provided the spur for meditations on the relationship between faith and reason. To speak of the Enlightenment is to speak of a movement that was complex and multifaceted, consisting of the acts, influence, and writings of individuals who were diverse in their views and commitments, sometimes religiously devout but also often aggressively anti-religious. In one canonical discussion, Immanuel Kant's 'What is Enlightenment?' (1784), the philosopher dares every individual to exert their own faculties of reason and, in the name of freedom, not to take anything on faith. The rejection of authority, dogma, tradition, and convention is so thorough that Kant vows not to tolerate 'a book that has understanding for me, a pastor who has a conscience for me, a doctor who judges my diet for me'.[22] As might be expected, Catholic writers responded with a vindication of faith and a critique of the limits of an overreaching rationality, especially when it came to mysteries such as the Blessed Sacrament. The Catholic theologian Sylvester Jenks argued, 'Human Reason is the best thing in nature, if rightly managed; and the worst, if a proud wilful creature have the keeping of it.'[23] In addition, Jenks's axiom represents a defence of reason that may not be expected, but that is an integral part of the Catholic understanding of the human person and God's creation. There would be no repudiation of reason, which was viewed as one of God's greatest gifts, in order to elevate an irrational faith. Nor would Catholics allow faith to be sequestered in a separate sphere from reason as a private, emotional, or solely ethical phenomenon. Faith and reason had to be, as in John Paul II's later formulation, 'like two wings on which the human spirit rises to the contemplation of truth',[24] a truth that culminates in the true God becoming truly incarnate in the 'humble hidden state' described by Alban Butler. John Gother thus firmly believed in turning to a manger on a winter's night to seek enlightenment from 'the rays of the true light' that has 'dispelled the darkness of this sacred time'. Amid the transformations in the experience of English Catholics, their Janus-faced integration of memories and

---

[21] For nineteenth-century debates on faith and reason in Catholic theology, see Joseph Fitzer, *Romance and the Rock* (Minneapolis: Fortress Press, 1989).

[22] Immanuel Kant, 'An Answer to the Question: What is Enlightenment?', in James Schmidt (ed.), *What is Enlightenment: Eighteenth-Century Answers and Twentieth-Century Questions* (Berkeley and Los Angeles: University of California Press, 1996), 58.

[23] Sylvester Jenks, *The Blind Obedience of an Humble Penitent: The Best Cure for Scruples* (1699), 43.

[24] John Paul II, *Fides et Ratio* (Boston: Pauline Books, 1998), 7.

promises, and their continued pilgrimage through their homeland, Gother petitioned that by 'knowing the mysteries of this light on earth, we may come to the possession of his joys in heaven'.[25] Written at the end of the seventeenth century, said throughout the eighteenth century, and republished at the turn of the nineteenth century, Gother's Christmas prayer expresses familiar needs for humility, perseverance, and hope:

By thy coming,
 By thy nativity,
 By all the mercies of this day, deliver us, O Jesus.
 We, sinners, beseech thee,
 That thou would vouchsafe to give us thy grace, whereby we may become thy true disciples.
 That in all things we may take thee for our pattern, and be ever mindful of following thy example.
 That we may learn to renounce all our pride, and follow thy humility.
 That we may suffer, with thy patience, whatever evils befall us.
 That in a cheerful silence we may readily submit to whatever humiliations God has appointed for us.
 That having undertaken to be our advocate, thou would vouchsafe to plead for us, and obtain for us this day the pardon of all our sins.
 That thou would give a blessing to thy Church, and deliver it from all abuses.
 That thou would give a blessing to this nation, and delivering it from all vice and error, make it to thyself a holy people.
 That thou would give a blessing to us who are here assembled in memory of thy nativity, and powerfully assist us with thy grace, according as our several necessities require.... Amen.[26]

---

[25] John Gother, *Gother's Prayers for Sundays and Festivals* (Wolverhampton, 1800), 35.
[26] Ibid. 30–1.

# John Gother

Gother stands between the resilient Recusant culture of the Reformation period and the quieter, reflective spirituality of English Catholicism that emerged following the 1688 Revolution. Born in Southampton, he was raised Protestant and heard all of what William Cobbett would later call the recriminatory 'magpie-sayings' against Catholics. Nevertheless, Gother converted in 1667 and soon after studied at the English College in Lisbon for the priesthood. He came to London in 1681 at a tumultuous time in English history amid the fallout from Titus Oates's 'Popish Plot' and the attempt to exclude James, the Catholic brother of Charles II, from the throne. Gother himself would make James II's reign even more of a tumult with the publication of *A Papist Misrepresented and Represented* (1685), a critical work of apologetics that attempted to debunk popular images of 'papist' beliefs and practices and to replace them with a clear sense of Catholic doctrine, worship, and morality. Stereotypes, fraught with political weight in the 1680s, were not easily swept away, and Gother found himself exchanging polemical pamphlets with no less than eight major Protestant writers, including the most prominent critic of Catholicism, Edward Stillingfleet, Bishop of Worcester from 1689, in what was known as the 'Representing' controversy. Political change overtook theological debate, however, as James II went into exile. Gother, too, withdrew from the public eye after 1688 and spent the remainder of his life as a chaplain in Northamptonshire to the family of George Holman, whose father-in-law had been executed as a result of Oates's machinations. He made his two major contributions to the coming century of Catholic life from this retreat. First, Gother received into the Church the son of Holman's housekeeper. This young man, named Richard Challoner, became the vicar apostolic of the London District, and guided the English Catholic Church through the eighteenth century. Second, Gother wrote a series of devotional works, mostly labelled 'instructions', that not only addressed elements of Catholic worship but also gave counsel to Catholics in all walks of life and for all areas of human experience. Developing a tradition that reached back to St Francis de Sales, these reflections for Christians living in the world focused on the threats to a devout life, not so much from apostasy or persecution, but rather from worry, complacency, and busyness. Gother's writings shaped Catholic spirituality through English Catholicism's Victorian 'Second Spring' and remain poignant in our own distracted age. For the soundness of his thought and the grace of his style, Charles Butler compared him favourably to Jonathan Swift, and John Dryden reportedly labelled him a master of the English language. Gother died at sea, and his remains were laid to rest in the chapel of the English College at Lisbon, near the altar of St Thomas à Becket.

## The Catholic Misrepresented

The Father of Lies is the author of misrepresenting. He first made the experiment of this black art in Paradise; having no surer way of bringing God's precept into contempt, and making our first parents transgress, than by misrepresenting the command which their Maker had laid on them. And so unhappily successful he was in this his first attempt, that this has been his chief stratagem ever since, in all business of difficulty and concern; esteeming that his best means for preserving and propagating wickedness amongst men, by which he first won them to lose their innocence. And therefore there has nothing of good yet come into the world, nothing been sent from Heaven, but what has met with this opposition; the common enemy having employed all his endeavours of bringing it into discredit, and rendering it infamous, by misrepresenting it. Of this there are frequent instances in the Old Law, and more in the New. The truth of it was experienced on the person of Christ himself, who, though he was the Son of God, the immaculate Lamb, yet was he not out of the reach of calumny, and exempt from being misrepresented. See how he was painted by malicious men, the Sons of Belial, Ministers of Satan: *a profane and wicked man, a breaker of the Sabbath, a glutton, a friend and companion of publicans and sinners, a fool, a conjurer, a traitor, a seducer, a tumultuous person, a Samaritan, full of the Devil; he hath Belzebub, and, by the Prince of the Devils, casteth he out devils* (Mark 3: 22). There being no other way of frighting the people from embracing the truth and following the Son of God, but by thus disfiguring him to the multitude, reporting light to be darkness, and God to be the Devil. The disciples of Christ everywhere met with the like encounters.... Neither did these calumnies, these wicked misrepresentations stop here; he that said, *The disciple is not above his master, if they have called the master of the house Belzebub; how much more shall they call them of his household?* did not only foretell what was to happen to his followers then present, but also to the faithful that were to succeed them, and to his Church in future ages; they being all to expect the like fate; that though they should be never so just to God and their neighbour, upright in their ways, and live in the fear of God, and the observance of his laws; yet must they certainly be reviled and hated by the world, made a byword to the people, and have the repute of idiots, seducers, and be a scandal to all nations. And has not this been verified in all ages? (1)

## The Catholic Re-Presented: 'Worshipping' Saints

He [the Catholic] believes, there's only one God, and that it is a most damnable idolatry to make gods of men, either living or dead. His Church teaches him indeed, and he believes, that it is good and profitable to desire the intercession of the saints reigning with Christ in Heaven; but that they are either God, or his Redeemer, he is no where taught; but detests all such doctrine. He confesses that we are all redeemed by the blood of Christ alone, and that he is our only mediator of redemption: but as for mediators of intercession (that is, such as we may desire lawfully, to *pray for us*) he does not doubt, but it is acceptable to God, we should have many. Moses was such a mediator for the Israelites; Job for his three friends; Stephen for his persecutors. The Romans were thus desired by St Paul to be his mediators; so were the Corinthians, so the Ephesians; so almost every sick man desires the congregation to be his mediator; that is, to be remembered in their prayers. And so he desires the blessed in Heaven to be his mediators; that is, that they would *pray to God for him*. And in this, he does not at all neglect coming to God, or rob him of his honour; but directing all his prayers up to him, and making him the ultimate object of all his petitions, he only desires sometimes the just on earth, sometimes those in Heaven, to join their prayers to his, that so the number of petitioners, being increased, the petition may find better acceptance in the sight of God. (2)

## The Catholic Re-Presented: The Virgin Mary

He believes it damnable to think the Virgin Mary more powerful in Heaven than Christ: Or that she can in any thing command him: He honours her indeed, as one that was chosen to be *Mother of God*, and *blessed amongst all women*: And believes her to be most acceptable to God, in her intercession for us: But owning her still as a creature, and that all she has of excellency or bliss is the gift of God, proceeding from his mere goodness. Neither does he at any time say even so much as one prayer to her, but what is directed more principally to God; being offered up as a thankful memorial of Christ's Incarnation, and an acknowledgement of the blessedness of Jesus the fruit of her womb. And this without imagining that there's any more dishonouring of God in his reciting the angelical salutation, than in the first pronouncing it by the Angel Gabriel and Elizabeth: Or that his frequent repetition of it is any more an idle superstition, than it was in David to repeat the same words over twenty times in the 136<sup>th</sup> Psalm. (3)

## The Catholic Re-Presented: The Eucharist

He believes it unlawful to commit idolatry and most damnable to worship or adore any breaden god, or to give divine honour to any elements of bread and wine. He worships only one God, who made Heaven and Earth, and his only Son Jesus Christ our Redeemer; who, being in all things equal to his Father, in truth and omnipotency, he believes, made his words good pronounced at his last supper; really giving his body and blood to his apostles: the substance of bread and wine, being by his powerful words changed into his own body and blood; the species only or accidents of the bread and wine remaining as before. The same he believes of the most holy Sacrament of the Eucharist, consecrated now by priests; that it really contains the body of Christ, which was delivered for us; and his blood, which was shed for the remission of sins. Which being there united with the Divinity, he confesses Whole Christ to be present. And him he adores and acknowledges his Redeemer, and not any bread or wine. And for the believing of this mystery, he does not at all think it meet for any Christian to appeal from Christ's words to his own senses or reason for the examining the truth of what he has said; but rather to submit his senses and reason to Christ's words in the obsequiousness of faith. (4)

## The Catholic Re-Presented: Worshipping in Latin

He is commanded to assist at the church service, and to hear Mass, and in this he is instructed; not to understand the words, but to know what is done: For the Mass being a Sacrifice, wherein is daily commemorated the death and passion of Christ, by an oblation made by the priest of the body and blood of the Immaculate Lamb under the symbols of bread and wine according to his own institution: it is not the business of the congregation present to employ their ears in attending to the words; but their hearts in contemplation of the divine mysteries: by raising up fervent affections of love, thanksgiving, compassion, hope, sorrow for sins, resolutions of amendment, etc. that thus having their heart and intention united with the priests, they may be partakers of his prayers, and of the sacrifice he is then offering, than which he believes nothing is more acceptable to God or beneficial to true believers. And for the raising of these affections in his soul and filling his heart with the ecstasies of love and devotion, he thinks in this case, there's little need of words; a true faith, without these, is all sufficient. Who could but have burst forth into tears of love and thanksgiving, if he had been present while our Saviour was tied to the pillar, scourged and tormented, though he opened not his mouth to the bystanders, nor spoke a word? Who would have needed a sermon to have been filled with grief and compassion, if he had seen his Saviour exposed to the scorn of the Jews, when he was made a bloody spectacle by Pilate, with *Ecce homo, Lo the Man*? Who would have stood cold and senseless upon Mount Calvary, under the Cross, when his Redeemer was hanging on it, though he had not heard or not understood a word that he spoke? Does any one think that those holy women, who followed their Lord in these sad passages and were witnesses of his sufferings wanted holy affections in their souls, because he spoke not; or were they scandalized at his silence? (5)

## The Catholic Re-Presented: Scandal

He is a member of a Church, which, according to the ninth article of the Apostles Creed, he believes to be holy; and this not only in name, but also in doctrine; and for the witness of her sanctity, he appeals to her councils, catechisms, pulpits, and spiritual books of direction; in which the main design is to imprint in the hearts of the faithful this comprehensive maxim of Christianity: *That they ought to love God above all things, with their whole heart and soul and their neighbours as themselves.* And that none flatter themselves with a confidence to be saved by faith alone without living soberly, justly and piously.... He doubts not at all but that as many as live according to the direction of his Church, and in observance of her doctrine, live holily in the service and fear of God and with an humble confidence in the merits and passion of their Redeemer, may hope to be received after this Life into eternal Bliss. But that all in communion with his Church do not live thus holily and in the fear of God, he knows it is too, too evident; there being many in all places wholly forgetful of their duty, giving themselves up to all sorts of vice, and guilty of most horrid crimes. And though he is not bound to believe all to be truth that is charged upon them by adversaries; there being no narrative of any of those devilish contrivances and practices laid to them wherein passion and fury have not made great additions; wherein things dubious are not improved into certainties, suspicions into realities, fears and jealousies into substantial plots, and down-right lies and recorded perjuries into pulpit, nay Gospel truths, yet he really thinks, that there has been men of his profession of every rank and degree, learned and unlearned, high and low, secular and ecclesiastic, that have been scandalous in their lives, wicked in their designs, without the fear of God in their hearts, or hope of their own salvation. But what then? Is the whole Church to be condemned for the vicious lives of some of her professors and her doctrine to stand guilty of as many villainies as those commit who neglect to follow it? If so, let the men of that society, judgement, or persuasion, who are not in the like circumstances, fling the first stone. Certainly if this way of passing sentence be once allowed as just and reasonable, there never was, nor ever will be, any religion or Church of God upon the earth. (6)

## A Prayer at the Elevation of the Host

I love thee, dear Jesus, the Saviour of my soul, who died on the Cross a sacrifice for the sins of the whole world. I most firmly believe that by virtue of consecration thou, Lord, true God and true man, art really present in a most wonderful manner, on the altar. I believe thou art here present, who art the assured hope, and only salvation of sinners; who art the sovereign remedy of all our necessities, the comfort in our troubles, and support in our distress. (7)

## The Ritual Meaning of the Mass

I think it may not be improper here to give a short glance at the chief ceremonies used at Mass; because those who understand enough ... may make some reflections on them such as may be a great help to direct them in their devotion.

First then, *bowing down* is a posture often used by the priest ... as often as he says such prayers, in which he *acknowledges his unworthiness, humbly makes his offering to Almighty God, begs for mercy, etc.* And this he is ordered to do that by this external humiliation, he may be put in mind of that interior humility of spirit, with which he ought ever to perform those actions; as likewise to direct all present then to humble themselves before Almighty God while they see the priest thus bowing down.

2. *Kneeling* is generally in the Mass an act of adoration, by which the priest gives sovereign worship to Christ our Redeemer really present in the Eucharist. And therefore this the priest performs with all the powers of his soul, adoring before his Lord, and shows the faithful how they ought ever to adore in spirit, as often as they see the priest kneeling before the Holy Eucharist. He kneels likewise once in the middle of the creed when he pronounces these words: *Et homo factus est: And he was made man.* And once at the end of St John's Gospel, when he says: *Et Verbum Caro factum est; And the Word was made flesh.* Both times to signify the Second Person of the Blessed Trinity coming down from Heaven to take on him our nature so to become our Redeemer: in acknowledgement of which mystery, all Christians ought to bow, both priest and people, so to testify their sense of that infinite mercy, and give thanks for it.

3. *Striking the Breast* is a ceremony delivered in Scripture as an expression of a sincere repentance in the poor publican. And this the priest uses as often as he professes a repentance for his sins, as in the *confiteor*; or begs for mercy; as at *Agnus Dei*: Or confesses his unworthiness, as at *Domine non sum dignus.* And if he does this, not as using a bare ceremony, but with a truly humble and contrite heart, there's no question, it is what is very Christian and may serve likewise to move the faithful to a hearty contrition and sincere acknowledgement of their unworthiness as often as they practise the like action. And if they would thus seriously return to the heart, as often as they strike their breast, they might reasonably hope with the publican to go home justified.

4. *Turning to the People* is what the priest does as often as he gives a blessing to them; in saying, *Dominus vobiscum; Our Lord be with you, etc.* or desires their prayers, as at *Orate Fratres; brethren pray, etc.* For as when he makes his offerings and prayers to God, he stands with his face to the altar, which is the place of worship; so when he addresses himself to the people, he turns to them.

5. *Making the sign of the Cross* is used in blessing the bread and wine as an acknowledgement of our belief that all grace and benediction is to come to us through the merits and passion of Christ crucified.

6. *Kissing the altar* is what the priest does before he blesses the offering, or the people, etc. to signify again that all peace and blessing is purchased for us by Christ's suffering on the Cross, which is represented by the altar: And that all Good is to come to us from His sacred merits. (8)

## The Moral Meaning of the Mass

To those who know how to govern their thoughts and are well acquainted with the way of the spirit, hearing Mass is but one continued exercise of the soul in all the acts of Christian virtues...This is done by an inward light communicated by Almighty God, not only to men of learning; but often to such, who being otherwise weak and ignorant, have nothing but humility, and seeking God with sincere hearts to prepare them for these favours of Heaven.

All these when they go to hear Mass, go as to a school of virtue, where they are to meet their Divine Master, by whom they are to be instructed in all the rules of a Christian life, to be reproached of all their failings and encouraged in all those great duties, which are required of them.

1. They behold in this mystery, Christ our Lord in the flames of divine love, offering himself a sacrifice every day to the glory of his Father. Which is a lesson to them that if they design truly to belong to God, they ought daily to offer themselves to him, to make their lives a perpetual sacrifice and endeavour to live no more to themselves but to him.

2. They see an excess of that other branch of charity, which regards our neighbour in the Holy Eucharist, where Christ gives himself to the faithful under the form of bread and nourishment, by means of which they may be changed and transformed into him. And this is a rule to them, of the love they ought to bear to their neighbour: and a reproach, as often as they consider how interest and self love makes them neglect this great duty and lay a ground for misunderstandings, complaints and quarrels.

3. They see him there in a state of humility under the Sacramental Species: This is to them a condemnation of all pride, and by his example, suppresses all vain esteem they can have of themselves.

4. They behold in him a wonderful patience: bearing not only with the blasphemies of unbelievers, but also with the sacrileges of unworthy receivers. This confounds their excessive niceness, who cannot, without disturbance, bear the least injury or contempt.

5. They consider him there in a state of poverty: This condemns all thoughts of covetousness; and encourages them to cast off all vain solicitude; and submit to inconveniences without murmuring.

6. They see him there as it were in a state of penance, covered with those sensible accidents, as with sackcloth and ashes, and thus offering himself to his Eternal Father as an Host of Propitiation for our sins: This shows them how to repent of their sins; and with what charity they ought to pray for all those who are separated from God by their offences and are under the tyranny of vicious habits.

7. They see him there an advocate for all even for those who have offended him. This forcibly moves them to cast off all sorts of animosities, ill-will, or hatred from their hearts, and to let no kind of injuries be a confinement to their charity, which ought to be, like their Master's, extended to all.

Infinite other lessons of this kind they hear from their Divine Master in this school of piety; such as the world cannot understand. Whilst placing themselves at his feet, like Holy *Magdalen*, with humility they say to him in their hearts, *I will hear what our Lord shall speak.* (9)

## Guidance for Anxious and Scrupulous Christians

These stand in need of a skilful hand to support them under their disturbance and prevent their falling a prey to the Devil's malice, who is busy in improving their disquiets, that by their interior confusion he may make them unfit for their best duties, rob them of all comfort, weaken their faith and hope and persuade them to desist from praying and any farther endeavours of amendment, since all they have hitherto done is to no purpose. This is his design generally against those souls, whose solid principles make him despair of ever drawing them into vice; and therefore he abuses their pious inclinations, by perplexing their thoughts with unprofitable fears, so to hinder them at least from making any advance; and hoping for farther success, since where-ever anxiety seizes, he looks for a prey.

For disappointing this malice and preventing all miscarriage, these Christians ought to remember, this life is not a state of perfection, but of weakness, and of trials, and that as long as they are in it, they must not expect to be as angels, but be contented to be as men; that is, frail, uncertain, and infirm: That as it is unreasonable to expect here the peace, security, and happiness of Heaven; so it is likewise, to look for the perfection of it: That to afflict themselves because they are not privileged against all sin in this sinful life is the same indiscretion as to grieve because they are subject to pains and distempers in this state of corruption. (10)

## Guidance for Busy and Worried Christians

Now though the number of careless Christians may be much the greater who look not into the obligations of their state or perform them with such indifference that it is plain their concern is only to satisfy the eyes of men, but not to answer their duty to justice, which God has laid upon them, yet their number is very great too who have their hearts so wholly possessed with worldly business that their solicitude in this stifles so much their concern for eternity, that it may be truly said, 'They are men of this world and forget they were created for a better.'

Now in this matter are to be distinguished two ranks of Christians. The one of those whose solicitude is occasioned by excess of business, which gives little liberty to their thoughts for considering and providing for eternity. The other of those whose constitution is so worldly that whatever their business be, whether little or great, their whole soul is taken up in it; and are so bent on their ordinary and home affairs, many of which are of themselves indifferent, that their concern in these takes off their concern for eternity, so that they can scarce find time for prayer; and whenever they perform it, it is with such a crowd of other thoughts, that they scarce know what they do and are even then rather working and contriving for this world, than praying for their establishment in a better. To both these we must say something.

And as to the former sort of Christians, it cannot be expected that any can live so exempt from solicitude in this world, but that in business of great concern, in time of surprising misfortunes, disappointments, and common afflictions of this life, their minds will be subject to that distraction and confusion, as will prove a hindrance to all exercises of devotion. This cannot be altogether prevented, because of the narrowness of human spirit, which being seized violently with any one thing, cannot apply itself with freedom to any other. Though there be likewise great difference in this; because those who are fully convinced of the uncertainty and vanity of all that is sublunary, or belongs to earth, and have concluded their only happiness to be in the possession of God, are not so easily surprised at disappointments, nor so wholly seized with trouble, as others, who have not yet learnt this lesson so well, but are admirers and fond of the world. But whatever this difference be, they are all under the same obligation of endeavouring to calm their spirits with all possible speed, since in such disturbance they are not capable of performing any Christian duty well, as it ought to be.

But if the case be so, that the solicitude of Christians be not accidental, but habitual; that is, be occasioned by an almost perpetual hurry of affairs, here the obligation is very different from those above-mentioned. For then they are under a necessity of quitting some part of their usual business, or else of gaining such a command of themselves that they can keep their minds composed for the quiet performance of such duties as belong to God, and likewise find leisure for the discharge of this obligation. The reason is, because all Christians by their profession are bound to answer the end for which they were created in the constant performance of the homage due to God, and making provision while they are in this world, for an eternal well-being in the next. And whatever proves, in fact, inconsistent with this general duty, becomes, upon this, unlawful, and is inconsistent with their being truly Christians. And here there is no consideration to be had of their profession or business being lawful; however lawful and just it may be in itself; yet if it puts them out of a condition of serving God, and saving their souls, it is by this rendered unlawful to them. Because there is an evident injustice in the omission of that, which, before all things, they are bound to seek, and for the gaining of which, they were placed in this world and had a being given them. . . .

Providence has ordered it, that whatever labour is necessary for life, may be thus sanctified; since all labour of the hands gives liberty to the mind for considering upon eternity, and necessarily admits of such intermissions, as gives those concerned, sufficient opportunities of performing the duties of the soul, if they are but careful to make use of them. And for such other professions, where the mind is more engaged, if they carry on their business no farther than necessity of life or common decency requires, this will be no stop to the affairs of the soul, because the mind or time will not be so taken up, but there may be still liberty for all duties. And it is seldom that worldly business becomes fatal to the soul, but when Christians quite outgoing all bounds of nature and reason, are overcome by some passion or other and bend all the faculties of their souls upon satisfying their ambition, their prodigality, the desire of appearing great, or their covetous humour. For when passion comes to govern, then the mind is no longer regulated by principles of reason and faith, but these being stifled, moderation and order are no more respected, but all must be carried on according to the violence of inclination; and if the stock can but be increased it is not considered how this stands with the interest of the soul; but this, like a poor inconsiderable thing, must shift as well as it can. This is the solicitude that wars against Heaven. . . .

As for the other sort of Christians, who, whether in great or little affairs, perform all with that solicitude, that they scarce know what the freedom of spirit is, I must confess their constitution is unhappy and very much indisposes them for the practice of a Christian life. The first instruction for these, is to put them upon considering the difficulties and dangers of their state. They are to reflect that whatever their business be in this life, they have still a much greater business on their hands, even that for which they were born, of preparing their souls for life everlasting. ... The second instruction must be for them to consider the particular difficulty they have in this more than others; for that their natural temper, which bends them with so much earnestness down to the earth, puts Heaven out of their sight, confines their solicitude to worldly affairs and indisposes them for all duties of devotion; so that they can but seldom find leisure for them, whilst every little business appears so weighty as to be sufficient motive for excusing their prayers; and whenever they go about them, it is with a heart so worldly, that their thoughts, even then, have more of earth than Heaven. (11)

## Guidance for those Wrestling with Sinful Habits

I say to all who through an ill custom are slaves to any particular vice, that if God touches their hearts with the sincere desires of a true conversion, they must remember, they have a great and difficult work upon their hands, such as requires both time, labour, and more than ordinary patience for its accomplishment; and that their repentance cannot be sincere, if they think of doing no more than what others do for the obtaining pardon of an accidental or occasional sin.

For in such a sin there is no more necessary, than a hearty sorrow for the offence committed, and a compliance with such other conditions as are annexed to this sorrow; but in the case of habitual sin, there can be no sincere repentance, but such as not only grieves at the guilt contracted, but likewise considers that great weakness, to which he is subject, resolves to make war against his own inclinations so as to be in hopes of overcoming them, as also to avoid the occasions of his sin. ...

But which way is he to go about it? The most effectual would be to seek some place of retirement, in which being separated from company and his usual provocations to sin, he might wholly apply himself to such exercises of piety and mortification, as might be proper for convincing him of the evil of his former state and seasoning his soul with better principles, such as will make him resolute in going through all the labours and difficulties of a change. This, under the direction of a good guide, is certainly the surest way for coming to the desired end; because of the great advantages the penitent has in being removed from usual dangers and receiving all necessary information and encouragement. ...

And here he must remember not to be discouraged, if he finds not a sudden change, but that his evil continues obstinate and seems not to abate notwithstanding all his endeavours. For he must be mindful what his disorder is, that it is habitual, not to be overcome but by a change of the whole interior man; that as it came to this head by degrees, so time must be allowed for breaking its force and regaining that command of himself, which he has lost. That this is all driving up hill and making head against the stream, which is not to be done by one push, but must be effected by labour and patience. That having been long subject to the Devil's tyranny, he will be more than ordinarily industrious in keeping his hold, and, by his troublesome assaults, endeavour to put him out of all hopes of ever accomplishing his designs. That the Divine Justice may permit these difficulties, in punishment of his former sins, and to make him sensible that it is no small thing to have so long forsaken his God. That the Divine Mercy may concur in this to make him know how to value virtue and grace by the difficulty of their purchase and oblige him to be more solicitous in preserving them, when once obtained. Upon these considerations he ought to hold on with courage, patience and perseverance, and not be tired with the labour of his undertaking, nor disheartened with the little advance he makes in it; but still continue with hopes, that obstinate endeavours, under the favour of Heaven, will at length master an obstinate evil. (12)

## Guidance for Parents

First, they are to remember their general duty; that their children are their charge, of which they must render an account to God; and for this end, they are bound to be very careful of them in their infancy; to give them good education as they come to the use of reason; be watchful of all their ways in their youth; be industrious in making due provision for them; be discreet in disposing of them and settling them in a Christian state of life; and as long as they live, be ever solicitous in giving all the good advice their circumstances shall require. (13)

## Fair Trade

Is not this a strange character of a Christian world, that believing truth and justice to be the way to the eternal truth, there is scarce such a thing to be found amongst them as a confidence of any being true and just; but in all business there is as general a distrust, as if there were no faith amongst them? The hardness of customers makes shopkeepers swear and lie; and therefore are customers hard, because they know shopkeepers will swear and lie. Both have something to mend, and I think those who keep shop may safely begin without danger of being much losers by it. For I cannot but believe that if a person were so exact to truth, that those who come to buy could have a confidence in him, that he would neither demand an unreasonable price, nor put off things for good, which are not so, this would increase the number of customers, and by moderate gain come to equal their heaps, who use all unwarrantable means for imposing on those who come to buy: And in case it should not, yet there would be the comfort of a good conscience, which with the hopes of God's blessing, would make abundant recompense for whatever advantage their neighbours have over them and is the fruit of their injustice. (14)

## A Prayer for Times of Distress

Enlighten me, O good Jesus, with the clearness of inward light, and chase away all darkness from my heart. Put a stop to all my wandering thoughts, and break the force of all those temptations which violently assault me. Stretch forth thy powerful arm and fight for me. Put to flight the wild beasts, my passions, which seek to destroy me. Command the winds and tempests. Say to the sea, be still; and behold, a calm will follow; there shall be a peace by the power of thy Word. (15)

NOTES AND SOURCES

1. John Gother, *A Papist Misrepresented, and Represented: or, A Twofold Character of Popery* (1685), 3–4.

2. Ibid. 15–16.

3. Ibid. 7–18.

4. Ibid. 19–20.

5. Ibid. 60–1.

6. Ibid. 75–7.

7. John Gother, *Instructions and Devotions for Hearing Mass* (1725), 26.

8. Ibid. 90–3.

9. Ibid. 93–6.

10. John Gother, *Instructions for Particular States* (1689), 4–5.

11. Ibid. 136–9, 143–4, 144–5, 146–7.

12. Ibid. 241–6.

13. Ibid. 323–4.

14. John Gother, *Instructions for Masters, Traders, Labourers* (1699), 32–3.

15. John Gother, *Instructions and Devotions for the Afflicted and Sick* (1705), 69–70.

# Edward Hawarden                                          1622–1735

In 2006, Father Aidan Nichols, OP, was named the John Paul II Memorial Visiting Lecturer, the first lectureship in Catholic theology at Oxford since the Reformation; Edward Hawarden nearly beat him to the punch. The Lancashire-born Hawarden was the head of a delegation of learned Douai priests appointed to fulfil James II's plan to convert Magdalen College into a bastion of Catholic education. The plan fizzled out with the 1688 Revolution, and Hawarden returned to Douai where he earned the degree of Doctor of Divinity and served as vice-president. He was involved but exonerated in the divisive Jansenist controversy at Douai before returning to England in 1707. After serving the English mission in Lancashire and Durham, it was in London that Hawarden produced his most influential works. Most prominently, this included a refutation of Samuel Clarke's denial of the coequality of the Three Divine Persons—a defence of Trinitarian orthodoxy that led Oxford University to thank Hawarden formally.

## The Trinity, Scripture, and Tradition

Catholics, besides the words of Scripture considered barely in their literal and known sense, have a special regard to the faith of Christians in all past ages. They are very well assured, that Christian ears could never endure this blasphemy: that the Son and the Holy Spirit are things, which God freely made and can unmake at pleasure. And, under this light, they consider all Scripture texts, relating to the Son and to the Holy Spirit. Which texts, if viewed under this light, are evidently demonstrative. And Catholics have such a regard to universal and apostolical tradition; they are so accustomed to join faith and the reading of the Holy Scripture together, that they account this to be the natural signification of the words. (1)

## The Trinity, Faith, and Reason

A Trinity of Divine Persons, each of which, though not *self-existent*, is *necessarily existent*, and is the *supreme and self-existent God*; how incomprehensible soever, is not a contradiction, but a mystery only. Of which, without revelation, we could never have had any certain knowledge.

That there is one divine and *self-existent* Person, reason informs us. But three Divine Persons, we know only by faith. Reason tells us that there is a Person, who is *God from no other*. And faith teaches us that there are two Persons who are *God from God*. (2)

NOTES AND SOURCES

1. Edward Hawarden, *An Answer to Dr. Clark, and Mr Whiston, concerning the Divinity of the Son and of the Holy Spirit* (London, 1729), p. vii.

2. Ibid. 35.

# John Dryden                                                        1631–1700

The twentieth-century novelist Graham Greene marvelled at Dryden's capacity for responding deeply to the demands of his world: 'The great figure of Dryden comprises the whole of the late seventeenth-century scene: like some infinitely subtle meteorological instrument, he was open to every wind: he registered the triumph of Cromwell, the hopes of the Restoration, the Catholicism of James, the final disillusionment. When he died...he left the new age, the quieter, more rational age, curiously empty.' Many critics of Dryden have seen too much mutability in the poet's adjustments to the day's climate and labelled his changes of mind, especially his final adoption of Catholicism, as conversions of convenience that followed the path of preferment and patronage in conforming to the beliefs of the powerful. Unable to reconcile his writing of an anti-Catholic drama titled *The Spanish Friar* (1680) amid the Popish Plot and Exclusion Crisis with his translation of the hagiographic *Life of St Francis Xavier* (1688) for James II, Elizabeth Inchbald could not accept the theological sincerity of 'one who might have done honour' to the Roman Catholic Church. Yet his conversion to Catholicism was a studied and carefully deliberated step in his life, and it produced a masterpiece of English poetry, *The Hind and the Panther* (1687). This allegorical piece, which features a dialogue between denominations (Catholicism the hind, Anglicanism the panther, and a menagerie of other Protestant dissenters), is a reflection of the times and its author—complex, ironic, in turns harshly polemical and then hopeful that discourse can assuage violence. It also represents the paradox of Dryden's faith that meshes scepticism and belief: the poem shows a distrust of personal judgement and a recognition of the limits of rationality leading to a full embrace of Rome's authority and tradition. This culminating vision, however, was at the end of a long journey for Dryden. His Northamptonshire family raised him in a Puritan home. Following his classical education at Westminster School and then Trinity College, Cambridge, he found employment in Cromwell's civil service, composed an elegiac poem for his death, and walked in his funeral procession alongside Milton. Yet he also flourished after the 1660 Restoration of Charles II, composing panegyrics to the new king, establishing himself as a leading dramatist, and crafting his influential essay *Of Dramatic Poetry* (1668). His appointment as poet laureate and royal historiographer to Charles II took him even deeper into the ideological conflicts of his times, and his critics could not separate his 1685 conversion from his temporal advancement. Yet, in the face of financial hardship and possible persecution, Dryden did not follow others in abandoning his faith or his Jacobite loyalties after the 1688 Revolution. He turned to the theatre again for income, but a public figure unsympathetic to the new regime faced restrictions in writing for the politically charged stage. Translation was safer, and not unfruitful, ground. His translation of *The Works of Virgil* (1697) was a cultural landmark, and his versions of hymns such as *Veni Creator Spiritus* retain their place in the English Catholic canon. Despite his controversial political and religious reputation, his body was eventually laid to rest alongside Chaucer and Spenser in Westminster Abbey, the nation's shrine to poetic achievement.

## The Sacred Arts and the Resurrection

When in mid-air, the golden trump shall sound,
To raise the nations under ground;
When in the Valley of Jehosaphat,
The Judging God shall close the Book of Fate;
And there the last assizes keep,
For those who wake, and those who sleep;
When rattling bones together fly,
From the four corners of the sky,
When sinews o'er the skeletons are spread,
Those clothed with flesh, and life inspires the dead;
The sacred poets first shall hear the sound,
And foremost from the tomb shall bound:
For they are covered with the lightest ground
And straight, with in-born vigour, on the wing,
Like mounting larks, to the new morning sing.
There Thou, Sweet Saint, before the choir shalt go,
As harbinger of Heav'n, the way to show,
The way which thou so well hast learned below. (1)

## The Hind: A Symbol of the Catholic Church

A milk white Hind, immortal and unchanged,
Fed on the lawns, and in the forest ranged;
Without unspotted, innocent within,
She feared no danger, for she knew no sin.
Yet had she oft been chased with horns and hounds,
And Scythian shafts; and many winged wounds
Aimed at Her heart; was often forced to fly,
And doomed to death, though fated not to die. (2)

## The Convert's Rest

What weight of ancient witness can prevail
If private reason hold the public scale?
But, gracious God, how well dost thou provide
For erring judgements an unerring guide!
Thy throne is darkness in th'abyss of light,
A blaze of glory that forbids the sight;

O teach me to believe Thee thus concealed,
And search no farther than thy self revealed;
But her alone for my director take
Whom thou hast promised never to forsake!
My thoughtless youth was winged with vain desires,
My manhood, long misled by wandring fires,
Followed false lights; and when their glimpse was gone,
My pride struck out new sparkles of her own.
Such was I, such by nature still I am,
Be thine the glory, and be mine the shame.
Good life be now my task: my doubts are done... (3)

## Religious Toleration

Of all the tyrannies on human kind
The worst is that which persecutes the mind.
Let us but weigh at what offence we strike,
'tis but because we cannot think alike.
In punishing of this, we overthrow
The laws of nations and of nature too.
Beasts are the subjects of tyrannic sway,
Where still the stronger on the weaker prey.
Man only of a softer mould is made;
Not for his fellows' ruin, but their aid:
Created kind, beneficent and free,
The noble image of the Deity. (4)

## The Four Marks of the Church: One, Holy, Catholic, and Apostolic

Behold what marks of majesty she brings;
Richer than ancient heirs of Eastern kings:
Her right hand holds the sceptre and the keys,
To show whom she commands, and who obeys:
With these to bind, or set the sinner free
With that t'assert spiritual royalty.
One in herself not rent by schism, but sound,
Entire, one solid shining diamond,
Not sparkles shattered into sects like you,
One is the church, and must be to be true:
One central principle of unity,
As undivided, so from errours free,
As one in faith, so one in sanctity.
. . .
Thus one, thus pure, behold her largely spread
Like the fair ocean from her mother bed;
From East to West triumphantly she rides,

All shores are watered by her wealthy tides:
The Gospel's sound diffused from pole to pole,
Where winds can carry, and where waves can roll.
The self same doctrine of the sacred page
Conveyed to ev'ry clime in ev'ry age.

. . .

Despair at our foundations then to strike
Till you can prove your faith Apostolic;
A limpid stream drawn from the native source;
Succession lawful in a lineal course.
Prove any church opposed to this our head,
So one, so pure, so unconfin'dly spread,
Under one chief of the spiritual state,
The members all combined, and all subordinate.
Show such a seamless coat, from schism so free,
In no communion joined with heresy:
If such a one you find, let truth prevail:
Till when your weights will in the balance fail:
A church unprincipled kicks up the scale. (5)


## Answered Prayers

Our vows are heard betimes! and Heaven takes care
To grant, before we can conclude the prayer:
Preventing angels met it half the way,
And sent us back to praise, who came to pray. (6)


## God is Abroad

Though poets are not prophets, to foreknow
What plants will take the blight, and what will grow,
By tracing Heav'n his footsteps may be found:
Behold! how awfully He walks the round!
God is abroad, and wondrous in his ways,
The rise of empires, and their fall surveys;
More (might I say) than with an usual eye,
He sees his bleeding Church in ruin lie,
And hears the souls of saints beneath his altar cry. (7)


## A Royal Dedication: *The Life of St Francis Xavier*

I know not, Madam, whether I may presume to tell the world, that your Majesty
has chosen this great saint for one of your celestial patrons, though I am sure you
will never be ashamed of owning so glorious an intercessor; not even in a country,
where the doctrine of the holy Church is questioned, and those religious addresses
ridiculed. Your Majesty, I doubt not, has the inward satisfaction of knowing, that
such pious prayers have not been unprofitable to you, and the nation may one day

come to understand, how happy it will be for them to have a son of prayers ruling over them: Not that we are wholly to depend on this particular blessing, as a thing of certainty, though we hope, and pray for its continuance. The ways of Divine Providence are incomprehensible, and we know not in what times, or by what methods, God will restore his Church in England, or what farther trials and afflictions we are yet to undergo. Only this we know, that if a religion be of God, it can never fail, but the acceptable time we must patiently expect, and endeavour by our lives not to undeserve. I am sure if we take the example of our sovereigns, we shall place our confidence in God alone: we shall be assiduous in our devotions, moderate in our expectations, humble in our carriage, and forgiving of our enemies. (8)

## St Francis Xavier on Firmly Believing

I went about, with my bell in my hand...and gathering together all I met, both men and children, I instructed them in the Christian doctrine: The children learnt it easily by heart, in the compass of a month, and when they understood it, I charged them to teach it their fathers and mothers, all of their own family, and even their neighbours.

On Sundays I assembled the men and women, little boys and girls in the chapel; all came to my appointment, with an incredible joy, and most ardent desire to hear the Word of God. I began with the confessing God to be one in nature, and trine in Persons. I afterwards repeated, distinctly, and with an audible voice, the *Lords Prayer*, the *Angelical Salutation*, and the *Apostles Creed*. All of them together repeated after me; and it is hardly to be imagined, what pleasure they took in it. This being done, I repeated the *Creed* singly; and insisting on every particular article, asked if they certainly believed it? They all protested to me with loud cries, and their hands across their breasts, that they firmly believed it. My practice is to make them repeat the *Creed* oftener than the other prayers; and I declare to them, at the same time, that they who believe the contents of it are true Christians. (9)

## St Francis Xavier's Address to the Learned

I have often thoughts to run over all the Universities of Europe, and principally that of Paris, and to cry aloud to those who abound more in learning than in charity, *Ah how many Souls are lost to Heaven, through your default!* It were to be wished, that those people would apply themselves as diligently to the salvation of souls, as they do to the study of sciences; to the end they might render to Almighty God a good account of their learning, and the talents which he has bestowed on them: Many, without doubt, moved with thoughts like these, would make a spiritual retreat, and give themselves the leisure of meditating on heavenly things, that they might listen to the voice of God. They would renounce their passions, and trampling under foot all worldly vanities, would put themselves in condition of following the motions of the Divine Will. They would say from the bottom of their hearts, *Behold me in readiness, O my Lord, send me wheresoever thou shalt please, even to the Indies if thou command'st me.*

Good God, how much more happily would those learned men then live, than now they do! with how much more assurance of their salvation! and in the hour of death, when they are ready to stand forth, before the dreadful Judgement Seat, how much greater reason would they have, to hope well of God's eternal mercy, because they might say, *O Lord, thou hast given me five Talents, and behold I have added other five.* (10)

## St Francis Xavier on the Works of Mercy

Above all things have care of perfecting your self; and of discharging faithfully, what you owe to God, and your own conscience. For by this means you will become most capable of serving your neighbour, and of gaining souls. Take pleasure in the most abject employments of your ministry; that by exercising them, you may acquire humility, and daily advance in that virtue.

Be sure yourself to teach the ignorant those prayers, which every Christian ought to have by heart; and lay not on any other person, an employment, so little ostentatious. Give your self the trouble of hearing the children and slaves repeat them word by word, after you. Do the same thing to the children of the Christian natives of the country: they who behold you thus exercised, will be edified by your modesty. And as modest persons easily attract the esteem of others, they will judge you proper to instruct themselves, in the mysteries of Christian religion.

You shall frequently visit the poor in the hospitals, and from time to time exhort them to confess themselves, and to communicate; giving them to understand, that Confession is the remedy for past sins, and the Communion a preservative against relapses: That both of them destroy the cause of the miseries of which they complain, by reason that the ills they suffer, are only the punishment of their offences. On this account, when they are willing to confess, you shall hear their Confessions, with all the leisure you can afford them. After this care taken of their souls you are not to be unmindful of their bodies, but recommend the distressed with all diligence and affection, to the administrators of the hospital, and procure them, by other means, all relief within your power.

You shall also visit the prisoners, and excite them to make a general Confession of their lives. They have more need than others, to be stirred up to it, because among that sort of people, there are few to be found, who ever made an exact Confession. Pray the Brotherhood of Mercy, to have pity on those wretches, and labour with the judges for their enlargement; in the mean time providing for the most necessitous, who oftentimes have not wherewithal to subsist. (11)

## St Francis Xavier's Living Books

Wheresoever you shall be, even though you only pass through a place, and stay but little in it, endeavour to make some acquaintance, and enquire of those who have the name of honest and experienced men, not only what crimes are most frequently committed in that town, and what deceits most used in traffic, as I have already taught you ... but farther learn the inclinations of the people, the customs of the country, the form of government, the received opinions, and all things respecting the commerce of human life. For believe me, the knowledge of those things, is very profitable to a missioner, for the speedy curing of spiritual diseases, and to have always at hand, wherewithal to give ease to such as come before you.

You will understand from thence, on what point you are most to insist in preaching, and what chiefly to recommend in Confessions. This knowledge will make, that nothing shall be new to you, nothing shall surprise, or amaze you; it will furnish you with the address of conducting souls, and even with authority over them. The men of the world are accustomed to despise the religious as people who understand it not. But if they find one, who knows how to behave himself in conversation and has practised men, they will admire him as an extraordinary person; they will give themselves up to him, they will find no difficulty, even in doing violence to their own inclinations, under his direction, and will freely execute what he enjoins, though never so repugnant to their corrupt nature. Behold the wonderful fruit of knowing well the world; so that you are not at this present, to take less pains in acquiring this knowledge, than formerly you have done, in learning philosophy, and divinity. For what remains, this science is neither to be learnt from ancient manuscripts, nor printed books; it is in living books, and the conversation of knowing men, that you must study it: With it, you shall do more good, than if you dealt amongst the people, all the arguments of the doctors, and all the subtleties of the school....

I do not forbid you, nevertheless, to consult the holy Scriptures on requisite occasions, nor the Fathers of the Church, nor the canons, nor books of piety, nor treatises of morality; they may furnish you with solid proofs for the establishment of Christian truths, with sovereign remedies against temptations, and heroical examples of virtue. But all this will appear too cold and be to no purpose, if souls be not disposed to profit by them; and they cannot profit but by the ways I have prescribed: So, that the duty of a preacher, is to sound the bottom of human hearts, to have an exact knowledge of the world, to make a faithful picture of man, and set it in so true a light, that every one may know it for his own. (12)

## When Did We See Thee?

Sure she had guests sometimes to entertain,
Guests in disguise, of her Great Master's train:
Her Lord himself might come, for ought we know;
Since in a servant's form he lived below:
Beneath her roof, he might be pleased to stay:
Or some benighted angel, in his way
Might ease his wings; and seeing Heav'n appear
In its best work of mercy, think it there,
Where all the deeds of charity and love
Were in as constant method, as above:
All carried on; all of a piece with theirs;
As free her alms, as diligent her cares;
As loud her praises, and as warm her prayers. (13)

## *Veni Creator Spiritus*—Come Creator Spirit

Creator Spirit, by whose aid
The world's foundations first were laid,
Come visit ev'ry pious mind;
Come pour thy joys on human kind:

From sin, and sorrow set us free;
And make thy temples worthy Thee.

O, Source of uncreated light,
The Father's promised *Paraclite!*
Thrice Holy Fount, thrice Holy Fire,
Our hearts with Heav'nly love inspire;
Come, and thy sacred unction bring
To sanctify us, while we sing!

Plenteous of grace, descend from high,
Rich in thy sev'n-fold energy!
Thou strength of his Almighty Hand,
Whose pow'r does Heav'n and Earth command:
Proceeding Spirit, our defence,
Who do'st the gift of tongues dispense,
And crown'st thy gift, with eloquence!

Refine and purge our earthy parts;
But, oh, inflame and fire our hearts!
Our frailties help, our vice control;
Submit the senses to the soul;
And when rebellious they are grown,
Then, lay thy hand, and hold 'em down.

Chase from our minds th'Infernal Foe;
And peace, the fruit of love, bestow:
And, lest our feet should step astray,
Protect, and guide us in the way.

Make us eternal truths receive,
And practise, all that we believe:
Give us thy self, that we may see
The Father and the Son, by thee.

Immortal honour, endless fame
Attend th'Almighty Father's name:
The Saviour Son, be glorified,
Who for lost man's redemption died:
And equal adoration be
Eternal Paraclete, to thee. (14)

NOTES AND SOURCES

1. John Dryden, 'To the Pious Memory of the Accomplisht Young Lady Mrs Anne Killigrew', in *Poems by Mrs Anne Killigrew* (London, 1686).
2. John Dryden, *The Hind and the Panther, A Poem* (London, 1687), 1–2.
3. Ibid. 5.
4. Ibid. 14–15.
5. Ibid. 62–3, 66–7.

6. John Dryden, 'Britannia Rediviva' (London, 1688), 1.

7. Ibid. 3–4.

8. John Dryden, 'Dedication to the Queen', in *The Life of St Francis Xavier* (London, 1688).

9. Dominique Bouhours, trans. John Dryden, *The Life of St Francis Xavier* (London, 1688), 107–8.

10. Ibid. 156–7.

11. Ibid. 359–60.

12. Ibid. 383–4, 386.

13. John Dryden, *Eleonora: A Panegyrical Poem Dedicated to the Memory of the Late Countess of Abingdon* (London, 1692), 4–5.

14. John Dryden, 'Veni Creator Spiritus, Translated in Paraphrase', in *Examen Poeticum* (London, 1693), 307–9.

# Edward Scarisbrick (alias Neville) SJ                    1639–1709

The life of the Lancashire-born Jesuit priest, Edward Scarisbrick (alias Neville), was marked by the extremes of the age. His family sent many young men into the Jesuits, and Edward followed this vocation as a student, ordinand, and later teacher at St Omer's. He returned to the mission in Lancashire only to be among those targeted in Titus Oates's 'Popish Plot'—a supposedly Jesuit-led conspiracy against the life of Charles II that generated a fanatical anti-Catholic fever throughout England in the late 1670s. In a few years, however, Scarisbrick was a royal chaplain to James II, preaching on such subjects as 'Catholic Loyalty'. The wheel of fortune would continue to spin quickly for Scarisbrick—the 1688 Revolution forced him into exile in France, and he ended his days back in Lancashire in 1709. His sermon before James II on 'Spiritual Leprosy' is attuned to the consequences of such extremes, contrasting the intended glory of human beings with their degradation by sin, a condition so critical that only the incarnation of God the Son could provide healing.

## The Dignity of the Human Person

To the end then we may have a true and right prospective of the horrid form of a soul, disfigured by sin, I will place the same before you in a more pleasant prospect of its native worth and dignity. Man, according to his own nature, is of a noble race, stamped at his creation according to the likeness of his Maker; and though moulded of clay and earth, yet by the divine breath received an immortal substance, a spiritual being, a life-giving soul; which being the best part, and not much inferior to the angels, raised him above the grosser region of sense and matter, and invested him with the sovereignty of this lower world. Grace yet still improved his fortune. For his nature, by a strange union of love, being espoused to the Divinity, he ascends to a higher Rank. He is adopted the Son of God, designed heir of the Kingdom of Heaven; and by consequence, being of so noble a condition and race, ought never to degenerate from the worth of his extraction. Acknowledge then, O Christian Soul, your dignity, consider who is your head, of what mystical body you are a member: Call to mind, that from all eternity you were predestinated to be a holy, pure, and an elected people, a royal priesthood without spot or blemish; to whom Christ, that he might distinguish you from all other baser and viler sects, hath given a new being in the font of Baptism, hath washed you with his sacred blood, inspired into you not a breath of life, as in your creation, but his ever holy and vivifying Spirit. O that it were in my power to describe unto you, as it were in passing, the beauty of an innocent and just soul, embellished with the ornaments of sanctifying grace. All things in Heaven and Earth fall short thereof; the sacred Scripture seems to labour in finding out rich comparisons, noble titles whereby to give a right idea of so amiable an object; such a soul is called in one place, the *Temple of the living God*, in another, the *Sanctuary of the Holy Ghost*, in a third place, the *Seat of Wisdom*, elsewhere the *Throne of the sacred Trinity*. Now again she is compared to a *Spouse*, set forth on the day of her nuptials, with all the state and pomp imaginable; then to a *Queen* adorned with the royal robes of gold, with a *Sceptre* of immortality in her hand, and a *Crown* of glory on her head; till at length by participation of the divine attributes, she is even styled a little God. *Ego dixi, dij estis vos et filii excelsi omnes* ['I have said: You are gods, and all of you the sons of the most High' (Ps. 81: 6)]. But her chief glory is from within, according to that, *Omnis decor filiae regis ab intus* ['All the glory of the king's daughter is within' (Ps. 44: 14)]; invisible, it is true, to the eyes of mortals, but yet nothing is so taking and charming to those of immortal and pure spirits. The understanding, like a sun, is always shining with the bright rays of supernatural truths, the memory looking back with gratitude upon past favours and benefits, the will, as a phoenix, consuming in chaste and holy desires. As in Heaven, so nothing here finds admittance, but what is pure and clean. Irregular motions and appetites are either quiet or silent; or if they tend to mutinies or rebellion, they are presently checked, and forced to remain in a due subordination to reason, and to follow the train of princely virtues. In a word, nothing comes so home to a true and full description of her, as what Ezekiel gives us, under the person of the King of Tyrus, *Tu signaculum similitudinis, plenus sapientia et decore, in deliciis Paradisi fuisti, omnis lapis pretiosus operimentum tuum* ['Thou wast the seal of resemblance, full of wisdom and perfect in beauty. Thou wast in the pleasures of the paradise of God: every precious stone was thy covering' (Ezek. 28: 12–13)]. (1)

## Christ, the Physician of Souls

Almighty God, the great and omnipotent physician of our souls, is so passionately charitable, that he undertakes the cure himself; he visiteth in person the patient, affording him his corporal presence in our assumed nature; he doth not only prescribe the medicine, but will stand likewise to the cost of the cure, and that after a strange manner, by taking upon him our infirmities, our miseries and grief: *Verè languores nostros tulit, et dolores nostros ipse portavit* ['Surely he hath borne our infirmities and carried our sorrows' (Isa. 53: 4)]. (2)

NOTES AND SOURCES

1.  Edward Scarisbrike, SJ, 'Sermon XXVII: A Sermon Preach'd before Her Majesty the Queen-Dowager, The Thirteenth Sunday after Pentecost, 1686', in *A Select Collection of Catholick Sermons*, 2 vols. (London, 1741), ii. 429–62; 434–6.

2.  Ibid. 457.

# Philip Leigh (alias Layton or Metcalfe) SJ          1650–1717

Pilgrims have travelled to St Winefride's Well in the North Wales town of Holywell since the Middle Ages. From all of Britain and beyond, they came through penal times to the place where a pious, young Welsh maiden was assaulted and martyred by a corrupt, lustful prince. The Lancashire-born Jesuit Philip Leigh helped preserve this tradition in *The Life and Miracles of St Wenefride* (1712). Leigh (who also went by the names Metcalfe and Layton to escape persecution) was educated at St Omer's and the English College in Rome, served the English Mission in Durham and Wales, and finished his service at Holywell. His edition records the history of St Winefride (often spelled Wenefride or Winifred in English and Gwenffrewi in Welsh), the curative properties of the well, and the prayers that were said at the shrine. At this holy site, often referred to as 'the British Lourdes', the pilgrimages and prayers continue today.

## The Story of St Winefride

Oh! That Christians had such a horror, and destestation of mortal sin to look upon it as more hideous and frightful than a violent death. St Winefride was of that settled opinion, she had two sorts of deaths waiting for an answer, a separation of the soul from the body or a separation of the soul from God, she did not balance upon the matter, but undauntedly and heroically replied how, by her parents' approbation, she was holily espoused *to the Son of God*, who infinitely exceeds all power and beauty upon earth, that she would be faithful and constant in her pure affections, and rather lose her life, than to admit any corrival. *Neither shall your menaces, and terrors*, (said she) *draw me from the sweetness of His love, nor so overawe me, as to make me recede in the least, from executing what I have promised.* As it happens sometimes, that despised carnal love turns into rage, so it fared with barbarous Cradocus, who seeing himself scorned (as he thought) gave such a deadly blow to the virgin's neck, that the first stroke severed the head from the body, which falling upon the descent of the hill rolled down to the church, where the congregation was kneeling before the altar. As they were terrified with the bloody object of her head, so they were astonished to behold a clear and rapid spring gushing out of that spot of ground her head had first fallen upon, which to this very day, is visited from all parts, by devout pilgrims. The place of her martyrdom had before her death the name of the *Dry Valley*, or *Barren Bottom*, which was changed into the title of *Finhon*, which in old Welsh, signifies, a *Fountain*, or *Well*. It was also observed that the stones of the well were tinctured with drops, as it were of blood, to perpetuate the memory of what she had shed for the love of Christ, and in process of time, it was taken notice of that the moss growing round the well had a very fragrant smell as an emblem of the odour of her angelical virtues. (1)

## The Miracles of St Winefride's Well

I could bring a *cloud of witnesses* (to use Saint Paul's expression) asserting other undeniable miracles, wrought by Saint Winefride's intercession, not in an obscure corner, but in the face of the sun. I solemnly declare, that I leave behind twice as many wonders, happening in the last century, of which many were eyewitnesses at the holy fountain. Holy Well seems to resemble, in some sort, the Probatica Pond, where, in five porches, there lay *a great Multitude of Sick Persons, of blind, lame, and withered*. In the travelling season the town appears populous, crowded with zealous pilgrims, from all parts of Britain. The well itself receives a succession of visitants from sunrise till late at night. The many hand-barrows and crutches, which have been hung at the pillars, demonstrate the mercies of God, and the powerful intercession of the Virgin-Martyr. They are soon removed by those who envy the glory of our Saint. I forbear to recount at large the recovery of blindish eyes, of barren women becoming fruitful, of inveterate violent convulsions suddenly ceasing, of deaf persons favoured with hearing, of stubborn devils cast out of *possessed* people (certainly the immortal spirits, who suffer the eternal torments of Hell, could not be forced away by the material elements of a cold bath).... St Augustine, in his twelfth book of the *City of God*, writing of a blind man, who received sight, and of other miracles, when St Ambrose translated the holy bodies of Saints Gervasius and Protasius, thought it sufficient conviction against the incredulous scoffing heathens, that... *A vast concourse of people were able to attest the truth of them;* which is exactly our present case. (2)

## Litany and Prayer to St Winefride

Lord, have mercy upon us.
Christ, have mercy upon us.
Lord, have mercy upon us.
God the Father of Heaven, have mercy upon us.
God the Son, Redeemer of Mankind, have mercy upon us.
God the Holy Ghost, have mercy upon us.
Holy Trinity, one God, have mercy upon us.
Holy Mary, pray for us.
Holy Mother of God,
Holy Virgin of Virgins,
O Blessed St Winefride,
O humble and mild virgin,
O glorious spouse of Christ,
O devout and charitable virgin,
O sweet comforter of the afflicted,
O singular example of chastity,
O radiant star.
O fairest flower of the British nation,
O admirable and elected vessel,
O mirror of chastity,
O mirror of devotion,
O mirror of piety,
O bright lamb of sanctity,
O golden image of angelical purity,
O hope and safety of distressed pilgrims, pray for us.
That we may be delivered from all iniquity, O holy virgin and martyr, pray
    for us.
That we may be delivered from all disordered passions of the mind,
That we may be delivered from the deceits of the world, flesh, and Devil,
That we may be delivered from all occasions of sin,
That we may be delivered from plague, famine and war,
That we may be delivered from the wrath of God and eternal damnation,
That we and all sinners may have true contrition, and full remission of
    our sins,

That all schismatics, heretics, and infidels, may be converted to the Holy
  Catholic and Apostolical Faith.
That we may always hate sin, and overcome all temptations,
That we may despise all worldly vanities and delights,
That we all may ever fear God, and fulfil his holy will,
That we may have both spiritual and corporal health,
That we may devoutly affect chastity and purity of life,
That we may fervently love humility and mildness.
That we may delight in pious prayer, fasting, and charitable alms,
That we may discreetly and fervently continue in the exercise of godliness,
That we may cheerfully and constantly suffer for the love of Christ,
That the souls in Purgatory, and all afflicted persons, may obtain heavenly
  consolations,
That our benefactors, and all that labour to save souls, may be blessed with
  abundance of grace, and everlasting life,
That we may enjoy true peace, and endless felicity,
That God of his abundant mercy will vouchsafe to bless this our pilgrimage,
That by thy pious intercession it may be to the perfect health of our souls and
  bodies,
That thou wilt vouchsafe to grant our requests,
O Blessed Winefride.

Let us Pray.

O Blessed St Winefride O Glorious Virgin and Martyr, who hast admirably
beautified with the purple of thy blood the rare purity of thy innocent life,
whom God has so specially chosen, so highly privileged, and so wonderfully
restored to life again, gracing thee with the honour of a living martyr, causing
a fountain miraculously to spring, bearing a perpetual memory of thy name,
for the relief of all diseased and distressed pilgrims, who shall devoutly beg
thy powerful intercession, O Blessed St Winefride, hear the prayers, and
receive the humble supplications, of thy poor devoted pilgrims, and obtain
that by thy pious intercession God of his infinite mercy will be pleased to
grant us a full pardon and remission of our sins, and a blessing to this our
pilgrimage; and that we may increase and persevere in God's grace, and enjoy
him eternally in Heaven. This we beg of thee, O blessed virgin and martyr for
Jesus Christ our Lord and Saviour's sake. Amen. (3)

NOTES AND SOURCES

1. [Philip Leigh], *The Life and Miracles of Saint Wenefride* (n.p., 1712), 26–9. For an earlier version of the life
   of St Winefride, see pp. 13–15.

2. Ibid. 174–7.

3. [Philip Leigh], *The Litanies of S. Wenefride, Virgin and Martyr* (n.p., 1712), 3–5, 8.

# Jane Barker                                      1652–1732

It is remarkable that history has virtually forgotten a woman as remarkable as Jane Barker. Her
name deserves a place of honour among eighteenth-century writers: her experimental and

introspective 'Galesian' trilogy of novels (1713–26) captured the challenges of being a woman of letters; and, alternately playful and polemic, her poetry swings from forthright emotion to complex conceit, and represents a neglected voice in English Catholic verse. Born into a staunchly royalist family in Northamptonshire and raised at a Lincolnshire manor leased by her family, her education was informal but wide-ranging, as she studied with her much beloved older brother Edward, an Oxford graduate and would-be doctor whose early death affected Barker deeply. A spinster to her death, she nevertheless exchanged her poetry with a coterie of male friends in Cambridge and found that a large selection of her poems was published, without her knowledge, in *Poetical Recreations* (1688). The decade in which her poetry was first published was eventful, beginning with the death of her father, proceeding with her conversion to Catholicism, and ending with her following James II into exile. Even though she returned to the family home in 1704 after an operation for cataracts that may have done her eyesight more harm than good, she did not compromise her Jacobite convictions. Her novel *Exilius* (1715), her manuscript 'Poems Referring to the Times' (1701) presented to James III, and her verse narrative about the faith and politics of a female protagonist named 'Fidelia' all convey an artistic resistance to the new order established under William and Mary. Her faith in the Catholic Church, however, should not be reduced simply to a faith in James even though she believed a relic of the Stuart king had cured a tumour in her breast and later chose to die in Saint-Germain. Her religious poems contemplating nature and family relationships show a reflective exploration of the mysteries of human life, and her translation of the spiritual writing of Fénelon—an influential figure for eighteenth-century English Catholics—brings a linguistic intensity to traditional Lenten devotions.

## The Celibate Life

Since, O ye Pow'rs, ye have bestowed on me
So great a kindness for virginity,
Suffer me not to fall into the pow'rs
Of men's almost omnipotent amours;
But in this happy life let me remain,
Fearless of twenty five and all its train,
Of slights or scorns, or being called Old Maid,
Those goblins which so many have betrayed:
Like harmless kids, that are pursued by men,
For safety run into a lion's den.
Ah lovely state how strange it is to see,
What mad conceptions some have made of thee,
As though thy being was all wretchedness,
Or foul deformity i'th' ugliest dress;
Whereas thy beauty's pure, celestial,
Thy thoughts divine, thy words angelical:
And such ought all thy votaries to be,
Or else they're so, but for necessity.
A virgin bears the impress of all good,
In that dread name all virtue's understood:
So equal all her looks, her mien, her dress,

That nought but modesty seems in excess.
And when she any treats or visits make,
'tis not for tattle, but for friendship's sake;
Her neighb'ring poor she does adopt her heirs,
And less she cares for her own good than theirs;
And by obedience testifies she can
Be's good a subject as the stoutest man.
She to her Church such filial duty pays,
That one would think she'd lived i'th' pristine days.
Her closet, where she does much time bestow,
Is both her library and chapel too,
Where she enjoys society alone,
I'th' Great Three-One—
She drives her whole life's business to these ends,
To serve her God, enjoy her books and friends. (1)

## Sitting by a Rivulet: An Image of Eternity

Ah lovely stream, how fitly may'st thou be,
   By thy *immutability*,
Thy gentle motion and *perennity*,
   To us the emblem of *eternity*:
   And to us thou do'st no less
   A kind of *omnipresence* too express.
   For always at the *ocean* thou
Art always here, and at thy *fountain* too;
   Always thou go'st thy proper course,
   *Spontaneously*, and yet by force,
   Each Wave forcing his *precursor* on;
   Yet each one runs with equal haste,
   As though each feared to be the last.
   With mutual strife, void of contention,
In Troops they march, till thousands, thousands past.
   Yet gentle stream, thou'rt still the same,
   Always going, never gone;
   Yet do'st all constancy disclaim,
Wildly dancing to thine own murmuring tuneful song;
   Old as time, as love and beauty young. (2)

## Enlightened Eyes and Dark Nights

Farewell, O *eyes*, which I ne'er saw before,
And 'tis my int'rest ne'er to see ye more;
Though th' *deprivation* of your light,
I'm sure, will make it doubly night;
Yet rather I'll lose my way i'th' dark than stay;

For here I'm sure my *soul* will lose her way.
Oh' tis not dark enough, I wish it were,
Some rays are still on my eyes' *atmosphere*;
Which give sufficient light, I find,
Still to continue me stark blind;
For to eyes that's dazzl'd with too *radiant* light,
Darkness proves best restorative o'th' light. (3)

## The Death of a Brother

Ask me not why the *rose* doth fade,
*Lilies* look pale, and *flowers* die;
Question not why the *myrtle shade*
Her wonted shadows doth deny.

Seek not to know from whence begun
The sadness of the *nightingale*:
Nor why the *heliotrope* and *sun*,
Their constant *amity* do fail.

The *turtles* grief look not upon,
Nor reason why the *palm-trees* mourn;
When, widow-like, they're left alone,
Nor *phoenix* why her self doth burn.

For since *he's* dead, which life did give
To all these things, which here I name;
They fade, change, wither, cease to live,
Pine and consume into a flame. (4)

## A Station of the Cross: The Veil of Veronica

Behold the best action that was done in favour of the suffering Jesus! For (as tradition holds) this devout woman Veronica, being in her house, heard the clamour of the multitude, composed of people and soldiers, conducting our Lord to punishment. She rose up hastily, and looking out at her door, saw in the midst of the throng, Jesus, who casting a ray from his divine eyes, made her, by the light of faith, know him to be the Son of God, and her Redeemer. At which being extremely transported, she took off her veil, and ran into the midst amongst the soldiers and officers of justice, (without minding their affronts, blows, or pushes) until she came to our Saviour, and in spite of all opposition, she adored him, and with her veil in triple folds, wiped and cleaned his face, obscured with a cloud, even the sins of the world. This was an action so heroic as cannot be paralleled, nor sufficiently praised; that she should venture among such an incensed throng of all sorts, without considering the force of the soldiers, or the rudeness of the mob, or the pretended mask of justice, which they wore, in having those officers of judicature with them; that she should venture at such a time, when all the world was combined against him, a time when God his Father had abandoned him into the hands of sinners; at a time when the angels of peace wept, without power to help him; at a time when his apostles quitted, betrayed, and denied him; at a time when neither his afflicted Mother, or any other friend, could succour him; at a time when the whole City of Jerusalem persecuted him to death, and deemed it a crime to take any notice of him, or think him a good man. Then it was that the holy Veronica, this brave heroine, adored him as her God, for which no doubt she wears an immortal crown of glory. Wherefore our Saviour gave her the richest present he ever made to any creature; for he gave her the divine figure of his face impressed on each fold of her veil. O Veronica, extend this veil throughout the whole universe, that all mankind may see the disconsolate countenance of a suffering God. Preach, by this image, the passion of Jesus Christ in more places, and farther distant than ever the voice of the apostles reached; and thereby teach Christians courage and affection towards their Saviour, that in the time of persecution, some may, by thy example, assist him in assisting his Church, or the suffering members of it. For my own part, I will always endeavour, at least, to commemorate and wish it in my power to imitate this heroic action of the pious Veronica. (5)

## A Penitential Psalm: *De Profundis*

1. Out of the deep have I called unto thee, O Lord: Lord, hear my voice.

2. O let thine ears consider well: the voice of my complaint.

3. If thou, Lord, wilt be extreme to mark what is done amiss: O Lord, who may abide it?

4. For there is mercy with thee: Therefore shalt thou be feared.

5. I look for the Lord, my soul doth wait for him: In his word is my trust.

6. My Soul fleeth unto the Lord: Before the morning watch, I say, before the morning watch.

7. O *Israel*, trust in the Lord, for with the Lord there is mercy: And with him is plenteous redemption.

8. And he shall redeem *Israel*: From all his sins. (6)

## A Hymn for the Ascension

Come let us sing the praises of this day,
On which from Olivet, Christ brought away
Millions, which long in expectation lay.

Th' Eternal Father led the Blessed to meet
Him, and their new co-habitants to greet;
And ev'ry one had leave to kiss his feet.

All with their crowns and coronets adored
This mankind's Saviour, this their *God-Man* Lord,

And praised those suff'rings they had so deplored.

All that the Cherubims or Angels sung,
Or played on harps, with new *Te Deums* strung,
Were praises of the Cross, and him who thereon hung.

Each wound he had, darted forth rays so bright,
As almost dazzled their angelic sight,
And quite out-shone the most celestial light.

And then with mighty pomp, the Trinity
Bestowed their crown on his humanity,
And all again adored this Unity.

Hence a new source of happiness began,
To *Abraham's* Seed, from *Bersheba* to *Dan*,
And *Adam's* race now bless *the Fall of Man*. (7)

NOTES AND SOURCES

1.  Jane Barker, 'A Virgin Life', in *Poetical Recreations* (London, 1688), 12–13.
2.  Jane Barker, 'Sitting by a Rivulet', ibid. 24–7; 24.
3.  Jane Barker, 'Coming In—From a Dark Night', ibid. 58.
4.  Jane Barker, 'On the Death of my Brother. A Sonnet', ibid. 107.
5.  François Fénelon, trans. Jane Barker, *The Christian Pilgrimage: Or, a Companion for the Holy Season of Lent* (London, 1718), 80–3.
6.  François Fénelon, trans. Jane Barker, 'Psalm 130. De Profundis', in *The Christian Pilgrimage: Or, a Companion for the Holy Season of Lent* (London, 1718), 131.
7.  Jane Barker, 'Hymn on the Ascension', ibid. 115–16.

# Thomas Ward                                    1652–1708

If there were irenic voices among English Catholics in the eighteenth century, that of Thomas Ward, who literally fought for Papal claims, was not one of them. Born in 1652 as the son of a Yorkshire farmer, his theological studies led him to leave his native Presbyterianism for Roman Catholicism. He subsequently travelled to the continent and saw active military service in the Papal guard. When he returned to England in 1685 to join in the religious and political controversy surrounding James II, his pen name was 'the Roman Catholic soldier'. His combative approach appeared in his *Errata to the Protestant Bible* (1688), which was later republished by John Lingard and defended by John Milner. His most enduring work, however, was the polemical and vitriolic *England's Reformation: A Poem* (1710), which attacked the disordered lives of the monarchs 'Harry', 'Ned', and 'Bess' for disordering the nation. With its four cantos treating everything from psalm translations to ordination rites, the poem even features a *Hamlet*-like visit of Henry VIII to Elizabeth (though this father's ghost comes from Hell not Purgatory as in Shakespeare's play). Given the sense of cultural and architectural loss conveyed in this contribution to English Catholic satire (something like Pope's *Dunciad* set amid Early Modern religious and political strife), it is not surprising that the epigraphs in A.W. Pugin's anti-modern manifesto, *Contrasts* (1836), come from *England's Reformation*.

## The Trauma of the Reformation

Thus was the Church of *England* broke
By schism from its native stock,
And since has withered and decayed,
As branches rent from tree do fade;
And thus it was our King became
The Church's head with power supreme,
A power ecclesiastical
O'er bishops, councils, popes, and all
The powers on earth ecclesiastic,
Whether foreign or domestic.

A power so vast, and so egregious,
As turned to laics vowed religious:
Judged whom they pleased for heretics,
Then burned them with faggot-sticks:
Th'Ancient cannons it abrogated,
And points of faith annihilated,
Altered the Church's liturgies,
And did her rituals suppress.
It framed new forms of *ordination*,
Such as before were ne'er in fashion.
Its Holy Sacraments abolished,
And consecrated kirks demolished;
Transformed the choirs into stables,
And altars into fuddling tables:
The Mass abolished, and the Mass-days,
Turned fasts to feasts, and feasts to fast-days.
In place of all which they devise
New creeds, new prayers, new homilies.
*Harry* the Eighth set out the first creed.
*Ned* made the second, *Bess* the worst creed.
Of common-prayer-books, *Ned* made two,
And homilies composed a few:
*Bess* mends his prayer-books and made more
New homilies, above a score.
Each prince thus as he gets the crown,
Makes a religion of his own. (1)

## The Dissolution of the Monasteries

Abbeys six hundred forty five,
(If we may history believe,)
They levelled to foundations, and
Unjustly seized all their *land*.

Chanteries and chapels they threw o'er
Twenty three hundred sev'nty four.
Good *hospitals* one hundred ten,
Which long had kept poor pious men,
They seized into their impious hands,
And turned *poor* saints to vagabonds,
And *colleges* almost one hundred
Into their ancient chaos turned.
Scarce stone on stone, or brick on brick,
Was left of any one fabric,
Save here and there a bit of wall,
To show a glorious abbey's fall,
And the old foot-steps yet of stones,
To meet the ground it covered once.

. . .

Where once the *lark* on fluttering wing;
Called drowsy brothers up to sing,
*Lauds, Matins, Thanks* to God above,
Now not a tongue is heard to move,
Unless of *owls* and birds of night,
Or dismal shrieks of haunting sprite.
Those sacred *cells*, where *votaries* were
In peaceful contemplative prayer,
Are lurking dens of wild beasts made,
And foxes howl where hermits prayed.

Oh! Lofty towers, and sacred piles,
That once adorned our happy isles,
Who can record your *overturning*
But in deep sighs and bitter mourning?
Besides the lines my papers bear,
Let injured justice take her share,
And sigh through all the liquid air;
'till the whole world perceives the noise,
And falls to listen to the voice;
Then let it *form* such words, that *all*
May understand, and weep your fall,
And the sad fate of all your saints,
And innocent inhabitants,
Who were so violently hurled
From blest abodes, to cursed world. (2)

NOTES AND SOURCES

1. Thomas Ward, *England's Reformation: A Poem in Four Cantos* (London, 1715), 45–6.
2. Ibid. 52–3.

# (Mary Howard) Mary of the Holy Cross OSC            1653–1735

The life of Mary Howard, later known as Sister Mary of the Holy Cross, improbably recalls the sufferings of so many virginal medieval saints who pitted their faith against the lustful gaze of a powerful king. Yet Howard did not lose her life from refusing the entreaties of a monarch, but rather found it. Born to a noble, Protestant Berkshire family, Mary was raised with all the world could offer and, at 18, became the epitome of grace and beauty. At a play, this did not escape the attention of Charles II, whose potential interest led her and her family to remove her to France. Yet here, while residing in a Benedictine convent to learn French, Mary converted to Roman Catholicism and discerned her vocation to the religious life. Despite the heated opposition of her family, this determined young woman entered the English convent of Poor Clares at Rouen at the age of 22. Completing her renunciation of the world of fashion and intrigue for that of devotion and prayer, she would become the abbess in 1702. Her biographer, Alban Butler, wrote, 'In her we see that fervour makes even the greatest austerities and labours light and sweet.' These selections, which Butler published from her numerous manuscript instructions on the religious life, demonstrate the qualities of humility, patience, and compassion that this unlikely shepherd of souls showed for her fellow imitators of Christ and St Clare.

## Praying the Divine Office

This is the principal service of God, there being nothing on earth which represents more perfectly the state of the blessed in Heaven, than to praise him with fervour and cheerfulness. For it is written: *Happy are they who dwell in the House of God, to bless and praise him eternally.* It is the perpetual employment of the angels and religious persons, being angels on earth, ought as much as possible, to imitate the angels of Heaven. O my Soul, praise thy Lord and thy God, to whom belong all praise and glory, in Heaven and on earth. O God of glory and majesty, from thy throne proceedeth a voice, which says to all the inhabitants of the celestial Jerusalem: Give praise and benediction to God, all you that are here. O that every moment of my life I might praise thee, bless thee, give thee thanks for thy great glory. O most great, most glorious, most bountiful Lord God, I adore thee from the centre of my nothing. Give me Grace, that I may always offer to thee the sacrifice of praise with fervour of spirit, that so it may be acceptable to thee. Stay, I beseech thee, the powers of my soul, especially my wandering imagination, that in the beginning, continuance, and end of this angelical exercise, I always keep myself in thy divine presence. (1)

## Aspiring to the Company of the Angels

O my God, I wish I had all the awe and respect with which the angels and twenty-four elders are penetrated, when they prostrate themselves before the Lamb. Strike me with an holy fear, and let me be plunged in adoration of the greatness of thy sovereign majesty, and penetrated with a sense of my own baseness, to the end, that if I cannot, like them, offer thee, a pure heart, all burning with love, I may at least offer thee an humble heart, and assist in thy presence with as great reverence, attention, devotion, and humility, as I am able. When will it be, O sovereign majesty, that I shall praise thee like the angels? When shall I love thee perfectly? Happy are they who praise thee eternally. Make me of this number by thine infinite mercy. O blessed St Collet, who like a celestial nightingale, spent all thy strength in singing the praises of thy Creator, whilst here below, and art now keeping a concert with the choirs of angels in the celestial Jerusalem, pray for me, that I may so love and praise God in this life, that I may one day enter into the temple of glory, to praise and bless him eternally in thy happy company. Amen. (2)

## Conduct in Church

The Sisters must be diligent and ready in going to the choir at the first sound of the bell, leaving imperfect the work they are about, rather than staying to finish it. The holy Scripture speaking of the most pure and elevated among the celestial spirits, maketh an abridgement of all their greatness and privileges, by saying, that they assist always before the throne of God. Nothing can be greater than such an honour. The sisters must therefore repair diligently, and with great joy into this sanctuary, there to adore the Holy of Holies. What a consolation for a soul full of faith and love, to be always present before our Lord, to prostrate herself at the feet of Jesus Christ, to pour out her heart in his presence, whilst the whole world is overwhelmed with affliction and misery.

They must keep their sight under a strict guard in all places, but particularly in the choir, and at all prayer. It is an excellent means to keep their thoughts and hearts recollected, and to cut off an infinity of distractions. Happy that soul which closes her eyes to exterior and perishable things, that she may never, if possible, lose sight of her sovereign and only true good.

They must stand upright and handsomely in the choir, remembering that Jesus Christ beholds them, also his holy angels. Let them consider how these blessed spirits abase themselves with reverence and respect before the infinite majesty of God; how they tremble in his presence. And shall poor dust and ashes dare to stand in an irreligious posture before her Lord and Master? The infinite mercies of Jesus Christ, and his astonishing humiliation in the holy Eucharist, far from diminishing, ought to increase our respect. The more his love makes him forget what he is, the more ought we to bear in mind what we are, and what he is.

They must keep strict silence in the church, and this as well with their bodies and limbs, as with their tongues. This has always been esteemed a thing so sacred that, as the Scripture tells us, when the Temple of *Solomon* was built, God commanded that there should not be heard so much as the sound of an hammer, or any other instrument. Every one must therefore carefully avoid making any noise, both out of respect to the presence of Jesus Christ; and also not to give the least occasion of distraction to their Sisters.

They must go out of the church with great gravity and modesty. For a religious person, that comes conversing with God, ought to appear rather as an angel, than as a human creature, all penetrated with his divine presence, sanctity and modesty ought to shine in their exterior. These virtues will render them accessible to all, respected by all. (3)

## Prayer after Communion

O Soul of Jesus Christ, sanctify me. Blood of Jesus Christ, cleanse me. Body of Jesus Christ, save me. (4)

## Devotion to St Michael

Obtain for me, ardent Seraphims, some sparks of your flames; Blessed Cherubims, some irradiations of your light; holy Thrones, a participation of your peace; excellent Dominations, a courageous empire over all my passions; Sacred Virtues, a share of your strength against the enemies of Jesus Christ; Awful Powers, your authority over devils; glorious Principalities, your zeal for the honour of the most High God; Holy Archangels, your ardour for the defence and propagation of the Church, and the sanctity of its mysteries; Blessed Angels, your charitable care for the salvation of men; and you seven Princes, who stand always before the throne of God, and the Lamb, make me break with you the same bread of Heaven, in the contemplation of the same God, and may I be like you, all inflamed, and entirely transformed into love. O invincible defenders of the reign of Jesus Christ, all penetrated with zeal for his glory, and for the establishment of his worship, let me breathe nothing but his mysteries, his maxims, his virtues, and his divine spirit. May I subject to Him all my powers, and the very centre of my heart, that having glorified Him on earth with an homage of adoration and obedience like yours, I may contemplate Him one day in the splendour of a blessed immortality, and present Him, with you, eternal canticles of praise and love. Amen. (5)

## Giving of Love

O my most sweet Lord Jesus, give me this love. Draw to thyself all the powers of my soul. I ask of thee, O Lord, no earthly treasures, no worldly goods or glory. I beg only the riches of thy pure love, that in all things I may seek thee alone, prize thee above all, be content with thee alone, who art to me all in all. O love of my God, the life of my soul, the crown of my head, the centre of all my affections. To thee I consecrate all my actions. To thee I dedicate irrevocably all my labours and desires; all I am or have. I will not live, my God, but to love thee; I will not breathe, but to glorify thee. O that I could break forth without intermission, into seraphic acts of thy love, O my most amiable Lord! O that I could continue to repeat them each moment of my life! Particularly, may I die in the highest raptures of this love. (6)

## Charity in Chief Points

We must have a tender cordial love for all, accompanied with respect, preventing each other in every service, shunning all disputes, as the seed of dissention, always ready to leave our own will and judgement to conform to others, to bear each other's ways and humours, never complaining of any one's behaviour, and behaving toward all with sweetness, by which we may change antipathy into love. (7)

## Humility

To be poor and proud is abominable before God and men. We must therefore have a mean opinion of ourselves in all things, be ready sincerely to take upon ourselves any fault, of which we are accused, to acknowledge it, and make satisfaction; bow to each other, when we pass by, esteeming ourselves happy to serve any one, and unworthy to be served by any one; bear a great respect and love to all, as to the spouses of Jesus Christ. (8)

## Dying Words

Now the hour is come that there is no comfort but in Jesus Christ. Talk not to me of this or that devotion. Jesus Christ is my whole support. All good is due only to his grace. I am a poor weak creature. (9)

NOTES AND SOURCES

1. Alban Butler, *A Short Account of the Life and Virtues of the Venerable and Religious Mother, Mary of the Holy Cross, Abbess of the English Poor Clares at Roüen* (London, 1767), 164–5.
2. Ibid. 165–6.
3. Ibid. 166–9.
4. Ibid. 174.
5. Ibid. 177–8.
6. Ibid. 179.
7. Ibid. 185.
8. Ibid. 186.
9. Ibid. 193.

## Sylvester Jenks (alias Metcalfe)      1656–1714

The humane writing of the Shropshire-born priest and theologian, Sylvester Jenks (alias Metcalfe), demonstrates the intelligence and insight that he brought to English Catholic culture of the early eighteenth century. As a student and later a professor of philosophy at Douai, Jenks encountered the controversial influence of Jansenism, a heretical interpretation of St Augustine that emphasized predestination, God's irresistible will over and against human freedom, the depravity of the human condition, draconian rigour in morality, and a severe stringency in approaching the sacraments. It is often characterized as a Catholic Calvinism. Anticipating St Thérèse of Liseux's recommendation of a 'Little Way' of loving and contemplating God, Jenks elevates humility against this dour school of thought. For those struggling in despair to meet Jansenism's impossible standards, he recalls the Good News that God is love and that He can be approached freely as a friend whose grace and mercy are open to all sinners. Epistemologically humble, Jenks also warns against an over-reaching rationality that can obscure this love and its expression in the sacraments. If history had been kinder to Jenks—he was appointed to be a royal chaplain just before the 1688 Revolution and elected to a bishopric just before his death—his voice may have had an even greater place in English and European religious history.

## A Theologian's Thanksgiving

I humbly thank my God, I am a Catholic: *I believe in God*, etc. *I believe in the Holy Ghost; the Holy Catholic Church*, etc. And, in my daily prayers, I humbly beg, that I may always be so happy as to *have* grace, without *understanding* it; rather than once be so uncomfortably miserable as to *understand* it without *having* it. (1)

## Human Freedom against Jansenism's Predestination

God's predetermination never hinders us from freely determining our selves. He does not take our work out of our hands, but only joins with us to help us in determining our selves. He cannot help us, unless we co-operate with him. To *help* us, is not to do it *for* us, but to do it *with* us. And then, by the essential prerogative of universal and first cause, in the very same moment, my determination of my self, is his effect as well as mine; and is not his, before it is mine; no more than I am his, before I am my own. . . .

Predetermination is as ready to the will as noon day light to the eye. A man, who has good eyes, may freely shut them against the brightest light, and refuse the benefit of it. But, on the other hand, he is as free to open his eyes; and then, in the very moment, the light is as ready for him, and as much at his service, as if it were at his command. (2)

## God is Love

To make it plainly appear that the love of God above all things is the greatest duty of a Christian, one would think it were enough to show that it is a duty which comprises all our other duties; that it is the total sum of Christianity; and that, without the least hyperbole, it is the *whole duty of man*; because all other precepts whatsoever only are so many branches of this *Great Commandment*, which is the root of all the rest. . . .

If we draw the prospect nigher, we shall find an infinite variety of pressing motives which enforce our obligation. Every single excellence of the object we adore is all divine. No shadow there of any blemish to obscure those charms, which challenge our affection. Nothing in our God but what is infinitely amiable, and deserving infinitely more than *all* the love that we are able to return. Since therefore all and every one of his innumerable excellences are unlimited and boundless; since they all and every one deserve a suitable esteem; since they command our love as much as they deserve it: hence it follows clearly, that our duty is as boundless as their merit; and that, as St Bernard says, *There is no other measure of our love, than loving without measure.* (3)

## Hope over Despair

The greatest mystery of Christian morality consists in the equal balancing of hope and fear, betwixt God's mercy and his justice; that we may neither be secure in sin, because he is so merciful; nor yet despond, because he is so just. Presumption and despair are the two rocks between which all Christians ought to steer an even course; and so avoid the one as not to dash upon the other. It is perhaps the greatest secret of the Devil's art. He first inclines us to presume; and we no sooner see the danger of it; but he tempts us to despair. Thus he commences; thus he finishes his work. . . .

If when a sinner struggles with his chains, endeavours to break loose, and the more he struggles, the more he finds himself engaged (which the All-seeing Wisdom frequently permits, to humble a proud soul); if then these two great truths were settled in his mind: to wit, that God *can* free him, if He will, and that He *will* not fail to free him, if he please; O! with what pleasure would he relish the assurance of this loving confidence! With how much transport of a joyful mind would he recite those words of St Paul, *I know in whom I have believed*; I know in whom I put my trust; I know, and *am persuaded, He is able* to deliver me. I am assured, He is not only *powerful* but *merciful*; and therefore I am certain He both *can* and *will* assist me....

Must I *despair*? Yes, yes: It is absolutely *necessary* for me to *despair* of my *own* strength, that I may seriously *begin* to *hope* in nothing else but *Him* who *gives grace to the humble, and resists the proud*. And may I by his grace *persevere* all my life, *improving* each day more and more, *in this despair*, which is the reason why I *hope* more *now* than any other time. (4)

## The Loving Friendship of God

True friendship naturally inspires a loving confidence in our friend. The more we love him, the more we confide in him. And if we love him very much, we are apt to have so much confidence in him, as to think it almost impossible for him to find in his heart to hurt us. If this be so, even amongst us mortals, notwithstanding our ill nature and our being subject to mistake, surely the self-same reason is of much more force, when it is applied to God. Our friends on earth may be mistaken, and suspect our love; or else may possibly be so ill natured as to slight it, though they know it. But our God can neither be ill natured to us, nor mistaken in us: If we love him, we may be assured, he always knows it, and he never slights it.

It is St Augustine's maxim: *Love, and do what you will*. Do but *love* God, and whatever you *do*, under the direction and influence of this love, will never disturb your peace. Do but *love* him heartily, and then you will never purposely and deliberately design to offend him: your chief design will always be to please him: and, whatsoever frailties or surprises happen, as long as this design subsists, you need not doubt but that they always will be pardonable. Do but *love* him above all things, and all your imperfections, whatsoever they are, will only serve to humble you, they never will incline you to despair. (5)

## The Meaning of Transubstantiation

The enemies of Christ's divinity abhor the faith of it as contrary to sense, because all those who saw him, plainly saw he was a man; and opposite to reason, because it seems to them impossible either for immensity to be comprehended in the compass of a man or for one person to subsist in two natures. The enemies of transubstantiation urge the same arguments against it. They say it is contrary to sense, because all those who see it, plainly see it is bread; and opposite to reason, because it seems to them impossible either for *Christ*'s body to be comprehended in so small a compass or for one body to be at the same time in two places. Never was St Paul's advice more seasonable than in this age of ours. He tells us, that it is our duty *to cast down imaginations, and every high thing that exalts itself against the knowledge of God, bringing into captivity every thought to the obedience of Christ*. I must confess it is natural enough to entertain a doubtful thought of what is far above the reach of reason.... The mysteries of faith would be no longer mysteries, if reason comprehended them. Much less would they deserve that name, if sense discovered them. We commonly say, that *Seeing is believing*; and amongst men acquainted with the cheats of a deceitful world, we find the wisest are the slowest in believing what they do not see. But yet the word of God has so much credit with us that we confidently trust him farther than we see him. And when we hear him say, *This is my body*, we *believe* it though we do not *see* it. Nor is it any wonder that we boldly venture to believe such things as are beyond the reach of sense; more than it is that we believe such points as are above the reach of reason. (6)

NOTES AND SOURCES

1. Sylvester Jenks, *A Short Review of the Book of Jansenius* (n.p., 1710), 152–3.

2. Ibid. 77–8, 79.

3. Sylvester Jenks, *A Contrite and Humble Heart* (n.p., 1693), 3–5.

4. Ibid. 109–10, 114–15, 195–6.

5. Sylvester Jenks, *The Blind Obedience of an Humble Penitent. The Best Cure for Scruples* (n.p., 1699), 29–31.

6. Sylvester Jenks, *Three Sermons upon the Sacrament* (London, 1688), 3–4, 5–6.

# Thomas Tyldesley and Nicholas Blundell   1657–1715; 1669–1737

Tyldesley's and Blundell's journals, which were published in the nineteenth century, give insight into the awkward sense of tranquillity punctuated by harassment and of contentment mixed with frustration that characterized the everyday lives of two English Catholic gentlemen in eighteenth-century Lancashire. Both writers came from families intertwined with the most contentious religious and political events in English history. Tyldesley's grandfather was 'the Cavalier', Sir Thomas Tyldesley, one of Charles I's leading military men. For the English Civil War Society in their historical recreations of the seventeenth century, his spirit still animates a regiment to combat the Puritan Roundheads. With a comparable family history, Blundell could boast an Elizabethan ancestor who died under imprisonment for harbouring a priest; a Cavalier grandfather with a captain's commission under Tyldesley; and a Jesuit uncle who was arrested by Titus Oates while attempting to controvert Oates's spurious accusations against St Omer's. Both diarists were educated at St Omer's before settling into their lives as country squires. Tyldesley's account of life at Myerscough Lodge and Fox Hall in Blackpool gives a sense of proscribed ambition as he made due with restraints on his social and political life because of his religion. A Jacobite whose home was reputed to harbour recusant priests and royalists, Tyldesley died in 1715 before the first Jacobite Rebellion. Blundell weathered the rebellion hiding in the priest's hole at Crosby Hall, his ancestral home near Liverpool. He recorded, 'I set in a streat [narrow] place for a fat man.' Most of Blundell's concerns partook of the 'fat' of life as he worries about the year's batch of cider and the price of goods. Nevertheless, he had to sail to the Continent following the conflicts in Preston before returning to what his biographer has called his 'little world'. These entries reveal insights into their devotional life, as Tyldesley marks each of his birthdays with a prayer and attends a Mass celebrated by Edward Hawarden. As a squire balancing the demands of his de facto parish, Blundell finds himself in another narrow place as he negotiates the relationship between the priest he supported, the local Catholic community, and his wife.

## Tyldesley's Journal: Birthday Thanksgivings

April 3 [1712].—Blessed be the holy and undivided Trinity for ever more, for the merciful preserving and bringing me to the age of 55 years; Amen.

April 3 [1713].—For His great mercy of permitting me life to this day, the Great Divinity of 3 Persons and one God be for ever and ever glorified, honoured, and praised, world without end, Amen. Went to Aldcliffe to prayers; the remainder of the day in the house.

April 3 [1714].—For the great preservation and blessing the merciful, omnipotent, and glorious God has bestowed upon me, poor mortal, in this winter, delivering me from two angry fits of the gout, a fever for 5 weeks, and a fever fit—Ill for 12 or 14 days, may his glorious and blessed Name ever be sanctified by me, mine, and all who here after shall read this, for his blessings have been according to his great love and pity, above every thing but his great mercy. Went to Doctor Ha[wa]rden to X [Mass]. Returned back to dinner. (1)

## Blundell: The Qualities of a Good Priest

To Mr Barnes, to be left at Mr. Nelsons an Apothecary in Great Wild Street London. Feb. 4th. 1706/7

Sir,
    Though you be a stranger to me yet I presume to address myself to you, being you are not ignorant of the subject I write about which is to desire you will, with what convenient speed you can, furnish us with one of yours, that you think will be proper. You have formerly been informed how we desire he should be qualified, so shall be brief on that subject, only say in few words that we desire a man of wit and conversation, one that can preach well and is willing to take pains amongst the poor Catholics, of which we have a great many, and one that is of a good humour and will be easy contented with tolerable good fare . . . Sir your speedy answer to this would much oblige.
    Your Humble Servant
Nicholas Blundell (2)

## To Mr Barnes. Feb. 17th 1707/8

I ought long since to have returned you thanks for the good man you sent us viz: Mr Aldred who is qualified according as desired and is extremely to my liking and gives very great satisfaction to the Catholics hereabouts who are very numerous, but cannot say my wife carries to him so civilly as she ought, which causes him to be dissatisfied and not willing long to continue in my Family. However, he being so well approved of both by myself and all the neighbourhood, I am not willing he should part far, so have taken care that another house not far distant from hence be provided for him, and many of my neighbours have made their petition both to Mr Babthorpe and myself that he may be fixed there, and that is now also my petition to you . . . the neighbours have not only petitioned for his stay, but have on their own accord promised considerably towards his maintenance which, with what I shall do, will I hope, maintain him sufficiently. (3)

NOTES AND SOURCES

1. Thomas Tyldesley, *The Tyldesley Diary*, ed. Joseph Gillow and Anthony Hewitson (Preston, 1873), 17, 83, 141–2.
2. Nicholas Blundell, *Blundell's Diary and Letter Book 1702–1728*, ed. Margaret Blundell (Liverpool: Liverpool University Press, 1952), 77.
3. Ibid. 79.

# Christopher Tootell 1662–1727

Christopher Tootell, the Lancaster-born priest and uncle to the historian Hugh Tootell (Charles Dodd), served at Ladywell, Fernyhalgh (near Preston) from 1699 until his death in 1727 and recorded the shrine's history in his *Traditional Account of Our Lady's Well and Chapel in Fernyhalgh* (1723). Since the late medieval period, 'Ladye Well' was an important place of pilgrimage and prayer, dedicated to the Blessed Virgin Mary and believed to possess healing powers. The chapel at the well was destroyed with the dissolution of the monasteries, but rebuilt in the late seventeenth century. As important as the shrine and well were devotionally, this sequestered locale may have been at times even more important educationally. The legendary recusant schoolteacher, Alice Harrison or 'Dame Alice', established her long-enduring Catholic school here in 1708 after she was received into the Church by Edward Melling, Tootell's nephew and successor at Fernyhalgh. Perhaps influenced by her own conversion against the strident objections of her family, Harrison opened the school not only to Catholics from across England but also to Protestants. Lessons included a daily trip to say prayers at the well—an experience that would shape the spiritual lives of the school's illustrious pupils, which included Alban Butler and future presidents of Douai and Ushaw colleges. One former student, Peter Newby, would also open a school near the site so that the educational efforts and devotion at this shrine truly represented a tradition.

## Our Lady's Well in Fernyhalgh

A virtuous and wealthy merchant in great distress upon the Irish sea, had recourse to him for safety, whom the winds and sea obey; and made a vow, in case he escaped the danger, to acknowledge the favour of his preservation by some remarkable work of piety. After this, the storm began to cease, and a favourable gale wafted his ship unto the coast of Lancashire, where, whilst he thankfully reflected on his merciful deliverance, and was in pain to know by what pious work his vow might be acceptably fulfilled, a miraculous voice admonished him to seek a place called Fernyhalgh, and there to build a chapel, where he should find a crab-tree bearing fruit without cores, and under it a spring. In compliance with this direction, he spared no pains in travelling about and seeking for the place called Fernyhalgh, but all in vain, until at last he came to Preston; where having taken up his lodgings late at night, the housemaid came in from milking, and excused her late return, occasioned by loss of time in seeking and following the strayed cow as far as Fernyhalgh. This accidental notice of the place he sought for, revived the weary traveller, and sent him full of joy to take his rest. In the morning a guide conducted him to Fernyhalgh, where he continued his search until he found the crab-tree, and the spring foretold him; as also an unexpected, and until then undiscovered image of the Blessed Virgin Mary, which occasioned the spring to be called Our Lady's Well, and the chapel he built hard by it, to be dedicated in her name to God's honour and service, and likewise called Our Lady's Chapel in Fernyhalgh.

But after the suppression of chantries and free chapels, its principal timber was removed and applied to the building of a house.... Nevertheless, the ancient devotion of neighbouring Catholics did not fail with the old chapel, but survived its ruin, and continued in their constant assemblies, and praying together at the well, on Sundays and holidays, and especially on the Feasts of Our Lady, even in the severest times of persecution.

Of these devotees, several have piously believed and thankfully acknowledged special benefit and help received by means of their frequent visiting and constant praying at Our Lady's Well. And others not only practised, but also recommended to posterity, a more than ordinary devotion to the Blessed Virgin Mary at Fernyhalgh in contriving, erecting, and finishing a house of prayer there, in the year of our Lord 1684 and 5.—Ad majorem Dei gloriam, Deiparaeque Virginis Gloriam. [To the greater glory of God, and the glory of the Virgin Mother of God.] Amen. (1)

NOTES AND SOURCES

1.   Christopher Tootell, 'A Traditional Account of our Lady's Well and Chapel in Fernyhalgh', *Catholicon*, 3 (Oct. 1816), 129–30.

# Hugh Tootell (alias Charles Dodd)      1671–1743

The twentieth-century German critic Walter Benjamin said that the conscientious historian must strive 'to deliver tradition anew from the conformism which is on the point of overwhelming it'. Hugh Tootell, in his life's masterwork *The Church History of England, From 1500–1688* (1737–42) attempted this in retelling the history of the Reformation from the English Catholic perspective. Tootell unapologetically challenged the conventional wisdom that saw the Reformation as a progressive and inevitable march out of the Dark Ages and accused Catholics of any number of horrible beliefs and seditious practices. A Lancashire native, he was tutored by his uncle, Christopher Tootell, before studying with Edward Hawarden at Douai and earning a bachelor of divinity from St Gregory's Seminary in Paris. He originally assumed his pen name, Charles Dodd, to save his family from suffering a penal fine for educating Catholic youth abroad. Tootell travelled extensively in Europe and served on the English mission before settling in as the chaplain to Robert Throckmorton of Harvington Hall in Worcestershire, an Elizabethan manor house whose series of priest holes (hiding places for fugitive priests) provided a fit setting for finishing his historical work. Not only did the narrative of the *Church History* represent an important alternative view of the past, its appendices replete with primary source documents and its descriptions of English Catholics neglected in other history books proved important resources. In a testament to Tootell's influence, a nineteenth-century republication of the voluminous work included John Lingard among its subscribers.

## The Use and Abuse of Plots

As it is the nature of all plots, when well contrived, to be dark, and intricate; so it is necessary for the generality of readers to be provided with a key to unlock some secrets; the want whereof would make them incapable of passing a true judgement either of causes, or persons. And first as to plots in general: some have been pleased to observe, that plots, whether real or fictitious, are not detrimental to government; but, on the contrary, very useful for many of those purposes persons are bent upon who seek after a good establishment in this life. Seditious practices, say they, like cracks in an edifice, have no good aspect; yet they commonly discover the root of the evil, and put the ministry in the way of securing the government by proper remedies. This is the natural consequence of a real plot. And even when it is all fiction and contrivance, it is attended with several politic advantages. It is a means of making some sort of persons become odious to the generality of the nation. It gives a handle for raising taxes upon a whole nation, but especially upon malcontents and delinquents. It is a plentiful harvest for politicians and avaricious persons, who raise their fortune upon the ruins of those that are under oppression and frowned upon by the court. Such sort of sham-plots are no new things. They have been set afoot in all reigns: nor can it be denied to have been the case of Catholics in almost every reign since the beginning of the Reformation. Whenever their adversaries were apprehensive of their flourishing, there was commonly some contrivance to blacken them and weaken their interest. For instances of this kind, the history of our nation affords several very remarkable ones.... By a strange sort of logic, a Catholic and a rebel have been passed current for the same thing; and so they are commonly misrepresented both in private conversation, in the pulpit, and at the bar. (1)

## Church, State, and Lived Religion

We may observe how gradually the reformers proceeded in their attacks against the Church of Rome and in many respects against religion in general. Henry VIII (who began the attack with reviving the old controversy between England and Rome concerning appeals in matters of discipline) lays claim to an independence even in matters of faith; and the see of Rome is deprived of all those perquisites and allowances, which were judged convenient towards supporting the dignity of him who was supreme pastor of God's church, viz. Annates, peter-pence, and other benevolences, which the monarchs of England had ever bestowed upon the Holy See, for the purpose mentioned. Then, having banished the pope's authority, he falls upon his own clergy at home and declares himself to be the fountain of all their power and jurisdiction, both temporal and spiritual; and that all their synodical sanctions and decrees concerning errors, abuses, etc. were void, and of no account without his concurrence and approbation. By this step the church was swallowed up in the state, and the whole affair of religion placed upon the same foot with trade and manufactures. Afterwards, by seizure of the abbey-lands, impropriated tithes, colleges, hospitals, chapels, etc. he drove his supposed enemies from their encampment and deprived them of subsistence. Edward VI still made farther advances. Besides completing the work his father had left unfinished, as to the seizure of colleges, hospitals, etc. he strips all the cathedrals and parochial churches of their plate and rich ornaments; orders a new liturgy, and new articles of religion to be drawn up, which was never heard of or practised in the nation; and, that the clergy might be rendered incapable of obstructing the designs of the court, as his father had deprived the bishops of their power, so he enslaves their persons and obliges them to hold their sees only *quam diu se bene gesserint* [as long as they conduct themselves well]. And now lastly, Queen Elizabeth pursues this noble scheme of reforming, by depriving the bishoprics of many of their fairest manors upon the pretence of allowing an equivalent out of impropriated tithes. A method both then and ever since complained of by their own clergy....I cannot tell whether the supreme governing party, from 1641 to 1660, may be honoured with the title of reformers. If so, they finished Henry VIII's project very completely by seizing the lands belonging to bishops, deans, chapters, etc. and might have clinched the whole affair of reforming, if, in imitation of their brethren in Holland, and other places, they had stripped the parochial clergy of all their tithes and only allowed them a subsistence by way of contribution. This would have been an effectual way of taming the ecclesiastical body, made them wholly dependent and susceptible of any impression. It would then be in their choice either to starve or to embrace any creed the civil power would be pleased to impose them. I may perhaps mistake the intention of the lay-reformers; but I am confident, I have not misreported matter of fact....

Catholics will be apt to infer that as the substance of the Reformation was carried on upon human considerations, *viz.* to secure the queen's title and possession of church lands; so the same spirit is discoverable in every branch of it. For why do they fast, and abstain from flesh? To promote fishing and increase the number of mariners for sea service. Why do they make use of sacraments? Not as the channels of grace, but only outwards tokens of their inclinations. Why do they frequent the church, pray, and give alms? Not that these performances are capable of effecting any thing towards appeasing God's wrath or procuring his favour; but merely for the sake of outward discipline and church economy. Why do they admit persons to exercise the ministerial function? Not that they look upon them qualified by any divine power or character, but only by deputation from the civil power, to which they are subject in every branch of their office. By this means the church is not only reformed, but lost and melted away in the state, to whose politic ends both preaching, praying, fasting, alms, and the use of the very sacraments are become subservient upon every occasion. (2)

NOTES AND SOURCES

1.   Charles Dodd (Hugh Tootell), *The Church History of England*, 3 vols. (Brussels [London], 1737–42), ii. 17–18.
2.   Ibid. 9–10, 30.

# Alexander Pope                                    1688–1744

Newman saw in Pope a potential 'rival to Shakespeare' but was disappointed by the religious vision of this 'unsatisfactory' Catholic. Pope himself complained that his family thought he only produced 'ungodly verses'. There is much to be said for these evaluations. Newman specifically objected to *Essay on Man* (1734–5), which has been labelled Deistic for the unknowable distance and indifference attributed to the Divine in the famous couplet, 'Know then thyself, presume not God to scan; | The proper study of mankind is man.' While this criticism may oversimplify God's role in the poem's vision of nature and morality, Pope leaves, nevertheless, little or no room for Christian revelation or redemption. The viciousness of his satires, chiefly in *The Dunciad* (1729, 1742, 1743), and his involvement in the fashions of the day also speak of a certain 'worldliness', which was the chief spiritual concern of contemporary Catholic divines such as John Gother or Richard Challoner. Pope, however, cannot be separated from his Catholicism, even if that often seems to be his own desire. As the son of a London linen merchant who was a convert to Catholicism and a mother with a Catholic background, his early education, indeed his only formal education, came from priests and at small, technically illegal, Catholic schools in London. The verbal echoes in his early Biblical poems, *The Messiah* (1712) and Psalm XCI (1717), derive from the Catholic Douai-Rheims translation of Scripture, not the authorized King James version. His translation of 'The Hymn of St Francis Xavier' (1711) was done at the request of the family chaplain of Pope's Jacobite friend, John Caryll, who himself suggested Pope write a mock epic about the spat between two prominent Catholic families that became *The Rape of the Lock* (1712). Caryll was just one part of Pope's Catholic social network that also included Teresa and Martha Blount (the latter addressed in the birthday blessing below), who represented significant female interests in his life and who resided at the recusant manor house of Mapledurham near Reading. Perhaps most significantly, Pope's Catholicism contributed to his sense of being an outsider in English society. Not only was he a 'Papist', the onset of Pott's disease in his youth stunted his growth and left him painfully disabled for the rest of his life. His climb to the top of English literary society was thus a particularly sweet victory. In this vein, the poet, who as a boy had to relocate farther from Westminster because of the penal laws, used the income from his enormously successful translation of Homer to build an enviable villa, garden, and grotto in Twickenham that was the pinnacle of neoclassical design. That its pagan 'Grotto of Inspiration' also featured the *arma Christi*, which depicts the crown of thorns and the five wounds of Christ, again shows Pope's contradictions. He died at Twickenham in 1744, received the last rites, and was buried next to his parents. His original villa does not remain, but the grotto can be found in the vicinity of St Mary's University College, founded in 1850 by Cardinal Wiseman to educate teachers to serve the Catholic poor.

## Hymn of St Francis Xavier

Thou art my God, sole object of my love;
Not for the hope of endless joys above;
Not for the fear of endless pains below,
Which they who love thee not must undergo.

For me, and such as me, thou deign'st to bear
An ignominious cross, the nails, the spear:
A thorny crown transpierced thy sacred brow,
While bloody sweats from ev'ry member flow.

For me in tortures thou resignd'st thy breath,
Embraced me on the cross, and saved me by thy death.
And can these suff'rings fail my heart to move?
What but thyself can now deserve my love?

Such as then was, and is, thy love to me,
Such is, and shall be still, my love to thee—
To thee, Redeemer! mercy's sacred spring!
My God, my Father, Maker, and my King! (1)

## *The Messiah*: An Advent Verse

Rapt into future times, the Bard begun;
A *Virgin* shall conceive, a *Virgin* bear a Son!
From *Jesse*'s root behold a branch arise,
Whose sacred flow'r with fragrance fills the skies.
Th'aethereal Spirit o'er its leaves shall move,
And on its top descends the mystic Dove.
Ye Heav'ns from high the dewy nectar pour,
And in soft silence shed the kindly show'r!
The sick and weak the healing plant shall aid,
From storms a shelter, and from heat a shade.
All crimes shall cease, and ancient fraud shall fail;
Returning Justice lift aloft her scale;
Peace o'er the world her olive wand extend,
And white-robed Innocence from Heav'n descend.
Swift fly the years, and rise th'expected morn!
Oh spring to light, auspicious babe, be born!
. . .
Hark! a glad voice the lonely desert cheers:
Prepare the Way! a God, a God appears;
A God, a God! the vocal hills reply,
The rocks proclaim th'approaching Deity.
Lo earth receives him from the bending skies!
Sink down ye mountains, and ye valleys rise:
With heads declined, ye cedars, homage pay;
Be smooth ye rocks, ye rapid floods give way!
The SAVIOUR comes! by ancient bards foretold:
Hear him ye deaf, and all ye blind behold!
He from thick films shall purge the visual ray,
And on the sightless eye-ball pour the day.
'Tis he th'obstructed paths of sound shall clear,
And bid new music charm th'unfolding ear;
The dumb shall sing, the lame his crutch forgo,
And leap exulting like the bounding roe;
No sigh, no murmur the wide world shall hear,
From ev'ry face he wipes off ev'ry tear,
In adamantine chains shall death be bound,
And hell's grim tyrant feel th'eternal wound.
As the good shepherd tends his fleecy care,
Seeks freshest pastures and the purest air,
Explores the lost, the wand'ring sheep directs,
By day o'er sees them, and by night protects,
The tender lambs he raises in his arms,
Feeds from his hand, and in his bosom warms:
Mankind shall thus his guardian care engage,
The promised Father of the future age. (2)

## Sacred Music and St Cecilia

Music the fiercest griefs can charm,
And Fate's severest rage disarm:
Music can soften pain to ease,
And make despair and madness please:
Our joys below it can improve,
And antedate the bliss above.
 This the divine Cecilia found,
And to her Maker's praise confined the sound.
When the full organ joins the tuneful choir,
 Th' immortal Pow'rs incline their ear;
Born on the swelling notes our souls aspire,
While solemn airs improve the sacred fire;
 And angels lean from Heav'n to hear!
Of Orpheus now no more let poets tell,
To bright Cecilia greater pow'r is giv'n;
 His numbers raised a shade from Hell,
 Hers lift the soul to Heav'n. (3)

## Psalm 91: The Believer's Hope

He who beneath thy shelt'ring wing resides,
Whom thy hand leads, and whom thy glory guides,
To Heav'n familiar his bold vows shall send,
And fearless say to God—*Thou* art my friend!
'Tis Thou shalt save him from insidious wrongs,
And the sharp arrows of censorious tongues.
When gath'ring tempests swell the raging main,
When thunder roars, and lightning blasts the plain,
Amidst the wrack of nature undismayed,
Safe shall he lie, and hope beneath thy shade.
By day no perils shall the just affright,
No dismal dreams or groaning ghosts by night.
His God shall guard him in the fighting field,
And o'er his breast extend his saving shield:
The whistling darts shall turn their points away,
And fires around him innocently play.
Thousands on ev'ry side shall yield their breath;
And twice ten thousand bite the ground in death;
While he, serene in thought, shall calm survey
The sinners fall, and bless the vengeful day!
 Heav'n is thy hope: thy refuge fixed above;
No harms can reach thee, and no force shall move.
I see protecting myriads round thee fly,
And all the bright militia of the sky.

These in thy dangers timely aid shall bring,
Raise in their arms, and waft thee on their wing,
These shall perform th'almighty orders given,
Direct each step, and smooth the path to Heaven.
Thou on the fiery basilisk shalt tread,
And fearless crush the swelling aspic's head,
Rouse the huge dragon, with a spurn, from rest,
And fix thy foot upon the Lion's crest.
Lo *I*, his *God!* in all his toils am near:
I see him ever, and will ever hear:
When he the rage of sinners shall sustain,
I share his griefs, and feel my self his pain:
When foes conspiring rise against his rest,
I'll stretch my arm, and snatch him to my breast.
Him will I heap with honours, and with praise,
And glut with full satiety of days;
Him with my glories crown; and when he dies,
To him reveal my joys, and open all my skies. (4)

## A Birthday Blessing

Oh be thou blessed with all that Heav'n can send,
Long health, long youth, long pleasure, and a friend:
Not with those toys the female world admire,
Riches that vex, and vanities that tire.
With added years if life bring nothing new,
But like a sieve let ev'ry blessing through;
Some joy still lost, as each vain year runs o'er,
And all we gain, some sad reflection more;
Is that a birth-day? 'tis alas! too clear,
'Tis but the fun'ral of the former year.
   Let joy or ease, let affluence or content,
And the gay conscience of a life well spent,
Calm ev'ry thought, inspirit ev'ry grace,
Glow in thy heart, and smile upon thy face.
Let day improve on day, and year on year,
Without a pain, a trouble, or a fear;
Till death unfelt that tender frame destroy,
In some soft dream, or ecstasy of joy:
Peaceful sleep out the Sabbath of the tomb,
And wake to raptures in a life to come. (5)

## Hope

Hope humbly then; with trembling pinions soar;
Wait the great teacher, Death, and God adore!
What future bliss, he gives not thee to know,
But gives that Hope to be thy blessing now.

Hope springs eternal in the human breast:
Man never is, but always to be blest:
The soul uneasy, and confined at home,
Rests, and expatiates, in a life to come. (6)

## Overambitious Science

Go, wond'rous creature! mount where Science guides,
Go measure earth, weigh air, and state the tides,
Instruct the planets in what orbs to run,
Correct old Time, and regulate the Sun;
Go, soar with Plato to th' empyreal sphere,
To the first Good, first Perfect, and first Fair;
Or tread the mazy round his follow'rs trod,
And quitting sense call imitating God,
As Eastern priests in giddy circles run,
And turn their heads, to imitate the Sun.
Go, teach Eternal Wisdom how to rule;
Then drop into thyself, and be a fool! (7)

## To a Victim of Breast Cancer

Here rests a woman, good without pretence,
Blest with plain reason and with sober sense;
No conquests she, but o'er herself desired;
No arts essayed, but not to be admired:
Passion and pride were to her soul unknown,
Convinced that virtue only is our own.
So unaffected, so composed a mind,
So firm, yet soft, so strong, yet so refined,
Heav'n, as its purest gold, by tortures tried;
The saint sustained it, but the woman died. (8)

NOTES AND SOURCES

1. Alexander Pope, 'Hymn of St Francis Xavier', in 'An Original Juvenile Composition of Mr. Pope', *Gentleman's Magazine*, 61/4 (Oct. 1791), 892.

2. Alexander Pope, 'Messiah. A Sacred Eclogue', *The Spectator*, 378 (14 May 1712), in *The Spectator*, v (London, 1757), 342–4.

3. Alexander Pope, *Ode for Musick [on St Cecilia's Day]* (London, 1713), 7–8.

4. Alexander Pope, 'Psalm XCI', in *Poems on Several Occasions* (London, 1717), 209–11.

5. Alexander Pope, 'To Mrs. M.B. on her Birth-day', in *The Works of Alexander Pope*, vi, ed. William Warburton (London, 1751), 79–80.

6. Alexander Pope, *An Essay on Man* (London, 1734), 11. I. 87–94.

7. Ibid., 22. II. 19–30.

8. Alexander Pope, 'Epitaph. On Mrs. Elizabeth [Who Dyed of a Cancer in her Breast]', in *Miscellaneous Poems, By Several Hands*, ed. D. Lewis (London: J. Watts, 1730), 89.

# Bishop Richard Challoner                                          1691–1781

There is a gentle irony in the labels, the 'Age of Challoner' or the 'Church of Challoner', which are frequently used to describe English Catholicism of the eighteenth century. Challoner was without the rhetorical flourish or effulgent personality that evokes similar sobriquets for Dryden, Pope, or Johnson. Rather, the designation recognizes the indefatigable application of the writer whose works consolidated a tradition of English Catholic devotion as well as the unrelenting dedication of the London vicar apostolic whose service helped to transform a far-flung mission into a stable Church and community. His origins were humble, and he owes his conversion at a young age to John Gother. These two great spiritual writers were brought together at Warkworth Manor in Northamptonshire after Gother's exile from London following the 1688 Revolution and Challoner's mother's turn to housekeeping after the death of his father. Under Gother's direction, Challoner left for Douai in 1705 and flourished there as a student, prefect, vice-president, and professor before leaving for the English mission in London in 1730. He nearly returned to Douai as its president in 1738, but he had shouldered the workload of the London vicar apostolic, Benjamin Petre, and was subsequently impressed as his coadjutor and named a bishop. As the vicar apostolic, de facto from 1741 and de jure following Petre's 1758 death, Challoner did not seem to resent the change in his career and energetically devoted himself to the care of his sprawling district. He was most comfortable among the emerging Catholic middle-class of London and was particularly active among the poor, even providing rudimentary medical treatments. He also tried to promote the type of discipline and erudition among the clergy that he demanded of himself in a rigid daily routine of writing, prayer, and service. Amid the hustle of a conscientious vicar apostolic's duties, very few could have maintained the literary pace of the man nicknamed 'Book' at Douai. Yet making room for contemplation amid the world's distractions was one of the key themes in his more than sixty works that recalled the nation's Catholic past in *Memoirs of Missionary Priests* (1741–2) and *Britannia Sancta* (1745) as well as translated texts from the broader Catholic tradition such as St Augustine's *Confessions* (1739) and *The Imitation of Christ* (1737). From *Think Well On't* (1728) to the collection of prayers and devotions that defined the age's spirituality—*The Garden of the Soul* (1740), Challoner's works provided what Eamon Duffy has called 'plain speech directed towards positive action' and distilled a spiritual tradition continuous with St Francis de Sales and St Vincent de Paul. Challoner did not share the aristocracy's anxious need to reclaim Catholics' standing in national society, but he did oversee the general establishment of Catholics as unthreatening, though sometimes still unwelcome, neighbours to Anglicans and dissenters. For this reason, it was particularly tragic that in the last year of his life, Challoner had to flee London during the 1780 Gordon Riots and return to find many of the areas he served badly damaged in the 'no popery' upheaval. Nevertheless, after this violence and a debilitating stroke, Challoner's last utterance, when pointing to a donation to be distributed to the poor, was one word: 'Charity'.

## Introduction to the Devotional Life

The devil, who very well knows that such souls as apply themselves seriously to mental prayer will be none of his, makes all possible efforts to divert Christians from this application by a thousand impostures; and to frighten them with phantoms of imaginary difficulties. But this very opposition of his ought to convince us of the great importance of this exercise and to make us more eager to pursue it, in spite of all his lies and deceits. He pretends the practice of mental prayer is not for all, but only for such as live in convents or colleges; that it requires wit and learning; and that the exercise of it is very difficult. But all this is nothing but a delusion, it is all imposition and lies. Mental prayer, by the way of meditation, is very easy, even to the meanest capacities. It requires nothing but a good will and a sincere desire of conversing with God, by thinking of him and loving him. In effect, the great business of mental prayer is *thinking* and *loving*: and who is there that can even live without *thinking* and *loving*? But then in mental prayer, the *thinking* and *loving* are not confined to such narrow limits, or mean objects, as the thoughts and affections of worldlings are, which lie always grovelling upon the earth. But it has an immense field, opened for its entertainment, of great and everlasting truths, and such as are both highly moving, and of infinite importance to us all; and of great and eternal goods, together with the way to make them all our own. (1)

## A Morning Offering

At your first waking in the morning make the sign of the cross, saying, *In the name of the Father, and of the Son, and of the Holy Ghost*, Amen. *Blessed be the holy and undivided Trinity, now, and for ever*, Amen. Then adore God, and make an offering of your whole being to him for that day and for ever....

Whilst you are dressing and washing yourself, entertain some pious thoughts, and by devout aspirations beg of God to clothe your soul with heavenly virtues, and to wash you clean from all stains of sin. Then say....

I desire to spend this day in thy divine service; and therefore I now offer up to thee all the thoughts, words and actions of this day, that they may all be consecrated to thee by a pure intention of thy greater glory, in union with that pure intention, with which my Lord *Jesus Christ* performed all his actions in his mortal life. I beg that my whole soul, with all its powers, may be ever thine; that my memory may be always recollected in thee; that my understanding may always be enlightened by thy truth, and my will always enflamed by thy love. O! that every breath that I shall take this day might be an act of praise and love of thee; as the blessed in Heaven are every moment praising and loving thee! (2)

## A Petition to the Blessed Virgin Mary

Anth. O Holy Mary, succour the miserable, help the faint-hearted, comfort the afflicted, pray for the people, intercede for the clergy, make supplication for the devout female sex: let all be sensible of thy help, who celebrate thy holy commemoration.

V. Pray for us, O holy mother of God.
R. That we may be made worthy of the promises of Christ.
Let us Pray.

Grant, we beseech thee, O Lord God, that we thy servants may enjoy perpetual health of mind and body; and by the glorious intercession of blessed Mary, ever Virgin, may be delivered from present sorrows, and come to eternal joys, through our Lord Jesus Christ. (3)

## A Prayer for Expectant Mothers

O Lord God Almighty, Creator of Heaven and earth, who hast made us all out of nothing, and redeemed us by the precious blood of thy only Son; look down upon thy poor handmaid here prostrate before thee, humbly imploring thy mercy, and begging thy blessing for herself and her child, which thou hast given her to conceive. Preserve, I beseech thee, the work of thy hands, and defend both me and the tender fruit of my womb from all perils and all evils. Grant me in due time a happy delivery and bring my child safe to the font of baptism, that it may be there happily dedicated to thee, to love and serve thee faithfully for ever. (4)

## The Life of St Helena

Our Island has too good a title to the birth of this holy empress, by immemorial possession and ancient tradition, asserted by all our own historians ... not to give her a place amongst our British Saints. She was born towards the middle of the third century; as some say at York (where there is an ancient church dedicated in her honour), as others affirm at London (the walls of which city she is said to have built, where divers of her medals have been found), or as others will have it at Colchester, said to have taken its name from her father Coel, a British Prince.[1] Her excellent endowments, both of body and mind, recommended her so far to Constantius Chlorus, afterwards Emperor, that he took her to wife; to whom she brought forth the great Constantine, about the year 274. ...

Helena (whom at [Constantine's] first accession to the Empire he had called to his court and declared Augusta or Empress) if she was not beforehand with him, was certainly not long behind in embracing the Christian faith and solid piety, which improved in such manner her natural talents of wit, courage and magnificence as to make her a most perfect pattern of virtue, most worthy of the imitation of princes and great ones. She became not only a Christian, but a most fervent Christian. ...

Her piety particularly showed it self in the Holy Land; to which she took a journey by divine instinct to honour the places sanctified by the mysteries of our redemption. These had been profaned by the infidels, who had built a temple of Venus, in the very place where our Lord suffered on mount Calvary, had erected a statue of Jupiter over his sepulchre, and a temple of Adonis at the place of his birth at Bethlehem. All these the good Empress demolished, and in their stead built those most noble christian churches of the holy sepulchre, or of the cross and resurrection, of our Lord's Nativity at Bethlehem, and of his Ascension on Mount Olivet. ...

But we must not here forget what all antiquity has celebrated as the most glorious of St Helena's achievements in the Holy Land, which was the discovery she there made of the Cross of Christ. This blessed instrument of our redemption had lain long concealed and buried deep in the ground in the place where our Lord was crucified. And no one now living could give the Empress, who earnestly desired to find it, any tidings of it, till at length, having sought it in vain in all parts of Jerusalem, she was

---

[1]  The 'Old King Cole' of nursery rhyme fame.

moved by a divine inspiration to dig for it in the place where she had demolished the temple of Venus, in which at last she discovered the grotto of the sepulchre and not far off three crosses with the title which had been fixed to the cross of our Lord, and the nails which had pierced his sacred hands and feet.... The pious Empress transported with joy at the finding of this treasure ... claimed one part for herself, which she afterwards carried to her son Constantine, together with the nails by which our Saviour was crucified. The other part she enclosed in a case of silver, and deposited in the church of Jerusalem, where it was kept with great veneration and visited by pious Christians from all parts of the world. (5)

## A Prayer for Peace

Anth. Give peace, O Lord, in our days; for there is no other to fight for us, but thou our God.

V. Let peace be made in thy strength.
R. And plenty in thy towers.
Let us pray.

O God, from whom are holy desires, right counsels, and just works, give to thy servants that peace which the world cannot give; that both our hearts may be addicted to thy commandments, and the fear of enemies being taken away, the times may be quiet under thy protection. Through our Lord Jesus Christ. Amen. (6)

## The Death of Thomas à Becket

Archbishop Theobald died in the year 1162, and immediately the Chancellor [Thomas à Becket] was pitched upon to be his successor.... Upon this he was made priest (for he was only deacon before) on Whitsun-Saturday 1162; and on Trinity-Sunday was consecrated archbishop. It was wonderful to see what a change the divine grace made in his soul on this occasion. He presently put off the courtier and put on the prelate, and became in every respect a new man, and a perfect model of all pastoral virtues. He embraced a laborious and penitential life, wore a rough hair shirt next to his skin, arose every morning at two o'clock, and, after reciting his office, washed the feet of thirteen poor men, begging their prayers and giving each of them alms. This done, he took a short repose, and then employed the rest of the morning in reading and meditating on the holy Scriptures, an exercise in which he took great delight.... It is not to be expressed what numbers he daily relieved with food, raiment and other necessaries; what care he took of the sick; and with what vigour he maintained the causes of the weak, against such as sought to oppress them. He reprehended the vices of great ones with a liberty and courage becoming his station, yet tempered with prudence and discretion. And he showed upon all occasions a steady zeal and invincible fortitude in the cause of God and his Church.

This zeal by degrees drew upon our Saint the king's indignation. This prince was not pleased, that upon being made archbishop he had resigned the office of chancellor. But he was much more offended when he found him intent on recovering out of his hands, or out of the hands of his favourites, the possessions or rights which belonged to the church of Canterbury, which they had unjustly usurped. And that he constantly opposed the violences and rapines of the grandees of the court. Particularly he took it ill that he resisted an abuse, that had been introduced, by which the revenues of vacant churches were seized on by the prince; and on this account the bishoprics and abbeys were kept a long time vacant, to increase the revenue of the crown....

Whilst the saint was at Sens, many fruitless attempts were made, as well by the Pope, who employed several legates for that purpose, as by the French king, to accommodate matters between King Henry and the Archbishop. But that Prince still insisted on the customs, as he called them, of his kingdom, which were highly prejudicial to the church; and the saint would by no means consent even to connive at such iniquities. Thus matters went, till at length after seven years banishment, the king relenting, St Thomas was called home, but, as it proved, to die a Martyr....

St Thomas had been but a short time in England, discharging there the office of a zealous pastor, when some of his enemies going over to Normandy...accused him...of disturbing the kingdom and of attempting many things prejudicial to the authority of his Majesty. Upon which, the King, without staying to examine the truth, in the violence of his passion, cursed all those that eat of his bread and had not the courage to revenge his cause and rid him of one priest, who would not suffer him, as he said, to be at peace in his own kingdom. These murdering words, of which the King quickly repented, gave occasion to four of the most resolute of his courtiers to depart immediately for England in order to dispatch the Archbishop....

On the twenty ninth of December, the day after the feast of Holy Innocents, the assassins arrived at Canterbury. And first going to the Archbishop's palace, they loaded him with injuries, which he bore with a wonderful patience and meekness; and whereas they also told him their design was upon his life, he replied, 'He had for this long while made a sacrifice of his life to God; to whom he committed his whole cause; and that if they were come to kill him, he was prepared for them and would not flinch or turn his back in the combat of his Lord.' Then putting his hand to that part of his head where they afterwards gave him his death's wound, *It is here*, said he, *It is here, I wait for you*. With this they went out in a fury and putting on their armour, returned immediately to execute their wickedness. By this time the Archbishop was gone to the church, it being the time of Vespers or Evensong, where his ecclesiastics that were about him would have shut the doors and barricaded them against the violence of those murderers. But the Saint would not suffer it, telling them the church was not to be turned into a castle or camp and therefore ought not to be barricaded. The assassins therefore came in with their drawn swords, crying out, *where is the Traitor? where is the Traitor?* To which words when no one answered, some of them said, *where is the Archbishop?* And then the Saint advanced towards them with an undaunted courage saying, *Here am I, the Archbishop, but no traitor. Thou must now die*, said one of them, *thou canst not escape our hands. I am ready to die*, said the saint, *for my God, for the cause of justice, and for the liberty of the Church, but I charge you in the name of Almighty God, the sovereign Judge, that you hurt none of my monks, of my clergy, or my people.* Then kneeling down he recommended himself and the Church's cause to God, to the prayers of the blessed Virgin, and of the saints, especially of St Dennis the Martyr; and begged God's mercy for his murderers. Of these Tracy, or as others say, Fitz-Orson began the tragedy by offering to discharge a violent blow on the saint's head. . . . Two of the others with equal violence striking him on the head with their broad swords cast him down to the ground, and when he was just expiring, the fourth cut off with one blow the top of his head and drew out his brains on the pavement. Thus was the servant of God martyred in the fifty-second year of his age, in the year 1170. He was buried privately by the monks the next morning, who upon stripping him in order to put on his pontifical robes, found a long and rough hair-shirt next to his skin. . . .

St Thomas was canonized by Pope Alexander the third, in the year 1173. His festivity was ordered to be kept on the twenty ninth of December, and his translation on the seventh of July. His shrine was the richest in the kingdom and the pilgrimage to his tomb the most frequented of any in England. These riches were all sacrilegiously carried off in the times of King Henry VIII, and the relics of the saint were burnt to ashes. (7)

## Seeking God and His Church

The great business of a Christian, and the only end for which God made man, is to know, love, and to serve his Maker in this life, according to that religion which he has instituted, and so to secure to his soul a happy being hereafter in the eternal enjoyment of the Sovereign Good. This is the *one thing necessary* (Luke 10: 42). If this be secured, all is well; if this miscarry, all is lost. It must be therefore of the utmost importance to find out this true way of serving God according to his appointment by making a diligent search which, among this great variety of sects, is the religion of divine institution; and, having found it out, to follow this true way of God and walk according to its directions and precepts.

Whosoever believes a God and a revealed religion must be convinced of the importance of this search. For whosoever believes a God, must believe him to be the Truth, and that he can approve of nothing but the Truth. And whosoever believes that this God of Truth has revealed to man the religion by which and in which he would be worshipped, must also believe that it is the indispensable duty of man in consequence of the will and ordinance of his Maker, to seek out and embrace this true way of worship, which he has revealed . . .

The author is sensible that the things of this world all seem to stand against the Old Religion in this nation: The general prejudice of the people, the penal laws, the authority of the magistrate, the interest of the clergy, the eloquence of the pulpit, the learning of the universities, the favour of men in power, the influence of education; in a word, all temporal considerations of honour, profit and pleasure are visibly on the Protestant side. To balance these worldly advantages, which are apt to have a powerful influence on men's minds, he presents his Catholic reader with a set of motives of a superior nature, which will satisfy him, that if he has the world against him, he has at least God and his Truth on his side. (8)

## The Death of St Margaret Clitherow

On the 26th of March (some say the 25th) of this [1586] or the foregoing year, for authors are divided about the time, Mrs. Margaret Clitherow, whose Maiden Name was Middleton, a gentlewoman of a good family in Yorkshire, was pressed to death at York. She was prosecuted, under that violent persecution raised in those times, by the Earl of Huntington, Lord President of the North. The crime she was charged with was relieving and harbouring priests. She refused to plead that she might not bring others into danger by her conviction or be accessory to the jurymen's sins in condemning the innocent. And therefore, as the law appoints in such cases, she was pressed to death. She bore this cruel torment with invincible patience, often repeating in the way to execution that, 'This Way to Heaven was as short as any other.' Her husband was forced into banishment. Her little children, who wept and lamented for their mother, were taken up, and being questioned concerning the articles of their religion, and answering as they had been taught by them, were severely whipped; and the eldest, who was but twelve years old, was cast into prison. Her life was written by the Reverend and Learned Mr. John Mush, her director, who, after many years labouring with great fruit in the English mission, after having suffered prisons and chains, and received even the sentence of death for his Faith, died at length in his bed, in a good old age, in 1617. (9)

## Last Words of the Elizabethan Martyr Margaret Ward

After eight days she was brought to the bar where, being asked by the judges if she was guilty of that treachery to the Queen and to the laws of the realm of furnishing the means by which a traitor of a priest, as they were pleased to call him, had escaped from justice? She answered, with a cheerful countenance in the affirmative: *And that she never, in her life, had done any thing of which she less repented, than of the delivering that innocent lamb from the hands of those bloody wolves.* They sought to terrify her by their threats and to oblige her to confess where the priest was, but in vain; and therefore they proceeded to pronounce sentence of death upon her, as in cases of felony. But, withal, they told her that the Queen was merciful, and that if she would ask pardon of her Majesty and would promise to go to Church, she would be set at liberty, otherwise she must look for nothing but certain death.

She answered, *That as to the Queen she had never offended her Majesty, and that it was not just to confess a fault, by asking pardon for it, where there was none. That as to what she had done in favouring the priest's escape, she believed the Queen herself, if she had the bowels of a woman, would have done as much, if she had known the ill treatment he underwent. That as to the going to their Church, she had, for many years, been convinced that it was not lawful for her so to do, and that she found no reason now to change her mind and would not act against her conscience; and therefore they might proceed, if they pleased, to the execution of the sentence pronounced against her. For that death, for such a cause, would be very welcome to her; and that she was willing to lay down not one life only, but many, if she had them, rather than betray her conscience, or act against her duty to God and his holy religion.*

She was executed at Tyburn, August 30, 1588, showing to the end a wonderful constancy and alacrity, by which the spectators were much moved and greatly edified. (10)

## The Unexamined Life

Consider those words of the prophet Jeremiah: *With desolation is the whole earth laid desolate, because there is no one who thinks in his Heart* (Jer. 12: 11). And reflect how true it is that the want of consideration on the great truths of Christianity is the chief source of all our evils. Alas! The greatest part of men seldom or never think either of their first beginning, or last end. They neither consider who brought them into the world, nor for what; nor reflect on that eternity, into which they are just about to step. Hence all their pursuits are earthly and temporal, as if they were only made for this life, or were to be always here. Death, Judgement, Heaven and Hell, make but little impression upon them, because they don't give them leisure to sink deep into their souls by the means of serious consideration. (11)

## Human Nature

Every Christian by nature, and inasmuch as he is a man, is the most perfect of all visible creatures, endowed with understanding and reason; composed of a body whose structure is admirable and as a spiritual and immortal soul, created to the image and likeness of God, and capable of the eternal enjoyment of him; enriched with a free-will; and advanced by his Creator, to the dignity of Lord and Master of all other creatures; though not designed to meet with his happiness in any of them, but in the Creator alone. Ah! my soul, hast thou hitherto been sensible of the dignity of thy nature? Hast thou not too often like brute beasts looked no farther than this earth, that is, these present material and sensible things? Hast thou not too often made thyself a slave to creatures, which were only made to serve thee? (12)

## God

God is everywhere. *If I ascend into Heaven*, says the Psalmist, *thou art there; if I descend into Hell, thou art there* (Ps. 138: 8). He fills both Heaven and earth, and there is no created thing whatsoever, in which he is not truly and perfectly present. In him we live, in him we move, our very being is in him. As the birds wherever they fly meet with the air, which encompasses them on all sides; and the fishes swimming in the ocean every where meet with the waters; so we, wherever we are, or wherever we go, meet with God. We have him always with us. He is more intimately present to our very souls, than our souls are to our bodies. (13)

## Hell

The Fires of Hell, with all the rest of the exterior torments which are endured there, are terrible indeed, but in no ways comparable to the interior pains of the soul: that *poena damni*, or eternal loss of God and of all that is good; that extremity of anguish, which follows from this loss; that rueful remorse of a bitter but fruitless repentance, attended with everlasting despair and rage; that complication of all those racking tortures in the inward powers and faculties of the soul, are torments incomparably greater than any thing that can be suffered in the body.

In particular that pain of loss, which in the judgement of divines, is the greatest of all the torments of Hell—though worldlings here have difficulty of conceiving how this can be. Alas! poor sinners, so weak is their notion of eternal goods and so deeply are they immersed in the things of this world, amusing themselves with the variety of created objects, which divert their thoughts from God's sovereign goodness, that they cannot imagine that this loss of God can be so great and dismal a torment as the saints and servants of God, who are guided by better lights, all agree it is. But the case will be quite altered when they shall find themselves in Hell. There they shall be convinced by their own woeful experience what a misery it is to have lost their God. To have lost him totally, to have lost him irrevocably, to have lost him eternally, to have lost him in himself, to have lost him in all his creatures. To be eternally banished from him, who was their only happiness, their last end, and sovereign good, the overflowing fountain of all good; and in losing him, to have lost all that is good, and that for ever. As long as sinners are in this mortal life, they many ways partake of the goodness of God, *who makes his sun to rise upon the good and bad, and rain upon the just and unjust.* All that is agreeable in this world, all that is delightful in creatures, all that is comfortable in life, is all in some measure a participation of the divine goodness. No wonder then that the sinner, while he so many ways partakes of the goodness of God, should not in this life be sensible of what it is to be totally and eternally deprived of him. But in Hell alas! those unhappy wretches shall find that in losing their God, they have also lost all kind of good or comfort, which any of his creatures heretofore afforded. Instead of which, they find all things now conspiring against them, nor any way left of diverting the dreadful thought of this loss, which is always present to their minds and gripes them with inexpressible torments. (14)

## Heaven

If God's justice be so terrible in regard to his enemies, how much more still his mercy, his goodness, his bounty declare itself in favour of his friends. Mercy and goodness are his favourite attributes, in which he most delights. His *mercies*, says the royal prophet, *are above all his works* (Ps. 144: 9). What then must this blessed Kingdom be, which in his goodness he has prepared for his beloved children, for the manifestation of his riches, his glory and magnificence for all eternity. A Kingdom, which the Son of God himself hath purchased for us at no less price than that of his own most precious blood. No wonder then that the Apostle cries out, *That neither eye hath seen, nor ear heard, nor hath it entered into the heart of man, what God hath prepared for those that love him.* No wonder that this beatitude is defined by divines, *as a perfect and everlasting state, replenished with all that is good, without the least mixture of evil* (1 Cor. 2: 9). A general and universal good, filling brimful the vast capacity of our affections and desires, and eternally securing us from any fear or danger of want or change. Ah! Here it is that the servants of God, as the *Psalmist* declares *Shall be inebriated with the plenty of God's House, and shall be made to drink of the torrent of his pleasure*; even of that *fountain of life*, which is with him, and flows from him, into the happy souls for ever and ever (Ps. 35: 9–10).

Although this blessed Kingdom abounds with all that can be imagined good and delightful, yet that there is one sovereign Good, in the sight, love and enjoyment of which consists the essential beatitude of the soul. And that is God himself, whom the blessed ever see face to face, and by the contemplation of this infinite beauty, are set on fire with seraphic flames of love, and by a most pure and amiable union, are transformed in a manner into God himself; as when brass or iron in the furnace is perfectly penetrated by the fire, it loseth its own nature and becometh all flame and fire. Ah happy creatures! What can be wanting to complete your joys, who are in perfect possession of your God, the overflowing source of all good, who have within and without you the vast ocean of boundless felicity? O! The excessive bounty of our God, who giveth his servants in reward of their loyalty so complete a good, which is nothing less than himself, the immense joy of angels. O! Shall not that suffice, my soul, to make thee happy, which makes God himself happy.

The glory and beauty of the heavenly Jerusalem, which the Holy Scripture, to accommodate itself to our weakness, represents to us under the notion of such things, which we most admire here below. So St John in the *Apocalypse*, describing this blessed City, tells us that its walls are of precious stones, and its streets of pure and transparent gold. That these streets are watered with the River of the Water of Life, resplendent as crystal, which flows from the throne of God; and that on the banks of this river on both sides grows the Tree of Life; that there shall be no night nor any sun or moon, but that the Lord God shall be its light for ever. O blessed Jerusalem! O how glorious are the things that are said of thee, O City of God! But what wonder: for if our great God has given us such and so noble a palace here below in this place of banishment, beautified with this sun, moon and stars, accomplished and furnished with this infinite variety of plants, flowers, trees, and living creatures of so many sorts, all subservient to man; if, I say, he has so richly provided for us in this Vale of Tears and region of the Shade of Death, what must our eternal habitation be in the Land of the Living? If here he is so bountiful even to his enemies, in giving them so commodious, so noble a dwelling, what may his friends and servants expect in his eternal Kingdom, in which and by which, he designs to manifest to them his greatness and glory for endless ages in an everlasting banquet, which he has there prepared for his elect? Blessed by all creatures be his goodness for ever.

The blessed inhabitants of this heavenly Kingdom, those millions of millions of angels, of whom the prophet *Daniel*, having seen God Almighty in a vision, tells us that *thousands of thousands administered unto him; and tens of thousands of hundreds of thousands stood before him* (Dan. 7: 10); that infinite multitude of saints and martyrs, and other servants of God of both sexes, gathered out of all nations, tribes and tongues; and above them all, the blessed Virgin Mother of God, Queen of Saints and Angels. Their number is innumerable. But O! Who can express the happiness of enjoying this blessed company? They are all most noble, most glorious, most wise, most holy. They are all of blood royal, all kings and queens, all children and heirs of the most high God—ever beautiful, and ever young, crowned with wreaths of immortal glory, and shining much more brightly than the sun. Their love and charity for one another is more than can be conceived. They have all but one heart, one will and one soul. So the joy and satisfaction of every one is multiplied to as many-fold as there are blessed souls and angels in Heaven, by the inexpressible delight that each one takes in the happiness of all and every one of the rest. Christians, let us imitate their virtues here, that we may come to their happy society hereafter, and with them eternally sing to our God the immortal Songs of *Sion*. (15)

## A Prayer for the Kingdom of God

O Father of lights, and God of all truth, purge the whole world from all errors, abuses, corruptions and vices. Beat down the standard of Satan, and set up every where the standard of Christ. Abolish the reign of sin, and establish the kingdom of grace in all hearts. Let humility triumph over pride and ambition; charity over hatred, envy and malice; purity and temperance over lust and excess; meekness over passion; and disinterestedness and poverty of spirit over covetousness and love of this perishable world. Let the Gospel of Jesus Christ, both in its belief and practice, prevail throughout all the universe.

Grant to us thy peace, O Lord, in the days of our mortality, even that peace which thy Son bequeathed as a legacy to his disciples: a perpetual peace with thee; a perpetual peace with one another; and a perpetual peace within ourselves. Grant that all Christian princes and states may love, cherish and maintain an inviolable peace among themselves. Give them a right sense of the dreadful evils that attend on wars. Give them an everlasting horror of all that bloodshed, of the devastations and ruin of so many territories, of the innumerable sacrileges, and the eternal loss of so many thousand souls, as are the dismal consequences of war. Turn their hearts to another kind of warfare: teach them to fight for a heavenly kingdom.

Remove, O Lord, thy wrath, which we have reason to apprehend actually hanging over our heads for our sins. Deliver all Christian people from the dreadful evil of mortal sin. Make all sinners sensible of their misery. Give them the grace of a sincere conversion to thee and a truly penitential spirit, and discharge them from all their bonds. Preserve all Christendom, and in particular this nation, from all the evils that threaten impenitent sinners such as plagues, famines, earthquakes, fires, inundations, mortality of cattle, sudden and unprovided death, and thy many other judgements here and eternal damnation hereafter. Comfort all that are under any affliction, sickness, or violence of pain. Support all that are under temptation. Reconcile all that are at variance. Deliver all that are in slavery or captivity. Defend all that are in danger. Grant a relief to all in their respective necessities. Give a happy passage to all that are in their agony. Grant thy blessing to our friends and benefactors and to all those for whom we are particularly bound to pray; and have mercy on all our enemies. Give eternal rest to all the faithful departed and bring us all to everlasting life, through Jesus Christ thy Son Amen. (16)

## An Evening Offering

Before you go to bed, read a chapter in the Scripture or some spiritual book. Forecast with yourself the subject of the next morning's meditation and think upon it whilst you are undressing yourself. When you compose yourself in your bed, think on your grave and how quickly death (of which sleep is an image) will be with you, and what your sentiments will then be of all worldly vanities.

Offer up to God your sleep, submitting to it with a pure intention of his holy will, and that by this repose of nature you may recover new vigour to serve him. Wish that every breath you are to take this night might be an act of praise and love of the divine Majesty, like the happy breathings of the angels and saints, who never sleep. And so compose yourself to rest in the arms of your Saviour. (17)

NOTES AND SOURCES

1. Richard Challoner, *Considerations upon Christian Truths and Christian Duties Digested into Meditations for Every Day in the Year* (n.p., 1754). pp. v–vi.

2. Richard Challoner, *The Garden of the Soul: or, A Manual of Spiritual Exercises and Instructions* (London, 1755), 19–20, 24–5.

3. Ibid. 128–9.

4. Ibid. 282–3.

5. Richard Challoner, *Britannia Sancta, or, The Lives of the Most Celebrated British, English, Scottish, and Irish Saints*, 2 vols. (London, 1745), ii. 84–6.

6. Challoner, *The Garden of the Soul*, 129–30.

7. Challoner, *Britannia Sancta*, ii. 326–7, 331–5.

8. Richard Challoner, *The Grounds of the Old Religion* (Augusta, 1742), pp. i–iv.

9. Richard Challoner, *Memoirs of Missionary Priests*, 2 vols. (n.p., 1741–2), i. 189.

10. Ibid., i. 226–7.

11. Richard Challoner, *Think Well On't; or Reflections on the Great Truths of the Christian Religion* (London, 1734), 5–6.

12. Ibid. 20–1.

13. Ibid. 137.

14. Ibid. 82–5.

15. Ibid. 93–8.

16. Challoner, *The Garden of the Soul*, 302–4.

17. Ibid. 165–6.

# Alban Butler                                          1710–1773

A mark of success for a religious writer is for his work to overshadow his own fame and for its vitality to outlive him. While Alban Butler may not be a household name, *Butler's Lives of the Saints* has proved a treasured book for generation after generation. Born in Northhampton-shire, Butler was educated at Dame Alice's school at Lady Well, Fernyhalgh, where he most likely crossed paths with Hugh Tootell, the other great English Catholic historian of the early eighteenth century. As a student in Lancashire and then at Douai, Butler showed a proclivity for learning and piety and was known for sacrificing his sleep for his devotion to books and to prayer. At Douai, he was ordained priest, named a professor, and elected vice-president before leaving to serve on the English mission in 1749. He had helped Richard Challoner research his *Memoirs of Missionary Priests* (1741), an antecedent to Butler's own hagiographic undertaking. Written for the ordinary English Catholic, the four volumes of *Lives of the Fathers, Martyrs and other Saints* (1756–9) required a life's work of historic and linguistic erudition to gather stories from the sacred history of Christianity for every day of the year. His nephew and biographer, Charles Butler, expressed the power of his writings:

The chief merit of his works is that they make virtue and devotion amiable. He preaches penance, but he shows its rewards; he exhorts to compunction, but he shows the sweetness of pious sorrow; he enforces humility, but he shows the blessedness of an humble heart; he recommends solitude, but he shows that God *is* where the world is not. No one reads his work who does not perceive the happiness, even in this world, of a holy life, or who does not wish to die the death of a saint.

While such holy effects have resulted in innumerable editions in many languages, its style and its historical scope even gained the *Lives* the unlikely appreciation of Edward Gibbon. Butler had planned additional works such as biographies of John Fisher and Thomas More, a treatise on natural and revealed religion, and a travel narrative of the Grand Tour, but other duties called. From 1766, he served as the president of St Omer's, where he died in 1773. While any traces of his grave did not outlast the French Revolution, his *Lives* has been an enduring memorial to a man that has been compared to St Francis de Sales.

## The Benefits of Spiritual Reading

As in corporal distempers a total loss of appetite which no medicines can restore forebodes certain decay and death, so in the spiritual life of the soul a neglect or disrelish of pious reading and instruction is a most fatal symptom. What hopes can we entertain of a person to whom the science of virtue, and of eternal salvation, doth not seem interesting or worth his application? 'It is impossible', says St Chrysostom, 'that a man should be saved who neglects assiduous pious reading or consideration. Handicraftsmen will rather suffer hunger and all other hardships than lose the instruments of their trade, knowing them to be the means of their subsistence.' No less criminal and dangerous is the disposition of those who misspend their precious moments in reading romances and play-books, which fill the mind with a worldly spirit, with a love of vanity, pleasure, idleness, and trifling; which destroy and lay waste all the generous sentiments of virtue in the heart, and sow there the seeds of every vice, which extend their baneful roots over the whole soil. Who seeks nourishment from poisons? What food is to the body, that our thoughts and reflections are to the mind. By them the affections of the soul are nourished. The chameleon changes its colour as it is affected by sadness, anger, or joy; or by the colour upon which it sits; and we see an insect borrow its lustre and hue from the plant or leaf upon which it feeds. In like manner what our meditations and affections are, such will our souls become, either holy and spiritual or earthly and carnal. By pious reading the mind is instructed and enlightened, and the affections of the heart are purified and inflamed. It is recommended by St Paul as the summary of spiritual advice.

Devout persons never want a spur to assiduous reading or meditation. They are insatiable in this exercise, and, according to the golden motto of Thomas à Kempis, they find their chief delight *in a closet with a good book.* Worldly and tepid Christians stand certainly in the utmost need of this help to virtue. The world is a whirlpool of business, pleasure, and sin. Its torrent is always beating upon their hearts, ready to break in and bury them under its flood, unless frequent pious reading and consideration oppose a strong fence to its waves. The more deeply a person is immersed in its tumultuous cares, so much the greater ought to be his solicitude to find leisure to breathe after the fatigues and dissipation of business and company. To plunge his heart, by secret prayer, in the ocean of the divine immensity and by pious reading, to afford his soul some spiritual reflection, as the wearied husbandman, returning from his labour, recruits his spent vigour and exhausted strength by allowing his body necessary refreshment and repose.... Though we cannot imitate all the actions of saints, we can learn from them to practise humility, patience, and other virtues in a manner suiting our circumstances and state of life; and can pray that we may receive a share in the benedictions and glory of the saints. As they who have seen a beautiful flower-garden, gather a nosegay to smell at the whole day; so ought we in reading to cull out some flowers by selecting certain pious reflections and sentiments with which we are most affected. And these we should often renew during the day, lest we resemble a man who having looked at himself in the glass goes away, and forgets what he had seen of himself. (1)

## The Epiphany: The Magi's Faith before Christ's Nativity

So far from being shocked at the poverty of the place, and at his unkingly appearance, their faith rises and gathers strength on the sight of obstacles which, humanly speaking, should extinguish it. It captivates their understanding; it penetrates these curtains of poverty, infancy, weakness, and abjection; it casts them on their faces, as unworthy to look up to this star, this God of Jacob. They confess him under this guise to be the only and eternal God. They own the excess of his goodness in becoming man, and the excess of human misery, which requires for its relief so great a humiliation of the Lord of glory.... Where shall we find such a faith in Israel? I mean among the Christians of our days. The wise men knew by the light of faith that he came not to bestow on us earthly riches, but to banish our love and fondness for them and to subdue our pride. They had already learned the maxims of Christ and had imbibed his spirit. Whereas Christians are for the greatest part such strangers to it and so devoted to the world and its corrupt maxims, that they blush at poverty and humiliation and will give no admittance in their hearts to the humility and the cross of Jesus Christ. (2)

## The Meekness of St Francis de Sales

Meekness was the favourite virtue of St Francis de Sales. He once was heard to say that he had employed three years in studying it in the school of Jesus Christ and that his heart was still far from being satisfied with the progress he had made. If he, who was meekness itself, imagined nevertheless that he had possessed so little of it, what shall we say of those, who upon every trifling occasion betray the bitterness of their hearts in angry words and actions of impatience and outrage? Our saint was often tried in the practice of this virtue, especially when the hurry of business and the crowds that thronged on him for relief in their various necessities, scarce allowed him a moment to breathe. He has left us his thoughts upon this situation, which his extreme affability rendered very frequent to him. 'God', says he, 'makes use of this occasion to try whether our hearts are sufficiently strengthened to bear every attack. I have myself been sometimes in this situation. But I have made a covenant with my heart and with my tongue in order to confine them within the bounds of duty. I considered those persons who crowd in one upon the other as children who run into the embraces of their father; as the hen refuseth not protection to her little ones when they gather around her, but on the contrary extendeth her wings so as to cover them all. My heart, I thought, was in like manner expanded, in proportion as the numbers of these poor people increased. The most powerful remedy against sudden movements of impatience and passion is a sweet and amiable silence. However little one speaks, self-love will have a share in it, and some word will escape that may sour the heart and disturb its peace for a considerable time. When nothing is said and cheerfulness preserved, the storm subsides, anger and indiscretion are put to flight, and nothing remains but a joy pure and lasting.... The person who possesses Christian meekness is affectionate and tender towards every one. He is disposed to forgive and excuse the frailties of others. The goodness of his heart appears in a sweet affability that influences his words and actions and presents every object to his view in the most charitable and pleasing light. He never admits in his discourse any harsh expression, much less any term that is haughty or rude. An amiable serenity is always painted on his countenance, which remarkably distinguishes him from those violent characters, who with looks full of fury know only how to refuse, or who when they grant, do it with so bad a grace, that they lose all the merit of the favour they bestow.' (3)

## St Gregory the Great

It was before his advancement to the see of Rome, or even to the government of his monastery, that [St Gregory] first ... projected the conversion of the English nation. This great blessing took its rise from the following occasion. Gregory happened one day to walk through the market and here taking notice that certain youths of fine features and complexion were exposed to sale, he enquired what countrymen they were and was answered that they came from Britain. He asked if the people of that country were Christians or heathens and was told they were still heathens. Then Gregory fetching a deep sigh, said: 'It was a lamentable consideration that the prince of darkness should be master of so much beauty and have so comely persons in his possession, and that so fine an outside should have nothing of God's grace to furnish it within.' (4)

## St Joseph's Attending to our Lord

Aelred, our countryman, abbot of Rievaulx, in his sermon on losing the child Jesus in the temple, observes that this his conduct to his parents is a true representation of that which he shows us, whilst he often withdraws himself for a short time from us to make us seek him the more earnestly. He thus describes the sentiments of his holy parents on this occasion: 'Let us consider what was the happiness of that blessed company in the way to Jerusalem to whom it was granted to behold his face, to hear his sweet words, to see in him the signs of divine wisdom and virtue, and in their mutual discourse to receive the influence of his saving truths and example. The old and young admire him. I believe boys of his age were struck with astonishment at the gravity of his manners and words. I believe such rays of grace darted from his blessed countenance as drew on him the eyes, ears, and hearts of every one. And what tears do they shed when he is not with them.' He goes on considering what must be the grief of his parents when they had lost him, what their sentiments and how earnest their search, but what their joy when they found him again. 'Discover to me,' says he, 'O my Lady, mother of my God, what were your sentiments, what your astonishment and your joy when you saw him again, and sitting not amongst boys, but amidst the doctors of the law? When you saw every one's eyes fixed on him, every one's ears listening to him, great and small, learned and unlearned, intent only on his words and motions. You now say: "I have found him whom I love. I will hold him, and will no more let him part from me." Hold him, sweet Lady, hold him fast. Rush on his neck, dwell on his embraces, and compensate the three days absence by multiplied delights in your present enjoyment of him. You tell him that you and his father sought him in grief. For what did you grieve? Not for fear of hunger or want in him whom you knew to be God, but I believe you grieved to see yourself deprived of the delights of his presence even for a short time. For the Lord Jesus is so sweet to those who taste him that his shortest absence is a subject of the greatest grief to them.' This mystery is an emblem of the devout soul, and Jesus sometimes withdrawing himself and leaving her in dryness that she may be more earnest in seeking him. But above all, how eagerly ought the soul which has lost God by sin seek him again and how bitterly ought she to deplore her extreme misfortune?

The holy family of Jesus, Mary and Joseph presents to us the most perfect model of heavenly conversation on earth. How did those two seraphim, Mary and Joseph, live in their poor cottage? They always enjoyed the presence of Jesus, always burning with the most ardent love for him, inviolably attached to his sacred person, always employed and living only for him. What were their transports in beholding him, their devotion in listening to him, and their joy in possessing him? O heavenly life! O anticipation of the heavenly bliss! O divine conversation! We may imitate them, and share some degree of this advantage, by conversing often with Jesus, and by the contemplation of his most amiable goodness kindling the fire of his holy love in our breasts. The effects of this love, if it be sincere, will necessarily appear in our putting on his spirit, and imitating his example and virtues; and in our studying to walk continually in the divine presence, finding God every where, and esteeming all the time lost which we do not spend with God, or for his honour. (5)

## The Contemplative Life of St Cuthbert

He laboured assiduously among the people to bring them off from several heathenish customs and superstitious practices which still obtained among them. For this purpose ... he often went out, sometimes on horseback, but oftener on foot, to preach the way of life to such as were gone astray. Parochial churches being at this time very scarce in the country, it was the custom for the country people to flock about a priest or ecclesiastical person when he came into any village for the sake of his instructions, hearkening willingly to his words, and more willingly practising the good lessons he taught them. St Cuthbert excelled all others by a most persuasive and moving eloquence, and such a brightness appeared in his angelical face in delivering the word of God to the people, that none of them durst conceal from him any part of their misbehaviour, but all laid their conscience open before him and endeavoured by his injunctions and counsels to expiate the sins they had confessed by worthy fruits of penance. He chiefly visited those villages and hamlets at a distance, which being situate among high and craggy mountains, and inhabited by the most rustic ignorant and savage people, were the less frequented by other teachers. After St Cuthbert had lived many years at Melrose, St Eata, abbot also of Lindisfarne, removed him thither and appointed him prior of that larger monastery. By the perfect habit of mortification and prayer the saint had attained to so eminent a spirit of contemplation that he seemed rather an angel than a man. He often spent whole nights in prayer, and sometimes to resist sleep, worked or walked about the island whilst he prayed. If he heard others complain that they had been disturbed in their sleep he used to say that he should think himself obliged to any one that awaked him out of his sleep, that he might sing the praises of his Creator and labour for his honour. His very countenance excited those who saw him to a love of virtue. He was so much addicted to compunction and inflamed with heavenly desires, that he could never say Mass without tears. He often moved penitents who confessed to him their sins to abundant tears by the torrents of his own which he shed for them. His zeal in correcting sinners was always sweetened with tender charity and meekness....

The life of St Cuthbert was almost a continual prayer. There was no business, no company, no place how public soever which did not afford him an opportunity and even a fresh motive to pray. Not content to pass the day in this exercise, he continued it constantly for several hours of the night, which was to him a time of light and interior delights. Whatever he saw seemed to speak to him of God and to invite him to his love. His conversation was on God or heavenly things, and he would have regretted a single moment which had not been employed with God or for his honour as utterly lost. The inestimable riches which he found in God showed him how precious every moment is in which he had it in his power to enjoy the divine converse. The immensity of God who is present in us and in all creatures, and whom millions of worlds cannot confine or contain; his eternity to which all time co-exists, and which has neither beginning, end, nor succession; the unfathomed abyss of his judgements; the sweetness of his providence; his adorable sanctity; his justice, wisdom, goodness, mercy and love, especially as displayed in the wonderful mystery of the Incarnation, and in the doctrine, actions and sufferings of our Blessed Redeemer; in a word, all the incomprehensible attributes of the Divinity, and the mysteries of his grace and mercy, successively filled his mind and heart and kindled in his soul the most sweet and ardent affections, in which his thirst and his delight, which were always fresh and always insatiable, gave him a kind of anticipated taste of paradise. For holy contemplation discovers to a soul a new most wonderful world, whose beauty, riches and pure delights astonish and transport her out of herself. (6)

## The Quiet Enthusiasm of St Philip Neri

St Philip was one of the best scholars of the age, but being desirous to approach nearer and nearer to Jesus Christ, whose sweet attractions he continually felt in his soul, at twenty-three years of age he sold even his books for the relief of the poor. Often in prayer he was so overwhelmed with spiritual joy and sweetness as not to be able to stand. Sometimes he was heard as he lay prostrate on the ground to cry out: 'Enough, O Lord, enough. Withhold a little at present, I beseech you, the torrent of your sweetness.' And another time: 'Depart from me, O Lord, depart from me. I am yet a mortal man and am not able to bear such an abundance of celestial joy. Behold I die, my dear Lord, unless you succour me.' He used often to say: 'O God, seeing you are so infinitely amiable, why have you given us but one heart to love you, and this so little and so narrow?' It is believed that if God had not, on such occasions, abated or withdrawn his consolations, he must have died through excess of joy, as he himself averred. Humility made him most industrious to conceal his knowledge or science, and much more the extraordinary gifts of grace. For he in all things sought his own contempt. Had not his heart been perfectly empty of itself, the divine love could never have found room in it to overflow in such abundance. So impetuous and so sensible was this love in his breast that it frequently discovered itself in a wonderful manner in his countenance and in the violent palpitation of his heart.... The divine love so much dilated the breast of our saint in an extraordinary rapture that the gristle which joined the fourth and fifth ribs on the left side was broken, which accident allowed the heart and the larger vessels more play, in which condition he lived fifty years. In the midst of a great city, he led for some years almost the life of a hermit. For a long time he ate only bread with a few olives, herbs or an apple, drank only water, and lay on the bare floor. His earnest desire of loving God more perfectly, by being united to him in glory, made him languish continually after that blessed hour when his soul should be freed from the prison of his body, and taking her flight to its origin and centre, should drown itself in the ocean of all good. He was wont to say, that to one that truly loveth God, nothing can happen more grievous than delays of his enjoyment, and than life itself. But then the will of God, and the love of penance and suffering made this delay itself a subject of comfort in which he also rejoiced with St Paul, in as much as by living on earth he was able still to labour in bringing souls to God. His insatiable zeal for the salvation of others drew him often to the exchange and other public places in the city to seek opportunities of gaining some soul to God, or at least of preventing some sin, in which he did wonders. And whilst yet a layman quite changed the face of several public places. He often visited the hospitals, there to comfort, exhort and serve the sick. He lamented to see the custom of waiting on poor sick persons disused in the world, a practice extremely conducive to inspire sentiments of humility and charity....

St Philip, inflamed with the love of God and a desire of praising him worthily, after offering him all the affections of his soul and the homages of all his creatures, seeing in their poverty and inability nothing equal to his infinite greatness, comforted himself in finding in the Mass a means of glorifying him by a victim worthy of himself. This he offered to him with inexpressible joy, devotion and humility, to praise and honour his holy name, to be a sacrifice of perfect thanksgiving for his infinite benefits, of expiation for sin, and of impetration to obtain all graces. Hence in this sacrifice he satiated the ardent desires of his zeal, and found such an excess of overflowing love and sweetness. (7)

## The Assumption of the Blessed Virgin Mary

The Assumption of the Virgin Mary is the greatest of all the festivals which the Church celebrates in her honour. It is the consummation of all the other great mysteries, by which her life was rendered most wonderful. It is the birth day of her true greatness and glory, and the crowning of all the virtues of her whole life, which we admire single in her other festivals. It is for all these gifts conferred on her that we are on this day to praise and thank Him who is the author of them, but especially for that glory with which he hath crowned her. In this we must join our homages and joy with all the blessed spirits in Heaven. What must have been their exultation and triumph on this occasion! With what honour do we think God himself received his mother into his kingdom! What glory did he bestow on her whom he exalted above the highest Cherubim and placed on a throne raised above all the choirs of his blessed spirits! The Seraphim, angels, and all the other glorious inhabitants of his kingdom, seeing the graces with which she was adorned and the dazzling beauty and lustre with which she shone forth as she mounted on high from the earth, cried out in amaze: *Who is she that cometh up from the desert flowing with charms and delights leaning upon her beloved?* Accustomed as they were to the wonders of Heaven, in which God displayeth the magnificence of his power and greatness, they are nevertheless astonished to behold the glory of Mary; and much more so, to see the earth which had been loaded with maledictions and covered with monsters of abomination and horror, now produce so great a treasure and send to them so rich a present. They pronounce it blessed for having given her birth, but their Heaven much more so in now receiving her for eternity. But ought we not rather to stop our inquiries in silent raptures of admiration and praise, than presume to pursue them in an object which is the astonishment of the highest angels? (8)

## St Augustine, Faith, and Reason

[St Augustine's] vanity was soothed and flattered by the Manichees who pretended to try everything by the test of bare reason and scoffing at all those who paid a due deference to the authority of the Catholic Church, as if they shackled reason and walked in trammels. It was by this artifice that he was seduced and caught in their nets. They promised to show him everything by demonstration, banishing all mystery and calling faith weakness, credulity, and ignorance. 'They said that, setting aside *dreadful* authority, they would lead men to God, and free them from all errour by reason alone'.... St Augustine afterward, upon mature consideration, found that it is highly rational, with regard to supernatural truths, to acquiesce in the testimony of God, manifested by an authority of the church derived from him, guided by his unerring Spirit, in conserving unviolated his divine revelation, of which we have the strongest assurance given us by the same revelation, confirmed to us by evident miracles, and other motives of credibility, to which, upon an impartial review, no one can prudently refuse assent. Modern Socinians and others, who boast mightily of making reason their only guide, are driven by their own principles into the most glaring inconsistencies and monstrous absurdities against reason itself, as St Augustine afterward discovered of the ancient Manichees. Whereas reason leads us as it were by the hand to divine revelation, which far from opposing it, shows its insufficiency in things that lie beyond its reach and offers its own noon-day light to direct us safely to the most necessary and important truths. (9)

## The Festival of the Rosary

The Rosary is a practice of devotion, in which, by fifteen Our Fathers, and one hundred and fifty Hail Marys, the faithful are taught to honour our divine

Redeemer in the fifteen principal mysteries of his sacred life, and of his holy Mother. It is therefore an abridgement of the gospel, a history of the life, sufferings, and triumphant victory of Jesus Christ, and an exposition of what he did in the flesh, which he assumed for our salvation. It ought certainly to be the principal object of the devotion of every Christian always to bear in mind these holy mysteries, to return to God a perpetual homage of love, praise, and thanksgiving for them, to implore his mercy through them, to make them the subject of his assiduous meditation, and to mould his affections, regulate his life, and form his spirit by the holy impressions which they make on his soul. The Rosary is a method of doing this, most easy in itself, and adapted to the slowest or meanest capacity; and at the same time most sublime and faithful in the exercise of all the highest acts of prayer, contemplation, and all interior virtues. (10)

## Guardian Angels

Amongst the adorable dispensations of the divine mercy in favour of men, it is not the least that he has been pleased to establish a communion or spiritual commerce between us on earth and his holy angels, whose companions we hope one day to be in the kingdom of his glory. This communion is entertained on our side by the religious veneration with which we honour them as God's faithful, holy, and glorious ministering spirits and beg their charitable succour and intercession with God; on their side by their solicitude and prayers for us, and the many good offices they do us. The providence of God, always infinitely wise, infinitely holy, and infinitely gracious, vouchsafes to employ superior created beings in the execution of his will in various dispensations towards other inferior creatures.... One of the most merciful appointments of God relating to this economy established by him between the blessed angels and men, is, that he commissions chosen high spirits to be particular guardians to each of us. In this providence are displayed the infinite majesty, wisdom and power of God, and the excess of his goodness towards his creatures. Also a deep foundation is laid of the greatest charity and the highest mutual joy in each other between the angels and the elect for all eternity in their happy society of Heaven....

We must not only respect, but gratefully and devoutly love and honour our tutelary spirit. He is a faithful guardian, a true friend, a watchful shepherd and a powerful protector. He is a high spirit of Heaven, and a courtier of the immortal king of glory. Yet his tender charity, goodness and compassion move him, through the divine appointment, to employ his whole power in guarding and defending us. He often protects our bodies, as the devils have sometimes power to hurt them. But what does not he do for our souls? He instructs, encourages, secretly exhorts, and reproves us. He defends us against our enemy, often discovers his stratagems, averts many dangers, and comforts and supports us in our trials, and in the terrible hour of our death. He invisibly performs for us the offices which that angel who led the Jews into the promised land did for them; and which Raphael performed to the younger Toby, in his journey to Rages. For he is our good and sure guide through the dangers of this life to eternal glory. What return shall we make by gratitude, confidence, respect and obedience to this our faithful Raphael, our good angel! What praise and thanks do not we owe to God for so inestimable a benefit! (11)

## The Humble Leadership of St Edward the Confessor

A man must be grounded in perfect humility and has need of an extraordinary strength and grace to bear the weight of honour and not suffer his heart to cleave to it. The height of dignity exposes souls to great dangers, as the highest trees are assailed by the greatest storms. So that a much greater virtue is required to command than to obey. And a Christian ought to learn from the example which Christ has set us, that it is often the safest way to endeavour to fly such posts and that no one ought to receive a place of honour, without being well assured that it is the will of God that calls him to it, and without being resolved to live upon that pinnacle always in fear and trembling, by having constantly the weight of his obligations and the fear of the divine judgements before his eyes. Those who open a door to any secret ambition in their hearts are justly abandoned by God, who says of them: *The kings have reigned, but not by me: they have been princes, and I knew it not.* St Edward was called to the crown by the right door and placed by God on the throne of his ancestors, and had no views but to the advancement of the divine honour, and to the comfort and relief of a distressed people. So far was he from the least spark of ambition that he declared he would by no means accept the greatest monarchy, if it were to cost the blood of a single man. The very enemies of the royal family rejoiced to see Edward seated on the throne. All were most desirous, after so much tyranny, wars, and bloodshed, to have a saint for king, in whom piety, justice, universal benevolence, and goodness would reign and direct all public councils. (12)

## All Saints

In this and all other festivals of the saints, God is the only object of supreme worship, and the whole of that inferior veneration which is paid to the saints is directed to give sovereign honour to God alone, whose gifts their graces are. And our addresses to them are only petitions to holy fellow-creatures for the assistance of their prayers to God for us. When therefore we honour the saints, in them and through them we honour God, and Christ true God and true Man, the Redeemer and Saviour of mankind, the King of the saints, and the source of all their sanctity and glory. In his blood they have washed their robes. From him they derive all their purity, whiteness, and lustre. We consider their virtues as copies taken from him the great original, as streams from his fountain, or as images of his virtues produced by the effusion of his spirit and grace in them. His divine life is their great exemplar and prototype, and in the characteristical virtues of each saint, some of his most eminent virtues are particularly set forth: his hidden life in the solitude of the anchorites; his spotless purity in the virgins; his patience or charity in some; his divine zeal in others; in them all in some degree his plenitude of all virtue and sanctity. Nor are the virtues of the saints only transcripts and copies of the life or spirit of Christ, they are also the fruit of his redemption, entirely his gifts and graces. And when we honour the saints, we honour and praise Him who is the author of all their good. So that all festivals of saints are instituted to honour God and our Blessed Redeemer. (13)

## Saints in the World

By the frequent use of the sacraments, assiduous prayer, pious reading or meditation, and the practice of devout aspirations, we must unite our souls to God. This
crucifixion of self-love and union of our hearts to God are the two general means
by which the Spirit of Christ must be formed and daily improved in us, and by
which we shall be imitators of the saints. This task requires earnest application,
and some consideration and leisure from business.... Against this great application to the means of our sanctification, some object the dissipation and hurry of
the world in which they live. They doubt not but they could do this if they were
monks or hermits. All this is mere illusion. Instead of confessing their own sloth to
be the source of their disorders, they charge their faults on their state and
circumstances in the world. But we have all the reason in the world to conclude
that the conduct of such persons would be more scandalous and irregular in a
monastery than it is in the world. Every thing is a danger to him who carries the
danger about with him. But can any one pretend that seculars can be excused from
the obligation of subduing their passions, retrenching sin, and aiming at perfection? Are they not bound to save their souls; that is, to be saints? God who
commands all to aim at perfection, yet whose will it is at the same time that to
live in the world should be the general state of mankind, is not contrary to himself.
That all places in the world should be filled is God's express command, also that
the duties of every station in it be faithfully complied with. He requires not then
that men abandon their employs in the world, but that by a disengagement of
heart and a religious motive or intention, they sanctify them. Thus has every
lawful station in the world been adorned with saints. God obliges not men in the
world to leave their business. On the contrary, he commands them diligently to
discharge every branch of their temporal stewardship. The tradesman is bound to
attend to his shop, the husbandman to his tillage, the servant to his work, the
master to the care of his household and estates. These are essential duties which
men owe to God, to the public, to themselves, and to their children and families; a
neglect of which, whatever else they do, will suffice to damn them. But then they
must always reserve to themselves leisure for spiritual and religious duties. They
must also sanctify all the duties of their profession.... The Christian who would
please God must carefully exclude in his actions all interested views of self-love
and direct all things he does purely to the glory of God, desiring only to
accomplish his holy will in the most perfect manner. Thus a spirit of divine love
and zeal, of compunction, penance, patience, and other virtues, will animate and
sanctify his labour and all that he does. (14)

## The Immaculate Conception of the Blessed Virgin Mary

The Immaculate Conception of the holy Mother of God was not only in itself a
great and glorious mystery, but likewise joyful to mankind. Certain glimmerings
of the benefit of our Redemption had gone before from the fall of Adam in several
revelations, types, and figures, in which the distant prospect of this wonderful
mercy filled the patriarchs and other saints of the Old Law with comfort and holy
joy. But the conception of Mary displayed the first rays of its approaching light

and may be said to have been its rising morning, or the dawning of its day. In this mystery she appeared pure and glorious, shining among the daughters of Adam as *a lily among thorns* (Cant. 2: 2). To her from the moment of her conception God said: *Thou art all beautiful, my love, and there is no spot in thee* (Cant. 4: 7). She was the *enclosed garden*, which the serpent could never enter, and *the sealed fountain* which he never defiled (Cant. 4: 12). She was the Throne and the Tabernacle of the true Solomon, and the Ark of the Testament to contain, not corruptible manna, but the Author of the incorruptible life of our souls. Saluting her with these epithets, in exultation and praise, let us sing with the church: 'This is the Conception of the glorious Virgin Mary, of the seed of Abraham, sprung from the tribe of Juda, illustrious of the house of David, whose life, by its brightness, illustrates all churches.' (15)

## Christmas

To sanctify this feast, we ought to consecrate it to devotion and principally to the exercises of adoration, praise and love. This is the tribute we must offer to our new born Saviour when we visit him in spirit with the good shepherds. With them we must enter the stable and contemplate this mystery with a lively faith, by which under the veils of this infant body we discover the infinite majesty of our God. And in this mystery we shall discern a prodigy of omnipotence to excite our praise, and a prodigy of love to kindle in our souls the affections of ardent love of God.

To contemplate immensity shut up in a little body, omnipotence clothed with weakness, the eternal God born in time, the joy of angels bathed in tears, is something far more wonderful than to consider God creating a world out of nothing, moving the Heavens, and weighing the universe with a finger. This is a mystery altogether unutterable, to be adored in silence and in raptures of admiration, not to be declared by words. 'How can any one speak of the wonder which is here wrought amongst us?' says St Fulgentius. 'A man of God, a creature of his Creator, one who is finite and was born in time of Him who is immense and eternal.' Here, He who is wonderful in all his works, has outdone what creatures could have known to be possible to Omnipotence itself, had they not seen it accomplished. Another eminent servant of God cries out upon this mystery: 'O Lord our God, how admirable is thy name over all the earth! Truly Thou art a God working wonders. I am not now astonished at the creation of the world, at the Heavens, at the earth, at the succession of days and seasons. But I wonder to see God enclosed in the womb of a virgin, the Omnipotent lain in a manger, the eternal Word clothed with flesh.' Ought we not to invite the heavenly spirits to exert their might in praising the Lord for this incomprehensible effort of his power, goodness and wisdom? To glorify their God in this state of humiliation which his infinite love has moved him to put on to save sinful man? *Adore him, all you his angels. . . .* O! what must have been their sentiments when they saw a stable converted into Heaven by the wonderful presence of its king and beheld that divine infant, knowing his weak hands to be those which framed the universe and bordered the Heavens with light, and that by Him both the heavens and the earth subsist? Are they not more astonished to contemplate him in this humble hidden state than seated on the throne of his glory? In the most profound sentiments of adoration and love they sound forth his praises in the loudest strains, and with their melody fill not only the Heavens, but also the earth. Shall not man, for whom this whole mystery is wrought, and who is so much favoured, and so highly privileged and ennobled by the same, burn with an holy ardour to perform his part in this duty and make the best return he is able of gratitude, adoration and praise? ... In our devotions, also acts of love ought to challenge a principal part, the incarnation of the Son of God being the mystery of love; or properly a kind of ecstasy of love, in which God strips himself as it were of the rays of his glory to visit us, to become our brother, and to make himself in all things like to us.

Love is the tribute which God challenges of us in a particular manner in this mystery. This is the return which he requires of us for all he has done and suffered for us. He says to us: *Son, give me thy heart.* To love him is our sovereign happiness, and the highest dignity and honour to which a creature can aspire. (16)

NOTES AND SOURCES

1. Alban Butler, *The Lives of the Fathers, Martyrs, and other Principal Saints*, 4 vols. (London, 1756). i, pp. iii–iv, ix.
2. Ibid., i. 41.
3. Alban Butler, *The Lives of the Fathers, Martyrs, and other Principal Saints*, 12 vols. (Dublin, John Exshaw, 1779), i. 430–1.
4. Alban Butler, *The Lives of the Fathers, Martyrs, and other Principal Saints*, 4 vols. (London: 1756), i. 437.
5. Alban Butler, *The Lives of the Fathers, Martyrs, and other Principal Saints*, 12 vols. (Dublin, John Exshaw, 1779), iii. 218–19, 221.
6. Ibid. 223–4, 228–9.
7. Alban Butler, *The Lives of the Fathers, Martyrs, and other Principal Saints*, 4 vols. (London, 1756), ii. 456–7, 469.
8. Alban Butler, *The Lives of the Fathers, Martyrs, and other Principal Saints*, 4 vols. (London, 1757). iii, 497–9.
9. Ibid. 682–8.
10. Ibid. 24.
11. Alban Butler, *The Lives of the Fathers, Martyrs, and other Principal Saints*, 4 vols. (London, 1759), iv. 33–4, 40–1.
12. Ibid. 248.
13. Ibid. 459–61.
14. Ibid. 469–71.
15. Alban Butler, *The Lives of the Fathers, Martyrs, and other Principal Saints*, 12 vols. (Dublin, 1780). xii. 177–8.
16. Ibid. 319–21.

# Thomas West (alias Daniel) SJ                                    1720–1779

The services by priests on the English mission were not always directly religious, nor was their guidance always primarily spiritual. This is true of the Scottish-born Jesuit Thomas West (alias Thomas Daniel). He was educated in Edinburgh and seems to have travelled extensively as a merchant before studying at St Omer's and then Liège. It is notable that he was received into the Society of Antiquaries in 1751 before entering the Society of Jesus. His assignments on the English Mission around Ulverston, Kendal, and other parts of the Northwest allowed him to fulfil both vocations. In 1778, he published his *Guide to the Lakes*, which the poet of the Lake District, William Wordsworth, described as 'eminently serviceable to the Tourist for nearly 50 years'. Capturing and contributing to the growing popularity of the Lakes' 'picturesque' qualities, West conducted visitors to 'stations' where they could attain the most beautiful views and appreciate Creation with the eyes of a landscape painter. The *Guide* went through eleven editions by 1821 and was superseded by Wordsworth's own *Guide through the District of the Lakes*. In this work, Wordsworth drew not only on West's guide to the landscape but also his contribution to the history of Wordsworth's 'native Country'. *The Antiquities of Furness; or, an Account of the Royal Abbey of St Mary, in the Vale of Nightshade, near Dalton in Furness* (1774) included an exploration of the Reformation's effects on the countryside and the populace surrounding Furness Abbey in present-day Cumbria. Currently a national heritage site, the striking red sandstone ruins of the former Cistercian abbey still leave visitors, in the phrase of Wordsworth, surveying the way 'havoc tired and rash undoing' have left

> a structure famed
> Beyond its neighbourhood, the antique walls
> Of that large abbey which within the Vale
> Of Nightshade, to St Mary's honour built,
> Stands yet, a mouldering pile, with fractured arch,
> Belfry, and images, and living trees,
> A holy scene!

## Peaceful and Pastoral Monasticism in England

The introduction of monks into England is spoken of as a masterpiece of policy in the court of Rome, as endeavouring thereby to secure her authority by an increase of property, which would arise to her from the pious donations and offerings of the faithful, and the founding of many religious houses to be occupied by such as were from the nature of their institute attached to the holy see and might occasionally serve every purpose of spiritual tyranny; and it is alleged that the monks, by the austerity of their religion and morals, fascinated the minds of the people, and by their pretension to extraordinary sanctity secured a submission to all their decisions and an implicit obedience to their doctrines. This is a heavy charge, and, if well grounded, should have prevented the monastic rule from ever taking effect in any kingdom, or occasioned its ruin as soon as the discovery was made or the charge found. But notwithstanding what has been so often and repeatedly offered, we find monasteries were established in this island long before the era of Augustine the monk, the time when her close connection with Rome is said to have taken place. We are informed by Gildas, who was himself a monk of the famous monastery of Bangor, in Flintshire, that monasteries in Britain were of a higher antiquity than the connection with the Holy See, supposing, with Rowland and others, these to have taken place at the coming of St Augustine into England. Venerable Bede, who flourished about a hundred and thirty years after the destruction of the monastery of Bangor, says that the monks of that house were divided into seven classes, each class having its respective employment; and the learned primate Ussher speaks of it as a school of Christian learning for the improvement of Christian knowledge and supplying the faithful with fit pastors; and adds, that it afterwards became the famous monastery of Bangor ys Coed. In all this, we hear nothing of foreign connections, of sinister inventions, of hypocrisy. When the Saxons took occasion to butcher twelve hundred of the monks and utterly erase the monastery, they were not found in arms, but in prayer, for the defence of themselves and their country against those invaders. The monastic institute, in the early periods, seems to have been favourable to the cause of Christianity. (1)

## The Piety of Pre-modern English Catholics

It might here be observed, that the same spirit appeared in the two succeeding reigns as there did in this; in which period, of less than ninety years, three hundred religious houses were founded, being just so many spiritual corporations instituted for the support of religion, the perpetuating the rights of the church, the maintaining of ecclesiastical discipline, the encouragement of piety, and the advancement of goodly learning; by all which the kingdom must have received some advantages, the direct and principle object of these pious institutions. Whatever inconvenience afterward accrued to the government and people under the reigns of impotent princes, yet were they not the necessary consequence of such institutions, but of the intriguing ambition of artful and designing men, such as have often disturbed, and sometimes subverted, the best establishments to answer the vilest purposes; and for enhancing power to themselves and enslaving their fellow subjects. What improvements have been made in the polity of state and religion since, I leave to the reader's judgement, but let every illiberal reflection cease, which would stain with ignominy, or contempt, the leading principle of these good men, who to the best of their understanding laid the foundation of our present happy establishment here, after many struggles even unto blood. Let us allow them the honour of having planned many good things and invented many useful constitutions both in church and state. Let us thank them for what they have done well and improve upon what remains, that posterity may not with more justice blame the refinement of the present age, than the managers now with charity do ridicule the rude polity and flaming piety of a noble and illustrious race of men. (2)

## Injustices Committed in the Dissolution of the Monasteries

In the reign of Henry VIII there were extant the most honourable marks of our forefathers' piety, monuments erected to the honour of God, to the propagation of virtue, the encouragement of learning, and help of the poor, since the highest period of Christianity, religious houses, monasteries, abbeys, priories. . . . In 1536, all houses of 200l. per annum, and under, were, with consent of parliament, given to the king and suppressed, in number 376. The following year, the remaining number were also suppressed, with 96 colleges, 110 hospitals, and 2374 chantries and free chapels. Thus the stately edifices and immense wealth, which had been the work of many ages to accumulate, were defaced, destroyed, dissipated, and squandered away in a moment; the annual revenues of which amounted to 160,000l. being more than one third of all the church revenues in the kingdom; besides the sums made of every article that had a name, even to the hedge-row trees, which were valued and sold. No wonder then that such sacrilegious rapine astonished the whole Christian world, but the king's passions admitted of no alternative. A parliament was summoned, which by its unlimited power might legalise these acts of cruelty and oppression by a transcendent decree. The act, however, was drawn up with such care and circumspection, as to remove all suspicion of hard usage and forced surrenders; and the king was to be solicited by the parties to accept of their surrender, as is seen in the surrender deed of the abbey of Furness. The whole was varnished over with a vast prospect of advantage to the public. The nobility were taught to believe that they should have large shares in the spoils, either by free gifts, easy purchases, or advantageous exchanges. The gentry were flattered with the hopes of a very considerable rise in honour and estate, nor were they disappointed, for a considerable part of the abbey lands were granted out by lease, or otherwise, before the meeting of parliament. And thus it was that the minister secured his scheme by interesting many of the nobility and commons in support of it. (3)

## The Countryside and the Dissolution of the Monasteries

The dissolution of the abbey greatly affected both the civil and domestic state of Low Furness, which for the space of four hundred years had been improving either by the labour of the monks at their first coming, and during the first fervour of their institute, or by the encouragement afterwards given to their tenants and vassals. But to this, the dissolution gave a sudden check. The large demands for provisions of all kinds, occasioned by constant hospitality, and the frequent concourse of company resorting to the abbey, dropped at once. The boons and rents in kind were now no longer paid. A small acknowledgement in money was all that was required, or could be expected, from so small a tract of insulated land. Thus agriculture received a fatal blow. The means were first neglected, then forgot. The fertile fields and spacious lawns, which had given a name to Plain Furness, waved no more with the rich harvest of silver wheat. (4)

NOTES AND SOURCES

1. Thomas West, SJ, *The Antiquities of Furness; or, an Account of the Royal Abbey of St Mary, in the Vale of Nightshade, near Dalton in Furness* (London, 1774), 16–17.

2. Ibid. 20.

3. Ibid. 115–16.

4. Ibid. 121.

# Joseph Reeve SJ                                    1733–1820

In the writing of Joseph Reeve, there is a sustained attempt to translate and communicate glory. To do so often meant reaching into the past. The Jesuit Reeve, who was educated at St Omer's College and later became a teacher of humanities there for eight years, wrote a historical narrative about the 1762 forced relocation of that institution to Liège due to the French parliament's persecution of the Society. He did not follow the college on to Bruges when the Jesuits were suppressed in 1773. Instead, from 1767 until his 1820 death, he served as chaplain to the Catholic Clifford family at Ugbrooke Park in Devon. Even as he celebrated the survival of this pre-Reformation Catholic manor house whose grandeur still attracts the public today, he turned his attention to the lost glory of the nearby coastal Torre Abbey, which belonged to the Norbertines before the Reformation. He also composed an abridged scriptural history and church history. Some of his recovery projects made less immediate sense: for example, he undertook translations of the great English writing of Addison, Dryden, and Pope *into Latin*. His more successful work, however, derived from bringing the religious humanism of St Augustine *into English*. His *Practical Discourses* (1788, 1793) meditate on how men and women living in eighteenth-century England can come to approach knowledge of the mysterious, infinite, and transcendent characteristics of God. His eulogist captured the continued resonance of Reeve's writings: *'Though dead, he speaks*, and movingly exhorts us to serve Our Creator in holiness and justice during the remainder of our existence.'

## Recalling the Lessons of Torre Abbey

Shall Brixham's strand glow in th'historic page,
And brighter Torr no poet's pen engage?
Tho' hallow'd mitres glitter there no more,
The friendly Abbey still adorns the shore.
There verdant meads, there hills and wood conspire
To charm the sight and fan the Muse's fire.
Wide-stretching rocks majestically bold
Th'embosomed bay within the land infold,
There Britain's fleets secure at anchor lie,
Hear tempests howl, and all their rage defy.
There meek religion's ancient temple rose,
How great, how fall'n, the mournful ruin shows.
Of sacrilege behold what heaps appear,
Nor blush to drop the tributary tear.
Here stood the font; here on high columns raised
The dome extended; there the altar blazed.
The shattered aisles, with clust'ring ivy hung,
The yawning arch, in rude confusion flung,
Sad-striking remnants of a former age,
To pity now might melt the spoiler's rage.
Lo! sunk to rest the wearied vot'ry sleeps,
While o'er his urn the gloomy cypress weeps.
Here silent pause, here draw the pensive sigh,
Here musing learn to live, here learn to die. (1)

## The Whole of Knowledge

Let the proud philosopher examine the whole creation through in his search after knowledge, let him be skilled in every art and science, let him study nature in all its works, let him dive into the deep recesses of the sea, and sift the bowels of the earth, let him trace the shining orbs and planets in their vast revolutions through the Heavens and number the stars of the firmament. But should he rest there and lift up his mind to nothing higher, something will be still wanting to dignify his knowledge and to make it profitable unto eternal life. *For though I should be master of every science*, says St Paul; *though I should be able to disclose the most hidden secrets, and with the certainty of a prophet foretell future events, yet without charity I am nothing in the sight of God*. The humble peasant, whose only study is to know, to serve, and honour God by a right intention in all he does, is in the order of grace not only a better, but also a wiser man. The invisible perfections of our great Creator are made manifest to us by the visible beauties of the creation, says the same Apostle to the Romans, and from viewing the things that are made, we rise to the knowledge of Him who made them, even so as to adore his eternal power and divinity. (2)

## The Little Way

A devout consideration of the divine perfections is within the reach of the meanest capacity. Every Christian, however destitute of human learning, has the capacity of knowing God, of confessing his providence, of admiring his justice, of loving his goodness, and of adoring his wisdom. In the humble performance of our prayers and other spiritual duties we need no shining talents, no sublime variety of thought, nor any eminent gift of contemplation. To enable us to love and serve God, it is not necessary that we should possess either power, or riches, or learning. Such qualities may entitle us indeed to some notice in the world, but without humility, without piety and charity, they are of little value in the sight of God.

To those, who are little in their own eyes, our heavenly Father communicates his favours more abundantly, and while he resists the proud, on the humble only he bestows the grace of true wisdom. I give thee thanks, O Father, Lord of Heaven and earth, says our blessed Saviour, because thou hast hidden these things from the wise and prudent and hast revealed them to little ones. (3)

## The Presence of God

To enjoy the presence of God in the manner that is suited to our mortal state, it is not necessary to ascend in spirit into Heaven, as if he resided no where else. To converse with him, to warm our affections for him, to communicate our sentiments to him, and to unite our hearts intimately with him, we have but to rouse our faith, and we shall find him always by us, always with us, and always in us. *For he is not at any distance from each one of us*, says St Paul, *in him we live, in him we move, and in him we have our very being*.

A fish swimming in the sea is not so thoroughly encompassed by the watery deep, as we are by the divine immensity: for the sea has its bounds, immensity has none. Whichever way we move, and to whatever point we direct our steps, it is still within the ocean of that boundless immensity of God, which surrounds and invests us on every side. God by his essence is not only diffused around us in the light we see and in the air we breathe, he is moreover infused into our very souls within us. He penetrates our whole substance, he infolds and carries us in his bosom: so that we cannot move a hand or foot, which he is not witness of, nor form a passing thought, which he does not see, nor speak so much as a single word, which he does not hear. The immensity of God therefore constitutes the most intimate and the most perfect connection that can possibly exist between the Creator and his creatures. (4)

## The Goal of our Restless Hearts

Great God, how ineffable is this thy goodness, how wonderful thy love! Thou hast created us with no other design, than to make us happy with thyself. Thou hast enlightened our minds to know thee, thou hast moved our wills to love thee, thou hast dilated our hearts to receive thee, thou hast cleansed and sanctified our souls to possess thee. O Lord, thou art the God of our salvation. Thou inspirest us with holy desires, that we may seek thee; thou helpest our endeavours, that we may serve thee; thou directest our steps, that we may find thee; and when we have the happiness to find, it is then thou teachest, how sweet thy service is to those who love thee. (5)

## The Enlightenment of Divine Wisdom

O divine Wisdom, come timely to our aid and dispel the clouds of infidelity that gather from every quarter round us. Come, and point out our way through the dark and intricate mazes, that divide and perplex our progress. Under thy direction we shall never err, under thy guidance we shall never stray. Under the influence of thy divine rays enlightened will be our reason, considerate will be our words, and prudent will be our steps in the pursuit of our last end. For they, who are actuated with thy spirit, always keep their last end in view and steadily pursue it. (6)

## The Excess of God

By the light God has stamped upon us we are enabled to form the most noble and the most sublime ideas of his divinity. But however noble and sublime our ideas may be of him, they fall infinitely short of what he is in himself. God is great, God is holy, God is powerful, God is wise; but his wisdom, his power, his holiness, and his greatness infinitely surpass every idea we can form of them. For our ideas are always suited to the capacity of our understanding, which being imperfect and limited by nature, can never comprehend the infinite and unbounded essence of divine perfection. When from the magnificent works of the creation we raise our thoughts to the invisible Creator of them, or when, as the holy Scripture represents him, we contemplate the self-existing Lord of all things, sitting upon his throne of glory and shaking the heavens with the splendour of his majesty, or directing the motion of the stars and planets in the firmament by his omnipotence, or pressing upon the hills and mountains of the earth, and bending them down with the journeys of his eternity, we conceive but little of his plenitude of perfection. For God is not only all that which his prophets have so sublimely spoken of him, but he is infinitely more. He is infinitely more majestic, more beautiful, more holy and more perfect than the most enlightened mind of man can possibly conceive. Hence the holy Fathers in speaking of the nature of God unanimously agree, that it is easier to say what he is not, than to say what he is. For of him we can say no more than what he has been pleased to reveal, and even in that we can speak no otherwise than conformably to the language, which he has taught us in the inspired writings. (7)

NOTES AND SOURCES

1.  Joseph Reeve, SJ, 'Ugbrooke Park: A Poem', in *Miscellaneous Poetry in English and Latin* (London, 1794), 4–5.

2.  Joseph Reeve, SJ, *Practical Discourses upon the Perfections and Wonderful Works of God*, 2 vols. (Exeter, 1793), i. 3–4.

3.  Ibid. 15–16.
4.  Ibid. 78–9.
5.  Ibid. 223.
6.  Ibid. 164.
7.  Ibid. 285–7.

## Charles Plowden SJ                                                    1743–1821

Charles Plowden's 1790 sermon at the consecration of America's first bishop, John Carroll of Baltimore (1735–1815), not only celebrates that important occasion but also represents the personal and ecclesiastical connections between the Catholic Church in England and the new nation's Catholics. Until Carroll's installation in the new see, all Catholics in the American colonies were governed from a distance by the London vicar apostolic. The ties were more extensive as Carroll and his friend and fellow Jesuit Plowden were both educated at English institutions on the Continent. They underwent hardship together when the Austrian authorities arrested them at the English college at Bruges as part of the 1773 suppression of the Jesuit order. Their relationship would also survive the American Revolution as Carroll unsuccessfully attempted to persuade Plowden to lead the fledgling American college that would become the great Jesuit seat of learning in the heart of the United States capital, Georgetown University. Instead Plowden would go on to become a chaplain to the Weld family in Dorset, a prominent opponent of the Cisalpine movement, and the provincial and rector of Stonyhurst after the restoration of the Jesuits. So when, at Lulworth Castle's Chapel of St Mary's, Plowden commemorates the consecration of a new bishop by an older nation who would not have their hierarchy restored until 1850, he is also speaking of the way faith and friendship endure and transcend the trials of history.

## English Catholicism and the United States

Our blessed Lord and Redeemer, having defeated the powers of hell, by the triumph of the cross, formed to himself a kingdom on earth, which was to consist of the chosen of every nation; because all nations were now become his own, by right of conquest. The sun of justice, which rose from the east, has in its progress enlightened every region of the globe: and the kingdom of Christ, the Church, under the government of his Vicar and of pastors deputed by him, has successively embraced the whole world. Ages succeed ages; empires subvert empires. But the empire of Jesus Christ perseveres ever one and the same, ever persecuted and ever conquering. Because all human revolutions are entirely subservient to it, and the formation of the kingdom of Christ is the ultimate object of the whole dispensation of providence in the government of this world. Never, perhaps, was this truth more sensibly evinced than in the late violent convulsions, by which the hand of the Almighty has dismembered the great British empire and has called forth into existence a new empire in the Western world, the destinies of which, we trust, are founded in his tenderest mercies. For although this great event may appear to us to have been the work, the sport of human passions, yet the earliest and most precious fruit of it has been the extension of the kingdom of Christ, the propagation of Catholic religion, which, heretofore fettered by restraining laws, is now enlarged from bondage, and is left at liberty to exert the full energy of divine truth....

It is to be observed, that if Britain infected them with error, we have the consolation to know, that their Catholicity is also derived immediately from us; and as we, in former ages, received the faith of Rome from the great St Gregory and our Apostle St Augustine; so now, at the interval of twelve hundred years, our venerable prelate, the heir of the virtues and labours of our Apostle, will, this day, by commission from the successor of St Gregory, consecrate the first Father and Bishop of the new church.... Glorious is this day, my brethren, for the church of God, which sees new nations crowding into her bosom; glorious for the prelate elect, who goes forth to conquer these nations for Jesus Christ, not by the efforts of human power, but in the might of those weapons which have ever triumphed in this divine warfare. He is not armed with the strength of this world, but he is powerful in piety, powerful in zeal, powerful in evangelical poverty and firm reliance on the protection of that God who sends him. Glorious is this event... honourable and comforting is this awful solemnity to his and our common benefactor, the founder of this holy sanctuary, which shall be revered through succeeding ages, even by churches yet un-named, as the privileged, the happy spot, from whence their episcopacy and hierarchy took their immediate rise. And this precious distinction will be justly attributed to the protection and favour of the glorious mother of God. (1)

NOTES AND SOURCES

1. Charles Plowden, *A Short Account of the Establishment of the New See of Baltimore, in Maryland, and of Consecrating the Right Reverend Dr. John Carroll, First Bishop thereof, on the Feast of the Assumption, 1790* (London, 1791), 7–10.

# Peter Newby                                      1745–1827

The eventful and in many ways frustrated life of the poet and educator, Peter Newby, shows the restrictions and promise of Catholic life in England on the cusp of Emancipation. Newby was born near Kendal in Horncop Hall, a house where Mass was clandestinely celebrated. He followed a fairly typical course in his early years, gaining an education first at Dame Alice Harrison's school at Fernyhalgh and then at Douai. Yet when he realized he did not have a vocation to the priesthood, he was an educated young man whose prospects were heavily restricted due to the penal laws. Subsequently, he took a job on a slave ship out of Liverpool and spent two years in West Africa and Jamaica. The lasting effect of what he would later call 'scenes that would have shocked even apathy itself and made the sternest stoic weep' were recorded in his 1788 anti-slavery poem *Almoona, or, The African's Revenge*. After his return in 1766, he turned to education, first as an assistant to the Anglican schoolmaster Batholomew Booth and later as schoolmaster at his own academy near the former site of Dame Harrison's school in Fernyhalgh, Lancashire. This despite the fact that Catholic schools were illegal until 1791. During this time, he also married and fathered five children. When the school closed its doors in 1797, he started an unsuccessful printing business in Preston dedicated largely to Catholic books. Left to eke out an existence from private tutoring, he ended up receiving aid from the Broughton Catholic Charitable Society, which he himself had helped to found. All of these foundering hopes and ambivalent enterprises are expressed in his poetry, published in the 1773 *Six Pastorals* and two-volume 1790 *Poems*. The anxieties and simple humanity of a man known as 'the poet of Preston' do not dovetail either with the composed neoclassical balance or the forceful romantic surges characteristic of his age's literature. In their familial and local attachments and their unease about the poet's place in English society, they do, however, convey the difficulties and consolations of English Catholic life before the turn of the nineteenth century.

## Contemplating Nature

Whether we view the branching deer
    Swiftly rebounding o'er the mead;
Or the mild sheep, senseless of fear,
    Climbing the cliff's high head:
Whether some gentle river's murm'ring fall
    Strikes on our ears, embrowned with aged woods;
Or, in some pleasant, wild, romantic vale,
    A winding current flows in stronger floods;
Still the grand views of nature are complete,
    And every change is beautiful and great.

These are thy works, author of light;
    This sweet variety thy plan,
Formed for the rapturous delight
    Of thine image—Man!
Shall then the good and virtuous heart refrain,
    When contemplation blazons ev'ry view,
When it beholds thy mild, benignant reign,
    To pay the homage to thy goodness due?
No, Virtue cries, 'Thy Godhead we'll obey,
Each night we'll praise thee, and adore each day.' (1)

## Solitude and Contemplation

With thee thy votary e'er shall choose
Beneath the aged oaks to muse,
Who, wide, their friendly arms extend,
From scorching sun-beams to defend
    My solitary way;
Or, length'ning far the ev'ning shade,
Romantic make each curving glade,
    To close the waning day.

Or let me sit, in pensive thought,
    Near a slow, creeping stream,
My mind, with resignation fraught,
    Wrapt in some solemn theme.
Then as its gliding course I see,
Secreted from the world with thee,
Let me reflect; thus pass my days,

And to my God my homage raise,
    With fervency and zeal;
Its murmurs, as it flows along,
And babbles to my plaintive song,
    My list'ning heart shall feel. (2)

## Religious Liberty for Catholics

FREEDOM! thou genius of my native isle,
Thou guardian goddess of each gen'rous mind,
Wishful I long to meet thy open smile,
And in my breast thy happy influence find.
Hail! heav'n-born maid! whose countenance benign,
On which all graces and all virtues shine,
Diffuses wide an universal joy
Where e'er thy liberal dictates spread their sway,
Whose roseat charms were never known to cloy,
For independence marks thy envied sway.
Hail! heav'n-born maid! oh! might'st thou dwell
with me,
Who in the land of freedom am not free!
   ...
Yes, rise, ye lib'ral souls, who greatly soar
Above the vulgar, plead their noble cause—
Freedom, enamoured, will your names adore,
Who help t'expunge those shameful Penal Laws
That hang with gloominess o'er all their days—
And merit ev'ry good man's warmest praise.
Nations around with plaudits shall repay
The deed, and emulate th' example shown,
While grateful thousands to your hearts convey
The blessings begged from heav'n's all-seeing throne.
You will exult to see your neighbours blest,
And genuine joy shall warm each gen'rous breast.

But if vain, idle fears, must still disgrace,
And narrow prejudices clog the mind,
Grant me, at least, my neighbour to embrace,
Fond of his virtues, to his errors blind;
His principles shall never weigh with me—
My brothers in my countrymen I see.
But yet, thou greatest bliss that man can know,
At whose sweet name my soul is all on fire,
Who mak'st my longing hopes with transports glow,
And give up ev'ry other fond desire,
Oh! come, at length, propitious smile on me,
Give me new life, and tell me I am free.

Else better dwell on some far distant shore,
Where FREEDOM roams at large, and plants her shed,
Where nature scatters, from her bounteous store,
Rich scraps of land, where wand'ring flocks are fed.
There, master of myself, from insults free,
I might enjoy the sweets of LIBERTY.
The pleasures of this clime I would forgo,
The sycophantic smile, the servile air—
I only then should with my God to know,
And freely would resign each worldly care:
There, undisturbed, my altar I could raise,
And as I pleased th' Almighty I could praise. (3)

NOTES AND SOURCES

1.  Peter Newby, 'Ode to Morning', in *Poems*, 2 vols. (Liverpool, 1790), i. 6–9, 8–9.

2.  Peter Newby, 'Ode to Solitude', ibid., i. 10–14, 11.

3.  Peter Newby, 'Ode III. Religious Liberty', ibid., i. 91–4; 91, 93–4.

## Joseph Berington                                                   1746–1827

The historian Eamon Duffy has argued that Berington was the 'one man' who formulated the
theoretical framework of the English Catholic Cisalpine movement, now sometimes referred
to as the 'English Catholic Enlightenment', and that later 'supporters rallied to the banner he
had raised'. There has not been neutral ground in assessing Berington and his work as he was
assailed by Bishop Milner and others in his own day for heterodox theological teaching and
considered as a possible 'prophet of ecumenism' in our own. The Herefordshire-born Berington was educated and ordained at Douai, where he was a professor of philosophy until his
censure by Alban Butler for advancing anti-scholastic and materialistic metaphysical principles. He returned to the English mission and served as Sir John Throckmorton's chaplain from
1793 until his death. His works show an incredible range, including a controversial history of
English Catholicism, a survey of Patristic doctrine, medieval historiography, and apologetic
and polemical works addressed to both Catholic and non-Catholic audiences. There are
discernible themes that unite them, however. Berington tended to distance Catholicism
from any medieval characteristics and called for a return of Christianity to a primitive form
that was simple, clear, and reasonable. Such characteristics accorded not only with Enlightenment rationality—the following critique of materialism takes the form of a letter *to* not
*against* the Unitarian sage and scientist Joseph Priestley—but also mainstream English
Protestantism. His position tended to limit the authority of the Papacy, and, following
nationalizing Gallican ecclesiastical models, craft a culturally English model of the Church.
This in turn promoted a social and political programme as Berington and others believed such
conciliation would lead to toleration and reintegration into society through legislative relief
from the penal laws. Berington, however, remains an elusively complex individual and
thinker. He challenged the popular Evangelical writer Hannah More for her anti-Catholicism,
asking her to 'have the goodness to drop the insulting words, *Papist*, popery, and *Romanist*'
from her theological tracts. In addition, he was also the first Catholic priest in England to
eschew unobtrusive brown dress in favour of wearing black clerical attire in public.

## The Progress of the Reformation

In Germany, another spirit brooded in the public mind, indicating discontent, impatience of grievances, and an anxious, but undefined, wish of change. Their complaints had often been heard, but no redress had been obtained. With the rest of Europe they complained that the power exercised by the Roman bishops was exorbitant and oppressive; that their legates and other agents were rapacious and arrogant; that the manners of the higher and lower clergy and of the monks were disorderly and dissolute; and they loudly demanded, as their fathers had done, a Reformation of the Church in its head and in its members. It would have been well had these complaints been patiently heard and wisely redressed. This unfortunately was not the case, and not many years later, that *revolution* followed, which, in the Christian world, produced a series of events, which were to many the source of manifold evils, and to some of partial good. The cause of literature was, eventually, benefited. But could it have been thus benefited by this alone? Or was the character of the northern nations really become so torpid that nothing short of a general combustion blown up by the breath of a Saxon friar could have roused their minds into action?

I believe, that the effect might not have been so rapid: but when I look to the state of Italy, as it then was, and to the state of France, as it soon would be—I can say with confidence that genuine literature and the polite arts must shortly have revisited all the European kingdoms, even though no such revolution, as has been called the *Reformation*, had intervened, to inflame and convulse the moral state of Christendom. In that case, it is pleasing to recollect that—without civil or religious strife, and without those seeds of animosity being engendered, which no time is likely to eradicate—we should have seen abuses corrected; ignorance dispelled; rights maintained; learning restored; the arts keeping possession of our temples; and, in our own country, those noble edifices, the monuments of the generous piety of our ancestors, preserved from destruction, and made the asylums not of monkish indolence, but of studious ease, modest worth, and Christian philosophy. (1)

## True Wealth and Empire

The wealth of England and its power have, surely, been promoted by its commerce with other nations, and by its manufactures at home. But they also have been the sources of many evils, and our present depravity of manners takes its principal strength from them....

Before the love of gain had extended commerce, and luxury had quickened the loom and the anvil, England was less rich. But had we fewer honest citizens, and fewer patriots? Indeed, were we less populous? The country is drained of its inhabitants to supply the losses, which disease, contracted from a thousand causes, never fails to make in the crowded cities. The country, after all, is the only nursery, where strong bodies and sound minds are bred. Were our barren wastes enclosed, and the plough permitted to break their useless sod; we should see the wondrous productions of Deucalion and Pyrra realized before our eyes. Men and women would spring up where rocks and barrenness had before dwelt. I would rather see agriculture extended, than cities built. The event would compensate for the loss of empire. It would do more. The empire we have lost would be re-produced at home; and were India severed from us as America has been, in our own fields we should find all its boasted riches. (2)

## Body and Soul

My opinion is, with the world in general, that man does really consist of two parts, as essentially different from one another, as *matter* and *spirit*. These two are joined together in the strictest bonds of union. This union is the source of the most fertile and most wonderful harmony in nature. A substance, simple and *highly* active, sensitive, perceptive, cogitative and rational, is united to a being, compounded and *inferiorly* active, insensitive, imperceptive, uncogitative and irrational. From this surprising union arises a reciprocal commerce between the two substances, a sort of action and re-action, which constitutes the life of organized-animated beings....

As to the nature of that link, by which soul and body are united, it must be resolved into the will of their creator. It was his will, that there should exist such a being as man; and man was to be an aggregate of two distinct substances. He could not be merely *spirit*, because he was designed to communicate with, and to preside over a world of matter; nor could he be solely *body*, because being such, he would not have risen much above the dust he trod on. He might perhaps have vegetated a man-plant, by organization alone, exalted above the flowers of the field, or the trees of the forest; but in such a state he could never have felt either pain or pleasure, have perceived, have thought, or have reasoned; nor could therefore any system have been realized, of worth or harmony, wherein no master-wheel should be found to ennoble and animate the whole. Thus it was seen good that man should exist. That is, that a soul and body should be conjoined in the closest ties of reciprocal influence, and that they should remain so till the principal bodily organs became unfit to perform their allotted functions. Any action, in either of the partners, *absolutely* independent, would be contrary to their laws of union; because it could not be the action of a man, who by nature consists of soul and body. Before the soul can proceed to action, the bodily organs must be duly formed and modified. They then receive impressions from their proper objects, and then begin the first mental operations. In process of time other powers are gradually expanded, as their relative causes rise into action.

It was wisely pre-ordained, that a being, destined to commence his course from material objects, and from thence gradually to proceed to a world of higher order and excellence, should also in a similar scale acquire his experience and knowledge, beginning from the humble ideas of sense, and advancing progressively to the summit of science, perfection, and virtue, through the numberless degrees, which lie between the two extreme points. Nor is it any debasement to the exalted powers of the soul that their first display and after-exertion, should have been made dependent of the bodily organs; that they should mutually correspond in the exactest proportion of growth and maturity; and that finally they should fade and die off in the same ratio, as man descends towards the grave. All this only serves to evince their fixed destination. It points out a system of the most perfect harmony, wherein part must tally with part, and the whole accord, or the inevitable consequence is, discord, disorder, and dissolution. (3)

# Why I am a Catholic

I will now say *why I am a Catholic*. First, however, let me observe, that the distinction between Catholic and Christian, in their proper acceptation, is a distinction without a difference. It prevails, however, and has long prevailed to a certain extent since, as early as the fourth century, (though before well known) a Spanish Bishop, reasoning against the Novatians, who had separated themselves from the Church, says: 'Christian is my name; Catholic is my surname.' It served, therefore, to denote those, who adhered to, and were members of that great society, which in the creed is called the Catholic Church.

I am a Catholic then because I am a Christian; and I reason in the following manner:—1. Having been conducted, as has been stated, to the threshold of divine Faith, am I not bound to receive, as undoubted truths, whatever God, in his goodness, has taught me by his Son, without demur and without wavering; not enquiring whether they accord with my preconceived notions, or with the relations and analogies of things conceived in my mind?

2. Would not such demur, and wavering, and such enquiry, argue pride, and a culpable want of confidence in that Being, whose wisdom, and power, and goodness, and love for his creatures, we know to be without bounds?

3. But how am I to learn what truths those are which God has revealed?

4. Am I to learn them—for eighteen hundred years have now elapsed since first they were delivered—am I to learn them from those records, called the Books of the New Testament, wherein are deposited many words and actions of our Saviour's life and conversation, as likewise many rules of belief and practice—or may those truths be collected from any other source?

5. To satisfy this difficulty, should I not enquire, whether any rule has been prescribed, which it is my duty to follow, and, by following which, I shall learn, in perfect security, the truths in question. Conscious, that, without such rule to guide me, I must be liable, from the very character of mind, to fall into misconceptions and error.

6. I now turn to those Scriptures, and perusing them with respectful caution, I find that, in giving his last instructions to his apostles, Christ bids them *Go*, and *teach* all nations, *teaching* them to observe *all things whatsoever* he had commanded; and he promises to *be with them all days, even to the end of the world* (Matt. 28: 20). In the gospel of St Mark, I find the same injunction repeated with the threat that he who *believeth not* the gospel, which shall be *preached* to every creature, shall be *condemned* (Mark 16: 15–16).

7. This is the ordinance or rule which I sought, and by it, I plainly see, two things are established. First, an *authority* which is to point out to me, by *teaching*, what I am to believe, and, secondly, a *duty*, if I will be saved, of listening to and obeying that authority.

8. But I cannot discover, that any command is given of committing to writing what our Saviour had taught, nor any reference made to books that might be written. *Go and teach* is the simple mandate: and as, during the lives of the Apostles, there was no written word that could be a rule, under what new injunction, is the rule of *teaching* set aside, and that of Scripture-interpretation substituted?

9. The authority then, of which I speak, was first lodged with the Apostles, to whom it was directly committed. But as they, in a few years, would be called away from their labours, and Christ promised that he would be with them to the end of the world, must not this promise include them and their successors in the ministry of the gospel?

10. Should it be restricted to the few years of the lives of the apostles, would Heaven, I humbly ask, have sufficiently provided for the perpetuity of that faith, the foundations of which had been laid at such a vast expense of supernatural means?

11. In the successors, then, of the Apostles, I conclude, was to be lodged, when they were gone, the same authority of teaching; and to the faithful was to descend, under the same menace of condemnation, the duty of receiving what they should be thus taught.

12. Still, this being allowed me, must it not be proved—in order to ascertain the genuine character of these teachers—that the line of their succession from the Apostles, during eighteen hundred years, has not been broken; and moreover, that nothing, at any time, has been added to, nor taken from, that deposit of sacred truths, which was originally committed to the Apostles?

13. Doubtless, this must be proved. First, then, I look to the promise of Christ, that he would be with pastors of his Church to the end of the world. Secondly I turn to the annals of history, in which is recorded the succession of those pastors—the object of my research—and I particularly select the succession of the Bishops of Rome. Thirdly I institute a similar enquiry, through a similar research, on the points of belief.

14. The result of this investigation is that a line of succession, in that Church, may be traced, distinctly and incontrovertibly; and that, whether I take the whole code of belief, or, which is more easily accomplished, select any one article; state it, as it is now publicly taught; and pursue it through the popular books of instruction, and the writings of those, who, in every age, have recorded its doctrine— I am, invariably, brought to one conclusion, that the Catholic belief of the nineteenth century does, in no point, differ from the belief of the early ages, that is, from the belief of the Apostles.

15. Here I rest in perfect security. My reason has led me to a guide, and to that guide I submit my judgement on all those points, which it has pleased God to reveal and his Church proposes to my belief.—I have said, *why I am a Catholic.* (4)

NOTES AND SOURCES

1. Joseph Berington, *A Literary History of the Middle Ages* (London, 1814), 516–17.

2. Joseph Berington, *An Essay on the Depravity of the Nation, with a View to the Promotion of Sunday Schools* (Birmingham, 1788), 15–16.

3. Joseph Berington, *Letters on Materialism and Hartley's Theory of the Human Mind, Addressed to Dr. Priestley* (London, 1776), 71, 78–80.

4. *The Faith of Catholics, Confirmed by Scripture and Attested by the Fathers of the First Five Centuries*, ed. Joseph Berington and J. Kirk (London, 1813), pp. xxiv–xxviii.

# Charles Butler                                            1750–1832

Before launching a polemical attack on Charles Butler, the Revd Henry Philpotts (later the Anglican Bishop of Exeter) pauses to pay 'respect' to him 'as a Scholar, a Gentleman, and ... a sincere Christian'. Such a remark was not uncommon, since no lawyer, perhaps, has ever been as studiously, rigorously, and unremittingly civil as Butler. For him, however, it was more than just a personal virtue; such moderation was needed, he believed, to assuage Protestant fears about 'papists' and end social and legal prejudice against English Catholics. As a leading member of the Cisalpine movement, he was one of English Catholicism's pre-eminent men of letters and one of the nation's most renowned lawyers. Educated at Douai, he was the nephew and biographer of Alban Butler. In that life of the author of the *Lives of the Saints* (1756–9), he published the moving last letter of Butler's mother that gives rare insight into the spiritual life of one of the many women responsible for shaping the eighteenth-century Church, albeit often from behind the scenes. He studied law under Catholic conveyancers and was entered at Lincoln's Inn before becoming, in 1791, the first Catholic barrister since the 1688 Revolution. As secretary to the Catholic Committee, he was involved in crafting the 1791 Relief Act that made this possible, including a divisive but ultimately unsuccessful provision that would have designated Catholics as 'Protesting Catholic Dissenters'. Such interventions— as well as his editing of Coke's *The Institute of the Laws of England* (1787) and writing historical works, biblical criticism, political pamphlets on Catholic Emancipation, and biographies—did gain Butler ecumenical esteem, but he also faced confrontations both within and without the Catholic fold. Bishop Milner was a constant combatant as the two differed on everything from the extent of Papal authority to the way to conduct a journal, as evidenced in Butler's short-lived but high-minded *Catholic Gentleman's Magazine* (1818–19). Against Philpott's praise of Butler's 'tone and temper', the poet Samuel Taylor Coleridge suspected 'courteous Butler' as 'Rome's smooth Go-between' who traded in 'half-truths'. Coleridge's estimate was influenced by Butler's *The Book of the Roman Catholic Church* (1825), a thorough, polite, and systematic answer to the poet laureate Robert Southey's attack on the 'Papal system' in his *Book of the Church* (1824). Much of Butler's energy was geared towards achieving Catholic Emancipation. He not only lived to see this in 1829, but in 1831 he was the first Catholic to be appointed a King's Counsel since the reign of James II.

## Catholic versus Papist

Sir,
    The title which you give to the chapter of your work, which I have now to consider, is, 'View of the *Papal* System': The words *Popery, Papal* and *Papist* being particularly offensive to Roman Catholics, in the sense in which these words are generally used by our adversaries, I have altered it, by substituting the word 'Roman Catholic' for the word 'Papal'. In the oath, which the legislature has prescribed to us, we are styled 'Roman Catholics'. On this account it has always been a rule with me, to denote, in my publications, the religious denomination of Christians to which I belong, by the appellation of 'Roman Catholics'.

    But, is it not in strictness entitled to this honourable appellation? Speaking of the Arians, St Augustine observes, that 'they called theirs the Catholic Church, and wished others so to call it. But', continues this great man, 'if any stranger comes into their cities, and inquires of them for a catholic church, to which churches do they themselves point? Certainly not to their own.' May *I* not ask, whether, if a stranger were to inquire, even from a prelate of your church, where the Catholics assembled for divine worship, he would point to his own cathedral, or to any of his parochial churches? Would he not point to the place of worship in which those, whom the law terms Roman Catholics, are used to assemble? Would not the same answer be given if the inquiry was made of any Protestant in any other condition of life? Would not this be the case all over the world? And does it not incontrovertibly show the universal feelings of persons of every creed, that mine is the church, catholic, or the church, universally diffused? (1)

# A Defence of Catholic Devotion

'The saints, reigning with Christ, offer up their prayers to God for man. It is a good and useful supplication to invoke them; and to have recourse to their prayers, help and assistance to obtain favours from God, through his Son Jesus Christ our Lord, above, who is our Redeemer and Saviour.' This is the decree of the council of Trent. The catechism, published in pursuance of its decrees, teaches that 'God and the Saints are not to be prayed to in the same manner; for we pray to God that He himself would give us good things, and deliver us from evil things: but we beg of the saints, because they are pleasing to God, that they would be our advocates, and obtain from God what we stand in need of.' Consult Bossuet's *Exposition of Faith* under this article; read *the catechisms*, which we successively put into the hands of children, youth, and persons grown up. Examine *all our writers*, either profound or popular, you will meet with the same doctrine. Open our *prayer books*, you will find that, when we address God the Father, God the Son, God the Holy Ghost, or the Holy Trinity, we say to them, '*Have mercy on us*'; and that, when we address the Blessed Virgin, the saints, or the angels, the descent is infinite, and we say to them, '*Pray for us*'.

What do we think of those who give to the Virgin Mary, to the saints, or to the angels, the honour due to God? Open Mr Gother's *Papist Misrepresented*, abridged by Doctor Challoner,—the editions of which abridgement are count-less—you will find in them these strong expressions: 'Cursed is he that believes the saints in Heaven to be his redeemers; that prays to them as such; or that gives God's honour to them, or to any creature whatsoever. Amen.' 'Cursed is every goddess-worshipper, that believes the blessed Virgin Mary to be any more than a creature; that worships her, or puts his trust in her, more than in God; that believes she is above her Son, or that she can, in any thing, command Him. Amen.'

Does not the Greek Church, do not all the oriental Churches, which separated from the church of Rome before the Reformation, invoke the Virgin Mary, the other saints, and the angels? Does not Martin Luther exclaim, 'Who can deny that God works great miracles at the tombs of the saints? I therefore, with the whole Catholic Church, hold that the saints are to be honoured and invoked by us. Let no one omit to call upon the Blessed Virgin, the angels, and saints, that they may intercede for them at the hour of death.' Do not several distinguished divines of your Church maintain the same doctrine? Is it not approved by Leibniz? Finally, does not Doctor Thorndike warn his brethren 'not to lead people by the nose to believe, that they can prove papists to be idolaters, when they cannot.'

Then permit me to ask, whether the authorities which I have cited, do not give a true and clear exposition of the doctrine of the Catholic Church, upon this important subject? Whether the doctrine be idolatrous or superstitious? Whether the practice of it do not fill the mind with soothing reflections? With thoughts that increase charity and animate piety? You cannot find a virtuous Catholic, who will not own to you that he considers the hours, thus spent by him, to be among the most pleasing of his life.

Pursuing the same method, in respect to the cross and relics of the saints, I shall transcribe the decree of the Council of Trent upon them: 'Although the images of Christ, the Virgin Mother of God, and the other saints, are to be kept and retained, particularly in churches, and due honour and veneration paid to them, yet we are not to believe, that there is any divinity or power in them, for which we respect them, or that any thing is to be asked from them, or that trust is to be placed in them, as the heathens of old trusted in their idols.' Consult all the authors mentioned in the former part of this letter, you will find the same language. Open our *catechisms*, you will find it asked, 'May we pray to relics or images?' You will find it answered, 'No! by no means, for they have no life or sense to hear or help us.' Then, open Gother's *Papist Misrepresented*, you will read, 'Cursed is he that commits idolatry, that prays to images or relics, or worships them for God.'

In an old English 'Treatise on the Ten Commandments', printed in Westminster Abbey before the Reformation, in 1496, by Winken de Worde, it is said, 'Worship not the image, nor the stock, stone, or tree; but worship him that died on the tree for thy sin and thy sake, so that thou kneel, if thou wilt, *before* the image, but not *to* the image; for it seeth thee not, it heareth thee not, it understandeth thee not; for, if thou do it, *for* the image, or *to* the image, thou doeth idolatry.'

Such is the doctrine of the Catholic Church, on those subjects.

We venerate the Cross, as a memorial of the passion and death of the Author of our salvation. We venerate the images, paintings and relics, of the saints, as memorials, that bring their virtues and rewards to our minds and hearts. We also venerate their relics, as portions of their holy bodies, which will be glorified through all eternity.

In all this, can you find out anything reprehensible? (2)

## Purgatory and Prayers for the Dead

As to the existence of Purgatory, for the belief of which the Roman Catholics have been so often and so harshly reviled,—Do not all, who call themselves 'rational Protestants', think with us, that, (to use the language of doctor Johnson), 'the generality of mankind are neither so obstinately wicked, as to deserve everlasting punishment; nor so good, as to merit being admitted into the society of the blessed spirits; and that God is, therefore, generously pleased to allow a middle state, where they may be purified by a certain degree of suffering.' With those who profess this doctrine, does not your own opinion accord? And what is this but the very doctrine of the Roman Catholic Church respecting Purgatory?

As to prayers for the dead. The council of Trent has decreed, 'that there is a Purgatory, and that the souls detained in it *are helped* by the suffrages of the faithful'.

The nature and extent of these suffrages are thus explained by St Augustine: 'When the sacrifice of the altar, or alms, are offered for the dead, then, in regard to those whose lives were very good, such sacrifices may be deemed acts of thanksgiving. In regard to the imperfect, they may be deemed acts of propitiation; and though they bring no aid to the very bad, they may give some comfort to the living.'

Tradition, in favour of the Catholic doctrine of Purgatory, is so strong, that Calvin confesses explicitly, that 'during 1,300 years before his time, (1,600 before ours), it had been the practice to pray for the dead, in the hope of procuring them relief'. You yourself will scarcely venture to assert, that there is any thing substantially wrong in this devotion, when you recollect, that Archbishop Cranmer said a Solemn Mass for the soul of Henry II of France; that bishop Ridley preached, and that eight other prelates assisted at it in their copes.

How does it soothe the affliction of the surviving husband, wife, parent, or child, to pray for the souls of those, whose loss they deplore! and to think that they benefit them by their prayers! Does not this communion between the living and the dead call forth the kindest feelings of the heart? those charities which endear man to man, and multiply the circles of benevolence? Is not, therefore, even humanely speaking, the doctrine of the Roman Catholic Church, respecting prayers for the dead, good and profitable? (3)

## What Was Lost in the Reformation?

Twice (if not thrice) did the Roman Catholic religion rescue the inhabitants of England from paganism. She instructed them in the divine truths of the Gospel; introduced civilization among them; was, after the Norman Conquest, their only protection against the oppressions of their conqueror; and, during a long subsequent period, their only defence against the tyranny of the barons. To her, you owe your *magna charta*, the important statute, *de tallagio non concedendo*,[2] and several other statutes, regulations and forms, which are the groundwork and bulwark of your constitution. A numerous clergy instructed them in moral duty. Numerous portions, both of men and women, whose institutes were holy, furnished the young with means of education, the old with comfortable retreats, and all with the opportunities of serving God in honour and integrity. Throughout England the Roman Catholic religion only was acknowledged, so that the Reformation found the whole nation one flock under one shepherd. Almost every village contained a church, to which the faithful, at stated hours, regularly flocked for the celebration of the eternal sacrifices, for morning and evening prayer, and for exhortation and instruction. In a multitude of places, the silence of the night was interrupted by pious psalmody. Surely these circumstances were not only great religious, but great political blessings. England was covered with edifices raised by the sublimest science and dedicated to the most noble and most salutary purposes. Commerce prospered. Agriculture, literature, every useful and ornamental art and science was excellently cultivated and was in a state of gradual improvement. The monarch was illustrious among the most illustrious potentates of Europe and held the balance between its preponderating princes. His court was splendid; the treasury overflowed with wealth; THERE WAS NO DEBT; and, (one fourth part of the tithes in every place being set apart for the maintenance of the poor), THERE WAS NO POOR LAW.

Such was the *temporal prosperity* of England at the dawn of the Reformation. Will it suffer on a comparison of it with the condition of England at any subsequent era? Or even with its present? (4)

---

[2] The 'statute concerning tallage', or royal taxation collected without assent, attributed to the reign of Edward I.

# On Mystical Theology

Mystical theology is defined to be an union of the soul with God,—so intimate, that her essence is, in a manner, transformed into the essence of God, and, in consequence of it, she beholds him, not intuitively, as he is seen by the blessed in Heaven, but, in a divine light; and she believes in him, hopes in him, and loves him, not by particular or discursive acts, but in silent affection and adoration....

But for the passage into it, the most heroic exertions and sacrifices are necessary. The soul must completely die to the world and herself and obtain a complete victory over all that draws, or even has a remote tendency to draw her from God. Persecution from the world at large, from those who are most dear to her, repeated mortifications and bitter external and internal trials of every kind, are the means, which God generally uses, to effect her final purification; but, by far the severest trial with which he visits her, is the Spiritual Night, as it is termed by those writers, through which he generally makes her pass. In that state, she is assailed by the strongest temptations. She often seems to herself to be on the brink of yielding to them, and sometimes fears she has yielded. The most blasphemous thoughts, the most irregular ideas crowd her mind. She feels, or rather apprehends she feels a complacency in them. God seems to her to abandon her; she no longer beholds in him her father, her redeemer, the shepherd who leads to the green pasture or the living water. She views him armed with terrors, conceives herself an object of his wrath, and, in indescribable anguish, fears it will be her everlasting lot. Still, she perseveres. In the midst of this agonising suffering, she is invariably patient, invariably humble, invariably resigned, and, even when she seems to herself to sink under the harrowing impression of her being an eternal object of divine wrath, and fears all is lost, (her last and heaviest trial), she habitually trusts herself to his mercy and abandons herself to his holy will. Then, she is nailed to the sacred Cross: she dies to the world, to herself, to all that is not God, and her sacrifice is complete.

But, as these writers assure us, in the midst of this severe visitation, God is ever near her, and enriches her with the most pure and exalted virtues. She acquires an habitual conformity to his holy will, a perfect indifference to all actions and objects except as they please or displease him. On him alone, she is occupied, with him alone, she is filled, she loves him for himself; and the divine transformation, so beautifully described by St Paul, when he exclaims,—'It is not I that live, it is Christ that liveth in me' (Gal. 2: 20), then ensues.

Such are the spiritual favours, which, in this hour of desolation, while she herself is not only unconscious of them, but actually fears herself an object of wrath, this humble and afflicted soul is said by these writers to receive from the unbounded mercy of God, and such, they inform us, are the exalted gifts with which her perseverance is crowned. Often, she continues for several years in the state of trial, and the spiritualists who describe it, speak of it as exceeding every species of corporal pain.

But her hour of reward at length arrives:—God then showers on her an abundance of those sacred favours, which the same writers inform us, no tongue can adequately tell, and those only can conceive, who have had some experience of them. Wonderfully her intellect is enlightened on divine subjects, her will animated by divine love, her memory radiated by the recollection of the divine mercies. Her appetites are so governed by the Holy Spirit, as to be subservient to her religious perfection, her very corporal existence partakes of the holy jubilation of her soul, and rejoiceth, with her, in God her saviour. She beholds, not intuitively as they are beholden by the angels and saints, but in a divine light, the adorable essence, the sacred mysteries of the trinity and incarnation, the unspeakable perfections of God, and the wisdom and justice of his ways with man. He admits her to habitual and intimate communications with him. 'Frequent', says the author of the *Imitation of Christ*, 'are the visits of God to such a soul, sweet his conversation with her, grateful the consolations, unspeakable the peace which he brings to her, wonderful the familiarity which he vouchsafes her.' Her joy is pure and passeth understanding. Surrounded by the light and power of divine love, she lives, and feels, and moves in God alone. (5)

## Catholic Journalism

Dedicated to the Catholic cause, and earnestly desirous of promoting its interests by every means in our power, the present publication—formed on a similar plan, but accommodated to the concerns of Catholics—is now respectfully presented to the British public—to that portion of it, in particular, which is within the Catholic pale. Without trespassing too much on the indulgence of our readers, we beg leave to state to them, in a few words, the general outlines of the plan on which we mean to conduct it.

Each month that passes over us will principally engage our attention. The public and private events which then particularly interest the Catholic body, the prejudices then particularly working against us, the circumstances then particularly operating in our favour, every object of our immediate hope or immediate fear, will always occupy our first thoughts; and we shall anxiously endeavour to lay before our readers all the information on these subjects, that active and extensive research can procure. We shall notice the most important publications that shall appear against us, or in our favour. We ourselves mean occasionally to take the field; and when a respectable adversary appears, and the Catholic cause seems to demand it from us, we shall not fear to oppose to him the lance of stern defiance, or gentle courtesy.

Our readers must be sensible of the many hostile publications with which the press incessantly assails us, some of which are entitled to an answer, but none entitled to a book. On these we shall ever fix a watchful eye; and when we shall think them worthy of animadversion, we shall animadvert on them in the manner which they deserve: but we shall never exceed the limits of legitimate defence; and our readers may be assured, that neither a sentiment nor a word shall ever be found in our pages, which a Christian or a gentleman would not avow. *A good Christian is never outdone in good manners.* This was a frequent saying of St Francis of Sales. It affords a lesson which we shall religiously strive to observe. The disputes among ourselves we shall always be unwilling to notice. When it becomes necessary, we shall most anxiously strive to do it in a manner that will rather compose the difference, than increase the agitation. *Paci deditum est opus nostrum:* Ours shall ever be pages of peace. (6)

## Last Letter of Mrs Ann Butler

My Dear Children,

Since it pleases almighty God to take me out of this world, as no doubt wisely foreseeing I am no longer a useful parent to you, (for no person ought to be thought necessary in this world, when God thinks proper to take them out); so, I hope, you will offer the loss of me, with a resignation suitable to the religion you are of, and offer yourselves. He who makes you orphans so young, without a parent to take care of you, will take you into his protection and fatherly care, if you do love and serve him, who is the Author of all goodness. Above all things prepare yourselves, while you are young, to suffer patiently what afflictions he shall think proper to lay upon you; for it is by this he trieth his best servants. In the first place, give him thanks for your education in the true faith, (which many thousands want): and then I beg of you earnestly to petition his direction, what state of life you shall undertake, whether it be for religion, or to get your livings in the world. No doubt but you may be saved either way, if you do your duty to God, your neighbour, and yourselves. And I beg of you to make constant resolutions, rather to die a thousand times if possible, than quit your faith; and always have in your thoughts, what you would think of were you as nigh death as I now think myself. There is no preparation for a good death, but a good life.—Do not omit your prayers, and to make an act of contrition and examination of conscience every night, and frequent the blessed Sacraments of the Church. I am so weak, I can say no more to you; but I pray God bless and direct you, and your friends to take care of you. Lastly, I beg of you never to forget to pray for your poor father and mother when they are not capable of helping themselves:—so I take leave of you, hoping to meet you in Heaven to be happy for all eternity—

Your affectionate mother,

Ann Butler (7)

NOTES AND SOURCES

1. Charles Butler, *The Book of the Roman-Catholic Church* (London, 1825), 99–100.
2. Ibid. 100–4.
3. Ibid. 104–6.
4. Ibid. 170–1.
5. Charles Butler, *On Mystical Theology or the Science of Sacred Contemplation* (n.p., 1810), 2, 4–6.
6. Charles Butler, *Catholic Gentleman's Magazine*, 1 (1818), 3.
7. Charles Butler, *An Account of the Life and Writings of the Rev. Alban Butler* (London, 1799), 4–5.

# James Archer                                      1751–1834

The Georgian Church's most eloquent and renowned preacher began his career in a pub. After his 1780 ordination at Douai, James Archer first served at London's Ship Inn, which had long served as a place of worship for Catholics during penal times. It had been while working there as a boy that Bishop Challoner recognized his abilities and sent him on to Douai. His future was more august as he preached, from 1791 onwards, in the more opulent Bavarian chapel, one of the several tolerated embassy Catholic churches that served as de facto London parishes. His popular sermons, which were collected and frequently republished, demonstrate a sustained commitment to a religious humanism that explains and justifies religious doctrine on the basis of human nature. Such a universalizing approach, which reclaimed the Enlightenment term 'universal benevolence' for the Christian Gospel, allowed him to reach a broad ecumenical audience, as did his own personal reputation for sociability and conviviality. He was not naive, however, about the religious divisions in England as one of his first sermons freshly reacted to the Gordon Riots and meditated on how 'the hour of trial...lays open the intricate folds of conscience, and shows whether we are really citizens of Heaven, or still wedded to the pomps, the vanities, and enjoyments, of the earth.' While his openness and social exuberance were sometimes criticized, Archer was created a Doctor of Divinity by Pope Pius VII in 1821 for his contributions to Catholic letters and devotion.

## Humanity's Restless Heart

Man is a being possessed of an immortal soul. He has a mind capable of elevating itself, even to the contemplation of the Deity; and the desires of his heart, vast and unbounded like the immortal principle whence they proceed, are never to be satisfied but by the possession of an infinite good. When he obtains all he coveted on earth, he is still uneasy. There remains a void not yet filled up. His desires increase with his enjoyments; and, after hurrying on from one pursuit to another, he sits down breathless and fatigued with his fruitless labour, and confesses that all is vanity and affliction of spirit. (1)

## What is Devotion?

Devotion...is that habitual disposition of soul which is formed by divine love. It commands several acts of the mind, and excites various emotions in the heart, which all centre in the Supreme Being and tend to divine and immortal objects. The constituent parts of devotion are: first, a continual sense of the presence of God; secondly, sentiments of gratitude for his benefits; thirdly, ardent desires of being inseparably united to him; and lastly, a placid resignation to every appointment of his all-wise and beneficent providence....

Those...mistake the nature of devotion who consider it as a gloomy and melancholy temper of mind, which looks with an indignant eye on all that is pleasing or amusing in life. It is quite otherwise, my brethren. Devotion is ever easy and cheerful. Most certainly the devout man abstains from every unlawful pleasure: he checks also every intemperate fondness for pleasures which in themselves are innocent, but which, if pursued too eagerly, may enervate his mind, or divert his attention from more important occupations. In a word, devotion will not suffer amusement to be our principal object, but readily allows that share of it which is requisite to relaxation of mind and body and to the relieving of the heart from its cares. It admits likewise, and recommends a decent conformity of dress and manners, according to our respective situations in life, with the established customs and fashions of the age in which we live, provided they be consistent with purity and innocence. Do not think, my beloved, that in religion all is sorrow and dejection. Quite the contrary. Those do a material injury to religion, who present it under an unpleasing and forbidding form. By clothing it with unnecessary austerity, they disfigure its natural features, and do away all its enchanting graces. They terrify weak minds and deter them from embracing it; whereas there is nothing in the spirit of religion which is adverse to a cheerful enjoyment of our situation in the world.

It is also a mistaken notion to believe that devotion nourishes a spirit of severity in judging of the manners and characters of others. Devotion has long been injured by this reproach, insomuch that as I have already observed, to have the character of being devout, and to pass for censorious, and fond of detraction, appears to many persons to be nearly the same thing. I know not whether persons given to devotion, are, in reality, more addicted to this snarling and uncharitable-ness than other people. But this I know, if they be censorious, it is not true devotion that makes them so. Its first principle is universal benevolence. Candour, meekness, and humility are ever its attendants. It is gentle, liberal, generous, and unassuming. Severe to itself only, it makes to others every allowance which humanity can suggest. If your devotion be not accompanied with these amiable qualities; if it embitter your sentiments, or infuse acrimony into your language; depend upon it, some evil passion yet lurks in your hearts.

Be careful, therefore, henceforth to remove from your devotion these defects, and every other defect. Give that dignity to true piety, and labour to procure for it that esteem, to which it is justly entitled. Thus you will put to silence the ignorance of foolish men: thus you will gain your neighbour to Christ Jesus, and find your own hearts enlarged in the service of God. (2)

## Prayer's Enlightenment

Truly, if you be not blind to your own dearest interests, prayer will ever be your joy in prosperity, and your relief and consolation in distress. A Christian is essentially a man of prayer: to converse with Heaven is the darling occupation of his life. The Church of Christ, in this state of earthly banishment expresses, without intermission, in plaintive accents her longing after immortality and distinguishes her children by the ardent sighs which they continually send up towards their celestial inheritance....

Here a new prospect is opened before us. Our nature indeed, even in its degraded and fallen state, preserved still some of the beautiful traits which were in the beginning impressed upon it by the hand of the Creator. Its august ruins bore testimony to its former magnificence. We could discover in them the plan of an edifice, which was designed to be an ornament of nature for endless ages. The vast desires of the human heart, which after trying the whole range of created objects, could rest in none of them, in none could taste any complete satisfaction, proclaimed the excellence of its destination. But revelation has thrown a new and brighter evidence on these consoling truths; has caused the dawn of that light which is yet inaccessible, to shed its beams on the minds of the disciples of Jesus, and gladden their hearts; has opened the eyes of mortal men to behold the regions of immortal bliss, and invites them to aspire to the participation of infinite joys and glories. A true Christian therefore is a citizen of Heaven. All his projects and labours terminate in the securing of a permanent possession in the kingdom of Jesus. His eye is ever turned towards the blessed Jerusalem. His heart continually pants after its enjoyments. And what is the sentiment of these affections, but the exercise of prayer? In prayer, our faith dwells among divine and immortal objects: in prayer, hope draws, as it were, near to them, lays hold of them, and makes them its own; in prayer we exert that noble power of love with which our hearts are actuated, by fervent aspirations towards these exquisite delights; awaiting, with longing expectation, the rising of that auspicious day, when we shall no longer be subjected to the vicissitudes of human things, but be dissolved, and be with Christ in the plenitude of unalterable felicity. (3)

## Why Catholics Make the Sign of the Cross

Our faith in the three Divine Persons of the adorable Trinity is the foundation of all our hopes, the source of our merits, the principle of our holiness, and the beginning and the root of our justification. It is the small seed mentioned in the Gospel, which, taken root in the heart, at length shoots forth branches which reach the highest Heavens, and will bear those delicious fruits which we are to gather throughout eternity. It is on this account, that the words by which we generally express it, *In the name of the Father, and of the Son, and of the Holy Ghost*, are, and have ever been, considered in our religion, as most sacred, august, and venerable. By the appointment of our divine Redeemer, these words enter into the administration of all the sacraments of the new law. If we are regenerated by the saving waters of Baptism, it is in the name of the Father, Son, and Holy Ghost. If we are strengthened by divine grace in confirmation; if our sins are remitted in the sacrament of penance; if we are consecrated for the ministry of the Gospel; all this is done in the name of the same most holy and adorable Trinity. The same sacred name is invoked when we receive a blessing from the pastors and prelates of the church. And when we announce to you the words of eternal life, we begin always by acknowledging our dependence on the Father, who is the source of truth and wisdom, the Son, who brought life and immortality to light, and the Holy Ghost, whose grace and influence alone can make these truths fructify in our hearts; in order that we may ever remember that Christianity brings with it no blessing, no justification or salvation, but by faith in the blessed Trinity.

For the same reason, my brethren, was introduced that pious practice of never beginning or executing any work of importance, without signing ourselves with the sign of the cross and pronouncing those sacred words. We acknowledge by that practice, that the merit of the action we perform must be derived from our faith; and that, without it, our labours would be fruitless, and of no estimation in the sight of God. The first Christians, as we learn from Tertullian, made constant use of the sign of the cross. He informs us, that on every occasion, and in every occupation of life, at their going out or coming in, at their getting up or lying down, at their meals, at their business, they made this sacred sign on their foreheads. Of this practice the Catholic Church has been ever tenacious. I know that weak and uninformed persons, empty and superficial reasoners, light and giddy minds, affect a sneer and laugh at such a practice. But we regard not their derision. If ridicule were the test of truth, then every thing most sacred must be rejected. Surely, in the eye of unprejudiced reason, nothing can be more conformable to the spirit of a Christian, nothing more immediately directed to the glory of our Creator, than to enter upon each action by invoking his adorable name and imprinting on our foreheads the glorious sign of our Redemption. Hence also the church of Christ is ever careful to close all the inspired hymns and canticles, which she sings to her divine Spouse, with the doxology, or *Glory be to the Father, and to the Son, and to the Holy Ghost*. And with the same divine theme she terminates all her hymns and prayers. (4)

## Suffering and Sanctification among English Catholics

Figure to yourselves a situation the most distressing; and you will find saints, who by that situation have worked out their salvation.

The earliest periods of Christianity present to us innumerable bright examples, which abundantly confirm the truth of this reflection. The Church of Christ was never more eminent for the fervour of its piety, nor more beautiful in the purity of its morals, than when under a cloud of affliction. Those ages in which it was exposed to all the fury of inhuman persecutors, were the ages of its triumph. In the course of time, when peace was restored to it, the morals of its members became gradually more corrupt. Its days were less pure and innocent, in proportion as they glided on with more smoothness and tranquillity; and religion has in latter times been pierced with more cruel anguish by the degeneracy of her children, in the time of their prosperity, than ever she could feel, while she saw the sword of persecution daily tinged with their blood.

This consideration should be to you, my beloved, particularly consoling. You, like the first Christians, have much to suffer in this country on account of your attachment to a religion, which, during the course of many centuries, exerted its beneficent influence over this island in civilizing human manners; in diffusing over men's minds the light of heavenly wisdom; in softening their hearts to all the gentle and tender virtues of compassion, benevolence, and brotherly love; and strengthening all the bands of social life. Even in a land which glories in its freedom, that religion, under whose auspices our forefathers procured, maintained, and defended all our civil liberties, is rendered obnoxious to the greater part of your fellow citizens; and the profession of it deprives you of many of the rights and privileges of your countrymen. At the same time, ignorance, prejudice, or malice, disfigures your tenets by the grossest misrepresentations, and attributes to you the most infamous principles and doctrines; accuses you of authorizing a breach of faith in your contracts with persons of a different religious communion; of idolatry; of a vindictive, persecuting, bloody-minded disposition, all which you have been taught by your religion to detest and reprobate.

Be animated, therefore, by the same spirit which inspired the apostles and martyrs in the first ages of the Church; and then the difficulties with which you have to struggle will only serve to increase your fervour and enforce your adherence to that faith, which you are evidently convinced is grounded on divine revelation. While you are ever ready to give an answer to every one that asks you a reason of that faith which is in you, be careful to let your belief regulate your actions. Give conspicuous proofs of the purity and sanctity of your religion, by your ardent piety, by the innocence of your manners, by the tender charity and sincere affection with which you embrace all your fellow creatures without distinction of opinions or persuasions. The inward testimony of conscience will console and speak peace to your hearts, while you are exposed to temporal afflictions for obeying its dictates. Though despised and ridiculed, though persecuted by the ignorance or passions of men;

instead of conceiving any rancour against your enemies, you will rather compassionate their delusion, looking forward with joy towards that future world where truth shall emerge from the obscurity with which it is now overshadowed—shall appear in all its lustre and native beauty, to command the love and veneration of every heart. It was thus that the patience and meekness of the primitive Christians triumphed over persecution and gave the strongest evidence that their religion was established and supported by heavenly wisdom and power. (5)

## The Unity of the Human Race

The first voice of reason, the earliest cries of nature, and that exquisite pleasure which warms our hearts when we do a benevolent action, pressingly invite us to love and assist one another. We are held together by the most endearing tie. We are all relations and brethren. We are all one common origin, are made of the same substance, formed by the same creative power; and we tend to the same destination and last end. We are, moreover, united together by the bands of civil society. Formed for social life, we stand in need one of another. We have each of us many natural wants, which of ourselves we cannot supply. The supreme Ruler of the universe, who openeth his hand, and filleth with blessing every living creature, in providing abundantly for all the inhabitants of the earth, hath not bestowed separately upon each individual, that which is sufficient for him, so that he can enjoy it, as it were, concentrated within himself, and detached from any community. But, to some hath imparted an abundance of one kind of blessings; to others, blessings of another kind; to the end that his creatures, by communicating to each other their respective advantages, might be formed together into one compact body; of which each member depends upon another, each is necessary to the others, and all jointly contribute to the harmony, to the happiness, and perfection, of the whole. It is evident, therefore, that the blessings which we individually possess are not intended for ourselves exclusively, but are designed to be shared with those of our fellow-creatures who are unprovided with the same blessings. Hence our affluence, wisdom, prudence, education, genius, abilities, interest, authority, and power, our strength, health, and all our faculties of body and mind, are bestowed upon us by Providence, that we may make them instrumental in promoting the happiness of our neighbours, and relieving their spiritual and corporal necessities. The obligation, consequently, of assisting each other, is legible in the very frame of our being, is demonstrated by the view of our natural condition on the earth. (6)

## Reason and Revelation

We find equal matter for astonishment, my brethren, in observing the growth and rapid progress of infidelity in these our days. At this period of the world, when the religion of Jesus, planted in Judea by the eternal word of God, enforced by miracles, supported by prophecies, beautiful in the structure and harmony of all its parts, pure in its morality, beneficial in all its influences, elevated and sublime in its doctrines and precepts, watered by the blood of the martyrs, made illustrious by the distinguished characters and heroic virtues of thousands, whom it has formed to everything great and good; when this religion has triumphed over idolatry, and extended its dominion to the ends of the earth; when kings, nations, and empires have submitted to its power, flourished under its auspices, and gloried in protecting and defending it; at this period of the world, at a time too which is distinguished by the appellation of the enlightened age; men born and educated in the bosom of Christianity, make it their glory to oppose it, to attack it, to ridicule and laugh it to scorn, to withdraw their assent from its doctrines, and refuse submission to its injunctions, is considered as a becoming use of reason, a mark of courage and strength of mind, a noble freedom of thought....

In defending revelation, I wish not to depreciate human reason, much less to establish Christianity on its ruins. Reason is the most beautiful ornament of our nature, the distinguishing excellence of our being. We were gifted with it by our bountiful Creator, that by its light we might direct our steps through life and determine the part we should act with respect to all the concerns of this world; and particularly those most important of all concerns, the goods and evils of eternity. Hence St Paul tells the Romans that their submission to the law of Christ must be *reasonable*. Indeed, were the doctrines which are delivered as revealed truths demonstratively repugnant to reason, we should be bound to reject them, because the Deity is incapable of acting in contradiction with himself. He is the author of reason; therefore that which is contrary to reason cannot have been revealed by him. (7)

## The Nobility and Freedom of a Christian

The dignity of a Christian, whether we judge of it from the estimation in which he is held by the Supreme judge of merit or from the superiority to which he is exalted above all distinctions of this world, is, indisputably, the greatest that can be conferred on any created being. Since God is the fountain of all honour and greatness, the excellencies of created beings are so many emanations from him. His creatures are great and excellent, in proportion as they stand in a nearer relation to him. Hence it follows, that to be made his friends, his associates, the objects of his esteem and of his tenderest love, is the most exalted degree of dignity and excellence to which a finite and imperfect being is capable of arriving. And these distinctions Christianity confers. A Christian is the friend, the favourite, the adopted son of God, heir of God, and coheir with Jesus Christ, to whose dominion *all principality, and power, and virtue, and domination, and every name that is named, not only in this world, but also in that which is to come*, are eternally subjected (Eph. 1: 21–2).

With relation to the things of this world, a true Christian is a man raised above the earth; no longer agitated by the little revolutions and vicissitudes of human things; no longer to be dejected by the frowns of adversity, or transported beyond the bounds of moderation by the smiles of prosperity. His treasure, and all that he loves, is in Heaven, where no fraud or violence can enter. He is free, even in captivity and chains; ever master of himself; ever possessed of absolute sway over all the passions of his own heart. He does good actions, not catching at human applause, but to approve himself to his Creator; he does good actions with equal alacrity, in the obscurity of retirement, and when exposed to the notice of his fellow-creatures. But he wishes rather for the retired shade, because he fears lest the breath of human applause should tarnish his virtues and well knows that his Lord views with delight every deed of goodness, how much soever despised, disregarded, or forgotten by the giddy and thoughtless inhabitants of the earth.

He fears not death. Death appears to him disarmed of all its terrors. Why should he fear it? It is the gate which opens into everlasting life. He rejoices in the hope that the period which puts an end to his mortal existence, will be the moment in which he is introduced to the society of all that is beautiful, wise, and happy. This is true greatness; this is nobility; this is dignity indeed! (8)

NOTES AND SOURCES

1. James Archer, 'The Nativity', in *Sermons on Various Moral and Religious Subjects*, i, 2nd edn. (London, 1794), 101.
2. James Archer, 'On Devotion', ibid., ii, 3rd edn. (London, 1817), 5, 15–17.
3. James Archer, 'On the Necessity and Advantages of Prayer', James Archer, 'On Devotion', ibid., ii. 36, 38–40.
4. James Archer, 'On the Incomprehensibility of Some Doctrines of the Christian Religion', ibid., ii. 99–101.
5. James Archer, 'On Afflictions', ibid., ii. 251–4.
6. James Archer, 'On Fraternal Charity', ibid., ii. 262–3.
7. James Archer, 'On the Evidence and Comforts of Christianity', ibid., i, 2nd edn. (London, 1794), 218–20, 223–4.
8. Ibid. 236–9.

# Bishop John Milner                                    1752–1826

Bishop Milner hated cheese—he would walk out of his way to avoid smells from a cheese shop; would leave the table if an offending cheddar were served. He nearly lost a lifelong friendship when presented with a round of Swiss by his future biographer's parents. In short, he was not a man of moderate opinion nor did he hesitate to act on his views. On the one hand, this trenchancy earned him both the nickname in Rome of the 'English Athanasius' and the admiration of Newman, who called him the 'champion of God's ark in an evil time'. On the other hand, it brought the vicar apostolic of the Midland district into a lifelong conflict with representatives of the Cisalpine movement such as Charles Butler and Joseph Berington. Born in London as the son of a tailor who suffered from mental illness, he was enrolled at Sedgley Park in 1765 before Bishop Challoner recommended him for Douai. Upon ordination, he returned briefly to the English mission in London before taking an appointment in Winchester. The themes of Milner's career first emerged here. Milner would become a leading voice in the controversies over the place of Catholics in England between the 1780 Gordon Riots and the 1829 Catholic Emancipation Act, and he generally believed that the future of English Catholicism had to be based on a restoration of its past glories, a devotional attachment to the traditions of the Church in Europe, and a strict adherence to doctrinal orthodoxy and Church authority. He wrote a tome on the antiquities of the Winchester area that earned him a place in the Society of Antiquaries. His championing of Gothic architecture in his writings, and in his construction of a new church on that model, made him a forerunner of the Gothic Revival, and, like Pugin, he was an unhesitating controversialist. His enduring work, *The End of Religious Controversy* (written in 1803, published in 1818), portrayed an epistolary exchange among representatives of several denominations whose 'end' is their conversion to Catholicism. He attempted to have Rome condemn John Lingard's *History of England*—a 'bad book'—for insufficiently revering the Catholic past and was, in turn, ordered by Rome to cease writing for *The Orthodox Journal* because of his vitriolic attacks on Lingard and any Catholic, including his hierarchical colleagues, associated with Cisalpinism. However, the man whom Newman imagined as prophesying the restoration of the hierarchy in his famous 1852 'Second Spring' sermon at Oscott should not be seen solely among these internecine conflicts. On behalf of the Irish bishops in England, Milner successfully resisted a version of Catholic Emancipation that would have given the government a 'veto' over the appointment of Catholic bishops. From the time Oscott College came under his direction in 1808, he transformed the floundering institution into a centre of English Catholic learning. He built there the first chapel in England dedicated to the Sacred Heart, and he was largely responsible for bringing this public devotion into the country. Milner's translation of St Teresa of Avila's meditations—done at the request of Mary Augustina More (d. 1807), an Augustinian prioress in Bruges and descendant of Thomas More—also embodies this intense and emotional spirituality that, according to Newman, was able to 'soften and melt the frost which stiffened the Catholicism of his day' to make way for the 'tender and fervent aspirations of Continental piety'.

## Reading St Teresa of Avila in an Enlightened Age

I was prepared to meet with those tender sentiments of devotion, and those pure maxims of heavenly doctrine, which the Church ascribes to our saint in the prayer appointed for her festival. To my surprise, however, on perusing it, I discovered that pathetic strain of eloquence, and that quickness and sublimity of imagination which are to be found in few devotional treatises. In short, I was convinced it deserved to be generally known, and that it was not more calculated to gratify the devotion of the pious, than to produce... the conversion of sinners....

In an age which seems to threaten a second grand defection from the Church, under the delusive idea of reforming errors and abuses, a work of the old stamp, like this, calculated to oppose the prevailing torrent by opposing that spirit of irreligion from which it flows, naturally seeks for protection in a lineal descendant of that illustrious martyr, the rescuer, in his age, of his country from infamy, who endeavoured to extinguish the flames of the first Reformation with his blood, and whose Christian use of the great talents, with which he was entrusted, has proved, that men are not always wicked in proportion to the means they have of being so.

There is danger, Madam, to all that is rational and good from too much speculation and refinement, as well as from stupid ignorance. Hence the Apostle of the Gentiles admonishes us, *not to be more wise than it behoveth to be wise, but to be wise unto sobriety* (Rom. 12: 3). In speaking of the ancient philosophers he had before said, that *they evaporated in their own thoughts... and professing themselves to be wise, they become fools* (Rom. 1: 21–2). The present enlightened age, as it is pleased to term itself, has reasoned till it has hardly a principle left to reason upon. Politicians have reformed their political constitutions till all the evils of anarchy have poured in upon them. The fashionable religionists of the day have reformed Christianity till they have degraded Christ himself from his throne and worn down his supernatural religion to a system that stands in need of no messiah at all. And even a great proportion of Catholics themselves, in the present day, are evidently tired of that necessary confinement of thought and practice, which is essential to their being enclosed in the *one Sheepfold* of the *one Shepherd* (John 10: 16), and pant for every kind of Reformation, except that of their morality. (1)

## St Teresa on the Wounding Dart of Divine Love

O My Lord and my God, it is a great consolation to a soul that suffers, in her absence from thee, to know that thou are present every where. But of what service is this truth to her, when the ardour of her love to thee, O my God, increases, and the violence of her pain redoubles! For then her understanding grows obscure, and her reason confused, so that she becomes quite insensible of this important maxim. The only thoughts that then possess her, are, that she is unfortunately separated from thee, and that she can no where discover a remedy for her calamity. For the heart that is deeply wounded with divine love seeks for no counsel or comfort but from him that has inflamed it, knowing that it is from him alone it can receive the assuagement of its pain. When thou pleasest, O my Saviour, thou dost presently heal the wound thou hast made, but till then it is vain to look for any remedy or comfort, but in the knowledge of our sufferings answering so good an end.

O Thou, true lover of our souls, with what goodness, with what sweetness, with what delight, with what heavenly caresses, with what demonstrations of an infinite love dost thou cure our wounds, by means of the same love that has caused them! O my God, thou only comforter of my pains, how foolish is it in me to imagine, that human remedies can soothe a breast that is on fire with the love of thee! Who can penetrate to the depth of this wound of love? Who can tell from whence it comes, or how at once a pain so severe and yet so delicious, can be removed? How can it be expected that a wound, inflicted by the Almighty, should be closed by the contemptible efforts of human art?

It is with reason the spouse, in the Canticles, says, *My Beloved to me, and I to my Beloved* (Cant. 2: 16). She says first, *My Beloved to me*, because it is not possible that so divine a thing as this happy union is, should take its beginning from so base an origin as my affections are. But why, O thou spouse of my soul, if my affections be so base, why do they not rest in creatures? Why do they constantly mount up to the Creator? How comes it also to be said, *I to my beloved*, no less than *My beloved to me*? It is thou indeed, my true lover, that dost begin this sweet contest of love, which is first carried on by a total absence of all the powers of my soul, whilst they impatient seek after thee. Thus resembling the spouse in the Canticles, by running, as it were, through the streets and public places and conjuring the daughters of Jerusalem to indicate to them where they can find their God. But this contest of love being once begun, against whom do these powers of my soul strive, but against him who has taken possession of that fortress of the soul which they before held, and, who in subduing them, has only in view, that they should be forced to acknowledge their own misery and insufficiency when deprived of him; and thus, by taking from him the graces they stand in need of, they should, in some sort, subdue again their conqueror? For, by thus renouncing all confidence in their own strength, they derive an effectual strength from him, and in confessing themselves conquered they become truly conquerors. O my soul, what an admirable conflict of this nature hast thou sustained! and how strictly has the saying of the spouse in the Canticles, *My beloved to me, and I to my beloved*, been verified in thy regard! Who will now attempt to extinguish these united flames, which in fact are no longer two fires but one. (2)

## St Teresa on Divine Love

O how short-sighted is the wisdom, and how uncertain the prudence of mankind! Do thou, O my God, by thy heavenly wisdom, provide me with the necessary means for serving thee according to thy own will, and not according to mine. Do not inflict the severe punishment upon me of granting me my requests, when they are not conformable to the designs of thy love, which I wish ever to be the very principle of my life. Let me die to myself; and let one who is greater than I, who loves me better than I love myself, for ever live in me, that I may learn how to serve him. Let him live in me, and thus give me life. Let him reign in me, that thus I may become his servant. For this is the only liberty I crave. Alas, how can that soul be truly free that is not in subjection to the Most High! and what more wretched slavery can she be reduced to, than to lose the protection of her Creator! Happy those who find themselves so strongly bound to thee by the ties of thy love that it is not in their power to disengage themselves from thee. *Love is strong as death and hard as hell* (Cant. 8: 6) ... I choose rather to live and die in the hope of this happy eternity, than to possess all created beings, and all worldly advantages, which must so soon have an end. Forsake me not, O God, for my trust is in thee. O let me not be confounded for ever. O grant that I may always faithfully serve thee, and in every thing else do with me what thou wilt. (3)

## The Spiritual Symbolism of St George

To come now to the emblem of St George, who is represented in fierce combat with a dragon.... though there is no mention of the combat which our saint maintained against any corporeal dragon, there are frequent allusions to that spiritual victory which he gained over *that old Serpent, called the Devil and Satan* (Rev. 12: 9), according to the figure and language of scripture. Thus, in the first legend of St George, ... after an account of our martyrs being brought into the temple of Apollo, in order to join in the idolatrous sacrifice there performed, and of his forcing the demon of the place to acknowledge his own weakness, and the power of the true God, by which miracle the imaginary Empress Alexandria is said to have been converted, and of his baffling all the arts and cruelty of his persecutors, it is added in the conclusion: 'There are the trophies gained in the well-fought battles of this noble conqueror, these are his glorious achievements and combats against his enemies.' But it is chiefly in an historical panegyric ... that this mystical description of the spiritual battles and conquests of the 'soldier of Christ', as the martyr George is every where called, is to be met with in the most ample form. Speaking of the conversions wrought by the sight of the patient sufferings of St George, our author exclaims: 'All these were rescued by him from the very jaws of the dragon. O the insatiable jaws of the devil'; and after much the same expressions, as those quoted above concerning the 'spiritual trophies and spoils gained by his victorious warrior', he adds, 'George, whilst yet in the body, slew his incorporeal enemy'. These and such like passages, in the current legends and panegyrics of the times, must be allowed to have been more than sufficient for the artists who invented the different symbols of the saints, to represent our martyr under the striking figure of an armed warrior foiling, with his lance, a furious dragon. What confirms this explanation is that the emblem in question is not peculiar to St George, but is attributed to several other martyrs, especially of the military order, who were celebrated for their constancy in suffering torments, and in overcoming various temptations of the spiritual enemy. (4)

## The Religious Sublimity of Gothic Architecture

A most curious and interesting fact, however, in my opinion, for the investigation of architectural antiquaries, is, to ascertain the true principles of the sublime and beautiful, as applied to those sacred fabrics which are the undoubted masterpieces and glory of the pointed order. It is in vain that Sir Christopher Wren and Mr. Evelyn ... stigmatize these structures, as being 'congestions of heavy, dark, melancholy, monkish piles, without any just proportion, use, or beauty'. For it is confessedly true, that every man who has an eye to see, and a soul to feel, on entering into York Minster and chapterhouse, or into King's College or Windsor chapel, or into the cathedrals of Lincoln or Winchester, is irresistibly struck with mingled impressions of awe and pleasure, which no other buildings are capable of producing; and however he may approve of the Grecian architecture for the purposes of civil and social life, yet he instinctively experiences in the former a frame of mind that fits him for prayer and contemplation, which all the boasted regularity and magnificence of Sir Christopher's and the nation's pride, I mean St Paul's cathedral, cannot communicate, at least in the same degree.

To explain in detail the principles on which the above mentioned effects are produced would be to describe the whole structure of an ancient cathedral; and, at the same time, to form the best panegyric on the architects who raised them. This, however, it is not my present intention to do, but merely to enumerate a few of these principles which are more obvious. In the first place, then, it is well known that height and length are amongst the primary sources of the sublime. It is equally agreed that these are the proportions which our ancient architects chiefly affected in their religious structures. But besides the real effect of these proportions, which were generally carried as far as they were capable of, the mind was farther impressed by an artificial height and length, which were the natural produce of the style employed. For the aspiring form of the pointed arches, the lofty pediments, and the tapering pinnacles with which our cathedrals are adorned, contribute perhaps still more to give an idea of height than their real elevation. In like manner, the perspective of uniform columns, ribs, and arches, repeated at equal distances, as they are seen in the isles of those fabrics, produces an artificial infinite in the mind of the spectator, when the same extent of plain surface would perhaps hardly affect it at all. For a similar reason, I think the effect of the ancient cathedrals is greatly helped by the variety of their constituent parts and ornaments, though I suppose them all to be executed in one uniform style. The eye is quickly satiated by any object, however great and magnificent, which it can take in all at once, as the mind is with what it can completely comprehend; but when the former, having wandered through the intricate and interminable length of a pointed vault in an ancient cathedral, discovers two parallel lines of equal length and richness with it; then proceeding, it discovers the transepts, the side chapels, the choir, the sanctuary, and the Lady chapel, all equally interesting for their design and execution, and all of them calculated for different purposes: the eye, I say, is certainly much more entertained, and the mind more dilated and gratified, than can possibly be effected by any single view, even though our modern architects should succeed in their attempts to make one entire sweep of the contents of a cathedral, to show it all at a single view, and to make one vast empty room of the whole.

It is not necessary for me to dwell upon the effect of that solemn gloom which reigns in these venerable structures, from the studied exclusion of too glaring a light, or upon that glowing effect produced by appropriate painting and carving in the windows, or other parts of them, or upon the essential beauty and just proportions in which they are raised, where the infinite variety of ribs, arches, bosses, and other ornaments, all grow out of the main columns, with the regularity of nature in the vegetable kingdom, and also with her wise contrivance to combine strength with beauty. I say, it is not necessary for me to dwell upon these points, because, however they may be carped at by interested men, they are obvious of themselves and admitted by all persons of candour and sentiment. There is one circumstance, however, to which these venerable structures are indebted for the impression they make that is not so evident at first sight, and which therefore I here mention, namely, the arrangement and disposition of their several parts, in due subordination to that which is their principal member, by which means that unity of design so necessary in every composition is maintained in them. This principal member in our cathedral churches is the choir and sanctuary, destined for the performance of the service and mysteries of religion; and all the other portions of the sacred fabric will be found subservient, and as it were converging, to this, as to their centre. On the same account, the most exquisite productions of art, and the greatest profusion of wealth, were uniformly bestowed on this particular part. We may judge from hence what must be the effect of destroying the altar-screen of a cathedral, and removing the altar itself, according to a modern instance, under an idea of improving its appearance. It is like removing the head from the human figure, or placing it on some other member, for the purpose of increasing its beauty. (5)

## Miracles at St Winefride's Well

To announce a miracle in these days of infidelity, or rather Sadducism, must subject the person who announces it to the censure of many, and the ridicule of more. I reflect, however, that the very miracles recorded in the gospel were subject to the same ordeal....

Still it may be hoped, that this miraculous cure, by being more generally known, will produce those good effects upon a certain number of sincere and humble souls, which it has already produced upon some, and which it was certainly designed by Almighty God to produce, independently of the immediate benefit of the subject of it. For every known miracle is the voice of God proclaiming to men his infinite power, goodness, and providence in their regard. It calls therefore for a renewal of our profound homage, of our ardent love, and of our entire confidence in him, under all accidents and sufferings that we do or may experience. Every miracle is moreover a divine sanction of the religious worship or devout practices, for the sake of which, or by means of which, such supernatural communication with man has taken place. Hence the present miraculous cure, obtained of Almighty God by the prayers of the Blessed Virgin Mary and of St Winefride, who had been invoked for this purpose, at a place particularly consecrated to the memory of the latter more than a thousand years ago, ought to confirm us in our faith, and particularly in that article of it which declares, that 'the Saints reigning with Christ offer up their prayers for mankind'. It ought to excite our fervour in begging the aid of their intercession with our common Lord; being assured that these our brethren and fellow-citizens have not lost either the will or the power to assist us, by entering into the regions of eternal charity, and by becoming the courtiers of the great King, but that, as a Holy Father assures us: 'Whilst they are secure of their own happiness, they are solicitous about ours.' (6)

## Explaining Devotion to the Sacred Heart of Jesus

From what has been here said and quoted, it will be gathered that the object of this devotion is not the material heart of our blessed Saviour; but the same, as it constitutes a most noble and essential part of his humanity, as it is the peculiar seat of his immense charity, and as it is hypostatically united with the Divinity itself. In fact, it is the incomprehensible, infinite love of this incarnate God for us poor mortals, which made him 'obedient unto death, even the death of the cross', and which still detains him our willing captive and victim in the adorable Sacrifice of the Altar, that is the principal object of this devotion; as, indeed, its ultimate end is to inflame our hearts with a reciprocal love for this most amiable and loving Redeemer, conformably with the first injunction of his *great commandment* of love, 'Thou shalt love the Lord thy God with all thy heart' (Matt. 22: 37); and in compliance with the earnest desire which he testifies where he says: 'I am come to cast fire on the earth; and what do I desire but that it be enkindled' (Luke 12: 49). (7)

## Devotion to the Sacred Heart of Jesus

### DEVOUT SALUTATIONS TO THE SACRED HUMANITY OF JESUS CHRIST

Eternal Son of the living God, who, in the excess of thy mercy and love, didst take upon thee our human nature, to suffer in it the punishment due to my sins, what grateful homage and love do I not owe to this sacred humanity, sacrificed wholly and in each part for my salvation! I salute thee then, O precious body of Christ, suffering cold and want at thy birth—hunger and fatigue during thy life—and a bloody scourging, which rendered thee 'like a leper, and as one struck by God' (Isa. 53: 4), before thy death.

R. *I salute and adore thee, thou dear suffering body of my Lord and Redeemer Jesus Christ.*

Prostrate before you, I salute and adore you, O sacred feet of my Redeemer, so often wearied, during his mortal course, in 'seeking the lost sheep of the house of Israel' (Matt. 15: 24), and at length transfixed with torturing nails to the wood of the cross.
R. *I salute and adore you, O bleeding feet of my Saviour Jesus Christ.*

I salute and adore you, omnipotent hands of my gracious Master, which healed the sick, and wrought other miracles for his people, and, in return, were nailed by them to the instrument of his torture, in order to exhaust his life by lengthened sufferings.
R. *I salute and adore you, O bountiful hands of my Saviour Jesus Christ, bleeding on the cross.*

I salute and adore you, O venerable head and countenance of the Word Incarnate, on which the angels look with awe, but which by his sinful creatures were buffeted, and blindfolded, and spit upon, and crowned with thorns.
R. *I salute and adore thee, O divine countenance of my awful Judge, and I beseech thee, that, instead of thy terrible frown, I may meet with thy gracious smile, when thou shalt unveil thyself to me.*

I salute and adore thee, O sacred spirit of the divine Jesus, which, from the moment of his conception, foresaw and accepted of all the ignominies and pains he successively endured; oppressed with sorrow even unto death, in the Garden of Gethsemane, and left by the Eternal Father to the extremity of interior and exterior torment, till their violence exhausted and took away his breath.
R. *I salute and adore thee, O most afflicted spirit of my willing victim Jesus Christ, and beg of thee that I may henceforward love him with all my soul and all my mind.*

I salute and adore thee, O glowing heart of my best friend Jesus Christ, that wert laid open at his death, to give me, with the last drop of his life's blood, the final proof of his boundless love for me.

R. *I salute and adore thee, O precious Heart of Jesus, that loved me unto death. Grant that I may love thee with all my heart now and for evermore.* Amen.

### THE SHORT LITANY OF THE SACRED HEART

Lord, have mercy on us.
 R. *Lord, have mercy on us.*
Christ, have mercy on us.
 R. *Christ, have mercy on us.*
Christ, hear us.
 R. *Christ, graciously hear us.*
O God, the Father of our Lord Jesus Christ, *Have mercy on us.*
O God the Son, the Redeemer of mankind, *Have mercy on us.*
O God the Holy Ghost, the Comforter of the just, *Have mercy on us.*
O Sacred Trinity, three Persons in one God, *Have mercy on us.*
Sacred heart of Jesus.
 R. *Grant us grace to love thee.*
Sacred Heart of Jesus, hypostatically united with the Eternal Word,
Sacred Heart of Jesus, furnace of divine love,
Sacred Heart of Jesus, mirror of meekness and humility,
Sacred Heart of Jesus, source of true contrition,
Sacred Heart of Jesus, the treasury of all graces,
Sacred Heart of Jesus, *sorrowful in the Garden unto death,*
Sacred Heart of Jesus, fainting under his bloody sweat,
Sacred Heart of Jesus, *saturated with affronts* (Lam. 3: 30),
Sacred Heart of Jesus, *obedient unto the death of the cross* (Phil. 2: 8),
Sacred Heart of Jesus, pierced with the soldier's spear,

Sacred Heart of Jesus, the refuge of sinners,
Sacred Heart of Jesus, the consolation of the afflicted,
Sacred Heart of Jesus, the hope of the dying,
Sacred Heart of Jesus, the joy of the elect,

From insensibility of thy infinite love for us, *Deliver us, O Heart of Jesus*.
From the ingratitude of wilfully offending thee, *Deliver us, O Heart of Jesus*.
From the misery of being separated from thee in time and eternity, *Deliver us, O Heart of Jesus*.
O Jesus, meek and humble of heart.
      R. *O Jesus, make our hearts like unto thy heart.*

*Let us pray.*

O Jesus Christ, who, from the full treasury of thy Sacred Heart, didst draw the inestimable graces which thou dispensest to thy faithful lovers, grant that, mortifying our pride and self-love, we may become true imitators of thy meekness and humility, and becoming every day more sensible of thy excessive love, in making thyself our companion in thy Incarnation, our victim in thy Passion and Death, and our food in thy Real Presence on our altars, we may henceforward return thee, to the best of our power, love for love during this our present state, and be immersed hereafter in the abyss of thy divine love, who with the Father and the Holy Ghost livest and reignest one God, world without end. *Amen.* (8)


# How Came I Here?

If you can for a few minutes, irreligious worldling, turn your mind from trifling concerns of little moment to yourself to one of the utmost consequence, and which immediately relates to your own welfare, let me exhort you to question yourself in some such manner as the following: 'How came I here? The world had existed some thousands of years, and I had no being in it. Who drew me out of the abyss of nothing and bestowed upon me this excellent body, this capacious mind? I am deeply conscious that I could not give a being to myself; and when I enquire of the objects which surround me on the earth, and of the vast bodies which roll over my head in the heavens, each of them exclaim to me, in the language of St Augustine: *It was not I that made thee: we are all equally the workmanship of an eternal, omnipotent, and infinitely benevolent being.*' What heart, impressed with these truths, can avoid paying a constant and explicit homage, in acts of humility, thanksgiving, and love, to this its beneficent Creator, its God? And yet there always have been, and there are now, in greater numbers than heretofore, men who ridicule the expression of these noble sentiments, that is to say, the exercise even of natural religion, as superstition and a degradation of our nature. Whereas, in real truth, it is our intercourse with the Deity, that is to say, religion, which ennobles our nature and constitutes its final cause of existence. Without religion, how little superior is man to the beasts of the field! They eat, and drink, and play, and propagate their species to do the same after them: and for what more than this does man exist, if he does not serve his God and provide for a happiness hereafter, which he finds is not to be enjoyed here on earth. (9)

## Belief in God Leads to the Church

Admitting, however, the obligation of worshipping my Creator, these men will sometimes say: 'What necessity is there of my being shut up in a particular building, or of my joining with other people in the performance of it? Is not the whole universe the temple of the Deity? And is not the homage of a sincere heart more acceptable to him that any exterior rites or forms whatsoever?' It is true the immensity of God *fills the heavens and the earth*, as he himself declares. It is true, he requires to be *worshipped in spirit and in truth*, as our Divine Saviour expressly tells us. Nevertheless in the very passages of scripture here quoted, and in many others...the Almighty is pleased to sanction and appoint social and public worship to be offered up to him in certain places appropriated to this purpose. Accordingly I find the Holy Patriarchs, from the beginning of the world, worshipping God in an exterior and public manner and dedicating certain places and things to the honour of his Divine Majesty. I afterwards find the great legislator of God's people constructing an ark and a tabernacle of the most costly materials for the public exercise of their religion, according to express revelations made to him concerning these matters. And lastly, I behold the inspired Solomon, exhausting his royal treasures in building and ornamenting a house, which the Almighty deigns to choose as *a house of sacrifice* for himself, and dedicating it with the utmost pomp and solemnity of religion. The fact is, he who *knoweth what is in man* foresaw that, unless we are reminded, at stated times, of the duty which we owe to him, and unless we are excited by the example of our fellow creatures, by the pomp and solemnity of the worship itself, and by other exterior means, we should either totally neglect this worship, or we should comply with it in the most tepid and unworthy manner. I must add, that the disciples of Christ have not been behind hand with the ancient people of God in the solemnity and splendour of their religious worship, or magnificence of the churches which they built for the performance of it. Our Catholic ancestors, in particular, filled this land with the riches and most beautiful edifices for the service of religion, a small part of which are still to be seen. On these and their appurtenances they lavished their wealth, being content with comparatively homely habitations, furniture, and fare for their own use. (10)

## Catholic Complacency

In the first part of my discourse I addressed myself chiefly to deists and other irreligious sophists, and in the second part of it to my fellow Christians of the different new-invented systems. It now remains for me, in this concluding portion of it, to say a few words particularly adapted to the Catholic part of my audience. Infinite thanks then, my dear fellow members in Jesus Christ, are due from you to the pure mercy of God which has preserved you in the safe tranquillity of his holy ark, the Catholic church, whilst you see, with your own eyes, those Christians who have abandoned it *tossed to and fro and carried about by every wind of doctrine*. The best proof of your security from error in the bosom of this Church is that, whereas you know well that persons of other communions are in the frequent habit of seeking to enter into it, at the awful conscience-speaking article of death and of sending for your pastors for this purpose, there is no instance known, there is none upon record, of a well instructed Catholic seeking to die in any religion but his own! Infinite thanks, again, are due from you to the pure mercy of God for the numerous and inestimable practical helps for working out your salvation which this Church affords you, in the communion of saints; in the seven sacraments, those living fountains of grace, so admirably adapted by infinite wisdom to your several necessities and stations of life; and finally, in the adorable sacrifice of the new law, so infinitely superior to the types of it in the old law; which sacrifice, you know, constitutes the most essential part of your public worship. But, my fellow Catholics, to come to the point which I announced in the division of my sermon, will any of these advantages or all of them together avail you of themselves to please God or to save your souls? May you argue with the Pharisees: 'We are the children of Abraham and therefore we shall inherit the promises of Abraham?' No, my brethren. For Christ answers them and you: 'If you are the children of Abraham, do the works of Abraham.' In other, more explicit words, he tells you: 'If you will enter into life keep the commandments'; not one or two of the commandments, but all and every one of them. There is no place, in the region of infinite purity and infinite happiness, for pride, or avarice, or lust, or anger, or intemperance, or envy, or sloth. Should you be found guilty of any one of these vices, or of a single act of them, unrepented of, at the all-important moment of your entering into eternity (as judging from their lives, we may safely say, too many Catholics will be found) the religious advantages which God has conferred upon you will be the cause of your heavier condemnation. 'It will be more tolerable to Tyre and Sidon' than to you 'at that day'. In a word, the exterior of religion, however necessary, will not avail you without the interior vital part of it which is comprised in truly 'loving God with all your heart, with all your soul, with all your mind, and with all your strength, and your neighbour as yourselves'; and, as the beloved disciple assures us, this 'love must not consist in words only, but in deed and in effect'. (11)

## Seek a Guide

When ... will there be an end of the objections and cavils of men, whose pride, ambition, or interest leads them to deny the plainest truths? You have seen those which the ingenuity and learning of the Porteus's, Seckers, and Tillotsons have raised against the unchangeable Catholic rule and interpreter of faith. Say, is there anything sufficiently clear and certain in them to oppose to the luminous and sure principles, on which the Catholic method is placed? Do they afford you a sure footing to support you against all doubts and fears on the score of your religion, especially under the apprehension of approaching dissolution? If you answer affirmatively, I have nothing more to say; but if you cannot so answer, and, if you justly dread undertaking your voyage to eternity on the presumption of your private judgement, a presumption which you have clearly seen has led so many other rash Christians to certain shipwreck, follow the example of those who have happily arrived at the port which you are in quest of. In other words, listen to the advice of the holy patriarch to his son: *Then Tobias answered his father—I know not the way, etc.; then his father said—Seek thee a faithful guide* (Tobit 5: 4). You will no sooner have sacrificed your own wavering judgement, and have submitted to follow the guide, whom your heavenly Father has provided for you, than you will feel a deep conviction that you are in the right and secure way; and very soon you will be enabled to join with the happy converts of ancient and modern times, in this hymn of praise: 'I give Thee thanks, O God, my Enlightener and Deliverer; for that Thou hast opened the eyes of my soul to know Thee. Alas! too late have I known Thee, O ancient and eternal Truth! too late have I known Thee' (St Augustine, *Confessions*). (12)

## Adhering to the Crucifix

Hence, if you should become a Catholic, as I pray God you may, I shall never ask you if you have a pious picture or relic or so much as a crucifix in your possession. But then, I trust, after the declarations I have made, that you will not account me an idolater should you see such things in my oratory or study, or should you observe how tenacious I am of my crucifix in particular. Your faith and devotion may not stand in need of such memorials, but mine, alas! do. I am too apt to forget what my Saviour has done and suffered for me, but the sight of His representation often brings this to my memory and affects my best sentiments. Hence, I would rather part with most of the books in my library than with the figure of my crucified Lord. (13)

NOTES AND SOURCES

1. John Milner, *The Exclamations of the Soul to God: or, The Meditations of St Teresa after Communion* (London, 1790), pp. ii–iii, vi–viii.

2. Ibid. 69–74.

3. Ibid. 79–80, 84.

4. John Milner, *An Historical and Critical Inquiry into the Existence and Character of Saint George, Patron of England* (London, 1792), 29–32.

5. John Milner, *Essays on Gothic Architecture* (London, 1800), pp. xvi–xx.

6. John Milner, *Authentic Documents Relative to the Miraculous Cure of Winefrid White, of the Town of Woverhampton, at Holywel, in Flintshire on the 28th of June 1805* (London, 1805), 38–40.

7. John Milner, *Bishop Milner's Devotion to the Sacred Heart of Jesus* (London, 1867), 10–11.

8. Ibid. 21–7.

9. John Milner, *The Substance of a Sermon, Preached at the Blessing of the Catholic Chapel of St Chad in the Town of Birmingham on Sunday, December 17, 1809* (Birmingham, 1809), 7–8.

10. Ibid. 9–11.

11. Ibid. 46–8.

12. John Milner, *The End of Religious Controversy* (London: Catholic Truth Society, 1912), 143–4.

13. Ibid. 322–3.

# Elizabeth Inchbald

1753–1821

Elizabeth Inchbald dazzles even at the distance of 200 years. Witty and beautiful, politically daring and religiously devout, she acted, edited, and wrote novels and plays on the way to becoming one of the most fascinating literary women of the British romantic period. Born and raised near Bury St Edmunds, Inchbald (née Simpson) ran away from home at age 19 to seek a living as a London stage actress. She faced two handicaps in this venture: an unwillingness to compromise herself (she reportedly poured a jug of scalding water on a licentious theatre manager) and a stammer. Nevertheless, she acted for seventeen years, marrying the Catholic actor Joseph Inchbald and gaining the friendship of two stars of the stage, Sarah Siddons and her Douai-educated brother John Philip Kemble. After the death of her husband in 1779, Inchbald found more success in writing, beginning with a farce called *The Mogul Tale* (1784) that would be followed by many other popular comedies. Her first novel, *A Simple Story* (1791), gained the admiration of Maria Edgeworth and Madame de Staël among others and, with its unlikely love story between a laicized priest and his Protestant ward, can be considered a forerunner of the twentieth-century 'Catholic Novel'. Many may know Inchbald's name from another novel, Jane Austen's *Mansfield Park*, in which the staging of her adaptation of a revolutionary German play sends the Bertram household into chaos. Indeed, her politics were radical, and *Nature and Art* (1796) is known as a Jacobin novel of the type written by William Godwin, a revolutionary philosopher and her close friend. Jacobinism and Catholicism seem an unlikely pairing, but both shaped Inchbald's views. Her early life was informed by a family friendship with the prominent Catholic Gage family, and she had Catholic friends such as Kemble and the controversial biblical critic Alexander Geddes. Literary scholars will never forgive William Poynter, her confessor, who counselled her to destroy her four-volume memoirs which may have made her the Pepys of her age. She was most regular in her devotion later in life, and she settled into a Kensington boarding home that was a former Catholic school and safehaven for French émigrés. She appears to have known many English Catholics who also had to flee the French Revolution, and her ability to see multiple sides of the issues seems to drive her reconciliatory message in her only tragedy *The Massacre* (written in 1793, published 1833). That play, too controversial to be performed in her lifetime, captures her political commitments and her sympathy with sufferers, but no single genre—not her sparkling comedies, her intense novels, or the judicious dramatic commentary from her voluminous edited collections *British Theatre* (1806–09) and *Modern Theatre* (1811)—could quite contain all of her independent, quicksilver personality.

## *The Massacre:* Friendship over Sectarian Violence

*Tri[castin]. [Laying hold of his hand.]* Dugas, hesitate an instant, and consider once—once call to mind, before you drag me and my wretched family to immediate death, that you and I are fellow-creatures—we are countrymen—nay more, townsmen—and, till this unhappy period, have always lived like neighbours. Many little acts of friendship have passed between us—such, my neighbour, as ought not to be forgotten in an hour of tribulation like this. Oh! by the many times we have exchanged like friendly salutation of 'good morrow', or the kind farewell of 'good night'—the numerous times that, at the hospitable board, we have wished each other, in our cheerful glasses, 'health and a happy day!'—by all these little kindnesses, which have their weight, with minds susceptible, do not imbrue your hand in your neighbour's blood. (1)

## The Embers of Religious Strife

It was the custom, till within a very few years, to perform this tragedy constantly on the 5$^{\text{th}}$ of November, in honour of the landing of the Prince of Orange, afterwards King William—but as that political fire, which once gave brightness to its gloomy scenes, no longer blazes, it is now seldom acted, and never with strong marks of approbation.

As Rowe was a good man, a religious man, his chief delight the study of divinity and ecclesiastical history, with such propensities, and such a capacious mind to improve by them, it is to be deplored that he should hope to compliment a Christian king, and strictly pious as William was known to be, by a calumnious representation of his declared enemy. That title alone should have made the character of his royal adversary sacred. (2)

## The Challenge of Goodness to a Dramatist

The failure of many past dramatists, in the perfection of their art, has chiefly arisen from their bestowing spirit, fire, and ever powerful emotion of the soul, upon the wicked, and making all their good people insipid. Such is the case in this comedy.—Lord Lovell, Lady Allworth, and every amiable character, is a dull one; whilst the amusement of the public is to depend upon the mean and the base.

It is certainly a more difficult task for a writer to give violent exertions of the mind to the good, than to the evil-disposed persons of his drama. The life of the vicious man is one continued round of agitation, whilst the man of virtue has not only fewer turbulent passions, but a higher degree of control over those by which he is assailed; nor can they ever amount, in his breast, to those grand exhibitions for a theatre—remorse, or despair.

But, as the virtuous are the most placid, the higher skill of an author is shown, in depicting these characters under sensations which awaken interest, and yet do not impair their moral disposition. (3)

NOTES AND SOURCES

1. Elizabeth Inchbald, 'The Massacre', in *Memoirs of Mrs. Inchbald*, ed. James Boaden (London, 1833), 373.
2. Elizabeth Inchbald, 'Remarks on *Tamerlane* by Nicholas Rowe', in *The British Theatre*, x (London, 1808), 4.
3. Elizabeth Inchbald, 'Remarks on *A New Way to Pay Old Debts* by Philip Massinger', ibid., vi (London, 1808), 4.

# Bishop William Poynter                                    1762–1827

After his death, the heart of William Poynter was deposited beneath the altar in the chapel of St Edmund's College, Ware; thus, his ultimate place of rest also represents the ultimate site of those acts of sacrifice and mediation that characterized his life. Along with the students at Douai, of which he was an alumnus and professor, Poynter was imprisoned by the French Revolutionary authorities in 1793. Students would later testify to the fortifying effect of seeing Poynter daily scale the walled ramparts of their prison in Doullens to say the divine office. Upon his return to England in 1795, he served first as vice-president and then president of St Edmund's College. He managed to retain this position while serving as a bishop and coadjutor of the London district until 1812 when he became the vicar apostolic. In these positions of prominence, he found himself amid the internal struggle over what concessions should be made to the British government in exchange for Catholic Emancipation. Poynter attempted to mediate between the English bishops and the Cisalpine Catholic Committee's conciliatory position and the uncompromising wariness of the Irish bishops and bishop John Milner. Both Milner's friends and foes could agree that opposing him was not an enviable position, and Poynter's experience was no different. If these often fierce internal battles were not enough, he also interceded in post-Napoleonic France for English Catholics whose property had been confiscated in the Revolution. After many years of difficult negotiations across the Channel, he partially succeeded, only to see British authorities seize the compensatory funds on the grounds that they would go to 'superstitious' usage. It has been speculated that the funds were diverted to the construction of Marble Arch in London or the Regent's Palace in Brighton. Amid this maelstrom, Poynter wrote extensively, and his publications included his recollections of the final days of Douai, a theological controversy with a radical Irish priest, and a prayer book for Catholic sailors and soldiers. His meditations on the essential meaning of Christianity and the relationship between faith and reason derive from Poynter's contribution to the recurring theme of both Catholic and Protestant nineteenth-century apologetic theology—providing evidences for Christian belief.

## What is Christianity?

Christianity is that form of religion, which was taught and instituted by Christ. It embraces the *doctrines* of faith, which Christ revealed; the supernatural *moral precepts*, which he delivered; the *sacred rites*, which he instituted; and the *form of constitution*, which he founded, for the government of his Church. Its doctrines are most sublime, and consoling; and, at the same time, most true and certain. Its moral precepts are most pure and perfect, prescribing the renunciation of all sin and the exercise of every virtue. Its religious rites are most holy and salutary, being the divinely established means of offering an acceptable worship to God, and of communicating the graces of sanctification to the souls of men. To those who embrace the Christian Religion with sincerity and observe its injunctions with fidelity, it imparts peace and spiritual consolation in life and ensures the enjoyment of a glorious immortality after death.

Christianity is the work of God; a magnificent work, in the establishment and support of which, he has displayed his power, his wisdom, his mercy and goodness, even in a stronger light than in the creation and preservation of the world. Its end is the glory of God, and the renovation and eternal happiness of man. (1)

## Faith and Reason

Nothing can be more unreasonable than to seek the certain knowledge of truths and facts by means which are not naturally and specifically adapted to the object of inquiry; or to deny the truth of any doctrine, or the existence of any fact, because it cannot be demonstrated, or established by arguments or testimonies, which have no analogy or connection with them. Would it be reasonable, to deny the metaphysical doctrines of the spirituality or immortality of the soul, because they cannot be proved by the testimony of the senses? Or to deny that the battle of Hastings was ever fought, or that there ever existed such a person as William the Conqueror, because these historical facts cannot be demonstrated like a mathematical problem, by lines and angles? Or to deny the existence of colour because it cannot be perceived by the eye? To attempt to prove such objects by such means, would be to pervert the order of nature, and to subvert the grounds of certitude....

Is then the light of reason to be extinguished by revelation? Is the total exercise of natural reason to be prohibited in the search of religious truths? No, certainly not. The truths which are the objects of reason and of revelation are distinct, and are grounded on distinct motives of assent. Reason and revelation have their separate provinces, in which they may respectively exercise their rights.

Revelation leaves reason free to range over the vast field of nature and to pursue the study of natural and moral truth by the principles of natural science. Revelation brings a new light to the human mind, by infusing a sublime knowledge of supernatural truths and by giving additional testimony, perfection, and sanction to the truths and precepts of the moral law of nature. But revelation opposes no obstacle to discoveries and improvements in the natural sciences. Indeed, have not civilization and literature been introduced into many countries by those who introduced the belief of the doctrines of revelation? Has not reason been improved, to the highest degree, in minds enlightened with the knowledge of revealed truths? Were an Origen, a St Chrysostom, a St Augustine, a St Jerome, in former ages; or a Bossuet, a Fénelon, a Pascal, a Descartes, in later times, impeded in the improvement of their natural talents, or in the acquisition of natural sciences, by their belief of the doctrines of revelation? Have not the ministers and professors of revealed religion been the greatest encouragers and promoters of the arts and sciences in all ages? Revelation, as well as good sense, commends the use and condemns the misuse of the powers of reason.

In the search of religious and revealed truths, reason is by no means prohibited the use and exercise of her powers, provided she employ them about those objects, which lie within her proper jurisdiction, and she do not wander our of her own province. But if reason attempt to demonstrate the *truth* or *falsehood* of the doctrines and mysteries of revelation, by discussing the *intrinsic* nature of the objects of these doctrines and mysteries, or by philosophical arguments drawn from self-evident principles of *natural* science, with which they have no connection, reason does go out of her province. She acts unreasonably, by attempting to demonstrate that by *intrinsic* evidence, which is not the object of it; any more than colour is the object of the ear, or sound of the eye, or the existence of an historical fact is the object of a mathematical demonstration. (2)

NOTES AND SOURCES

1. William Poynter, *Christianity, or, The Evidences and Characters of the Christian Religion* (London, 1835), pp. iii–iv.

2. Ibid. 6, 20–1.

# John Chetwode Eustace 1762–1815

For an aristocratic young man in the eighteenth century, making a 'Grand Tour' of the natural and historic sites of continental Europe was a necessary rite of passage and a keystone to a proper education. During this tour, religious considerations were inevitable as Protestant Englishmen balanced the architectural and artistic achievements in Catholic countries against perceptions of 'papist' backwardness in morality and politics. *A Classical Tour through Italy* (1813) by Eustace—a Catholic priest, tutor, and travel writer—sought to make the 'Grand Tour' an occasion to appreciate rather than deprecate English Catholics. Born in Ireland but raised in Staffordshire, Eustace resided with the Benedictines at Douai before being ordained at Maynooth. While he did serve as a chaplain in Norfolk for a time, Eustace spent most of his life as a tutor and accompanied his pupils to Europe. In the *Classical Tour*, which went through eight editions between 1813 and 1841, Eustace did not hide that Catholicism was his 'sincere and undisguised belief and profession', attesting his 'affectionate attachment to the ancient Faith' and admiration for the 'affecting lessons, the holy examples, and the majestic rites of the Catholic Church'. Eustace's Cisalpine allegiances and Whig politics made this enthusiasm for the English reading public more palatable, as he could describe the Vatican with awe on one page and question the Pope's infallibility on another. A man of eloquence and charm, Eustace enjoyed literary fame until his 1815 death from malaria during another Italian tour.

## Rome: The Eternal City

In the whole universe, there are only two cities interesting alike to every member of the great Christian commonwealth, to every citizen of the civilized world, whatever may be his tribe or nation—Rome and Jerusalem. The former calls up every classic recollection, the latter awakens every sentiment of devotion; the one brings before our eyes all the splendours of the present world; the other, all the glories of the world to come. By a singular dispensation of Providence, the names and influence of these two illustrious capitals are combined in the same grand dispensation; and as Jerusalem was ordained to receive, Rome was destined to propagate 'the light that leads to Heaven'. The cross which Jerusalem erected on Mount Calvary, Rome fixed on the diadem of emperors, and the prophetic songs of Mount Sion have resounded from the seven hills to the extremities of the universe.—How natural then the emotion which the traveller feels, when he first beholds the distant domes of a city, of such figure in the history of the universe, of such weight in the destinies of mankind, so familiar to the imagination of the child, so interesting to the feelings of the man! (1)

## Awe and the Vatican

As you enter you behold the most extensive hall ever constructed by human art, expanded in magnificent perspective before you; advancing up the nave you are delighted with the beauty of the variegated marble under your feet, and the splendour of the golden vault over your head. The lofty Corinthian pilasters with their bold entablature, the intermediate niches with their statues, the arches that communicate with the aisles, and the graceful figures that recline on the curves of those arches charm your eye in succession as you pass along. But how great your astonishment when you reach the foot of the altar and standing in the centre of the church, contemplate the four superb vistas that open around you; and then raise your eyes to the dome, at the prodigious elevation of four hundred feet, extended like a firmament over your head, and presenting in glowing mosaic the companies of the just, the choirs of celestial spirits, and the whole hierarchy of Heaven arrayed in the presence of the Eternal, whose 'throne high raised above all height' crowns the awful scene....

Under the high altar of St Peter's is the tomb of that apostle, formerly called the Confession of St Peter, an appellation which it has communicated to the altar and its canopy....The pavement of the area is upon a level with the *Sacre grotte*, though the regular entrance into those subterraneous recesses is under one of the great pillars that support the dome.

The *Sacre grotte* are the remains of the ancient church built by Constantine, the pavement of which was respected and preserved with all possible care during the demolition of the old and the construction of the new Basilica. They consist of several long winding galleries extending in various directions under the present building. They are venerable for their antiquity and contents, and if Addison never visited Westminster abbey, or trod its gloomy cloisters without strong impressions of religious awe, I may be pardoned when I acknowledge that I felt myself penetrated with holy terror, while, conducted by a priest in his surplice with a lighted torch in his hand, I ranged through these dormitories of the dead, lined with the urns of emperors and pontiffs, and almost paved with the remains of saints and martyrs. The intrepid Otho, the turbulent Alexander, and the polished Christina, lie mouldering near the hallowed ashes of the apostles Peter and Paul, of the holy pontiffs Linus, Silvester and Adrian. The low vault closes over their porphyry tombs, and silence and darkness brood uninterrupted around them. My awe increased as I approached the monument of the apostles themselves. Others may behold the mausoleum of an emperor or a consul, a poet or an orator, with enthusiasm; for my part, I contemplated the sepulchre of these Christian heroes with heart-felt veneration. What, if a bold achievement, an useful invention, a well-fought battle or a well-told tale can entitle a man to the admiration of posterity and shed a blaze of glory over his remains, surely, the courage, the constancy, the cruel sufferings, the triumphant death of these holy champions, must excite our admiration and our gratitude, ennoble the spot where their relics repose, and sanctify the very dust that imbibed their sacred blood. They enlightened the world by their doctrine, they reformed it by their example, they devoted their lives to the propagation of truth, and they sealed their testimony with their blood. They are therefore the patriots of the world at large, the common benefactors of mankind, and in the truest and noblest sense, heroes and conquerors. How natural then for a Christian not only to cherish their names but to extend his grateful veneration to their ashes and their monuments. (2)

NOTES AND SOURCES

1. John Chetwode Eustace, *A Classical Tour through Italy*, i (London, 1813), 201–2.

2. Ibid. 348, 351–3.

# John Lingard                                                      1771–1851

Contemporaries both hailed John Lingard 'among the most eminent of our English historians' and denounced him as a Catholic priest whose voluminous and painstakingly researched accounts of English history were 'venomous with the most sanctified appearance of impartiality'. Born in Winchester, Lingard was among the students of Douai who fled the French Revolution in 1793. After his ordination in 1795, he served as vice-president of Crook Hall, the home of the northern refugees from Douai, and for a year from 1810 was President of the transplanted college at Ushaw. However, after these academic beginnings, the rest of his life was spent in pastoral ministry and study in the mission at Hornby, Lancashire. His prolific writings ranged from biblical translation to hymn-writing, including his enduring reworking of the hymn *Ave Maris Stella*—'Hail, Queen of Heaven, the Ocean Star'. Yet he was most renowned for his extensive historical writing and for his historiographical method. Lingard saw impartiality, candour, and fairness as his religious duty as a historian, leading him to champion the consultation of primary sources and original documents over inherited prejudice and stereotypes. His greatest work, *History of England* (1819–1830), was read widely in Britain, translated for European audiences, adapted by William Cobbett for his *History of the Protestant Reformation in England* (1824–7), and continued by Hillaire Belloc in the twentieth century. The honours in his own lifetime included Pius VII's conferral of the degrees of doctor of divinity, civil law, and canon law, becoming an associate to the Royal Society of Literature, election to a corresponding membership of the Académie Française, and a possible creation as a cardinal *in petto* by Leo XII that was not confirmed before the Pope's death. Lingard strongly defended Catholic doctrine and practice in extended controversy with Shute Barrington (1734–1826), the Anglican Bishop of Durham, who had claimed that all Catholic images and statuary in churches necessarily led to idolatry. Lingard gained an unlikely last word in this debate when a posthumous commemorative statue of Barrington by the sculptor Francis Leggatt Chantrey (1781–1841) was installed in Durham Cathedral in 1833. His historical account of Reformation upheaval highlights the social and political as much as the religious in lamenting violations of English custom, law, and liberty in the name of power.

## Catholics not Idolaters

*Thou shalt not make to thyself any graven image, nor the likeness of any thing that is in Heaven above, or in earth beneath.* 'It is in vain', he [the Bishop of Durham] tells us, 'to allege that images are used as the aids and not the objects of devotion. It is impossible to preserve the distinction in the minds of the people. Abuse is unavoidable. Idolatry is the inevitable consequence.' In favour of this accusation, so unfounded in fact, so injurious to the feelings of a people as zealous for the honour of God as the Bishop of Durham himself, the only thing that can be said is, that it has been often and vehemently urged by the adversaries of the Church of Rome. It has also been often and victoriously refuted. But, probably, the reading of the bishop has been principally confined to our accusers, and has been seldom extended to our apologists. The opinions, which in his youth he imbibed from the bigotry and prejudice of controvertists, he still cherishes in his old age, and condemns us as idolaters, when he might any day, by an easy experiment, convince himself of the falsity of the accusation. Let him interrogate the first Catholic child of ten years of age, whom he may chance to meet in the streets, whether it be lawful to worship images? And he will receive the answer: 'No, by no means; for they can "neither hear, nor see, nor help us." ' This is the lesson which is impressed on our minds in our infancy; and it is so consonant to religion and common sense, that, I believe, it is never effaced. I may certainly claim a more extensive acquaintance with Catholics than the bishop of Durham; but I never yet met with any so ignorant, as to pay adoration to either images or pictures.

The bishop proceeds to observe that this practice 'is repugnant to the letter of God's commandments'. But, as to the letter of the commandments, it may be observed, that the practice of Catholics is not more repugnant to it than the practice of Protestants. Taken literally, the commandments prohibit, without exception or qualification, the making of any graven thing, or the likeness of any thing that is in Heaven above or on the earth beneath. If we are to be judged by the letter of the law, let our adversaries submit to the same trial; and let the Bishop of Durham justify, if he can, the graven things, and the likenesses of things in Heaven above and on the earth beneath, which still exist in his cathedral. It was formerly ornamented by the ingenuity of the sculptor and the painter; and of these ornaments, if many have been effaced by the Gothic fanaticism of the first reformers, many are still preserved by the pious care of their posterity. Aware of this difficulty, he has prudently inserted in his edition of the commandment, the words, 'for the purpose of religious worship'; an explanation which I cordially approve, as it perfectly agrees with the Catholic doctrine. 'This commandment', says our catechism, 'forbids the making of images so as to adore and serve them: that is, it forbids making them our Gods.' If then Catholics be idolaters, tell me, what is the bishop of Durham? (1)

## Religious Imagery

It is our doctrine that pious pictures and images ought not to be treated with disrespect, under the false pretence that they are idols; and this doctrine, repro- bated as it formerly was with contempt and detestation, is now, I observe, gradually making its way into the creed of the Established Church, in proportion as the fanaticism of the first reformers subsides, and reason and common sense recover their authority. The piety of our fathers, two centuries ago, would have condemned the works of Raphael and Michael Angelo to the flames and the mattock, had they discovered them in their churches; but modern Protestants have learned that they can pray in the presence of a painting or a statue without experiencing any impediment to their devotion or any temptation to idolatry. It is unfortunate that similar sentiments did not animate their progenitors. We should not now have to lament our inferiority in the elegant productions of the chisel and the pencil; nor would our native artists be compelled to visit foreign countries that they may study the master-pieces of the painter and the statuary. It is, indeed, true, that besides the prohibition of disrespect, our church also maintains it to be lawful to treat them with respect, in as much as they are the representations of our Blessed Redeemer, and of his faithful followers; and this respect has been by our adversaries, with as much injustice as ingenuity, transubstantiated into an idola- trous worship. I could, however, wish they would, once at least, inform us in what idolatry consists? Is it in paying divine worship to images? Such worship we condemn as sincerely as themselves. The respect which we allow is of a much inferior, a very different, description. It is the same as a subject may pay to the effigy of his sovereign, such as nature prompts a child to pay to the portrait of a deceased parent. Or is any respect whatsoever idolatrous? Then the Christians of the east were idolaters, when they were accustomed to burn incense before the statues of the Christian emperors. The peers of the United Kingdom are idolaters, as often as they make a reverence to the vacant throne. The Protestants of the Established Church are idolaters, as often as they kneel before the consecrated bread and wine. (2)

## This Is My Body

According to the Catholic belief, the bread and wine in the sacrament of the Eucharist, are made verily and indeed, the body and blood of Christ. This doctrine is grounded on the express words of our blessed Lord in the institution of the sacrament: *This is my body. This is my blood.* The natural import of these words is so very obvious, that I shall content myself with only one observation: that if Christ had wished to inculcate the Catholic doctrine, he could not have done it in terms better adapted to the purpose; and if he meant to inculcate the doctrine of the Church of England, he could hardly have selected words more likely to lead his disciples into error.

In opposition to this statement, the Bishop of Durham contends that the words of Christ are to be taken not in their literal, but in a figurative sense. Now to me it appears that the presumption is in favour of the literal meaning. If, as our adversaries maintain, it be from the scriptures, that each individual is to cull the articles of his creed, it is but reasonable to conceive that the Holy Spirit will have delivered these articles in the sacred volumes in terms the most natural and intelligible. To have described the more important points of Christian belief and Christian practice, in figurative or metaphorical language, susceptible of a thousand different meanings, would have been to sow the seeds of disunion and to perplex the mind of the sincere inquirer. We may therefore lay it down as a canon of scriptural interpretation that the literal should be considered as the true meaning, unless there be the clearest evidence of the contrary. The neglect of this canon has opened a door to every species of religious innovation. It has enabled men to explain away all the mysteries of Christianity and even to justify a subscription to the truth of doctrines, which at the same time, they suspect, perhaps believe, to be false.

It should moreover be observed that the doctrine which maintains the literal meaning of the words, *this is my body; this is my blood,* is not of recent invention or confined to the breasts of a few individuals. It was the uniform belief of the whole Christian church at the time of the Reformation. It had been the belief of the whole church for several centuries, according to the confession of our adversaries. According to our opinion, it had been so from the time of the apostles. At the present day, it is the belief of the great majority of Christians. It is believed by the Church of Rome, and all the western churches in communion with her. It is believed by all the Lutheran churches, though they are separated from her. It is believed by all the oriental churches, whether they admit, or reject her communion.... Certainly an opinion of such antiquity, and such almost universal diffusion in the Christian church, is deserving of respect and should not be abandoned, but on the strongest grounds. (3)

## The Trial and Death of Thomas More

After the condemnation, but before the execution of Fisher, sir Thomas More was placed a prisoner at the bar of that court, in which he had formerly presided as judge with universal applause. To make the greater impression, he was conducted on foot through the most frequented streets, from the Tower to Westminster Hall. He appeared in a coarse woollen gown. His hair, which had lately become grey, his face which, though cheerful, was pale and emaciated, and the staff, with which he supported his feeble steps, announced the length and rigour of his confinement; and a general feeling of horror and sympathy ran through the spectators. Henry dreaded the effect of his eloquence and authority; and therefore, to distract his attention and overpower his memory, the indictment had been framed of enormous length and unexampled exaggeration, multiplying the charges without measure, and clothing each charge with a load of words, beneath which it was difficult to discover its real meaning....

As soon as the sentence had been pronounced, More attempted, and, after two interruptions, was suffered to address the court. He would now, he said, openly avow, what he had hitherto concealed from every human being, his conviction that the oath of supremacy was unlawful. It was, indeed, painful to him to differ from the noble lords whom he saw on the bench, but his conscience compelled him to bear testimony to the truth. This world, however, had always been a scene of dissension; and he still cherished a hope that the day would come, when both he and they, like Stephen and Saul, would be of the same sentiment in Heaven. As he turned from the bar, his son threw himself on his knees and begged his father's blessing; and as he walked back to the Tower, his daughter Margaret twice rushed through the guards, folded him in her arms, and unable to speak, bathed him with her tears.

He met his fate with constancy, even with cheerfulness. When he was told that the king, as a special favour, had commuted his punishment to decapitation, 'God', he replied, 'preserve all my friends from such favours.' On the scaffold the executioner asked his forgiveness. He kissed him, saying: 'Thou wilt render me to-day the greatest service in the power of any mortal: but' (putting an angel into his hand) 'my neck is so short that I fear thou wilt gain little credit in the way of thy profession.' As he was not permitted to address the spectators, he contented himself with declaring that he died a faithful subject to the king, and a true Catholic before God. His head was fixed on London bridge. (4)

# Henry VIII

As the king advanced in age, his vices gradually developed themselves. After the death of Wolsey, they were indulged without restraint. He became as rapacious as he was prodigal; as obstinate as he was capricious; as fickle in his friendships, as he was merciless in his resentments. Though liberal of his confidence, he soon grew suspicious of those whom he had ever trusted; and, as if he possessed no other right to the crown than that which he derived from the very questionable claim of his father, he viewed with an evil eye every remote descendant of the Plantagenets; and eagerly embraced the slightest pretexts to remove those whom his jealousy represented as future rivals to himself or his posterity. In pride and vanity he was perhaps without a parallel. Inflated with the praises of interested admirers, he despised the judgement of others; acted as if he deemed himself infallible in matters of policy and religion; and seemed to look upon dissent from his opinion as equivalent to a breach of allegiance. In his estimation, to submit and to obey were the great, the paramount duties of subjects; and this persuasion steeled his breast against remorse for the blood which he shed, and led him to trample without scruple on the liberties of the nation.

When he ascended the throne, there still existed a spirit of freedom, which on more than one occasion defeated the arbitrary measures of the court, though directed by an able minister and supported by the authority of the sovereign. But in the lapse of a few years that spirit had fled, and before the death of Henry, the king of England had grown into a despot, the people had shrunk into a nation of slaves. The causes of this important change in the relations between the sovereign and his subjects, may be found not so much in the abilities or passions of the former, as in the obsequiousness of his parliaments, the assumption of the ecclesiastical supremacy, and the servility of the two religious parties which divided the nation....

Henry acquired and exercised the most despotic sway over the lives, the fortunes and the liberties of his subjects. Happily the forms of a free government were still suffered to exist. Into these forms a spirit of resistance to arbitrary power gradually infused itself. The pretensions of the crown were opposed by the claims of the people, and the result of a long and arduous struggle was that constitution, which for more than a century has excited the envy and the admiration of Europe. (5)

## The Abuse of the Penal Laws

From the defeat of the armada till the death of the queen, during the lapse of fourteen years, the Catholics groaned under the pressure of incessant persecution. Sixty-one clergymen, forty-seven laymen, and two gentlewomen, suffered capital punishment for some or other of the spiritual felonies and treasons, which had been lately created. Generally the court dispensed with the examination of witnesses. By artful and ensnaring questions, an avowal was drawn from the prisoner that he had been reconciled, or had harboured a priest, or had been ordained beyond the sea, or that he admitted the ecclesiastical supremacy of the pope, or rejected that of the queen. Any one of these crimes was sufficient to consign him to the scaffold. Life, indeed, was always offered, on the condition of conformity to the established worship, but the offer was generally refused. The refusal was followed by death, and the butchery, with very few exceptions, was performed on the victim, while he was yet in perfect possession of his senses....

In addition to these sufferings must be mentioned the domiciliary visits in search of Catholic clergymen, which have formerly been described. At first they were events of rare occurrence, but now they were repeated frequently in the year, often on the slightest suspicion: on the arrival of a stranger; on the groundless information of an enemy, a discharged servant, or a discontented tenant; sometimes for the sole purpose of plunder; and sometimes through the hope of reward as the forfeiture of the estate followed the apprehension of the priest. This, in the memorials of the age, is described as the most intolerable of grievances. It was in vain that the Catholic gentleman withdrew himself from the eyes of the public, and sought an asylum in solitude. His house afforded him no security. Even in the bosom of his family he passed his time in alarm and solicitude; and was exposed at every moment to the capricious visits of men, whose pride was flattered by the wanton exercise of authority over their betters, or whose fanaticism taught them to believe that they rendered a service to God by insulting and oppressing the idolatrous papist. (6)

## Elizabeth and Religious Liberty

The historians, who celebrate the golden days of Elizabeth, have described, with a glowing pencil, the happiness of the people under her sway. To them might be opposed the dismal picture of national misery, drawn by the Catholic writers of the same period. But both have taken too contracted a view of the subject. Religious dissension had divided the nation into opposite parties of almost equal numbers, the oppressors and the oppressed. Under the operation of the penal statutes, many ancient and opulent families had been ground to the dust. New families had sprung up in their place, and these, as they shared the plunder, naturally eulogized the system to which they owed their wealth and their ascendancy. But their prosperity was not the prosperity of the nation. It was that of one half obtained at the expense of the other.

It is evident that neither Elizabeth nor her ministers understood the benefits of civil and religious liberty. The prerogatives which she so highly prized have long since withered away. The bloody code which she enacted against the rights of conscience has ceased to stain the pages of the statute-book, and the result has proved that the abolition of despotism and intolerance adds no less to the stability of the throne, than to the happiness of the people. (7)

## *Ave Maris Stella*—Hail, Queen of Heaven, the Ocean Star

HAIL, Queen of Heaven, the ocean star,
    Guide of the wanderer here below,
Thrown on life's surge, we claim thy care,
    Save us from peril and from woe.
            Mother of Christ, Star of the sea,
            Pray for the wanderer, pray for me.

O gentle, chaste, and spotless maid,
    We sinners make our prayers through thee;
Remind thy Son that he has paid
    The price of our iniquity.
            Virgin, most pure, Star of the sea,
            Pray for the sinner, pray for me.

Sojourners in this vale of tears,
    To thee, blest advocate, we cry,
Pity our sorrows, calm our fears,
    And soothe with hope our misery.
            Refuge in grief, Star of the sea,
            Pray for the mourner, pray for me.

And while to him who reigns above,
    In Godhead One, in persons Three,
The source of life, of grace, of love,
    Homage we pay on bended knee—
            Do thou, bright Queen, Star of the sea,
            Pray for thy children, pray for me. (8)

NOTES AND SOURCES

1.  John Lingard, *Remarks on a Charge Delivered to the Clergy of the Diocese of Durham by Shute, Bishop of Durham, at the Ordinary Visitation of the Diocese in the year 1806*, in *A Collection of Tracts, on Several Subjects, Connected with the Civil and Religious Principles of Catholics* (London, 1826), 1–35; 10–11.

2. John Lingard, *A General Vindication of the Remarks on the Charge of the Bishop of Durham*, ibid. 59–107; 70–1.

3. John Lingard, *Remarks on the Doctrine of the Bishop of Durham with Respect to the Holy Eucharist*, in *A Collection of Tracts, on Several Subjects, Connected with the Civil and Religious Principles of Catholics* (London, 1826), 215–42; 215–17.

4. John Lingard, *A History of England*, iv (London, 1820), 218–21.

5. Ibid. 357–8, 367.

6. Ibid., v (London, 1823), 513–14, 516–17.

7. Ibid. 625.

8. John Lingard, 'Hail, Queen of Heaven', in *St Dominic's Hymn-Book* (London, 1885), 37.

## William Eusebius Andrews                                    1773–1837

In the early nineteenth century, English Catholics strove to establish a journal that would connect Catholics across the nation and advocate their political campaign for Catholic Emancipation. No single figure was as active or as controversial in this early flowering of Catholic journalism as the indefatigable and irrepressible William Eusebius Andrews. Born to convert parents in Norwich, Andrews was first an apprentice and then a managing editor for the *Norfolk Chronicle* before entering the fray of the London press in 1813. His first and most successful venture was *The Orthodox Journal* (1813–20), of which he was the editor and publisher. While Charles Butler promised to fill his periodical, *The Catholic Gentleman's Magazine* (1818–19), with 'pages of peace', Andrews made no such claim or any such effort. His journal embodied the type of pugilistic, partisan prose that could be found in such journals as Leigh Hunt's *Examiner* (1808–21). In addition to those outside the fold harbouring anti-Catholic prejudice, Butler and other Cisalpine Catholics were the frequent targets of Andrews's fulminations. Andrews and John Milner, a supporter and frequent contributor to *The Orthodox Journal*, generally agreed, but they did clash over politics. Andrews made common cause with the radicals and reformers, and he grew angry with fellow Catholics who shied away from the movement to reform parliament following the 1819 Peterloo Massacre. Daniel O'Connell's willingness to accept a Catholic Emancipation bill that also disenfranchised the Irish poor likewise elicited venom from Andrews. His combination of traditional theology with populist politics made him a unique figure in his day, as did his tirelessness in the face of penury and poor health. He restarted the *Orthodox Journal* several times (1823–4; 1829–30; 1832–8), launched *The Truth Teller* in London and New York (1824–9), began *The Catholic Advocate of Civil and Religious Liberty* (1820–1), and commenced a serial critique of John Foxe's anti-Catholic *Book of Martyrs* on the auspicious day of the fifth of November (1824–6). He even found time to establish two societies: the ecumenical, working-class 'Friends of Civil and Religious Liberty' and the charitable 'Catholic Club', whose membership of artisans and tradesmen anticipated the guilds later promoted by Eric Gill and G. K. Chesterton—perhaps the only other Catholic journalist with a personality comprehensive enough to match that of Andrews.

## No Popery!?

HONEST ENGLISHMEN.... listen to the voice of reason, and execrate this hellish cry. You have all the vile, and factious, and intolerant, and seditious, and murder-ous, and impious, joined in this cry!—Those who thus unite, are leagued against three fourths of Christendom, and are opposed to the greatest men of present and former times. Recollect, that, from the professors of Catholicism, (nicknamed Popery), you derive all that is illustrious in the fame of ancestry; all that is chivalrous in the annals of arms; all that is noble in the records of humanity; all that is great in the archives of arts, science and literature. From those men you have received all that is magnificent in your temples, sublime in doctrines, wonderful in sanctity, and sacred in religion! . .

ENGLISHMEN! remember your Augustines, your Swithins, your Bedes, your Walkelins, your Wykehams, your Egberts, your Alfreds, your Edgars and your Edwards; if that remembrance be forgotten, England's brightest annals sink into oblivion! Remember that some of these great and illustrious men were missionaries from the Pope who first converted your pagan ancestors to the faith; and that whilst you cry *No-Popery*, you have the name of *Pope Gregory* (who deputed the glorious Augustine to convert your nation) enrolled in the calendar of saints prefixed to your Common Prayer Book!!! What was the religion of Constantine, Charlemagne, Alfred and Edward? That which is nicknamed Popery! Who obtained for England the Charter of her Liberties, and the seal of her independence? An Archbishop, with the Barons of Runnymede, professors of Popery! Who introduced trial by jury and the common law of England? Professors of Popery! Who invented the compass and the art of printing? Professors of Popery! Who framed the free constitution of the Spanish Goths? Professors of Popery! Who preserved the Bible, the Fathers, and the Classics? Professors of Popery! Who compiled the various polyglots, before Walton? Professors of Popery! Who were the founders, not only of the great universities in England, but of those most renowned throughout the world? Professors of Popery! Who were the great masters of architecture, of painting, of music, and of all the arts and sciences? Professors of Popery! Who were the renowned poets, the historians, the jurists, the soldiers, the men of deep research and profound literature? Professors of Popery! Who were the martyrs who bled for the truth of religion? Professors of Popery! Who were the saints who exalted human nature and made man little less than angels? Professors of Popery? Who were the Fathers who *defended* and illustrated Christianity, and silenced the advocates of error? Professors of Popery! Who were the men who preached the glad tidings of Redemption from pole to pole and established the incorruptible faith of Christ from North to South and from East to West? Professors of Popery! Who confounded the vain wisdom of the world, silenced the silly eloquence of pretended philosophy, struck dumb the oracles of paganism, annihilated the altars of infidelity and impiety, and, on their ruins, erected the glorious standard of the Cross of Christ? They were all professors of what is nicknamed Popery! (1)

## Unjust Prejudice against Catholics

'Among other diabolical outrages,' says the *Book of Martyrs*, '[Nero] ordered that the city of Rome should be set on fire, which was done by his officers, guards, and servants. While the city was in flames he went up to the tower of Maecenas, played upon his harp, sung the song of the burning of Troy and declared, "That he wished the ruin of all things before his death." Among the noble buildings burnt was the circus, or place appropriated to horse races; it was half a mile in length, of an oval form, with rows of seats rising above each other, and capable of receiving, with ease, upwards of 100,000 spectators. Many other palaces and houses were consumed; and several thousands of the people perished in the flames, were smothered, or burned beneath the ruins. This dreadful conflagration continued several days; when Nero, finding that his conduct was greatly blamed, and a severe odium cast upon him, determined to lay the whole upon the Christians, at once to excuse himself and have an opportunity of witnessing new cruelties. The barbarities exercised upon the Christians during the first persecutions were such as even excited the commiseration of the Romans themselves. Nero even refined upon cruelty and contrived all manner of punishments for the Christians. In particular he had some sewed up in the skins of wild beasts and then worried by dogs till they expired; and others dressed in shirts made stiff by wax, fixed to axle trees, and set on fire in his gardens. This persecution was general throughout the whole Roman empire; but it rather increased than diminished the spirit of Christianity.' The fire lasted six days together, and of fourteen wards of quarters of the city, only four escaped. Of the tortures practised on the Christians Juvenal says,

> Death was their doom, on stakes impaled upright,
> Smeared o'er with wax, and set on fire to light,
> The streets, and make a dreadful blaze by night.

Now, if the present editors of Foxe's *Book of Martyrs* consider this conduct of Nero in charging the primitive Christians with setting fire to Rome, to cast the odium upon them, as base and infamous; what, we ask, can they think of the 'Protestant ascendancy-men', in Charles the second's reign, who as basely attempted to fix the dreadful fire of London in 1666 on the Catholics in order to excite the hatred of the ignorant multitude against them? Nay, more than this, these Christian calumniators raised a monumental pillar to commemorate the dire calamity, and round the pedestal of this column they placed the following inscription: 'THIS PILLAR IS SET UP IN PERPETUAL REMEMBRANCE OF THE BURNING OF THIS PROTESTANT CITY, BY THE POPISH FACTION, IN SEPTEMBER, A.D. 1666, FOR THE DESTRUCTION OF THE PROTESTANT RELIGION AND OF OLD ENGLISH LIBERTY, AND FOR THE INTRODUCTION OF POPERY AND SLAVERY.'—Thus, without a shadow of a shade of proof, did these Protestants accuse their Catholic neighbours of setting fire to the city of London, when it was evidently a stroke of the Divine hand; and they next erect a monument to perpetuate the slander to future ages. (2)

## St Alban and St Margaret Clitherow

We now come to the account given by Foxe of '*Alban, the first British martyr.*' This account we shall give in the words of the Protestant martyrologist, before we proceed with our comments. He says, 'Alban, from whom, St Alban's, in Hertfordshire, received its name, was the first British martyr. He was originally a pagan, and being of a very humane disposition, he sheltered a Christian ecclesiastic, named Amphibalus, who was pursued on account of his religion. The pious example, and edifying discourses of the refugee, made a great impression on the mind of Alban; he longed to become a member of a religion which charmed him; the fugitive minister, happy in the opportunity, took great pains to instruct him; and before his discovery, perfected Alban's conversion. Alban now took a firm resolution to preserve the sentiments of a Christian, or to die the death of a martyr. The enemies of Amphibalus having intelligence where he was secreted, came to the house of Alban, in order to apprehend him. The noble host, desirous of protecting his guest, changed clothes with him in order to facilitate his escape; and when the soldiers came, offered himself up as the person for whom they were seeking. Being accordingly carried before the governor, the deceit was immediately discovered; and Amphibalus being absent, that officer determined to wreak his vengeance upon Alban. With this view he commanded the prisoner to advance to the altar and sacrifice to the pagan deities. The brave Alban, however, refused to comply with the idolatrous injunction and boldly professed himself to be a Christian. The governor therefore ordered him to be scourged, which punishment he bore with great fortitude, seeming to acquire new resolution from his sufferings. He was then beheaded. The Venerable Bede states, that, upon this occasion, the executioner suddenly became a convert to Christianity and entreated permission either to die for Alban or with him. Obtaining the latter request, they were beheaded by a soldier, who voluntarily undertook the task. This happened on the 23$^{rd}$ of June, A.D. 287, at Verulam, now St Alban's, in Hertfordshire where a magnificent church was erected to his memory about the time of Constantine the great. This edifice was destroyed in the Saxon wars, but was rebuilt by Offa, king of Mercia, and a monastery erected adjoining it, some remains of which are still visible.'

   In this account there are many points to notice, as they will clearly show that this protomartyr of England was a Catholic saint, and not a Protestant one. It is not a little singular besides, that the imputed offence for which Mrs. Clitherow suffered under 'Protestant-ascendancy'... is the same as that for which St Alban was martyred under Pagan ascendancy, namely, having 'sheltered a Christian ecclesiastic'. And what adds still more to the singularity of this coincidence is, that as St Alban was the *first* martyr in England under pagan ascendancy, so was Mrs. Clitherow the *first* martyr for the Catholic faith under the remorseless and unprincipled Elizabeth, on her commencing to persecute that religion which she swore at her coronation to protect and follow. Thus then, if Alban be worthy of the rank of a martyr, and John Foxe has recorded him as such, Mrs. Clitherow is entitled to the same rank, since both were Catholics; both humanely protected a persecuted fugitive for conscience sake; and both refused to violate their consciences, when called upon to do so by their judges. Alban was desired to sacrifice to pagan deities, which he refused; and Mrs. Clitherow, when placed at the bar, refused to plead guilty, because she knew that no sufficient proof could be brought against her; or not guilty, because she knew such a plea was equivalent to falsehood. The only difference between the two cases is, as we have before said, that Alban was a martyr to the intolerance of pagan ascendancy; and Mrs. Clitherow felt the cruel hand of 'Protestant-ascendancy'. The one was a man, whose sufferings were mild and merciful, compared to the other, a woman, whose death was as barbarous as it was before unheard of. (3)

## Social Justice for the Industrial Revolution

Among the various melancholy reflections arising from the dire distress and unparalleled misery into which the labouring classes in the manufacturing districts are at this time plunged, that which is the predominating feeling in my mind is the calm indifference with which that distress is viewed by the guilty authors of it, who live and revel on the public plunder, and who profligately squander away the public money. It appears from a report of a debate which took place in the Collective, that a Mr. James asked very pithily and very properly, 'Why spend nine thousand pounds on three pictures, while the people are starving?' How was this met? By coughing. He recited cases of individuals eating cats and carrion, and how was it met? By coughing....

No; such nonsense as this is not to be borne with any longer. The Catholics have now but to be firm, spirited, and patriotic, and they will have an opportunity ere long afforded them of rescuing the wretched people from a state of degradation and woe, such as was never before known. It is a painful thing that Catholics should not see that in this case and at this time, their interest goes along with their duty; it is not by writing heretical definitions of allegiance, although sanctioned by a young-hearted, hoary-headed, forensic theologian, that the Catholic aristocracy are to work advantageously for the people; but it is by coming forward and making common cause with them in getting relieved from corrupt representation, unjust taxation, and heartless profligacy. (4)

## The Rights of Man

Because, during the revolution, philosophical intolerants have given to the world horrible comments on the rights of man, much more by their actions than by their theoretical visions, we must not therefore conclude that man has not any rights. The voice of religion, of morality, of natural and positive justice, of universal reason, of common opinion, of conscience, is sufficiently loud for me to think myself dispensed with the proof.

To exclaim then without restriction against the rights of man, or, what is much worse, to explain them as those who stile themselves *liberales* do, like miscreants and assassins, or, which is not so deplorable, like visionary theorists is to outrage the truth. The latter is often found between the two extremes. The very common manner of judging of human things by the abuses made of them, sometimes by the wicked and sometimes by fools, is vicious. If man has natural, religious, political and civil rights, which is incontestable, we ought to recognise them frankly, and, on the other side, we ought also to combine them with the duties which we have towards God, and towards our fellow creatures, or rather with the rights which God exercises over us, and with the common rights which each man has over another. There are some who recognize these rights in theory, but who, being in power, frequently make no scruple to elude, violate and insult them in practice. (5)

## The Voice of the People

That the voice of the people is the voice of God is a maxim so powerfully enforced by the establishment of the Christian faith in all climes and in all ages, that no man in his rational senses will have the hardihood, I think, to contest it. When our blessed Saviour was brought before the high priest of the Jews and questioned about his doctrine, he did not answer the haughty interrogator, but he referred him to the people, as witnesses to what he had taught. 'I have spoken *openly* to the *world*.' Said Christ: 'I have always taught in the synagogue and in the temple, whither all the Jews resort; and *in secret* I have spoken nothing. Why askest thou *me?* Ask them who have heard what I have spoken to them. Behold, they know what things I have said.' Here then we have the example of the divine Redeemer of mankind referring the constituted authorities of his country to the public voice for an account of his doctrine and conduct, declaring that the latter had been open and undisguised, and that secrecy and intrigue formed no part of the law which he came to establish. This disinterested and magnanimous behaviour of Christ before the court of the high priest, and his refusal to submit to the inquisitorial proceedings of the Sanhedrin, furnish a sublime lesson to the ministers of the Catholic church, but more especially to those who are placed as missioners among the children of error and ignorance, how to regulate their conduct, especially as it regards their connection with those in power. The reply of our Saviour, instead of calling forth the admiration of the man who had been appointed to guide and direct the people of Israel, aroused the insolence of his underlings, one of whom gave Christ a blow, saying, 'Answerest thou the high priest so?' To which Jesus, with the greatest composure and dignity, replied, 'If I have spoken evil, give testimony of the evil; but if well, why strikest thou me?' Here again our Saviour appealed to public opinion against the tyrannical injustice of this creature of the high priest and showed that indignities and oppression are not always to be borne without reproof. Imitating the example of their divine Master, the apostles directed their labours towards the people and preached Christ crucified in the temple, and other public places; and when they were urged by the authorities of the state to give over their appeals to public opinion, they resolutely refused to listen to the proposals, but continued to lay down the maxims of truth, to which the people gave willing ear and became, as it were, the visible voice of God, bearing to the votaries of the powers of darkness the omnipotence of that word which the apostles and their disciples preached to them. In the first ages of the church, so forcibly did the voice of truth operate on the public mind, that the rulers of the world were instigated by the father of lies to exert all the means, which force and oppression had placed in their hands, to stem the current of public opinion. (6)

NOTES AND SOURCES

1.  William Eusebius Andrews, *The Truthteller*, 39 (8 July 1826), 18–20.
2.  William Eusebius Andrews, *A Critical and Historical Review of Fox's Book of Martyrs Shewing the Inaccuracies, Falsehoods, and Misrepresentations in that Work of Deception*, ii (1824), 23.
3.  Ibid., vii (1824), 98–9.
4.  William Eusebius Andrews, 'A Plain Catholic', *The Truthteller*, 30 (6 May 1826), 166–7.
5.  William Eusebius Andrews, 'The Rights of Man', *Orthodox Journal*, 8/86 (July 1820), 274.
6.  William Eusebius Andrews, 'Vox populi, Vox Dei', *Orthodox Journal*, 8/88 (September 1820), 333–4.

# George Leo Haydock                                    1774–1849

*'Tristitia vestra vertetur in gaudium*—Your sorrow shall be made very joyful unto you': this was the motto of the Haydock family that the Elizabethan martyr George Haydock inscribed in his Newgate prison walls before being executed at Tyburn. They also describe the efforts of his descendant, George Leo Haydock, to serve God and his Church in trying circumstances. Born to a recusant and formerly Jacobite family near Preston, Haydock was among the last

generation of students at Douai. With great pathos, he later recorded the progress of the French Revolution, the eventual seizure of the venerable institution, and his own flight to England in the 1790s. His lament at leaving over 200 volumes of books behind—taking with him only a copy of the *Imitation of Christ*—show the scholarly and bibliophile tendencies that did accompany him to Old Hall and then Crook Hall, the re-establishments of Douai that became St Edmund and Ushaw College respectively. Following his ordination in Durham, he was sent on the English mission to Ugthorpe in Yorkshire, inauspiciously known as the 'Purgatory' of the mission because of its impoverishment and neglect. Haydock seems to have made the most of it, however, building a new chapel in 1810 and completing in 1814 his new edition of the Douai Bible, which remained in circulation in England and America well into the nineteenth century. This project must have influenced his 'translation' of continental Catholic devotional practices, such as the Litany of Loreto, for English-speaking readers of Scripture. While disputes over finances led him to be transferred to Lancashire and a tempo-rary suspension of his faculties from 1831 to 1839, he died in 1849 while serving the mission in Penrith where he was later memorialized with a tablet bearing the family motto. These selections record not only Haydock's experience of moving across the Channel but also the transnational passages of his surrounding Catholic community. His sister relates to the Haydock family the flight of her fellow Augustinian nuns from the French Revolution. Nicholas Alain Gilbert (1762–1821), a French émigré priest who served Ugthorpe's neighbouring mis-sion at Whitby from 1803 until the 1815 defeat of Napoleon, developed local devotions that were later published and edited by Haydock. Haydock's closing entry describing a call to minister to the sick not only shows his perseverance late in life but also gives a glimpse into the life of the Catholic poor whose voices are not often heard in the historical record.

## Douai and the Beginning of the French Revolution

Freed from restraint, and under the circumstances from the means of restraint, the undisciplined soldiery, and the more undisciplined mob, perambulated the vari-ous streets and visited in succession the houses of the principal citizens, and by their significant menaces, compelled them to join in their frantic cries of *vive la nation*, and then exacted beer and provisions as the price of their further forbearance.

From these unpleasant visitations it might have been expected that the English secular college, consisting almost entirely of English students, would have been exempted. They were not their subjects; they were not personally interested in their changes and revolutions; they were not partisans of any of the factions which then ruled or attempted to rule; they were mere strangers enjoying there an asylum and a refuge which had been denied them at home. What mattered it to them whether this desirable protection were extended to them under an absolute or a limited monarchy, which last seemed to be the expressed want and wish of the day? But no! a lawless rabble acts and does not argue. The sovereign people were determined that their obstrusive aggressions should be made impartially. In the plenitude of their assumed power they thundered at the College door requiring immediate admittance. Some delay occurred, during which the superiors wisely instructed the younger students to receive the deluded multitude with some English cheers, such as boys know how to give, to propitiate them in somewise, and to prevent further violence. Accordingly, after some further demur the mob forced an entrance into the College, and crossing the ambulacrum, rushed into the quadrangular court directly opposite, where, to their astonishment and apparent gratification, they were met by a laughing array of boys, who, throwing their hats up into the air, received them with loud huzzars, and vociferated at the top of their lungs the fashionable cry of the day, *vive la nation*.

This cry, at that time, by no means denoted an acquiescence in the fatal measures which marked and disgraced the subsequent eras of the revolution. It then imported merely the downfall and dismission of arbitrary power, not inherent originally in the French constitution, but assumed and usurped in the lapse of time and arrogantly proclaimed when Louis XIV had the audacity to announce *La France c'est moi*.

The nation in its strength arose at last to depose this hateful absolute power, and, as it was said, with the concurrence in some measure of its present king. This, at least, is certain, that the *states-general* were summoned by him to assemble and deliberate on the pressing emergencies that caused them to be convoked and to apply a remedy to evils too deeply felt to be denied. Such a partial return to the paths of liberty and a participation in the government, was hailed with pleasure by the people of England, who watched with intense curiosity and interest the throes of a mighty nation bursting its trammels, and beginning to trample upon an odious despotism.

The first acts of a nation striking in its own defence and evincing by the destruction of the infamous Bastille its determination to be free, were highly popular in England. Great hopes were excited; great results were anticipated. So that when these uninvited strangers arrived in the College, it was not thought inconsistent with any duty to welcome their arrival by joining in the shouts of liberty and well-wishing to the nation. This kind of reception, more favourable than they had anticipated, had a magical effect upon the invaders. So far from resorting to violence or personal ill-treatment, they subsided at once into a sort of suavity of behaviour and comical amenity and added greatly to the amusement of the boys by their grimaces, antic gestures and dances, which were mischievously applauded by loud incessant peals of laughter; and the mob accepting with the modest assurance of Frenchmen these unmistakeable tokens of merriment as a compliment paid to their own powers of pleasing were consequently highly gratified, and expressed in warm terms their satisfaction at the mode of their reception. They then departed, after partaking at their own request of the College beer, taking with them some of the boys whose appearance or behaviour had particularly attracted their attention.

It was laughable to witness the motley and ludicrous appearance of these chosen companions of the military. Supported on each side by the arms of the now friendly soldiers, they were hugged and petted and held up to the admiration of all good citizens. They were then saddled with military accoutrements, had cocked hats placed on their heads and naked swords in their hands, and in this quaint guise they were hailed and applauded by the uproarious shouts of the surrounding multitude. Fortunately, laughter succeeded to preceding violence. Even the insurgent bands bent on mischief, whom they occasionally met in their progress through the streets, stood still awhile, contemplating with delight the unexpected display, and then summoning all their energies joined heartily in the public merriment, uniting at one time the grimaces and antics of the monkey with something of the ferocity of the bear dance. It was impossible for a bystander not to be gratified with the bearing of these students, their steadiness and self-possession, and at times with their radiant, honest faces beaming with fun and frolic. After the scenes of horror and violence which the town had witnessed without the power of repressing them, the burst of innocent and harmless mirth escaping from the lips of these boys was quite refreshing and had a most composing effect; a gleam of sunshine streaming athwart a lurid sky. (1)

## The Seizure of Douai during the French Revolution

On hearing this decree, the first idea that suggested itself to us was to escape from the premises in the dark, in the almost forlorn hope of finding some means of passing the town's gates on the morrow. This, at the first attempt, was discovered to be an impracticable measure. The next was to call up those who had retired to rest, and in conjunction with them to secure as much of our wardrobes, etc., public and private, as we could convey away unnoticed. The officer was very urgent that we should hasten our departure without any solicitude about our clothing or other effects, giving us his assurance that all should be safely sent after us. To this notification, taking it for what it was worth, we paid no attention, but collected what we could in the very few moments allowed us for assembling. Some clothes, which were afterwards found to be eminently useful, were procured from the tailors' apartments, and a small amount of silver utensils, which, to avoid suspicion, had not been removed from daily use. When the patience of those appointed to escort us, which was by no means extraordinary, was exhausted, word was given to us to pass instantly into the streets, and thence, enclosed by two serried ranks of military, who were rigidly strict in the performance of their charge, we were marched quickly into the Scotch college, which having entered, our claims to our own establishment were declared to be extinct. In effect, it had been confiscated. From that fatal night we may date the final downfall of the noble English Secular College of Douai.

Stripped of the support of all thy various aid of instruction and everything that had hallowed thy previous existence, poor *alma mater*, thine was a cruel and unmerited doom; but thou hadst, and deservedst to have, many sincere mourners. The end was *qualis ab incepto* [of the same character as the beginning]. Nursed and cradled in adversity and unremitting suffering, pursued throughout almost thy entire duration by the merciless laws and refined barbarity of a merciless princess, and harassed by the atrocious and insatiate hostility of succeeding governments, who thought they did an agreeable thing to God by hunting thy noblest sons to a cruel death—all those unnatural but vain attempts to crush out thy very existence thou couldst bear and didst bear. But when the sanguinary laws that had been created against thee had at length been cancelled, or greatly modified, then in almost the first moments of thy peaceful rest, in the very dawn of thy hopes, in the midst of thy aspirations after labour untrammelled by fears of prison or death, a storm arose from an unexpected quarter in which thou hadst hitherto been kindly fostered, cherished, and protected. Not France, once the soul of honour and unbending integrity, dealt thee thy death-blow, but the most worthless of her sons, profiting by the explosion of a sanguinary revolution, rose like the Seine to the surface, and wresting the reins of government from feeble hands, rioted then in every excess that can degrade the name of man. Their envenomed darts were ever aimed at a noble quarry, and thou, in common with the best, sankest under them. Thy virtues were the occasion of thy fall. Never stain nor spot has tarnished thy unblemished escutcheon. Farewell, then, kind *alma mater*; farewell, a long farewell. (2)

## Letter from Sr. Stanislaus Haydock: On Fleeing the Revolution

*Sept.* 8, 1794. My dearest Sister—I am ashamed of myself for my past negligence in not writing to you or dear mother before this. It has not, I do assure you, proceeded from want of affection, for that would be an unpardonable piece of ingratitude, which I hope never to be guilty of. You desired to know the particulars of our journey; to comply with your request I will inform you as well as I can. We left dear Louvain that lamentable day, the 28th of June. We were forced to quit our beloved convent, 47 in number; 21 nuns, 4 priests, 12 lay-sisters, 4 pensioners, 3 servants, and a young lady. We had 4 wagons to be crushed into, so you may imagine we were finely crowded. We came through Holland, and continued in our wagons till we arrived at Breda, where we stayed one night and were very civilly treated. From thence we went in a barge to Rotterdam. I think our misery in the barge exceeded that of the wagons. At Rotterdam we stayed a week, very uncomfortable indeed; thence we took shipping, which was going from one misery to another still greater. We were not far advanced when, in a dangerous spot, the captain got in two Dutch pilots who ran us aground, where we were obliged to remain near a day and a night with the ship very much sunk on one side, so that we could not stand without holding by something to support ourselves. We had contrary winds almost all the way, which prolonged us near eight days on sea. The miseries and distresses which we suffered there from sickness, etc., were greater than I can describe. We landed at Gravesend, where we rested ourselves one night, being, as you may imagine, most heartily tired. The day after we set off again by water for Hammersmith, where we arrived all safe, but wearied out of our lives. We are here very different indeed to what we were at Louvain. We are obliged to be three or four in a room, very much pinched for place, and many other inconveniences. However, we must resign ourselves to the will of God. I doubt not but He will support us under the pressure of our afflictions. It is the greatest cross He could have sent us excepting being under the French.... According to inclination nothing would give me so great pleasure as once more to see you and dear mother, my uncles and aunts, friends and acquaintances. But that's out of the question, therefore, I must make a sacrifice of that satisfaction. You will be very much surprised to receive this letter from the hand of my dearly beloved George. We have great reason to be content with him; indeed, I must say he has behaved most affectionately to me.... At Hammersmith we wear our habit and keep our order as well as circumstances will permit, though not quite as we have been accustomed to at dear Louvain. We don't rise at midnight, but at 5 o'clock in the morning, which I find much harder as you know I always loved my bed and do so still.... I thought, perhaps, you might have some thoughts of coming to see me, and though, I do assure you, it would be a true and sincere pleasure to me, yet I do not wish it at present, because I could have very little enjoyment of you; it is not now with us as it was at Louvain. There we could entertain our friends comfortably with lodging and board, but not so now.... I remain, my dear sister, your loving and beloved—Stanislaus Haydocke. (3)

## On the Litany of Loreto: Its Foundations in Scripture

We address ourselves to God, and humbly beseech the most favoured of all his creatures to obtain, through her only Son, all blessings for us. Her titles are of four kinds. First, as Mother of God; and consequently, of divine grace, Jesus Christ the author of it. Her dignity of *mother* and *virgin*, causes us to extol her miraculous *purity*. Hence, also she is styled *amiable* or lovely, and truly *admirable*. Second, as *virgin* she is pronounced to be adorned with all suitable accomplishments, *prudent*, and deserving our *veneration* and the *renown* of all generations. Those who refuse, show that they do not belong to that happy society, which, in every age, has complied with this prophecy (Luke 1: 48). Her *power* with her son is boundless; from him she has learnt sentiments of *mercy* and *fidelity*. Who ever invoked her and was disappointed? Third, several mystical titles are used to denote her *dignity*. *Mirror* or 'looking-glass' *of justice*, intimates that she ever showed the brightest pattern of perfection. *Seat of wisdom*, in whom the wisdom of God was pleased to dwell for nine months, and replenish her with wisdom. *Cause of our joy* by bringing forth the Saviour of the world, who makes peace in Heaven and on earth. She is a *vessel* of election more than St Paul, (Acts 9: 15) to whom God applies this title. For she was chosen to be his instrument in doing the greatest wonders of grace—a *spiritual vessel* enabled by the Holy Spirit to become the Mother of God, and of course, a *vessel of honour* selected by the pure bounty of God, while he casts away vessels of dishonour (Rom. 9: 21). She is *a vessel of singular devotion*. For never did any pure creature evince so great a love and obedience to God, which is true devotion. *Mystical rose*, most beautiful and aromatic, sending forth the *good odour of Christ*, which we ought all to do. Divine wisdom says of itself, *I was exalted as a rose plant* (Ecclus. 24: 18). *Tower of David, which is built with bulwarks, etc.* (Cant. 4: 4), *Tower of Ivory. Thy neck*, says the spouse, *is as a tower of ivory* (Cant. 7: 4), on account of her spotless purity, and that security which she affords by her fervent prayers, to the saints and penitents on earth. *House of gold*, the dwelling place of the King of kings, from whom she received the gold of charity. For as gold is the most precious of metals, so is charity the Queen of virtues, for which the Blessed Virgin was most resplendent, and agreeable to God; like a palace of gold for the king of Heaven. *Ark of the Covenant* on the terms of the gospel *which is established* by her son *on better promises* (Heb. 8: 6) than the old one. The ark contained the two tables of the Law, given on Mount Sinai, in the midst of thunder and lightning, to move all to observe it carefully. *Gate of Heaven*, which has been opened to us by Jesus, and to which, she greatly facilitates our admission, by her prayers. *Morning Star*, which precedes the rising sun: so Mary appearing in the world, gave an earnest of the sun of justice coming to make the first fine day of grace, for all who had, till then, been sitting in the shades of death. *Health of the weak, etc.* From *the Tower of David, all the armour of valiant men*, and suitable medicines may be supplied. Mary affords a *refuge* to penitent sinners and obtains *comfort* and *help for Christians*. Fourth, her prerogatives, above all the *Angels* and *Saints*, cause the Church to honour her in a special manner, with *hyperdulia* or 'a greater service', styling her, *Queen* of the different orders, as her son is *King* of the Saints, and *Lord of Lords*.

These titles are due to her sacred person and eminent virtues. They tend to increase our confidence in her intercession, and engage her to patronize us the more. By them, we also honour her divine son, as the good woman did when in the midst of Christ's enemies, she exclaimed, *Blessed is the womb which bore Thee.* Only let us not forget the approbation and advice given by Jesus on this occasion. *Yea rather, blessed are they who hear the word of God, and keep it* (Luke 11: 28) as his mother did always. (4)

## Scriptural Litany to the Blessed Virgin Mary

Holy Mary, *Pray for us.*
Mary, daughter of David,
Mary, the joy of Israel,
Mary, the glory of Jerusalem,
Mary, the honour of thy people,
Mary, promised to the fathers,
Mary, announced by the prophets,
Mary, who, by the power of thy Son, hast crushed the head of the old serpent,
Mary, ever Virgin,
Mary, who didst find grace with God,
Mary, to whom the Angel Gabriel was sent from Heaven,
Mary, full of grace,
Mary, blessed among women,
Mary, who didst profess thyself the hand-maid of the Lord,
Mary, whose humble state God did regard,
Mary, upon whom the Holy Ghost came down,
Mary, whom the power of the Most High, did over-shadow,
Mary, who didst visit thy cousin Elizabeth,
Mary, by whose Son, John was sanctified in his mother's womb,
Mary, who wouldst obey Caesar's decree,
Mary, who distant from home and poor, didst bring forth thy first-born Son,
Mary, of whom Jesus was born,
Mary, who didst lay down thy Son in a manger,
Mary, who didst behold the shepherds and the wise men coming to adore thy
      Son,
Mary, who didst subject thyself to the law of purification,
Mary, who didst carry Jesus to Jerusalem, to present him to the Lord,
Mary, who with thy Son didst flee to Egypt,
Mary, who didst seek Jesus for three days, sorrowing,
Mary, who didst find him in the temple, and wast in admiration seeing him
      in the midst of the doctors,
Mary, who didst faithfully keep all the words concerning thy Son, and
      ponder them in thy heart,
Mary, to whom the infant Jesus was subject,
Mary, whose heart was moved with compassion, when they wanted wine at
      Cana,

Mary, at whose request Jesus wrought his first miracle,
Mary, for whose sake Jesus began to manifest his power, before his time was
    come,
Mary, who hast recommended a perfect obedience to all the words of thy
    Son,
Mary, who didst stand by the cross of thy Son,
Mary, whose soul was pierced through by a sword of grief,
Mary, who wast by Jesus on the cross appointed mother of the disciple whom
    he loved,
Mary, to whom Jesus before his death recommended the beloved disciple, to
    be thy Son,
Mary, who after the ascension of thy Son didst continue with the apostles in
    prayer,
Mary, to whom He that is mighty, hath done great things,
Mary, whom all generations shall call blessed: *Pray for us.*

Blessed art thou, Mary, who hast believed:
*For those things shall be accomplished that were spoken to thee by the Lord.*

*Let us pray.*
Pour forth, we beseech thee, O Lord, thy grace into our hearts, out of thy
tender mercy; and by the prayers of Mary, the most pure mother of thy Son,
sanctify our bodies, by the virtue of chastity, and our souls, by humility and
love: through the same *Jesus Christ, our Lord.* Amen. (5)


## The Mass and the Passion of Christ

*As often as you eat this bread and drink this cup, you do show the Lord's death, till
he come* at the last day: for so long, in spite of all the efforts of Satan, the Mass will
be celebrated (1 Cor. 11: 26). It sets before us, in the most impressive manner, the
stations of our Saviour's passion, and subsequent glory. *If He shall lay down his life
for sin, he shall see a long-lived seed* of Christians, *and he shall divide the spoils of
the strong* adversaries of the Gospel (Isa. 53: 10, 12). It would therefore be a very
excellent method of hearing Mass to accompany our suffering Lord (in spirit)
from his agony in the garden, to his ascension, in the following manner:

| | |
|---|---|
| 1. The Priest comes to the altar and begins the Psalm *Judica.* | Jesus leaves his disciples and prays to his Father in his agony. |
| 2. All confess their sins, bowing, to God and their fellow-creatures. | Jesus laden with the sins of the world, falls on the ground. |
| 3. The Priest goes up to the altar and kisses it. | Jesus goes to meet his enemies and receives the traitor's kiss. |
| 4. He reads the Introit, or entrance. | Jesus is dragged before Annas, the late High Priest |
| 5. He thrice repeats *Kyrie* to each of the Divine Persons, says the *Gloria,* and | Jesus is denied thrice by Peter. He graciously looks upon him, for the glory |

| | |
|---|---|
| turns to the people with *Dominus vobiscum.* | of his name, to move him to a speedy repentance. |
| 6. He goes to the side of the altar and reads the prayer and lesson, or epistle. | Jesus is sent to Caiphas, accused and unjustly condemned, as guilty of blasphemy. |
| 7. He bows down and says, in silence, *Cleanse my heart.* | Jesus is falsely accused before Pilate, and keeps silence. |
| 8. He has the book removed to the other side and reads the gospel. | Jesus shows in the court of Herod, an example of all gospel virtues, meekness, etc. |
| 9. In the middle, he recites the Creed. | Jesus witnesseth the truth before Pilate. |
| 10. He uncovers the chalice. | Jesus is stripped and scourged. |
| 11. He offers up the bread. | Jesus says, *I am ready for scourges* (Ps. 37: 18). |
| 12. He offers up the wine. | The blood of Christ streams on the ground. |
| 13. He washes his fingers at the side of the altar. | Jesus is pronounced just by Pilate, who vainly washes his hands. |
| 14. He bows down in the middle of it. | Jesus is crowned with thorns as a mock king. |
| 15. He says *Orate fratres.* Pray Brethren. | Jesus is brought out *Ecce homo.* Behold the man. |
| 16. He prays in silence. | Jesus receives sentence of death, with submission. |
| 17. He says the preface aloud, with the *Sanctus.* | Jesus carries his Cross while angels sing Alleluia Holy, etc. |
| 18. He begins the canon, which is always the same, and said with a low voice. | Jesus is led away to Mt. Calvary, and in silence, offers up all his sufferings for our salvation. |
| 19. He prays at the *Memento* for himself and friends. | Jesus requests the pious women to weep for themselves and children. |
| 20. He spreads his hands over the bread and wine. | Jesus is stretched naked on the cross, to be nailed to it. |
| 21. He consecrates the bread and elevates the host to be adored. | Jesus is raised above the heads of the people a victim for all. |
| 22. He does the same with the chalice. From this to the Com. Corresponds with the time which Jesus spent alive on the Cross. | Jesus pours forth his blood for us. The words which are spoken aloud, put us in mind of the seven speeches of Christ crucified. |
| 23. The Priest receives the body and blood of Christ. | Jesus dies for mankind. *Ye do show our Lord's death* (1 Cor. 11: 26). |
| 24. He purifies and covers the chalice. | Jesus in clean linen, is consigned to the tomb. |

| 25. He turns twice to the people with *Dominus vobiscum.* | Jesus appears and gives peace to his disciples repeatedly. |
| 26. He gives his blessing. | Jesus lifts his hand to bless (Luke 24: 50). |
| 27. He reads the last gospel proving Christ's divinity. | Jesus ascends to Heaven and sits at the right hand of the Father (Acts 1). |

Those who cannot read well, may at these pauses, think; and often repeat during this holy service, the petitions of the Lord's prayer, the Glory, etc. or, 'O sacred banquet! in which Christ is received, the memory of his Passion renewed; the soul is filled with Grace; and a pledge is given to us of future glory!' Or, 'O saving victim, etc.' They may also make short acts of faith, hope, and charity, contrition, and other virtues suggested by the subject. Thus we have accompanied our Saviour through the stages of his Passion. (6)

## An Act of Hope

O my God, nothing is hard or impossible to thee, because thy power is infinite; and there is nothing that thou art not willing to do in favour of us poor mortals, because thy mercy and goodness for us are infinite. Thou hast made us to thy own image and likeness, and thou lovest the work of thy hands; thou hast redeemed us by the precious blood of thy only Son; and for his sake thou art ever opening thy hand to pour out thy graces upon us; never forsaking us, if we forsake not thee; and still calling upon unhappy sinners that have forsaken thee to return to thee. Thou hast promised mercy to such as sincerely seek it, grace to such as heartily pray for it, and eternal salvation, through Jesus Christ, to such as persevere to the end in thy fear and love. Upon these strong grounds I build all my hopes; and relying upon the assistance of thy grace, and the merits of my Saviour Jesus Christ, I trust to find mercy in the forgiveness of my sins, and so to pass the remainder of this mortal life in thy divine service, that I may come hereafter to enjoy thee in a happy eternity. In thee, O Lord, is my hope, O let me never be confounded. (7)

## The Sick Call

I must confess I am not in my best fashion, and hence I have excused myself from saying afternoon prayers at the chapel—the first time these nearly ten years. Seeing the little fruit, I could not refrain from tears, particularly as the third Sunday in September is the feast of the seven sorrows of the Blessed Virgin, and I could hardly get through the *Stabat Mater*, which you may find most affecting at page 15 of the new Hymn Book which I gave you, *The most afflicted Mother stood, etc.* I had other subjects of sorrow to dwell upon. Last Wednesday week a tramp, 27 years old, who with her mother became serious (at my instigation perhaps) about six years ago, and who was at communion a month before at Cockermouth, where the cholera is raging (as in many parts of England and Europe), fell down on the moor and was found with her mother and brother by a gentleman. He gave them 1s. to get some brandy, and they were conveyed to a public-house about eight miles from Penrith. They were placed by the overseer, Wilson, in an outhouse intended for calves or pigs, without a door or a stool, on straw. The doctor did not think she would live twelve hours then, yet I was not informed till Saturday.... She wished very much to see me. Accordingly I hired a horse, and was two hours on the road going. I set off at two and got home about seven, much shaken, though I went slowly.... But I must stay at my post, though unworthy and almost useless... Your snug parlour would not be comfortable if I thought I was not working while it was day for me—night is coming. My schoolfellow, Rev. Thomas Gillow, four years older, has resigned on account of old age. Most at my time of life have indeed retired to prepare more immediately for eternity. Still, if God give ability He requires us to labour to the end. (8)

NOTES AND SOURCES

1. George Leo Haydock, *The Haydock Papers: A Glimpse into English Catholic Life*, ed. Joseph Gillow (London, 1888), 94–8.

2. Ibid. 119–20.

3. Stanislaus Haydock, *The Haydock Papers: A Glimpse into English Catholic Life*, ed. Joseph Gillow (London, 1888), 181–3.

4. George Leo Haydock, *A Key to the Roman Catholic Office* (Whitby, 1823), 54–7.

5. N. A. Gilbert, *The Method of Sanctifying the Sabbath Days at Whitby, Scarborough, and co. with a Paraphrase on Some Psalms* (York, 1824), 42–4.

6. Haydock, *A Key to the Roman Catholic Office*, 70–3.

7. Gilbert, *The Method of Sanctifying the Sabbath Days*, 9–10.

8. Haydock, *The Haydock Papers*, 242–3.

# Arthur Clifford                                                    1777–1830

The first major event in the life of Clifford could have produced a far different effect. As a student, he was one of the 'Douai *trente-deux*', the thirty-two Douai faculty, students, and neighbouring monks imprisoned in 1793 by Revolutionary forces as France and England headed into a prolonged war. Many Catholic monasteries suffered the same fate as Douai and, in the process, brought their treasures from the past, including their libraries' manuscripts, into the public eye. These two aspects of the 1790s shaped Clifford's life in unexpected ways. Later in life, he resided in Paris for many years and worked as an editor for Giovanni Antonio Galignani (1757–1821), the Italian-born publisher who dedicated his life to improving French–English relations. In addition to contributing to the Paris-based, English-language newspaper *Galignani's Messenger*, Clifford also helped produce travel guides for the French capital and other European countries. Clifford seems to have harboured bitterness towards neither the French nor England's religious past. Having discovered a gilt box covered in 'literary dust' in his family seat of Tixall Hall in Staffordshire, Clifford published Reformation-era papers and manuscripts from the Clifford and Aston families under the titles *Tixall Letters* (1815) and *Tixall Poetry* (1813). These included the letters of Sir Walter Aston (1583–1639), who converted to Catholicism while serving as Charles I's ambassador to Spain, and the poetry of his son Herbert Aston (1614–89). 'They were all Roman Catholics,' Clifford wrote of the Astons in 1813, 'and, what is remarkable, they are all, in the male line at least, become extinct. Their very names and dwellings have perished!' All that now remains of the recusant manor Tixall Hall is a sixteenth-century gatehouse—now available for holiday lets—and Clifford's works.

## A Prayer to the Almighty amid the Ruins of History

To want, and pining misery dear,
And loved by all the country near,
When, as successive ages rolled,
The steel-clad knight, or baron bold,
In arms, and well-fought fields grown gray,
Here calmly closed life's parting day.
For heroes, here their eyes have closed,
And statesmen from their toils reposed;
And sages, won by nature's charms,
Have wooed her to their longing arms;
*And poets, here have struck the lyre—*
*And caught the soul-inflaming fire,*
*Which, as it thrilled their nerves along,*
*And woke the hidden powers of song,*
*To distant times again addrest,*
*Shall raise the mind, and warm the breast.*

Now sinks the fading orb of night,
The stars withdraw their twinkling light,
And seem in fancy's ear to say,
We too are fated to decay.

O thou! Almighty Power Supreme!
Whose bounty gives this nightly beam,
Who pourest on the wondering soul,
This boundless blaze from pole to pole—
Though hid from my imploring eye,
Thy works declare thee ever nigh.
O teach me clearly to conceive,
O teach me firmly to believe,
That, from this wreck of mortal things,
To which our sense so fondly clings,
That, from this dark, bewildered state,
Entangled in the maze of fate,
A fair, harmonious scene shall rise—
When, opened to our anxious eyes,
Cleared from all mist of doubt, and fear,
Thy perfect justice shall appear.
Guide me through life's perplexing way,
Cheer me with hope's auspicious ray.
May simple joys my cares beguile,
May love and friendship on me smile;
Till my rapt soul, from earth set free,
Shall seek eternal rest in Thee. (1)

## St Monica's Maternal Love

Ye tender soft-paired mother springs,
That trickling steal from those new op'ning eyes,
Where Monica, love's siren, sings,
To enchant her Austin into Paradise;
Kind fallacies, that have so well outdone
The logic of your over subtle son:

If such fertile parent showers
Revived in him the eternal spring of bliss;
If those seed pearl-blooms of yours
Brought him such harvest home of happiness;
Oh, drop my barren soul one fruitful tear,
Or let it glean some pregnant sorrow there.

Then earthly parents all adieu,
Now only Heaven must be of kin to me;
I'll be conceived and born anew,
And only tears shall be my pedigree.
Thrice happy generation! To be styled,
Of Austin's mother pearls the adopted child. (2)

NOTES AND SOURCES

1. Arthur Clifford, 'A Midnight Meditation among the Ruins of Tixall', in *Tixall Poetry* (Edinburgh, 1813), pp. xxxix–xl.

2. 'Herbert Aston', 'A Sigh to St Monica's Teares', ibid. 52–3.

# Henry Weedall                              1788–1859

'Every one is made for his day,' pronounced Newman in Henry Weedall's funeral sermon, 'he does his work *in* his day; what he does is not the work of any other day, but of his own day; his work is necessary in order to the work of that next day which is *not* his, as a stepping-stone on which we, who come next, are to raise our own work.' These are fit words to describe a man who dedicated himself to Catholic education. Born in London and educated at Sedgley Park in Staffordshire, Weedall was among the handful of students at Oscott College when it came under the control of Bishop John Milner in 1808. His life was forever intertwined with Milner, and with Oscott, as it was there he was ordained, taught, and served first as vice-president in 1818 and then president in 1826. Though he was short and slight with bad eyesight and accompanying painful headaches, he was nevertheless active, gregarious, learned, and witty. As an example of what Newman would call his 'natural playfulness of thought and manner', he could be seen in the 1830s scurrying up ladders and scaling scaffolding to show visitors the progress on Oscott's new buildings and chapel. Largely the result of the exertions of Weedall and Bishop Thomas Walsh, the Oxbridge-style quadrangle and Pugin's effulgent neo-Gothic chapel provided an august centre for English Catholic spiritual and intellectual life that would house generations of seminarians and host the 1852 first provincial synod of the re-established hierarchy at which Newman gave his famous 'Second Spring' sermon. Weedall narrowly dodged being numbered among those bishops as, in 1840, he was appointed vicar-apostolic to the Northern district; however, his health and the resistance of some of the Northern clergy—which he encouraged—resulted in his successful plea of *noli episcopari*. After being reassigned to Leamington Spa and St Chad's in Birmingham, he returned to the presidency of Oscott in 1853 where he ended his days. Weedall was known for his eloquence (though not his brevity) from the pulpit, and his biographer, F. C. Husenbeth, called preaching his 'grand distinguishing talent'. It is also fitting that the Oscott chantry named for Weedall, who was created a Doctor of Divinity in 1821 by Pope Leo XII and a monsignor by Pius IX, features an impressive statue of *Sedes Sapientiae*—Our Lady, Seat of Wisdom.

## The Dedication of Oscott's Church Bell

Dear Christians, and you my respected brethren and beloved friends who are to form the future inmates of this establishment, this is the great lesson which the bell is intended frequently to preach to us. It will break in upon our occupations, whether serious or gay, whether lawful or unlawful. Like the voice of Christ to Martha, it will remind us of the inutility of much that we are doing, perhaps even of its sinfulness. It will discourse, wisely and forcibly, of the value of the soul, and of the importance of attending to its salvation, of the shortness of time and the awful length of eternity. It will sound like the solemn warnings of the last trumpet, and teach us to prepare whilst preparation is practicable. It will entone the Angelical Salutation three times each day, and bid us bend our heads, and humble our hearts in the adoration of the adorable mystery of the Incarnation. It will regulate a variety of duties, as its ancient inscription purports:

> Laudo Deum verum. Plebem voco. Congrego Clerum.
> Defunctos ploro. Pestum fugo. Festa decoro.
> [I praise the true God. I call the people. I gather the clergy.
> I mourn the dead. I put disease to flight. I celebrate the Holy Days.]

It will summon us to prayer, morning and evening; it will notify in deeper tones the celebration of the awful mysteries. It will remind us of the duty of praying for the dead, it will encourage us to pray in seasons of danger, it will multiply its admonitions on our holy sabbaths, and give a cheerful solemnity to the days consecrated to a more particular worship. And oh! if a good God shall vouchsafe to listen to the prayers of the Church and to give his additional blessing to that which will, this day, be solemnly invoked, how may we hope to see piety increase and religion flourish amongst us. (1)

## Oscott and the Meaning of Catholic Education

May not we without offence indulge the joyous emotion, and felicitate ourselves and the Catholics of this district, on the humble portion of good which the divine blessing has enabled us to achieve, and the impulse which this building is calculated to give to our holy religion, a religion which is identified with all that is venerable and ancient in the country; with all that is true in faith and morals; with all that is sound in principle and politics; with all that is beautiful in art, and science, and philosophy; with all that is honourable, and just, and becoming in the ethics of life; with all that supports the social system, and prepares the soul for an eternal one; which works out pre-eminently the glory of God, and peace, and charity, and good-will to men. (2)

## Charity

Perhaps, upon no subject is this instruction so necessary as on the present, because there is no one virtue of our age which combines more apparent compliance with less real practice. We see great and splendid efforts of humanity, but seldom behold them ripening into charity; and religion is often doomed to weep over the abortions of nature, when she fain would have recognized the offspring of grace.

Whatever may be the general opinion of mankind as to the correctness of such an assertion, I am persuaded, my beloved brethren, and the wise and the good will agree with me, that it rests on irrefragable argument, drawn from the solidest maxims and purest practices of Christianity. The cause of the failure may be traced to that delusive system which characterizes the religion of the day. The object of this system is to destroy the broad line of distinction between the natural and the supernatural virtues; to raise the one to a level with the other; and to dignify the *man* at the expense of the *Christian*. Thus for example, the attachments of kindred, of affection, of interest, or an attention to the general civilities of life, are too often mistaken for the divine virtue of fraternal love; moderation and forbearance for mortification and patience; connubial decorum for chastity; the excess of patriotism or the intemperance of bigotry are misnamed zeal and justice, and the refined sensibility of a false honour, though it enlist in its cause all the angry passions, is trumpeted forth as a branch of those sacred duties which by the laws of God every individual owes to himself. It is on this equalizing principle also that humanity and charity are so often confounded together; from which strange admixture there arises a second evil, as prejudicial to the interests of the poor as to the diffusion of real charity. For considering the subject, as too often we are inclined, a mere exercise of the benevolent affections, seeing no obligation in question, but only a counsel, acknowledging no claims in the poor but those of pity, looking only to the proportion of relief actually afforded, and not to the immensity of their wants, regarding only what has been done, and not what ought to have been done,—we are too apt to sit down in the plenitude of self-approbation as rich in charity when we are poor and pitiful, and to assume to ourselves the full credit of a gratuitous action when the gospel would teach us we feel far below our duty. (3)

## The Distribution of Wealth

If the earth is intended for the support of men, and it be fully adequate to supply the wants of all, it follows by a necessary consequence, that there does somewhere exist a fund for this purpose, an ample fund which may be, and ought to be applied to relieve the wants of the poor. But where does this fund exist? Either with the rich or with the poor. Not with the poor, for in that case they would cease to be poor. Then it exists with the rich, in the superfluities of the rich. Here must the poor apply and the rich will refuse at their peril. For let it not be thought that the unequal distribution of wealth, which appears in the world was intended solely for the advantage of the rich. He sees but one side of the beautiful scheme of Providence, and understands not even that, who fancies that a just and merciful God would have reduced one half of mankind to a dependence on the other, without a view to some advantage resulting to both. No, my friends, it was indeed becoming the wisdom of God to ordain this inequality among mankind, because our nature and relative condition rendered necessary a gradation in rank and subordination in society; but it was also becoming his loving and paternal solicitude not to leave these poor dependents to perish, or even to owe their subsistence to the casual benevolence of the rich, but to provide against these possible evils by the imperious law of charity, which enjoins *an equality*, so that, as the Apostle observes, *the abundance of the rich may supply the wants of the poor: as it is written, He that had much had nothing over: and he that had little, had no want* (2 Cor. 8: 14, 15; Exod. 16: 18). (4)

## The Dangers of Consumerism

But perhaps you may say you have no superfluities—that when the provisions are completed, there will remain no surplus for charity. Not in the ruinous combination of extravagance and luxury, I believe it; not on the plan of satisfying the many factitious wants that clamour around us. But, my brethren, we needs must recollect that although religion is bountiful to our real wants, it will show no indulgence to our artificial ones. If then we would be as careful of our souls as we too often are of our miserable gains, we must examine with rigid exactness the whole system of our expenditure. We must dare to question the justice of those demands which folly and fashion unceasingly urge; and however painful the sacrifice, we must strike off with a desperate economy every item suggested by prodigality, ambition, sensuality, or pride. Run through the whole length of your establishment and say whether every expense is regulated by the moderation of the gospel. Does temperance or does appetite preside at your tables? Have vanity or extravagance no share in the purveyance? Is there no unnecessary waste? No crumbs that bestrew your floor, and no thought to collect them for the hungry orphan? Are your horses and your servants proportioned to your rank? Might no retrenchment be made in the costliness of your furniture, none in the splendour of your dress? Might not the frequency of your excursions be diminished, excursions more for pleasure than for profit? Do the idle and the vicious never feed upon the patrimony of the poor? Is it never hazarded at the card or the gaming table? Never wasted at the assembly or the theatre, or thoughtlessly distributed amongst the innumerable channels of trifling, dangerous, or guilty pleasures? Unreasonably then do you plead you have no superfluities, till this necessary reduction be previously made. But be candid, my brethren, and acknowledge that when you spoke of superfluities, you had measured them by the unreasonable wants of nature, and not by the simplicity of a Christian. Many there are, my brethren, and for the interests of humanity we could wish them fewer who make pretensions to a uniform practice of charity, and profess to reserve a portion of their goods for this purpose. But does any accident occur, some temporary pressure oblige them to retrench, their benevolent fund is the first to go. Alas! charity in their estimation is the most obvious superfluity; and whilst appetite and pleasure are indulged in all their accustomed desires, the widow and her boy are turned adrift upon the world with 'her fragment of bread and her bottle of water', to seek shelter and protection from another hand, and perhaps too, like Agar in the deserts of Bersabee, to meet with both from some angel of the wilderness (Gen. 21).

Yet I know it will be said, for it is frequently declared, that the very extravagance complained of is silently beneficial to mankind, that the profusion of the rich is the fortune of the poor, and even that luxury is the very best practical method of charity. My brethren, we are not assembled to discuss a point of political economy, nor will I trespass here upon the civil part of the question; it may be very sound policy, but it is wretched morality. A scheme which is radically bad, can never be sanctified in its effects, and if luxury, pride, and effeminacy be of this description, it is little to say that they are productive of accidental good. It is dignifying the basest passions of the soul at the expense of the noblest, it is degrading our virtues to the rank of a marketable commodity, and making our vices the medium of purchase. It is throwing open that road which Divine Wisdom has made narrow, and emblazoning our title to Heaven on the very records of our disgrace. But granting that some benefit is derived to the poor from the dissemination of wealth, does it fall, think ye, where most it is due? Does it spread to the hovels of indigence, and not rather to the abodes of comparative abundance? Does it go to rejoice the heart of the aged and infirm, the sick and the imprisoned, to feed the hungry and to clothe the naked, and not rather to swell the coffers of plenteous mediocrity, where, after having glutted the enjoyment of the rich, it generates wants unknown to a simpler age, and encourages among the middling classes that mimicry of wealth so subversive of the end and happiness of society? (5)

## Worshipping with the Heart

Let us begin with the virtue of religion. Of this a principal duty is worship. Reason teaches us to worship God. The natural law prescribes that we should do it frequently. The divine law specifies a day; and the ecclesiastical law extends and modifies the precept in many determinate ways. Now if at the stated periods a person repair to the temple of God, behave with exterior decency, listen to the accustomed offices, and recite with faithful lips the ordinary forms of prayer, he has complied indeed with the letter of the law, and may appear to some to have satisfied his obligations. But if his worship has stopped here, it has been but a pitiful worship. God has not been really worshipped, he has not been supplicated; such a man has fulfilled no duty, he has uttered no prayer. What then was wanting? Why the essence was wanting, the spirit was wanting, the interior, the heart. And what does this enjoin more, you may ask? Oh it enjoins nothing, I love to reply, but it prompts to every thing. It deals in no injunction. It awaits not the cold formality of a precept in the enthusiasm it enkindles, and the vigour it excites. It suggests to the soul which it animates, rapid and forcible ideas of the majesty of God, his infinite attributes and eternal perfections, his immensity, his power, his wisdom; his beauty, his glory, his justice, his mercy, his love. It then turns her views upon herself. It shows her her littleness, her insignificance, her dependence. She is lost, and confounded, and humbled to the dust. She adores with the prostration of the soul and trembles as she adores. It then reminds her that this great and powerful Being, infinitely happy within himself, has yet deigned to think of her; to give her a portion of his existence, itself an immeasurable favour; to create worlds for her happiness, whilst her he has created for no world, but for the everlasting enjoyment of himself. Her powers are engrossed in devotion. She fain would express her feelings. She would borrow the hearts and the tongues of all created beings and would give heart and tongue to those who have them not, to help her to bless and to praise the Lord. She rejoices to meet her brethren in the temple of God, to join the solemn invitatories of thanksgiving and prayer. But here her confusion is increased. Every object that bespeaks the love of God and of his son Jesus Christ, bespeaks also her ingratitude and guilt. It reminds her what she was, what she might have been, what she is: that she was an enemy of God, that she might have been justly rejected, but that she is redeemed. But oh! when she considers how she was redeemed: that it was the only Son of God who purchased her redemption; purchased it by his humiliations, his sufferings, his torments, and death; torments and death beyond human endurance, or human conception; that by mysteries ineffable and divine, he has contrived to perpetuate in his church the memory of these incomprehensible favours, and to represent himself on the altar as her physician, her friend, her father, and her God. Oh! it is then that language cannot paint her feelings. It is then that the soul is bursting with agony, but an agony sweeter to her than an ocean of worldly delights. Faith, hope, love and sorrow alternately predominating, or raising their mingled emotions, depict on the countenance the spirit of prayer. No languid looks, no indolent posture, no vacant, restless, or indecent gaze, but all is modesty, humility, devotion, and love. If ever a contrary feeling arise, it is a feeling of indignation that Christians should value so little the exceeding great love of their Saviour, and that amid the profusion of graces and mercies that are squandered around them, they should yet be seen stipulating with their God for their conveniences, their gratifications, and their little paltry passions, as if the whole of their hearts were too much in exchange for his. (6)

## Confession as a Humane Sacrament

Confession is represented as a burden inconsistent with the liberty of the Gospel, unbecoming the dignity of man, fettering the intercourse between the sinner and his God, and impeding, rather than promoting, the efforts of repentance. To those who have honestly taken such views of the subject, I would beg leave to reply. Look well to your own hearts on this delicate question and see whether you are not fostering a presumptuous pride, under pretext of vindicating the dignity of the Christian. It is not for the sinner to prescribe terms to his Creator, on which to re-purchase favour and forgiveness. Such a spirit is the spirit of Naaman, when enjoined to *go and wash* for his leprosy, in the *waters of the Jordan*. 'What', said the proud man, *have we not rivers at home? Are not the Abana, and the Pharphar, rivers of Damascus, better than all the waters of Israel, that I may wash in them and be made clean?' So he turned and was going away with indignation. And his servants came to him and said, 'Father, if the prophet had bid thee do some great thing, surely thou shouldst have done it. How much rather what he now hath said to thee, "Wash and thou shalt be clean?"'* (4 Kings 5: 12–13) What these considerate servants said to their master, that I say to my erring brethren. If Christ had prescribed to the sinner conditions of reconciliation a thousand times more humiliating than that of acknowledging his offences in the secrecy of confession; yet so loathsome is the leprosy of sin, and so alarming, so painful is a state of hostility with God, and so dismal the prospect of being eternally separated from him, that we should cheerfully accept of any alternative, gratefully comply with any conditions, rather than live his enemy, and hazard the loss of our immortal souls. *If he had bid thee do some great thing, surely thou shouldst have done it. How much rather what he now hath said to thee, 'Wash and thou shalt be clean.'*

But you exaggerate the difficulties of the subject. Confession is not the torturing process which you may have imagined. There is nothing arbitrary in the institutions of Jesus Christ. They all bear the stamp of infinite wisdom, accommodating itself to the state and condition of his creatures. And be you well assured, that *he who knows what is in man*, has also, in this instance, provided the most effectual remedy against the slothfulness, the insensibility, the pride and ignorance of his nature. So far from diverting the sinner from the proper objects of his solicitude, confession conducts him into the paths of true repentance, encourages his efforts, and sustains his steps. (7)

NOTES AND SOURCES

1. Henry Weedall, quoted in F. C. Husenbeth, *The Life of the Right Reverend Monsignor Weedall, D.D.* (London, 1860), 183–4.

2. Ibid. 187–8.

3. Henry Weedall, *A Sermon Preached in the Roman Catholic Chapel of St Chad, Chadwell Street, Birmingham, on Sunday, December 31, 1815 for the Benefit of the Catholic Sunday School* (Birmingham, 1816), 4–5.

4. Ibid. 6–7.

5. Ibid. 13–15.

6. Henry Weedall, *The Spirit and the Truth of Religion, Deduced from Reason and Scripture, A Sermon, Preached on the Anniversary of the Opening of the Catholic Chapel at Sheffield on Thursday, April 30, 1818* (London, 1818), 12–15.

7. Henry Weedall, *A Vindication of the Catholic Doctrine and Discipline of Confession, A Homily* (Leamington, 1846), 26–8.

# William Joseph Walter                                     1789–1846

Though he was a man whose vocation was preserving and retelling the past, William Joseph Walter has been himself virtually forgotten. He did much, however, to make the English Catholic tradition accessible to a modern readership in both England and America. After residing at St Edmund's College as a student and professor, Walter made his way in life with his pen, translating French works by Chateaubriand and Cochin and editing collections of poetry and prose by Robert Southwell. The latter projects were recommended to Walter by the fiercely anti-Catholic Poet Laureate Robert Southey who, at a literary gathering at the Lake poet's home in Keswick, reportedly expressed his surprise that 'Catholics should so neglect' their 'early writers and particularly the beautiful productions of Southwell'. This editorial reclamation came after Walter's 1816 account of a recovered medieval manuscript by a Fountains Abbey monk called *Clavis Scientiae, or Bretayne's Skyll-Kay of Knowing*, another journey into the English Catholic poetic past. Given the contemporary taste for forgeries of ancient poetry from the British isles by Chatterton and MacPherson, the current unknown status of this manuscript, and the fact that Walter appears to have 'puffed' the work in an English Catholic periodical as meeting demand for English Catholic antiquities, it is possible that the work was Walter's own attempt to invent an English Dante. His most significant and reliable work, however, came after his 1839 emigration to Philadelphia where he published a life of Thomas More. He subsequently and unsuccessfully tried to start a Catholic library series for the US Catholic market with works on Mary Queen of Scots, St John Chrysostom, and others. He died in 1846 after dedicating his last work to Newman—an appropriate close as Walter's emphasis on transformative individual emotion and the recovery of the past prefigure the religious romanticism of the 'Second Spring'.

## The Exemplary Life of St Thomas More

That examples of past ages move us more than those of our own time, may, probably, be in part ascribed to the reverence we feel for antiquity, and to the mysterious veneration which hangs around the memory of the illustrious dead. Objects that are viewed through the medium of a softening distance, lose many of those blemishes and inequalities, which approximation allows us to discover. There are some characters, however, which have borne with them to the tomb so few of the failings of our nature, that they have no need of this illusion of antiquity to invest them with an interest not their own. In this number may be ranked the subject of our memoir. (1)

## St Thomas More's Wit

Sir Thomas now withdrew his attention altogether from public affairs, and devoted his leisure to study and devotion. He completed different controversial works which he had begun during his chancellorship and gave them to the public.... These works show the extent of More's learning, and his tact in polemic warfare; and have often been resorted to by later divines, as arsenals stored with materials for the defence of the faith. How far wit and humour are suitable weapons in a contest involving interests so solemn and important, we shall not stop to examine; but if it be allowed the champion of truth to employ them, certain it is that More has wielded them with vigour and address. The contrast between the lighter warfare, and the solemn and touching passages which stand in juxtaposition, has a very singular effect. Take an example or two. He has a well-conducted argument, terminating in the following forcible sentence: 'Therefore, to tell me to leave the truth as taught in the known church, and seek it in an unknown, is to persuade me to renounce the light of the sun in order to pick my way by a rush-light.' (2)

## The Final Meeting of More and His Daughter

Scarcely had he set his foot upon the wharf, where the Tower guards were drawn up to receive him, when a person made her way through the assembled throng, arrested the procession, and in an instant clung round his neck. It was his Margaret, his good angel, who had been eagerly watching for his landing, her heart having told her that this would be the last opportunity of seeing her dear father in this world. No sooner had she caught a glance of him, and saw the axe borne before, with the edge towards him—the certain sign of what was to follow— than she rushed forward, 'and without care for herself, passing through the midst of the guard, who with bills and halberts compassed him around, there openly in the sight of them all embraced him, took him about the neck, and kissed him, unable to utter any other word than "Oh my father! Oh my father!"' Before the face of his judges, More had stood calm, cheerful, triumphant; but this was an appeal to the tenderest feelings of his heart for which he was little prepared. But, 'pleased with her most natural and dear affection toward him, he gave her his fatherly blessing, telling her that God's holy will must be done; that she knew full well all the secrets of his heart, and that, like him, she must conform to the decrees of Heaven and be patient.' They parted. But 'scarcely had she gone ten steps, when, not satisfied with the former farewell, like one who had forgotten herself, ravished with the entire love of so worthy a father, she again rushed through the closing guards, hung about his neck, and divers times kissed him.' More's philosophy was not proof against this second attack; he spoke not a word, but the tears streamed from his eyes. These sorrows were infectious: 'Yea, there were very few in the crowd, who could not refrain from weeping at this sight; no, not the guards themselves.'

In so trying a moment, More realized the full force of that admonition of the Psalmist: *Cast thy burthen upon the Lord, and He will support thee!*

Nor had Margaret come unattended to fulfil this melancholy office of love. She was accompanied by her brother, and by Margaret More's ward, who imitated Mrs. Roper's example, and embraced their father, friend, and protector; as also did Margaret's 'faithful maid servant, Dorothy Colley', of whose testimony of affection More afterwards observed, 'that it was homely, but very lovingly done.'

History has recorded few things so affecting as this last interview between More and his daughter. As we read, and remember the blameless, and even lofty character of their domestic life, the school, the playful and unreserved intercourse of the father and his children, their severer studies, their religious exercises, the truly moral feeling which regulated the employments of every hour, the charity to others, and the perfect union among themselves; as we recollect all this, we are led to see how far the taking counsel with things impure can stifle in the heart the sense of justice and humanity, and are enabled to estimate the amount of selfishness, insensibility, and crime, chargeable to the monarch who could deprive his people of examples so pure, so generous, so ennobling. (3)

## Robert Southwell's Message to Posterity

Now is the time in which many of our forefathers desired to live—a time when they might not only profit the Church by the example of their life, and the virtue of their preaching, but also—and how much did they desire it!—by the effusion of their blood. When England was Catholic, she had many glorious confessors. It is for the honour and benefit of our country that it should be well stored with a number of martyrs; and we have now, God be thanked!, such martyr-makers in authority, as mean, if they have their will, to make saints enough to furnish all our churches with treasure, when it shall please God to restore them to their true honours; and doubt not but either they, or their posterity, shall see the very prisons of execution become places of reverence and devotion; and the scattered bones of those that in this cause have suffered, though now thought unworthy of Christian burial, then shrined in gold, and held in the highest respect. (4)

## Imitating the Love of St Mary Magdalene

O Christian soul! take Mary for thy mirror; follow her affection, that like effects may follow thy own. Learn, O sinful man, of this once sinful woman, that sinners may find Christ, if their sins be amended. Learn, that whom sin loses, love recovers; whom faintness of faith chases away, firmness of hope recalls; and that which no other mortal force, favour or policy can compass, the continued tears of a constant love are able to attain. Learn of Mary, for Christ to fear no encounters; out of Christ, to desire no comfort; and with the love of Christ, to over-rule the love of all things. Rise early in the morning of thy good resolves, and let them not sleep in sloth, when diligence may perform them. Run, with repentance, to thy sinful heart, which should have been a temple, but through thy fault has proved no better than a tomb for Christ; since, having no life in thee to feel him, he seemed to thee as if he had been dead. Roll away the stone of thy former hardness, remove all the heavy loads that oppress thee in sin, and look into thy soul whether thou canst there find the Lord. If he be not within thee, stand weeping without, and seek him till he be found. Let faith be thine eye, hope thy guide, and love thy light. (5)

NOTES AND SOURCES

1.  William Joseph Walter, *Sir Thomas More: His Life and Times* (London, 1840), 1.

2.  Ibid. 203–4.

3.  Ibid. 334–6. For More's letter to his daughter, see pp. 62–3. For Margaret Roper's writings, see pp. 50–2.

4.  Robert Southwell, *An Epistle of Comfort to the Reverend Priests, and to the Honourable, Worshipful, and Others of the Lay Sort, Restrained in Durance for the Catholic Faith,* in *The Prose Works of Robert Southwell,* ed. William Joseph Walter (London, 1828), 124–99; 197. For a broader selection of Southwell's writing, see pp. 151–8.

5.  Robert Southwell, *Mary Madalen's Teares,* ibid. 11–84; 81–2.

# (Domenico Giovanni Luigi Barberi)     1792–1849
# Blessed Dominic of the Mother of God CP

Prayer has a way of blurring the boundaries of citizenship. An orphaned Italian shepherd boy named Domenico Barberi, born in the closing years of the French Revolution, played such a crucial role in the English Catholic revival that he is often known as 'The Apostle of England'. The same spirit that drew Barberi away from farmwork in Viterbo also turned him towards England. In 1814, even before he was ordained or received as a cleric into the Discalced Clerks of the Most Holy Cross and Passion (generally known as the Passionists), Barberi had a mystical experience in which he felt a vocation from Christ to be a missionary to England. At the time, he could not even locate England on the map, but his daily prayers were directed towards England until he set foot there in 1840. In the meantime, his years were filled with teaching, writing philosophy and theology ('Ten years of learning, twenty of meditation, and an hour of composition,' he prescribed, 'if you want to make a work worthy of admiration'), helping the sick during a cholera outbreak, and serving as a rector and provincial to the Passionists. His arrival in Staffordshire to establish a Passionist community in Aston Hall was part of an eventful round of exuberant, if not always fluent, preaching and pastoral work that lasted nearly a decade. He had a strong influence on those in the Oxford Movement, and John Henry Newman—who commemorated Barberi both in *Loss and Gain* (1848) and *Apologia Pro Vita Sua* (1864)—was the most famous and dramatic, but not the only, convert he received into the Church. If his mission to England seems to have begun in a miraculous way, his death was likewise wondrous. In his meditation written in the prophetic style of Jeremiah called *Lamentation for England* (1831), Barberi offers his own life for the revival of the faith in England. In 1849, a year before the restoration of the English hierarchy, England's unlikely herald of the ancient faith died in the most modern of settings—a Reading hotel room at a railway station following a heart attack on the train from London. He was beatified in 1963 by Pope Paul VI, and his shrine is in Sutton, near Liverpool.

## A Life Offered for the English Revival

Have mercy then on England; and behold, O Lord, if thou wilt accomplish this, new temples shall be raised to the honour of thy name, and new altars. Sacrifices also shall be offered acceptable unto thee, even the sacrifice of Jesus in the Eucharist; and in these holy temples shall thy infinite majesty be praised and adored. Jesus thy son shall once more be loved and praised; and Mary also shall be praised and invocated. Vouchsafe then, O Lord, to accomplish with thy powerful arm this thing, which thou hast inspired me to beg of thee. I shall never be fully happy until I behold the completion of these my desires, I shall not die contented unless I behold brought back to the fold of thy church the nations which for many years and ages have dwelt far off from thee. But if it be thy will that I die before I see this accomplished, I shall die contented only if I am assured that it shall one day come to pass after my death. Yes, O Lord, I am ready to die this instant, or to suffer the heaviest temporal calamity, on this condition, that England shall return to the true faith. I ask not, O Lord, to be the instrument of so great a work, no, to thee I leave it to choose who shall be the minister of thy mercies. Only do I beg of thee the salvation of my dear brethren. 'Fratres meos quaero' [I seek my brethren (Gen. 37: 16)]. This alone do I entreat thee, this alone is all I desire. Comforted then by the sweet hope that thou vouchsafest to grant to me, I will remain tranquil, waiting in silence for that grace from thee which I have asked of thee, 'Bonum est praestolari cum silentio salutare Dei' [It is good to wait with silence for the salvation of God (Lam. 3: 26)]. (1)

NOTES AND SOURCES

1.  Dominic Barberi (Padre Dominico della Madre di Dio), *The Lamentation of England*, trans. Ambrose Lisle March Phillipps de Lisle (Leicester, 1831), 18–19.

## (George Spencer) Ignatius of St Paul CP                1799–1864

George Spencer may have become a Catholic prior to the 'Second Spring', but his spiritual transformation, unique personality, and contributions to England's spiritual life are not out-shone by those later converts. Spencer came from the most illustrious of backgrounds. He was the youngest son in the family of the second Earl Spencer, whose descendants include Winston Churchill and Diana, Princess of Wales. He was educated at Eton and Trinity College, Cambridge. He was ordained an Anglican priest and became the rector at his family's Althorp estate. A life of such privilege and comfort may not often produce a Christian Diogenes, but Spencer devoted his life to the pursuit of religious truth in the faith that such a candid and sincere inquiry would ultimately lead to Christian unity. This commitment led him, in 1830, to leave his former life and become a Catholic. As a priest he would serve in the West Midlands, but his broader mission has earned him the title 'Apostle of Prayer for England'. Spencer spearheaded campaigns to pray for the conversion of England in Italy, Ireland, and France, but, for him, the means of conversion and the basis of ecumenical unity had to be an open and prayerful dialogue directed towards discovering truth. This task took him to Oscott College, where he served as spiritual director and professor, and culminated in his entering the Passionist Congregation at Aston Hall that was founded by his friend and mentor, Blessed Dominic Barberi. The remainder of his life was devoted to preaching and praying for England across Europe and, at home, to supporting the Passionist congregation of nuns founded by his fellow convert Elizabeth Prout (1820–64) that, radically, disposed of economic and class distinctions, ministered to Manchester's industrial poor, and housed girls working in factories. Spencer died in 1864, and, in 1973, his remains were transferred to a new shrine alongside Barberi and Prout in the Church of St Anne and Blessed Dominic in Sutton. There is currently a cause for the canonization of both Spencer and Prout, who walked with prayer, truth, and charity amid the sweetness and light of nineteenth-century high culture as well as through what Francis Thompson called darkest England's 'immense, soundless, bitter ocean' of social degradation.

## A Search for Truth

The result of all these discussions with different sects of Protestants was a conviction that no one of us had a correct view of Christianity. We all appeared right thus: in acknowledging Christ as the Son of God, whose doctrines and commandments we were to follow as the way to happiness, both in time and eternity; but it seemed as if the form of doctrine and discipline established by the Apostles had been lost sight of all through the church. I wished therefore to see Christians in general united in the resolution to find the way of truth and peace, convinced that God would not fail to point it out to them. Whether or not others would seek his blessing with me, I had great confidence that, before long, God would clear up my doubts, and therefore my mind was not made uneasy by them.

After this period, I entertained the opinion that the Reforms had done wrong in separating from the original body of the Church; at any rate I was convinced that Protestants who succeeded them were bound to make attempts at reunion with it. I still conceived that many errors and corruptions had been introduced amongst Catholics, and I did not imagine that I could ever conform to their faith, or join in all their practices, without some alterations on their part; but I trusted that the time might not be distant when God would inspire all Christians with a spirit of peace and concord, which would make Protestants anxiously seek to be reunited to their brethren, and Catholics willing to listen to reason and to correct those abuses in faith and discipline which kept their brethren from joining them. To the procuring such a happy termination to the miserable schisms which had rent the Church I determined to devote my life. I now lost no opportunity of conversation with Protestants or Catholics. My object with both was to awaken them to a desire of unity with each other; to satisfy myself more clearly where was the exact path of truth in which it was desirable that we should all walk together; and then to persuade all to correct their respective errors, in conformity with the perfect rule, which I had no doubt the Lord would in due time point out to me, and to all who were at length willing to enter with me on these discussions with candour, they would at once begin to see the errors which to me appeared so palpable in their system; but I was greatly surprised to find them all so fixed in their principles, that they gave me no prospect of reunion except on condition of others submitting unreservedly to them; and, at the same time, I could see in their ordinary conduct and manner of disputing with me nothing to make me suspect them of insincerity, or of want of sufficient information of the grounds of their belief. These repeated conversations increased more and more my desire to discover this true road, which I saw that I, at least for one, was ignorant of; but I still imagined that I could see such plain marks of difference between the Catholic Church of the present day and the Church of the primitive ages as described in Scripture, that I repeatedly put aside the impression which the arguments of Catholics, and yet more my observation of their character, made upon me; and I still held up my head in the controversy....

On Sunday, the 24th of January, 1830, I preached in my church, and in the evening took leave of my family for the week, intending to return on the Saturday following to my ordinary duties at home. But our Lord ordered better for me. During the week I spent on this visit I passed many hours daily in conversations with Phillipps, and was satisfied beyond all my expectations with the answers he gave me to the different questions I proposed about the principal tenets and practices of Catholics. During the week, we were in company with several other Protestants, and among them some distinguished clergymen of the Church of England, who occasionally joined in our discussions. I was struck with observing how the advantage always appeared on his side in the arguments which took place between them, notwithstanding their superior age and experience, and I saw how weak was the cause in behalf of which I had hitherto been engaged. I felt ashamed of arguing any longer against what I began to see clearly could not be fairly disproved. I now openly declared myself completely shaken, and though I determined to take no decided step till I was entirely convinced, I determined to give myself no rest till I was satisfied and had little doubt now of what the result would be. But yet I thought not how soon God would make the truth clear to me. I was to return home, as I have said, on the Saturday. Phillipps agreed to accompany me on the day previous to Leicester, where we might have farther conversation with Father Caestryck, the Catholic Missionary established in that place. I imagined that I might probably take some weeks longer for consideration. But Mr. Caestryck's conversation that afternoon overcame all my opposition. He explained to me and made me see that the way to come at the knowledge of true religion is not to contend, as men are disposed to do, about each individual point, but to submit implicitly to the authority of Christ, and of those to whom he has committed the charge of his flock. He set before me the undeniable but wonderful fact of the agreement of the Catholic Church all over the world in one faith, under one head. He showed me that the assertions of Protestants that the Catholic Church had altered her doctrines were not supported by evidence. He pointed out the wonderful unbroken chain of the Roman Pontiffs. He observed to me how in all ages the Church, under their guidance, had exercised an authority undisputed by her children, of cutting off from her communion all who opposed her faith and disobeyed her discipline. I saw that her assumption of this power was consistent with Christ's commission to his apostles to teach all men to the end to the world; and his declaration that those who would not hear the pastors of his Church rejected him. What right then, thought I, had Luther and his companions to set themselves against the united voice of the Church? I saw that he rebelled against the authority of God when he set himself up as an independent guide. He was bound to obey the Catholic Church. How should I then not be equally bound to return to it? And need I fear that I should be led into error, by trusting myself to those guides to whom Christ himself thus directed me? No! I thought this impossible. Full of these impressions, I left Mr, Caestryck's house to go to my inn, whence I was to return home next morning. Phillipps accompanied me and took this last occasion to impress on me the awful importance of the decision which I was called upon to make. At length I answered, 'I am overcome. There is no doubt of the truth. One more Sunday I will preach to my congregation and then put myself into Mr. Foley's hands and conclude this business.'

It may be thought with what joyful ardour he embraced this declaration and warned me to declare my sentiments faithfully in these my last discourses. The next minute led me to the reflection: Have I any right to stand in that pulpit, being once convinced that the Church is heretical to which it belongs? Am I safe in exposing myself to the danger which may attend one day's travelling, while I turn my back on the Church of God, which now calls me to unite myself to her for ever? I said to Phillipps, if this step is right for me to take next week, it is my duty to take it now. My resolution is made; tomorrow I will be received into the Church. We lost no time in dispatching a messenger to my father, to inform him of this unexpected event. As I was forming my last resolution, the thought of him came across me. Will it not be said that I endanger his very life by so sudden and severe a shock? Ought I not, in deference and in tenderness towards him, at least, to go home and break it gently to him? The words of our Lord rose before me, and answered all my doubts: 'He that hateth not father and mother, and brothers, and sisters, and houses, and lands, and his own life, too, cannot be my disciple.' To thee Lord, then, I trusted for the support and comfort of my dear father under the trial, which in obedience to his call, I was about to inflict upon him. I had no further anxiety to disturb me. God alone knows the peace and joy with which I laid me down that night to rest. The next day, at nine o'clock, the Church received me for her child. (1)

NOTES AND SOURCES

1. George Spencer, *A Short Account of the Conversion of the Hon. and Rev. G. Spencer to the Catholic Faith* (London, [1838–41]), 5–11.

# Nicholas Patrick Stephen Cardinal Wiseman     1802–1865

'Then truly is this day to us a day of joy and exaltation of spirit, the crowning day of long hopes, and the opening day of bright prospects.' These celebratory words are taken from Wiseman's most famous writing, his 1850 pastoral letter announcing the restoration of bishops to England as replacements for the vicars apostolic, the accompanying change from districts to dioceses, and his own new position of cardinal archbishop to guide the reorganized flock. Following on from the 1829 Catholic Emancipation Act, which by allowing Catholics to sit in parliament had legitimated their place in the United Kingdom, the return of the hierarchy legitimated English Catholics' place in the Universal Church and meant that they were no longer a 'mission'. While Catholics may have appreciated the joy in Wiseman's letter, his words resonated differently in the public's ears. Wiseman's title as the Archbishop of *Westminster*, at the very heart of the nation's political and religious identity, and his address from 'Without the Flaminian Gate' (a Romish landmark perceived as resolutely and imperially foreign) set off the crisis of the 'Papal Aggression', a widespread anti-Catholic backlash on the common street corner, Fleet Street, and Downing Street. Expressing what was widely seen as a Catholic intrusion from Italy, Queen Victoria is reported to have asked, 'Am I Queen of England or am I not?' The furore was essentially a miscommunication, a disjunction between Rome's language and England's preconceptions, that Wiseman did much to assuage in a series of sermons and pamphlets appealing to the English sense of 'fair play' and asserting the spiritual and charitable aspirations of the new bishops. The cultural distance between Rome and England is one that Wiseman devoted his whole life to bridging. Born to Irish parents in Seville, he excelled at his studies at Ushaw College from 1810 until he and a small group of students left in 1818 to reclaim the English College in Rome, which had been abandoned since 1798 because of conflicts with French Revolutionary and Napoleonic forces. He excelled there as well, earning a Doctor of Divinity, lecturing and publishing on biblical philology, and later becoming rector. His responsibilities and projects included welcoming English visitors to Rome as well as giving lectures in England on such topics as the theology of the Eucharist and the relationship between science and religion. He returned to England in 1840 as bishop, coadjutor to the vicar apostolic in the Central district, and the president of Oscott College. After 1850, the reaction to the 'Papal Aggression' crisis was not the only difficulty to confront Wiseman. Added to the inevitable territorial conflicts that came with the new diocesan structure, Wiseman's own 'Ultramontane' attachments to Rome met with opposition from the remaining 'Cisalpine' figures in English Catholicism who suspected him as foreign and authoritarian. He was generally respected, however, for his immense learning, his engaging writing (his novel 1855 *Fabiola* was a popular success), his care for the poor, and his advancement of Catholic education. He died in 1865 having shepherded English Catholics through a triumphant but still unsettling transition. The first Archbishop of Westminster's remains were eventually laid to rest in a new Westminster Cathedral that was still under construction.

## Return to the English College, Rome

Long-standing desires, then, were about to be satisfied at last; and some degree of recent apprehension was going to be allayed, and welcome rest after long travel was promised; when, at the end of the road which looks straight onwards from the Milvian Bridge, we could see the open gate of Rome.

That noble entrance was by no means then what it is now. On the outside, the gates of the Borghese villa did not stand near; but the visitor had to walk a long way under the wall of the city, overhanging his path, till a narrow gate led him into a long close alley, the first of the villa. But within the Flaminian Gate, the obelisk indeed was there, as were the two twin churches beyond, closing, by their porticoes and domes, the wedges of houses between the three great divergent streets; but that was all.... Still it was one of the grandest approaches to any modern city, and one that did not altogether deceive you. The slow pace of a *vettura* along the Corso gave an opportunity of admiring the magnificent palaces that flank it on both sides, till a turn to the right brings you into the square, of which the column of Antoninus forms the centre, and then a twist to the left places you before a row of pillars which likewise bears his imperial name, but in addition a more modern one, unpleasant to travellers' ears—that of Custom House. Even this most distasteful department of civilised government contrives in Rome to get lodged in a classical monument of ancient taste.

From this point, after its disagreeable ceremonial had been completed, all reckoning was lost. A long narrow street, and the Pantheon burst full into view; then a labyrinth of tortuous ways, through which a glimpse of a church, or palace-front might be caught occasionally askew; then the small square opened on the eye, which, were it ten times larger, would be oppressed by the majestic, over-whelming mass of the Farnese palace, as completely Michelangelesque in brick as the Moses is in marble, when another turn and a few yards of distance placed us at the door of the 'venerable English College'. Had a dream, after all, bewildered one's mind, or at least closed the eager journey, and more especially its last hours, during which the tension of anxious expectation had wrought up the mind to a thousand fancies? No description had preceded actual sight. No traveller, since the beginning of the century, or even from an earlier period, had visited it or mentioned it. It had been sealed up as a tomb for a generation; and not one of those who were descending from the unwieldy vehicle at its door had collected, from the few lingering patriarchs, once its inmates, who yet survived at home, any recollections by which a picture of the place might have been prepared in the imagination. Having come so far, somewhat in the spirit of sacrifice, in some expectation of having to 'rough it', as pioneers for less venturesome followers, it seemed incredible that we should have fallen upon such pleasant places as the seat of future life and occupation. Wide and lofty vaulted corridors; a noble staircase leading to vast and airy halls succeeding one another; a spacious garden, glowing with the lemon and orange, and presenting to one's first approach a perspective in fresco by Pozzi, one engraved by him in his celebrated work on perspective; a library airy, cheerful, and large, whose shelves, however, exhibited a specimen of what antiquarians call 'opus tumultuarium' [a hastily arranged work], in the piled up disorganised volumes, from folio to duodecimo, that crammed them; a refec-tory wainscoted in polished walnut, and above that, painted, by the same hand, with St George and the Dragon, ready to drop on to the floor from the groined ceiling; still better, a chapel, unfurnished indeed, but illuminated from floor to roof with the saints of England, and celestial glories, leading to the altar that had to become the very hearthstone of new domestic attachments, and the centre of many yet untasted joys;—such were the first features of our future abode, as, alone and undirected, we wandered through the solemn building, and made it, after years of silence, re-echo to the sound of English voices, and give back the bounding tread of those who had returned to claim their own.... One felt at once at home; it was nobody else's house; it was English ground, a part of fatherland, a restored inheritance. (1)

## Catholic Emancipation

And first—to begin with the very outset of Pius's Pontificate—he was elected March 31, 1829; and, scarcely a month later, it was my pleasing duty to communicate to him the gladsome tidings of Catholic Emancipation. This great and just measure received the royal assent on the 23rd of April following. It need hardly be remarked, that such a message was one of unbounded joy, and might well have been communicated to the Head of the Catholic Church in the words by which the arrival of paschal time is announced to him every year: 'Pater sancte, annuntio vobis gaudium magnum' [Holy Father, I announce to you a great joy]. To him, who was not only most intelligent, but alive to all that passed throughout Christendom, the full meaning of this measure was of course apparent. But generally it was not so. In foreign countries, the condition of Catholics in Great Britain was but little understood. . . .

We then proceeded to make preparations for our festival, on the usual Roman plan. The front of our house was covered with an elegant architectural design in variegated lamps, and an orchestra was erected opposite for festive music. In the morning of the appointed day, a *Te Deum*, attended by the various British colleges, was performed; in the afternoon a banquet on a munificent scale was given at his villa near St Paul's, by Monsignor Nicolai, the learned illustrator of that Basilica; and in the evening we returned home to see the upturned faces of multitudes reflecting the brilliant 'lamps of architecture' that tapestried our venerable walls. But the words 'Emancipazione Cattolica', which were emblazoned in lamps along the front, were read by the people with difficulty, and interpreted by conjecture; so that many came and admired, but went away, unenlightened by the blaze that had dazzled them, into the darkness visible of surrounding streets.

In fact, the first two words, long and formidable to untutored lips was no household word in Italy, nor was there any imaginable connection in ordinary persons' minds between it and its adjective, nor between the two and England. But to us and our guests there was surely a magic in the words, that spoke to our hearts, and awakened the sweet music, more cheering than that of our orchestra, and kindled up a brighter illumination in our minds than that upon our walls. We had left our country young, and hardly conscious of the wrongs which galled our elders, we should return to it in possession of our rights; and thus have hardly experienced more sense of injury than they who have been born since that happy era. . . . Still, if wrongs had not been keenly felt, the act of justice so honourable to one's country, and the sense of relief from degrading trammels, made every British Catholic heart rejoice in Rome, when the news reached us, that the struggle of years had been crowned with triumph, and that the laurels of a peaceful Waterloo had graced the same brows as were crowned by the wreaths of our last great sanguinary victory. It was, however, the future, and not the present, that gladdened that hour, the birth-hour of great and enduring events. . . . The day that prepared such a prospect for a country divided in religion, may well be considered a bright one in the brief annals of the Pontificate within which it fell. (2)

## A Guide to Biblical Criticism

Every teacher has his own peculiar method of conveying instruction, resulting from his character, his intention, his principles, his situation; and it is obvious, that any explanation of his words, at variance with his well-known methods and character, cannot for a moment be admitted. Any interpretation of a passage in Plato, which supposed him to abandon his inductive and discursive method, and argue in a synthetical and formal manner, or which made him represent Socrates as a haughty overbearing despot in discussion, would be instantly rejected, as incompatible with the known character and principles of that philosopher. In like manner, any explanation of words spoken by our Blessed Saviour, which should be at variance with his usual and constant method of instructing, or which should suppose him to be ought but meek, humble, conciliating, and charitable, must be unhesitatingly rejected. (3)

## Reconciling Contrasts in Christ

It will be readily allowed, that nothing can be more beautifully consistent than the character of our Saviour. And yet what forms its principal and distinguishing peculiarity is the superhuman manner in which traits of the most opposite nature, and apparently of the most unharmonizing qualities, blend together, in such just proportion as to make one perfect and consistent whole. In him we have an independence which renders him superior to all the world, yet a humility which subjects him to the meanest of its inhabitants; an intrepid firmness in reproof, and a nervous eloquence in condemning, which humbles and crushes the most daring, yet a sweetness and gentleness in instructing, which encourages and wins the timid and the prejudiced; a fortitude which could support the most excruciating tortures, yet a meekness which could suppress the slightest expression of triumph. There is not one passage in his entire life, which refuses to harmonize with the rest, however different it may appear, at first sight, from his usual conduct; there is no apparent shade in his character which does not beautifully mingle in with its brightest colours. Hence is there not a single transaction of our Lord's, upon earth, which may not be dwelt upon by the Christian teacher, as a lesson of conduct, the most perfect and most instructive,—not one where the Christian apologist could not rest, to point out to the unbeliever a beauty and a sublimity more than human. (4)

## The Unity of Knowledge

When I consider how many different men have laboured almost unwittingly to produce the results I have laid before you ... when I see them thus, all like emmets bearing their small particular loads, or removing some little obstruction, and crossing and recrossing one the other, as though in total confusion, and to the utter derangement of each other's projects; and yet when I discover that from all this there results a plan of exceeding regularity, order, and beauty; it doth seem to me as though I read therein signs of a higher instinct, and of a directing influence over the thoughtless counsels of men, which can bring them unto great and useful purposes. And such methinks is to be found in the history of all sound learning. For, as a day appearing now and then of brighter and warmer sunshine doth foreshow that the full burst of summer's glory is about to break upon the earth, so do certain privileged minds, by some mysterious communication, ever foresee, as it were, or rather feel sometime beforehand, and announce the approach of some great and new system of truth; as did Bacon, of philosophy; and Leibniz, of our science; and Plato, of a holier manifestation. Then arise, and come in from all sides, we know not how, workmen and patient labourers, like those who cast down faggots under a foundation, or raise stones thereon; whom no one takes for the architects or builders of the house, for they know and comprehend nought of its plans or objects; and yet every stone which they place fitteth aright, and adds to the usefulness and beauty of its parts. And so, after this fashion, by the work of many conjoined, though not combined in any plan, a science is builded up in fair proportions, and seemeth to stand well and in its proper place among the others already raised; and so at length cometh to be a joint, as it were, in the general fitness of things, and a maxim in the universal truth, and a tone or accord in the harmony of nature.

Now I cannot persuade myself that there is not an overseeing eye in this ordering of things dissimilar to one great end, when I see that this great end is the confirmation of God's holy word; but rather of this seeming human industry I would say with the divine poet:—

> Then turns
> The Primal Mover with a smile of joy
> On such great work of nature; and imbreathes
> New spirit replete with virtue, that what here
> Active it finds, to its own substance draws;
> And forms an individual soul that lives,
> And feels, and bends reflective on itself.
> —DANTE, *Purgatorio.* xxv.

Not that He partaketh in the errors and follies of such as labour in these pursuits, but as he useth the evils of this world for the most holy purposes, and unfolds often therefrom the most magnificent passages of His blessed providence, so may He here overrule and guide even the ill-intended labours of many, and so dispose thereof, as that a new and beautiful light may come forth upon His truths, when such is most truly needed.

Thus would I consider the rise and development of any new science, as entering essentially into the established order of God's moral government; just as the appearance, from time to time, of the new stars in the firmament, according to what astronomers tell us, must be a preordained event in the annals of creation. And if you agree with me in these reflections, you will also methinks feel as I do, that in tracing the history of any pursuit, we are not so much indulging a fond curiosity, or following the progress of man's ingenuity, as watching the beautiful courses whereby God hath gradually removed the veil from before some hidden knowledge, first lifting up one corner thereof, then another, till the whole is rolled away: and you will with me delight in studying the purposes and applications thereby intended, both towards our humble instruction and His increasing glory. (5)

## Knowing and Respecting Creation

It would, of course, be impossible to bring every branch of the natural sciences so completely into contact with sacred studies, as these whereof we have treated, nor can it be necessary to do so. For there is one way in which they all can be made subservient to the interests of religion, by viewing them as the appointed channels by which a true perception and estimate of the Divine perfections are meant to pass into the understanding; as the glass wherein the embodied forms of every great and beautiful attribute of the Supreme Being may best be contemplated; and as the impression upon the mind of the great seal of creation, whereon have been engraved, by an Almighty hand, mystical characters of deepest wisdom, omnipotent spells of productive power, and emblems most expressive of an all-embracing, all-preserving love. And even as the engraver, when he hath cut some way into his gem, doth make proof thereof upon the tender wax; and, if he find not the image perfect, is not thereby disheartened, so long as it presents each time a progressive approach to its intended type, but returns again and again unto his peaceful task; so, if we find not that, at once, we bear upon ourselves the clear and deep impress of this glorious signet, must not we fear to proceed with our labours, but go on, ever striving to approach nearer and nearer the attainment of a perfect representation. A few years will probably bring forward new arguments for the great facts whereof we have treated, which will render all that you have heard but of small value. Those that come after us will, peradventure, smile at the small comprehension granted to our age, of nature and her operations:—we must be content, amidst our imperfect knowledge, with having striven after that which is more full.

For, if the works of God are the true, though faint, image of himself, they must, in some way, partake of his immensity; and, as the contemplation of his own unshadowed beauty will be the unsating, everlasting food of unembodied spirits, so may we say, that a similar proportion hath been observed between the examination of his image reflected on his works, and the faculties of our present condition; inasmuch as therein is matter for meditation ever deeper, for discovery ever ampler, for admiration ever holier. And so God, not being able to give to the beauties of his work that infinity which is reserved to the attributes they exhibit, has bestowed upon them that quality which best supplies and represents it; for, by making our knowledge of them progressive, he has made them inexhaustible. (6)

## Knowledge and Belief

I may naturally be asked, what addition I consider myself to have made to the evidences of Christianity. Now, to this question I should reply with most measured reserve. I hold those evidences to be something too inwardly and deeply seated in the heart, to have their sum increased or diminished easily by the power of outward considerations. However we may require and use such proofs of its truths, as learned men have ably collected, when reasoning with the opponents of Christianity, I believe no one is conscious of clinging to its sublime doctrines and its consoling promises, on the ground of such logical demonstration; even as an able theorist shall show you many cogent reasons, founded on the social and natural laws, why ye should love your parents, and yet both he and you know that not for those reasons have you loved them, but from a far holier and more inward impulse. And so, when we once have embraced true religion, its motives, or evidences, need not longer be sought in the reasonings of books; they become incorporated with our holiest affections; they result from our finding the necessity for our happiness, of the truths they uphold; in our there discovering the key to the secrets of our nature, the solution of all mental problems, the reconciliation of all contradictions in our anomalous condition, the answer to all the solemn questions of our restless consciousness.

Thus is religion like a plant, which drives its roots into the centre of the soul; having in them fine and subtle fibres, that pierce and penetrate into the solidest framework of a well-built mind, and strong knotty arms that entangle themselves among the softest and purest of our feelings. And if without it also put forth shoots and tendrils innumerable, wherewith, as with hands, it apprehends and keeps hold of mundane and visible objects, it is rather for their benefit and ornament than from any want of such support! nor does it from them derive its natural and necessary vitality. (7)

## A Life of Learning

I know not why any one who possesses but ordinary abilities, may not hope, by persevering diligence, somewhat to enlarge the evidences of truth. There are humble departments in this as in every other art; there are calm, retired walks, which lead not beyond the precincts of domestic privacy, over which the timid may wander, and without exposure to the public gaze, gather sweet and lowly herbs, that shall be as fragrant on the altar of God, as the costly perfume which Bezaleel and Oholiab compounded with so much art. The painted shell which the child picks up on the hill side, may well be sometimes as good evidence of a great catastrophe, as the huge bones of sea-monsters, which the naturalist digs out of the limestone rock; a little medal may attest the destruction of an empire, as certainly as the obelisk or triumphal arch....

But whosoever shall try to cultivate a wider field, and follow, from day to day, as humbly we have striven here to do, the constant progress of every science, careful ever to note the influence which it exercises on his more sacred knowledge, shall have therein such pure joy, and such growing comfort, as the disappointing eagerness of mere human learning may not supply. Such a one I know not unto whom to liken, save to one who unites an enthusiastic love of nature's charms, to a sufficient acquaintance with her laws, and spends his days in a garden of the choicest bloom. And here he seeth one gorgeous flower, that has unclasped all its beauty to the glorious sun; and there another is just about to disclose its modester blossom, not yet fully unfolded: and beside them, there is one only in the hand-stem, giving but slender promise of much display; and yet he waiteth patiently, well knowing that the law is fixed whereby it too shall pay, in due season, its tribute to the light and heat that feed it. Even so, the other doth likewise behold one science after the other, when its appointed hour is come, and its ripening influences have prevailed, unclose some form which shall add to the varied harmony of universal truth, which shall recompense, to the full, the genial power that hath given it life, and, however barren it may have seemed at first, produce something that may adorn the temple and altar of God's worship. (8)

## The Mustard Seed and the Kingdom

The kingdom of Heaven here mentioned is undoubtedly the Church or religion of Christ. Its beginnings were small and inconsiderable, its means of propagation insignificant; and yet, in a few years, it astonished the world by the immensity of its growth; for it even became as the vine, whereof the Psalmist says, that 'it filled the land, the shadow of it covered the hills, and the branches thereof the cedars of God. It stretched forth its branches unto the sea, and its boughs unto the river' (Ps. 79: 10–12). Such, no doubt, is the primary and most obvious application of this excellent parable, which may be considered as the counterpart of that vision interpreted by Daniel, wherein a little stone, cut out of the mountain without hands, threw down the statue that represented the great successive empires of the world, and, covering their place, 'became a great mountain, and filled the whole earth' (Dan. 2: 35). But the image so happily chosen by our Saviour, may suggest a more enlarged and varied contemplation of the growth of Christianity in its moral structure, as well as in its outward relations; by which I mean, that the religion of Christ will be found to possess a marvellous power of developing, when a proper occasion presents itself, germs of great principles latent within it, adapted to the circumstances in which Providence shall place it.…

But gladly do I turn from the consideration of others to that of ourselves. Were not we but a few years ago as a grain of mustard-seed in our island? May we not say that had not the Lord left us a seed, we should have been, in the completeness of our destruction, even as Sodom and Gomorrah? Were we not as a spark trodden under foot, which all men despised? And what have we done that we should so quickly have grown to be a great people? Who hath given us the power, quietly and unperceived to creep out above the earth, and to put forth our leaves and our branches, till our head has been lifted up? Who hath fanned us till our glow returned, and we have spread, and have communicated to many others our own fire? Who but the God of Israel who alone doth wonderful things? We are in union with His kingdom to which the promise of fruit hath been made. The power of man may dismember it, and maim it till it shall seem to have well nigh destroyed it; but let only one small fibre remain in the ground, and in the words of Job, 'If its root be old in the earth, and its stock be dead in the dust; at the scent of water it shall spring, and bring forth leaves, as when it was first planted' (Job 14: 8, 9).

And so it is yet almost in the recollection of the aged, how our priests crept forth from their lurking places in the night, to administer the rites of our religion to their timid flocks, in private chambers, or in the concealment of the garret. Still more the time is yet remembered by the young amongst us, when four walls and a roof were considered abundantly sufficient to constitute a temple to the Lord of Hosts, nor durst we aspire after more. But the time soon came when the God of our Fathers looked down upon our affliction, and visited us in His mercies. He led us forth from our bondage, He wonderfully nourished and increased us, He inspired us with nobler thoughts and feelings, and gave us a yearning after the glory of His house. He sent us our Ooliabs and Beseleels, furnished with skill and with zeal to undertake and execute things not unworthy of our desires; He infused a generous spirit into our rich and our poor; He gave to pastors a firm reliance on His providence, and to the flocks a grace to peril and even sacrifice somewhat for the accomplishment of His work; and lo! not one sanctuary only, but many simultaneously arise over the land, that make us regret the less the lost inheritance of our fathers. And this even so, as that each successive edifice shall be in majesty and grandeur, superior to its predecessor, as befits monuments which shall declare to future generations the gradual development of the Catholic spirit in our own. For with each shall there be a corresponding expansion of the Catholic heart, in feeling and in love; a warmer devotion, and a bolder practice; a more fearless approximation to the form and spirit of religion in Catholic countries; and a return, within all legitimate bounds, to the early associations of our native land. (9)

## The English Way, the Way of the Cross

My Brethren, the Catholic ritual for the first approach of a new Bishop to his See, exhorts that the streets through which he shall pass be festooned with garlands, and his path strewn with flowers. For us, no doubt, it has been better that our road should have been hedged with thorns, and our way sown with briars. The more deeply and broadly any work bears the impression of the Cross, the more surely does it come to us sealed of God. The episcopal dignity is an elevation of fearful duties and responsibilities: and it can never feel so safe, as when the height chosen for it by Providence is on Calvary, rather than on Thabor. Then do you, my dear Catholic children, lift up your heads, in humble hope, in proportion as affliction and tribulation assail you. Leave to the powerful protection of a gracious and gentle Sovereign, who loves all her faithful subjects alike, the guardianship of your civil and religious freedom once granted you; trust to the good sense of your countrymen for a better understanding of your principles, your actions, and your motives; but look up to God alone, for the only blessing which can make the hierarchy of your Church in this country, fruitful in heavenly gifts for your souls, and an instrument of eternal salvation. (10)

## 'Papal Aggression': England and the Universal Church

And so small as the Catholic Church may appear in this kingdom, it will now be considered as a 'branch' not of an imaginary Church with which it has no visible connection, but of a communion of Churches united firmly to one trunk, and growing from one only root.

From this communion arises one of the great consolations of our present condition. On every side the union which charity, as well as faith gives us with the Catholicity of the world, is powerfully showing itself, by the overflowing abundance of prayer, which every part of Europe is raising from us....Every Catholic country is alive to our present arduous position, and the storm that has assailed us. From the multitudes assembled in the great churches of cities, to the rural population of villages, from the bishop of ancient see, to the mountain curate, the Catholic continent, and the neighbouring island, all feel with us, hope with us, sympathize with us, and what is more pray with and for us. Even in the cloistered retreats of consecrated virgins, where the great events of this world knock in vain at the door for admission, the distant agitation of our little church has pushed its vibration, along with the golden cords of Catholic unity, into the silent cell, and prayer and communions are offered up, with all the fervour of pure hearts, for us, my Brethren, of England. From every quarter the same words reach us 'we are praying earnestly for you'; yes, from strangers (if Catholics *can* be strangers), from those whose face we have none of us seen. How comforting must all this be to us, who believe our present work to be the work of God! How like His work indeed is this of prayer! Addresses to the throne of God for protection, not to that of earthly domination; watching, before the altar instead of town-hall demonstrations; multiplied communions in place of hand-bills and placards; novenas and public adorations of the Most Holy, instead of clamours and abusive cries....As for us, my Brethren, let us continue in our old way; trust to God to protect what we believe to be His; and as when he freed Peter from prison He inspired the whole Church to pray without ceasing for him (Acts 12: 5), so let us believe, that a similar inspiration to all His Church now, to pray for our deliverance from present tribulation, is a happy earnest of our approaching consolation. (11)

## The New Archbishop's Westminster

The diocese, indeed, of Westminster embraces a large district, but Westminster proper consists of two very different parts. One comprises the stately Abbey, with its adjacent palaces and its Royal parks. To this portion the duties and occupation of the Dean and Chapter are mainly confined; and they shall range there undisturbed. To the venerable old Church I may repair, as I have been wont to do. But perhaps the Dean and Chapter are not aware that, were I disposed to claim more than the right to tread the Catholic pavement of that noble building, and breathe its air of ancient consecration, another might step in with a prior claim. For successive generations there has existed ever, in the Benedictine order, an Abbot of Westminster, the representative, in religious dignity, of those who erected, and beautified, and governed that church and cloister. Have they ever been disturbed by this 'titular?' Have they heard of any claim or protest on his part, touching their temporalities? Then let them fear no greater aggression now. Like him, I may visit, as I have said, the old Abbey, and say my prayer by the shrine of good St Edward; and meditate on the olden times, when the Church filled without a coronation, and multitudes hourly worshipped without a service.

But in their temporal rights, or their quiet possession of any dignity and title, they will not suffer. Whenever I go in, I will pay my entrance-fee, like other liege subjects, and resign myself meekly to the guidance of the beadle, and listen, without rebuke, when he points out to my admiration detestable monuments, or shows me a hole in the wall for a confessional.

Yet this splendid monument, its treasures of art, and its fitting endowments, form not the part of Westminster which will concern me. For there is another part which stands in frightful contrast, though in immediate contact, with this magnificence. In ancient times, the existence of an Abbey on any spot, with a large staff of clergy, and ample revenues, would have sufficed to create around it a little paradise of comfort, cheerfulness, and ease. This, however, is not now the case. Close under the Abbey of Westminster there lie concealed labyrinths of lanes and courts, and alleys and slums, nests of ignorance, vice, depravity, and crime, as well as of squalor, wretchedness, and disease; whose atmosphere is typhus, whose ventilation is cholera; in which swarms a huge and almost countless population, in great measure, nominally at least, Catholic; haunts of filth, which no sewage committee can reach—dark corners, which no lighting-board can brighten. This is the part of Westminster which alone I covet, and which I shall be glad to claim and to visit, as a blessed pasture in which sheep of holy Church are to be tended, in which a Bishop's godly work has to be done, of consoling, converting, and preserving. And if, as I humbly trust in God, it shall be seen, that this special culture, arising from the establishment of our Hierarchy, bears fruits of order, peacefulness, decency, religion, and virtue, it may be that the Holy See shall not be thought to have acted unwisely, when it bound up the very soul and salvation of a chief pastor with those of a city, whereof the name indeed is glorious, but the purlieus infamous—in which the very grandeur of its public edifices is as a shadow, to screen from the public eye sin and misery the most appalling. If the wealth of the Abbey be stagnant and not diffusive, if it in no way rescue the neighbouring population from the depths in which it is sunk, let there be no jealousy of any one who, by whatever name, is ready to make the latter his care, without interfering with the former. (12)

NOTES AND SOURCES

1. Nicholas Wiseman, *Recollections of the Last Four Popes and of Rome in their Times* (London, 1858), 7–11.
2. Ibid. 391–7.
3. Nicholas Wiseman, *The Real Presence of the Body and Blood of Our Lord Jesus Christ in the Blessed Eucharist* (London, 1934), 30.
4. Ibid. 138–9.
5. Nicholas Wiseman, *Twelve Lectures on the Connexion between Science and Religion*, 5th edn. (London, 1853), i. 59–62.
6. Ibid. 353–4.
7. Ibid., ii. 264–6.
8. Ibid. 295–8.
9. Nicholas Wiseman, 'On the Developments of Christ's Teaching [St Mary's Catholic Church, Derby October 9, 1839]', in *Sermons Preached on Various Occasions* (Dublin, 1889), 213–37; 214–15, 233–5.
10. Nicholas Cardinal Wiseman, 'Lecture I', in *Three Lectures on the Catholic Hierarchy* (London, 1850), 16.
11. Nicholas Wiseman, 'Lecture II', ibid. 15–16.
12. Nicholas Wiseman, *An Appeal to the Reason and Good Feeling of the English People on the Subject of the Catholic Hierarchy* (London, 1850), 30–1.

# (Margaret Mary Hallahan) Margaret of the Mother of God OP     1803–1868

The persevering sanctity of Margaret Hallahan demonstrates both the suffering and the service that characterized the life of Irish Catholics in nineteenth-century England. Somers Town in London was full of Irish and French Catholic immigrants in 1803 when Hallahan was born. Her hard urban life became even harder when the 9-year-old's Irish parents died. Orphaned, she became a servant for over twenty years when a period spent in the Catholic atmosphere of Bruges led her to seek her true family in the religious life. She pledged herself to the Third Order of St Dominic in 1834 and unsuccessfully attempted to establish a community of English Tertiaries in Bruges. Afterwards she served as a headmistress of a girls' school in Coventry under Bishop William Ullathorne. With his help, her next attempt to establish a community of Dominican sisters proved more successful and the Congregation of Saint Catherine of Siena spread to other sites across England. With a reputation for a will and judgement sharpened by her early experiences of hardship, she dedicated her life and her community to caring for the sick and the orphaned. She was even undeterred by a spinal disease that plagued her final years. William James in *Varieties of Religious Experience* (1902) grouped her with St Francis, St Ignatius Loyola, and St Bernard as 'spiritual heroes' because their 'sense of mystery in things, their passion, their goodness' make the 'strong men of this world and no other seem as dry as sticks, as hard and crude as blocks of stone or brickbats.' These selections from Hallahan's biography capture the brusque clarity of a woman whose approach to the spiritual life was summarized in her motto: 'God alone'. The diocesan stage of her cause for beatification was completed in 1957.

## Hallahan's Short Insights into a Life with God

She had the faculty of putting a great truth in a short sentence, with a force that made it as clear as if it had been expanded in a treatise, whilst no treatise could give it the same cogency. A collection of her pithy sayings would make an admirable manual of spiritual proverbs. Let me give a few more examples of these sayings, uttered as occasion called them forth: 'Penance,' she said, 'ought not to sadden or depress. If it does, it is a sign of something wrong in the soul; for the function of penance is to unlock the soul and set it free'; 'There are no penances that search the soul like those that God sends'; 'When God sends you a trial, no one but God can relieve it. You must be directed, but only God can enable you to go through with it; and the more you keep it between God and yourself, the better it will be for you'; 'If you rid yourself of human respect, it will not only free your mind, but will improve your health by removing the strain upon you'; 'There is no deep love of God without a childlike, reverential fear'; 'Nothing makes a soul clear-sighted like humility'; 'You can only love God as far as you are humble'; 'So long as I keep my eye on God all is well, but if I lose sight of Him, I am troubled indeed'; 'Contemplation does not consist in saying many prayers, but in setting your heart on God.' (1)

## The Simplicity and Proximity of Christ

If one word suffice for your prayer, ... keep to that word, and whatever short sentence will unite your heart with God. He is not found in multiplicity, but in simplicity of thoughts and words. We meditate to find God, but if our soul goes to Him immediately, we put ourselves in prayer, we need no images, for we have the reality. I never could reason or make an imaginary scene in my life, and that is why the Exercises of St Ignatius do not suit me. Whilst I was trying to form a scene, I could ask for grace and mercy for the whole world, and for myself too. We are not all formed alike, and God is glorified by the variety of His creatures, so that, however holy one practice may be for one soul, it would not lead another to God, and yet all are good and holy. If our dear Lord lives in the centre of the soul, (as He really does,) what need have His spouses to look for him elsewhere? There He is, to hear and to grant all we ask; again, when we are before our God in the Adorable Sacrament of the Altar, *what need we anything else but to look and ask?* (2)

## There He Is!

A little tract on devotion to the Sacred heart was once put into [Hallahan's] hands, in which occurred the following words, being, in part, a translation from St Catherine of Siena: '*There He is*—all God, all man, hidden under the whiteness of a little piece of bread.' She read it just before the celebration of the Forty Hours, and a few days afterwards returned it to the Sister who had given it to her, saying, 'I have something to thank you for. Your "*There He is*" has never been out of my head all the Forty Hours. I have never once entered the church without saying to myself, "There He is, there He is!"' and as she spoke the tears were in her eyes. It became one of her favourite ejaculations; and one day, long afterwards, when leaving the choir where the Blessed Sacrament was exposed, she touched the same Religious on the arm, and indicating the altar by a quiet gesture, whispered to her, as if in confidence, 'There He is!' (3)

## The Business of Scruples

Cease all that self-examination, ... it keeps you always more busy with yourself than with God. There are innumerable wants in the Church, many souls to convert, and many indifferent Catholics who want the last grace to bring them to their duties. Think of all these things, and leave yourself in the hands of God with a perfect spirit of abandonment. I should be weary of myself, and lose all courage, were I to occupy myself with myself. Keep the eye of your soul on our only good God. Be sure it is self-love and self-seeking that is occupying you now. There is too great an eagerness to have all things, self into the bargain, *quite right*; and if self mingles with it, our Lord is sure to upset it for our greater good. There is but one perfect Being—God, and all His works. Let us be content with our own nothingness. (4)

## The Gifts of Christmas Day

My very dear Children,

A very happy Christmas to you all, and I hope you will bring joy and happiness to many, for we may truly say, unto them a child is born!—after so many years without the real Presence to have our Lord once more amongst them, and to be born again daily in the Holy Sacrifice of the Mass. If Catholics had real faith, they would walk miles to hear Mass; but the more God does for us, the more lazy we are in His service. 'He comes to His own, and His own receive Him not'; but let us, my very dear children, receive Him with open arms and loving hearts; let us warm His tender limbs with our acts of love and true devotion; let humility be one of the principal gifts we ask of Him, for, in this age of pride and luxury, a humble soul must be very near and dear to God. I hope, in time, should God enable us to do it, that Christmas may bring many souls into God's Church. It is a great condescension of our dear Lord to employ us in the same work that He came from Heaven to accomplish—the salvation of souls. Let us work for this end, for it must be the most pleasing to our good God, for He has prepared Heaven for His children, and wills that none should be lost or lose their blessed home; so, if we love God, we must love souls, and work for them too, as our Lord did. It requires sacrifice, and of this He gave one continued example. He lived a life of continual sacrifices, and died a sacrifice of love for souls on the altar of the Cross. This must animate us to work and to suffer. It is all very well to be fine in our words, and speak of the good of saving souls, but this will not save us. We are called to the Apostolate as far as women can be, and this is what our Reverend Master-General impressed on us, and we must work and suffer, pray and love, and do all we can, with our dear hidden Lord to help us, to save souls. Yes, my very dear Sisters, Jesus comes from His home of peace and glory to seek lost man: let us, then, do the same with courage and generosity. He has put the work in your hands by giving you His little ones to teach. Do it, then, and do it for Jesus' love and Jesus' grace, and blessing will be your reward.—Your mother in Jesus,

Margaret, Of the Mother of God (5)

## Leatare Sunday: Seeking Christ Always

My very dear Children,

I must not let *Laetare* Sunday pass without wishing you a happy and holy celebration of the holy season of Passiontide, and a full share in the merits of the Passion and death of our Divine Lord and Spouse. Yes, my dear Sisters and children, I cannot wish you anything better than a closer union with your Jesus, and a clinging to His Cross. If you aim at this, all things will be alike to you, for you will see him in all things, and will only seek to please Him and do His holy will. We have much to pray for and much to do, to try and repair the daily and hourly insults offered to God, to His holy Mother, to our holy Church, and to her visible Head. We are living, not in ages of faith, but in an age of infidelity and crime; and we know not if we may not hear of things quite appalling to nature. Let us then be always ready, with our lamps trimmed to meet our Divine Lord. He may come at the first or second watch, we know not; but certain it is He will come, and we know not the day nor the hour, nor where, nor when. Be then always ready to meet your Spouse. I wish you all a happy feast tomorrow, and hope you will enjoy yourselves as much as you can. The way to enjoy all things is to live only for God; *to be all for him*, and He *all for you*, in all places and at all times. If we love God and seek Him only, we find Him and His blessed peace everywhere. To serve God is to reign; we are then free, holy, and happy; and if we do not serve Him *everywhere*, we do not serve Him *anywhere*. (6)

## A Lenten Reflection on the Wounds of Our Lord

My dearest Children in Jesus,

As the great week of our redemption is at hand, I feel more in spirit with you than I can well express, and never do I go before God but I beg Him that this His great, His generous outpouring of His most Precious Blood may be the sanctification of you all. For what will all these great mysteries avail us, if we do not apply them to ourselves, and so imbibe the graces and treasures that flow from the sacred wounds of our Bleeding Bridegroom? May we not truly say, 'A Spouse of Blood Thou art to me!' But if Jesus is a Spouse of Blood to us, and for us, let us not cause that blood to flow again by opening the wound of His sacred side (the wound of love, by excellence) by our imperfect thoughts, words, or looks. O dear Sisters, did we see Jesus hanging on the cross with all His wounds open, and the cold bleak wind blowing into them, our first thoughts would be, what could we do to comfort Him. Let the same feeling animate them now, and let us comfort, and console, and bind up the wounds of our dear Lord, God, and Spouse, by being, in deed and in truth, perfect religious, by the modesty and recollection of our looks. And if the interior be absorbed in God, the whole exterior will show it. It is not in the downcast eye, for many with keeping the eyes down see most; but it is in keeping the eyes of the soul close shut to all but God that true recollection consists. Try to attain this, and you will bind up the wounds of Jesus in many ways; for it is to those who are so closely united to Him that He looks for help, comfort, and relief in this moment of His Passion, which is renewed daily, hourly, and momentarily by a guilty world. May the Blood of Jesus be poured on you all for your sanctification, is the prayer of your devoted Mother in Jesus,

Margaret, Of the Mother of God (7)

## An Invitation to the Holy Spirit

My very dear Children,

May the Holy Spirit fill all your souls on this great day, that nothing of nature may remain. It is a Feast on which we may obtain all that our heart can desire, if we will but ask with humility. 'Come, Holy Ghost!' What can we wish for more than *the Spirit of God*? For if we have His Spirit we have love, humility, poverty, obedience, chastity. *Come, Holy Ghost!* Come, and with you bring forbearance, docility, kindness, and deference. *Come, oh come, Holy Spirit of God!* and fill our souls with all that can make us dear to Thee, to each other, and to all creatures for the love of Thee. Do, my very dear Sisters, aim at living according to the Spirit of God. Remember His Divine Spirit is ever with you; you cannot hide yourself from Him whose eye is ever on you to mark what is done for the love of Him. (8)

## All Saints' Day

Do not look back, but go forward with courage and fervour. God forgives the past, and will bless our weakest endeavours; so that on this great feast we have everything to encourage us. We are sinners, so were the saints; we are lukewarm, so were the saints; we have to fight with our corrupt nature, so had the saints; and we shall be saints too, if we will, for the same grace, the same love of our Divine Lord, the same helps in every way are ready and given to us, if we will but make use of them as the saints did. Be ye faithful, my very dear children, and be faithful unto death, for it is only this fidelity which will obtain for you the crown of life. (9)

NOTES AND SOURCES

1. William Ullathorne, 'Preface', in Augusta Theodosia Drane, *Life of Mother Margaret Mary Hallahan, Foundress of the English Congregation of St Catherine of Siena* (London: Longmans, Green & Co., 1929), p. ix.
2. Mary Margaret Hallahan, quoted in Drane, *Life of Mother Margaret Mary Hallahan*, 257–8.
3. Drane, *Life of Mother Margaret Mary Hallahan*, 258–9.
4. Mary Margaret Hallahan, quoted ibid. 266–7.
5. Ibid. 397–8.
6. Ibid. 399–400.
7. Ibid. 400–1.
8. Ibid. 404–5.
9. Ibid. 408.

## George Duncombe Cox                                    1807–1840

It is tempting to label George Duncombe Cox a Catholic John Keats. While Cox cannot approximate the great Romantic poet's artistic quality, their lives show some striking similarities. Born in Durham, Cox was educated in medicine and practised as a doctor after graduating from the University of Edinburgh in 1835. He had strong religious and cultural interests as well, starting in 1840 the short-lived Edinburgh-based *The Phoenix*, another attempt to advance the Catholic cause among the public in the British Isles through the periodical press. Struck down by illness, Cox died at the young age of 33. His 1834 collection of poems is now very rare but remains a moving meditation on the fragility and dignity of human life. Drawn from his own encounters with the sick and the dying and perhaps his own sense of mortality, he attempts to capture a world ravaged by disease and death while yet illuminated with faith and beauty.

### Hearing Heaven in the Nightingale's Song

The sound of evening music
    Vibrates along the mind,
And strikes a chord of feeling
    Too sweet to be defined.

When, with the moonlight rising,
    The nightingale's sweet voice,
We doubt, and know not whether
    To sorrow or rejoice.

Her song has too much sweetness
    To be the voice of pain,
But yet she seems to murmur
    O'er hopes indulged in vain.

'Tis said that as she's sitting
    Upon the midnight spray,
She weeps her ravished young ones
    That death has torn away.

Oh, man is like the warbler
    That pours the flood of song—
His chaunt of joy is fleeting,
    His dirge of grief is long.

He mourns o'er hope in ruins,
    O'er bliss that is no more;
The youth-bloom that must perish
    The noon of life before.

Like her he moans in darkness;
    But, after night, a morn
Shall rise and shine for ever
    To cheer the sorrow-worn.

There, by the living waters,
    And the life-bearing tree,
Shall man drink deep of beauty,
    Through fresh eternity.

There, lofty angels soaring
    Through thought's celestial sky,
Shall contemplate God's wisdom
    With an enraptured eye.

In joy too overpowering,
    A mild, but chastening grief,
As shades along the sunshine,
    Oft gives the heart relief.

And man thus mourns in Heaven;
    For happy tears shall flow
In pity for the love
    That gave a God to woe.

There is the cross triumphant,
    The thorny crown there blooms,
And Christ's dear blood is flowing
    Beyond the land of tombs.

His blood—the living waters;
    His cross—the tree of life;
His crown—the blessed crowning
    With an immortal leaf.

Let Angels be the eagles
    That sweep the skies above;
But Man shall there transfigure
    The warbling bird of love.

Bright Soul! Break through thy bondage,
    And all thy chains be riven;
Then shalt thou sing and sorrow—
    The nightingale of Heaven. (1)

## Remembering our Mortality

Remember, man, thou art but dust,
And unto dust thou shalt return;
And in this vale of tears thou must
Unceasing sigh, and weep, and mourn.

The sword of victory turns to rust,
The fires of war our cities burn:
Remember thou art also dust,
And that thou shalt to dust return.

Time strikes the hero, breaks his bust,
Nor even spares his funeral urn:
For he was made to fall to dust,
As all things shall to dust return.

In him who dies not, place thy trust,
And oft in sorrow to him turn;
Rememb'ring thou art sprung of dust,
Only to ashes to return. (2)

NOTES AND SOURCES

1.  George Duncombe Cox, 'Evening Song of the Nightingale', in *Poems* (Edinburgh, 1834), 44–7.

2.  George Duncombe Cox, '*Memento Homo Quia Pulvis Es, et in Pulverem Reverteris*', ibid. 75–6.

# Augustus Welby Northmore Pugin                    1812–1852

Pugin's father, Augustus Charles, trained him in own profession of architecture, but failed to instruct him in the Catholic faith in which he himself had been raised. Augustus Welby was received into the Church in 1834 and thereafter devoted himself to serving her by his art. The beauty of medieval architecture played its part in drawing him to the Church, but he always insisted that his conversion was not merely aesthetic: 'Although I will allow the change has been brought about in me owing to my *studies of ancient art* yet I have still higher reasons which I can satisfactorily account for if required for my belief.' It has been well said of Pugin that he achieved more in his short life of forty years than most men manage if they survive to be 100. He was the leader and inspirer of the Gothic revival in England, the architect of countless Catholic churches, cathedrals, monasteries, and seminaries, the designer of many of the interiors of the Houses of Parliament, and a tireless propagandist for not only the architecture but also the social doctrine and order of the Middle Ages. In his book, *Contrasts*, published two years after his conversion, he sets off, among other things, Bentham's modern scientific system for dealing with the homeless (the *panopticon*, which incarcerates them and places them under constant surveillance) with the monastic hospices of the Gothic age in which, for the love of Christ, beggars and tramps were fed, clothed, and housed with compassion. Of his greatest masterpiece, St Giles, Cheadle, Newman said: 'It is...the most splendid building I ever saw. It is coloured inside every inch in the most sumptuous way....the windows are all beautifully stained. The Chapel of the Blessed Sacrament is, on entering, a blaze of light—and I could not help saying to myself *Porta Coeli*.' Overwork and the incompetence of doctors ruined his health. Pugin was declared insane and consigned to Bethlehem Hospital in London, that Bedlam whose historical development from hospice and religious house to hellish place of confinement perfectly illustrates the arguments of *Contrasts*. At the end he was allowed to die in the home he had designed for himself and his family on the cliffs above Ramsgate and was buried in the cemetery of St Augustine's Abbey, another of his architectural wonders.

## The Church as Patron of the Arts

The Church is the true mechanics' institute, the oldest and the best. *She was the great and never failing school in which all the great artists of the days of faith were formed.* Under her guidance they directed the most wonderful efforts of her skill to the glory of God; and let our fervent prayer ever be, that the Church may again, as in days of old, cultivate the talents of her children to the advancement of religion and the welfare of their own souls;—for without such results talents are vain, and the greatest efforts of art sink to the level of an abomination. (1)

## Building a City for God

The greatest privilege possessed by man is to be allowed, while on earth, to contribute to the glory of God. A man who builds a church draws down a blessing on himself both for this life and that of the world to come, and likewise imparts under God the means of every blessing to his fellow creatures; hence we cannot feel surprised at the vast number of religious buildings erected by our Catholic forefathers in the days of faith, or at their endeavours to render those structures, by their arrangement and decoration, as suitable as their means could accomplish for their holy and important destination. It must have been an edifying sight to have overlooked some ancient city raised when religion formed a leading impulse in the mind of man, and when the honour and worship of the Author of all good was considered of greater importance than the achievement of the most lucrative commercial speculation. There stood the mother church, the great cathedral, vast in height, rising above all the towers of the parochial churches which surrounded her; next in scale and grandeur might have been discerned the abbatial and collegiate churches with their vast and solemn buildings; each street had its temple raised for the true worship of God, *variously beautiful in design, but each a fine example of Christian art.* Even the bridges and approaches were not destitute of religious buildings, and many a beautiful chapel and oratory was corbelled out on massive piers over the stream that flowed beneath.

The great object I have in directing your attention to such a Catholic city is to illustrate the principle of decorative propriety in ecclesiastical buildings. We have here various edifices of various dimensions, various degrees of richness, various in arrangement, yet each bears on its very face the stamp of Catholic; cathedral or abbey, church or oratory, they all show that they are dedicated to the one true faith, raised by men actuated by one great motive, the truly Catholic principle of dedicating the best they possessed to God. (2)

## The Simple Witness of the English Parish Church

An old English parish church, as originally used for the ancient worship, was one of the most beautiful and appropriate buildings that the mind of man could conceive; every portion of it answered both a useful and mystical purpose. There stood the tower, not formed of *detached and misapplied* portions of architectural detail stuck over one another to make up a height, but solid buttresses and walls rising from a massive base, and gradually diminishing and enriching as they rise, till they were terminated in a Heaven-pointing spire surrounded by clusters of pinnacles, and forming a beautiful and instructive emblem of a Christian's brightest hopes. These towers served a double purpose, for in them hung the solemn sounding bells to summon the people to the offices of the church, and by their lofty elevation they served as beacons to direct their footsteps to the sacred spot. Then the southern porch, destined for the performance of many rites,—the spacious nave and aisles for the faithful,—the oaken canopy carved with images of the heavenly host, and painted with quaint and appropriate devices,—the impressive doom or judgement pictured over the great chancel arch,—the fretted screen and rood loft,—the mystical separation between the sacrifice and the people, with the emblem of redemption carried on high and surrounded with glory,—the great altar, rich in hangings, placed far from irreverent gaze, and with the brilliant eastern window terminating this long perspective; while the chantry and guild chapels, pious foundations of families and confraternities, contributed greatly to increase the solemnity of the glorious pile. Such is but a faint outline of the national edifices which have been abandoned for pewed and galleried assembly rooms, decorated only with gas fittings and stoves, and without so much as one holy or soul-stirring emblem about them. (3)

## The Laity and Gregorian Chant

England can never be Catholicized by the destruction of her cathedrals, the conversion of the liturgy into a song-book, and the erection of churches, whose appearance is something between a dancing-room and a mechanics' institute, and I do greatly mistake the souls of Englishmen, if this miserable system is ever permitted to take root in this land; for, although some weak persons may be led away by novelties, yet there is a general feeling of solid devotion, and a growing appreciation of the glories of Catholic antiquity that will effectually preserve us from the encroachment of modern innovations. And, although there is every reasonable hope, that in due time this country will again receive Catholic truth in all its fullness, yet such a result can only be accomplished by our rising to the high standard of ancient excellence and solemnity, and not by lowering the externals of religion to the worldly spirit of this degenerate age....

　　There does exist a *want of reality* in the present services of the churches, as they are performed in this, and many other countries; and from what does it proceed, but the *corrupt and artificial state of ecclesiastical music.* Owing to the complicated nature of modern figured compositions, both the clergy and the people have been precluded from taking any real part in the service of Almighty God. They are reduced to the position of *listeners,* instead of *worshippers*; so that, in lieu of the grand and edifying spectacle of priests and people uniting in one great act of adoration and praise, the service is transferred to a set of hired musicians, frequently heretics and infidels, who *perform* in a gallery, while the congregation are either amused or wearied, and the clergy who are present generally take advantage of these interminable fugues to say their own office, which has no reference whatever to the great act of sacrifice at which they are ostensibly assisting. Thus the unity of this, the most majestic, the most solemn act of Christian worship, is destroyed, and in many places, it has degenerated into a mere musical entertainment for the audience, and at which they assist with no more devotion than in a common theatre....

How easy in this age of printing to multiply Choral-books *ad infinitum*. How simple to print music for the five Gregorian Masses, so as to bring them within the reach of the humblest individual. If these were taught in every school, and inculcated in every Catholic family, our churches would soon present the cheering, the *inspiring* spectacle of a mass of people united, not only in heart, but in *voice*, in the worship of their Creator; and this not in modern and unhallowed sounds, but in the very words sung by the angels in Heaven when the Redeemer was born; and in words to which the old vaults, raised to the honour of God centuries ago, have often re-echoed with the returning festivals; and in words which, protected by Catholic authority, will descend, by Catholic tradition, to ages yet unborn. May the Almighty God in his mercy open the hearts of our rulers to these important truths. May he inspire our ecclesiastics with the spirit of reviving the solemn offices, which alone embody the spirit of the liturgy and set forth the majesty of the divine mysteries. May He grant us to see a restoration, not only of the external glory of His temple, but of the reverent service which is alone suited to its ancient symbolism; and may our churches—which, for the most part, are so many stumbling blocks to our separated countrymen, from the discrepancy between the fabric and the service—be purged from the disgrace of these modern performances, and become as shining beacons, not alone by the altitude of their spires, but by the purity and *reality* of the divine offices celebrated in them. (4)

## Finding the Faith of our Fathers

Regarding, therefore, the state of religion for the last three centuries as a punishment for the unfaithfulness of the English Church, we cannot but feel grateful that, notwithstanding all the repeated efforts and successes of the bitterest puritans, so many traces of the ancient paths have yet been preserved, to guide those who are now striving to regain the holy place. There is something surely providential in the retention of the ancient titles and dignities: the daily chant of the divine office in the cathedrals and colleges; the dedication of churches in honour of the ancient saints; the consecration of ground for the burial of the dead; the preservation of the chapel and order of England's patron, St George; the Catholic character of many portions of the liturgy, with its calendar of fasts and festivals; the solemn service and anointing of the sovereign at the coronation. These, and many more, seem so many pledges that God will not be angry with this land for ever. For there is no other instance of a country having fallen into the miserable state of Protestantism, having retained so much that is calculated to awaken in the breasts of her children a love and reverence for the past, and to lead them back to union with the see of blessed Peter, from whence the day-star of truth first beamed upon us....

It is almost inconceivable that men, who had been educated in the principles of the ancient faith, who had partaken of the sacraments of the Church, and knelt at its altars, should have demolished, for the sake of stone, timber, and lead, edifices whose beauty and skill would have secured them from injury even in this generation, and which should have possessed in their eyes the highest claim on their veneration; and we can only account for the atrocities which accompanied the ascendancy of Protestantism in England, by supposing the perpetrators blinded to the enormity of their own actions by the punishment of God. To hear of the choirs of vast churches stript and roofless; tombs of prelates and nobles ransacked for lead; brass rent from graves; the consecrated vessels of the sanctuary profaned and melted; the bones of saints and martyrs burnt; the images of our Divine Redeemer trodden under foot, dragged about and consumed; vestments converted to domestic use; monastic libraries pillaged and burnt; and all this without foreign foe or invasion, in once and then but lately Catholic England, and perpetrated by men who had been born and bred in the Catholic Church,—seems like a fearful dream, and almost incredible; and now the sad recital of destruction alone, moves us more than even the record of ancient glory. We lament over the prostrate pillars and scattered fragments of some once noble pile; we raise the fallen cross; bare the ancient legend on the wall; collect the fragments from the shattered panes, and clear the accumulating soil from moulded base and tomb. The study of Catholic antiquity is so associated with ancient piety and holy recollections, that the soul is insensibly drawn from the contemplation of material objects to spiritual truths.

An Englishman needs not controversial writings to lead him to the faith of his fathers. It is written on the wall, on the window, on the pavement, by the highway. Let him but look on the tombs of those who occupy the most honourable position in the history of his country,—the devout, the noble, the valiant, and the wise,— and he will behold them with clasped hands invoking the saints of Holy Church, whilst the legend round the slabs begs the prayers of the passers-by for their souls' repose. At Canterbury he beholds the pallium, emblem of the jurisdiction conferred by St Gregory on the blessed Augustine, first primate of this land; at York, the keys of Peter, with triple crowns, are carved on buttress, parapet, and wall. Scarcely one village church or crumbling ruin that does not bear some badge of ancient faith and glory. Now the crosses on the walls tell of anointings with holy chrism and solemn dedication; the sculptured font, of sacraments seven, and regeneration in the laver of grace. The legend on the bell inspires veneration for these consecrated heralds of the Church. The chalice and host over priestly tomb teaches of altar and sacrifice. The iron-clasped ambry, sculptured in the wall, bears record of holy Eucharist reserved for ghostly food; the stoups in porch, and Galilee of hallowed water, and purification before prayer; while window, niche, spandrel, and tower set forth, by pious effigies, that glorious company of angels, prophets, apostles, martyrs, and confessors, who, glorified in Heaven, watch over and intercede for the faithful upon earth.

The Cross—that emblem of a Christian's hopes—still surmounts spire and gable. In flaming red it waves from the masts of our navy, over the towers of the sovereign's palace, and is blazoned on London's shield.

The order of St George, our patron saint, founded by King Edward of famous memory, is yet the highest honour that can be conferred by sovereigns on the subject; and his chapel is glorious, and his feast kept solemnly. Our cities, towns, and localities, the rocky islands which surround our shores, are yet designated by the names of those saints of old through whose lives, martyrdoms, or benefactions, they have become famous.

The various seasons of the year are distinguished by the *masses* of these holy tides. Scarcely is there one noble house or family whose honourable bearings are not identical with those blazoned on ancient church or window, or chantry tomb, which are so many witnesses of the pious deeds and faith of their noble ancestry.

Nay, more, our sovereign is solemnly crowned before the shrine of the saintly Edward, exhorted to follow in the footsteps of that pious king, and anointed with oil poured from the same spoon that was held by Canterbury's prelates eight centuries ago.

In short, Catholicism is so interwoven with every thing sacred, honourable, or glorious in England, that three centuries of Puritanism, indifference, and infidelity, have not been able effectually to separate it. It clings to this land, and develops itself from time to time, as the better feelings of a naturally honourable man who had been betrayed into sin. What! an Englishman and a Protestant! Oh, worse than parricide, to sever those holy ties that bind him to the past, to deprive himself of that sweet communion of soul with those holy men, now blessed spirits with God, who brought this island from pagan obscurity to the brightness of Christian light, who covered its once dreary face with the noblest monuments of piety and skill, who gave those lands which yet educate our youth, support the learned, and from whom we received all we have yet left that is glorious, even to our political government and privileges. (5)

## The Glories of Medieval Architecture

Do not all the features and details of the churches erected during the middle ages set forth their origin, and, at the same time, exhibit the triumphs of Christian truth? Like the religion itself, their foundations are in the cross, and they rise from it in majesty and glory. The lofty nave and choir, with still loftier towers, crowned by clusters of pinnacles and spires, all directed towards Heaven, beautiful emblems of the Christian's brightest hope, the shame of the pagan; the cross, raised on high in glory—a token of mercy and forgiveness—crowning the sacred edifice and placed between the anger of God and the sins of the city.

The images of holy martyrs, each bearing the instrument of the cruel death by which pagan foolishness hoped to exterminate, with their lives, the truths they witnessed, fill every niche that line the arched recesses of the doorways. Above them are forms of cherubims and the heavenly host, mingled with patriarchs and prophets. Over the great entrance, is the doom or final judgement, the divine majesty, the joys of the blessed spirits, the despair of the condemned. What subjects for contemplation do not these majestic portals present to the Christian, as he approaches the house of prayer! and well are they calculated to awaken those sentiments of reverence and devotion, suited to the holy place. But if the exterior of the temple be so soul-stirring, what a burst of glory meets the eye, on entering a long majestic line of pillars rising into lofty and fretted vaulting! The eye is lost in the intricacies of the aisles and lateral chapels; each window beams with sacred instructions, and sparkles with glowing and sacred tints; the pavement is a rich enamel, interspersed with brass memorials of departed souls. Every capital and base are fashioned to represent some holy mystery; the great rood loft, with its lights and images, through the centre arch of which, in distant perspective, may be seen the high altar blazing with gold and jewels, surmounted by a golden dove, the earthly tabernacle of the Highest; before which, burn three unextinguished lamps. It is, indeed, a sacred place. The modulated light, the gleaming tapers, the tombs of the faithful, the various altars, the venerable images of the just—all conspire to fill the mind with veneration, and to impress it with the sublimity of Christian worship. And when the deep intonations of the bells from the lofty campaniles, which summon the people to the house of prayer, have ceased, and the solemn chant of the choir swells through the vast edifice,—cold, indeed, must be the heart of that man who does not cry out with the Psalmist, *Domine dilexi decorem tuae, et locum habitationis gloriae tuae* [I have loved, O Lord, the beauty of thy house: and the place where thy glory dwelleth (Ps. 25: 8)]. (6)

## Resources for Reviving Sacred Architecture

Before true taste and Christian feelings can be revived, all the present and popular ideas on the subject must be utterly changed. Men must learn that the period hitherto called dark and ignorant far excelled our age in wisdom, that art ceased when it is said to have been revived, that superstition was piety, and bigotry faith. The most celebrated names and characters must give place to others at present scarcely known, and the *famous edifices* of modern Europe sink into masses of deformity by the side of the neglected and mouldering piles of Catholic antiquity. If the renunciation of preconceived opinions on these subjects, and the consequent loss of the present enjoyment derived from them, be considered as a great sacrifice, does not the new and glorious field that is opened offer far more than an equivalent? What delight to trace a race of native artists hitherto unknown, in whose despised and neglected productions the most mystical feeling and chaste execution is to be found, and in whose beautiful compositions the originals of many of the most celebrated pictures of more modern schools are to be traced; what exquisite remains of the sculptor's skill lie buried under the green mounds that mark the site of once noble churches; what originality of conception and masterly execution do not the details of many rural and parochial churches exhibit! There is no need of visiting the distant shores of Greece and Egypt to make discoveries in art. England alone abounds in hidden and unknown antiquities of surpassing interest....

In the first place, I will commence with the cathedrals, the most splendid monuments of past days which remain, and, therefore, the most deserving of first consideration.

No person thoroughly acquainted with ecclesiastical antiquities, and who has travelled over this country for the purpose of attentively examining those wonderful edifices, which, though shorn of more than half their beauties, still proudly stand pre-eminent over all other structures that the puny hand of modern times has raised beside them, but must have felt the emotions of astonishment and admiration, that their first view has raised within him, rapidly give place to regret and disgust at the vast portion of them that has been wantonly defaced, and for the miserable unfitness of the present tenants for the vast and noble edifices they occupy....

The various chapels, each with its altars, were served by different priests, who at successive hours of the morning, commencing at six, said masses, that all classes and occupations might be enabled to devote some portion of the day to religious duties. The cloisters formed a quiet and sheltered deambulatory for the meditation of the ecclesiastics; and the chapter-house was a noble chamber, where they frequently met and settled on spiritual and temporal affairs relating to their office.

These churches were closed only for a few hours during the night, in order that they might form the place from whence private prayers and supplications might continually be offered up. But of what use are these churches now? Do their doors stand ever open to admit the devout? No, excepting the brief space of time set apart twice a-day to keep up the form of worship, the gates are fast closed, nor is it possible to obtain admittance within the edifice without a fee to the guardian of the keys. Ask the reason of this, and the answer will be, that if the churches were left open they would be completely defaced, and even become the scene of the grossest pollutions. If this be true, which I fear it is, what, I ask, must be the moral and religious state of a country, where the churches are obliged to be fastened up to prevent their being desecrated and destroyed by the people? How must the ancient devotion and piety have departed? Indeed, so utterly are all feelings of private devotion lost in these churches, that were an individual to kneel in any other time than that actually set apart for Divine service, or in any other part of the edifice but that which is enclosed, he would be considered as a person not sound in his intellects, and probably be ordered out of the building. No, cathedrals are visited from far different motives, by the different classes of persons who go to them. The first are those who, being connected with or living near a cathedral, attend regularly every Sunday by rote. The second are those who, not having any taste for prayers, but who have some ear for music, drop in, as it is termed, to hear the anthem. The third class are persons who go to see the church. They are tourists; they go to see everything that is to be seen. Therefore they see the church,—*id est* ['There it is'], they walk around, read the epitaphs, think it very pretty, very romantic, very old, suppose it was built in superstitious times, pace the length of the nave, write their names on a pillar, and whisk out, as they have a great deal more to see and very little time. (7)

## Religious Freedom and the English Reformation

Had there been a shadow of political freedom left in England, there can be no doubt that, with such a body of ecclesiastical rulers, the old religion would have been maintained, but such was the annihilating power of the crown in those days, and so utterly unknown were the principles of toleration and religious freedom, that the religious notions of the sovereign were the only standard by which the worship and faith of the whole nation were to be regulated, and hence the queen proceeded to require an external conformity to the new liturgy and articles from the entire mass of her subjects, and to enforce the same by fines, impositions, confiscations, and even death. And this diabolical system, for we can give it no other appellation, is what fools yet designate as the glorious free principles of the Reformation, principles which, if now in force, would consign the very speaker of such sentiments, as those of freedom, to the nearest jail. A system of coercion utterly repulsive and unbearable to a free nation. Religious freedom is totally distinct from the English Reformation. It is a new idea, unknown to our ancestors who lived in those times. There was no freedom under Henry; no freedom under Edward; no freedom under Mary; no freedom under Elizabeth; no freedom under a long line of their successors, nor would there be now but that knowledge, instruction, and truth have been so diffused by the increased facilities of our age, that notwithstanding all the prejudices of custom, and love of tyrannical power, the public opinion of this and other nations has forced from the reluctant legislature their deliverance from the curse of religious restrictions, which even in these days some seek to revive. It would, however, be most unjust to attach the odium of the persecution of the Catholic body, under Elizabeth and her successors, to the principles of the Church of England; and equally so to attribute the miserable executions of the preceding reign to the Catholic faith. *They were produced by one common cause—the tyranny of the state,* working its direful machinery in either direction as the humour or idea of the Sovereign might direct. (8)

## The Modern Church: Militant and Ever Recusant

From the enmity of the worldly powers we have *nothing* to fear; from their favour and protection *everything.* We neither ask for temporal aid or temporal honour: the faithful will provide the first, the second is not worth having. Nor has the Sovereign in her gift so noble a title to respect as that which the very office of a bishop, duly performed, imparts to the ecclesiastic who holds it.

But, God forbid that our ecclesiastical rulers should ever be again mixed up with the intrigues of a minister or the adulation of an audience-chamber. In the eye of the law, our bishops will only rank as English citizens and subjects; they will bear the ordinary burdens of tax and rate; be exempt from any odious exemptions and privileges, and amenable to the common law of the land. But to us they will be the ministers of divine and ecclesiastical authority upon earth; they will receive our obedience and respect; we shall look on them as imbued with the holiest powers; they will consecrate the churches we raise for the worship of Almighty God, and the cemeteries where we shall repose when dead; they will anoint the altars of sacrifice with the holy chrism; they will impart the Holy Spirit in the sacrament of orders to successive generations of ecclesiastics, brought up under their guidance in their seminaries and colleges. They will be true pastors and shepherds of souls, and fathers of the poor. Denuded of their worldly magnificence, that I have shown to have been in former ages so fearful a snare, they will devote their entire lives and energies to the sacred duties of their office. (9)

## The Restoration of the English Hierarchy

If ever there was a time or occasion when we might hope for unity in the Catholic body, this is one. If there could be imagined a moving cause so powerful as to break up local prejudices, party feelings and unworthy division, it is this restoration of ecclesiastical government, and gathering our shattered and separated fragments into a real church. If there ever was a magnetic power to draw gold from misers, to make niggards liberal, and sluggards active, it is now. If ever there was an event which was calculated to promote unity of action and unity of soul, to make men confess their past sins, and to make good resolutions for the future, to make them liberal to religion, and devout and thankful to God, animating them with a true spirit of the faith they profess, and lead them to discard for ever paganism and its wretched incongruities, and to labour with heart and soul for the revival of the true architecture created by the Christian religion itself, it is the foundation of this English Hierarchy which should be our delight and our glory, and which should now become one of the earnest objects of our lives and actions to support and maintain in all *freedom, honour, and integrity, in sæcula sæculorum.* Amen. (10)

NOTES AND SOURCES

1. A. W. Pugin, *The True Principles of Christian Architecture* (London, 1841), 33.

2. Ibid. 42–3.

3. Ibid. 49–51.

4. A. W. Pugin, *An Earnest Appeal for the Revival of the Ancient Plain Song* (London, 1850), 4–5, 10.

5. A. W. Pugin, *An Apology for the Revival of Christian Architecture in England* (London, 1843), 47–50.

6. A. W. Pugin, *Contrasts: Or a Parallel between the Noble Edifices of the Middle Ages and Corresponding Buildings of the Present Day* (London, 1841), 4–5.

7. Ibid. 16–17, 35–6.

8. A. W. Pugin, *An Earnest Address on the Establishment of the Hierarchy* (London, 1851), 8–9.

9. Ibid. 30.

10. Ibid. 32.

# PART 3

## 1850–1999

Mosaic of the Mother of God in the altarpiece of the Lady Chapel in Westminster Cathedral, c. 1912, designed by Robert Anning Bell. Photograph courtesy of Brother Lawrence Lew OP.

# An English Spring

In July 1852, in his sermon before the bishops assembled at Oscott College for their first synod, Newman described the restoration of the Catholic hierarchy in England as a 'Second Spring', but he suggested it might turn out to be a Spring of English instability rather than of Italian serenity, 'an uncertain, anxious time of hope and fear, of joy and suffering, of bright promise and budding hopes, yet withal, of keen blasts, and cold showers, and sudden storms'.[1] The realism Newman displayed on this occasion is characteristic of the man. No Catholic thinker in the modern age has been less inclined to be a devotee of progress than this doctor of development, none more sceptical of promises of springtimes in the Church, or of Utopias in the world. The author of the *Parochial and Plain Sermons*, with their searing honesty about fallen humanity's moral fragility, knew that in this life the Church and all her members are engaged in ceaseless spiritual combat. At the opening of the seminary at Olton in 1873, he preached on 'The Infidelity of the Future', and confessed he thought that 'the trials which lie before us are such as would appal and make dizzy even such courageous hearts as St Athanasius, St Gregory I, or St Gregory VII'.[2] From Christ's first coming to His second, the history of the Church is strangely blended of light and dark, with signs of faith's ascendancy in one quarter accompanied by evidences elsewhere of the apostasy that heralds the end of time. As Newman says in the notes of one of his sermons: 'In every age things are so like the last day as to remind us that perhaps it is coming; but still not so like that we know.'[3]

From 1850, the Catholic Church in England seemed to enjoy an Italian sort of Spring, of bright promise and budding hopes. Protestant England's violent reaction to the 'Papal Aggression'—the passing of bills in Parliament and the burning of effigies in the street—played itself out without arresting the advance of the Church. Everywhere, so it seemed, both spiritually and physically, almighty God was 'building up what was destroyed and planting what was desolate' (cf. Ezek. 36: 36). Even ten years before the restoration of the hierarchy, and five years before Newman's conversion, Ambrose Phillipps de Lisle could say that 'Catholicity in England is proceeding at a railroad pace'.[4] In that same year, Pugin was building seventeen Catholic churches,[5] and in the decades that followed, other architects would continue to build, though not always in Pugin's style, for parishes, schools, seminaries, and monasteries. Throughout the nineteenth century, and up to the middle of the twentieth, infused with new life by Irish immigration and successive waves of conversions, the Catholic Church in England steadily grew to strength in

---

[1] See pp. 453–6 below.
[2] <http://www.newmanreader.org/works/ninesermons/sermon9.html>.
[3] See p. 467 below.
[4] Louis Allen, 'Letters of Phillipps de Lisle to Montalembert', *Dublin Review*, 228 (1954), 57; cited in Edward Norman, *The English Catholic Church in the Nineteenth Century* (Oxford: Clarendon Press, 1984), 201.
[5] Cf. Edward Norman, *The English Catholic Church in the Nineteenth Century* (Oxford: Clarendon Press, 1984), 201.

number and to vitality in mission. The return of Our Lady's Dowry to communion with the Vicar of her Son did not seem a fanciful prospect, and to that end generations of priests were trained daily to labour and, on Sundays at Benediction, expressly to pray.

The material and spiritual Second Spring of English Catholicism included a literary renaissance of immense fruitfulness.[6] Its most striking quality was its diversity, not only in genre but in the persons of the writers and their lives. But then this was a *Catholic* literary revival, and where anything truly Catholic is concerned, as James Joyce said, 'Here comes *everybody*'.[7] The vast majority of the writers were converts, of whom John Henry Newman, Henry Edward Manning, Ronald Knox, and G. K. Chesterton are the best known, but some were cradle Catholics, such as Hilaire Belloc, Bede Jarrett, and Herbert Vaughan. Most were men, but women, too, produced work that ranks high in the English Catholic canon: for example, Caryll Houselander, Alice Meynell, and Maisie Ward. The faithful in all states of life had a part to play: bishops like Ullathorne and Manning wrote books of theology and spiritual doctrine, and many priests, both secular and religious, bequeathed English Catholicism not only sermons and works of divinity, but also poetry, novels, literary criticism, and social commentary. Long before anyone talked about the 'apostolate of the laity' or 'Catholic Action', Catholic lay folk were active in all kinds of literature and every species of journalism. Some enjoyed success and acclaim even by the measure of the world (Tolkien, Waugh, Greene), while others died apparent failures, outcasts from conventional society (Lionel Johnson). Many of the disturbed and disturbing men of the Eighteen Nineties found the truth, with forgiveness and healing, in the Catholic Church. Oscar Wilde stated the principle that in the eleventh hour he put into practice: 'The Catholic Church is for saints and sinners alone. For respectable people the Anglican Church will do.'[8]

Three kinds of writing stand out in the work of the men and women selected for inclusion in this volume: poetry, the novel, and apologetics. One author is among the greatest English poets of the nineteenth century: Gerard Manley Hopkins. Francis Thompson, too, has a music all of his own and a grandeur of vision, a scope of interest, rivalling anything to be found in poets outside the

---

[6] In *The Catholic Revival in English Literature, 1845–1961* (Leominster: Gracewing, 2003), Father Ian Ker sets himself the goal, which he attains, of 'making real the extent to which Catholicism informed and shaped a considerable and impressive corpus of literature in the nineteenth and twentieth centuries' (p. 7). In the mid-twentieth century, Frank Sheed, the publisher of many of the most distinguished Catholic writers of England, North America, and continental Europe produced a useful series of sketches, *Sidelights on the Catholic Revival* (London: Sheed & Ward, 1941). France in the same period, as well as producing great Catholic philosophers such as Maritain and Gilson and theologians of both the Thomist and the *ressourcement* schools, gave Christendom Péguy and Claudel in poetry (in theatre, too, in Claudel's case) and Bernanos, Green, and Mauriac in the novel (see H. Serry, *Naissance de l'intellectuel catholique* (Paris: La Découverte, 2004) ). For the German Catholic literary revival in the mid-twentieth century, see Helena M. Tomko, *Sacramental Realism: Gertrud von le Fort and German Catholic Literature in the Weimar Republic and Third Reich (1924–46)* (London: Maney, 2007). In the same period, even Scandinavia with its tiny Catholic population had Catholic writers of international renown such as the Norwegian novelist Sigrid Undset, who won the Nobel Prize for literature in 1928, and the Danish man of letters, Jens Johannes Jørgensen.

[7] See Anthony Burgess, *Here Comes Everybody: An Introduction to James Joyce for the Ordinary Reader* (Feltham: Hamlyn, 1982).

[8] Cited by Richard Ellmann, *Oscar Wilde* (London: Hamish Hamilton, 1987), 548.

Church. Among more recent writers, John Bradburne, who died a martyr in Zimbabwe, is a poet to be named without embarrassment of exaggeration in the company of Hopkins and Thompson. As for the novel, there is an excess of riches in Catholic use of this form. Greene and Waugh are masters of the craft, and Tolkien one of the most widely read of all English writers; then there are Baring, and Benson, and Chesterton, and many others less well known such as Lady Georgiana Fullerton and Dr William Barry. Finally, and most importantly, we must mention the great English tradition of apologetics. All of our writers had a general and remote intention to give a reason for the hope that was in them (cf. 1 Peter 3: 15), but some—Belloc, Chesterton, Knox, Lunn, McNabb, Martindale, and Sheed—were immediately committed to the task, and took their defence of the faith not only into print, but to Speakers' Corner and the airwaves of the BBC, and into town halls up and down the country.

What attributes are common to the men and women in the third part of this anthology? The first is their adherence, in the brokenness of their lives and personalities, to the one true faith of the Catholic Church. The Modernists are not included, for Modernism, as Pope St Pius X said, is 'the synthesis of all heresies', the replacement of the objective truth of Divine Revelation with subjective experience and sentiment, the very opposite of what is Catholic.[9] The men and women represented here struggled with every kind of passion to which wounded human nature is prone, but there is none who by formal heresy lost the good of the intellect and made that capitulation to the world which is Modernism, or, as Newman called it a generation before, 'Liberalism in Religion'.[10] 'It is always easy to let the age have its head', said Chesterton in *Orthodoxy*, 'the difficult thing is to keep one's own. It is always easy to be a Modernist; as it is easy to be a snob.'[11] For all their frailties, and despite their myriad differences in personality and outlook, our authors did not make that final facile surrender.

The second attribute follows directly from the first: these authors all bear witness to the reality of the Incarnation of the eternal Word, which with the Blessed Trinity is the chief object of the Catholic faith. They see the truths repudiated by the Reformation—the hallowed matter of the sacramental system, the visibility of the Church built on Peter, and the intercession of Mary and the saints—as so many outworkings and unfoldings of the primal mystery of the Word made flesh. As Father Martindale explains in an extract below, to refuse the human and fleshly instruments of redemption is to aspire to a religion more spiritual than the one God has actually given us, more spiritual than God has created us human beings to be.[12] Whether they were blessed with the faith from childhood or gave it their assent by conversion, the poets and preachers of this anthology perceived the truth of the Incarnation in its fully Catholic proportions, and by their eloquence helped to reassert the classic principle, 'The flesh is the hinge of salvation', which Pope John Paul II has more recently expounded, in the context of marriage and human sexuality, in his 'Theology of the Body'. The

---

[9] Cf. Pope St Pius X, *Pascendi dominici gregis* (1907); *My Words Will Not Pass Away* (Rizal: Sintag-tala, 1974), 264.

[10] See pp. 456–7 below.

[11] G. K. Chesterton, *Orthodoxy*, new edn. (London & Glasgow: Collins, 1961), 100.

[12] See pp. 601–2 below.

God-man's redemption of the whole man is the object of Catholic faith, the goal of the Sacraments, the foundation of Catholic morality, and the intention for which the humblest believer asks God for His help.

The third quality found in a very large number of these authors, a quality as much of mind as of heart, is humour, or more exactly good humour, something close to what Aristotle and St Thomas called *eutrapelia* (playfulness).[13] Though in itself it belongs to the natural order, the sense of humour of a man engraced by Christ becomes a fruit of the Holy Spirit; it is the gladness of heart of someone whose mind is enlivened by truth—*gaudium, laetitia, iucunditas, hilaritas*, in the vocabulary of the Middle Ages. Some of our authors were by temperament inclined to melancholy; others were explosively choleric; but somehow, in most of them, if not in all, we get a glimpse of what Chesterton called 'the gigantic secret of the Christian', namely, *joy*—joy bubbling over into merriment.[14] Chesterton himself is one of its best embodiments, but in many others, too, there is that firm resolve which lies at the heart of true comedy, namely, the refusal to take oneself and the world's fads and fancies too seriously, the noble refusal that only a will perfected by charity and an intellect illuminated by faith can make with any chance of success. In Newman, and later in Knox, it shows itself in the form of satire. In Evelyn Waugh, when he falls into savage sarcasm, Catholic *iucunditas*, that best of things, becomes the worst of things, but in his greatest work, for example in *Helena*, his own favourite among his novels, it is ordered and attractive. Throughout the century and a half here surveyed, in sermons and letters of direction, in apologetics and fiction, good humour keeps breaking through. Even Newman's gloss on the concept of a Second Spring, an *English* Spring, derives from one of the chief sources of English humour, that most absurd of all things, our *weather*.

What began in 1850 has turned out to be a typical English Spring. English Catholicity is no longer speeding 'at railroad pace'; sometimes, were it not for their belief in the Church's indefectibility, Catholics in England might be tempted to feel it had been derailed. But, as Hopkins perceived even in his darkest hours, 'there lives the dearest freshness deep down things', in the Church as well as in the natural world, and 'though the last lights off the black West went | Oh, morning, at the brown brink eastward, springs | Because the Holy Ghost over the bent | World broods with warm breast and with ah! bright wings'.[15] The Holy Ghost, no merely created or human principle, is the 'soul' of the Body of which the incarnate Son Himself is Head, and by those two missions, of the Son and the Spirit, the Church is protected from the storms of the world: 'The gates of Hell shall not prevail against her' (Matt. 16: 18).

It was not only in 'The Second Spring' that Newman displayed the realism of his theological vision and the Englishness of his interest in the weather. When asking himself why the month of May should be dedicated to the Mother of God, he has the same kind of thought. First, he acknowledges that the natural beauty of the month, the 'gladness and joyousness of external nature', is 'a fit attendant on our

---

[13] Cf. St Thomas Aquinas, *Summa theologiae* 2a2ae q. 168, a. 2.

[14] Cf. G. K. Chesterton, *Orthodoxy*, new edn. (London & Glasgow, 1961), 159.

[15] Cf. Hopkins's poem, 'God's grandeur', p. 519 below.

devotion to her who is the Mystical Rose and the House of Gold'. But then, countering the objection, 'True, but in this climate we have sometimes a bleak, inclement May', he makes the point that May is 'the month that *begins* and heralds in the summer', a month of promise:

May, then, is the month, if not of fulfilment, at least of promise, and is not this the very aspect in which we most suitably regard the Blessed Virgin, Holy Mary, to whom this month is dedicated? The prophet says, 'There shall come forth a rod out of the root of Jesse, and a flower shall rise out of His root' (Is 11: 1). Who is the flower but our blessed Lord? Who is the rod, or beautiful stalk or stem out of which the flower grows, but Mary, Mother of our Lord, Mary, Mother of God? It was prophesied that God should come upon earth. When the time was now full, how was it announced? It was announced by the angel coming to Mary. 'Hail, full of grace,' said Gabriel, 'the Lord is with thee; blessed art thou among women'. She then was the sure *promise* of the coming Saviour, and therefore May is by a special title her month.[16]

Mary is herself the 'bright promise' and the sign of hope for Christ's faithful in every age and in every land, as she was when the divine Head of the Church first came in the flesh, flesh He took from her, in the fullness of time in Nazareth of Galilee. This is the doctrine proclaimed by the Second Vatican Council in the eighth chapter of its Dogmatic Constitution on the Church, *Lumen gentium*:

[T]he Mother of Jesus in the glory which she possesses in body and soul in Heaven is the image and beginning of the Church as she is to be perfected in the world to come. Likewise she shines forth on earth, to the coming of the day of the Lord (cf 2 Pet 3: 10), a sign of certain hope and consolation to the pilgrim People of God.[17]

Orthodoxy of faith, loving devotion to the incarnate Word, and the good humour of hope, like everything else that is Christian, have their best and purest embodiment in Our Lady. It is she, then, the faithful Virgin, the Mother of the incarnate Word, 'the cause of our joy', who can be trusted to lead England, her dowry, towards the Catholic fullness of faith, and thus to a new burgeoning of that real but delicate season, the Second Spring. This was Newman's conviction, expressed by him in prayer:

Shine on us, dear Lady, with thy bright countenance, like the sun in his strength, O *stella matutina*, O harbinger of peace, till our year is one perpetual May. From thy sweet eyes, from thy pure smile, from thy majestic brow, let ten thousand influences rain down, not to confound or overwhelm, but to persuade, to win over thine enemies. O Mary, my hope, O Mother undefiled, fulfil to us the promise of this Spring.[18]

---

[16] John Henry Newman, *Meditations and Devotions*, new edn. (Burns & Oates, 1964), 105–6.

[17] The Second Vatican Council, *Lumen gentium*, n. 68.

[18] Cf. p. 454 below.

# Blessed John Henry Cardinal Newman 1801–1890

Newman's reception into the Church in 1845 is the spiritual centre of nineteenth-century English Catholicism. By his example and writings he moved many Englishmen and women, in the successive generations making up the century and his own long life, to find in the Catholic Church the 'One Fold of the Redeemer', thereby giving new energies to the Church in what he called her English 'Second Spring'. As a boy, in the autumn of 1816, following illness and the collapse of his father's bank, he had experienced an intellectual and spiritual conversion that left an indelible mark upon him: 'I fell under the influences of a definite creed, and received into my intellect impressions of dogma which, through God's mercy, have never been effaced or obscured'. The following year, he went up to Trinity College, Oxford, and in 1822 won a fellowship by examination at Oriel College. Two years later he was admitted to Anglican orders and appointed curate of St Clement's, Oxford. Later, as Vicar of the University Church of St Mary the Virgin, Newman worked with John Keble and Edward Bouverie Pusey to restore what he then believed was the Catholic identity of the Church of England. In 1833, the same year in which Keble preached his 'Assize Sermon', Newman wrote the first of the 'Tracts for the Times', which he and his friends used to propagate their views on Catholicity and Apostolicity. As Newman came to see it, Anglicanism represented the *via media* between opposed extremes, the mean of apostolic virtue between the defects of Protestantism and the excesses of Roman Catholicism. His reading of the Fathers led him to question the truth of this opinion. Wiseman's article on the Donatist schism and his own study of the Arian controversy helped him to see that in the early centuries the middle position was occupied by moderate heresy, whereas Rome remained secure and stable as the principle of truth from which all excesses and defects were measured. His confidence in Anglicanism was shaken still more by the vehement reaction to Tract 90, in which he argued for a Catholic interpretation of the Thirty-Nine Articles, and by the plans for a joint Anglican-Lutheran-Calvinist bishopric in Jerusalem. In 1842 he settled with a group of friends in a row of cottages in the village of Littlemore, just outside Oxford. It was there in September 1843, after his resignation from St Mary's, that he preached his last sermon as an Anglican; there that he wrote the *Essay on the Development of Christian Doctrine*, showing that the Catholic beliefs and practices that were so objectionable to Protestants were but the unfolding of the original deposit of Divine Revelation; and it was in Littlemore, too, on 9 October 1845 that Blessed Dominic Barberi received him into the Catholic Church. For part of 1846 he and his newly converted friends lived at the old Oscott College, to which he gave the name 'Maryvale'. In the autumn of 1846 he left to study for the priesthood in Rome and was ordained there on 30 May 1847. His year in Rome gave him the opportunity to learn more about the Oratory of St Philip Neri. Wiseman had suggested that its simple idea of secular priests living the common life in an apostolate uniting pastoral work with study would be appropriate for Oxford men used to collegiate existence. In addition, the spirit of St Philip attracted Newman and came decisively to shape his developing Catholic mind. After a short novitiate, Newman was made superior of the new English Oratory, and at First Vespers of Candlemas, 1 February 1848, the community was established at Maryvale. From these early years of his priestly and Oratorian life come Newman's conversion novel, *Loss and Gain*, the *Discourses to Mixed Congregations*, and *Anglican Difficulties*. His denunciation of the ex-Dominican Achilli, who had turned Protestant after being found guilty of sexual assault, led to Newman facing a trial for criminal libel, from which he emerged with a moral victory and a notional fine. From 1854 to 1858, at the invitation of Archbishop Cullen of Armagh, he served as Rector of the new Catholic University in Dublin, an assignment that occasioned the papers and lectures making up *The Idea of a University*. In 1859 he founded the Oratory School, which still flourishes, though now in the Thames Valley rather than in Birmingham. Challenging the lazy idea that Newman became a Catholic 'to find peace and an end of argument', Chesterton once pointed out that Newman 'had far more quarrels after he had gone over to Rome'—more quarrels but fewer compromises. Certainly, the late 1850s and the whole of the 1860s were a time of almost unceasing conflict for Newman: a dispute between the Birmingham and London Oratories leading to their juridical separation in 1856; controversy over the article, 'On Consulting the Faithful in Matters of Doctrine'; the writing of the *Apologia*, his spiritual autobiography, in response to Charles Kingsley's accusation that Newman, and indeed the Catholic clergy in general, preferred cunning to truth; and a struggle with Manning and the English Ultramontanes over, among other things, the founding of an Oxford Oratory and the wider question of Catholics sending their sons to the university. The Vatican Council's definition of papal infallibility, from 1867 as a prospect and after 1870 as a fact, was the cause of yet more strife for him, both with the Ultramontanes and with Protestants such as W. E. Gladstone. Newman said that he believed in papal infallibility from the day he became a Catholic, but he thought the definition was inopportune and might be a deterrent to converts. As soon as the Council had proclaimed the definition, he accepted it without hesitation. For the last thirteen years of his life, a relative peace descended at last upon him. In 1877 Trinity, always so dear to him, elected him to an honorary fellowship, and in 1879 Pope Leo XIII made him Cardinal-Deacon of St George in Velabro, an occasion that provided him with the opportunity, in the customary *biglietto* speech, of reaffirming his lifelong opposition to 'liberalism in religion'. The Cardinal's health began to break down in the second half of 1886, and on 11 August 1890 he died of congestion of the lungs at the Birmingham Oratory. He was buried at Rednal in the grave of his friend and confrère, Ambrose St John. On 2 November 2008, his relics, what few of them could be found, were solemnly transferred to a tomb in the Birmingham Oratory in readiness for his beatification, which took place in September 2010 on the occasion of Pope Benedict XVI's visit to England. Archbishop David Mathew's judgement of Newman, 'perhaps the greatest English influence on Catholic thought', is beyond denial, and indeed it may be that some future Pope will make him what many believe him unofficially already to be, the second English Doctor of the Church.

## The Second Spring

It is an innovation, a miracle, I may say, in the course of human events. The physical world revolves year by year, and begins again; but the political order of things does not renew itself, does not return; it continues, but it proceeds; there is no retrogression. This is so well understood by men of the day, that with them progress is idolized as another name for good. The past never returns—it is never good;—if we are to escape existing ills, it must be by going forward. The past is out of date; the past is dead. As well may the dead live to us, well may the dead profit us, as the past return. *This*, then, is the cause of this national transport, this national cry, which encompasses us. The past *has* returned, the dead lives. Thrones are overturned, and are never restored; states live and die, and then are matter only for history. Babylon was great, and Tyre, and Egypt, and Nineve, and shall never be great again. The English Church was, and the English Church was not, and the English Church is once again. This is the portent, worthy of a cry. It is the coming in of a Second Spring; it is a restoration in the moral world, such as that which yearly takes place in the physical . . .

What! those few scattered worshippers, the Roman Catholics, to form a Church! Shall the past be rolled back? Shall the grave open? Shall the Saxons live again to God? Shall the shepherds, watching their poor flocks by night, be visited by a multitude of the heavenly army, and hear how their Lord has been new-born in their own city? Yes; for grace can, where nature cannot. The world grows old, but the Church is ever young. She can, in any time, at her Lord's will, 'inherit the Gentiles, and inhabit the desolate cities'. 'Arise, Jerusalem, for thy light is come, and the glory of the Lord is risen upon thee. Behold, darkness shall cover the earth, and a mist the people; but the Lord shall arise upon thee, and His glory shall be seen upon thee. Lift up thine eyes round about, and see; all these are gathered together, they come to thee; thy sons shall come from afar, and thy daughters shall rise up at thy side.' 'Arise, make haste, my love, my dove, my beautiful one, and come. For the winter is now past, and the rain is over and gone. The flowers have appeared in our land . . . the fig-tree hath put forth her green figs; the vines in flower yield their sweet smell. Arise, my love, my beautiful one, and come.' It is the time for thy Visitation. Arise, Mary, and go forth in thy strength into that north country, which once was thine own, and take possession of a land which knows thee not. Arise, Mother of God, and with thy thrilling voice, speak to those who labour with child, and are in pain, till the babe of grace leaps within them! Shine on us, dear Lady, with thy bright countenance, like the sun in his strength, O stella matutina, O harbinger of peace, till our year is one perpetual May. From thy sweet eyes, from thy pure smile, from thy majestic brow, let ten thousand influences rain down, not to confound or overwhelm, but to persuade, to win over thine enemies. O Mary, my hope, O Mother undefiled, fulfil to us the promise of this Spring.

Westminster and Nottingham, Beverley and Hexham, Northampton and Shrewsbury, if the world lasts, shall be names as musical to the ear, as stirring to the heart, as the glories we have lost; and saints shall rise out of them, if God so will, and Doctors once again shall give the law to Israel, and Preachers call to penance and to justice, as at the beginning. Yes, my Fathers and Brothers, and if it be God's blessed will, not saints alone, not doctors only, not preachers only, shall be ours—but martyrs, too, shall reconsecrate the soil to God. We know not what is before us, ere we win our own; we are engaged in a great, a joyful work, but in proportion to God's grace is the fury of His enemies. They have welcomed us as the lion greets his prey. Perhaps they may be familiarized in time with our appearance, but perhaps they may be irritated the more. To set up the Church again in England is too great an act to be done in a corner. We have had reason to expect that such a boon would not be given to us without a cross. It is not God's way that great blessings should descend without the sacrifice first of great suffer-ings. If the truth is to be spread to any wide extent among this people, how can we dream, how can we hope, that trial and trouble shall not accompany its going forth? And we have already, if it may be said without presumption, to commence our work withal, a large store of merits. We have no slight outfit for our opening warfare. Can we religiously suppose that the blood of our martyrs, three centuries ago and since, shall never receive its recompense? Those priests, secular and regular, did they suffer for no end? or rather, for an end which is not yet accomplished? The long imprisonment, the fetid dungeon, the weary suspense, the tyrannous trial, the barbarous sentence, the savage execution, the rack, the gibbet, the knife, the cauldron, the numberless tortures of those holy victims, O my God, are they to have no reward? Are thy martyrs to cry from under thine altar for their loving vengeance on this guilty people, and to cry in vain? Shall they lose life, and not gain a better life for the children of those who persecuted them? Is this thy way, O my God, righteous and true? Is it according to thy promise, O King of saints, if I may dare talk to thee of justice? Did not thou thyself pray for thine enemies upon the cross, and convert them? Did not thy first Martyr win thy great Apostle, then a persecutor, by his loving prayer? And in that day of trial and desolation for England, when hearts were pierced through and through with Mary's woe, at the crucifixion of thy body mystical, was not every tear that flowed, and every drop of blood that was shed, the seeds of a future harvest, when they who sowed in sorrow were to reap in joy?

And as that suffering of the Martyrs is not yet recompensed, so, perchance, it is not yet exhausted. Something, for what we know, remains to be undergone, to complete the necessary sacrifice. May God forbid it, for this poor nation's sake! But still could we be surprised, my Fathers and my Brothers, if the winter even now should not yet be quite over? Have we any right to take it strange, if, in this English land, the spring-time of the Church should turn out to be an English spring, an uncertain, anxious time of hope and fear, of joy and suffering,—of bright promise and budding hopes, yet withal, of keen blasts, and cold showers, and sudden storms?

One thing alone I know,—that according to our need, so will be our strength. One thing I am sure of, that the more the enemy rages against us, so much the more will the Saints in Heaven plead for us; the more fearful are our trials from the world, the more present to us will be our Mother Mary, and our good Patrons and Angel Guardians; the more malicious are the devices of men against us, the louder cry of supplication will ascend from the bosom of the whole Church to God for us. We shall not be left orphans; we shall have within us the strength of the Paraclete, promised to the Church and to every member of it. My Fathers, my Brothers in the priesthood, I speak from my heart when I declare my conviction, that there is no one among you here present but, if God so willed, would readily become a martyr for His sake. I do not say you would wish it; I do not say that the natural will would not pray that that chalice might pass away; I do not speak of what you can do by any strength of yours;—but in the strength of God, in the grace of the Spirit, in the armour of justice, by the consolations and peace of the Church, by the blessing of the Apostles Peter and Paul, and in the name of Christ, you would do what nature cannot do. By the intercession of the Saints on high, by the penances and good works and the prayers of the people of God on earth, you would be forcibly borne up as upon the waves of the mighty deep, and carried on out of yourselves by the fulness of grace, whether nature wished it or no. I do not mean violently, or with unseemly struggle, but calmly, gracefully, sweetly, joyously, you would mount up and ride forth to the battle, as on the rush of Angels' wings, as your fathers did before you, and gained the prize. You, who day by day offer up the Immaculate Lamb of God, you who hold in your hands the Incarnate Word under the visible tokens which He has ordained, you who again and again drain the chalice of the Great Victim, who is to make you fear? what is to startle you? what to seduce you? who is to stop you, whether you are to suffer or to do, whether to lay the foundations of the Church in tears, or to put the crown upon the work in jubilation? (1)

## Divine Revelation and the Authority of the Church

The most obvious answer ... to the question, why we yield to the authority of the Church in the questions and developments of faith, is, that some authority there must be if there is a revelation given, and other authority there is none but she. A revelation is not given, if there be no authority to decide what it is that is given. In the words of St Peter to her Divine Master and Lord, 'To whom shall we go?' Nor must it be forgotten in confirmation, that Scripture expressly calls the Church 'the pillar and ground of the Truth', and promises her as by covenant that 'the Spirit of the Lord that is upon her, and His words which He has put in her mouth shall not depart out of her mouth, nor out of the mouth of her seed, nor out of the mouth of her seed's seed, from henceforth and for ever'. (2)

## Resisting Liberalism in Religion

For thirty, forty, fifty years I have resisted to the best of my powers the spirit of liberalism in religion. Never did Holy Church need champions against it more sorely than now, when, alas! it is an error overspreading, as a snare, the whole earth; and on this great occasion, when it is natural for one who is in my place to look out upon the world, and upon Holy Church as in it, and upon her future, it will not, I hope, be considered out of place, if I renew the protest against it which I have made so often.

Liberalism in religion is the doctrine that there is no positive truth in religion, but that one creed is as good as another, and this is the teaching which is gaining substance and force daily. It is inconsistent with any recognition of any religion, as *true*. It teaches that all are to be tolerated, for all are matters of opinion. Revealed religion is not a truth, but a sentiment and a taste; not an objective fact, not miraculous; and it is the right of each individual to make it say just what strikes his fancy. Devotion is not necessarily founded on faith. Men may go to Protestant Churches and to Catholic, may get good from both and belong to neither. They may fraternize together in spiritual thoughts and feelings, without having any views at all of doctrine in common, or seeing the need of them. Since, then, religion is so personal a peculiarity and so private a possession, we must of necessity ignore it in the intercourse of man with man. If a man puts on a new religion every morning, what is that to you? It is as impertinent to think about a man's religion as about his sources of income or his management of his family. Religion is in no sense the bond of society ...

I lament it deeply, because I foresee that it may be the ruin of many souls; but I have no fear at all that it really can do aught of serious harm to the Word of God, to Holy Church, to our Almighty King, the Lion of the tribe of Judah, Faithful and True, or to His Vicar on earth. Christianity has been too often in what seemed deadly peril, that we should fear for it any new trial now. So far is certain; on the other hand, what is uncertain, and in these great contests commonly is uncertain, and what is commonly a great surprise, when it is witnessed, is the particular mode by which, in the event, Providence rescues and saves His elect inheritance. Sometimes our enemy is turned into a friend; sometimes he is despoiled of that special virulence of evil which was so threatening; sometimes he falls to pieces of himself; sometimes he does just so much as is beneficial, and then is removed. Commonly the Church has nothing more to do than to go on in her own proper duties, in confidence and peace; to stand still and to see the salvation of God. (3)

## Conscience

Conscience is not a long-sighted selfishness, nor a desire to be consistent with oneself; but it is a messenger from Him, who, both in nature and in grace, speaks to us behind a veil, and teaches and rules us by His representatives. Conscience is the aboriginal Vicar of Christ, a prophet in its informations, a monarch in its peremptoriness, a priest in its blessings and anathemas, and, even though the eternal priesthood throughout the Church could cease to be, in it the sacerdotal principle would remain and would have a sway. (4)

## Becoming a Catholic

The prime, I may say the only reason for becoming a Catholic, is that the Roman Communion is the only True Church, the Ark of Salvation. This does not mean that no one is saved who is not within that Church, but that there is no other Communion or Polity which has the promises, and that those who are saved, though not in the One Church, are saved, not by virtue of 'the Law or Sect which they profess', as the Thirty-Nine Articles say, but because they do not know better, and earnestly *desire* to know the truth, and in consequence are visited by a superabundant mercy of God which He has not promised and covenanted. (5)

## Gerontius's Profession of Faith

*Sanctus fortis, Sanctus Deus,*
*De profundis oro te,*
*Miserere, Judex meus,*
*Parce mihi, Domine.*
Firmly I believe and truly
God is Three, and God is One;
And I next acknowledge duly
Manhood taken by the Son.
And I trust and hope most fully
In that Manhood crucified;
And each thought and deed unruly
Do to death, as He has died.
Simply to His grace and wholly
Light and life and strength belong.
And I love, supremely, solely,
Him the holy, Him the strong.
*Sanctus fortis, Sanctus Deus,*

*De profundis, oro te,*
*Miserere, Judex meus,*
*Parce mihi, Domine.*
And I hold in veneration,
For the love of Him alone,
Holy Church, as His creation,
And her teachings, as His own.
And I take with joy whatever
Now besets me, pain or fear,
And with a strong will I sever
All the ties which bind me here.
Adoration aye be given,
With and through the angelic host,
To the God of earth and heaven,
Father, Son, and Holy Ghost.
*Sanctus fortis, Sanctus Deus,*
*De profundis, oro te,*
*Miserere, Judex meus,*
*Mortis in discrimine.* (6)

## The Trinitarian God of Love

1. What mind of man can imagine the love which the Eternal Father bears towards the Only Begotten Son? It has been from everlasting,—and it is infinite; so great is it that divines call the Holy Ghost by the name of that love, as if to express its infinitude and perfection. Yet reflect, O my soul, and bow down before the awful mystery, that, as the Father loves the Son, so doth the Son love thee, if thou art one of His elect; for He says expressly, 'As the Father hath loved me, I also have loved you. Abide in my love.' What mystery in the whole circle of revealed truths is greater than this?

2. The love which the Son bears to thee, a creature, is like that which the Father bears to the uncreated Son. O wonderful mystery! *This*, then, is the history of what else is so strange: that He should have taken my flesh and died for me. The former mystery anticipates the latter; that latter does but fulfil the former. Did He not love me so inexpressibly, He would not have suffered for me. I understand now why He died for me, because He loved me as a father loves his son—not as a human father merely, but as the Eternal Father the Eternal Son. I see now the meaning of that else inexplicable humiliation: He preferred to regain me rather than to create new worlds.

3. How constant is He in His affection! He has loved us from the time of Adam. He has said from the beginning, 'I will never leave thee nor forsake thee.' He did not forsake us in our sin. He did not forsake me. He found me out and regained me. He made a point of it—He resolved to restore me, in spite of myself, to that blessedness which I was so obstinately set against. And now what does He ask of me, but that, as He has loved me with an everlasting love, so I should love Him in such poor measures as I can show.

O mystery of mysteries, that the ineffable love of Father to Son should be the love of the Son to us! Why was it, O Lord? What good thing didst thou see in me a sinner? Why wast thou set on me? 'What is man, that thou art mindful of him, and the son of man that thou visitest him?' This poor flesh of mine, this weak sinful soul, which has no life except in thy grace, thou didst set thy love upon it. Complete thy work, O Lord, and as thou hast loved me from the beginning, so make me to love thee unto the end. (7)

## Original Sin

To consider the world in its length and breadth, its various history, the many races of man, their starts, their fortunes, their mutual alienation, their conflicts; and then their ways, habits, governments, forms of worship; their enterprises, their aimless courses, their random achievements and acquirements, the impotent conclusion of long-standing facts, the tokens so faint and broken of a superintending design, the blind evolution of what turn out to be great powers or truths, the progress of things, as if from unreasoning elements, not towards final causes, the greatness and littleness of man, his far-reaching aims, his short duration, the curtain hung over his futurity, the disappointments of life, the defeat of good, the success of evil, physical pain, mental anguish, the prevalence and intensity of sin, the pervading idolatries, the corruptions, the dreary hopeless irreligion, that condition of the whole race, so fearfully yet exactly described in the Apostle's words, 'having no hope and without God in the world',—all this is a vision to dizzy and appal; and inflicts upon the mind the sense of a profound mystery, which is absolutely beyond human solution.

What shall be said to this heart-piercing, reason-bewildering fact? I can only answer, that either there is no Creator, or this living society of men is in a true sense discarded from His presence. Did I see a boy of good make and mind, with the tokens on him of a refined nature, cast upon the world without provision, unable to say whence he came, his birthplace or his family connections, I should conclude that there was some mystery connected with his history, and that he was one, of whom, from one cause or other, his parents were ashamed. Thus only should I be able to account for the contrast between the promise and the condition of his being. And so I argue about the world;—*if* there be a God, *since* there is a God, the human race is implicated in some terrible aboriginal calamity. It is out of joint with the purposes of its Creator. This is a fact, a fact as true as the fact of its existence; and thus the doctrine of what is theologically called Original Sin becomes to me almost as certain as that the world exists, and as the existence of God. (8)

## The Mental Sufferings of Our Lord in His Passion

Sin is the mortal enemy of the All-holy, so that He and it cannot be together; and as the All-holy drives it from His presence into the outer darkness, so, if God could be less than God, it is sin that would have power to make Him less. And here observe, my brethren, that when once Almighty Love, by taking flesh, entered this created system, and submitted Himself to its laws, then forthwith this antagonist of good and truth, taking advantage of the opportunity, flew at that flesh which He had taken, and fixed on it, and was its death. The envy of the Pharisees, the treachery of Judas, and the madness of the people, were but the instrument or the expression of the enmity which sin felt towards Eternal Purity as soon as, in infinite mercy towards men, He put Himself within its reach. Sin could not touch His Divine Majesty; but it could assail Him in that way in which He allowed Himself to be assailed, that is, through the medium of His humanity. And in the issue, in the death of God incarnate, you are but taught, my brethren, what sin is in itself, and what it was which then was falling, in its hour and in its strength, upon His human nature, when He allowed that nature to be so filled with horror and dismay at the very anticipation.

There, then, in that most awful hour, knelt the Saviour of the world, putting off the defences of His divinity, dismissing His reluctant Angels, who in myriads were ready at His call, and opening His arms, baring His breast, sinless as He was, to the assault of His foe,—of a foe whose breath was a pestilence, and whose embrace was an agony. There He knelt, motionless and still, while the vile and horrible fiend clad His spirit in a robe steeped in all that is hateful and heinous in human crime, which clung close round His heart, and filled His conscience, and found its way into every sense and pore of His mind, and spread over Him a moral leprosy, till He almost felt Himself to be that which He never could be, and which His foe would fain have made Him. Oh, the horror, when He looked, and did not know Himself, and felt as a foul and loathsome sinner, from His vivid perception of that mass of corruption which poured over His head and ran down even to the skirts of His garments! Oh, the distraction, when He found His eyes, and hands, and feet, and lips, and heart, as if the members of the Evil One, and not of God! Are these the hands of the Immaculate Lamb of God, once innocent, but now red with ten thousand barbarous deeds of blood? are these His lips, not uttering prayer, and praise, and holy blessings, but as if defiled with oaths, and blasphemies, and doctrines of devils? or His eyes, profaned as they are by all the evil visions and idolatrous fascinations for which men have abandoned their adorable Creator? And His ears, they ring with sounds of revelry and of strife; and His heart is frozen with avarice, and cruelty, and unbelief; and His very memory is laden with every sin which has been committed since the fall, in all regions of the earth, with the pride of the old giants, and the lusts of the five cities, and the obduracy of Egypt, and the ambition of Babel, and the unthankfulness and scorn of Israel. Oh, who does not know the misery of a haunting thought which comes again and again, in spite of rejection, to annoy, if it cannot seduce? or of some odious and sickening imagination, in no sense one's own, but forced upon the mind from without? or of evil knowledge, gained with or without a man's fault, but which he would give a great price to be rid of at once and for ever? And adversaries such as these gather around thee, Blessed Lord, in millions now; they come in troops more numerous than the locust or the palmer-worm, or the plagues of hail, and flies, and frogs, which were sent against Pharaoh. Of the living and of the dead and of the as yet unborn, of the lost and of the saved, of thy people and of strangers, of sinners and of saints, all sins are there. Thy dearest are there, thy saints and thy chosen are upon thee; thy three Apostles, Peter, James, and John; but not as comforters, but as accusers, like the friends of Job, 'sprinkling dust towards Heaven', and heaping curses on thy head. All are there but one; one only is not there, one only; for she who had no part in sin, she only could console thee, and therefore she is not nigh. She will be near thee on the Cross, she is separated from thee in the garden. She has been thy companion and thy confidant through thy life, she interchanged with thee the pure thoughts and holy meditations of thirty years; but her virgin ear may not take in, nor may her immaculate heart conceive, what now is in vision before thee. None was equal to the weight but God; sometimes before thy saints thou hast brought the image of a single sin, as it appears in the light of thy countenance, or of venial sins, not mortal; and they have told us that the sight did all but kill them, nay, would have killed them, had it not been instantly withdrawn. The Mother of God, for all her sanctity, nay by reason of it, could not have borne even one brood of that innumerable progeny of Satan which now compasses thee about. It is the long history of a world, and God alone can bear the load of it. Hopes blighted, vows broken, lights quenched, warnings scorned, opportunities lost; the innocent betrayed, the young hardened, the penitent relapsing, the just overcome, the aged failing; the sophistry of misbelief, the wilfulness of passion, the obduracy of pride, the tyranny of habit, the canker of remorse, the wasting fever of care, the anguish of shame, the pining of disappointment, the sickness of despair; such cruel, such pitiable spectacles, such heartrending, revolting, detestable, maddening scenes; nay, the haggard faces, the convulsed lips, the flushed cheek, the dark brow of the willing slaves of evil, they are all before Him now; they are upon Him and in Him. They are with Him instead of that ineffable peace which has inhabited His soul since the moment of His conception. They are upon Him, they are all but His own; He cries to His Father as if He were the criminal, not the victim; His agony takes the form of guilt and compunction. He is doing penance, He is making confession, He is exercising contrition, with a reality and a virtue infinitely greater than that of all saints and penitents together; for He is the One Victim for us all, the sole Satisfaction, the real Penitent, all but the real sinner.

He rises languidly from the earth, and turns around to meet the traitor and his band, now quickly nearing the deep shade. He turns, and lo there is blood upon His garment and in His footprints. Whence come these first-fruits of the Passion of the Lamb? No soldier's scourge has touched His shoulders, nor the hangman's nails His hands and feet. My brethren, He has bled before His time; He has shed blood; yes, and it is His agonizing soul which has broken up His framework of flesh and poured it forth. His passion has begun from within. That tormented Heart, the seat of tenderness and love, began at length to labour and to beat with vehemence beyond its nature; 'the foundations of the great deep were broken up'; the red streams rushed forth so copious and fierce as to overflow the veins, and bursting through the pores, they stood in a thick dew over His whole skin; then forming into drops, they rolled down full and heavy, and drenched the ground.

'O Heart of Jesus, all Love, I offer thee these humble prayers for myself, and for all those who unite themselves with me in Spirit to adore thee. O holiest Heart of Jesus most lovely, I intend to renew and to offer to thee these acts of adoration and these prayers, for myself a wretched sinner, and for all those who are associated with me in thy adoration, through all moments while I breathe, even to the end of my life. I recommend to thee, O my Jesus, Holy Church, thy dear spouse and our true Mother, all just souls and all poor sinners, the afflicted, the dying, and all mankind. Let not thy Blood be shed for them in vain. Finally, deign to apply it in relief of the souls in Purgatory, of those in particular who have practised in the course of their life this holy devotion of adoring thee.' (9)

## The Sacred Heart of Jesus

In explanation of the doctrine I say:

We believe Our Lord is *One* Person: there is One Lord, One Christ, One Emmanuel. And, since He has two natures, divine and human, He is at once without beginning and with beginning, Son of God and Son of Mary; He cannot, never could suffer, yet He did suffer on the Cross. Moreover, on account of that ineffable oneness of Person, we may say of Him, God is man, and man is God: God was born of Mary, and the Son of Man is in Heaven (John 3: 13)—God purchased us with His own blood (Acts 20: 28) and a man shall judge the world (Acts 17: 31). Hence, from the same absolute oneness of Person, we may (reverently) speak of God's Mother, God's flesh, God's face, God's hands. Hence too, when we worship the Eternal Word Incarnate, we cannot *help* by one and the same act worshipping His human nature, as being one with Him, not separate; else, we should not be worshipping Him at all; for we must worship Him *as He is*, and His human nature is united to Him after the manner of an attribute, and, as in worshipping His infinite Wisdom and Goodness, we worship Him, so in like manner, as to all that is His, we cannot divide Him into two, or worship Him at all, without at the same time worshipping His manhood and all that appertains to His manhood, because His manhood is inseparably one with His Person.

Therefore, when we say that we worship that manhood, we really mean that we worship His Divine Person *through* His manhood—in order to plead with Him His gracious Incarnation. And, when we worship His Body and Blood in the Holy Eucharist, we worship His Person *through* His Body and Blood, in order to plead His sufferings in our behalf, which are the symbol and means of our reconciliation. And, if we worship His Divine Heart, still it is the Second Person of the Holy Trinity that we worship, *through* that Heart which is one with Him, and which is the Symbol of that over-flowing compassion towards us which is human while it is divine. (10)

## Devotion to Our Lady and the True Divinity of her Son

Arianism had admitted that Our Lord was both the God of the Evangelical Covenant, and the actual Creator of the Universe; but even this was not enough, because it did not confess Him to be the One, Everlasting, Infinite, Supreme Being, but as one who was made by the Supreme. It was not enough in accordance with that heresy to proclaim Him as having an ineffable origin before all worlds; not enough to place Him high above all creatures as the type of all the works of God's Hands; not enough to make Him the King of all Saints, the Intercessor for man with God, the Object of worship, the Image of the Father; not enough, because it was not all, and between all and anything short of all, there was an infinite interval. The highest of creatures is levelled with the lowest in comparison of the One Creator Himself. That is, the Nicene Council recognized the eventful principle, that, while we believe and profess any being to be made of a created nature, such a being is really no God to us, though honoured by us with whatever high titles and with whatever homage. Arius or Asterius did all but confess that Christ was the Almighty; they said much more than St Bernard or St Alphonso have since said of the Blessed Mary; yet they left Him a creature and were found wanting. Thus there was 'a wonder in Heaven': a throne was seen, far above all other created powers, mediatorial, intercessory; a title archetypal; a crown bright as the morning star; a glory issuing from the Eternal Throne; robes pure as the heavens; and a sceptre over all; and who was the predestined heir of that Majesty? Since it was not high enough for the Highest, who was that Wisdom, and what was her name, 'the

Mother of fair love, and fear, and holy hope', 'exalted like a palm-tree in Engaddi, and a rose-plant in Jericho', 'created from the beginning before the world' in God's everlasting counsels, and 'in Jerusalem her power'? The vision is found in the Apocalypse, a Woman clothed with the sun, and the moon under her feet, and upon her head a crown of twelve stars. The votaries of Mary do not exceed the true faith, unless the blasphemers of her Son came up to it. The Church of Rome is not idolatrous, unless Arianism is orthodoxy. (11)

A tower in its simplest idea is a fabric for defence against enemies. David, King of Israel, built for this purpose a notable tower; and as he is a figure or type of Our Lord, so is his tower a figure denoting Our Lord's Virgin Mother. She is called the *Tower* of David because she had so signally fulfilled the office of defending her Divine Son from the assaults of His foes. It is customary with those who are not Catholics to fancy that the honours we pay to her interfere with the supreme worship which we pay to Him; that in Catholic teaching she eclipses Him. But this is the very reverse of the truth. For if Mary's glory is so very great, how cannot His be greater still who is the Lord and God of Mary? He is infinitely above His Mother; and all that grace which filled her is but the overflowings and superfluities of His incomprehensible Sanctity. And history teaches us the same lesson. Look at the Protestant countries which threw off all devotion to her three centuries ago, under the notion that to put her from their thoughts would be exalting the praises of her Son. Has that consequence really followed from their profane conduct towards her? Just the reverse—the countries, Germany, Switzerland, England, which so acted, have in great measure ceased to worship Him, and have given up their belief in His Divinity while the Catholic Church, wherever she is to be found, adores Christ as true God and true Man, as firmly as ever she did; and strange indeed would it be, if it ever happened otherwise. Thus Mary is the 'Tower of David'. (12)

## Purgatory

*[The angel speaks to the soul of Gerontius]*

> When then—if such thy lot—thou seest thy Judge,
> The sight of Him will kindle in thy heart
> All tender, gracious, reverential thoughts.
> Thou wilt be sick with love, and yearn for Him,
> And feel as though thou couldst but pity Him,
> That one so sweet should e'er have placed Himself
> At disadvantage such, as to be used
> So vilely by a being so vile as thee.
> There is a pleading in His pensive eyes
> Will pierce thee to the quick, and trouble thee.
> And thou wilt hate and loathe thyself; for, though
> Now sinless, thou wilt feel that thou hast sinn'd,
> As never thou didst feel; and wilt desire
> To slink away, and hide thee from His sight:
> And yet wilt have a longing aye to dwell
> Within the beauty of His countenance.
> And these two pains, so counter and so keen,—

The longing for Him, when thou seest Him not;
The shame of self at thought of seeing Him,—
Will be thy veriest, sharpest purgatory. (13)

## The Communion of Saints

We believe in a family of God, of which the saints are the heavenly members and we the earthly—yet one family embracing earth and Heaven. We believe we have access to the heavenly members, and are at liberty to converse with them—and that we can ask them for benefits, and they can gain them for us. We believe at the same time that they are so different from us, and so much above us, that our *natural* feelings towards them would be awe, fear, and dismay, such as we should have on seeing a ghost, or as Daniel's when he fell down and quaked at the vision of the Angel—these feelings being changed into loving admiration and familiar devotion, by our belief in the Communion of Saints. Moreover, we believe them present with us as truly as our fellow-men are present. (14)

## Jesus our Daily Sacrifice

Our Lord not only offered Himself as a Sacrifice on the Cross, but He makes Himself a perpetual, a daily sacrifice, to the end of time. In the Holy Mass that One Sacrifice on the Cross once offered is renewed, continued, applied to our benefit. He seems to say, my Cross was raised up 1800 years ago, and only for a few hours—and very few of my servants were present there—but I intend to bring millions into my Church. For their sakes, then, I will perpetuate my Sacrifice, that each of them may be as though they had severally been present on Calvary. I will offer myself up day by day to the Father, that every one of my followers may have the opportunity to offer his petitions to Him, sanctified and recommended by the all-meritorious virtue of my Passion. Thus I will be a Priest for ever, after the order of Melchisedech—my priests shall stand at the Altar—but not they, but I rather, will offer. I will not let them offer mere bread and wine, but I myself will be present upon the Altar instead, and I will offer up myself invisibly, while they perform the outward rite. And thus the Lamb that was slain once for all, though He is ascended on high, ever remains a victim from His miraculous presence in Holy Mass under the figure and appearance of mere earthly and visible symbols. (15)

## The Consolation of Christ's Bodily Presence in the Eucharist

[At Maryvale] I am writing next room to the Chapel—It is such an incomprehensible blessing to have Christ in bodily presence in one's house, within one's walls, as swallows up all other privileges and destroys, or should destroy, every pain. To know that He is close by—to be able again and again through the day to go in to Him . . . (16)

## The Church's Mission: The Salvation of Souls

The Church aims, not at making a show, but at doing a work. She regards this world, and all that is in it, as a mere shadow, as dust and ashes, compared with the value of one single soul. She holds that, unless she can, in her own way, do good to souls, it is no use her doing anything; she holds that it were better for sun and moon to drop from heaven, for the earth to fail, and for all the many millions who are upon it to die of starvation in extremest agony, so far as temporal affliction goes, than that one soul, I will not say, should be lost, but should commit one single venial sin, should tell one wilful untruth, though it harmed no one, or steal one poor farthing without excuse. She considers the action of this world and the action of the soul simply incommensurate, viewed in their respective spheres; she would rather save the soul of one single wild bandit of Calabria, or whining beggar of Palermo, than draw a hundred lines of railroad through the length and breadth of Italy, or carry out a sanitary reform, in its fullest details, in every city of Sicily, except so far as these great national works tended to some spiritual good beyond them.

Such is the Church, O ye men of the world, and now you know her. Such she is, such she will be; and, though she aims at your good, it is in her own way, and if you oppose her, she defies you. She has her mission, and do it she will, whether she be in rags, or in fine linen; whether with awkward or with refined carriage; whether by means of uncultivated intellects, or with the grace of accomplishments. Not that, in fact, she is not the source of numberless temporal and moral blessings to you also; the history of ages testifies it; but she makes no promises; she is sent to seek the lost; that is her first object, and she will fulfil it, whatever comes of it. (17)

## The Saints' Sense of Sin

It is indeed most true that the holier a man is, and the higher in the Kingdom of Heaven, so much the greater need has he to look carefully to his footing, lest he stumble and be lost; and a deep conviction of this necessity has been the sole preservation of the Saints. Had they not feared, they never would have persevered. Hence, like St Paul, they are always full of their sin and their peril. You would think them the most polluted of sinners, and the most unstable of penitents. Such was the blessed martyr Ignatius, who, when on his way to his death, said, 'Now I begin to be Christ's disciple'. Such was the great Basil, who was ever ascribing the calamities of the Church and of his country to the wrath of Heaven upon his own sins. Such was St Gregory, who submitted to his elevation to the Popedom, as if it were his spiritual death. Such too was my own dear Father St Philip, who was ever showing, in the midst of the gifts he received from God, the anxiety and jealousy with which he regarded himself and his prospects. 'Every day', says his biographer, 'he used to make a protest to God with the Blessed Sacrament in his hands, saying, "Lord, beware of me today, lest I should betray thee, and do thee all the mischief in the world".' At other times he would say, 'The wound in Christ's side is large, but, if God did not guard me, I should make it larger'. In his last illness, 'Lord, if I recover, so far as I am concerned, I shall do more evil than ever, because I have promised so many times before to change my life, and have not kept my word, so that I despair of myself'. He would shed abundance of tears and say, 'I have never done one good action'. When he saw young persons, he began considering how much time they had before them to do good in, and said, 'O, happy you! O, happy you!' He often said, 'I am past hope', and, when urged, he added, 'but I trust in God'. When a penitent of his called him a saint, he turned to her with a face full of anger, and said, 'Begone with you, I am a devil, not a saint'. When another said to him, 'Father, a temptation has come to me to think you are not what the world takes you for', he answered, 'Be sure of this, that I am a man like my neighbours, and nothing more'. (18)

## A Short Road to Perfection

We must bear in mind what is meant by perfection. It does not mean any extraordinary service, anything out of the way, or especially heroic—not all have the opportunity of heroic acts, of sufferings—but it means what the word perfection ordinarily means. By perfect we mean that which has no flaw in it, that which is complete, that which is consistent, that which is sound—we mean the opposite to imperfect. As we know well what *im*perfection in religious service means, we know by the contrast what is meant by perfection.

He, then, is perfect who does the work of the day perfectly, and we need not go beyond this to seek for perfection. You need not go out of the *round* of the day. I insist on this because I think it will simplify our views, and fix our exertions on a definite aim. If you ask me what you are to do in order to be perfect, I say, first— Do not lie in bed beyond the due time of rising; give your first thoughts to God; make a good visit to the Blessed Sacrament; say the Angelus devoutly; eat and drink to God's glory; say the Rosary well; be recollected; keep out bad thoughts; make your evening meditation well; examine yourself daily; go to bed in good time, and you are already perfect. (19)

## The Death of the Christian

O my Lord and Saviour, support me in that hour in the strong arms of thy Sacraments, and by the fresh fragrance of thy consolations. Let the absolving words be said over me, and the holy oil sign and seal me, and thy own Body be my food, and thy Blood my sprinkling; and let my sweet Mother Mary breathe on me, and my Angel whisper peace to me, and my glorious Saints, and my own dear Father, Philip, smile on me; that in them all, and through them all, I may receive the gift of perseverance, and die, as I desire to live, in thy faith, in thy Church, in thy service, and in thy love. (20)

## The Second Coming

1. Introd.—*Modicum* etc., 'A little while'–the disciples were perplexed.

2. Our Lord spoke as if He were to come again soon. And certainly many of His disciples thought He would. They thought not exactly that He would end the world, but that He would come to end the present state of it, to judge the wicked and introduce a holier world. Nay, at one time even the apostles.

3. But no one knows when, not even the angels.

4. It seems to have been Our Lord's wish that His coming should always appear near.

5. He gave indeed signs of His coming, but every age of the world has those signs in a measure.

6. The signs were the falling away and the coming of some great enemy of the Truth called Antichrist, who should bind together all the powers of the world; that as there was war between the good and bad angels in Heaven, so between the servants of Christ and Antichrist on earth.

7. This then is our state. In every age things are so like the last day as to remind us that perhaps it is coming; but still not so like that we know.

8. Every age is a semblance, a type in part of what then at last will be in fulness. (21)

NOTES AND SOURCES

1. John Henry Newman, 'The Second Spring', in *Sermons Preached on Various Occasions*, new edn. (London: Longmans, Green & Co., 1908), 168–81.

2. John Henry Newman, *An Essay on the Development of Christian Doctrine* (London: Longmans, Green & Co., 1909), 88–9.

3. John Henry Newman, 'The Biglietto Speech', in *Addresses to Cardinal Newman with his Replies etc., 1878–1881*, ed. W. P. Neville, Cong. Orat. (New York: Longmans, Green & Co., 1905), 64–70.

4. John Henry Newman, *Certain Difficulties Felt by Anglicans in Catholic Teaching*, vol. ii, new edn. (London: Longmans, Green & Co., 1897), 248–9.

5. John Henry Newman, Letter to Miss Rowe, 16 September 1873 in *Letters and Diaries of John Henry Newman*, edited at the Birmingham Oratory with notes and an introduction by Charles Stephen Dessain of the same Oratory, vol. xxvi: *Aftermaths, January 1872 to December 1873* (Oxford: Clarendon Press, 1974), 364.

6. John Henry Newman, *The Dream of Gerontius*, in *Verses on Various Occasions* (London: Burns & Oates, 1868), 296–8.

7. John Henry Newman, 'Meditations on Christian Doctrine', in *Meditations and Devotions*, new edn. (London: Burns & Oates, 1964), 7–8.

8. John Henry Newman, *Apologia pro vita sua*, Being a History of his Religious Opinions (London: Longmans, Green, Reader, & Dyer, 1879), 241–3.

9. John Henry Newman, 'The Mental Sufferings of Our Lord in his Passion', in *Discourses Addressed to Mixed Congregations* (London, 1906), 335–41.

10. John Henry Newman, Letter to Mrs Henry Wilberforce, 21 October 1873, in *Letters and Diaries*, xxvi. 378.

11. John Henry Newman, *An Essay on the Development of Christian Doctrine* (London: Longmans, Green & Co., 1878), 143–4.

12. John Henry Newman, 'Meditations on the Litany of Loretto, for the Month of May', in *Meditations and Devotions*, 144–5.

13. Newman, *The Dream of Gerontius*, 329–30.

14. John Henry Newman, Letter to Edward Berdoe, 2 October 1865, in *Letters and Diaries*, xxii: *Between Pusey and the Extremists, July 1865 to December 1866* (London: Nelson, 1972), 64.

15. John Henry Newman, 'Twelve Meditations and Intercessions for Good Friday', in *Meditations and Devotions*, 223.

16. John Henry Newman, Letter to Henry Wilberforce, in *Letters and Diaries*, xii: *Littlemore to Rome, October 1845 to December 1846* (London: Nelson, 1961), 129.

17. Newman, *Certain Difficulties*, 239–41.

18. John Henry Newman, 'Perseverance in Grace', in *Discourses Addressed to Mixed Congregations*, 138–9.

19. Newman, *Meditations and Devotions*, 285–6.

20. John Henry Newman, 'God's Will, the End of Life', in *Discourses Addressed to Mixed Congregations*, 123.

21. John Henry Newman, *Sermon Notes of John Henry Cardinal Newman 1849–1878*, edited by Fathers of the Birmingham Oratory, with an Introduction and Notes by James Tolhurst DD, new edn. (Leominster: Gracewing & University of Notre Dame Press, 2000), 225.

# Canon Frederick Oakeley                              1802–1880

Frederick Oakeley was the son of a baronet, and, after private tuition, matriculated at Christ Church, Oxford. He was elected to a fellowship at Balliol, and in 1837, on the recommendation of Dr Pusey, was appointed preacher at the Chapel Royal, Whitehall. For a time he was an Evangelical, but, through the influence of William George 'Ideal' Ward, he began to identify himself with the Tractarians. In 1839 he was appointed as minister of the Margaret Chapel in the West End of London, which would later become All Saints, Margaret Street. Increasingly drawn to Rome, Oakeley joined Newman's community in September 1845, and, three weeks after Newman's reception on 9 October, he himself was received at the little Catholic chapel in St Clement's, Oxford. After two years of study at St Edmund's College, Ware, he was ordained priest and served on the staff of St George's Cathedral in Southwark. In 1850 he was appointed rector of the mission at St John's, Islington, where he remained till his death. In 1852 he became a Canon of Westminster Cathedral. He was much loved for his kindness and gentle humour. His Irish parishioners christened him 'our Father O'Kelly'. He retained his friendship with his old Balliol pupil, Archibald Campbell Tait, who became Archbishop of Canterbury in 1868. His translation of *Adeste fideles*, 'O come all ye faithful', is sung every Christmas by Christians of many traditions. Canon Oakeley is buried at Kensal Green.

### The Offertory: *Accept, Holy Father, almighty, eternal God, this Immaculate Host*

*Catechumen*: Why is the term 'Immaculate Host' (or Victim) applied to the material of the Sacrifice before consecration?

*Priest*: Your question is a very apt one. The term can only be employed by anticipation. Although the subject of the oblation is as yet bread and wine only, yet the priest herein offers the whole substance and future action of the Mass.

C: Why does the priest make the sign of the Cross before depositing the holy bread on the altar?

P: To signify that the oblation has its effect from the Cross and Passion of our Redeemer.

C: What is signified by the Sacred Host lying on the corporal?

P: The meek submission of our blessed Lord to the will of His eternal Father in the Garden of Gethsemane. 'He fell upon His face', as we read in St Matthew 26: 39. (1)

NOTES AND SOURCES

1. Frederick Oakeley, *The Order and Ceremonial of the Most Holy and Adorable Sacrifice of the Mass*, Explained in a Dialogue between a Priest and a Catechumen (London: James Burns, 1848), 35.

# Archbishop William Bernard Ullathorne OSB        1806–1889

William Ullathorne was the snuff-taking, straight-talking Yorkshireman, born of old Catholic yeoman stock, who went from being a cabin boy to a Benedictine monk, a missionary in Australia, and the first Catholic Bishop of Birmingham. Like many young lads, he felt the call of the sea, and for a couple of years served on board the *Leghorn*, sailing into the Baltic, and *Anne's Resolution* out of Scarborough. Attending Mass with one of his shipmates, while they were docked in a Baltic port, moved him to the serious practice of his faith. In 1823 he entered the Benedictine school at Downside; a year later, he received the habit in the monastery. After ordination to the priesthood in 1831, he went to Australia in 1832 to work with Bishop William Morris, also a monk of Downside. For the next ten years he was tireless in ministering to the colonists and convicts, and can justly be called one of the founders of the Church in Australia. His pamphlet, *The Horrors of Transportation*, exposed the disastrous policies of the British government in administering its colonies in the antipodes. When his health began to fail, he returned to England. In 1845 he was appointed Vicar Apostolic of the Western District and, two years later, of the Central District. In 1850, on the restoration of the hierarchy, a cause of which he had been one of the leading advocates, he was appointed the first Bishop of Birmingham. He gave his sympathy and practical assistance to John Henry Newman and the other Oxford converts, and made their enthusiasms intelligible to the 'old Catholics' of the Midlands and the North. He took part in many of the great social and religious controversies of the Victorian age, and attended the First Vatican Council. In his common sense, forthrightness, and moral toughness, he embodied not only the qualities of character in which Yorkshiremen take pride but also the virtues that had sustained the 'old Catholics' throughout the preceding two centuries. There is therefore no reason to doubt the truth of the story told of him on his deathbed: as the priest was reading the prayers in the Ritual that ask Almighty God for protection from the Evil One, he was heard to say in the brogue of his native county, 'The devil is a jackass'.

## Mary's Womb: The Temple of Jesus the Priest

From the moment of His conception He had already made His oblation, for as St Paul says: 'Coming into the world, He said, A body thou hast fitted to me. Holocausts for sin did not please thee. Behold, I come. In the head of the book it stands written of me: that I should do thy will, O God' (Heb. 10: 5–7). And Mary was that most pure temple in which the great High Priest made His offering. There He first offered up that blood, there He first offered up that Flesh, of which He said at a later time: 'If you eat my flesh and drink my blood, you shall have life. As the Father lives in me, and I live by the Father, so he who eats me, the same shall live by me' (John 6: 55–8). But now it is in a far more intimate and constant way that Jesus lives by Mary, and Mary lives by Jesus. Oh, who can tell that mystery of life? Who can comprehend that union between the two hearts of Jesus and Mary? Everyone can understand how much he has been enriched through the heart of his mother, and how his noblest sentiments have been derived from her. But who can understand how Jesus enriched the heart of Mary in that incomparable union? For, next to that union by which Jesus is God and man in one person, there is no union so intimate as that of a mother with a child. The saints are His brethren by adoption, but Mary is His Mother by nature. They have affinity with Him, but she holds with Him the first degree of consanguinity. Her graces, then, are of quite another order than those which sanctified the very holiest of the saints. And, as St Thomas says, through the operations of her maternity, she touches more nearly on the confines of divinity. And which of the Seraphs could ever say to the Lord omnipotent: Thou art my Son; this day have I conceived thee? (1)

## The Dogma of the Immaculate Conception

It is nothing new. It is but an explication of the grace, and of the supereminent purity which the Church has always attributed to the Blessed Virgin. It is but an explication of that high sense in which was ever blessed and ever virgin. For the Immaculate Conception is but the expression of the ever-virginal integrity of her soul. If the Church had said anything tending to diminish the idea which she has ever entertained of the sancity of that sublime creature, then she would have uttered something new, but what she has spoken is contained in that idea, as a consequence is contained in its principle, or as a particular in its universal. It was always held implicitly or of pious belief; it is now held explicitly and proclaimed of Catholic faith...

Whether...we would consider the power of Jesus over creation, sin, death, or the devil, we shall find the highest example of its exercise in Mary. Or whether we would consider His condescension, love, and goodness to His creatures, we have still the most beautiful instance in Mary. Or whether we would consider the depths of the riches which He won upon His Cross, and the generosity with which He pours out those inexhaustible treasures, we shall find their most profuse expenditure was on His Immaculate Mother. Or whether we search the conditions of union with Jesus, we can contemplate them here in their most rare and absolute perfection. For to Mary alone of all saints can we add a perfecting clause to the Psalmist's words: 'With the holy thou shalt be holy, and with the elect thou shalt be elected' (Ps 17: 26–7), and with the immaculate thou shalt be immaculate. Or, if we would contemplate the final end of all God's works, His praise and glory in His saints, it is Mary who renders Him the greatest praise and glory, and her primal graces are the deep foundation from which that towering glory springs.

In short, the Immaculate Conception of Mary is a summary of all the truths of the Gospel, displays all the graces of her Son, strikes down countless errors, and puts sin, and the author of sin, beneath her stainless feet. (2)

## The Humility of Christ in His Passion

The Passion of Our Lord presents all the great virtues in their perfection for our imitation, whether self-denial, poverty of spirit, obedience, silence, humility, purity, patience, prayer, resignation, contempt of the world, or charity. But among all these virtues He pre-eminently appears as the Master of humility. His Passion is the book of humility, His Cross is the throne of humility, the terrible way from the Mount of Olives to Mount Calvary is the substantive exposition of the words: 'Learn of me, for I am meek and humble of heart'. (3)

## The Resurrection and Ascension of Our Lord

The Resurrection of our divine Redeemer from the grave, His Ascension from earth to Heaven, His seat in our human nature at the right hand of the Father, with all His wounds glorified, and His power over the souls of the humble, who draw their humility from Him, are the crowning of His Sacrifice, the sublime demonstration of His divinity, and the encouragement of all who love and suffer for His sake. 'He humbled Himself, becoming obedient unto death, even the death of the Cross. For which cause God also hath exalted Him, and hath given Him a name which is above all names; that in the name of Jesus every knee shall bow, of those that are in Heaven, on earth, and under the earth. And that every tongue should confess that the Lord Jesus Christ is in the glory of God the Father' (Phil 2: 8–11). (4)

## Charity: The Form of the Virtues

What ... can be said of the Christian virtues, especially when they live by the grace and inspiration of celestial charity, but that they emanate in their principle from the sanctity of God, are given to the soul upon the measure of her condition, and are distributed through all her powers, and worked into her life by the labours of the will? They make the soul luminous with the light of justice, harmonious with the beautiful order of their action, noble through obedience to the Eternal Love. When God sets charity in order within us, all the virtues receive the fire of her life, and God reigns through her gentle power as the queen of the soul. By reason of her origin, this divine virtue is most pure; minds defiled cannot defile her, but she removes the stains of error whithersoever she comes. She is of such potency that anger and discontent disappear in her presence; of such fortitude, that she grows stronger in adversities; of such liberty, that oppression only increases her freedom; of such altitude, that no human power can reach her, but she graciously descends to the humble. By partaking of this divine virtue, what was deformed receives a beautiful form, what was dead is restored to life and love, what was depraved is rectified, what was weak recovers health, and what was averse from God in us is happily reconciled. If the beginning of the Christian virtues is from God, their path is on the way to God, and they finally rest the soul in God. The heathens imagined a heaven of gods that came to the help or the injury of man. The True God came, and the false gods vanished. He brought us truth and justice, and the grace of all the virtues that take His name. Become one of us, except in our sin, He practised and taught the perfection of these virtues, and they changed the world. He still teaches them, still gives the grace to everyone who has good will to obey His voice. Wherefore the grace of these virtues is from the bosom of God, their examples are in the Eternal Word of God made man, and their inspiration is from the Holy Spirit. (5)

## The Difficulties of Virtue: Indulging the Imagination

The indulging of the imagination upon one's self is very weakening to the soul, obscures the present light, absorbs and troubles the force of the will, takes it off from working generously with the grace of God, diverts its attention from its true object, relaxes the virtues, discourages the soul with vain and useless alarms, and weighs the spirit down with sadness. Thus the soul makes her own fears, very far from the fear of God; her own difficulties, such as God has never made; and her own disheartenments, where God would have her lift her heart to Him. This is neither humility nor the way to humility: it is all the vapour of self-love. It is not self-knowledge, but delusion. One stroke of light from God will pierce through the whole mist, reveal the soul to herself, show her how she has been nursing self-love, and compel her to confess that she is nothing without God, and must go to Him for light and strength. Take off your imagination from yourself, and nine-tenths of your difficulties will be removed. You will then become subject to the light of God; you will lift up your mind to the great motives of your enterprise, and pray with clear intention for the divine help to advance with courage on the way to God ...

With respect to the management of the imagination, Our Lord has given us a rule that is applicable to many things. 'Be not solicitous for tomorrow, for the morrow will provide for itself. Sufficient for the day is the evil thereof' (Matt. 6: 34). Although the literal sense of this admonition relates to the things of the body, the rule is equally applicable to the things of the soul. Do not imagine difficulties before they come. To imagine them is to make them. You have the light and help of the present hour and duty, but not of the future. 'You know not', says St James, 'what tomorrow will bring forth' (Jas. 4: 14). Tomorrow will have its providence as well as today. The trial of tomorrow is not the trial of today, and the light and help of today is not the light and help of tomorrow. To lay the burden of the future on the present is what God never intended. He gives to each day its duty, and to each day its help. To load the present hour with the burden of the future, that never comes as anticipated, is both to encumber the present duty and weary the mind, and to derange the order of Divine Providence in your conduct. Thus that is made heavy which God has made easy. (6)

## The Definition of Papal Infallibility: Ullathorne's Explanation for his People

It has been most widely, but most erroneously, asserted by the adversaries of our faith, and possibly even some Catholics may have imbibed the notion, that this definition makes the Pope infallible in all his words and actions, and even to the extent of whatsoever he thinks. Nay, some have been so absurd as to say that it makes him sinless. But this is not the doctrine of the definition, nor is it the teaching of the Church. The definition does not extend infallibility to the private teaching of the Pope, still less to his conversation, or to his ordinary actions, or to his political functions, or to his judgement of causes as between man and man. To nothing of this kind does it reach; they are excluded by the very terms. It is only when he exercises a certain office in a certain way that he is declared to speak without error. Mark the words of the definition; they say, 'when he speaks *ex cathedra*, that is to say', continues the text, '*when* in discharge of the office of Pastor and Doctor of all Christians, by virtue of his supreme apostolic authority he defines'. And again, it is only when he *defines* 'a doctrine regarding faith or morals'. We might as well say that a judge is always delivering sentence, or that the Sovereign is always giving the force of law to acts of Parliament, as say that the Pope is always exercising his infallibility. The occasions for such an exercise of authority are comparatively few, and occur but now and then. As the judge only from the bench, and after the causes has been heard, pronounces that sentence which must be obeyed; as the Sovereign only from the throne of authority gives those acts, after their discussion in Parliament, the confirming sanction makes them law, so the Pope, only after due investigation made as to what is or what is not contained in the deposit of Catholic teaching, pronounces *ex cathedra*, from his apostolic chair or throne, what is to be believed, because it always has been received, as an article of Catholic tradition. The means which he employs for investigating what is the Catholic truth are enumerated in the decree itself. The Council says: 'According to the exigencies of times and circumstances, the Roman Pontiffs sometimes assembling Ecumenical Councils, or asking the mind of the Church scattered throughout the world, sometimes by particular synods, sometimes using other helps which divine Providence supplied, defined those things as to be held which with the help of God they had recognized as conformable with the sacred Scriptures and Apostolic Traditions.' The past is guarantee for the future, and prescribes the general principles and rules by which the Popes are guided. Scripture and Tradition are the fountains of their judgements. Into these they inquire, consulting according to the gravity of the case. In some cases the Catholic Tradition is so obvious that they require but little if any consultations; others are of greater gravity, and involve a certain obscurity. Such was that of the Immaculate Conception before its definition, which led the Pope to consult the whole episcopate before taking the final step. Again, in this case of defining his infallibility, the Pope has the sense of a General Council. But in every case of an infallible definition, it is always the Vicar of Christ who unites his apostolic authority to the Catholic Tradition.

Hence it is also stated in the decree, that it is not 'new doctrine' or any new revelation, but 'the deposit of faith delivered to the Apostles', which, not by inspiration, but by the guiding assistance of the Holy Ghost, they are able to keep inviolable, and to expound without error.

On the other hand, it is part and parcel of the definition of Papal infallibility, that 'the definitions of the Roman Pontiff are irreformable of themselves, and not from the consent of the Church'.

A little reflection will make this evident. The authority of the Roman Pontiff is not derived from the Church, but from Christ. It comes from above, not from below, and it is the supreme authority over the Church. The less cannot overrule the greater authority, and those who are subject to the supreme authority cannot reform its decisions. We must not be here misled by the example of temporal authority constituted by men: this power is constituted by God; and He can as easily make His Vicar infallible as His Church. Nay, for that matter, humanly speaking, it is easier to make one man infallible than a multitude. Christ constituted His Vicar as the representative of His authority; to Peter, thus constituted, He promised by His prayer an unfailing faith, and with that unfailing faith He enjoined him to confirm his brethren. But if the consent of the Church were needed for the validity of his definitions, it would not be the Vicar of Christ who confirmed his brethren, but his brethren who confirmed him. The very idea is destructive of the Papal infallibility. (7)

## The Bishop of Birmingham and the Curé of Ars: The Revival of the Catholic Church in England

On May 14, 1854, the Curé d'Ars received a visit from Bishop Ullathorne of Birmingham. 'I was speaking of prayer for England,' the Bishop writes, 'and was describing in a few words the difficulties and sufferings of our poor Catholics for their faith, when suddenly [the Curé] interrupted me by opening those eyes—cast into shadow by their depth, when listening or reflecting—and streaming their full light on me in a manner I can never forget, he said, in a voice as firm and full of confidence as though he were making an act of faith: *Mais, Monseigneur, je crois que l'Église d'Angleterre retournera à son ancienne splendour* ('I believe that the Church in England will recover her ancient splendour'). I am sure he firmly believes this, from whatever source he has derived the impression. (8)

NOTES AND SOURCES

1. William Bernard Ullathorne, *The Immaculate Conception of the Mother of God: An Exposition* (London: Richardson & Son, 1855), 9–10.

2. Ibid. 204, 210.

3. William Bernard Ullathorne, *The Groundwork of the Christian Virtues* (London: Burns & Oates, 1882), 209–10.

4. Ibid. 213.

5. Ibid. 51–2.

6. Ibid. 67.

7. Cuthbert Butler OSB, *The Vatican Council, 1869–1870: Based on Bishop Ullathorne's Letters*, ed. Christopher Butler OSB (London: Collins, 1962), 456–8.

8. Francis Trochu, *The Curé d'Ars, St Jean-Marie-Baptiste Vianney (1786–1859), according to the Acts of the Process of Canonization and numerous hitherto unpublished documents*, trans. Dom Ernest Graf OSB, of St Mary's Abbey Buckfast (London: Burns, Oates & Washbourne, 1927), 510–11.

# Henry Edward Cardinal Manning          1808–1892

The distortions of his first biographer, E. S. Purcell, the calumnies in Lytton Strachey's carica-ture, and the lack of a biography based on primary sources have kept Manning's intellectual and moral greatness hidden from the generations that have come after him; the works of Alan McClelland, David Newsome, and James Pereiro stand almost alone in their reclamation of the Cardinal whom Belloc regarded as the greatest of all the Oxford converts. Born into a family of merchant bankers, Manning was educated at Harrow, took a double first at Balliol, was elected to a fellowship at Merton, and entered the ordained ministry of the Church of England. In 1833 he was appointed curate of John Sargent, the rector of Lavington in Sussex; by Easter of that same year he was engaged to Caroline Sargent, his rector's daughter, and a few months later, after the death of John Sargent in May, he was presented to the living. Caroline died, childless, in 1837. At the age of 32, Manning was made Archdeacon of Chiche-ster. His later preoccupations as a Catholic bishop were foreshadowed in the 'charges' he gave in his Anglican office on questions both of social justice and of theological orthodoxy. After the Privy Council delivered the judgement that the Revd G. C. Gorham's denial of baptismal regeneration was not contrary to the doctrine of the Church of England, Manning resigned his living, and on 6 April 1851 he was received into the Catholic Church. Within ten weeks, and without the benefit of a sojourn in the seminary, Manning was ordained to the priesthood by Cardinal Wiseman; however, he was not altogether dispensed from further study and spent the first three years of his priesthood at the *Accademia dei Nobili Ecclesiastici* in Rome. Admiring the former archdeacon's powers of reasoning and seemingly boundless capacity for hard work, Wiseman entrusted Manning with tasks of mounting influence: as founder and first superior of the Oblates of St Charles, inspector of the diocesan schools, canon of Westminster, and provost of the chapter. On Wiseman's death, Blessed Pope Pius IX appointed him to succeed him as Archbishop of Westminster. For the next nearly thirty years, Manning led his diocese and the Church in England with administrative efficiency, and with a boldness of vision that has left a permanent mark on the Catholic culture of this country. His teaching on social justice, his practical love of the poor, and his intervention to end the Dock Strike in 1889 gave the English people a lesson in Catholic social doctrine that has never been surpassed in its clarity and moral force. The paradoxes of his sympathies are proof, not of inconsistency, but of the proper breadth of a Catholic mind and heart: the patrician convert and patriotic Englishman was a loyal friend of Ireland and the Irish clergy; the Ultramontane defender of Papal infallibility and the unique claims of the Catholic Church had a high admiration for General Booth, the founder of the Salvation Army; the opponent of the entry of Catholics into the old universities delighted in reminiscing with his old Oxford friends. The often criticized leading role that he played at the First Vatican Council, in promoting the definitions of Papal infallibility and primacy in jurisdiction, was inspired, not by private ambition, but by a conviction of truth and a sense of the urgency of the Church's struggle with a modern world ever more violently hostile to Christian faith and morality. In the reputation manufactured for him by Lytton Strachey, Manning seemed remote and cold; in the reality of his friendships, he was remembered as warm and affectionate. One day during the strike of 1889, when Ben Tillett, the dockers' leader, returned to his lodgings in the East End, he found Manning, dressed without finery in the black of an ordinary clergyman and reading the latest Sherlock Holmes story in the *Strand* magazine. His question for Tillett was a simple one: 'What can I do to help?' The poet Lionel Johnson said of Manning at his death, thinking especially of his championing of the working man: 'For thousands, ere he won the holiest home, | Earth was made homelier by this Prince of Rome.' One hundred thousand mourners came to view his body. London would not see such sorrow among so many till the funeral nine years later of Queen Victoria. Henry Edward Manning, Cardinal of the Roman Church, is buried in Westminster Cathedral with the prayer book of his wife, to whom on his deathbed he said he owed all the good he had done, all the good he had been.

## Why I Am a Catholic

I know that I am; I know that I have the light of reason, the dictate of conscience, the power of will; I know that I did not make all things, nor even myself. A necessity of my reason compels me to believe in One higher and greater than I, from whom I come, and to whose image I am made. My perfection and welfare consist in knowing Him, in being conformed to Him. I am sure that He is good, and that He desires my happiness; and that, therefore, He has not hid Himself from me, but has made Himself known, to the end that I may love Him and be like Him. I find that the light of the knowledge of God has filled the world, and has been ever growing by fresh accessions of light, waxing brighter and clearer until it culminated 'in the face of Jesus Christ'. In Him God and man were perfectly revealed. In Himself, in His words and in His commandments, I find the most perfect knowledge of God that the world has ever known; the most perfect knowledge of himself that man has ever reached; the most perfect law of morals towards God and towards man that men have ever received. All this is to be found in Christianity alone. Christianity is, therefore, the fullness of the revelation of God. Moreover, I find that the maximum of human and historical evidence proves this true and perfect Christianity to be coincident and identical with the world-wide and immutable faith of the Catholic and Roman Church. On these foundations—four square and imperishable—rests the faith to which God in mercy has called me, in which I hope to live and to die; for which I also hope that, by God's grace, I should be willing to give my life. (1)

## Peter Abides Always

With those who are out of the Church, Peter is a historical name, a person in the past, a subject of Patristic learning, a symbol of unity and authority. To Catholics,

Peter teaches and rules at this hour. His prerogatives are wielded by successor, but the powers are his. He is the source of jurisdiction, the organ of truth, the centre of unity. Pontiffs come and go, but Peter abides always. As one of the greatest of his successors has said: 'Simon may die, but Peter lives forever.' . . .

If there be, then, any truth evidently declared in Scripture and in universal tradition, in the writings of Fathers, and in the decrees of Councils, it is that which may be summed up in the following propositions:

1. That to Peter, first and alone, was given by our divine Lord the plenitude of all power, both of teaching and of ruling, together with the charge of the whole flock on earth.

2. That this power was so given to him that he was able to act alone and supremely, apart from the other Apostles; whereas the other Apostles were unable to act except in subordination to him.

3. That to him a special assistance was granted to sustain him in the knowledge and declaration of the faith, and a special office committed to him to confirm and to sustain the faith of the Apostles; so that the deposit of faith was doubly secured, first in the person of Peter, and next in the college of the Apostles in union with him.

4. That this divine foundation and institution of the Church is perpetual; that Peter lives on in his successors, and the college of the Apostles in the episcopate; so that both the Chair of Peter is indefectible and infallible, and also the episcopate in union with it. (2)

## The Catholic Church in England: Her Witness to Faith in the Incarnation

It is a great glory to the Catholic Church in England to stand out almost alone in the broad light of day, and in the face of the English people, as the witness for the full and explicit faith of the Incarnation; as the witness for the Sacred Heart of Jesus; as the witness of its love and of its tenderness, and of the one Name by which alone we can be saved. To be the full, explicit, and inflexible witness for all these divine things—for the person of Jesus, for the sole divine personality of the incarnate Son, for the dignity of His Immaculate Mother, and for the sympathy and tenderness of His Sacred Heart—to be the witness for all this is a joy and a glory. England has to make a reparation. The doctrine of the Incarnation . . . is indeed in the heart of the English people. But it is gravely threatened, and in every generation that passes I fear its light is becoming fainter and fainter, and the faith of men in that mystery is growing less and less. And why? Because the divine defences of that truth have been ruined in England. There are two outworks of the faith of the Incarnation. Like as we see in warfare, the outworks which defend the citadel must be taken before the citadel can be assailed. So it is with the faith. The two outworks which protect the Incarnation are the worship or devotion which we give to the Blessed Mother of God and the divine adoration of Jesus in the Most Holy Sacrament. Three hundred years ago the very name of the Mother of God was cast out. Her chapels were ruined, her festivals were abolished, her rosary was taken from her children. Every memorial of her was effaced. The little ones of England who had been trained up till then with her beads in their hands were thenceforth to know nothing of her as their Mother. Too effectually has this work been done. But more than this: the altars were pulled down. The very name of sacrifice was effaced. The festivals in honour of the Blessed Sacrament were abolished. The word 'priest'—everything that told of the Holy Mass, everything that manifested the presence of Jesus on the altar, the tabernacle, and the light that burnt before it—all these things were taken away. And when these two outworks were destroyed, the citadel itself was assailed. The doctrine of the Incarnation has been battered ever since, and to this day its light has been fading in England.

And therefore I believe that the work of grace which God has revived in the midst of us in these days is a providential warning. I believe that this restoration of the light of the Sacred Heart, come whence it may, and I know not whence it came, has been ordained to revive with an intense fervour and with a sevenfold ardour our devotion to the Person, the name, the Passion of our Divine Redeemer. It is come to restore the faith to England: first, in the Incarnation; secondly, in the presence of Jesus upon the altar; thirdly, in a joyful recognition that the title of Mother of God is truly the right of her who bore into this world the Divine Infant, God the Son incarnate.

A great grace, then, has been poured out upon us and upon the people of England, and there will come a time, hastened by these things, when thousands and ten thousands of hearts will return again to the true Mother of their faith. I believe that in the confusions we hear around us the announcement may be heard that the light of the Incarnation will spread once more over England in renewed splendours from sea to sea.

But, dear brethren, in the midst of this visitation of grace let us not be without a holy fear. If Jesus be now among us, he has come to put us on our trial: 'His fan is in His hand, and He will thoroughly purge His floor, and gather the wheat into His garner, and the chaff He will burn up with unquenchable fire' (Matt. 3: 12). (3)

## The Last Things: The Eternal Glory of the Sacred Heart

'As in Adam all die, so also in Christ shall all be made alive. But everyone in his own order: the first fruits, Christ; then they that are Christ's, who have believed in His coming. Afterwards the end, when He shall have delivered up the Kingdom to God and the Father, when He shall have brought to nought all principality and power and virtue, for He must reign until He hath put all His enemies under His feet ... And when all things shall be subdued unto Him, then the Son also Himself shall be subject unto Him, then the Son also Himself shall be subject unto Him that put all things under Him, that God may be all in all' (1 Cor. 15: 22–6, 28).

The temporal reign of the Son will then be accomplished. This dead world and all its elements will be dissolved with burning heat. The new heaven and the new earth will be revealed. The Mystical Body will be gathered from warfare on earth, and from expiation in Purgatory, into the Paradise of God. All will be consummated; the number of the elect will be full; the last saint, the last penitent will have been gathered by the angels from the four winds of Heaven. All will then be sealed with an eternal conformity to the Sacred Heart. And in that day, between Him and us, there will be no veil forever: our eyes will be no more 'holden that we cannot know Him'. They will be opened in that day when He shall drink the fruit of the

Vine new with us in the Kingdom of God. We shall not then break any more the Bread of Life in the Sacraments, but we shall see Him, the Substance and the Reality, the Word incarnate, the King in His beauty, and to all eternity we shall behold Him, and by and through Him we shall see God. The Sacrament of the Altar will be transfigured into the presence, real, personal, and visible, of Jesus upon the throne of His glory. The tabernacle of God will be open, and we shall see Him with the piercing intuition of the light of glory, for to the glorified intelligence all is transparent and luminous, as the light of noon. There will be seen, with open face and forever, all that we believe in now: the eternal glory of the Sacred Heart, the object of our divine worship, the original to which we are made, the fountain of eternal life. (4)

## The Universal Call to Holiness

The saints now before the Throne in the kingdom of glory are only the ripe and perfect fruit which has been gathered from the mystical vine; and we are the unripe and imperfect fruit hanging in their stead. You are all bound to be saints. The little children among us are the most like saints on earth; for they are the freshest from the waters of regeneration, and as yet the world has not stained them, and their own will has not departed from God. They are in their baptismal innocence. And our Divine Saviour took a little child and set him in the midst even of Apostles, and said, 'Unless you become as one of these, you shall not enter the kingdom of heaven'. We are, then, surrounded by saints. We think that saints are like the great mountains, or like the cedars of Lebanon, in the kingdom of God—seldom to be seen and afar off. There are saints standing amongst us, and we know them not. They do not know it themselves; for sanctity sees only its own imperfections. And you were once like the saints; you were once children fresh in the innocence of grace; for you were then humble, and unstained, and docile, and obedient. And there are other saints to be found on earth. In the multitude of the poor there are to be found the friends of Jesus and the followers of His poverty, and they are saints. (5)

## Transubstantiation

The words we [priests] speak are not ours, but His; not human, but divine. 'This is my Body' has no equal, except 'Let the light be'. These words created the light. The other words do not create; but they constitute, or bring upon the altar, the presence of the incarnate Word. They elevate the bread and the wine from the natural to the supernatural order. This is a power, not creative, but of omnipotence. The bread and wine are no longer subject to the conditions or law of nature as to their substance, but only as to their sensible phenomena. A divine change passes upon them, and yet not a natural change, for they pass away as to their substance, and yet abide as to their sensible effects. There is no such change in the order of nature, for there the whole natural substance and accidents either abide, or go together. Here the phenomena or sensible species and effects abide, as if they were in the natural order. The substance passes away in the supernatural order of the new creation. The words 'Let the light be', had their effect in the first creation of nature. The words, 'This is my Body', have their effect on the first creation and in the second, in both the old creation and the new. They stand next in order to the words, 'The Holy Ghost shall come upon thee, and the power of the Highest shall overshadow thee; therefore, that Holy (One) which shall be born of thee shall be called the Son of God' (Luke 1: 35). For this cause, the action of consecration and the action of the Incarnation are related to each other. Next to the Incarnation there is no action so transcendent, so purely divine, as the consecration and the Holy Sacrifice. It is the continuity of the Incarnation and Oblation of the incarnate Son. The voice that speaks the words is human; the words and effects are of the almighty power of God. (6)

## The Priest's Call to Sanctity: The Motive and the Means

St John Chrysostom says that the hand that consecrates ought to be purer than the solar light, and if the hand of the priest, what should be his eyes which gaze upon the Divine Presence, veiled but hardly hidden, and the lips which say, 'This is my Body', and the ears that hear our own familiar voice uttering these words of the new creation of God? But if such should be the sanctity of the body, what should be the purity of the soul of the priest: in his intellect, with all its powers, faculties, memory, and imagination; in his heart, with all its affections and desires; in his conscience, with all its discernment and sovereign commands; and in his will, with all its inflexible resolves and steadfast reign over his whole outward and inward life? . . .

It is of divine faith that God does not command impossibilities. And also that, to him that uses the grace he has, more grace is given. The priesthood is indeed a high estate and an arduous work. Men may shrink from it laudably, from humility, self-mistrust, and holy fear. But when the indelible character has been once impressed upon them, to waver and to doubt is like Peter upon the sea when the winds and the sea were boisterous. Our Lord in him rebukes our cowardice: 'O thou of little faith, wherefore didst thou doubt?' And these words ought to be forever in our ears. If we begin to sink, it is because we have begun to doubt. And then we begin to look here and there, backwards and forwards, and to think that safety and rest and sanctity is to be found in this state and the other, and anywhere but in our own. This is want of humble faith. If we would only use the grace we have, we should never fail; and in using it, the grace would be increased, or doubled, or multiplied tenfold in reward of humility and fidelity, and simple trust in our Divine Master. No man has so many talents to trade with, till his Master comes again, as a priest [does]. And no man can therefore lay up for himself so great a reward. Of our Blessed Mother alone it can be said that she corresponded with every light and inspiration and grace of the Holy Ghost, and that promptly and adequately, so that the increase of her grace cannot be measured, and is called an immensity. But every priest, though far below her because of our original sin and faults and falls, and of our tardy and inadequate correspondence with our great and innumerable graces, every priest may gain and store up in himself a great depth of sanctification, always increasing through life, and accumulating more and more unto the end. . . .

'One thing have I asked of the Lord, that will I seek after, that I may dwell in the house of the Lord all the days of my life, that I may see the delights of the Lord, and may visit His temple, for He hath hidden me in His tabernacle' (Ps. 26: 4–6). The 'one thing' of a priest's life is to dwell near Our Lord on the altar, to bear the key of the tabernacle, and to be as a disciple *ad latus Domini*, by the side of his Lord. The title *alter Christus* is both a joy and rebuke. If we be identified with Our Lord, He will dwell in us and reign in us. 'The charity of Christ urgeth us'—that is, His love to us urges us to love Him, to serve Him with all our inward life, for He died for us to this end, 'that we should no longer live unto ourselves'. 'With Christ I am nailed to the Cross, and I live, now not I, but Christ liveth in me' (Gal. 2: 19–20).

If the presence of Jesus penetrates throughout the soul, if it pervades the intellect, the will, the affection, He lives in us, and we, by Him, should live a supernatural life. All our freedom would still be perfect, but His mind and His inspirations would reign over us. We should think His thoughts, speak His words, do His acts. What a multitude of sweetness it would bring into our whole life, if we, as priests, could say, 'I live, not I, but Christ liveth in me'. The world would have nothing in us; we should neither seek it nor fear it. The consciousness of our predestination and vocation, and justification and adoption, and of our second and higher vocation to be in a special manner and measure conformed to the image of the Son by partaking of His priesthood, would be a perpetual motive to all perfection....

Holiness consists not in doing uncommon things, but in doing all common things with an uncommon fervour. No life was ever more full of work and of its interruptions than the life of Our Lord and His Apostles. They were surrounded by the multitude, and 'there were many coming and going, and they had not so much as time to eat' (Mark 6: 31). Nevertheless, a busy life needs a punctual and sustained habit of prayer. It is neither piety nor charity for a priest to shorten his preparation before Mass or his thanksgiving after it because people are waiting for him. He must first wait upon God, and then he may serve his neighbour. The hour and a half of a priest's Mass is both his own and not his own. It is the first fruits of his day. They belong to God: he has the *usufruct* [use], not the *dominium* [ownership], of them. He cannot alienate them. (7)

## The Priest's Daily Mass

'When the morning came, Jesus stood on the shore' (John 21: 4). The day begins with the presence of Jesus; the altar is the shore of the eternal world, and Jesus comes at our word. In the Holy Mass we know Him, and yet our eyes are holden. He is in another form. We cannot see Him, but we know that it is the Lord. He makes ready for us, and gives to us the Bread of Life. If we were to spend a whole life in preparation, one such divine contact with His presence would be an overpayment of all our prayer and penance and purification of heart. [St Gregory of Nazianzus says: 'Extreme old age would not be a long preparation for the priesthood'.] But He comes to us, not once in our life only, but morning by morning. Every day begins with Him. (8)

## Cooperating with the Holy Spirit

All day long the Spirit of God is in your hearts; all hours of the day He is calling on you to correspond with the will of God, that by it you may be sanctified. But do you correspond with it? You know that if you strike a note of music, all the octave notes will vibrate. Does your heart vibrate in correspondence and harmony with the voice of the Holy Ghost, prompting you to holy thoughts, good works, charitable actions, peace with all men, prayer and piety towards God? No grace that God gives ever fails of its effect, except through our fault. The seeds that fall upon the barren sand can bear no fruit; that which is cast upon the sea cannot strike a root; that which falls upon a mind which is like the troubled sea, or upon a heart which is like the barren sand, will bear no spiritual fruit. Nevertheless, the grace of God in itself is always fruitful; it never fails of its effect, unless we mar it. Are you, then, corresponding with the exuberant graces, which God is always bestowing upon you? Think of what you have received from your childhood. The lights that have come down on you from Heaven all your life long are not more abundant than the graces of the Holy Spirit, which have been bestowed upon you to impart the knowledge of self and the knowledge of God. The showers that water the earth are not more exuberant than the graces of sanctity which God has poured out into your hearts. How have you corresponded with them? Learn, then, brethren; let us all learn, for we all alike have need—and what I say to you I say first to myself—let us learn to have a delicate conscience, to understand promptly, and to correspond, if we can, proportionately; not to receive great graces languidly, and squander one half of them, and correspond faintly with the rest. Try with your whole soul and strength to rise up and to obey, when the grace of God calls you to any higher state or to any better action. (9)

## Love of God in Darkness

The bond of our union with God is the love of God above all things. He that dwelleth in charity dwelleth in God, and God in him. Here is the link of gold which binds the soul to God. Keep that link fast, and do not be afraid when the consciousness of your past sins and of your many temptations seems to come down upon you and to overwhelm you as a flood. In those darkest times, be sure that if you love God you are still united with Him. It is not when we walk in the brightness of the noonday only that we are united with Him. The purest union with God is when we walk with Him in the darkness, without consolation and without joy; having no other guide; our hand in His hand; going on like children, not knowing whither; but obeying the inspirations of God to do or not to do as He wills: out in the bleak cold sky, with no joy in our prayers and no rest of heart, in constant inward fears, with temptations all around, but always faithful to the guidance of the Spirit of God. 'Whosoever are led by the Spirit of God, they are the sons of God' (Rom. 8: 14). There are two axioms in the Kingdom of God which shall never fail: no penitent soul can perish, and no soul that loves God can be lost. (10)

## The Programme of Social Reform

Political economy is not a matter of values and exchanges, or of free contracts only, but of human life in all its social needs and welfare. It is impossible to discuss how many hours a day a man or a woman shall work, until we have first laid down how many hours in the day are needed that a man live a human life, and how much time in the day is needed that a woman may fulfil the duties of domestic life. To put labour and wages first, and human or domestic life second, is to invert the order of God and nature, and to ruin the society of man at its foundation . . .

The right of uniting for mutual protection and support is a natural and legitimate right inherent in capital and labour—in employers and employed. Such unions are most fruitful and peaceful when masters and men unite in one common confraternity or guild. When they are separate and independent, they ought freely to confer, face to face, in any contention arising between them, and failing to agree, they ought to refer their contention to councils of conciliation freely chosen by each side...

I do not believe that the powerful relations of employers and employed will ever be safely and solidly secured until the just and due proportion between profits and wages shall have been fixed, recognized, laid down, and publicly known to govern all free contracts between capital and labour. (11)

NOTES AND SOURCES

1. Henry Edward Manning, *Why I Became A Catholic: Or Religio Viatoris* (London: Burns & Oates, n.d.), 85–6.

2. Henry Edward Manning, *Petri Privilegium: Three Pastoral Letters to the Clergy of the Diocese* (London: Longmans, Green & Co., 1971), 16, 17–18.

3. Henry Edward Manning, *The Glories of the Sacred Heart* (London: Burns & Oates, 1876), 28–31.

4. Ibid. 278–9.

5. Henry Edward Manning, *The Internal Mission of the Holy Ghost*, 2nd edn. (London: Burns & Oates, 1875), 185–6.

6. Henry Edward Manning, *The Eternal Priesthood*, new edn. (London: Burns & Oates, 1907), 14–16.

7. Ibid. 18, 54–5, 56–8, 81–2.

8. Ibid. 89.

9. Manning, *The Internal Mission of the Holy Ghost*, 25–6.

10. Ibid. 163.

11. Henry Edward Manning, *The Dignity and Rights of Labour: And Other Writings on Social Questions* (London: Burns, Oates & Washbourne, 1934), 64–6.

# Lady Georgiana Fullerton                    1812–1885

Georgiana Fullerton was one of the first Catholic novelists in England and an apostle of practical charity. She was the daughter of Lord Granville Leveson-Gower, the first Earl Granville, and the granddaughter of the Duke of Devonshire; her brother, the second Earl, was Gladstone's foreign secretary. Well educated in languages and music (she was a piano pupil of Liszt), she married a member of the Irish gentry, Alexander George Fullerton, then an attaché at the British embassy in Paris, where her father was ambassador. In 1843 Alexander was received into the Catholic Church, to be followed three years later, after her father's death, by Georgiana. Apart from novels such as *Grantley Manor* and *Too Strange Not to be True*, Lady Fullerton wrote short stories, poetry, and biographies. The thoroughness of her historical research led to her being called as a witness in the process for the beatification of the English Martyrs. After the death of their son from a brain tumour in 1855, Alexander and Georgiana became Franciscan tertiaries and devoted the rest of their lives to the corporal and spiritual works of mercy. Georgiana helped to bring the Sisters of St Vincent de Paul to England, and with Frances Margaret Taylor founded a community, the Poor Servants of the Mother of God Incarnate, for women who could not afford the dowries then required for women's religious life. Father Faber gave her spiritual direction, and, on her death, Cardinal Newman said that, since becoming a Catholic, he had 'looked upon her with reverence and admiration for her saintly life'. Lady Fullerton died at her house in Bournemouth and is buried at the Convent of the Sacred Heart in Roehampton.

## 'For You and Many': Jesus Loves Us

He loved *me*, He delivered Himself up for *me*. O my Lord Jesus Christ, how that scene of the Last Supper does away with Satan's lies. He has so often whispered to your creatures that there is no hope of salvation for them; he has deluded them with that dreadful falsehood. Jesus, the Son of the Immaculate Mother, the Son of the eternal God, offers Himself, is willing to die for her whose pride, whose terrible pride, whose sensuality, whose littleness, whose meanness, whose vanity, whose hypocrisy, He knows. (1)

## The Language of the Church

Unto all lands thy sound has gone,
With still small voice or clarion tone,
Thou glorious old-Church Latin tongue,
Familiar still the Saints among!
It floats on the chill midnight air,
It ushers in the morn with prayer,
It blends with the soft vesper bell,
And whispers in the convent cell;
Sower of truth's eternal seed,
Tongue of the one unchanging creed
Confess'd, where'er the Martyrs bled,
By myriads of the sainted dead;
In every clime beneath the skies
Where Mass is said, where altars rise,
Distant and lone so'er they be:
From pole to pole, from sea to sea,
In high cathedral's sculptured nave,
Or lofty dome, or humble cave,
There does the Church her *Sanctus* sing,
And *Gloria in excelsis* ring;
Throughout the world, in ceaseless round,
The *Credo's* thrilling accents sound.
*Domine non sum dignus* leads
The suppliant cry a sinner needs;
And *Ecce agnus Dei* tells
That Christ on earthly altars dwells.
*Ora pro nobis* swells the prayer
Angels in golden censers bear;
*Salve Regina* hails the star
By Kings and Prophets seen afar.
Still does the *De Profundis* rise;
The *Stabat Mater* breathes its sighs.
The glad *Te Deum's* notes upraise

Of joyful hearts th'enraptured praise:
Each solemn rite, each sacred hour,
Still claims thy words of love and power,
Sower of truth's eternal seed,
Tongue of the one unchanging creed! (2)

## Praying Always: Prayers for the Whole Day

### GOING OUT OF MY HOUSE

*Angele Dei qui custos es mei, me tibi commissam pietate superna illumina, custodi, rege, et guberna.* [Angel of God, my guardian dear, to whom His love commits me here, ever this day be at my side, to light and guard, to rule and guide.]

### COMING HOME

Glory be to the Father, and to the Son, and to the Holy Ghost, as it was in the beginning, is now, and ever shall be, world without end. Amen.

### GOING INTO A HOUSE

Refrain my tongue from evil and my lips that they speak no guile.

### COMING OUT OF A HOUSE

Have mercy upon me, O God, according to thy great mercies, and according to the multitude of thy tender mercies blot out all my offences.

### GOING INTO A ROOM

O Sacred Heart of Jesus, I implore thy grace to love thee daily more and more.

### COMING OUT OF A ROOM

O Mary, conceived without sin, pray for us who have recourse to thee.

### GOING INTO A CHURCH

Blessed be Jesus in the Most Holy Sacrament of the Altar.

### TAKING HOLY WATER

O precious Blood of Jesus, cleanse me from all my sins.

### GENUFLECTING TO THE BLESSED SACRAMENT

O Sacred Heart of Jesus, I implore the grace to love thee daily more and more.

### BEFORE A STATUE OF THE IMMACULATE CONCEPTION

*Tota pulchra es, Maria, and macula originalis non est in te.* [All lovely art thou, O Mary, and the stain of Original Sin is not in thee.]

### BEFORE A MATER DOLOROSA

Mother of Sorrows, pray for me now and at the hour of my death. Or:

*Sancta Mater, istud agas*
*Crucifixi fige plagas*
*Corde meo valide.*

[Holy Mother, pierce me through.
In my heart each wound renew
Of my Saviour crucified.]

### BEFORE A CRUCIFIX

Behold, O kind and most sweet Jesus, I cast myself upon my knees in thy sight, and with the most fervent desire of my soul, I pray and beseech Thee that Thou wouldst impress upon my heart lively sentiments of faith, hope and charity, with true contrition for my sins, and a firm purpose of amendment, while with deep affection and grief of soul I ponder within myself and mentally contemplate thy five wounds, having before my eyes that which David, thy prophet, spoke of thee, my Jesus: 'They have pierced my hands and my feet; they have numbered all my bones.' Or:

*O Crux, ave, spes unica,*
*Hoc Passionis tempore,*
*Piis adauge gratiam*
*Reisque dele crimina.*

[Hail Cross, thou only hope of man,
Hail on this holy Passion day!
To saints increase the grace they have;
From sinners purge their guilt away.]

### BEFORE AN IMAGE OF OUR LADY AND CHILD

The first words, or the whole, of the Hail Mary.

### BEFORE THE IMAGE OF A SAINT

Saint...pray for me now and at the hour of my death.

### GOING OUT OF A CHURCH

Lord, now lettest thou thy servant depart in peace, or *Deus meus et omnia* [My God, and my all].

### PASSING BEFORE A CHURCH

I have loved the place where thy glory dwelleth. *Adoremus in aeternum Sanctissimum Sacramentum.* [Let us adore forever the Most Holy Sacrament.]

### GOING UP OR DOWNSTAIRS

*Deus in adiutorium meum intende. Domine, ad adiuvandum me festina.* [O God, incline unto my aid. O Lord, make haste to help me.]

### OPENING A LETTER

God be merciful to me, a sinner.

CLOSING ONE

*Deus meus et omnia.* [My God, and my all.] If it is for a charitable object, *Propter te, Deus meus.* [For thee, my God]. If it is a refusal, 'Hail Mary', also a Hail Mary for every beggar or petitioner I refuse, or 'God have mercy on her (or him) and on me a poor sinner.'

BEGINNING TO READ

*Deus in adiutorium meum intende.* [O God, incline unto my aid.]

CLOSING THE BOOK

*Domine, ad adiuvandum me festina.* [O Lord, make haste to help me.]

BEGINNING TO WRITE

*Veni, sancte Spiritus,*
*Et emitte caelitus*
*Lucis tuae radium.*

[Come, thou holy Paraclete,
And from thy celestial seat
Send thy light and brilliancy.]

LEAVING OFF [WRITING]

*Deus meus et omnia.* [My God, and my all].

GOING INTO A ROOM FOR CHARITABLE AFFAIRS, OR TO SEE A POOR PERSON, OR TO HAVE
A CONVERSATION WITH SOMEONE

*Veni, Pater pauperum,*
*Veni, dator munerum,*
*Veni, lumen cordium.*

[Father of the poor, draw near,
Giver of all gifts, be here,
Come, the soul's true radiancy.]

COMING FROM IT

Have mercy upon me, O God, according to thy great mercies, or *Deo gratias* [Thanks be to God], or God be merciful to me a sinner.

GRACE BEFORE MEALS

My God, make me thankful, and keep me from sin.

AFTER A MEAL

*Deo gratias* [Thanks be to God]. Blessed be God for all His mercies.

### LAST EJACULATIONS AT NIGHT

My God, into thy hands I commend my spirit, for thou hast redeemed me, O Lord, thou God of truth.

### FIRST IN THE MORNING

O Sacred Heart [of Jesus, I place all my trust in thee.] Immaculate Heart of Mary, pray for me.

### WHEN THE CLOCK STRIKES

May the most just, most amiable will of God, be in all things done and praised and exalted above all forever. (3)

NOTES AND SOURCES

1. Georgiana Fullerton, Retreat Notes, *The Inner Life of Lady Georgiana Fullerton* (London: Burns & Oates, n.d.), 231.

2. Georgiana Fullerton, *The Gold-digger and Other Verses* (London: Burns & Oates, 1872), 81–2.

3. Fullerton, Retreat Notes, 271–5.

## Edward Caswall, Cong. Orat. 1814–1878

Edward Caswall, convert clergyman and Oratorian priest, was a poet whose hymns are sung by both Protestants and Catholics throughout the English-speaking world. The son of a clergyman, he was educated at Marlborough and Brasenose College, Oxford. After taking Anglican orders, he became the incumbent of a parish in the diocese of Salisbury. In 1841 he married Louisa Stuart Walker, and in 1845, with his wife, he made a tour of the continent, which left him with a feeling of profound attraction to the Catholic Church. He resigned his living in March 1846, and, with his wife, was received into the Church a year later. After Louisa's death in 1849, he joined the Birmingham Oratory, whose founder and father, Blessed John Henry Newman, had by his writings influenced Caswall's decision to become a Catholic. He was ordained priest in 1852. As an Anglican, he had published humorous works and a collection of sermons, but as a Catholic, he devoted himself chiefly to poetry and the translation of the Latin hymns of the Breviary. He is buried with his Oratorian brethren at Rednal.

### Christ's Twofold Parentage

Christ has two Parents, in a twofold scheme,
A twofold birth sublime;
A Father, from eternity supreme,
A Mother, born in time.

He from His Father, by a termless birth,
Without a Mother came;
Created highest Heav'n, this lower earth,
And all the starry frame.

He from His Mother, in the midst of years,
Without a Father born,
Drain'd to the dregs the chalice of our tears,
Then died in pain and scorn.

O peerless mystery of depth and height,
In one same Person seen !
O finite closely knit with Infinite !
Celestial with terrene !

Jesu, by thy eternal Father's might,
Hear thou my trembling prayer;
Thou who art God of God, and Light of Light,
Omnipotent to spare !

Jesu, by thy sweet Mother's tender love,
Look tenderly on me;
Remember, mighty as thou art above,
I am one flesh with thee! (1)

## Christmas

See, amid the winter's snow,
Born for us on earth below,
See, the tender Lamb appears,
Promis'd from eternal years !
   *Hail, thou ever-blessed morn !*
   *Hail, Redemption's happy dawn!*
   *Sing through all Jerusalem,*
   *Christ is born in Bethlehem!*

Lo, within a manger lies
He who built the starry skies;
He, who thron'd in height sublime,
Sits amid the Cherubim!
   *Hail, thou ever-blessed morn* etc.

Say, ye holy Shepherds, say,
What your joyful news to-day;
Wherefore have ye left your sheep
On the lonely mountain steep ?
   *Hail, thou ever-blessed morn* etc.

'As we watch'd at dead of night,
Lo, we saw a wondrous light;
Angels singing peace on earth,
Told us of the Saviour's birth.'
   *Hail, thou ever-blessed morn* etc.

Sacred Infant all divine,
What a tender love was thine;
Thus to come from highest bliss,
Down to such a world as this!
   *Hail, thou ever-blessed morn* etc.

Teach, O teach us, Holy Child,
By Thy face so meek and mild,
Teach us to resemble Thee,
In Thy sweet humility !
   *Hail, thou ever-blessed morn* etc.

Virgin Mother, Mary blest,
By the joys that fill thy breast,
Pray for us that we may prove
Worthy of our Saviour's love.
   *Hail, thou ever-blessed morn* etc. (2)


## The Sacred Humanity of Our Lord

It is my sweetest comfort, Lord,
   And will forever be,
To muse upon the gracious truth
   Of thy humanity.

O joy, there sitteth in our flesh,
   Upon a throne of light,
One of a human mother born,
   In blazing Godhead bright.

Though earth's foundations should be moved
   Down to their lowest deep;
Though the whole sunder'd universe
   Into destruction sweep,

For ever God, for ever man,
   My Jesus shall endure;
And fix'd on Him, my hope remains
   Eternally secure. (3)


## Corpus Christi, Lauds: *Verbum supernum prodiens*

The Word, descending from above,
   Though with the Father still on high,

Went forth upon His work of love,
   And soon to life's last eve drew nigh.

He shortly to a death accursed
   By a disciple shall be given;
But, to His twelve disciples, first
   He gives Himself, the Bread from Heaven.

Himself in either kind He gave;
   He gave His Flesh, He gave His Blood;
Of flesh and blood all men are made;
   And He of man would be the Food.

At birth our brother He became;
   At meat Himself as good He gives
To ransom us He died in shame;
   As our reward, in bliss He lives.

O saving Victim! Opening wide
   The gate of Heav'n to man below.
Sore press our foes from every side;
   Thine aid supply, thy strength bestow.

To thy great Name be endless praise,
   Immortal Godhead, One in Three,
Oh, grant us endless length of days,
   In our true native land, with thee. (4)

## From the Office of the Holy Ghost

### MATINS

May the Spirit of glory
   His grace on us pour,
Whose presence o'ershadow'd
   The Virgin of yore,
When she the Archangel's
   Glad embassy heard,
And conceived in the flesh
   The ineffable Word.

### PRIME

Pure offspring of Mary's
   Immaculate womb,
Lifted up on the Cross,
   Laid low in the tomb,
Lo! Christ from His bondage
   Doth quickly arise,

And in sight of His brethren
  Ascend to the skies.

TERCE

His brethren He wills not
  As orphans to leave,
And on Pentecost morn
  His Spirit doth give,
Descending in power
  Their hearts to inspire,
In semblance of tongues
  Of miraculous fire.

SEXT

Straight wholly replenish'd
  From Wisdom's high throne,
Earth's languages all
  Are to them as their own;
And nothing accounting
  Of danger or death,
They speed through the nations
  The Catholic faith.

NONE

O Spirit of charity,
  Virtue and might,
Anointed by whom
  They fought the good fight.
Our sevenfold treasure,
  And life-spring divine,
Dread Finger of God,
  All glory be thine.

VESPERS

So lovingly named
  By the lips of the Lord,
Our teacher and guide
  And Consoler adored;
From Satan, from sin,
  And from all evil things,
The shelter bestow
  Of thy fostering wings.

COMPLINE

Thy splendour enlighten
  Our minds with its ray;

Thy guidance direct us
   Along the true way;
So when at the solemn
   Tribunal we stand,
May the Saviour set us
   Upon His right hand.

COMMENDATION

This honour and worship,
   My Paraclete dear,
I render to thee
   With devotion sincere,
And in hope by thy grace
   When I slumber to rest
To merit a place
   In the land of the blest. (5)

## The Most Holy Sacrifice of the Mass

When the Patriarch was returning
   Crown'd with triumph from the fray,
Him the peaceful king of Salem
   Came to meet upon his way;
Meekly bearing bread and wine,
   Holy Priesthood's awful sign.

On the truth thus dimly shadow'd,
   Later days a lustre shed;
When the great High Priest eternal,
   Under forms of wine and bread,
For the world's immortal food,
   Gave His Flesh and gave His Blood.

Wond'rous gift ! The Word who fashion'd
   All things by His might divine,
Bread into His Body changes,
   Into His own Blood the wine;
What though sense no change perceives,
   Faith admires, adores, believes.

He who once to die a Victim
   On the Cross, did not refuse,
Day by day, upon our altars,
   That same Sacrifice renews;
Through His holy priesthood's hands
   Faithful to His last commands.

While the people all uniting
  In the Sacrifice sublime,
Offer Christ to His high Father,
  Offer up themselves with Him;
Then together with the priest
  On the living Victim feast. (6)

## The Rock of Peter

Yes, there are times
When through my being's depth,
Shoots an ecstatic thrill
Of bounding gratitude for mercies past;
  To think that now,
From sophistry's black web,
From deadly subtle snare
Of heresy, I am escaped at last.

O happy I!
Who, spent by baffling surge,
Have now at length my foot
  Upon the Rock of Peter firmly set;
Round which the waves
Tumultuous rage in vain;
Vainly have raged of old,
And still in vain shall rage through ages yet.

Now let the hills
Be swept into the sea;
Let the floods lift their voice;
And mountains shake before the roaring deep;
  I on the Rock
Of ages safe from harm,
Will lay me down in peace,
And all amid the wrack securely sleep.

Thou o'er my head
Lulling the fretful sea,
Star of the deep, shine down,
Still evermore the same in storms or calms,
  And send sweet dreams
Of Paradise to me,
Taking my happy rest
Safe in my everlasting Father's arms. (7)

## Dependence on Internal and External Grace

O Lord, behold a sinner kneel
　Before thy gracious throne,
Confessing what he truly is,
　Left to himself alone.

Didst thou remove the inward stay
　Of thy supporting power,
No sin there is I might not do
　Within a single hour.

Or leaving me the grace I have,
　Didst thou a moment cease
To curb those outward elements
　That war against my peace,

How quickly would my nature run
　The way temptation led;
Become to sin again alive,
　Again to virtue dead.

Within, without, I lean on thee;
　On thee for aid rely;
Oh still my outward life protect,
　My inward life supply. (8)

NOTES AND SOURCES

1. Edward Caswall, *Hymns and Poems, Original and Translated*, new edn. (London: Burns & Oates, 1908), 279–80.
2. Ibid. 280–1.
3. Ibid. 276.
4. Ibid. 65.
5. Ibid. 134–6.
6. Ibid. 159–60.
7. Ibid. 453–4.
8. Ibid. 248.

# (Wilfrid) Frederick William Faber　　　　　1814–1863

Father Faber's memorial is the Brompton Oratory, whose vast congregations, now as at the beginning, are as catholic as the Church and as the sympathies of its founder. He was the scourge of the conventionalism of Victorian piety, but his own family, of partly Huguenot blood, was an icon of Establishment respectability. His father was secretary to the Prince-Bishop of Durham, Shute Barrington, and his uncle an Evangelical theologian and Master of Sherburn hospital. After Harrow, he went up to Oxford, where he won a scholarship at University College, attended the services at St Mary's, and soon made himself, as he put it, an 'acolyth' of the vicar, John Henry Newman. Towards the end of his second year, his Evangelicalism reclaimed him for a time, but hearing Pusey's Septuagesima sermon in 1836 changed his mind, and he began to identify himself with the Tractarians. Poetry was his great love, and with Wordsworth, older than him by almost two generations, he established a friendship of surprising equality of respect. Ordained to the Anglican ministry, he became Rector of Elton in Huntingdonshire. Just over a month after Newman's conversion, he decided to make his submission to the Church. He preached a sermon to his parishioners explaining his reasons, then took off his surplice and threw it on the floor. As he left the village, the people shouted from their windows, 'God bless you, Mr Faber, wherever you go'. Once received, Faber and his friends set themselves up as a religious community, won the patronage of the Earl of Shrewsbury, and, from a house on his land, Cotton Hall near Cheadle, set about converting the neighbourhood to the Catholic faith, and with remarkable success: 150 were received in the space of four months. Early in 1847 Faber and his 'Wilfridians' joined Newman's Oratory in Birmingham, but the clash of chemistry between the two men led to the establishment, under Faber's leadership, of a separate and eventually independent Oratorian community in London. The hymns of Father Faber have become the anthems of English-speaking Catholic identity. One of his prose works, *The Foot of the Cross*, in French translation, was read by St Thérèse of Lisieux and inspired one of her 'pious recreations' (religious plays for performance in Carmel). As a preacher, Faber never lost the fire he had as an evangelical; indeed, not long after his conversion he said that the more 'Roman' he became, the more he seemed to recover, 'only in a safe way and with makeweights', his 'old boyish evangelical feelings'. Once on a mission, when he realized he was failing to get through to the people in the pews, he cried out, 'How can I touch your hearts? I have prayed to Jesus, I have prayed to Mary. Whom shall I pray to next?' Then, on his knees, he went on, 'I will pray to *you*, my dear Irish children, to have mercy on your own souls', and the whole congregation fell to its knees with him. Faber's difficulties with Newman, his weaknesses of character, and the embarrassment that modern sophisticates feel in relation to his hymnody have obscured the insights of his spiritual doctrine and the quality of much of his verse. Faber is long overdue for reappraisal. If his writings edified St Thérèse, a Doctor of the Church and the 'greatest saint of modern times', as St Pius X called her, they have something to teach us all.

## Our Heavenly Father

My God! how wonderful Thou art,
  Thy Majesty how bright,
How beautiful thy Mercy-Seat
  In depths of burning light!

How dread are thine eternal years,
  O everlasting Lord!
By prostrate spirits day and night
  Incessantly adored.

How beautiful, how beautiful
  The sight of thee must be,
Thine endless wisdom, boundless power,
  And awful purity!

Oh how I fear thee, living God!
    With deepest, tenderest fears,
And worship thee with trembling hope,
    And penitential tears.

Yet I may love thee too, O Lord!
    Almighty as thou art,
For thou hast stooped to ask of me
    The love of my poor heart.

Oh then this worse than worthless heart
    In pity deign to take,
And make it love thee, for thyself
    And for thy glory's sake.

No earthly father loves like thee,
    No mother half so mild
Bears and forbears, as thou hast done,
    With me thy sinful child.

Only to sit and think of God,
    Oh what a joy it is!
To think the thought, to breathe the Name,
    Earth has no higher bliss.

Father of Jesus, love's Reward!
    What rapture will it be,
Prostrate before thy Throne to lie,
And gaze and gaze on thee! (1)


## The Divine Mercy

Mercy is the tranquillity of His omnipotence and the sweetness of His omnipresence, the fruit of His eternity and the companion of His immensity, the chief satisfaction of His justice, the triumph of His wisdom, and the patient perseverance of His love. Wherever we go, there is mercy, the peaceful, active, broad, deep, endless mercy of our heavenly Father. If we work by day, we work in mercy's light, and we sleep at night in the lap of our Father's mercy. The courts of Heaven gleam with its outpoured prolific beauty. Earth is covered with it, as the waters cover the bed of the stormy sea. Purgatory is as it were its own separate creation, and is lighted by its gentle moonlight, gleaming there soft and silvery through night and day. Even the realm of hopeless exile is less palpably dark than it would be, did not some excesses of mercy's light enter even there. (2)

## The Incarnation, the Church, and the Sacraments: God Seeks Our Love

A creature the Creator cannot be, but He will have a created nature, and make it unspeakably one with His divine person, so that He may be more like one of us, and heighten our reverence by the trembling freedoms of our familiarity, if only He may so enjoy vast augmentations of human love. If because we fell, He changed the manner of His coming, if rather than abandon His coming He plunged His Mother and Himself in a very ocean of sorrows, if, without humbling us by telling us of the change, He contentedly took shame for glory, suffering for joy, suffering for a kingdom, the Cross instead of the crown, what did it all but show but that He would still have our love, and that with ingenious compassion, which could only be divine, He would take the advantage of our miseries to exalt us all the more, and so win more abundant love? If He came only because we had fallen, if He condescended to be but a remedy for an evil, if He stooped to fight our battle in person, and in human flesh, with our triumphant enemy, if the Incarnation was an interference to prevent His own world from being stolen from Him, if it was a fresh invention out of the boundless resources of the divine pity, then still what does it mean but that He would have not let us go, He would not let us lose ourselves, because in His strangely persevering goodness He would not lose our love?

So again what is the Church but His way of rendering the blessings of His Incarnation omnipresent and everlasting? What is the Baptism of infants but a securing prematurely, and as it were against all reason, the eternal love of their unconscious souls? What is Confession, but mercy made common, justice almost eluded, the most made out of the least? These are human words, but they express something true. What is the Sacrament of Confirmation but an act of jealousy, lest the world should steal from God what He had already got? What is the Sacrament of Matrimony, but a taking of the stuff and substance of human life, its common sorrows and joys, its daily smiles and tears, the wear and tear of its rough and smooth, and elevating it all by a sort of heavenly transfiguration into a ceaseless fountain of supernatural and meritorious love? What is Extreme Unction, but an expression of affectionate nervousness, if we may so speak, of our dearest Lord, lest we should fail Him just at the last, when so many risks are run? What is the Sacrament of Order, but systematizing and ensuring a succession of daily miracles, such as consecrations, absolutions, exorcisms, and benedictions, each one of which is to create, and then to fertilize, and then to beautify, a little world of love for Him? Ask the Divine Solitary of the tabernacle why He lives His hermit life amongst us, and what could His answer be but this—I wait, to show love to and to receive it? But wide as He has made the ample bosom of His Church, and though He has multiplied with a commonness, which almost injures reverence, the potent Sacraments, this is not enough. None must slip through, if He can but help it. None must be lost except in His despite. There must be something still left, which needs no priest, something as wide as air and as free, which men may have when they cannot have, or at the needful moment cannot find, the Sacraments of His own loving institution.

One thing there is, and one only, and we are not surely now surprised to find that one thing: love. If need be, love can baptize without water, can confirm without chrism, can absolve without ordination, can almost communicate without a Host. For, great as are the Sacraments, love is a higher emanation of that priesthood which is forever according to the order of Melchizedek. (3)

## The Incarnation and the Divine Perfections

The deepest and most profitable devotion to the Incarnation is that which never loses sight for a single moment of our Blessed Lord's Divinity; and the richest as well as the safest devotion to the Divine Perfections is that which contemplates them in connection with the mysteries of the Incarnation....

To some the Divine Attributes lie always in the light of the Most Holy Trinity, and they can read God best by the splendour cast upon Him by the Eternal Generation of the Son or the Unbeginning Procession of the Spirit. To others again the treasures of the Godhead are unlocked by a series of shocks or sweet surprises, as is the case when we allow the mystery of the Incarnation to unfold for us the hidden recesses of the Godhead.

Thus the littleness of the Babe of Bethlehem, touched in our hearts by the faith in His Divinity, sends us by a kind of impulse far into the understanding of His infinity. The shame of Calvary lets us deeper down into His essential glory, than we should else have had the momentum to penetrate; for the abysses of God are waters in which it is hard for nature to sink. Of itself it only floats like driftwood on the surface. The thirst and fatigue of Jesus at the well of Jacob throw a light around Him as Creator, which has a startling clearness, and compels an instantaneous worship of speechless tears. This is the characteristic of devotion to the Divine Perfections through the Incarnation, that it impels us by these shocks deeper into the hiding-places of the Immense Majesty than we should otherwise have been able to go. (4)

## Making Christ's Mysteries Our Own

The grand thing at which we must aim is to bring it to pass that Our Lord's mysteries, His Passion and Childhood especially, should be continually in our thoughts. They should not be in the least like some past history, about which we may feel poetical, or sentimental, or have favourite views. But they should be as if they were living, contemporaneous, going on perpetually before our eyes, and in which we ourselves are actors. This is the difference between the mysteries of the Incarnate Word in the New Testament, and the glorious manifestations of God in the Old Testament. These last are our lesson; the first are our life. They do not simply remain written there, and shine. They live, they put forth attractions, they give power, they hold grace, they transform. The vitality of the Incarnation has gone into them...So by assiduous meditation, by sorrowing love or by rejoicing love, must we wear our way into the mysteries of Jesus, assimilating them to ourselves, living in them, feeling with them, until their mere character of history has added to itself the reality of a worship, and His Heart as it were beats in ours, as another, better, and supernatural life. (5)

## The Virginity of Our Lady and the Worship of the Heavenly Father

Even the virginity of Our Lord's earthly Mother is a kind of worship of His Heavenly Father, as if to have had a created father would have dimmed the Father's glory in the Eternal Generation. Thus did Mary's virginity rise up for ever in voiceless waves of exquisite incense, or like the fragrance of a spice-tree shaken by the wind, before the Paternity on high, an incense of which she herself in silent ecstasy was ever conscious, and which the Babe watched as it rose at all hours, gently forcing its way to the distant throne, like the spiral smoke-wreaths of the sweet gums climbing the altar to the Blessed Sacrament; and He watched it with His Infant eyes with an ineffably tender jubilee. But even independently of these mysteries, the whole spirit of the Sacred Infancy is always taking us by the hand and leading us softly up to the Eternal Father. (6)

## Our Lady's Expectation

Like the dawning of the morning,
On the mountain's golden heights,
Like the breaking of the moonbeams
On the gloom of cloudy nights,
Like a secret told by angels,
Getting known upon the earth,
Is the Mother's Expectation
Of Messias' speedy birth!

Thou wert happy, blessed Mother!
With the very bliss of Heaven,
Since the angel's salutation
In thy raptured ear was given;
Since the Ave of that midnight,
When thou wert anointed Queen,
Like a river overflowing
Hath the grace within thee been.

On the mountains of Judea,
Like the chariot of the Lord,
Thou wert lifted in thy spirit
By the uncreated Word;
Gifts and graces flowed upon thee
In a sweet celestial strife,
And the growing of thy Burden
Was the lightening of thy life.

And what wonders have been in thee
All the day and all the night,

While the angels fell before thee,
To adore the Light of Light.
While the glory of the Father
Hath been in thee as a home,
And the sceptre of creation
Hath been wielded in thy womb.

And the sweet strains of the psalmist
Were a joy beyond control,
And the visions of the prophets
Burnt like transports in thy soul;
But the Burden that was growing,
And was felt so tenderly,
It was Heaven, it was Heaven,
Come before its time to thee.

Oh the feeling of thy Burden,
It was touch and taste and sight;
It was newer still and newer,
All those nine months, day and night.
Like a treasure unexhausted,
Like a vision unconfess'd,
Like a rapture unforgotten,
It lay ever at thy breast.

Every moment did that Burden
Press upon thee with new grace;
Happy Mother! thou art longing
To behold the Saviour's Face!
Oh, His Human Face and Features
Must be passing sweet to see;
Thou hast seen them, happy Mother!
Ah then, show them now to me.

Thou hast waited, child of David!
And thy waiting now is o'er!
Thou hast seen Him, blessed Mother!
And wilt see Him evermore!
O His Human Face and Features!
They were passing sweet to see
Thou beholdest them this moment;
Mother, show them now to me. (7)

## St Joseph, Our Father

There are many saints above
Who love us with true love,
Many angels ever nigh;

But Joseph! none there be,
Oh none, who love like thee,—
Dearest of Saints! be near us when we die.

Thou wert guardian of our Lord,
Foster-father of the Word,
Who in thine arms did lie:
If we his brothers be,
We are foster-sons to thee,—
Dearest of Saints! be near us when we die.

Thou wert Mary's earthly guide,
For ever at her side,
Oh for her sake hear our cry;
For we follow in thy way,
Loving Mary as we may;—
Dearest of Saints! be near us when we die.

Thou to Mary's virgin love
Wert the image of the Dove,
Who was her Spouse on high;
Bring us gifts from Him, dear Saint!
Bring us comfort when we faint;
Dearest of Saints! be near us when we die!

Thou wert a shadow thrown,
From the Father's summit lone,
Over Mary's life to lie;
Oh be thy shadow cast
O'er our present and our past
Dearest of Saints! be near us when we die!

Sadly o'er the desert sand,
Into Egypt's darksome land,
As an exile didst thou fly;
And we are exiles too,
With a world to travel through;
Dearest of Saints! be near us when we die!

When thy gentle years were run,
On the bosom of thy Son,
Like an infant didst thou lie:
Oh by thy happy death,
In that tranquil Nazareth,
Dearest of Saints! be near us when we die! (8)

## The Cold of the Christmas Cave

The winter's night will almost freeze the Precious Blood within His veins. But what is the whole world but a polar sea, a wilderness of savage ice with the arctic sunshine glinting off from it in unfertile brightness, a restless glacier creeping onwards with its huge talons, but whose progress is little better than spiritual desolation? The Sacred Heart of the Babe of Bethlehem has come to be the vast central fire of the frozen world. It is to break the bands of the long frost, to loosen the bosom of the earth, and to cover it with fruits and flowers. (9)

## Corpus Christi

Jesus! My Lord, my God, my All!
How can I love thee as I ought?
And how revere this wondrous gift,
So far surpassing hope or thought?
Sweet Sacrament! we thee adore!
Oh make us love thee more and more!

Had I but Mary's sinless heart
To love thee with, my dearest King!
Oh with what bursts of fervent praise
Thy goodness, Jesus, would I sing!
Sweet Sacrament! we thee adore!
Oh make us love thee more and more!

Ah see! within a creature's hand
The vast Creator deigns to be,
Reposing infant-like, as though
On Joseph's arm, or Mary's knee.
Sweet Sacrament! we thee adore!
Oh make us love thee more and more!

Thy Body, Soul, and Godhead, all!
O mystery of love divine!
I cannot compass all I have,
For all thou hast and art are mine!
Sweet Sacrament! we thee adore!
Oh make us love thee more and more!

Sound, sound His praises higher still,
And come, ye angels, to our aid,
'Tis God! 'tis God! the very God
Whose power both men and angels made!
Sweet Sacrament! we thee adore!
Oh make us love thee more and more!

Ring joyously, ye solemn bells!
And wave, oh wave, ye censers bright!
'Tis Jesus cometh, Mary's Son,
And God of God, and Light of Light!
Sweet Sacrament! we thee adore!
Oh make us love thee more and more!

O earth! grow flowers beneath His feet,
And thou, O sun, shine bright this day!
He comes! He comes! O Heaven on earth!
Our Jesus comes upon His way!
Sweet Sacrament! we thee adore!
Oh make us love thee more and more!

He comes! He comes! the Lord of Hosts,
Borne on His throne triumphantly!
We see thee, and we know thee, Lord;
And yearn to shed our blood for thee.
Sweet Sacrament! we thee adore!
Oh make us love thee more and more!

Our hearts leap up; our trembling song
Grows fainter still; we can no more;
Silence! and let us weep—and die
Of very love, while we adore.
Great Sacrament of love divine!
All, all we have or are be thine! (10)

## Come to Jesus

Souls of men! why will ye scatter
Like a crowd of frightened sheep?
Foolish hearts! why will ye wander
From a love so true and deep?

Was there ever kindest shepherd
Half so gentle, half so sweet
As the Saviour who would have us
Come and gather round His Feet?

It is God: His love looks mighty,
But is mightier than it seems:
'Tis our Father: and His fondness
Goes far out beyond our dreams.

There's a wideness in God's mercy,
Like the wideness of the sea:
There's a kindness in His justice,
Which is more than liberty.

There is no place where earth's sorrows
Are more felt than up in Heaven;
There is no place where earth's failings
Have such kindly judgement given.

There is welcome for the sinner
And more graces for the good;
There is mercy with the Saviour;
There is healing in His Blood.

There is grace enough for thousands
Of new worlds as great as this;
There is room for fresh creations
In that upper home of bliss.

For the love of God is broader
Than the measures of man's mind;
And the Heart of the Eternal
Is most wonderfully kind.

But we make His love too narrow
By false limits of our own;
And we magnify His strictness
With a zeal He will not own.

There is plentiful redemption
In the Blood that has been shed;
There is joy for all the members
In the sorrows of the Head.

'Tis not all we owe to Jesus;
It is something more than all;
Greater good because of evil,
Larger mercy through the fall.

Pining Souls! come nearer Jesus,
And oh come not doubting thus,
But with faith that trusts more bravely
His huge tenderness for us.

If our love were but more simple,
We should take Him at His word;
And our lives would be all sunshine
In the sweetness of Our Lord. (11)

## At the Hour of our Death: Our Blessed Lady

The Most Holy Mother of God... [has] a very peculiar and distinct jurisdiction over deathbeds. The Church points this out to us again and again, in hymns and antiphons, as well as in the Hail Mary. The revelations of the saints, the teaching of devotional writers, and the universal sense of the faithful unite in proclaiming the power which God has given her in this particular respect. Some have spoken of it as the reward which Jesus has bestowed upon her for her heroic presence with her broken heart on Calvary. Others have said that it belonged to her as Queen of Mercy, because the hour of death is so wonderfully mercy's hour. All agree that deathbeds form a department of the Church, if we may speak so familiarly, which belongs to her officially. We should therefore be out of harmony with the Church, if this consideration did not practically enter into our devotion to our blessed Lady. The experience of all who grow in holiness is that they grow also in tenderest devotion and deepest reverence for our blessed Mother. We are always learning her anew, and so beginning to love her, as if what we had felt for her before was hardly worthy of the name of love. As the rest of our devotion to her grows, so also must our dependence on her aid in our last hour grow within our hearts. We shall pray to her more fervently about it. We shall make compacts with her, to which we shall assume her consent, that either by herself or by her angels she will fortify us by her presence at that dread moment. We shall entrust our fears to her, and leave to the management of her maternal solicitude every one of those circumstances of death, the very least detail of which is to us of such surpassing interest. (12)

## Kindness and its Power to Convert

We often begin our own repentance by acts of kindness, or through them. Probably the majority of repentances have begun in the reception of acts of kindness, which, if not unexpected, touched men by the sense of their being so undeserved. Doubtless the terrors of the Lord are often the beginning of that wisdom, which we name conversion, but men must be frightened in a kind way, or the fright will only make them unbelievers. Kindness has converted more sinners than zeal, eloquence, or learning, and these three last have never converted anyone, unless they were kind also. (13)

## Fidelity to the Duties of Daily Life

Your temptation is to postpone your duties as a mother to the exercises of the spiritual life... I want you to see that your fault is all from self-love.

First, God imposes your duties as a mother upon you, whereas you choose and impose your spiritual exercises on yourself.

Secondly, your disposition prefers the spiritual exercises to being teased with the children, and in a spirit of immortification you take what you like best, and neglect what you like least. So that it is your own will and your own choice that you are worshipping all through, and not the sweet adorable will of God.

Now I do not want you to go into excess, nor to neglect the spiritual life, but I want you fully to understand, 1. That the spiritual life consists far more in the interior spirit in which you do things than in the things themselves which you do. 2.

That it consists rather in the circumstances which Providence has placed you than in devotions or prayers. 3. That the fact that your external duties are less pleasant to you is a sign that you must more than ever give yourself to them, as a practice or mortification; and 4. That duties which concern the salvation of others are of greater moment when they *are* duties than spiritual exercises and private devotions.

I know how weak and ill you are, and I do not want to exact from you what you may have neither health nor spirits to bear. But I want you, 1., to have the children more with you; 2. to look after their faults more; 3. to talk to them more of God, Jesus Christ, our Blessed Mother and the angels; to take more pains to attach them to you and to win their love; and 5. to consider a quarter of an hour so spent of fifty times more spiritual consequence than hours of mental prayer.

Think all this over. I think you have been much in fault about it, and I dread your falling into a delusion which will spoil the whole of your spirituality.

See what an unkind letter I have written when you are so ill and suffering! But I am so very anxious about you that you will attribute it to my deep interest in you. Be sure you will have prayers here. But to please God and to do His will is the great thing, and to do it at the expense of our own is the greatest thing of all. (14)

## Faith of our Fathers

Faith of our Fathers! living still
In spite of dungeon, fire, and sword
Oh how our hearts beat high with joy
Whene'er we hear that glorious word:
Faith of our Fathers! Holy Faith!
We will be true to thee till death.

Our Fathers, chained in prisons dark,
Were still in heart and conscience free:
How sweet would be their children's fate,
If they, like them, could die for thee!
Faith of our Fathers! Holy Faith!
We will be true to thee till death.

Faith of our Fathers! Mary's prayers
Shall win our country back to thee;
And through the truth that comes from God
England shall then indeed be free.
Faith of our Fathers! Holy Faith!
We will be true to thee till death.

Faith of our Fathers! we will love
Both friend and foe in all our strife:
And preach thee too, as love knows how,
By kindly words and virtuous life:
Faith of our Fathers! Holy Faith!
We will be true to thee till death. (15)

NOTES AND SOURCES

1. Frederick William Faber, *Hymns* (London: Richardson & Son, 1862), 22–4.

2. Frederick William Faber, *Creator and Creature, or The Wonders of Divine Love* (London: Burns & Oates, n.d.), 164.

3. Ibid. 122–3.

4. Frederick William Faber, *Bethlehem* (London: Burns & Oates, 1860), 236–7, 238.

5. Frederick William Faber, *The Foot of the Cross, or The Sorrows of Mary* (London: Burns & Oates, n.d.), 143–4.

6. Faber, *Bethlehem*, 461–2.

7. Faber, *Hymns*, 135–7.

8. Ibid. 176–7.

9. Faber, *Bethlehem*, 132.

10. Faber, *Hymns*, 107–9.

11. Ibid. 289–91.

12. Frederick William Faber, *Spiritual Conferences* (London: Burns & Oates, 1859), 118–19.

13. Ibid. 6.

14. Frederick William Faber, Letter 108, to Mrs M., 28 September 1854, in John Edward Bowden, *The Life and Letters of Frederick William Faber* (London: Thomas Richardson & Son, 1869), 434–5.

15. Faber, *Hymns*, 265.

# Coventry Kersey Deighton Patmore 1823–1896

Coventry Patmore was the son of Peter George Patmore, who was himself a writer and the friend of Lamb, Hazlitt, and Leigh Hunt. Educated at home, he discovered and was enthralled by Dante, Chaucer, and Shakespeare. Despite his early success as a published poet, his father's financial losses forced him to seek regular employment, and for twenty years he worked as an assistant librarian at the British Museum. In 1847 he married Emily Augusta Andrews, who bore him three sons and three daughters. The happiness of his married life with Emily inspired his verse novel, *The Angel in the House* which sold over a quarter of a million copies. After Emily's death in 1862, he travelled to Rome with his friend, Aubrey de Vere, and there met a wealthy Catholic lady, Marianne Byles. After being received into the Church, he was married to Marianne by Henry Edward (later Cardinal) Manning. He bought an estate in Sussex and transformed himself, as Shane Leslie put it, from troubadour to 'fine old English gentleman'. After struggling for many years with temptations to doubt, especially about devotion to Our Lady, he went to Lourdes in 1877 and received, 'without any emotion or enthusiasm', the grace of a new tranquillity in believing. In 1878 he published his greatest work, *The Unknown Eros*, which explores the mystery of love, both divine and human. After the death of the second Mrs Patmore, he married Harriet Georgina Robson, who presented him, in his sixty-first year, with a son, Francis Epiphanius. His eldest daughter Emily became a nun and died a holy death, with her father at her side.

## The Body

Creation's and Creator's crowning good;
Wall of infinitude;

Foundation of the sky,
In Heaven forecast
And long'd for from eternity,
Though laid the last;
Reverberating dome,
Of music cunningly built home
Against the void and indolent disgrace
Of unresponsive space;
Little, sequester'd pleasure-house
For God and for His Spouse;
Elaborately, yea, past conceiving, fair,
Since, from the graced decorum of the hair,
Ev'n to the tingling, sweet
Soles of the simple, earth-confiding feet,
And from the inmost heart
Outwards unto the thin
Silk curtains of the skin,
Every least part
Astonish'd hears
And sweet replies to some like region of the spheres;
Form'd for a dignity prophets but darkly name,
Lest shameless men cry 'Shame!'
So rich with wealth conceal'd
That Heaven and Hell fight chiefly for this field;
Clinging to everything that pleases thee
With indefectible fidelity;
Alas, so true
To all thy friendships that no grace
Thee from thy sin can wholly disembrace;
Which thus 'bides with thee as the Jebusite,
That, <u>maugre</u> all God's promises could do,          [= despite]
The chosen People never conquer'd quite;
Who therefore lived with them,
And that by formal truce and as of right,
In metropolitan Jerusalem.
For which false fealty
Thou needs must, for a season, lie
In the grave's arms, foul and unshriven,
Albeit, in Heaven,
Thy crimson-throbbing Glow
Into its old abode aye pants to go,
And does with envy see
Enoch, Elijah, and the Lady, she
Who left the roses in her body's lieu.
O, if the pleasures I have known in thee
But my poor faith's poor first-fruits be,
What quintessential, keen, ethereal bliss
Then shall be his

Who has thy birth-time's consecrating dew
For death's sweet chrism retain'd,
Quick, tender, virginal, and unprofaned! (1)

## Fatherhood

My little Son, who look'd from thoughtful eyes
And moved and spoke in quiet grown-up wise,
Having my law the seventh time disobey'd,
I struck him, and dismiss'd
With hard words and unkiss'd,
His Mother, who was patient, being dead.
Then, fearing lest his grief should hinder sleep,
I visited his bed,
But found him slumbering deep,
With darken'd eyelids, and their lashes yet
From his late sobbing wet.
And I, with moan,
Kissing away his tears, left others of my own;
For, on a table drawn beside his head,
He had put, within his reach,
A box of counters and a red-vein'd stone,
A piece of glass abraded by the beach
And six or seven shells,
A bottle with bluebells
And two French copper coins, ranged there with careful art,
To comfort his sad heart.
So when that night I pray'd
To God, I wept, and said:
Ah, when at last we lie with tranced breath,
Not vexing Thee in death,
And thou rememberest of what toys
We made our joys,
How weakly understood,
Thy great commanded good,
Then, fatherly not less
Than I whom Thou hast moulded from the clay
Thou'lt leave Thy wrath, and say,
'I will be sorry for their childishness.' (2)

NOTES AND SOURCES

1. Coventry Patmore, 'To the Body', from *The Unknown Eros: Selected Poems of Coventry Patmore*, ed. with
   an introduction by Derek Patmore (London: Chatto & Windus, 1931), 73–5.
2. Coventry Patmore, 'The Toys', ibid. 10–11.

# Thomas Edward Bridgett CSSR                    1829–1899

Bridgett was the third son of the seven children of a Derbyshire mill owner. His father was a Baptist and his mother a Unitarian, but, while at Tonbridge School, he was baptized as an Anglican. As an undergraduate at St John's, Cambridge, he was attracted in turn by the broad and high movements in the Established Church. Reading Kenelm Digby and hearing Newman's lectures on *Anglican Difficulties* moved him to become a Catholic, and he was received by Father Stanton at the London Oratory on 12 June 1850. Later the same year he joined the Redemptorist Order. After seminary training in the Netherlands and ordination to the priesthood, he spent the rest of his life on the English mission. For nearly thirty years he was a member of the Redemptorist community at Clapham. His writings were chiefly historical and apologetical. The most important of them are his biographies of St John Fisher and St Thomas More, *Our Lady's Dowry* (1875), and *The History of the Holy Eucharist in Great Britain* (1881). He was a scrupulously careful scholar, and for his biography of More did much research on manuscripts in the recently established Public Record Office.

## Our Lady's Dowry

'The contemplation of the great mystery of the Incarnation', wrote Thomas Arundel, Archbishop of Canterbury, in 1399, 'has drawn all Christian nations to venerate her from whom come the first beginnings of our redemption. But we English, being the servants of her special inheritance and her own Dowry, as we are commonly called, ought to surpass others in the fervour of our praises and devotions.' (1)

## The Immaculate Virgin

The earliest Christian writers in England exhausted every epithet and title they could find to express the immaculate purity and perfect sanctity of the Blessed Mother of God. Venerable Bede quotes the words of the Irish poet Sedulius:

> To her we sing
> Who bore in time the world's eternal King,
> And peerless in the human race has found
> A mother's joy by virgin honours crown'd.

To Bede she is *Genitrix incorrupta*, the *Virgo incomparabiliter benedicta*—the Mother undefiled, the Virgin blessed beyond compare...St Aldhelm calls her 'the garden enclosed', 'the fountain sealed up', 'the one dove amid the threescore queens', and many other titles culled from the mystic Canticle of Canticles. The grave Alcuin writes verses in which he names her 'his sweet love, his honour, the great hope of his salvation, the Queen of Heaven, the flower of the field, the lily of the world, the fountain of life'.

A MS now in the University Library at Cambridge, called the Book of Cerne, and which belonged to Ethelwald, Bishop of Sherbourne in 760, contains the following prayer to the Blessed Virgin, a clear monument both of the faith and the devotion of the Anglo-Saxons in the time of Venerable Bede: 'Holy Mother of God, Virgin ever blest, glorious and noble, chaste and inviolate, O Mary Immaculate, chosen and beloved of God, endowed with singular sanctity, worthy of all praise, thou who art the advocate for the sins [peril] of the whole world: O listen,

listen, listen to us, O Holy Mary. Pray for us, disdain not to help us. For we are confident and know for certain that thou canst obtain all thou willest from thy Son, Our Lord Jesus Christ, God Almighty, the King of Ages, who liveth with the Father and the Holy Ghost, for ever and ever. Amen.' (2)

## Votive Masses of Our Lady

The origin of the Votive Masses of the Blessed Virgin is generally attributed to an Englishman, Alcuin. Froben, his editor, remarks, however, that Alcuin, according to his own assertion, merely extracted them from the Missal of his monastery at Tours. This is true. Yet Alcuin does not say that he had not been their first author, and certainly he composed one in honour of St Boniface, whose martyrdom had lately taken place. In any case, it was Alcuin who propagated them throughout Europe. 'I send you', he writes, 'a Missal chart, that you may be able on different days to direct your prayers to God, according to your devotion; sometimes in honour of the Holy Trinity, sometimes in earnest desire of wisdom, sometimes for the tears of penance, sometimes for perfect charity; or, again, if you wish to secure the prayers of the angels or of all saints. Also, should anyone wish to pray for his own sins, or for a loving friend, or for several friends, or for his brethren who are departing from this world; or when anyone wishes specially to implore the intercession of the Blessed Virgin Mary, Mother of God, or to invoke the merciful assistance of your most holy father, Boniface.' (3)

## The Evening *Salve* in Medieval England

In the statutes of St Mary Magdalen College, Oxford, Bishop Wayneflete says: 'Our pleasure is that on every Saturday throughout the year, and on all the eves of the feasts of the Blessed Virgin, after Compline, all and each of the fellows and scholars and ministers of our chapel do devoutly perform among themselves in the common hall, by note, an antiphon in honour of the glorious Virgin. By the statues for the collegiate church of Whittington College, London, it is ordained that even on ferial days, throughout the year, about or after sunset, when the poor labourers and those who live near the church are giving up work and business, when there is no reasonable hindrance, the chaplains, clerks, and choristers of the college who are at home, after the ringing of a small bell set apart for that office, shall meet in the chapel of St Mary, in the said church, and there sing to the honour of our Saviour and His Mother an antiphon with versicles and prayer. To keep up this custom many guilds were established. Stow tells us of one such called the 'Salve' in St Magnus church, near London Bridge, which was flourishing in AD 1343. Certain citizens, 'of their great devotion to the honour of God and His glorious Mother, Our Lady Mary the Virgin, began and caused to be made a chauntry to sing an anthem to Our Lady called *Salve Regina* every evening; and thereon ordained five burning wax lights at the time of the said anthem, in the honour of the five principal joys of Our Lady aforesaid ... and thereupon many other good people of the parish ... proffered to be aiders to support the said lights, and the said anthem to be continually sung, paying every person every week a halfpenny; and so that hereafter with the gifts a chaplain to say Mass for all benefactors.' This of course is only one specimen of a beautiful devotion practised throughout England. To many of my readers will have already occurred the memory of Chaucer's beautiful picture of the village school and of the boys learning to sing Our Lady's antiphon. (4)

## Prayers at the Elevation of the Sacred Host

The author of the *Ancren Riwle*, composed at the beginning of the thirteenth century, says: 'In the Mass, when the priest elevates God's Body, say these verses standing: *Ecce salus mundi*, "Behold the salvation of the world, the Word of the Father, a true Victim, living flesh, whole Godhead, very man", and then fall down with this greeting: *Ave principium nostrae creationis! Ave pretium nostrae redemptionis! Ave viaticum nostrae peregrinationis!* [Hail, principle of our creation! Hail, price of our redemption! Hail, journey-food for our pilgrimage!] But what room is there in me that my God should come to me, He who made Heaven and earth? Is it so, O Lord my God? Is there in me anything which may contain thee? Who will give me that thou wilt indeed come into my heart to inebriate it?' (5)

## The Last Mass of St Dunstan

On Ascension Day 988 [according to his biographer] Dunstan preached as he had never preached before, and as his Master, when about to suffer, had spoken of peace and charity to His disciples, and had given His Flesh and Blood for their spiritual food, so too did Dunstan commend to God the Church which had been committed to him, raising it to Heaven by his words and absolving it from sin by apostolic authority. And offering the Sacrifice of the Lamb of God, he reconciled it to God. But before the Holy Communion, having given as usual the blessing to the people, he was touched by the Holy Ghost, and pronounced the form of benediction with unusual grace. Then, having commended peace and charity to all, while they looked on him as on an angel of God, he exclaimed: 'Farewell for ever.' (6)

## Henry III's Devotion to Mass

The piety that Edward I thought to transmit to his children he had inherited from his father, Henry III, of whom Walsingham gives the following account: 'Every day he was wont to hear three Masses with music (*cum nota*), and, not satisfied with that, was present at many Low Masses, and when the priest elevated the Lord's Body, he used to support the priest's hand and kiss it. (7)

NOTES AND SOURCES

1. Thomas Edward Bridgett, *Our Lady's Dowry, or How England Gained and Lost That Title: A Compilation* (London: Burns & Oates, 1875), 1.

2. Ibid. 23–4.

3. Ibid. 154.

4. Ibid. 169–70.

5. Thomas Edward Bridgett, *A History of the Holy Eucharist in Great Britain*, new edn. with notes by H. Thurston SJ (London: Burns & Oates, 1908), 100.

6. Ibid. 112.

7. Ibid. 251.

# Herbert Alfred Henry Joseph Thomas Cardinal Vaughan

1832–1903

If there were space, many pages in this anthology might be devoted to the family of Herbert Vaughan. He was the eldest of the thirteen children of Colonel John Francis Vaughan and his first wife, Elizabeth Louisa Rolls, a fervent convert who prayed for an hour each day before the Blessed Sacrament asking God to give her family the grace of a vocation. Her prayers were answered. Six of the sons became priests (three of them bishops), and all five of the daughters entered religious life. Bernard, the Jesuit son, said of his mother that 'she made Heaven such a reality to us that we felt that we knew more about it, and liked it in a way far better even than our own home, where, until she died, her children were wildly, supremely happy'. Herbert Vaughan was in every respect the nobleman: in appearance and by family, and in the moral qualities of his soul. He was tall, majestic in bearing, and in his youth, according to Shane Leslie, was judged by his friends to be 'about the handsomest man in England'. He was a good shot and a sound horseman. But as priest and bishop, this scion of the recusant aristocracy, this seeming squirearch of the old school, displayed an astonishing breadth of sympathy and an unflagging apostolic zeal. He was the founder of St Joseph's College for missionaries at Mill Hill, and sent priests to work with the emancipated slaves in the American South. He spent twenty years as the Bishop of Salford, opening missions and building schools and orphanages. Against his own will, he succeeded his friend and mentor, Cardinal Manning, as Archbishop of Westminster. At the time of Viscount Halifax's discussions with the Abbé Portal, sensing the dangers of a false irenicism, he suggested to the Holy See that it should examine the question of Anglican Orders, and from the commission that was then established came the Apostolic Letter *Apostolicae curae*. Westminster Cathedral is his personal achievement. He chose both its architect, John Francis Bentley, and its Byzantine style; and his funeral Mass in 1903 was the first official function to take place in the completed building. For thirty-five years, he enjoyed a friendship of warm affection, unblemished purity, and practical collaboration with Lady Herbert of Lea, who after his death preserved the letters from which we take the extracts below. Cardinal Vaughan was buried on the Calvary ridge at St Joseph's, but in 2005 the body was moved to a tomb in his cathedral.

## Spiritual Dryness

I am not surprised you have been going through a time of desolation and spiritual dryness. You will have these periods, and they are useful to prove your love and the strength of grace acting upon a will that receives no support from the sensible affections. You must be very patient under it, and not for a moment subtract from prayer or give yourself more to activity in its place. We only said to trust Him more; to aid ourselves by reading and by prayer, and He will accomplish what is beyond our power to attain. I shall say Mass for you tomorrow, that we may both grow during the next year more and more fervent in His service, more and more dead to self, more and more purified from earthly motives, and more and more helpful to one another. (1)

## The Last Things

I received the last Sacraments on the 19 and thought St Joseph would have come for me, but he saw I was not ready then. Perhaps I may be on the 25 [March]—perhaps later. A good son delights to enjoy the presence of a good father, to share his company, his interests and even his nature, and his happiness. We are always saying 'Our Father who art in Heaven', and then secretly adding, 'but whatever you do, leave me where I am'. Do we believe? We weep and wail over the death of those we love, because we do not sensibly believe that they have gone home to their real Father and to all their best friends. Of course, I know that Our Father wishes us to do all we can by ordinary and natural means, to prolong our life of work and probation, and I have nothing to reproach myself with in this matter. I have got a good male nurse and every care needful. But a man over seventy has a right to look with a certain yearning towards the end. And we who are 'slaves' have our own little rights and hopes, which our Mother and St Joseph will keep an eye on ... You may be sure if I get home before you, I will do more for you there than I ever could on earth. (2)

## O Blessed Trinity!

How can I thank you for all your charity and kindness? Only by praying for you and helping you all I can towards that Eternal Life which we live for here below. *O Beata Trinitas!* To be, to know, and to love forever in that incomprehensible mystery of Love: this is happiness to look forward to. This is enough to make us both work and account all pains and losses here as nought for the greatness and intensity of the gain. Here is gold indeed, not for silver but for dross and earth. What utter fools we are to hesitate as we often do! (3)

NOTES AND SOURCES

1. Herbert Vaughan, New Year's Eve 1869, in *Letters of Herbert Cardinal Vaughan to Lady Herbert of Lea, 1867 to 1903*, ed. Shane Leslie (London: Burns & Oates, 1942), 137.
2. Herbert Vaughan, 22 March 1903, ibid. 453. The Cardinal died on 19 June 1903.
3. Herbert Vaughan, 26 December 1868, ibid. 133–4.

# (Arthur) Bertrand Wilberforce OP 1839–1904

Arthur Wilberforce, Bertrand as he became in religion, was the son of Newman's friend, Henry, and the grandson of the great abolitionist, William. When his father was received into the Church in 1850, he and the other children were conditionally baptized. From his mother, he said later in life, he had received, even as a little Anglican, an influence that was nothing but Catholic. He was sent to Ushaw for the diocesan priesthood, but after ordination as a deacon he decided to join the Dominicans. Despite his poor health, and even in his final illness, he travelled up and down the country preaching in parishes and religious houses. He was remembered for the sweetness of his voice, his gentleness, heroic kindness, sense of humour, and extreme unpunctuality—though his confrère Father Vincent McNabb suspected that what in others was a fault was in him a mystical perfection, because 'Father Bertrand's mind ranged mostly in eternity'. Before anything else he preached the mercy of God. 'Yes,' he said when criticized for devoting so many sermons to that subject, 'that is what draws sinners. You should be careful to have sermons of that kind at all stages of the mission, so that sinners may be touched and won.'

## Real Catholics

Once, when visiting an ancient church in the south of England, he was accosted by a strange gentleman who asked him if he were the vicar of the parish.

'No,' [Father Bertrand] replied. 'by the mercy of God, I have the great honour of being a Catholic priest.'

'Ah,' said the other, 'I suppose you mean *Roman* Catholic.'

'There is not the least necessity for using the word, since there are no Catholics who are *not* Roman.'

'Humph,' answered the gentleman, who turned out to be a curate belonging to the neighbourhood, 'that is a matter of opinion, I suppose.'

'On the contrary,' said Father Bertrand, 'it is a matter of divine revelation', upon which the stranger withdrew. (1)

## Modesty, Continency, and Chastity

Modesty, Continency, and Chastity make a man perfect in himself. Modesty is that nice orderly conduct that comes from remembering we are never alone, but always in God's presence; Continency makes us moderate in all lawful pleasures; and Chastity gathers up all the affections of the soul, and fixes them on God, making us avoid any kind of pleasure that we know would offend Him. (2)

## Taking up the Cross

To take up the Cross of Christ is not one action done once for all; it consists in distasteful small duties....

If I seem to be left, even by God, I become more conformed to His image who cried out in desolation on the Cross, which was His deathbed, 'My God, my God, why hast thou forsaken me?' (3)

## Unending Struggle

We *must* not be cast down because we fail and fail and fail. We all do the same, I suppose. At least, I do certainly. But one thing I am determined on—never to give up and show the white feather. (4)

## Final Perseverance

I wish you strength from the eternal Father, wisdom from the only-begotten Son, love from the co-equal Spirit, and may God continue in you His good work, and bestow on you that gift we cannot merit, but on which all depends, final perseverance. What a blessing that that is not and cannot be in our hands, for how likely should we be to fall! But we can trust His love, and are in His merciful hands. (5)

## Maxims on Prayer

We must remember that we pray not to please ourselves but God, and to do His holy will. If we keep this great principle in our minds and guide ourselves by it, we shall pray whether we feel inclined or not....

Prayer is to raise the mind and heart, that is, the will, to God. We raise the mind to Him by thinking of Him, and the will by desiring His light and help, even though no word is said....

There is no lesson harder and more important in the spiritual life, than to disregard utterly all feelings, and not be guided by them at all....

The great thing is to try and look at God, and not at ourselves. If we look at ourselves, we shall be disgusted. If we look at God, we shall be filled with hope, love, and joy....

Talking to God familiarly pleases Him most, because He loves us and loves to hear us prattle, rather than that we should read stilted things to Him. A father loves the talk of his children better than fine things dictated by a governess. (6)

## Hail Mary

Every Hail Mary is a petition to Our Lady to come and help us with the soothing unction of her presence at the hour of our death. Recite this prayer in preparation for death, day by day; and when nature fears, cry out loud, 'Pray for us now, and at the hour of our death!' (7)

## Confession

Do not be nervous about Confession. Remember that you kneel at the feet of Our Lord and speak to Him, and try to forget His minister, a poor sinful man who goes every week to Confession himself, but who has power from Our Lord, as minister of the Sacrament, to forgive your sins in the name and by the authority of Christ our Saviour. (8)

## Bad Thoughts

When thoughts pass through the imagination, or dwell there for a considerable time, there is no sin, however bad the thought is, as long as the will does not consent. It is not well to examine this much, because that is the way to encourage scruples. It is enough if you ask yourself, 'Am I certain I gave consent?', and if you are not certain, then you may conclude that there was not full consent at least, even though there might have been some weakness and want of prompt control of the thoughts. (9)

## Suffering: The Loss of One's Reason

If He wants you to live with disordered brain, why not, as well as with disordered liver? What matter? The image of God is in the soul. If that is in grace, why care if He desires the brain of 'His own' to be disordered? I feel no difficulty myself in this. I do pray that, if I should go mad, it may be evident to all that I am, so that no scandal may be given. I do not think that I should much mind, if it were God's will: Burgess Hill is a very pleasant place! But do not allow your imagination to dwell on it. Say, once for all, 'whatever is thy will I thank thee for.' After all, if He did will me to go mad, He, if I love Him, is bound by His gracious promise to make it 'work together unto good'. Again, if I went really mad, I could not sin, and sin is the only unmixed evil. (10)

## Suffering: Beautification by Love

God allows His friends to suffer that they may be polished and beautified, that their love may be purified, and so that they may not only go straight to Heaven, but may also have a far higher place in His Kingdom than if they had not suffered much and so many things. It is not in anger but love. (11)

## Real Presence, Real Absence

He used to say, 'I do not care about visiting Protestant churches; the Real Absence is so painfully obvious.' (12)

## Holy Communion and Death

Both Holy Communion and death lead me to Jesus Christ—the one to Him veiled, the other to Him visible. (13)

## Purgatory

It is very unkind and uncharitable to think that people go straight to Heaven, and because we love them to leave them without help in Purgatory. But it is happy to think of them there, because, though they suffer, they love God purely, they cannot sin, they are certain of Heaven. (14)

## Hope

Hope is not a Cardinal Virtue, but much more, one of the three Theological Virtues, that is, one of the virtues that join the soul to God. It is a supernatural virtue and as necessary as faith. Hope is the certain expectation that God in His mercy, through the merits of Christ, will give us life everlasting. It is our own nothingness that makes us put all our hope in God only, so that the fact of having done nothing for God need not tempt anyone to despair, because God is the God of the present: He looks to what you are now. If you thought yourself good, and that you deserved Heaven, that would be the perilous thing. (15)

NOTES AND SOURCES

1. H. M. Capes OSD, *The Life and Letters of Father Bertrand Wilberforce of the Order of Preachers* (London: Sands, 1912), 180–1.

2. *Some Maxims of Father Bertrand Wilberforce OP* (London: Catholic Truth Society, 1912), 23.

3. Ibid. 15, 26.

4. Capes, *Life and Letters*, 98.
5. Ibid. 186.
6. *Some Maxims*, 4–8.
7. Ibid. 19.
8. Capes, *Life and Letters*, 141.
9. Ibid. 153.
10. Ibid. 196.
11. Ibid. 261.
12. Ibid. 182.
13. *Some Maxims*, 26.
14. Ibid. 18.
15. Capes, *Life and Letters*, 177.

# Gerard Manley Hopkins SJ                           1844–1889

Hopkins's poetry surpasses the work of all the other poets of the nineteenth century in the deep grounding of its metaphysics, the grandeur of its theological vision, the gruelling honesty of its humanity, and the inventiveness of its language and forms. Born in Stratford, Essex, into the large family of a prosperous actuary, Hopkins was a rebellious schoolboy at Highgate before in 1863 going up on an exhibition to Balliol, where he read Ruskin, had tutorials with Jowett and Pater, and established what would be a lifelong friendship with Robert Bridges. On 21 October 1866 he was received into the Catholic Church by Blessed John Henry Newman. After leaving Oxford, he taught at Newman's Oratory School in Birmingham, and while there decided that God was calling him to be a Jesuit. Convinced that the writing of poetry was incompatible with the religious life, he burned most of the poems he had composed since his schooldays. While doing his philosophy at St Mary's Hall in Lancashire, he discovered the metaphysics of Duns Scotus, who attracted him by his interest in particularity ('thisness', *haecceitas*). After three years of theology at St Beuno's in North Wales, he was ordained to the priesthood on 27 September 1877. A series of teaching and parochial assignments in London, Oxford, and Lancashire was followed by his appointment as Professor of Classics at University College, Dublin, where he suffered from depression, wrote his 'terrible' sonnets, and died of peritonitis on 11 June 1889. He is buried in the Jesuit section of Prospect cemetery at Glasnevin. In his struggles with interior darkness and the wounds of his own personality, Hopkins looked beyond the consolations of art to a transcendent, theological aesthetic, 'God's better beauty, grace'. His poems remained in manuscript until Robert Bridges had them published in 1918.

## God's Grandeur

The world is charged with the grandeur of God.
  It will flame out, like shining from shook foil;
  It gathers to a greatness, like the ooze of oil
Crushed. Why do men then now not reck his rod?
Generations have trod, have trod, have trod;
  And all is seared with trade; bleared, smeared with toil;
  And wears man's smudge and shares man's smell: the soil
Is bare now, nor can foot feel, being shod.

And for all this, nature is never spent;
   There lives the dearest freshness deep down things;
And though the last lights off the black West went
   Oh, morning, at the brown brink eastward, springs—
Because the Holy Ghost over the bent
   World broods with warm breast and with ah! bright wings. (1)

## The Religion of Christ

Religion is the highest of the moral virtues, and sacrifice the highest act of religion. Also self-sacrifice is the purest charity. Christ was the most religious of men, to offer sacrifice was the chief purpose of His life, and that the sacrifice of Himself.

Reigning in Heaven, He could not worship the Father,[1] but when He became man and entered upon His new nature, the first thing He did in it was to adore God in it. As entering church we bless ourselves, as waking in the morning we are told to lift our hearts to God, so Christ no sooner found Himself in human nature than He blessed and hallowed it by saluting His heavenly Father, raising His new Heart to Him, and offering all His new being to His honour. That offering was accepted, but He was told that the sacrifice must be accomplished on the Cross of shame, and so from the first His sorrow was always in His sight. Every moment of His life He was unflinchingly renewing or keeping up His first offer, offering His Body to crucifixion, His Blood to be shed. This was Christ's Sacrifice, and how unspeakably dear to the eternal Father was this devotion of His only-begotten Son! This, then, is why Christ's Blood is so precious in the eternal Father's eyes. (2)

## The Windhover: To Christ Our Lord

I caught this morning morning's minion, king-
   dom of daylight's dauphin, dapple-dawn-drawn Falcon, in
     his riding
   Of the rolling level underneath him steady air, and striding
High there, how he rung upon the rein of a wimpling wing
In his ecstasy! then off, off forth on swing,
   As a skate's heel sweeps smooth on a bow-bend: the hurl and
     gliding
   Rebuffed the big wind. My heart in hiding
Stirred for a bird,—the achieve of; the mastery of the thing!

Brute beauty and valour and act, oh, air, pride, plume, here
   Buckle! AND the fire that breaks from thee then, a billion
Times told lovelier, more dangerous, O my chevalier!

---

[1] In a note, Hopkins's editor, Father Christopher Devlin SJ, explains this statement: '. . . because, as God, the Son is equal to the Father. Therefore "the Word was made flesh" in order to express the love of His Father through adoration' (*The Sermons and Devotional Writings of Gerard Manley Hopkins* (London: Oxford University Press, 1959), 275).

> No wonder of it: shéer plód makes plough down sillion
> Shine, and blue-bleak embers, ah my dear,
>     Fall, gall themselves, and gash gold-vermillion. (3)

## The God-Man

He was your maker in time past; hereafter He will be your judge. Make Him your hero now. Take some time to think of Him; praise Him in your hearts. You can over your work or on your road praise Him, saying over and over again: Glory be to Christ's body; Glory to the body of the Word made flesh; Glory to the body suckled at the Blessed Virgin's breasts; Glory to Christ's body in its beauty; Glory to Christ's body in its weariness; Glory to Christ's body in its Passion, Death, and Burial; Glory to Christ's body risen; Glory to Christ's body in the Blessed Sacrament; Glory to Christ's soul; Glory to His genius and wisdom; Glory to His unsearchable thoughts; Glory to His saving words; Glory to His Sacred Heart; Glory to its courage and manliness; Glory to its meekness and mercy; Glory to its every heartbeat, to its joys and sorrows, wishes, fears; Glory in all things to Jesus Christ, God and man. (4)

## The Missions of the Son and the Holy Ghost

Christ came into this world to glorify God His Father; the Holy Ghost came to glorify Christ. Christ made God known by appearing in human shape; the Word took flesh and dwelt amongst us; the Holy Ghost makes Christ known by living in His Church, He makes His temple in Christian hearts and dwells within us. Christ glorified the Father by His Death and Resurrection; the Holy Ghost glorifies Christ by the persecutions and the triumphs of the Catholic Church. Christ was Himself but one and lived and died but once; but the Holy Ghost makes of every Christian another Christ, an AfterChrist, lives a million lives in every age, is the courage of the martyrs, the wisdom of the doctors, the purity of the virgins, is breathed into each at Baptism, may be quenched by sin in one soul, but then is kindled in another, passes like a restless breath from heart to heart and is the spirit and life of all the Church: what the soul is to the human body that, St Austin says, the Holy Ghost is to the Church Catholic, Christ's Body Mystical. If the Holy Ghost is our spirit and our life, if He is our universal soul, no wonder, my brethren, no wonder He is our Paraclete in a way, too, that Christ alone could never be. (5)

## Duns Scotus's Oxford

> Towery city and branchy between towers;
> Cuckoo-echoing, bell-swarmèd, lark-charmèd, rook-racked,
>     river-rounded;
> The dapple-eared lily below thee; that country and town did
> Once encounter in, here coped and poisèd powers;
>
> Thou hast a base and brickish skirt there, sours
> That neighbour-nature thy grey beauty is grounded

Best in; graceless growth, thou hast confounded
Rural rural keeping—folk, flocks, and flowers.

Yet ah! this air I gather and I release
He lived on; these weeds and waters, these walls are what
He haunted who of all men most sways my spirits to peace;

Of realty the rarest-veinèd unraveller; a not
Rivalled insight, be rival Italy or Greece;
Who fired France for Mary without spot. (6)

## The Blessed Virgin compared to the Air we Breathe

Wild air, world-mothering air,
Nestling me everywhere,
That each eyelash or hair
Girdles; goes home betwixt
The fleeciest, frailest-flixed
Snowflake; that's fairly mixed
With, riddles, and is rife
In every least thing's life;
This needful, never spent,
And nursing element;
My more than meat and drink,
My meal at every wink;
This air, which, by life's law,
My lung must draw and draw
Now but to breathe its praise,
Minds me in many ways
Of her who not only
Gave God's infinity
Dwindled to infancy
Welcome in womb and breast,
Birth, milk, and all the rest
But mothers each new grace
That does now reach our race—
Mary Immaculate,
Merely a woman, yet
Whose presence, power is
Great as no goddess's
Was deemèd, dreamèd; who
This one work has to do—
Let all God's glory through,
God's glory which would go
Through her and from her flow
Off, and no way but so.
    I say that we are wound

With mercy round and round
As if with air: the same
Is Mary, more by name.
She, wild web, wondrous robe,
Mantles the guilty globe,
Since God has let dispense
Her prayers his providence:
Nay, more than almoner,
The sweet alms' self is her
And men are meant to share
Her life as life does air.
    If I have understood,
She holds high motherhood
Towards all our ghostly good
And plays in grace her part
About man's beating heart,
Laying, like air's fine flood,
The deathdance in his blood;
Yet no part but what will
Be Christ our Saviour still.
Of her flesh he took flesh:
He does take fresh and fresh,
Though much the mystery how,
Not flesh but spirit now
And makes, O marvellous!
New Nazareths in us,
Where she shall yet conceive
Him, morning, noon, and eve;
New Bethlems, and he born
There, evening, noon, and morn—
Bethlem or Nazareth,
Men here may draw like breath
More Christ and baffle death;
Who, born so, comes to be
New self and nobler me
In each one and each one
More makes, when all is done,
Both God's and Mary's Son.
    Again, look overhead
How air is azurèd;
O how! Nay do but stand
Where you can lift your hand
Skywards: rich, rich it laps
Round the four fingergaps.
Yet such a sapphire-shot,
Charged, steepèd sky will not
Stain light. Yea, mark you this:
It does no prejudice.

The glass-blue days are those
When every colour glows,
Each shape and shadow shows.
Blue be it: this blue heaven
The seven or seven times seven
Hued sunbeam will transmit
Perfect, not alter it.
Or if there does some soft,
On things aloof, aloft,
Bloom breathe, that one breath more
Earth is the fairer for.
Whereas did air not make
This bath of blue and slake
His fire, the sun would shake,
A blear and blinding ball
With blackness bound, and all
The thick stars round him roll
Flashing like flecks of coal,
Quartz-fret, or sparks of salt,
In grimy vasty vault.
  So God was God of old:
A mother came to mould
Those limbs like ours which are
What must make our daystar
Much dearer to mankind;
Whose glory bare would blind
Or less would win man's mind.
Through her we may see him
Made sweeter, not made dim,
And her hand leaves his light
Sifted to suit our sight.
  Be thou then, O thou dear
Mother, my atmosphere;
My happier world, wherein
To wend and meet no sin;
Above me, round me lie
Fronting my froward eye
With sweet and scarless sky;
Stir in my ears, speak there
Of God's love, O live air,
Of patience, penance, prayer:
World-mothering air, air wild,
Wound with thee, in thee isled,
Fold home, fast fold thy child. (7)

## The Rosary

It is dwelling on Christ's life in Mary His Mother's company, calling her to witness
how good He is, how merciful, how afflicted, how glorified by God, and so forth. (8)

## To what serves Mortal Beauty?

To what serves mortal beauty—dangerous; does set danc-
ing blood—the O-seal-that-so  feature, flung prouder form
Than Purcell tune lets tread to? See: it does this: keeps warm
Men's wits to the things that are; what good means—where a
    glance
Master more may than gaze,  gaze out of countenance.
Those lovely lads once, wet-fresh  windfalls of war's storm,
How then should Gregory, a father,  have gleanèd else from
    swarm-
èed Rome? But God to a nation  dealt that day's dear chance.
To man, that needs would worship block or barren stone,
Our law says: Love what are  love's worthiest, were all known;
World's loveliest—men' s selves. Self flashes off frame and
    face
    What do then? how meet beauty?  Merely meet it; own,
Home at heart, heaven's sweet gift;  then leave, let that alone.
Yea, wish that though, wish all,  God's better beauty, grace. (9)

## Carrion Comfort

Not, I'll not, carrion comfort, Despair, not feast on thee;
Not untwist—slack they may be—these last strands of man
In me ór, most weary, cry *I can no more.* I can;
Can something, hope, wish day come, not choose not to be.

But ah, but O thou terrible, why wouldst thou rude on me
Thy wring-world right foot rock? lay a lionlimb against me?
    scan
With darksome devouring eyes my bruisèd bones? and fan,
O in turns of tempest, me heaped there; me frantic to avoid
    thee and flee?
Why? That my chaff might fly; my grain lie, sheer and clear.
Nay in all that toil, that coil, since (seems) I kissed the rod,
Hand rather, my heart lo! lapped strength, stole joy, would
    laugh, chéer.
Cheer whom though? the hero whose heaven-handling flung
    me, fóot tród
Me? or me that fought him? O which one? is it each one?
    That night, that year
Of now done darkness I wretch lay wrestling with (my God!)
    my God. (10)

## That Nature is a Heraclitean Fire and of the Comfort of the Resurrection

Cloud-puffball, torn tufts, tossed pillows  flaunt forth, then
    chevy on an air-
built thoroughfare: heaven-roysterers, in gay-gangs  they
    throng; they glitter in marches.
Down roughcast, down dazzling whitewash,  wherever an
    elm arches,
Shivelights and shadowtackle in long  lashes lace, lance, and
    pair.
Delightfully the bright wind boisterous  ropes, wrestles, beats
    earth bare
Of yestertempest's creases; in pool and rutpeel parches
Squandering ooze to squeezed  dough, crust, dust; stanches,
    starches
Squadroned masks and manmarks  treadmire toil there
Footfretted in it. Million-fuelèd,  nature's bonfire burns on.
But quench her bonniest, dearest  to her, her clearest-selvèd
    spark
Man, how fast his firedint,  his mark on mind, is gone!
Both are in an unfathomable, all is in an enormous dark
Drowned. O pity and indig  nation! Manshape, that shone
Sheer off, disseveral, a star,  death blots black out; nor mark
    Is any of him at all so stark
But vastness blurs and time  beats level. Enough! the Resur-
    rection,
A heart's-clarion! Away grief's gasping,  joyless days, de-
    jection.
    Across my foundering deck shone
A beacon, an eternal beam.  Flesh fade, and mortal trash
Fall to the residuary worm;  world's wildfire, leave but ash:
    In a flash, at a trumpet crash,
I am all at once what Christ is,  since he was what I am, and
This Jack, joke, poor potsherd,  patch, matchwood, immortal
diamond,
                Is immortal diamond. (11)

## From 'The Wreck of the Deutschland': The Conversion of England

Dame, at our door
Drowned, and among our shoals,
Remember us in the roads, the heaven-haven of the
    reward:
    Our King back, Oh, upon English souls!
Let him easter in us, be a dayspring to the dimness of us,

Be a crimson-cresseted east,
   More brightening her, rare-dear Britain, as his reign rolls,
      Pride, rose, prince, hero of us, high-priest,
Our hearts' charity's hearth's fire, our thoughts' chivalry's
      throng's Lord. (12)

NOTES AND SOURCES

1. Gerard Manley Hopkins, *The Poems of Gerard Manley Hopkins*, ed. W. H. Gardner and N. H. MacKenzie, new edn. (London: Oxford University Press, 1970), 66.

2. Gerard Manley Hopkins, Sermon for 6 July 1879, the Feast of the Precious Blood, St Clement's Chapel, Oxford, in *The Sermons and Devotional Writings of Gerard Manley Hopkins* (London: Oxford University Press, 1959), 14–15.

3. Hopkins, *Poems*, 69.

4. Gerard Manley Hopkins, Sermon for 23 November 1879, St Joseph's, Bedford Leigh, in *Sermons and Devotional Writings*, 38.

5. Gerard Manley Hopkins, Sermon for 15 May, the Fourth Sunday after Easter, St Francis Xavier's, Liverpool, in *Sermons and Devotional Writings*, 99–100.

6. Hopkins, *Poems*, 79.

7. Ibid. 93–7.

8. Gerard Manley Hopkins, Sermon for 18 Sunday after Pentecost, St Joseph's, Bedford Leigh, in *Sermons and Devotional Writings*, 29.

9. Hopkins, *Poems*, 98.

10. Ibid. 99–100.

11. Ibid. 105–6.

12. Ibid. 63. 'The Wreck of the Deutschland' was inspired by the drowning in the Thames Estuary of five Franciscan nuns, exiled from Germany by the Falck Laws, on the midnight and morning of 7 December 1875.

# Joseph Rickaby SJ                                    1845–1932

Joseph Rickaby's long life connects the English Jesuits of Hopkins's time with the generation of D'Arcy and Martindale. Born in Yorkshire, he took his undergraduate degree at the University of London before going on to join the Society of Jesus. His work was chiefly that of a teacher of philosophy and theology, though he also published collections of retreat conferences. His greatest achievement is his annotated and abridged translation of St Thomas's *Summa contra Gentiles*. He wrote with grace and a lightness of touch about the weightiest of subjects. His final days were spent at St Beuno's in North Wales.

## The Mother in the House

'As the sun rising on the world in the high places of God, so is the beauty of a good woman the adornment of her house . . . Foundations abide forever on a solid rock, and the commandments of God abide in the heart of a holy woman' (Ecclus. 26: 21, 24). It has pleased God to put a *good woman* in His house, which is the Church. He created her and endowed her from the first in goodness, natural and supernatural: that was the grace of her Immaculate Conception. He chose her for Mother of His Only-begotten made man, and in gracing her with motherhood,

He still preserved her maidenhood: that was the grace of the Virgin Birth and the Divine Maternity. In the Holy Family she was Mother: she was mistress of the Holy House at Nazareth, out of which grew the Universal Church. She stood in her Mother's place by the side of her dying Son, and He bequeathed her, His one human treasure, to John and in John to all His beloved disciples, to be cared for and to care for them as their Mother. Clearly, she was chief of the knot of holy women who were with the Apostles on the day of Pentecost. As the House of God opened out, and was enlarged, and became thronged, her place was found by the hearth, at the very centre of the mysteries of Christianity. The theology of the Word incarnate, defined at Nicea and Ephesus, was the theology of Mary *Theotokos*. 'Going into the house', men 'found the Child with Mary His Mother' (Matt. 2: 11). The Child would be lonely, the house desolate, were the Mother taken away. And not the Eldest born only would be lonely, but also the other children (cf. Luke 2: 7; Ps. 88: 27; Rom. 8: 29; Col. 1: 15–18; Apoc. 13: 17). A Mother, a 'good woman' in the house, is an essential of our spiritual life. For a Catholic to cease to have recourse to Mary would be to compromise salvation. Happily, no Catholic from infancy thinks of doing such a thing. But converts are not always converted to Mary, and till they are converted to her they are not safe. (1)

## Christ's Suffering in His Mystical Body

Our Lord's sufferings in His natural body ended with His death, but there is a cross and passion in His Mystical Body which He must endure till the day of judgement, and this He portions out age by age among His friends. Receiving his portion with gladness, St Paul wrote: 'Now I rejoice in my sufferings, and make up in my flesh what was wanting of the sufferings of Christ' (Col. 1: 24). (2)

## Death and Resurrection

For all purposes of this life, man is completely overthrown on the day that he lies back, dead. Doughty warrior he may have been, but this day he is totally defeated: all resistance has ceased, you may take his spoils, and carry away everything that once was his. His very body no longer belongs to him: a lawyer will tell you it is no man's property. If he had no soul, he would be routed indeed. But his soul has escaped, fled somewhere from that field of final overthrow. This is the victory of death—so far as human forces go, absolute and irreversible. The one fact that reverses it is the Resurrection of Jesus Christ, God and Man, which Resurrection means no bare series of ghostly visions, but the return of His body, dead and buried, from the tomb to life. 'And in Christ all shall be brought to life, each in his own order: the first-fruits Christ, then they that are Christ's, at His coming: then the end' (1 Cor. 15: 22–4). With this in view, any man living in the grace of God, and hoping to die in the same, may look forward to the dissolution of his body with equanimity. As St John Chrysostom puts it: 'God being about to rebuild your house removes the inhabitant while the demolition takes place, that you may not be incommoded by the dust and disorder. Then when the new edifice is ready to receive you, you shall return'. This doctrine, and the hope which it inspires, is essential to Christianity, and marks off the Christian from the pagan man, ancient or modern. (3)

## The *Spiritual Exercises*: The Meditation on Hell

A man is never an entire failure until he goes to Hell. On the shore of eternity God has set up two lights for us to steer by and so bring our bark safe into port. There is the blue light of Heaven and the red light of Hell. Of the two, we should regard rather the light of the place that we are making for, whichever it be. But the red light carries further, and may be seen at times in a storm when the blue light is obscured. Satan labours to put out both lights, but especially the red light, knowing better what that means. To trim the red light is to make a good meditation on Hell. It is worth every man's while to do that at times...

'Depart from me, ye cursed, into everlasting fire' (Matt. 25: 41). This is too terrible a sentence to come from any merely human lips. No creature is fit to be trusted with such a weapon as everlasting fire. It requires the wisdom of God to wield it, along with all God's justice and all God's mercy. No priest nor Pope can pronounce this sentence, nor ecumenical council, nor any nor all of the angels in Heaven. Christ has left to His Church the power to absolve from sin, and to condemn to spiritual penalties, but not to condemn to penalties in the world to come, still less to everlasting punishment. Only Jesus Christ, my God and Saviour, can ever condemn me to everlasting fire. I would not trust anyone else with such power, but I can trust Him. That is my comfort when I think of this terrible sentence, that it is *His* sentence. He will never condemn without consideration and every allowance made. He will condemn none but the contumacious rebel who richly deserves it, as even in the Church on earth excommunication is fulminated only upon the contumacious.

'A guilty deed is the death of the soul, but to despair is to go down into Hell' (St Isidore). A man is drowned: his hat floats to the surface and goes down the stream, as a thing cast away. A soul is lost, and all its endowments with it. Floating as it were on the upper surface of the pool of fire, we discern the natural goods of the souls engulfed there: wealth, social position, genius, beauty, honours, so many excellencies lost, because, while possessed, they were enjoyed and gloried in, but not well used. (4)

## Heaven: Our True and Everlasting Home

One mark of a great man is the faculty of making himself vastly amiable when he wishes. It was said of the first Napoleon that he could thus overpower anyone at an interview. What are we to expect when God wishes to lay Himself out to be amiable, as a father at home and at leisure for his children? 'The door is shut' (Matt. 25: 10), not only to keep the wicked out, but for the everlasting security of the blessed within the home. There is no place like home, and therefore no place like Heaven, our true and everlasting home. The day of labour is over: the evening hour has come, and the labourers are paid (cf. Matt. 20: 8): the everlasting Sabbath has set in (cf. Heb. 4: 9). There is no more need for the sun to rise (cf. Apoc. 21: 23), as man shall never again 'go out to his labour' (Ps. 102: 23), nor for the moon, for 'there shall be no night there' (Apoc. 21: 25). God our Father will be at home for all His children: He will be, so to speak, at leisure for them. The work of their probation and sanctification is over, and nothing remains but for their Father to pour out upon them the fullness of His unrestrained paternal love. He is theirs, their 'God forever and ever' (Ps. 47: 14). Not one child of the family is absent, not one false brother has been let in. Great and small, they all have the range of their Father's house: they all *see* His face; they all have 'His name on their foreheads' (Apoc. 22: 4): 'This is the glory of all his saints' (Ps. 149: 9). 'Son, thou art always with me, and all mine is thine' (Luke 15: 31). ' . . . Good Jesus, Word of the Father, brightness of the Father's glory, on whom angels long to look, teach me to do thy will, that, guided by thy good Spirit, I may arrive at that blessed city, where is eternal day and one common spirit, where is assured security and secure eternity, and eternal tranquillity and tranquil happiness, and happy sweetness and sweet delight, where thou, God with the Father and the Holy Ghost, livest and reignest world without end. Amen' (St Gregory the Great on the Penitential Psalms). (5)

NOTES AND SOURCES

1. Joseph Rickaby, *Waters That Go Softly, Or Thoughts for Time of Retreat* (London: Burns & Oates, 1906), 73–4.

2. Ibid. 136.

3. Ibid. 145–6.

4. Ibid. 32–7.

5. Ibid. 171–3.

## Francis Neil Aidan Cardinal Gasquet OSB     1846–1929

Son of a French father and a Scottish mother, Gasquet went to school at Downside, and, having decided to join the community there, did his novitiate at Belmont. After several years teaching mathematics and history in the school, he was elected prior of the abbey, but in 1885 the breakdown of his health forced him to resign. As a diversion during convalescence, he took up historical research, which was thereafter to be his life's work. The favourable reception of his publications on the Protestant Reformation in England led to his appointment to the commission on Anglican Orders set up by Pope Leo XIII. From now to his death he served the Benedictines and the Church on the national and international stage: as Abbot-President of the English Benedictine Congregation, president of the commission for the revision of the Vulgate, member of Roman Congregations, and prefect of the Vatican archives. He also played a part in the Holy See's acceptance of a special envoy of the British government at the beginning of the First World War. At his last consistory, Pope St Pius X made him a cardinal-deacon; he was later promoted to be cardinal-priest. At his own request he was buried at Downside.

### The Guilds of the Middle Ages

By whichever name we call them, and assuming the religious basis which underlay the whole social life in the fifteenth century, the character and purpose of these medieval guilds cannot in reality be misunderstood. Broadly speaking, they were the benefit societies and the provident associations of the Middle Ages. They undertook towards their members the duties now frequently performed by burial clubs, by hospitals, by almshouses, and by guardians of the poor. Not infrequently they acted for the public good of the community in the mending of roads and the

repair of bridges, and for the private good of their members, in the same way that
insurance companies today compensate for loss by fire or accident. (1)

## Religious Instruction in Medieval England

From the time of the constitution of Archbishop Peckham at the Synod of Oxford
in 1281, to the time of the religious changes, there is every reason to suppose that
the ordinance contained in the followed words was observed in every parish
church in the country: 'We order', says the Constitution, 'that every priest having
the charge of a flock do, four times in each year (that is, once each quarter) on one
or more solemn feast days, either himself or by someone else, instruct the people
in the vulgar language simply and without any fantastical admixture of subtle
distinctions, in the articles of the Creed, the Ten Commandments, the Evangelical
Precepts, the seven works of mercy, the seven deadly sins with their offshoots, the
seven principal virtues, and the seven Sacraments.'

This means that the whole range of Christian teaching, dogmatic and moral,
was to be explained to the people four times in every year; and in order that there
should be no doubt about the matter, the Synod proceeds to set out in considerable detail each of the points upon which the priest was to instruct his people.
During the fourteenth and fifteenth centuries the great number of manuals
intended to help the clergy in the execution of this law attest the fact that it was
fully recognized and very generally complied with. (2)

## The Contented Catholicity of the English
## People in Early Tudor Times

A Venetian traveller at the beginning of the sixteenth century bears witness to the
influence of religion upon the English people of that time. His opinion is all the
more valuable, inasmuch as he appeals to the experience of his master, who was
also the companion of his travels, to confirm his own impressions, and as he was
fully alive to the weak points in the English character ... In regard to the religious
practices of the people, this intelligent foreigner says, 'They all attend Mass every
day, and say many *Paternosters* in public. The women carry long rosaries in their
hands, and any who can read take the Office of Our Lady with them, and with
some companion recite it in church verse by verse, in a low voice, after the manner
of churchmen. On Sundays they always hear Mass in their parish church and give
liberal alms, because they may not offer less than a piece of money of which
fourteen are equivalent to a golden ducat. Neither do they omit any form
incumbent on good Christians.'

In these days perhaps the suggestion that the English people commonly in the
early sixteenth century were present daily at morning Mass is likely to be received
with caution, and classed among the strange tales proverbially told by travellers,
then as now. It is, however, confirmed by another Venetian who visited England
some few years later, and who asserts that every morning 'at daybreak he went to
Mass arm-in-arm with some English nobleman or other'. And, indeed, the same
desire of the people to be present daily at the Sacrifice of the Mass is attested by
Archbishop Cranmer when, after the change had come, he holds up to ridicule the
traditional observances previously in vogue. What he specially objected to was the

common practice of those who run, as he says, 'from altar to altar, and from sacring, as they call it, to sacring, peeping, tooting, and gazing at that thing which the priest held up in his hands . . . and saying, 'This day I have seen my Maker', and 'I cannot be quiet except I see my Maker once a day'. . . .

At the close of the fifteenth century, Church work was in every sense of the word a popular work, and the wills, inventories, and churchwardens' accounts prove beyond question that the people generally contributed generously according to their means, and that theirs was the initiative, and theirs the energetic administration by which the whole was accomplished . . . Those who had no money to give brought articles of jewellery, such as rings, brooches, buckles, and the like, or articles of dress or of domestic utility, to be converted into vestments, banners, and altar hangings to adorn the images and shrines, to make the sacred vessels of God's house, or to be sold for like purposes. For the same end, and to secure the perpetuity of lamps before the Blessed Sacrament, or lights before the altars of saints, people gave houses and lands into the care of the parish officials, or made over to them cattle and sheep to be held in trust, which, when let out at a rent, formed a permanent endowment for the furtherance of these sacred purposes. (3)

NOTES AND SOURCES

1. Francis Aidan Gasquet OSB, *The Eve of the Reformation: Studies in the Religious Life and Thought of the English People in the Period Preceding the Rejection of the Roman Jurisdiction by Henry VIII* (London: John C. Nimmo, 1900), 363–4.

2. Ibid. 280.

3. Ibid. 324–8.

# Alice Christiana Gertrude Meynell     1847–1922

Alice Meynell was the daughter of Thomas James Thompson, a man of private means and the friend of Charles Dickens. He educated his children by lessons at home and grand tours abroad. On 20 July 1868, Alice was received into the Catholic Church at St George's, Worcester. A few years earlier her mother had taken the same step; her sister followed her, and her father was received before his death. The Jesuit who instructed her, Father Augustus Dignam, fell in love with her, and, at his own request, asked his superiors to send him abroad. The separation moved Alice to write some of her finest poems, including 'Renouncement'. Her first collection appeared under the title *Preludes* in 1875. In 1876 she met a young Catholic journalist, Wilfrid Meynell, and married him the following year at the Servite church on the Fulham Road. There were eight children of the marriage. Alice and Wilfrid collaborated in writing for magazines, including *Merry England*, to which in 1887 Francis Thompson, then a vagrant on the streets of London, submitted a few poems and essays for publication. The Meynells took Thompson into their family and gave him their affection and every kind of practical support. As the devoted mother of eight children, Alice was always busy with domestic duties, but at the same time poured out essays, reviews, and verse. Her essays appeared in, among other publications, *The Dublin Review*. She was a friend of Tennyson and admired by, among others, Coventry Patmore and George Meredith, both of whom fell in love with her, as did Francis Thompson. Chesterton called a 'very great lady' who was always interested 'in the intimate and individual story'.

## Advent Meditation

*Rorate coeli desuper, et nubes pluant Justum,*
*Aperiatur terra, et germinet Salvatorem.*
[Drop down dew, ye heavens, from above, and let the clouds rain the just;
Let the earth be opened, and bud forth a Saviour.]

No sudden thing of glory and fear
Was the Lord's coming; but the dear
   Slow Nature's days followed each other
   To form the Saviour from His Mother
—One of the children of the year.

The earth, the rain, received the trust,
—The sun and dews, to frame the Just.
   He drew His daily life from these,
   According to His own decrees
Who makes man from the fertile dust.

Sweet summer and the winter wild,
These brought Him forth, the Undefiled.
   The happy Springs renewed again
   His daily bread, the growing grain,
The food and raiment of the Child. (1)

## Unto Us a Son Is Given

Given, not lent,
And not withdrawn—once sent,
This Infant of mankind, this One,
Is still the little welcome Son.

New every year,
New born and newly dear,
He comes with tidings and a song,
The ages long, the ages long;

Even as the cold
Keen winter grows not old,
As childhood is so fresh foreseen,
And spring in the familiar green—

Sudden as sweet
Come the unexpected feet.
All joy is young, and new all art,
And He, too, whom we have by heart. (2)

## The Crucifixion

Oh, man's capacity
For spiritual sorrow, corporal pain!
Who has explored the deepmost of that sea,
With heavy links of a far-fathoming chain?

That melancholy lead,
Let down in guilty and in innocent hold,
Yea into childish hands deliverèd,
Leaves the sequestered floor unreached, untold.

One only has explored
The deepmost; but He did not die of it.
Not yet, not yet He died. Man's human Lord
Touched the extreme; it is not infinite.

But over the abyss
Of God's capacity for woe He stayed
One hesitating hour; what gulf was this?
Forsaken He went down, and was afraid. (3)

## The Newer Vainglory

Two men went up to pray; and one gave thanks,
    Not with himself—aloud,
With proclamation, calling on the ranks
    Of an attentive crowd.

'Thank God, I clap not my own humble breast,
    But other ruffians' backs,
Imputing crime—such is my tolerant haste—
    To any man that lacks.

'For I am tolerant, generous, keep no rules,
    And the age honours me.
Thank God, I am not as these rigid fools,
    Even as this Pharisee.' (4)

## The Capuchins of Pantasaph

With large aprons tied over their brown habits, the Lay Brothers work upon their
land, planting parsnips in rows, or tending a prosperous bee-farm. A young Friar,
who sang the High Mass yesterday, is gaily hanging the washed linen in the sun. A
printing press, and a machine which slices turnips, are at work in an outhouse, and
the yard thereby is guarded by a St Bernard, whose single evil deed was that under

one of the obscure impulses of a dog's heart—atoned for by long and self-conscious remorse—he bit the poet [Francis Thompson]; and tried, says one of the friars, to make doggerel of him...

Every midnight the sweet contralto bells call the community, who get up gaily to this difficult service. Of all duties this one never grows easy or familiar, and therefore never habitual. It is something to have found but one act aloof from habit. It is not merely that the friars overcome the habit of sleep. The subtler point is that they can never acquire the habit of sacrificing sleep. What art, what literature, or what life but would gain a secret security by such a point of perpetual freshness and perpetual initiative? It is not possible to get up at midnight without a will that is new night by night. So should the writer's work be done, and, with an intention perpetually unique, the poet's. (5)

NOTES AND SOURCES

1. Alice Meynell, *The Poems of Alice Meynell* (London: Oxford University Press, 1940), 11.

2. Ibid. 95.

3. Ibid. 116.

4. Ibid. 117.

5. Alice Meynell, *Essays* (London: Burns & Oates, 1914), 121–4.

## Canon William Francis Barry                      1849–1930

Canon Barry is a fine example of that rare breed, the pastor-scholar. Born in London of Irish parents, he studied for the priesthood at Oscott and the English College. He lived long enough to see both the ending of Papal temporal power on 20 September 1870, with the white flag waving over St Peter's, and the signing of the Lateran Pact on 11 February 1929. Ordained for the Archdiocese of Birmingham in 1873, he taught philosophy at Olton and theology at Oscott, and was on the mission for forty-one years, first at Dorchester-upon-Thames and later at Leamington Spa. He wrote in many genres: theology, philosophy, history, novels, and *belles lettres*. *The Tradition of Scripture*, from which the first of our extracts comes, is an introduction to biblical studies for students.

## St John's Gospel: The Centre of the New Testament

St John is the centre to which the Synoptics and St Paul converge. He crowns the one group of writings; he sustains the other. He furnishes the link which binds Our Lord and the Church together—and thus the Fourth Gospel is typical, and a wedding song for the New Covenant, as the Canticle of Solomon was for Israel. He mediates between the extremes of Ebionite and Gnostic. He is last of Apostles and first of divines. Maintaining that the Logos became flesh, this great evangelist interprets Jesus to all time, and by so doing completes the Scriptures that 'bear witness' to Him. Wonderful how repeatedly that word falls upon the page! The manhood, but also the Godhead: 'That which was from the beginning, that which we have heard, that which we have seen with our eyes, that which we beheld and our hands handled, concerning the Word of life, and the life was manifested, and we have seen and bear witness' (1 John 1: 1–2). Under stress of the conviction which fills him, the Beloved Disciple breaks down in his speech, but in its very stammerings it is all the more persuasive.

For St John knows that Jesus is the Messiah, and that He is the Logos, the wisdom and the power of God. It shines in dark places, brings out their evil, discovers their good. The Ebionite knew Christ according to the flesh, but there his knowledge ended. The Gnostic would never own that Jesus Christ was come in the flesh; he dissolved Jesus into principalities and powers, until on one side was the Unknowable, the Deep of Silence, on the other a phantom crucified in appearance and no true man. These divergencies of error the Fourth Gospel cuts up by the roots. And in so doing, it gives us the norm, secure and unfailing, upon which we must interpret the whole Bible, if we would not go astray. To 'dissolve Jesus', and to break the Scriptures into fragments, opposed or irreconcilable, are manifestations of the same false method. To see in Christ Our Lord a mere Galilean peasant is the natural consequence of reducing the Old Testament to a human record, not inspired and not miraculous. The offence of the Cross bears a strange likeness to the scandal which many have made for themselves out of words they had not rightly construed, or a toleration of the imperfect which they judged unbecoming in the Supreme. To such it may be answered, 'I heard a voice saying, Shall mortal man be more just than God? Shall a man be more pure than his Maker? Behold, He put no trust in His servants, and His angels He charged with folly; how much less in them that dwell in houses of clay, whose foundation is in the dust!' (Job 4: 17–19).

From the prophets, interpreting the Law by a God-given revelation, Israel through synagogue and priesthood received its Old Testament. From the Apostles its larger canon passed on to the Church, and no book which now forms part of the Bible was finally acknowledged except in deference to their judgement, as the Christian Tradition apprehended it. With our sacred books their religious meaning was handed down. In the text itself, devoutly preserved, though much of it seemed dark and something here and there difficult, a provision was made for better understanding when the world should be prepared. So long as every doubtful passage was referred to the judgement-seat of Christ, an imperfect instrument like allegory could do no lasting harm. The consent of the Fathers is by no means a fiction. Amid ceaseless warfare those teachers wrought the lines upon which our Creed has been elicited from the words of Scripture and the conscience of the faithful, gathered together in the Holy Ghost. Beautiful and majestic as a theory, binding all ages in one, never to be exhausted by meditation, that Creed has also proved itself a doctrine of life, apart from which there is no other wherein to put our trust. Israel waits for the Messiah; fidelity does not comprehend Him; the Church believes and adores.

Two quotations may sum up the whole matter. The first from St Paul to Timothy: 'Abide thou in the things which thou hast learned and hast been assured of, knowing of whom thou hast learned them ... Every Scripture inspired of God is also profitable for reproof, for correction, for instruction which is in righteousness' (2 Tim. 3: 14, 16). The second from St John's Gospel: 'Many other signs did Jesus in the presence of the disciples which are not written in this book, but these are written that ye may believe that Jesus is the Christ, the Son of God, and that believing ye may have life in his name' (20: 30 f.). (1)

# Pope St Pius X

He could not rely on the forces of the world; they had turned against him. To the enemies who are bent on destroying Catholicism it may well appear that never before did they reckon so many chances in their favour. Liberals, Freemasons, Positivists, Socialists, Modernists, a motley but united array, these gathering hosts were encamped over against St Peter's shrine, in the Holy City, keeping holiday to celebrate their victorious advance. The Pope was beleaguered in the Vatican. A great painter who could indeed dip his pencil 'in the gloom of thunder and eclipse' might have shown us that solitary, saint-like apparition, clad in white raiment, lifting pure hands and beseeching eyes in prayer beneath a stormy sky, not daunted by the tumult and the shouting, saddened yet steadfast in the presence of anarchy, which boasts itself under discordant names and flags of rebellion as pledged to the liberty it will not share with Catholics, and the progress it is making in civilization falsely so-called. Pius X prayed, and did not surrender. He was in that day of rebuke and blasphemy the champion of religious freedom. There is tragedy in the picture of a Vatican so beleaguered, but there is pathos, too; for these new Liberals, who were exalting the Slave-State, with its compulsory secular education, its collective despotism, its seizure of public and private re-sources, have almost persuaded their victims that the Pope is the people's enemy. Such has been the amazing condition of the French and Latin world. If the Vatican were taken, absolute secular governments would control and exploit that world from end to end. (2)

NOTES AND SOURCES

1. William Francis Barry, *The Tradition of Scripture: Its Origin, Authority, and Interpretation* (Longmans, Green & Co., 1908), 264–6.

2. William Francis Barry, *The Coming Age and the Catholic Church: A Forecast* (London: Cassell, 1929), 8–9.

## Herbert Henry Charles Thurston SJ        1856–1939

Father Thurston was a kind of ecclesiastical Google for pre-internet England. In the first half of the twentieth century, if you were a Catholic and wanted to find out more about surprising mystics and unlikely liturgies, as well as the origins of familiar prayers and the lives of the genuinely saintly, you turned to the writings of Father Thurston: 760 articles produced for *The Month* during his nearly fifty years of editorship, 180 entries in the *Catholic Encyclopaedia*, many tracts for the Catholic Truth Society, and a dozen or so books. The only son of a doctor, he had an entirely Jesuit education in France and England before he himself entered the Society in 1874. He did his theology at St Beuno's and was ordained in 1890. After 1918, when many of the war-bereaved were resorting to mediums and séances for consolation, Father Thurston's learning, common sense, and evident devotion to the truth helped to hold back the advance of spiritualism. Although his priestly life was spent almost entirely in writing and research, he had a broad pastoral appeal as a confessor and instructor of converts. He had a lifelong love of cricket, and, like his Dominican contemporary, Vincent McNabb, did most of his travelling round London on foot. His name lives on for the Google generation through the online availability of the *Catholic Encyclopaedia*.[2]

---

[2]  <http://www.newadvent.org/cathen/>.

## The Cross: Sorrow and Victory—*The Dream of the Rood*

I am not disputing—no one can dispute—that the Cross has been to the Christians of every age an emblem of hope and victory. In the very service of Good Friday itself, amidst all the signs of mourning, this note rings out gloriously in one of the noblest hymns of the liturgy, the *Vexilla Regis*, but nothing at the same time can be more untrue to say that the aspect in which the early Christians '*invariably* viewed the Cross was that of triumph and exultation, of victory and of rapture' [Dean Farrar].[3]

The same tone may be traced in the still earlier fragments of St Melito of Sardis,[4] but I prefer to direct attention to one of the most ancient monuments of literature in this country, the *Dream of the Rood*, by the Northumbrian poet, Cynewulf, who lived in the eighth century.[5] A portion of the poem is carved in runic characters upon the Ruthwell cross. The strangely modern feeling which breathes in this composition must strike every reader. The Holy Rood is represented as describing its own anguish when it bore the Saviour of the world. The Cross explains first how it had grown to maturity at the edge of the wood, and how it was cut down to serve for a shameful purpose, a gibbet for evil-doers:

> Then mankind's Lord drew nigh,
> With mighty courage hasting Him to mount on me and die;
> Though all earth shook, I durst not bend or break without His word;
> Firm I must stand, nor fall and crush the gazing foes abhorred.
> Then the young Hero dighted Him; Almighty God was He;
> Steadfast and very stout of heart mounted the shameful tree,
> Brave in the sight of many there when man He fain would free.
> I trembled while He clasped me round, yet groundward durst not bend,
> I must not fall to lap of earth, but stand fast to the end.
>
> A rood upreared, I lifted high the great King, Lord of Heaven;
> I durst not stoop; they pierced me through with dark nails sharply driven;
> (The wounds are plain to see here yet, the open wounds that yawn),
> Yet nothing, nowise, durst I do of scathe to anyone.
> They put us both to shame, us twain. I was all wet with blood
> Shed from His side when He had sent His spirit forth to God.

I cannot quote the whole of this charming poem, but must refer the reader to the original. The four lines following, however, are too noteworthy in their Catholic spirit to be passed over:

---

[3] Frederick William Farrar (1831–1903) was Dean of Canterbury, author of the novel, *Eric, or Little by Little*, and a philologist in the modern German style. He admired the work of Charles Darwin and arranged for him to be buried in Westminster Abbey. Thurston is quoting one of Dean Farrar's sermons.

[4] St Melito, who was Bishop of Sardis in Asia Minor, died towards the end of the second century.

[5] The authorship of the *Dream* is still not known with any certainty. Cynewulf remains a likely candidate.

Lo, then, the Prince of Glory, He did greatly honour me;
The Lord of Heaven did set me high o'er every forest-tree.
E'en as His Mother, Mary's self, Almighty God had mind
To honour in the sight of men, above all womankind. (1)


## The Paschal Candle

The writers of the Middle Ages...work out in detail, according to their wont, the points of resemblance between type and antitype, between lighted pillars of wax and the person of Christ Our Lord. Indeed, it may be said that the figure lends itself in many respects with peculiar appropriateness to the elaboration of this comparison. Already the *Exsultet* reminds us how 'this [fire], though it be divided, yet loseth it not anything in the communication of its light, feeding itself from the melted wax, which the bee hath produced to make the substance of this precious torch'. Even in such wise Christ could give Himself to be the light and life of many human souls, and yet remain in Himself entire and unchanged.

Similarly, the wax of which the candle was formed, suggested to medieval minds a vivid image of the virginal conception of our blessed Lady, to whom there is explicit reference in many older forms of the *Exsultet*. The bee's singular privilege of chastity was a legend universally accepted in the Middle Ages, and supported by no less an authority than that of the pagan poet Virgil. Hence the clean wax of which the candle was made, typified the sacred flesh of Jesus Christ, which He had taken from the most pure substance of His Virgin Mother. No wonder that the pious thought of the early rubricians went on to recognize in the wick of the candle an image of the human soul of Christ, without which his sacred flesh was inert and lifeless, and to see in the blessed flame which crowned it a figure of the divine personality of the Word, coming down from Heaven to give life to the world. Whether this flame was the new fire 'struck from the veins of flint', from the rock which was Christ, as the present ceremonial prescribes, or whether, as we learn was the custom amongst Teutonic peoples in the ninth century, the fire literally came from Heaven, being obtained from the heat of the sun's rays through a burning glass, or whether, as in the oldest forms of the Roman Ritual, the light was that hidden and mystically buried with our Saviour on Good Friday, the singular aptness of the symbolism in each case need hardly be insisted upon. That the candle should be lighted at intervals from Easter to Ascension Day, and that it should have embedded in it five grains of incense, emblematic of the five Sacred Wounds, which St Thomas was bidden to touch and examine, as the precious jewels which marked that glorified body, was only a development of the idea identifying this Paschal light with the risen life of our Saviour. Taking it all in all, there is perhaps no more perfect specimen of Christian symbolism to be found in the whole of Catholic liturgy than that of the Paschal candle. (2)

NOTES AND SOURCES

1. Herbert Thurston, *Lent and Holy Week: Chapters on Catholic Observance and Ritual* (London: Longmans, Green & Co., 1904), 401–3.

2. Ibid. 410–12.

# (Edward Joseph Aloysius) Cuthbert Butler OSB     1858–1934

Cuthbert Butler promoted as a scholar, and practised as a monk, a Benedictinism of great purity and balance, while failing as an abbot to give it the communal expression for which he longed. He was born in Dublin, the son of a professor in Newman's Irish Catholic university. He went from the school at Downside into the Benedictine novitiate at Belmont, where he acquired what was to be a lifelong devotion to the spiritual doctrine of Augustine Baker and the traditional asceticism of manual labour. After his return to Downside, he was ordained priest in 1884, and in 1896 became Master of Benet House, Cambridge, the hall for Downside monks studying at the university. With his wide knowledge and intense love of early monasticism, Butler found it troubling that the English Benedictine Congregation had developed into a federation of monasteries whose chief object seemed to be pastoral, the provision of priests for parishes, rather than strictly monastic. In 1900 his concerns were met, at least in part, by the granting of autonomy as abbeys to the various houses of the Congregation. In 1906, he was elected second abbot of Downside, and set himself the task, by teaching and example, to give primacy to the liturgy and, in the spirit of Dom Augustine Baker, to the practice of mental prayer. In 1922, the failure of his efforts to reduce Downside's parochial commitments led to his resignation and transfer to Ealing Abbey, where he spent the remainder of his life. At Cambridge he had produced an edition of Palladius's *Lausiac History* and on his return to Downside had published an edition of the Holy Rule as well as a collection of essays on *Benedictine Monachism*. In retirement he published *Western Mysticism*, a biography of Bishop Ullathorne, and a history of the First Vatican Council based on Ullathorne's letters.

## Are We All Called to the Mystical Life?

Let us...consider the claim of the mystics in the light of Christian theology, beginning with the New Testament. Such texts as the following at once meet us: 'If a man love me, he will keep my words, and my Father will love him, and we will come unto him and make our abode with him' (John 14: 23). The indwelling of the Holy Ghost in the souls of the just is affirmed by St Paul in a number of places: 'Know ye not that ye are the temple of God, and that the Spirit of God dwelleth in you?' (1 Cor. 3: 16). 'Know ye not that your members are the temple of the Holy Ghost who is in you, whom ye have from God?' (1 Cor. 6: 19).

In Catholic theology, and I believe in old-fashioned Protestant theology, these texts are taken as being literally true—in the regenerate soul in a state of grace God dwells, and in an especial manner the Holy Ghost. Thus St Thomas says: 'The Holy Ghost inhabits the mind by His substance' [*Summa contra Gentiles* 4, 18]. The effect of this indwelling is further described by St Paul: 'the love of God hath been shed abroad in our hearts through the Holy Ghost who hath been given unto us' (Rom. 5: 5); and along with love the other virtues, too, and the seven Gifts of the Holy Ghost, which make the twelve Fruits of the Spirit grow in the soul. All this results in a wondrous beautifying of the soul. On this subject Fathers, theologians, preachers wax eloquent; they find it difficult to depict the spiritual beauty of the soul in the state of God's grace and friendship, inhabited by the Holy Ghost, and adorned with His Gifts. They adopt the words of 2 Peter, 'partakers of

the divine nature' (1: 4) and rise to the idea of 'deification': 'All those in whom the
Holy Ghost abides become deified by this reason alone' [St Athanasius].

And not only in the order of grace, but in that of nature is God present in every
soul: 'He is not far from each one of us, for in Him we live and move and have our
being' (Acts 17: 27). As the theologians say, God is present in all creatures in a
threefold way: by essence, by power, by presence or inhabitation, and He is in a
special way present in spiritual beings. According to the Catholic sense of divine
immanence, God working in man is more intimately present in him than man is
even in himself. This reminds us of Augustine: 'Thou art more inward to me than
my most inward part.'

When these elements of Christian doctrine are kept in view, it appears that the
claim of the mystics is hardly more than this: that what is accepted by Christian
belief as realities of faith in the case of all souls in the state of grace, becomes
consciously realized in the mystic vision. It involves hardly more than momentary
liftings of the veil that keeps hidden from the mind's eye the soul's supernatural
estate. It is an experimental perception of the presence of God in the soul, who at
all times is there.

If it be said that on this showing what would be surprising is not that the
mystical experience should sometimes take place, but rather that it should so
seldom take place: should it not be expected to be a more ordinary experience of
the spiritual life devotedly lived? To such questions the answer must be the same
as that to all questions and difficulties concerning God's distribution of graces and
favours, whether in the supernatural order or the natural: We do not know. Our
only answer can be that confession of ignorance with which St Paul concludes the
discussion of these mysterious subjects: 'O the depth of the riches both of the
wisdom and of the knowledge of God!'

There is an answer given in the *Imitation of Christ*: 'This is the reason why there
are found so few contemplative persons, because few know how to separate
themselves wholly from created and perishing things' (3, 31). And this would be
the answer of St John of the Cross, that few are willing to pay the full price in
renunciation at which alone the mystic experience can be purchased; few are
prepared to make the Ascent of Mount Carmel with him. (1)

NOTES AND SOURCES

1. Cuthbert Butler, *Western Mysticism: The Teaching of SS. Augustine, Gregory, and Bernard on Contemplation and the Contemplative Life* (London: Constable, 1922), 301–3.

# Francis Joseph Thompson                                              1859–1907

What St Benedict Joseph Labre is in Catholic sanctity, Francis Thompson is in Catholic
literature: a vagrant and perpetual pilgrim, a troubled soul, a spiritual child, a prophet at
odds with his age; he is also a poet with a voice unlike any other in our language. Born into a
family of converts in that very Catholic town which is Preston, he was sent to study for the
priesthood at Ushaw College, Durham. Having been told he was unsuitable for ordination, he
started medical training at Owens College, Manchester, but, after illness and failure in
examinations, he left in 1883. An attempt at a commercial career also ended in failure; the
army rejected him. After quarrelling with his father, he went off to London, where he lived on

the streets and indulged the addiction to opium he had acquired as a medical student. Encouraged by his first mentor in poetry, Canon (later Bishop) John Carroll, and using a poste restante address, he submitted some poems to *Merry England*, the magazine edited by Wilfrid Meynell. Struck by the freshness and power of Thompson's writing, Meynell sought him out, found him in a desperate condition, and placed him in a private sanatorium. Apparently cured of the addiction, he then spent a year with the Norbertines at Storrington. Having returned to live in lodgings in London, he worked with the Meynells on their journals. In 1892 he started taking opium again and was sent by the Meynells for a visit to the Capuchins at Pantasaph in North Wales, which he left for London in 1896. Emotional entanglements led to another return to opium in 1900. He died at dawn on 13 November 1907 in the Hospital of SS John & Elizabeth in London, and is buried at Kensal Green. Chesterton said that none of his contemporaries could understand 'his sky-scraping humility, his mountains of mystical detail, his occasional and unashamed weakness, his sudden and sacred blasphemies', and that 'perhaps the shortest definition of the Victorian age' is to say that Francis Thompson stood outside it.

## The Kingdom of God

O world invisible, we view thee,
O world intangible, we touch thee,
O world unknowable, we know thee,
Inapprehensible, we clutch thee!

Does the fish soar to find the ocean,
The eagle plunge to find the air—
That we ask of the stars in motion
If they have rumour of thee there?

Not where the wheeling systems darken,
And our benumbed conceiving soars!—
The drift of pinions, would we hearken,
Beats at our own clay-shuttered doors.

The angels keep their ancient places,
Turn but a stone, and start a wing!
'Tis ye, 'tis your estrangèd faces,
That miss the many-splendoured thing.

But (when so sad thou canst not sadder)
Cry, and upon thy so sore loss
Shall shine the traffic of Jacob's ladder
Pitched betwixt Heaven and Charing Cross.

Yea, in the night, my Soul, my daughter,
Cry, clinging Heaven by the hems;
And lo! Christ walking on the water
Not of Gennesareth, but Thames. (1)

## The Hound of Heaven

I fled Him, down the nights and down the days;
I fled Him, down the arches of the years;
I fled Him, down the labyrinthine ways
   Of my own mind; and in the mist of tears
I hid from Him, and under running laughter.
    Up vistaed hopes I sped;
    And shot, precipitated,
Adown Titanic glooms of chasmèd fears,
From those strong Feet that followed, followed after.
    But with unhurrying chase,
    And unperturbèd pace,
Deliberate speed, majestic instancy,
    They beat—and a Voice beat
    More instant than the Feet—
'All things betray thee, who betrayest Me.'

    I pleaded, outlaw-wise,
By many a hearted casement, curtained red,
Trellised with intertwining charities;
(For, though I knew His love Who followèd,
    Yet was I sore adread
Lest, having Him, I must have naught beside.)
But, if one little casement parted wide,
The gust of his approach would clash it to:
Fear wist not to evade, as Love wist to pursue.
Across the margent of the world I fled,
And troubled the gold gateways of the stars,
Smiting for shelter on their clangèd bars;
    Fretted to dulcet jars
And silvern chatter the pale ports o' the moon.
I said to dawn: Be sudden—to Eve: Be soon;
With thy young skiey blossoms heap me over
    From this tremendous Lover
Float thy vague veil about me, lest He see!
    I tempted all His servitors, but to find
My own betrayal in their constancy,
In faith to Him their fickleness to me,
    Their traitorous trueness, and their loyal deceit.
To all swift things for swiftness did I sue;
    Clung to the whistling mane of every wind.
    But whether they swept, smoothly fleet,
    The long savannahs of the blue;
Or whether, Thunder-driven,
    They clanged his chariot 'thwart a heaven,
Plashy with flying lightnings round the spurn o' their feet:—

Fear wist not to evade as Love wist to pursue.
   Still with unhurrying chase,
   And unperturbèd pace,
Deliberate speed, majestic instancy,
   Came on the following Feet,
   And a Voice above their beat—
'Naught shelters thee, who wilt not shelter Me.' (2)

## The Passion of Mary

O Lady Mary, thy bright crown
   Is no mere crown of majesty;
For with the reflex of His own
   Resplendent thorns Christ circled thee.

The red rose of this Passion-tide
   Doth take a deeper hue from thee,
In the five wounds of Jesus dyed,
   And in thy bleeding thoughts, Mary!

The soldier struck a triple stroke,
   That smote thy Jesus on the tree:
He broke the Heart of Hearts, and broke
   The Saint's and Mother's hearts in thee.

Thy Son went up the angels' ways,
   His passion ended; but, ah me!
*Thou* found'st the road of further days
   A longer way of Calvary:

On the hard cross of hope deferred
   Thou hung'st in loving agony,
Until the mortal-dreaded word
   Which chills *our* mirth, spake mirth to thee.

The angel Death from this cold tomb
   Of life did roll the stone away;
And He thou barest in thy womb
   Caught thee at last into the day,
Before the living throne of whom
   The Lights of Heaven burning pray.

### *L'Envoy*

O thou who dwellest in the day!
   Behold I pace amidst the gloom:
Darkness is ever round my way
   With little space for sunbeam-room.

Yet Christian sadness is divine
    Even as thy patient sadness was:
The salt tears in our life's dark wine
    Fell in it from the saving cross.

Bitter the bread of our repast;
    Yet doth a sweet the bitter leaven:
Our sorrow is the shadow cast
    Around it by the light of Heaven.
    O light in Light, shine down from Heaven! (3)


## The Church and Poetry

The Church, which was once the mother of poets no less than of saints, during the
last two centuries has relinquished to aliens the chief glories of poetry, if the chief
glories of holiness she has preserved for her own. The palm and the laurel,
Dominic and Dante, sanctity and song, grew together in her soil: she has retained
the palm, but forgone the laurel. Poetry in its widest sense, [that is to say, taken as
the general animating spirit of the Fine Arts,] and when not professedly irreligious, has been too much and too long either misprised or distrusted; too much
and too generally the feeling has been that it is at best superfluous, at worst
pernicious, most often dangerous. Once poetry was, as she should be, the lesser
sister and helpmate of the Church; the minister to the mind, as the Church to the
soul. But poetry sinned, poetry fell; and, in place of lovingly reclaiming her,
Catholicism cast her from the door to follow the feet of her pagan seducer. The
separation has been ill for poetry; it has not been well for religion. (4)


## St Thomas More

Ah, happy Fool of Christ! unawed
By familiar sanctities,
You served Your Lord at holy ease
Dear jester in the Courts of God!
In whose spirit, enchanting yet,
Wisdom and love, together met,
Laughed on each other for content!
That an inward merriment,
An inviolate soul of pleasure,
To your motions taught a measure
All your days; which tyrant king,
Nor bonds, nor any bitter thing
Could embitter or perturb;
No daughter's tears, nor, more acerb,
A daughter's frail declension from
Thy serene example, come

Between thee and thy much content.
Nor could the last sharp argument
Turn thee from thy sweetest folly;
To the keen accolade and holy
Thou didst bend low a sprightly knee,
And jest Death out of gravity
As a too sad-visaged friend;
So, jocund, passing to the end
Of thy laughing martyrdom,
And now from travel art gone home
Where, since gain of thee was given,
Surely there is more mirth in Heaven! (5)

NOTES AND SOURCES

1. Francis Thompson, 'The Kingdom of God', in *The Works of Francis Thompson*, ii: *Poems* (London: Burns & Dates, 1913), 226–7.

2. Francis Thompson, 'The Hound of Heaven', ibid. i, 107–8.

3. Francis Thompson, 'The Passion of Mary', ibid. 171–2.

4. Francis Thompson, 'Shelley', in *The Works of Francis Thompson*, iii: *Prose* (London: Burns & Oates, 1913), 1.

5. Francis Thompson, 'To the English Martyrs', in *Works*, ii, 131–5.

# Bede Camm OSB                    1864–1942

Bede Camm was a convert clergyman and Benedictine who, by his popular historical works, introduced the lives of the martyrs and the Catholic culture of penal times to a wide readership in the first quarter of the twentieth century. Educated at Westminster, Keble, and Cuddesdon, he took Anglican orders and served a curacy in Kensington. In 1890 he was received into the Catholic Church and not longer afterwards joined the Benedictine community at Maredsous in Belgium, a foundation made by the German abbey of Beuron, and was ordained to the priesthood there in 1895. Having for a number of years lived with another Beuronese community, at Erdington in Birmingham, in 1913 he transferred his stability to Downside. In the same year he assisted in the reception into the Catholic Church of the Anglican monks of Caldey and the nuns of Milford Haven. During the Great War he served as a chaplain to the British Army in the Middle East. From 1919 to 1931 he was Master of Benet House, Cambridge. He died in 1942 and is buried at Downside.

## Pope St Gregory the Great: The Apostle of the English

True it is that Gregory never trod these shores, but nonetheless we recognize that the instinct of our Saxon fathers who claimed him as their apostle was a true one. They knew how he had longed to rescue them from the wrath of God, and to teach them to sing the celestial Alleluia; they loved to recount how he had indeed set out for England but had been recalled ere he had gone four days' journey, in order that he might rule over the flock of Christ. And then, when raised aloft upon Peter's chair, he had still borne our country in his heart, still laboured for its conversion, hoping, as he himself wrote to Augustine, that he might share in the reward of his labours, since he had so earnestly desired to share in the toil. And thus the love and gratitude of our fathers ring out in the words of their great doctor and historian. 'We may, and we ought, to call the blessed Grgeory our Apostle,' writes St Bede, 'for though to others he was not an apostle, nevertheless he is to us, for we are the seal of his apostleship in the Lord.' And so the English Church, assembled in solemn synod in the seventh century, decreed that the feast of this blessed Pope, her apostle, should ever be kept as a day of obligation, and that the names of Gregory and Augustine should ever be solemnly invoked in the Litanies of the Saints. And we remember with emotion the name of that English prince [Caedwalla, died 689] who, renouncing his pagan faith, journeyed in pilgrimage to the threshold of the apostle, in order that he might there receive at the hands of the Successor of St Peter the sacrament of regeneration; and dying there, still clad in his chrisom robe, was laid to rest at the feet of the great Gregory, the apostle of his race. There they found him in the seventeenth century, at the time of the rebuilding of the Vatican basilica—truly a touching emblem of England's ancient faith and ancient love. (1)

## 15 August 1918: British Soldiers on Pilgrimage in Jerusalem

The crypt [of the church of St Anne] is cut in the rock, and it is there that the Jerusalem tradition tells us our blessed Lady was born. Around the church and the great adjacent buildings (seminaries for the Greek Catholic clergy) are fair gardens and courts, and here too are to be found the subterranean remains of the Pool of Bethesda where Our Lord healed the paralytic...

The pilgrims reached the church three-quarters of an hour too soon. The difficulty was overcome by putting the sermon before the Mass, and thus after a hymn had been sung, I made my way through the throng and preached from the altar-steps. It was an impressive sight that met one's eyes as one looked round. The big church was literally packed with men. The general and the officers had seats in the nave, but the choir, sanctuary, nave, and aisles, were thronged with men, some sitting on the ground, others standing pressed together so closely that the priest had the greatest difficulty in getting to the altar. All carried their messtins and haversacks, for they were to lunch in the grounds after the Mass. I shall never forget that great throng of bronzed men, who had been through so many dangers, endured so many hardships in order to deliver Jerusalem from the infidel, and had now come on Mary's crowning day to render thanks to God at the tombs of Jesus and His Mother.

It was wonderful to hear them singing the familiar hymns during the Mass that followed. I have never heard anything like that 'Faith of our Fathers' shouted from fifteen hundred lusty throats, and it was even more wonderful to kneel in the hush and the stillness that fell on that great crowd when the bell rang out and the Host was raised. I don't wonder that the celebrant, Austrian though he was, burst into tears and could hardly go on with the Mass. He told us afterwards that he had never been so moved in his life, and he wrote a detailed account of the pilgrimage [for] Rome, which (as I found later on) had delighted the Holy Father, and done good in many ways there. Indeed, it was difficult enough to refrain from tears. 'Faith of our Fathers, holy faith, | We will be true to thee till death,' they sang, and in a few weeks' time, how many had found that death in the great advance through Galilee and Syria. How many more, alas, were to find it in the very hour of victory, mown down by the fatal epidemic which claimed many more lives than had the Turkish bullets. (2)

NOTES AND SOURCES

1. Bede Camm, *Tyburn and the English Martyrs: Conferences given at Tyburn during a Solemn Triduum in Honour of the English Martyrs, May 1–4, 1904*, new edn. (London: Burns, Oates & Washbourne, 1924), 23–4.

2. Bede Camm, *Pilgrim Paths in Latin Lands* (London: MacDonald & Evans, 1923), 145–7.

# (Henry Palmer) John Chapman OSB     1865–1933

The son of a canon of Ely, Chapman took a first in Greats at Christ Church and was ordained as an Anglican deacon. On 7 December 1890 he was received into the Catholic Church by Father Kenelm Digby Best at the London Oratory. He entered the Benedictine Abbey of Maredsous in Belgium in 1892, was ordained priest there in 1895, but was then 'lent' to the monastery at Erdington near Birmingham. After a brief return to Maredsous, he was asked in 1913 to be superior of the newly converted community on Caldey. He served for most of the First World War as a military chaplain, and in 1919 took up a post on the Vulgate Commission in Rome. Having for some time been affiliated to Downside Abbey, he was invited in 1922 to become its Claustral Prior, and in 1929 fourth Abbot.

## Prayer

Prayer, in the sense of union with God, is the most crucifying thing there is. One must do it for God's sake; but one will not get any satisfaction out of it, in the sense of feeling, 'I am good at prayer', 'I have an infallible method'. That would be disastrous, since what we want to learn is precisely our own weakness, powerlessness, unworthiness. Nor ought one to expect 'a sense of the reality of the supernatural' of which you speak. And one should wish for no prayer, except precisely the prayer that God gives us—probably very distracted and unsatisfactory in every way!

On the other hand, the only way to pray is to pray; and the way to pray well is to pray much. If one has no time for this, then one must at least pray regularly. But the less one prays, the worse it goes. And if circumstances do not permit even regularity, then one must put up with the fact that when does try to pray, one can't pray—and our prayer will probably consist of telling this to God.

As to beginning afresh, or where you left off, I don't think you have any choice! You simply have to begin wherever you find yourself. Make any acts you want to make and feel you ought to make; but do not force yourself into *feelings* of any kind.

You say very naturally that you do not know what to do if you have a quarter of an hour alone in church. Yes, I suspect the only thing to do is to shut out the church and everything else, and just give yourself to God and beg Him to have mercy on you, and offer Him all your distractions.

As to religious matters being 'confused and overwhelming', I daresay they may remain so—in a sense—, but if you get the right simple relation to God by prayer, you have got into the centre of the wheel, where the revolving does not matter. We can't get rid of the worries of this world, or of the questionings of the intellect; but we can laugh at and despise them so far as they are worries. . . .

The rule is simply:—*Pray as you can, and do not try to pray as you can't.* Take yourself as you find yourself, and start from that. (1)

## The Fear of Death

You ask why you are afraid of death. It is only human. St Teresa describes her mental and even bodily sufferings, caused by her violent desire to die and to 'be with Christ'. And yet, she says, she still had the human fear of death. And Our Lord chose to suffer this fear of death for our sakes. The separation of body and soul is a wrench. On the other hand, I know quite well what you mean about the feeling,—when you try to realize death—that there is nothing beyond.

The reason is plainly because *one cannot imagine it.* One tries to imagine a purely spiritual imagination of the soul without the body; and naturally one imagines a blank. And then one feels:—'There is no life after death'; and then one says to oneself:—'I am doubting the faith, I am sinning against faith'.

All the time, one is only unreasonable,—trying to imagine what can be intellectually conceived, but not pictured.

It is different, I think, if you think of death naturally; not unnaturally.

(1) To die is a violence (as I said) from one point of view; but from another, it is *natural.* And to most people it seems natural to die, when they are dying. Consequently it is easy to imagine yourself on your sick bed, very sick, and faintly hearing prayers around you, and receiving the Sacraments, and gently losing consciousness, and sleeping in God's arms. (This is actually the way death comes to most people,—quite easily and pleasantly.) And looked at in this way, it does not *feel* like an extinction, the going out of a candle; it seems, on the contrary, impossible to feel that this is the end of one's personality. But what comes next? We leave that to God,—we do not try to *imagine* it.

(2) Only in prayer can you get near it—if the world ever falls away, and leaves you in infinity—which you can only describe as nothingness, though it is everything.

The moral of all this is,—do not try to *imagine* 'after death', for imagination is only of material and sensible things. Only try to realize what it is to be with God. (2)

## Providence and the Present Moment

The only thing that matters is *now.* I mean that we have to be exactly in God's Will—united actively and passively with what He has arranged for us to be and to do, so that every moment we are quite simply in touch with God, because we are wishing to do what He wants of us, and to be as we find He wishes us to be. There is no other perfection than this. Tomorrow and yesterday are quite of secondary importance....

The only thing is to take life as it comes, with the greatest simplicity. Providence arranges everything, so all is right in the end. Meanwhile, if we worry, we must try also to take that fact with simplicity, however paradoxical it sounds. (3)

## Temptations against the Faith

Thank God for all your troubles, even for 'temptations' against faith. These are the hardest of all, only they are *not* temptations. For they only mean a feeling as though you did not believe. When one finds this feeling painful and unbearable, this is a proof that one does believe, and very much. (4)

NOTES AND SOURCES

1. John Chapman, Letter XII, To One Living in the World, 11 April 1927, in *The Spiritual Letters of Dom John Chapman OSB, Fourth Abbot of Downside*, ed. with an introductory memoir by Dom Roger Hudleston OSB of the same abbey (London: Sheed & Ward, 1935), 52–3.
2. John Chapman, Letter LVI: To a Benedictine Nun, 25 May 1929, ibid. 138–40; Letter XI: To One Living in the World, 20 January 1925, ibid. 52.
3. John Chapman, Letter XXXVIII: To a Lady Living in the World, 4 September 1932, ibid. 109; Letter LIX: To a Benedictine Nun, 19 June 1926, ibid. 149.
4. John Chapman, Letter LXV: To a Benedictine Nun, 21 November 1930, ibid. 161.

# (Margaret) Laurentia McLachlan OSB     1866–1953

Dame Laurentia, born in Scotland, but a Benedictine nun in Worcestershire for over seventy years, was in the tradition of such great medieval abbesses as St Hildegard, uniting scholarship (in Dame Laurentia's case, the study of Gregorian chant and monastic history) with wise and compassionate leadership of her community (the nuns of Stanbrook). Her extraordinary capacity for friendship far beyond the cloister was made famous by her devoted disciple, Dame Felicitas Corrigan, in the book, *The Nun, the Infidel, and the Superman*, which was later adapted for stage and screen. George Bernard Shaw, the most improbable of all her friends, said of her that she was the 'enclosed nun with the unenclosed mind'.

## Dame Laurentia's Last Days

Heaven was only next door, and she lay 'a very tired old sheep', as she smilingly put it, waiting for the door to open. During the days which followed, each one saw her alone. There was no formality, no strict order of rank, no dramatic leave-taking. All demonstrations of grief were sedulously avoided, as were any last behests or bequests. She made one exception to the general rule, however, in favour of a young nun whose solemn profession was likely to be deferred in the event of the Abbess's death. In characteristic monosyllables she made her a simple *au revoir*:

'Child, I am going to God. That is what I came for—what we all came for—to go to God. I am sorry I shall not be alive for your profession, but, Child, *I shall be there*. Give yourself wholly to God, to be entirely consecrated, sanctified, glorified.'

On Wednesday August 19, Dame Laurentia sent a message to summon her Prioress after Matins.

'I have sent for you now,' she said, 'because I want to talk to you, and I think I may not be able to speak tomorrow.'

She then spoke tender words of gratitude to the nun who had borne an exacting office with selfless devotion through unusually difficult years; she expressed her happiness at leaving a community so united in heart and mind; and finally, looking back across the centuries of God's watchful providence over the monastery, she bequeathed her last message.

'He will take care of you, for He loves this house. You must keep up the old traditions of Cambrai and Stanbrook. Keep abreast of the times, but never be modern nuns. Keep up the Stanbrook spirit.'

So she bade farewell. From that moment, although she remained conscious to the last, she was unable to speak. None who lived through those last days will ever forget the atmosphere of deep peace which pervaded the whole house.

> But such a tide as moving seems asleep,
> Too full for sound or foam,
> When that which drew from out the boundless deep
> Turns again home. (1)

NOTES AND SOURCES

1. A Benedictine of Stanbrook, *In a Great Tradition*, tribute to Dame Laurentia McLachlan, Abbess of Stanbrook (London: John Murray, 1956), 303–4.

# Lionel Pigot Johnson                                                    1867–1902

The son and brother of army officers, Johnson—small in build and always frail in health—pledged himself early to the cause of literature; writers constituted, so he thought, a 'third order of priesthood'. He was a scholar of Winchester and New College, where he came under the influence of Walter Pater and took a first in Greats. He was received into the Church at St Etheldreda's, Ely Place, on the feast of St Alban 1891. He was one of the 'Decadents' of the eighteen-nineties, the friend of Yeats and Dowson, and was responsible for introducing Oscar Wilde to Lord Alfred Douglas. For all his physical and moral infirmities, he applied his undoubted erudition to many subjects, and took a scholarly interest in Ireland and all things Celtic. His life was shortened by alcoholism. He died after falling and fracturing his skull, and is buried at Kensal Green.

## Ash Wednesday

### TO THE REV. FATHER STRAPPINI SJ

Ashen cross traced on brow,
Iron cross hid in breast,
Have power, bring patience, now:
Bid passion be at rest.

O sad, dear days of Lent,
Now lengthen your grey hours:
If so we may repent,
Before the time of flowers.

Majestical, austere,
The sanctuaries look stern:
All silent, all severe,
Save where the lone lamps burn.

Imprisoned there above
The world's indifferency:
Still waits Eternal Love,
With wounds from Calvary.

Come, mourning companies;
Come, to sad Christ draw near;
Come, sin's confederacies,
Lay down your malice here.

Here is the healing place,
And here the place of peace:
Sorrow is sweet with grace
Here, and here sin hath cease. (1)

## *Te martyrum candidatus*

TO THE VERY REV. JOHN CANON O'HANLON

Ah, see the fair chivalry come, the companions of Christ!
White horsemen, who ride on white horses, the Knights of God!
They, for their Lord and their Lover who sacrificed
All, save the sweetness of treading, where He first trod.

These through the darkness of death, the dominion of night,
Swept, and they woke in white places at morning tide:
They saw with their eyes, and sang for joy of the sight,
They saw with their eyes the Eyes of the Crucified.

Now, whithersoever He goeth, with Him they go:
White horsemen, who ride on white horses, oh fair to see!
They ride, where the Rivers of Paradise flash and flow,
White horsemen, with Christ their Captain: for ever He! (2)

NOTES AND SOURCES

1. Lionel Johnson, *The Complete Poems of Lionel Johnson*, ed. Iain Fletcher (London: Unicorn Press, 1953), 97.
2. Ibid. 214–15.

# (Joseph) Vincent McNabb OP       1868–1943

Vincent McNabb was an Ulsterman, the Belfast-born son of a sea captain. He said he was happy to inherit Ireland as mother and take England as wife. He joined the English province of the Order of Preachers in 1885, was ordained priest for it in 1891, and did higher studies in Louvain from 1891 to 1894. Within the order, his was a typically English Dominican life: several years of teaching philosophy and theology, priorships at Woodchester, Leicester, and Hawkesyard, and finally a long assignment at St Dominic's in London. In other respects, his life was extraordinary. He defended the faith at Speakers' Corner, and in pubs and church halls throughout the country. He walked everywhere and slept on the floor of his cell. He treasured the friendship, while also shaping the lives, of the greatest Catholic writers of his day (Hilaire Belloc, the Chestertons, Maurice Baring). He expounded, in practice as well as in theory, the economic philosophy known as Distributism, which he would have said was simply an application of the principles of Catholic social doctrine: distributing property widely for the security of marriage and the family. He united rocklike faith and radical asceticism with warm sympathy for the human beings of all sorts who crossed his path, especially children and the poor. Belloc said of him after his death: 'I have known, seen, and felt holiness in person'.

## The Incarnation

St Luke opens his second chapter on the world's romance by a statement of mere matter of fact. Of course, the Incarnation is, happily, a matter of fact; but it is a matter of divine fact. St John says as laconically as St Luke: *Verbum caro* FACTUM *est*. In writing this, my mind will persist in translating it: The Word-made-flesh is a FACT. (1)

## Union with Christ Suffering

Most humbly, my beloved Saviour, I bow myself before thee. I am a worm and no man. I alone deserve to suffer. I alone shrink from suffering. I was with thee in thy days of joy, singing 'Hosanna', and I wished to make thee King. Now in thine hour of suffering I am far from thee. I look upon thy Cross as scandal and thy pain as waste. Give me only wisdom to know the power of thy suffering and to bring that power into every part of my life, that I may pass through suffering and death to everlasting life. (2)

## Mary: All Gift, All Mercy

This lady, in her loveliness fair as the moon, and in her strength 'terrible as an army in battle array', is one of God's consummate mercies to men. There is nothing in all her beauty of body and soul that is not a gift, and an acknowledged gift, of God. Yet each gift of God to her was part of the riches of His mercy to us. (3)

## The Virgin Birth

The Virgin Birth is *possible*, if there is a God. An Omnipotent Being who can do all things and yet cannot do some things is hardly worth our attack or defence. Atheists and agnostics score easily off those Christians who admit the existence of God and deny the Virgin Birth...

The idea of the Virgin Birth was foreign to the Jewish atmosphere. It still is foreign to the Jewish atmosphere. To me it seems almost a miracle that the *idea* of Virgin Birth should have entered into the mind of a simple Galilean maid. Her thoughts, if they were directed towards the Messiah, would naturally lead her to consider solely the natural motherhood within marriage which was the dream of Jewish women. Even the idea of our blessed Lady, Mother and Maid, had a virgin birth. It is a revelation from God. (4)

## Our Lady of Sorrows

Oh, my beloved Mother, teach me the great way of sympathy with thy Son, remembering how thou didst stand by His Cross. Give me to stand when the world wishes me to move into the ways of sin. Let me stand quite still by the side of redemptive Truth. Teach me how to love, and it will be enough for this poor sinner. For, with Love in my heart, I should not be afraid to face life and death, and to find my Saviour after death. (5)

## Our Lord's Last Two Gifts

His two last gifts were His Body and Blood, and His Mother. And He gives her to St John, who had all the privileges of the Supper. (6)

## Mother of the Eucharist

In Catholic England the Blessed Sacrament was kept within a silver or golden dove that hung in midair before the High Altar. Was not our blessed Lady this pure silver-white dove, within whose womb Our Lord lay? (7)

## The Real Presence

There is SOMEONE there. This is the drawing power of the Blessed Sacrament. Someone, not a statue, a symbol, but a being; a body and soul; a heart; hands such as clasp daily; eyes such as give us daily tokens of love; and a great Heart burning with love for *us*. A FRIEND. (8)

## The Eucharistic Mystery: Sign and Reality

Jesus is really, not mystically, present.

Jesus is mystically, not really, slain.

Jesus is under the accidents not as in a sign, but with a sign, i.e. the species of bread and wine.

His death is merely signified, not His Presence. (9)

## Transubstantiation

Transubstantiation is a word standing for a doctrine. As a word, it dates from the tenth or eleventh century. As a doctrine, it dates from the words: 'This is my Body.' Simple folk who know little of the derivation or of the meaning of the word, know the doctrine; just as few know the derivation or meaning of 'Bellis perennis', yet fewer still do not know a daisy. These same simple folk who distinguish between the sun, and the light or beauty of the sun, or between bread and the touch or taste of bread, have no difficulty in distinguishing between a thing and the qualities or appearance of a thing. In other words, they have no difficulty in understanding the doctrine of Transubstantiation. (10)

## Confession to a Priest: Why It's Necessary

If our life were led absolutely without mortal sin, we should not be obliged to go to Confession. The statutory rule is that once a year you are expected to present yourself.

But if we have sinned grievously, we are obliged to present ourselves to the officials of the Church of Christ. Why? What is the beautiful philosophy behind that? No sin, especially no great sin, is just a harm done to the individual who commits it. I believe myself that the future of the human race is bound up with that idea. The soul that is conscious of a grievous sin is conscious of a great harm done to the community—to someone else. That common hurt should now be forgiven. What a profound thought that is! Almost the most unselfish thought about sin.

There is a kind of heroic sinner who is not influenced by the effect of sin on himself, but is deeply stirred at the thought of hurting someone else. You cannot frighten such as them by telling them of the effect—even the eternal effect—on themselves. It is very difficult in time to realize eternity. To them Hell is not a threat, it is just a rude word. It seems to fasten them in their sin. But let them realize they are hurting someone they love—that moves them. If they are such persons that they don't love anybody, I don't know what is to be done!

That is one of the most profound ideas about the divine institution of the Sacrament of Penance. It is an institution manifestly divine. No human thought could have instituted it. Nobody is as addicted to Confession as I am. I have been dogging it since my seventh year—every week; sometimes several times a week, my soul tortured by its sin. I always speak with thankfulness of having received those great mercies. I often feel more grateful to God for Confession than for Holy Communion. The sense of relief and peace is more intense. That is why I speak of it—poor miserable sinner who has dogged God in His mercies in that way.

I have felt of late that Confession of our sins to the Church is a divine institution to bring to our mind that we belong to the Church. We cannot go alone to God. We belong to His Mystical Body, the Church; by even our most secret sins, if they be grievous, we have injured the Mystical Body of Jesus Christ and must ask forgiveness of His Mystical Body, too. That is sound theology. Some people think the more we can eliminate the Church the better. That is all wrong. We are borne to Christ Our Lord by others. (11)

## Marriage

As you are not yet married, and as marriage is the fundamental state of life as well as the unity of the commonwealth, make up your mind whether you are called to this state. If you make up your mind to marry, do not marry merely a good wife: marry a good mother to your children. A wife that is a good mother to your children is the Angel of the House; the other sort is the very devil.

Before asking her hand and her heart, tell her how to test you. Advise her to ask herself not whether you would make her a good husband, but whether you would make a good father to her and your children. A wife that is not house-wife, and a husband that is not a good house-band are heading for Admiralty, Probate, and Divorce!

If you do not feel called to the state of marriage vows, there is another state of vows—where mysticism and asceticism prove themselves the redemption of economics. (12)

## Openness to Life

The normal effect of child-bearing within wedlock is to unlock the parents' hearts, throwing them open more and more, not only to their own children but to others, and even to our lesser kinfolk, the animals, that are so often the companions or the helpmates of man. (13)

The Church's teaching on Birth Control may be summarized thus. 'The only Birth Control which is not sinful is that in which both husband and wife willingly agree to abstain from marital intercourse.' This voluntary and agreed abstention may be temporary, as in so many wedded lives of today, or it may be perpetual, as in the case of St Edward the Confessor.

The Church does not teach that all wedded folk must beget children, nor that all must beget as many children as possible. She wisely leaves this matter to be decided by the mutual agreement of the husband and wife who by their wedlock have given to their partner power over their body. But she promulgates, as a divine law, the absolute prohibition of any sexual intercourse which is voluntarily robbed of its relationship to begetting offspring. For this reason she forbids by the divine law the use of contraceptives which have no other end than the reconciliation of sexual intercourse with the prevention of offspring. In promulgating this principle as a divine law the Church is consistent with her high view of the Sacrament of Marriage. Her doctrine of the indissolubility of marriage means that, provided all the conditions of a valid marriage have been observed, the resultant marriage has passed beyond the power of the Church to unmake. So, too, the conditions under which marital intercourse may or may not take place are not in the power of the Church to make or unmake. They belong to the great virtue of Justice between two human beings and God, which the Church is commissioned to safeguard, but not to change. (14)

## The Necessity of Prayer

Well, dear children in Jesus Christ, prayer is absolutely necessary. When we have attained to the use of reason, we cannot be saved without prayer. I need not say, therefore, that there are a great number of ways of praying. Our dear Lord said we should pray always. Everything we are doing should be either a prayer in itself or can be made into a prayer. Any action that is not in itself wrong can be done in union with God and His divine will.

The Apostles saw Our Lord praying, and they were so struck that they asked Him to teach them to pray. 'John taught his disciples. Would you teach us?' They had really been praying when they asked Him, because that asking was a prayer, though they did not know it.

He answered their request at once. They never thought He would give them this wonderful prayer, the 'Our Father'. That prayer instructs us at once that anything can be made into a prayer. We can pray 'Thy will be done' about everything that comes into our lives. If at the back of our minds we do not want God's will to be done, then our words are not a prayer. If we try to twist God's will round to our will, it is no use praying, 'Thy will be done'. We are really asking God to come round to our point of view. And yet, in our heart, as we say those words, we really do want to come round to His point of view. I am quite sure that God's Intelligence Department understands exactly what we mean, and even though it seems as if we want our own will, He understands when we pray 'Thy will be done' that we are wishing we could accept His will for us. St Augustine said that even when God refuses the desire of our heart, He never refuses the heart of our desire. That is very beautiful, and it is right. I am sure there is no such thing as unanswered prayer. All prayers are answered. Sometimes the answer doesn't suit, that's all. We think God hasn't answered us, when He has answered us bountifully. We ask Him to make us good, and He tries to make us saints, but we go about grousing and saying that He never answers our prayers!

I often wonder why people set so much store by one particular form of prayer. Prayer can be in everything. When the Angel Gabriel came to Our Lady, I am quite sure he found her on her knees (she would not be dressed up as she is in the pictures, in brocaded silk), but whether she was praying or scrubbing the floor I have not quite made up my theological mind.

The most necessary form of prayer is that of our dear Lord, doing good to our neighbour for the love of God. Our dear Lord accentuated that by saying that if we have anything against our neighbour we must forgive him; and if our neighbour has anything against us, we must go off to him to be forgiven. Then we can make our act a prayer.

It is quite easy to make anything that we do, that is not sin, into a prayer. In that way, it is hard for ordinary Catholics not to pray. Some particular forms of prayer may be hard, but to pray is not hard. If loving God is hard, ah, then it is hard to pray. But it is very hard not to love God, if we know anything about Him. (15)

## Distractions

I always say, some people haven't distractions, and that is entirely their own fault! It is almost a grave fault. Some people have distracted heads, and they do not distract their hearts at all. Perhaps one should have a distracted heart. It should burn within us. There is the prayer of Quiet and Peace, but that is not the sort of thing we should desire in this world. We must not pray because we like it; devotion doesn't mean just the consciousness of being nice and comfortable. Real devotion means promptitude of the will to follow the Divine Will. Some of the best prayers make us feel extraordinarily uncomfortable. I don't want to make you feel comfortable, but to make you feel right, reassured—to urge you to go on, and not to give up.

If distractions come from disorders in your life, give those up; don't give up prayer. Give up the thing that is stealing into your heart, pushing the right things out. Our dear Lord says, 'Come in and shut the door.' That means shutting out such distractions as arise from our disorderly affections. The tragedy of the Pharisee's prayer was that he had a distracted life. That is when distractions really matter. The weeds growing up in our heart are carefully tended. We are terrified of plucking them up. If we have a distracted life and are struggling terribly to put an end to it, we are pretty certain to have distracted prayers. I feel sure that the great fights in all souls begin in a moment of prayer. Something dawns upon us that we must do.

Our blessed Lord's prayer in the Garden was not a comfortable prayer. In His sacred humanity, He allowed distracted prayer to have its place. He redeemed us at great cost, and the cost is expressed by the distraction in His human will. It seems almost a distracted prayer—just one phrase seems to come, like a theme of a fugue, again and again.

I feel quite certain that if we have to put an end to our distracted life, one of the best battlefields is the battlefield of prayer. Let us come to pray. Let us enter into our room and shut the door, the human door to the human world, and let us pray to our Father in secret.

You know, dear children in Jesus Christ, when we really pray for spiritual things, necessary for our state of life, those prayers are always answered. It has been my experience that God answers those in the most amazing way. I always say that I have never seen any miracles, but I have seen again and again answers to prayer, to the right kind of prayer, for the right spiritual thing. I have seen those prayers answered immediately. Other things God sometimes answers by refusing. If a child asks for poisoned food, it is not given it. God gives us something else. He is answering the heart of the desire.

Don't let us, then, be too much distracted by distractions. Let us try to put an end to distractions merely in the intelligence. It is very difficult to think and to keep our attention fixed. St Francis de Sales said we could only keep our attention for a quarter of an hour. St Thomas Aquinas, who knew much more about prayer, said we could only keep it during one Credo. He was a great master of prayer himself. His last few years were spent in frequent ecstasy. (16)

## Praying for Perseverance

I myself pray God most earnestly—and I beseech you to pray—that I may die a Roman Catholic. I have constantly scandalized people by asking that as a great favour. I ask a roomful of children, 'Well, children, will you say a Hail Mary that Father Vincent McNabb may die a Roman Catholic?' My request is often greeted with laughter. I thank God for the laughter that has greeted one of the sincerest wishes of my heart. (17)

Another thought I want to put before you is that the essential prayer for us poor wayfarers striving to get into the supernatural is the prayer of petition, and the essential prayer is the prayer for final perseverance. We will not get that unless in some way or other we ask for it. Hence the great value of the 'Hail Mary'. It is a simple explicit prayer for the one thing we must petition for, 'pray for us sinners, now, and at the hour of our death'. That is the great essential prayer. (18)

## The Preaching of Platitudes

I have devoted my life to the preaching of platitudes; it is one of the satisfactions of my life. I like the old things—sun and moon, fresh air, bread and butter, work, friendship, avoiding the occasions of sin. Sometimes the devil would say to me, 'Now, Father Vincent, people don't like those sorts of things, give them something modern.' My Guardian Angel says, 'It isn't your duty to be modern. You must give something true.' (19)

## Death and the Lady We Love

Even the longest life is a very short day. Some of us are already hearing the bells toll to evensong and have reached the age when all bells are tolling for evensong. It is a tradition for us Dominicans to die singing the *Salve Regina*. We sing to the Lady we love. I hope I shall hear that when I am dying. They will say, 'Father Vincent is dying, Father Cantor, start the *Salve*.' If I have sufficient consciousness, I will probably join in. We meet death singing to our Mother as the darkness of this world passes into the dawning light of the next. (20)

> O Blessed Virgin Mary, Mother of Seven Sorrows,
> Yet Cause of my Joy,
> Beseech thy divine Son,
> That this great sinner and tom-fool
> May have the grace to die
> Without having a long face
> Or being a wet blanket. (21)

NOTES AND SOURCES

1. Vincent McNabb, *Some Mysteries of Jesus Christ* (London: Burns, Oates & Washbourne, 1941), 8.
2. Quoted in Ferdinand Valentine OP, *Father Vincent McNabb: The Portrait of a Great Dominican* (London: Burns & Oates, 1955), 223.
3. Vincent McNabb, *Mary of Nazareth* (London: Burns, Oates & Washbourne, 1939), p. xiv.
4. Ibid. 4.
5. Quoted in Valentine, *Father Vincent McNabb*, 223.
6. McNabb, *Mary of Nazareth*, 32.
7. Ibid. 50.
8. Vincent McNabb, *God's Good Cheer* (London: Burns, Oates & Washbourne, 1937), 9.
9. Ibid. 11.
10. Ibid. 5.
11. *A Vincent McNabb Anthology*, selected by Francis Edward Nugent (London: Blackfriars, 1955), 212–14.
12. Vincent McNabb, *Nazareth or Social Chaos* (London: Burns, Oates & Washbourne, 1933), 97–8.
13. Vincent McNabb, *Eleven, Thank God! Memories of a Catholic Mother* (London: Sheed & Ward, 1940), 19.
14. Vincent McNabb, 'The Crime of Birth Control', *Blackfriars*, 2 (1921), 215.
15. Vincent McNabb, *Stars of Comfort: Retreat Conferences* (London: Burns & Oates, 1957), 24–6.
16. Vincent McNabb, *The Craft of Prayer* (London: Burns, Oates & Washbourne, 1935), 72–4.
17. Cited in Valentine, *Father Vincent McNabb*, 233.
18. McNabb, *Stars of Comfort*, 28.
19. Cited in Valentine, *Father Vincent McNabb*, 226.
20. Cited ibid. 236.
21. Quoted ibid. 248.

# Joseph Hilaire Pierre René Belloc    1870–1953

Despite the Frenchness of his name, father, place of birth, and military service, Hilaire Belloc was rooted in the soil of Sussex and the Weald. After seven years at Newman's Oratory School in Birmingham, and a further five years attempting farming and draughtsmanship, walking across America, and serving in the French artillery, he went up to Oxford and gained a first in history at

Balliol: 'Balliol made me, Balliol fed me', he said, 'Whatever I had she gave me again'. His failure to win a prize fellowship at All Souls left him with a lifelong dislike of dons and forced him to make his living by writing—he always insisted that he wrote for money, not out of love of writing. For the next nearly fifty years he poured out poetry (comic and satirical verse as well as sonnets and lyrics), biography and history (especially military), travelogues full of digressions on everything (*The Path to Rome, The Cruise of the Nona, The Four Men*), and apologetics for the Catholic faith. His prose is robust and clear, and does its job of communicating thought without adornment or fuss. Whenever he recognized such qualities in other writers, he was generous in his praise: P. G. Wodehouse, for example, he regarded as simply the greatest master in his time of the craft of writing. In *The Servile State*, Belloc attacks Socialism and Capitalism as twin attempts to enslave the mass of men by depriving them of property and thus of freedom. His vision of a social order made up of propertied peasants and artisans supporting themselves and their families by the direct fruits of their labour, without servile dependence on the state or big business, helped to inspire the Distributist movement in which Belloc, Chesterton, and Fr Vincent McNabb played leading roles in the 1920s. In 1906 he became the Liberal Member of Parliament for South Salford. When he addressed his first meeting in the constituency during the election, he told his audience that he was a Catholic, that he attended Mass every day, and, showing them his rosary, that every day he told his beads. 'If you reject me on account of my religion,' he concluded, 'I shall thank God that He has spared me the indignity of being your representative.' In 1913, with Cecil and Gilbert Chesterton, he exposed the involvement of members of the Liberal government in insider trading in the Marconi Company. Two years earlier, with the same brothers, he had founded the weekly *Eye Witness*, which was to become *The New Witness* and finally *GK's Weekly*. His American wife, Elodie, died young in 1914, leaving him five children to bring up: he kept her room as a shrine, making the sign of the Cross on the always locked door as he passed it, and wore black for the rest of his life. He is famed for his friendship with Gilbert Chesterton, composing with him in the eyes of many a single entity, what Shaw called the 'Chesterbelloc'. But the two men, in everything except the faith they defended with such effect, were as different as could be, and especially in the making of enemies. The men whom Chesterton challenged could not help loving him, but when Belloc went to battle, he wounded and was wounded. His arguments are like the swing of a mace or a blast from the guns of his beloved artillery. His book on *The Jews*, as well as a thousand throw-away lines, acquired him the reputation of anti-Semitism, but he described that evil as a 'lunacy', and, despite his tub-thumping words about 'the Jewish question', Belloc remained the tireless critic of the causes of so much of twentieth-century anti-Semitism: the pseudo-science of racial purity, and the sentimental cult of the 'northern spirit'. For all his swagger, Belloc had the heart of a penitent, a constant struggler; his chief enemy was himself, as he was always ready to confess. Ronald Knox, preaching at his Requiem, remembered 'the punctilious care with which he would bestow charity on a beggar', and the way in which 'the very overtones of his unpretentious piety brought back to us memories of the faith, and of the Mass, and of our blessed Lady, to which English ears had grown unaccustomed'. Knox concluded with the words of St Paul: '"I have fought the good fight, I have finished the race, I have redeemed my pledge"—that is what Hilaire Belloc would wish us to say of him, and there are few of whom it could be said so truly.'

## The Faith

If the ordnance map tells me that it is eleven miles to Wookey Hole, then, my mood of lassitude as I walk through the rain at night making it *feel* like thirty, I use the will and say: 'No, my intelligence has been convinced, and I compel myself to use it against my mood. It is *eleven*, and though I feel in the depth of my being to have gone twenty miles and more, I *know* it is not yet eleven I have gone.

I am by all my nature of mind sceptical, by all my nature of body exceedingly sensual. So sensual that the virtues restrictive of sense are but phrases to me. But I accept these phrases as true and act upon them as well as a struggling man can. And as to the doubt of the soul I discover it to be false: a mood: not a conclusion. My conclusion—and that of all men who have ever once *seen* it—is the Faith. Corporate, organized, a personality, teaching. A thing, not a theory. It.

To you, who have the blessing of profound religious emotion, this statement may seem too desiccate. It is indeed not enthusiastic. It lacks meat. It is my misfortune. In youth I had it: even till lately. Grief has drawn the juices from it. I am alone and unfed. The more do I affirm the Sanctity, the Unity, the Infallibility of the Catholic Church. By my very isolation do I the more affirm it as a man in a desert knows that water is right for man, or as a wounded dog not able to walk yet knows the way home...

But beyond this there will come in time, if I save my soul, the flesh of these bones, which bones alone I can describe and teach I know—without feeling (an odd thing in such a connection) the reality of Beatitude, which is the goal of Catholic living. (1)

## The One True Church: Belloc's Letter to the Anglican Dean of St Paul's, W. R. Inge

What is the Catholic Church? It is that which replies, co-ordinates, establishes. It is that within which is right order; outside, the puerilities and despairs. It is the possession of perspective in the survey of the world. It is a grasp upon reality. Here alone is promise, and here alone a foundation.

Those of us who boast so stable an endowment make no claim thereby to personal peace; we are not saved thereby alone. But we are of so glorious a company that we receive support, and have communion. The Mother of God is also ours. Our dead are with us. Even in these our earthly miseries we always hear the distant something of an eternal music, and smell a native air. There is a standard set for us whereto our whole selves respond, which is that of an inherited and endless life, quite full, in our own country...

One thing in this world is different from all other. It has a personality and a force. It is recognized, and (when recognized) most violently loved or hated. It is the Catholic Church. Within that household the human spirit has roof and hearth. Outside it, is the Night.

> *In hac urbe lux sollennis,*
> *Ver aeternum, pax perennis*
> *Et aeterna gaudia....*

There is a city full, as are all cities, of halt and maimed, blind and evil and the rest; but it is the City of God. There are not two such Cities on earth. There is One. (2)

## The Prophet Lost in the Hills of Evening

> Strong God which made the topmost stars
> To circulate and keep their course,

Remember me, whom all the bars
　　Of sense and dreadful fate enforce.

Above me in your heights and tall,
　　Impassable the summits freeze,
Below the haunted waters call
　　Impassable beyond the trees.

I hunger and I have no bread.
　　My gourd is empty of the wine.
Surely the footsteps of the dead
　　Are shuffling softly close to mine!

It darkens. I have lost the ford.
　　There is a change on all things made.
The rocks have evil faces, Lord,
　　And I am awfully afraid.

Remember me: the Voids of Hell
　　Expand enormous all around.
Strong friend of souls, Emmanuel,
　　Redeem me from accursed ground.

The long descent of wasted days,
　　To these at last have led me down;
Remember that I filled with praise
The meaningless and doubtful ways
　　That lead to an eternal town.

I challenged and I kept the faith,
　　The bleeding path alone I trod;
It darkens. Stand about my wraith,
　　And harbour me—almighty God. (3)

## A Remaining Christmas

The people of the house, when they have dined, and their guests, with the priest who
is to say Mass for them, sit up till near midnight. There is brought in a very large log of
oak . . . This log of oak is the Christmas or Yule log, and the rule is that it must be too
heavy for one man to lift; so two men come, bringing it in from outside, the master of
the house and his servant. They cast it down upon the fire in the great hearth of the
dining room, and the superstition is that, if it burns all night and is found still
smouldering in the morning, the home will be prosperous for the coming year.

　　With that they all go up to the chapel, and there the three night Masses are said,
one after the other, and those of the household take their Communion.

　　Next morning they sleep late, and the great Christmas dinner is at midday. It is
a turkey, and a plum pudding, with holly in it, and everything conventional, and
therefore satisfactory, is done. Crackers are pulled, the brandy is lit and poured

over the pudding till the holly crackles in the flame, and the curtains are drawn a moment that the flames be seen. This Christmas feast, so great that it may be said almost to fill the day, they may reprove who will, but for my part I applaud...

This house where such good things are done year by year has suffered all the things that every age has suffered. It has known the sudden separation of wife and husband, the sudden fall of young men under arms who will never more come home, the scattering of the living and their precarious return, the increase and the loss of fortune, all those terrors and all those lessenings and haltings and failures of hope which make up the life of man. But its Christmas binds it to its own past and promises its future, making the house an undying thing of which those subject to mortality within it are members, sharing in its continuous survival.

It is not wonderful that of such a house verse should be written. Many verses have been so written commemorating and praising this house. The last verse written of it I may quote here by way of ending:

> Stand forever among human houses,
>   House of the Resurrection, House of Birth;
> House of the rooted hearts and long carouses,
>   Stand and be famous over all the Earth. (4)

## Ballade to Our Lady of Czestochowa

Lady and Queen and Mystery manifold
And very Regent of the untroubled sky,
Whom in a dream Saint Hilda did behold
And heard a woodland music passing by:
You shall receive me when the clouds are high
With evening and the sheep attain the fold.
This is the faith that I have held and hold,
And this is that in which I mean to die.

Steep are the seas and savaging and cold
In broken waters terrible to try;
And vast against the winter night the wold,
And harbourless for any sail to lie.
But you shall lead me to the lights, and I
Shall hymn you in a harbour story told.
This is the faith that I have held and hold,
And this is that in which I mean to die.

Help of the half-defeated, House of gold,
Shrine of the Sword, and Tower of Ivory;
Splendour apart, supreme and aureoled,
The Battler's vision and the World's reply.
You shall restore me, O my last Ally,
To vengeance and the glories of the bold.
This is the faith that I have held and hold,
And this is that in which I mean to die.

*Envoi*

Prince of the degradations, bought and sold,
These verses, written in your crumbling sty,
Proclaim the faith that I have held and hold
And publish that in which I mean to die. (5)

## Courtesy

Of Courtesy, it is much less
Than Courage of Heart or Holiness,
Yet in my Walks it seems to me
That the Grace of God is in Courtesy.

On Monks I did in Storrington fall,
They took me straight into their Hall;
I saw Three Pictures on a wall,
And Courtesy was in them all.

The first the Annunciation;
The second the Visitation;
The third the Consolation,
Of God that was Our Lady's Son.

The first was Saint Gabriel;
On Wings a-flame from Heaven he fell;
And as he went upon one knee
He shone with Heavenly Courtesy.

Our Lady out of Nazareth rode—
It was Her month of heavy load;
Yet was Her face both great and kind,
For Courtesy was in Her Mind.

The third it was our Little Lord,
Whom all the Kings in arms adored;
He was so small you could not see
His large intent of Courtesy.

Our Lord, that was Our Lady's Son,
Go bless you, People, one by one;
My Rhyme is written, my work is done. (6)

## Intimations of Beatitude

I went out on to the balcony, where men and women were talking in subdued tones. There, alone, I sat and watched the night coming up into these Tuscan hills.

The first moon since that waning in Lorraine (how many nights ago, how many marches!) hung in the sky, a full crescent, growing into brightness and glory as she assumed her reign. The one star of the west called out his silent companions in their order; the mountains merged into a fainter confusion; Heaven and the infinite air became the natural seat of any spirit that watched this spell. The fire-flies darted in the depths of vineyards and of trees below; then the noise of the grasshoppers brought back suddenly the gardens of home, and whatever benediction surrounds our childhood. Some promise of eternal pleasures and of rest deserved haunted the village of Silano.

In very early youth the soul can still remember its immortal habitation, and clouds and the edges of hills are of another kind from ours, and every scent and colour has a savour of Paradise. What that quality may be no language can tell, nor have men made any words, no, nor any music, to recall it—only in a transient way and elusive the recollection of what youth was, and purity, flashes on us in phrases of the poets, and is gone before we can fix it in our minds—oh! my friends, if we could but recall it! Whatever those sounds may be that are beyond our sounds, and whatever are those keen lives which remain alive there under memory— whatever is Youth—Youth came up that valley at evening, borne upon a southern air. If we deserve or attain beatitude, such things shall at last be our settled state; and their now sudden influence upon the soul in short ecstasies is the proof that they stand outside time, and are not subject to decay. (7)

## Heresy

Heresy ... means the warping of a system by 'exception', by 'picking out' one part of the structure, and implies that the scheme is marred by taking away one part of it, denying one part of it, and either leaving the void unfilled or filling it with some new affirmation ... The denial of a scheme wholesale is not heresy, and has not the creative power of a heresy. It is of the essence of heresy that it leaves standing a great part of the structure it attacks. On this account it can appeal to believers and continues to affect their lives through deflecting them from their original characters. Wherefore it is said of heresies that 'they survive by the truths they retain'. (8)

## Song of the Pelagian Heresy for the Strengthening of Men's Backs and the very Robust Outthrusting of Doubtful Doctrine and the Uncertain Intellectual

Pelagius lived in Kardanoel
    And taught a doctrine there
How whether you went to Heaven or Hell,
    It was your own affair.
How, whether you found eternal joy
    Or sank forever to burn,
It had nothing to do with the Church, my boy,
But was your own concern.

*[Semi-chorus]*

Oh, he didn't believe
In Adam and Eve,
  He put no faith therein!
His doubts began
With the fall of man,
  And he laughed at original sin!

[Chorus]
With my row-ti-tow, ti-oodly-ow,
  He laughed at original sin!

Whereat the Bishop of old Auxerre
  (Germanus was his name)
He tore great handfuls out of his hair,
  And he called Pelagius Shame:
And then with his stout Episcopal staff
  So thoroughly thwacked and banged
The heretics all, both short and tall,
  They rather had been hanged.

[Semi-chorus]
Oh, he thwacked them hard, and he banged them long
  Upon each and all occasions,
Till they bellowed in chorus, loud and strong,
  Their orthodox persuasions!

[Chorus]
With my row-ti-tow, ti-oodly-ow,
  Their orthodox persuasions!

Now the Faith is old and the Devil is bold
  Exceedingly bold, indeed;
And the masses of doubt that are floating about
  Would smother a mortal creed.
But we that sit in a sturdy youth,
  And still can drink strong ale,
Oh—let us put it away to infallible truth,
Which always shall prevail!

[Semi-chorus]
And thank the Lord
For the temporal sword,
  And for howling heretics, too;
And whatever good things
Our Christendom brings,
  But especially barley-brew!

[Chorus]
With my row-ti-tow, ti-oodly-ow,
  Especially barley-brew! (9)

## Bereavement and the Faith

[*To Mrs Wansbrough, on the death of her father*] I beg you not to over-grieve. The advantage of the faith in this principal trial of human life is that the faith is reality, and that through it all falls into a right perspective. That is not a consolation—mere consolation is a drug and to be despised—it is the strength of truth. We know how important life is (and no one knows that outside the faith), but we also know that we are immortal, and that those we love are immortal, and that the necessary condition, before eternity, is loss and change, and that we can regard them in the light of their final revelation and of re-union with what we love. I do not say this because I would make less the enormity of these blows. I know them as well as anyone, and I reeled under them. But with the faith they can be borne; they take on their right value. They are not final. I am going to have a Mass said for your father at once. He was a good and constantly kind friend to me, and I always came back to his home with expectation. Very many can say the same. I am only one. God bless you, my dear, and keep you well and secure in the business of this sad world till you also attain felicity for ever. (10)

## Remedying the Evils of Capitalism: The Choice between Socialism and Distributism

If you are suffering because property[6] is restricted to a few, you can alter that factor in the problem *either* by putting property into the hands of many, *or* by putting it into the hands of none. There is no third course.

In the concrete, to put property in the hands of 'none' means to vest it in the hands of political officers. If you say that the evils proceeding from Capitalism are due to the institution of property itself, and not to the dispossession of the many by the few, then you must forbid the private possession of the means of production by any particular and private part of the community. But someone must control the means of production, or we should have nothing to eat. So in practice this doctrine means the management of the means of production by those who are the public officers of the community. Whether these public officers are themselves controlled by the community or no has nothing to do with this solution on its economic side. The essential point to grasp is that the only alternative to private property is public property. Somebody must see to the ploughing and must control the ploughs; otherwise no ploughing will be done.

It is equally obvious that, if you conclude property in itself to be no evil but only the small number of its owners, then your remedy is to increase the number of those owners...

The first model we call Socialism or the Collectivist State; the second we call the Proprietary or Distributive State...

The Capitalist State breeds a Collectivist Theory which *in action* produces something utterly different from collectivism: to wit, the Servile State. (11)

---

[6] In a footnote, Belloc explains that by the word 'property' he means 'property in the means of production'.

## The Servile State

The future of industrial society, and in particular of English society, left to its own direction, is a future in which subsistence and security shall be guaranteed for the Proletariat, but shall be guaranteed at the expense of the old political freedom, and by the establishment of that Proletariat in a status really, though not nominally, servile. At the same time, the Owners will be guaranteed in their profits, the whole machinery of production in the smoothness of its working, and that stability which has been lost under the Captialist phase of society will be found once more.

The internal strains which have threatened society during its Capitalist phase will be relaxed and eliminated, and the community will settle down upon that servile basis which was its foundation before the advent of the Christian faith, from which that faith slowly weaned it, and to which in the decay of that faith it naturally returns. (12)

NOTES AND SOURCES

1. Hilaire Belloc, Letter to G. K. Chesterton, August 1922, cited in Robert Speaight, *The Life of Hilaire Belloc* (London: Hollis & Carter, 1957), 374–5.

2. Hilaire Belloc, *Essays of a Catholic Layman in England* (London: Sheed & Ward, 1931), 304–5, 157.

3. Hilaire Belloc, *Sonnets and Verse* (London: Duckworth, 1923), 63–4.

4. Hilaire Belloc, *A Conversation with an Angel* (London & Toronto: Cape, 1931), 280–5.

5. Belloc, *Sonnets and Verse*, 136–7.

6. Ibid. 51–2.

7. Hilaire Belloc, *The Path to Rome* (London: Nelson, n.d.), 314–16.

8. Hilaire Belloc, *The Great Heresies*, new edn. (London: Catholic Book Club, n.d.), 5–7.

9. Hilaire Belloc, *The Four Men: A Farrago*, new edn. (London: Nelson, 1948), 92–5.

10. Hilaire Belloc, Letter to Mrs Wansbrough, 13 December 1927, in *Letters from Hilaire Belloc*, selected and edited by Robert Speaight (London: Hollis & Carter, 1958), 191.

11. Hilaire Belloc, *The Servile State* (London & Edinburgh: T. N. Foulis, 1912), 99–101.

12. Ibid. 183.

# Robert Hugh Benson                                     1871–1914

Hugh Benson was the youngest son of Edward White Benson, Archbishop of Canterbury, and brother of Edward Frederic, the humorous novelist, and Arthur Christopher, master at Eton and author of the words of 'Land of Hope and Glory'. After Eton and Trinity College, Cambridge, Hugh was ordained as an Anglican priest by his own father. After a short time as a member of the Anglican religious community at Mirfield, he was received into the Catholic Church in 1903, ordained priest in 1904, and made Monsignor in 1911. He devoted most of his ten years of priesthood to an apostolate of literature and preaching. As well as historical novels set in the centuries of persecution, he wrote novels set in his own Edwardian times and directed against the fads of the age, including spiritualism; futuristic novels about the coming of Antichrist and the conversion of the world to the Catholic Church; devotional poetry, dramas, and works of apologetics. For all the nervous intensity of his novels and his character, Benson's redeeming quality, said Father Martindale, was 'the grace of humour'.

## Rome: Learning the Lesson of the Incarnation

I sat under priest-professors who shouted, laughed, and joyously demonstrated before six nations in one lecture room. I saw the picture of the 'Father of princes and kings and Lord of the world' exposed in the streets on his name-day, surrounded by flowers and oil lamps, in the manner in which, two centuries ago, other lords of the world were honoured. I went down into the Catacombs on St Cecilia's day and St Valentine's, and smelled the box and the myrtle underfoot that did reverence to the fragrance of their memories, as centuries ago they had done reverence to victors in another kind of contest. In one sentence, I began to understand that 'the Word was made flesh and dwelt among us'; that as He took the created substance of a Virgin to fashion for Himself a natural body, so still He takes the created substance of men—their thoughts, their expressions, and their methods—to make for Himself that Mystical Body by which He is with us always; in short, I perceived that 'there is nothing secular but sin'. Catholicism, then, is 'materialistic'? Certainly: it is as materialistic as the Creation and the Incarnation, neither more nor less. (1)

## 'I Thirst'

Up to the present the deepest point of Christ's humiliation has been His cry to His Father, that call for help by the Sacred Humanity which by His own will was left derelict, His confession to the world that His soul was in darkness. Now, however, He descends a still deeper step of humiliation, and calls for help, to man.

Christ asks man for help!

All through His life He had offered help: He had fed hungry souls and hungry bodies. He had opened blind eyes and deaf ears, and lifted up the hands that hung down, and strengthened the feeble knees. He had stood in the Temple and called to all that thirsted to come and drink. Now, in return, He asks for drink, and accepts it. So David, too, in the stress of battle had cried, 'Oh, that some man would give me a drink of the water out of the cistern that is in Bethlehem' (2 Kgs. 23: 15). For both David and David's Son were strong enough to condescend to weakness.

In the age-long Calvary of the world's history, Jesus cries on man to help Him, and the Giver of all humiliates Himself to ask.

Truly He makes every other appeal first. To the selfish undeveloped soul He speaks in the voice of Sinai, 'Thou shalt not'. To a soul that has made a little progress He offers encouragement and promises. 'Blessed is such and such a man, for he shall receive a reward.' But here and there are souls that are deaf to Hell and Heaven alike, to whom the future means little or nothing, souls that are too reckless to fear Hell, too loveless to desire Heaven. And to those He utters His final heart-piercing appeal. 'If you will not accept help from me, give at least help to me. If you will not drink from my hands, give me at least drink from yours. *I thirst.*'

It is an amazing thought that men should have reduced Him to this, and it is a suggestive thought that men who will not respond for their own sakes, will, sometimes, respond for His.

'See,' cries Jesus Christ, 'you have given up the search; you have turned away from the door and will not knock. You will not take the trouble to ask. So it is I who have to do these things. Behold, it is I who go seeking the lost; it is I who stand at the door and knock. It is I who ask, who am become a beggar ... Have mercy on me, O my friends, for the Lord hath afflicted me. I no longer offer water, but I ask it, for without it I die.'

It is good for us, sometimes, to look at the spiritual life from another standpoint altogether. There come moments and even periods in our lives when religion becomes an intolerable burden; when the search is so long and fruitless that we sicken of it; when no door opens, however vehemently we knock; when we ask, and there is no Voice that answers. At times like this we lose heart altogether. It seems to us even that our own desires are not worth satisfying; that religion, like every instinct of our nature, reaches an end beyond which there is no going; that desire has, in fact, failed, and that we are not even ambitious of attaining Heaven. The truth is that we are limited beings, and that the 'divine discontent', the desire for the infinite, the endless passion for God, is as much a grace from God as the power to reach to Him and win Him. It is not only that God is our reward, and Our Lord, but He must actually be our Way by which we come to Him: we cannot even long for Him without His help.

It is when we are wearied out then by desiring, when desire itself has failed, that Jesus speaks to us in this Fifth Word from the Cross. (2)

## Easter Sunday Mass

[*It is Easter Sunday morning in Sussex, in the 1580s. Anthony and Isabel Norris, the children of a Puritan father, have just been received into the Catholic Church. Now brother and sister are attending Holy Mass in the chapel of their Catholic neighbours, the Maxwells of Great Keynes.*]

Then at last the morning came, and Christ was risen beyond a doubt. Just before the sun came up, when all the sky was luminous to meet him, the two again passed up and round the corner, and into the little door in the angle. There was the same shaded candle or two, for the house was yet dark within, and they passed up and on together through the sitting room into the chapel where each had made a first Confession the night before, and had together been received into the Catholic Church. Now it was all fragrant with flowers and herbs; a pair of tall lilies leaned their delicate heads towards the altar, as if to listen for the soundless coming in the name of the Lord; underfoot, all about the altar, lay sprigs of sweet herbs, rosemary, thyme, lavender, bay-leaves, with white blossoms scattered over them—a soft carpet for the Pierced Feet, not like those rustling palm-swords over which He rode to death last week. The black oak chest that supported the altar-stone was glorious in its vesture of cloth-of-gold, and against the white-hung wall at the back, behind the silver candlesticks, leaned the gold plate of the house, to do honour to the King. And presently there stood there the radiant rustling figure of the priest, his personality sheathed and obliterated beneath the splendid symbolism of his vestments, stiff and chinking with jewels as he moved.

The glorious Mass of Easter Day began. *Immolatus est Christus; itaque epulemur*, St Paul cried from the south corner of the altar to the two converts, 'Christ our Passover is sacrificed for us; let us keep the feast, but not with the old leaven' ...

[*The Mass continues to the Canon.*] Then a hush fell, and presently in the stillness came riding the Personages who stand in Heaven about the Throne: first, the Queen Mother herself, glorious within and without, moving in clothing of wrought gold, high above all others; then the great princes of the blood royal, who are admitted to drink of the King's own cup, and sit beside Him on their thrones, Peter and Paul and the rest, with rugged faces and scarred hands, and with them great mitred figures—Linus, Cletus, and Clement, with their companions.

And then another space and a tingling silence. The crows bow down like corn before the wind; the far-off trumpets are silent, and He comes, He comes!

On He moves, treading underfoot the laws He has made, yet borne up by them as on the Sea of Galilee. He who inhabits eternity at an instant is made present. He who transcends space is immanent in material kind. He who never leaves the Father's side rests on His white linen carpet, held, yet unconfined, in the midst of the little gold things and embroidery and candle-flames and lilies, while the fragrance of the herbs rises about Him. There rests the gracious King. Before this bending group the rest of the pageant dies into silence and nothingness outside the radiant circle of His presence. There is His immediate priest-herald, who has marked out this halting-place for the Prince, bowing before Him, striving by gestures to interpret and fulfil the silence that words must always leave empty. Here, behind, are the adoring human hearts, each looking with closed eyes into the face of the Fairest of the children of men, each crying silently words of adoration, welcome, and utter love.

The moments pass. The court ceremonies are performed. The Virgins that follow the Lamb—Felicitas, Perpetua, Agatha, and the rest—step forward smiling, and take their part; the eternal Father is invoked again in the Son's own words; and at length the King, descending yet one further step of infinite humility, flings back the last vesture of His outward royalty, and casts Himself in a passion of haste and desire into the still and invisible depths of these two quivering hearts, made in His own image, that lift themselves in an agony of love to meet Him . . .

Meanwhile, the Easter morning is deepening outside, the sun is rising above the yew hedge, and the dew flashes drop by drop into a diamond and vanishes; the thrush that stirred and murmured last night is pouring out his song, and the larks that rose into the moonlight are running to and fro in the long meadow grass . . . And presently they come, the tall lad and his sister, silent and together, out into the radiant sunlight, and the joy of the morning, and the singing thrush and the jewels of dew, and the sweet swaying lilies are shamed and put to silence by the joy upon their faces and in their hearts. (3)

## The Age of Antichrist: Martyrdom

[*It is the end time. Antichrist has come in the person of Julian Felsenburgh, the President of Europe, who has established world peace and humanitarianism in place of true religion. Persecution of the Church has begun. The English priest, Percy Franklin, has an audience with the Pope, who bears the name John.*]

Percy sat back, trembling.

'Yes, my son. And what do you think should be done?'

Percy flung out his hands. 'Holy Father, the Mass, prayer, the Rosary. These first and last. The world denies their power: it is on their power that Christians must throw all their weight. All things in Jesus Christ—in Jesus Christ, first and last. Nothing else can avail. He must do all, for we can do nothing.

The white head bowed. Then it rose erect. 'Yes, my son ... But as long as Jesus Christ deigns to use us, we must be used. He is Prophet and King as well as Priest. We then, too, must be prophet and king as well as priest. What of prophecy and royalty?'

The voice thrilled Percy like a trumpet.

'Yes, Holiness ... For prophecy, then, let us preach charity; for royalty, let us reign on crosses. We must love and suffer ...' He drew one sobbing breath. 'Your Holiness has preached charity always. Let charity then issue in good deeds. Let us be foremost in them; let us engage in trade honestly, in family life chastely, in government uprightly. And as for suffering—ah, Holiness!'

His old scheme leaped back to his mind, and stood poised there convincing and imperious.

'Yes, my son, speak plainly.'

'Your Holiness, it is old, old as Rome, every fool has desired it: a new order, Holiness, a new order', he stammered.

The white hand dropped the paper-weight. The Pope leaned forward, looking intently at the priest.

'Yes, my son?'

Percy threw himself on his knees.

'A new order, Holiness. No habit or badge, subject to Your Holiness only, freer than Jesuits, poorer than Franciscans, more mortified than Carthusians: men and women alike, the three vows with the intention of martyrdom. The Pantheon for their church; each bishop responsible for their sustenance, a lieutenant for each country ... Holiness, it is the thought of a fool ... And Christ Crucified for their patron.'

The Pope stood up abruptly, so abruptly that Cardinal Martin sprang up, too, apprehensive and terrified. It seemed that this young man had gone too far.

Then the Pope sat down again, extending his hand.

'God bless you, my son. You have leave to go ... Will Your Eminence stay for a few minutes?' [*Later the Pope institutes just such an order.*] (4)

## The Pope Responds to Antichrist's New World Order

The murmur died suddenly to a rustle and a silence. There was a ripple of sinking heads along the seats as the door beside the canopy opened, and a moment later, John, *Pater patrum*, was on his throne ...

'We are not unmindful of the blessings of peace and unity, nor do we forget that the appearance of these things has been the fruit of much that we have condemned. It is this appearance of peace that has deceived many, causing them to doubt the promise of the Prince of Peace that it is through Him alone that we have access to the Father. That true peace, passing understanding, concerns not only the relations of men between themselves, but, supremely, the relations of men with their Maker, and it is in this necessary point that the efforts of the world are found wanting. It is not indeed to be wondered at that in a world which has rejected God this necessary matter should be forgotten. Men have thought, led astray by seducers, that the unity of nations was the greatest prize of this life, forgetting the words of our Saviour, who said that He came to bring not peace but a sword, and that it is through many tribulations that we enter God's Kingdom.

First, then, there should be established the peace of man with God, and after that the unity of man with man will follow. "Seek ye first", said Jesus Christ, "the Kingdom of God, and then all these things shall be added unto you." ' (5)

NOTES AND SOURCES

1. Robert Hugh Benson, *Confessions of a Convert*, new edn. (Sevenoaks: Fisher Press, 1991), 114–15.
2. Robert Hugh Benson, *The Friendship of Christ* (London: Longmans, Green & Co., 1913), 139–41.
3. Robert Hugh Benson, *By What Authority?* (New York: P. J. Kenedy, n.d.), 338–41.
4. Robert Hugh Benson, *The Lord of the World* (London: Burns, Oates & Washbourne, 1928), 125–6.
5. Ibid. 140–2.

# Robert Henry Joseph Steuart SJ                    1874–1948

Robert Steuart was born into a Scottish family that had long been Catholic, and spent a happy childhood at Ballechin, the family's country house in Perthshire. By the age of 13 an earlier enthusiasm for the priesthood had given way to a determination to join the Navy, but the Navy rejected him because of his annual 'hay-asthma', and so, like many others before him, he accepted the Army as second best. His short time at the military college at Woolwich was marked by wild excesses in his social life and failure in the classroom. His father's angry response, 'You fool!', sparked the response, 'I'll go and be a Jesuit!'–'not seriously', he said later, 'but bitterly and unreflectively, as a man might say, "I'll blow my brains out!" '. However, he persevered with his resolution, and in February 1893 entered the Society. During the First World War he served as chaplain to a Highland regiment and was four times mentioned in dispatches. He later wrote a memoir of his life in the trenches, *March, Kind Comrade*. After the war, till his death, he held a number of appointments in the Society, including superior of St Aloysius, Oxford, and of Farm Street. He is remembered as a man of dry humour, fierce honesty about his personal weaknesses and limitations, a compassionate spiritual director, a challenging preacher of the Exercises, and the author of books that appealed to an English Catholic audience longing for spiritual reading that was as humane as it was orthodox. The inspiration of his doctrine was St John of the Cross, and the chief object of his meditation and teaching our mystical incorporation into Christ. He encouraged others to do what he tried, with God's help, to do himself, namely, as Father Martindale put it, 'to "live by faith", and to be sure that God was loving him though he could not feel that that could possibly be true'.

## The Resurrection of Our Lord

His Resurrection, by which He had made good all His claims and had completed the work that His Father had given Him to do, demonstrated to [His disciples] as nothing else could have done, how death might be life, and disgrace be honour, and the gibbet be a throne, and the mocking crown of thorns be the diadem of everlasting empire.

We should never, indeed, be able to acquiesce in these antinomies were it not for His Resurrection—not merely because that was the proof of His truth which He had previously offered, but also because such a reversal as it implies of the accepted values of life and death, and of all their images and equivalents, is in itself a divine seal set upon His word, for therein is embodied what perhaps we may call the secret of God's eternal estimate of all things and events of time, of which, even through the dark glass of our temporal existence, we may catch some small glimpse...Their hearts, indeed, 'burned within them' as they listened, because their obtuseness was less their fault than their misfortune, and when they heard the truth from His own lips their hearts recognized it, as afterwards they recognized Himself in the breaking of bread.

The fact of the Resurrection is for us the key to the truth, to the God-like understanding of all things, right and wrong, and better and best, for it is the 'acted expression', as far as we can now apprehend it, of His divine mind. For the same reason it provides, too, the clue to the only solution of those painful mysteries which in this life have no other explanation, and resist all other evidence, than that of faith. Because of it we should find it easy to believe, and to act upon the belief, that in all circumstances and in all places, and happen what may to us of good or of evil, ever 'His hand leadeth us and His right hand holdeth us'. (1)

## The Mystical Body

The doctrine of the mystical incorporation of the Christian with Christ may well be considered as the foundation and summing up of the entire Christian system both in theory and in practice. In it are involved the dogmas of the divinity and humanity of Christ and our own adoptive sonship of God: of our elevation to the supernatural plane of life which we call the state of sanctifying or habitual grace: of the possibility of meriting before God by our good works and of recovery from actual sin by repentance: of the efficacy of prayer and of the Sacraments: of the final resurrection of our bodies—in a word, the whole complexus of revealed truths, and all the privileges, promises, and sanctions by which, or for the sake of which, the Christian life is ordered...

What...is meant by the doctrine of the Mystical Incorporation with Christ is that by the Sacrament of Baptism there is effected between Christ and the baptized person a true, if ineffable, union (what Mother Julian of Norwich calls 'a ghostly one-ing') in virtue of which the subject of the Sacrament, without losing his own identity, takes upon himself in the eyes of God identity with Christ Himself. 'I live, now not I, but Christ liveth in me', says St Paul: meaning that I am supernaturally alive or not alive, in God's eyes, according as looking at me He sees, or does not see, me as Christ and Christ as me. (2)

## The Prayer of Petition

If I ask for things that must be right, such as charity, self-control, perseverance, the virtues, how is it that I don't get them? In this particular matter we must remember that the mere possession of a virtue means nothing in God's eyes; the only value in its possession is the effort I put into the getting of it—the effort I make to be and do what God wants me to be and do, even if I never attain what I strive for. God can—for special purposes—eliminate faults, but there is no merit to the person. The real merit is when I strive and make efforts. I can't make these efforts without grace, and I pray, I shall get this grace. Grace does not do away with the effort but makes it possible; it is not possible without it. This is the importance of the Prayer of Petition....

When the Church says that prayer is always granted, the meaning is that some spiritual gain accrues to us through our prayer. The value of temporal things doesn't last, but the spiritual things are eternal, their value does not alter. Our Lord said, 'Ask and it shall be given you, seek and you shall find; knock and it shall be opened to you'; but He also said, 'Seek first the Kingdom of God'—before all these material things. We must put the right things in the right place; and we should remember that we do not always ask for the right thing. God, who is Goodness itself, can only give us the good thing. So I mustn't doubt that though the actual thing I asked for I didn't get, my prayer was granted. The evil powers are always trying to make us take the shadow of things for the substance. From habit we test things from their unreality aspect, and we think things are wrong if they don't fit into our ways. Every time a person in contact with God puts up a prayer, it is granted, but it may not be granted in a way that a person can see, but as God sees. With God there is no past and no future; He lives in an utterly unimaginable state of being always *present*. I have just to believe that every time I put myself into communication with Him, there comes to me a real answer to my prayer, but in a shape perhaps that I cannot now recognize, or in a region to which I have not access as yet. My prayer, clothed by me in a material garb, is granted by God in its spiritual value. We have to occupy ourselves for the time being with what are only shadows of the realities. Not till we are free from the limitations of temporal existence shall we see things as they really are. So we must overhaul our prayers, and re-enforce in each the statement, 'Thy will be done' in this particular thing for which I ask. The one thing I want, the real significance of my prayer, is: 'Thy will be done.' It is the general aspect of prayer that wants correcting. If I seek first the Kingdom of God, then all the material things I want will have their supernatural value. It needs faith; but we are Christians, and doesn't that mean that we accept all the implications of Christianity? God is All, and when we realize this, all the bewildering details of life fall into place. (3)

## The Prayer of Silence

The normal progress of Affective Prayer is towards greater and greater simplification. The soul, obeying the instinct of the mind, merges all acts into one act which embraces all the others. What do all my acts thread on to? One thing only—adoration to God. I hold myself simply before Him in a silent attitude of adoration—all the ingredients of adoration converging in this one act. This is the proper attitude of the human being; this opens the way to Contemplation...

There may perhaps come into the mind—in relation to this prayer—a thought, a temptation, that one is doing nothing; and in consequence objections are sometimes brought against it. But this is not so; and the objections perhaps arise owing to forgetfulness that through supernatural grace we are already on God's plane. If I am a Christian and a Catholic, and know that the one thing that matters is that I should love God, then my prayer will take this form of just holding myself before Him—just being conscious that I am looking towards God, and God towards me. And if the thought should come—how can such a thing happen to *me*?—I must remember who I am. Am I not incorporated with Christ in Baptism? Do I not receive Him in His sacrament? Have I not the Holy Spirit of God dwelling in my soul? Then put all such ideas from the mind; it is quite natural that God should seize you in that way. God says: 'Come unto me, all you who are burdened, and I will refresh you.'

Let me then—without fear of making a mistake about it—try to put myself before God without words. God loves me with a love that transcends all translation into the terms of human love. All that He asks is that I should not forget Him—not be unaware of Him. It is not necessary to talk nor to explain things, I must just hold the thought: there is God, and here am I—that is all that matters. Here am I, like an empty jug wanting to be filled by Him; empty, but for the one desire that God will come and fill me with Himself. (4)

## The Death of a Deserter

Shortly after five I called him. He was to die at six o'clock. He dressed in silence, but without the smallest sign of agitation. I remember how careful he was about the adjustment of his puttees. He then renewed his Confession and received Communion once more.

After his breakfast he smoked a cigarette, but refused all stimulant, and we remained talking quietly until the sergeant, as had been arranged, put in his head to warn us that the time was drawing near. He then handed me a letter for his wife, and asked me particularly to remember that to the best of his belief he had no debts, and that he bore no grudge to anyone. I knew to what he referred.

A few minutes more and the door opened to admit the APM, accompanied by a medical officer, the prisoner's own company sergeant-major, and three military police. The prisoner came at once to attention and saluted the officers. The sergeant then formally identified him; the policemen tied a bandage over his eyes and fastened his hands behind him, and the medical officer pinned a small square of lint over his heart, to serve as a mark for the firing party.

Then, with the APM leading, we went out. The place of execution was only a few yards away—three sides of a square, solidly built of sandbags, and in the centre a stout post. I kept my hand upon his arm as we walked, and I can vouch for it that he never faltered or trembled.

Arrived within the square he was bound securely to the post, and I had time to hear him make his act of contrition and give him absolution once more, to put the crucifix to his steady lips, to press his hand in good-bye, and to get 'God bless you, Father', from him, before the APM motioned to me to stand aside.

It was a misty morning, and the white fog magnified the sounds that rose from the just-awakened camps about us. Some trucks clanked noisily on a siding below, and there was a stamping of horses and a rattle of chains from the standings across the road above us. Shouts and whistles and the thousand confused rumours of a busy camp reached us, and in the distance a mellow baritone voice was singing 'The Roses of Picardy'. With these familiar sounds of everyday life in his ears and the bite of the sharp morning air on his face, in full health and strength and youth, he died.

At a sign from the APM, the firing party, which up till then had been with their backs to the condemned man, faced about to him. At a second sign they took aim; at a third they fired; and the bound figure crumpled and slid down as far as the ropes would let him go. Instantly the officer in command called his men to attention, formed fours, and marched them off; and the medical officer, stepping forward to examine the body, reported five bullets through his heart.

The cemetery lay a few hundred yards away, and less than a quarter of an hour from the time that the dead man and I had sat talking together in the hut, the earth had been pressed down over him in his grave, and I was signing the label for the identifying peg at his head. That, and a pool of bright red blood steaming in the hollow of the stretcher, was all the trace that he had left.

He had paid the just penalty of his offence, but I ask no better than that I may meet my death, when I must, as gallantly as did that deserter. (5)

## Typical Sayings of Father Steuart

I will be saint for a minute—and the many dots join together until it is one continuous line.

The saints have not got the attitude, 'Don't come near me!'

Often our Crosses come to us on two legs.

Don't think of God as sitting at a desk making ticks against us. (6)

NOTES AND SOURCES

1. R. H. J. Steuart, *In Divers Manners* (London: Longmans, Green & Co., 1938), 97–9.
2. R. H. J. Steuart, *The Two Voices: Spiritual Conferences of R. H. J. Steuart SJ*, ed. with a memoir by C. C. Martindale SJ (London: Burns & Oates, 1952), 197–8.
3. Ibid. 245–6, 247–8.
4. Ibid. 263–5.
5. R. H. J. Steuart, *March, Kind Comrade* (London: Sheed & Ward, 1931), 101–3.
6. R. H. J. Steuart, *Spiritual Teaching of Father Steuart SJ*, ed. K. Kendall (London: Burns & Oates, 1952), 128.

# Maurice Baring                                                    1874–1945

Born into one of the great banking families of Europe, the eighth of the ten children of Lord Revelstoke, Maurice Baring remained grateful for a childhood and youth of unshadowed happiness. After Eton and Cambridge (and Oxford), and five years as a diplomat, he worked as a correspondent of the *Morning Post* during the Russo-Japanese war. A gifted linguist, he became fluent in Russian, translated Pushkin, and edited the *Oxford Book of Russian Verse*. Of his reception into the Church at the London Oratory in 1909 he said that it was 'the only action of my life which I am quite certain I have never regretted'. For his service during the First World War, when he assisted General Trenchard in the development of the Royal Flying Corps and the establishment of the Royal Air Force, he was awarded the OBE. After the war he devoted himself to the writing of novels, such as *C*, *Cat's Cradle*, and *Daphne Adeane*, in which, as Father Ian Ker has said, 'Catholicism is shown to offer the way of rendering personal suffering redemptive in a world where human love is ultimately doomed'. But his interests and writing also embraced short stories, poetry, military history, literary criticism, biography, drama, and parodies. He was the friend of many of the great English Catholics of the first half of the century. In James Gunn's painting in the National Portrait Gallery, he stands, cigarette in hand, looking down with affection and amusement at Chesterton scribbling at a desk and Belloc glowering beside him. Without any pretensions to scholarship, Baring is conspicuous, even among his glittering contemporaries, for the breadth of his culture. The whole of ancient and modern European literature was at his finger-tips. His knowledge and love of music and the theatre took in everything from Wagner to Dan Leno. And yet, for all his brilliance of mind, he remained childlike at heart, modest, playful, with a subversive sense of humour directed generally to himself. His last years, spent with Lord and Lady Lovat in Scotland, were, despite the extreme discomforts of Parkinson's disease, a time of peace and contentment.

## Candlemass

The town is half awake; the nave, the choir,
Are dark, and all is dim within, without;
But every chapel fringed with the devout
Is bright with February flowers of fire.
At Mass, a thousand years ago in Rome,
Thus Priest, thus Server at the altar bowed;
Thus knelt, thus blessed itself the kneeling crowd,
At Dawn, within the secret catacomb.
Thus shall they meet for Mass, until the day
The glory of the world shall pass away.
And beauty far above all human reach,
And power, and wealth beyond all mortal price,
And glory that outsoars all thought, all speech,
Speak in the whispered words of sacrifice. (1)

## The Balm of Sacrifice

[*Fanny, who is not a Catholic, and describes herself as a pagan, consults Father Rendall about her desire to marry Francis, with whom she had fallen in love in 1916, just before her husband, Michael, went missing in action. After the Armistice, having lived together, she and Francis make up their minds to marry, when news comes that Michael is alive and well, and will return tomorrow.*]

'You, who like pagan sentiments, [says Father Rendall], do you remember what Antigone said to Creon, when she performed the funeral rites for her brother after Creon had forbidden it? "Not did I think that thou, a mortal man, couldst by a breath cancel the immutable unwritten laws of God. They are not of today nor of yesterday.'"

'But that is just it [replies Fanny]. I say I *am* obeying the unwritten law. Antigone was accused of breaking the formal law of man. It is laws of man I am breaking—the conventions of the world—of society.'

'On the contrary, the laws of man will allow you to divorce as much and as often as you please. It is the law of God you are breaking. The law that Antigone broke was the man-made law—a fortuitous, cruel, and unjust law—made for a special spiteful purpose; and she said expressly that the law she broke was not ordained of Zeus nor enacted by Justice. The law she kept was the law of God. The law you wish to break is the law of God: "Thou shalt not commit adultery." '

'But I have broken that already . . . so surely it doesn't matter what I do now. It's too late.'

'According to our belief, it is never too late; and according to our belief, it matters immensely.'

'That's the vicious circle again. According to your creed.'

'You must make up your mind whether you are appealing to Caesar or to God, and you mustn't confuse your tributes.'

They were already further than Victoria Gate.

'I must go back,' said Fanny, 'I will think it over. Thank you for all you have done and said. You have been most kind. Even if I don't take your advice—and it is most probable, it would indeed be a miracle, I think, if I did take it—you have helped me; you have been very kind, and I am sorry, as they say at the exchanges, to have troubled you.'

'May I ask you one last question? 'said Father Rendall.

'Yes, of course.'

'You say you are a pagan. What is, in your opinion, the fundamental idea of paganism? What is the essence of Greek tragedy?'

'Sacrifice', said Fanny without hesitation.

'There!' said Father Rendall, 'Now believe me that in every act of sacrifice we make there is a *balm*, and in every act of self that we make there is an aftertaste of fire, smoke, dust, and ash. Goodbye.' And he looked at her with steady compassion.

'Goodbye,'she said, 'and pray for me.'

[*She decides to end her affair with Francis, and vows to 'live for others, for Michael and the children, and try and make them happy.' She feels the sense of balm of which Father Rendall had spoken.*] (2)

## *Vita nuova*: Baring's Conversion

### I

I found the clue I sought not, in the night,
While wandering in a pathless maze of gloom;
The sky was hid behind huge shapes of doom;
There was no moon, nor any star in sight,

My hopes, my dreams, and my faithless creeds were slain,
Like corpses on a battlefield they lay;
The world was but a graveyard dark with clay;
The stifling cloud denied one drop of rain;

When from the giddy marge of the abyss,
I cried aloud in agony and fear,
When, suddenly, it seemed my single tear
Stretched and became a shining bridge to bliss.

I stood before a topless gate. Within
I guessed the light, I dared not enter in.

### II

One day I heard a whisper: 'Wherefore wait?
Why linger in a separated porch?

Why nurse the flicker of a severed torch?
The fire is there, ablaze beyond the gate.

Why tremble, foolish soul? Why hesitate?
However faint the knock, it will be heard.'
I knocked, and swiftly came the answering word,
Which bade me enter to my own estate.

I found myself in a familiar place;
And there my broken soul began to mend;
I knew the smile of every long-lost face—

They whom I had forgot remembered me;
I knelt, I knew—it was too bright to see—
The welcome of a King who was my friend.

III

My treasure and my resting-place are found,
My mother-land, my immemorial home;
Beyond the reefs of treasonable foam,
I know the lights that flash upon the sound.

Lightning may strike, and hurricane may blow,
Whatever shall befall, I cannot fear:
Whether the hour be far away or near,
That tranquil harbour shines and waits, I know.

I know. There is no mortal word to say;
For what there is to speak is vast and dim;
But haply, if God please, beyond the day.

Delivered from the bars and bonds of speech,
Made strong with language which the angels teach,
I'll share my secret with the Seraphim. (3)

## Body and Soul

My body is a broken toy
Which nobody can mend.
Unfit for either play or ploy,
My Body is a broken toy,
But all things end.
The siege of Troy
Came one day to an end.
My body is a broken toy
Which nobody can mend.

My soul is an immortal toy
Which nobody can mar.

Though rusted from the world's alloy
It glitters like a star. (4)

NOTES AND SOURCES

1. Maurice Baring, 'Candlemass', *Blackfriars*, 4 (1923), 782.
2. Maurice Baring, *Daphne Adeane* (London: Heinemann, 1926), 301–3, 324.
3. Maurice Baring, *Collected Poems* (London: Heinemann, 1925), 65–7.
4. Quoted by Baring's great-niece, Emma Letley, in *Maurice Baring: A Citizen of Europe* (London: Constable, 1991), 227.

# Gilbert Keith Chesterton                                    1874–1936

Chesterton's end is in his beginning. His life's work was an endeavour always to be, or at least to become again, the child he used to be. He wanted to keep hold not simply of his childhood's happiness, but of its perceptions, its wonder at reality, the perceptions and wonder that were at the heart of its happiness. The doctrine that he most extensively proclaimed and consistently put into practice is a variation on what his contemporary, and the patron of his parish church, St Thérèse of Lisieux, called the 'little way' of spiritual childhood. Childhood for Chesterton was not a dull track towards the exciting highway of adulthood, but 'the white and solid road and the worthy beginning of the life of man'. Asked for his reason for becoming a Catholic in 1922, he would answer without hesitation, 'To get rid of my sins'—in the Sacrament of Penance, the Sacrament, he said, that restores innocence and makes a man a little child again. After the happiness of the early years in Kensington, after the schooling and the friendships at St Paul's, after the attempt at a training in art at the Slade, what did he become? He was content to call himself a journalist, but there is no reason why we should be. He seems to be so much more: illustrator, theatrical designer (for toy theatres), writer of novels (including the Father Brown mysteries), poet (short verse, drinking songs, and his narrative masterpiece, *The Ballad of the White Horse*), dramatist, biographer (Watts, Browning, Cobbett, Aquinas), historian, literary critic, debater and public speaker, the champion of Distributism and sane economics, the scourge of birth control, suicide, divorce, eugenics, and other evils, 'gifted defender of the Catholic faith' (as Pope Pius XI called him on his death). GK would not want us to scruple over the journalist tag. He would point out that men hired, as hacks are hired, to report and comment on everything ('All human life is there') have the universe as their special subject, and as a professional class do in fact tend to range far and wide in their interests. However, few scribblers have had minds so cosmic in their capacity as his. Perhaps the best of all titles for Chesterton is the one awarded him by Walter de la Mare, 'Knight of the Holy Ghost'. *Knight* he was for sure: from his boyhood, he aspired to chivalry, and if you leaf through the books and magazines he owned and treated as drawing paper, you will find the knight to be one of the favourite subjects of his doodling. On the day of his marriage to Frances Blogg, he bought a revolver with cartridges, not he assures us in his autobiography with any murderous intent towards himself or his wife, but with the chivalrous aim of protecting her from 'the pirates doubtless infesting the Norfolk Broads', to which they travelled for their honeymoon. He was a constant fighter in the intellectual and moral order, but the thrust of his rapier in debate, though it disarmed, never dishonoured his opponents.

(His judgement of Thomas Hardy, 'the village atheist brooding over the village idiot', seems to be the sole exception: it hurt Hardy, and GK later regretted having said it.) Knight *of the Holy Ghost*, indeed: for the Spirit of charity breathes through his words and actions; unlike his friend Hilaire Belloc, he was incapable of making enemies and endeared himself even to those, such as Bernard Shaw and H. G. Wells, with whom he emphatically and publicly disagreed. It is that heroism of kindness, the stubborn determination to find some element of truth and goodness in what his adversaries were trying to say or to be, which qualifies him, in the opinion of many, to be a suitable candidate for the honours of the Church's altars. Whatever judgement ecclesiastical authority might one day make, Gilbert Keith Chesterton, the poet of Christmas, does seem to be a man who took Our Lord at His word, and received the Kingdom with the heart of a child.

## The Wonder of Childhood

What was wonderful about childhood is that anything in it was a wonder. It was not merely a world full of miracles; it was a miraculous world. What gives me this shock is almost anything I really recall, not the things I should think most worth recalling....

Stevenson, whom I so warmly admire ... talks of the child as normally in a dazed day-dream, in which he cannot distinguish fancy from fact. Now children and adults are both fanciful at times, but that is not what, in my mind and memory, distinguishes adults from children. Mine is a memory of a sort of white light on everything, cuttings things out very clearly, and rather emphasizing their solidity. The point is that the white light had a sort of wonder in it, as if the world were as new as myself, but not that the world was anything but a real world. (1)

## Youthful Darkness Broken by Gratitude

With little help from philosophy and no real help from religion, I invented a rudimentary and makeshift mystical theory of my own. It was substantially this: that even mere existence, reduced to its most primary limits, was extraordinary enough to be exciting. Anything was magnificent as compared with nothing...I hung on to the remains of religion by one thin thread of thanks. I thanked whatever gods might be, not like Swinburne, because no life lived forever, but because any life lived at all; not, like Henley, for my unconquerable soul (for I have never been so optimistic about my own soul as all that), but for my own soul and my own body, even if they could be conquered. This way of looking at things, with a sort of mystical minimum of gratitude, was of course to some extent assisted by those few of the fashionable writers who were not pessimists, especially by Walt Whitman, by Browning and by Stevenson: Browning's 'God must be glad one loves his world so much', or Stevenson's 'belief in the ultimate decency of things'. But I do not think it is too much to say that I took it in a way of my own, even if it was a way I could not see clearly or make very clear. What I meant, whether or no I managed to say it, was this: that no man knows how much he is an optimist, even when he calls himself a pessimist, because he has not really measured the depths of his debt to whatever created him and enabled him to call himself anything. At the back of our brains, so to speak, there was a forgotten blaze or burst of astonishment at our own existence. The object of artistic and spiritual life was to dig for this submerged sunrise of wonder, so that a man sitting in a chair might suddenly understand that he was actually alive, and be happy. (2)

## The Catholic Church: The Champion of Reason

The Catholic Church comes forward as the one and only real champion of reason. There was ... a hundred years ago a school of free-thinkers which attacked Rome by an appeal to reason. But most of the recent free-thinkers are, by their own account rather than by ours, falling from reason even more than from Rome. One of the best and most brilliant of them, Mr Bernard Shaw, said only the other day that he could never entirely agree with the Catholic Church because of its extreme rationalism. In this perception he is at least quite rational; that is, as we poor rationalists would say, he is quite right. The Church is larger than the world, and she rightly resisted the narrow rationalists who maintained that everything in all the world could be approached in exactly the same way that is used for particular material things in this world. But she never said those things were not to be approached, or that reason was not the proper way to approach them, or that anybody had any right to be unreasonable in approaching anything. She defends the wisdom of the world as the way of dealing with the world; she defends common sense and consistent thinking and the perception that two and two make four. And today she is alone in defending them. (3)

## Father Brown Exposes the Superstitions of the Unbeliever

He stood up abruptly, his face heavy with a sort of frown, and went on talking almost as if he were alone. 'It's the first effect of not believing in God that you lose your common sense and can't see things as they are. Anything that anybody talks about, and says there's a good deal in it, extends itself indefinitely like a vista in a nightmare. And a dog is an omen, and a cat is a mystery, and a pig is a mascot, and a beetle is a scarab, calling up all the menagerie of polytheism from Egypt and old India—Dog Anubis and great green-eyed Pasht, and all the holy howling Bulls of Bashan, reeling back to the bestial god of the beginning, escaping into elephants and snakes and crocodiles—and all because you are frightened of four words: 'He was made man'. (4)

## Thomist Realism: Eggs are Eggs

The philosophy of St Thomas stands founded on the universal common conviction that eggs are eggs. The Hegelian may say that an egg is really a hen, because it is a part of an endless process of Becoming; the Berkeleian may hold that poached eggs only exist as a dream exists; since it is quite as easy to call the dream the cause of the eggs as the eggs the cause of the dream; the Pragmatist may believe that we get the best out of scrambled eggs by forgetting that they ever were eggs, and only remembering the scramble. But no pupil of St Thomas needs to addle his brains in order adequately to addle his eggs; to put his head at any peculiar angle in looking at eggs, or squinting at eggs, or winking the other eye in order to see a new simplification of eggs. The Thomist stands in the broad daylight of the brotherhood of men, in their common consciousness that eggs are not hens or dreams or mere practical assumptions; but things attested by the Authority of the Senses, which is from God. (5)

## The Convert

After one moment when I bowed my head
And the whole world turned over and came upright,
And I came out where the old road shone white,
I walked the ways and heard what all men said,
Forests of tongues, like autumn leaves unshed,
Being not unlovable, but strange and light;
Old riddles and new creeds, not in despite
But softly, as men smile about the dead.

The sages have a hundred maps to give
That trace their crawling cosmos like a tree,
They rattle reason out through many a sieve
That stores the sand and lets the gold go free:
And all these things are less than dust to me
Because my name is Lazarus and I live. (6)

## Conversion: The Reasons

The difficulty of explaining 'why I am a Catholic' is that there are ten thousand reasons all amounting to one reason: that Catholicism is true. I could fill all my space with separate sentences each beginning with the words, 'It is the only thing that...' As, for instance, (1) It is the only thing that really prevents a sin from being a secret. (2) It is the only thing in which the superior cannot be superior, in the sense of supercilious. (3) It is the only thing that frees a man from the degrading slavery of being a child of his age. (4) It is the only thing that talks as if it were the truth; as if it were a real messenger refusing to tamper with a real message. (5) It is the only type of Christianity that really contains every type of man, even the respectable man. (6) It is the only large attempt to change the world from the inside; working through wills and not laws... (7)

## Conversion: Confession

When people ask me, or indeed anybody else, 'Why did you join the Church of Rome?', the first essential answer, if it is partly an elliptical answer, is 'To get rid of my sins'. For there is no other religious system that does *really* profess to get rid of people's sins. It is confirmed by the logic, which to many seems startling, by which the Church deduces that sin confessed and adequately repented is actually abolished, and that the sinner does really begin again as if he had never sinned... When a Catholic comes from Confession, he does truly, by definition, step out again into that dawn of his own beginning and look with new eyes across the world to a Crystal Palace that is really of crystal. He believes that in that dim corner, and in that brief ritual, God has really re-made him in His own image. He is now a new experiment of the Creator. He is as much a new experiment as he was when he was really only five years old. He stands, as I said, in the white light at the worthy beginning of the life of a man. The accumulations of time can no longer terrify. He may be grey and gouty, but he is only five minutes old. (8)

## The Consubstantial Trinity: The God of Love

If there is one question which the enlightened and liberal have the habit of deriding and holding up as a dreadful example of barren dogma and senseless sectarian strife, it is this Athanasian question of the co-eternity of the Divine Son. On the other hand, if there is one thing that the same liberals always offer us as a piece of pure and simple Christianity, untroubled by doctrinal disputes, it is the single sentence, 'God is love'. Yet the two statements are almost identical; at least, one is very nearly nonsense without the other. The barren dogma is only the logical way of stating the beautiful sentiment. For if there be a being without beginning, existing before all things, was He loving when there was nothing to be loved? If through that unthinkable eternity He is lonely, what is the meaning of saying He is love? The only explanation of such a mystery is the mystical conception that in His own nature there was something analogous to self-expression, something of what begets and beholds what it has begotten. Without some such idea, it is really illogical to complicate the ultimate essence of deity with an idea like love. If the moderns really want a simple religion of love, they must look for it in the Athanasian Creed. The truth is that the trumpet of true Christianity, the challenge of the charities and simplicities of Bethlehem or Christmas Day, never rang out more arrestingly and unmistakably than in the defiance of Athanasius to the cold compromise of the Arians. It was emphatically he who was fighting for a God of Love against a God of colourless and remote cosmic control, the God of the Stoics and the agnostics. It was emphatically he who was fighting for the Holy Child against the grey deity of the Pharisees and the Sadducees. He was fighting for that very balance of beautiful interdependence and intimacy, in the very Trinity of the Divine Nature, that draws our hearts to the Trinity of the Holy Family. His dogma, if the phrase be not misunderstood, turns even God into a Holy Family. (9)

## Brother Thomas of the Creator

Granted all the grandeur of Augustine's contribution to Christianity, there was in a sense a more subtle danger in Augustine the Platonist than even in Augustine the Manichee. There came from it a mood which unconsciously committed the heresy of dividing the substance of the Trinity. It thought of God too exclusively as a Spirit who purifies or a Saviour who redeems, and too little as a Creator who creates. That is why men like Aquinas thought it right to correct Plato by an appeal to Aristotle: Aristotle who took things as he found them, just as Aquinas accepted things as God created them. In all the work of St Thomas the world of positive creation is perpetually present. Humanly speaking, it was he who saved the human element in Christian theology, if he used for convenience certain elements in heathen philosophy. Only, as has already been urged, the human element is also the Christian one. (10)

# The Fall

The Fall is a view of life. It is not only the only enlightening, but the only encouraging view of life. It holds, as against the only real alternative philosophies, those of the Buddhist or the Pessimist or the Promethean, that we have misused a good world, and not merely been entrapped into a bad one. It refers evil back to the wrong use of the will, and thus declares that it can eventually be righted by the right use of the will. Every other creed except that one is some form of surrender to fate. A man who holds this view of life will find it giving light on a thousand things, on which mere evolutionary ethics have not a word to say. For instance, on the colossal contrast between the completeness of man's machines and the continued corruption of his motives; on the fact that no social progress really seems to leave self behind; on the fact that the first and not the last men of any school or revolution are generally the best and purest; as William Penn was better than a Quaker millionaire or Washington better than an American oil magnate; on that proverb that says: 'The price of liberty is eternal vigilance', which is only what the theologians say of every other virtue, and is itself only a way of stating the truth of original sin; on those extremes of good and evil by which man exceeds all the animals by the measure of Heaven and hell; on that sublime sense of loss that is in the very sound of all great poetry, and nowhere more than in the poetry of pagans and sceptics: 'We look before and after, and pine for what is not'; which cries against all prigs and progressives out of the very depths and abysses of the broken heart of man, that happiness is not only a hope, but also in some strange manner a memory; and that we are all kings in exile. (11)

# Aristotle and the Incarnation: Chesterton's Book on St Thomas Aquinas

It was Aquinas who baptized Aristotle, when Aristotle could not have baptized Aquinas; it was a purely Christian miracle which raised the great pagan from the dead. And this is proved in three ways (as St Thomas himself might say), which it will be well to summarize as a sort of summary of this book.

First, in the life of St Thomas, it is proved in the fact that only his huge and solid orthodoxy could have supported so many things which then seemed to be unorthodox. Charity covers a multitude of sins; and in that sense orthodoxy covers a multitude of heresies; or things which are hastily mistaken for heresies. It was precisely because his personal Catholicism was so convincing that his impersonal Aristotelianism was given the benefit of the doubt. He did not smell of the faggot because he did smell of the firebrand; of the firebrand he had so instantly and instinctively snatched up, under a real assault on essential Catholic ethics. A typically cynical modern phrase refers to the man who is so good that he is good for nothing. St Thomas was so good that he was good for everything; that his warrant held good for what others considered the most wild and daring speculations, ending in the worship of nothing. Whether or no he baptized Aristotle, he was truly the godfather of Aristotle, he was his sponsor; he swore that the old Greek would do no harm; and the whole world trusted his word.

Second, in the philosophy of St Thomas, it is proved by the fact that everything depended on the new Christian *motive* for the study of facts, as distinct from truths. The Thomist philosophy began with the lowest roots of thought, the senses and the truisms of reason; and a Pagan sage might have scorned such things, as he scorned the servile arts. But the materialism, which is merely cynicism in a Pagan, can be Christian humility in a Christian. St Thomas was willing to begin by recording the facts and sensations of the material world, just as he would have been willing to begin by washing up the plates and dishes in the monastery. The point of his Aristotelianism was that even if common sense about concrete things really was a sort of servile labour, he must not be ashamed to be *servus servorum Dei*. Among heathens the mere sceptic might become the mere cynic; Diogenes in his tub had always a touch of the tub-thumper; but even the dirt of the cynics was dignified into dust and ashes among the saints. If we miss that, we miss the whole meaning of the greatest revolution in history. There was a new *motive* for beginning with the most material, and even with the meanest things.

Third, in the theology of St Thomas, it is proved by the tremendous truth that supports all that theology; or any other Christian theology. There really was a new reason for regarding the senses, and the sensations of the body, and the experiences of the common man, with a reverence at which great Aristotle would have stared, and no man in the ancient world could have begun to understand. The Body was no longer what it was when Plato and Porphyry and the old mystics had left it for dead. It had hung upon a gibbet. It had risen from a tomb. It was no longer possible for the soul to despise the senses, which had been the organs of something that was more than man. Plato might despise the flesh; but God had not despised it. The senses had truly become sanctified; as they are blessed one by one at a Catholic baptism. 'Seeing is believing' was no longer the platitude of a mere idiot, or common individual, as in Plato's world; it was mixed up with real conditions of real belief. Those revolving mirrors that send messages to the brain of man, that light that breaks upon the brain, these had truly revealed to God Himself the path to Bethany or the light on the high rock of Jerusalem. These ears that resound with common noises had reported also to the secret knowledge of God the noise of the crowd that strewed palms and the crowd that cried for Crucifixion. After the Incarnation had become the idea that is central in our civilization, it was inevitable that there should be a return to materialism, in the sense of the serious value of matter and the making of the body. When once Christ had risen, it was inevitable that Aristotle should rise again. (12)

## The Christlike Francis

In speaking the ease with which truth may be made to look like its own shadow or sham, [Cardinal Newman] said, 'And if Antichrist is like Christ, Christ, I suppose, is like Antichrist.' Mere religious sentiment might well be shocked at the end of the sentence, but nobody could object to it except the logician who said that Caesar and Pompey were very much alike, especially Pompey. It may give a much milder shock if I say here, what most of us have forgotten, that if St Francis was like Christ, Christ was to that extent like St Francis. And my present point is that it is really very enlightening to realize that Christ was like St Francis. What I mean is this: that if men find certain riddles and hard sayings in the story of Galilee, and if they find the answers to those riddles in the story of Assisi, it really does show that a secret has been handed down in one religious tradition and no other. It shows that the casket that was locked in Palestine can be unlocked in Umbria, for the Church is the keeper of the keys. (13)

## Christmas: The Child-God

Any agnostic or atheist whose childhood has known a real Christmas has ever afterwards, whether he likes it or not, an association in his mind between two ideas that most of mankind must regard as remote from each other: the idea of a baby and the idea of unknown strength that sustains the stars. His instincts and imagination can still connect them, when his reason can no longer see the need of the connection; for him there will always be some savour of religion about the mere picture of a mother and a baby; some hint of mercy and softening about the mere mention of the dreadful name of God. (14)

## Christmas: The Virgin Mother

If the world wanted what is called a non-controversial aspect of Christianity, it would probably select Christmas. Yet it is obviously bound up with what is supposed to be a controversial aspect (I could never at any stage of my opinions imagine why): the respect paid to the Blessed Virgin. When I was a boy, a more Puritan generation objected to a statue upon my parish church representing the Virgin and Child. After much controversy, they compromised by taking away the Child. One would think that this was even more corrupted with Mariolatry, unless the mother was counted less dangerous when deprived of a sort of weapon. But the practical difficulty is also a parable. You cannot chip away the statue of a mother from all round that of a new-born child. You cannot suspend the new-born child in mid-air; indeed, you cannot really have a statue of a new-born child at all. Similarly, you cannot suspend the idea of a new-born child in the void or think of him without thinking of his mother. You cannot visit the child without visiting the mother; you cannot in common human life approach the child except through the mother. If we are to think of Christ in this aspect at all, the other idea follows as it is followed in history. We must either leave Christ out of Christmas, or Christmas out of Christ, or we must admit, if only as we admit it in an old picture, that those holy heads are too near together for the haloes not to mingle and cross. (15)

### *Regina angelorum*

Our Lady went into a strange country,
    Our Lady, for she was ours,
And had run on the little hills behind the houses
    And pulled small flowers;
But she rose up and went into a strange country
    With strange thrones and powers.

And there were giants in the land she walked in,
    Tall as their toppling towns,

With heads so high in Heaven, the constellations
   Served them for crowns;
And their feet might have forded like a brook the abysses
   Where Babel drowns.

They were girt about with the wings of the morning and evening,
   Furled and unfurled,
Round the speckled sky when our small spinning planet
   Like a top is twirled;
And the swords they waved were the unending comets
   That shall end the world.

And moving in innocence and in accident,
   She turned the face
That none has ever looked on without loving
   On the Lords of Space;
And one hailed her with her name in our own country
   That is full of grace.

Our Lady went into a strange country
   And they crowned her for a queen,
For she needed never to be stayed or questioned
   But only seen;
And they were broken down under unbearable beauty
   As we have been.

But ever she walked till away in the last high places,
   One great light shone
From the pillared throne of the king of all that country
   Who sat thereon;
And she cried aloud as she cried under the gibbet
   For she saw her Son.

Our Lady wears a crown in a strange country,
   The crown he gave,
But she has not forgotten to call to her old companions
   To call and crave;
And to hear her calling a man might arise and thunder
   On the doors of the grave. (16)

## Mad, Bad, or God

Mahomet did not make [the claim to be God] any more than Micah or Malachi. Confucius did not make it any more than Plato or Marcus Aurelius. Buddha never said he was Brahma. Zoroaster no more claimed to be Ormuz than to be Ahriman. The truth is that, in the common run of cases, it is just as we should expect it to be, in common sense and certainly in Christian philosophy . . . Normally speaking, the greater a man is, the less likely he is to make the very greatest claim. Outside the unique case we are considering, the only kind of man who ever does make that kind of claim is a very small man, a secretive or self-centred monomaniac ... It is by rather an unlucky metaphor that we talk of a madman as cracked, for in a sense he is not cracked enough. He is cramped rather than cracked; there are not enough holes in his head to ventilate it. This impossibility of letting in daylight on a delusion does sometimes cover and conceal a delusion of divinity. It can be found, not among prophets and sages and founders of religions, but only among a low set of lunatics. But this is exactly where the argument becomes intensely interesting, because the argument proves too much. For nobody supposes that Jesus of Nazareth was *that* sort of person. No modern critic in his five wits thinks that the preacher of the Sermon the Mount was a horrible half-witted imbecile that might be scrawling stars on the walls of a cell. No atheist or blasphemer believes that the author of the Parable of the Prodigal Son was a monster with one mad idea like a Cyclops with one eye. Upon any possible historical criticism, He must be put higher in the scale of human beings than that. Yet by all analogy we have really to put Him there or else in the highest place of all. (17)

## The Cry of Dereliction

If there be any sound that can produce a silence, we may surely be silent about the end and the extremity, when a cry was driven out of that darkness in words dreadfully distinct and dreadfully unintelligible, which man shall never understand in all the eternity they have purchased for him; and for one annihilating instant an abyss that is not for our thoughts had opened even in the unity of the absolute, and God had been forsaken by God. (18)

## The Eucharistic Congress: Dublin, 1932

As the Congress drew to its end, the patch of glowing weather which had been stretched like a golden canopy, strangely and almost insecurely, began to show signs of strain or schism. There was a hint of storm in the still heat, and here and there random splashes of rain. It was naturally a topic of anxious talk, and it gave birth to one great saying, which I shall always remember as one of those tremendous oracles that sometimes come from the innocent. A priest told me that he had heard a very poor threadbare working woman saying in a tram, with a resignation perhaps slightly touched with tartness: 'Well, if it rains now, He'll have brought it on Himself.' (19)

## Rome and Reality

At the moment when Religion lost touch with Rome, it changed instantly and internally, from top to bottom, in its very substance and the stuff of which it was made. It changed in substance; it did not necessarily change in form or features or externals. It might do the same things; but it could not be the same thing. It might go on saying the same things; but it was not the same thing that was saying them. At the very beginning, indeed, the situation was almost exactly like that. Henry VIII was a Catholic in everything except that he was not a Catholic. He observed everything down to the last bead and candle; he accepted everything down to the last deduction from a definition; he accepted everything except Rome. And in that instant of refusal, his religion became a different religion; a different sort of religion; a different sort of thing. In that instant it began to change; and it has not stopped changing yet. (20)

## Why I Despise Birth Control

I despise Birth Control first because it is a weak and wobbly and cowardly word. It is also an entirely meaningless word, and is used so as to curry favour even with those who would at first recoil from its real meaning. The proceeding these quack doctors recommend does not *control* any birth. It only makes sure that there shall never be any birth to control. It cannot for instance, determine sex, or even make any selection in the style of the pseudo-science of Eugenics. Normal people can only act so as to produce birth, and these people can only act so as to prevent birth. But these people know perfectly well as I do that the very word Birth Prevention would strike a chill into the public, the instant it was blazoned on headlines, or proclaimed on platforms, or scattered in advertisements like any other quack medicine. They dare not call it by its name, because its name is very bad advertising. Therefore they use a conventional and unmeaning word, which may make the quack medicine sound more innocuous.

Second, I despise Birth Control because it is a weak and wobbly and cowardly thing. It is not even a step along the muddy road they call Eugenics; it is a flat refusal to take the first and most obvious step along the road of Eugenics. Once grant that their philosophy is right, and their course of action is obvious; and they dare not take it; they dare not even declare it. If there is no authority in things which Christendom has called moral, because their origins were mystical, then they are clearly free to ignore all the difference between animals and men, and treat men as we treat animals. They need not palter with the stale and timid compromise and convention called Birth Control. Nobody applies it to the cat. The obvious course for Eugenists is to act towards babies as they act towards kittens. Let all the babies be born, and then let us drown those we do not like. I cannot see any objection to it, except the moral or mystical sort of objection that we advance against Birth Prevention. And that would be real and even reasonable Eugenics, for we could then select the best, or at least the healthiest, and sacrifice what are called the unfit. By the weak compromise of Birth Prevention, we are very probably sacrificing the fit and only producing the unfit. The births we prevent may be the births of the best and most beautiful children; those we allow, the weakest or worst. Indeed, it is probable; for the habit discourages the early parentage of young and vigorous people; and lets them put off the experience to later years, mostly from mercenary motives. Until I see a real pioneer and progressive leader coming out with a good, bold, scientific programme for drowning babies, I will not join the movement.

But there is a third reason for my contempt, much deeper and therefore more difficult to express; in which is rooted all my reasons for being anything I am or attempt to be; and above all, for being a Distributist. Perhaps the nearest to a description of it is to say this: that my contempt boils over into bad behaviour when I hear the common suggestion that a birth is avoided because people want to be 'free' to go to the cinema or buy a gramophone or a loud-speaker. What makes me want to walk over such people like doormats is that they use the word 'free'. By every act of that sort they chain themselves to the most servile and mechanical system yet tolerated by men. The cinema is a machine for unrolling certain regular patterns called pictures, expressing the most vulgar millionaires' notion of the taste of the most vulgar millions. The gramophone is a machine for recording such tunes as certain shops and other organizations choose to sell. The wireless is better, but even that is marked by the modern mark of all three: the impotence of the receptive party. The amateur cannot challenge the actor; the householder will find it vain to go and shout into the gramophone; the mob cannot pelt the modern speaker, especially when he is a loud-speaker. It is all a central mechanism giving out to men exactly what their masters think they should have.

Now a child is the very sign and sacrament of personal freedom. He is a fresh free will added to the wills of the world; he is something that his parents have freely chosen to produce, and which they freely agree to protect. They can feel that any amusement he gives (which is often considerable) really comes from him and from them and from nobody else. He has been born without the intervention of any master or lord. He is a creation and a contribution; he is their own creative contribution to creation. He is also a much more beautiful, wonderful, amusing, and astonishing thing than any of the stale stories or jingling jazz tunes turned out by the machines. When men no longer feel that he is so, they have lost the appreciation of primary things, and therefore all sense of proportion about the world. People who prefer the mechanical pleasures, to such a miracle, are jaded and enslaved. They are preferring the very dregs of life to the first fountains of life. They are preferring the last, crooked, indirect, borrowed, repeated and exhausted things of our dying Capitalist civilization, to the reality which is the only rejuvenation of all civilization. It is they who are hugging the chains of their old slavery; it is the child who is ready for the new world. (21)

## A Second Childhood

When all my days are ending
And I have no song to sing,
I think I shall not be too old
To stare at everything;
As I stared once at a nursery door
Or a tall tree and a swing.

Wherein God's ponderous mercy hangs
On all my sins and me,
Because He does not take away
The terror from the tree
And stones still shine along the road
That are and cannot be.

Men grow too old for love, my love,
Men grow too old for wine,
But I shall not grow too old to see
Unearthly daylight shine,
Changing my chamber's dust to snow
Till I doubt if it be mine.

Behold, the crowning mercies melt,
The first surprises stay;
And in my dross is dropped a gift
For which I dare not pray:
That a man may grow used to grief and joy
But not to night and day.

Men grow too old for love, my love,
Men grow too old for lies;
But I shall not grow too old to see
Enormous night arise,
A cloud that is larger than the world
And a monster made of eyes.

Nor am I worthy to unloose
The latchet of my shoe;
Or shake the dust off my feet
Or the staff that bears me through
On ground that is too good to last,
Too solid to be true.

Men grow too old to woo, my love,
Men grow too old to wed:
But I shall not grow too old to see
Hung crazily overhead
Incredible rafters when I wake
And find I am not dead.

A thrill of thunder in my hair:
Though blackening clouds be plain,
Still I am stung and startled
By the first drop of the rain:
Romance and pride and passion pass
And these are what remain.

Strange crawling carpets of the grass,
Wide windows of the sky:
So in this perilous grace of God
With all my sins go I:
And things grow new though I grow old,
Though I grow old and die. (22)

## The Key-Man

This story [his autobiography] can only end as any detective story should end, with its own particular questions answered and its own primary problem solved. Thousands of totally different stories, with totally different problems, have ended in the same place with their problems solved. But for me my end is my beginning, as

Maurice Baring quoted of Mary Stuart, and this overwhelming conviction that there is one key which can unlock all doors brings back to me my first glimpse of the glorious gift of the senses, and the sensational experience of sensation. And there starts up again before me, standing sharp and clear in shape as of old, the figure of a man who crosses a bridge and who carries a key, as I saw him when I first looked into fairyland through the window of my father's peepshow. But I know that he who is called Pontifex, the Builder of the Bridge, is called also Claviger, the Bearer of the Key, and that such keys were given him to bind and loose when he was a poor fisher in a far province, beside a small and almost secret sea. (23)

NOTES AND SOURCES

1. G. K. Chesterton, *Autobiography* (London: Hutchinson, 1937), 38, 48–9.

2. Ibid. 93–5.

3. G. K. Chesterton, Introduction to Fulton J. Sheen, *God and Intelligence in Modern Philosophy: A Critical Study in the Light of the Philosophy of St Thomas* (London: Longmans, Green & Co., 1925), pp. vii–ix.

4. G. K. Chesterton, 'The Oracle of the Dog', from *The Incredulity of Father Brown*, in *The Father Brown Stories* (London: Cassell, 1947), 368.

5. G. K. Chesterton, *St Thomas Aquinas* (London: Hodder & Stoughton, 1933), 175.

6. G. K. Chesterton, 'The Convert', in *The Collected Poems of G. K. Chesterton*, new edn. (London: Methuen, 1948), 387.

7. G. K. Chesterton, 'Why I am a Catholic', in George J. Marlin et al. (eds.), *The Collected Works of G. K. Chesterton*, vol. iii (San Francisco, 1990), 127.

8. Chesterton, *Autobiography*, 329.

9. G. K. Chesterton, *The Everlasting Man*, new edn. (San Francisco: Ignatius Press, 1993), 227–8.

10. G. K. Chesterton, *St Thomas Aquinas* (London: Hodder & Stoughton, 1933), 96.

11. G. K. Chesterton, *The Thing* (London: Sheed & Ward, 1938), 227–8.

12. Chesterton, *St Thomas Aquinas*, 136–9.

13. G. K. Chesterton, *St Francis of Assisi* (London: Hodder & Soughton, 1924), 134–5.

14. G. K. Chesterton, *The Everlasting Man*, new edn. (San Francisco: Ignatius Press, 1993), 170.

15. Ibid. 171.

16. G. K. Chesterton, *Regina Angelorum* (written in 1925), in *The Queen of Seven Swords (London: Sheed & Ward, 1926), 18–19.*

17. Chesterton, *The Everlasting Man*, 212.

18. Ibid. 202–3.

19. G. K. Chesterton, *Christendom in Dublin* (London: Sheed & Ward, 1932), 59.

20. G. K. Chesterton, *The Well and the Shallows*, in *The Collected Works of G. K. Chesterton*, vol. iii, with introduction and notes by James J. Thompson Jr (San Francisco, 1990), 367–8.

21. Ibid. 439–41.

22. G. K. Chesterton, *The Ballad of St Barbara and Other Verses* (London: Cecil Palmer, 1922), 40–2.

23. Chesterton, *Autobiography*, 342–3.

# (Martin) Anscar Vonier OSB 1875–1938

Dom Vonier was a German with a French-sounding name who spent most of his life in England. His mastery of English prose and his contributions to English monasticism and theology not merely permit but require his inclusion in this anthology. After early training, profession, and ordination at Buckfast Abbey, he studied for a doctorate in philosophy at Sant'Anselmo in Rome. While crossing the Atlantic on monastic business, he himself was saved, but his abbot lost, when their ship was wrecked off Cartagena. Six weeks later, on 14 September 1906, he was elected second abbot of Buckfast. Convinced that Providence had spared his life for some great purpose, he began the immense task of rebuilding the great abbey church destroyed at the Protestant Reformation. The work was done by the monks and took thirty-two years to complete. As well as being master-builder of his church and father to his monks, Vonier taught philosophy and theology to the juniors, and was in great demand throughout the country as preacher and retreat master. As a theologian, Vonier wrote, with admirable clarity and in close adherence to the mind of St Thomas, on all the great dogmas of the faith, especially the Incarnation (*The Personality of Christ*) and the Blessed Sacrament (*A Key to the Doctrine of the Eucharist*).

## Communicating the Beauty of the Faith

Our Faith must be beautiful if it is to hold souls. Far from us the illusion that it is sufficient to tell our people what to believe and what to do as one gives medicine to a sick person, tasteless or perhaps even unpalatable! Perhaps we priests too readily become the victims of certain well-worn phrases which seem to be the product of lazy shepherds, and which appear to make every dogma just a blow on the head which the believer should receive thankfully. Some piece of doctrine is given him, not as bread to eat and to enjoy, but as a stone to carry about. Far from us, I say, such facile belief in our people's readiness to be contented believers; they are hungering and thirsting for the beauties of their Faith, and unless we meet them in their legitimate desires our true contact with souls becomes less and less every year. (1)

## Sharing in Causality: Doing Good to Others

The Catholic view . . . is that the greatest and highest communication of God is the participation of causality. Not only is He the cause of all things and all good, but He makes His creatures also to be, in their respective degree, causes of things and causes of good; and in our metaphysics, as well as in our piety, we go by this principle, that the highest creature is also the most powerful creature, and that the more God loves a spiritual being, the more means He gives to that being of doing good to others. (2)

## The Angels

If the Church blesses a bridge over a river, she confidently expects that an angel will be deputed to the keeping of that bridge. The Church prays God to join His angel to the chariot on which her blessing has been bestowed. The angels are called down to the house of the sick, into the home of the newly wed, into the rooms where Christ's little ones are being taught their faith and their letters. There seems to be no end to those angelic possibilities in the sense of the Catholic Church. Everywhere the evil spirits are driven away, and the good spirits are made to take their place. (3)

It is a favourite theme with St Thomas Aquinas to represent the whole physical world as being entrusted by God to the keeping of the angels. The stars in their courses are watched by the mighty spirits; nations are committed to the care of a heavenly prince; and there is no part of the universe which does not feel the breath of those whose mind beholds the countenance of God. An all-pervading principle governs the theology of the spirit ministry—namely, an inferior thing in creation is invariably under the tutelage of a higher thing. To this great law there is no exception. The universe is held together with the golden threads of spirit power as well as with the coarser sinews of natural energy. (4)

[The guardian angels are] Providence in practice, and therefore they become one of the main factors in the world's course. (5)

An immense amount of angelic work for man's benefit must be of the defensive kind; man could never know, unless it were revealed to him, from what evils he has been saved. The spirits fight for us to a great extent without our knowledge, their mission is essentially one of guardianship of a lower being, and it is carried out quite independently of that lower being's participation or recognition. It is truly a trust, and the spirit is responsible for the full discharge of that trust to the heavenly Father by whom it was committed to him. (6)

The sins of men are not signs that men are not guarded by good spirits, for, as St Thomas says so well [1a q. 113, a. 1, ad 3], we can act against the good instigations of the spirit that is outside us as we can against the good instincts that are within us. The good instincts remain as a great reality in spite of our prevarication; so likewise the angelic inspiration remains in spite of our voluntary deafness to it. Nor could it be said that the spirits work in vain, even with those who are lost. Not only are we to suppose, again with St Thomas [q. 113, a. 4, ad 3], that the most perverted of men are kept from greater evils by their heavenly guardians, but the evil committed by one man is kept in check by those spirits of sanctity, lest it work havoc in other men. (7)

## The Fall of the Angels

When Christ speaks of the reward of the elect, He represents it in the form of an invitation to take possession of the Kingdom that had been prepared from the foundation of the world. The chastisement of the wicked He speaks of as everlasting fire prepared for the devil and his angels. This terrible penal arrangement is not said to be, like the gracious provision for merit, *a constitutione mundi*, from the foundation of the world. Satan and his followers were not created evil; there was no thought in God's first providence of an *ignis aeternus*. No Christian doubts the existence of evil powers in the spirit world, but no Christian considers those evil powers to be anything but a miscarriage, through the creature's act, of the Creator's first plan. There is no evil principle having, so to speak, an estate by itself; all evil is an apostasy of a being that was primarily good; all evil is a bad use of the good things of God. (8)

## The Dynamism of the Hypostatic Union

The merely static view of the presence of Divinity in Christ through Hypostatic Union might easily lead to a concept of Christ's Personality that accentuates the duality of the natures in Him at the expense of the union of the two natures. With all due reverence, might I be allowed to say that there is a danger of our thinking of Christ 'in layers', with the consequent feeling of unreality? The older theology was as firm a believer in the differences of the two natures in Christ, the divine and the human; but the two natures were not exclusive levels of life in Christ's Personality; there is a most intimate compenetration of activities in the two natures, the divine nature using the human nature as its *instrumentum conjunctum* ['united instrument'], as my mind uses my hand, according to the favourite simile of St Thomas. The identification of the two natures, and their fusion into one entity, is the old Eutychian heresy, the most subtle aberration of man trying to understand the psychology of Christ. St Thomas has shown how it is possible to conceive a compenetration of the two natures that is not a fusion, viz. in the compenetration of mutual activities.

The Son of Man stands before us in the fullness of Divine Power; and Divinity, far from diminishing His manhood, has given that humanity undreamed of fullness and strength, that will make every heart in this world and in the next find shelter in Him, as the birds of the air find shelter in a mighty tree. (9)

## Transubstantiation

The uninitiated may be startled when he hears St Thomas declare that the Body of Christ in the Sacrament is not in a place, as He is in Heaven in a place, yet such is the emphatic and unswerving teaching of St Thomas. For the great Doctor it is simply unthinkable—nay, it implies a metaphysical contradiction—that the Body of Christ should ever be considered as moving simultaneously from place to place, or as overcoming, in some miraculous manner, all spatial hindrances. Transubstantiation is infinitely simpler. Wherever bread is found, wherever wine is found, their hidden substance is transubstantiated into the hidden substance of Christ's Body and Blood, in the same way in which it was done at the Last Supper. This is what St Thomas means when he says that the Body of Christ is not in a place but in a sacrament. The thing, the Body of Christ, is not taken hold of, hurried through space, and put into a definite place on a definite altar; this is not Eucharist at all. But the divine invocation, as the words of consecration are so often called by the Fathers, makes the substance of a definite bread and the substance of a definite cup of wine into a new thing, and what is that new thing? It is simply that thing which is in Heaven, the Body and Blood of Christ, but which, not for one instant, has left Heaven. (10)

## Adoration of Christ's Person in the Eucharist

When we go to the altar of the Blessed Sacrament, we speak to Our Lord; at Benediction we glorify the Son of God; the exposition throne is the seat of His Majesty. Many people think that this piety towards the person of Christ in the Eucharist is really a substantial alteration in the ways of Catholicism; one has even read books in which it was asserted that under the guidance of the Holy Ghost the Eucharistic mentality of the Church is being transformed, the person of Christ replacing the Sacrament of Christ. Put in this wise the assertion is, of course, nonsense...In virtue of concomitance the whole person of Christ is under the consecrated Elements ... As it is a theological, dogmatic fact that the whole person of Christ is in the Eucharistic elements, this modern piety is fully justified, it is sacramental, it is archaic, if we like. Christ Himself said: 'He that eateth *me*', and therefore this personal element expressed in the 'me' could be translated at any time into personal worship. (11)

## Thinking about Immortality and Believing in the Resurrection

Christians ought to dread nothing more than a diminution of their faith in Christ's bodily Resurrection, for as Christians, and in virtue of our mystical incorporation with the Incarnate God, all our hopes of personal immortality are based on Christ's Resurrection. We do not ignore other motives; nowhere are such motives searched into, and probed, and held with greater reverence than in Catholic schools of theology; yet when all has been said, the mental satisfaction derived from such speculations is as nothing when compared with the over-powering conviction that comes to us from the constant contemplation of the sweet mystery of Easter. To speak and think lightly of the mystery of Christ's bodily rising from the dead, and to rely merely on the philosophical grounds of belief in our soul's immortality, is indeed to sell our birthright for a pottage of lentils. I will not enter here into the question whether it is possible for the human reason, in the long run, to hold as a deliberate conviction any doctrine as to man's personal immortality, and at the same time reject the dogma of Christ's Resurrection. I do not believe that faith in survival after death could have deep roots in a mind that recoils from faith in Christ's Resurrection. All I need say here is that the doctrine of Christ's Resurrection, being a specifically Christian doctrine, is of such nature as to give us an unshakable assurance of our personal immortality; so that for us temptations of doubt and despair are best overcome, not so much by investigations into the philosophical grounds of the soul's survival, as by meditating humbly on the Paschal mystery. (12)

## The Resurrection of the Body and Life Everlasting

Resurrection means, above all things, restoration of life, continuation through God's act of that life which had been interrupted by death. The dead are made to live again. 'And as in Adam all die, so also in Christ all shall be made alive. But everyone in his own order: the firstfruits, Christ; then they that are of Christ, who have believed in His coming' (1 Cor. 15: 22, 23). The risen Christ had evidently the same life before and after His resurrection. It is true that His life after the Resurrection had qualities of glory which the life before His Crucifixion did not possess. Yet substantially it is the same life, before and after. He laid down His life for us, and He took it up again for us. The everlasting merit of Christ's mortal career lies in this, that now, in His risen state, there pulsates in Him that very life which He took from His Blessed Mother ... Death with regard to God, 'who quickeneth the dead, and calleth those things that are not, as those that are' (Rom. 4: 7), can never be more than a state of sleep. In raising up the dead, He brings back to them that consciousness which was part of their former lives; they are like men awaking from a long sleep ... It is surely of deep significance that even with regard to the final resurrection, the resurrection from the dust, the dead are called sleepers by Holy Writ...By all the principles of Catholic theology, the human beings who have been in their graves for a thousand years are neither nearer to, nor farther away from, life than was the daughter of Jairus, who had died just before Jesus arrived in the house. To believe in God's power to raise up the dead maid whose corpse still forms an apparent, cohesive whole, and to hesitate in one's belief in God's power to raise to life those whose ashes have been scattered to the winds, would be almost childishly illogical. To divine omniscience it cannot matter whether the ultimate elements of man's natural self are to be found. The return to life of a dead body is neither more nor less possible whatever the state or condition of that body, whatever the degree of disintegration. Is not death this very thing, the final unfitness of a bodily organism for life? A corpse is as distant from the source of life as the ashes inside a funeral urn; and whosoever is in the grave may be said to be only a sleeper with regard to God's omnipotent power to restore life; it is no more difficult for God to give life to the dead of past ages than to the son of the widow who is just being carried to his grave. We have St Paul's authority for saying that the bodies of the innumerable Christians who are in their graves will be raised to life as easily as the dead body of Christ, who is only 'the firstfruits of them that sleep' (1 Cor. 15: 20). To my mind the question of the resurrection of the dead is wonderfully simplified if once we grasp clearly this idea of the restoration to personal life which ceased to flow when death supervened. (13)

## The Hierarchy of Heaven

Our heavenly kingdom is essentially an hierarchical world, where each blessed one fills a great role, has his proper niche of splendour; and the whole labour of sanctification is to shape us all for that very place in the divine edifice which from all eternity Christ decreed to be ours.

> Many a blow and biting sculpture
> Polished well those stones elect,
> In their places now compacted
> By the heavenly Architect,
> Who therewith hath willed forever
> That His palace should be decked. (14)

NOTES AND SOURCES

1. Anscar Vonier, 'The Doctrinal Power of the Liturgy of the Catholic Church', in *Sketches and Studies in Theology* (London: Burns, Oates & Washbourne, 1940), 150.
2. Anscar Vonier, *The Collected Works of Abbot Vonier*, iii: *The Soul and the Spiritual Life* (London: Burns & Oates, 1953), 168.
3. Anscar Vonier, 'The Angels', in *The Teaching of the Catholic Church: A Summary of Catholic Doctrine*, ed. G. D. Smith (London: Burns, Oates & Washbourne, 1948), 252.
4. Ibid. 268.
5. Vonier, *Collected Works*, iii. 166.
6. Vonier, 'The Angels', 271.
7. Ibid. 270–1.
8. Ibid. 276.

9. Anscar Vonier, *The Personality of Christ*, in *Collected Works*, i: *The Incarnation and Redemption* (London: Burns & Oates, 1952), 140–1.

10. Anscar Vonier, *A Key to the Doctrine of the Eucharist* (London: Burns, Oates & Washbourne, 1925), 186–7.

11. Anscar Vonier, 'The Relationship between Mass and Benediction', in *Sketches and Studies in Theology*, 124–5.

12. Vonier, *Collected Works*, i. 52–3.

13. Ibid., iii. 369–70.

14. Ibid. 336.

# William Edwin Orchard

1877–1955

Even to people who know London well, it comes as a surprise to find a Ukrainian Catholic Cathedral in Duke Street, in the heart of Mayfair. What is even more surprising is that, before becoming a cathedral, this late-nineteenth-century building was a Congregationalist chapel, the King's Weigh House, and the setting, for twenty years or so, of some of the most spectacularly high-church liturgy in the capital, combined with revivalist preaching and the promotion of pacifism. The man responsible for this remarkable ecclesiastical experiment, the Revd Dr W. E. Orchard, left school at the age of 12 to work with his father on the railway at Euston Station. The influence of a Presbyterian minister moved him to conversion, and to the desire for ordination as a minister. He educated himself in the biblical languages, and after training at Westminster College, Cambridge, was ordained for ministry at the Presbyterian church in Enfield. In 1914 he was appointed to the King's Weigh House, and set about introducing the devotions and furnishings of a Catholic church, including daily Benediction, as well as acquiring what he believed were valid priestly orders from a wandering schismatic bishop. On one occasion, decked out in cassock and biretta, he was stopped by a woman who asked whether it was a Catholic church: 'Madam,' he replied, 'honesty obliges me to admit that it isn't. But I'm doing my best to make it one. I think you are probably looking for Farm Street.' In 1932 he resigned from the King's Weigh House, and on 2 June was received into the Catholic Church. Three years later he was ordained *sub conditione* as a Catholic priest. He continued to write and give lectures, but his ecclesiastical superiors forbade him to publicize his pacifist opinions. For the last twelve years of his life he served as chaplain to a religious community in Gloucestershire, and is buried in the Dominican cemetery at Woodchester.

## Hell and Human Freedom

The doctrine of Hell is the proof of how far the Catholic Church feels compelled to go in the interests of human freedom. It maintains that no one will ever be compelled to surrender to God; to dwell in His presence, if he does not want to; to go to Heaven, if that is not where he would be at home. It holds that it is in the power of human freedom to decide to be eternally free of this whole business of God, worship, religion; to spend its eternal existence in rebellion, at an infinite distance from what it hates and fears, and with the guarantee that it shall never be bothered by these things again; and that conditions of perfect knowledge, clear vision, and unalterable decision will be provided for this purpose by the event which is called the Last Judgement. Only, on the other hand, Catholic teaching maintains that this alternative is Hell; no soul can there be happy, be other than tortured by its own unfulfilled and outraged nature, or there be other than enslaved to itself; and that this friction between what it ultimately needs and what it finally desires lights what are described as dreadful fires. Strictly speaking, however, God sends no one there; each one goes to his own place, which he himself freely chooses. What constitutes the fires of Hell must ultimately be identified with what constitutes the light of Heaven; the blessed who love the light enjoy what others find torment. What, however, most particularly needs to be remembered is that the people who are most in danger of Hell are not the heathen who have never seen the light of Christianity, nor those who have, but who sincerely cannot see that it is light, whether it has been discoloured for them by misrepresentation or by their own prejudices. It is those who are in danger who, having seen the light, have said to darkness, 'Be thou my light'; and most of all those who have believed in the light as it shines most clearly in the Catholic Church, but have been inwardly unfaithful, mortally sinful, and finally impenitent; for we are told they shall have their portion with the hypocrites: 'There shall be weeping and the gnashing of teeth'. The doctrine of Hell is, therefore, rightly defended by the Catholic Church as dealing with a reality, and proclaimed as something to be so avoided that the best thing to do is to go to the opposite extreme. Further it can be claimed that Hell is the creation, not only of Sovereign Might and Justice, but of Love; for Hell is that which the loveless make for themselves out of the love of God. (1)

## The Logical Conclusion and Only Hope: The Catholic Faith

Lack of perspective, individualistic selfishness, failure to realize the depths to be avoided and the heights to be gained: these are the real hindrances to accepting the claims of the Catholic Church. If we would be human, we must be rational; if rational, ethical; if ethical, evangelical; if evangelical, Catholic; if Catholic, Roman: that is the logic of progress, freedom, light. If one rejects the Roman claims one must eventually reject Catholicism; if Catholicism is rejected, then gradually go doctrine, Sacraments, Scripture, Christ, God, man; Hell, then Heaven; the next world, then this; faith goes, then hope, then love. This is the logic of denial, darkness, death. (2)

NOTES AND SOURCES

1. W. E. Orchard, *From Faith to Faith: An Autobiography of Religious Development* (London: Putnam, 1933), 306–7.

2. Ibid.

## Cyril Charles Martindale SJ                                    1879–1963

Father Martindale was the most prolific Jesuit author of his generation. The son of a knighted officer of the Indian Civil Service, he was received into the Catholic Church on leaving Harrow. Shortly afterwards, he entered the Jesuit novitiate. After philosophy at St Mary's Hall, Stonyhurst, he matriculated at the Jesuits' hall at Oxford, where he won Firsts in Mods and Greats and many prizes; he was widely regarded as the most brilliant Oxford classicist of his day. After ordination in Dublin in 1911, he returned to the university to lecture. During the First World War, he ministered to the wounded soldiers in the military hospital in the Examination Schools. After the War he began a missionary apostolate, at home and abroad, of a range that was extraordinary even by the standards of the Society. He worked with university students, with the poor at clubs and settlements in the East End of London, on the Permanent Committee of the International Eucharistic Congresses, for the establishment of the Apostleship of the Sea, and in the instruction of converts of all sorts and conditions. He wrote, preached, and broadcasted with grace, humour, and dogmatic precision. He had the gift of writing the kind of book no one had dreamt of attempting before: for example, Catholic apologetics in the form of novels (*Jock, Jack, and the Corporal*) and saints' lives stripped of preciousness and unreality. For the duration of the Second World War, he was detained in occupied Denmark. Despite suffering a series of heart attacks, he made what the Danes themselves acknowledged was a historic contribution to the development of Catholic life in Scandinavia. After the War, he was stationed at Farm Street, where, despite poor health, he was able to return to much of his pre-war priestly work. Father Basset says of him that even in his ripe old age he was 'entirely absorbed with the needs of the present moment, above all the need to bring the message of the Incarnation to a suffering world. Classless, selfless, restless, his mind was forever composing variations on this central theme.' In his last letter, reporting his eighth reception of Extreme Unction, he said: 'I'm pretty ill, and, in fact, one night they said the Prayers for the Dying for me. I find it hard to be brought back, but the Lord's will is the most lovable of all.'

## Christianity is Christ: The Witness of St Paul

The tiny phrase 'in Christ' occurs one hundred and sixty-four times in the letters of St Paul, and hardly elsewhere in the New Testament. 'To me,' he confessed, 'life *is* Christ', and if 'death', as he continued, was in any sense a 'gain', that would be simply because, having died, he would then *see* Christ whom now unseen he was serving with all his will and work (cf. Phil. 1: 21). And if he lived 'in Christ', so, correspondingly, 'I live, *I* no longer, but Christ is living in me'. The two lives, Christ's and the Christian's, were quite simply interpenetrative. (1)

## The Sacraments and the Incarnation

God will not save human nature apart from human nature. The material side of the transaction of our saving might have been minimized. God might have saved us by a prayer, a hope, by just one act of love. He might have remained invisible to eye, inaudible to ear. But He did not. He took our human nature—the whole of it. Nothing that is in us, was *not* in Him. Jesus Christ was true God, and true man. In Him was that twofold nature, in one person. And indeed in His human nature was that double principle that is in ours—there was body, and there was soul. In Jesus Christ are forever joined the visible and the invisible, the Infinite and the created, limited thing that man is; man, in short, and God. Since, then, the Incarnation, no one can possibly criticize a religion because it is not wholly 'spiritual'. We are not wholly spiritual; Christ is not wholly spiritual. The religion that we need, the religion that He gives, will not be totally unlike what we are, and what He is. Christ did not treat us as though we were stones, nor yet as if we were angels. He became man, because we are men, and *as* man He, perfect man, will treat us...

The Church, existing as it does upon this earth for the sake of men who live on the earth and not for disembodied souls, still less for angels, is so constructed as to suit the situation. It is visible, yet invisible. It has its way in, and its way out. It has quite definite frontiers. It has a perfectly unmistakable form of government... I need but add that, the nature of its Founder being what it is, and the nature of the Church being what it is, and our nature being such as we have described it, you cannot possibly be surprised if what goes on within the Church is in keeping with all the rest. The object of the Church being the salvation and sanctification of ourselves, the method of the Church will include and not disdain a material element. Even beforehand, we might have expected this, nay, felt sure that it would be so. In the concrete, this method will turn out to be the Sacramental System...

Let me but add that we should be glad this is so. Had Our Lord given us a wholly 'spiritual' religion (if such a thing is conceivable), we might have reproached Him for neglecting those bodies of ours, which minister to us so much good pleasure, and provide for us such great difficulties. We might have grieved that He had done nothing for our social instinct, that always, in every department, forces us to create some social unit or other. Again, knowing ourselves all too well, we might have felt that the ideal, just because so disembodied, would prove to be beyond us; we would be sure that the weight of our bodily humanity would sooner or later drag us down. After all, we must eat and drink; men marry; they mingle with their fellows—if we can in no way co-ordinate all this with what is spiritual, catch it up, use it, see how it is legitimate, and can be made of value—we are practically being asked to despair of human life. On the other hand, if we see that no part of human nature is neglected by Our Lord, we are, as I said, not only grateful but most humbly grateful, seeing that what has so often supplied material for sin is judged, by Christ, as nonetheless able to be given a lofty task, the sublimest duty—that of co-operating with grace, nay, being used by grace and in its interests. And once and for all, we see that God scorns nothing that He has made: that Jesus Christ was man, not despising or hating His manhood; that His Church understands, as He does, all that is 'in man'; and that as the eternal Son of God assumed a human nature, never to lay it down, so too in our very bodies, and helped by bodily things, we are to enter into that supernatural union with God through Christ, wherein is to consist our everlasting joy. (2)

## The Words of the Missal: God's Largesse

God's action is not feeble, but forceful; the Missal invites us to see that it is not niggardly, an affair of doles, but open-handed, lavish. There are three words especially that we can consider. One is, precisely, *largiri*, to 'lavish', to do things 'largely'; another, *satiari*, and another, *repleri*, which mean to receive till you have *enough*, to absorb, till you are filled...

Under the words lies the doctrine, first, that all grace is a free gift. We do not earn it; we do not first give to God, so that He 'pays us back'; His goodness to us is sheer 'largesse'. Then comes the idea that even in giving us what is undeserved, God does it on a large scale; He does not just 'dole it out'. We ask so often during Mass for this or that *te largiente*—'from thy free and most generous gift'—that we will not quote that little phrase separately, but we may just contrast it with other 'giving' words, such as the simplest of all, *da nobis*, 'give to us'; *concede*, 'yield', that is, come to an agreement with us; grant to us; *praebe*, 'hand to us'; *indulge*, 'be kind enough to allow us', in fact, 'indulgently allow us'. The word we are thinking of implies not only free gift but *lavish* gift... 'Lavish on us the reward that is eternal bliss' (Fourth Collect, Ember Saturday in Advent); it is His *grace* that makes this lavish gift, and *is* it (Secret, First Mass of Christmas)...We may conclude by quoting the beginning of the Prayer for the Eleventh Sunday after Pentecost: 'Almighty, eternal God, who in the abundance of thy loving kindness dost go beyond not only the merits of thy suppliants, but their prayers!' So totally removed from the petty, so *grand*, is the Missal. (3)

## The Words of the Missal: Sharing in God's Life

When the prayer for Palm Sunday asks that we may be 'consorts' of Our Lord's Resurrection, just as the *Stabat Mater* asks that we may be consorts in His Passion, the words mean much more than merely a request that we may also suffer, and also rise again—'along with' Christ, so to say. Our sufferings are to be intertwined with His and so too our risen life—and better than intertwined; for two lives do not meet and interact merely like two threads that are twisted together and knotted and consolidated into one thread. The thing is more organic than that!

'May the receiving of thy Sacrament *restore* us...and cause us to cross over into sharing—*consortium*—in the mystery of salvation' (Postcommunion, Ember Friday in Advent). 'May we be made fellow-sharers in the heavenly remedy' (Postcommunion, Monday after the Second Sunday in Lent)...Besides all this, we are continually reminded that the *thing* in which our 'participation' occurs—for after all, that is an abstract word—is the divine life of all the Blessed Trinity—a definite 'transaction' takes place, *commercia*, in which we, offering something to God, namely, our ready wills, which are the most personal part of ourselves, receive in return something that God alone can give, namely, His own life.

'O God, who by the mysterious transaction of this sacrifice dost make us to participate in One Supreme Divinity' (Secret, Fourth Sunday after Easter...). 'Through this most holy transaction, may we be found to exist in His nature in whom, along with thyself, exists our own humanity' (Secret, First Mass of Christmas; the words are almost more audacious that we should dare to write!). 'Even as the Selfsame hath shone forth, born man, yet true God, so may this earthly substance confer upon us that which is divine' (Secret, Second Mass of Christmas). It is *His* 'new light' that has shone on to human eyes and into human hearts (Preface for Christmas and Epiphany). It is *His* new birth, by means of flesh, that is to set us free (Collect, Third Mass of Christmas). It is He who is both the originator of our new birth and the giver, in consequence, of our true immortality (Postcommunion, ibid.). It is 'among His members' that we pray to be accounted, in whose flesh and blood we have communicated (Postcommunion, Saturday after the Third Sunday of Lent); and at the end of the third prayer for the Blessing of Palms we ask that 'in Him, and by means of Him whose *limbs* thou hast willed us to become', we may win our victory and achieve our resurrection, a resurrection which is a 'participation' in His own. (4)

NOTES AND SOURCES

1. C. C. Martindale, *Christianity is Christ: Five Courses of Sermons* (London: Sheed & Ward, 1935), 169–70.

2. C. C. Martindale, 'The Sacramental System', in *The Teaching of the Catholic Church*, ed. G. D. Smith (London: Burns, Oates & Washbourne, 1952), 737–9.

3. C. C. Martindale, *The Words of the Missal* (London: Sheed & Ward, 1932), 49–53.

4. Ibid. 151–2.

# Alfred Noyes 1880–1958

In the age of Eliot and Pound, this outspokenly anti-modern poet, the champion of traditional forms and subject matter, won an enthusiastic readership in both England and North America. Noyes's first wife died suddenly in 1926. The following year he became a Catholic and married into one of the old English Catholic families, the Weld-Blundells. During the First World War he worked for the Foreign Office; in the Second, he lived in Canada and the United States. It was here that his eyesight began to deteriorate, in the end rendering him blind. In 1949 he and his family returned to England to live on the Isle of Wight. He is buried there at St Saviour's Catholic church, Totland.

## The Assumption

Before earth saw Him she had felt and known
    The small soft feet that thrust like buds in Spring.
The body of Our Lord was all her own
    Once. From the Cross her arms received her King.

Think you that she, who bore Him on her breast,
    Had not the Word still living in her heart?
Or that, because once voice had called her blest
    Her inmost soul had lost the better part?

*Henceforth all generations...* Ah, but that
    You think was but an ancient song she knew!
Millions this night will sing Magnificat,
    And bring at least one strange prediction true.

Think you His Heaven, that deep transcendent state,
    Floats like Murillo's picture in the air?
Or that her life, so heavenly consecrate,
    Had no essential habitation there?

Think you He looked upon her dying face,
    And throned above His burning seraphim,
Felt no especial tenderness or grace
    For her whose life-blood once had throbbed in Him?

Proof of His filial love, His body on earth
    Still lives and breathes, and tells us, night and day,
That earth and Heaven were mingled in His birth
    Through her, who kneels beside us when we pray.

Kneels to the Word made flesh; her living faith
    Kneels to incarnate Love, 'not lent but given',
Assumed to her on earth, and after death
    Assuming her to His own Heart in Heaven. (1)

NOTES AND SOURCES

1. Alfred Noyes, *Collected Poems*, new edn. (London: John Murray, 1963), 416.

# (Cyril) Bede Jarrett OP                                         1881–1934

Bede Jarrett so strengthened and enlarged the mission of the English Dominicans that he can be regarded as almost, after St Dominic, the Order's second founder in England. He was born into a military family and educated at Stonyhurst. He received the Dominican habit on the Feast of Our Lady of Ransom, 1898. Having studied philosophy and theology at Woodchester and Hawkesyard, he became the first Dominican in modern times to read for a degree at Oxford, taking a double first in Classical Moderations and Modern History. Fr Bernard Vaughan, in a speech at the time, referred to him as 'the first swallow of the Dominican summer'. After a further year of study in Louvain, he began parish work at St Dominic's in London. At the early age of 33, he became prior of the same house, and two years later was appointed provincial, a post he retained to his death. His achievements as provincial are breathtaking. He transferred the Dominican school for boys to Laxton, established a house in Edinburgh, launched missions in South Africa and Persia, and assisted the Dominican sisters in their amalgamation. On 15 August 1921, on the seventh centenary of the Dominicans' first arrival in Oxford, he re-founded the Oxford priory after a gap of four centuries. When the foundation stone was laid, he said: 'We're beginning without a penny, but we shall build as the money comes in.' Eight years later, the church was consecrated, free of debt. Alongside these practical works, he maintained the traditional Dominican life of study, lecturing, and preaching, wrote countless books and articles, instructed converts, and counselled souls. His confrère, Fr Bernard Delany, recalls that he was 'scarcely ever known to be absent from a community duty'. 'There was no sense of hustle or fuss about him, no fidgety nervousness, no suggestion of strain or overwork.' He seemed like an 'inspired boy', mature yet with 'all the charm and grace of youth'. He died after a short illness at the age of 52.

## Deification

This very strong expression is used by St Augustine and many of the Fathers to describe one of the effects of grace. By grace we are deified, i.e. made into gods. Right at the beginning of all the woes of humanity when, in the Garden of Eden, Adam and Eve first were tempted, the lying spirit promised that the reward of disobedience would be that they should become 'as gods'. The result of sin could hardly be that, so man, made only a little lower than the angels, can at times find himself rebuked by the very beasts. Yet the promise became in the end fulfilled, since the Incarnation really effected that transformation, and God, by becoming human, made man himself divine. St Peter, in his second epistle (1: 4), insinuates the same truth when he describes the great promises of Christ making us 'partakers of the divine nature'. The work, then, of grace is something superhuman and divine. Creation pours into us the divine gift of existence and therefore makes us partakers in the divine being, for existence implies a participation in the being of God. The indwelling of the Blessed Trinity, then, does even more, for by it we participate not only in the divine being, but in the divine nature, and fulfil the prophecy of Our Lord, 'Ye are gods'. Justification, therefore, is a higher gift than creation, since it does more for us.

This divine participation is what is implied in many texts which allude to the Sacrament of Baptism, for the purpose of Baptism is just that, to make us children of God. The phrases concerning 'new birth' and 'being born again' all are intended to convey the same idea, that the soul by means of this Sacrament is lifted above its normal existence and lives a new life. This life is lived 'with Christ in God', i.e. it is a sort of entrance within the charmed circle of the Trinity, or, more accurately, it is that the Blessed Trinity inhabits our soul and enters into our own small life, which at once therefore takes on a new and higher importance. In it henceforth there can be nothing small or mean. For the same reason Our Lord speaks of it to the Samaritan woman as '*the* gift of God', beside which all His other benefactions fade into nothingness. Again, it is a 'fountain of living water'; it is a 'refreshment'; it is 'life' itself. Not the stagnant water that remains in a pool in some dark wood, but a stream gushing out from its source, fertilizing the ground on every side, soaking through to all the thirsty roots about it, giving freshness and vitality to the whole district through which it wanders. Life indeed it bears as its great gift; and so does sanctifying grace carry within it the fertilizing power needed by the soul.

The participation in the divine nature is therefore no mere metaphor, but is a real fact. The indwelling of God makes the soul like to God. I find myself influenced by the people with whom I live, picking up their expressions, copying their tricks and habits, following out their thoughts, absorbing their principles, growing daily like them. With God at the centre of my life the same effect is produced, and slowly, patiently, almost unconsciously, I find myself infected by His spirit. What he loves becomes my ideal; what he hates, my detestation. But it is even closer than this, no mere concord of wills nor harmony of ideas, a real and true elevation to the life of God. Grace is formally in God, at the back, so to say, of His divine nature, the inner essence of Himself. By receiving it, therefore, I receive something of God, and begin to be able to perform divine actions. I can begin to know God even as I am known, to taste His sweetness, and by His favour to have personal, experimental knowledge of Himself. To act divinely is only possible to those who are made divine. This, then, becomes the formal union with God, its term, its end, its purpose. Deified, therefore, we become in our essence by grace, in our intelligence by its light, in our will by charity. (1)

## What the Blessed Trinity Thinks of Us

One shouldn't expatiate on what folk think of us, but only at the odd comments the Three-in-One might make in their eternal conversation: 'Hubert, all right, you know, but rather foolish, the way he won't let Us deal with him. Frightfully pig-headed and all that. Doesn't give a fellow the chance to make him really what he could be, but is bothering what he's got to do. As though he were anything! Scruples and all that bunkum! Terrified of a hearty breakfast! Frightened of brawn! As though that mattered, when it's under obedience. Rather silly of the Novice Master to have let him starve himself to start with. He'll jolly well have to feed to get sane again. But if he'd only realize that he's got to be passive in Our hands, he'd have a happier time than he has, and fruitfuller, too. Between You and Me, he's got the makings of a rather charming saintlet. But he won't let himself be led. He will want to put everything right. Yet his character is attractive—a mixture of My humour and My love of high things. He's got the go and the grit and the guts, but he lacks sense!'

That's more or less what I overheard of the *arcana Dei* the last time but one I had an ecstasy; I give it you for what it's worth. Anyhow let the 'dear physician' [St Luke] on his feast day heal you of your worries with the cool strength of his touch. May he show you, as in his Gospel he loves to do, the innermost recesses of the prayer of Christ! May he show you how to lie limp in the everlasting arms, *removens prohibens*, getting rid of self more and more, and leaving all to the Wisdom, Love, and Power of God. (2)

## St Dominic's Devotion to Our Lady and His Prayer

His friars were 'her' friars, needing and receiving her especial help. Visions were seen, it was reported, of his sons preaching from books held before them by Our Lady's hands; she corrected them, protected them, blessed them sleeping; and was seen in Cambridge to send fire on them when they prayed; at death comforted them. The spirit of the saint descended, then, on his children, says Gérard de Frachet, to sum up all his record of devotion, 'so that studying and praying and sleeping they had her before their eyes, and she turned her eyes of mercy ever towards them'.

For St Dominic, then, prayer was the simple converse of the soul with God; and converse is the easier, fuller, when it is between two friends. The more, then, the mind can realize the friendship with God which is the essence of religion, the more facile is the heart's opening of itself, for the problem of prayer is always how to make God the friend not only accepted and believed in, but form part of the familiar circumstances of life. Everything that could help to produce this truth vividly was made use of: vocal prayer, gestures, beads; and, since he found that a dialogue of speech and silence, a chorus of praise, could be more easily secured by a devotion to the sacramental Presence, it was round the altar that he grouped his interests. The Mass was the highest expression of it; the crucifix its homeliest representation. The Gospels most wonderfully depict that perfect life and character, and show up against background of hill and lake and field and village and cobbled streets the moving figure of the true and loyal friend. Hence the Mass became his most particular devotion; the crucifix his daily companion, his 'ever open book'; and the New Testament his favourite study, carried always, learnt by heart, made the textbook of life. 'He spoke only of and to God,' said a follower of Dominic; and we feel that he did this naturally because God was the central object of his daily work and nightly watching. As Dante observingly notes of him, he was the 'athlete' of Christ, 'kindly to his friends, fierce to his foes'; he was the 'torrential' preacher just because he was 'fast-knit to Christ', and he was knit fast to Christ by means of his vivid and intensely personal prayer. (3)

## The Death of St Aelred of Rievaulx

In a portion of his cell a chapel was arranged, an altar and a crucifix above it, and the figures of his most beloved saints about it. A fire was lit in the cell; over this he crouched in his great pain; stone, kidney trouble, all manner of diseases assailed him. His comfort lay in the Mass, and in his well-beloved books, the psalter with his own marginal annotations, the Gospel of St John, and the *Confessions* of St Augustine—his dearest author, whose writings were the foundation of his own, whose *Confessions* could always make him cry, and who was referred to by the monks chaffingly whenever they quoted him to St Aelred as 'your St

Augustine'. These three had always been the staple food of his thought and prayer. With these and his prayers, he would spend his days save when the monks came to talk to him. As the early days of 1167 advanced he had to give up sitting on his bench at the entrance of that part of his cell which had been fitted up as an oratory, 'thinking how he was but dust'. Instead he had to keep to his bed. On 5 January he was anointed by Abbot Roger of Byland. His pains steadily increased. When death actually came, it could not come quickly enough for him: *Festinate*, he kept repeating. 'Make haste, make haste, for Christ's love.' This he added in his own Northumbrian Saxon tongue, dwelling on the words, 'For Christ's love'. It seemed sweeter to him in English; the very words were music to him, 'Christ's love', 'Christ's love'. Walter Daniel, who wrote his life, was with him, and pointing to the oratory, said to the dying abbot: 'My Lord, look at the cross; let thy eye be where thy heart is'. Aelred burst out anew: 'Thou art my God and my Lord. Thou art my refuge and my Saviour. Thou art my glory and my hope for eternity. Into thy hands I commend my spirit.' It was 12 January 1167 when he died. (4)

## Women in the Middle Ages: An Influential Sermon

Humbert of Romans, who ruled the Dominican Order as Master-General during the middle period of St Thomas's life, has left us a sermon which was intended to form a model for other friars when preaching to women, and to furnish ideas to be adapted by them to the circumstances of their audience. In it we have this characteristic passage:

Note that God gave women many prerogatives, not only over other living things but even over man himself, and this by nature, by grace, and by glory. In the world of *nature*, she excelled man by her origin, for man He made of the vile earth, but woman He made in Paradise. Man He formed of the slime, but woman of man's rib. She was not made of a lower limb of man—as, for example, of his foot—lest man should esteem her his servant, but from his midmost part, that he should hold her to be his fellow, as Adam himself said, 'the woman whom thou gavest as my helpmate'. In the world of *grace*, she excelled man, for God, who could have taken flesh of a man, did not do so, but took flesh of a woman. Again, we do not read of any man trying to prevent the Passion of Our Lord, but we do read of a woman who tried, namely, Pilate's wife, who tried to dissuade her husband from so great a crime because she had suffered much in a dream because of Christ. Again, at His Resurrection, it was to a woman He first appeared, namely, to Mary Magdalen. In the world of *glory*, for the King in that country is no mere man, but a mere woman is its Queen. It is not a mere man who is set above the angels and all the rest of the heavenly court, but a mere woman is, nor is anyone who is merely man as powerful there as is a mere woman. Thus is woman's nature in Our Lady raised above man's in worth, and dignity, and power, and this should lead women to love God and to hate evil.

It is quite evident that this sermon of Master Humbert was extensively used. The ideas in it are commonly to be found in many medieval sermons. (5)

NOTES AND SOURCES

1. Bede Jarrett, *The Abiding Presence of the Holy Ghost in the Soul* (London: Burns, Oates & Washbourne, 1957), 69–71.

2. Bede Jarrett, Letter to Hubert van Zeller OSB, 29 September 1928, in *Letters of Bede Jarrett: Letters and Other Papers from the English Dominican Archives*, selected by Bede Bailey OP, and ed. Simon Tugwell OP and Dom Aidan Bellenger (Stratton-on-the-Fosse: Downside Abbey, 1989), 136.

3. Bede Jarrett, *Life of St Dominic (1170–1221)* (London: Burns, Oates & Washbourne, 1934), 113–14.

4. Bede Jarrett, 'St Aelred of Rievaulx', in Maisie Ward (ed.), *The English Way: Studies in English Sanctity from St Bede to Newman* (London: Sheed & Ward, 1933), 101–2.

5. Bede Jarrett, *Social Theories of the Middle Ages, 1200–1500* (London: Ernest Benn, 1926), 71–2.

# Arthur Eric Rowton Gill                                    1882–1940

A large part of the human race is familiar with the work of Eric Gill through the printing types *Gill sans* and *Perpetua*, which he designed, and which Mr Bill Gates has bequeathed to every owner of a computer. But though lettering was where he started out as an artist, or 'responsible workman' as he preferred to say, Gill produced his greatest work in sculpture (through direct carving on stone) and engraving; the most beautiful example of the former is probably his set of Stations of the Cross for Westminster Cathedral. He was born the son of a clergyman, but in 1913, with his wife and children, was received into the Catholic Church. He later became a Dominican tertiary. The influence of Dominican thinking about art and society, especially in the form of the Distributism preached by his friend, Fr Vincent McNabb, inspired him to live with his family in a community of craftsmen, and later to fire broadsides, in articles and collections of essays, against the 'art-nonsense' propagated by the aesthetes and the injustices perpetrated by the industrialists. In his lifetime he was notorious for his eccentricity, not least his refusal to wear conventional clothes, and, as revealed in Fiona McCarthy's biography, the eroticism that is evident almost everywhere in his work went to perverse extremes in his private life. In his writings Gill insists upon the Thomistic distinction between the virtue of prudence, which makes a man good, and the virtue of art, which makes his work good. By this measure we can admire the greatness of his art, while feeling sorrow at his weaknesses. Gill's chosen epitaph captures the blend in him of the medieval and the modern, of spiritual struggle and artistic dedication: 'Remember EG, the stoneworker, 1936. Woe is me.'

## Art and Prudence

An act that is good, or thought to be good, with regard to oneself is called a *prudent* act.
An act that is good, or thought to be good, with regard to a thing to be made is called *art*.
A man whose acts are conformed to his own good is called a *prudent man*.
A man whose acts are conformed to the good of things is called an *artist*.
Skill in doing good to oneself is called *prudence*.
Skill in doing good to things is called *art*.
Prudence is the means to happiness in oneself.
Art is the means to pleasure in what is not oneself.
To have happiness is the object of prudence.
Happiness in oneself is a good and is the object of the will. Happiness is subjective.
To have pleasure in things is the object of art.
Pleasure in things is a good, and is the object of the intelligence.

Pleasure is objective.

Great intelligence is not necessary for prudence (happiness).

Great prudence is not necessary for intelligence (pleasure).

A fool may be a saint.

A villain may be an artist.

A fool may be a villain.

A saint may be an artist.

But a fool cannot be an artist, nor a villain a saint . . .

Prudence is the application of ethics to practice.

Art is the application of aesthetics to practice.

The practice of prudence is called morals.

The practice of art is called craft or craftsmanship.

Happiness, being man's goal, his final goal, it behoves a man to be a prudent man; for prudence has man's final happiness for its object.

But happiness is a state of mind.

It is that state of mind in which what is desired is known.

Final happiness is the state of mind in which the desired good is the known good—

In which the desired God is the known God.

When what is desired is known, it is said to be *seen*.

Final happiness is to see God.

This is called the Beatific Vision.

Happiness is, therefore, not a state of bliss merely;

It is a state of bliss in knowledge.

But knowledge is necessarily knowledge of something—not of *no* thing.

Happiness is in a knowledge of that thing or those things that are pleasing.

Happiness is in knowledge of those things that are pleasing to the mind.

Those things are pleasing to the mind which are in themselves good.

God alone is good.

So those things are pleasing to the mind which are of God or in God.

Here below we may see God in all things (that is earthly happiness).

We may see through all things to God.

The state of Heaven is that in which we see all things in God.

We see through God to all things.

The prudent man acts so that he may achieve the blissful state of heavenly happiness.

But that state is one in which he has knowledge of all things in God—
　　*gaudium de veritate*.

Happiness is therefore not separable from pleasure in things.

Prudence is therefore not separable from art.

As making has need of doing—so prudence has need of art.

The achieving of happiness in oneself is the business of prudence.

The supplying of pleasure in things is the business of art. (1)

NOTES AND SOURCES

1. Eric Gill, *Beauty Looks After Herself* (London: Sheed & Ward, 1933), 12–15.

# Siegfried Sassoon                                        1886–1967

Sassoon was the Fox-hunting Man of the Weald who became the Infantry Officer on the Western Front, and at the end of his life, after decades of emotional turmoil, found peace in the faith and life of the Catholic Church. Born into a great Anglo-Jewish family, he was educated at Marlborough and Clare College, Cambridge, from which he went down to enjoy the life of a country gentleman, hunting, playing cricket, and writing poetry. Having enlisted as a private soldier, he was commissioned in the Royal Welch Fusiliers (the same regiment as Robert Graves and David Jones) in 1915 and sent to France. Rescuing a wounded soldier under heavy fire won him the MC, but his later attack on the conduct of the war, though theoretically deserving of a prison cell (or worse), landed him in a hospital bed, to be treated, as the authorities saw it, for shell shock. After the war, apart from dabbling in Labour party politics and a spell as literary editor of the *Daily Herald*, he spent the remainder of his life as a man of letters, writing, among other things, his classics of fictionalized and factual autobiography, *Memoirs of a Fox-hunting Man*, *Memoirs of an Infantry Officer*, and *The Old Century and Seven Years More*. In 1957 he was received into the Catholic Church. Dame Felicitas Corrigan, with her community at Stanbrook, became his chief spiritual support; she said that his conversion was 'the harvest of a quiet mind and fruit of spiritual victory'. The poems printed below come from this final, Catholic chapter of his life. He is buried in the churchyard at Mells in Somerset, near to his friend, Monsignor Ronald Knox.

### *Arbor vitae* 1959

For grace in me divined
This metaphor I find:
    A tree.
How can that be?

This tree all winter through
Found no green work to do—
    No life
Therein ran rife.

But with an awoken year
What surge of sap is here—
    What flood
In branch and bud.

So grace in me can hide—
Be darkened and denied—
    Then once again
Vesture my every vein. (1)

## A Prayer at Pentecost 1960

Master musician, Life, I have overheard you,
Labouring in litanies of heart to word you.
Be noteless now. Our duologue is done.

Spirit, who speak'st by silences, remake me;
To light of unresistant faith, awake me,
That with resolved requiem I be one. (2)

## Compline, May 1962

Much weariness I plead, by daylong duties brought;
Much world-bewilderment from tired and troubled thought.
Now for my need, let child simplicity be sought.

Below the Crucifix I watch my candle shine—
I, O so earthbound, O so darkly undivine.
Light of our living souls, be lit this night in mine. (3)

## A Prayer in Old Age, 23<sup>rd</sup> September 1964

Bring no expectance of a heaven unearned
No hunger for beatitude to be
Until the lesson of my life is learned
Through what Thou didst for me.

Bring no assurance of redeemed rest
No intimation of awarded grace
Only contrition, cleavingly confessed
To Thy forgiving face.

I ask one world of everlasting loss
In all I am, that other world to win.
My nothingness must kneel below Thy Cross.
There let new life begin. (4)

NOTES AND SOURCES

1. *Siegfried Sassoon: Poet's Pilgrimage*, assembled with an introduction by Dame Felicitas Corrigan OSB (London: Victor Gollancz, 1973), 188.
2. Ibid. 190.
3. Ibid. 227.
4. Ibid. 233.

# Vernon Cecil Johnson 1886–1969

Vernon Johnson received the grace of conversion and the call to the priesthood through the prayers and writing of St Thérèse, and devoted the whole of his Catholic and priestly life to the expounding of her message. Educated at Charterhouse and Trinity College, Oxford, Johnson studied for the Anglican ministry at Ely Theological College. After ordination and a curacy in Brighton, he joined the Anglican Franciscans, then known as the Society of the Divine Compassion. The reading of the Little Flower's autobiography inspired him to visit Lisieux, and it was there, on his first trip abroad and in his first encounter with the Catholic Church, that he began the spiritual journey that would end four years later with his reception by Father Vincent McNabb OP. In 1933, after studying at the Beda, he was ordained for the Archdiocese of Westminster, and in 1941 he succeeded his friend, Ronald Knox, as Catholic chaplain to Oxford University. He also worked with the Catholic Missionary Society, in the parish of St James's, Spanish Place, and as chaplain of Sudbury Hill convent. The Association of Priests and Laity of St Thérèse of the Child Jesus, founded by him in 1939, still exists and publishes the magazine, *Sicut Parvuli*.

## Why I Became a Catholic

The supreme reason, behind all others, was that I could not resist the claim of the Catholic Church to be the one true Church founded by Our Lord Jesus Christ to guard and teach the truth to all men till the end of time. She alone claims to be infallibly guided by the Holy Spirit in her teaching: she alone possesses the authority and unity necessary for such a divine vocation, and she alone, in the Papacy, gives any effective and working meaning to the position of St Peter in Scripture. It was the positive fact of the Catholic Church from which I could not escape.

Thus the state of the Church of England was a very secondary difficulty and only served to confirm my growing belief in the Catholic Church. The Prayer Book controversy was, to me, more a symptom than anything else; though serious, it was never so serious, to me, as Modernism. Modernism, I saw, as I came to understand it better, was clearly destroying the true conception of, and belief in, the personality of Christ and His Godhead—the foundation truth of the Christian religion. (1)

## The Little Way of St Thérèse: Little Sacrifices

We all try to escape little sacrifices, and we find we cannot do so: hence that inner conflict which makes us depressed and nervy, and sick at heart. We are conscious of continual calls to a higher standard of spiritual life, of invitations to be less indulgent of ourselves and of our personal comfort, to be more disciplined in the use of our time, to be less subservient to human respect, and therefore to be less worldly. These are calls to make little sacrifices, and so they are painful to our human nature, and the immediate suffering obscures the ultimate spiritual gain. We are afraid, and we fail to respond.

At other times the occasions are provided by calls on our time through the interruptions of others, interruptions sometimes unavoidable but sometimes quite unnecessary; the call to sacrifice our own point of view where no principle is involved, for the sake of peace; the failure of the hopes we had placed in others; their lack of gratitude and lack of response; the spoiling by other people's mistakes or lack of vision of what we imagine God's plan to be. From such occasions as these there is no escape; we have to accept them in one way or another, and more often than not we do so in the wrong way. Knowing that they are going to hurt our self-love, we instinctively try to protect ourselves by making them minister to it. We let them rankle in our minds, wrap ourselves up in a garment of self-pity, and become irritable and discontented.

From all this St Thérèse liberates us. She shows us that these occasions of sacrifice, so far from being something to be avoided, are providentially arranged by Our Lord, and carefully proportioned by Him to our powers; they are opportunities which we can grasp to prove our love and so give Him joy. (2)

## The Little Way of St Thérèse: Small Actions

St Thérèse gathers in every single action and incident in human life, and claims it for Our Lord. 'Jesus tells us that the smallest actions done for His love are those which charm His Heart. If it were necessary to do great things, we should be deserving of pity, but we are fortunate indeed, since Jesus lets Himself be led captive by the smallest action.'

St Thérèse does not say the *small* actions, but the *smallest*... She gives us an example. 'I endeavoured', she says, 'above all, to practise little hidden acts of virtue, such as folding the mantles which the Sisters had forgotten, and being on the alert to render them help.' *Folding the mantles which the Sisters had forgotten*—that is what the smallest actions meant in the convent life of St Thérèse. In our spiritual snobbery we smile at it as petty and trifling; it would have been more practical to make the Sisters do it themselves; but while the smile is still on our lips, we begin to see that it was the coalescing of just such little actions as these which produced the colossal phenomenon of St Thérèse of the Child Jesus...

If we do everything to please Our Lord, we shall find ourselves becoming more and more alert to help others and far more conscious of the endless little opportunities around us, the value of which we had never realized before. To find time for a visit to Our Lord in the Blessed Sacrament will become perfectly easy, whereas before it required a superhuman effort. We shall be able to carry on happily though the midst of the smallest details of the day, because through them we have found the way out of ourselves into the heart of God, and into the hearts of our fellow men. (3)

## The Little Way: Suffering in the Mystical Body

To offer Him, and herself in Him, that He might offer Himself and suffer in her, and that so the whole redemptive activity of the Merciful Love of Calvary might be worked out in her own soul—that is what St Thérèse means by offering herself as a little victim of the Merciful Love of God: little, because the more wholly she surrenders herself to the grace of her Baptism with the simple dependence of a little child, the more complete will be her offering, her conformity with Christ.

But it is not only for her own soul's sake that she will thus make her offering as she takes her stand at the foot of the Cross; she will offer herself also for the salvation of others. Our Lord has willed that we as members of His Mystical Body should make one thing, or, as St Thomas says, 'one mystical person' with Him, and thus should be able to appropriate the sacrificial activity of Him who is our

Head, so that He offers and suffers in us. It follows then that we appropriate that sacrificial activity in all the fullness of its application, not only for ourselves, but for all the members of the Mystical Body, and indeed for the whole human race, for God will have all men to be saved and to come to the knowledge of the truth. Thus it is that we are able to share by participation in Our Lord's redemptive work for the salvation of mankind. Thus Christ is fulfilled only through the sufferings of us, His members. 'I ... fill up those things that are wanting of the sufferings of Christ, in my flesh, for His Body, which is the Church', says St Paul (cf Col. 1: 24). 'I resolved to remain continuously in spirit at the foot of the Cross, that I might receive the divine dew of salvation and pour it forth upon souls', says St Thérèse.

Christ can no longer suffer in His natural body; He does so in His Mystical Body. 'The Church fills up those sufferings that are still lacking to the whole Christ ... Her Passion is the extension of Christ's own Passion and therefore an extension of His redemptive victory. By our willing acceptance of suffering, therefore, Christ continues to suffer in us, and to work out to its completion through the centuries the effect of His redemptive act for the salvation of the human race performed once for all on Calvary' (Dom Bruno Webb). Such is the theology of the profound doctrine of vicarious suffering underlying the simple language of the Little Flower, when she says that she will remain continually in spirit at the foot of the Cross in order to receive and pour forth the divine dew of salvation upon souls. (4)

NOTES AND SOURCES

1. Vernon Johnson, *One Lord, One Faith: An Explanation* (London: Sheed & Ward, 1929), 7–8.

2. Vernon Johnson, *Spiritual Childhood: A Study of St Teresa's Teaching* (London: Sheed & Ward, 1953), 122–4.

3. Ibid. 132–4.

4. Ibid. 168–9.


# Sir Arnold Henry Moore Lunn                    1888–1974

Arnold Lunn excelled as an apologist for two activities of high danger and rewards: skiing, and adherence to the faith and practice of the Catholic Church. He was the son of Sir Henry Lunn, who laboured in Madras in the twin professions of missionary doctor and travel agent. After Harrow, he went up to Balliol, where, like many other Oxford men through the centuries, he attained glory everywhere except in the Examination Schools. He was secretary of the Union, edited *The Isis*, and founded the Oxford University Mountaineering and Alpine Clubs. His father's travel agency interests introduced him to the Swiss Alps. When he was barely 20, he crossed the Bernese Oberland on skis. A fall on the mountains in 1909 shattered his right leg and shortened it by three inches. This permanent disability did not keep him from the slopes, and in 1924 he made the first ski ascent of the Eiger. He was the inventor of the modern slalom, and introduced downhill and slalom racing to the 1936 Olympic Games. During the Great War he served in France with the Quaker ambulance unit. In the early 1920s, he wrote an essay on *A Spiritual Aeneid*, the conversion story of his Balliol contemporary, Ronald Knox. The book had caused exasperation in the Protestant Lunn, who sought, as he put it, 'catharsis' in writing about it. From this first essay came *Roman Converts*, which examines the paths to Rome of Knox, Newman, Manning, Chesterton, and Tyrrell. Lunn sent a copy to Knox, and from that contact came an exchange of letters, later published as *Difficulties*, with Knox defending and Lunn attacking the Roman claims. The final upshot of the disputation was

Knox's receiving of Lunn into the Church in July 1933. As a Catholic, he used his skills as an apologist, or 'advocate', as he liked to say, in debates with the likes of J. B. S. Haldane and Professor Joad. In the Second World War Lunn worked for the Ministry of Information, and as a press correspondent. He was a passionate opponent of both National Socialism and Communism. In 1952 he received a knighthood for his services to skiing and Anglo-Swiss relations.

## Catholicism: True Rationalism

St Thomas Aquinas began with accepting the existence of the external world, and deduced therefrom the fact that God exists. The moderns begin by denying the existence of God and end by doubting the existence of the external world. The wheel has completed the full circle, and reason has been disowned by the rationalists.

I quote with pleasure the following definition of rationalism from a Memorandum of the Rationalist Press Association:

Rationalism may be defined as the mental attitude which unreservedly accepts the supremacy of reason, and aims at establishing system of philosophy and ethics verifiable by experience and independent of all arbitrary assumptions of authority.

I congratulate the RPA on formulating a definition of rationalism which a Catholic can accept with conviction, for the Catholic accepts the supremacy of reason. He believes that Catholic philosophy is 'verifiable by experience', and he certainly holds that the Catholic faith is 'independent of all arbitrary assumptions of authority'. The authority of the Church, so far from being arbitrary, can be justified by the appeal to reason.

The Catholic, contrary to what is popularly believed, does not appeal to faith or to authority to support the Catholic claims. He claims to show by reason that God exists. He examines the Bible and, treating it purely as a human document, shows that the Resurrection is a reasonable hypothesis, the only plausible solution to the greatest of all historical problems. He appeals to reason in support of his view that Christ founded a Church, and that the Catholic Church alone can produce legitimate title deeds. The Catholic does not appeal to authority to support his belief in authority, among other reasons because the great medieval theologians had learned from Aristotle not to argue in a circle. It is only when the Catholic has established by reason the existence of an infallible Church that he surrenders his private judgement to the judgement of the Church, on those points, and on those points only, on which the Church speaks with the voice of God. In all other questions private judgement still remains supreme. (1)

## Apologetics: The Inconsistency of Bertrand Russell

If [as Russell says] man's 'loves and beliefs' are but the outcome of an 'accidental collocation of atoms', then our beliefs are the by-product of forces alien to reason and are therefore not the result of any logical process. We have, therefore, no means of knowing whether in fact our beliefs *are* the outcome of an 'accidental collocation of atoms'. Bertrand Russell, in fact, is busily engaged in sawing away the branch on which he is sitting, for the only rational consequence of accepting materialism is the suspicion that we have no rational grounds for accepting any belief, including materialism. (2)

## Non-Catholic Infallibilists

A friend of mine summed up one of the suasions which influenced her conversion in the remark, 'I was tired of being my own Pope'. A most un-English sentiment, for an Englishman's home is his Vatican.

In England the Catholic is an agnostic in relation to the 'Infallibilists' with whom he is surrounded. I am always meeting Popes, in the train up to town, in my club and on the snow. My friend Mr Pooter, for instance, is a convinced Infallibilist. He *knows* that religion consists not in making fusses about candles, but in tactful assistance to lame dogs confronted by stiles. The doctrinal pronouncements of my old friend, Fuddlebeigh, are couched in similar strain. 'Between you and me,' he is fond of saying, 'it doesn't matter a damn what a chap believes provided that he is a good chap. What's yours?'...

The Church might make more headway against this universal Popery if our Pastorals could be re-written in the style of a business prospectus: 'Our aim is the rationalization of competing infallibilities by means of an international merger. Our policy may be summed up in one sentence: Better and fewer Popes.' (3)

## Mountaineering and Religion: The Pope's Suggestion

It is foolish to invite the ridicule of the discerning by making claims for mountaineering which cannot be substantiated. Mountaineering is neither a substitute for religion nor a civic duty. It is a sport, for we climb, not to benefit the human race, but to amuse ourselves. Insofar as mountaineering is something more than a sport, we must base this claim on the fact that it is carried out in surroundings which suggest spiritual truths even to the unspiritual. Ruskin compared mountains to cathedrals, and the comparison is sound, for one does not worship cathedrals, though one may worship in the cathedrals of man or among the cathedrals of nature.

All evil, as a great medieval thinker remarked, is the result of mistaking means for ends. Mountaineering is not an end in itself, but a means to an end. 'For it is true', as the first mountaineer to ascend the throne of Peter (Pius XI) remarked:

For it is true that, of all innocent pleasures, none more than this one (excepting where unnecessary risks are taken) may be considered as being helpful mentally and physically, because, through the efforts required for climbing in the rarefied mountain air, energy is renewed; and owing to the difficulties overcome, the climber thereby becomes better equipped and strengthened to resist the difficulties encountered in life, and by admiring the beauties and grandeur of the scenery as seen from the mighty peaks of the Alps his spirit is uplifted to the Creator of all. (4)

NOTES AND SOURCES

1. Arnold Lunn, *Now I See* (London: Sheed & Ward, 1934), 131–2.
2. Arnold Lunn, *And Yet So New* (London: Sheed & Ward, 1958), 223–4.
3. Arnold Lunn, *Within that City* (London: Sheed & Ward, 1936), 60–1.

4. Arnold Lunn, 'Alpine Mysticism and "Cold Philosophy" ', in Douglas Woodruff (ed.), *For Hilaire Belloc: Essays in Honour of His 72nd Birthday* (London: Sheed & Ward, 1942), 71–2.

## Monsignor Ronald Arbuthnott Knox          1888–1957

Ronald Knox, one of the best-known Catholic priests in twentieth-century England, was born into one of the great clerical dynasties of the Anglican Establishment. His father was the son of a clergyman and himself became Bishop of Manchester. Even in a family of lofty intellect, Ronnie was regarded as 'unusually brilliant' and was reading Virgil by the age of 6. A glittering career at Eton and Balliol was followed by the taking of Anglican orders and appointment as chaplain of Trinity College, Oxford. In the last years before the Great War, he came to prominence as one of the outriders on the extreme wing of the Anglo-Catholic movement. He was much sought after as a preacher, and in his writing began to display the gifts that make him one of the master parodists and satirists of modern English literature. In *Reunion All Round*, a tract written in the style of Swift, he mocked the indifferentism of the fledgling ecumenical movement by proposing that the comprehensiveness of the Church of England should be widened to make room for all beliefs, including Islam and atheism. The prospect of death in the trenches moved several of his Oxford friends and protégés to turn from the vagueness of official Anglicanism and the frivolities of Anglo-Catholicism to the divine solidity of the Catholic Church. He himself was received in 1917. After theological studies at St Edmund's, Ware, he was ordained to the priesthood in 1919. He taught at Ware till 1926, when he was made Catholic chaplain to the University of Oxford. To make money for the chaplaincy, and for his own amusement, he began to write detective stories and, with Agatha Christie and G. K. Chesterton among others, was one of the founders of the Detection Club. He resigned from the Oxford chaplaincy in 1939 in order to concentrate on writing, in particular his translation of the Bible. He spent the war as the chaplain to a convent school evacuated to Shropshire, an assignment that inspired *The Mass in Slow Motion* and *The Creed in Slow Motion*, both masterpieces of doctrinal pedagogy, which convey lofty dogmatic truths in language and with a humour calculated to appeal to schoolgirls. He disliked foreign travel and did very little of it. When asked why he, a Monsignor of the Roman Church, had never visited the Eternal City, he replied that he was a bad sailor, and so preferred to keep away from the engine room. His last years were spent quietly living with the Asquiths in Mells in Somerset.

## Proving God's Existence: The Question Why?

It's an inveterate habit of man to ask, 'Why?' Most of us have been told off about it in the nursery, and discouraged from doing it. I remember once travelling in a train with a small boy who pointed to the clock in Banbury station and asked, 'What does the clock say?' And the mother said, 'It's a quarter to two.' And the small boy said, 'Why is it a quarter to two?' A child like that grows up into a scientist, and spends its whole life asking why. All our science comes from the human habit of asking for the reason of everything, our ineradicable belief that very event must have a cause. And when we've pushed that habit as far as it will go, all we have done is to weave long chains of causes, each one depending on the next. Why did you twist your ankle? Because the low gate into the garden was shut when you didn't expect it to be. Why was it shut? To keep the little pigs out. Why were the little pigs running loose? Because there wasn't enough feed for them if they were put in a sty. Why wasn't there enough feed for them? Because ships get torpedoed in the Atlantic. Why do ships get torpedoed in the Atlantic? Because we are at war with Germany. Why are we at war with Germany? And so on. The series of causes stretches back and back, and you never get to the end of it. But, you see, it can't really be infinite. Because an infinite series of causes all depending on one another wouldn't be a sufficient explanation of anything. Somewhere, at the end of that chain, there must be a First Cause which is not caused by anything which went before it. And that First Cause is God. His face looks down at us, as we try to run away from Him, looks down this long avenue of causality, and reminds us that He made us; we did not make ourselves. (1)

## Understanding the Dogma of the Blessed Trinity

We've got to go right back, and think of God existing altogether outside time, independently of any worlds, or any angels for that matter. From all eternity there has been a multiplicity of life within the unity of the Godhead. God the Father, from all eternity, has spoken a Word, or, if you prefer to put it in a rather more luminous way, from all eternity He has thought a thought of Himself. When you or I think, the thought has no existence outside our own minds, but when the eternal Mind thinks of itself, it produces a Thought as eternal as itself, and that Thought is, like the eternal Mind, a Person. And so you get two persons within the Blessed Trinity, the eternal Mind and its eternal Thought. And now, you can't imagine two divine persons as existing side by side, can you, without their having some relation to each other, some attitude to each other, and what that attitude will be it is not difficult to guess; they will love one another. And this Love, which springs at once from the eternal Mind and its eternal Thought, binding them to one another, is the Holy Spirit. That is why we say that the Holy Spirit proceeds from the Father and the Son. He is the conscious response of Love which springs up between Them; He goes out from each of Them to the other. That is not intended to be an explanation of the doctrine of the Blessed Trinity, because you cannot explain a mystery. But I think that is as near as our minds will get to understanding what the doctrine of the Trinity is about. (2)

## True God and True Man

Jesus Christ was both human and divine, but in different ways. His nature was human, His person was divine. That is what we mean by the Hypostatic Union. When we say the Litany of the Sacred Heart, we say, 'Heart of Jesus, hypostatically united to the Word of God', not knowing very much it means. Hypo is something you use for developing photographs, and statics are a kind of higher mathematics, but all that doesn't help us much. Hypostatically united means personally united. It means that Jesus Christ has a human nature, but in person He is divine.

A divine person with a human nature—and therefore a divine person with two natures, one human and one divine. Our Lord couldn't stop being God when he became man. He was still reigning as God in Heaven, when Our Lady was wrapping Him up in His swaddling-clothes at Bethlehem. You say, 'That's very confusing'. I should just think it was. Nothing I can suggest in the way of illustration can really be of any use, simply because the Hypostatic Union is something unlike anything else in existence; it is a closer, more intimate union than anything we can imagine. Our Lady is united to God by love; how close that bond is! But in the Incarnation you have a union closer than love itself. The same person on earth may hold two different positions, two different titles, as the King was both King of England and Emperor of India; but in the Incarnation it is not a question of two different titles, two different positions; it is a question of two natures, two modes of being. You read stories sometimes of people possessed by devils, and having to be exorcized, and in those stories it seems as if the devil managed to take complete control of the possessed person, spoke with his voice, looked out with his eyes, thought with his mind. But always, even in such a case as that, the human personality is there, must be there, even though it's driven (so to speak) into a corner. But in the incarnate Christ, though there is a human mind, a human soul, there is no human personality. The person you see at Bethlehem or on Calvary is God. Nothing in our human experience can be used to illustrate that mystery. But it is a mystery, not a contradiction.

You'll find as you grow up, and get talking to Protestants more and find out what they think about religion, that they are nearly all wrong about what we've been saying this afternoon. They will start by telling you that they believe Our Lord was God, but when you question them a little more closely, you'll find that most of them think He was a very good man, so good that he was allowed (I'm going to be irreverent again) to enjoy a kind of honorary rank as God. Some of them think it happened when He was baptized, if you remember, in the Jordan, and the Holy Ghost came down on Him there in the form of a dove. That, they will tell you, is when Our Lord started to be God. But, you see, it's all nonsense really.

If the Baby who lay in the crib at Bethlehem was a human person, then it was a human person who hung on the Cross, and your sins and mine have never been properly atoned for, if that's so, because human sin is an infinite offence to the majesty of God, and you can't atone for an infinite offence by a finite act of reparation. No, God's only Son, wishing to make reparation in full for our fault, took a human nature upon Him, because that was the only way in which it was possible for Him to suffer. It was like the action of some rich man who makes himself responsible for the debts of a bankrupt, because he thinks those debts ought to be paid. Like that, only different from that, because the condescension was much greater, because the price He paid cost Him much more, it cost Him His life. 'Greater love hath no man than this', He tells us, 'that a man should lay down his life for his friends.' No *man*, but, being God, He revealed to us a love even greater than the love He spoke of. Being God, he took a human life in order to be able to lay it down; and to lay it down for us, who were not His friends, but His enemies. (3)

## The Effect of Christmas

I think you can say that there are three qualities, I won't say which have been made known to us, but which show up in a new light, as the result of the Christian revelation: humility, charity, and purity. They are all words derived from the

Latin; but if a Roman of Julius Caesar's time could come back to earth, I don't think we could mention them to him without finding ourselves at cross purposes.

Humility—if you look up that word in the Latin dictionary, you will get a surprise. You will find that it means 'lowness, meanness, insignificance, littleness of mind, baseness, abjectness', and it has no other sense until you come on to the Christian authors. And yet how instinctively we recognize the worth of it today, even those of us who wouldn't call ourselves in any sense Christians! To be sure, there are all sorts of inferior substitutes for it which owe little or nothing to the influence of Bethlehem; there is the mock modesty which prompts us to underrate our own achievements simply as a matter of good manners; we don't want to make a bad impression of boastfulness on the people we meet. There is the calculating, affected humility of Uriah Heep; you demean yourself before important people because you know which side your bread is buttered. But real humility, how it shines when it catches the light! The man who can take an affront and feel it is no more than he deserves; who takes it for granted that his successful rival was the better candidate; who can work to other men's plans when they run contrary to his own advice, the advice which was not asked for, or went unregarded—how we admire such a man, even when we think that he carries his good qualities to a fault! And the reason for our admiration—the historical reason for our admiration—is because we have been told about a God who for us men and for our salvation came down from Heaven, and took upon Himself the nature of a slave for our sakes.

And charity—if you look that up in the Latin dictionary, you find that it means affection for your family or your close friends. How should it mean anything more, to people who hadn't read the parable of the Good Samaritan? Once again, not everything that is done in the name of charity is real charity. There is the ostentatiousness which likes to see its name on a subscription-list; there is the love of interference which is ever eager to manage other people's lives for them. But, when you have made all allowances for that, charity towards complete strangers has become a habit with us. It has filled the world with hospitals and orphanages and almshouses, and all because of Bethlehem; there was no name for such things before Jesus Christ came. Because Jesus Christ came to redeem us when we were strangers who had no claim on him, brought redemption to everybody near and far, we too, even you and I, are ashamed to button up our pockets.

And then—purity. The Romans, of course, use the word often enough, but I don't think they meant any more by it than cleanness of body; no one seems to have bothered much about purity of mind. And yet Our Lord tells us that all sins, even the sins of sense, take their origin in the mind. How hard it is, nowadays, to persuade people that there is such a thing as purity! They get it mixed up with mere ignorance of sex; or with prudery, that loves the sensation of being shocked; or with the morbid horror of sex which is found, sometimes, in ill-adjusted natures. But there is such a thing as real purity, which sees the facts of life as they are, and has too much sense of the rich, living thing marriage is, of the bright, delicate thing virginity is, to sully either with brooding thoughts, or with sniggering jocularity. That, too, we owe to Bethlehem; to the memory of that virgin motherhood which saved us all. All that we owe to Christmas. (4)

## Holy Saturday

After the Mass of Holy Saturday, when you are sitting in your room, perhaps with some favourite book in front of you, there is a sudden knock at the door. 'Come in', you shout cheerily, half turning to greet the visitor. The door is opened by a priest in cotta and stole, who, after a brief Latin salutation, sprinkles the treasured volume with holy water, and withdraws. What sacred thoughts ought to be ours on this occasion?

For myself, I like to think of some old patriarch in Limbo, King David, let us say, waiting, through long centuries of twilight for his permit to enter Heaven. Waiting, not under the stroke of divine chastisement, but with a patience beyond all imagining; alone there, with his memories and his hopes, like a watchman waiting for dawn. The Spirit of Christ is in him, making known to him the sufferings which Christ's cause brings with it, and the glory that crowns them; when is it to be? And how is the time to be recognized? All at once, the door of his prison swings open, and in a blaze of light he sees the figure so often, in his poetic imaginings, ah, how dimly foreshadowed, the martyred Christ, wounds shining on hands and feet! Christ is risen, and David, walking up after his likeness, finds there everlasting content. (5)

## The Ascension of Our Lord

Our High Priest we call Him, for it is the business of a priest to mediate between man and God; and no one could do that perfectly except He who is both God and Man. And it is His humanness that we chiefly remember, when we think about the mystery of His Ascension... 'It is not as if our high priest was incapable of feeling for us in our humiliations; He has been through every trial, fashioned as we are, only sinless' (Heb. 4: 15). Since He went up into Heaven, a cloud has concealed Him from our sight; it has not concealed us from His. He knows our individual needs, and can feel for them, because He has had such needs Himself. Oh, it is foolish of us, no doubt, to ask for sympathy in that way; we know, of course, that the divine nature is all-merciful—how else could it be divine? But somehow it makes it easier for us to focus our minds on the lovingness of God, if we can tell ourselves that Jesus Christ is in the bosom of the Father—Jesus Christ, who rested His head, at the Last Supper, on the bosom of a human friend. He has known all our trials, borne all the weaknesses that are a true part of our nature, been helpless in Mary's arms, hung desolate on the Cross. 'Gall and wormwood', we say to him with Jeremias, 'gall and wormwood, keep all this well in memory' (Lam. 3: 19), and our gall and wormwood becomes less bitter to us, because we know that He remembers. (6)

## 'Hail, Holy Queen'

*Hail, holy Queen*—crowned in heaven by the piety of your ascended Son, crowned on earth by the gratitude of a million suppliants. How little you regarded your royal lineage as a daughter of the house of David! 'Hearken, O daughter, and consider, incline thy ear, and forget thy people and thy father's house: instead of thy fathers thou shalt have children, whom thou mayest make princes in all lands'—you are crowned, not by some accident of birth, for the sake of those who went before you, but by the loving homage of all those saints who derive from you their spiritual succession. Hail, holy Queen, still remembering in the courts of Heaven your low estate, the anxieties of womanhood and the simple cares of home!

*Mother of Mercy*—if it be true that we inherit from our parents not our bodily features only, but something also of the stuff of our minds, the make-up of our temperaments, then He, whose sacred humanity was perfectly human, must have received from you some gift of human tenderness. At least, as His Mother, you brought into the world Incarnate Mercy; at least, by your own compassion you have won the title, *Mater Misericordiae*! (7)

## Pope Pius XI and the Kingship of Christ

He does not belong to the ordinary tradition of ecclesiastical Rome. Until he was sixty, he was known as a librarian and a scholar; he lived in an international and, I think you may say, an interdenominational world of scholarship. He is, for example, the only Pope since the Reformation and long before it who knows what Oxford looks like, except from pictures. He was librarian at Milan; a friend of mine reading recently at the Ambrosian library came across a slip of paper in a book with some MS notes on it, signed 'A. Ratti'. Quite suddenly at the age of sixty he was sent out as nuncio to Poland—to all that there was of Poland, when the Russian Revolution had already happened, and the war was not yet over. The story is that he was chosen for that post because he was the only priest in the Church of Christ thought capable of learning Polish in a fortnight. His position lasted after the war; and he was in Warsaw at what was probably the most thrilling moment of history since Versailles; the moment at which the Red Army swept through Polish territory and were at the very gates of the capital, which seemed doomed to fall. The Government was preparing to leave; it was suggested to the embassies that they should leave, too; nobody was quite certain what to expect of Bolshevism in its moment of military triumph. Monsignor Ratti insisted on staying; the American, Italian, and Danish envoys—no others—remained to follow his example and share his fate. He saw, on the feast of the Assumption, Pilsudski and Weygand roll back the Bolshevist armies from the gates of Warsaw in defeat.

Then, almost immediately, just when he seemed the only man who could comb out the tangle of Eastern European politics, he was recalled to Italy and made Cardinal Archbishop of Milan. It was under his very eyes that all the early struggles between the Italian Communists and the growing strength of the Fascists took place, within the walls of his own cathedral city. He had not held that position for a year when he was summoned to Rome for the conclave after the death of Benedict XV; and from that conclave he never returned. He would never climb in the Alps, he would never poke about in the Bodleian, again.

In the course of that providential career he had seen more than it is given to most Popes to see. His background was a background of European culture; and circumstances had suddenly thrust under his eyes, after his sixtieth year, vivid impressions of that struggle between two great forces in Europe, nationalism and international Socialism, which the rest of the world hardly expected as yet. When he was crowned Pope, he insisted on giving his blessing to the world from the balcony of St Peter's, a thing no Pope had done since the loss of the temporal power. Even so early, he had made up his mind that the Papacy must come out of its retirement, and make itself felt as a moral force in the world. And I think he introduced this feast of the Kingship of Christ with the same idea in view. He saw that the minds of men, of young men especially, all over Europe, would be caught by a wave of conflicting loyalties, which would drown the voice of conscience, and produce everywhere unscrupulous wars between class and class, the threat of equally unscrupulous wars between nations. To save the world, if he could, from that frenzy of reckless idealism, he would recall it to the contemplation of a very simple truth. The truth, I mean, that the claim of Christ comes first, before the claims of party, before the claims of nationality. *Pax Christi in regno Christi*; peace and justice were duties which man owed to God more elementary than any duties to his fellow men. All that, before the conflict between the Church and Fascism, before the revolution in Spain, before the name of Hitler had ever been set up in the type-room of a foreign newspaper. The institution of this feast was not a gesture of authoritarianism against democracy. It was a gesture of Christian truth against a world which was on the point of going mad with political propaganda. (8)

## The Incarnation and the Eucharist

Has He done nothing . . . to make it easier for us to find Him? Why, yes, surely; in the mystery of His Incarnation, so full of His condescension, this is perhaps the greatest condescension of all—that He who is without limit should be limited, as Incarnate, to one position in space. When Moses drew near to the burning bush, when Elias heard from his cave a whisper of the divine voice, God manifested His presence in a special way, but that was all. When Our Lady bent over the crib at Bethlehem, God was *there*. It was not necessary for her to say, 'Where is thy pasture ground, where now is thy resting-place?'—He lay in her arms, He fed at her breast. It was no use for the scornful unbeliever to challenge St John or St Andrew with the old question, 'Where is thy God?' —those first apostles could say, and did say, 'Come and see'. For thirty-three years of human history it was possible to say, 'There is God! Look where He feeds, with publicans and sinners! Look, where He lies in the forepart of a ship which the waves threaten with destruction!'

Yes, for thirty-three years: but afterwards? We can make our pilgrimage to the holy places, pass along the roads which were once trodden by divine feet, mount the hill on which Our Lord suffered, worship, perhaps, at His very tomb. But it is all a story of yesteryear; what use is it (we complain) that God should draw near to us in space, if He does not also draw near to us in time? It is not enough that *our* God should make Himself present to *us*; why does not *my* God make Himself present to *me*?

As we know, God has foreseen that complaint of ours, and has condescended to make provision for it. Everything else about the Blessed Sacrament may be obscure to us; we do not see Our Lord as He is, we cannot fathom the mystery of that change which is effected in the consecrated elements, we have no clue to the manner in which Holy Communion imparts its virtue to our souls. But one thing we can say, without bewilderment or ambiguity—God is here. Like those two disciples when they heard St John the Baptist acclaim the Lamb of God, who should take away the sins of the world, we, taught by the Church that all salvation is to be found in Christ, are eager to know more of Him, to see Him in the most representative light possible, to catch a glimpse of Him in the setting, in the surroundings which most truly manifest His character. 'Master', we ask Him, 'where dost thou live?' And He points to the tabernacle with the invitation, 'Come and see.' (9)

## Forgiving and Loving

[The saints] really do love their fellow man as such; they feel the same thrill of pleasure when they see a man coming down the road which you and I feel when we see a friend coming down the road. Mankind is their kindred, the world is their parish. And, consequently, one who shows bitter enmity towards a saint, speaks evil of him, persecutes him, is to the saint simply a friend who is being tiresome; it's a sort of tiff between lovers which is bound to blow over. (10)

## The Priest: The Living Instrument of Jesus Christ

When a priest baptizes or absolves, he stands there, sits there, only to unseal the fountains of grace in answer to the faith and penitence which knock to receive them. But when he stands at the altar, the priest does something more; he takes upon himself the person of Christ, re-enacting in his name the ceremony which he performed on the night before His Passion. A priest clad in the sacred vestments (says the author of the *Imitation*) is the vice-gerent of Christ Himself (cf Book 4, ch. 5). He uses Our Lord's own words, identifies himself with the offering which Our Lord continually makes before the Father of His own Body and Blood. How is it that men can be found with the assurance, with the presumption, to do that?

The difficulty is solved for us by one golden phrase of St John Chrysostom's. 'When you see a priest offering the sacrifice', he says. 'do not think as if it were *he* doing this; it is the hand of Christ, invisibly stretched forth.' The hand of Christ invisibly stretched forth—that is the image we must conjure up if we are to think of the Mass as what it really is. The philosopher Aristotle, in defining the position of a slave, uses the words, 'A slave is a living tool'. And that is what a priest is, a living tool of Jesus Christ. He lends his hands to be Christ's hands, his voice to be Christ's voice, his thoughts to be Christ's thoughts; there is, there should be, nothing of himself in it from first to last, except where the Church graciously permits him to dwell for a moment in silence on his own special intentions, for the good estate of the living and the dead. Those who are not of our religion are puzzled sometimes, or even scandalized, by witnessing the ceremonies of the Mass; it is all, they say, so mechanical. But you see, it *ought* to be mechanical. They are watching, not a man, but a living tool; it turns this way and that, bends, straightens itself, gesticulates, all in obedience to a preconceived order—Christ's order, not ours. The Mass is best said—we Catholics know it—when it is said so that you do not notice how it is said; we do not expect eccentricities from a tool of Christ. (11)

## 'St George for Merry England!'

England will not be merry until England is Catholic. That word 'merry' is not so simple as it sounds. It is a difficult word, for example, to translate into any foreign language. It is typical of our modern conditions that we hardly ever use it nowadays, except when we call a person 'merry', meaning that he was slightly drunk. It survives, chiefly, in old-fashioned formulas such as Merry England, or a Merry Christmas. Merry does not mean drunk, or uproarious, or frivolous. It means that a man is light-hearted, that his mind is at ease, that he is in a good humour, that he is ready to share a bit of fun with his neighbours. There is humility in the word, and innocence, and comradeship. And such a frame of mind as that is not to be secured, by grown-up people, through a continuous whirl of excitements, or a long course of dissipations. It comes from within.

A country cannot be merry while it forgets God. And a country cannot be merry for long, or with safety, if it tries to be Christian without being Catholic. England is not, of course, even today, a country of atheists. But there is a very large fraction of our fellow countrymen—I do not think you can put it much lower than four-fifths—which does not go to church. And most of these people do not think about God if they can help it—that is what I call 'forgetting God'. They try to satisfy themselves with this world; and that is a thing which you cannot do; almighty God does not mean us to do it; he wants us to draw us back to Himself. The man who confines his outlook to this world is worried all the time, at the back of his mind, by the old riddle of existence; the troubles, the sufferings, the tragedies of the world keep flicking him like briers as he goes along: problems of conduct—which is the right thing to do, and why should I do it?—stick to him like burrs and force themselves upon his notice. You may forget your cares for a time, you may drown them occasionally with your pleasures, but you can never banish them. A man will never be light-hearted in this world unless he is thinking of the next world; this world is too chequered an affair for that.

And in the long run, even a Christian nation cannot be merry unless it is a Catholic nation. For these non-Catholic Christianities—why, I do not know, but as a matter of observation it is true—always go hand-in-hand with some kind of Puritanism that interferes with man's innocent enjoyments. Sometimes they want to make us all into teetotallers, sometimes they are out against boxing, or racing, or the stage; sometimes they insist that we shall sit indoors all Sunday afternoon and go to sleep. Wherever Protestant opinion really rules a country, you always find legislation of one sort or another which is designed to stop people being merry. It sounds distant and old-fashioned to us, but that is because Protestantism has lost its grip on the country. In the United States, where the Protestants, though few in number, are rich and powerful, the thing goes on to this day. And when Protestantism does lose its grip, a reaction sets in, a reaction against Puritanism, which instead of making people merry makes them dissolute. A false religion, no less than lack of religion, will destroy, in the end, a nation's peace of mind.

Let us comfort ourselves, then, those of us who love England, with the thought that in trying to convert England we are not trying to alter her into something that is strange and foreign: we are trying to make her once more merry England—that which she was and that which traditionally she ought to be. Those who hate our religion are fond of pointing us to the example of Catholic nations abroad, of which they draw a very unfair picture, and then say: 'Look at Belgium—do you want England to be like that? Look at Spain—do you want England to be like that?' But the truth is that, for better or worse, England will never be quite like any other country. You may love her, you may hate her, but you must take her as she stands.

Those native virtues that now grow wild in her hedgerows will only bloom the stronger and the fairer when the faith cultivates them. The more England becomes Catholic, the more English she will become.

Let us, then, on this feast of our patron, pray earnestly and resolve always to pray earnestly for the conversion of the country we love. Let us ask his prayers, and the prayers of our blessed Lady and the English martyrs, that the tide of conversions we see chronicled year by year may flow still more strong, and still more deep, till at last the heart of the country reawakes, and remembers, and returns to her ancient love. It will hardly be in our time, I suppose, that the change comes; but even now we can stand, like Moses on Mount Nebo, and see beneath us the promised land that is one day to be our Catholic heritage. Let us stand together, strong in the faith of that vision, and resolve that through no fault of ours, that high endeavour to which we are pledged shall fall short of a swift and a lasting achievement. May the prayers of St George protect this country that is dedicated to his honour, and bring all those who do him honour to that true country of ours which is in Heaven. (12)

NOTES AND SOURCES

1. Ronald Knox, *The Creed in Slow Motion* (London: Sheed & Ward, 1950), 11–12.

2. Ibid. 144–7.

3. Ibid. 52–4.

4. Ronald Knox, *The Pastoral Sermons of Ronald A. Knox*, ed. Philip Caraman SJ (London: Burns & Oates, 1960), 364–8.

5. Ibid. 383.

6. Ibid. 407.

7. Ronald Knox, *A Retreat for Priests* (London: Sheed & Ward, 1946), 176.

8. Knox, *The Pastoral Sermons of Ronald A. Knox*, 456–8.

9. Ibid. 218–19.

10. Ibid. 51–2.

11. Ibid. 342–3.

12. Ronald Knox, *Occasional Sermons of Ronald A. Knox*, ed. Philip Caraman SJ (London: Burns & Oates, 1960), 12–14.

# Martin Cyril D'Arcy SJ     1888–1976

Martin D'Arcy was a Jesuit philosopher and theologian of insight and fluent style, an effective apologist for the faith by means of broadcasting, and the mentor of many of the best-known converts of the twentieth century, including Monsignor Ronald Knox, Edith Sitwell, and Evelyn Waugh. Knox treasured his friendship with D'Arcy to the point of saying that, as far as he was concerned, Heaven would include being able to walk round Christ Church Meadow with Father D'Arcy. The youngest of the four sons of a barrister, he was educated at Stonyhurst and, after his Jesuit novitiate at Roehampton, he went to read Greats at Pope's (later Campion) Hall, Oxford, gained a first, and won many prizes. After his four years of theology, he was ordained and sent to Rome for higher studies in philosophy, but he did not settle there, and so, after a year of further reading at Farm Street, his superiors sent him back to Campion Hall to lecture and tutor in philosophy. So notorious did he become for success in making converts that a character in Muriel Spark's novel, *The Girls of Slender Means*, can 'never make up his mind between suicide and an equally drastic course of action known as Father D'Arcy'. D'Arcy's books include *The Nature of Belief* (1931), *The Pain of this World and the Providence of God* (1935), and *The Mind and Heart of Love* (1945), the last being a response to the Swedish Lutheran, Anders Nygren, who had claimed that Catholic theology has allowed a 'Greek' doctrine of *eros*, the love of self-fulfilment, to corrupt New Testament *agape*, the love of self-giving. D'Arcy's striking appearance—ascetical face, scrawny neck in gaping Roman collar, and wildly distracted hair—captured the attention of painters and sculptors, the best portrait of all being by Augustus John. Post-conciliar changes, especially in the liturgy, confused and depressed him. Feeling, as he said at the time, sick in soul, he lamented 'the modern copying of Protestantism and Iconoclasm', the huge exodus from his beloved Society, and the twisting of the liturgy by 'semi-sophisticated barbarians'. In his last years he spent much of his time in the United States, where he found friendship and a greater sympathy for his theological outlook than he encountered in England. He died at the Hospital of St John and St Elizabeth and, with many others in this anthology, was buried at Kensal Green.

## Apologetics by Beauty

Apologists are bound by the very nature of the attack upon the Church to take objection after objection, to confine themselves to one point and prove the falsity of the objection and the credibility of the doctrine attacked. But apologists are permitted to use also another method, to paint the everlasting beauty of 'the city set on a hill'. They can say with Christ, 'Come and see', and as the onlooker looks, he will find his mind captivated by the truth; he will cry out, 'The finger of God is here', and the all too human rival religions and copies of Christianity will, without hesitation or controversy, be set aside as counterfeit. (1)

## Faith and Reason: Believing on God's Authority

What happens...in the passage from reason to faith, is not the black-out of reason but the enlightening of it. The evidence before us we had interpreted according to our own way of looking at it. That interpretation might be prejudiced or fair, but at its best, just because it is human and limited, it is like that of a sceptic judging Chartres Cathedral. By faith we are enabled to see the plan of life, not from our point of view but from that of its author, and it comes home to us as the only way of life, the only truth, and the pledge of peace. As such you see that faith in God differs from all other beliefs. *They* keep on the same plane of human weakness and uncertainty, and that is why we can rightly question at times the orders or doctrines which we are asked to believe. But faith in a divine revelation must be complete and final. It is like love in this, that the lover surrenders himself and identifies all that he is with the beloved. But, whereas human love can be betrayed, Truth, which brings the whole of life into a whole new order of significance, and is guaranteed by God Himself, cannot betray us; in fact, so enlightened is the mind that it sees the evidence as clearly as a loving child can recognize the familiar traits and gestures of its mother.

Now you may disagree with what I've said, and I've not been trying to prove to you in detail the truth of the Christian religion. But what I do hope is that I've made clear to you that faith, however mistaken, is not founded on unreason. It is much less unreasonable than what you yourselves are doing constantly, that is, allowing yourselves to be influenced or converted by the views of another. When a man becomes a Darwinian or Marxist or Freudian, or follows the direction of some authority on gardening or football or cooking, he is taking over another's point of view. His pattern is changed, and he is thinking along with the person who changed it. I ask you to recognize that God Himself may have let Himself be known, and given us the clue to life. If you are so graced as to be able to catch hold of that truth and identify yourself with it, then it may overwhelm you with its evidence, and lead you, quite reasonably, to commit your ways unto Him and make His word the final arbiter of your destiny. (2)

## The Sacred Heart

Millions have been helped to love God better by devotion to the Heart of Christ. The heart is an old and natural symbol of love, and we say to one another, 'Dear heart'. 'Heart speaks to heart', as Scripture tells us. But what gives the special characteristics to this devotion is that Christ suffered for our iniquity, and that a lance pierced His side on the Cross, and from His side flowed blood and water. Hence we think of Christ with a wounded heart, wounded by man's coldness and hostility.

There is a deep mystery hidden in this devotion, for not only is the heart a living symbol of Christ's love, which brings, too, His humanity close to us, but it is as if we were hidden within the wounds of Christ, so that we enter into His life. It was said of St Paul, *Cor Pauli erat cor Christi*, 'the heart of Paul was the heart of Christ'. St Paul thought and loved like Christ, but also as Christ, who lived in him. In some mysterious way, by the gift of grace, the Holy Spirit dwells in us and makes us one with Christ, as the Holy Spirit is the living link between the Father and the Son. 'As thou, Father, in me, and I in thee, that they also may be one in us.'

This mysterious identification of the members of the Mystical Body with Christ helps to explain a devotion to the Sacred Heart which seems to imply that Christ is still being wounded. We feel sure that Christ cannot be indifferent to us now, and that there is a deep truth in the saying of Pascal that Christ is in agony until the end of the world. But we also know that Christ now is in glory, that He 'sitteth at the right hand of God, the Father almighty', and that He can suffer no more in that body which was raised from the dead. But He can suffer as the Head in His Mystical Body, that is, in His members. In some inexplicable way, we in our turn re-live the life of Christ, and meet His Nativity, His Childhood, His Gethsemane, and His Golgotha. We 'make up what is wanting in the sufferings of Christ'; we carry His Cross, and in a minor key we co-redeem and make reparation to God and, in His name and grace, give glory to His Father. And what we do, He does, so that in some inexplicable way He re-lives in us all His sorrow of the world and becomes sin without sinning. By this redeeming, ever proceeding act, Christ gathers all the positive experiences of time and transfigures them. They thus make up a part of that immortal inheritance, His Kingdom, which Christ is to hand to His Father at the end of time. (3)

## 'Our Tainted Nature's Solitary Boast'

The Mother of God is the foreword, the living type, of that perfect humanity which her Son came to re-constitute. As Charles Péguy wrote: 'She in her youthful splendour is already that new universe which the Church is to be'; or, in the words of Claudel: 'It is from her, set there before His gaze, that the Eternal takes the measure of all things'. From her lips comes the Magnificat, the pure song of praise of the new creation, the work of Our Lord God made man and dwelling among us. Hence the Church likes to hide behind her in its prayers and make God look through her at His scapegrace children. (4)

## Sharing in God's Own Life

The Son of God has made reparation for sin in His victimized body, and that sacrifice being acceptable has brought as its reward the transfiguration of that body and the uplifting with it of all mankind, if they but choose to belong to Christ. The human nature of Christ is glorified and full of grace, and other finite individuals are graced, too, but how? The answer is simple, but divine in its conception and in its working out, for it is by incorporation in Christ, by communion with the all-holy Body and Blood of the Redeemer.

A mother feeds her babe from the breast, and her milk is the nourishment which is transformed into the flesh of the child. Christ, too, feeds us, and with His own Body and Blood, but this food is not assimilated to that life of ours so much lower in comparison with His. We are transformed into Him and become identical with that higher principle of life that is part of that new Body of His which grows with the extension of the Church, and is not yet, as St Paul tells us, complete. It is meet that a higher form of life should assume a lower form of life into its own being, and so Christ can truly say, in the words put on His lips by St Augustine: 'I am the nourishment of great souls. Grow, and you shall be able to feed on me, but you will not change me into you, as with bodily food; it is you that will be changed into me.' In the Catacombs a favourite design is of a young unbearded shepherd who leads his flock *in pascua*: the *pascua* are the Body and Blood of the Shepherd, who gives His life for His sheep.

And so, without absorption, without any shade of pantheism, the Christian is made a sharer in the divine nature. The Father, the Son, and the Holy Ghost have one divine incommunicable nature, and the Son also has a human nature hypostatically united to His divinity, and moreover, a Mystical Body united through His human nature to Himself, but composed of free, independent human persons. The link, as has been said, is the human nature of Christ. By that human nature which is personally united to God, free, independent persons are also united to God, since that flesh and that blood assume the lower life of man into Christ, without detriment to the *individual*. Justly, the Church in the epistle for the feast of the Resurrection takes St Paul's words, with their significant allusion to bread, the species of the Eucharist: 'Purge out the old leaven that you may be a new paste as you are unleavened, for Christ our Pasch is sacrificed. Therefore... let us feast with the unleavened bread of sincerity and truth' (1 Cor. 5: 7). (5)

## The Holy Sacrifice of the Mass: The Twofold Consecration

That the Mass is a sacrificial act is clear, for all the requisites are present—Priest, Victim, and oblation in a visible rite. But now straightway the question arises, How is a victim present? There is no act of immolation, no new blood-letting. As the Council of Trent asserts, the Mass is an unbloody sacrifice. The answer is shown to us in the Last Supper. There Our Lord, by means of the bread and wine, represented the immolation to come. Behind the appearances were His true Body and Blood, so that the Passion was represented symbolically by the separate consecration and the Victim really offered. Similarly, in the separate consecrations at Mass, there is a symbolical immolation which serves as a visible liturgical action necessary for a true sacrifice. But that action is only symbolical or mystical; no new *real* victimizing of the flesh and blood of Christ takes place, bloody or unbloody. And the reason is simple: if the Body and Blood of Christ are there present on the altar, they are there in a glorious state, *and in a Victim state*. The Victim being present, the rite representing a victim, the Victim being offered, all the requisites for sacrifice are there....

The Mass, therefore, may be said to be the holy place to which all the most sublime truths of the Christian faith converge and whence they issue. The sacrificial and propitiatory aspect of the Redemption is perpetuated by the presence of the Victim of Calvary. By offering up this Victim, the world concurs with the wish of Christ to save it, and adds the assent which was necessary as a condition to make the living act of reparation by Christ efficacious. It follows, therefore, that the fruits of the Redemption are laid at the disposal of the faithful in the Mass. Secondly, the primary effect of the Redemption—namely, elevation into a supernatural order of union with Christ and so with the Blessed Trinity—is condition and consummation of the Mass. For only those who are so united with Christ as to be one with him can offer a sacrifice which will be identical with that of Calvary. Were it not in some sort Christ who continued to offer, the Mass would be a new sacrifice and supplement that of Calvary, if such a thing were possible. In fact, it is impossible, for a new sacrifice, being human, would be incommensurate with that of the Son of God. Consequently, the Mass is subordinated to that of Calvary and yet can be said to be identical with it, inasmuch as the participation of the members in the infinite act of the Head is a subordinate act, whose value is derived from the virtue of that Head. The point is that the offerers of the Mass are participants of the grace of Jesus Christ and, in a limited though an exact sense, divine themselves. And the manner in which they are sharers of the divine nature is by their incorporation with Christ, by becoming 'one flesh and one spirit' with Him in the Communion, which ends the sacrificial action of the Mass, as the Resurrection was the complement of the Passion. (6)

## Immortal Mind

Mind releases us from being a cipher, a mere numerical identity, and we become spectators of all time and space. This faculty of standing outside ourselves...is the greatest gift of spirit and the sure sign of the presence of something immaterial. It is the source of our freedom and personality, as it enables us to stand above the drift of our body and our instincts, our habits and conventions. Because of it we can direct our mind to reality as such, think of what is absolute and not merely relative to our individual interests, distinguish truth from falsehood and love others for themselves.

'Within be fed, without be rich no more. So shalt thou feed on death, that feeds on men. And death once dead, there's no more dying then.' The new world which starts within one's mind and begins to live, is, as Shakespeare says, the death of death. That is why the primal argument for immortality is based on the fact that mind and matter are opposites. It is matter which perishes. There is a constant coming and going, advent and decrease. The shapes and forms which matter takes are all composite, a unity of parts. When the parts begin to fall away, dissolution follows. The transformations in nature are possible because new associations and unities are formed, and it is the function of science to discover the elements and their possible combinations and to state the laws which govern these changes. Even our life of the senses fades, memory nods, and no matter whether we paint the 'outward walls so costly gay', there is but 'short a lease', and 'worms, inheritors of this excess' shall 'eat up thy charge'. Only the mind and its subject can survive because the law of dissolution does not hold for it.

I have used the word 'dissolution' as a synonym for death, and for a reason. We think of death as the close of our temporal story, but in reality it is the decay, the falling apart of the elements which make up our bodily organism. Death can have no meaning when applied to what is immaterial; it essentially involves the idea of debris, of parts which have fallen asunder. The dead stoat has lost its organic unity, and the matter of which it is composed is undergoing a change; the fingers bitten by frostbite mortify, and the dead flesh may have to be cut away. But such dismemberment can have no application, save by metaphor, to mind and spirit. Imagine taking the mind to pieces, as one might a clock, dismantling it as one would a room. Because of the unsuitability of such a metaphor, we prefer usually to use an image which suggests suddenness and total obliteration. We speak of the mind as like a candle which is lit and can be extinguished, or a breath which is and is not. Mind has no parts; it cannot be weighed and measured; it cannot suffer the pains of decay nor be divided like an inheritance. When we are saying that we are thinking badly, we mean that we are unable to think correctly or consecutively. When we say that our mind is tired, we mean that its instrument, the brain, does not function properly, or that our attention is weakened by bodily fatigue. In the sad process of senile decay, it is not the mind which fails but the memory and the associations; the feeble know what they know, truth is still truth to them, but they forget from one moment to another, and phantasmagoria confuses the poor mind and stampedes its proper functioning...

Mind cannot be totally conditioned by matter. On examination we find that its characteristics are the opposite of material. What we mean by death concerns what is composed of parts and capable of decay and dissolution. Mind is indissoluble and cannot die. Its immortality is therefore assured. (7)

## Risen Body

St Paul expressly implies that the body which we shall possess is the effect of a 'life-giving spirit'. The steps in his argument are that Christ rose from the dead with a glorified body; Christ has given us His own life. This life is a 'life-giving spirit', and as His own body had conferred upon it incorruptibility, so too the new supernatural 'life-giving spirit' in us will animate a body fit to function as co-partner in the uninterrupted, perfect life which it is to enjoy in eternity...

In what sense, it may be asked, can this risen body ... be called identical with the body which is ours in this life? The question is often asked in derision, and everyone knows the scoffing jest that cannibals make it very hard for their victims to enjoy their former bodies when they rise again. The general doctrine is, as usual, clearly expressed by St Thomas Aquinas: 'What does not bar numerical identity in a man while he lives on uninterruptedly, clearly can be no bar to the identity of the risen man with the man that was. In a man's body, while he lives, there are not always the same parts in respect of matter, but only in respect of species. In respect of matter there is a flux and reflux of parts; still that fact does not bar the man's numerical identity from the beginning to the end of his life' (*Summa contra gentiles* 4, 81). Here St Thomas puts his finger on the relevant point, for, as he says, a man remains one with himself insofar as, despite all the changes which occur within him, he is the same *man*, with the same *human* body; the change of 'parts' does not affect the specific identity. Clearly this is so. Much happens to the body within an hour, let alone a day, as the work of loss and repair goes on without any trade-union hours. What is remarkable...is the perseverance of the structure or inscape, the artistry of the soul which converts all that it receives into the form, invisible and visible, which is its own. As in some medieval chasuble or cope the embroidery may have been so often restored that scarcely any part of the original needlework remains, yet the design preserves its original clarity. When, then, the complete man is restored, and the phrase of corruption has passed into the permanent state of incorruption, thanks to the life-giving power of the spirit which lives in Christ, the identity of this new self with its past will be clearer than that of any Cinderella who had been changed into a queen...

Not only, therefore, will the blessed in Heaven enjoy the company of 'Christ and His Mother and all His hallows'. But through that same body and its senses which gave to our hearts so many wounds of joy will those same joys return. In this life, those joys live on in memory; they made a feast with us and then departed, and the greater the love the more painful the farewells which had to be made. But God, who has done what is so much greater, turned sin and death into a triumph and restored the dead to life, will not withhold what is less, namely, to restore the experiences which made us what we are and bound friends to us by affection and vow. Nor will those experiences be just memories, for memories mean that something has been lost and that we are spiritual orphans. 'I will not leave you orphans; I will come to you.' The Last Supper, as St John narrates it, records what seemed to be the saddest parting in history, but was not to be so. The vine-branch was not to be separated from the Vine, the living members from Him who was the Resurrection and the Life. In the day of the reward we will not have to ask for anything, for all things, all joys and all loves, will be ours. Memories will give up their dead, and the past will live again in this fullness of life. (8)

## The Nuptial Mystery

Love means union, and between human beings finds an end in marriage, since human nature consists of body as well as of soul. Now the Son of God took to Himself a human nature and used that as the means of making us sharers in the divine nature. The perfect mode of union, therefore, between God and man, love in its supreme expression, the standard and pattern to be imitated in the hierarchy of creatures, will find its analogy in human love in marriage. No metaphor here, but a secret cousinship, between the perfect and the imperfect, and the imperfect will receive its full explanation and interpretation when God reveals Himself, and shows that all creation revolves round Christ and was made in His setting. Therefore, St Paul, speaking of human marriage, does not invert the right order when he startles his readers with the abrupt ending, that a man shall cleave to his wife, and they shall be two in one flesh, not because of the natural law, but because marriage is a sacrament, the symbol, the institution on a lower plane of the supreme union between Christ and His Church. And so we may justifiably attribute to the union between Christ and His new members all that is perfect in the reality of marriage and then sublimate it, and see it as the inadequate but admirably suited image of the boundless love of Christ for mankind. (9)

NOTES AND SOURCES

1. Martin Cyril D'Arcy, *The Mass and Redemption* (London: Burns, Oates & Washbourne, 1926), p. vi.
2. Martin Cyril D'Arcy, *Belief and Reason* (London: Burns, Oates & Washbourne, 1944), 39–40.
3. Martin Cyril D'Arcy, *Of God and Man: Thoughts on Faith and Morals* (Dublin: Clonmore & Reynolds, 1964), 153–4.
4. Ibid. 164.
5. D'Arcy, *The Mass and Redemption*, 13–15.
6. Ibid. 67–8, 113–14.
7. Martin Cyril D'Arcy, *Death and Life* (London: Longmans, Green & Co., 1942), 34–7.
8. Ibid. 175–7.
9. D'Arcy, *The Mass and Redemption*, 27–8.

# Henry Christopher Dawson                    1889–1970

Christopher Dawson, despite the unrivalled breadth of his learning, never received from the British academic establishment the recognition he deserved. Educated at Winchester and Trinity College, Oxford, Dawson was received into the Catholic Church in 1914. From 1925 to 1933 he worked as a part-time lecturer in the history of culture at University College, Exeter. During the Second World War, Cardinal Hinsley and the Anglican Bishop Bell, because of their admiration for his work, involved him in the Sword of the Spirit movement. In 1958 he was appointed as the first Chauncey Stillman Professor of Roman Catholic Studies at Harvard, where he remained until 1962, when the breakdown of his health forced him to return to England. His discipline was that of a cultural historian and sociologist, a 'meta-historian', as he liked to call himself, whose understanding of human history was informed by the philosophical and theological wisdom of the Catholic tradition.

## St Augustine on Sex

His fundamental attitude to sex is extraordinarily rational and even scientific. 'What food is to the conservation of the individual,' he writes, 'that sexual intercourse is to the conservation of the race.' Hence, insofar as the sexual appetite is directed to its true end, it is as healthy and good as the desire for food. But, on the other hand, any attempt on the part of the individual to separate the pleasure which he derives from the satisfaction of his sexual appetite from its social purpose is essentially immoral. And since the purpose of sex is social, it requires an appropriate social organ for its fulfilment. This organ is the family, the union of man and wife, 'which is the first natural bond of human society'. Nevertheless, St Augustine teaches that the institution of marriage does not rest solely on its fulfilment of its primary function—the procreation of children. If so, there would be no permanence in a childless marriage. It has a 'second good', the power of friendship, which has its root in the essentially social character of human nature. The union of male and female is necessary not only for the procreation of children, but also for mutual help, 'so that when the warmth of youth has passed away, there yet lives in full vigour the order of charity between husband and wife'. In other words, marriage has a spiritual as well as a physical foundation, and it is the union of these two principles, both alike social and natural, which determines the character of the family and the origin of all social morality.

Thus the resistance of Catholicism to the hedonism and individualism of the new morality rests not on an irrational system of taboo, but on a solid foundation of biological and sociological principle. It condemns contraception as an unnatural attempt to divorce the sexual activity from its biological function; it forbids irregular sexual intercourse, because it involves the separation of sex from its proper social organ; and it is opposed to divorce and remarriage, because they destroy the permanence of the marriage bond and thus break down the organization of the family as the primary sociological unit.

And for the same reasons the Church maintains the original and inalienable rights of the family against the claims of the modern state to override them. Leo XIII writes: 'No human law can abolish the natural and original right of marriage, ordained by God's authority from the beginning... hence we have the family, the society of a man's house, a society limited in numbers, but no less a true society anterior to every kind of state and nation, invested with rights and duties of its own totally independent of the civil community' (*Rerum Novarum*).

Hence, as Leo XIII pointed out elsewhere, in his encyclical on marriage (*Arcanum Divinum*), the alteration by the state of the fundamental laws that govern marriage and family life will ultimately lead to the ruin of society itself. No doubt the state will gain in power and prestige as the family declines, but state and society are not identical. In fact, the state is often most omnipotent and universal in its claims at the moment when society is dying, as we see in the last age of the Roman Empire. As the vital energy of society declined, the machinery of bureaucratic administration grew more vast and more complicated, until the wretched provincial was often glad to abandon his household and take refuge in the desert or among the barbarians in order to escape from the intolerable pressure exercised by the ubiquitous agents of the bureaucracy.

At the present day we have reason to ask ourselves whether modern civilization is not threatened with a similar danger owing to the absorption of the whole of human life in the artificial order of bureaucracy and industrialism. The introduction of the new moral code would remove the last obstacle to the complete mechanization of society and lead to the final supersession of the independent family by the state. No amount of governmental organization can supply the place of the natural reserves of vitality on which social health depends. If the Catholic theory of society is true, the supersession of the family means not progress, but the death of society, the end of our age and the passing of European civilization. (1)

## The Dark Ages: Death and Resurrection

The writings of St Gregory the Great reflect the appalling sufferings and the profound pessimism of the age. He even welcomes the pestilence that was devastating the West as a refuge from the horrors that surrounded him.

When we consider the way in which other men have died, we find a solace in reflecting on the form of death that threatens us. What mutilations, what cruelties have we seen inflicted upon men, for which death is the only cure and in the midst of which life was a torture!

He sees Ezekiel's prophecy of the seething pot fulfilled in the fate of Rome:

Of this city it is well said, 'The meat is boiled away and the bones in the midst thereof' ... For where is the Senate? Where is the People? The bones are all dissolved, the flesh is consumed, all the pomp of the dignities of this world is gone. The whole mass is boiled away ...

But the worst had not yet come. In the seventh century the Arabs conquered Byzantine Africa, the most civilized province of the West, and the great African Church, the glory of Latin Christianity, disappears from history. Early in the eighth century the tide of Muslim invasion swept over Christian Spain and threatened Gaul itself. Christendom had become an island isolated between the Muslim south and the Barbarian north.

Yet it was in this age of universal ruin and destruction that the foundations of the new Europe were being laid by men like St Gregory, who had no idea of building up a new social order, but who laboured for the salvation of men in a dying world because the time was short. And it was just this indifference to temporal results which gave the Papacy the power to become a rallying-point for the forces of life in the general decadence of European civilization. In the words of the inscription which Pope John III set up in the Church of the Most Holy Apostles: 'In a straitened age, the Pope showed himself more generous and disdained to be cast down though the world failed.'

At the very moment of the fall of the Empire in the West, St Augustine, in his great book *Of the City of God*, had set forth the programme which was to inspire the ideals of the new age. He viewed all history as the evolution of two opposite principles embodied in two hostile societies, the heavenly and the earthly cities, Zion and Babylon. The one had no final realization on earth, it was *in via*, its *patria* was heavenly and eternal; the other found its realization in earthly prosperity, in the wisdom and glory of man; it was its own end and justification. The State, it is true, was not condemned as such. Insofar as it was Christian, it subserved the ends of the heavenly city. But it was a subordinate society, the servant and not the master; it was the spiritual society that was supreme. The moment that the state came into conflict with the higher power, the moment that it set itself up as an end in itself, it became identified with the earthly city and lost all claims to a higher sanction than the law of force and self-interest. Without justice, what is a great kingdom but a great robbery, *magnum latrocinium*? Conquering or being conquered does no one either good or harm. It is pure waste of energy, the game of fools for an empty prize. The terrestrial world is unsubstantial and transitory, the only reality worth striving for is that which is eternal—the heavenly Jerusalem, 'the vision of peace'. (2)

## The Christian Culture of Anglo-Saxon England

The appearance of the new Anglo-Saxon culture of the seventh century is perhaps the most important event between the age of Justinian and that of Charlemagne, for it reacted with profound effect on the whole continental development. In its origins it was equally indebted to...two forces...the Celtic monastic movement and the Roman Benedictine mission. Northern England was common ground to them both, and it was here that the new Christian culture arose in the years between 650 and 680 owing to the interaction and fusion of the two different elements. Christianity had been introduced into Northumbria by the Roman Paulinus, who baptized King Edwin in 627 and established the metropolitan see at the old Roman city of York, but the defeat of Edwin by the heathen Penda and the Welsh Cadwallon led to the temporary ruin of the Anglian Church. It was re-established by King Oswald in 634 with the help of St Aidan and the Celtic missionaries whom he brought from Iona to Lindisfarne, and throughout his reign Celtic influence reigned supreme. It was not until the Synod of Whitby in 664 that the Roman party finally triumphed, owing to the intervention of St Wilfrid, who dedicated his long and stormy life to the service of the Roman unity. It is to him and his fellow-worker, St Benedict Biscop, that the establishment of Benedictine monasticism in northern England is due. Nor was their activity solely of ecclesiastical importance, for they were the missionaries of culture as well as of religion, and they were responsible for the rise of the new Anglian art. They brought back from their many journeys to Rome and Gaul skilled craftsmen and architects, as well as books, pictures, vestments and musicians, and their abbeys of Ripon and Hexham, Wearmouth and Jarrow, were the great centres of the new culture. At the same time in the south, similar work was being carried out by the Greek-Syrian archbishop, Theodore, and the African abbot, Hadrian, who were sent from Rome in 668. In them we can trace a new wave of higher culture from the East, which does much to explain the rise of Anglo-Saxon scholarship and the superiority of the Latin of Bede and Alcuin to the barbarous style of Gregory of Tours or the Celtic author of the *Hisperica famina*...Nevertheless, behind all these foreign influences, there lies a foundation of native culture. The same age and district that produced the Anglian crosses also saw the rise of Anglo-Saxon literature. It was the age in which the old pagan story of Beowulf received its literary form, and even more characteristic of the time were the Christian poets, Caedmon, the shepherd of Whitby abbey, whose romantic story is preserved by Bede, and Cynewulf, the author of several surving poems, including *Andreas, Elene, Juliana*, and, perhaps, also of the noble *Dream of the Rood*, a quotation from which is sculptured on the Rothwell cross. (3)

## The Anglo-Saxon Contribution to the Carolingian Renaissance: Latinity and Liturgy

In France and Italy, where Latin was a living language, it had become contaminated with the barbarized vernacular. In England it was a learned language, founded upon the study of classical models, and its cultivation was encouraged by that enthusiasm for the Roman tradition which had inspired Anglo-Saxon culture since the days of St Wilfrid and Benedict Biscop.

It was the chief representative of this Anglican culture, Alcuin, the head of the school of York, who became the link between what M. Halphen has termed the Anglo-Saxon 'pre-Renaissance' and the new Carolingian movement. He entered Charles's service in 782 as the director of the Palace school, and thenceforward exercised a decisive influence on Charles's educational policy and on the whole literary movement. Alcuin was no literary genius; he was essentially a schoolmaster and grammarian who based his teaching on the old classical curriculum of the seven liberal arts, according to the tradition of Boethius and Cassiodorus and Isidore and Bede. But it was just such a schoolmaster that the age required, and thanks to the support of his royal pupil, he was able to realize his educational ideas on an imperial scale and to make the school of the Palace the standard of culture for the greater part of Western Europe. It was to him, apparently, that Charles entrusted the work of revising the Bible and the service books and thus of initiating the Carolingian liturgical reform which is the foundation of the liturgy of the medieval Church. The Roman rite had already been adopted by the Anglo-Saxon Church under Benedictine influence, and it now became the universal rite of the Carolingian Empire, displacing the old Gallican use, which together with the allied Ambrosian and Mozarabic rites had obtained throughout the West, save in Rome and its suburbicarian jurisdiction. But the new Carolingian liturgy still retained traces of Gallican influence, and in this way a considerable Gallican element has entered the Roman liturgy itself.

The influence of Alcuin and the Anglo-Saxon culture is also to be seen in the reform of the script, which is one of the characteristic achievements of the Carolingian age. The new Christian culture of England and Ireland owed its existence to the transmission and multiplication of manuscripts, and had attained a high level of calligraphy. Consequently it was to England, even more than to Italy, that the Carolingian scholars turned for more correct texts, not only of the Bible and the Roman liturgy, but also for the works of classical writers, and both Anglo-Saxon and Irish scholars and copyists flocked to the palace school and the great continental abbeys. (4)

## Natural Law

There is an eternal law that governs all things and is, as it were, the reason of the universe. In this order man participates consciously insofar as he is a rational and moral being, and it is the source from which all human laws derive their ultimate sanction. As St Augustine says in a famous passage in *The City of God*: 'Since God, from whom is all being, form, and order, has left neither Heaven nor earth, nor angel nor man, nor the lowest of creatures, neither the bird's feather, nor the flower of the grass, nor the leaf of the tree without its due harmony of parts, and without, as it were, a certain peace, it cannot be believed that he should have willed the kingdoms of men and their government and subjection to be outside the laws of His Providence.'

It is true that St Augustine recognized only too clearly that man's history is a black record, and that even the relative peace and order that had been conferred on the ancient world by the Roman Empire had been purchased only by a vast expenditure of blood and human suffering. The Empire was, in fact, not the creation of justice, but of the will to power. Nevertheless, insofar as it was not satisfied with power alone, but aspired to rule by law, it recognized the principle of justice which implies the existence of moral principles and of the eternal laws on which they are based.

This is the meaning of natural law in the traditional Catholic sense. It is a very simple doctrine since it merely asserts—to use the words of St Thomas—that 'there is in men a certain natural law, which is a participation of the eternal law by which men discern good and evil.' Without this power of discernment man would not be a reasonable being. But this does not mean that it provides a ready-made code of rules which everyone everywhere admits. The moral sense varies according to the measure of the understanding, and differences of education and culture and character affect the one no less than the other. Hence St Thomas admits that the natural law may be obscured or perverted by social causes; as an example he quotes Caesar on the Germans, who did not regard robbery as unjust so long as it was carried on outside the frontiers of the State, but rather as a laudable form of youth activity. But although man's moral consciousness is limited and conditioned by social factors, it is never entirely extinguished; just as man remains a rational being even in a state of barbarism, which seems to the civilized man to be little higher than that of an animal. And as every man by his reason has some knowledge of truth, so every man by nature has some knowledge of good and evil, which makes it possible for him to adhere to or deviate from the universal order...

How did this sacred and secular tradition come to be abandoned—as for the most part it has been abandoned—by the modern world? Its enemies come from very different camps, yet their agreement on this issue is something more than an accident and corresponds to a very deep cleavage in European thought. On the one hand, it had its origin in one element of Protestant and specifically Lutheran thought, i.e. the doctrine of the total depravity of human nature and the dualism, or rather the contradiction of nature and grace, which leaves the former a helpless prey to the powers of evil, until it is rescued by the violent irruption of divine grace...The profound pessimism of Luther saw in nature nothing but the kingdom of death and the law of nature as a law of wrath and punishment, and thus his extreme supernaturalism prepared the way for the secularization of the world and the abolition of objective standards.

But the revolt against natural law did not only spring from the otherworldliness of Luther and the Reformers. It found an even more powerful support in the worldliness of the Renaissance statesmen and thinkers. Already before the Reformation, Machiavelli had produced his Intelligent Man's Guide to Politics, which studies the art of government as a non-moral technique for the acquisition and maintenance of power, thus depriving the state of its religious character as the temporal organ of divine justice, and making the interests of the state the supreme law by which all political acts must be judged.

This is the source of the 'new jurisprudence' which took the place of the common law of Christendom, and which, as Leo XIII explained in his political encyclicals [e.g., *Immortale Dei*, and *Libertas praestantissimum*] undermined the moral foundations of western civilization. (5)

NOTES AND SOURCES

1. Christopher Dawson, 'Christianity and Sex', in *Enquiries into Religion and Culture* (London: Sheed & Ward, 1933), 267–8.

2. Christopher Dawson, *The Making of Europe: An Introduction to the History of European Unity*, new edn. (London: Sheed & Ward, 1948), 150–2.

3. Ibid. 163–4.

4. Ibid. 177–8.

5. Christopher Dawson, *The Judgement of the Nations* (London: Sheed & Ward, 1943), 92–5.

# Mary Josephine 'Maisie' Ward          1889–1975

Maisie Ward grew up in a household of high culture, and of multiple connections with the Catholic writers of late Victorian and Edwardian England. She was the daughter of Wilfrid Philip Ward, editor of the *Dublin Review* and biographer of Wiseman and Newman, and granddaughter of William George ('Ideal') Ward. Her mother, the novelist Josephine Mary Ward, was the daughter of James Hope-Scott of Abbotsford, the convert husband of Sir Walter Scott's granddaughter, Charlotte Harriet Jane Lockhart. Chesterton, Belloc, and von Hügel were friends of the family. In 1926 she married the young Australian lawyer, Frank Sheed, with whom she had worked in the Catholic Evidence Guild, and bore him two children, Rosemary, who became a translator, and Wilfrid, novelist and essayist. Frank and Maisie founded the publishing house Sheed & Ward, which introduced the Catholic literary revival, in England and on the continent, to a wide readership in the English-speaking world. The New York side of the business was set up in the 1930s, and during the Second World War Maisie moved the family to live permanently in the USA, while Frank shuttled back and forth across the Atlantic. Maisie was a woman of seemingly unlimited energy: she wrote prolifically, travelled all over the world to lecture, and sought to give practical expression to Catholic social doctrine by, among other things, supporting Dorothy Day, founder of the Catholic Worker movement, attempting to run farms according to the principles of Distributism, and working with others to establish the Catholic Housing Aid Society in England. She wrote biographies of Browning, Chesterton, Houselander, and the young Newman, a book of meditations on the mysteries of the Rosary—using the paintings of Fra Angelico as a starting-point—and an introduction to the Four Gospels and Acts. *The English Way*, edited by Maisie in 1933, did by way of essays something similar to what this anthology is attempting through texts and biographies, to chart the course of 'English sanctity' from St Bede to Cardinal Newman. In the 1950s and 60s, Sheed and Ward translated and published the work of the continental *nouveaux théologiens*, who played such a prominent part at the Second Vatican Council.

## The English Way

Christianity is the religion of the Incarnation of Godhead in humanity, of the Absolute in the relative, of Eternity in time. Because it is universal, it is in every country, but because it is sacramental it is intensely local, found in each country in a special and unique fashion, not a spirit only but a spirit clothed in material form. St Gregory, as we know, once counselled St Augustine not to destroy the temples which had been used for pagan worship but to consecrate them to Christ. So, too, the Englishman was not to be changed *for* but *into* the Christian. (1)

## Explaining the Rosary

*The beads are there for the sake of the prayers, and the prayers are there for the sake of the mysteries.*

Take first the beads: on the lowest, a convenient method of counting. My husband sometimes says he wishes our ten fingers could be blessed and indulgenced, for they so often serve when the rosary has been left at home or in the pocket of another coat.

Next above their use for counting we may put, perhaps, their value as a help to concentration. Sir Walter Scott used to fell trees when he was writing a novel. It was the best way, he said, to get his plots and his characters to move and live; he compared it to a woman's knitting... Without entirely understanding the relation between body and soul that causes this special connection between thought and some mechanical activity, we know that it exists. Pascal put the matter rather oddly when speaking of using the rosary, taking holy water, etc. He said, *Abêtissez-vous*, which has been translated (even more oddly) 'stupefy yourself'. This, of course, is not what he meant, and he goes on to explain it better as 'winning over the machine', or the mechanical side of our nature, so that it helps instead of hindering the direction the spirit desires to take. The best translation might be, 'Don't mistake yourself for a pure spirit'. Use the lower faculties as well as the higher. The world around is one huge distraction from prayer; the very holding, the very slipping through our fingers of the beads, can be a powerful counter-distraction—on a bus, in the subway, in the street, in a foxhole...

On a higher level this use of the beads is a part of the whole philosophy of the Church about man's nature. We are not pure spirit but composite beings made of spirit *and* matter. And so we need, if our prayer is to be true to our nature, to use material things: images either set before the eyes or fashioned in the imagination, the cross at the end of the beads, the blessing that makes them sacred, the prayers that we say on them.

For *the beads are there for the sake of the prayers.*

The prayers are first the Apostles' Creed, then the Our Father on the large beads, the Hail Mary on the small beads, which come in groups of ten called decades, the *Gloria [Patri]* on the spaces that follow the decades.

The prayers of the Rosary arouse criticism from Protestants and even from a few Catholics. Obviously we repeat the same words again and again—and the text that condemns 'vain repetition' is quoted against us. It is rather 'vain mouthings' that this text condemns—words used with no soul in them. Repetition need not be soulless: a wife never tires of hearing her husband say, 'I love you', a mother never tires of her child's first words, repeated often because he knows no others.

But, in fact, with the Rosary *the prayers are there for the sake of the mysteries.*

The fifteen mysteries of the Rosary fall into three groups—Joyful, Sorrowful, Glorious—each group containing five mysteries.[7] The Five Joyful Mysteries are the Annunciation, the Visitation, the Nativity, the Presentation, the Finding of Our Lord in the Temple; the five Sorrowful, the Agony in the Garden, the Scourging at the Pillar, the Crowning with Thorns, the Carrying of the Cross, the Crucifixion; the five Glorious, the Resurrection, the Ascension, the Descent of the Holy Ghost, the Assumption, the Coronation...

We have all repeated hundreds of times, when learning our catechism, that a mystery is a truth which is above reason, revealed by God... The fact that it is

---

[7] In the Apostolic Letter *Rosarium Virginis Mariae*, promulgated on 16 October 2002, at the beginning of the twenty-fifth year of his pontificate, Pope John Paul II added five Mysteries of Light, covering the life of Our Lord from His Baptism to His Institution of the Eucharist, to the fifteen Mysteries of His Joy, Sorrow, and Glory.

above reason does not mean that we can know nothing about it, but that we can never know everything about it. 'If any man thirst,' Our Lord cried to the Jews, 'let him come to me and drink.' The Rosary is one of the great proofs that the ordinary Catholic has in fact accepted this invitation to drink from the well of the divine mysteries. Day by day he quenches his spiritual and intellectual thirst at a well that is inexhaustible. Thanks to the Rosary, his practice is better than his theory. For the Rosary properly said is a meditation upon, or a contemplation of, the mysteries of our redemption. And just as the liturgy carries the scheme of the redemption extended through the year, the Rosary carries it briefly through each week...

Because the scheme of man's redemption meant that God became man, the Rosary is at once deeply divine and deeply human. We can say, as a friend of mine tells me she does, one day thinking of it in relation to the Holy Trinity, another day as it casts light on the social problems of our age in relation to which we Catholics have to act Christ's part, a third day trying to weave the mysteries into the liturgical season. 'Sometimes,' she added, 'I don't get beyond one mystery.'

These ways are, it will be seen, a mixture of meditation and a sort of simple contemplation. By meditation we mean considering something thoughtfully, passing from point to point, usually ending with a resolution and a prayer for help to keep it. (In mundane matters we often meditate. Shall I, for example, buy a new hat? I look in the shop window; I compare prices; I consider the state of my purse; finally, I resolve for or against.)

Contemplation does not go from step to step like meditation. It is more in the nature of a simple, steadfast gazing of the soul at God, through the medium, it may be, of some individual mystery.

Coming on earth and living as man, God not only showed us something of His divine nature; He also cast light for us on our human nature. Many of us feel today that one of the great difficulties of life is a sort of bewilderment. Everything we read and hear is confused. The people we read about in books, the people we meet in daily life, seem almost to be disintegrating, so uncertain are they of the purpose and meaning of their being and existence. When God became man, it was not only to come to our aid with all the power of His Godhead; it was to reveal to us the true way of human life by living it. One method of studying this human and divine life is the Rosary, and we can slant the rays of its light now in one direction, now in another. We can think solely of what was happening in the Stable or on the Cross; we can look through these events into Heaven; we can relate them with our own lives....

St Philip at the Last Supper asked Our Lord how they were to find the way to follow Him to Heaven, and Our Lord replied, 'I am the Way'. And now the Church tells us that in Our Lady is 'all grace of the way'. It must be so because she bore Christ and brought Him into the world. It must be so because she is the Mother of the Mystical Body, the Mother of each one of us.

While with heart and mind we seek always to find Christ, our Way to Heaven, we have to walk daily the ways of this world: of our life from morning till night, and from night till morning.

We often need grace of the way when it is hard to walk. We need hope of life and of virtue when our hope fails in the maze of this world. In the Rosary we rejoice, sorrow and triumph with Our Lady as she walks the same path we have to walk. But now she has reached the end, and we can think of her, too, restfully, as a 'fair flower by the water brooks', giving to us the Water of Life. So the Church, telling us to rejoice on all Our Lady's feasts, gives us on this feast [Our Lady of the Rosary] this thought in particular—grace of the way:

> Maria regnans in Patria
> Ora pro nobis in via.
> [Mary, reigning in the Fatherland,
> Pray for us who are still on the way.]

For in thee is all Grace of the Way, and we shall find thee at our journey's end. (2)

## The Second Joyful Mystery: The Visitation of Our Lady

Our Lord in this mystery has not only taken a human nature from Mary but has left Himself helpless, powerless in the darkness of her womb to be taken where she wills. It is the beginning of a divine economy of grace whereby God saves mankind by giving Himself into the power of men. The Curé d'Ars, marvelling over the Blessed Sacrament, said: 'I bear Him to the right, and He stays to the right; I bear Him to the left, and He stays to the left.'

Alone of all creatures Mary was utterly worthy of her trust. Henceforward, wherever she went she would bring Jesus. It is noteworthy how in the Church when any special devotion to Our Lady is started it develops into devotion to the Blessed Sacrament—at Lourdes, for instance. Pilgrims came at first for the grotto and were chiefly healed there. But later the great moment became that of the procession of the Blessed Sacrament—the Gospel invocations, 'Lord, if thou wilt, thou canst make me whole!' 'Lord, that I may see; Lord, that I may hear!' And now cures follow the lowering of the monstrance onto the sick man's head. So, too, Father Thurston says that Benediction originated in the singing of laude, or canticles, to Our Lady. Presently these were sung before the Blessed Sacrament was exposed, and finally the blessing by the priest with the Host transformed the service into Benediction.

In this mystery Mary had brought Jesus with her. Elizabeth, too, was carrying a child—John the Baptist. The Gospel tells us that John leaped in his mother's womb, and Elizabeth was filled with the Holy Ghost: the Church tells us that at that instant he received supernatural life, in fulfilment of what the angel had foretold to Zachary, his father: 'And He shall be filled with the Holy Ghost even from His Mother's womb.' Our Lord was conceived, John was born, with sanctifying grace in the soul and thus freed from the worst effect of Adam's fall, for they were so close to the Redeemer whose death was bringing new life to all mankind.

These few verses of the Gospels contain material for endless meditation. We shall never exhaust Mary's Magnificat, which contains the clue to all our social problems and the key to true human living. To begin by 'magnifying' God and rejoicing in Him is the path to recognizing our own nothingness. Because Our Lady was utterly humble, all generations would call her blessed. Only to the humble can God safely entrust His gifts: 'He hath put down the mighty from their seat and hath exalted the humble.' Later on, in the Sermon on the Mount, Our Lord would bless those who hunger and thirst after justice. Already Our Lady knows that to be filled we must first hunger. 'He hath filled the hungry with good things; the rich He hath sent empty away.' Surely everyone should learn the Magnificat by heart. (3)

## New Adam and New Eve on Calvary

The Fathers of the Church were fond of drawing the parallel between Adam and Christ here on Calvary or Golgotha—a name that means place of the skull. Tradition says it was the place of Adam's burial; legends picture the Cross made out of the wood of the tree of the knowledge of good and evil.

*Adam* had been given the supernatural life for the human race. He lost it through disobedience, choosing his own will instead of God's, choosing brief pleasure instead of eternal joy.

*Christ* won back the supernatural life for the human race. He chose obedience to the will of God even unto death. He chose suffering to win for man eternal happiness.

*Adam*, after he had sinned, knew that he was naked and fashioned himself a garment.

*Christ* allowed the stripping of His garments, the utter loss of human dignity, the extreme of poverty.

*Adam* believed the tempter—'Ye shall be as gods'—and disobeyed God in the attempt to become divine.

*Christ*, by His obedience to God, has made us able, by obedience, actually to be 'as gods', 'partakers of the divine nature'.

The Fathers draw also the parallel between Eve and Our Lady.

*Eve* tempted Adam to sin and so brought about the fall.

*Our Lady* brought her Son into the world for its redemption. She stood at the foot of the Cross, sharing in that redeeming work.

Humanity began in the garden of pleasure. *Eve*, taken from Adam's side, was its mother.

Mary, the Mother of God, is the mother of all the living who live with the new life of her Son. The new humanity—the Mystical Body—came forth from the pierced side of Christ on the Cross of pain. *Mary* is its Mother. Christ gave her to all mankind in the person of St John when He said: 'Woman, behold thy son.' And to St John: 'Behold thy mother.' (4)

NOTES AND SOURCES

1. Maisie Ward, Foreword to M. C. D'Arcy SJ et al., *The English Way: Studies in English Sanctity from St Bede to Newman* (London: Sheed & Ward, 1933), 7.

2. Maisie Ward, *The Splendour of the Rosary: With Prayers by Caryll Houselander and Pictures by Fra Angelico* (New York: Sheed & Ward, 1945), 7–16, 54–5.

3. Ibid. 68–70.

4. Ibid. 117–18.

# John Ronald Reuel Tolkien                    1892–1973

Of the millions who read and love *The Lord of the Rings* only a few realize that its author was a Catholic of simple piety and lifelong practice, and that his stories were the achievement of an intellect and imagination enlightened by the faith of the Church. Ronald Tolkien was born of parents originating from Birmingham but resident in Bloemfontein, South Africa, where his father worked as a bank manager. In 1895, while Ronald and his younger brother were visiting England with their mother, their father died of rheumatic fever, leaving his widow with little money to support herself and her two young sons. Her poverty was made even more acute in 1900 when conversion to the Catholic faith caused her extended family to disown her. When she died four years later, her sons, on her own instructions, were made the wards of Father Francis Morgan of the Birmingham Oratory. Despite the sorrow of losing his parents, and the constraints of living as a lodger, first with relatives and later with a friend of Father Francis, Tolkien had a happy and highly successful school career at King Edward's Birmingham, where, having received a thorough training in the grammar and syntax of Latin and Greek, he went on to explore the Germanic languages of the Middle Ages: Old and Middle English, Old Norse, and Gothic. At Exeter College, Oxford, to which he won an exhibition in 1910, he transferred, after Classical Moderations, to the Honour School of English, specializing in philology and achieving a first. In March 1916 he married Edith Bratt, a fatherless girl with whom he had fallen in love when he was 16. They were to have four children. In June 1916 Tolkien was commissioned in the Lancashire Fusiliers and saw action at the battle of the Somme. One of his closest school friends was killed on the first day of the battle, and another later in the same year. He himself contracted trench fever in October 1916, and was sent back to England. After the armistice he returned to Oxford and worked on the staff of the new Oxford Dictionary. In 1920 he was appointed Reader in English at Leeds and threw himself into building up the philological side of his department's teaching and research. His edition of *Sir Gawain and the Green Knight* was to become the standard text of the poem in twentieth-century Middle English scholarship. In 1925 he was elected to the Rawlinson and Bosworth Chair of Anglo-Saxon in Oxford, and it was there that he spent most of the rest of his life. Despite important work on *Beowulf* and the *Ancrene wisse*, Tolkien now turned from the study of the historical languages and literature of Anglo-Saxon and medieval England to the construction of the imagined languages and history of 'Middle Earth'. The first published expression of this mythopoeia was *The Hobbit* (1937). *The Lord of the Rings*, which continues the story begun in *The Hobbit* of the magic ring found by Bilbo Baggins, was published in three volumes in 1954 and 1955. Tolkien read the book, as he wrote it, to his friend C. S. Lewis and the other members of the group known as 'The Inklings'. Despite the sharply divided reactions of the critics over the years, *The Lord of the Rings* has not only gained a readership of unparalleled immensity and enthusiasm, but has also inspired the genre of 'fantasy' literature. The movie adaptation, directed by Peter Jackson in three parts (2001–3), was one of the most financially successful productions in the history of the cinema. Tolkien's life as an Oxford don and family man was unchanged by the success of his books. After retirement from the Merton Chair of English Language and Literature, to which he had been elected in 1945, he moved for a time to Bournemouth, but, after the death of his wife in 1971, he returned to live in rooms at Merton College. Ronald and Edith are buried together in Wolvercote cemetery in Oxford.

# Guardian Angels

Remember your guardian angel. Not a plump lady with swan-wings! But—at least this is my notion and feeling—as souls with free will we are, as it were, so placed as to face (or to be able to face) God. But God is (so to speak) also behind us, supporting, nourishing us (as being creatures). The bright point of power where that life-line, that spiritual umbilical cord touches: there is our angel, facing two ways, to God behind us in the direction we cannot see, and to us. But, of course, do not grow weary of facing God, in your free right and strength (both provided 'from behind', as I say). If you cannot achieve inward peace, and it is given to few to do so (least of all to me) in tribulation, do not forget that the aspiration for it is not a vanity, but a concrete act. I am sorry to talk like this, and so haltingly. But I can do no more for you, dearest . . . (1)

## This Fallen World

Fr C[arter, parish priest of St Gregory's, Oxford] gave a pretty stirring little sermon, based on Rogation Days . . . in which he suggested we were all a lot of untutored robots for not saying grace; and did not suggest but categorically pronounced Oxford to deserve to be wiped out with fire and blood in the wrath of God for the abominations and wickedness there perpetrated. We all woke up. I am afraid it is all too horribly true. But I wonder if it is *specially* true now? A small knowledge of history depresses one with the sense of the everlasting mass and weight of human iniquity: old, old, dreary, endless, repetitive, unchanging, incurable wickedness. All towns, all villages, all habitations of men—sinks! And at the same time one knows that there is always good: much more hidden, much less clearly discerned, seldom breaking out into recognizable, visible, beauties of word or deed or face—not even when in fact sanctity, far greater than the visible, advertised wickedness, is really there. But I fear that in the individual lives of all but a few, the balance is debit—we do so little that is positive good, even if we negatively avoid what is actively evil. It must be terrible to be a priest! (2)

## The Blessed Sacrament

Out of the darkness of my life, so much frustrated, I put before you the one great thing to love on earth: the Blessed Sacrament . . . There you will find romance, glory, honour, fidelity, and the true way of all your loves on earth, and more than that: Death: by the divine paradox, that which ends life, and demands the surrender of all, and yet by the taste (or foretaste) of which alone can what you seek in your earthly relationships (love, faithfulness, joy) be maintained, or take on that complexion of reality, of eternal endurance, which every man's heart desires. . . .

The only cure for sagging or fainting faith is Communion. Though always Itself, perfect and complete and inviolate, the Blessed Sacrament does not operate completely and once for all in any of us. Like the act of faith it must be continuous and grow by exercise. Frequency is of the highest effect. Seven times a week is more nourishing than seven times at intervals. Also I can recommend this as an exercise (alas, only too easy to find opportunity): make your Communion in circumstances that affront your taste. Choose a snuffling or gabbling priest, or a proud and vulgar friar; and a church full of the usual bourgeois crowd, ill-behaved children—from those who yell to those products of Catholic schools who the moment the tabernacle is opened sit back and yawn—open-necked and dirty youths, women in trousers and often with hair unkempt and uncovered. Go to

Communion *with* them (and pray for them). It will be just the same (or better than that) as a Mass said beautifully by a visibly holy man, and shared by a few devout and decorous people. (It could not be worse than the mess of the feeding of the five thousand—after which Our Lord propounded the feeding that was to come.)

I myself am convinced by the Petrine claims, nor, looking around the world, does there seem much doubt which (if Christianity is true) is the True Church, the temple of the Spirit dying but living, corrupt but holy, self-reforming and re-arising. But for me that Church of which the Pope is the acknowledged head on earth has as chief claim that it is the one that has (and still does) ever defended the Blessed Sacrament, and given it most honour, and put it (as Christ plainly intended) in the prime place. 'Feed my sheep' was His last charge to St Peter, and since His words are always first to be understood literally, I suppose them to refer primarily to the Bread of Life. It was against this that the W[estern] European revolt (or Reformation) was really launched—'the blasphemous fable of the Mass'—and faith/works a mere red herring. I suppose the greatest reform of our time was that carried out by St Pius X [his encouragement of frequent Communion and his lowering of the age for First Communion]: surpassing anything, however needed, that the [Second Vatican] Council will achieve. I wonder what state the Church would now be but for it ...

I am one who came up out of Egypt, and pray God none of my seed shall return thither. I witnessed (half-comprehending) the heroic sufferings and early death in extreme poverty of my mother, who brought me into the Church, and received the astonishing charity of Francis Morgan. But I fell in love with the Blessed Sacrament from the beginning—and by the mercy of God never have fallen out again, but alas, I indeed did not live up to it ... Out of wickedness and sloth I almost ceased to practise my religion—especially at Leeds, and at 22 Northmoor Road. Not for me the Hound of Heaven, but the never-ceasing appeal of the Tabernacle, and the sense of starving hunger. I regret those days bitterly (and suffer for them with such patience as I can be given); most of all because I failed as a father. Now I pray for you all, unceasingly, that the Healer (the *Haelend*, as the Saviour was usually called in Old English) shall heal my defects, and that none of you shall ever cease to cry, *Benedictus qui venit in nomine Domini*. (3)

## Our Lady

I think I know exactly what you mean by the order of grace, and, of course, by your references to Our Lady, upon which all my own small perception of beauty, both in majesty and simplicity, is founded. (4)

## The Truth of the Church and the Sins of her Members

The temptation to 'unbelief' (which really means rejection of Our Lord and His claims) is always there within us. The stronger the inner temptation the more readily and severely shall we be 'scandalized' by others. I think I am as sensitive as you (or any other Christian) to the 'scandals', both of clergy and laity. I have suffered grievously in my life from stupid, tired, dimmed, and even bad priests; but I now know enough about myself to be aware that I should not leave the

Church (which for me would be leaving the allegiance of Our Lord) for any such reasons. I should leave because I did not believe, and should not believe any more, even if I had never met anyone in orders who was not both wise and saintly. I should deny the Blessed Sacrament, that is: call Our Lord a fraud to His face. (5)

## The Courtesy of Heaven: Tolkien's Modern Version of *Pearl*

[Pearl, *an alliterative poem of fourteenth-century England attributed to the anonymous author of* Sir Gawain and the Green Knight, *is a story told by a man who, having lost his 'Pearl' (probably his young daughter), is transported in a dream to a beautiful garden in which this very Pearl appears to him, and assures him that she is in bliss, and is now the bride of the Lamb. He asks whether she has taken the place of Our Lady as Queen of Heaven. She replies by showing her own devotion to the Mother of God, and explaining to the narrator that in Heaven it is courtesy, not competition, that reigns over all.*]

'O courteous Queen', that damsel said,
Kneeling on earth with uplifted face,
'Mother immaculate, and fairest maid,
Blessed beginner of every grace!'
Uprising then her prayer she stayed,
And there she spoke to me a space:
'Here many the prize they have gained are paid,
But usurpers, sir, here have no place.
That empress' realm doth heaven embrace,
And earth and hell she holds in fee,
From their heritage yet will none displace,
For she is the Queen of Courtesy.

The court where the living God doth reign
Hath a virtue of its own being,
That each who may thereto attain
Of all the realm is queen or king,
Yet never shall other's right obtain,
But in other's good each glorying
And wishing each crown worth five again,
If amended might be so fair a thing.
But my Lady of whom did Jesu spring,
O'er us high she holds her empery,
And none that grieves of our following,
For she is the Queen of Courtesy.

In courtesy we are members all
Of Jesus Christ, Saint Paul doth write:
As head, arm, leg, and navel small
To their body doth loyalty true unite,
So as limbs to their Master mystical
All Christian souls belong by right.

Now among your limbs can you find at all
Any tie or bond of hate or spite?
Your head doth not feel affront or slight
On your arm or finger though ring it see;
So we all proceed in love's delight
To king and queen by courtesy.' (6)

## The Lord of the Rings

*The Lord of the Rings* is, of course, a fundamentally religious and Catholic work:
unconsciously so at first, but consciously in the revision. That is why I have not
put in, or have cut out, practically all references to anything like 'religion', to cults
or practices, in the imaginary world. For the religious element is absorbed into the
story and the symbolism. However, that is very clumsily put, and sounds more
self-important than I feel. For, as a matter of fact, I have consciously planned very
little; and should chiefly be grateful for having been brought up (since I was eight)
in a faith that has nourished me and taught me all the little that I know; and that I
owe to my mother, who clung to her conversion and died young, largely through
the hardships of poverty resulting from it. (7)

## Sacred Myth-Making

The heart of man is not compound of lies,
But draws some wisdom from the only Wise,
And still recalls him. Though now long estranged,
Man is not wholly lost nor wholly changed.
Dis-graced he may be, yet is not dethroned,
And keeps the rags of lordship once he owned,
His world-dominion by creative act:
Not his to worship the great Artefact,
Man, sub-creator, the refracted light
Through whom is splintered from a single White
To many hues, and endlessly combined
In living shapes that move from mind to mind.
Though all the crannies of the world we filled
With elves and goblins, though we dared to build
Gods and their houses out of dark and light,
And sow the seeds of dragons, 'twas our right
(Used or misused). The right has not decayed.
We make still by the law in which we're made....

In Paradise perchance the eye may stray
From gazing upon everlasting Day
To see the day-illumined, and renew
From mirrored truth the likeness of the True.
Then looking on the Blessed Land 'twill see
That all is as it is, and yet made free:

Salvation changes not, nor yet destroys,
Garden nor gardener, children nor their toys.
Evil it will not see, for evil lies
Not in God's picture but in crooked eyes,
Not in the source but in malicious choice,
And not in sound but in the tuneless voice.
In Paradise they no more look awry;
And though they make anew, they make no lie.
Be sure they still will make, not being dead,
And poets shall have flames upon their head,
And harps whereon their faultless fingers fall:
There each shall choose for ever from the All. (8)

NOTES AND SOURCES

1. J. R. R. Tolkien, from a letter to his son, Christopher, 8 January 1944, in *Letters of J. R. R. Tolkien: A Selection*, ed. Humphrey Carpenter with the assistance of Christopher Tolkien (London: George, Allen & Unwin, 1981), 66.

2. J. R. R. Tolkien, from a letter to his son, Christopher, 14 May 1944, ibid. 80.

3. J. R. R. Tolkien, from a letter to his son, Michael, 6–8 March 1941, ibid. 53–4; from a letter to his son, Michael, 1 November 1963, ibid. 338–40.

4. J. R. R. Tolkien, from a letter to Father Robert Murray SJ, 2 December 1953, ibid. 172.

5. J. R. R. Tolkien, from a letter to his son, Michael, 1 November 1963, ibid. 338.

6. *Sir Gawain and the Green Knight, Pearl, and Sir Orfeo*, trans. J. R. R. Tolkien, new edn. (New York: Ballantyne Books, 1980), 111–12.

7. J. R. R. Tolkien, from a letter to Father Robert Murray SJ, 2 December 1953, in *Letters of J. R. R. Tolkien*, 172.

8. J. R. R. Tolkien, 'Mythopoeia', in *Tree and Leaf, including the Poem Mythopoeia*, introduction by Christopher Tolkien (Boston: Houghton Mifflin, 1989), 98–9, 100–1.

# John Cameron Andrieu Bingham Michael Morton    1893–1979

J. B. 'Johnnie' Morton's fifty years with the *Daily Express* bridge the journalistic worlds of G. K. Chesterton and Richard Ingrams. After Harrow and Oxford, he fought through a large part of the First World War, first as a private soldier and later as an officer. After suffering shell-shock on the Somme, he was transferred to Military Intelligence, a career move he described as 'a fate which may befall the best of us'. In 1922 he was received into the Catholic Church, and in the same year joined the staff of the *Express*. The humour and satire of his *Beachcomber* column had as their inspiration his high intelligence and distaste for modern culture, but also his Catholic faith and commitment to Judaeo-Christian morality. The inhabitants of the world of Beachcomber—the mad scientist Dr Strabismus (Whom God Preserve), the effete poet Roland Milk, Prodnose the pedant—are personalities worthy of immortal remembrance, as are many of Morton's one-liners. 'Wagner', he once said, 'is the Puccini of music', and he defined a 'bomb-shell' as 'the omission of a cricketer from a team'. He wrote books of many kinds: novels, history (especially French), and biography (including a life of St Thérèse of Lisieux). If you had met him in a Fleet Street pub, you would have seen a short, stocky man, with the complexion and rough tweeds of a farmer and a crew cut of the style of his friend and hiking companion, Hilaire Belloc. After the death of his wife in 1974 and his involuntary retirement from the *Express* in 1975, he suffered depression and died in a nursing home in Worthing.

# Christmas Song

High Queen and Hope of those whose weary eyes
Watched in the winter darkness long ago,
Guard us who stumble on to where He lies;
Hungry are all our hearts for Paradise,
We broken men that seek Him through the snow.

Mother of all the desolate sons of men,
Sword of the fallen, gaze in pity down;
Show us the ancient star returned again
And guide our footsteps over field and fen.
To that Great Light wherein our sorrows drown. (1)

# The Battle of Vienna, 1683: Sobieski Saves Christendom

Kara Mustapha did what he could. He attempted to re-organize the scattered units, to persuade them to stand firm. But he could not put courage into an army that was beaten as soon as the Polish cavalry formed for the charge. Too often, on too many fields, they had learnt the folly of resistance. Fear became public, and those not involved in the actual fighting of the last moments were only too anxious to save their skins, and perhaps some booty or other amassed during the advance to Vienna. By six o'clock Sobieski drew rein before the gorgeous tent of the Vizier; outside it a slave still held ready the horse upon which his master was to have rallied his men. One of the golden stirrups was at once sent to the Queen as a token of victory. Those Janissaries who were still in the trenches, and had been carrying on their work all through the day, attempted, when they learnt the truth, to turn their guns upon the victorious allies. But it was too late, and the remnant of them were either killed or captured. Meanwhile, Louis of Baden's dragoons entered the town by what was left of the Scottish gate. It was the sixtieth day since the Turks had pitched their camp under the walls.

There followed a remarkable instance of the hold Sobieski held over the assortment of troops which he commanded upon this memorable day. Since it was by no means unlikely that Kara Mustapha would be able to rally enough men for a counter-attack, the King insisted upon the strictest discipline. There was to be no looting and no disorder, under pain of death. Exhausted though his men were, there must be no relaxation until all danger was over. It should be remembered that these orders were issued to men who had fought all day in almost unendurable heat, and among whom the rich plunder of the Turkish camp was a byword. Yet when the prize was before them, they found themselves working on the same old treadmill of pickets, fatigues, and parties of reconnaissance. While they stood to arms through the night, too weary to pursue the retreating enemy, the remains of Mahomet's vast army were flying pell-mell along the roads to the Hungarian border.

Thus was Vienna relieved, and all our inheritance saved by the sword of the Polish king. (2)

NOTES AND SOURCES

1. J. B. Morton, *By the Way* (London: Sheed & Ward, 1936), 375.
2. J. B. Morton, *Sobieski, King of Poland* (London: Eyre & Spottiswoode, 1932), 199–200.

# Walter David Michael Jones                    1895–1974

David Jones was the Catholic Blake of the twentieth century, a visionary Londoner whose mind roamed the universe, but, while Blake ventured, in Thomas Merton's words, among 'almost all of the heterodox and heretical mystical systems that ever flourished in the West', Jones stayed firm in orthodoxy. Born in Brockley, David Jones was always fluent in his mother's Rotherhithe Cockney, but longed to speak his father's Flintshire Welsh. He showed an early aptitude for drawing and painting, and at the age of 14 entered Camberwell Art School. Early in 1915 he joined the Royal Welch Fusiliers and served on the Western front. His life in the trenches left a permanent mark on his later painting and poetry, and to the end he retained a fierce loyalty to his comrades and regiment. After the war he was received into the Catholic Church by Father John O'Connor. Through O'Connor, Jones came into contact with the sculptor, Eric Gill, and joined the latter's Guild of St Joseph and St Dominic in Ditchling, moving with them to live at Capel-y-ffin in South Wales from 1924 to 1927. Having learnt the art of engraving with the Guild, Jones achieved considerable success as an illustrator. However, as time went on, he developed his style of water-colour painting and what he liked to call 'painted inscriptions'. In 1937 he published an account of his wartime experiences, *In Parenthesis*. It was written in an unclassifiable modernist style, a kind of prose-poem that brings into synthesis the voices (with all their profanities) of Tommy Atkins and Dai Greatcoat, medieval Welsh literature, Arthurian romance, and the liturgy of the Catholic Church. T. S. Eliot and W. B. Yeats praised it, and in 1938 it won the Hawthornden prize. *The Anathémata* appeared in 1952. Inspired in part by a visit to Palestine, during which he was struck by the historic parallels between the modern British and the ancient Roman occupations of the region, the book draws on materials from early British history and mythology and the history and myths of the Mediterranean region to explore the possibility of small cultures resisting the power of empire. The poem received mixed reviews in the press, but was acclaimed by W. H. Auden, Kathleen Raine, and William Carlos Williams. For the rest of his life, Jones worked on a long poem, of which *The Anathémata* was intended to form part. David Jones died in Harrow in 1974, having earlier that year been made a Companion of Honour by the Queen. Perhaps his greatest achievement as a poet is his vision of the Church's traditional liturgy as the consummation of the cosmos. The ceremonial acts and ritual words of the priest in the Sacrifice of the Mass not only re-present the mysteries of salvation, but also recapitulate the types and shadows of those mysteries in the literatures and religions of the world, in the history, especially military, of mankind, and in the particularities of the natural world.

## The Nativity of Our Lord

> What says his *mabinogi*?
>> Son of Mair, wife of jobbing carpenter
>> *in via nascitur*[8]
> lapped in hay, *parvule*.
> But what does his Boast say?
>> *Alpha es et O*
>>> that which

---

[8] [David Jones's note] See the Homily of St Gregory, Pope, said at Matins for Christmas Day.

the whole world cannot hold.
Atheling to the heaven-king.
Shepherd of Greekland.
Harrower of Annwn.
Freer of the Waters.
Chief Physician and
*dux et pontifex.*
Gwledig Nefoedd *and*
Walda of *every* land
*et vocabitur* WONDERFUL. (1)

## The Kensington Mass

His hands conjoined
   *super altare*
his full chin crumpled
   to the pectoral folds of
his newly washed focale
he begins the suffrage:
   ORAMUS TE DOMINE
pleading that the merits of
   the Blessed departed
the veterani in their celestial castrum
& colonia 'in hevyn on hicht'
might assist him at the work
he is about to make

but in especial he asks the adjuvance of
   these athletes of God
tokens of whom are cisted
   immediately beneath
& central to
   the Stone of Oblation
at which he now stands.
He inclines lower yet
   and with a gravitas & pietas
that can be felt
   lightly & swiftly his lips
press, in medio, the uppermost of the
three-fold, fine abbed fair cloths
   of Eblana flax
that must pall
   the mensa Domini
these are indeed 'his own raiment'.
As he says the words: sanctorum tuorum, quorum reliquiae
HIC SVNT his apparelled amice hunches a little with the
thrust forward & more downward head of him. He has no

need of the rubric's nudge: *osculatur altare in medio*.
for what bodily act other
  would serve here?
Creaturely of necessity
  for we are creatures
Our own salutation
  were it possible
could be no other than the rubrics *osculatur*
  were it Argive Helen's chiton hem
or the hem of the garment
  of gilt interthreaded green
  wide laticlaved of murex
the long tunica of
  our own Elen of the Army-paths
whose outward splendour of form
was informed by an instress
  of great noblesse. (2)

## The Grail Mass

Inclined in the midst of the instruments
and invoking the life-giving persons
and in honour of the former witnesses
*et istorum*, dusty in the cist
he kisses the place of sepulture.

He turns to ask of the living.
Those round about answer him.
He turns again and immediately
      toward the tokens.

He continues and in silence
inclined over the waiting creatures
of tillage and of shower.

Ceres and Liber and
the dancing naiad
have heard his: Come who makes holy
and now and so still
      between the horns of the *mensa*
they wait awhile
his: ratify, accept, approve.

You are his special signs
And you'll be doubly *signa*
Before he's at the *Unde et memores*.

O no, not flee away
but wait his word
not to th'infernal jail
   (as blind makers
In harmonic numbers tell)
Not troop off, not you, nor
Peor's baalim
   but wait on him.
Yes, brutish you
   But you his forerunners
each of you, his *figura*.

Need peculiar powers forgo their stalls?
He's no douser of dim tapers
and why should Anubis hasten
except to glast the freeing of the waters.
So stay
   But when they sing
QUI VENIT
here all of you
   kneel
every Lar of you
   numen or tutelar
from *terra*, *pontus* and the air
or from the strait bathysphere.
   Now constellate
are all your brights
   of this lifted Lode.
What light else
   brighted you ever?

He stands upright now in the weeds
of the young-time, of the sap-years.
   Under his fair-worked apparels
the tubular blacks of the mean years
of the dead time.
   In file of two
the patrician tunicas
move up in support.
   (They've stitched the laticlave so
since the year that measures all the years.)
He hunches free of wrist
   the gothic folds
(O, give us a Roman planet any day!)
Loudly he clears his throat
brother ass must neigh for all his May Day rosette
the belly murmurs though it serve Melchisedec.

Full and clear he rounds his vowels
when he says *Per omnia*
but his full chin crumples to the pectoral folds
at *Gratias agamus.*

And now he sings out
   and alone
the gleemen and the Powers take the cue
he has the Nine Bright Shiners at his beck
when he stands substitute to the Man in the Mock. (3)

## The *Memento*

You that shall spread your hands over the things offered
make *memento* of us
and where the gloss reads *jungit manus*[9] count us among his
argonauts whose argosy you plead,[10] under the sign of the
things you offer.
                  Extend your hands
all you *orantes*
             for the iron-dark shore
is to our lee
over the lead-dark sea
and schisted Ocrinum looms in fairish visibility
and white-plumed riders shoreward go
                  and
THE BIRDS DECLARE IT
             that wing white and low
that also leeward[11] go
           go leeward to the tor-lands
where the tin-veins maculate the fire-rocks.
The birds
              have a home
in those rocks. (4)

---

[9] [David Jones's note] In the Canon of the Mass at the beginning of the prayer *Hanc igitur oblationem*, the rubric directs the priest to spread his hands over the offerings, and after the words, 'that we be…counted within the flock of thy elect' a further rubric, *Jungit manus*, directs him to join his hands together.

[10] [David Jones's note] What is pleaded in the Mass is precisely the argosy or voyage of the Redeemer, consisting of His entire sufferings and His Death, His conquest of Hades, His Resurrection, and His return in triumph to Heaven. It is this that is offered to the Trinity (cf. 'Myself to myself' as in the *Havamal* is said of Odin) on behalf of us argonauts and of the whole argosy of mankind, and, in some sense, of all sentient beings, and, perhaps, of insentient too, for, as Paul says, 'The whole of nature, as we know, groans in a common travail all the while' (Rom. 8: 22, Knox translation).

[11] [David Jones's note] Leeward is to be pronounced lew-ard.

## Flanders: First Sight of the Mass

It was after the Somme, I think, when I had returned to France from being wounded. Anyway when or where it was I can't exactly place. But as I was always cold, one of my main occupations was to hunt for any wood that was dry and could be used to make decent fire. We were in some support trenches and I said to the people I was with, 'I'm going off to find some decent firewood'. Just a little way back that is between our support trench and the reserve line I noticed what had been a farm building now a wreckage in the main, owing to shell fire. No individual of any sort was about and I noticed that one bit of this wreckage a byre or outhouse of some sort still stood and its roofing appeared to be intact and its walling undamaged at least from a little distance.

I thought now that looks to be most likely the very place where there might be not only wooden objects of one sort or another, broken cart-wheels, or other discarded bits of timber, but, with a bit of luck, a wood-store perfectly dry and cut ready for use. So I went to investigate and when I came close to the wall I found there were signs of its having been more knocked about than appeared from a few hundred yards away, but there was no door or opening of any sort on that side, but I found a crack against which I put my eye expecting to see either empty darkness and that I should have to go round to the other side of the little building to find an entrance. But what I saw through the small gap in the wall was not the dim emptiness I had expected but the back of a sacerdos in a gilt-hued *planeta*, two points of flickering candlelight no doubt lent an extra sense of goldness to the vestment and a golden warmth seemed, by the same agency, to lend the white altar cloths and the white linen of the celebrant's alb and amice and maniple (the latter, I notice, has been abandoned, without a word of explanation, by these blasted reformers). You can imagine what a great marvel it was for me to see through that chink in the wall, and kneeling in the hay beneath the improvised *mensa* were a few huddled figures in khaki.

Only a very few, for of course most of the R.W.F. [Royal Welch Fusiliers] were of some Nonconformist sect and the Londoners mostly C. of E. But there was a big-bodied Irishman and an Italian naturalized Englishman, represented under the forms of Bomber Mulligan and Runner Meotti in *In Paren[thesis]*...I can't recall at what part of the Mass it was as I looked through that squint-hole and I didn't think I ought to stay long as it seemed rather like an uninitiated bloke prying on the Mysteries of a Cult. But it made a big impression on me. For one thing I was astonished how close to the Front Line the priest had decided to make the Oblation and I was also impressed to see Old Sweat Mulligan, a somewhat fearsome figure, a real pugilistic, hard-drinking Goidelic Celt, kneeling there in the smoky candlelight. And one strong impression I had (and this I have often thought about over this last ten years of change when clerics of all sorts declare that the turning-round of the *mensa* and the use of the vernacular and much besides made the faithful more at one with the sacred minister and so get back nearer to the Coena Domini) for at that spying unintentionally on the Mass in Flanders in the Forward Zone I felt immediately that oneness between the Offerant and those toughs that clustered round him in the dim-lit byre—a thing I had never felt remotely as a Protestant at the Office of Holy Communion in spite of the insistence of Protestant theology on the 'priesthood of the laity'. (5)

## Liturgical Reform

In using the bits [for Rebecca's inscription] from the Mass of Corpus Christi, I wondered what on earth they'll do with that sublime composition when they sing it in the vernacular. How *can* you give the total oneness of the firm theological statement and the splendid poetry of *Dogma datur Christianis quod in carnem transit panis*, to mention but two lines? And the Christmas Preface (that the idiots eliminated from the Corpus Christi Mass some few years back)—it can't be done.

I feel bloody sorry for our hierarchy actually, for whatever they decide they will be blamed by both parties, by those who are all agog for thorough and complete vernacularization and by those (some almost equally tedious) who see no point in any change at all. I say 'equally tedious' because there are some who just want, out of mere custom, to have no change—rather like those cavalry officers of the First World War who were totally blind to the requirements of trench warfare and who, like Haig himself, as late as 1916 said that one machine-gun to a company was ample. That sort of attitude is ludicrous, and *some* of the stalwart resisters to liturgical change are a bit like that...

I think our boys are making the same mistake as those classical dons who used to say that the teaching of the Greek and Latin languages was maintained because it taught men to think clearly, to write clear English, to become competent civil servants or what not. Apart from being largely balls, the reasons are utile and so-called 'practical'. What the dons ought to have said was that the classics were an integral part of our Western heritage and should be fought for on that ground alone. Our Church leaders have even more reason to guard that heritage—for it is saturated with the sacral. It's not a matter of knowledge but of love. It's a terrible thought that the language of the West, of the Western liturgy, and inevitably the Roman chant, might become virtually extinct. (6)

## The Prayers of the Lonely

When it was quite dark and there was no sound at all except of a difficult breathing coming up from the earth, and intermittently the half-cries of those who would call strongly from their several and lonely places, on

that Creature of Water, or on
some creature of their own kind by name, as on
gentle Margaret on
Amy, on Gwenfrewi
on Bella on Donnabelle
on Aunt Birch on
Ned
long dead, on dead old Elfed, on great-uncle George, on Brigit the Kildare maid that kindled the fires for Billy of Clonmor in the *hortus* of Iverna. On Joan the maid that keeled the pots beyond the baize doors at Mrs Jack Horners. Or on those Bright ones to whose particular cults they were dedicate.

On God the Father of Heaven because with Him there is neither wounding nor unwounding. On God the Word because by Him we know the wound and the salve, on God the Life Giver because His workings are never according to plan and because of the balm under His Wing, and because by Him even the GOC in C's diversion before the Mill can shine with the splendour of order. The Sanctifier and bright Lord who is glorious in operation, the dispositioner, the effector of all transubstantiations, who sets the traverse wall according to the measure of the angel with the reed, who knows best how to gather his epiklesis from that open plain, who transmutes their cheerless blasphemy into a lover's word, who spoke by Balaam and by Balaam's ass, who spoke also by Sgt. Bullcock.

On the Lamb because He was slain.
On the Word seen by men because He was familiar with the wounding iron.
On the Son of Man because He could not carry the cross-beam of his *stauros*.
On the Son of Mary, because, like Perédur, He left His Mother to go for a soldier, for He would be a *miles* too.
On Mary because of her secret piercing, and because, but for her pliant *Fiat mihi*, no womb-burden to joust with the fiend in the lists of Hierosolyma, in His fragile habergeon: HUMANA NATURA.[12]
On the Angel in skins because the soldiers asked him a question.
On the key-man, the sword-bearer, because he lied to a nosey girl and warmed his hands at a corporal's brazier...
On the God of the philosophers who is not in the fire, but who yet can make fire.
On Enoch's shining companion who walks by your side like an intimate confederate, who chooses suddenly, so that the bearers look in vain for your body, who takes you alive to be his perpetual friend.
On Abraham's God who conditions his vows, who elects his own, who plucks out by tribe and sub-tribe and gens and family. (7)

NOTES AND SOURCES

1. David Jones, *Anathémata: Fragments of an Attempted Writing* (London: Faber, 1952), 207–8. [David Jones's note] Boast... Wonderful. (A) Cf 'Cnut rules the land, as Xst the shepherd of Greece, the heavens'. (B) Annwn, annoon, the Celtic hades. (C) Penfeddyg meaning Chief Physician was the title of Peredur (Percival), who 'freed the waters'... (D) Gwledig Nefoedd, goo-led-ig nev-oithe, Ruler of the Heavens. Taliesin addresses God as *gwledig nef a phob tud*, 'ruler of Heaven and of every country' or people. Historically the title Gwledig was used only of territorial rulers of importace, and its use is confined to the sub- and Post-Roman period in Britain.

2. David Jones, 'The Grail Mass', in *The Roman Quarry and Other Sequences*, ed. Harman Grisewood and René Hague (London: Agenda Editions, 1981), 88–9.

3. Ibid. 106–8.

4. Jones, *Anathémata*, 106–7.

5. David Jones, Letter to René Hague, 9–15 July 1971, in *Dai Greatcoat: A Self-Portrait of David Jones in his Letters*, ed. René Hague (London: Faber, 1980), 248–9.

6. David Jones, Letter to Harman Grisewood, 6 July 1964, ibid. 207–8.

7. David Jones, *The Sleeping Lord and Other Fragments* (London: Faber, 1974), 107–8.

[12] [David Jones' note] Cf. Langland's *Piers Plowman* B text, Passus xviii, lines 22–23.

# (Michael Clive) David Knowles OSB                    1896–1974

David Knowles was a Benedictine of classic inclination who fell into that most un-Benedictine state which is canonical punishment for disobedience. After Downside school, he went up to Christ's College, Cambridge, where he took a first in both parts of the Classical Tripos. He entered the Downside novitiate in 1914, and was ordained priest in 1922. Inspired by the monastic theology of his first abbot, Dom Cuthbert Butler, Knowles became convinced that God was calling him to live a more strictly contemplative observance of the Rule than is generally possible in the English Congregation with its long history of taking monks from the cloister into the classroom and the parish. In 1934 Rome rejected his plans for a new community, a judgement that he decided he could not accept. He was transferred to Ealing Priory, but a nervous breakdown on the eve of the Second World War led him to leave Downside without permission, an act that provoked his suspension canonical. Having become a Fellow of Peterhouse in 1944, he was appointed Regius Professor of Modern History at Cambridge in 1954, and held the chair till he retired in 1963. Through the good offices of Abbot Christopher Butler, the suspension was lifted, and he lived the last years of his life as an officially exclaustrated monk of Downside. His greatest works of scholarship are in the history of English monasticism, but he also wrote with insight about the Church's tradition of mystical theology and, surprisingly, the American Civil War, the passion of his boyhood and the subject of his first published book. In 1968 he wrote a noble defence of *Humanae vitae*.

## *Humanae vitae*

Sexual experience, though normally the entry to married life, is not for human beings, far less for Christians, the be-all and end-all of marriage. It has its place, but it passes. In the words of Our Lord, there is neither marrying nor giving in marriage in the life beyond this life, though the love of two persons, two souls in him, will remain. But in so far as physical, sexual love is present, it is present for a function, that of giving new life. It is therefore the teaching of the Church, not that of Paul VI apart from the Church, 'that any use whatever of marriage must retain its natural potential to procreate human life'.

His Holiness has, as we have been told in sincere and moving words, read much, spoken much, thought much, and, what is more, prayed and suffered much, and devout souls throughout the Church have prayed with him and offered the Holy Sacrifice for his intention. We know, and he knew better, what a tremendous and agonizing responsibility was his; indeed, a greater responsibility can rarely, if ever, have confronted a pope; and he knew that he would be, like his Master, a 'sign of contradiction'. We are told that he gradually saw more and more clearly what he must say. He answered on the spiritual level, transcending all debates on natural law and asserting, though in ampler terms, the constant teaching of the Church of which he is the head. Is any Catholic, believing in Christ's promise to Peter and in the guidance of the Holy Spirit, prepared to assert that he answered not only inopportunely and unwisely, but faultily and erroneously?

We must not allow ourselves to be confused or shaken by noise of words and the dust of dispute. The simple teaching of the Church has been lost sight of behind appeals to science, to conscience, to freedom, and to what not. These have nothing to do with the spiritual issue at stake, that of the law of God and the clear teaching of the Church on Christian purity in marriage. Protests and petitions are wholly irrelevant. There is no need for dialogues and confrontations and the techniques of teaching. Has any reader or any speaker loved Our Lord the better for them? The decision and its fulfilment may indeed be hard for many married people. They will have their reward a hundredfold. But it is not they who are causing all the disturbance. I speak to Catholics, who look to Our Lord and Our Lady for help and example in their daily life, and who believe that the Holy Spirit dwells in the Church, in the successor of St Peter and in their own souls. Do those who argue about the rights of conscience, the limits of infallibility, the claims of science, or the non-existence of natural law find that their prayer, their hidden love of Our Lord, His Cross and His Mother, grow within them as it grew within the disciples on the road to Emmaus? Does their spiritual life and the simplicity of their faith grow deeper? Do they in the fullest sense rejoice in their faith and in their love of Our Lord? The coldness, the hardness, the aridity of their words wake no echo in the reader's heart. Silence and prayer and quiet thought alone can restore peace. And peace can come only through union, in faith and filial obedience, with the Vicar of Christ. (1)

## St Wulstan of Worcester

Only one Englishman remained in the position he had held in 1066; not under a cloud, but with his reputation enhanced. Wulstan, Bishop of Worcester, survived the Conquest, and survived it for almost thirty years, and while he acquiesced in the fact, and indeed supported the Conqueror, and was trusted both by him and his new Primate, Lanfranc, he remained a centre of English thought and literature till his death...

And Wulstan was English by nature. Hard as they are to define, certain bold national characteristics are recognized by everyone when they are present in strength in some great national character. Geoffrey Chaucer, Thomas More, William Shakespeare, and Samuel Johnson are as clearly English as Jeanne d'Arc and Blaise Pascal are French, and John of the Cross and Ignatius Loyola Spanish. And different as Wulstan is from More and Johnson, he is clearly of their stock.

Like Shakespeare, Wulstan was born in the heart of England. His native village, whether Long Itchington or Bishop's Itchington, is within a few miles of the oak which boasts that it is the centre of England, and within a few miles of the spire of Stratford-on-Avon. From the high ground there one looks over the vale of Evesham to the Malverns and Cotswolds that Wulstan knew so well on his bishop's visitations. He found his schooling, too, in the heart of England—first in the abbey of Evesham, which, with those round it, had not suffered from the decline that came to many in England at that time; and then in the abbey of Peterborough, which, so a chronicler tells us, was still called 'golden town' because of its beauty and prosperity. Soon after his return home, he followed his father and mother to Worcester, where both had entered monasteries, and became a member of the bishop's household. The bishop chose him for ordination, and for a short time he was the parish priest of Hawkesbury in Gloucestershire; then he became a monk in the cathedral priory of Worcester, which had been founded c. 970 by St Oswald, the master of Wulstan's own father. The priory was small, and Wulstan, after passing through the offices of schoolmaster, precentor, and sacristan, became prior at the age of forty. Under his rule the priory prospered temporally and spiritually; he won back many a village in the Severn valley which had been seized by the great laymen of the district, and he increased the number of monks; we are told that as prior he used to stand daily at the door of the church to give counsel to all who wished it; he preached to the people and baptized the children of the poor; men came from afar as penitents to him, and among them the great, such as Earl Harold...

Wulstan, one month before his death, had told his monks—as has many another saint, down to St Thérèse of Lisieux—that he would be nearer to them when dead than when alive. He kept his promise, and almost at once the monks of Worcester began to receive from him cures of bodily and spiritual ills. The first attempt at canonization was made fifty years after his death, but it came to nothing. Fifty years later, in 1201-2, so many miracles took place that the bishop—the zealous and holy Malger—approached Innocent III. A commission was set up, including the Archbishop of Canterbury and the Bishop of Ely, and the members reported to Rome the genuineness of the miracles, sending to Innocent with their report Coleman's *Life of Wulstan*. The canonization took place on April 21st 1203, and the great Pope himself composed the prayer which is still read at Mass in the English missal:

Pour forth into our hearts, O Lord, the spirit of thy love, that, by the intercession of blessed Wulstan, thy confessor and pontiff, we may deserve to enjoy thy sweetness in eternal bliss...(2)

## Julian of Norwich

Julian of Norwich is, in qualities of mind and heart, one of the most remarkable—perhaps the most remarkable—Englishwoman of her age. Her mind can wrestle with the deepest mysteries of theology and life, and has absorbed (or discovered for itself) much of the abstruse technical phraseology of the schools. At the same time she shows herself a generous and loving woman with an extraordinary delicacy of feeling, and she is able to express in language which goes directly home to the heart, and yet is in no way rough or oversimple, for she had also a vivid pictorial memory and a wide range of words. In her sobriety, as in her depth, she deserves to rank very high among the women mystics of the Middle Ages. (3)

## The Destruction of Catholic England:
## The Witness of *The Rites of Durham*

The lights did 'burn continually both day and night' in the great cressets before the high altar, 'In token that the house was always watching to God', and the sound of bells at midnight 'in the lantern called the new work', clear in the magical silence of midsummer or borne fitfully across the Wear in winter storms, gave assurance to the townspeople and the countryside 'in the deep night that all was well'. In the great church itself the shrines of St Cuthbert and of Bede the Venerable took the mind back to the earliest days of the faith in Northumbria, while the silver pyx with its lights bore witness to a presence more sacred than that of the Temple.

Throughout the days and years sunlight and taperlight had rested upon the blue and gold and crimson and cream and silver of the vestments and vessels. The old conservative did not live to see the final desecration, when thousands of Scottish prisoners, famished, sick and dying, tore down the screens and tabernacle work for firewood, and filled the cathedral with flame and smoke, but he had seen the shrine and the pyx disappear. The glory had departed from Durham, for the ark of God had been taken away. (4)

NOTES AND SOURCES

1. David Knowles, *Peter Has Spoken: The Encyclical without Ambiguity* (London: Catholic Truth Society, 1968), 11 f.

2. David Knowles, 'St Wulstan of Worcester', in Maisie Ward (ed.), *The English Way: Studies in English Sanctity from St Bede to Newman* (London: Sheed & Ward, 1933), 66–7, 77.

3. David Knowles, *The English Mystical Tradition*, new edn. (London: Burns & Oates, 1964), 135.

4. David Knowles, *The Religious Orders in England*, iii: *The Tudor Age*, corrected new impression (Cambridge: Cambridge University Press, 1971), 136–7.

# Francis Joseph Sheed                        1897–1981

Frank Sheed was not only an energetic apologist for the faith by his writing and public speaking, but also the publisher of a large number of the twentieth-century authors in this anthology. He was born in Australia and studied law there before coming to London in the 1920s. With his wife, Maisie Ward, he founded the publishing house of Sheed & Ward, which introduced the leading Catholic authors of the twentieth century, continental as well as British, to a wide readership in the English-speaking world. Sheed finally made his home in the USA, where, as in England, he became prominent in the apostolate of apologetics, especially in the Catholic Evidence Guild. In *The Church and I*, published in the seventies, towards the end of his long life, the confident apologist betrays a certain bewilderment at the strange opinions of the times. In response to a left-wing cleric, active in opposition to the Vietnam war, who 'flipped aside' contraception, abortion, and infallibility as 'Mickey Mouse questions', Sheed comments: 'I wonder how Mickey Mouse would cartoon the million infant Americans slain in the womb in the Eastern United States alone during legalized abortion's first year—Vietnam's slaughter does not match that.'

## The Catholic Intellect

For the soul's full functioning, we need a Catholic intellect as well as a Catholic will. We have a Catholic will when we love God and obey God, love the Church and obey the Church. We have a Catholic intellect when we live consciously in the presence of the realities that God through His Church has revealed. A good working test of a Catholic will is that we should do what the Church says. But for a Catholic intellect, we must also see what the Church sees. This means that when we look out upon the Universe we see the same Universe that the Church sees; and the enormous advantage of this is that the Universe the Church sees is the real Universe, because she is the Church of God. Seeing what she sees means seeing what is there. And just as loving what is good is sanctity, or the health of the will, so seeing what is there is sanity, or the health of the intellect. (1)

## Mystery

As used by theologians, the word does not mean a truth of which we cannot know anything; it means a truth of which we cannot know everything. Mystery there *must* be once we touch the nature of God. He is the Infinite, the Immeasurable, the Limitless. We are finite, measured, limited on all sides. It is impossible that we should totally contain God in our minds so as totally to comprehend Him. But by His loving kindness we are endowed with a nature that can know something of Him—some little by its own powers, vastly more by what He tells us of Himself in the mysteries He has revealed. (2)

## Creation: The Work of the Blessed Trinity

We must see the universe and everything in it (ourselves included) as held in existence from moment to moment by nothing save God's continuing will to hold it (including us) there. This is the plain truth about all created things: not to see it is to be in error, tragic or comic or sheerly farcical, about ourselves and everything else. The failure to see it, is what causes man to play such fantastic tricks before high heaven as make the angels weep. So far this is no more than a summary of the truth already stated about the presence of God in all things. But we can now add something enormous. The God who is thus continuously present in us as in all things is the Blessed Trinity. At the very centre of our being, Father, Son, and Holy Ghost are living their infinite life of knowing and loving.

Thus the formula for everything from Adam to the Archangel is nothingness made into something and kept in being by the infinite power of the Blessed Trinity. Note especially the phrase 'made into something'. Things are not simply thoughts in the mind of God. He has given them real existence, real be-ing. He does not simply think them: He has made them. The universe is not a system of ideas thought by God, it is a system of things made by God. The universe really *is*.

But not as God is. Here we may pause to … distinguish between the absolute being of God and the relative being of created things, what philosophers call the analogy of being. God alone wholly *is* with all that '*is*' can mean. You can say of the universe that it is, but you cannot leave it there: you have to keep adding words, and every word you add subtracts. Thus you must say of the universe: 'It is, because …'; 'It is, but it was not'; 'It is, but it might not have been'; 'It is, so long as …'; 'It is this or that—e.g., man or cat, little or big'. Every one of these and a thousand other additions one must make to the simple statement 'It is' are limitations, subtracting something from the fullness of what 'is' can mean. Each thing *is*, but dependently, but conditionally, but as this or that limited selection of limited excellences. It is, but relatively, partially. But when you have said of God He is, in the first place you have said everything, and in the second if you still want to add words—e.g., He is infinite, He is omnipotent, He is all-good, He is omniscient—the added words subtract nothing, but merely draw out for consideration some special perfection already contained in the fullness of *is*. Nothing else is, with all that *is* can mean. It is only some of what *is* can mean. Nothing else is good with all that goodness can mean. Only God is absolute Good, absolute *is*.

Because it is created of nothing the universe does not add to God. God plus the universe does not total up to something greater than God, in some such way as we might feel that a man plus his image in the mirror is not greater than the man. The created universe contains nothing that is not the result of His power, a power needed not only to bring it into existence, but to maintain it in existence. Nothing else is in the finite save what God puts there and keeps there. (3)

## Original Sin

Here we come to one of the most mysterious of the doctrines that treat directly of man, the doctrine of Original Sin, which is bound up with the truth that Adam's sin involved the whole race. In some profoundly dark way Adam's sin is in his descendants as real sin: they are not only affected by the results of his sin, they are somehow involved in the guilt of it: 'a multitude, through one man's disobedience, became guilty' (Rom. 5: 19).

It is in us not as an actual sin, a personal sin, as it was in Adam who actually committed it, but as a habitual sin, a state of unrighteousness, which most theologians equate with the absence of the supernatural life which should, had Adam not sinned, have been there. Thus the Council of Trent says that 'unrighteousness follows natural birth precisely as righteousness follows regeneration'— in other words we are born into unrighteousness (absence of sanctifying grace) just as we should have been born into sanctifying grace but for Adam's sin, just as . . . we are reborn into sanctifying grace by baptism.

But wherein lies our guilt? That this privation of grace should be in us as an effect of sin, we can see. But how is it sin? It is, as we have seen, not a personal sin. But if it is not personal, how is it ours? Because of that other element in us, our nature. It was a state of sinfulness in Adam's nature, and Adam's nature was the source of our nature. Theologians teach that it is transmitted by the natural way of sexual generation: it comes to us because we are *ex semine Adae*, of Adam's seed. If we could see more clearly into the relation of person and nature within ourselves, and into the relation of each man's nature with the nature of those through whom and ultimately from whom it comes to him, there would be no mystery. Lacking that clear vision, we find it darkly mysterious. To me it seems that the twelfth-century writer Odo of Cambrai came very close to the limit of lucidity in his work *De peccato originali*. 'The sin wherewith we sinned in Adam is natural in me, personal in Adam. In Adam it is graver, in me less grave; for in him I sinned, not as who I am but as what I am. It was not I that sinned in him, but what I am; I sinned in him as man not as Odo, as substance not as person. Because the substance does not exist save in the person, the sin of the substance is the sin of the person, yet not personal. That sin is personal which I commit as who I am not as what I am, by which I sin as Odo not as man, by which I sin as person not as nature.' (4)

## The Incarnation

God the Son was a Person, a Someone, possessing the nature of God in its fullness, and this in the eternity of the Divine Being. At a certain point in time He took to Himself and made His own a human nature. Thus we have the unique instance of one single person with two natures, divine and human. To the question 'Who are you?' Christ would have but one answer. He is the Second Person of the Blessed Trinity, God the Son, the Word. But to the question 'What are you?' Christ Our Lord would have two answers, for He has two natures; He is God, and He is man.

Note the consequences for Our Lord's actions. Nature decides what the person can do. This one Person had two natures, two sources of action from which He could draw. He had the Divine Nature, and so could do all that goes with being God. He had a human nature, and so could do all that goes with being God. He had a human nature, and so could do all that goes with being man. But whether He was doing the things of God in His Divine Nature or doing the things of man in His human nature, in either event it was the Person who was doing them; and there was but one Person, and He was God.

Thus Christ Our Lord, having a human nature, was able to perform a human act; but He who performed it was a divine Person. Being able to perform a human act, He could offer it in expiation of the human act of Adam. But because He was a divine Person, His human act had a value which no act of a merely human person could have had.

And this same union in Him of human and divine which was the ground of His work of expiation, was the ground of His work of reconciliation, too. If the human race were to be brought back from servitude to sonship, here was the man who in Himself was Son and not servant; if the human race were once more to be at one with God, here in Christ Jesus humanity was already united with the Godhead in a union of inconceivable closeness. Christ Our Lord was the atonement before He made the atonement. He alone could perform an act at once human and divine. Thus He could offer to God an act of obedience in love which as human could rightly be set against humanity's sin of rebellion in self-love, and which as divine must have all the value needed, or immeasurably more than all the value needed, to satisfy for it. (5)

## Resurrection, Ascension, and Sacrifice

Realize that the Resurrection was not simply a convenient way for Our Lord to return to His Apostles and give them final instructions, nor His Ascension simply a convenient way of letting them know definitely and beyond question or peradventure that He had left this world. Resurrection and Ascension belong organically to the Sacrifice He offered for us. The Sacrifice, insofar as it is the offering to God of a victim slain, was complete upon Calvary. But in the total conception of sacrifice, it is not sufficient—as Cain found long before—that a victim be offered to God; it is essential that the offering be accepted by God; and given that the nature of man requires that sacrifice be an action externally visible, it belongs to the perfection of sacrifice that God's acceptance should be as externally visible as humanity's offering. It is in this sense that Resurrection and Ascension belong organically to the Sacrifice. By the miracle of the Resurrection, God at once shows His acceptance of the Priest as a true priest of a true sacrifice *and* perfects the Victim offered to Him, so that whereas it was offered mortal and corruptible it has gained immortality and incorruptibility. By the Ascension God accepts the offered Victim by actually taking it to Himself. Humanity, offered to God in Christ the Victim, is now forever at the right hand of the Father.

This is the significance of the prayer at Mass which comes a little before the Consecration: 'Receive, O Holy Trinity, this oblation which we offer thee in memory of the Passion, Resurrection, and Ascension of Our Lord', and of the prayer which follows the Consecration immediately: 'We offer to God's most excellent Majesty, the pure Victim, the holy Victim, the spotless Victim: and we offer it in commemoration not only of Christ's blessed Passion but also of His Resurrection from the dead, and likewise of His glorious Ascension. (6)

## The Communion of Saints

Because we are members of Christ's Body we are one with Him: and also we are one with one another. In a body, one member can help another: if the foot be hurt, the hand can tend it. So in the Mystical Body: one man can help another, by prayer and teaching and sacrifice. Here upon earth our prayers for one another are thus fruitful: we can pray for the souls in Purgatory: the souls in Heaven can pray for us. It has to some been a difficulty that death should be no barrier to this stream of prayer. That one living Christian should pray for another, or ask another to pray for him, has always seemed obviously right. But within the Body of Christ, death makes no difference. The soul of one who has left this world is not less a member of the same body as we, but is living more intensely with the life of Christ which we also share. If we should have asked him to pray for us during his life, we do so now more than ever. One striking characteristic of the Catholic Church is that real friendships do exist between her children still upon earth and one or other of the saints in Heaven. Sin is a barrier between souls: death is not. There is this constant flow of prayer throughout the whole body: for we are not members simply of one society, we are members of one thing—a living thing. (7)

## The Mystical Body of Christ

If we are to live in Christ, and He is to live in us, then there must be some such relationship between us and Him as that between a person and the cells of his body. It is in this sense that the Church is the Body of Christ. It is not merely an organization, something to which we resort for the gifts our souls need; it is an organism, a living body with its own life-secret and its own life-stream. But He whose Body it is, is Christ, so that He is the life-secret; and the life-stream flows from Him to every cell in the Body, so that, in so far as we are alive, it is with His life. We are living in Him because He is living in us.

This then is the reality of the Church, men bound together into one by the one life-stream flowing from the Head which is Christ. So St Paul can say to the Romans, 'We, though many in number, form one body in Christ' (Rom. 12: 5); and to the Ephesians, 'God has put everything under His dominion, and made Him the head to which the whole Church is joined, so that the Church is His body, the completion of Him who everywhere and in all things is complete' (1: 22–3); and to the Galatians, 'All you who have been baptized in Christ's name have put on the person of Christ; no more Jew or Gentile; no more slave and freeman; no more male and female; you are all one person in Jesus Christ' (3: 27–8) . . .

Everything that we have learnt about the Church must be re-translated into this new language of organic union with Christ. Baptism, as we have just seen, no longer means merely entry into the Church, or even merely rebirth into the supernatural life. It means rebirth into Christ. By our rebirth in baptism we are incorporated with Christ as by our birth in the natural order we are incorporated with Adam. By our incorporation with Christ we share alike in the satisfaction that He offered for sin, and the supernatural union with God that He merited.

Redemption was won for all men on Calvary; it is made actual in each man at Baptism. By Baptism we die, as He did, and rise again, as He did. 'You, by Baptism, have been united with His burial, united, too, with His Resurrection ... in giving life to Him, God gave life to you too, when you lay dead in your sins' (Col. 2: 12–13) ...

Our incorporation with Christ is so real that, in the phrase of St Thomas, 'His sufferings avail for us as if we had suffered them ourselves' (*Summa theologiae* 3a q. 69): the words are the natural development of St Paul's phrase (Gal. 2: 19): 'with Christ I hang upon the Cross'. Thus, the satisfaction He made is ours because we are in Him. The supernatural union with God which is the purpose and crown of Redemption is likewise ours because we are in Him. We have seen why Our Lord said I *am* the Life. We can also see why He said I *am* the Way. He not only opens the way for us and points the way to us: He *is* the Way. What we must do is enter into Him and abide in Him. That is salvation. United thus organically with His sacred humanity, we are united with His Person, that is to say with the Second Person of the Blessed Trinity, and so with the Triune God. In our life in Him, the breach between man and God is healed and the relation of oneness restored. It is the formula of restoration He had uttered at the Last Supper: 'I am in my Father, and you in me, and I in you.'

Redemption, then, finds a new statement in terms of the Mystical Body; so does the work of the Holy Ghost ... The Holy Spirit comes to us *because* we are inbuilt into Christ in whom He is. The life which is Christ's—and ours because His—is the operation of the Holy Spirit in His human nature. Therefore we may speak of life in the Body as Christ living in us, or the Holy Spirit living in us. Our Lord speaks of both in-livings, and so does St Paul. In one passage (Rom. 8: 9–11) he has them both—'Christ lives in you', 'the Spirit dwells in you', 'a man *cannot* belong to Christ unless he has the Spirit of Christ'. Just as both live in us, both operate in us: 'All this is the work of one and the same Spirit' (1 Cor. 12: 11): 'So effectually does His [Christ's] power manifest itself in me.'

It is because of the indwelling and operation of the Holy Spirit in Christ Our Lord that we cannot be incorporated in Christ without having the same indwelling and operation. 'Your bodies belong to the body of Christ', says St Paul (1 Cor. 6: 15), and a few verses later, 'Your bodies are the shrines of the Holy Spirit'.

For this twofold presence, the Church has found various phrases: Christ is the Source, the Holy Spirit the operative principle: Christ is the Head of the Body, the Holy Spirit the Soul. There is one lovely variant of this last phrase used by St Thomas and again by Pope Leo XIII (*Divinum illud munus*): the Holy Spirit is the Heart. (8)

## Sanctifying Grace

Everything hangs on this, that sanctifying grace is a real transformation of the soul. Where Luther taught that the soul in grace is wearing the garment of Christ's merits, the Church teaches that the very substance of the soul is renewed, the soul is affected in its very being, so that it may well be called a new creation: it has a new life in it, a life with its own vital 'organs' and operations, so that it can now perform actions at the level of its new being, actions which because they are supernatural can merit a supernatural reward. Thus it is that St Paul speaks of us as 'in Christ a new creature' (2 Cor. 5: 17), 'the new man, who according to God is created in justice and holiness of truth'.

Yet it remains the same soul, with the same faculties: soul and faculties are not destroyed that some new thing may take their place, but elevated to a new level of life and the operations that go with it. Grace does not destroy nature, but is built into it, and from within elevates it. The intellect has the new power of faith, the will the new powers of hope and charity. The point is so important that one must take the risk of labouring it. A rough analogy may help: the wire in an electric light bulb, when connected with the battery, is luminous, so much so that, looking at it, we seem to see only light, and no wire, and might be tempted to think that the wire was gone, and that the light had taken its place. But it is the same wire, only luminous. And if the connection with the source of power be broken, we see that it is the same wire. The soul in grace is luminous, but it does not cease to be the soul.

With what is the soul luminous? With Sanctifying Grace; with the Theological Virtues, Faith, Hope, and Charity; with the Moral Virtues, Prudence, Justice, Temperance, Fortitude; with the Gifts of the Holy Ghost, Knowledge, Understanding, Wisdom, Counsel, Fortitude, Piety, and Fear of the Lord...(9)

## Heaven

Scripture tells us three things very clearly: (1) The happiness of Heaven is perfect—broken by no present sorrow and no fear of future ceasing. It is happiness of the whole being, the soul's every power acting at its very highest. (2) The happiness of Heaven is indescribable and unimaginable. 'Eye hath not seen, nor hath ear heard, nor hath it entered into the heart of man what things God hath prepared for them that love Him' (1 Cor. 2: 9). The language made by man from his experiences of this life has no power to convey the experiences of the next. The pictures of joy built by our imagination, fed upon the joys of this life, are poor shadows of the joy of Heaven.

(3) But if by imagination we can take no grip on Heaven's happiness, by the faculty of intellect—acting upon the Revelation of God—we can know something of it. In Heaven we shall see God 'face to face'; we shall 'know as we are known', so says Scripture (1 Cor. 13: 12). Which means that we shall know God, not, as we know things here below, by an idea in the mind, but direct, God Himself present in our very soul and realized by us as present, realized at the very highest point of intensity. This is what theology calls the Beatific Vision. 'We shall be made like to Him,' says St John, 'for we shall see Him as He is' (1 John 3: 2)...

So much for the essential of Heaven—the direct apprehension of the Blessed Trinity. Bound up with that is a fellowship with all the other citizens of Heaven; fellowship with Christ Our Lord—the Second Person of the Trinity made man—with His Mother, with the angels and saints. So that Heaven is not only our relationship with God come to maturity, but also our relationship with all the lovers of God—with all created beings, that is, who have achieved the purpose for which God made them. (10)

NOTES AND SOURCES

1. Frank Joseph Sheed, *Theology and Sanity* (London: Sheed & Ward, 1948), 3.
2. Frank Joseph Sheed, *A Map of Life: A Simple Study of the Catholic Faith* (London: Sheed & Ward, 1933), 77 f.
3. Sheed, *Theology and Sanity*, 87–9.
4. Ibid. 140–1.
5. Ibid. 169–70.
6. Ibid. 190.
7. Sheed, *A Map of Life*, 65–6.
8. Sheed, *Theology and Sanity*, 225–8.
9. Ibid. 295–6.
10. Sheed, *A Map of Life*, 140–2.

# Cecily Hallack

1898–1938

Cecily Hallack was a tall, beautiful woman, vivacious and outward-going, whose good humour and generosity were undiminished by lifelong financial worries and increasingly poor health. The daughter of a Congregationalist minister, she was received into the Church at the age of 20, and not long afterwards became a Franciscan tertiary. She wrote prolifically—novels, short stories, poetry, and books for children. Her greatest work is *Adventure of the Amethyst*, at once a children's novel and an adult essay in apologetics. It tells the story of the Lovell children, who meet an elderly, wheelchair-bound bishop, 'Monseigneur', who with immense gentleness and prudence introduces them, step by step, to the Catholic religion, and helps dispose them for receiving the gift of faith. In her final years Cecily Hallack lived in a house in Sussex provided for her by the monks of Downside. She died of a brain tumour, and is buried in the cemetery of the Observant Franciscans in Crawley.

## Ready for Anything: The Sacrament of Confirmation and the Gifts of the Holy Spirit

Monseigneur instructed them for Confirmation and gave them that new Sacrament before they went to school. They did not need much instruction, because they knew it was the Sacrament in which they received the Gifts of the Holy Ghost, so that they would be ready to stand up for their faith against the world.

'Confirmation enlists you in the Regular Army of the Church', said Monseigneur. 'I don't say you wouldn't fight for the Faith now, just as any brave and loyal person would fight for their home if it was attacked. But Confirmation enrols you as a regular and gives you your supernatural equipment.'

He told them that the Sacrament of Confirmation was given with chrism, and that they could remember how the Roman soldiers used to rub themselves with oil to make them supple and quick in moving, and also difficult for the enemy to catch hold of. The chrism of Confirmation would make them quick to avoid sin, and in fighting it, and hard for the devil to hold, even for a moment.

And he said that it equipped them with the virtues which were the special Gifts of the Holy Ghost—Wisdom, Understanding, Counsel, Fortitude, Knowledge, Piety, and the Fear of the Lord.

'Not', he said, 'that you will know how to act with them straightaway, any more than a raw recruit knows how to handle his sword the moment he is invested with it. But that you have them if you will begin to practise using them.'

'What is the difference between, Wisdom, Understanding, Counsel, and Knowledge, sir?' asked Hugh.

'Wisdom', Monseigneur said, 'is an illumination of the Holy Ghost which shows revealed truths to us in all their grandeur to the greater joy of our souls. You may know there are mountains in Switzerland, but if you, when you go to look at them, can see them by the light of dawn or sunset or moonlight, it makes a lot of difference. You can't understand how tremendous they are until you see them in the best of light. Understanding explains itself. It brings us to see better *why* God's laws are to be trusted and obeyed, because it gives us the light to see how good God is. Counsel means showing us *how* to do right in everyday life. And Knowledge...well, haven't you sometimes felt, when you heard something explained, about God and the spiritual world, that you had always known it? We knew it by a bit of knowledge that grace hid in our soul, ready to recognize that truth when we heard it. But in Confirmation God gives us a kind of instinctive knowledge of anything we shall need to know in our warfare in the world. So that when we have no one to tell us what to do, if we simply try and think what would be right to do, we shall know right from wrong.'

'Fortitude is what I have always wanted to have,' said Rose. 'I used to try to be brave, but I always knew I got frightened. Now when I have to be brave, I shall know I have got fortitude.'

'That's the way,' said Monseigneur. (1)

## After Communion

Jesus, my God, you are here safe in my heart. Mother Mary and all the angels and saints are adoring you there. I know that hearing Holy Mass and receiving you in Communion is the greatest thing I can possibly do to please you and to help the whole world.

Now I am closer to you than little St John the Baptist was when he played with you.

Dear God, my Father in Heaven, the Holy Ghost is making me full of love and thanks to you. He is offering to you from my heart your beloved Son Jesus.

With Jesus there, my heart is a little heaven. (2)

NOTES AND SOURCES

1. Cecily Hallack, *Adventure of the Amethyst* (London: Macmillan, 1937), 329–31.

2. Cecily Hallack, *The Small Person's Confession and Communion Book* (London: Macmillan, 1934), 20.

# Frances Caryll Houselander                    1901–1954

Caryll Houselander was a Catholic, not from the cradle or by adult conversion, but, as she liked to say, from her 'rocking-horse': she was received into the Church at the age of 6, when a family friend encouraged her mother to have the children brought up as Catholics. Her education was nothing if not ecumenical: a Jewish kindergarten followed by schools run by nuns, Protestants, and the state. For a number of years she fell away from the practice of her faith and explored other religious traditions, including Russian Orthodoxy. In this same period, she fell in love with Sidney Reilly, the fighter pilot and British spy, who was executed by the Soviets in 1925. Having trained at art colleges, she worked as a book illustrator and interior designer, and, for a church furnishing firm, as a carver of crib figures and Stations of the Cross. From 1942, because of her insights into the conflicts of the human soul and her own long history of mental suffering, doctors began to send her their patients for psychotherapy, an experience that led to the writing of her book, *Guilt*. Dr Eric Strauss, the psychiatrist and neurologist, said of her work with disturbed children that 'she loved them back to life'. She wrote poetry, a novel, and books of children's stories. Her chief contribution to the spiritual tradition of Catholic England was her series of short works of spirituality. Though her writing career spanned only ten years of her life, the profundity of her theological perception, expressed in language at once homely and poetic, places her high in the canon of English Catholic writing. 'She seemed', said Monsignor Knox, 'to see everything for the first time, and the driest of doctrinal considerations shone out like a restored picture when she had finished with it'.

## The Rest of the Infant Jesus

The Infant Christ is the whole Christ. Christ was not more God, more Christ, more man, on the Cross than He was in His Mother's womb. His first tear, His first smile, His first breath, His first pulsation in the womb of His Mother, could have redeemed the world.

In fact, Christ chose the life of growth and work and suffering and the death on the Cross which we know, but, by His own choice, all this was to depend on a human being giving herself to Him in His infancy, giving her own humanity to the actual making of that infant's humanity and giving Him her life in which to rest.

If all in whom Christ lives at all, in whom He is an infant—which means anyone whose soul is alive at all—surrendered themselves to Him, resting in Him, that He might rest in them, in each one of them the world's redemption would begin as it began in Mary, the Mother of God.

Christ is formed in us and we are formed into Christ when we rest in Him and He rests in us.

In Advent Christ rested in Mary—still, silent, helpless, utterly dependent. The Creator trusted Himself to His creature.

He trusted the expression of His love to her, the expression of God's love for the world, and of His love of His Father. Just as the work of His love would be trusted to us, in His life in us.

He was dumb, her voice was His voice. He was still, her footsteps were His journeys. He was blind, her eyes were His seeing. His hands were folded, her hands did the work of His hands. His life was her life, His heart beat was the beating of her heart.

This was a foreshadowing of what the Incarnation would mean for us; for in us too, Christ rests as He rested in Mary. From the moment when the Christ life is conceived in us, our life is intended for one thing, the expression of His love, His love for God and for the world. Our words are to be the words that He wants to speak, we must go wherever He wants to go, we must see and look at whatever He wants to see and look at, the work that our hands do must be the work that His hands want to do, our life the living of His life, our loves the loving of His heart.

But there is the other aspect of this Advent of Christ's. While He remained hidden in Mary, His rest was a tremendous activity, He was making her into Himself, making Himself from her; from her eyes He was making the eyes that would weep over Jerusalem, that would shine upon the wild flowers, that would close in death and open in the morning of Resurrection. From her hands He was making the hands that would heal and raise the dead and be nailed to the Cross. From her heart He was making the Heart whose love would redeem the world.

The same thing happens when, allowing the Infant Christ to rest in us, we wait patiently on His own timing of His growth in us, and give Him just what He asks, the extremely simple things that are ourselves, our hands and feet, our eyes and ears, our words, our thoughts, our love. Not only does He grow in us, but we are formed into Him. (1)

## Jesus in the Womb, Jesus in the Host

By His own will Christ was dependent on Mary during Advent: He was absolutely helpless; He could go nowhere but where she chose to take Him; He could not speak; her breathing was His breath; His heart beat in the beating of her heart.

Today Christ is dependent upon men. In the Host He is literally put into a man's hands. A man must carry Him to the dying, must take Him into the prisons, workhouses, and hospitals, must carry Him in a tiny pyx over the heart on to the field of battle, must give Him to little children and 'lay Him by' in His 'leaflight' house of gold.

The modern world's feverish struggle for unbridled, often unlicensed, freedom is answered by the bound, enclosed helplessness and dependence of Christ— Christ in the womb, Christ in the Host, Christ in the Tomb. (2)

## Herod's Fear of the Child and St Thérèse's Little Way

Herod ordered the children to be killed because he was afraid that any one of them might be Christ.

Any child might be Christ!—the fear of Herod is the fear of every tyrant, the hope of every Christian, and the most significant fact in the modern world.

Any child might be Christ; yes, and Herod in his attempt to destroy that one Child, to eradicate the threat of the Infant from his nation, baptized a host of children in their own blood and made a legion of little 'Christs', who should come unseen with heavenly weapons, flocking to the tattered and blood-soaked standard of innocence through all the ages of mankind.

What processions of little children the Holy Innocents, and with them the Guardian Angels, have followed across the world in our own times, and are following now! from the day when, thirty years ago, Russian children were driven before the Red Army, to be tossed alive into open graves in the steppes, until now.

From Czechoslovakia, France, Belgium, Holland, Java, Korea, Greece, Poland, Estonia, Latvia, Lithuania, Rumania, Bulgaria, Albania, China, Finland, Hungary, Austria, Serbia, Croatia, Slovenia, Bosnia, Montenegro, and Macedonia, children have been persecuted and driven out or killed by tyrants, who, whether they bear the name of one ideology or another, can equally be identified with Herod.

Who can doubt that the angels and Innocents meet these little victims of the Godless to speed their way to God?

And on earth, the answer to Herod is still the Incarnation; still the Birth of the Infant Christ, the life of the world in the least and the littlest.

The characteristic of modern sanctity crystallizes the answer of Christ to Herod now. It is the sanctity of spiritual childhood, that sanctity which St Teresa [Thérèse] of Lisieux has defined—holiness that means becoming a child, not just any child, but the Christ-child.

That which St Teresa calls her 'little way' has set fire to and illuminated the world: it has entered into millions of homes. It is a flame of love blown on the great wind of the Spirit, but one which has kindled many very humble little fires. It burns in the hearth of poor homes, in the mercy of nightlights in the rooms of sleeping children, in the lamp set for a welcome in the cottage window. It is both the Star of Bethlehem and a candle in the hand of love. The Spirit has borne it and bears it still, not only on the mighty wind, but on the zephyr that carries the warm sunlight and the smell of wild flowers gently through the rooms of the house.

It is the light that illumines where reason stops short, and the breath that blows the smoking flax to flame.

Yet it is a mystery, almost a miracle, that the present-day world should have responded—more, surrendered—to that young French nun. For she is, or rather seems to be, what most people, and especially most English people, dislike. She was sentimental, so much so that some have asked whether she may be an outlet for the inhibited sentimentality that is a symptom of one of the several epidemic psychological diseases of this age.

The exaggerated repudiation of sentimentality does not cover the depth of feeling that its votaries pretend that it does; on the contrary, it is a pitifully transparent symptom of emotional impotence. Impotence of the deep and tender feeling which not only gives grace and poetry to life but gives balance to the whole personality.

Not only are there many psychologically sick people who can only suffer and even only love vicariously through theatres and books, but there are many more who, while repudiating sentimentality with tell-tale violence, will flock to see child prodigies on the films in order to obtain the faintly sickening solace of tears, produced by synthetic sentimentality. In many people that sap which drives the tender green shoot into the light and causes the dry wood to blossom has dried up.

Could there be such an explanation for the world-wide acceptance of 'The Little Flower of Jesus' and her shower of roses?

I think not; because these roses grow out of the dark and bitter wood of the Cross.

St Teresa expressed herself in a way which belittled her own greatness. Her constant reiteration of the word 'little', her indiscriminate scattering of sugary adjectives all over her autobiography, hides the bones of suffering that she is really speaking about, like a pretty printed cloth thrown over a skeleton.

Consequently, many think that her 'little way' means her 'easy way' and so miss the whole point of her message.

She did not teach the way of Spiritual Childishness, but of Spiritual Childhood. She did not simply become a child, but a Christ-child, the child of God, whose suffering is the suffering of the Cross, whose love is the love of the Cross.

Her own life was neither easy nor ordinary; it had the quality of iron. She suffered to the limit in mind and body and spirit. She suffered beyond the pitch of human endurance from the exploitation of her unselfishness; she knew as much as that other Carmelite, St John of the Cross, of the dark night of the soul, and far less of sweetness than he. She knew the desolation of Christ's cry on the Cross: 'My God, my God, why hast thou forsaken me?'

She did not value her extraordinary sufferings more than her ordinary ones; she estimated the minute irritating things of every day as being of equal value to the tragic things in her life. She knew that the nervous irritability of an exhausted body, tortured by the rattling of a rosary in the silence, had the same kind of power to redeem as the pains of her death.

No one has ever realized the value of little things as she did; for no one has ever realized more that the Christ-Child suffered in her, and that the Christ-Child can suffer nothing that is not in the redeeming Passion of Infinite Love.

It is this sentimental, passionate little nun, St Teresa of Lisieux, who, in her own life, has defined the sanctity of today, the answer to the Herods of today: it is the sanctity of Spiritual Childhood.

To overcome the world we must become children. To become children we must fold our consciousness upon the Divine Infant who is the centre of our being; who is our being itself; and all that we are must be absorbed in Him; whatever remains of self must be the cradle in which He lies. This is the answer to Herod in all times, the answer of St Teresa of Lisieux in our time: 'the Little Way of Spiritual Childhood', which is the oneing of the soul with God, in the Passion of the Infant Christ. (3)

## The Fear of Death

The fear [of death for those dear to us and ourselves] does not show any want of faith; faith does not ask of us to be inhuman. Our Lord experienced all the fears you are experiencing, in the Agony in the Garden; moreover He showed, by weeping in public, extreme grief over death, even in the case of Lazarus, whom He was about to raise from the dead. He never rebuked anyone for mourning over the dead; on the contrary, He was so moved by their grief that He several times restored the dead to life—the daughter of Jairus, the widow's son, etc—from sheer compassion.

From this fact one may learn that first of all there is not the least imperfection or want of faith in the feeling of fear in this way, or in shrinking from these things. Actually, since pain and death are both primarily results of sin, there is something essentially right in hating and fearing them in themselves. But a second deduction from what I have said above about Our Lord is that His compassion is such that if He can spare us these sufferings, even by a miracle, He will; and from this, yet another, and the most important conclusion of all: namely, God (for Christ is God)—God will never allow any pain or illness or death for anyone, *unless* it is essential and necessary for our ultimate joy: unless, because of the multitudinous circumstances of our life, known only to God (not known to anyone else, even ourselves), this particular suffering has become the *only* way through which we can arrive at ultimate lasting happiness.

So we can pray with great confidence because we *know* that God Himself *wants* to spare us; and if He can, without taking away our final happiness, He will.

I think it is very helpful to reflect that God loves those whom we love, far *more* than we do—infinitely more. We love at all only because our hearts dimly reflect His. We know and realize a fragment of what goes on in the hearts of our nearest and dearest: God knows every nerve and fibre.

I have personally found it helpful to accept fear, to say, 'Yes, I am afraid: for as long as this suspense (or whatever it is) lasts, I *shall* be afraid. I accept it as perfectly just and right.' Some people might not be helped by this thought, but I have been, profoundly and often, myself...

There is no want of faith in fear of death—in fact, it is right to fear it and shrink from it, since death has come into the world through sin. It is against nature and against God's will; the instinctive shrinking from it which all healthy-minded people feel, is right and goes to prove how we all are really made in the image of God. It is also part of our redemption to fear it is. It *is* a punishment. But the fear can gradually be tempered by hope, and reduced as we grow in Christhood and in love for God, because Christ, by surrendering Himself in His human nature to death, has made it not only a punishment but a doorway to life. Also, *He* has already died your death and overcome it!

On the purely natural plane, fear of death usually shows natural vitality and health. As we get weaker and iller, we fear it less and less, and hundreds of doctors, priests, and nurses testify the fact that death, when it comes, is nearly *always*, merciful and easy. For a Catholic, the Holy Viaticum brings Our Lord Himself to help and make it easier still, and sheer physical weakness helps!

But no amount of reasoning helps about this fear, I know. Like all the rest, the best is to accept it.

God is showing you a very great favour in giving you such big suffering for His children. I am sure you are among those chosen few who are being asked to reach out invisibly to all those who are in such bitter need of spiritual help today—and this is so *much* more than any specific little good work or 'Catholic Action' you could do.

Accept it all as Our Lord did His own Passion in Gethsemane. He experienced all this fear, asked to be let off, and when He wasn't He surrendered every fibre of His being to God's will. Repeat *His* prayer, in His power, in the power of His *risen* love, which is yours if you choose to use it: 'Not my will—but thine.'

Of course I realize how heroic all this sounds and what a *lot* it asks of your poor human nature, but in it is the seed of peace: and do not forget that, in our Christ-life as in His historical life, the Resurrection *must* follow swiftly on the Crucifixion. (4)

## Christ in Us

The meaning of the Mystical Body of Christ is that Christ lives in all Christians. The practical result of this, for us, is that now on earth the whole of Christ's life is always being lived; the things that happened to Him on earth are happening to Him now in His members. The things that He did on earth He is doing now through us....

Only Our Lady has ever lived all the aspects and phases and moments completely.

In some He is newly born.

In some He is a child.

In some He is homeless.

In some He is ignored, unrecognized, mocked, betrayed.

In some He is hungry; in some He is naked; in some He is helpless....

He remains being tempted in all those who are tempted: in those who are in mortal sin, He is in the tomb.

We should never come to a sinner without the reverence that we would take to the Holy Sepulchre.

Pilgrims have travelled on foot for years to kiss the Holy Sepulchre, which is empty. In sinners we can kneel at the tomb in which the dead Christ lies.

Christ is in Gethsemane in all those who are crushed by fear, by shame, by the sense of guilt, by the neurotic type of scruple, by the sensitive awareness of the tragedy of the world and of sin as its cause. He is present in all those who are afraid of the sacrifice asked of them and who seek help and sympathy and the prayers of others.

The incidents of His life are reproduced over and over again in innumerable ways. (5)

## This War is the Passion

For us, the war is the Passion of Christ. There is no need now to dwell on its cruelty; we shall not be able to forget that. To the natural eye it seems that out of this war nothing could possibly result but bitterness, hatred, and ruin, and indeed nothing else could result from it were it not for one person—Jesus Christ, Our Lord.

Because He has made us 'other Christs', because His life continues in each one of us, there is nothing that any one of us can suffer which is not the Passion He suffered. Our redemption, though it was achieved completely by Our Lord, does, by a special loving mercy of His, go on in us. It is one unbroken act which goes on in the Mystical Body of Christ on earth, which we are. (6)

NOTES AND SOURCES

1. Caryll Houselander, *The Passion of the Infant Christ* (London: Sheed & Ward, 1949), 21–3.

2. Caryll Houselander, *The Reed of God* (London: Sheed & Ward, 1945), 31.

3. Houselander, *The Passion of the Infant Christ*, 89–93.

4. Caryll Houselander, *The Letters of Caryll Houselander: Her Spiritual Legacy* (New York: Sheed & Ward, 1965), 166–7, 178–9.

5. Houselander, *The Reed of God*, 104, 114, 115–16.

6. Caryll Houselander, *This War is the Passion* (London: Sheed & Ward, 1945), 1.

# William Abel Pantin                    1902–1973

Billy Pantin is remembered as one of the most learned and most lovable Oxford dons of recent times. Born into a family of scholars, he was educated at Westminster and Christ

Church, took a first in Modern History, and held a lectureship at Manchester before returning to Oxford as Fellow and Tutor in Modern History at Oriel. For much of the Second World War he was the only fellow in residence, and more or less ran the college. In 1946 he was appointed Keeper of the University Archives at the Bodleian Library. He became a Catholic while still at school, and brought his faith, piety, and scholarly interest in Benedictine monasticism together when he was made a *confrater* at Ampleforth. Later in life he became absorbed in the history of the Benedictine colleges of Oxford. His rooms, with floors, tables, and chairs as well as walls covered with books and maps, became, said the *Times* in its obituary, 'an academic peepshow'. It concluded: 'The mixture of freshness and informality with erudition, which made him a successful tutor and lecturer, came out in his conversation. He was a charming host, an apt and witty after-dinner speaker, and a good colleague.'

## The Catholic England of the Middle Ages

The thing that strikes me most about the Catholic England of the Middle Ages is that it contrived to be so intensely English and so intensely Catholic at the same time. That is a very important point; it is, in the first place, an antidote or answer to that exaggerated, exclusive nationalism and racialism that the Holy Father [Pope Pius XI] condemns every day. We may not, here in England, be in much danger of adopting these extreme forms of this doctrine . . . But I think there are a good many people who, consciously or unconsciously, are prejudiced against the Church by the idea that to be a Catholic is not quite compatible with being a real Englishman. They seem to think that because a man is in communion with the Apostolic See, he becomes a kind of spiritual alien. And they imply that everything that is best in the English character and civilization and constitution dates from the break with Rome. The answer to that is to look at medieval England. England—for there really was an England then, not just a portion of Great Britain—was most English when she was most Catholic, when she was most part of an international religion and culture. Grace does not destroy nature, it makes the most of it. *Non eripit mortalia, qui regna dat coelestia.* And in spite of centuries of schism and growing unbelief, I believe that English civilization is still based in its Catholic past . . . remember that to be Catholic is to be normal, the normal condition of civilized man in general and of Englishmen in particular. (1)

## Catholic Canterbury: The Pre-Conquest Saints

The conversion of the Anglo-Saxons was a contrast to the conversion of the Roman empire, for it was in its early stages remarkably bloodless; when trouble came, it was from pagan reaction in the North or pagan invasions. That is why the great founders and builders of the Anglo-Saxon Church were confessors, men like St Augustine, St Theodore, St Dunstan, the saints of Canterbury in fact, who do in this way represent the quintessence of medieval English sanctity. There were martyrs, but they were mostly of a different type, either, on the one hand, those produced for export, so to speak, like the English apostles of Germany and Scandinavia, or else belonging to that remarkable type, the martyr kings, who are so characteristic of early English hagiology.

There are a surprising number of these martyr kings: St Oswald and St Edwin of Northumbria, victims of Penda, the pagan king of Mercia; St Edmund of East

Anglia, of course, the victim of the Danish invaders; and a large number, it must be admitted, who were the victims of the treachery or rivalry of their fellow Christians: St Oswin and St Alkmund of Northumbria, St Kenelm and St Wistan of Mercia, St Ethelbert of East Anglia, St Edward in Wessex, the princes St Ethelbert and St Ethelred in Kent. Perhaps in some of these cults we can see the same admiring pity or sense of pathos for a tragic end, which later led to the attempted canonization of Simon de Montfort, Henry VI, and even of Edward II and Thomas of Lancaster. (2)

## Catholic Canterbury: The Daughter of Rome

Canterbury, being a direct colony of the Roman Church, is in a remarkable way a conscious imitation of Rome, a 'new Rome' of the North. The Roman missionaries, St Augustine and his companions, seem to have done their best to reproduce what they were familiar with at Rome, here at Canterbury, in the arrangement and dedication of the churches, and so forth... At Rome the Pope's cathedral church inside the walls is the basilica of St Saviour, commonly called St John Lateran; at Canterbury, too, the cathedral inside the Roman walls is the basilica of St Saviour, commonly called Christ Church. At Rome, outside the walls, are the tombs and basilicas of the two Apostles, St Peter's at the Vatican, and St Paul's; at Canterbury, outside the walls is the monastery of St Peter and St Paul, later known as St Augustine's. At Rome, and therefore at Canterbury, burial within the walls is forbidden; the first Archbishops of Canterbury are buried outside the walls, in the monastery of St Peter and St Paul, which thus, like its Roman prototypes, comes to have the tombs of its own apostles, St Augustine and the rest. In the same monastery and its cemetery are buried also abbots and members of the Kentish royal family. St Ethelbert is the Kentish Constantine, retiring gracefully from the royal city to make room for the church. At Canterbury, the Roman models are necessarily simplified and telescoped into one; the single monastery of St Peter and St Paul, with its cemetery beside the Roman road to Sandwich, has to stand for both the Roman basilicas of the two Apostles, and for all the cemeteries that line the roads outside Rome. (3)

## Catholic Canterbury: The Communion of Saints in a Charter

The twelfth century brought two new saints of the greatest importance, St Anselm and St Thomas, and the fame and miracles of St Thomas drew pilgrims from everywhere. A process of centralization can be seen at work, in pilgrimages as in everything else; a few great pilgrimages of international reputation seem to take the place of the innumerable local cults that we see in the *Notationes de sanctis*... But it must not be thought that St Thomas drove out the older cults at Canterbury. Each time a monk of Christ Church entered the choir for Matins or left it after Compline, he had to make a visit to the shrines of St Dunstan and St Alfege that stood on each side of the high altar. The devotion to these saints takes a very quaint form in one Canterbury charter, which gives as its list of witnesses: 'Our Lord Jesus Christ and St Mary Ever-Virgin, and St Thomas the Martyr, and St Dunstan and St Alfege, and all the saints of our Church, and

Robert the porter, and Martin the seneschal, and Gilbert of the hall…and many others'. (4)

NOTES AND SOURCES

1. William Pantin, speech at the Catholic Truth Society Congress, Brighton 1938, cited in Conrad Pepler OP, *The English Religious Heritage* (London: Blackfriars, 1958), 11–12.

2. William Pantin, 'The Pre-Conquest Saints of Canterbury', in *For Hilaire Belloc: Essays in Honour of his 72nd Birthday* (London: Sheed & Ward, 1942), 148–9.

3. Ibid. 151.

4. Ibid. 168–9.

# Archbishop David James Mathew 1902–1975

Visitors to Oxford in the 1960s and 70s often encountered Archbishop David Mathew and his brother, Father Gervase OP, walking arm in arm down the Broad, each in a clerical dress that was as sensationally dishevelled as it was traditionally correct. Those years, spent with Lord and Lady Camoys at Stonor, were the last chapter of a life of extreme diversity, which had included service as a midshipman in the Great War, history at Balliol, studies for the priesthood at the Beda, ordination on patrimony, a curacy in Cardiff docks, a chaplaincy in London, auxiliary episcopate in wartime Westminster, diplomacy for the Holy See in Africa, military episcopate out of Aldershot, and work on the preparatory commission for Vatican II. Somehow, amidst all his practical duties, David Mathew was able to publish many works of historical scholarship, all of them spiced with deadpan humour. His Requiem was sung in Westminster Cathedral, and he is buried at Downside. As Fr Fergus Kerr OP has said, the eccentricity of the two brothers could be disconcerting to some, 'but many others found in their love for one another, and in the absolute simplicity of their religion, a touchstone of fidelity'.

## The Martyrdom of St John Fisher

It was on the Thursday after *Dominica in Albis* [Low Sunday], in that Eastertide of 1534, that he was brought down to the Tower. Through this week in the liturgical calm of the Paschal season, the proper of the Mass had remained unchanging. 'And there are three that give testimony on earth,' the meaning would come to him as his failing eyes peered towards the missal with the Lady Margaret's portcullis on the cover, 'the Spirit and the Water and the Blood'. How strongly would the Epistle sound forth as a demand and a warning. *Et tres sunt qui testimonium dant in terra: spiritus et aqua et sanguis.* It was a not unfitting prelude to the leadership of the white-robed army, *te martyrum candidatus*. As the gates of the Tower of London closed behind him, the bishop had marked out his future. The imprisonment lasted for a year, and finally, on 22 June 1535, the Bishop of Rochester was put to death for his refusal to accept the Royal Supremacy, and for his statement that 'the king our sovereign Lord is not supreme head in earth of the Church of England'. In the previous month he had received the title of Cardinal Priest of the church of St Vitalis, so that Peter's approval sealed his action. He died that the English provinces might still remain within the unity of Catholic faith…

The details of his last hours show again the workings of a life's simplicity. 'The twenty-second day of June next following,' so runs the Rastell fragment, 'about five o'clock in the morning, the Lieutenant of the Tower came to this holy man in his bed asleep and waked him and showed him . . . that the king's pleasure was that he should suffer in that forenoon. "Well," quoth the bishop, "if this be your errand hither, it is no news unto me; I have looked daily for it. I pray you what is it o'clock?" "It is", quoth the Lieutenant, "about five." "What time", quoth the bishop, "must be mine hour to go out hence?" "About ten of the clock," said the Lieutenant. "Well, then," quoth the bishop, "I pray you, let me sleep an hour or twine. For I may say to you, I slept not much this night, not for fear of death, I tell you, but by reason of my great sickness and weakness." With which answer, the Lieutenant departed from him till about nine o'clock, at which time he came again to the bishop's chamber, and found him upward, putting on of his clothes, and showed him that he was come for him. "Well," quoth the bishop, "I will make as convenient haste as my weak and sickly aged body will give me leave. And, I pray you, reach me there my furred tippet to put about my neck." "Oh, my Lord," quoth the Lieutenant to him, "what need you to be now so careful of your health? Your time is very short, little more than half an hour." "I think none otherwise," quoth the bishop, "but, I pray you, yet give me leave to put on my furred tippet, to keep me warm for the while until the very time of execution, for I tell you truth, though I have, I thank Our Lord, a very good stomach and willing mind to die at this present, and I trust in His goodness and mercy He will still continue it and increase it, yet will I not hinder my health in the meantime not a minute of an hour, but will preserve it in the mean season with all such discrete ways and means as almighty God of His gracious goodness hath provided for me." Then was he carried down out of his chamber between twain in a chair, and so to the Tower gate.'

The next passage appears in the early English life, attributed to Richard Hall, and therefore has only such authority as that work will carry. 'But as he was mounting up the stairs,' so runs this extract, 'the southeast sun shined very bright in his face, whereupon he said to himself these words, lifting up his hands, *Accedite ad eum et illuminamini et facies vestrae non confundentur* ['Come ye to Him and be enlightened, and your faces shall not be confounded', Ps. 33: 6]. How significant are these words, 'Come ye to Him and be enlightened'. But for the last words on the scaffold we have an eye-witness's authority: 'Then spake he . . . in effect as follows,' the Rastell fragment continues, 'Christian people, I am come hither to die for the faith of Christ's Catholic Church.'

A carol, very familiar to the thought of Bishop Fisher's time, reflects in dawn-clear phrases the England and the cause for which he died. In the first reference to Our Lord the intimate religion of the little shrines and churches lies revealed:

> For in this rose contained was
> Heaven and earth in little space,
> *Res miranda.*

The miracle of the Incarnation is suggested, the nearness of Bethlehem, the lowing cattle, God's presence in tranquillity in the fields. And then the last couplet brings to mind the spirit of the bishop's martyrdom.

> Leave we all this worldly mirth,
> And follow we this joyful birth.
> *Transeamus.* (1)

## The Restoration of the Hierarchy

On 29 September 1850, Pope Pius IX restored the English hierarchy by the Letters Apostolic, *Universalis Ecclesiae*, and erected one metropolitan see [Westminster] and twelve suffragan bishoprics [Beverley, Birmingham, Clifton, Hexham, Liverpool, Newport and Menevia, Northampton, Nottingham, Plymouth, Salford, Shrewsbury, and Southwark]. Nicholas Wiseman became Cardinal priest of the title of Santa Pudentiana and Archbishop of Westminster.

His return from Rome was leisurely and splendid, as his cardinalitial carriage with the arms on the panels rolled from the States of the Church into Tuscany; to Florence, where the footmen met His Eminence with torches; then through the Lombard plain and into the Austrian dominions. It was at Vienna that he first saw the *Times* leader which dealt with the appointment. His letter from the Flaminian Gate of Rome had been published in England before he was aware of the storm which the restoration of the hierarchy had aroused. Its rich and enthusiastic phrasing, while angering the Protestants beyond measure, caused disquiet among the reserved, tenacious, careful Catholics of the older school. In London there were public demonstrations, and effigies of the new Cardinal were burned in the streets. Lord John Russell, the Prime Minister, took up the agitation, naturally determined that capital should not be made out of this event by the opposition. The Cardinal's immediate return, and the publication of *The Appeal to the English People* did much to restore the situation. In this letter his apostolic charity for his own flock, and especially for the poor, was shown clearly in all the capably worded and coloured writing.

The Duke of Norfolk supported the public agitation, while his eldest son, Lord Arundel and Surrey, the friend of Montalembert and Faber, came forward in the Lower House in defence of the Cardinal. Another Catholic peer protested against 'this edict of the Court of Rome', and in 1851 the Ecclesiastical Titles Bill was passed. This measure imposed a fine of £100 upon any Catholic bishop who assumed the title of a territorial see. It remained a dead letter, and was repealed some twenty years later.

The indignation subsided rapidly, and public interest faded. A considerable section of opinion...had always viewed the matter calmly, and had deplored the introduction of the Bill. The stream of converts flowed again after the Gorham Judgement, and the new hierarchy held their first synod at Birmingham in 1852. (2)

NOTES AND SOURCES

1. David Mathew, 'Blessed John Fisher', in Maisie Ward (ed.), *The English Way: Studies in English Sanctity from St Bede to Newman* (London: Sheed & Ward, 1933), 205–8.
2. David Mathew, *Catholicism in England, 1535–1935: Portrait of a Minority—Its Culture and Tradition*, new edn. (London: Catholic Book Club, 1938), 197–8.

# Evelyn Arthur St John Waugh                    1903–1966

Evelyn Waugh liked to say that his family's 'trade' was literature: his father, Arthur, worked as a publisher, and his older brother, Alec, was a novelist. At Lancing, despite a feeling of having been abandoned to an unfashionable school without family associations, he learnt to draw and paint, excelled as a debater, edited the school magazine, and won a history scholarship to Hertford College, Oxford. There he fell in with a set of brilliant Etonians and plunged into a life of pleasure. He left Oxford with huge debts, a third class degree, and a firm resolve to 'draw, decorate, design, and illustrate'. He tried art school and schoolmastering before finally entering the family trade with a biography of *Rossetti* and his first novel, *Decline and Fall* (1928), which received enthusiastic reviews in the press. He married Evelyn Gardner in 1929, but, following her adultery, divorced her in 1930. On Michaelmas Day, the same year, Father Martin D'Arcy SJ received him into the Catholic Church. His novels of this period, *Vile Bodies* (1930) and *A Handful of Dust* (1934), satirize the nihilism of a society that rejects Christianity and lives only to gratify the senses. In the 1930s he wrote travel books and worked abroad for the papers, reporting on Hailie Selassie's coronation for *The Times* and the Italian invasion of Abyssinia for the *Daily Mail*. His biography of *Edmund Campion*, which appeared in 1935, was the first explicit expression in a book of his faith and won for him the Hawthornden prize. In 1937, after the annulment of his first marriage, he married Laura Herbert, from a family of aristocratic Catholic converts. Installed in a fine old house in Gloucestershire, the wedding present of his wife's grandmother, he continued writing books (*Scoop, Robbery under Law*) and contributing articles and reviews to a wide range of newspapers and periodicals. On the outbreak of war, he obtained a commission in the Marines, transferred to the newly formed Commandos, and saw action in West Africa (a disastrous attempt to land General de Gaulle at Dakar), Libya, and Crete. After transfer to the Royal Horse Guards in 1942, he spent two depressing years on postings in Britain before joining Fitzroy Maclean's mission to Yugoslavia. He ended the war demoralized by the incompetence and cowardice he had witnessed at first hand (he himself displayed extraordinary courage in battle), and by the compromise of collaborating with the Communists in the overthrow of their Antichrist twins, the National Socialists. The initial exhilaration and final disillusionment of his wartime service are recorded in the *Sword of Honour* trilogy of novels (1952–1961). The success of *Brideshead Revisited* (1945), which is widely regarded as one of the greatest English Catholic novels, gave him financial security and made him a best-selling author in the United States. On visits to America in the late 1940s Waugh was struck by the vitality and confidence of its Catholic life, and became convinced that the Church was entering an 'American epoch' of bright promise. He regarded his novel *Helena* (1950) on the life of the mother of Constantine as his best book and was therefore immensely disappointed by its failure with the critics and the general public. In 1954, on a sea voyage to Ceylon, he displayed extreme symptoms of psychosis and began to fear that he had been possessed by a demon. On his return to London, Waugh's friend, Father Philip Caraman SJ, introduced him to the Catholic psychiatrist, Dr Eric Strauss, who diagnosed bromide poisoning, the result of trying to cure his insomnia with a mixture of bromide and alcohol. Strauss gave him a prescription for a different sleeping draught, and the voices stopped that night. Out of this frightening episode came the novel, *The Ordeal of Gilbert Pinfold* (1957). His last four years of life were darkened by the postconciliar changes in the liturgy, whose transcendent beauty he felt had been destroyed. On the day of his death, Easter Sunday 1966, he was in good spirits at home, and was able to attend Mass celebrated by Father Caraman in the traditional form. Some time before lunch his wife found him dead from a massive heart attack. He is buried in the churchyard at Combe Florey in Somerset.

## The Bosh of Gnosticism and the Particularities of the Incarnation

*[At a soirée for grand Roman ladies, the still pagan Helena hears her former tutor, Marcias, now a Gnostic sage, deliver a lecture about Aeons, Sophia, the Demiurge*

*etc. etc. After an unsatisfactory exchange with him at the meeting, Helena consults Lactantius, the Christian apologist and tutor of Crispus, her grandson.*]

The voice rippled on, and when Helena at length had hold of herself, was at the peroration. The hostess said her words of thanks: '...I am sure we are all a great deal clearer than we were on this important topic...the lecturer has kindly consented to answer any questions...'

No one spoke immediately; then: 'I was not quite sure whether you said that the Demiurge was an Aeon.'

'No, madam. It was one of the aims of my poor discourse to demonstrate that he was not.'

'Oh...thank you.'

Minervina nodded as though to say: 'I could have told you that, and I should have done so rather more sharply.'

There was further pause; then in clear, schoolroom tone, Helena said: 'What I should like to know is: When and where did all this happen? And how do you know?'

Minervina frowned. Marcias replied: 'These things are beyond time and space. Their truth is integral to their proposition and by nature transcends material proof.'

'Then, please, how do you know?'

'By a life-time of patient and humble study, your Majesty.'

'But study of what?'

'That, I fear, would take a life-time to particularize.'

A little murmur of appreciation greeted this neat reply and on the crest of it the hostess rose to dismiss the meeting. The ladies rustled forward towards the lecturer, but he, deprecating their flattery, came to meet Helena. 'I was told your Majesty might do me the honour of coming.'

'I scarcely hoped you had recognized me. I am afraid the lecture was far above my head...'

'But your question just now. "When? Where? How do you know?"—was a child's question.'

'That is why your religion would never do for me, Marcias. If I ever found a teacher, it would have to be one who called little children to him.'

'That, alas, is not the spirit of the time. We live in a very old world today. We know too much. We should have to forget everything and be born again to answer your questions...'

That evening Helena sent for Lactantius and said: 'I went to the lecture this afternoon. I found I knew the man quite well. He used to belong to my father in Britain. He's put on a lot of weight since then. I couldn't understand a word he said. It's all bosh, isn't it?'

'All complete bosh, your Majesty.'

'So I supposed. Just wanted to make sure. Tell me, Lactantius, this god of yours. If I asked you when and where he could be seen, what would you say?'

'I should say that as a man he died two hundred and seventy-eight years ago in the town now called Aelia Capitolina in Palestine.'

'Well, that's a straight answer anyway. How do you know?'

'We have the accounts written by witnesses. Besides that there is the living memory of the Church. We have knowledge handed down from father to son, invisible places marked by memory—the cave where he was born, the tomb where his body was laid, the grave of Peter. One day all these things will be made public. Now they are kept a secret. If you want to visit the holy places, you must find the right man. He can tell you, so many paces to the East from such and such a stone, where the shadow falls at sunrise on such and such a day. A few families know these things, and they see to it that their children learn the instructions. One day when the Church is free and open there will be no need for such devices.'

'Well, that's all most interesting. Thank you. Lactantius.' (1)

## The Finding of the True Cross

Helena's many prayers received unequal answers. Constantine was at long last baptized and died in the expectation of an immediate, triumphal entry to Paradise. Britain for a time became Christian, and 136 parish churches, a great part of them in the old lands of the Trinovantes, were dedicated to Helena. The Holy Places have been alternately honoured and desecrated, lost and won, bought and bargained for, throughout the centuries.

But the wood has endured. In splinters and shavings, gorgeously encased, it has travelled the world over and found a joyous welcome among every race.

For it states a fact.

Hounds are checked, hunting wild. A horn calls clear through the covert. Helena casts them back on the scent.

Above all the babble of the age and ours, she makes one blunt assertion. And there alone lies Hope. (2)

## Low Mass and Conversion

When I first came into the Church I was drawn, not by splendid ceremonies but by the spectacle of the priest as a craftsman. He had an important job to do which none but he was qualified for. He and his apprentice stumped up to the altar with their tools and set to work without a glance to those behind them, still less with any intention to make a personal impression on them.

'Participate'—the cant word—does not mean to make a row as the Germans suppose. One participates in a work of art when one studies it with reverence and understanding. (3)

## The Real Presence

[It is England during the Second World War. Charles Ryder, an army officer on active service, discovers that he and his men are encamped close to Brideshead, the home of the Marchmains, a noble Catholic family that Charles has known since he was an undergraduate in Oxford and the friend of Sebastian, the younger son. When he first came to the house, he was without religion. Now, after many years away from Brideshead and the Marchmains, he returns, and as a Catholic.]

There was one part of the house I had not yet visited, and I went there now. The chapel showed no ill-effects of its long neglect; the art-nouveau paint was as fresh and bright as ever; the art-nouveau lamp burned once more before the altar. I said a prayer, an ancient, newly-learned form of words, and left, turning towards the camp; and as I walked back, and the cook-house bugle sounded ahead of me, I thought:

'The builders did not know the uses to which their work would descend; they made a new house with the stones of the old castle; year by year, generation after generation, they enriched and extended it; year by year the great harvest of timber in the park grew to ripeness; until in sudden frost, came the age of Hooper; the place was desolate and the work all brought to nothing; *Quomodo sedet sola civitas*. Vanity of vanities, all is vanity.

'And yet,' I thought, stepping out more briskly towards the camp, where the bugles after a pause had taken up the second call and were sounding, 'Pick-em-up, pick-em-up, hot potatoes', 'and yet that is not the last word; it is not even an apt word; it is a dead word from ten years back.

'Something quite remote from anything the builders intended, has come out of their work, and out of the fierce little human tragedy in which I played; something none of us thought about at the time; a small red flame—a beaten-copper lamp of deplorable design relit before the beaten-copper doors of a tabernacle; the flame which the old knights saw from their tombs, which they saw put out; that flame burns again for other soldiers, far from home, farther, in heart, than Acre or Jerusalem. It could not have been lit but for the builders and the tragedians, and there I found it this morning, burning anew among the old stones.'

I quickened my pace and reached the hut which served us for our ante-room.

'You're looking unusually cheerful today,' said the second-in-command. (4)

## The Last Journey of St Edmund Campion and his Companions

Then they [Campion, St Alexander Briant, and St Ralph Sherwin] were slowly dragged through the mud and rain, up Cheapside, past St Martin le Grand and Newgate, along Holborn to Tyburn. [William] Charke [clergyman and controversialist] plodded along beside the hurdle, still eager to thrash out to the last word the question of Justification by Faith alone, but Campion seemed not to notice him; over Newgate Arch stood a figure of Our Lady which had so far survived the Anglican hammers. Campion saluted her as he passed. Here and there along the road a Catholic would push himself through the crowd and ask Campion's blessing. One witness...followed close at hand and stood by the scaffold. He records how one gentleman, 'either for pity or affection, most courteously wiped' Campion's 'face, all spattered with mire and dirt, as he was drawn most miserably through thick and thin; for which charity, or haply some sudden moved affection, God reward him and bless him'.

The scene at Tyburn was tumultuous. Sir Thomas More had stepped out into the summer sunshine, to meet death quietly and politely at a single stroke of the axe. Every circumstance of Campion's execution was vile and gross.

Sir Francis Knollys, Lord Howard, Sir Henry Lee, and other gentlemen of fashion were already waiting beside the scaffold. When the procession arrived, they were disputing whether the motion of the sun from east to west was violent or natural; they postponed the discussion to watch Campion, bedraggled and mud-stained, mount the cart which stood below the gallows. The noose was put over his neck. The noise of the crowd was continuous, and only those in his immediate neighbourhood could hear him as he began to speak. He had it in mind to make some religious exhortation.

'*Spectaculum facti sumus Deo, angelis et hominibus*', he began. 'These are the words of St Paul, Englished thus, "We are made a spectacle unto God, unto His angels and unto men", verified this day in me, whom am here a spectacle unto my Lord God, a spectacle unto His angels and unto you men.'

But he was not allowed to continue. Sir Francis Knollys interrupted, shouting up at him to confess his treason.

'As to the treasons which have been laid to my charge,' he said, 'and for which I am come here to suffer, I desire you all to bear witness with me that I am thereof altogether innocent.'

One of the Council cried that it was too late to deny what had been proved in the court.

'Well, my Lord,' he replied, 'I am a Catholic man and a priest; in that faith I have lived, and in that faith I intend to die. If you esteem my religion treason, then am I guilty; as for other treason I never committed any, God is my judge. But you have now what you desire. I beseech you to have patience, and suffer me to speak a word or two for discharge of my conscience'...

In a few halting sentences he made himself heard above the clamour. He forgave the jury and asked forgiveness of any whose names he might have compromised during his examination [under torture]...

Then a schoolmaster named Hearne stood forward and read a proclamation in the Queen's name, that the execution they were to witness that morning was for treason and not for religion. Campion stood in prayer. The Lords of the Council still shouted up questions to him about the Bull of Excommunication, but now Campion would not answer and stood with his head bowed and his hands folded on his breast. An Anglican clergyman attempted to direct his prayers, but he answered gently, 'Sir, you and I are not one in religion, wherefore I pray you content yourself. I bar none of prayer, but I only desire them that are of the household of faith to pray with me, and in mine agony to say one creed.'

They called to him to pray in English, but he replied with great mildness that 'he would pray God in a language which they both well understood.'

There was more noise; the Councillors demanded that he should ask the Queen's forgiveness.

'Wherein have I offended her? In this I am innocent. This is my last speech; in this give me credit—I have and do pray for her.'

Still the courtiers were not satisfied. Lord Howard demanded to know what Queen he prayed for.

'Yea, for Elizabeth your Queen and my Queen, unto whom I wish a long quiet reign with all prosperity.'

The cart was then driven from under him, the eager crowd swayed forward, and Campion was left hanging, until, unconscious, perhaps already dead, he was cut down, and the butcher began his work. (5)

NOTES AND SOURCES

1. Evelyn Waugh, *Helena*, new edn. (Harmondsworth: Penguin, 1963), 83–5.

2. Ibid. 158–9.

3.  Evelyn Waugh, *The Diaries of Evelyn Waugh*, ed. Michael Davie (London: Weidenfeld & Nicholson, 1976), 792–3.

4.  Evelyn Waugh, *Brideshead Revisited: The Sacred and Profane Memories of Captain Charles Ryder*, rev. edn. (Harmondsworth: Penguin, 1962), 330–1.

5.  Evelyn Waugh, *Edmund Campion*, new edn. (London: Hollis & Carter, 1947), 201–4. For more on the life of St Edmund Campion, see pp. 112–7 above.

# Henry Graham Greene                                    1904–1991

Was Graham Greene a Catholic writer? The question is hard to answer. He was a Catholic by conversion, but not always, particularly towards the end of his life, by manifest conviction. Some critics find his novels *too* Catholic. For example, the South African novelist and Nobel laureate J. M. Coetzee has complained that Greene and many of his characters seem to think that 'Catholics have unique access to an ancient body of wisdom, and that English Catholics in especial, members of a once persecuted sect, are as a result inherent outsiders'. Regardless of whether English Catholics are entitled to such claims, Coetzee's invocation of the 'Byronic outsider' is apt. Greene's biography is comparable to Childe Harold's or Don Juan's: embroiling himself in love affairs and political affairs, wandering to the ends of the earth, brooding on the mysteries of man and the cosmos, and creating autobiographically inflected characters who did all these things and more. His early life already showed signs of emotional turbulence, as he struggled with the complications of being a pupil at the school, Berkhamsted, of which his father was headmaster. He even attempted suicide, borrowing ideas for overdosing from a Dorothy L. Sayers murder mystery, and playing Russian Roulette with his brother's revolver. His parents sent him for psychoanalysis, which gave him occasional escapes from school, but no lasting peace of soul. Following graduation from Balliol College, Oxford, he attempted to make a living as a novelist and journalist in London and Nottingham, where he became a Catholic in 1926. His conversion was influenced by his fiancé and later wife, Vivienne Dayrell-Browning, herself a convert. The life and teachings of the Church seized his imagination, as evidenced in his cycle of 'Catholic novels'—*Brighton Rock* (1938), *The Power and the Glory* (1940), *The Heart of the Matter* (1948), and *The End of the Affair* (1951)— as well as *The Lawless Roads* (1939), his travel narrative offering an English Catholic view of religious persecution in Mexico. The rest of Greene's life is not easily summarized. He worked for MI6 during and after the Second World War; separated from Vivienne and conducted long-running affairs with married women; travelled to countries at war or under political repression (Sierra Leone, Vietnam, Poland, Russia, China, Cuba, and Haiti); enjoyed a friendship of mutual affection and respect with Evelyn Waugh; and wrote highly regarded reviews, essays, and screenplays including the *film noir* classic, *The Third Man* (1949). His beliefs are not easily summarized either. In 1954, when *The Power and the Glory* was denounced to the Holy Office, he wrote a letter to Cardinal Montini, later Pope Paul VI, protesting his 'profound and filial devotion to the person of the Sovereign Pontiff', but the portrayal of loss of faith in the 1961 novel, *A Burnt Out Case*, seemed to Evelyn Waugh to reflect Greene's own spiritual crisis. Indeed, in the last years of his life, with his hostility towards the Papacy and his attraction to heterodox opinions, he does not seem to be a man who believed 'firmly and truly'. However, by arrangements made several months beforehand, he received the last rites of the Church, and at the funeral Mass his friend, Father Durán, the model for *Monsignor Quixote*, insisted that he died a true believer. Sharing Péguy's opinion that the sinner was at the heart of Christianity, Greene's novels display the interior suffering of complex characters confronting the seeming ubiquity of evil. The passages selected below from *The End of the Affair* depict the hard-won hope of a convert adulteress, Sarah Miles, torn between her longing to escape a loveless marriage to the dull civil servant Henry Miles and her promise to God to renounce her passion for Maurice Bendrix. Greene is always wrestling with the great dogmas of the faith, but he never seems to find them a source of light and strength. Ralph McInerny's conclusion is the right one: Graham Greene was 'a Catholic writer—*of a sort*'.

## Sarah Miles Confronts the Love of God

I said to God, 'So that's it. I begin to believe in you, and if I believe in you I shall hate you. I have free will to break my promise, haven't I, but I haven't the power to gain anything from breaking it. You let me telephone, but then you close the door in my face. You let me sin, but you take away the fruits of my sin. You let me try to escape with D., but you don't allow me to enjoy it. You make me drive love out, and then you say there's no lust for you either. What do you expect me to do now, God? Where do I go from here?'

When I was at school I learnt about a King—one of the Henrys, the one who had Becket murdered—and he swore when he saw his birthplace burnt by his enemies that because God had done that to him, 'because You have robbed me of the town I love most, the place where I was born and bred, I will rob You of that which You love most in me.' Odd how I've remembered that prayer after sixteen years. A King swore it on his horse seven hundred years ago, and I pray it now, in a hotel room at Bigwell-on-Sea—Bigwell Regis. I'm going to rob you, God, of what you love most in me. I've never known the Lord's Prayer by heart, but I remember that one—is it a prayer? Of what you love most in me.

What do you love most? If I believed in you, I suppose I'd believe in the immortal soul, but is that what you love? Can you really see it there under the skin? Even a God can't love something that doesn't exist, he can't love something he cannot see. When he looks at me, does he see something that I can't see? It must be lovely if he is able to love it. That's asking me to believe too much, that there's anything lovely in me. I want men to admire me, but that's a trick you learn at school—a movement of the eyes, a tone of voice, a touch of the hand on the shoulder or the head. If they think you admire them, they will admire you because of your good taste, and when they admire you, you have an illusion for a moment that there's something to admire. All my life I've tried to live in that illusion—a soothing drug that allows me to forget that I'm a bitch and a fake. But what are you supposed to love then in the bitch and the fake? Where do you find that immortal soul they talked about? Where do you see this lovely thing in me—in me, of all people? I can understand you can find it in Henry—my Henry, I mean. He's gentle and good and patient. You can find it in Maurice who thinks he hates, and loves, loves all the time. Even his enemies. But in this bitch and fake where do you find anything to love?

Tell me that, God, and I'll set about robbing you of it for ever.

How did the King keep his promise? I wish I could remember. I can remember nothing more about him than that he let the monks scourge him over the tomb of Becket. That doesn't sound like the answer. It must have happened before. (1)

## Sarah Miles and the Incarnation

It was very hot today and it dripped with rain. So I went into the dark church at the corner of Park Road to sit down for a while. Henry was at home and I didn't want to see him. I try to remember to be kind at breakfast, kind at lunch when he's home, kind at dinner, and sometimes I forget and he's kind back. Two people being kind to each other for a lifetime. When I came in and sat down and looked round I realized it was a Roman church, full of plaster statues and bad art, realistic art. I hated the statues, the crucifix, all the emphasis on the human body. I was trying to escape from the human body and all it needed. I thought I could believe in some kind of a God that bore no relation to ourselves, something vague, amorphous, cosmic, to which I had promised something and which had given me something in return—stretching out of the vague into the concrete human life, like a powerful vapour moving among the chairs and walls. One day I too would become part of that vapour—I would escape myself for ever. And then I came into that dark church in Park Road and saw the bodies standing around me on all the altars—the hideous plaster statues with their complacent faces, and I remembered that they believed in the resurrection of the body, the body I wanted destroyed for ever. I had done so much injury with this body. How could I want to preserve any of it for eternity, and suddenly I remembered a phrase of Richard's—about human beings inventing doctrines to satisfy their desires, and I thought how wrong he is. If I were to invent a doctrine it would be that the body was never born again, that it rotted with last year's vermin....

And of course on the altar there was a body too—such a familiar body, more familiar than Maurice's, that it had never struck me before as a body with all the parts of a body, even the parts the loin-cloth concealed. I remembered one in a Spanish church I had visited with Henry, where the blood ran down in scarlet paint from the eyes and the hands. It had sickened me. Henry wanted me to admire the twelfth-century pillars, but I was sick and I wanted to get out into the open air. I thought, these people love cruelty. A vapour couldn't shock you with blood and cries.

When I came out into the plaza I said to Henry, 'I can't bear all these painted wounds.' Henry was very reasonable—he's always reasonable. He said, 'Of course it's a very materialistic faith. A lot of magic...'

'Is magic materialistic?' I asked.

'Yes. Eye of newt and toe of frog, finger of birth-strangled babe. You can't have anything more materialistic than that. In the Mass they still believe in transubstantiation.'

I knew all about that, but I had an idea that it more or less died out at the Reformation, except for the poor of course. Henry put me right (how often has Henry rearranged my muddled thoughts). 'Materialism isn't only an attitude for the poor,' he said. 'Some of the finest brains have been materialist, Pascal, Newman. So subtle in some directions: so crudely superstitious in others. One day we may know why: it may be a glandular deficiency.'

So today I looked at that material body on that material cross, and I wondered, how could the world have nailed a vapour there? A vapour of course felt no pain and no pleasure. It was only my superstition that imagined it could answer my prayers. Dear God, I had said. I should have said, Dear Vapour. I said I hate you, but can one hate a vapour? I could hate that figure on the Cross with its claim to my gratitude—'I've suffered this for you', but a vapour...And yet Richard believed in less even than a vapour. He hated a fable, he fought against a fable, he took a fable seriously. I couldn't hate Hansel and Gretel, I couldn't hate their sugar house as he hated the legend of Heaven. When I was a child I could hate the wicked queen in Snow White, but Richard didn't hate his fairy-tale Devil. The Devil didn't exist and God didn't exist, but all his hatred was for the good fairy-tale, not for the wicked one. Why? I looked up at that over-familiar body, stretched in imaginary pain, the head drooping like a man asleep. I thought, sometimes I've hated Maurice, but would I have hated him if I hadn't loved him too? Oh God, if I could really hate you, what would that mean?

Am I a materialist after all, I wondered? Have I some glandular deficiency that I am so uninterested in the really important unsuperstitious things and causes— like the Charity Commission and the index of living and better calories for the working class? Am I a materialist because I believe in the independent existence of that man with the bowler, the metal of the cross, these hands I can't pray with? Suppose God did exist, suppose He was a body like that, what's wrong in believing that His body existed as much as mine? Could anybody love Him or hate Him if He hadn't got a body? I can't love a vapour that was Maurice. That's coarse, that's beastly, that's materialist, I know, but why shouldn't I be beastly and coarse and materialist. I walked out of the church in a flaming rage, and in defiance of Henry and all the reasonable and the detached I did what I had seen people do in Spanish churches: I dipped my finger in the so-called holy water and made a kind of cross on my forehead. (2)

## The Mexican 'Reformation'

In July 1926, Father Miguel Pro landed at Veracruz. He was twenty-five years old and a Jesuit. He came back to his own country from a foreign seminary much as Campion returned to England from Douai. We know how he was dressed when a year and a half later he came out into the prison yard to be shot, and he may well have worn the same disguise when he landed (the equivalent of Campion's doublet and hose): a dark lounge suit, soft collar and tie, a bright cardigan. Most priests wear their mufti with a kind of uneasiness, but Pro was a good actor.

He needed to be. Within two months of Pro's landing, President Calles had begun the fiercest persecution of religion anywhere since the reign of Elizabeth. The churches were closed, Mass had to be said secretly in private houses, to administer the Sacraments was a serious offence. Nevertheless, Pro gave Communion daily to some three hundred people, confessions were heard in half-built houses in darkness, retreats were held in garages. Pro escaped the plain-clothes police again and again. Once he found them at the entrance to a house where he was supposed to say Mass; he posed as a police officer, showing an imaginary badge and remarking, 'There's a cat bagged in here,' and passed into the house and out again with his cassock under his arm. Followed by detectives when he left a Catholic house and with only fifty yards' start, he disappeared altogether from their sight round a corner—the only man they overtook was a lover out with his girl. The prisons were filling up, priests were being shot, yet on three successive first Fridays Pro gave the Sacrament to nine hundred, thirteen hundred, and fifteen hundred people.

They got him, of course, at last (they had got him earlier if only they had known it, but they let him go). This time they made no mistake, or else the biggest mistake of all.... The American ambassador thought he could do more good by not intervening and left next day with the President and Will Rogers, the humorist, on a Pullman tour.... Pro was photographed by the official photographer, praying for his enemies by the pitted wall, receiving the *coup de grâce*; the photographs were sent to the Press—to show the firmness of the Government—but within a few weeks it became a penal offence to possess them, for they had had an effect which Calles had not foreseen.

For Mexico remained Catholic; it was only the governing class—politicians and *pistoleros*—which was anti-Catholic. (3)


## Not Peace, but a Sword

There was a large cockroach dead on the floor of my room and a sour smell from the water-closet. Thunder came rolling up from Texas and rain splashed and dug and churned the unmade roads. I tried to read myself to sleep with *Barchester Towers* ('St Ewold's is not a rich piece of preferment—it is worth some three or four hundred a year at most, and has generally been held by a clergyman attached to the cathedral choir...'), but I couldn't concentrate. The world is all of a piece, of course; it is engaged everywhere in the same subterranean struggle, lying like a tiny neutral state, with whom no one ever observes his treaties, between the two eternities of pain and—God knows the opposite of pain, not we. It is a Belgium fought over by friend and enemy alike. There is no peace anywhere where there is human life, but there are, I told myself, quiet and active sectors of the line. Russia, Spain, Mexico—there's no fraternization on Christmas morning in those parts. The horror may be the same, it is an intrinsic part of human life in every place: it attacks you in the Strand or the tropics; but where the eagles are gathered together, it is not unnatural to expect to find the Son of Man as well. So many years have passed in England since the war began between faith and anarchy: we live in an ugly indifference. Over here lay the grave of Pro, Tabasco with every church destroyed, and Chiapas, where the Mass was forbidden. The advertisements for aerated waters and patent medicines line the modern highway which leads to the front line and the tourists go back and forth, their cars laden with serapes and big hats, and their minds sprightly with the legend of a happy and picturesque Mexico.

'He was content to be a High Churchman,' I read of Mr. Arabin, under the bare globe, on the hard iron bedstead, 'if he could be so on principles of his own, and could strike out a course showing a marked difference from those with whom he consorted.' Trollope's gentle irony, the sense of breakfasts at the archdeacon's, dining room-prayers, and somewhere in the far distance, beyond the Barchester spires, a doubt about everything. A drunken voice sang in Spanish and the rain fell over the dreary Nuevo León plain, and I thought of Father Pro coming into this country in disguise—the badly cut suit and the striped tie and the brown shoes; then the secret Masses, the confessions at street corners, the police hunts and the daring evasions—the long rainy season and afterwards the dry and then the rains again, and, when they cleared, arrest and death, unshaven, crying, 'Hail Christ the King' in the yard of the prison. They had killed Campion, they said, for treason, not for his religion, and they said the same of Pro in 1927. The war doesn't change its character in a few centuries; it moves as slowly as evolution through a thousand years—it takes more than ten centuries to change one muscle—and Pro speaks with the psychology of Thomas of Canterbury, who also was in love with the good death, 'The victims are many; the number of martyrs grows every day. Oh, if only I should draw a winning number.'

The rain came down and the lights went out in the United States, and Mr Arabin made his tentative efforts at love in the flower garden. (4)

## Our Lady of Guadalupe

Guadalupe—a quarter of an hour's tram ride from the cathedral, in a suburb which retains the shape and air of a village as some parts of London do—is the most important shrine in Mexico, the centre of a whole nation's devotion. There isn't a town of any size which doesn't contain a church of Guadalupe with a facsimile of the famous relic.

The plain formal eighteenth-century church stands in a little plaza where a market is held every day of the week—ices and fruit, little sweet corncakes cooked while you watch and wrapped up in coloured paper like crackers, the blue Guadalupe glass, the colour of poison bottles, small crude toys. Outside the Chapel of the Well, a spring which is said to have flowed from under the feet of the Virgin, are stacks of empty whisky bottles in which to carry away the brackish healing water. Within the church the miraculous serape hangs above the altar, the dark-skinned Indian Virgin bending her head with a grace and kindliness you will find nowhere in mortal Mexico.

She appeared first at Amecameca, fifty miles away, but no one paid her any attention; then on December 9 1531, an Indian peasant, Juan Diego, was climbing Tepayac hill, at the foot of which the shrine now stands. The Virgin appeared to him among the rocks—there was music suddenly and light—she called him 'my son' and told him to carry a message to the Bishop Zumárraga that he was to build a shrine on that spot where she might watch and love the Indians....

It is as well to remember how revolutionary this vision must have seemed. It was only ten years since Mexico City had fallen to Cortés, the country was not yet subdued, and it is doubtful what kind of greeting the average Spanish adventurer would have given an Indian who claimed to have been addressed as 'my son' by the Mother of God. The legend, one is told by Mexican politicians, was invented by the Church to enslave the Indian mind, but if indeed it had been invented at that period by the Church, it would have been with a very different purpose. This Virgin claimed a Church where she might love her Indians and guard them from the Spanish conqueror. The legend gave the Indian self-respect; it gave him a hold over his conqueror; it was a liberating, not an enslaving, legend. (5)

## The Thing

One visitor replying to a polite formal enquiry of the Pope [Pius XII] said that there were two Masses he would always remember: one was at 5:30 in the morning at a side altar, in a small Franciscan monastery in Apulia, the Host raised in Padre Pio's hands marked with the black ugly dried patches of the stigmata: the other was the Pope's Jubilee Mass in Rome, the enormous crowd pressed into St Peter's, and men and women cheering and weeping as the Pope passed up the nave, boys flinging their Scout hats into the air: the fine transparent features like those on a coin going by, the hand raised in a resolute blessing, the smile of 'deep affection', and later the Pope alone at the altar, when the Cardinals who served him had stepped aside, moving with grace and precision through the motions of the Mass, doing what every priest does every day, the servant of the servants of God, and not impossibly, one feels, a saint.

But how much more difficult sanctity must be under the Michelangelo frescoes, among the applauding crowds, through the daily audiences with the bicyclists and the tram conductors, the nuns and the ambassadors, than in the stony fields of Apulia where Pio is confined. It is the strength of the Church in Italy that it can produce such extremes, and exactly the same thought came to one kneeling among a dozen women one early morning in the Franciscan monastery, and pressed among the cheering crowds in St Peter's. It was not after all the question, can this Thing survive? It was, how can this Thing ever be defeated? (6)

NOTES AND SOURCES

1. Graham Greene, *The End of the Affair* (New York: Penguin, 1979), 80–1.

2. Ibid. 87–90.

3. Graham Greene, *The Lawless Roads* (London: William Heinemann & the Bodley Head, 1978), 8–10.

4. Ibid. 26–8.

5. Ibid. 94–5.

6. Graham Greene, 'The Paradox of a Pope', in *Collected Essays* (New York: Viking, 1969), 380–96.


# John Carmel Cardinal Heenan                                    1905–1975

John Heenan was a priest and bishop of complete Catholic fidelity, simple piety, and boundless apostolic energy, but died, as Cardinal Archbishop of Westminster, worn out by his labours during the revolutionary changes in society and the Church of the late sixties and early seventies. An Essex boy, the youngest of the five children of Irish parents, he was educated for the priesthood at Ushaw and the English College, Rome, where he gained doctorates in philosophy and theology from the Gregorian University. After ordination in 1930 and the completion of his studies in Rome, he served as a curate in his home diocese of Brentwood. The new Archbishop of Westminster, Arthur Hinsley, who had been his rector in Rome, made use of Heenan's intellectual gifts in the drafting of speeches and supported his courageous plan to visit Stalinist Russia, in disguise, to report on the realities of life under a violently oppressive atheistic Communist regime. From 1937 to 1947 he was a parish priest in East Ham, where, despite an increasing number of engagements as a public speaker and broadcaster, he devoted himself to his people as they endured the successive tribulations of unemployment, the Blitz, and post-war austerity. His book *The People's Priest* (1951), the fruit of these years, is his *regula pastoralis* for parish priests, and remains a classic. In 1947 he became superior of the Catholic Missionary Society, a team of diocesan priests who toured the country preaching missions and giving lectures in universities and town halls. In 1951 he was consecrated and enthroned as Bishop of Leeds, but was then translated to Liverpool in

1957, and finally to Westminster in 1963, a year after the opening of the Second Vatican Council. When asked in a television interview which of the Church's teachings he found it hardest to accept, he replied without a pause, 'That God loves me'. The answer was typical of his humility, and of his concentration, amidst all the confusions of his times, on the one thing needful.

## Memories of Ushaw College

During May the whole school used to march into the chapel of Our Lady of Help (the Ushaw Madonna) singing the Magnificat. It was an Ushaw tradition to foster in the alumni a manly devotion to the Mother of God. Far removed from sentimentality, it is a source of strength to a priest. Manliness was characteristic of most of the typically Ushaw virtues. We lived hard, but for a male community we were astonishingly well mannered. The toughest boy would open a door for his companion to pass through before him. Courtesy is the mark of mutual respect. Years later I was to learn of the Ushaw custom also founded on respect and what today—but most certainly not in those days—might be called love. On the annual school reunion all expenses were shared. Thus, coming from London, I was no worse off than those who only had to take a twopenny bus. This sharing of expenses was designed to enable the poorest or most remote member of the school to attend the reunion without embarrassment. (1)

## Priestly Life: Visiting the Blessed Sacrament

The priest's whole life circles around the tabernacle. But it is useful to make a rule never to pass the church without making a courtesy call on the Master. Going out to visit parishioners, it is worthwhile to enter the church for a minute or two to ask for guidance and a blessing. If we are to pray without ceasing, it is necessary to make all our work a prayer. This can be done in no other way than by constantly reminding ourselves of God's presence while we are about our work. The church is the priest's workshop. It should always be the point of our departure and return. (2)

## Priestly Life: The Missal's Prayers of Preparation before Mass

Most priests soon lose any taste for verbose forms of prayer. But the little prayer to Our Lady asking her to stand by us and all priests wherever in the world they may be offering the Holy Sacrifice, because she 'stood by her sweet Son as He hung on the Cross', cannot fail to uplift the priest who is so soon to celebrate. Then comes the declaration of intention before Mass. Some priests learn this by heart and recite it as they are going from the sacristy to the altar. Their final plea to God is for 'joy with peace, a reform of life, time for true repentance, grace and consolation of the Holy Spirit, and perseverance in good work'. (3)

## The Priest and the Dying

We must be careful not to regard our duty to the dying as though it were only a question of giving them Holy Viaticum, Extreme Unction, and the Last Blessing. This, of course, is the most important part of our ministry. But it is not all that is required of us. In the Ritual which we carry about with us we find after the formula of the blessing *In articulo mortis* the prayers for the commendation of a soul. It should be our endeavour whenever possible to be with our people at the very last. This may mean that we shall pay several visits in a single day to a person who is dying. It will also mean that we shall have to neglect many other tasks we had intended to do. Nobody chooses his own time for dying. It follows that whenever death comes it is bound to interfere with some programme we had arranged.

Take the prayers in the Ritual, and see what the Church expects from her pastors. She imagines that, when the last moments come, the father of the flock will be by the side of his children. The priest should invite all the family to gather round the bedside with him when he begins the Litany. When the death agony seems to be imminent—the priest who has formed the habit of being with the dying will usually have little difficulty in deciding the appropriate moment—the strong and consoling words of the Church should be recited:

Go forth, Christian soul, out of this world in the name of God the Father almighty who created thee; in the name of Jesus Christ, the Son of the living God, who suffered for thee; in the name of the Holy Ghost, who sanctified thee; in the name of the glorious and holy Virgin Mary, Mother of God; in the name of Blessed Joseph, the spouse of the same glorious Virgin; in the name of the angels and archangels . . .

No matter to what inconvenience he may need to put himself the priest who loves his flock will count no cost too great which enables him to see a soul safely into eternity. Besides the main effect of easing the soul in the loneliness of the death agony the priest's tender care will often result in the conversion of those around the bedside who might never be moved by the most eloquent sermon. No man can say what blessings fall upon a parish whose priest has ushered grateful souls into God's presence. Who can measure the power of their prayers with God? (4)

NOTES AND SOURCES

1. John C. Heenan, *Not the Whole Truth*, new edn. (London: Hodder & Stoughton, 1973), 45.

2. John C. Heenan, *The People's Priest* (London: Sheed & Ward, 1951), 31.

3. Ibid. 37.

4. Ibid. 48.

# (Claud) Hubert van Zeller OSB 1905–1984

Hubert van Zeller had friendships with the grandest names in English Catholicism, but his practice of monastic life was of Patristic austerity: apart from a toothbrush and a typewriter, he had no possessions, ate and fasted strictly according to the Rule, and, when he was seriously ill, had to be barred from choir under obedience. Born in Egypt and educated at Downside, his gratitude for the happiness of his childhood and youth is summed up in the titles of his books, *Willingly to School* and *One Foot in the Cradle*. After unsuccessful assignments as a schoolmaster, he spent twelve years as a chaplain to nuns in North Wales and the United States. He was an accomplished sculptor and draughtsman, and, in addition to many works of spirituality, produced the cartoon-book, *Cracks in the Cloister*, a kindly satire on monastic life in the age of *aggiornamento*. Perhaps the greatest earthly influence on him was not a Benedictine, but a Dominican, Father Bede Jarrett.

## Petitionary Prayer

We must make an act of faith about the greater value to God and to our own souls of that prayer which leaves Him an open field. The prayer which narrows to a pin-point request is likely to be inspired more by self than by grace. The same kind of faith must cover those occasions when we feel we are not honouring our obligations with regard to our friends, not praying for them by name and even forgetting that we have promised to help them with our prayers. We must refuse to be stampeded by scruple in this matter.

As the priest at the altar sweeps the particles from the paten into the chalice, leaving them there without trying to count them, so the soul should not worry about discriminating and enumerating. The intentions are contained in the movement of the prayer, in the comprehensive desire: they are all there, mingling with the Precious Blood.

As an abbot, singing the community High Mass on a feast-day for the brethren behind him in the choir, does not have to run his mind down the list, but takes the whole family of them from the prior to the most recent postulant in the sweep of his sacrifice, so should the soul know that in virtue of an intention previously formulated the promised prayers are adequately fulfilled. (1)

## Dryness in Prayer

God, by denying us satisfaction, both sharpens our hunger and enlarges our power of ultimate appreciation. The hunger may be felt or unfelt; it is the gratification of the appetite that matters. The soul that hungers for God will be satisfied in the end.

A man who has been away for years from his family, but who has regarded himself during all his wanderings as belonging to it, will find himself all the more appreciative of it when he gets back. He will know where his home really is. He may not have visualized his home, sentimentalized over it, or even thought a great deal about it, but all along his real self has been anchored in it.

We belong to God, we are at home in God. We may forget his claims on us by thinking of other things, but so long as we have the essential desire of our soul set towards Him, His grace is enlarging our capacity for divine love. The closer we keep in touch with Him by reiterated desire the greater the praise we give Him and the more surely we dispose ourselves for the union of our souls with Him. (2)

## The Duty of Prayer

There are always good reasons for evading the duty. I can cite lack of time, lack of training, lack of ability. The objections seem unanswerable. But they are wrong. There is no excuse for evading the duty of prayer.

Precisely because prayer is, as St Teresa insists, the one way of finding God, it is the target for the devil's attack. Like charity, for which again there is no substitute, and of which prayer is itself the highest expression, it can be whittled down to nothing.

If he cannot suppress our prayer activity by the straightforward temptation of laziness, the devil will try the more subtle temptation of false humility. He will try to convince us that we are so bad at it that it is a waste of time, and that dull people like ourselves must put their trust in the alternative activity of outward works.

In the matter of vocal prayer, it will be suggested that we are getting no good out of repeating phrases which routine has robbed of all devotion, and even of all meaning. In the matter of mental prayer, it will be suggested that we are so idle in the exercise that it is more likely to be an occasion of sin than an occasion of giving glory to God.

'Drop this fiction of yours about prayer', the devil will say to us, 'and admit honestly that you have been clinging to an empty formula, to an idea which is no more than a superstition. You have kept up your prayers until now only because you are afraid to confess to yourself what a waste of time it is. It is high time you switched over to the exercise of the Christian virtues instead' . . .

Certainly we are 'bad at prayer'; of course, we do not come fresh upon the prayer that we have made for years. No saint has yet claimed that he is good at prayer; there is no mind that can find novelty in what has become habitual. But these are no reasons for not practising prayer; rather they are reasons for persevering in it in faith.

So long as we want to give glory to God in prayer, we can count on the grace which makes good our shortcomings. Where God sees the firm intention of praying, He can dispense with the honour which actual attention may give Him. In the scheme of praise, sensible devotion is not nearly so important as the will to worship.

To give up prayer for the fear of offending God by our insufficiency and distractions is as absurd as to give up sleep for the fear of sleeping badly, or to give up eating for fear of eating the wrong things. (3)

## Temptation is Not Sin

Conflict is not sin, temptation is not sin, failure admitted and repented of is not, any longer, sin. Sin is occasioned by the refusal to admit the danger of sin. Sin is committed by the refusal to prolong the conflict. Sin is prolonged by the refusal to admit the failure. (4)

## Reverence for the Body

Learning from the Resurrection, a man should come to reverence the body where before he either hated it as an evil or feared it as a danger or used it as a means of gratification. The doctrine of the Incarnation teaches him the same lessons. We are baptized into the Mystical Body of Christ, we die in Him, and we rise again in Him.

The Christian's approach to the whole business of 'body' should mark him off at once from either the heathen or unbeliever. Our Lord, in His life as in His Church, impressing upon the faithful the necessity of looking upon the body as an integral part of man's nature: the Manichee regarding the body as inherently bad. Where the heathen or heretic ascetic proposes to himself the thought of death, the Christian ascetic has always before him the thought of life in Christ. Where the one makes it his resolve to refuse the body all that can keep alive its desires, the other makes it his resolve to refuse the body all that weaken its union with God.

Asceticism for one means the minimum of sustenance; asceticism for the other means the maximum of love.

But this idea can be misconceived, can be brought to a too facile birth. Though the maximum of love is the aim set before the Christian ascetic, it is no comfortable ideal that is projected: the means towards its realization may often have to be very uncomfortable indeed. Almost certainly the call to total love will mean the minimum of luxury; possibly it may even mean the minimum of comfort; in some cases it will mean nothing but the bare necessities.

So outwardly there may be little to show the difference between out-and-out ascetics, whether they be Christian or heathen. The difference will lie in the intention: one kind will treat penance as an excellence in itself, to be perfected at whatever cost to the body; the other will treat penance as an expression, as a means, as an attempt to co-operate in a work which is perfected in Christ and by Christ. If penance stops short at self, even at self-sanctification, it has not learned its Christian doctrine. (5)

## 'Passive' Penance

It is to be assumed as axiomatic...that the trials which God allows us in the nature of human existence are to be preferred before any which we could devise for ourselves. To these we must try to respond as voluntarily as to those which are voluntarily chosen. 'Passive' in this context does not mean inert, unco-operating, dead; it means, on the contrary, willing, yielding positively, being very much alive. The penance is 'passive' only in the sense that God is suffered to take the initiative.

Among such penances could be numbered the trials that come from one's temperament and training, from one's state of life, from one's contacts with others, from one's age and health and surrounding circumstances generally. Powerless to alter the conditions imposed by Divine Providence, we welcome the signified will of God. In faith we bow to His wisdom, take it for granted that His love is the explanation of the treatment which is being handed out to us, submit ourselves to whatever else may yet await us.

The more interior the faculty and intense its appetite, the greater the penance and the stronger the faith required to meet it. Thus God may try the intellect by allowing us to feel deluded, by involving us in every sort of doubt, by showing us the weakness of our judgement. He may try the will by allowing our love for Him to seem wasted, by meeting our desire for a return of affection from others with indifference or ingratitude or misunderstanding. He may try our memory with a knowledge of missed opportunity and a sense of resentful regret. He may try the imagination by letting us feel obsessed by temptations and dreads. He may try the physical side of our natures with sickness, exhaustion, loss of material goods, nerves, sleeplessness, and the inability to feel comfort in any outward thing.

Not one among the above catalogue of horrors is an active penance: all are trials coming from the permissive will of God, and not from personal selection. Such penance is *made*, however, by the soul: it is response to grace. A soul habitually on the alert to serve God by prayer and penance is in a state of positive receptivity which makes these 'passive' trials generative. The attitude is the same as Our Lady's *Fiat mihi secundum verbum tuum*. [Be it done unto me according to thy word.] (6)

NOTES AND SOURCES

1. Hubert van Zeller, *Approach to Prayer* (London: Sheed & Ward, 1958), 61.
2. Ibid. 118.
3. Ibid. 119–21.
4. Hubert van Zeller, *Approach to Penance* (London: Sheed & Ward, 1958), 42.
5. Ibid. 44–5.
6. Ibid. 51–3.

# (Anthony) Gervase Mathew OP 1905–1976

Gervase Mathew, the younger brother of Archbishop David Mathew, was an Oxford Dominican of prodigious polymathy. Born in Chelsea and educated privately, he took a third in Modern History at Balliol, and in 1928 joined the Dominicans. His teaching and writing ranged over many disciplines: classical antiquity, the Greek Fathers, Byzantine art, fourteenth-century English literature, and the archaeology of East Africa and Southern Arabia. He was the founder of Byzantine studies in Oxford and held a lectureship in it, for which he took no salary, till 1971. He also collaborated with his brother, Archbishop David, to whom he was devoted; among other things, they wrote together *The Reformation and the Contemplative Life* on the impact of the Protestant revolt on the Carthusian order. He was much in demand as a retreat master and confessor, and is remembered for his extraordinary kindness and gentleness: a confrère, preaching at his Requiem at Blackfriars, said that the harshest thing Father Gervase was ever heard to say about anyone was, 'He is a bit of a goose'. He survived his brother by four months.

## Dominican Spirituality

Dominican spirituality in its highest form remains one of the chief of the syntheses of St Thomas. It is not that it was created by him or even re-fashioned, but it was to attain to the expression of its final unity in the clear splendour of his thought... Forms of prayer and study which had already grown traditional in the order were at last welded in the twenty-fourth and twenty-fifth chapters in the third book of the *Contra gentiles*. The conception of a higher phase of prayer as remote and antithetic to the intellect could have no place in a Thomist system precisely since human prayer is the giving and the uniting of a man to God: *Deo autem assimilatur maxime creatura intellectualis per hoc quod intellectualis est* [The intellectual creature is especially assimilated to God by the fact that it is intellectual] (*Contra gentiles* bk. 3, ch. 23). It is from an exigency of nature that man finds his beatitude through intellectual vision. The impulse to know more perfectly is the corollary of love, for the lover is not content with a superficial knowledge of the beloved. The conception of prayer as a sudden immobile experience could have no place in a Thomist system; even ecstatic prayer cannot possess the immobility of God's essence and is still dynamized by finality. It remains one phase out of many phases in the soul's ascent to God. For in contrast to the neo-Platonizing theologians, St Thomas is intent upon the ascent of being and not on its cascade. To a Thomist all finite being is in movement insofar as it is in being, for the finite, precisely since it is not self-sufficient, must tend towards the self-sufficient, and precisely since it is only participant must retain the possibility of becoming and the desire to become. *Unde patet quod omnia appetunt divinam similitudinem* [It is clear that all things seek after the divine likeness] (*Contra gentiles* bk. 3, ch. 24).

It is the universality of this vision that has preserved Dominican spirituality undepartmentalized; contemplation has never been divorced from action. Even the Thomist prayer of quiet is practical as well as speculative, and has as its scope a better ruling of all the moral life. For the excellence of the gift of *intellectus* consists precisely in the consideration of the eternal and of the necessary not only as they are in themselves but also as the rules of human action. Mysticism is not a closed compartment in the Christian life. Mystic knowledge is regulated by faith, and to a Thomist the value of an advance in mystic prayer lies primarily in the advance in charity that it may presuppose. The doctrine of the Gifts remains the essential note in Thomist spiritual theory precisely since it provides the unbroken rhythm in the ascent to the divine. The contemplative will possess a higher degree of knowledge as he grows more connatural with the contemplated, and he has grown more connatural through the growth of charity and its corollary, the more patent presence of the Gifts. Speculative wisdom gives correct judgement after reason has made due search, but it pertains to the Gift of Wisdom to judge of God by kinship (cf. *Summa theologica* 2a2ae q. 45, a. 2). Precisely insofar as Dominican spirituality is Thomist it is integrated into a *Summa theologica* derived from the same principles governed by the same laws.

A specifically Dominican school in spirituality had been first created through the special purpose of the Order and the choice of means that it necessitated. Its theory had been synthesized by St Thomas; its application was due to the half-successful endeavour of many Dominicans now forgotten. It is probable that many in the Order have come to realize and embody the full idea of Dominican contemplation; it is doubtful if many of them have achieved the full ideal of Dominican activity. The interplay of natural talent and obedience has led inevitably to specialization in action if not in thought. A full expression of Dominican spirituality is often only possible to communities at the cost of the canalized energies of their members. It was a consequence that the wide use of personal dispensation characterized early Dominican legislation, and that variety was soon accepted as a means to unity; historically, Dominican spirituality has been marked by this individual variety in its application. The saints and *beati* of the Order have achieved sanctity in very different settings: in the *studia*, the anchorholds, or the parish houses, or the wandering life of the medieval preacher. Yet the constant effort to sustain among so much illusion the sense of the real has given their lives a special unity. Success in preaching as well as in study must presuppose the recognition of the immediate factors in each very concrete situation. At times, monastic spirituality has been the spirituality of a liturgy moving securely through a shadow world intent upon the world it shadowed. In a phrase of St Bede's, the literal has been to the allegorical as water is to wine. But Dominican spirituality has remained in practice the application of literal fact to literal fact. It is significant that the long traditions of Dominican exegesis have been concentrated on the literal sense of the texts. The Rosary is in itself a symbol; Dominican devotions have always centred in the detailed following of Christ's life on earth. It is this that has linked forever study and apostolate. St Dominic had desired to spend himself for men as Christ had spent Himself upon the Cross, and the greatest of the

Dominican schoolmen were to be aided by syllogism to the incarnate Word. At the last analysis all Dominican spirituality has remained the spontaneous following of Christ as Truth. (1)

## St Bede the Venerable

'For we being many are one bread, one body.' The Pauline conception of the Church remains apparent throughout the Christocentric trend of all Bede's thought. It is this that explains so much by which his work is differentiated, a sense of the individual significance of each human life and a formal courtesy of style alien to the literary convention of his age. For he knew that the men of whom he wrote were the threads from which Christ's seamless coat was woven, temples of the Holy Ghost and the vine-branches, the Resurrection and the Life. And it was this that brought him when already old to the study of the history of the Church, for to him Church history was the Fifth Evangel. Even 'the Ecclesiastical History of the English Nation' may be regarded as yet another essay in exegesis, a somewhat elaborate commentary on a sentence from the Epistles, 'who hath called you out of darkness into His marvellous light who in time past were not a people, but are now the people of God'. (2)

NOTES AND SOURCES

1. Gervase Mathew, 'Dominican Spirituality', *Blackfriars*, 17 (1936), 654–7.

2. Gervase Mathew, 'St Bede', in Maisie Ward (ed.), *The English Way: Studies in English Sanctity from St Bede to Newman* (London: Sheed & Ward, 1933), 17.

# (Lawrence Samuel) Gerald Vann OP          1906–1963

Gerald Vann entered the Dominican Order as a boy of 17 and was ordained priest in 1929. After further studies in Rome, he served on the staff, and as headmaster, of the Dominican school at Laxton, Northamptonshire. From 1952 to his death he devoted his time to writing, lecturing, and giving retreats. He also became well known in the USA, and from 1959 to 1962 spent a semester each year at the Catholic University of America in Washington DC. A confrère said of him after his death: 'He was a true son of St Dominic in that he never spared himself and was always alive to the needs of others. He who wrote so eloquently of pain suffered bitterly in his last months and grew even sweeter.'

## The Intelligibility of the Universe

The ultimate questions why and whither are not scientific questions, because they are not questions of empirically observable fact; but that does not mean that there is no answer to them. We must choose: either we must believe that the universe is ultimately unintelligible, because science cannot explain it; or we must accept an explanation which does make the universe intelligible, but which is not supplied by science. There is an intelligible answer; and there is only one. All the things that we know are fleeting; they come to be, and they pass away. They do not exist necessarily, therefore; they can either be or not be. And this is the same as saying that they do not exist of themselves; they exist at all only because they have received existence from something else. And ultimately therefore that something else must be a thing that does exist of itself; and because it exists of itself, it is rightly called Being Itself—not something that has existence but something that is existence. And if we go on to recognize the presence of design and order in the universe, we shall recognize that this Being is not an It but a He; and then we may be ready to learn more about Him from religion. We of the modern west are the only people in the whole history of the world who have refused to find an explanation of the universe in a divine mind and will; and it is worth wondering whether perhaps that refusal is not at the root of the chaos and misery in which we find ourselves. Without a sense of ultimate purpose, without intelligible answer to the ultimate why and whither, what else could we expect? (1)

## Why the Word Was Made Flesh

Why was the Word made flesh, why the agony and the Cross and the dereliction, if not in order that the inconceivable might become fact, that the Infinite Perfect might weep and sweat drops of sorrow for the sufferings of men, and so bring them back by the only way possible to the deepest knowledge of His love and so to love Him—and to become once again children—themselves. The Word was made flesh that God might suffer with His servants. Never think that is all over; that it was God indeed who wept over Jerusalem, but that for our days there can be no tears. We can write the history of the life of Christ; but God has no history. What was done in and by the humanity of Christ was done in time; but it is God who acts and suffers through the humanity and God is not in time. The tears were shed at a historical moment which is past, though it was not for that place and that moment only but for the whole past and future of the world that He wept. And just as each moment of the age-long process is equally present to the eternal 'Now', so too the sorrow that God suffers in the soul of Christ is not a distant memory but an eternal actuality. Did you think that God wept over Jerusalem but must be deaf to the cries of suffering that fill the whole world today? The Word was made flesh and dwelt amongst us that not a single cry or tear torn from the heart of humanity—yes, and the heart of nature, too—might be left unshared by the heart of God; and so we have seen His glory. (2)

## Crucifying Christ by Our Sins

In the simple prayer of sorrow that we learned as children preparing for Confession, we tell God we are sorry for our sins, 'because they have crucified my loving Saviour, Jesus Christ'. Christ did not die merely because of the sins that were then committed or that had been committed in the past: it was the total evil of the world, past, present, and future, that was responsible for Calvary. And as with the sin, so with the suffering that is the effect of sin: wherever you find it, there is the Cross. People say, 'You can't hurt God': they are wrong if they miss this point, that when I sin now, I as surely crucify God as did the soldiers on the hill of Golgotha, and similarly when I suffer now, God is as surely involved in that suffering as He was in the sorrows of the city over which He wept ... On the Cross Christ had knowledge of every suffering that was to come after; He was involved in it since He was suffering in order to heal or transform it, and so He was sharing in it, and offering it to His Father together with His own suffering, for the renewal of the world. The crucifixion was an event in time, but the Cross transcends time. (3)

## Grace Presupposes Nature

For St Thomas, grace is not at a tangent to nature: it works in and through nature. If a room is to be swept for God's greater glory, it must be swept with a broom, not a litany. A mood of sadness, he suggests, is to be cured by sleep and a good, hot bath (cf *Summa theologiae* 1a2ae q. 38, a. 5). Right action is action that is reasonable; and to think that we can live for God by despising our God-given reason is not only presumption but also something approaching blasphemy. (4)

## Christ in His Church

Christ is still in the world today. The Catholic believes that the Church is the prolongation in time of the life of Christ; and that the whole of the sacramental system, and the Mass in particular, is the divine means of bringing this life and power to man, as the teaching authority of the Church is the divine means of guarding and interpreting the revelation of God and so of guiding the reason of man. (5)

## The Vocation of Tears

The vocation of tears is not a luxury in the Church's life. There are vocations which bring it great blessings and enrich its life, but which it could no doubt do without. This is not one of them. If it had not been for the tears of Monica, the Church would have no St Augustine: the whole world today is an Augustine, waiting for the redemptive tears which will bring upon it the grace of God and restore it to life in Him.

There is a prayer in the Missal which begs for the gift of tears: it is a grace we all need for ourselves, and we ought to ask for it. (6)

## Holy Mass: My Sacrifice and Yours

The Mass is not just a memorial of Calvary; it is not a repetition of Calvary; it is the same essential act. The physical pain and the mental dereliction are over, but the Cross was the expression, through the humanity, of the eternal will-to-share, and the Mass is the same essential expression of that same will-to-share. God's Cross goes on. Not a sparrow falls to the ground, today as yesterday, but our heavenly Father has care of it. And through the humanity of the Son, it is a *redeeming* care.

But, as Pope Pius XII made clear in his encyclical *Mystici corporis*, in this redemptive process which goes on day by day the Head of the Mystical Body needs the members, needs the prayer and penance of the faithful. By sharing in the Mass we share in the Cross and the fruits of the Cross. But how do we share in the Mass? The Mass is first an offering. It is the self-offering of Christ, but of Christ the Head, and it is therefore the offering of the *totus Christus*, Christ together with the members of His Body. 'Brethren,', the priest says, 'pray that my sacrifice and yours may be acceptable': we are meant to share in the sacrifice by offering ourselves and our whole lives, our world, the lesser creation over which man is meant to have dominion, in and through the offering of Christ. Insofar as we offer fully and immolate fully, we shall share fully in the divine compassion and its healing effect. But what is the immolation we have to carry out? Immolation is renunciation and in the last resort self-renunciation, but that in its turn implies what Our Lord calls being poor in spirit, the ability 'to care and not to care', the ability to leave everything gladly or at least willingly in the hands of God. And we cannot do that fully, unless we free ourselves as far as possible from the tyranny of time. For us on earth there is no 'perfect simultaneous possession of endless life', but only the fleeting moment; hardly has beauty come to be but it is passing away, and joy eludes us like the running waters of a stream, so we cling and clutch, and try impotently to make the temporal present an eternal now...Blessed Henry Suso tells us: 'Be steadfast, and never rest content until thou hast obtained the Now of eternity as thy present possession in this life, so far as this is possible to human infirmity'. How is this to be done? By seeing all things and events in God, and God in all things and events, and therefore taking them all from His hands...

'Cast thy care upon the Lord' (Ps. 54: 23), we are told by the Psalmist. If we can find in the Mass, as we should, the power to put ourselves and all things unreservedly into God's hands, and to live in the present, we shall be sharing fully in the self-offering of Christ and at the same time shall be coming to an understanding of that paradox of utter caring and utter not-caring, of supreme sorrow and supreme joy; we shall be sharing in the sorrow and joy of Christ. (7)

## Thomist Politics

There are five points to be noted:

(1) where individualism asserts personality to the neglect of individual duties, and absolutism asserts the concept of the common good to the neglect of personal rights, Thomism stands for the rights of the person, but holds that these rights are fulfilled only through service of the common good;

(2) where liberal democracy asserts individual autonomy at the expense of authority legislating for the common good, and absolutism elevates authority legislating for the common good, and absolutism elevates authority to the extinction of personal freedom, Thomism withdraws some areas of life altogether from the secular power, lays the secular power itself under obedience to theological principles, demands decentralization of control in some matters and adequate representation of opinion in the rest, but safeguards unity and control of class interests by the monarchical principle;

(3) where individualism gives the State the exclusively negative role of non-interference and so plays into the hands of the money power, and nationalism, controlling economics, denies international duties and makes for hatred and war, Thomism would control money for the good of the nations as a whole;

(4) where individualism uses the contract theory to deny the natural foundations of citizenship, and absolutism by denying the contract destroys the rational foundations of citizenship, the Thomist distinction safeguards both;

(5) where individualism leads, through the policy of *laissez-faire*, to class warfare, and absolutism leads, through the policy of violence, to class extinction, Thomism harnesses all classes in a unified effort to achieve the good of all. (8)

NOTES AND SOURCES

1. Gerald Vann, *The Heart of Man* (London: Geoffrey Bles, 1944), 15–16.

2. Ibid. 34–5.

3. Gerald Vann, *The Son's Course* (London: Collins, 1959), 140.

4. Gerald Vann, *The Temptations of Christ* (New York: Sheed & Ward, 1957), 108.

5. Vann, *The Heart of Man*, 41.

6. Gerald Vann, *Eve and the Gryphon* (Oxford: Blackfriars Publications, 1946), 51.

7. Vann, *The Son's Course*, 147–9.

8. Gerald Vann, 'An Introduction to Thomist Politics', *Blackfriars*, 19 (1938), 336.

# Group Captain Leonard Cheshire VC                    1916–1992

Leonard Cheshire was a war hero, but is now best remembered, through the homes that bear his name, as an apostle of charity in the service of the dying and disabled. The son of an Oxford law don, he was educated at the Dragon and Stowe before going up to Oxford to read his father's own subject at Merton. He spent his three years enjoying himself in the traditional manner of pre-war undergraduates: breaking all known records for the speed of his return (in an Alfa Romeo) from Hyde Park Corner to Magdalen Bridge; getting to Paris and back, for the bet of a pint, with only 12/6 in his pocket; and going dog-racing with the college servants. He learnt to fly with the University Air Squadron, and just before the outbreak of war received a permanent commission in the Royal Air Force; throughout the Thirties he had become convinced of his duty to fight the evil coming out of National Socialist Germany. As a pilot in Bomber Command, he carried out an exceptionally large number of raids over the industrial cities of Germany, often volunteering for missions when it was not his turn. By his bravery, humour, and generosity of spirit, he inspired an intense devotion in his air crew. For bringing them back safely in a burning aircraft after a raid on Cologne, he was awarded the DSO. He ended the war as the RAF's most highly decorated pilot, and received the Victoria Cross for four and a half years of sustained courage in action: his reputation in Bomber Command, said the citation, was second to none. In 1945 he represented the British government on the American mission that dropped the atomic bomb on Nagasaki. After the war, having been demobilized with a disability pension because of what was diagnosed as an 'affective disorder', he attempted to set up a community for ex-servicemen, and to that end persuaded his aunt to sell him a twenty-five bedroom house, Le Court in Hampshire, on the basis of a hundred per cent mortgage. The project came to nothing, and Cheshire was left with huge debts. It was then that he received a phone call from the matron of the local hospital to say that Arthur Dykes, who had been pig-man at Le Court, was dying and had no one to look after him. Before long Le Court had become a refuge and place of comfort for the sick and disabled with nowhere else to go. In 1948, inspired by the reading of Vernon

Johnson's *One Lord, One Faith*, Cheshire became a Catholic. In the late Forties, while working for Barnes Wallis as a test pilot, he found an abandoned building near the test site, and set it up as a home for the disabled under the patronage of St Teresa [Thérèse] of Lisieux. In 1950 he contracted TB and was sent to a sanatorium in Midhurst for two years. He spent the time studying Scholastic theology and Scripture, and from his bed continued to direct the work of the home and indeed to establish two new ones. By 1955 there were six such Cheshire Homes. They are now to be found throughout the world. In 1959 he married Sue Ryder, who had done work similar to his own, mostly with displaced persons and the victims of the concentration camps: before their marriage, they composed a prayer vowing their service, 'unto death', of the sick and the dying. Cheshire's life and heroic works of charity were built on a foundation of prayer. At one time he considered a religious vocation with the Benedictines and Carthusians, and, despite not following that path, retained his connection with the Charterhouse by making an annual retreat at Parkminster. Early in 1992 Cheshire was diagnosed with motor neurone disease and died later in the year. In her Christmas message for 1992, Her Majesty the Queen mentioned her last meeting with Cheshire at a reception for members of the Order of Merit and remembered how he had spoken, not of his own suffering, but of 'his hopes and plans to make life better for others'.

## Conversion, Christmas, and the Mass

Christmas 1948. Reception into the Catholic Church . . . 'I, Geoffrey Leonard Cheshire, holding in my hand God's holy Gospels, and enlightened by divine grace, publicly declare that I accept the Faith which is taught by the Catholic, Apostolic, and Roman Church. I believe that Church to be the one true Church which Jesus Christ set up here on earth, to which I make my submission with all my heart.'

How victorious and triumphant it sounds! Would that one could declare it, not just before a small handful of Catholic friends, but before the whole wide world— before the friendly, the indifferent, the hostile, all and everybody alike. I, Geoffrey Leonard Cheshire, in making this, my Profession of Faith, declare that I have at long last been set free from the chains of error and doubt. I declare that I no longer have to guess at the truth about life and death—and all that lies beyond. That I no longer have to choose between this line of argument and that, between this religious denomination and the other; that I have now stumbled across the truth—the truth not as man supposes it to be, but as God knows and guarantees. And the truth has set me free. I declare that just as there is but one God and but one human race, so there is but one true Church and one true faith; that just as God is Father of the human race, so the Church has been appointed its Mother. I declare that were it otherwise, the forces of darkness would have finally prevailed, and the divisions of man triumphed over the oneness of God. Then would the human race remain forever just a race, and never become, as so sublimely desired, a family, God's very own, the completion of Him who everywhere and in everything is complete.

Finally, the ceremony is over. Fresh air and watery sun. Four or five people hurrying up with words of welcome and congratulation; all so sincere and obviously happy. Among them the baker's delivery man. A sudden overwhelming realization of what it means, even here on earth, to be received into such a family. Then, after a long and busy day, a stroll up and down outside the front door in search of peace and quiet. For tonight, of all nights, must not pass without due preparation. Never again will Christmas Eve be quite as this one; never again will there be first Midnight Mass to hear, and first Communion to receive. Overhead just the stars silently running their course; from the surrounding trees and woods hardly so much as the rustle of a leaf. Time, one could almost suppose, has come to a standstill, halted by the approach of eternity. It is the eve of Christmas, the anniversary of the night when the world was reconciled with God and at last found peace. 'While all things were in quiet silence, and the night was in the midst of her course, thy almighty Word, O Lord, came down from Heaven, from thy royal throne, and dwelt among us; and we saw His glory, the glory as of the Only-begotten of the Father, full of grace and truth.' Yes, and as then in the stable at Bethlehem, so today Christ comes down from Heaven to give His peace to the world—in the Mass.

'The Catholic religion', had said Father Clarke, 'is the worship of God through Jesus Christ Our Lord, and it is precisely in the Mass that this finds its focus. The Mass is the gathering up of man and his whole life and offering it to God in union with the sacrifice of Christ. In the Mass Christ is really and truly present—just as truly, though in a different manner, as He once was on the Cross of Calvary. When we are at present at Mass ourselves, provided our dispositions are what they ought to be, our whole lives are caught up in *His* life; our day gains a new significance; our actions—even the most seemingly worthless and indifferent—acquire an eternal value. (1)

## TB and the Holy Shroud

The imprint is perfect in every detail; not a single distortion, not a single smudge. There is no sign of decomposition, no sign of human intervention in the removal of the Shroud. The manner in which the body has left is altogether incomprehensible. It remains God's secret: and for us one more guarantee of the Resurrection. (2)

'Group Captain Cheshire, [said the doctor] you've got TB of the lungs. We'll get a bed ready for you, and once you're in it, there you'll have to stay.'

And stay I did—for the best part of two and a half years.

In the New Year, after I had been moved to Midhurst Sanatorium, Sussex, they took me across to the surgical block for a series of operations on my lung—a new experience to have to lie back and let others do the doing. On the eve of the first of them a life-sized reproduction of the Holy Face from the Shroud of Turin was put on the wall at the foot of my bed. And there, for a full month, I did little but lie and look at it. Here, too, was a new experience. For in front of me was no face such as artists depict, even the best of them, but one that stood in a class all of its own, one that bore the unmistakable stamp of authenticity—the face of the dead Christ, not painted by an artist's hand, but imprinted by some mysterious process of natural photography on the winding-sheet in which He had been buried. Here was not just a face worthy of a God who had become man out of love for man, who lived as only God can live, who had taught as only Truth Itself can teach, who had died and then risen from the dead as only the Author of Life could rise; here was a face which had plumbed to the very depths the mystery of suffering and death. As I gazed at it, I felt impelled to inquire into its origin, and as I inquired, I felt impelled not so much to go on looking (though that I certainly did), as to get up and act.

For here before my eyes was the Face of Victory, the face of One who acknowledges no defeat; who, though done to death, has yet conquered even this last enemy; who has seen in suffering and death, not mere misfortunes to be put up with as best they might, but as the very instruments of the world's salvation, even as the Heaven-sent means of redeeming a fallen humanity. Here was a face which summoned each and everybody, whether in the cloister or in the factory, whether in the forest or in the office, whether in the house or on a sick bed, to take his share in the battle, to be fellow conquerors with Him in the conquest of Heaven. Here was a face which spoke on behalf of all those who had already laid down their lives, of whatever nationality, better men than we who have survived, whose sufferings and courage cry out to us to carry on where they left off, not nation against nation, but the entire human race against our common enemy, against the forces of error and darkness, against divisions and prejudice, against all that bars the way to the eternal and boundless happiness for which man is destined. And here was a face which guaranteed victory in advance, which demanded only that we should stand firm where we were put and leave the rest to Him.

Before such a face as this, so ill used, yet so serene, so majestic yet so gentle, who could fail to be moved? Who could fail to see its reflection in the poor, the maimed, the sick, the dying, the unwanted, the lonely, in all those who suffer or are in need from whatever cause? And who, having seen all this, could be content to lie back and rest so long as anywhere in the world there remains but one human being in want or distress? (3)

NOTES AND SOURCES

1. Leonard Cheshire, *The Face of Victory* (London: Hutchinson, 1961), 152–5.

2. Leonard Cheshire, *The Holy Face: An Account of the Oldest Photograph in the World* (Newport: R. H. Johns, 1954), 10.

3. Cheshire, *The Face of Victory*, 165–7.

# John Bradburne                                    1921–1979

John Bradburne was by his own description the 'vagabond of God': a wanderer with his face set towards the Jerusalem above, a man who loved Christ by the gift of self even to martyrdom, the child of Mary, the friend of lepers, and one of the most prolific English religious poets of modern times. The son of a high church Anglican clergyman, he was educated at Greshams and served with heroism in the Gurkhas and Chindits in the Second World War. He was received into the Catholic Church on the feast of Christ the King in 1947, and then, in unconscious imitation of St Benedict Joseph Labre and Blessed Charles de Foucauld, he began a pilgrimage for the love of Christ that took him to Lourdes, Rome, and Jerusalem, to novitiate and postulancy in religious orders, to the streets of London as a busker and to the high seas as a stoker, to the Archbishop of Westminster's country house as caretaker, and finally to the leper colony in Mutemwa, Rhodesia, and the Third Order habit of St Francis, as a servant of the poorest of the poor. He was abducted and killed during the Rhodesian civil war and buried amid strange and beautiful signs seeming to confirm the sanctity already venerated in his lifetime. The Catholics of Zimbabwe hope and pray that he will be the first from that land to be raised by the Church to the honours of the altar.

## Three Wishes

First, to serve and live with lepers; the second, to die a martyr; the third, to be
buried in the Franciscan habit. (1)

## The Love of Solitude

Bereft of solitude my spirit stands
At point of being murdered by its lack,
My breathing bursts for freedom from the bands
Of converse binds my being front and back;
Being alone to me is company
With love the Fount of life in all that lives,
The Triune Lord accords in unity
Of solitary God as good He gives;
Consult the self-sufficiency of God
And leap from out the chains constraining man
To think him lord of every step he's trod,—
Call the tune, Piper, and enwall to plan:
Heavenly Pan, loose me from earthly bonds
Of cloying pleasure whereat joy desponds.


'In medio ecclesiae remain
Amidst your Mistress Miriam and reign.' (2)

## Greensleeves

It is important for a man
Who lives alone with love of God
To honour the monastic plan
In spite of no abbatial rod.

The more his mind's to keep his cell
The more he finds that dwelling gay,
If he has learnt to weigh it well
'El' will be all he'll need to pray.

But whosoever lives alone
With love of God must also love
His Mother—Queen upon the throne
Of hearts she cleans and weans above.

Green-sleeved are all the avenues
From English Spring to Spring at hand,
In jacarandas too my Muse
Delights in this Mashonaland.

No exile in the land of Ham
I sing the song that rang along to Walsingham. (3)

## To a Wandering Jew

Strange vagabond, who knows not what to seek
The rest you lack flies not thus far afield:
Much babel tumult renders hearing weak,
And, so replete with sights, your sight is sealed
Far out you stray to find your Inmost Soul,
While souls His Eloquence in stillness find—
Be still then! let God's Silence make you whole,
For He Alone can calm your troubled mind:
Your soul's Desire is nearest though unseen,
Your Haven of Perfection's close at hand,
And that wide wandering was fevered dream:
God's Love within you is your Native Land!
Then seek none other, never more depart—
For you are homeless save God keeps your heart.

The Joy of man's desiring is the Lord,
And where the Treasure is, there is the Heart:
What then, if having wandered far abroad
A man finds God at Home? will he depart
Again? to seek his Treasure far and wide,
When he has found the House where it is safe:
Will he reject his Saviour Crucified?
The Risen Christ lives (like a little waif)
Hidden, unheard, uncared for by the World
Which passes busily His Sacrament,
In quest of treasure which must soon be furled
(With all the perishable firmament)
And put away for ever, by that KING
Who hides our folly in His Suffering! (4)

## The Fatal Tree, The Cross of Life

To gain the knowledge of both good and evil
Wins not the power to distinguish well
But gives will's whilom freedom to the devil
Who fits it with a bias towards hell;
Though too such knowledge is a thing divine
Without God's grace it races after ill
Because we have been made to toe the line
That, tight-ropelike, runs up to Zion's Hill;

Wherefore the fatal tree must be uprooted
Boldly and in its place another set

That is the Cross which carries us, transmuted,
With Christ to be as gods and freer yet:
Calvary and the Easter-garden stand
In Paradise regained on Holy Land.

'I have said, ye are gods!' (5)

## Resurrexit sicut dixit

Considering the Sacrament
At the centre of Our Faith
We hail The King in the little tent
As The A and O, no wraith!

So light, so frail, so waferlike,
So seemingly the taste
Of earthly bread...but to Pat and Mike
He's the Risen Lord, embraced!

God grant the Faith may stay with us
As Christ Himself abides
While the Holy Tongue of the 'Oremus'
Gives way to the play, subsides.

The gorgon we decapitate,
The dragon put we down
Where the greensleeved Queen Immaculate
Stands firmly on his crown.

Assumpta est Maria
And ascended is Our King:
In Truth remain we freer
Than the pharisaic fling!

Though the heaven of the Pharisee
And the leaven of the scribe
Is swelling so from sea to sea
To Saint Peter's comes The Tribe.

Now Judah is our talisman,
New Jewry is our hope:
Pipe well, Thou great incarnate Pan,
And recreate the Pope.

Alleluia! Shalom! (6)

## The Real Presence

John's whole bearing in that little church made one know that the King was in the tabernacle, and could one but move the veil, one would see Him face to face. John knelt right down when he genuflected, something one felt drawn to imitate. (7)

## Loving Lepers

In that I've always loved to be alone
I've treated human beings much as lepers,
For this poetic justice may atone
My way with God's, whose ways are always helpers;
I did not ever dream that I might go
And dwell amidst a flock of eighty such
Nor did I scheme towards it ever. No
The Prospect looms not to my liking much;
Lepers warmly to treat as human beings
Is easy to the theorist afar,
Near to my heart from bondage be their freeings,
May it be flesh not stone, O Morning Star!
Miriam, shine, sweet Mistress, in thy name
Salvation, wake, lepers make leap, unlame! (8)

## The Death of the Lepers and the Resurrection of the Body

John was always at peace after seeing a leper safely 'home'. I never knew him to grieve over a death at Mutemwa. He spoke much of their high reward and of their new, glorious bodies. He often quoted Philippians 3: 21: 'He will transfigure these wretched bodies of ours into copies of His glorious body. He will do that by the same power with which He can subdue the whole universe.' (9)

NOTES AND SOURCES

1. John Dove SJ, *Strange Vagabond of God: The Story of John Bradburne* (Swords: Poolbeg Press, 1983), 159.

2. Ibid. 194–5.

3. John Bradburne, <http://www.johnbradburnepoems.com/view.php?id=BRAD0554>.

4. John Bradburne, <http://www.johnbradburnepoems.com/view.php?id=BRAD0872>.

5. John Bradburne, <http://www.johnbradburnepoems.com/view.php?id=BRAD0290>.

6. John Bradburne, <http://www.johnbradburnepoems.com/view.php?id=BRAD0639>.

7. The impressions of Pauline Hutchings, the wife of a Rhodesian farmer (Dove, *Strange Vagabond of God*, 227).

8. Ibid. 211–12.

9. Ibid. 245.

# (George Haliburton) Basil Cardinal Hume OSB     1923–1999

Basil Hume, the first Benedictine to become Archbishop of Westminster, was admired for his humility, good-humoured style of leadership, sincere love of the poor, and Benedictine devotion to prayer. The son of an Anglican father and a French Catholic mother, he was educated at

Ampleforth, entered the monastery there in 1941, read history at St Benet's in Oxford, and did his theology at Fribourg. After ordination to the priesthood in 1950, he became a master in the school, and from 1955 a housemaster, a job he loved. In 1963 he was elected Abbot of Ampleforth, and in 1976 was appointed by Pope Paul VI to succeed Cardinal Heenan as Archbishop of Westminster. His twenty-three years in Archbishop's House included many dramatic events, both in the Church and in the country and world at large, including Pope John Paul II's visit to Britain, the Falklands campaign, the miners' strike, the continuing 'troubles' in Northern Ireland, the famine in Ethiopia, the Gulf War, the death of Princess Diana, and, following the decision of the Church of England to ordain women, the reception of large numbers of Anglican clergymen into the Catholic Church. In the late eighties and early nineties, at the time of debates in Parliament on abortion and experimentation on human embryos, he spoke clearly and courageously in defence of human life from the first moment of fertilization and stated the fundamental principle of all morality: 'Moral choices do not depend on personal preference and private decision but on right reason and, I would add, divine order.' In an act without precedent, when he was already mortally ill, Her Majesty the Queen showed her affection and respect for him by appointing him to the Order of Merit; she is said to have referred to him as 'my Cardinal', something no English monarch had done for five centuries. Cardinal Hume led the Catholic Church towards the celebration in 2000 of the Great Jubilee of the Incarnation, but died six months before it began.

## Prayer

To pray is to make ourselves aware of God and in that awareness respond to Him. It is an attempt to raise our minds and hearts to God. Abbot Herbert [Basil Hume's predecessor as Abbot of Ampleforth] used to tell us that to try to pray was in fact to pray.

Prayer is an act of faith, hope, and charity. It is always an act of faith: 'Lord, we would have our eyes opened.' Our Lord, let me remind you, puts to us the question He put to the two blind men on the way to Jericho: 'What would you have me do for you?' 'Lord, we would have our eyes opened' (Matt. 20: 33). He puts to us the question He put to that other blind man whom, as St John records, He cured: 'Do you believe?' 'I do believe, Lord', the man answered, and falling down adored Him (John 9: 38).

Prayer is an act of charity, an act of love. 'You know all things, Lord, you know that I love you' (John 21: 17). It is an act of hope, because He puts to us the same question He put to certain of the Apostles (in the sixth chapter of St John): 'Would you, too, go away?' 'Lord, to whom would we go? Yours are the words of eternal life. We have learned to believe and are assured that you are the Christ, the Son of God' (John 6: 66 f). We, also, are tempted to go away, turn away, and then we remember that there is none other to whom we can go to find eternal life.

Prayer is the cry of the humble man, one who recognizes his inadequacy before God. 'Lord, be merciful to me a sinner' (cf. Luke 18: 13). 'It is not those who are healthy who have need of the physician, but those who are sick' (Matt. 9: 12). To pray is to acknowledge our dependence on God. And so we wonder why we should ask, when God is already aware of our needs. Because He told us Himself that we should ask: 'Ask, and you will receive' (Matt. 7: 7). Because our asking is part of the order of things that brings about the working of God's Providence. And if our request is not answered, we know it is because His wishes for us will always be greater than our ambitions. (1)

## Through Mary, to Jesus: Yesterday, Today, and Tomorrow

In the year 2000 we shall be celebrating in a most solemn manner the birth of Our Lord. The Church lives through Advent again—waiting and preparing. Mary is present and as Mother. She points to her Son, the Word that became flesh, to God who became man.

The birth of Mary constituted a new beginning for humanity. She was part of God's plan to put right the tragic result of sin in our own personal times and in our society as a whole. But sin never touched Mary, for she was conceived immaculate. She was born perfect—full of grace and, surely, gifted with all those human qualities which we instinctively admire. She was understanding, compassionate, affectionate, with a presence that inspired others weaker and more fragile than she was. I believe that all who met her were immediately drawn to her. She had an attractive personality. People wanted to be with her.

She had been fashioned by God to be the perfect Mother, for to be Mother was and is her special role. She was the Mother of Jesus, and now is the Mother of the Church. Indeed, her birth heralded, as it were, the birth of Jesus and the birth of the Church.

The Nativity scene is well imprinted on the minds of Christ's followers. The faithful have knelt often enough at the Crib and adored the image of the Child before them, the God whom they know and acknowledge as a result of their faith.

That belief in the fact that the Word became flesh, that the Second Person of the Blessed Trinity became man, is the basis of our Christian faith. Affirming this truth is important, too, to appreciate fully Mary's role as Mother of the Church and the part she must play in our lives. The Church was born on Calvary; its mission began at Pentecost. Mary was present on both occasions, and always in her role as Mother.

Calvary was that special 'hour' about which her Son often spoke, the hour of His glorification through Death and Resurrection, and of our redemption and salvation from sin. You remember how He said to her, 'Woman, behold thy Son', and to John, at that moment representing all humanity, 'Behold thy Mother'.

She points to Him, the Word that became flesh, to God the Son who became man, and she says to us what she told the waiters at Cana: 'Do whatever He tells you' (John 2: 5) (John 19: 26-7). (2)

NOTES AND SOURCES

1. Basil Hume, *Searching for God*, new edn. (London: Hodder & Stoughton, 1983), 155-6.

2. Basil Hume, *The Mystery of the Incarnation* (London: Darton, Longman & Todd, 1999), 132-3.

# Index